A

SELECTION OF CASES

ON THE

LAW OF CONTRACTS.

WITH REFERENCES AND CITATIONS.

By C. C. LANGDELL,

DANE PROFESSOR OF LAW IN HARVARD UNIVERSITY.

PREPARED FOR USE AS A TEXT-BOOK IN HARVARD LAW SCHOOL.

"It is ever good to rely upon the book at large, for many times *compendia sunt dispendia*, and *melius est petere fontes quam sectari rivulos*." — Co. Litt. 305 *b*.

"The advised and orderly reading over of the books at large, I absolutely determine to be the right way to enduring and perfect knowledge." — Pref. to 4 Rep.

THE LAWBOOK EXCHANGE, LTD.
Clark, New Jersey

ISBN 978-1-58477-001-5

Lawbook Exchange edition 1999, 2014

The quality of this reprint is equivalent to the quality of the original work.

THE LAWBOOK EXCHANGE, LTD.
33 Terminal Avenue
Clark, New Jersey 07066-1321

Please see our website for a selection of our other publications and fine facsimile reprints of classic works of legal history:
www.lawbookexchange.com

Library of Congress Cataloging-in-Publication Data

A selection of cases on the law of contracts : with references and citations / [compiled] by C.C. Langdell ; prepared for use as a text -book in Harvard Law School.
p. cm.
Originally published: Boston : Little, Brown & Co., 1871.
Includes bibliographical references and index.
ISBN 1-58477-001-5 (cloth : alk. paper)
1. Contracts—United States Cases. I. Langdell, C.C (Christopher Columbus), 1826-1906.
KF801.A7L3 1999
346.7302—dc21 99-28293
CIP

Printed in the United States of America on acid-free paper

A

SELECTION OF CASES

ON THE

LAW OF CONTRACTS.

WITH REFERENCES AND CITATIONS.

By C. C. LANGDELL,

DANE PROFESSOR OF LAW IN HARVARD UNIVERSITY.

PREPARED FOR USE AS A TEXT-BOOK IN HARVARD LAW SCHOOL.

"It is ever good to rely upon the book at large, for many times *compendia sunt dispendia*, and *melius est petere fontes quam sectari rivulos.*"—Co. Litt. 305 *b*.

"The advised and orderly reading over of the books at large, I absolutely determine to be the right way to enduring and perfect knowledge."—Pref. to 4 Rep.

BOSTON:

LITTLE, BROWN, AND COMPANY.

1871.

CAMBRIDGE:
PRESS OF JOHN WILSON AND SON.

PREFACE.

I CANNOT better explain the design of this volume than by stating the circumstances which led me to undertake its preparation.

I entered upon the duties of my present position, a year and a half ago, with a settled conviction that law could only be taught or learned effectively by means of cases in some form. I had entertained such an opinion ever since I knew any thing of the nature of law or of legal study; but it was chiefly through my experience as a learner that it was first formed, as well as subsequently strengthened and confirmed. Of teaching indeed, as a business, I was entirely without experience; nor had I given much consideration to that subject, except so far as proper methods of teaching are involved in proper methods of study.

Now, however, I was called upon to consider directly the subject of teaching, not theoretically but practically, in connection with a large school, with its more or less complicated organization, its daily routine, and daily duties. I was expected to take a large class of pupils, meet them regularly from day to day, and give them systematic instruction in such branches of law as had been assigned to me. To accomplish this successfully, it was necessary, first, that the efforts of the pupils should go hand in hand with mine, that is, that they should study with direct reference to my instruction; secondly, that the study thus required of them should be of the kind from which they might reap the greatest and most lasting benefit; thirdly, that the instruction should be of such a character that the pupils might at least derive a greater advantage from attending it than from devoting the same time to private study. How could this threefold object be accomplished? Only one mode occurred to me which seemed to hold out any reasonable prospect of success; and that was, to make a series of cases, carefully selected from the books of reports, the subject alike of study and instruction. But here I was met by what seemed at first to be an insuperable practical difficulty, namely, the want of books; for though it might be practicable, in case of private pupils having free access to a complete library, to refer them directly to the books of reports, such a course was quite out of the question with a large class, all of whom would want the same books at the same time. Nor would such a course be without great drawbacks and inconveniences, even in the case of a single pupil. As he would always have to go where the books were, and could only have access to them there during certain prescribed hours, it would be impossible for him to economize his time or work to the best advantage; and he would be liable to be constantly haunted by the apprehension that he was spending time, labor, and money in studying cases which would be inaccessible to him in after life.

It was with a view to removing these obstacles, that I was first led to inquire into the feasibility of preparing and publishing such a selection of cases as would be adapted to my purpose as a teacher. The most important element in that inquiry was the great and rapidly increasing number of reported cases in every department of law. In view of this fact, was there any satisfactory principle upon which such a selection could be made? It seemed to me that there was. Law, considered as a science, consists of certain principles or doctrines. To have such a mastery of these as to be able to apply them with constant facility and certainty to the ever-tangled skein of human affairs, is what constitutes a true lawyer; and hence to acquire that mastery should be the business of every earnest student of law. Each of these doctrines has arrived at its present state by slow degrees; in other words, it is a growth, extending in many cases through centuries. This growth is to be traced in the main through a series of cases; and much the shortest and best, if not the only way of mastering the doctrine effectually is by studying the cases in which it is embodied. But the cases which are useful and necessary for this purpose at the present day bear an exceedingly small proportion to all that have been reported. The vast majority are useless and worse than useless for any purpose of systematic study. Moreover, the number of fundamental legal doctrines is much less than is commonly supposed; the many different guises in which the same doctrine is constantly making its appearance, and the great extent to which legal treatises are a repetition of each other, being the cause of much misapprehension. If these doctrines could be so classified and arranged that each should be found in its proper place, and nowhere else, they would cease to be formidable from their number. It seemed to me, therefore, to be possible to take such a branch of the law as Contracts, for example, and, without exceeding comparatively moderate limits, to select, classify, and arrange all the cases which had contributed in any important degree to the growth, development, or establishment of any of its essential doctrines; and that such a work could not fail to be of material service to all who desire to study that branch of law systematically and in its original sources.

It is upon this principle that the present volume has been prepared. It begins the subject of Contracts, and embraces the important topics of Mutual Consent, Consideration, and Conditional Contracts. Though complete in itself, it is my expectation that it will be followed by other volumes upon the same plan; but I have as yet formed no definite opinion as to how far the design will be carried. A volume upon Sales of Personal Property is more than half completed, and will be published within a few months.

C. C. LANGDELL.

CAMBRIDGE, Oct. 1, 1871.

CONTENTS.

TABLE OF CASES.

SELECT CASES ON CONTRACTS.

CHAPTER I.

MUTUAL CONSENT.

"Est autem pactio duorum pluriumve in idem placitum consensus."
ULPIAN, D. 2, 14, 1, 2.

PAYNE *v.* CAVE.

IN THE KING'S BENCH, MAY 2, 1789.

[*Reported in* 3 *Term Reports,* 148.]

THIS was an action tried at the Sittings after last Term at Guildhall before Lord Kenyon, wherein the declaration stated that the plaintiff, on 22d September, 1788, was possessed of a certain worm-tub, and a pewter worm in the same, which were then and there about to be sold by public auction by one S. M., the agent of the plaintiff in that behalf, the conditions of which sale were to be the usual conditions of sale of goods sold by auction, &c., of all which premises the defendant afterwards, to wit, &c., had notice; and thereupon the defendant, in consideration that the plaintiff, at the special instance and request of the defendant, did then and there undertake and promise to perform the conditions of the said sale to be performed by the plaintiff as seller, &c., undertook, and then and there promised the plaintiff to perform the conditions of the sale to be performed on the part of the buyer, &c. And the plaintiff avers that the conditions of sale hereinafter mentioned, are usual conditions of sale of goods sold by auction, to wit, that the highest bidder should be the purchaser, and should deposit five shillings in the pound, and that if the lot purchased were not paid for and taken away in two days' time, it should be put up again and resold, &c. [stating all the conditions]. It then stated that the defendant became the purchaser of the lot in question for 40*l.* and was requested to pay the usual deposit, which he refused, &c. At the trial, the plaintiff's counsel opened the case thus: The goods were put up in one lot at an auction; there were several bidders, of whom the defendant was the last, who bid 40*l.*; the auctioneer dwelt on the bidding, on which the defendant said, "Why do you dwell? you will not get more." The auctioneer said that he was informed the worm weighed at least 1300 cwt., and was worth more than 40*l.*; the defendant then asked him whether he would warrant it to weigh so much, and receiving an answer in the negative, he then declared that he would not take it, and refused to pay for it. It was resold on a subsequent day's sale for 30*l.* to the defendant, against whom the action was brought for the difference. Lord Kenyon, being of opinion on this statement of the case, that the defendant was at liberty to withdraw his bidding any time before the hammer was knocked down, nonsuited the plaintiff.

Walton now moved to set aside the nonsuit, on the ground that the bidder was bound by the conditions of the sale to abide by his bidding, and could not retract. By the act of bidding he acceded to those conditions, one of which was, that the highest bidder should be the buyer. The hammer is suspended, not for the benefit of the bidder, or to give him an opportunity of repenting, but for the benefit of the seller; in the mean time, the person who bid last is a conditional purchaser, if nobody bids more. Otherwise, it is in the power of any person to injure the vendor, because all the former biddings are discharged by the last; and, as it happened in this very instance, the goods may thereby ultimately be sold for less than the person who was last outbid would have given for them. The case of Simon *v.* Motivos,[1] which was mentioned at the trial, does not apply. That turned on the Statute of Frauds.

The Court thought the nonsuit very proper. The auctioneer is the agent of the vendor, and the assent of both parties is necessary to make the contract binding; that is signified on the part of the seller by knocking down the hammer, which was not done here till the defendant had retracted. An auction is not unaptly called *locus pœnitentiæ.* Every bidding is nothing more than an offer on one side, which is not binding on either side till it is assented to. But according to what is now contended for, one party would be bound by the offer, and the other not, which can never be allowed. *Rule refused.*

[1] 3 Burr. 1921.

COOKE *v.* OXLEY.

IN THE KING'S BENCH, MAY 14, 1790.

[*Reported in* 3 *Term Reports*, 653.]

THIS was an action upon the case; and the third count in the declaration, upon which the verdict was taken, stated that on, &c., a certain discourse was had, &c., concerning the buying of two hundred and sixty-six hogsheads of tobacco; and on that discourse the defendant proposed to the plaintiff that the former should sell and deliver to the latter the said two hundred and sixty-six hogsheads [at a certain price]; whereupon the plaintiff desired the defendant to give him (the plaintiff) time to agree to or dissent from the proposal till the hour of four in the afternoon of that day, to which the defendant agreed; and thereupon the defendant proposed to the plaintiff to sell and deliver the same upon the terms aforesaid, *if the plaintiff would agree to purchase them upon the terms aforesaid, and would give notice thereof to the defendant before the hour of four in the afternoon of that day;* the plaintiff averred that he did agree to purchase the same upon the terms aforesaid, and did give notice thereof to the defendant before the hour of four in the afternoon of that day; he also averred that he requested the defendant *to deliver* to him the said hogsheads, and offered to pay to the defendant the said price for the same, yet that the defendant did not, &c.

A rule having been obtained to show cause why the judgment should not be arrested, on the ground that there was no consideration for the defendant's promise,

Erskine and *Wood* now showed cause. This was a bargain and sale on condition; and though the plaintiff might have rescinded the contract before four o'clock, yet, not having done so, the condition was complied with, and both parties were bound by the agreement. The declaration considered this as a complete bargain and sale; for the breach of the agreement is for not *delivering* the tobacco, and not for not selling it.

Lord KENYON, Ch. J. (stopping Bearcroft, who was to have argued in support of the rule): Nothing can be clearer than that, at the time of entering into this contract the engagement was all on one side; the other party was not bound; it was therefore *nudum pactum.*

BULLER, J. It is impossible to support this declaration in any point of view. In order to sustain a promise, there must be either a damage to the plaintiff, or an advantage to the defendant: but here was neither when the contract was first made. Then, as to the subsequent time, the promise can only be supported on the ground of a new contract made at four o'clock; but there is no pretence for that. It has been argued that this must be taken to be a complete sale from the time when the condition was complied with; but it was not complied with, for it is not stated that the defendant did agree at four o'clock to the terms of the sale; or even that the goods were kept till that time.

GROSE, J. The agreement was not binding on the plaintiff before four o'clock; and it is not stated that the parties came to any subsequent agreement; there is, therefore, no consideration for the promise.[1]

Rule absolute.[2]

ADAMS AND OTHERS *v.* LINDSELL AND ANOTHER.

IN THE KING'S BENCH, JUNE 5, 1818.

[*Reported in* 1 *Barnewall & Alderson*, 681.]

ACTION for non-delivery of wool according to agreement. At the trial at the last Lent Assizes for the county of Worcester, before Burrough, J., it appeared that the defendants, who were dealers in wool at St. Ives, in the county of Huntingdon, had, on Tuesday, the 2d of September, 1817, written the following letter to the plaintiffs, who were woollen manufacturers residing in Bromsgrove, *Worcestershire:* "We now offer you eight hundred tods of wether fleeces, of a good fair quality of our country wool, at 35*s.* 6*d.* per tod, to be delivered at Leicester, and to be paid for by two months' bill in two months, and to be weighed up by your agent within fourteen days, *receiving your answer in course of post.*"

1 "An offer which in its terms allows a certain time for acceptance, may be withdrawn during that time before acceptance. In the case of Cooke *v.* Oxley, the plaintiff in his declaration stated that the defendant proposed to the plaintiff to sell and deliver certain goods upon certain terms, if the plaintiff would agree to purchase them upon the terms aforesaid, and would give notice thereof to the defendant before the hour of four in the afternoon of that day; the plaintiff then averred that he did agree to purchase the goods aforesaid, and did give notice thereof to the defendant before the hour of four in the afternoon of that day, and proceeded to charge a breach by the defendant in not delivering; after verdict for the plaintiff, the declaration was held bad in arrest of judgment on the ground that it did not contain an allegation of a contract. It was said that the defendant was not bound to continue his offer until four o'clock because it was not made upon any consideration, and there was no averment that he in fact continued his offer at the time it was accepted, so that no agreement was alleged as a matter of fact. It may be remarked that the facts alleged, in the absence of proof of dissent by the defendant, might have been sufficient for a jury to infer the fact that the defendant's offer continued open when the plaintiff accepted it, so as to establish a complete agreement between them; but such fact could not be imported into the declaration without an allegation to that effect." Leake on Contracts, 21. For further criticisms upon Cooke *v.* Oxley, see Metcalf on Contracts, 19–23; Benjamin on Sale, 45–50. — ED.

2 This judgment was affirmed in the Exchequer Chamber; M. 32 G. 3.

This letter was misdirected by the defendants to Bromsgrove, *Leicestershire*, in consequence of which it was not received by the plaintiffs in Worcestershire till 7 P. M. on Friday, September 5th. On that evening the plaintiffs wrote an answer, agreeing to accept the wool on the terms proposed. The course of the post between St. Ives and Bromsgrove is through London, and consequently this answer was not received by the defendants till Tuesday, September 9th. On the Monday, September 8th, the defendants, not having, as they expected, received an answer on Sunday, September 7th (which, in case their letter had not been misdirected, would have been in the usual course of the post), sold the wool in question to another person. Under these circumstances, the learned Judge held that, the delay having been occasioned by the neglect of the defendants, the jury must take it that the answer did come back in due course of post; and that then the defendants were liable for the loss that had been sustained: and the plaintiffs accordingly recovered a verdict.

Jervis having in Easter Term obtained a rule *nisi* for a new trial, on the ground that there was no binding contract between the parties,

Dauncey, *Puller*, and *Richardson* showed cause. They contended that, at the moment of the acceptance of the offer of the defendants by the plaintiffs, the former became bound. And that was on Friday evening, when there had been no change of circumstances. They were then stopped by the Court, who called upon

Jervis and *Campbell* in support of the rule. They relied on Payne *v.* Cave,[1] and more particularly on Cooke *v.* Oxley.[2] In that case, Oxley, who had proposed to sell goods to Cooke, and given him a certain time, at his request, to determine whether he would buy them or not, was held not liable to the performance of the contract, even though Cooke, within the specified time, had determined to buy them, and given Oxley notice to that effect. So here the defendants who have proposed by letter to sell this wool, are not to be held liable, even though it be now admitted that the answer did come back in due course of post. Till the plaintiffs' answer was actually received, there could be no binding contract between the parties; and before then the defendants had retracted their offer by selling the wool to other persons. But

THE COURT said, that if that were so, no contract could ever be completed by the post. For if the defendants were not bound by their offer when accepted by the plaintiffs till the answer was received, then the plaintiffs ought not to be bound till after they had received the notification that the defendants had received their answer and assented to it. And so it might go on *ad infinitum*. The defendants must be considered in law as making, during every instant of the time their letter was travelling, the same identical offer to the plaintiffs; and then the

[1] 3 T. R. 148. [2] 3 T. R. 653.

contract is completed by the acceptance of it by the latter. Then as to the delay in notifying the acceptance, that arises entirely from the mistake of the defendants, and it therefore must be taken as against them, that the plaintiffs' answer was received in course of post.

Rule discharged.

ROUTLEDGE *v.* GRANT.

In the Common Pleas, May 13, 1828.

[*Reported in* 4 *Bingham*, 653.]

Assumpsit. The declaration stated (first count) that the plaintiff was possessed of a term in a dwelling-house, to expire 25th December, 1856; and that defendant agreed, on the 29th April, 1825, upon receiving a lease for twenty-one years, at 250*l.* a year rent, with the option of having the time extended to thirty-one years on giving six months' notice, and upon having possession on the 25th July then next, to pay plaintiff 2,750*l.*, and take the fixtures at a valuation.

Averment of plaintiff's readiness to grant the lease. Breach; refusal to accept it, and to take the fixtures at a valuation; and non-payment of the 2,750*l.*

The second count alleged the plaintiff to be entitled to a certain term, to wit, a term of thirty-two years, in the dwelling-house, under a certain contract between the plaintiff and Anthony Hermon, who was authorized in that behalf; and then stated the agreement with the defendant, and the breach, as before.

The third count alleged plaintiff to be possessed for the residue of a certain term, to expire 25th December, 1856; and the agreement, tender of lease to defendant, and breach, as before.

At the trial before Best, C. J., London Sittings after Michaelmas term, it appeared that, on the 18th March, 1825, the plaintiff received a note from the defendant touching the premises in these terms:—

MR. GRANT'S PROPOSAL.

To pay a premium of 2,750*l.*, upon receiving a lease for twenty-one years, with the option (upon giving six months' previous notice to the landlord or his agent) of having the time extended to thirty-one years, paying the same yearly rent as before, for such extended term of ten years beyond twenty-one years.—Rent, 250*l.*

Mr. Grant to pay for the fixtures at a valuation, possession to be given on or before 25th July next, to which time all taxes and outgoings are to be discharged by Mr. Routledge; and a definitive answer to be given within six weeks from the 18th March, 1825.

The plaintiff, who at this time had only a term of twelve years in the premises, had to apply to his landlord for a new lease before he was in a condition to accept the defendant's offer. The plaintiff, having come to an understanding with his landlord, wrote the following note to the defendant:—

Mr. Routledge begs to say that he accepts Mr. Grant's offer for his house, No. 59 St. James's Street, and that he will give Mr. Grant possession on the 1st of August next.

St. James's Street, 6th April, 1825.

Mr. R. will esteem it a particular favor if Mr. Grant will not, for the present, name the subject to any one.

The defendant returned the following answer:—

7th April, 1825.

SIR,—I received your note last night, and hasten to acquaint you, that, having considered as confidential the negotiation respecting your house, I had mentioned it to no one; but upon consulting with a friend this morning, in whose opinion I have more confidence than my own, I am advised, for some reasons which had not occurred to myself, not to think of taking a house in St. James's Street for a dwelling-house. May I therefore request you to permit me to withdraw the proposal I made to you about it? I am in hopes you will make no hesitation to do this, when you consider the spirit of candor and openness in which it was made to you. But should it be otherwise, as I am the last that would willingly act with inconsistency, I will willingly refer the question to friends for decision, and abide by their opinion of the case.

I have the honor to be, &c., ALEX. GRANT.

MR. THOMAS ROUTLEDGE.

To this the plaintiff replied as follows:—

8th April, 1825.

SIR,—In answer to your letter of yesterday, I beg to state, that, relying upon your performing the agreement for the purchase of my house in St. James's Street, I have taken another house, and made arrangements which I cannot, without great loss, relinquish. I hope, therefore, that you will not wish me to withdraw it. I am, &c.,

THOS. ROUTLEDGE.

ALEXANDER GRANT, Esquire.

The defendant rejoined:—

9th April, 1825.

SIR,—Your note of yesterday surprised me, being altogether at variance with your conversation with me two or three hours previous to your note, dated on the evening of 6th, in which, you must recollect, you one moment declared yourself off; and, finally, you went away to have the opinion of Mrs. Routledge about the answer you were to send me. How therefore you can, under such circumstances, suffer loss and inconvenience from my declining to proceed further in the treaty, I am at a loss to imagine; and I was in hopes you would have been satisfied with what I had stated in reply to your first note, to have had the liberality of letting the matter drop. But if that should not be your intention, I have only to add that you may proceed with your claim for "loss and inconvenience," as you may think most advisable. I am, &c.,

ALEX. GRANT.

MR. THOMAS ROUTLEDGE.

The plaintiff, after this, surrendered the existing lease to his landlord, and obtained from him a new one, dated 21st April, 1825, from the 25th December, 1824, for thirty-two years, for the same clear yearly rent of 250*l.*, payable quarterly; in which the covenants on the part of the lessee were similar to those in the former; and then wrote the defendant the following letter:—

SIR,—Upon referring to my letter to you of the 6th inst., accepting your offer for my house, No. 59 St. James's Street, I perceive that I, by mistake, stated that I would give possession on the 1st day of August next. By your offer, you state that possession is to be given on or before the 25th July next; and I inform you that I am ready to give you possession, according to your proposal.

I am, &c., THOS. ROUTLEDGE.

29th April, 1825.

This letter, on the day it was dated, was delivered at the defendant's house; and the keys, and a lease of the premises in question, according to the agreement, were tendered to him before the 25th July, but rejected.

The six weeks, from the 18th March, 1825, within which, by the defendant's proposal, a definitive answer was to be given, expired on the 1st May, 1825.

Upon these facts it was objected, first, that the plaintiff being allowed six weeks to accept or reject the defendant's offer, the defendant was entitled also, until it was accepted, to retract it, at any period before the expiration of the six weeks; that there was no acceptance of the terms proposed till the 29th of April, which came too late, the defendant having retracted his proposal on the 9th. Secondly, that the plaintiff had not, before the defendant withdrew his proposal, any such interest in the premises as he was alleged to have in the declaration, or as would have enabled him to accede to that proposal. The plaintiff was thereupon nonsuited, with leave to move the Court to set the nonsuit aside.

Taddy, Serjt., accordingly obtained a rule *nisi* to set aside this nonsuit, and

Wilde, Serjt., showed cause. There was no valid contract binding on both parties. By the terms of the defendant's proposal, the plaintiff had six weeks to accept or reject it, and the parties would not have been on an equal footing if the defendant had not the privilege of withdrawing his proposal during the same period; having finally withdrawn it on the 9th of April, the plaintiff's acceptance on the 29th came too late, the acceptance on the 6th being out of the question, as not acceding to the terms offered by the defendant. Kennedy *v.* Lee,[1] has decided that an acceptance varying in any degree from the terms of an offer, is in effect no acceptance; and Adams *v.* Lindsell[2] confirms the principle established in Cooke *v.* Oxley,[3] that a party who allows time for the acceptance of an offer may retract before it is accepted. But the plaintiff, at the time of the defendant's offer, and up to the period of his withdrawing it, had no such interest in the premises as that stated in the declaration, nor even such as could have enabled him to meet the proposal; he had only a term of twelve years when he agreed to grant thirty-one. On the ground of variance, therefore, the nonsuit cannot be impeached.

Taddy and *Jones*, Serjts., in support of the rule. The defendant's offer was made on good consideration; namely, that the plaintiff should procure him a term of thirty-one years in the premises; and a party cannot retract, during the time which he allows for deliberation, an offer made on good consideration. Cooke *v.* Oxley was determined on the ground that the bargain was *nudum pactum*, and therefore without consideration. Lord Kenyon said, "At the time of entering into the contract the engagement was all on one side; the other party was not bound; it was, therefore, *nudum pactum*." And Buller, J., put it on the ground that it ought to have been stated that the defendant (who was allowed till four o'clock to consider whether or not he would buy goods on the terms offered) "did agree at four o'clock to the terms of the sale:" from which it may be inferred that if such a statement had been made in the declaration and proved, the defendant would have been liable for refusing to perform his contract. In the present case there is a sufficient consideration, and a sufficient averment and proof of the plaintiff's agreeing to the terms of the contract before the expiration of the time limited. In Adams *v.* Lindsell the defendants were held to be bound by an offer to sell upon receiving an answer in course of post, although, by accident, the answer did not arrive till two days after the next post, and the defendants had, in the mean time, sold the goods to a third person.

With respect to the alleged variance,—it is sufficient that the plaintiff had a term at his disposal; the time when it was to expire was immaterial, and the allegation that it was to expire in 1856 may be rejected as surplusage.[4] . . .

It is sufficient if the party has at the time of the completion of the contract, that which he proposes to sell. And on the 29th of April, before which time there was no complete contract in the present case, the plaintiff was in possession of the term he agreed to dispose of.

Best, C. J. The nonsuit was right on both grounds. I put it on

[1] 3 Meriv. 454. [2] 1 B. & A. 681. [3] 3 T. R. 653.

[4] The learned counsel here stated the case of Carvick *v.* Blagrave, 1 Br. & Bing. 536, 4 B. Moore, 303.—Ed.

the same footing as I did at *Nisi Prius.* Here is a proposal by the defendant to take property on certain terms; namely, that he should be let into possession in July. In that proposal he gives the plaintiff six weeks to consider; but if six weeks are given on one side to accept an offer, the other has six weeks to put an end to it. One party cannot be bound without the other. This was expressly decided in Cooke *v.* Oxley, where the defendant proposed to sell, at a certain price, tobacco to the plaintiff, who desired to have till four in the afternoon of that day to agree to or dissent from the proposal; with which terms the defendant complied; and the plaintiff having afterwards sued him for non-delivery of the tobacco, Lord Kenyon put it on the true ground, by saying, "At the time of entering into this contract the engagement was all on one side; the other party was not bound." Buller, J., said, "It has been argued that this must be taken to be a complete sale from the time the condition was complied with: but it was not complied with; for it is not stated that the defendant did agree *at* four o'clock to the terms of the sale; or even that the goods were kept till that time." I put the present case on the same ground. At the time of entering into this contract the engagement was all on one side. In Payne *v.* Cave[1] it was holden that the defendant, who had bid at an auction, might retract his bidding any time before the hammer was down, and the Court said, "The auctioneer is the agent of the vendor, and the assent of both parties is necessary to make the contract binding; that is signified on the part of the seller by knocking down the hammer, which was not done here till the defendant had retracted. An auction is not unaptly called *locus pœnitentiæ.* Every bidding is nothing more than an offer on one side, which is not binding on either side till it is assented to. But, according to what is now contended for, one party would be bound by the offer, and the other not, which can never be allowed."

These cases have established the principle on which I decide; namely, that till both parties are agreed, either has a right to be off. The case of Adams *v.* Lindsell is supposed to break in on them; but I think it does not, because the Court put it on the circumstance that the offer was made by the post, and say, "If the defendants were not bound by their offer when accepted by the plaintiffs, till the answer was received, then the plaintiffs ought not to be bound till after they had received the notification that the defendants had received their answer and assented to it. And so it might go on *ad infinitum.* The defendants must be considered in law as making, during every instant of the time their letter was travelling, the same identical offer to the plaintiffs; and then the contract is completed by the acceptance of it by the latter." If they are to be considered as making the offer till it is accepted, the other may say, "make no further offer, because I shall not accept it;" and to place them on an equal footing, the party who offers should have

[1] 3 T. R. 148.

the power of retracting as well as the other of rejecting: therefore I cannot bring myself to admit that a man is bound when he says, "I will sell you goods upon certain terms, receiving your answer in course of post." However, it is not necessary to touch that decision, for the reasoning of the Court coincides with the principle on which we now determine. As the defendant repudiated the contract on the 9th of April, before the expiration of the six weeks, he had a right to say that the plaintiff should not enforce it afterwards.

But upon the question of variance, we are all of opinion that none of the counts apply. It is not necessary, perhaps, that the termini of the plaintiff's lease should be set out with precision; but the variance is fatal if the plaintiff has not, at least, an interest which will enable him to perform his contract. The variance is not in words, but in substance. The plaintiff had no such term as that stated in the first and third counts. In the second, he states he had a contract for a lease;—such a contract, to be valid, must be in writing, and he cannot be said to have had it unless he had it in writing. But there was no evidence of any such contract; and, therefore, upon both grounds, the rule must be discharged.

BURROUGH, J.,[1] coincided in discharging the rule on the ground of variance.

GASELEE, J. If this case had rested on the first point, I should have wished for time to consider it; but on the ground of variance, I have no doubt that this rule must be *Discharged.*

HEAD *v.* DIGGON

IN THE KING'S BENCH, MICH. TERM, 1828.

[*Reported in* 3 *Manning & Ryland,* 97.]

ASSUMPSIT. The declaration stated, that plaintiff bargained for, and bought from defendant, certain large quantities of wool, to wit, at and for a certain rate or price, to wit, at or for the rate or price of 9*l.* 10*s.* for each and every pack thereof; and thereupon, in consideration of the premises and that plaintiff had undertaken to accept and pay for said wool at and for, &c., defendant undertook that he would, within a reasonable time, deliver said wool. Averment, that a reasonable time had elapsed, and that plaintiff had always been ready and willing to receive and pay; whereof defendant had notice: Yet defendant did not deliver

[1] Park, J., was absent at Chambers.

within such reasonable time, or at any time. Whereby plaintiff lost great gains and profits. Second count, stating the consideration to be, that plaintiff *would buy*, receive and pay, and alleging a promise to sell and deliver, and a readiness to buy, accept, and pay. Third count, laying the promise to deliver on request. At the trial before Holroyd, J., at the last Assizes for the county of Suffolk, the following facts appeared. The plaintiff is a wool-factor in Bury St. Edmund's, the defendant is a fellmonger at Thetford. On Thursday, the 17th of April, 1828, the plaintiff went to the defendant's house at Thetford to treat for the purchase of wool. After some discussion about the price, the plaintiff requested of the defendant time to consider of his terms. The defendant said he would give him a week. The plaintiff replied that three or four days would be enough. The defendant then wrote the following paper: —

THETFORD, April 17, 1828.

Offered Mr. Head, of Bury, the under wool, with three days' grace from the above date: —

40 Sussex head and lamb,
40 Head ditto, } £9 10*s*.
17 Broad head,

As per sample; delivered in good condition.

FRAS. DIGGON.

On the following Monday the plaintiff went to the defendant to accept the wool, and to make arrangements for the delivery. The defendant said, that as the plaintiff had not seen him or written him on Sunday, he had given a price to one Fyson. The plaintiff said that Sunday was not a day of business. The defendant persisted in refusing to deliver the wool. Upon this evidence the learned Judge was of opinion that the plaintiff had failed in proving a contract binding on both parties, and on the authority of Cooke *v.* Oxley[1] directed a nonsuit, which

Storks, Serjt., now moved to set aside. It is true, that up to a certain period, one party was at liberty; but in Adams *v.* Lindsell[2] the defendant offered to sell certain goods to the plaintiff, receiving an answer by return of post. The letter being misdirected, the answer, signifying the acceptance of the offer, arrived two days later than it ought to have done. The defendant had on the preceding day sold the goods to a third person. The Court held that this was a binding contract, and that an action lay for non-delivery of the goods. Cooke *v.* Oxley, upon which the other side relies, was cited in Adams *v.* Lindsell, and may be considered as overruled by the latter decision. [Lord Tenterden, C. J. Must both parties be bound, or is it sufficient if one only is bound? You contend that the buyer was to be free during the three

[1] 3 T. R. 653. [2] 1 Barn. & Ald. 681.

days, and that the seller was to be bound. The declaration treats it as a complete contract, an absolute and unconditional bargain. Those counts are not proved. Whether a declaration could be framed to meet the facts, we are not called upon to decide.] The declaration applies to the contract at the period when, by the plaintiff's acceptance, it became complete.

Lord TENTERDEN, C. J. If the contract is to be taken as made only at the time when the plaintiff signified his acceptance of the offer, it is disproved by the circumstance that the defendant did not then agree.

BAYLEY, J. I am of the same opinion; and in Routledge v. Grant[1] it was held by the Court of Common Pleas, that unless both parties are bound, neither is bound. *Rule refused.*[2]

MARY ANN WILLIAMS v. WILLIAM CARWARDINE.

IN THE KING'S BENCH, APRIL 18, 1833.

[*Reported in 4 Barnewall & Adolphus*, 621.]

ASSUMPSIT to recover 20*l*., which the defendant promised to pay to any person who should give such information as might lead to the discovery of the murder of Walter Carwardine. Plea, general issue. At the trial before Park, J., at the last Spring Assizes for the county of

[1] 4 Bing. 653, 1 M. & Payne, 717.

[2] In Kennedy v. Lee, 3 Merivale, 454, which was cited by the defendant's counsel in Routledge v. Grant, Lord Eldon said, "I have always understood the law of the Court to be, with reference to this kind of contract, that if a person communicates his acceptance of an offer within a reasonable time after the offer is made, and if, within a reasonable time of the acceptance being communicated, no variation has been made by either party in the terms of the offer so made and accepted, the acceptance must be taken as simultaneous with the offer, and both together as constituting such an agreement as the Court will execute."

Pothier says (*Traité du Contrat de Vente*, No. 32): "In the contract of sale, as in other contracts, there may be consent of parties, not only between those who are present, but those who are absent, by letters or by an agent (*entremetteur*), *per epistolam, aut per nuntium.* In order to constitute consent in this case, it is necessary that the intention of the party who writes to another to propose the bargain, should continue until the time at which the letter reaches the other party, and at which the latter declares that he accepts the bargain. This intention is presumed to continue as long as nothing appears to the contrary; but if I write to a merchant at Leghorn a letter, in which I propose to purchase of him a certain quantity of merchandise at a certain price, and before my letter can have reached him I write him a second letter, by which I intimate that I no longer desire to make this purchase; or if before that time I die, or lose the use of my reason, although this merchant of Leghorn, at the receipt of my letter, in ignorance of the change of my intention, or my death or my insanity, an-

Hereford, the following appeared to be the facts of the case: One Walter Carwardine, the brother of the defendant, was seen on the evening of the 24th of March, 1831, at a public house at Hereford, and was not heard of again till his body was found on the 12th of April in the river Wye, about two miles from the city. An inquest was held on the body on the 13th of April and the following days till the 19th; and it appearing that the plaintiff was at a house with the deceased on the night he was supposed to have been murdered, she was examined before the magistrates, but did not then give any information which led to the apprehension of the real offender. On the 25th of April the defendant caused a handbill to be published, stating that whoever

swers that he accepts the proposed bargain, yet no contract of sale arises between us; for my intention not having continued until the time at which my letter was received and my proposal accepted, the consent or concurrence of our wills, necessary to form a contract of sale, has not occurred. This is the opinion of Barthole and of the other doctors cited by Bruneman, *ad legem* 1, *ff. de contractu emptionis,* who have with reason rejected the contrary opinion of the Gloss *ad dictam legem.* [It must be observed, however, that if my letter causes the merchant to be at any expense, in proceeding to execute the contract proposed; or if it occasions him any loss, as for example, if in the intermediate time between the receipt of my first and that of my second letter, the price of that particular kind of merchandise falls, and my first letter deprives him of an opportunity to sell it before the fall of the price; in all these cases I am bound to indemnify him, unless I prefer to agree to the bargain as proposed by my first letter. This obligation results from that rule of equity, that no person should suffer from the act of another: *Nemo ex alterius facto prægravari debet.* I ought therefore to indemnify him for the expense and loss which I occasion him by making a proposition, which I afterwards refuse to execute. For the same reason, if the merchant, on the receipt of my first letter, and before receiving the second which contains a revocation of it, or being in ignorance of my insanity or death, which prevents the conclusion of the bargain, charges to my account and forwards the merchandise; though, in that case, there cannot properly be a contract of sale between us, yet he will have a right to compel me or my heirs to execute the proposed contract, not in virtue of any contract of sale, but of my obligation to indemnify him, which results from the rule of equity above mentioned." — Ed.]

After reading the judgment in Kennedy v. Lee, it is refreshing to return to this writer (not, of course, to be judged of by the above translation), whose luminous method in the investigation of abstruse and complicated propositions appears almost to justify the proverbial boast of his countrymen with respect to the redeeming excellence of their language: "Ce qui n'est pas clair, n'est pas Français."

["According to Pothier, an offer of a contract sent by letter may be withdrawn by the mere sending of a subsequent letter stating a change of mind, provided only it is sent before the first can have arrived, although it may not arrive until after the first is received and answered; so that, although on receipt of the first letter, and in ignorance of the change of mind conveyed by the second, an answer is sent accepting the offer, there is no contract, because there is no agreement. The passage from Pothier to this effect (*Contrat de Vente,* s. 32) has been cited by some writers as in accordance with English law (see Chitty, Contr. 7th edit. 12; Head v. Diggon, 3 M. & R. 97, 100, n. c), but it is here submitted that it is inconsistent with the decisions above cited, and contrary to principle in regarding as the test of agreement the abstract intentions of the parties instead of the expressions of intention communicated between them." Leake on Contracts, 20 n. (d.) — Ed.]

would give such information as should lead to a discovery of the murder of Walter Carwardine, should, on conviction, receive a reward of 20*l.*; and any person concerned therein, or privy thereto (except the party who actually committed the offence), should be entitled to such reward, and every exertion used to procure a pardon; and it then added, that information was to be given, and application for the above reward was to be made, to William Carwardine, Holmer, near Hereford. Two persons were tried for the murder at the summer assizes, 1831, but acquitted. Soon after this, the plaintiff was severely beaten and bruised by one Williams; and on the 23d of August, 1831, believing she had not long to live, and to ease her conscience, she made a voluntary statement, containing information which led to the subsequent conviction of Williams. Upon this evidence it was contended, that as the plaintiff was not induced by the reward promised by the defendant, to give evidence, the law would not imply a contract by the defendant to pay her the 20*l.* The learned Judge was of opinion, that the plaintiff, having given the information which led to the conviction of the murderer, had performed the condition on which the 20*l.* was to become payable, and was therefore entitled to recover it; and he directed the jury to find a verdict for the plaintiff, but desired them to find specially whether she was induced to give the information by the offer of the promised reward. The jury found that she was not induced by the offer of the reward, but by other motives.

Curwood now moved for a new trial. There was no promise to pay the plaintiff the sum of 20*l.* That promise could only be enforced in favor of persons who should have been induced to make disclosures by the promise of reward. Here the jury have found that the plaintiff was induced by other motives to give the information. They have, therefore, negatived any contract on the part of the defendant with the plaintiff.

DENMAN, C. J. The plaintiff, by having given information which led to the conviction of the murderer of Walter Carwardine, has brought herself within the terms of the advertisement, and therefore is entitled to recover.

LITTLEDALE, J. The advertisement amounts to a general promise, to give a sum of money to any person who shall give information which might lead to the discovery of the offender. The plaintiff gave that information.

PARKE, J. There was a contract with any person who performed the condition mentioned in the advertisement.

PATTESON, J. I am of the same opinion. We cannot go into the plaintiff's motives. *Rule refused.*[1]

[1] "The publication of an advertisement offering a reward for information respecting a loss or a crime is an offer to any person who is able to give the information asked; and the acceptance of it by giving such information creates a valid contract." Leake

HYDE *v.* WRENCH.

IN CHANCERY, DECEMBER 8, 1840.

[*Reported in* 3 *Beavan*, 334.]

THIS case came on upon general demurrer to a bill for specific performance, which stated to the effect following:—

The defendant, being desirous of disposing of an estate, offered, by his agent, to sell it to the plaintiff for 1,200*l.*, which the plaintiff, by his agent, declined; and on the 6th of June the defendant wrote to his agent as follows: "I have to notice the refusal of your friend to give me 1,200*l.* for my farm; I will only make one more offer, which I shall not alter from; that is, 1,000*l.* lodged in the bank until Michaelmas, when title shall be made clear of expenses, land tax, &c. I expect a reply by return, as I have another application." This letter was forwarded to the plaintiff's agent, who immediately called on the defendant; and, previously to accepting the offer, offered to give the defendant 950*l.* for the purchase of the farm, but the defendant wished to have a few days to consider.

On the 11th of June the defendant wrote to the plaintiff's agent as follows: "I have written to my tenant for an answer to certain inquiries, and, the instant I receive his reply, will communicate with you, and endeavor to conclude the prospective purchase of my farm. I assure you I am not treating with any other person about said purchase."

The defendant afterwards promised he would give an answer about accepting the 950*l.* for the purchase on the 26th of June; and on the 27th he wrote to the plaintiff's agent, stating he was sorry he could not feel disposed to accept his offer for his farm at Luddenham at present.

This letter being received on the 29th of June, the plaintiff's agent on that day wrote to the defendant as follows: "I beg to acknowledge the receipt of your letter of the 27th instant, informing me that you are not disposed to accept the sum of 950*l.* for your farm at Luddenham. This being the case, I at once agree to the terms on which you offered the farm; viz., 1,000*l.* through your tenant, Mr. Kent, by your letter of the 6th instant. I shall be obliged by your instructing your solicitor to communicate with me without delay, as to the title, for the reason which I mentioned to you."

The bill stated, that the defendant "returned a verbal answer to the last-mentioned letter, to the effect he would see his solicitor thereon;"

on Contracts, 13. And see Denton *v.* G. N. Railway Company, 5 El. & Bl. 860; Smith *v.* Moore, 1 C. B. 438; Thatcher *v.* England, 3 C. B. 254; Lancaster *v.* Walsh, 4 M. & W. 16; Lockhart *v.* Barnard, 14 M. & W. 674; Gerhard *v.* Bates, 2 El. & Bl. 476; Neville *v.* Kelly, 12 C. B. N. S. 740.—ED.

and it charged that the defendant's offer for sale had not been withdrawn previous to its acceptance.

To this bill, filed by the alleged purchaser for a specific performance, the defendant filed a general demurrer.

Mr. *Kindersley* and Mr. *Keene*, in support of the demurrer. To constitute a valid agreement there must be a simple acceptance of the terms proposed. Holland *v.* Eyre.[1] The plaintiff, instead of accepting the alleged proposal for sale for 1,000*l.* on the 6th of June, rejected it, and made a counter proposal; this put an end to the defendant's offer, and left the proposal of the plaintiff alone under discussion; that has never been accepted, and the plaintiff could not, without the concurrence of the defendant, revive the defendant's original proposal.

Mr. *Pemberton* and Mr. *Freeling*, contra. So long as the offer of the defendant subsisted, it was competent to the plaintiff to accept it; the bill charges that the defendant's offer had not been withdrawn previous to its acceptance by the plaintiff; there, therefore, exists a valid subsisting contract. Kennedy *v.* Lee,[2] Johnson *v.* King,[3] were cited.

The MASTER *of the* ROLLS.[4]

Under the circumstances stated in this bill, I think there exists no valid binding contract between the parties for the purchase of the property. The defendant offered to sell it for 1,000*l.*, and if that had been at once unconditionally accepted, there would undoubtedly have been a perfect binding contract; instead of that the plaintiff made an offer of his own to purchase the property for 950*l.*, and he thereby rejected the offer previously made by the defendant. I think that it was not afterwards competent for him to revive the proposal of the defendant, by tendering an acceptance of it;[5] and that therefore there exists no obligation of any sort between the parties; the demurrer must be allowed.

[1] 2 Sim. & St. 194.

[2] 3 Mer. 454.

[3] 2 Bing. 270.

[4] Lord Langdale. — ED.

[5] "An agreement may undoubtedly be constituted by letters; but if, in the course of the treaty, an offer made by letter is verbally rejected, the party who makes it is relieved from his liability on that offer, unless he consent to renew the treaty on the same footing; the party who has rejected the offer cannot afterwards, at his own option, convert the same offer into an agreement by acceptance; for that purpose he must have the renewed consent of the party who made the first offer." Lord Langdale, M. R., in The Sheffield Canal Company *v.* The Sheffield & Rotherham Railway Company, 3 Railway and Canal Cases, 121. — ED.

POTTER *v.* SANDERS.

IN CHANCERY, JULY 10, 11, AND NOV. 4, 5, 1846.

[*Reported in* 6 *Hare*, 1.]

G. S. SANDERS was seised in fee of three closes of land, in Byfield, in the county of Worcester, subject to a mortgage of 500*l*., which he offered to sell at the price of 950*l*., upon the condition that the purchaser should not require a covenant for the production of certain title deeds, which Sanders was unable to obtain. Potter, being informed of this offer, wrote to Sanders a letter, dated the 20th of April, 1844, offering 800*l*. for the land, taking the title as it stood. In reply to this letter, Sanders wrote to Potter as follows:—

BEWLEY MILL, REDDITCH, April 23, 1844.

SIR,—I received your favor this morning, and in reply beg to say that I accept of your offer of 800*l*. for the land at Byfield. I have written to Mr. Gery by this post, who shall let you know when the deeds are ready, which I believe will be in a few days. Will that be convenient to you?

Yours, &c., G. S. SANDERS.

This letter was put into the post-office on the day of its date. Sanders also wrote to Gery a letter of the same date, as follows:—

DEAR SIR,—I have written to Mr. Potter to say that he shall have the land at Byfield for 800*l*. I have told him that I have no doubt but that you will have the conveyance ready in a few days. Can you do so? As I am short of cash, would you ask him if he would pay me 100*l*. as a deposit, *instanter*? Perhaps it would not inconvenience him, and it would be of great service to me. You could give him a proper receipt, signed by me, and which would make our bargain more firm. I suppose, as Mr. Potter intends to pay off the mortgage, it will be necessary for the mortgagees to sign the deed; and I have no doubt but that one of them will wish to be present at the settling, to receive the 500*l*. and interest. You need not tell Potter as from me, but hint to him, that if he does not complete the purchase without delay his chance will be gone.

Yours, &c., G. S. SANDERS.

While this correspondence was going on with Mr. Gery and Potter, Sanders was also in communication with another party, who was willing to purchase the land.

On the 8th of April, S. Gardner, as the agent of William Coates, applied to Sanders's father, who lived at Daventry, for the price of the land, and the father on the same day wrote to Sanders the following letter:—

DEAR GEORGE, — My principal reason for writing is to know the lowest price you will take for your land at Byfield. I have had a person to inquire after it to-day. He wishes for an answer immediately; so please to send me word directly on receipt of this. Yours, &c.,

THOMAS SANDERS.

This communication was answered by a letter from Sanders to his father, dated the 12th of April, 1844, as follows:—

MY DEAR FATHER, — Unluckily I did not send for my letters yesterday, so did not have your kind note till this morning. I hope the delay will not be of consequence. My lowest price for the Byfield land is 925*l.*; and I will pay for the conveyance, which will take the 25*l.* I should think the timber on the land is worth 50*l.*, and that the purchaser would have into the bargain. I must admit I should be glad to sell it, and will leave it to you to dispose of it, if possible, should the parties offer even a less sum; although I think it ought not to go under the 925*l.* Mr. Gery would be employed to convey, as he has already in his possession a draft of the deed. Yours, &c.,

G. S. SANDERS.

The father thereupon wrote the following letter, dated the 13th of April, 1844, to Gardner:—

I have heard from my son this morning. He is willing to take for his land 950*l.*, the timber included, or less, if the timber be valued. I shall be glad to hear from you as soon as convenient.

On the 23d of April, Sanders wrote to his father:—

MY DEAR FATHER, —Potter has written to offer me 800*l.* for the land at Byfield. Have you heard any thing from the party you wrote to me about? Perhaps if the party applying to you has no connection with Potter he would be induced to give more if he knew that I had received an offer from another party. I received Potter's letter this morning, and am now off to market, so have only time to say all are well.

In the morning of the 24th of April, 1844, an interview took place between Gardner and Sanders's father at the house of the latter, at Daventry, at which the father, on behalf of Sanders, agreed (absolutely, as the witnesses deposed) to sell to Gardner, as the agent of Coates, the three closes of land for 900*l.*; and the timber upon it to be taken at a valuation. Sanders was informed of this contract by the following letter from his father:—

In reply to yours, received this morning, I have to say, that, if you approve of it, I have sold your land at Byfield for 900*l.*; the timber upon it to be taken at a fair valuation, and the purchaser to pay for the conveyance, and you for the title. The purchaser is acquainted with the title, and will pay for the land at Midsummer or Michaelmas next: which you think proper. I have promised to give an answer on Saturday next, if I can learn from you before that time. I hope you will be pleased with what I have done.

The transactions after the 24th of April, 1846, were these: By a letter dated the 24th of April, but bearing the post-mark of the 26th, Sanders stated to Potter that his father had sold the land before the letter to Potter of the 23d of April was written. Sanders, in reply, was informed by Mr. Gery, in a letter of the 28th of April, that Potter insisted upon his contract, and that he (Mr. Gery), thought there was no alternative for Sanders but to submit to perform it. Sanders, in a letter to Mr. Gery, of the 30th of April, acquiesced in this view, and reiterated his request for the immediate payment of 100*l.* in part of the purchase-money. Other communications passed with reference to the performance of the contract and preparation of the conveyance, and on the 7th of May, Potter paid Sanders 100*l.* in part of his purchase-money of 800*l.* On the other hand, Sanders, on the 26th of April, replied to his father's letter of the 24th of April, thus:—

MY DEAR FATHER, — I am much pleased with the bargain you have made for me. I should wish the purchase to be completed at Midsummer. As Aplin will have to make the conveyance, the title is sure to be correct. Who is the purchaser?

On the 27th of April, a memorandum of agreement was drawn up in writing, and signed by Sanders's father, as the agent of Sanders, and Gardner as the agent of Coates, in the terms of the contract already stated,—with the additional provision that, at Midsummer, the purchase was to be completed and possession given to the purchaser.

At the time of the foregoing transactions neither Coates, nor Gardner his agent, had any notice of the contract which Sanders had made with Potter; but Gardner received notice of that contract early in May, and on the 14th of the same month formal notice thereof was given to Coates; and Coates and Sanders were informed that Potter insisted upon his right to have the contract performed.

By indentures, dated the 31st of May and the 1st of June, 1844, Sanders and the mortgagees, by his appointment, conveyed the land to Coates, in consideration of the payment by the latter of the purchase-money mentioned in the memorandum of agreement of the 27th of April.

The bill was filed by Potter against Sanders and Coates; and it prayed that Sanders might be decreed specifically to perform his contract with Potter for sale of the land, and that Coates might be declared to be a trustee for Potter, and that Coates and Sanders might be decreed to convey the premises to Potter; or if it should appear that Coates had no notice of the contract with Potter before the conveyance, then that an account might be taken of what was due to Potter from Sanders for principal and interest on the 100*l.*, and that Sanders might be ordered to pay the same and the costs of the suit to Potter.

Gardner, who was the agent of Coates, stated in his evidence, that on the 17th of April, 1844, he made an offer for the land to Sanders's father, who promised him the refusal for a week, and that he completed the contract on the 24th of April, on which day the week would expire.

At the hearing,

Mr. *Walker* and Mr. *Stinton*, for the plaintiff, cited Daniels *v.* Davison,[1] Farmer *v.* Robinson.[2]

Mr. *Beals*, for the defendant Sanders.

Mr. *Romilly* and Mr. *Fleming*, for the defendant Coates. There is a question whether the contract with Coates was not the prior contract; but the least favorable way of stating his case is to say that the equities are equal; and Coates having the legal estate, the Court will not interfere to dispossess him of it. The bill seeks the specific performance of a contract to which Coates is no party. This is contrary to the course of the Court. Why is Coates to be involved in a suit concerning a transaction with which he had nothing to do? Tasker *v.* Small,[3] Mole *v.* Smith,[4] Robertson *v.* The Great Western Railway Company,[5] Wood *v.* White,[6] Mason *v.* Franklin.[7] To sustain a suit for specific performance there must be mutuality; but here it is clear that Sanders could not maintain such a suit against Potter. How, then, can Potter sustain the suit against Sanders? and if he has not the right against Sanders he has not the right against Coates. Suppose a case in which a vendor had fraudulently contracted to sell the same estate to three different persons successively, and conveyed the estate to the third purchaser. The two first purchasers have their legal remedies upon their several contracts, but neither of them can call upon the third purchaser to transfer to him the legal estate. Suppose, again, a contract with one party who pays his purchase-money, but does not obtain a conveyance, and a second contract fraudulently made with another purchaser, who at the time of his contract has no notice of the first contract, and afterwards acquires the legal estate. The right of the first purchaser is not to a conveyance of the estate to himself as a purchaser, but only to stand as a mortgagee of the estate for the amount of his purchase-money. 5 Bythewood, by Jarman, 3d ed. p. 445, Allen *v.* Anthony,[8] Dawson *v.* Ellis.[9] The circumstance that the contract with Coates was parol only is not material; for a parol contract is a good defence in equity, although a decree for specific performance could not be made upon it. Hyde *v.* Wrench.[10] Here was a clear authority to the father to sell the estate, and a contract for sale made under that authority. The Court will not deprive Coates of the legal interest which he has

[1] 16 Ves. 249; s. c., 17 Ves. 433.
[2] 2 Campb. 339, n.
[3] 3 Myl. & Cr. 63.
[4] Jac. 490.
[5] 10 Sim. 314.
[6] 4 Myl. & Cr. 460.
[7] 1 Y. & C. C. C. 239.
[8] 1 Mer. 282.
[9] 1 J. & W. 524.
[10] 3 Beav. 334.

acquired in pursuance of that contract. Parken *v.* Whitby[1] was also cited, on the effect to be given to Gardner's deposition.

VICE-CHANCELLOR:[2] — After stating the facts which took place before and on the 24th of April, and the subsequent conveyance to Coates, —

The above facts are, I believe, sufficient to raise the question at issue between the parties; for I lay out of the case the argument at the bar founded upon the facts deposed to by Gardner, but not suggested in the pleadings, that the defendant's contract of the 24th of April is to be referred to the 17th of April. The answer is most explicit, that the defendant's contract was on the 24th, and upon that issue is joined. Neither the payment of the 100*l.*, which was made after notice of the defendant's agreement, nor the correspondence and communications which took place between the different parties after the 23d of April, appear to me to affect the question in the cause, except as they clearly show upon whom the costs of this suit ought to fall. On the 27th of April, 1844, the plaintiff received a letter from defendant Sanders, dated the 24th of April, but having the post-office mark of the 26th, — and which cannot by any possibility be correctly dated, in which he says, — not very candidly, — that when his letter of the 23d was written, his father had made the contract with Coates. Sanders was soon afterwards informed by a letter from Mr. Gery, that the plaintiff insisted upon the performance of the contract; and from that time he apparently considered the plaintiff entitled to the benefit of his contract. He desired Gery to proceed with the conveyance, suggested that a formal agreement in writing be prepared to make the matter safe; and on the 7th of May received from the plaintiff 100*l.* on account of his purchase. However, on or soon after the 14th of May, his views were altered, and he appears then to have considered the defendant Coates entitled to a performance of the contract entered into on his behalf. None of these matters, however fertile they may have been as topics for observation upon conduct, appear to me to affect the dry legal questions to which I am bound to confine myself.

The first question is, whether the plaintiff's contract has not priority, in point of time, over the verbal contract made with Coates on the 24th of April. If that question be answered in the affirmative, it will dispose of the whole case. For the property comprised in the contract would cease to belong to the vendor from the moment that contract was concluded; and I am quite clear (in the circumstances which I have detailed) that Coates can derive no advantage from the conveyance of the legal estate, taken after notice of the plaintiff's agreement for purchase, and whilst his own position was unaltered by payment of purchase-money or otherwise, under an agreement which, if the plaintiff's contract had priority, would be void from the beginning.

For the purpose of answering the question, whether the plaintiff's

[1] Turn. & Russ. 366. [2] Sir James Wigram. — ED.

contract had priority, I was at one moment inclined to direct an inquiry (the answer to which I felt certain I might anticipate), at what hour of the 24th of April the letter of the 23d was delivered at the plaintiff's residence in the regular course of post. I cannot doubt that it would be delivered before the verbal contract with Coates was made; and, if so, that would decide the case. But, upon further consideration, I think it unnecessary to direct that inquiry. The delivery of the letter on the 24th was merely the completion of an act by which the vendor had bound himself on the 23d. If the vendor had died on the 23d, after posting the letter of that date, I can scarcely entertain a doubt but that the plaintiff would in this court have been the owner of the estate, as against the heir of the vendor. But without carrying the point further, I think the vendor, when he put into the post-office the letter to the plaintiff of the 23d of April, did an act which, unless it was interrupted in its progress, concluded the contract between himself and the plaintiff. I cannot, in short, doubt but that the letter of the 23d was a revocation of the authority which the vendor had given to his father, to make a contract for him for the sale of the estate. Independently therefore of the consideration, that the contract with Coates of the 24th of April was a verbal contract only, I think the plaintiff is entitled to a decree.

In the preceding observations I have assumed that the agreement made with Coates on the 24th was absolute in the first instance. But from the contemporaneous letter of Sanders, the father, it may be doubted whether the agreement was not conditional; and if that were so, there can be no doubt that Sanders's letter, of the 23d of April, to the plaintiff, was received before Sanders could have assumed to confirm the agreement made by his father.

Mr. *Romilly* asked that the decree might provide for the payment by Sanders of the costs of Coates.

The *Vice-Chancellor* said that Coates was aware of the facts of the case when he took his conveyance. If Sanders had covenanted to indemnify Coates, he did not require the assistance of this Court to obtain his costs. If he had not such an express covenant, the Court would not imply one.

Decree for specific performance of the plaintiff's contract. All necessary parties to convey. Account of the purchase-money remaining due, and of the rents and profits. Costs against both defendants; but, if any part of such costs shall be recovered against Coates, Coates to be at liberty, in the name of the plaintiff, to recover such costs over against Sanders, Coates undertaking to indemnify the plaintiff in respect of the costs of such proceedings as he may take for that purpose.

DUNLOP *v.* HIGGINS.

In the House of Lords, February 21, 22, 24, 1848.

Dunlop and Others, *Appellants*.
Vincent Higgins and Others, *Respondents*.

[*Reported in* 1 *House of Lords Cases*, 381.]

This was an appeal against a decree of the Court of Session, made under the following circumstances: Messrs. Dunlop & Co. were iron masters in Glasgow, and Messrs. Higgins & Co. were iron merchants in Liverpool. Messrs. Higgins had written to Messrs. Dunlop respecting the price of iron, and received the following answer: "Glasgow, 22d January, 1845. We shall be glad to supply you with 2000 tons, pigs, at 65 shillings per ton, net, delivered here." Messrs. Higgins wrote the following reply: "Liverpool, 25th January, 1845. You say 65*s.* net, for 2000 tons pigs. Does this mean for our usual four months' bill? Please give us this information in course of post, as we have to decide with other parties on Wednesday next." On the 28th Messrs. Dunlop wrote, "Our quotation meant 65*s.* net, and not a four-months' bill." This letter was received by Messrs. Higgins on the 30th of January, and on the same day, and by post, but not by the first post of that day, they despatched an answer in these terms: "We will take the 2000 tons pigs you offer us. Your letter crossed ours of yesterday, but we shall be glad to have your answer respecting the additional 1000 tons. In your first letter you omitted to state any terms; hence the delay." This letter was dated "31st January." It was not delivered in Glasgow until 2 o'clock P. M. on the 1st of February, and, on the same day, Messrs. Dunlop sent the following reply: "Glasgow, 1st February, 1845. We have your letter of *yesterday*, but are sorry that we cannot now enter the 2000 tons pig-iron, our offer of the 28th not having been accepted in course." Messrs. Higgins wrote on the 2d February to say that they had erroneously dated their letter on the 31st January, that it was really written and posted on the 30th, in proof of which they referred to the post-mark. They did not, however, explain the delay which had taken place in its delivery. The iron was not furnished to them, and iron having risen very rapidly in the market, the question whether there had been a complete contract between these parties was brought before a court of law. Messrs. Higgins instituted a suit in the Court of Session for damages, as for breach of contract. The defence of Messrs. Dunlop was, that their letter of the 28th, offering the contract, not having been answered in due time, there had been no such acceptance as would convert that offer into a lawful and binding contract; that their letter having been delivered at Liverpool before eight o'clock in the morning of the 30th of January, Messrs. Higgins ought, according to the usual practice of merchants, to have answered it by the first post, which left Liverpool at three o'clock P. M. on that day. A letter so despatched would be due in Glasgow at two o'clock P. M. on the 31st of January; another post left Liverpool for Glasgow every day at one o'clock A. M., and letters to be despatched by that post must be put into the office during the preceding evening, and if any letter had been sent by that post on the morning of the 31st, it must have been delivered in Glasgow in the regular course of post at eight o'clock in the morning of the 1st of February. As no communication from Messrs. Higgins arrived by either of these posts, Messrs. Dunlop contended that they were entitled to treat their offer as not accepted, and that they were not bound to wait until the third post delivered in Glasgow at two o'clock P. M. of Saturday, the 1st of February (at which time Messrs. Higgins' letter did actually arrive), before they entered into other contracts, the taking of which would disable them from performing the contract they had offered to Messrs. Higgins.

The cause came before Lord Ivory, as Lord Ordinary, who directed an issue, which he settled in the following terms:—

"Whether, about the end of January, 1845, Messrs. Higgins purchased from Messrs. Dunlop 2000 tons of pig-iron, at the price of 65*s.* per ton, and whether Messrs. Dunlop wrongfully failed to deliver the same, to the damage, loss, and injury of the pursuers? Damages laid at 6,000*l.*" This issue was tried before the Lord Justice General, when it appeared that the letter of Messrs. Higgins, accepting the offer, was written on the 30th; that it was posted a short time after the closing of the bags for the despatch at three o'clock P. M. on that day, and consequently did not leave Liverpool till the despatch at one o'clock in the morning of the 31st; that, in consequence of the slippery state of the roads, the bag then sent did not arrive at Warrington till after the departure of the down train that ought to have conveyed it, and that this circumstance occasioned it to be delayed beyond the ordinary hour of delivery. The Lord Justice General told the jury "that he adopted the law as duly expounded in the case of Adams *v.* Lindsell,[1] and which is as follows: 'A., by a letter, offers to sell to B. certain specified goods, *receiving an answer by return of post;* the letter being misdirected, the answer notifying the acceptance of the offer arrived two days later than it ought to have done; on the day following that when it would have arrived, if the original letter had been properly directed, A. sold the goods to a third person,' and in which it was held 'that there was a contract binding the parties from the moment the offer was accepted, and that B. was entitled to recover against A. in an action for not completing his contract.'"

[1] 1 Barnewall & Alderson, 681.

The counsel for Messrs. Dunlop tendered the following exceptions: The first exception related to evidence, and alleged "that no evidence to show that the letter, purporting to be dated on the 31st, was really written on the 30th of January, ought to have been admitted." The other exceptions related to the charge, and were as follows: —

2. In so far as his Lordship directed the jury, in point of law, that if Messrs. Higgins posted their acceptance of the offer in due time according to the usage of trade, they are not responsible for any casualties in the post-office establishment.

3. In so far as his Lordship did not direct the jury, in point of law, that, if a merchant makes an offer to a party at a distance by post-letter, requiring to be answered within a certain time, and no answer arrives within such time as it should arrive, if the party had written and posted his letter within the time allowed, the offerer is free, though the answer may have been actually written and posted in due time, if he is not proved to be aware of accidental circumstances preventing the due arrival of the answer.

4. In so far as his Lordship did not direct the jury, in point of law, that, in the case above supposed, if an answer arrives, bearing a date beyond the time limited as above for making answer, and arrives by a mail, and is delivered at a time corresponding to such date, the offerer is entitled to consider himself free to deal with the goods as his own, either to sell or to hold, if he be not in the knowledge that the answer received was truly written of an earlier date, and delayed in its arrival by accident.

5. In so far as his Lordship did not direct the jury, in point of law, that, in case of failure to deliver goods sold at a stipulated price, and immediately deliverable, the true measure of damage is the difference between the stipulated price and the market price, on or about the day the contract is broken, or at or about the time when the purchaser might have supplied himself.

These exceptions were afterwards argued before the judges of the First Division, who pronounced an interlocutor, disallowing the exceptions; and that interlocutor was the subject of the present appeal.

Mr. *Bethell* and Mr. *Anderson*, for the appellants.

The question raised in this case is one of considerable importance, and the decision of it in accordance with the judgment of the court below, will have the effect of rendering the acceptance of contracts a matter of doubt and uncertainty. If the decision of the judges of the Court of Session is right, a contract is complete when the acceptance of the offer to enter into it is posted, although such acceptance may not reach the person who made the offer till long after the time at which, by the usage of trade, he is entitled to expect it. Such a decision, if unreversed, will leave the person making an offer under the necessity of waiting for an indefinite time in order to know whether his offer has been accepted. During all this time he will be restrained from freely dealing with his own property.

The exceptions here ought to have been sustained by the Court. The first of them relates to the evidence offered at the trial. That evidence was improperly admitted. The Court ought not to have received evidence to contradict a written document. When a letter is sent to a party, he has a right to assume that it is properly written, and is entitled to rely on its contents. He is at least entitled to do so as against the writer of the letter. The writer is not at liberty to show those contents to be erroneous: at all events he is not at liberty to do so after the person receiving it has acted upon it, and thus to affect the rights of that party, and to give himself rights to which, if the letter had been correctly written, he would not have been entitled. To admit such evidence is to unsettle all the rules of business, and to prevent commercial men acting with that certainty and confidence which are necessary for the proper conduct of commercial affairs.

[THE LORD CHANCELLOR. When a party sends a letter, actually sent on the 30th, but dated by mistake on the 31st, may he not show that that date has been put in by mistake?]

It might be difficult to maintain the simple negative of that question, but in considering the admissibility of such evidence, all the circumstances of the case must be referred to. In the present case, for instance, as the letter was received on a day after that of its date, and when, therefore, the person receiving it had no reason to suspect that the date was erroneously given, his rights ought not to be affected by a subsequent explanation; and the evidence intended to afford that explanation ought not therefore to have been admitted.

Then as to the second exception: if a letter sent is posted in due time, but is not received in due time, who is to bear the loss consequent upon its non-delivery? Certainly not the person to whom it is sent. The fact that it is sent by the post-office makes no difference in the matter. It is the same as if the letter was sent by a special messenger, in which case it is plain that the person sending the messenger would be responsible for any accident or delay. The appellants are not to be made responsible for the casualties of the post-office, and surely they cannot be made so in a case in which the persons sending an answer to an offer which they had made, totally disregarded the ordinary usages of commercial houses as to the time of sending such answer.

The clear principle, set forth in the third objection, is that which ought to be adopted in all cases of this kind. Where an individual makes an offer by post, stipulating for, or, by the nature of the business, having the right to expect, an answer by return of post, the offer can only endure for a limited time, and the making of it is accompanied by an implied stipulation that the answer shall be sent by return of post. If that implied stipulation is not satisfied, the person making the offer is released from it. When a person seeks to acquire a right, he is bound to act with a degree of strictness, such as may not be required where he is only endeavoring to excuse himself from a liability. The question of reasonableness of notice, which may be admitted in cases of bills of exchange, cannot be introduced in a case where one party seeks to enforce on another the acceptance of a contract. A bill of exchange is already a binding contract; no new right is acquired by notice; it is merely a necessary proceeding to enable the party giving it to enforce a right previously created.

Then as to the [fourth?] exception. In the case of a contract, the acceptance of the offer creates the contract; the acceptance implies that both parties have knowledge of all the circumstances. On principle, it is plain that the acceptance should be immediate, and that if there is a delay in making that acceptance known, the offerer is free. In order to make the contract perfect, there ought to have been a co-existing assent. Countess of Dunmore *v.* Alexander.[1] There, a lady having written to another to engage a servant for her, and then sent a second letter to countermand the first, and the two letters having been delivered to the servant simultaneously, it was held that there was not a complete contract, and that the servant was not entitled to wages. The Court of King's Bench, in Head *v.* Diggon,[2] acted upon the same principle. There, A. and B. being together, B. offered goods to A. at a certain price, and gave A. three days to make up his mind. The Court held that this was not an absolute bargain, and that within the three days B. had a right to retract.

Such are the principles which ought to govern this case. Then as to authority. It is curious enough that this exact question seems never to have arisen. That circumstance is some proof of the clearness of the principle which is applicable to such transactions, for had there been any question as to that principle, — had it been doubtful whether delay might be excused, and whether, in spite of delay, a party guilty of it might not still insist on a contract being complete, cases must have arisen as to the degree of laxity permitted by the law in the acceptance of contracts. None such is to be found. The case of Adams *v.* Lindsell,[3] was the authority adopted by the Lord Justice General in his direction to the jury: but that case does not justify his ruling. [THE LORD CHANCELLOR. If the letter of acceptance is sent in the usual way, is the sender still responsible for its due delivery?] If not, then both parties are free. One cannot be bound while the other is free. Each party takes an equal risk. But supposing delay is to be permitted, to what extent is it to be allowed? May the delay last one, two, or three days, or a week, or a fortnight, or a month? If any delay is to be permitted, the extent of it must be defined. Otherwise, all com-

[1] 9 Shaw & Dunlop, 190. [2] 3 Manning & Ryland, 97.
[3] 1 Barnewall & Alderson, 681.

mercial matters will be in a state of perpetual uncertainty. But, in fact, no delay is allowed. Each party is bound to write by return of post, and each is liable to the consequences of his own letter [not ?] arriving in time. Such appears to be the mercantile usage on the subject. When an offer is made by one merchant to send to another a particular commodity which varies in price, that offer is made subject to the obligation of its being answered by return of post. It is therefore an offer subject to a condition. It is conditional, in point both of time and manner of acceptance. As to time, the offer enures till it can be answered by return of post. If it is made on a condition, then it is clearly not binding till that condition shall be accepted. Here, too, the condition is a condition precedent. Nothing, therefore, can be substituted for it.

[THE LORD CHANCELLOR. Where is this condition imposed ?]

In mercantile usage, founded on law. The legal condition is to return an answer in a particular time. Mercantile usage has fixed that time as the return of post. No decision has ruled, as a point of legal principle, that, if an individual addressed fails in performing this condition, still that the person making the offer is bound. The principle of the Scotch law, as stated in M'Douall's Institutes, is the other way. It is there said,[1] "Conditional obligations, properly so termed, are presently binding and irrevocable, and only the effect is suspended, but sometimes the obligation is only to be contracted upon a condition which affects the very substance of it. Thus an offer has an implied condition of acceptance, whereby alone the consent of the other party accedes and converts the offer into a contract; so that it is not binding, but ambulatory or revocable, till it is accepted, and therefore either revocation by the offerer, or death of either party before acceptance, voids it. The same rule holds in mutual contracts, — the one party subscribing is not bound till the other subscribe likewise." The law of England is in conformity with the principle of the Scotch law.

As the revocation by either party before acceptance makes the offer void, the acceptance of the other side must be notified within a definite period of time; Stair's Institutes.[2] This rule of notification is a condition precedent in the English as well as the Scotch law. This principle was acted on by the Court of King's Bench in the case of Davison *v.* Mure.[3] That was the case of a ship which was captured by the Americans while under convoy. The condition there was that the master should make the best defence, and without it appeared to a court-martial that he had done so, he was not to be allowed to recover. It was held that this condition was a condition precedent. The same doctrine was applied by that Court to the condition in a policy of insurance against fire, that the party should obtain a certificate from the

[1] Bk. 1. tit. 4, p. 98, fol. ed.

[2] Tit. 2, § 8.

[3] 3 Douglas, 28.

rector of his parish, and a certain number of the inhabitants, before entitling himself to payment of his claim for loss; Worsley *v.* Wood.[1] If this is a condition precedent, then it must be exactly performed, and nothing can be substituted for it. In this respect there is a difference between a condition precedent and a condition subsequent. The former must be performed before an estate can vest; while the performance of the latter, which is intended to defeat an existing estate, may be dispensed with. The act of God, the king's enemies, or the impossibility of performance, will furnish an excuse as to a condition subsequent. This is a settled principle of our law, and the case of Brodie *v.* Todd[2] shows that the law of Scotland recognizes the same rule. In that case, Arnot, a merchant of Leith, agreed to purchase from Todd & Co. of Hull, goods which were to be paid for by his acceptance. They put the goods on board a vessel at Hull; enclosed a bill of lading and a draft for the price in a letter, advising Arnot of the shipment, and requesting him to return the draft accepted "in course." This letter was received by Arnot on the morning of the 24th of April, and if answered by him by return of post, the answer might have been received by Todd & Co. on the morning of the 26th. Arnot, however, did not answer it till that day, when he sent back the draft accepted. In the course of the 26th, Todd & Co., not having received the draft as expected, re-landed the goods. Arnot brought an action; and the question was, whether the request to return "in course," meant a return by the earliest post, and constituted a condition precedent. The Lords held that the words meant by return of post, and did constitute a condition precedent, and consequently that no action was maintainable by Arnot, since he had not complied with the condition on which the bargain was made. That case is completely decisive as to what is the doctrine of the Scotch law, and must govern the decision here.

[THE LORD CHANCELLOR. Is it not a question of fact, whether the posting of the letter, in this case, on the 30th of January, was not a compliance with the duty of the party? Here is no distinct stipulation,—it is all matter of inference. The question is, whether putting in the post is not a virtual acceptance, though by the accident of the post it does not arrive. In the case quoted, one whole day was allowed to intervene. But in this case, if putting the letter in the post is a compliance with the condition, there is an end of the question.]

That would be so, if it was a condition subsequent, for then something could be substituted for actual performance. But this is a condition precedent, and must be literally performed.

In considering this question Lord Jeffrey observed, "The party here only says, 'If I do not hear by return of post.' I have yet to learn that the return of post is like the return of the sun to the meridian at a particular time. I do not think that the use of such a phrase

[1] 6 Term Rep. 710. [2] 17 Fac. Col. Dec. 20, May, 1814.

is equivalent to the stipulation of a particular time. I am inclined to hold that the return of post means the actual return of the post. And the *species facti* here was, the letter accepting the offer having been sent in due time to the post-office, that it did [not?] come to hand at the hour at which, according to the usual time required for its transmission, it should have come. But the actual course of *that* post was not till the morning of the 1st February." And the learned Judge justifies his doctrine by referring to the case of the post coming by sea, where a general average time is fixed, but where return of post is not calculated by that average, but by the actual arrival of the post, and then he supposes a universal snow-storm affecting the delivery by land, and argues that if matter of that general notoriety would affect the question, so does any other accident to the post although not so generally known. But surely this is giving an entirely new interpretation to mercantile contracts, and is making accidental circumstances or natural delays, always counted upon, furnish ground for the construction of a delay occasioned by an accident which neither party anticipated. Besides, it is clear on the facts here, that had the letter been put into the early post of the 30th January, this accident would not have befallen it; so that the accidental delay in the post-office was really the consequence of the delay in posting the letter, and was so far attributable to the respondents.

They cannot, therefore, claim any advantage from their acceptance of the contract, which acceptance they did not notify, nor condemn the other parties for non-performance of a contract, the acceptance of which they did not know. It is the acceptance which completes the contract. The agreement is not suspended till the offerer has actually received notice of the acceptance, but only until he might have received notice, had that notice been forwarded at the earliest moment. This is the rule declared in Bell's Principles of the Law of Scotland,[1] and this rule must be applied to, and must govern the decision of the present case.

. . . .[2]

Mr. *Stuart Wortley* and Mr. *Hugh Hill*, for the respondents, were not called on.

THE LORD CHANCELLOR.[3] My Lords, every thing which learning or ingenuity can suggest on the part of the appellants, has undoubtedly been suggested on the part of the learned counsel who have just addressed the House; and if your Lordships concur in my view, that they have failed in making out their case, you will have the satisfaction of knowing that you have come to that conclusion after having had

[1] Page 35, § 78.

[2] The parts omitted relate to a question of damages depending upon the local law of Scotland. — ED.

[3] Lord Cottenham. — ED.

every thing suggested to you that by possibility could be advanced in favor of this appeal.

The case certainly appears to me one which requires great ingenuity on the part of the appellants, because I do not think that, in the facts of the case, there is any thing to warrant the appeal. The contest arises from an order sent from Liverpool to Glasgow, or rather a proposition sent from Glasgow to Liverpool, and accepted by the house at Liverpool. It is unnecessary to go earlier into the history of the case than the letter sent from Liverpool by Higgins, bearing date the 31st of January. A proposition had been made by the Glasgow house of Dunlop, Wilson, & Co., to sell 2000 tons of pig-iron. The answer is of that date of the 31st of January: "Gentlemen, we will take the 2000 tons, pigs, you offer us." Another part of the letter refers to other arrangements; but there is a distinct and positive offer to take the 2000 tons of pigs. To that letter there is annexed a postscript in which they say, "We have accepted your offer unconditionally; but we hope you will accede to our request as to delivery and mode of payment by two months' bill."

That, my Lords, therefore, is an unconditional acceptance, by the letter dated the 31st of January, which was proved to have been put into the post-office at Liverpool on the 30th; but it was not delivered, owing to the state of severe frost at that time, which delayed the mail from reaching Glasgow at the time at which, in the ordinary course, it would have arrived there. The letter having been put in on the 30th of January, it ought to have arrived at Glasgow on the following day, but it did not arrive till the 1st of February.

It appears that between the time of writing the offer and the 1st of February, the parties making the offer had changed their minds; and instead of being willing to sell 2000 tons of pig-iron on the terms proposed, they were anxious to be relieved from that stipulation; and on that day, the 1st of February, they say, "We have yours of yesterday, but are sorry that we cannot enter the 2000 tons of pig iron, our offer of the 28th not having been accepted in course."

Under these circumstances, the parties wishing to buy, and by their letter accepting the offer, instituted proceedings in the Court of Session for damages sustained by the non-performance of the contract. And the first question raised by the first exception, applies not to the summing up of the learned Judge, but to the admission of evidence by him; for connected with that admission of evidence is the first exception. I need hardly say but little on this point, but as it formed part of the proceedings on which the judgment must ultimately be pronounced, I will very shortly call your Lordships' attention to the proposition presented for your decision by that first exception.

My Lords, the exception states, "that the pursuers having admitted that they were bound to answer the defenders' offer of the 28th, by letter written and posted on the 30th, and the only answer received by the defenders being admitted to be dated on the 31st of January, and received in Glasgow by the mail which in due course ought to bring the Liverpool letters of the 31st, but not Liverpool letters of the 30th, it is not competent in a question as to the right of the defenders to withdraw or fall from the offer, to prove that the letter bearing date the 31st of January was written and despatched from Liverpool on the 30th, and prevented by accident from reaching Glasgow in due course, especially as it is not alleged that the defenders were aware (previous to the 3d of February) of any such accident having occurred."

The counsel for the pursuer answered that nothing had been stated, but that the pursuers were bound instantly to answer the defenders' offer of the 28th of January, and that, according to the practice of merchants, it was sufficient if that letter was answered on that day on which it was received.

The Lord Justice General did overrule the objection, and admitted the evidence.

The exception is that the learned Judge was wrong in permitting the pursuer to explain his mistake. The proposition is, that if a man is bound to answer a letter on a particular day, and by mistake puts a date in advance, he is to be bound by his error, whether it produces mischief to the other party or not. It is unnecessary to do more than state this proposition in order to induce you to assent to the view I take of the objection, and to come to the conclusion that the learned Judge was right in allowing the pursuer to go into evidence to show the mistake.

I pass on then to the fourth exception which is connected with this point, and which states that his Lordship did not direct the jury in point of law, that, in the case above supposed, if an answer arrives, bearing a date beyond the time limited as above for making answer, and arrives by a mail, and is delivered at a time corresponding to such date, the offerer is entitled to consider himself free to deal with the goods as his own, either to sell or to hold, if he was not in the knowledge that the answer received was duly written at an earlier date, and delayed in its arrival by accident; that is to say, that if a letter bears a date which, on the face of it, shows that it was written erroneously, nevertheless the party is bound by the date so written on the face of the letter, and you cannot go into the circumstances to explain how it happened that the letter did not arrive in time, but that you are bound to assume that it arrived on the day mentioned, and the party cannot give any evidence in explanation.

My Lords, that falls with the other exception, and the two together go for nothing. I merely state it for the purpose of asking your Lordships to concur in the opinion that I have formed — that the learned

Judge was correct in the mode in which he left the question to the jury, and consequently that on that point the bill of exceptions cannot be supported.

The next exception to be considered is the second, and that raises a more important question, though not one attended with much difficulty. The exception is, that his Lordship did direct the jury in point of law, that if the pursuers posted their acceptance of the offer in due time, according to the usage of trade, they are not responsible for any casualties in the post-office establishment.

Now, there may be some little ambiguity in the construction of that proposition. It proceeds on the assumption that, by the usage of trade, an answer ought to have been returned by the post, and that the 30th was the right day on which that answer ought to have been notified. Then comes the question, whether under those circumstances, that being the usage of trade, the fact of the letter being delayed, not by the act of the party sending it, but by an accident connected with the post, the party so putting the letter in on the right day is to lose the benefit which would have belonged to him if the letter had arrived in due course?

I cannot conceive, if that is the right construction of the direction of the learned Judge, how any doubt can exist on the point. If a party does all that he can do, that is all that is called for. If there is a usage of trade to accept such an offer, and to return an answer to such an offer, and to forward it by means of the post, and if the party accepting the offer puts his letter into the post on the correct day, has he not done every thing he was bound to do? How can he be responsible for that over which he has no control? It is not the same as if the date of the party's acceptance of the offer had been the subject of a special contract: as if the contract had been, "I make you this offer, but you must return me an answer on the 30th, and on the earliest post of that day." The usage of trade would require an answer on the day on which the offer was received, and Messrs. Higgins, therefore, did on the 30th, in proper time, return an answer by the right conveyance — the post-office.

If that was not correct, and if you were to have reference now to any usage constituting the contract between the parties a specific contract, it is quite clear to me that the rule of law would necessarily be that which has obtained by the usage of trade. It has been so decided in cases in England, and none has been cited from Scotland which controverts that proposition; but the cases in England put it beyond all doubt. It is not disputed — it is a very frequent occurrence, that a party having a bill of exchange, which he tenders for payment to the acceptor, and payment is refused, is bound to give the earliest notice to the drawer. That person may be resident many miles distant from him; if he puts a letter into the post at the right time, it has been held quite sufficient; he has done all that he is expected to do as far as he is concerned; he has put the letter into the post, and whether that letter be delivered or not, is a matter quite immaterial, because for accidents happening at the post-office he is not responsible.

My Lords, the case of Stocken *v.* Collin[1] is precisely a case of that nature, where the letter did not arrive in time. In that case Baron Parke says, "It was a question for the jury whether the letter was put into the post-office in time for delivery on the 28th. The post-office mark certainly raised a presumption to the contrary, but it was not conclusive. The jurors have believed the testimony of the witness who posted the letter, and the verdict was therefore right. If a party puts a notice of dishonor into the post, so that in due course of delivery it would arrive in time, he has done all that can be required of him, and it is no fault of his if delay occurs in the delivery." Baron Alderson says, "The party who sends the notice is not answerable for the blunder of the post-office. I remember to have held so in a case on the Norfolk Circuit, where a notice addressed to Norwich had been sent to Warwick. If the doctrine that the post-office is only the agent for the delivery of the notice, was correct, no one could safely avail himself of that mode of transmission. The real question is whether the party has been guilty of laches."

There is also the other case which has been referred to, which declares the same doctrine, the case of Adams *v.* Lindsell.[2] That is a case where the letter went, by the error of the party sending it, to the wrong place, but the party receiving it answered it, so far as he was concerned, in proper time. The party, however, who originally sent the offer not receiving the answer in proper time, thought he was discharged, and entered into a contract and sold the goods to somebody else. The question was, whether the party making the offer had a right to withdraw after notice of acceptance. He sold the goods after the party had written the letter of acceptance, but before it arrived he said, "I withdraw my offer." Therefore he said, "before I received your acceptance of my offer I had withdrawn it." And that raised the question when the acceptance took place, and what constituted the acceptance. It was argued, that "till the plaintiff's answer was actually received, there could be no binding contract between the parties, and that before then the defendants had retracted their offer by selling the wool to other persons." But the Court said, "If that were so, no contract could ever be completed by the post, for if the defendants were not bound by their offer when accepted by the plaintiffs till the answer was received, then the plaintiffs ought not to be bound till after they had received the notification that the defendants had received their answer and assented to it. And so it might go on *ad infinitum*. The defendants must be considered in law as making, during every

[1] 7 Meeson & Welsby, 515. [2] 1 Barnewall & Alderson, 681.

instant of the time their letter was travelling, the same identical offer to the plaintiffs, and then the contract is completed by the acceptance of it by the latter."

Those two cases leave no doubt at all on the subject. Common sense tells us that transactions cannot go on without such a rule, and these cases seem to be the leading cases on the subject, and we have heard no authority cited which in the least degree affects the principle on which they proceed. The law of Scotland appears to be the same as the law of England, for Mr. Bell's Commentary lays down the same rule as existing in Scotland, and nothing has been stated to us in contradiction of his opinion.

Now whether I take that proposition as conclusive upon the objection, or whether I consider it as a question entirely open, whether the putting the letter into the post was, or not, in time to constitute a valid acceptance, it appears to me that the learned Judge was right in the conclusion to which he came, that he was right in the mode in which he left the question to the jury, and that he was not bound to lay down the law in the manner alleged in the bill of exceptions.

The next exception is the third, which says, "In so far as his Lordship did not direct the jury in point of law, that if a merchant makes an offer to a party at a distance, by post letter, requiring to be answered within a certain time, and no answer arrives within such time as it should arrive, if the party had written and posted his letter within the time allowed, the offerer is free, though the answer may have actually been written and posted in due time, if he is not proved to be aware of accidental circumstances preventing the due arrival of the answer."

That, my Lords, raises first of all a proposition that does not arise in this case at all. It assumes a contract that requires an answer within a certain stipulated time, and it assumes (which is already disposed of by what I have said in answer to the second exception) that the putting a letter into the post is not a compliance with the requisition of the offer. But there is no special contract here, and therefore this exception cannot be maintained.

. . . .[1]

I believe that in these remarks I have exhausted the whole of the objections made; and my advice to your Lordships is to affirm the judgment of the Court from which this is appealed.

It was ordered that the interlocutor complained of should be affirmed, with costs.

[1] See *supra*, p. 31, n. 2.—ED.

OFFORD *v.* DAVIES AND ANOTHER.

IN THE COMMON PLEAS, JUNE 2, 1862.

[*Reported in 12 Common Bench Reports, New Series,* 748.]

THIS was an action upon a guaranty. The first count of the declaration stated, that, by a certain instrument in writing signed by the defendants, and addressed and delivered by the defendants to the plaintiff, the defendants undertook, promised, and agreed with the plaintiff in the words and figures following, that is to say: "We, the undersigned, in consideration of your discounting, at our request, bills of exchange for Messrs. Davies & Co., of Newtown, Montgomeryshire, drapers, hereby jointly and severally guarantee *for the space of twelve calendar months* the due payment of all such bills of exchange, to the extent of 600*l.* And we further jointly and severally undertake to make good any loss or expenses you may sustain or incur in consequence of advancing Messrs. Davies & Co. such moneys." Averment, that the plaintiff, relying on the said promise of the defendants, after the making of the said promise, and within the space of twelve calendar months thereafter, did discount divers bills of exchange for the said Messrs. Davies & Co., of Newtown aforesaid, certain of which bills of exchange became due and payable before the commencement of this suit, but were not then or at any other time duly paid, and the said bills respectively were dishonored; and that the plaintiff, after the making of the said promise, and within the said twelve calendar months, advanced to the said Messrs. Davies & Co. divers sums of money on and in respect of the discount of the said last-mentioned bills so dishonored as aforesaid, certain of which moneys were due and owing to the plaintiff before and at the time of the commencement of this suit; and that all things had happened and all times had elapsed necessary, &c.; yet that the defendants broke their said promise, and did not pay to the plaintiff, or to the respective holders for the time being of the said bills of exchange so dishonored as aforesaid, or to any other person entitled to receive the same, the respective sums of money payable by the said bills of exchange; nor did the defendants pay to the plaintiff the said sums of money so advanced by the plaintiff as aforesaid, or any part thereof; whereby the sums payable by the said bills of exchange so dishonored as aforesaid, became lost to the plaintiff, and he became liable to pay and take up certain of the said bills of exchange, and did pay and take up certain of the said bills of exchange, and was forced and obliged to and did expend certain moneys in endeavoring to obtain part of certain of the said bills of exchange, and the plaintiff lost the interest which he might have made of his moneys, if the said bills had been duly paid at maturity.

Fourth plea, to the first count, — so far as the same relates to the sums payable by the defendants in respect of the sums of money payable by the said bills of exchange, and the said sums so advanced, — that, after the making of the said guaranty, and before the plaintiff had discounted such bills of exchange, and before he had advanced such sums of money, the defendants countermanded the said guaranty, and requested the plaintiff not to discount such bills of exchange, and not to advance such moneys.

To this plea the plaintiff demurred; the ground of demurrer stated in the margin being "that the fourth plea offers no defence to that part of the declaration to which it is pleaded, for that a party giving a guaranty [for a definite period] has no power to countermand it without the assent of the person to whom it is given." Joinder.

Prentice (with whom was *Brandt*), in support of the demurrer. A guaranty like this, to secure advances for twelve months, is a contract which cannot be rescinded or countermanded within that time without the assent of the person to whom it is given. [BYLES, J. What consideration have these defendants received?] For any thing disclosed by the plea, the plaintiff might have altered his position in consequence of the guaranty, by having entered into a contract with Davies & Co., of Newtown, to discount their bills for twelve months. In Calvert *v.* Gordon, 1 M. & R. 497, 7 B. & C. 809, 3 M. & R. 124, it was held that the obligor of a bond conditioned for the faithful service of A. whilst in the employ of B., cannot discharge himself by giving notice that after a certain period he will be no longer answerable; nor can the personal representative of the obligor discharge himself by such a notice.[1] Lord Tenterden, in giving judgment in that case, says (3 M. & R. 128): "The only question raised by the defendant's second plea is, whether it is competent to the surety to put an end to his liability by giving a notice which is to take effect from the very day on which it is given. It would be a hardship upon the master if this could be done. It is said that it would be a hardship on the surety if this liability must necessarily continue during the whole time that the principal remains in his service; but, looking at the instrument itself, it would appear that it was the intention of the testator to enter into this unlimited engagement. It was competent to him to stipulate that he should be discharged from all future liability after a specified time, after notice given. This he has not done." Here, the defendants *have* stipulated that their liability shall discontinue at the end of twelve calendar months. What pretence is there for relieving them from that bargain? [BYLES, J. Sup-

[1] And see Gordon *v.* Calvert, 2 Sim. 253, 4 Russ. 581, where an injunction to restrain proceedings at law upon the bond was dissolved.

pose a man gives an open guaranty, with a stipulation that he will not withdraw it, — what is there to bind him to that?] If acted upon by the other party, it is submitted that that *would* be a binding contract. Hassell *v.* Long, 2 M. & Selw. 363, is an authority to the same effect as Calvert *v.* Gordon. In Pothier on Obligations, Part II. c. 6, § 7, art. 2, p. 442, it is said, "When the obligation to which a surety has acceded must from its nature exist a certain time, however long it may be, the surety cannot within that time demand that the principal debtor should discharge him from it; for as he knew, or ought to know, the nature of the obligation to which he acceded, he should have reckoned upon continuing obliged during the whole of the time." Again, Part III. c. 6, art. 4, p. 635: "Regularly, lapse of time does not extinguish obligations: persons who enter into an obligation oblige themselves and their heirs until the obligation is perfectly accomplished. But there may be a valid agreement that an obligation shall only continue to a certain time. For instance, I may become surety for a person upon condition that my undertaking shall not bind me after the expiration of three years."

E. James, Q. C. (with whom was *T. Jones*), contra. The cases upon bonds for guaranteeing the honesty of clerks or servants are inapplicable: there the contract attaches as soon as the clerk or servant enters the service, and it is not separable. This, however, is not a case of contract at all. It is a mere authority to discount, and a promise to indemnify the plaintiff in respect of each bill discounted; and it was perfectly competent to the defendants at any time to withdraw that authority as to future transactions of discount. This is more like the *mandatum pecuniæ credendæ* treated of by Pothier — on Obligations, Part II. c. 6, § 8, art. 1. If so, it is subject to all incidents of a mandate or authority. [WILLES, J. *Mandatum* does not mean a bare authority which may be revoked.] In Story on Agency, the learned author, having stated in § 463 that, "in general, the principal has a right to determine or revoke the authority given to his agent, at his own mere pleasure," proceeds in § 464: "The civil law contained an equally broad doctrine. Si mandavero exigendam pecuniam, deinde voluntatem mutavero, an sit mandati actio vel mihi, vel hæredi meo? Et ait Marcellus, cessare mandati actionem, quia extinctum est mandatum, finitâ voluntate.[1] The same principle has infused itself into the jurisprudence of modern Europe, as, indeed, it could not fail to do, since it is but an application of a maxim founded upon the natural rights of men in all ages, in regard to their own private concerns, where the law has not interfered to prohibit the exercise of them." "But," § 466, "let us suppose that the authority has been in part actually executed by the agent; in that case, the question will arise whether the principal can revoke the authority, either in the

[1] D. 17, 1, 12, 16. — ED.

whole or as to the part which remains unexecuted. The true principle would seem to be, that, if the authority admits of severance, or of being revoked as to the part which is unexecuted, either as to the agent or as to third persons, then and in such case the revocation will be good as to the part unexecuted, but not as to the part already executed." A mutual agreement to rescind can only be necessary where there is a mutual contract. But, in a case like this, where there is no complete contract until something is done by the mandatory, the assent of both parties cannot be required. Suppose Davies & Co., of Newtown, had become notoriously insolvent, would the defendants continue bound by their guaranty, if the plaintiffs, with notice of that fact, chose to go on discounting for them? [WILLIAMS, J. Suppose I guarantee the price of a carriage, to be built for a third party who, before the carriage is finished, and consequently before I am bound to pay for it, becomes insolvent, — may I recall my guaranty?] Not after the coach-builder has commenced the carriage. [ERLE, C. J. Before it ripens into a contract, either party may withdraw, and so put an end to the matter. But the moment the coach-builder has prepared the materials, he would probably be found by the jury to have contracted.] In an American work of considerable authority, Parsons on Contracts, p. 517, it is said, "A promise of guaranty is always revocable, at the pleasure of the guarantor, by sufficient notice, unless it be made to cover some specific transaction which is not yet exhausted, or unless it be founded upon a continuing consideration, the benefit of which the guarantor cannot or does not renounce. If the promise be to guarantee the payment of goods sold up to a certain amount, and, after a part has been delivered, the guaranty is revoked, it would seem that the revocation is good, unless it be founded upon a consideration which has been paid to the guarantor for the whole amount; or unless the seller has, in reliance on the guaranty, not only delivered a part to the buyer, but bound himself by a contract, enforceable at law, to deliver the residue." Brocklebank v. Moore, cor. Abbott, C. J., Guildhall Sittings after Trinity Term, 1823, referred to in 2 Stark. Evid., 3d edit. 510, n., is a direct authority that "a continuing guaranty is countermandable by parol." And the same principle is clearly deducible from Mason v. Pritchard, 12 East, 227. [WILLIAMS, J. That would have been applicable, if this had been a guaranty for 600*l.*, with no mention of the twelve calendar months.] The mention of twelve months would not compel the plaintiff to go on discounting for that period. In Holland v. Teed, 7 Hare, 50, under a guaranty given to a banking-house consisting of several partners, for the repayment of such bills drawn upon them by one of their customers as the bank might honor, and any advances they might make to the same customer, within a certain time, it was held that the guaranty ceased upon the death of one of the partners in the bank before the expiration of the time to which the guaranty was expressed to extend; that bills accepted before the death of the partner, and payable afterwards, were within the guaranty; and that the amount guaranteed could not be increased by any act of the continuing firm and the customer after the death of the partner, although such amount might be diminished by such act. [Byles, J. The case of a change in the firm is now provided for by the Mercantile Law Amendment Act, 19 & 20 Vict. c. 97, § 4. Erle, C. J. What meaning do you attribute to the words "at our request" in this guaranty?] As and when we request. The notice operated a retractation of the request, and any discount which took place after that notice was not a discount at the request of the defendants.

Brandt, in reply. The Court of Exchequer have decided in this term, in a case of Bradbury v. Morgan,[1] that the death of the surety does not operate a revocation of a continuing guaranty. If that be so, it is plain that the guaranty is not a mere *mandatum*, but a contract. In Gordon v. Calvert, 2 Sim. 253, 4 Russ. 581, the executrix of the deceased surety gave notice to Calvert & Co., the obligees, that she would no longer consider herself liable on the bond; but the Vice-Chancellor (Sir L. Shadwell) said, that, "by the original contract, the liability of the surety was to continue as long as Calvert & Co. kept Richard Edwards, or he chose to remain in their service; that after Calvert and Co. had received the plaintiff's letter they never gave her any intimation that they did not consider her as continuing liable under her husband's bond; that their conduct did not operate in any manner upon her; and that therefore the injunction ought to be dissolved." That shows that, in the opinion of that learned Judge, the assent of the three persons concerned and interested in the bargain would be requisite to its dissolution. The fourth plea does not allege that notice of revocation was given before any bills had been discounted by the plaintiffs. It must therefore be assumed that some discounts had taken place. [*T. Jones*. The fact undoubtedly is so.]

Cur. adv. vult.

Erle, C. J., now delivered the judgment of the Court.[2]

[1] Since reported, 31 Law J. Exch. 462; [1 H. & C. 249]. There the guaranty was in the following terms: "Messrs. Bradbury & Co.,—I request you will give credit in the usual way of your business to H. L.; and, in consideration of your doing so, I do hereby engage to guarantee the regular payment of the running balance of his account with you, *until I give you notice to the contrary*, to the extent of 100*l.*": and it was held, that the liability was not determined by the death of the surety, but that his executors were liable to Bradbury & Co. for goods sold and credit given to H. L. subsequently to the surety's death,—on the ground, (contrary to the doctrine laid down in Smith's Mercantile Law, 4th edit. 425, 6th edit. 477, and adopted in Williams on Executors, 5th edit. 1604) that the guaranty was a *contract* to be answerable to the extent stipulated for credit given to the principal debtor, until the creditors should receive a notice to put an end to it.

[2] The case was argued before Erle, C. J., Williams, J., Willes, J., and Byles, J.

The declaration alleged a contract by the defendants, in consideration that the plaintiff would at the request of the defendants discount bills for Davies & Co., not exceeding 600*l.*, the defendants promised to guarantee the repayment of such discounts *for twelve months*, and the discount, and no repayment. The plea was a revocation of the promise before the discount in question; and the demurrer raised the question whether the defendants had a right to revoke the promise. We are of opinion that they had, and that, consequently, the plea is good.

This promise by itself creates no obligation.[1] It is in effect conditioned to be binding if the plaintiff acts upon it, either to the benefit of the defendants or to the detriment of himself. But, until the condition has been at least in part fulfilled, the defendants have the power of revoking it. In the case of a simple guaranty for a proposed loan, the right of revocation before the proposal has been acted on did not appear to be disputed. Then are the rights of the parties affected either by the promise being expressed to be for twelve months, or by the fact that the same discounts had been made before that now in question, and repaid? We think not.

The promise to repay for twelve months creates no additional liability on the guarantor, but, on the contrary, fixes a limit in time beyond which his liability cannot extend. And, with respect to other discounts, which had been repaid, we consider each discount as a separate transaction, creating a liability on the defendant till it is repaid, and after repayment leaving the promise to have the same operation that it had before any discount was made, and no more.

Judgment for the defendants.

[1] "A great number of cases are of contracts not binding on both sides at the time when made, and in which the whole duty to be performed rests with one of the contracting parties. A guarantee falls under that class; when a person says, 'In case you choose to employ this man as your agent for a week, I will be responsible for all such sums as he shall receive during that time, and neglect to pay over to you,' the party indemnified is not therefore bound to employ the person designated by the guarantee; but if he do employ him, then the guarantee attaches and becomes binding on the party who gave it." Parke, B., Kenneway *v.* Treleavan, 5 M. & W. 498, 501. "Suppose I say, if you will furnish goods to a third person I will guarantee the payment: there you are not bound to furnish them; yet if you do furnish them in pursuance of the contract, you may sue me on my guarantee." Patteson, J., Morton *v.* Burn, 7 Ad. & El. 19, 23. And see Morrow *v.* Watts, 18 Penn. St. 118, 120, citing Clark *v.* Russel, 3 Watts, 216. — ED.

RAMSGATE VICTORIA HOTEL COMPANY LIMITED *v.* MONTEFIORE

SAME *v.* GOLDSMID.

IN THE EXCHEQUER, JANUARY 17, 1866.

[*Reported in Law Reports*, 1 *Exchequer*, 109.]

THESE were actions for non-acceptance of shares, and for calls; and cross-actions for recovery of deposit, and for damages for not duly allotting shares, turned into a special case.

The company was completely registered 6th June, 1864. By the second article of association it was provided that the company should continue incorporated, notwithstanding that the whole number of shares in the company might not be subscribed for or issued, and might commence and carry on business when, in the judgment of the board, a sufficient number of shares had been subscribed to justify them in so doing.

The prospectus of the company contained the following words: "Deposit on application 1*l.* per share, and 4*l.* on allotment." And it was further stated that if no allotment were made the deposit would be returned.

The defendant Montefiore, on the 8th of June, 1864, filled up, signed and sent to the directors the printed form of application annexed to the prospectus, which was as follows: —

GENTLEMEN, — Having paid to your bankers the sum of 50*l.*, I hereby request you will allot me fifty shares of 20*l.* each in the Ramsgate Victoria Hotel Company (Limited); and I hereby agree to accept such shares, or any smaller number that may be alloted to me, to pay the deposit and calls thereon, and to sign the articles of association of the company at such times and in such manner as you may appoint.

The defendant had so paid the sum of 50*l.*, and had taken from the bankers the following receipt: —

Received, the 8th of June, 1864, on account of the directors of the Ramsgate Victoria Hotel Company (Limited), the sum of 50*l.*, being the deposit paid in accordance with the terms of the prospectus, on an application for an allotment of fifty shares in the same undertaking.

On the 17th of August the secretary made out and submitted to the directors a list of applicants for shares up to that time, in which appeared the name of the defendant for fifty shares. The list was headed: "List of subscribers, August 17, 1864."

On the 2d of November the secretary again submitted a list of subscribers to the directors, but they did not deem it advisable to proceed to an immediate allotment, and entered a minute to that effect. On the 8th of November the defendant, having received no communication from the company, withdrew his application.

On the 23d of November the secretary prepared another list of subscribers, including the defendant's name. The directors made the first call, and by their direction the secretary wrote the following letter to the defendant: —

SIR, — I am instructed by the directors to acquaint you that, in compliance with your application, they have allotted to you fifty shares in this company, and have entered your name in the register of shareholders for the same; and I have to request that you will pay the balance of the first call, as noted below, on or before the 15th December, to the London and County Bank, 21 Lombard Street, E. C.

The defendant having refused to accept the shares or pay the call, the company brought the present action against him.

It was contended by the company that the last-mentioned list and those previously mentioned, or one of them, constituted a sufficient register of shares within the Companies' Act, 1862.

The directors had entered into an agreement for the purchase of the site of the hotel, paid the deposit, and commenced operations.

The facts with respect to Goldsmid were the same, except that he had never withdrawn his application, nor given any notice of his intention to do so.

Mellish, Q. C. (*Digby* with him), for the company, contended that, although in ordinary cases the assent of both parties, mutually communicated, was necessary to form a contract, yet on the authority of *Ex parte* Bloxam [1] and *Ex parte* Cookney [2] shares might be completely allotted without any communication to the applicant, or acceptance by him; that the facts above stated showed an allotment made on the 17th of August; but that, if not, the allotment in November was, considering the nature of the contract, made within a reasonable time, and, if so made, the letter of withdrawal was inoperative.

M. Chambers, Q. C. (*Cohen* with him), for the defendants, were not called on.

THE COURT (POLLOCK, C. B., MARTIN, CHANNELL, PIGOTT, BB.), observed that, in both cases cited, the question was as to the liability of an applicant for shares as a contributory, and they referred to the judgment of Turner, L. J., in *Ex parte* Bloxam,[3] as explaining the *ratio decidendi* in that case; they held that there was no allotment till November 23, that the allotment must be made within reasonable time, and that the interval from June to November was not reasonable, and therefore gave *Judgment for both the defendants.*

[1] 33 L. J. (Ch.) 519, 574.
[2] 3 De G. & J. 170; 28 L. J. (Ch.) 12.
[3] 33 L. J. (Ch.) 575, 576.

IN RE NATIONAL SAVINGS BANK ASSOCIATION.

HEBB'S CASE.

IN CHANCERY, MAY 1, 1867.

[*Reported in Law Reports*, 4 *Equity*, 9.]

THIS was an application by Henry Kirke Hebb, that his name might be removed from the list of contributories of the National Savings Bank Association, a company formed under the Joint Stock Companies' Act, 1856, and now being wound up under the Companies' Act, 1862.

On the 28th of August, 1857, Hebb signed and gave to the agent of the company at Lincoln an application for ten shares in a form provided by the company, and at the same time paid to the agent a deposit of 5*s*. per share, for which the agent gave him a receipt, with a memorandum that a duly authorized receipt would be forwarded from the head office within eight days.

On the 4th of September, 1857, the directors allotted ten shares to Hebb, and entered his name in the allotment book, and on the same day sent to their agent at Lincoln the letter of allotment with a receipt for the deposit signed by two directors, but the agent did not deliver the letter and receipt to Hebb until the 9th of September. In the mean time, on the 8th of September, Hebb wrote a letter to the directors, withdrawing his application, and requesting the return of the deposit.

On the 26th of August, 1858, Hebb having insisted upon repudiating the allotment and threatened to sue the company for the deposit, the directors paid him the deposit. The allotment was not formally cancelled, and Hebb's name remained on the register of shareholders, but he had no further communication from the company until June, 1866, when the company was ordered to be wound up.

Mr. *De Gex*, Q. C., for the applicant.

First. The applicant never became a shareholder within the meaning of the Joint Stock Companies' Act, 1856, § 19, inasmuch as he never accepted any shares, having withdrawn his application before its acceptance by the directors was communicated to him. A contract is not binding until the party who has made the proposal has received from the other party notice that the latter has accepted it. Routledge *v.* Grant.[1] So long as the letter of allotment remained in the hands of their agent the company might have cancelled the allotment, and the applicant could not have compelled them to give him the shares, and, on the other hand, he was entitled to withdraw his application.

[1] 4 Bing. 653.

[Mr. *Roxburgh*, Q. C., *amicus curiæ*. In Pellatt's Case,[1] although there was no decision upon the point, the Lords Justices expressed an opinion that notice of allotment was necessary to complete the contract, and that in Bloxam's Case[2] the decision must have been founded on the assumption that Bloxam knew of the allotment, though he had no formal notice.]

Secondly. If there was a binding contract, it was annulled when the deposit was returned, and it has been so treated by both parties ever since. It was competent to the company to annul it, and the directors could exercise this power on behalf of the company. *Ex parte* Beresford;[3] *Ex parte* Miles.[4] Where there is a *bonâ fide* dispute as to the validity of a contract to take shares, the directors may compromise it, or release the alleged shareholder from the contract. Lord Belhaven's Case.[5] And even if the directors had no such power, the consent of the shareholders would be presumed after the lapse of so many years. Brotherhood's Case.[6]

Mr. *Baggallay*, Q. C., and Mr. *J. Napier Higgins*, for the official liquidator.

First. The contract was complete as soon as the shares were allotted. The directors could not, either as against the applicant, or as against the other shareholders, have recalled the allotment, whether or not it had been notified to the applicant, and the applicant might at any time after the 4th of September, 1857, have enforced specific performance. It has never been decided that notice of acceptance is necessary to complete a contract. In Routledge *v.* Grant[7] there was no acceptance of the offer; in *Ex parte* Miles,[8] before any allotment was made both parties agreed to vary the contract; in Pellatt's Case[9] there was no decision on this point. In Dunlop *v.* Higgins[10] it was held that a contract was complete as soon as a letter was posted accepting the offer. [They also referred to Chitty on Contracts.][11]

Secondly. If the contract was binding, the applicant, having become a shareholder, could only be released by the consent of every shareholder. Spackman's Case;[12] Stanhope's Case.[13] In Lord Belhaven's Case[14] the deed of settlement expressly empowered the directors to compromise suits, and Lord Belhaven paid a sum of money to be released from the alleged contract; here there was no such power, and in fact there was no compromise.

Lord ROMILLY, M. R. I think that Mr. Hebb is not a contributory of this company. The mere writing of a line in a book is not in my

1 Law Rep. 2 Ch. 527.
2 33 L. J. (Ch.) 519, 574.
3 2 Mac. & G. 197.
4 34 L. J. (Ch.) 123.
5 3 D. J. & S. 41.
6 31 Beav. 365; on appeal, 8 Jur. (N. S.) 926.
7 4 Bing. 653.
8 34 L. J. (Ch.) 123.
9 Law Rep. 2 Ch. 527.
10 1 H. L. C. 381.
11 Pages 9 *et seq.*, (5th edit.).
12 11 Jur. (N. S.) 207.
13 Law Rep. 1 Ch. 161.
14 3 D. J. & S. 41.

opinion an irrevocable act; and if a person applies for shares in a company, and the directors write down his name in the allotment book, they may at any time before the allotment has been communicated to the allottee alter or cancel the allotment; if it were not so, a mere accident might irrevocably bind the company.

These applications for and allotments of shares must be treated upon the same principles as ordinary contracts between individuals. If A. writes to B. a letter offering to buy land of B. for a certain sum of money, and B. accepts the offer, and sends his servant with a letter containing his acceptance, I apprehend that until A. receives the letter, A. may withdraw his offer, and B. may stop his servant on the road and alter the terms of his acceptance, or withdraw it altogether; he is not bound by communicating the acceptance to his own agent. Dunlop *v.* Higgins[1] decides that the posting of a letter accepting an offer constitutes a binding contract, but the reason of that is, that the post-office is the common agent of both parties. In the present case, if Mr. Hebb had authorized the agent of the company to accept the allotment on his behalf there would have been a binding contract, but he gave no such authority, and, as he had withdrawn his original offer before he received the letter of the directors, the position of the parties was changed, and that letter became an offer which required the acceptance of Mr. Hebb to constitute a binding contract.

In Martin *v.* Mitchell[2] Sir T. Plumer says, "When one party, having entered into a contract that has not been signed by the other, afterwards repents, and refuses to proceed in it, I should have felt great difficulty in saying that he had not a *locus pœnitentiæ*, and was not at liberty to recede until the other had signed, or in some manner made it binding upon himself. How can the contract be complete before it is mutual? And can it be complete as to the one, and not as to the other?" I am of opinion that an offer does not bind the person who makes it until it has been accepted, and its acceptance has been communicated to him or his agent. Consequently, in my opinion Mr. Hebb never became a shareholder; but if he had once become a shareholder, I should have felt a difficulty in holding that he had been released from that position by the subsequent return of the deposit. His name must be removed from the list of contributories, and both he and the official liquidator must have their costs out of the estate.

[1] 1 H. L. C. 381.

[2] 2 Jac. & W. 413, 428.

ELIASON *ET AL.* *v.* HENSHAW.

SUPREME COURT OF THE UNITED STATES, FEB. 17, 20, 1819.

[*Reported in 4 Wheaton*, 225, 4 *Curtis*, 382.]

ERROR to the Circuit Court for the District of Columbia.

Jones and *Key*, for the plaintiff in error.

Swann, for the defendant in error.

WASHINGTON, J., delivered the opinion of the Court.

This is an action, brought by the defendant in error, to recover damages for the non-performance of an agreement, alleged to have been entered into by the plaintiffs in error, for the purchase of a quantity of flour at a stipulated price. The evidence of this contract, given in the court below, is stated in a bill of exceptions, and is to the following effect: A letter from the plaintiffs to the defendant, dated the 10th of February, 1813, in which they say: "Captain Conn informs us that you have a quantity of flour to dispose of. We are in the practice of purchasing flour at all times, in Georgetown and will be glad to serve you, either in receiving your flour in store when the markets are dull, and disposing of it when the markets will answer to advantage, or we will purchase at market price when delivered; if you are disposed to engage two or three hundred barrels at present, we will give you $9.50 per barrel, deliverable the first water in Georgetown, or any service we can. If you should want an advance, please write us by mail, and will send you part of the money in advance." In a postscript they add: "Please write by return of wagon whether you accept our offer." This letter was sent from the house at which the writer then was, about two miles from Harper's Ferry, to the defendant at his mill, at Mill Creek, distant about twenty miles from Harper's Ferry, by a wagoner then employed by the defendant to haul flour from his mill to Harper's Ferry, and then about to return home with his wagon. He delivered the letter to the defendant on the 14th of the same month, to which an answer, dated the succeeding day, was written by the defendant, addressed to the plaintiffs at Georgetown, and despatched by a mail which left Mill Creek on the 19th, being the first regular mail from that place to Georgetown. In this letter the writer says: "Your favor of the 10th instant was handed me by Mr. Chenoweth last evening. I take the earliest opportunity to answer it by post. Your proposal to engage 300 barrels of flour, delivered in Georgetown by the first water, at $9.50 per barrel, I accept, and shall send on the flour by the first boats that pass down from where my flour is stored on the river; as to any advance, will be unnecessary,—payment on delivery is all that is required."

On the 25th of the same month, the plaintiffs addressed to the defendant an answer to the above, dated at Georgetown, in which they acknowledge the receipt of it, and add: "Not having heard from you before, had quite given over the expectation of getting your flour, more particularly as we requested an answer by return of wagon the next day, and as we did not get it, had bought all we wanted."

The wagoner, by whom the plaintiffs' first letter was sent, informed them, when he received it, that he should not probably return to Harper's Ferry, and he did not in fact return in the defendant's employ. The flour was sent down to Georgetown some time in March, and the delivery of it to the plaintiffs was regularly tendered and refused.

Upon this evidence, the defendants in the Court below, the plaintiffs in error, moved that Court to instruct the jury, that, if they believed the said evidence to be true as stated, the plaintiff in this action was not entitled to recover the amount of the price of the 300 barrels of flour, at the rate of $9.50 per barrel. The Court being divided in opinion, the instruction prayed for was not given.

The question is, whether the Court below ought to have given the instruction to the jury, as the same was prayed for. If they ought, the judgment, which was in favor of the plaintiff in that court, must be reversed.

It is an undeniable principle of the law of contracts, that an offer of a bargain by one person to another imposes no obligation upon the former, until it is accepted by the latter according to the terms in which the offer was made. Any qualification of or departure from those terms invalidates the offer, unless the same be agreed to by the person who made it. Until the terms of the agreement have received the assent of both parties, the negotiation is open, and imposes no obligation upon either.

In this case, the plaintiffs in error offered to purchase from the defendant two or three hundred barrels of flour, to be delivered at Georgetown by the first water, and to pay for the same $9.50 per barrel. To the letter containing this offer they required an answer by the return of the wagon by which the letter was despatched. This wagon was at that time in the service of the defendant, and employed by him in hauling flour from his mill to Harper's Ferry, near to which place the plaintiffs then were. The meaning of the writers was obvious. They could easily calculate by the usual length of time which was employed by this wagon in travelling from Harper's Ferry to Mill Creek, and back again with a load of flour, about what time they should receive the desired answer; and, therefore, it was entirely unimportant whether it was sent by that or another wagon, or in any other manner, provided it was sent to Harper's Ferry, and was not delayed beyond the time which was ordinarily employed by wagons engaged in hauling flour from the defendant's mill to Harper's Ferry. Whatever uncertainty there might have been as to the time when the answer would be received, there was none as to the place to which it was to be sent; this was distinctly indicated by the mode pointed out for the conveyance of the answer. The place, therefore, to which the answer was to be sent constituted an essential part of the plaintiffs' offer.

It appears, however, from the bill of exceptions, that no answer to this letter was at any time sent to the plaintiffs at Harper's Ferry. Their offer, it is true, was accepted by the terms of a letter addressed Georgetown, and received by the plaintiffs at that place; but an acceptance communicated at a place different from that pointed out by the plaintiffs, and forming a part of their proposal, imposed no obligation binding upon them, unless they had acquiesced in it, which they declined doing.

It is no argument, that an answer was received at Georgetown; the plaintiffs in error had a right to dictate the terms upon which they would purchase the flour; and, unless they were complied with, they were not bound by them. All their arrangements may have been made with a view to the circumstance of place, and they were the only judges of its importance. There was, therefore, no contract concluded between these parties; and the Court ought, therefore, to have given the instruction to the jury which was asked for.

Judgment reversed. Cause remanded, with directions to award a *venire facias de novo.*

M'CULLOCH *v.* THE EAGLE INSURANCE COMPANY.

SUPREME JUDICIAL COURT OF MASSACHUSETTS, OCT. TERM, 1822.

[*Reported in* 1 *Pickering,* 278.]

THIS action, which was assumpsit, came before the Court upon a case stated. The material facts were as follows. On the 29th of December, 1820, the plaintiff, who lived at Kennebunk, in Maine, wrote to the defendants requesting to know on what terms they would insure $2500 on his brig Hesper and cargo from Martinico to the United States. The defendants, on the 1st of January, 1821, sent an answer, saying they would take the risk at two and a half per cent. This letter was received by the plaintiff on the 3d of January, on which day he wrote a reply, requesting the defendants to fill a policy on the terms proposed by them. The defendants on the 2d of January wrote again to the plaintiff, declining to take the risk, but the plaintiff had sent his letter of the 3d before he received the last letter of the defendants. All the letters were sent by mail, and were duly received by the parties respectively. The vessel was afterwards lost on the voyage.

The only question in the cause was, whether the correspondence of the parties constituted a contract by which the defendants were bound.

Prescott, for the plaintiff. It is important to have a contract for insurance take effect immediately. When the terms are agreed on, and a minute of them is made on the books of an insurance company, they consider both parties holden, in case a loss or arrival should happen before the policy is made out. The letter of the 1st of January was an engagement which was binding on the defendants until the plaintiff should express his refusal to accept their offer. It resembles a *pollicitation* in the civil law, which from the first is obligatory on the party making it, and, upon the assent of the person to whom it is made, becomes binding on both parties. The letter of the 3d of January was an assent on the part of the plaintiff, which was not defeated by the defendants' letter of the 2d. If this letter of the 2d had reached the plaintiff before his letter of the 3d had been written and put into the post-office, it might have been a revocation of the defendants' offer. It would resemble a stopping *in transitu*. If the defendants had carried their first letter to the plaintiff, and he had told them to fill a policy, the contract would have been complete. So if they had employed an agent at Kennebunk for that purpose, and the plaintiff had said the same thing to the agent. The putting the plaintiff's letter of the 3d into the post-office was a delivery to the defendants. [WILDE, J. If so, why was not the putting of the defendants' letter of the 2d into the post-office a delivery to the plaintiff?[1]] The countermand could be

[1] "In all engagements *inter absentes*, when the negotiations are carried on by letters or messages, an offer by one party, until it is made known to the other, is but an intention not expressed, *propositum in mente retentum:* If the messenger or letter can be overtaken before it arrives at its destination it may be revoked; but if the revocation does not arrive until after the offer is received *and accepted*, and especially not until it has been acted upon, then it is too late. For the revocation is but a simple act of the will, a *propositum*, not *res gesta*, an act done, until after it is known, and of course can have no more effect than an intention not expressed, but confined within the breast of the party. It is a remark of one of the most profound jurists of the last age, that an act of the will not known is in jurisprudence as if it did not exist. *Une volonté qui n'est pas connue est en jurisprudence comme si elle n'existait pas.* 6 Toull. *Droit Civil*, No. 29. . . . At the same time it is freely admitted that this is a question of general jurisprudence of no little intricacy, and that it is not easy to determine by any universal and inflexible rule when engagements entered into by letters or messengers, between persons residing at a distance from each other, become irrevocably binding on both parties. The question was pretty fully considered by the Court of King's Bench, in the case of Adams *v.* Lindsell, 1 Barn. & Ald. 681, and the decision was in conformity with the principle that I have adopted. But I infer from the reasoning

of no avail until it was received. It was not necessary that the defendants should have immediate notice of the plaintiff's assent. Their promise was binding or not, as the plaintiff should please. After the letter of the 3d was put into the post-office, the defendants would have had a remedy for the premium. Suppose that a merchant in Baltimore writes to one here, offering to sell him bank-shares at a certain price, and the merchant here immediately answers that he will take them: this is a contract as soon as the answer is put into the post-office; and if the Baltimore merchant, the next day after sending his first letter, should write that stocks had risen, and decline selling, it would not avail him.

Saltonstall, for the defendants. The letter of the 29th of December was merely an inquiry. It was nothing like a proposition. No answer to it would have made a contract. The defendants made an offer on the 1st of January, which was retracted on the 2d before it was accepted. Both parties assented to it at different times, but never together; so that there was never a mutual assent. When was the contract made? Not before the 3d, and at that time the offer was retracted. Eliason *v.* Henshaw, 4 Wheat. 228. One party is not bound until the other has had a reasonable time to give his assent. Both should be bound, or both have leave to retract. Cooke *v.* Oxley, 3 D. & E. 653, is a strong case to this effect. There is no case where one party is bound and the other not, except it be so expressed in the terms of the contract; as in the sale of a horse, with liberty to the purchaser to return it if he is not satisfied with it. When was the plaintiff bound? When he put his letter into the post-office? If he could have procured insurance to be made at Kennebunk, might he not have stopped the letter? It was not sufficient that an assent was in the mind of the plaintiff; it should have been made known to the other party. The case supposed respecting bank-shares is this same case.

Prescott, in reply. Suppose an agent of the defendants had carried the letter of the 1st of January, and had delivered it on the 3d, and

of Best, C. J., in the case of Routledge *v.* Grant, 4 Bing. 653, that this decision was not entirely satisfactory to the Court of Common Pleas, or at least it receives but a qualified approval. The same general question was presented to the Supreme Court of Massachusetts, in M'Culloch *v.* The Eagle Ins. Co., 1 Pick. 278, and to the Court of Errors in New York, in Mactier *v.* Frith, 6 Wend. 103, and these courts came to opposite conclusions. It has been found not free from difficulties by the civilians, and perhaps it will not be found an easy task to reconcile all their opinions. The subject has been examined by Pothier, *Contrat de Vente*, No. 32; by Toullier, *Droit Civil*, Vol. 6, No. 30, 31, and notes; Vol. 7, No. 321, and notes; and it was discussed by Merlin in a very elaborate argument before the Court of Cassation, with his usual logical acuteness and copiousness of learning. *Répertoire de Jurisprudence, Vente*, § 1, art. 3, No. 11, *bis*. To the general rule that has been stated there is one well-established exception. If the party who makes the offer dies or becomes insane before it is received and accepted, the offer is then a nullity, though accepted before the death is known." Ware, J., The Palo Alto, Daveis, 343, 357. Compare *supra*, p. 13, n. 2. — ED.

the plaintiff had told him that he accepted the offer. The letter of the 2d would have been on the way as now, but there would have been a good contract. In the case supposed of procuring insurance at Kennebunk, the plaintiff could not have stopped his letter after it was put into the post-office. If the defendants could prove his saying that he assented, it would have given them a right of action against him. The letter was merely notice of his assent.

PARKER, C. J., delivered the opinion of the Court. This action is brought to recover a sum alleged to have been insured by the defendants on the brig Hesper, belonging to the plaintiff, on a voyage from Martinico to her port of discharge, and another sum on her cargo. The usual evidence of such contract, a policy, never having been made, the only question submitted is, whether there was an agreement to insure; every thing else necessary to entitle the plaintiff to recover being agreed by the parties. And it is certain that, if a contract was made, the mere want of a policy will not prevent the plaintiff from recovering.

We are to inquire then, whether the correspondence between the parties, which is submitted to us, does constitute a contract binding upon both parties; if it does not, whatever might be the expectations of either, it is only an attempt to make a contract, which has failed. The letter from the plaintiff, of the 29th of December, contained an inquiry only, as to the rate of premium at which the insurance might be done in the defendants' office, and the plaintiff was entirely at liberty to accept or refuse the terms which were proposed in answer; even if he had made no reply to the defendants' letter, there would have been neither a breach of contract nor of civility. This answer was written on the 1st of January, and would reach the post-office in Kennebunk, the place of the plaintiff's residence, on the 3d. It was replied to on the day of the arrival by an acceptance of the terms, and a direction to make out the policy and deliver it to the plaintiff's agent in Boston, who was authorized to give a promissory note for the premium in common form. But on the 2d of January, before the defendants' letter to the plaintiff could have been received, another letter was written by the defendants, retracting the offer made in the former letter, and signifying a determination not to insure upon that vessel upon any terms. These letters crossed each other upon the road. It is contended by the plaintiff, that the bargain was complete at the moment he wrote and put into the mail his letter signifying his acceptance of the terms offered; by the defendants, that the treaty was open until they should have received that letter, and that in the mean time they had a right to withdraw their offer. We adopt the latter opinion as the most reasonable. The offer did not bind the plaintiff until it was accepted; and it could not be accepted, to the knowledge of the defendants, until the letter announcing the acceptance was received, or at most until the regular time for its arrival by mail had elapsed. Had the vessel arrived in safety at Kennebunk on the 2d or on the morning of the 3d, the plaintiff would not have accepted the offer, and was not bound to accept; so that the defendants would not have been entitled to any premium, and both must be bound in order to make the contract binding upon either, unless time is given by one to the other, in which case perhaps he may be bound, although the other is not; at least we should think this reasonable in mercantile contracts, though it was decided otherwise in the case of Cooke *v.* Oxley, 3 D. & E. 653. In that case the declaration stated, that the defendant proposed to the plaintiff to sell him tobacco at a certain price, and at the request of the plaintiff gave him until four o'clock P. M. to consent or disagree to the proposal. The plaintiff averred, that he did agree to purchase, and gave notice thereof to the defendant before four o'clock; that he offered to pay the price, and requested the defendant to deliver the tobacco, which he refused. The court, without hearing the counsel for the defendant, said that it was an engagement all on one side, and was therefore *nudum pactum;* and Buller, J., said there was neither damage to the plaintiff, nor advantage to the defendant, at the time when the contract was first made. The judgment was affirmed in the Exchequer Chamber. This was treated by the plaintiff's counsel as an actual sale upon condition, to avoid the Statute of Frauds; so that the real question in that case was, whether there was a bargain in fact amounting to a sale, as the question here is, whether there was an insurance in fact, the usual evidence of which only was left unfinished; and it is as necessary that the obligation should be mutual in this case as in that. See also Payne *v.* Cave, 3 D. & E. 148. It is suggested that the putting the letter into the mail was a completion of the bargain; but if the vessel had arrived, and the plaintiff had recalled his letter, or if he had sent on an express to announce his refusal to accept before the letter arrived, we think he would not have been held to pay the premium.

No authority has been cited on the side of the plaintiff to support his case, and we cannot perceive upon general principles any ground upon which he can recover. There seems to have been *locus pœnitentiæ* for both parties, no change of circumstances having occurred, nor any information being received, until the loss of the vessel was known, which was nearly three months after the correspondence ceased between the parties; during all which time the plaintiff might have got insured elsewhere if the risk was a fair one. Had the vessel arrived after the defendants' letter was received, and before it was answered, there can be no doubt the plaintiff might have declined entering into the bargain, because he then had made no contract; and so long as it continued open for the plaintiff, it must have been open for the defendants, and their revocation was made before the plaintiff had opportunity to accept.

It was suggested in the argument that the correspondence between these parties formed what is called in the civil law a *pollicitation*, a sort of contract which arises from a promise made by one party only, without any consent or acceptance by the other; but this is a peculiar kind of obligation, which exists only from an individual towards a body politic or government. Heinecc. sec. Ord. Pandect. Part 7, §§ 334, 335. In a note to the first of these sections the author says, "For although promises made otherwise always require the consent and acceptance of the other party, yet here" (that is, in promises made to the State) "the law itself accepts the promise for the State." *Plaintiff nonsuit.*[1]

MACTIER'S ADMINISTRATORS, *Appellants*, and FRITH, *Respondent*.

NEW YORK COURT OF ERRORS, DECEMBER, 1830.

[*Reported in* 6 *Wendell*, 103.]

APPEAL from Chancery. At New York, in the autumn of 1822, the respondent and Henry Mactier, the intestate, agreed to embark in a

[1] Since the above case was decided, the case of Adams v. Lindsell, 1 B. & A. 681, has been seen, which bears strongly upon this case, and might possibly, if it had been referred to in the argument, have occasioned a delay of judgment for farther consideration; and yet perhaps there is a material difference in the subject-matter of the two cases, of sufficient importance to warrant a different judgment. The case referred to was on a contract which was held to amount to a sale of goods; nothing more was necessary to complete it between the parties, than for the one to agree to sell, and the other to buy; there was no contingency, on the happening of which either could be released; and it was held, that as one offered to sell on certain terms, if he received an answer in due course of mail, and the other agreed to take upon those terms, the writing of the letter by the latter and putting it into the first mail perfected the bargain, so that there was nothing left to be done but a delivery of the goods purchased, which was not essential to complete the sale between the two; and the Court disregarded the case of Cooke v. Oxley, or thought it did not apply, stress being laid upon it by the counsel for the defendant. It was thought probably that the bargain being left open for one of the parties until four o'clock P. M., made the case of Cooke v. Oxley a different one in principle from that under consideration. And the case above reported differs from the case in B. & A., inasmuch as there was not in the latter any notice of a revocation of the offer to sell.

But a more material difference perhaps is, that a treaty respecting insurance is necessarily subject to contingencies while it is forming. An arrival of the vessel before the plaintiff wrote his letter of the 3d would certainly have put an end to it; and perhaps afterwards, if, before the defendants could have received any acceptance of their offer, notice had been given by the plaintiff that he did not choose to proceed in the contract. Whether it would be so, if intelligence of a loss had arrived between the offer of the defendants to insure, and the notice of acceptance by the plaintiff received, *quære*. Possibly so essential a change of circumstances, added to the certainty that the plaintiff could get no other insurance, would give him a claim upon the defendants. — *Reporter*.

commercial adventure, in which they were to be jointly and equally interested. Frith was to direct a shipment of 200 pipes of brandy from France to New York, to be consigned to Mactier, who was to ship to the respondent at Jacmel, in St. Domingo, provisions to the amount of the invoice cost of the brandy, and the respondent was to place the shippers of the brandy in funds by shipments of coffee to France, in French vessels, and the parties were to share equally in the result of the speculation all around.

In pursuance of this arrangement, Frith, on the 5th September, 1822, wrote Firebrace, Davidson, & Co., a mercantile house at Havre, to ship 200 pipes of brandy to New York to the consignment of Mactier. On the 24th December, Frith, who had returned to Jacmel, where he did business as a merchant, wrote a letter to Mactier on a variety of subjects, in which was contained a paragraph in these words: "I also have the pleasure of handing you copies of Messrs. Firebrace, Davidson & Co.'s letters regarding the brandy order. By-the-by, as your brother, before I left New York, declined taking the interest I offered him in this speculation, and wishing to confine myself in business as much as possible, so as to bring my concerns to a certain focus, *I would propose to you to take the adventure solely to your own account*, holding the value to cover the transaction to my account in New York." On the 17th January, 1823, Mactier wrote to Frith, acknowledging the receipt of his letter of the 24th ult.; thanks him for sending the copy of Firebrace, Davidson & Co.'s letter on the subject of the brandy order; says that he has received a letter from them, informing that the brandy would be shipped and leave Bordeaux about the 1st of December then past; and adds, "This has been from the first a favorite speculation with me, and am pleased to say it still promises a favorable result; but to render it complete, I am desirous the speculation should go forward in the way first proposed, thereby making it a treble operation. As you have, however, expressed a wish that I should take the adventure to my own account, *I shall delay coming to any determination till I again hear from you.* The prospect of war between France and Spain may defeat the object of this speculation, as far as relates to the shipment of provisions hence to Hayti, to be invested in coffee for France, *in which case I will at once decide to take the adventure to my own account.* Our London accounts, down to the 5th of December, speak confidently of a war between France and Spain,—a measure which, if carried into effect, would operate to *your disadvantage.*" Also, "The next arrival from Europe will probably decide the question of peace or war, and I will lose no time in communicating the same to you;" and also, "Let what will happen, I trust you will in no way be a sufferer." On the 7th March, 1823, Frith wrote Mactier, making no other allusion to the last letter of Mactier than the following: "I have received your esteemed favors of the 17th and 31st January, *and note their respective contents.*"

On the twelfth day of March, 1823, the ship La Claire arrived at New York, laden with the brandy in question, and was at the wharf on the morning of the 13th of March. A clerk of Mactier testified that he had a conversation with Mactier about the time the brandy arrived, perhaps the morning after, and Mactier then said *he should take it to himself.* A merchant of New York also testified, that Mactier consulted with him on the subject of some brandy which he expected to arrive; there was some offer for his taking it on his own account, and he appeared inclined to take it. From the state of things, he advised Mactier to take it, and there was a letter drafted by Mactier upon the subject, in which the merchant made some alterations. The letter stated that he, Mactier, should take the brandy to his own account. On the 17th of March, Mactier entered the brandy at the custom-house *as owner*, and not as consignee, took the usual oath, and gave a bond for the duties. On the twenty-second day of March, he sold 150 pipes of the brandy on the wharf to several commercial houses, and took their notes for the price of the same. The remaining 50 pipes were put in the public store, and remained there in bond, the liquidated duties not having been secured to be paid by Mactier. On the twenty-fifth day of March, Mactier wrote a letter, directed to Frith at Jacmel, in which he said: "I have now to advise the arrival of French ship La Claire with the 200 pipes of brandy, and that in consequence of the probability of war between France and Spain, and in compliance with the wish expressed in your regarded favor of the 24th December, and my answer thereto of the 17th January last, *I have decided to take this adventure to my own account.* I therefore credit you with the amount of the invoice," amounting to $\$14,254\frac{47}{100}$. To this letter was attached a postscript, dated the 31st of March. On the twenty-eighth day of March, Frith wrote a letter to Mactier, dated at Jacmel, in which, speaking of the brandy in question, he says: "With regard to this adventure, I would wish to confirm, if altogether satisfactory to you, what I mentioned to you some time ago, and which I omitted to repeat to you in my previous letter, in reply to your's of the 17th of January. I find the more one does in this country, in the present state of trade, the more one's affairs get shackled." Previous to the arrival of these two last letters at their respective places of direction, Mactier was dead, he having departed this life on the 10th of April, 1823. On the 21st of April, Frith again wrote a letter addressed to Mactier, in which he acknowledges the receipt of his letter of the twenty-fifth of March, says he has noted its contents, and requests Mactier to charter on his account a stanch, first-class vessel, and send out to Jacmel by her 400 barrels of flour, 150 barrels of pork, 150 barrels of beef, 100 barrels of mackerel, &c., &c. In the mean time, however, Mactier having died, administration of his goods, &c., was granted to A. N. Lawrence and another, who, in May,

1823, gave the requisite bonds to secure the duties on the 50 pipes of brandy which had not been bonded for by Mactier in his lifetime, except by the general bond on entering the goods at the custom-house, and took the 50 pipes from the public store and sold them at public auction.

The respondent, unwilling to come in as a general creditor of Mactier and receive a *pro rata* distribution, on the 1st April, 1824, filed his bill in the Court of Chancery, alleging that the brandy was shipped from France on his sole account, and that Mactier was only the consignee thereof. The respondent in his bill admits that he proposed to Mactier to become the purchaser of the brandy, but avers that after the receipt of his letter of the 17th January, he considered him as having declined his proposal, and that no other offer was subsequently made by the respondent. He sets forth a letter written to him by Mactier, on the thirteenth day of March, 1823, in which, speaking of the brandy ordered from France, he says: "I am looking daily for its arrival; it is to be regretted the order was not more promptly executed, as the delay I fear will operate to *our* disadvantage. We have London dates to the 30th January; war between France and Spain may now be considered inevitable; France has recalled her minister, and 100,000 Frenchmen have been ordered to march into Spain." He alleges that the letter of Mactier to him, of the 25th March, was not received until several days after the death of Mactier, and that his letter to Mactier of the 21st April was written in ignorance of the death of Mactier, and that he did not intend thereby, and he conceives he did not finally consummate, the sale as claimed. He avers that the promissory notes received by Mactier from the purchasers of the 150 pipes of brandy remained in Mactier's possession at the time of his death, not discounted or passed away; and that the same came into possession of, and were at maturity collected by, the defendants; that the defendants, by wrongfully and collusively representing themselves as entitled to the 50 pipes of brandy remaining in the public store, obtained possession of and sold the same; and that on the 2d July, 1823, he, by his attorney, claimed of the defendants the part of the shipment or invoice of brandy which remained unsold at the decease of Mactier; and also demanded the proceeds of that part of the invoice sold by Mactier, existing in notes or otherwise, and the proceeds of the part sold by the defendants. The bill concludes by praying an account of the sales of the brandy, and a decree directing the defendants to retain in their hands sufficient of the funds belonging to the estate of Mactier to pay and satisfy the respondent when his accounts shall be settled and adjudged upon by the Court.

The defendants put in their answer, insisting that the brandy, on its arrival at the port of New York, was the sole and exclusive property of Mactier; and that the portion thereof which came to their hands at his decease, and the proceeds of that part thereof which was sold by him in his lifetime, and which came to their hands, rightfully belonged to his estate, and was subject to be disposed of in a due course of administration. The defendants admit that they have in their hands $13,935 belonging to the estate of Mactier, after the payment of certain debts to the United States, and various other sums of money which they were directed to pay, have credit for the payment of, and are authorized to retain, by virtue of a decree of the Court of Chancery of the 14th June, 1823, in a cause wherein A. Mactier, senior, in behalf of himself and the creditors of Henry Mactier, deceased, is complainant, and themselves defendants; and they contend that such decree is in full force, and that by virtue thereof they are bound to pay the above-mentioned sum of money and such as may come to their hands *pro rata*, or equally among all the creditors of Henry Mactier, pursuant to such decree.

By the answer it was admitted that the defendants had found among the papers of Henry Mactier two invoices of the 200 pipes of brandy, similar in all respects, except that one states the shipment to have been made "to the address and for the account of Henry Mactier," and the other states it to have been made "for the account of the complainant to the address of Henry Mactier." The first of the invoices was used upon entering the brandy at the custom-house. It also appeared in evidence that on the first day of March, 1823, Mactier effected an insurance on *commissions* arising on a consignment from Bordeaux to New York, to the amount of $1500. In a petty cash-book of Mactier's there is the following entry: "1823, March 17, John A. Frith's sales of brandy, paid entry at custom-house, eighty cents." The clerk of Mactier, who made this entry, testified that the name of Frith, prefixed to the entry in the petty cash-book, does not necessarily prove that the brandy was Frith's, but it shows that he at that time supposed the brandy to be Frith's; if it had then belonged to Mactier, or if Mactier had decided to take it and any entry in the books had been made showing that fact, he would have entered it, "Sales of brandy Dr. for entering," &c. At the time of making the entry, he considered the fact of ownership contingent. Mactier afterwards directed the account to be opened in the books, charging the brandy to himself, the account to be "Sales of brandy." An entry was made in the day-book, of the twenty-eighth day of March, crediting Frith with the invoice amount of the brandy. Entries, he said, are sometimes made several days after the transaction; then the entry refers back to the true date of the transaction, mentioning the time. The entry was made by the thirty-first day of March. He also testified that the letter of the thirteenth of March, mentioned in the complainant's bill, was copied on the night of that day, but he had no recollection when it left the office; it possibly might not have gone until the La Claire arrived.

On the 20th May, 1825, Chancellor Sanford made an order of reference to a master to examine witnesses, and to report whether in his opinion the complainant was the owner of any part, and what part, of the shipment of brandy at the time of the sale of the same, or of any part thereof; and if so, whether as such owner he had a *lien*, by virtue of such ownership, on the brandy, or the proceeds thereof, in the hands of the defendants; and that if the master should be of the opinion that he was entitled as a special creditor, or had a lien, that then he should take and state an account, and report the amount due the complainant as such special creditor, or having a lien. Under this order witnesses were examined, and a mass of documentary evidence produced before the master, who, on the 10th October, 1825, reported that the complainant was not the owner of the shipment of brandy, neither at the time of the sale of the part thereof made by Mactier in his lifetime, or of the other part thereof made by the defendants as his administrators since his death, and had no lien on the brandy, or on the proceeds thereof in the hands of the administrators. To this report the complainant excepted, and the cause was heard upon the exceptions before Chancellor Walworth, who, in March, 1829, allowed the exception to that part of the master's report above stated (other exceptions to other parts of the report, which it has not been deemed essential to state, were disallowed), and decreed that the report be referred back to the master to alter and correct the same, and to take and state an account, and report the amount due the complainant, on the principle that he, as *survivor*, is entitled to the net proceeds of the adventure of brandy, so far as they can be traced and identified, and has a specific lien on the net proceeds of the 50 pipes of brandy sold by the administrators, and on the proceeds of the notes given for the 150 pipes which remained uncollected or not passed away at the time of Mactier's death, or on so much as is necessary to satisfy the balance due complainant for payment and disbursements on account of that adventure, after deducting from those proceeds the balance of the amount paid for duties and expenses, if any, over and above the amount of proceeds of the shipment of brandy which were received by Mactier in his lifetime. From this decree the defendants appealed. For the reasons of the Chancellor for the decree pronounced by him, see 1 Paige, 434.[1] The cause was argued here by

S. Boyd and *S. A. Talcott*, for the appellants.

S. Stevens and *G. Griffin*, for the respondent.

[1] The opinion of the Chancellor, so far as it relates to the questions discussed upon the appeal, is as follows (1 Paige, 439): "The material and important question in this cause relates to the shipment of brandy, which I will now consider. On looking into the testimony on this subject, and the correspondence between Frith and Mactier, I am satisfied the complainant never was the sole owner. But if he did not make a valid sale of his interest in that adventure previous to the death of Mactier,

The following opinions were delivered:—

By Mr. Justice MARCY. The object of the bill filed in this case is to obtain from the administrators of Mactier the proceeds of the 50

he has a specific lien upon the proceeds of the 50 pipes which were afterward sold by the administrators, and the proceeds of the notes received on the sale of the first 150 pipes, which had not been collected or negotiated previous to Mactier's death. I have no doubt the original transaction was substantially as stated in the answer of the administrators. The parties undertook an adventure in which they were to be equal sharers in profit and loss. A cargo of brandy was to be purchased in France on the credit of Frith, and consigned to Mactier at New York. On its arrival there, he was to sell it and remit the invoice cost in provisions consigned to Frith at Jacmel; from the sale of which the latter was to raise funds to furnish a shipment of coffee to his correspondent in France, to pay the original cost of the brandy. Under this agreement, it would be immaterial whether Mactier charged a selling commission on the brandy or not. If he charged a commission, it would have been countervailed by a similar charge on the sale of the provisions by Frith in the West Indies; but neither could be entitled to a *del credere* commission, as the sales would be at the risk of both. In pursuance of this agreement, on the 5th of September, 1822, while the complainant was on a visit to New York, he gave an order to Firebrace, Davidson, & Co., of Havre, for the shipment of 200 pipes of brandy, to be consigned to Mactier; but on his return to Hayti, he came to the conclusion to give up the adventure to Mactier, if the latter would consent to take it off his hands. Accordingly, on the 24th of December, he wrote to Mactier, proposing that he should take the adventure solely to his own account, holding the value to cover the transaction to the complainant's account in New York. If this proposition had been directly and explicitly accepted by Mactier, there could be no doubt as to the proceeds of the 150 pipes sold before his death. But it might be necessary to examine the question so much discussed on the argument, as to the right of Frith to stop *in transitu* the 50 pipes which remained in the public store, and which had not come to Mactier's hands, and the liquidated duties on which had not been secured at the time of his death. Having arrived at the conclusion that Mactier did not, in his answer of the 17th of January, 1823, intend to accept of that offer, and that it was not afterwards binding on Frith, I do not consider it necessary to express any opinion on the question as to his specific lien on the proceeds of the 50 pipes only.

"In Mactier's answer to the proposition of the 24th of December, he says the original adventure had from the first been a favorite speculation, and still promised a favorable result, and he was desirous it should go on in the way first proposed; but as Frith had expressed a wish that he should take the same on his own account, he should delay coming to any conclusion, till he again heard from the complainant. If he had stopped there, the answer could only have admitted of one construction; but he adds: 'The prospect of a war between France and Spain may defeat the object of this speculation, as far as relates to the shipment of provisions hence to Hayti, to be invested in coffee to be sent to France in French vessels; in which case, I will at once decide to take the adventure to my own account.'

"The defendants' counsel insist that this was a conditional acceptance of the offer of Frith; and as he did not dissent from it, both parties were bound by it as soon as it was ascertained there was such a prospect of war between France and Spain as to render it unsafe to go on with the original adventure. Whatever might have been the intention of Mactier, it was not such an acceptance of the offer of the 24th of December as to make that offer binding on Frith. And Mactier having declined to accept the adventure as proposed, he could not by any subsequent assent to the original offer make a valid contract for the purchase of the interest of Frith in the pipes of brandy which came to their possession after his death, and the amount of such notes taken on the sale of the 150 pipes on the 22d of March, 1823, as were uncollected and undisposed of at the death

brandy. It is evident this conditional acceptance of the offer was never acted on or assented to by Frith. For as late as the 28th of March, instead of assenting to a conditional sale, he again renews the original offer of the 24th of December, which was for an absolute sale.

"Mactier did not consider himself the absolute or probable owner of the brandy on the first of March, or he would not have insured the commissions he expected to receive on the sale. On the 13th of March, when he considered war between France and Spain as inevitable, he says nothing more on the subject of taking the speculation to himself, but speaks of the brandy as a matter in which they were jointly concerned. He says the offices refuse to insure on French vessels, and he fears the delay in the shipment of the brandy will operate to the disadvantage of himself and Frith. It is true the vessel arrived safe on the evening of that day; and soon after that, he began to talk with his clerk, and consult with his friends, as to the propriety or expediency of taking the brandy to himself. But he did not make up his mind until twelve days after the arrival of the vessel, and after he had ascertained the value of the brandy by an actual sale of three-fourths of the shipment. Under these circumstances, can it be supposed, if any disaster had happened to the vessel which was not covered or fully guarded against by the policy effected in France, or the brandy had come to a bad market, he would have considered himself bound by the indefinite and vague expressions contained in his letter of the 17th of January?

"On the 7th of March, Frith acknowledged the letter of the 17th of January, but said nothing about the brandy. This communication was received on the 7th of April, two or three days before Mactier's death. Another letter was written by Frith on the 28th of March, which was not received until long afterwards. In this he repeated the original offer contained in the letter of the 24th of December. As this letter never came to the knowledge of Mactier, and could not have reached this country until some time after his death, the master very correctly decided that Frith was not bound by the offer contained therein. But as Frith there states that he intended to have made the same offer in the letter of the 7th of March which Mactier did receive, the master considers it evidence of a mental assent to the conditional acceptance of the offer of the 24th of December; and that the letter of the 7th of March is to be taken as if it contained a renewal of the proposition of the 24th of December. If the mental assent of Frith was alone sufficient to close the bargain, so as to make it binding on both parties without any expression of such assent, I should not consider the expression in the letter of the 28th of March as evidence of that mental assent, but the contrary; because the offer in these letters is not the same contract as that contained in the letter of the 17th of January, but materially different. The first is an absolute sale, to take effect immediately; the other is conditional, to take place on a contingency, leaving Frith responsible for one-half of all risks in the mean time.

"The letter of the 28th of March is undoubtedly evidence that on the 7th of that month Frith wished to renew his offer to sell. To make a valid contract it is not only necessary that the minds of the contracting parties should meet on the subject of the contract, but they must communicate that fact to each other, so that both parties may know that their minds do meet. Why did the master decide that the letters of the 25th and 28th of March did not of themselves make a valid contract? Both minds met on the same point on the 28th of March, when the letter of Frith was written, and the invoice price of the brandy was credited to him by Mactier. But as the latter never heard of the letter, and the former never heard of the entry until after the death of Mactier, there was no contract made which was binding on either.

of Mactier, or at least so much thereof as may be necessary to pay the balance due the respondent for disbursements on account of the adventure. The question on which the decision in this case, as I apprehend, mainly depends, relates to the alleged sale of the brandy to Mactier. There are many definitions of what constitutes a contract, but all of them are of course substantially alike. Powell states a contract to be a transaction in which each party comes under an obligation to the other, and each reciprocally acquires a right to what is promised by the other. Powell on Cont. 4. In testing the validity of contracts many things are to be considered. The contract that the appellant sets up in this case is alleged by the respondent to be deficient in several essential requisites. When that was done which, on the assumption of there being parties capable of contracting, was necessary, as the respondent contends, to complete it, Mactier was dead. If the contract was only in progress of execution, and there remained but a single act to be done to complete it, his death rendered the performance of that act impossible; it suspended the proceedings at the very point where they were when it occurred.

The doctrine of relation was discussed on the argument, and its application urged on us. It was insisted that if nothing but a formal act was to be done, and it was done by the surviving party after the death of the other, and in ignorance of it, this act might be adjudged to relate to a period antecedent to the death of the party dying. If, as it was held in the Court below, the bargain in this case could not be closed until Frith received Mactier's letter accepting his offer to sell, the receiving that letter, it was said, might be considered as having relation to the time when it was sent, upon the principle that courts often resort to this doctrine of relation to prevent an injury resulting to a party from the act of God. Where an agent without competent authority makes a contract, a subsequent ratification by the principal relates back to the time when the agent acted. The ratification is

If the master had applied this same principle to the mental assent of Frith at the time he wrote the letter of the 7th of March, he would have found it equally fatal to the supposed bargain, founded on the offer intended to have been inserted therein. As Mactier never knew such an offer was intended to have been made, it is the same as if the offer had been inserted, but the letter had never reached him. He could not assent to an offer which he never heard of, and consequently there was no bargain.

"Having arrived at the conclusion that Frith did not, in fact, sell his interest in the adventure to Mactier, as survivor he is entitled to the net proceeds of the brandy so far as they can be traced and identified. He has a specific lien on the 50 pipes sold by the administrators, and on the proceeds of the notes given for the other 150 pipes which remained uncollected in the hands of Mactier at the time of his death; or on so much thereof as is necessary to satisfy the balance due him for disbursements on account of that adventure. The report must therefore be referred back to the master, to be corrected accordingly. And the question of costs on these exceptions, and all other questions, are to be reserved until the coming in of the master's amended report." — Ed.

equivalent to an original authority; it is considered in law as furnishing proof of an authority in the agent at the time he assumed to have it. If, however, he had disclosed his want of authority, but had settled the terms of the contract, in the belief that what he did would be ratified, the doctrine of relation would not apply; the bargain would take effect from the time of the ratification. The reason for the distinction which I apprehend to exist in the two cases is, that in the one acts are done which make a perfect contract, provided the actors had the authority they assumed to have; and the ratification of their acts by those from whom their power must have been derived, if they had it, is legal evidence that they did have it when they acted. In the other case, the fact being made known that there was not competent power in one of the actors, the very foundation on which alone the presumption of authority can rest, is destroyed. A presumption will not be called in to supply an impossibility. In a contract of sale all agree that there must be two minds, at least, concurring at the moment of its completion; but this cannot be if there be but one contracting party in existence. There is also, as I conceive, a difference between acts essential to perfect an agreement, and those which relate to the forms prescribed in certain instances as modes of proof. This difference is illustrated by those cases which were referred to on the argument concerning the enrolment of deeds. The enrolment is a formal act, but necessary to be done, to enable the party to prove the bargain and sale; but when it is done, it relates to the time when the indenture was executed. It is, as Lord Bacon calls it, but a perfective ceremony of the first deed of bargain and sale. *Regula* 14. So where chancery decrees the execution of a parol contract on the ground of part performance, the title certainly, as between the parties, vests from the time of the contract, and not from the performance of those acts that remove the bar created by the Statute of Frauds. The doctrine of relation may be permitted to operate on these *formal acts*, but it cannot be used, as it is proposed to use it here, to supply a *party* to a contract who does not exist at the time when the act is done which fixes to it the seal of validity; or, what is the same thing, it cannot carry back that act to a time when parties capable of contracting did in fact exist. This view of the subject is conformable to the civil law as well as the law of France. By these laws, the death of the party offering to sell is held to be a revocation of the offer, and an acceptance subsequent to that event is ineffectual to close the bargain. Pothier, *Traité du Contrat de Vente*, p. 1, § 2, art. 3, No. 32. My conclusion, in regard to this objection to the alleged contract, is, that if any act was required to be done, even by Frith, to complete the sale when Mactier died, that act could not be subsequently performed.

I am now to consider whether there was a contract before Mactier's death, which had the consent of the contracting parties so given and made known as to be binding on them. That a consent is necessary, all agree; but what shall constitute it in a given case may admit of much diversity of opinion. The consent of the parties in a contract of sale, as explained by Pothier, consists in the concurrence of the will of the vendor to sell a particular thing to the purchaser for a specified price, with the will of the purchaser to buy the same thing for that price. Pothier, *Traité du Contrat de Vente*, p. 1, § 2, art. 3, No. 31. Delvincourt, another eminent French writer on the civil code of France, says that, although it is impossible that there should be a contract without the consent of all parties, it is not indispensable that the wills of the parties should concur at the same instant, provided the will of the one that did not concur at first is declared before the will of the other is revoked. 5 *Cours de Code Civil*, 93. Although the will of the party making the offer may precede that of the party accepting, yet it must continue down to the time of the acceptance. Where parties are together chaffering about an article of merchandise, and one expresses a present willingness to accept of certain terms, that willingness is supposed to continue, unless it is revoked, to the close of their interview and negotiation on the same subject; and if during this time the other party says he will take the article on the terms proposed, the bargain is thereby closed. Pothier, *Tr. du Cont. de Vente*, p. 1, § 2, art. 3, No. 31. What I mean by its being closed is, that nothing mutual between the parties remains to be done to give to either a right to have it carried into effect; either can enforce it against the other, or recover damages for the nonfulfilment of it; but if there be conditions expressed or implied to be performed by the purchaser, he cannot compel the delivery until they are performed. If the price is to be immediately paid or security given, he cannot have the property until payment is made, or security given, or a tender thereof. Touchstone, 204, 5; Noy's Max., chap. 42; 2 Blackstone's Comm. 447.

Where the negotiation between the contracting parties, residing at a distance from each other, is conducted, as it usually is, by letters, it is necessary, in order that their minds may meet, that the will of the party making the proposition to sell should continue until his letter shall have reached the other, and he shall have signified, or at least had an opportunity to signify, his acceptance of the proposition. This Pothier holds to be the legal presumption, unless the contrary appears. His language is: *Cette volonté est présumé tant qu'il ne parait rien de contraire.* This doctrine, which presumes the continuance of a willingness to contract after it has been manifested by an offer, is not confined to the civil law and the codes of those nations which have constructed their systems with the materials drawn from that exhaustless store-house of jurisprudence: it is found in the common law; indeed, it exists of necessity wherever the power to contract exists in parties separated from each other. The rule of the common law is, that wherever the existence of a particular subject-matter or relation has been once proved, its continuance is presumed till proof be given to the contrary, or till a different presumption be afforded by the nature of the subject-matter. 16 East, 55. Stark. Ev. 1252. The case of Adams v. Lindsell, 1 Barn. & Ald. 681, proceeds upon and affirms the principle, that the willingness to contract thus manifested is presumed to continue for the time limited, and, if that be not indicated by the offer, until it is expressly revoked or countervailed by a contrary presumption. In that case it was said, "The defendants must be considered in law as making, during every instant of time their letter was travelling, the same identical offer to the plaintiffs; and then the contract is complete by the acceptance of it by the latter." Against the authority of the case of Adams v. Lindsell, we have urged on us a decision of a court of the highest respectability in one of our sister states. The case of M'Culloch v. The Eagle Ins. Co., 1 Pick. 278, conflicts in principle, according to my views of it, with the case decided by the King's Bench. I should have been pleased to see these tribunals harmonize upon a question of no small importance to the commercial world; and I have therefore deliberately weighed the ingenious attempts made to reconcile these decisions upon this point; but these attempts appear to me to have been unsuccessful. A refinement which would distinguish between a contract for insurance, and one for the sale of goods, in relation to the assent of the parties, might relieve us from the embarrassment which the different principles of these decisions is calculated to produce; but to apply such a distinction hereafter would doubtless involve courts in a still more distressing embarrassment. Distinctions which are not founded on a difference in the nature of things, are not entitled to indulgence; they tend to make the science of law a collection of arbitrary rules appealing to factitious reasons for their support, consequently difficult to be acquired, and often of uncertain application. The two cases referred to should have had applied to them the same rule of law, and we are required to say what that rule is, in deciding the case now under consideration.

The principle of the decision of the King's Bench is, simply that the acceptance of an offer made through the medium of a letter binds the bargain, if the party making the offer has not revoked it, as he has a right to do before it is accepted. The rule laid down by the Supreme Court of Massachusetts regards the contract as incomplete until the party making the offer is notified of the acceptance, or until the time when he should have received it, the party accepting having done what was incumbent on him to give notice. The Chancellor in deciding this case gave his sanction to the latter rule: "To make a valid contract," he says, "it is not only necessary that the minds of the contracting parties should meet on the subject of the contract, but they must know that fact."[1] The decision of the court of Massachusetts makes knowledge, by the party tendering the offer, of the other's acceptance, essential to the completion of the contract. If one party is not bound till he knows or might know, and therefore is presumed to know, that the other has accepted, the accepting party on the same principle ought not to be bound till he knows the offering party has not recalled the offer before knowledge of the acceptance. The principle of that case would bring the matter to the point stated by the Chancellor; viz., the parties must know that their minds meet on the subject of the contract. If a bargain can be completed between absent parties, it must be when one of them cannot know the fact whether it be or be not completed. It cannot begin to be obligatory on the one before it is on the other; there must be a precise time when the obligation attaches to both, and this time must happen when one of the parties cannot know that the obligation has attached to him; the obligation does not therefore arise from a knowledge of the present concurrence of the wills of the contracting parties. All the authorities state a contract, or an agreement (which is the same thing), to be *aggregatio mentium*. Why should not this *meeting of the minds*, which makes the contract, also indicate the moment when it becomes obligatory? I might rather ask, is it not, and must it not be, the moment when it does become obligatory? If the party making the offer is not bound until he knows of this meeting of minds, for the same reason the party accepting the offer ought not to be bound when

[1] This proposition, which is an extract from the Chancellor's opinion as printed in the Case presented to this Court, is somewhat modified in its terms, as it appears in the reports of the Court of Chancery. There it is said, "To make a valid contract, it is not only necessary that the minds of the contracting parties should meet on the subject of the contract, but they must communicate that fact to each other, so that both parties may know that their minds do meet." 1 Paige, 442. It is understood that the Chancellor has said that his views on this subject have been mistaken or misapprehended. Though the general proposition above quoted is advanced in his opinion, it is introduced in that part of it where he is considering the effect of Mactier's letter of the 25th, and Frith's of the 28th of March, and what Frith intended to insert in his letter of the 7th of March. Having considered the offer of Frith, made in his letter of the 24th December, disposed of by Mactier, in his answer of the 17th January, declining to accept it, he then looks at the letters of the 25th and 28th of March to see if a contract was concluded by them; and as Mactier died before his letter of the 25th reached Frith, and before Frith's letter of the 28th, renewing the offer, reached New York, he considered those letters did not of themselves make a valid contract. The remark of the Chancellor, which has been taken for a general proposition of law, is understood to have been made with a direct reference to the facts presented by these two letters. Taking this view of the Chancellor's observation, the principal point of difference between him and the Court for the Correction of Errors would seem to be, that he considered Mactier's letter of the 17th January as declining the offer, and therefore putting an end to it; and the Court considered that Mactier's answer held the offer under advisement, that it was so held down to the time when Mactier accepted it, and that Frith assented to its being thus held under advisement.

his acceptance is received, because he does not know of the meeting of the minds; for the offer may have been withdrawn before his acceptance was received. If more than a concurrence of minds upon a distinct proposition is required to make an obligatory contract, the definition of what constitutes a contract is not correct. Instead of being the meeting of the minds of the contracting parties, it should be a knowledge of this meeting. It was said on the argument, that if concurrence of minds alone would make a valid contract, one might be constructed out of mere volitions and uncommunicated wishes; I think such a result would not follow. The law does not regard bare volitions and pure mental abstractions. When it speaks of the operations of the mind, it means such as have been made manifest by overt acts; when it speaks of the meeting of minds, it refers to such a meeting as has been made known by proper acts; and when thus made known it is effective, although the parties who may claim the benefit of, or be bound by a contract thus made, may for a season remain ignorant of its being made.

Testing the rules of law laid down in the two cases to which I have referred by the authority of reason, and the practical results that are likely to flow from them, it does appear to me that we are not left at liberty to hesitate about the choice. If we are inclined, from the force of abstract reason, to prefer the rule laid down by the Court of King's Bench, that inclination will be greatly strengthened by a recurrence to the opinions of courts and jurists. The Common Pleas, in England, seem to me to have given their approval to the decision of Adams *v.* Lindsell, 4 Bing. 653. Judge Washington, in delivering the opinion of the court in Eliason *v.* Henshaw, 4 Wheaton, 228, said: "Until the terms of the agreement have received the assent of both parties, the negotiation is open, and imposes no obligation on either." The inference from this proposition is, that the assent of the parties to the terms of the agreement, and not their knowledge of it, completes the contract. It was decided in the Circuit Court of the United States for Pennsylvania, that contracts are formed by the offer on the one hand, and an acceptance on the other. After acceptance the contract is obligatory on both. Coxe's Dig. 192. In this case, knowledge of the acceptance is not brought into view as necessary to constitute the obligation. Both the Roman law and the French civil code, as we have seen by the references already made, contain a doctrine in accordance with the principle of these cases. I think I am therefore warranted in saying that the proposition may be considered as established, that the acceptance of a written offer of a contract of sale consummates the bargain, provided the offer is standing at the time of the acceptance.

What shall constitute an acceptance will depend in a great measure upon circumstances. The mere determination of the mind, unacted on, can never be an acceptance. Where the offer is by letter, the usual mode of acceptance is the sending of a letter announcing a consent to accept; where it is made by a messenger, a determination to accept, returned through him, or sent by another, would seem to be all the law requires, if the contract may be consummated without writing. There are other modes which are equally conclusive upon the parties: keeping silence, under certain circumstances, is an assent to a proposition; any thing that shall amount to a manifestation of a formed determination to accept, communicated or put in the proper way to be communicated to the party making the offer, would doubtless complete the contract; but a letter written would not be an acceptance, so long as it remained in the possession or under the control of the writer. An acceptance is the distinct act of one party to the contract, as much as the offer is of the other; the knowledge, by the party making the offer, of the determination of the party receiving it, is not an ingredient of an acceptance. It is not compounded of an assent by one party to the terms offered, and a knowledge of that assent by the other.

I will now apply this law to the facts of this case. Frith's offer to sell his interest in the brandy certainly continued till his letter of the 24th of December was received at New York, and Mactier had a fair opportunity to answer it. If the answer of the 17th of January had contained an unqualified acceptance, the bargain would have been closed when it was sent away for Jacmel; but the offer was not then accepted. There was a promise to accept upon a contingency; for Mactier says, after alluding to the prospect of a war between France and Spain, "in which case," that is, in case of such a war, "I will at once decide to take the adventure to my own account." This concluded nothing. If the event had actually happened, and Frith had insisted on enforcing this conditional acceptance, it would not have been in his power to do so. The most that Mactier said was, that if an expected event happened, he would do an act which would complete the bargain. The happening of the event could not, without the act, complete it. The Roman law regarded the tense of the verb used by the contracting parties to determine whether the bargain was concluded: *Verbum imperfecti temporis rem adhuc imperfectum significat.* There is a wide difference between a promise to give an assent to a proposition for a contract on the happening of a contingency, and the annunciation of a present assent to it. If the expected event happens, and the act promised is performed, the bargain is closed; but it is the promised acceptance, and not the happening of the event, that gives validity to the contract. If in this case the offer of Frith had been to Mactier to take the brandy on the happening of a French and Spanish war, and Mactier had promised to decide to take it in such an event, the simple fact of his taking it after the war would have enabled

Frith to treat him as the purchaser of it. Such an act would have been a valid acceptance; but a conditional acceptance of an unconditional offer, followed up by acts of the acceptor, after the condition was fulfilled on which the acceptance depended, might not be considered as completing the bargain, without the acquiescence of the party making the offer in those acts, because the minds of the parties would not have met on the precise terms of the contract.

To conclude the bargain, Mactier must have accepted the offer as tendered to him by Frith, and that acceptance must have been while the offer, in contemplation of law, was still held out to him. That there was an acceptance, or rather that Mactier did all that was incumbent on him to do to effect an acceptance, was not denied; but it was insisted, on the part of the respondent, that it was made after the offer was withdrawn. It will be necessary to consider when this acceptance took place, as preparatory to settling the fact of the continuance of the offer down to that time. There is not the slightest evidence of the determination on the part of Mactier to take the brandy before the 17th day of March. The insurance that he effected on his commissions on the 1st of March disproves the existence of such a determination on that day; but if the situation of the parties was changed, and Frith was now endeavoring to set up the contract, I am at a loss to conceive how Mactier's representatives could withstand the force of the facts which took place on the 17th of March. In answer to the offer, Mactier delayed coming to a determination thereon, but promised to accept it if there should be a war; on the 17th of March, when that event was considered settled, he entered the brandy as his own property, and told his clerk that he had determined to take it. But if there should be any doubt as to the effect of this conduct, there can be none as to his subsequent acts. By a letter dated the 25th, with a postscript of the 31st of March, he accepts the offer. This letter was immediately transmitted to Frith, and as soon as the 28th of March entries were made in his books, showing that he had become the purchaser. Enough was done by the 31st to constitute an acceptance of Frith's offer and to complete the bargain, if the offer can be considered as standing till that day.

An offer, when once made, continues, as I have heretofore shown, to the satisfaction of my own mind at least, until it is expressly revoked, or until circumstances authorize a presumption that it is revoked. The offer itself may show very clearly when the presumption of revocation attaches. Where it is made to be replied to by return mail, the party to whom it is addressed must at once perceive that it is not to stand for an acceptance to be transmitted after the mail. If an offer stands until it is expressly withdrawn, or is presumed to be withdrawn, whether it is held out to a party at a particular period or not, is a matter of fact. Then we are to determine, as a matter of fact, whether Frith's offer was held out for Mactier's acceptance until the 31st of March; if Frith intended it should stand so, and he viewed himself as tendering it to Mactier down to that time, we are bound to regard it as standing, unless his intention was the result of the fraudulent conduct of Mactier. The acts of Frith, after the death of Mactier, could do nothing towards completing an unfinished contract; but I think they may be fairly adverted to for the purpose of ascertaining his intentions in relation to the continuance of his offer. On the 7th of March he acknowledges Mactier's letter of the 17th of January, which did not decline, as it has been construed to do, the offer, but apprised him that it was kept under advisement; and by using the expression, "noting the contents," Frith is I think to be understood as yielding to the proposed delay. If a doubt as to this construction of that letter could spring up in the mind, it would be at once removed by the perusal of the letter of the 28th of the same month. In that he expresses a wish to confirm what he had said in the letter making the offer to sell, and declares that he had in a previous letter, which must mean that of the 7th, omitted to communicate the same thing. In answering Mactier's letter which contained the acceptance of his offer, he recognizes the bargain as closed, and gives directions as to investing the proceeds of the brandy. All the subsequent correspondence acquiesces in the sale. It appears to me to be impossible to say, after reading the letters of Frith written subsequent to his knowledge of Mactier's acceptance, that he did not consider the offer as held out to Mactier down to the time when it was accepted, and the bargain closed by that acceptance; and I think we must adjudge it to have been closed, unless the agreement was nugatory by reason that the thing to which it related had not an actual or potential existence when the contract was consummated.[1] . . .

Upon the view of the whole of this case, I entertain the opinion that the decree of the Chanceller ought to be reversed.

By Mr. Senator MAYNARD.[2] . . . To make a contract, there must be an agreement, — a meeting of the minds of the contracting parties. On the 28th of March the minds of these parties certainly did meet. On that day Frith wrote to Mactier, renewing and confirming his previous proposition to him "to take the adventure to his sole account," and on that day Mactier actually did take it to his "sole account." Here was an actual meeting of the minds of the parties on the subject of the contract, and a decisive act of one of them, giving it entire effect. If the meeting of the minds of the parties, accompanied by the only act necessary to give complete effect to the contemplated con-

[1] The remainder of the opinion relates to questions having no bearing upon the subject of "Mutual Consent." — ED.

[2] Concurring opinions were delivered by Senators Benton, Maynard, Oliver, and Throop; but it is not deemed necessary to include in this collection more than the following portion of the opinion of Senator Maynard. — ED.

tract, are all the circumstances requisite to constitute a valid contract, then there was in this instance a sale of the commodity in question. But his Honor, the Chancellor, has said that, "to make a valid contract, it is not only necessary that the minds of the contracting parties should meet, but they should know that fact." If this be a correct principle, and of universal application, then surely in this case there was no contract. The letter of Frith of the 28th of March, and all subsequently written by him, did not reach this country until after the death of Mactier. Can this principle be correct and universal? The parties were distant, and negotiating for the sale of a commodity in the possession of one of them. The adventure was agreed upon, and the brandy ordered on the 5th of September, "to be in New York by January following, or sooner, if possible." When Frith wrote his letter of December 24th, he must have believed that the brandy would have arrived at New York before his letter, or at all events before he could receive an answer. If such had been the fact, and the brandy had been in the actual possession of Mactier, to whom it was consigned, will it be contended that he must have forborne "to take the adventure" to himself, according to the proposition, until he had informed Frith that he would do so, and received intelligence from him that he was in possession of that information? I cannot believe that the principle can be carried to that extent. Nor can I perceive why it would not have been a valid contract, if the brandy had actually arrived at the receipt of Frith's proposition, if Mactier had immediately "taken the adventure to himself," and credited Frith with the value. If that would have been a contract, binding upon the parties, then it is not universally true that the minds of contracting parties must not only meet, but that they must know that they do meet, before the agreement becomes a contract. If this principle be correct and universal, it is difficult to conceive when a contract would ever be concluded between distant parties. An offer may be revoked at any time before it is accepted. When a party who has received an offer sends his acceptance, he does not know that the minds of the parties meet, because he knows that a revocation of the offer may be on its way. When the party who made the offer receives the acceptance, he cannot know that there is a meeting of minds, because he knows that the acceptance may have been revoked. And when the party accepting receives information that his acceptance is received and the offer confirmed, he is in equal uncertainty as to the meeting of minds, because there may have been a revocation of that confirmation. Such a negotiation would be endless, for the parties could never know that their minds met. The impossibility of arriving at certainty, and consequently the intrinsic difficulty of giving effect to this principle, shows that as a rule it must have some exceptions. One of these instances, it appears to me, must be where the parties are distant, and one of them has the power by his own act to give full effect to the contract, and he does that act in accordance with the mind of the other. In support of the Chancellor's opinion reference has been made to the case of M'Culloch *v.* Eagle Ins. Co., 1 Pick. 278; but I find nothing in that case decisive on this point. That was a case of revocation. On the 29th of December the plaintiff sent a letter by mail to the defendants, making inquiries how they would insure a vessel and cargo, but making no offer by which he could be bound. On the 1st of January the defendants wrote him that they would insure on certain terms, and the next day wrote him again, revoking that offer, and declining to effect any insurance. The plaintiff received the offer to insure on the 3d, and sent an acceptance before he received the revocation, which reached him in due course of the mail. The parties rested until the loss was ascertained; and the court held there was no contract; and surely there was not, because the offer to insure was revoked before it was accepted, and on that point the cause was decided. The case would have been very different if the plaintiff had requested the defendants to make out a policy upon his vessel and cargo at a specified premium, and deliver it to his agent, and the defendants had actually complied with his request. In the present case, Frith proposed to Mactier "to take the adventure solely to his own account," on certain terms. Mactier replied, not accepting, discouraging but not rejecting the proposition; holding it for further negotiation in one event, and promising absolutely to accede to it on the occurrence of another contingency. The proposition remained, neither rejected by one, nor revoked or modified by the other. The brandy arrived, preceded by information of the occurrence of the contingency on which Mactier had promised to take the adventure to himself. After a few days employed in consultation with his friends as to his obligation, he did accede to the proposition, and did all that was necessary to give effect to the contract. It is urged that the letters of Frith, which reached this country after the death of Mactier, cannot make a contract. Most certainly they cannot; but they furnish evidence that one had been made before, by proving an actual meeting of the minds of the parties, if a contract can be made without a mutual and reciprocal knowledge of such meeting. And if a contract cannot be made without that knowledge, those letters would not have constituted a contract, if they had reached this country in the lifetime of Mactier. They prove all now that they would have proved if the death had not occurred. They never would have proved that each party knew the minds met. They prove that the mind of Frith had undergone no change; that he continued the proposition; that his mind was the same on the 28th of March, when Mactier actually took the adventure to himself, as it was on the 24th of December, when he proposed to have him do it. A valid contract was therefore made by the act of Mactier on the 28th of March, if the same act would have made one on the 17th of January, when he wrote his reply to the proposition. . . .

Whereupon, on the question being put, Shall the decree of the Chancellor appealed from be reversed? Chief Justice SAVAGE and Justices SUTHERLAND and MARCY, and eighteen Senators, voted in the affirmative; and three Senators voted in the negative, — viz., Senators McCARTY, TODD, and WHEELER.

The decree of the Chancellor was accordingly reversed with costs.

AVERILL AND ANOTHER v. HEDGE.

SUPREME COURT OF ERRORS OF CONNECTICUT, JUNE, 1838.

[*Reported in* 12 *Connecticut Reports,* 424.]

THIS was an action of assumpsit, alleging that the defendant, who conducted business at Wareham, Mass., under the name of the "Washington Iron Company," promised to deliver to the plaintiffs a quantity of rods, shapes, and band-iron, in March, 1836.

The cause was tried at Hartford, February term, 1838, before WILLIAMS, C. J.

The plaintiffs claimed to have proved their case by a correspondence between the parties in the year 1836; particularly by a letter from the plaintiffs to the defendant, dated the 29th of February; the defendant's answer of the 2d of March; a letter from the plaintiffs, dated the 14th of March; and the answer of the defendant, also dated the 14th of March by mistake, in fact written the 16th of March; and the plaintiffs' reply thereto, dated the 19th of March. The whole correspondence between the parties was read in evidence; the substance of which was as follows: —

HARTFORD, 29th February, 1836. DEAR SIR, — Regarding the future disposal of your nails as settled, it would be improper to importune you further on that point. Perhaps however you will not object to sending us a supply of rods and shapes for our spring sales. Please to say on what terms you will send us ten or fifteen tons, assorted, by first packet in the spring. We shall also be glad to purchase our hollow ware of you on the same terms as heretofore. Shall be pleased to hear from you soon. [Signed, "J. & H. AVERILL," the plaintiffs; and addressed to JOHN THOMAS, Esq.]

WAREHAM, 2d March, 1836. On the writer's return from the South last evening, he found your favor of the 29th ult., to which we now reply. We will deliver to you in Hartford ten or fifteen tons of rods, shapes, and band-iron, as follows: say — shapes and band-iron, at $110 per gross ton, six months; and old sable rods, at $116, six months. Old sable iron is now quick at $110 per ton in Boston; and there is but very little iron there at any price. We will deliver you at Hartford a common assortment of hollow ware, at $28 per ton, six months. [Signed, "WASHINGTON IRON COMPANY, per JOHN THOMAS, Agent;" and addressed to the plaintiffs.]

HARTFORD, 14 March, 1836. DEAR SIR, — We have bought of Ripley & Averill their stock of hollow ware, with the understanding that we were to receive the benefit of their orders given you last July. The balance of this order we believe was in readiness last fall; but, owing to the early closing of our navigation, was not shipped. Will you ship us this lot of ware by first packet, on terms then agreed on with R. & A.? Please advise us by return mail if we may expect it. [Signed by plaintiffs, and addressed to JOHN THOMAS, Esq.]

WAREHAM, March 14, 1836. DEAR SIRS, — Your favor of the 14th inst. is at hand, and contents noted. We shall most cheerfully comply with your request to ship to you the balance of Ripley & Averill's order of hardware, not filled in consequence of the early frost last autumn; such being the understanding between yourselves and Mr. Ripley. We learn from our neighbors, engaged in the manufacture of this article, that they now hold it at $30 per ton, and shall not sell it at a less price through the season; and consequently we shall not consider ourselves holden to the offer made to you on the 2d inst., unless you signify your acceptance thereof by return mail, but shall furnish the balance of Ripley & Averill's order in conformity with the contracts made with them.

Do you accept of our proposal for supplying you with rods, shapes, and band-iron; and if so, what quantity of each shall we send you? [Signed, "WASHINGTON IRON COMPANY, per JOHN THOMAS, Agent;" and addressed to the plaintiffs.]

HARTFORD, March 19th, 1836. DEAR SIR, — Your favor of the 17th came to hand last evening, too late to be answered before this morning. We note and duly appreciate your prompt assent to send us the balance of R. & A.'s order for hollow ware, at old prices. In our future purchases of that article, we will buy of you at $28 per ton, six months, as offered in your favor of the 2d. We will also take the following shapes, &c., on your terms there given: 160 bundles of new sable or Swedes, different shapes, specified; also 40 bundles smaller shapes, to be of old sable, assorted; 120 bundles band iron, assorted; 60 bundles half-inch spike rods; 200 bundles P S I horse-nail rods, or a ton, if convenient, in 28lb. bundles, sending 5 tons in all. [Signed by the plaintiffs, and addressed to JOHN THOMAS, Esq.]

In a letter dated March 21st, 1836, addressed to John Thomas, Esq., the plaintiffs alter their order for band-iron, varying the sorts.

WAREHAM, April 2d, 1836. Your favors of the 19th and 21st reached here in the absence of the writer. We regret that you had not sooner signified your acceptance of our proposition of the 2d of March, touching supplies of shapes, band-iron, &c., as we had, prior to the reception of your favors above alluded to, entered into such engagements in other markets as rendered it impossible for us to supply you with those articles on any terms. [Signed "WASHINGTON IRON COMPANY, per JOHN THOMAS, Agent;" and addressed to the plaintiffs.]

On the 6th of April, 1836, the plaintiffs addressed a letter to the defendant's agent, remonstrating against his conduct in refusing to send them the iron ordered. The defendant's agent replied, by a letter dated the 8th of April, as follows: —

On 29th February you ask our terms for 10 or 15 tons of rods and shapes. On 2d March we give them to you per mail. On 14th March you again address us upon another subject; but although our proposition in ordinary course of mail must have been in your hands 10 to 12 days, yet no allusion was made to it. On 16th, after replying to yours of 14th, we ask if you accede to our proposition of the 2d. After this, we waited for your reply until the 22d, when, not having heard from you, we made such other arrangements as made it impossible for us to fill your orders of 19th or 21st, both which came together in the same mail on 23d. We did not intend the question proposed to you in ours of 16th as a renewal of our proposals of the 2d ult., nor do we believe that it will bear that construction; but nevertheless we should have filled your order had it been seasonably received.

This correspondence was conducted through the mail; upon the part of the defendant, by his avowed agent, John Thomas, and by the plaintiffs themselves, on their part. The plaintiffs resided in the city of Hartford, near the post-office.

The letter written by the defendant on the 16th of March, dated 14th, arrived at Hartford on the 18th of March, about 2 o'clock P. M. The plaintiffs' answer to the letter, dated the 19th of March, was post-marked the 20th; and the letter written by the plaintiffs on the 21st of March was post-marked on the day of its date; and both letters arrived at Wareham at the same time, viz., on the 23d of March.

The plaintiffs claimed, that during said month of March the price of the article, which was the subject of controversy, was constantly advancing in the market; and that they had sustained loss in their business by the non-compliance of the defendant with his contract.

The defendant introduced a witness to prove that letters mailed at Hartford for Wareham were, by the usual course of mail, sent by Providence, and would reach that place on the evening of the day after leaving Hartford, — but might be sent by Boston; although when sent by Boston, on the days that both mails went, a letter would be one day longer in reaching Wareham; — that a mail was sent every day from Hartford to Boston, and every day but Sunday from Hartford to Providence; — that the Providence mail usually left the post-office in Hartford about 5 o'clock every morning except Sunday, when no mail was sent, and Monday, when it left about 10 o'clock A. M. The mails were, in the course of business, closed one hour before they left the office. Upon the 14th of March, 1836, the Providence mail left the office at 25 minutes past 5 o'clock in the morning, and on the 21st at 6 minutes past 10 in the morning. The 20th was Sunday; and letters put into the office on Saturday evening and on Sunday evening would be forwarded by the same mail. The usual course of business at the post-office in Hartford was to stamp or post-mark all letters, not on the day they were forwarded, but the day they were received into the office, — unless received after 9 o'clock in the evening, when they were post-marked as of the succeeding day.

Upon the facts so proved and disclosed in the correspondence, the plaintiffs claimed that the proposal of the defendant, in his letter of the 2d of March, to furnish the plaintiffs with rods, shapes, and band-iron, was renewed by his letter written 16th of March, and dated 14th; and that the plaintiffs, by their answer of the 19th of March, in due time signified their assent to the proposal therein contained; and thus was the contract stated in the declaration completed.

These claims of the plaintiffs were all resisted and denied by the defendant.

The Court charged the jury, that in mercantile transactions of this character, affected as they must be by the constant fluctuations of markets, the utmost promptitude must be exacted consistent with a due regard to ordinary business; and that if the letter written by the plaintiffs, accepting the proposal of the defendant relative to said rods, bands, &c., was not delivered into the post-office in Hartford before the day it was post-marked, viz. the 20th of March, it was not sent in such reasonable time as to make their acceptance obligatory upon the defendant.

A verdict was thereupon returned for the defendant; and the plaintiffs moved for a new trial.

Hungerford, in support of the motion, contended, that by the plaintiffs' letter of the 19th of March, accepting the offer of the defendant, the contract was closed, and rendered binding upon the parties. In the first place, the plaintiffs were not bound to reply to this offer by return mail. The defendant had himself placed his proposals regarding hollow ware and iron upon different grounds. As to the former, it was a condition of the offer that the plaintiffs should signify their acceptance by return mail; but as to the latter, it was left open to be replied to in a reasonable time. Johnson & al. *v.* King, 2 Bing. 270. This was evidently the understanding of the parties. Secondly, the plaintiffs' letter of the 19th of March was in reasonable time. The plaintiffs' letter of acceptance was put into the post-office in season to go by the next regular mail after the return mail. The regular mail from Hartford to Wareham is by Providence. The defendant's letter of the 16th being received on Friday the 18th, the return mail was on Saturday the 19th. The next mail after the return mail was on Monday the 21st, there being no Providence mail on Sunday; and the plaintiffs' letter of the 19th was put into the post-office in season to go by Monday's mail. Thirdly, the plaintiffs had no advantage over the defendant in respect to any fluctuations in the market; for the defendant could revoke his offer at any time before it was accepted by the plaintiffs.

T. C. Perkins, contra, contended, 1. That the defendant had expressly limited his offer to a reply by return mail, with respect to the iron as well as the hollow ware. The original application of the plaintiffs, in their letter of the 29th of February, was for iron and hollow ware. The defendant, in his reply of the 2d of March, gives terms for iron and hollow ware; and in his letter of the 16th calls the attention of the plaintiffs to both these subjects; and in the same letter says he shall not consider himself bound by the offer made on the 2d, unless the plaintiffs signify their acceptance by return mail. Eliason *v.* Henshaw, 4 Wheat. 225.

2. That aside from any express condition, the plaintiffs were bound to communicate their acceptance by return mail, if practicable. Here they had abundant time for this purpose; viz., all the afternoon and evening of the 18th. In oral negotiations, the answer must be immediate, — *i.e.*, during the interview, — or it will not bind. If it were not so, the contract would be all on one side: the owner would be tied up from selling, while the applicant was not bound to buy; and the latter might wait for changes in the market, of which the former could not have the benefit. This inconvenience and damage would be cast on the owner without any consideration received. A negotiation by correspondence stands on the same ground. The party to whom an offer is made is bound to decide upon it as soon as it reaches him; and if he assents, to notify the other party immediately. Mactier's Admrs. *v.* Frith, 6 Wend. 103, 114, 122, 131.

3. That it is not necessary, in order to vindicate the charge, to claim that the plaintiffs should have replied by the first mail practicable. The charge allowed them for this purpose, not only the afternoon and evening of the 18th, but nearly the whole of the 19th. The question therefore is, whether the plaintiffs could hold back their answer until the 20th, watching the fluctuations in the market, and then bind the defendant by their acceptance. It is said the plaintiffs did communicate their answer by the first regular mail after the return mail. The first answer to this is, that a letter put into the post-office on the 19th might have gone by the Boston mail on the 20th (Sunday), and have reached Wareham sooner than by the Providence mail of Monday. But, secondly, this point does not depend solely on the time when the letter would arrive, but also, and principally, upon the time when the plaintiffs accepted the offer by putting their letter of acceptance into the post-office, thereby precluding themselves from further speculations on the markets. If this was not done, either on the day they received the defendant's letter, or on the day after, it was not done in reasonable time.

Bissell, J. From the correspondence between these parties, and which is made a part of the case, it appears, that on the 29th of February, 1836, the plaintiffs inquired of the defendant upon what terms he would supply them with ten or fifteen tons of rods, shapes, and band-iron. To this communication the defendant replied on the 2d of March, specifying the terms on which he would furnish the articles in question. On the 14th the plaintiffs wrote to the defendant on other business; but took no notice of his offer. The defendant replied on the 16th; and at the close of his letter he inquires of the plaintiffs whether they accept his proposal regarding the rods, shapes, and bands. This letter, it appears, arrived at Hartford on the 18th, about 2 o'clock afternoon. The plaintiffs accept the defendant's proposals in a letter dated on the 19th, but which the jury have found was not delivered into the post-office at Hartford until the 20th; and the 20th being Sunday, and no mail leaving Hartford on that day, the letter was not actually sent until the morning of the 21st. And it further appears that this letter, and also another from the plaintiffs, dated the 21st, reached the defendant on the 23d. It also appears that the defendant, having waited for the plaintiffs' answer until the 22d, and having heard nothing from them, then made such arrangements as rendered it impossible for him to comply with their order. It is further found, that on the 19th of March the Providence mail left the office at Hartford at 25 minutes past 5 o'clock; and that a letter forwarded by that mail would have reached the defendant on the evening of the following day.

The great question in the case is, whether upon these facts there has been such an acceptance of the defendant's offer as that he is bound by it.

The jury were instructed, that if the letter written by the plaintiffs, accepting the proposal of the defendant, was not delivered into the post-office at Hartford until the 20th of March, it was not sent in such reasonable time as to make their acceptance obligatory on the defendant.

Several questions, not immediately growing out of the charge, but which, if decided in favor of the defendant, make an end of the case, have been much discussed at the bar.

1. It has been contended that the proposal of the defendant, in his letter of the 2d, was not renewed by his letter of the 16th of March. Upon this point no opinion was given by the judge on the circuit, unless an opinion may be inferred from the ground on which he rested the case in his instructions to the jury. Nor is it essential that a decided opinion on the question should be expressed by this Court; because there are other grounds on which we are unanimously of opinion that the ruling of the judge below must be sustained.

Were this, however, a turning point in the case, we should probably be prepared to say, that the defendant's letter of the 16th of March does contain a distinct renewal of his former proposal. His language is certainly very strong to show that such was his intention. He says: "Do you accept of our proposal for supplying you with rods, shapes, and band-iron; and if so, what quantity of each shall we send you?" Now we cannot but think that the fair and obvious construction of this language is, that the defendant then stood ready to supply the articles upon the terms already specified. And such appears to have been his own view of the case, as is manifest from his subsequent letter of the 8th of April.

2. It has been urged, that admitting this letter to contain a renewal of the former proposal, yet, *by the terms of it*, the plaintiffs were bound to signify their acceptance by return of mail. The question, in this aspect of it, is manifestly independent of any mercantile usage. That the defendant had a right to attach this condition to his offer is undeniable. The question is, whether he has done so; and whether such is the true construction of his letter.

In his letter of the 2d of March, the defendant had offered to supply the plaintiffs an assortment of hollow ware at certain prices; and in regard to this offer, in his letter of the 16th, he says: "We shall not consider ourselves holden to the offer made you on the 2d inst., unless you signify your acceptance thereof by return of mail;" and he then puts the inquiry with regard to rods, shapes, and band-iron, that has been already mentioned. Now, it should be borne in mind, that the defendant's proposal, in regard to these articles, had already been before the plaintiffs for at least ten or twelve days; and one claim put forth by them on the trial was, that during the month of March the price of these articles was constantly advancing in the market. The question then arises, whether under these circumstances it was the intention of the defendant to give them further time; and whether such intention can be fairly inferred from the language of his communication. In regard to the hollow ware, there can be no question. The plaintiffs were positively required to signify their acceptance by return mail. And when, in the same letter and under similar circumstances, they are also required to decide upon the proposal in regard to the rods, &c., it is certainly not easy to see why the defendant should have made, or should have intended to make, a distinction between these classes of articles. Had the judge directed the jury that the defendant was not bound, unless the plaintiffs signified their acceptance by return of mail, we are by no means satisfied that the direction would have been wrong. As, however, he placed the case on grounds more favorable to the plaintiffs' claim, a decision upon this point is unnecessary. Any further discussion of it is therefore waived.

3. We come then to the inquiry, whether the instruction actually given to the jury is correct in point of law. And here it may be remarked, that it is very immaterial when the letter of the plaintiffs was

written: until *sent*, it was entirely in their power and under their control; and was no more an acceptance of the defendant's offer than a bare determination, locked up in their own bosoms and uncommunicated, would have been. And it surely will not be claimed that mere volitions, a mere determination to accept a proposal, constitute a contract. The plaintiffs then did not accept the defendant's proposition until the 20th, and for aught that appears [not] until the evening of that day. That they were bound to accept within a reasonable time was distinctly admitted in the argument; and if not admitted, the position is undeniable. The case of the plaintiffs then comes to this, and this is the precise ground of their claim: That they had a right to hold the defendant's offer under advisement for more than forty-eight hours, and to await the arrival of three mails from New York, advising them of the state of the commodity in the market; and having then determined to accept, the defendant was bound by his offer; and that this constitutes a valid mercantile contract. Now, in regard to such a claim, we can only say, that it appears to us to be in the highest degree unreasonable; and that we know of no principle, of no authority, from which it derives the slightest support.

Indeed, it seems to us to be subversive of the whole law of contracts. For it is most obvious, that, if during the interval the defendant was bound by his offer, there was an entire want of mutuality: the one party was bound, while the other was not. Had the proposition been made at a personal interview between the parties, there can be no pretence that it would have bound the defendant beyond the termination of the interview. The case of Cooke *v.* Oxley, 3 Term Rep. 653, is decisive on this point, and goes much further. There, A., having proposed to sell goods to B., gave him, at his request, a certain time to determine whether he would buy them or not; and it was held, that although B. determined within the time, A. was not bound. And Lord Kenyon there says: "Nothing can be clearer than that at the time of entering into this contract, the engagement was all on one side; the other party was not bound; it was, therefore, *nudum pactum.*" So also in the case of Payne *v.* Cave, 3 Term Rep. 148, it was decided that the bidder at an auction, under the usual conditions that the highest bidder shall be the purchaser, may retract his bidding at any time before the hammer is down.

Now, it is most manifest, that if the principle of these cases is to be applied to and govern the present, they are entirely decisive of it in favor of the defendant. It is however claimed, and perhaps justly, that the case of Cooke *v.* Oxley has been disregarded, if not overruled, by the more modern decisions; or at least that it has been holden not to apply to mercantile contracts, negotiated through the medium of the post-office. Thus, in the case of Adams *v.* Lindsell, 1 B. & A. 681, there was an offer to sell goods on certain specified terms, provided an acceptance of the offer was signified by return of mail. This was done; and it was held (the defendant not having retracted his offer in the mean time), that the contract was complete. It is not easy to reconcile this decision with that of Cooke *v.* Oxley, unless it can be distinguished on the ground that, as the offer was made through the mail, the party is to be considered as repeating the offer at every moment until the other party has had an opportunity of manifesting his acceptance. And this seems to have been the ground on which the case was placed by the Court of King's Bench. They say: "If the defendants were not bound by their offer, when accepted by the plaintiffs, till the answer was received, then the plaintiffs ought not to be bound till after they had received the notification that the defendant had received their answer, and was bound by it; and so it might go on *ad infinitum.* The defendants must be considered in law as making, during every instant of time their letter was travelling, the same identical offer to the plaintiffs; and then the contract is completed by the acceptance of it by the latter."

These positions are questioned, if not directly controverted, by Best, C. J., in the case of Routledge *v.* Grant, 4 Bing. 653. He says, "If they are to be considered as making the offer till it is accepted, the other may say, 'Make no further offer, because I shall not accept it;' and to place them on an equal footing, the party who offers should have the power of retracting, as well as the other of rejecting; therefore I cannot bring myself to admit that a man is bound when he says, 'I will sell you goods on certain terms, receiving your answer in course of post.'" He does not, however, profess to overrule the case of Adams *v.* Lindsell; nor was it necessary, as there were other grounds on which the rule in Routledge *v.* Grant was discharged.

In the case of M'Culloch *v.* The Eagle Ins. Co., 1 Pick. 281, decided by the Supreme Court of Massachusetts, the case of Cooke *v.* Oxley is cited with approbation and followed. And the decision there cannot easily be reconciled to the doctrines advanced in Adams *v.* Lindsell. For it was there held, that an offer to insure the plaintiff's vessel at a given premium, communicated by mail and promptly accepted, was not binding on the defendants, they having in the mean time written a letter retracting their offer. This decision proceeded upon the ground that the treaty was open until the plaintiff's letter notifying his acceptance, was received; and that, in the mean time, the defendants have a right to withdraw their offer. Parker, C. J., in giving the opinion of the Court, said, "The offer did not bind the plaintiff until it was accepted; and it could not be accepted, to the knowledge of the defendants, until the letter announcing the acceptance was received, or at most until the regular time for its arrival by mail had elapsed."

The case of Adams *v.* Lindsell is regarded as an authority, and followed, by the Supreme Court of Errors of the State of New York, in

Mactier *v.* Frith, 6 Wend. 103. And there the doctrine is asserted, that the acceptance of an offer, made through the medium of a letter, binds the bargain, if the party making the offer has not in the mean time revoked it. And the rule adopted in Massachusetts, that regards the contract as incomplete, until the party making the offer is notified of the acceptance, is rejected. The doctrine of Adams *v.* Lindsell and of Mactier *v.* Frith may perhaps be considered as receiving the implied sanction of the Supreme Court of the United States, in the case of Eliason *v.* Henshaw, 4 Wheat. 225; although a decision upon the precise point was unnecessary, the offer there not having been accepted according to the terms on which it was made.

We do not feel that the task is imposed upon us of reconciling these conflicting authorities, if indeed they do conflict; for within the principle of none of them can the claim of the plaintiffs be established.

In Mactier *v.* Frith, which goes as far as any of the cases on this subject, the rule is laid down, that the offer continues until the letter containing it is received, and the party has had a fair opportunity to answer it. And it is further said, that a letter written would not be an acceptance, so long as it remained in the possession or under the control of the writer. An offer then, made through a letter, is not continued beyond the time that the party has a "fair opportunity" to answer it. This is substantially the doctrine of the charge. And it is not only highly reasonable, but is supported by all the analogies of the law. Once establish the principle that a party to whom an offer is made, may hold it under consideration more than forty-eight hours, watching in the mean time the fluctuations of the market, and then bind the other party by his acceptance, and it is believed that you create a shock throughout the commercial community, utterly destructive of all mercantile confidence. No offers would be made by letter. It would be unsafe to make them.

It is only necessary to apply these principles to the case before us; and their application is exceedingly obvious. The proposal of the defendant, which had already been several days before the plaintiffs, was renewed early on the afternoon of the 18th. They show no act done by them signifying their acceptance, until the evening of the 20th. Was this within a reasonable time? Was this the first fair opportunity of manifesting their acceptance? We think this can hardly be claimed. Had the defendant had an agent in Hartford, through whom the offer was made, might the plaintiffs thus have delayed the communication of their acceptance to him? This would not be pretended. And can it vary the principle, that the offer, instead of being thus made, was made through the agency of the post-office? Had the offer of the defendant been promptly accepted, information of the acceptance would have reached the defendant on the evening of the 20th, in due course of mail. He waited until the 22d; and hearing nothing from the plaintiffs, he then virtually retracted his offer, by making such arrangements as made it impossible for him to fill their order. We think he was fully justified in so doing; and that upon every sound principle the rule in this case must be discharged.

In this opinion the other Judges concurred.

New trial not to be granted.

WILLIAM LORING AND ANOTHER v. CITY OF BOSTON.

SUPREME JUDICIAL COURT OF MASSACHUSETTS, MARCH TERM, 1844.

[*Reported in 7 Metcalf*, 409.]

ASSUMPSIT to recover a reward of $1000, offered by the defendants for the apprehension and conviction of incendiaries. Writ dated September 30th, 1841.

At the trial before Wilde, J., the following facts were proved: On the 26th of May, 1837, this advertisement was published in the daily papers in Boston: "$500 reward. The above reward is offered for the apprehension and conviction of any person who shall set fire to any building within the limits of the city. May 26, 1837. Samuel A. Eliot, Mayor." On the 27th of May, 1837, the following advertisement was published in the same papers: "$1000 reward. The frequent and successful repetition of incendiary attempts renders it necessary that the most vigorous efforts should be made to prevent their recurrence. In addition to the other precautions, the reward heretofore offered is doubled. One thousand dollars will be paid by the city for the conviction of any person engaged in these nefarious practices. May 27, 1837. Samuel A. Eliot, Mayor." These advertisements were continued in the papers but about a week; but there was no vote of the city government, or notice by the mayor, revoking the advertisements, or limiting the time during which they should be in force. Similar rewards for the detection of incendiaries had been before offered, and paid on the conviction of the offenders; and at the time of the trial of this case, a similar reward was daily published in the newspapers.

In January, 1841, there was an extensive fire on Washington Street, when the Amory House (so called) and several others were burnt. The plaintiffs suspected that Samuel Marriott, who then boarded in Boston, was concerned in burning said buildings. Soon after the fire said Marriott departed for New York. The plaintiffs declared to several persons their intention to pursue him and prosecute him, with the intention of gaining the reward of $1000 which had been offered as aforesaid. They pursued said Marriott to New York, carried with them a person to identify him, arrested him, and brought him back to Boston. They then complained of him to the county attorney, obtained other witnesses, procured him to be indicted and prosecuted for setting fire to the said Amory House. And at the March term, 1841, of the Municipal Court, on the apprehension and prosecution of said Marriott, and on the evidence given and procured by the plaintiffs, he was convicted of setting fire to said house, and sentenced to ten years' confinement in the State Prison.

William Barnicoat, called as a witness by the defendants, testified that he was chief-engineer of the fire department in Boston, in 1837 and for several years after; that alarms of fire were frequent before the said advertisement in May, 1837; but that from that time till the close of the year 1841, there were but few fires in the city.

As the only question in the case was, whether said offer of reward continued to be in force when the Amory House was burnt, the case was taken from the jury by consent of the parties, under an agreement that the defendants should be defaulted, or the plaintiffs become nonsuit, as the full Court should decide.

Peabody & J. P. Rogers, for the plaintiffs.

J. Pickering (City Solicitor), for the defendants.

SHAW, C. J. There is now no question of the correctness of the legal principle on which this action is founded. The offer of a reward for the detection of an offender, the recovery of property, and the like, is an offer or proposal, on the part of the person making it, to all persons, which any one capable of performing the service may accept at any time before it is revoked, and perform the service; and such offer on one side, and acceptance and performance of the service on the other, is a valid contract made on good consideration, which the law will enforce.[1] That this principle applies to the offer of a reward to the public at large, was settled in this Commonwealth in Symmes *v.* Frazier, 6 Mass. 344; and it has been frequently acted upon, and was recognized in the late case of Wentworth *v.* Day, 3 Met. 352.

The ground of defence is, that the advertisement, offering the reward of $1000 for the detection and conviction of persons setting fire to buildings in the city, was issued almost four years before the time at

[1] "The offer of a reward or compensation, either to a particular person or class of persons, or to any and all persons, is a conditional promise; and if any one to whom such offer is made shall perform the service before the offer is revoked, such performance is a good consideration, and the offer becomes a legal and binding contract. Of course, until the performance, the offer of a reward is a proposal merely, and not a contract, and therefore may be revoked at the pleasure of him who made it." Shaw, C. J., Freeman *v.* City of Boston, 5 Met. 56, 57. — ED.

which the plaintiffs arrested Marriott and prosecuted him to conviction; that this reward was so offered in reference to a special emergency in consequence of several alarming fires; that the advertisement was withdrawn and discontinued; that the recollection of it had passed away; that it was obsolete, and by most persons forgotten; and that it could not be regarded as a perpetually continuing offer on the part of the city.

We are then first to look at the terms of the advertisement, to see what the offer was. It is competent to the party offering such reward to propose his own terms; and no person can entitle himself to the promised reward without a compliance with all its terms. The first advertisement offering the reward demanded in this action was published March 26th, 1837, offering a reward of $500; and another on the day following, increasing it to $1000. No time is inserted in the notice, within which the service is to be done for which the reward is claimed. It is therefore relied on as an unlimited and continuing offer.

In the first place, it is to be considered that this is not an ordinance of the city government, of standing force and effect; it is an act temporary in its nature, emanating from the executive branch of the city government, done under the exigency of a special occasion indicated by its terms, and continued to be published but a short time. Although not limited in its terms, it is manifest, we think, that it could not have been intended to be perpetual, or to last ten or twenty years or more; and therefore must have been understood to have some limit. It was insisted, in the argument, that it had no limit but the Statute of Limitations. But it is obvious that the Statute of Limitations would not operate so as to make six years from the date of the offer a bar. The offer of a reward is a proposal made by one party, and does not become a contract until acted upon by the performance of the service by the other, which is the acceptance of such offer, and constitutes the agreement of minds essential to a contract. The six years, therefore, would begin to run only from the time of the service performed and the cause of action accrued, which might be ten, or twenty, or fifty years from the time of the offer, and would in fact leave the offer itself unlimited by time.

Supposing then, that by fair implication there must be some limit to this offer, and there being no limit in terms, then by a general rule of law it must be limited to a *reasonable time;* that is, the service must be done within a reasonable time after the offer made.

What is a reasonable time, when all the facts and circumstances are proved on which it depends, is a question of law. To determine it, we are first to consider the objects and purposes for which such reward is offered. The principal object obviously must be to awaken the attention of the public, to excite the vigilance and stimulate the exertions of police officers, watchmen, and citizens generally, to the detection and punishment of offenders. Possibly too it may operate to prevent offences, by alarming the fears of those who are under temptation to commit them, by inspiring the belief that the public are awake, that any suspicious movement is watched, and that the crime cannot be committed with impunity. To accomplish either of these objects, such offer of a reward must be notorious, known and kept in mind by the public at large; and for that purpose the publication of the offer, if not actually continued in newspapers, and placarded at conspicuous places, must have been recent. After the lapse of years, and after the publication of the offer has been long discontinued, it must be presumed to be forgotten by the public generally, and, if known at all, known only to a few individuals who may happen to meet with it in an old newspaper. The expectation of benefit then from such a promise of reward must in a great measure have ceased. Indeed, every consideration arising from the nature of the case confirms the belief that such offer of reward, for a special service of this nature, is not unlimited and perpetual in its duration, but must be limited to some reasonable time. The difficulty is in fixing it. One circumstance (perhaps a slight one) is, that the act is done by a board of officers, who themselves are annual officers. But as they act for the city, which is a permanent body, and exercise its authority for the time being, and as such a reward might be offered near the end of the year, we cannot necessarily limit it to the time for which the same board of mayor and aldermen have to serve; though it tends to mark the distinction between a temporary act of one branch and a permanent act of the whole city government.

We have already alluded to the fact of the discontinuance of the advertisement, as one of some weight. It is some notice to the public that the exigency has passed for which such offer of a reward was particularly intended. And though such discontinuance is not a revocation of the offer, it proves that those who made it no longer hold it forth conspicuously as a continuing offer; and it is not reasonable to regard it as a continuing offer for any considerable term of time afterwards.

But it is not necessary, perhaps not proper, to undertake to fix a precise time as reasonable time; it must depend on many circumstances. It is somewhat analogous to the case of notes payable on demand, where the question formerly was, within what time such note must be presented, and, in case of dishonor, notice be given, in order to charge the indorser. In the earliest reported case on the subject (Field *v.* Nickerson, 13 Mass. 131), the Court went no farther than to decide that eight months was not a reasonable time for that purpose.

Under the circumstances of the present case, the Court are of the opinion that three years and eight months is not a reasonable time.

within which, or rather to the extent of which, the offer in question can be considered as a continuing offer on the part of the city. In that length of time, the exigency under which it was made having passed, it must be presumed to have been forgotten by most of the officers and citizens of the community, and cannot be presumed to have been before the public as an actuating motive to vigilance and exertion on this subject; nor could it justly and reasonably have been so understood by the plaintiffs. We are therefore of opinion that the offer of the city had ceased before the plaintiffs accepted and acted upon it as such, and that consequently no contract existed upon which this action, founded on an alleged express promise, can be maintained.

Plaintiffs nonsuit.

HAMILTON v. LYCOMING MUTUAL INSURANCE CO.

Supreme Court of Pennsylvania, May Term, 1847.

[*Reported in 5 Pennsylvania State Reports*, 339.]

In error from the Common Pleas of Clinton.

May 29. Case stated for the opinion of the Court.

On the 22d of January, 1842, the plaintiff in error caused a survey to be made by the agent of defendants, of a building known as the Clinton Academy, and made a written application to the agent for an insurance. In this it was stated there was a flue in the house, secured by a sheet-iron collar. On the same day he executed and delivered to the agent a premium note, promising to pay in such sums as the directors might according to their charter demand. On this note the amount required to be paid in cash, together with the price of the policy, was paid; and the plaintiff received from the agent a certificate reciting the application, the note and the payments thereon, and stating that $1050 "will be insured on the property for five years from the date of the application, if the company approve the said application." The papers were transmitted to the company, and laid before the executive committee, who did not approve of the application, nor issue a policy; but the secretary wrote the agent that plaintiff must substitute an earthen collar for the sheet-iron one, and procure the consent or authority of the trustees of the building to his obtaining an insurance, and when the company were duly certified that these requisites were complied with, they would send him on the policy.

This consent was obtained in writing, and the required alterations made. The plaintiff informed the agent of these facts, and requested him to call and see the written assent, and that the requirements had been complied with. This request was constantly repeated during the summer, but not complied with, owing to a press of private engagements. The building was destroyed by fire in April, 1843. After this the agent wrote the defendants, stating the circumstances, and that it was merely through his own neglect he had not called on plaintiff, as requested, to see the alterations.

By the eleventh by-law, the duty of the agent was to make surveys and receive applications for insurance, and to transmit to the secretary all applications received and surveys made by him.

The facts as to plaintiff's interest were submitted, subject to the question of their relevancy. The building had been originally a church erected on land given for that purpose. A new church having rendered it almost unnecessary, the members of the congregation who had obtained a charter for a literary institution, in their individual capacities authorized plaintiff to repair the building, the expenses to be paid out of subscriptions, until which time plaintiff was to hold stock in the new corporation. He also held mechanics' liens for repairs made by himself, amounting to $1000. After repairing it, plaintiff occupied the building as an academy and dwelling-house. There was also religious worship occasionally had in the hall.

By the defendants' charter it was provided that all persons insuring became members of the corporation, whose affairs were to be managed by directors annually chosen by the members. And that every person, before he became a member by insuring, should, before he received his policy, deposit his note, part of which was payable in cash, and the residue at any time the directors should appoint. *Vide* acts 20th of March, 1840, p. 180; April 13, 1838, p. 363. By the act of 1842, p. 426, it was further provided that the company should have a lien for their premium notes on the insured property.

The Court (Woodward, P. J.) gave judgment for defendants for reasons, of which the following is but an outline. The charter intended policies to be the mode of defining the rights of the insured and their membership of the corporation. That there was a peculiar propriety for such a rule here, the members who were liable for the contracts of the company being scattered over the country, and liable to imposition if the naked agreement of the officers of the company bound it. The charter intending a policy as the final consummation of the contract, it was in this case incomplete. Nor would the neglect of the agent to call and examine the alterations be any discharge of the condition precedent of defendants [plaintiff?] sending to the company the written authority, by the trustees of the building, to effect the insurance. Under these circumstances, the company could not have enforced the payment of the note; the answer to that would have been, our contract is not yet closed. Supposing therefore the parol contract was binding on the corporation, it had not been fully entered into here.

The plaintiff in error (*propria persona*) submitted a written argument of forty-six pages. In the course of it, he said the defendants in the Court below put their whole defence on plaintiff's want of interest in the building, and authority to procure an insurance on it. That a corporation must be able to contract without seal, in the same manner as they were able to authorize a seal to be affixed to a contract; it being that precedent authority, of which the seal was evidence, which rendered it obligatory. This was declared in Bank v. Patterson, 7 Cranch, 299, which is affirmed in Rathbone v. Tioga, 2 Watts & Serg. 77, 80. To the same effect is Whitehall v. Whitehall, 3 Serg. & Rawle, 119; Danforth v. Schoharie, 12 Johns. 227; Hayden v. Middlesex, 10 Mass. 397; Fleckner v. Bank of the United States, 8 Wheat. 338; 2 Kent's Com. 289–291. There was nothing peculiar in the charter; and it, as well as the words of the certificate, implied that an insurance was effected from the date of the certificate and acceptance of the premium note.

The real question is, was there a contract? Now if a delivery of a policy would have been all that was necessary under the circumstances, that is conceded; for the policy would be but evidence of an antecedent contract. The formal papers required by the company were all executed; certain conditions were required; they were performed; after this, all that was left was the delivery of the policy; that was for them; and that they intended to do it, is shown by their retention of the money. If the consent of the trustees had been forwarded to the plaintiffs, the answer would have been,—See the agent; he transacts the business. The agent knew of the authority having been procured. There was no bargain to send that assent, but a requisition that before they sent the evidence of the contract they should know the fact was so.

The position that the plaintiff was not bound by his note is overthrown by Gray v. Foster, 10 Watts, 280. There, as in Armstrong v. M'Ghee, Addis. 261, it is ruled that acts indicating an assent of two minds are sufficient evidence of a contract. Of these there are enough to bind the plaintiff on his note.

Armstrong, contra. The reasoning of the Court below is the best argument for the defendant. The company were not bound until a policy issued. 2 Watts & Serg. 545. There were ample grounds for requiring this previous assent of the trustees of the property. By the charter, the premium notes are liens on the land of the insured, and it was for that purpose the company stipulated for it. The plaintiff had made the agent of the company his own agent to deliver this, and is bound by his neglect. 7 Watts & Serg. 348. But at all events there was no authority by an owner of the land competent to attach the lien of the note; hence the contract was not binding.

May 31. GIBSON, C. J. In commercial towns, where the members of the profession are familiar with the law of insurance, actions on mere agreements to insure, whether against fire or perils of the sea, are not uncommon. They are noticed in 1 Phillips on Insurance, § 3, p. 9; but it appears that the terms of the contract must have been settled by the concurrent assent of the parties, and that nothing must have remained to be done but to deliver the policy, else the risk will not have been begun; in other words, that the agreement must have had, at some particular instant, that *aggregatio mentium* which is indispensable in the constitution of every contract. But what are the tests of its presence? In M'Culloch *v.* The Eagle Ins. Co., 1 Pick. Rep. 278, the plaintiff wrote to learn the terms on which the defendant would be willing to insure his vessel on a particular voyage, and was answered that it should be done for a particular premium. He immediately sent an order for insurance on the terms proposed; but before it was written the defendant had despatched another letter, declining to take the risk; and it was held, that at no instant had there been a simultaneous expression of assent. On a principle somewhat analogous stands Cooke *v.* Oxley, 3 Term Rep. 653, in which it appears by the declaration that the defendant had offered the plaintiff a commodity at a particular price, provided the latter would give notice of his acceptance before a particular hour of the day; that the notice had been given within the time, but that the article had not been delivered; but judgment was arrested because the plaintiff had not laid a cause of action. This last case is resolvable into the principle, that either party may retract his offer while the matter is pending, just as a bid at auction may be retracted before the hammer is down. Such too is the principle of Routledge *v.* Grant, 3 Car. & P. 267; and it is a very practicable one where the negotiation is not carried on through the post-office. But the last case upon the point has overruled M'Culloch *v.* The Eagle Insurance Company. In Adams *v.* Lindsell, 1 Barn. & Ald. 681, the defendants had offered to sell the plaintiffs a parcel of wool on terms expressed in their letter, "receiving an answer in the course of post." The letter, being misdirected, did not go by course of post; but the plaintiffs wrote, as soon as it was received, that they would take the wool on the terms proposed. The defendants however, not having received the answer when they expected it, sold the wool to another. The Court said that, if a bargain could not be closed by letter before the answer was received, no contract could be completed through the medium of the post-office. That if the defendants were not bound by their offer when it was accepted, then the plaintiffs ought not to be bound till after they had received a notification that the defendants had received their answer and assented to it, and that so it might go on *ad infinitum*. That the defendants must be considered in law as making, during every instant their letter was travelling, the same offer to the plaintiffs, and that the contract was completed by the acceptance of it; and that, as the delay in notifying it arose from the mistake of the defendants themselves, it was to be taken against *them* that the answer had been received by course of post. I am unable to see how this conclusion can be resisted. The learned reporter of M'Culloch *v.* The Eagle Insurance Company has attempted to distinguish it from Adams *v.* Lindsell, principally on the ground that a treaty respecting insurance is necessarily subject to contingencies whilst it is forming. Undoubtedly. But the question remains: When is it entirely formed? Had their ship returned before the plaintiffs, in the former case, had answered, they would have been at liberty to decline the offer; but it follows not that they would have been at liberty to retract an actual acceptance before the defendant had received it. The truth is, the two cases are not to be reconciled; and the conclusion is inevitable, that an actual concurrence of assent, at any particular moment, is the ruling circumstance, the time of communicating it being comparatively unimportant.

But the contract before us was not negotiated by letter. The plaintiff applied to the defendants' agent for a policy on the Clinton Academy, then occupied by him; paid the requisite proportion of the premium; executed a premium note for the residue; and had a survey made according to the regulations at his own expense; all which was laid before the company, and referred to its executive committee. The secretary subsequently wrote to the agent, requiring the plaintiff to substitute an earthenware stove-pipe collar for his sheet-iron one, and to procure the assent of the trustees of the academy, who held the title, to the contract of insurance; and saying that, being duly certified that these things were done, he would send on the policy. The plaintiff accordingly made the substitution, procured the written assent of the trustees, told the agent what had been done, and repeatedly urged him to call at the plaintiff's house, and "attend to the matter." The agent replied, that "he must first bring him that paper of the trustees;" but, being requested to call and get it, he promised to do so, yet never did.

It is clear that the company is to be affected by the acts of its agent, within the scope of his authority, as acts done by itself. It appears by the eleventh by-law, that his business was to receive applications, take surveys and forward them, with the cash received and premium note, to the company; and it appears by the letter of the secretary, that it was the practice to negotiate the terms of insurance through him, standing in the attitude of an insurance broker. The case then stands thus: The company offered to effect insurance for a certain premium, on performance by the plaintiff of two conditions. These were performed, and the company had notice of it. The company was subsequently requested to call by its agent at the plaintiff's house, to see that the substitution was made, and receive the written assent of the trustees, which it promised to do but did not, and in the mean time the building was burnt down. There was no supineness on the part of the plaintiff, at least none which had not been induced by the agent; while the company, on the other hand, was chargeable with positive negligence. Now if I promise to reward a man if he will do me a particular service, and he does it, I am bound to reward him for it, though he had not engaged to do it. The nature of a conditional promise, resting on an executory consideration, was explained in Clark *v.* Russel, 3 Watts, 217; and it may be seen from it that the plaintiff, having actually performed what he had been requested to do, was entitled to have the policy. The terms of the contract were matured when the company had notice that its conditions were performed; and from that moment the risk was incurred. It would be unconscionable in it to insist upon its own omission to execute the policy, on the ground that the resolution of the trustees had not been handed to its agent, especially as he had prevented the plaintiff from tendering it by promising to call and get it. A parol agreement for a policy, therefore, was complete.

After the decision of the Supreme Court at Washington, in the Bank of Columbia *v.* Patterson's Administrators, 7 Cranch, 299, sanctioned by this Court in the Chestnut Hill and Spring House Turnpike Company *v.* Rutter, 4 Serg. & Rawle, 16, and by many courts in our sister states, it is too late to insist that a corporation can contract only by an instrument under its corporate seal. "When a corporation," said Judge Story, "is acting within the scope of the legitimate purpose of its institution, all parol contracts made by its authorized agents are express promises of the corporation; and all duties imposed on them by law, and all benefits conferred at their request, are implied promises for which an action lies." It has become a familiar principle, that a corporation may, by the instrumentality of its agents, contract within the sphere of its proper functions pretty much as a natural person may. The action in the very case of M'Culloch *v.* The Eagle Insurance Company, was founded, like the present, on a corporation's parol promise; and some years ago an action on an agreement for a policy against fire was tried before me, and a recovery had without objection on that ground, though the counsel retained by the corporation were among the soundest lawyers at the Philadelphia bar. We say, therefore, that the agreement was complete, and that the plaintiff is entitled to recover on it to the extent of the loss, if the sum insured will reach so far; to be liquidated, if the parties cannot agree, by a writ of inquiry of damages.

Judgment of the Common Pleas reversed, and judgment *quod recuperet* rendered by this Court.

THE BOSTON AND MAINE RAILROAD *v.* JOSEPH H. BARTLETT AND ANOTHER.

SUPREME JUDICIAL COURT OF MASSACHUSETTS, MARCH TERM, 1849.

[*Reported in* 3 *Cushing*, 224.]

THIS was a bill in equity for the specific performance of a contract in writing.

The plaintiffs alleged that the defendants, on the 1st of April, 1844, being the owners of certain land situated in Boston, and particularly described in the bill, "in consideration that said corporation would take into consideration the expediency of buying said land for their use as a corporation, signed a certain writing, dated April 1st, 1844," whereby they agreed to convey to the plaintiffs "the said lot of land for the sum of twenty thousand dollars, if the said corporation would take the same within thirty days from that date;" that afterwards, and within the thirty days, the defendants, at the request of the plaintiffs, "and in consideration that the said corporation agreed to keep in consideration the expediency of taking said land," &c., extended the said term of thirty days, by a writing underneath the written contract above mentioned, for thirty days from the expiration thereof; that, on the 29th of May, 1844, while the extended contract was in full force and unrescinded, the plaintiffs elected to take the land on the terms specified in the contract, and notified the defendants of their election, and offered to pay them the agreed price (producing the same in money) for a conveyance of the land, and requested the defendants to execute a conveyance thereof, which the plaintiffs tendered to them for that purpose; and that the defendants refused to execute such conveyance, or to perform the contract, and had ever since neglected and refused to perform the same.

The defendants demurred generally.

J. P. Healy, for the defendants, contended that there was no allegation in the bill of a consideration for the contract, as originally made, or as extended; and consequently that the same was not enforceable either at law or in equity. Howell *v.* George, 1 Madd. 1; 2 Story, Eq. § 787; Brownsmith *v.* Gilborne, 2 Str. 738; Colman *v.* Sarel, 3 Brown's C. 12; 1 Madd. C. Pr. 327; 1 Fonblanque, 42. The counsel also referred to 1 Harr. Dig. 603; Burnet *v.* Bisco, 4 Johns. 235; Tucker *v.* Woods, 12 Johns. 190; Bean *v.* Burbank, 4 Shepl. 458.

G. Minot (with whom was *R. Choate*), for the plaintiffs, suggested, that if the demurrer was sustained, it would not be for the reason stated, but on the authority of Cooke *v.* Oxley, 3 T. R. 653, and Tucker *v.* Woods, 12 Johns. 190, which are not now law. The question is one of mutuality rather than of consideration. The offer of the defendants was a continuing one, which might have been withdrawn at any time; but, when accepted, the effect was the same as if the offer had only been made the moment before. Such an offer requires no consideration. When accepted, there is promise for promise.

The case of Cooke *v.* Oxley is overruled by Adams *v.* Lindsell, 1 B. & Ald. 681; Mactier *v.* Frith, 6 Wend. 103; Peru *v.* Turner, 1 Fairf. 185; Kennedy *v.* Lee, 3 Merivale, 441; Averill *v.* Hedge, 12 Conn. 424; Carr *v.* Duval, 14 Pet. 77; 1 Sugden on Vendors, 164; M'Culloch *v.* Eagle Ins. Co., 1 Pick. 278. It is virtually overruled by the following cases decided by this Court: Thayer *v.* Middlesex Mut. Fire Ins. Co., 10 Pick. 326; Foster *v.* Boston, 22 Pick. 33; Bird *v.* Richardson, 8 Pick. 252. See also the remarks in 20 Am. Jurist, 17, on the case of Cooke *v.* Oxley, and the case of Hamilton *v.* Lycoming Mut. Ins. Co., 5 Barr, 339, in which it was virtually overruled.

Healy, in reply, said that in all the cases cited for the plaintiffs except the last, there was a consideration.

FLETCHER, J.[1] In support of the demurrer in this case, the only ground assumed and insisted on by the defendants is, that the agreement on their part was without consideration, and therefore not obligatory. In the view taken of the case by the Court, no importance is attached to the consideration set out in the bill; namely, "that the plaintiffs would take into consideration the expediency of buying the land." The argument for the defendants, that their agreement was not binding because without consideration, erroneously assumes that the writing executed by the defendants is to be considered as constituting a contract at the time it was made. The decision of the court in Maine in the case of Bean *v.* Burbank, 4 Shepl. 458, which was referred to for the defendants, seems to rest on the ground assumed by them in this case.

In the present case, though the writing signed by the defendants was but an offer, and an offer which might be revoked, yet, while it remained in force and unrevoked, it was a continuing offer during the time limited for acceptance; and, during the whole of that time, it was an offer every instant; but as soon as it was accepted it ceased to be an offer merely, and then ripened into a contract. The counsel for the defendants is most surely in the right, in saying that the writing when made was without consideration, and did not therefore form a contract. It was then but an offer to contract; and the parties making the offer most undoubtedly might have withdrawn it at any time before acceptance.

But when the offer was accepted, the minds of the parties met, and the contract was complete. There was then the meeting of the minds of the parties, which constitutes and is the definition of a contract.

[1] Wilde, J., did not sit in this case.

The acceptance by the plaintiffs constituted a sufficient legal consideration for the engagement on the part of the defendants. There was then nothing wanting, in order to perfect a valid contract on the part of the defendants. It was precisely as if the parties had met at the time of the acceptance, and the offer had then been made and accepted, and the bargain completed at once.

A different doctrine, however, prevails in France and Scotland and Holland. It is there held, that whenever an offer is made, granting to a party a certain time within which he is to be entitled to decide whether he will accept it or not, the party making such offer is not at liberty to withdraw it before the lapse of the appointed time. There are certainly very strong reasons in support of this doctrine. Highly respectable authors regard it as inconsistent with the plain principles of equity, that a person who has been induced to rely on such an engagement, should have no remedy in case of disappointment. But, whether wisely and equitably or not, the common law unyieldingly insists upon a consideration, or a paper with a seal attached.

The authorities, both English and American, in support of this view of the subject, are very numerous and decisive; but it is not deemed to be needful or expedient to refer particularly to them, as they are collected and commented on in several reports as well as in the text books. The case of Cooke *v.* Oxley, 3 Term Rep. 653, in which a different doctrine was held, has occasioned considerable discussion, and, in one or two instances, has probably influenced the decision. That case has been supposed to be inaccurately reported, and that in fact there was in that case no acceptance. But, however that may be, if the case has not been directly overruled, it has certainly in later cases been entirely disregarded, and cannot now be considered as of any authority.

As therefore, in the present case, the bill sets out a proposal in writing, and an acceptance and an offer to perform, on the part of the plaintiffs, within the time limited, and while the offer was in full force, all which is admitted by the demurrer, so that a valid contract in writing is shown to exist, the demurrer must be overruled.

WILLIAM H. TAYLOE, *Appellant*, *v.* THE MERCHANTS' FIRE INSURANCE COMPANY OF BALTIMORE.

SUPREME COURT OF THE UNITED STATES, JANUARY TERM, 1850.

[*Reported in* 18 *Curtis*, 191, 9 *Howard*, 390.]

THE case is stated in the opinion of the court.

Johnson, Attorney-General, for the appellant.

Lloyd and *Nelson*, contra.

NELSON, J., delivered the opinion of the court.

This is an appeal from a decree of the Circuit Court for the district of Maryland, which was rendered for the defendants.

The case in the court below was this. William H. Tayloė, of Richmond County, Virginia, applied to John Minor, the agent of the defendants, residing at Fredericksburg, in that State, for an insurance upon his dwelling-house, to the amount of $8000 for one year; and, as he was about leaving home for the State of Alabama, desired the agent to make the application in his behalf.

The application was made accordingly, under the date of 25th November, 1844, and an answer received from the secretary of the company, stating that the risk would be taken at seventy cents on the thousand dollars, the premium amounting to the sum of fifty-six dollars. The agent stated in the application to the company the reason why it had not been signed by Tayloe: that he had gone to the State of Alabama on business, and would not return till February following; and that he was desired to communicate to him at that place the answer of the company.

On receiving the answer, the agent mailed a letter directed to Tayloe, under date of the 2d of December, advising him of the terms of the insurance, and adding: "Should you desire to effect the insurance, send me your check payable to my order for $57, and the business is concluded." The additional dollar was added for the policy.

This letter, in consequence of a misdirection, did not reach Tayloe till the 20th of the month; who, on the next day, mailed a letter in answer to the agent, expressing his assent to the terms, and enclosing his check for the premium as requested. He also desired that the policy should be deposited in the bank for safe-keeping. This letter of acceptance was received on the 31st at Fredericksburg by the agent, who mailed a letter in answer the next day, communicating to Tayloe his refusal to carry into effect the insurance, on the ground that his acceptance came too late, the centre building of the dwelling-house in the mean time, on the 22d of the month, having been consumed by fire.

The company, on being advised of the facts, confirmed the view taken of the case by their agent; and refused to issue the policy, or pay the loss.

A bill was filed in the court below by the insured against the company, setting forth substantially the above facts, and praying that the defendants might be decreed to pay the loss, or for such other relief as the complainant might be entitled to.

I. Several objections have been taken to the right of the complainant to recover, which it will be necessary to notice; but the principal one is, that the contract of insurance was not complete at the time the loss happened, and therefore that the risk proposed to be assumed had never attached.

Two positions have been taken by the counsel for the company for the purpose of establishing this ground of defence.

1. The want of notice to the agent of the company of the acceptance of the terms of the insurance; and,

2. The non-payment of the premium.

The first position assumes that, where the company have made an offer through the mail to insure upon certain terms, the agreement is not consummated by the mere acceptance of the offer by the party to whom it is addressed; that the contract is still open and incomplete until the notice of acceptance is received; and that the company are at liberty to withdraw the offer at any time before the arrival of the notice; and this even without communicating notice of the withdrawal to the applicant; in other words, that the assent of the company, express or implied, after the acceptance of the terms proposed by the insured, is essential to a consummation of the contract.

The effect of this construction is, to leave the property of the insured uncovered until his acceptance of the offer has reached the company, and has received their assent; for if the contract is incomplete until notice of the acceptance, till then the company may retract the offer, as neither party is bound until the negotiation has resulted in a complete bargain between the parties.

In our apprehension, this view of the transaction is not in accordance with the usages and practice of these companies in taking risks; nor with the understanding of merchants and other business men dealing with them; nor with the principles of law, settled in analogous cases, governing contracts entered into by correspondence between parties residing at a distance.

On the contrary, we are of opinion that an offer under the circumstances stated, prescribing the terms of insurance, is intended and is to be deemed a valid undertaking on the part of the company, that they will be bound, according to the terms tendered, if an answer is transmitted in due course of mail accepting them; and that it cannot be withdrawn, unless the withdrawal reaches the party to whom it is addressed before his letter of reply announcing the acceptance has been transmitted.

This view of the effect of the correspondence seems to us to be but carrying out the intent of the parties, as plainly manifested by their acts and declarations.

On the acceptance of the terms proposed, transmitted by due course of mail to the company, the minds of both parties have met on the subject, in the mode contemplated at the time of entering upon the negotiation, and the contract becomes complete. The party to whom the proposal is addressed has a right to regard it as intended as a continuing offer until it shall have reached him, and shall be in due time accepted or rejected.

Such is the plain import of the offer. And besides, upon any other view, the proposal amounts to nothing, as the acceptance would be but the adoption of the terms tendered, to be in turn proposed by the applicant to the company for their approval or rejection. For if the contract is still open until the company is advised of an acceptance, it follows of course that the acceptance may be repudiated at any time before the notice is received. Nothing is effectually accomplished by an act of acceptance.

It is apparent, therefore, that such an interpretation of the acts of the parties would defeat the object which both had in view in entering upon the correspondence.

The fallacy of the argument, in our judgment, consists in the assumption that the contract cannot be consummated without a knowledge on the part of the company that the offer has been accepted. This is the point of the objection. But a little reflection will show that, in all cases of contracts entered into between parties at a distance by correspondence, it is impossible that both should have a knowledge of it the moment it becomes complete. This can only exist where both parties are present.

The position may be illustrated by the case before us. If the contract became complete, as we think it did, on the acceptance of the offer by the applicant on the 21st December, 1844, the company of course could have no knowledge of it until the letter of acceptance reached the agent on the 31st of the month; and, on the other hand, upon the hypothesis it was not complete until notice of the acceptance, and then became so, the applicant could have no knowledge of it at the time it took effect. In either aspect, and indeed in any aspect in which the case can be presented, one of the parties must be unadvised of the time when the contract takes effect, as its consummation must depend upon the act of one of them in the absence of the other.

The negotiation being carried on through the mail, the offer and acceptance cannot occur at the same moment of time; nor, for the same reason, can the meeting of the minds of the parties on the subject be known by each at the moment of concurrence; the acceptance must succeed the offer after the lapse of some interval of time; and if the process is to be carried further in order to complete the bargain, and notice of the acceptance must be received, the only effect is to reverse the position of the parties, changing the knowledge of the completion from the one party to the other.

It is obviously impossible, therefore, under the circumstances stated, ever to perfect a contract by correspondence, if a knowledge of both parties at the moment they become bound is an essential element in making out the obligation. And as it must take effect, if effect is given at all to an endeavor to enter into a contract by correspondence, in the absence of the knowledge of one of the parties at the time of its consummation, it seems to us more consistent with the acts and declarations of the parties, to consider it complete on the transmission of the acceptance of the offer in the way they themselves contemplated; instead of postponing its completion till notice of such acceptance has been received and assented to by the company.

For why make the offer, unless intended that an assent to its terms should bind them? And why require any further assent on their part, after an unconditional acceptance by the party to whom it is addressed?

We have said that this view is in accordance with the usages and practice of these companies, as well as with the general principles of law governing contracts entered into by absent parties.

In the instructions of this company to their agent at Fredericksburg, he is advised to transmit all applications for insurance to the office for consideration; and that upon the receipt of an answer, if the applicant accepts the terms, the contract is considered complete without waiting to communicate the acceptance to the company; and the policy to be thereafter issued is to bear date from the time of the acceptance.

The company desire no further communication on the subject, after they have settled upon the terms of the risk, and sent them for the inspection of the applicant, in order to the consummation of the bargain. The communication of the acceptance, by the agent afterwards, is to enable them to make out the policy. The contract is regarded as complete on the acceptance of the terms.

This appears also to have been the understanding of the agent; for, on communicating to the insured the terms received from the company, he observes: "Should you desire to effect the above insurance, send me your check payable to my order for fifty-seven dollars, and the business is concluded;" obviously enough importing that no other step would be necessary to give effect to the insurance of the property upon the terms stated.

The cases of Adams v. Lindsell, 1 Barn. & Ald. 681, and Mactier's Admrs. v. Frith, 6 Wend. 103, are authorities to show that the above view is in conformity with the general principles of law governing the formation of all contracts entered into, between parties residing at a distance, by means of correspondence.

The unqualified acceptance by the one of the terms proposed by the other, transmitted by due course of mail, is regarded as closing the bargain from the time of the transmission of the acceptance.

This is also the effect of the case of Eliason v. Henshaw, 4 Wheat. 228, in this court, though the point was not necessarily involved in the decision of the case. The acceptance there had not been according to the terms of the bargain proposed, for which reason the plaintiff failed.

2. The next position against the claim is the non-payment of the premium.

One of the conditions annexed to the policies of the company is, that no insurance will be considered as made or binding until the premium be actually paid; and one of the instructions to the agent was, that no credit should be given for premiums under any circumstances.

But the answer to this objection is, that the premium in judgment of law was actually paid at the time the contract became complete. The mode of payment had not been prescribed by the company, whether in specie, bills of a particular bank, or otherwise; the agent therefore was at liberty to exercise a discretion in the matter, and prescribe the mode of payment; and accordingly we find him directing in this case, that it may be paid by a check payable to his order for the amount. It is admitted that the insured had funds in the bank upon which it was drawn, at all times from the date of the check till it was received by the agent, sufficient to meet it; and that it would have been paid on presentment.

It is not doubted that, if the check for the premium had been received by the agent from the hands of the insured, it would have been sufficient; and in the view we have taken of the case, the transmission of it by mail, according to the directions given, amounts in judgment of law to the same thing. Doubtless if the check had been lost or destroyed in the transmission, the insured would have been bound to make it good; but the agent in this respect trusted to his responsibility, having full confidence in his ability and good faith in the transaction.[1] . . .

Upon the whole, without pursuing the examination further, we are of opinion that the decree of the court below should be reversed, and that the cause be remitted, with directions to the court to take such further proceedings therein as may be necessary to carry into effect the opinion of this court.

[1] The parts omitted relate to questions wholly foreign to the subject of "Mutual Consent." —ED.

VASSAR AND OTHERS v. CAMP AND OTHERS.

NEW YORK COURT OF APPEALS, SEPTEMBER TERM, 1854.

[*Reported in* 1 *Kernan,* 441.]

ACTION to recover damages for the breach of an alleged contract to deliver ten thousand bushels of barley.

On the trial of the cause at the Dutchess County Circuit, before Justice Barculo, it was proved that the plaintiffs were brewers, doing business at Poughkeepsie, and the defendants merchants and produce-dealers at Sackett's Harbor; that on the 22d of August, 1850, the defendants addressed and forwarded to the plaintiffs at Poughkeepsie, by mail, a letter dated on that day at Sackett's Harbor, in which they say: "We will undertake to deliver you at Albany, between the 1st and 20th October next, from 5,000 to 10,000 bushels of first quality Jefferson county barley of this year's growth, at 67½ cents per bushel, and weighing not less than 48 lbs. per bushel. It being understood that if this offer shall be accepted, speedy notice of the same be given us;" and that on the 26th of the same month, the plaintiffs wrote and forwarded to the defendants by mail a letter, in which they say: "Yours of the 22d inst. is before us, and in reply we accept of your offer for 10,000 bushels Jefferson county barley, and herewith enclose a contract for the same, signed by us, with duplicate; the latter you will execute and return by the next mail."

This letter contained a contract signed by the plaintiffs, and a duplicate thereof to be signed by the defendants, which duplicate was in the words following: "Sackett's Harbor, August 26, 1850. For and in consideration of one dollar to us in hand paid by M. Vassar & Co., the receipt whereof is hereby acknowledged, we hereby agree to deliver them in the city of Albany, on or before the 20th of October next, 10,000 bushels of first quality Jefferson county two-rowed barley, of this season's growth, to weigh not less than 48 pounds per bushel, at sixty-seven and a half cents per bushel (67½-100), cash on delivery. Measuring divided as usual."

On the 30th of August, the defendants forwarded to the plaintiffs by mail a letter dated that day, in which they say: "Your favor of the 26th instant reached us this day. By reference to our proposal you will perceive that it was not restricted to any one particular kind of barley, except 'first quality Jefferson county barley.' We have therefore enclosed the contracts you sent us, and send you others with our signature and a duplicate for you to sign and send us. We have extended the period of delivery to the 30th of October, as there will be at least ten days' delay from the date of your letter before we can receive and act upon your reply. As soon as received, we shall send amongst the farmers and secure the first lots, even at an extra price, and when not threshed out, shall caution them against breaking the barley as little as possible."

In this letter the defendants re-enclosed to the plaintiffs the contract and duplicate received from them, without signing the latter, and forwarded to the plaintiffs a proposed contract signed by the defendants, dated August 30th, 1850, in the same language as the duplicate above set forth, omitting the words "two-rowed," and inserting 30th of October instead of the 20th as the time for the delivery, with a duplicate thereof to be signed by the plaintiffs. This last-mentioned letter, with the enclosures, was received by the plaintiffs on the 3d or 4th of September; and they signed the duplicate received by them, enclosed it in a letter which they addressed to the defendants at Sackett's Harbor, and on the 4th of September deposited this letter, so addressed, in the post-office at Poughkeepsie. In this last-mentioned letter, as appears by a copy thereof retained by them, the plaintiffs said: "Yours of the 30th ultimo, enclosing contract for 10,000 bushels of barley, was received this morning, and herewith return the duplicate signed by us. Your correction in regard to its being purely of the two-rowed kind was perfectly right, although in our letter of the 26th inst. it did not occur to us that your county raised any other kind of barley to any very considerable extent. We have no objection to receiving either kind, provided it has been grown together; but if it comes separately we expect you will keep it apart, it being quite difficult to malt it when mixed, grown on different farms. We are glad to notice your remark respecting care in selecting good qualities, and especially the caution to your farmers towards breaking the kernels in the process of threshing."

On the 14th of September the defendants wrote to the plaintiffs, referring to the letter of the former of the 30th of August, stating that they had been daily expecting and awaiting a reply, but had received none, and that there had been so much delay that it would be then difficult to purchase in Jefferson county the proposed quantities of first quality barley, as purchasers had within a few days previous been among the farmers, and engaged a large portion of the crop, and requesting that the proposed contract forwarded to the plaintiffs on the 30th of August be returned. To this the plaintiffs, under date of 19th September, replied, stating what they had done on the 4th of September, as hereinbefore stated. By subsequent letters the plaintiffs insisted that there was a valid contract which the defendants should fulfil, which the latter denied.

The defendants gave evidence tending to prove that the letter of the 4th of September, with the counterpart of the contract signed by the plaintiffs, was never received by them, or their agents or clerks, and that they had no knowledge or notice that the plaintiffs had assented to or signed the same until the receipt of their letter of the 19th of September; and that the defendants were in a situation and ready to have performed the contract, and could have done so with profit, if they had received the counterpart signed by the plaintiffs, or had notice that they assented to the contract at any time prior to about the middle of September.

The plaintiffs gave evidence tending to prove that the letter of the 4th of September was received by mail at the post-office at Sackett's Harbor, and placed by the postmaster in the letter-box of the defendants in that office.

The jury, in response to written interrogatories submitted to them by the court, found "that the letter of the plaintiffs of the 4th of September, containing the counterpart, and addressed and deposited as hereinbefore stated, was transmitted by mail to the post-office at Sackett's Harbor, and was there deposited by the postmaster in the letter-box or drawer of the defendants in said office, on or about the 7th day of September aforesaid; and that there was no sufficient evidence that the defendants ever received such letter;" and also assessed the amount of damages in the event that the plaintiffs were entitled to recover. Thereupon the said justice ruled and decided that the contract was obligatory upon the defendants, and ordered judgment for the plaintiffs for the amount of the damages assessed; and the counsel for the defendants excepted. This judgment was affirmed by the Supreme Court at general term, in the second district. The defendants appealed to this court.

There were other questions litigated and decided, distinct from the question whether or not there was a valid contract; but they were peculiar to the facts of this case, and not of general interest.

J. A. Spencer, for the appellants.

C. Swan, for the respondents.

SELDEN, J. The first and most important question presented in this case is: Did the contract for the delivery of 10,000 bushels of barley at the city of Albany ever become obligatory upon the defendants; and if so, at what time?

It is insisted, on the part of the plaintiffs, that a contract was consummated by the correspondence between the parties, irrespective of either of the formal agreements signed by them respectively; that the proposition made by the defendants, under date of the 22d of August, was distinctly and unequivocally accepted by the plaintiffs in their letter of the 26th; and that the contract thus perfected, having been subsequently embodied in the agreement dated August 30th, takes effect from the 26th, when the offer was accepted. There are, however, two conclusive objections to this position. First. It is evident from the correspondence, that there was no concurrence of the parties as to the precise terms of the contract, until the mutual execution of the written agreement, dated August 30th. The letters on one side mentioned only "first quality Jefferson county barley," while those on the other spoke of "two-rowed" barley. That this discrepancy in the views of the parties continued up to and after the 26th, is proved by the enclosures in the plaintiffs' letter of that day. The general acceptance of the defendants' offer, in the commencement of that letter, is qualified by the terms of the written contract enclosed, showing how the plaintiffs understood the offer. The plaintiffs cannot be held to have assented by that letter to any contract, except that which was embodied in the written agreement enclosed, to which the letter itself referred. The two must clearly be construed together. But again, if the parties had entirely agreed upon the terms of the contract in their previous correspondence, the change in the written agreement of the 30th of August, in regard to the time for the delivery of the barley, made that a new contract to take effect from the time of its adoption, and superseded the previous arrangement.

The real question then is as to the validity of the agreement dated August 30th, and as to the time when it took effect, if at all. This agreement was signed by the defendants, and transmitted by them on the day of its date by mail to the plaintiffs, with a counterpart to be signed by the latter and returned. The plaintiffs received the documents on the 4th of September, signed and enclosed the counterpart, and deposited it in the mail the same day, addressed to the defendants at Sackett's Harbor, where they resided. Was any thing more necessary to complete the agreement; did the contract become obligatory upon the deposit of the counterpart in the mail, duly executed by the plaintiffs, or was its receipt by the defendants, or notice to them of its execution, essential to its validity?

This precise question has been so fully considered in several modern cases, that it would be a work of entire supererogation to discuss it here. It arose in England in the case of Adams *v.* Lindsell, 1 Barn. & Ald. 681. In that case an offer to sell wool was made through the mail. The offer was received by the plaintiffs on the 5th of September, who wrote and mailed their answer, accepting the offer, the same evening; but this answer was not received until the 9th of September by the defendants, who in the mean time, supposing their offer had not been accepted, had sold the wool to other parties. The action was for the non-delivery of the wool; and if the contract was regarded as consummated on the 5th of September, when the answer accepting the offer was mailed, the defendants were liable; but if not until its receipt on the 9th, then no liability attached. The court held unanimously that the contract became obligatory on the 5th, when the answer of the plaintiffs was deposited in the mail. In the case of Mactier *v.* Frith, 6 Wend. 103, the same question arose in this State, and was very elaborately discussed by our late Court of Errors. The court in that case, by an almost unanimous vote, affirmed the doctrine of Adams *v.* Lindsell, in opposition to that of M'Culloch *v.* The Eagle Ins. Co., 1 Pick. 278, in which the Supreme Court of Massachusetts had adopted a different rule. The decision in Mactier *v.* Frith has since been followed in our State in the case of Brisban *v.* Boyd, 4 Paige, 17; in the State of Connecticut, in the case of Averill *v.* Hedge, 12 Conn. 424; in Pennsylvania, in the case of Hamilton *v.* Lycoming Ins. Co., 5 Barr, 339; and in Georgia, in Levy *v.* Coke, 4 Georgia R. 1.

The question has also again arisen in England, and been passed upon by the House of Lords there, in the case of Dunlop *v.* Higgins, 12 Jurist, 295. In that case, the case of Adams *v.* Lindsell is referred to, and confirmed in the most decided and unequivocal terms. The doctrine of this case therefore, and that of Mactier *v.* Frith, 6 Wend. 103, must be considered as too firmly settled, both in this country and in England, to be shaken or doubted. It is moreover maintained, in the cases referred to, by the most satisfactory and conclusive reasoning.

But it is insisted by the defendants' counsel, that this case is taken out of the rule by the concluding clause in the defendants' letter of the 30th August, which is in these words: viz., "We have extended the period of delivery to the 30th of October, as there will be at least ten days' delay from the date of your letter before we can receive and act upon your reply. *As soon as received*, we shall send amongst the farmers and secure the first lots, even at an extra price, and where not threshed out, shall caution them against breaking the barley as little as possible." The idea advanced is, that this clause, taken in connection with that in the defendants' letter of the 22d August, in which they say, "It being understood that if this offer be accepted, speedy notice of the same be given us," is equivalent to an express condition that the defendants would be bound from the time when *they should receive* notice of the plaintiffs' acceptance, and not before. But this position gives, I think, a force and an interpretation to those clauses which was never intended, and which they will hardly bear. The clause in the letter of the 22d August cannot with propriety be supposed to refer to any other than a notice by mail, through which the whole negotiation was no doubt expected to be and was in fact conducted. When a notice is to be given by mail, in most cases, if not in all, it is sufficient for the party giving notice to deposit in the mail. He can do nothing more to insure its safe delivery, and is not responsible for its miscarriage. In regard to the clause in the letter of the 30th August, it appears to me plain that it was not intended and cannot be construed as fixing the time when the contract should become obligatory, but as expressive merely of the promptness with which the defendants *designed to act*, upon receiving notice that their offer was accepted. Something less equivocal than this should be required to change a fixed and settled rule of law.

My conclusion therefore is, that the contract was perfected, and became obligatory upon all the parties, on the 4th of September, when the counterpart was deposited in the mail, and not before. It being a contract purely prospective, having no relation to any thing past, the antedating has no effect whatever upon the time of its inception.

Denio, J. [After discussing the other questions.] I come therefore to the inquiry, whether there was in fact any contract really concluded between the parties for the sale or for the procuring and delivery of barley by the defendants to the plaintiffs. There cannot be any dispute about the facts. The correspondence prior to the 30th August is only material for the purpose of determining who the contracting parties were, and as explanatory to what afterwards took place; for the defendants, by their letter of that date, inserted in the proposed contract a substantial alteration of the terms which the plaintiffs had proposed, which prevented it from amounting to an acceptance of the contract which the plaintiffs had offered to enter into. That letter was therefore a fresh proposal, and amounted to nothing unless it should be assented to by the plaintiffs. On the day the plaintiffs received it by mail at Poughkeepsie, they subscribed the brief contract enclosed in it, which they re-enclosed in a letter addressed to the defendants at Sackett's Harbor. That letter with its enclosure arrived at its destination by due course of the mail, and was placed by the postmaster in the defendants' drawer at the post-office. It was afterwards lost, without actually reaching the hands of the defendants. I do not see the slightest reason to doubt the entire integrity of the defendants. They had no motive for suppressing the letter if they had received it, but a strong one for acknowledging and acting upon it. The loss of the letter was a misfortune by means of which some two thousand dollars were lost; and the question is upon which of these parties the law casts the burden of that loss. This depends upon the question whether a binding and operative executory contract resulted from the facts which have been mentioned; for if such a contract was effected, the plaintiffs were entitled to the benefit of it, though the breach on the part of the defendants was not wilful or designed, but was the result of accident and misfortune. Where two parties, both being present together, enter into negotiations looking to the making of a contract, the minds of both must ordinarily meet at the same time upon the same identical terms, or no contract is made. Where the parties reside at a distance from each other, and the negotiation is conducted by written correspondence, though there must be the assent of both parties to the same provisions, it is of course impracticable that such assent should be manifested simultaneously. One must state what he is willing to agree to, and the other must, when the proposition has reached him, assent to the same terms, and in some manner manifest that assent. Prior to the case which I am about to mention, the authorities were supposed to leave it doubtful whether a contract was created by the assent of the party to whom the proposal was made, until the evidence of such assent had actually come to the knowledge of the party who had made the proposal. That doubt was put at rest by the decision of the Court for the Correction of Errors, in Mactier *v.* Frith, 6 Wend. 106. Two persons were joint-owners of a cargo of brandy which had been shipped on their account in France for the port of New York. Frith, one of the parties, resided at St. Domingo; and Mactier, the other joint-owner, resided in New York. Frith, while the cargo was supposed to be at sea, wrote to Mactier, proposing that the latter should take the adventure solely on his own account. While that offer remained open, and after the brandy had arrived in New York, Mactier wrote to Frith that he had decided to take the adventure on his own account, and had credited him, Frith, with the invoice. The letter was forwarded; but before it could reach Frith, Mactier died, and a controversy arose between Frith and the representatives of Mactier as to the ownership of Frith's original share of the cargo. The determination of this controversy depended upon the question whether a contract of sale had been consummated before Mactier died. The court held, reversing a decree of the Chancellor, that such a contract had been concluded. The principle established was, that it was only necessary that there should be a concurrence of the minds of the parties upon a distinct proposition, manifested by an overt act; that the sending of a letter announcing a consent to the proposal was a sufficient manifestation, and consummated the contract from the time it was sent. The court therefore held that the property in the brandies passed in Mactier's lifetime.

It would answer no useful purpose to review the antecedent authorities which were examined and considered in that case. Being a judgment of the court of last resort, it is high evidence of the law, and necessarily decides the question now before us, unless there is a material distinction in principle between the two cases. The contract in the case of Frith *v.* Mactier was an executed one; but the alleged agreement here was executory. I do not perceive that this constitutes a distinction favorable to the defendants. If such facts would constitute a contract which would pass the title to property, there is no good reason for holding that it would not be sufficient to bring into existence an executory undertaking, binding the parties by way of agreement.

The defendants' counsel, however, maintains that by a fair construction of the proposition made by the defendants in their letter of the 30th of August, it was made a condition that the contract should not become operative until the plaintiffs' assent had actually come to the knowledge of the defendants. Notwithstanding the rule of law which I have considered as settled by the judgment of the Court of Errors, I do not doubt but that a party proposing to contract may make it a condition that no bargain shall arise or be consummated until the affirmative answer of the party shall be actually received by the party proposing. The question then is, whether such a condition is found in this letter. It is not so stated in terms. By the next preceding letter of the plaintiffs they had proposed the 20th of October as the time for the delivery of the barley. The defendants changed the time by extending it ten days, till the 30th of October. For this change they give the following reason: "We have extended the period of delivery to the 30th of October, as there will be at least ten days' delay from the date of your letter before we can receive and act upon your reply." There is nothing in this, as it seems to me, indicative of an intention to shift the consequences of a miscarriage of a letter from the plaintiffs to the defendants. It is apparent that no idea of the loss or miscarriage of the plaintiffs' expected letter was in the minds of the defendants. They counted on the fidelity of the mails and of the officers of the post-office; and as a delay in completing the contract had arisen from the modification of the terms, they proposed a later period for the delivery of the barley, corresponding with that delay. To create a distinction which should be sufficient to take a case out of the rule of law to which I have referred, the condition should be explicitly stated, so that the party to whom the proposal is made may, should he think proper, despatch a messenger, or take some other method of performing the condition by bringing the acceptance home to the knowledge of the other party. But the letter proceeds: "As soon as received, that is, [the answer], we shall send among the farmers and secure the first lot," &c. This remark conveyed no intimation to the plaintiffs that a condition was intended to be annexed, which would change the ordinary rule of law. It seems to have been made in order to show the plaintiffs the kind of diligence and energy with which they intended to execute the contract. They had placed the time of delivery so remote as to afford them time to purchase and forward the barley after the receipt of the acceptance, taking into account the ordinary delays of the mail. That the mail was contemplated as the medium of transmission is perfectly plain from all the letters, and especially from the subsequent ones written by the defendants, in which they suggest that the miscarriage has been occasioned by an error in that department. Such delays the defendants took into consideration and provided for, but they made no suggestion as to what was to be the consequence of the miscarriage of a letter, simply because no such circumstance had crossed their minds. Upon the whole case, I am of opinion that the contract became operative when the plaintiffs signed the duplicate contract and placed it in the post-office addressed to the plaintiffs, and that the accident by which the letter failed to come to the actual knowledge of the defendants was the misfortune of the defendants and not of the plaintiffs. I am consequently in favor of affirming the judgment of the Supreme Court.

Judgment accordingly.[1]

[1] See Duncan v. Topham, 8 C. B. 225, *accord.*—Ed.

ABRAM FITCH AND PROSSER JONES, *Appellants*, v. ADRASTUS SNEDAKER, *Respondent*.

NEW YORK COURT OF APPEALS, JUNE TERM, 1868.

[*Reported in* 38 *New York Reports*, 248.]

WOODRUFF, J.[1] On the 14th of October, 1859, the defendant caused a notice to be published, offering a reward of $200 . . . "to any person or persons who will give such information as shall lead to the apprehension and conviction of the person or persons guilty of the murder of" a certain unknown female.

On the 15th day of October, before the plaintiffs had seen or heard of the offer of this reward, one Fee was arrested and put in jail; and though not in terms so stated, the case warrants the inference that, by means of the evidence given by the plaintiffs on his trial and their efforts to procure testimony, Fee was convicted.

This action is brought to recover the reward so offered. On the trial the plaintiffs proved the publication of the notice, and then proposed to prove that they gave information before the notice was known to them, which led to the arrest of Fee. This evidence was excluded. The plaintiffs then offered to prove that, with a view to this reward, they spent time and money, made disclosures to the district attorney, to the grand jury and to the court on the trial after Fee was in jail, and that, without their effort, evidence, and exertion, no indictment or conviction could have been had. This evidence was excluded.

The court thereupon directed a nonsuit.

It is entirely clear that, in order to entitle any person to the reward offered in this case, he must give such information as shall lead to both apprehension and conviction. That is, both must happen, and happen as a consequence of the information given. No person could claim the reward whose information caused the apprehension, until conviction followed: both are conditions precedent. No one could therefore claim the reward, who gave no information whatever until after the apprehension, although the information he afterward gave was the evidence upon which conviction was had, and however clear that, had the information been concealed or suppressed, there could have been no conviction. This is according to the plain terms of the offer of the reward, and is held in Jones v. The Phœnix Bank, 8 N. Y. 228; Thatcher v. England, 3 Com. Bench, 254.

In the last case it was distinctly held that, under an offer of reward, payable "on recovery of property stolen and conviction of the offender," a person who was active in arresting the thief and finding and restoring

[1] Clerke, J., delivered a short concurring opinion. — ED.

part of the stolen property, giving information to the magistrates, tracing to London other of the property, and producing pawnbrokers with whom the prisoner had pledged it, and who incurred much trouble and expense in bringing together witnesses for the prosecution, was not entitled to the reward, as it appeared that another person gave the first information as to the party committing the robbery.

In the present case, the plaintiff, after the advertisement of the defendant's offer of a reward came to his knowledge, did nothing towards procuring the arrest, nor which led thereto, for at that time Fee had already been arrested.

The cases above referred to therefore establish that, if no information came from the plaintiffs which led to the arrest of Fee, the plaintiffs are not entitled to recover, however much the information they subsequently gave, and the efforts they made to procure evidence, may have contributed to or even have caused his conviction; and therefore evidence that it was their efforts and information which led to his conviction was wholly immaterial, if they did not prove that they had given information which led to his apprehension, and was properly rejected.

The question in this case is simple. A murderer having been arrested and imprisoned in consequence of information given by plaintiff before he is aware that a reward is offered for such apprehension, is he entitled to claim the reward in case conviction follows?

The ruling on the trial, excluding all evidence of information given by the plaintiffs before they heard of this reward, necessarily answers this question in the negative.

The case of Williams *v.* Carwardine (4 Barn. & Ad. 621, and same case at the assizes, 5 Carr. & Payne, 566) holds that a person who gives information according to the terms of an offered reward is entitled to the money, although it distinctly appears that the informer had suppressed the information for five months, and was led to inform, not by the promised reward, but by other motives. The court said the plaintiff had proved performance of the condition upon which the money was payable, and that established her title; that the court would not look into her motives. It does not appear by the reports of this case whether or not the plaintiff had ever seen the notice or handbill posted by the defendant, offering the reward; it does not therefore reach the precise point involved in the present appeal.

I perceive, however, no reason for applying to an offer of reward for the apprehension of a criminal any other rules than are applicable to any other offer by one, accepted or acted upon by another, and so relied upon as constituting a contract.

The form of action in all such cases is assumpsit. The defendant is proceeded against as upon his contract to pay, and the first question is, Was there a contract between the parties?

To the existence of a contract there must be mutual assent, or, in another form, offer and consent to the offer. The motive inducing consent may be immaterial, but the consent is vital. Without that there is no contract. How then can there be consent or assent to that of which the party has never heard? On the fifteenth day of October, 1859, the murderer, Fee, had, in consequence of information given by the plaintiffs, been apprehended and lodged in jail. But the plaintiffs did not, in giving that information, manifest any assent to the defendant's offer, nor act in any sense in reliance thereon; they did not know of its existence. The information was voluntary, and in every sense (material to this case) gratuitous. The offer could only operate upon the plaintiffs after they heard of it. It was prospective to those who will in the future give information, &c.

An offer cannot become a contract unless acted upon or assented to. Such is the elementary rule in defining what is essential to a contract. Chitty on Con., 5th Am. ed., Perkins's notes, p. 10, 9 and 2, and cases cited. Nothing was here done to procure or lead to Fee's apprehension in view of this reward. Indeed, if we were at liberty to look at the evidence on the first trial, it would appear that Fee was arrested before the defendant offered the reward.

I think the evidence was properly excluded and the nonsuit necessarily followed.

The judgment should be affirmed.

Judgment affirmed.[1]

COUNTESS OF DUNMORE AND HUSBAND, *Advocators.* ELIZABETH ALEXANDER, *Respondent.*

COURT OF SESSION IN SCOTLAND, DECEMBER 15, 1830.

[*Reported in* 9 *Shaw and Dunlop*, 190.]

THE Countess of Dunmore, being about to change a servant, and having heard that Elizabeth Alexander was to leave the service of Lady Agnew of Lochnaw, wrote to her ladyship, mentioning the circumstance; stating that the wages she gave were £12 12*s.* per annum, and requesting to be informed as to Alexander's character. Lady Agnew, in answer, stated that she could recommend Alexander, who would gratefully accept the proposed wages; and her ladyship added as follows: "If Lady Dunmore decides upon taking Betty Alexander, perhaps she will have the goodness to mention whether she expects her at the new or the old term." On the 5th of November, the Coun-

[1] See Neville *v.* Kelly, 12 C. B. N. S. 740. — ED.

tess wrote to Lady Agnew, requesting that she would "have the goodness to engage Betty Alexander for her at the £12 12*s.* a year, but she wishes to have her at the new term, or as soon after as possible, because her present one must go at that time." The letter went through the post-office to Lochnaw; but as Lady Agnew had gone to Glasserton-house, it was sent to her there. Upon receiving it, Lady Agnew desired her housekeeper, Mrs. Moore (who had accompanied her), to notify the Countess's answer to Alexander, which was done by Moore making an addition on the letter itself and putting it into the post-office, addressed to Betty Alexander at Lochnaw. In the mean while, on the 6th of November (the day after writing the above letter), the Countess addressed another letter to Lady Agnew, intimating that she no longer needed Alexander. This second letter, which was also addressed to Lochnaw, was sent to Lady Agnew at Glasserton-house, and was received immediately after the other had been despatched to the post-office; but Lady Agnew sent the second one by express to the post-office, and both the letters arrived at Lochnaw together, and were delivered at the same moment to Alexander. Lady Dunmore having declined to receive her, or pay her wages, Alexander raised an action against her in June, 1827, before the Sheriff of Sterlingshire, for wages and board-wages for six months, from Martinmas, 1826, to Whit-Sunday, 1827, at which time she had got a new situation.

In support of this demand, she maintained that there had been a completed contract, and that Lady Dunmore was not entitled to resile. On the other hand, her Ladyship contended, that as the two letters had been received by Alexander at one and the same time, she was made aware that her services would not be required, and therefore she could not allege a concluded contract.

The Sheriff Substitute, after finding the above facts, pronounced an interlocutor in these terms: "Finds that Lady Agnew's card, formerly referred to, cannot from its terms be interpreted or considered otherwise than as an offer, on the part of the pursuer, to engage as a servant with the noble defender on the terms proposed in a communication, to which this card is obviously an answer;—finds it doubtful whether the noble defender's reply to Lady Agnew, contained in the card libelled on, uncommunicated in any way to the pursuer, can be held to be a legal acceptance of the offer;—but finds it very clear, abstractedly from the specialties of the present case, that the said card, communicated, in the manner it has been done, to the pursuer by Lady Agnew through Mrs. Moore, must be held to be a legal acceptance of the offer, an actual engagement of the pursuer, and a completion of the contract, from which neither party was entitled to resile;—therefore finds that the issue of this case depends on the solution of the question, whether a party who accepts of an offer is entitled at the same moment, *unico contextu*, or with the same breath, to retract his acceptance. And the Sheriff Substitute being of opinion that the instant an offer is accepted of the contract is completed, it is not in the power of either party to retract or resile;—that from the moment of acceptance, as expressed by Mr. Bell in treating of the contract of sale, there is between the parties *in idem placitum concursus et conventio*, which constitutes the contract;—finds that, as in the present instance the contract was completed by the transmission of the card libelled on to the pursuer, the engagement between the parties was rendered indissoluble without the consent of both, and that it was consequently beyond the power of the noble defender at any time, however short the interval, to retract the acceptance, or resile from the engagement;—on these grounds repels the defences, and decerns against the noble defenders in terms of the conclusion of the libel."

The Sheriff Depute having adhered, the Countess advocated; and the Lord Ordinary, having ordered cases, "advocated the cause, approved of the findings in point of fact in the Sheriff's interlocutor; but altered the judgment of the Sheriff, sustained the defences, assoilzied the advocators," and found no expenses due.[1]

Alexander reclaimed.

[1] The Sheriff, in his interlocutor of 15 February, 1828, has stated the facts correctly, but his judgment seems inconsistent with the facts he has found. He puts his opinion on the ground that the contract was only completed by the communication to the pursuer of Mrs. Moore's letters; yet he conceives there was some interval betwixt her knowledge of the consent and of the recall which rendered the latter ineffectual. But as the letters were delivered to the pursuer by the same person and at the same moment, while it is impossible to know which was first read, they must be held as one communication, and the notification of recall being simultaneous with that of the consent must do it away altogether.

The pursuer in this court has not attempted to support the Sheriff's view. But assuming that the Lady Agnew's letter of the 2d of November contained an offer on the part of the pursuer, and that Lady Dunmore's letter of the 5th was an acceptance of that offer, she contends that the contract was completed, so as to bar resiling, either by the writing or putting that letter into the post-office, or at least by its being received by Lady Agnew.

The Lord Ordinary thinks it doubtful if the letter of the 2d can be held as an offer made on the pursuer's part, or any thing but an answer to Lady Dunmore's inquiries. But at any rate it seems clear, from the terms of her letter of the 5th, that Lady Dunmore did not understand it as such, and that she did not mean her letter as an acceptance communicated to Lady Agnew, as acting for the pursuer. The letter plainly gives a commission to Lady Agnew to act as the writer's mandatory in engaging the pursuer, conceiving that the contract was still to be made. Now, having given such a commission, it was in the power of Lady Dunmore to give contrary instructions to her mandatory; and if these were received in such time that the mandatory was able to recall any step that she had taken before the contract was completed, no obligation could be incurred.

Even if the letter of the 5th could be viewed as an acceptance, it seems impossible to hold that it was sent to Lady Agnew as mandatory of the pursuer, so that the receipt of it by her completed the bargain. The writer plainly constitutes Lady Agnew as her mandatory in what was to be done, although it may be possible to hold

LORD BALGRAY. The admission that the two letters were simultaneously received puts an end to the case. Had the one arrived in the morning, and the other in the evening of the same day, it would have been different. Lady Dunmore conveys a request to Lady Agnew to engage Alexander, which request she recalls by a subsequent letter, that arrives in time to be forwarded to Alexander as soon as the first. This, therefore, is just the same as if a man had put an order into the post-office, desiring his agent to buy stock for him. He afterwards changes his mind, but cannot recover his letter from the post-office. He therefore writes a second letter countermanding the first. They both arrive together, and the result is, that no purchase can be made to bind the principal.

LORD CRAIGIE. I take a different view. Lady Agnew, acting for the servant, writes to Lady Dunmore, stating Alexander's readiness to accept the proposed wages, recommending her on account of her char-

that, by "engaging the pursuer," she meant that she should communicate to her the acceptance contained in her letter; and this communication was therefore necessary to perfect the location.

But the pursuer, on the authority of a passage in Mr. Bell's work, maintains that it is not necessary, in order to complete a consensual contract, that the acceptance should be communicated to the offerer, because the offerer having previously consented, the mere consent of the person to whom the offer is made constitutes the *consensus in idem placitum*, which is all that is requisite to perfect his engagement. But if the learned author's meaning is to be taken in the extensive sense here contended for, so as to bar the acceptor from resiling, it does not seem to be supported by sufficient authority. From the reason assigned, the mere existence of a consent in the acceptor's mind would have the effect to bind him, — a thing which might admit of being proved by a reference to oath. The pursuer indeed disclaims going this length, and contents herself with maintaining that any clear expression of the consent will be sufficient.

But surely the expression of consent made to a third person altogether unconnected with the offerer will not do, nor will the writing of a letter of acceptance be sufficient, if this letter is never sent. The Lord Ordinary conceives that if, after writing such a letter, the author should add a postscript, stating, that on further consideration, or in consequence of new intelligence, he did not choose to accept the offer, and if, from the letter's referring to other matters, he still thought it necessary to send it, the acceptance would be effectually recalled. But if this be the case, the same effect must follow when a second letter retracting the offer is transmitted by the same post, so as to be received at the same time, or where a communication to this effect is made by express or otherwise to the offerer before the acceptance reaches him. In short, each party may resile, so long as his offer or acceptance has not been communicated to the other party.

The pursuer may have suffered from the disappointment of her expectations; but the same hardship would have been felt, had Lady Dunmore written no letter but the last, in which case however the pursuer could have had no claim. The different ranks of the parties, and the great importance of the sum claimed to the one in comparison with the other, leads naturally to the giving all possible weight to the pursuer's argument. But any plea of favor of this kind is in a great measure done away by the very discreditable account which she has given as to her receipt of the letters, particularly in her deposition when examined as a haver in the Inferior Court.

acter, and concluding thus: "If Lady Dunmore decides on taking Betty Alexander, perhaps she will have the goodness to mention whether she expects her at the new or old term." Now, what is the answer of the Countess? A request to Lady Agnew to engage the servant at the wages mentioned, accompanied with a notice that "she wishes to have her at the new term," &c. Lady Agnew was thus the mandatory for both parties, the mistress and the servant; she was on the same footing as a person in the well-known situation of broker for both buyer and seller. Every letter between the principals, relative to an offer or an acceptance respectively, was, as soon as it reached Lady Agnew, the same as delivered for behoof of the party on whose account it was written. I hold, therefore, that when Lady Dunmore's letter reached Lady Agnew, the contract of hiring Alexander was complete,—the offer on the part of Alexander being met by an intimated acceptance on the part of the Countess. No subsequent letter from the Countess to Lady Agnew could annul what had passed by the mere circumstance of its being delivered, at the same time with the first, into the hands of Alexander. I do not think the servant could have retracted after the first letter reached Lady Agnew; and if she was bound, it seems clear that the Countess could not be free.

LORD GILLIES. I am decidedly of the opinion first expressed. Lady Agnew received a letter desiring her to engage a servant for Lady Dunmore. She proceeds to take steps towards this by putting a letter into the post-office for the purpose of making the engagement. But, before this letter reaches its destination, her authority to hire the servant is recalled; and, by the help of an express, she forwards the recall, so that it is eventually delivered through the same post with the former letter, and both reach the servant at once. They thus neutralize each other, precisely as in the case put by Lord Balgray, of an order and a countermand being sent through one post to an agent. I am therefore for adhering.

LORD PRESIDENT. I concur with the majority. There was no completed contract here, and Lady Dunmore was at liberty to resile as she did.

ALEXANDER THOMSON AND OTHERS (KEIR'S TRUSTEES), *Pursuers.* JAMES JAMES, *Defender.*

COURT OF SESSION IN SCOTLAND, JULY 12, 1855.

[*Reported in* 18 *Dunlop,* 1.]

THE pursuers, Mr. Thomson and others, were trustees appointed by the late Mr. Keir of Renniston. The lands of Renniston having been advertised for sale, the defender, Mr. James, on 21st November, 1853, made an offer for the purchase of the estate by a letter addressed to Mr. Thomson as follows: "Provided that a good and marketable title is given, I offer you £6400 (six thousand four hundred pounds) for the lands of Renniston; the purchase-money to be paid at such a time as may be hereafter mutually agreed upon."

On 24th November, 1853, Mr. Thomson replied to Mr. James, recommending that he should increase his offer by £50; and therefore stating, that before writing the parties interested in the sale, he should be glad to hear from Mr. James with the least possible delay, with an increase in his offer, and the terms of payment and interest he proposed.

In reply Mr. James wrote as follows on 26th November, 1853:—

DEAR SIR,—I am in receipt of your letter of the 24th instant regarding Renniston. The price which I have offered, viz. £6400, is in my opinion above the value of the property, and I cannot therefore increase it by the £50 as you propose; at the same time, I agree to be at half the expense of conveyance and stamps, and to the other conditions which you stipulate, except that I must insist upon a search, which I learn can now be had at much less expense than formerly. As regards the term of payment, I would propose Whit-Sunday next, and that my entry to the rents should be accordingly: this would save all questions as to rate of interest. Upon hearing from you that these terms are to be acceded to, the form necessary in such transactions will be gone through. I am, &c.

Mr. Thomson's reply was as follows:—

EDINBURGH, 28th Nov. 1853. DEAR SIR,—I am in receipt of yours of 26th, which I shall communicate to the parties, and give you their decision with the least possible delay. If, for the sake of £50, you don't get the place, or run the risk of a competition, all I can say is, you must not blame me. I remain, &c.

And on 1st December, 1853, Mr. Thomson again wrote to Mr. James as follows:—

DEAR SIR,—Annexed I beg to send copy of your offer for the lands of Renniston, dated 26th November, and I hereby accept the same, the price being six thousand four hundred pounds, payable at Whit-Sunday, eighteen hundred and fifty-four, and under the other stipulations referred to by you, as contained in my letter to you of 24th November, with this only alteration, that if you shall still wish for a search, it shall be furnished, though I humbly think, in the circumstances, you ought not to put the sellers to that expense. You had better instruct your agent to examine the titles now, so as to prevent any delay afterwards. Your entry to the lands is to be at Whit-Sunday next. I am, &c.

This acceptance of Mr. James's offer was posted at Edinburgh on 1st December. But of same date and on the morning of the same day, the defender posted a letter at Jedburgh, addressed to Mr. Thomson, withdrawing his offer for the purchase of Renniston. Both letters were delivered on the 2d December, 1853.

In these circumstances, the pursuers, holding that the defender had not the power to withdraw his offer, raised the present action of implement against him. They founded upon the correspondence, and particularly the letters of 26th November and 1st December, 1853, as constituting a valid contract of sale binding upon both parties.

The defender pleaded: That the offer having been withdrawn by him before it was accepted, and before any acceptance was intimated or delivered to him, any acceptance thereafter written out could not constitute a contract by or with him or binding upon him.

It was thought expedient to ascertain precisely the hours at which the letters of 1st December had been posted, and would reach their destination. A joint minute was accordingly lodged by the parties, stating, in regard to the letter from Mr. Thomson to the defender, dated 1st December, 1853: 1. That it must have been posted at the Castle Street receiving-office between half-past two and half-past four P. M. on the 1st December, 1853; 2. That it would be brought to the head office in Edinburgh at 5 P. M. on the same day; 3. That the hours of despatch from the General Post Office, Edinburgh, to Kelso, on the 1st December, 1853, were 7.15 A. M., and 4.45 P. M.; 4. That the letter referred to would be despatched from the General Post Office, Edinburgh, at 7.15 on the morning of the 2d December, 1853. In regard to the letter from Mr. James to Mr. Thomson, dated 1st December, 1853: 1. That it must have been posted at Jedburgh before three P. M., and despatched *via* Kelso at that hour; 2. That it must have arrived at the General Post Office, Edinburgh, the same night at 8.19; 3. That it would not be sent out for delivery till seven o'clock in the morning of 2d December.

In these circumstances the Lord Ordinary pronounced the following interlocutor: "The Lord Ordinary, having heard the counsel for the parties on the closed record, and on the motion by the pursuers for decree in their favor without farther inquiry, refuses the said motion, and appoints the case to be enrolled in the motion-roll, in order that the mode of settling the disputed facts may be settled."[1]

[1] The Lord Ordinary is of opinion that the letters libelled on, — viz., the letter of the defender to Mr. Thomson of 26th November, 1853, and the letter by

The pursuers reclaimed, and pleaded: That the offer was in general terms, and did not stipulate that the offerer should not be barred from retracting until the acceptance should actually reach him. It was immaterial, therefore, to inquire into details. It was sufficient that the defender's letter of retractation did not reach Mr. Thomson before the acceptance was posted. Nor could any unnecessary delay on the

the latter to the former, of 1st December thereafter, — were sufficient to constitute a binding contract of sale between the parties, provided the offer contained in the former of these letters was not recalled before it was accepted of by the latter. The defender, in making his offer, did not limit its binding effect to any specific period; and there was no such delay in the acceptance of that offer as rendered it inoperative at the time when it was accepted, if it had not been previously retracted.

On the other hand, the defender, as he did not state that he would remain bound by his offer for any definite period, was entitled, as the Lord Ordinary thinks, to retract that offer at any time before it was accepted of. And he maintains that, availing himself of that privilege, he retracted that offer on the 1st of December by his letter to Mr. Thomson of that date. Thus the question arises, whether the retractation of the offer by the one party, or the acceptance of it by the other, was the earlier in point of time.

The difficulty in determining this question appears to the Lord Ordinary to arise from the uncertainty as to which of the letters was first put into the post-office. If, at the time when Mr. Thomson's letter of acceptance was put into the post-office in Edinburgh, the defender's letter of retractation had not been placed in the post-office at Jedburgh, the bargain would appear to have been completed; because it appears to be settled, that when a written acceptance of such an offer is put into the post-office (in a case where the parties made the post-office the medium of conveying their communications), the contract of sale is thereby completed; and that the receipt of the acceptance by the offerer is not necessary in such a case; *vide* the case of Higgins, 2d July, 1847, D. ix. 1407, affirmed on appeal, 24th February, 1848, Bell, vi. 195; and it appears to the Lord Ordinary that on the same principle, when a written retractation of such an offer is put into the post-office before the offer is accepted, the offer is thenceforth recalled, and is no longer binding, and that the receipt of the retractation by the other party is not necessary for producing that effect.

At the debate, the parties, although they did not dispute that both the retractation and the acceptance were posted on the same day, — viz., the 1st of December, — were not agreed as to which of them was first posted; and in the hope of having this matter settled without judicial inquiry, the Lord Ordinary directed the parties to state in a minute what they were agreed upon as to the precise times of posting the letters. They accordingly lodged the joint minute No. 30 of process, and the statement in it is so far precise as to establish that the letter of retractation was put into the post-office at Jedburgh before three o'clock P.M., and the letter of acceptance was not put into the post-office in Edinburgh before half-past two o'clock P.M., on the 1st of December; but although both the letters were thus confessedly posted between half-past two and three o'clock of the same day, it is still left uncertain which of the two was first posted; and although the question of time is thus limited to a matter of minutes, yet the Lord Ordinary thinks that on principle the difference must be made the subject of inquiry, as if the dispute had related to hours or days. The pursuers, however, insist that they are entitled to decree in their favor without farther inquiry, on the admitted facts of the case, in respect that as they maintain the letter of retractation could have no effect until it was delivered; and they crave judgment on this point. It follows from what the Lord Ordinary has already stated, that he must refuse that motion.

part of the pursuer in accepting the offer be pleaded against him. Therefore the question arose purely, whether, notwithstanding the letter of retractation, the defender's offer was binding on him.

In posting the letter of acceptance within a reasonable time, the pursuer had done all that was required of him. Farther, by posting the letter he had put it out of his power to regain possession of it. The post-office then became not his messenger, but the messenger or servant of the person to whom the letter was addressed. The pursuer had lost all control over it, and could not have regained possession of it even if he had so desired. So far therefore as the pursuer was concerned, the letter of acceptance was delivered to the offerer by the act of posting.

But it was said that here there was no *concursus voluntatum*, and that such *concursus* was, according to the civilians, essential to the validity of every contract. But if by that was meant a concourse of wills, the existence of which was known to both parties at the same moment, in such a case as the present that was an impossibility. The principles laid down by civilians as necessary to the formation of a binding contract had no reference to the modes of communication by post, which did not then exist. That mode of transacting business being now universal, its conditions must be held to be imported into all such contracts taking place between parties living at a distance from each other. The fact of this being a purchase of heritage made no difference in the present case.

This is not a metaphysical question, but a question of Scotch law, to be decided, not according as Bartolus and Brunneman would have solved it, but according to principles of equity and justice, although civil law considerations might aid in the solution of it. The opinions of those writers, Bartolus, Brunneman, Baldus, &c., who may properly be called commentators, are not of great authority. They differ from the opinions expressed by Accursius, the author of the Gloss. These writers are not of high repute.[1] As one follows the other, their opinions do not rise higher than their source, and, as mere *dicta*, are therefore of little weight. These observations, however, do not apply to the later jurists, amongst whom may be classed Pothier, Toullier, and Heineccius.

Questions like the present were treated by the commentators not so much as questions of law as metaphysical questions — the speculations of learned men, but not intended for legislation nor for the guidance of law courts. They were not used as the foundation of practical law. But it was otherwise when Pothier wrote, for the jurists of that day refer to the actual decisions of the courts. No doubt they drew from the old commentators as sources of their opinion, but they wrote upon law as a practical science, and difficulties had appeared of applying

[1] Butler's *Horæ Juridicæ*, p. 98; Dictionnaire Universelle, *voce* Baldus.

that definition *consensus duorum pluriumvæ voluntatum in idem placitum* in the way in which the older commentators had gone. Pothier[1] is obliged to confess that there is not only contrary authority in the commentators, but, in order to get rid of the difficulty, he superinduces the view he takes of the contract of sale, which is inconsistent with the general opinion to which he has come in the first part of his text, putting two cases, in the one of which the acceptor has to be indemnified, as if there had been an obligation resting on the offerer, and in the second of which he is to have implement of the offer.

Thus the question must be disposed of on principles of equity and justice. The best way to solve it would be to sacrifice the words of the definition, and make a rule applicable to the transaction, and thus do justice to both parties, unless the principles of equity and justice must yield to the definition which the jurists have given, and all definitions are dangerous when attempted to be reduced to practice. Pothier had begun to express this difficulty, and Toullier[2] agrees with it. Warnköenig[3] follows Toullier. But these are not authorities on which the court ought to rely, unless no better can be got; for they are not safe, not merely because their opinions rest on an insecure foundation, merely adopting the general definition, but because there may be founded on them matter of great error, even according to their own stating of the question. Thus they put the three cases of voluntary revocation by the offerer, death, and insanity, all on the same principle. They deal with them as destroying or excluding completion of the contract altogether. Now the case of death is not so treated in modern law.[4] But there is a wide distinction in fact and nature between these three things. It may be, that on death or insanity there is something which destroys previous consent; but it cannot be said that the result stands on the same principle as where a party exercises his own will and withdraws his consent. In the one case it is voluntary. In the case of death or insanity it is beyond his power. The destruction by death or insanity of a previous consent is not brought about by the will of the party. It is not a revocation of consent as civilians treat it. Consent may be destroyed, but it is not a revocation, and stands on a different principle. To satisfy this definition, it would be sufficient, without any sign or letter, or any thing to signify to the acceptor that he had changed his purpose, for the offerer to show that there was no *consensus* between his mind and that of the acceptor, and that he had changed his mind. That is not the doctrine of modern law.

We get no satisfaction out of the older authorities, but we do find guides in the more modern authorities. Sugden (Lord St. Leonards),[5]

1 Pothier, *Traité du Contrat de Vente,* 1, 2, 3, 32.

2 Toullier, vol. vi. iii. 3, 39.

3 Warnköenig, p. 59.

4 Potter *v.* Sanders, 6 Hare's Chancery Cases, p. 1.

5 Sugden on Vendors and Purchasers (1851), p. 82, § 12.

who is an authority not to be repudiated, says that an acceptance by an owner of an offer by a letter will bind him from the time he posts his letter, although it is not received by the purchaser till the following day; and would be binding if the vendor died on the same day on which he posted his letter.[1] See also Dart's Compendium.[2]

American authorities take up the question, not on metaphysical principle, but on the principles of justice, as applicable to a different state of society from what it was when the commentators wrote.[3]

The English case of Adams[4] is a case of general doctrine, and is so referred to in most of the subsequent cases. It was not determined on a specialty. It is referred to by the Chancellor in the Scotch case of Higgins[5] as fixing that general principle. Where a party makes an offer limiting the time within which it shall be accepted, or when the offer is of such a nature that the law allows a certain time for its acceptance, the offerer is not entitled to resile or withdraw his offer within the time which he allows, or which the law gives the party for accepting it.

A party may reserve the right to retract the offer, or he may say, that although you have a certain time by law to accept, I shall also have such time to withdraw. That is his privilege, and he may so protect himself; but the party who is to accept is in a different situation. He is entitled to rely on an unqualified offer spontaneously sent to him. As in this case where no right to retract the offer is reserved, he is not to assume that the offerer secretly intends, notwithstanding, to retract that offer. He acts upon it. He accepts it; and he does so, because on principle and in equity he is entitled to act on it. The offerer has parted with his consent by the offer. He has put it in the power of the other party to receive it. It is no longer his to withdraw. The offerer had no power to retract until there was a reasonable time for an answer.[6]

The defender pleaded: That there was not here a completed contract of sale by the letters founded on. There were certain particulars important to be kept in view.

1. The contract here attempted to be enforced bears to be a contract for the sale of a landed estate. To such a contract, by the law of Scotland, writing is indispensable, — and writing such as binds both

[1] Potter, as above.

[2] Dart's Compendium of the Law of Sale, p. 118; Story on Contracts, 376, 377, § 384.

[3] Duer on Insurance.

[4] Adams v. Lindsell, 1 Barn. & Ald., 5th June, 1818, p. 682.

[5] Higgins v. Dunlop, 2d July, 1847, D. ix. p. 1407.

[6] Stair, i. 10, 2, 3; Erskine, iii. 3, 88; Bell's Com., i. 326, 327; Bell's Principles, §§ 73, 74, 75; Head v. Diggon, 3 M. & R. 97; Kent's Com., ii. 477; Routledge v. Grant, 18th Jan. 1828, Car. and Payne, iii. 267; Crawford, 18th Nov. 1807, F. C. M., *voce* Movables, No. 2.

parties at the same time. Facts and circumstances will not suffice; nor can they supply the place of writing. There must be a written acceptance subscribed and delivered. Until that is done there is *locus pœnitentiæ* on either side.[1]

2. In this case the offer requires that the offerer shall hear from the party to whom it is made,—indicating clearly that receipt of the acceptance was to be the *punctum temporis* when the bargain would be concluded.

3. Before the acceptance reached the offerer, the offer was retracted, and the retractation had reached the acceptor.

4. There is another specialty (which is disputed, and is not material in the present argument), viz., that the retractation was *de facto* put into the post before the acceptance; although in one view it may be necessary to fall back upon it, in which case the defender undertakes to prove it.

By what rule or principle is the question to be solved? The pursuers say, not by strict metaphysical principles of law, but by equity, that the court are to sacrifice the definition of the civil law, and make a rule founded on equity, as in mercantile law. On the other hand, the defender submits that the case is to be solved on the strict philosophical rule which is the foundation of the civil law and law of Scotland.

The rule of law is given in the Digest, *De Pactis*, in the words of Ulpianus,[2] who gives the ground of the rule,—that the meeting of the acts of the will must take place, like the meeting of two physical bodies, in one place. There must be *duorum pluriumvæ in idem placitum consensus*. To satisfy this definition, the concourse of the wills of both or all the contracting parties must be simultaneous. When both parties are in the same place,—*inter præsentes*,—the application of the rule is easy. In such a case, in order to complete the contract, the act of the will of each must be made known to the other. If, therefore, acceptance of the offer be made by a sign which is not understood by the offerer, there is no contract. So, if the offer be made in writing, and the party to whom it is made writes an acceptance and does not deliver it, there is no contract, because there is no *concursus* of wills. *Inter præsentes*, therefore, there is no contract until the act of the will of each is known to the other.

From the same definition it may be further deduced, that consent may be given *inter absentes*, *per nuntium*, or *per epistolam*. And this is quite consistent, provided you have an equivalent to what the law requires *inter præsentes*. This is well stated by a French civilian, Pardessus, who says, "There is required not only that the offer be known to the party to whom it is made, and the acceptance to the offerer,—but that up to the moment of the acceptance being made known, when the concourse of wills takes place, the will of the offerer

[1] Stair, i. 10, 9. [2] Ulpianus, Digest, ii. 14, 1.

shall have continued. Nothing farther is necessary then. No notification of receipt of the acceptance is required."[1]

This rule solves many of the difficulties which the opposite doctrine creates, because it gives a *punctum temporis*, viz., when the acceptance is known to the offerer, which at once seals the contract. That is also the rule of our law, founded on the civil law, which is the basis of our law of sale. No doubt the rule must in certain circumstances necessarily suffer modification. Either party may have so contracted as to put themselves out of the rule, or a principle may have grown up out of commercial law and practice which modifies it. 1. The offer may be gratuitous, in which acceptance may be presumed; or 2. The offerer may agree to remain bound for a certain defined time; or 3. Circumstances or usages of trade may introduce such a condition by implication. But apart from these specialties, such is this rule — giving the offerer a right to retract till the acceptance is known to him.

The highest and best authorities on such a matter are not the civilians or the commentators on the Roman law, but jurists properly so called, who treat of the law of nature. These writers are all clear, that to make a completed contract, acceptance must be known to the offerer.[2] Again, other things besides revocation prevent or obstruct the completion of the contract. The death or insanity of the offerer before acceptance is known to him will have this effect, and are placed in the same category with retractation by all the writers. Wherever matters are in such a situation that death or insanity of the offerer prevents the completion of the contract, there revocation does so. Yet in such a case there is only implied retractation. In the present case the retractation was direct and explicit.

In this matter the law of England is of no authority. Among other differences, the law of England holds that death or insanity does not put an end to the contract. The law of Scotland holds that it does. And so indeed in the whole law of sale the English law differs from ours. Then there is a marked difference between the two laws as to mandate. The law of England holds that death of the mandant immediately puts an end to the mandate, whether it be known to the mandatory or not. The law of Scotland holds differently. Therefore, as an authority in this case, the law of England must be rejected.

With regard to our own law there is not a vestige of authority in the writers on Scots law adverse to the doctrine of the civil law already quoted, or to the writers on the law of nations. The case of Crawford[3] has nothing to do with the doctrine of mutual contract. It was a case of specific appropriation. And as to the analogy of mandate — although

[1] Pardessus, *Droit Commercial*, vol. ii. p. 233 and 250 (2d ed.).

[2] Grotius, ii. 11, § 15; Pufendorff, iii. 6, § 15; Heineccius, Collected Works, vol. viii. p. 284; and Wolfius (Vattel's Abridgment), vol. iii. §§ 714, 715.

[3] Crawford, 18th Nov. 1807, Mor. App. i., *voce* Movables, No. 2.

analogy is a dangerous mode of reasoning — the distinction must be kept in mind between the case of a contract between mandant and mandatory, and of contracts between mandatory and third parties. In regard to the former the law is peculiar.[1] As to contracts between mandatory and third parties there is no peculiarity; in the law of mandate the general rules of the law of mutual contract apply.

Then as to the commentators on the civil law, their authority is uniform. From Bartolus, who in his age was considered the *speculum et lucerna juris*, and is so called by Cujacius, downwards, the rule is laid down without exception as above stated. But it is said that, according to modern writers, the definition of strict law is to be sacrificed, and the principles of equity are to be introduced. That may be true as to the common law of England, but not so as to the law of any other civilized country in Europe. Besides, what is meant in this sense by principle of equity but consuetude making law? It is not that equity is to be allowed to control the law, and there is no ground for equity to be brought in here. Modern civilians are all in favor of the rule.[2]

Now here there is a proposal made, through the medium of the post, to buy a landed estate. That proposal is retracted. No damage is alleged or claimed. The only counterpart of this offer, so as to make a contract, is acceptance. But acceptance is ineffectual until delivered — apart from the question of the knowledge of that acceptance, delivery is essential — to make it binding on the acceptor. Accordingly it is said to be delivered by being put into the box at a post-office, from which it could not be got back. The post-office is to be regarded merely as a messenger. The post-office regulations are merely for public convenience, and may be altered. They are not matter of law, but merely an accidental fact. But a letter may be got back, or may not reach its destination; or it may be anticipated by a swifter messenger, or there may be other modes of conveying intelligence contradicting the letter, or destroying its contents. The decision in the case of the Countess of Dunmore[3] negatives the doctrine that the posting of an acceptance is *eo ipso* completion of the contract. Therefore acceptance is not binding on the acceptor until it reach the party to whom it is addressed. It therefore could not, during that interval, bind the offerer. He had still right and power to resile. An offer is not an offer until it is received. An acceptance is not an acceptance until it is received. And the moment at which the contract is completed is that at which the acceptance is received by the offerer; because until then there is no expression of the acceptor's will effectual

[1] Lord Glenlee's opinion in Pollock v. Paterson, 10th December, 1811, F. C., p. 378.

[2] Pothier, *Traité de Vente*, i. 2, 3, § 32 (sub.); Toullier, *Droit Civil*, vol. vi. p. 745, § 714; Pardessus; Warnköenig, vol. ii. pp. 69, 70.

[3] Alexander v. Countess of Dunmore, 15th Dec. 1830.

to bind him. On these grounds the defence that there was here no completed contract ought to be sustained.[1]

LORD PRESIDENT. This action has been brought by the trustees of Mr. Keir of Renniston against Mr. James of Samieston to obtain implement of a contract said to have been completed by certain letters or missives for the purchase and sale of the estate of Renniston.

The facts as averred are few and simple. On 26th November, 1853, Mr. James wrote, and transmitted by post from the country, a letter addressed to Mr. Thomson (one of the pursuers) making an offer or proposal for the purchase of Renniston at £6400. That letter was received by Mr. Thomson in Edinburgh on the 28th of November, and was acknowledged on the same day by a letter in which Mr. Thomson said he would communicate with the parties, and give their decision with the least possible delay; and on 1st December Mr. Thomson posted at Edinburgh a written acceptance of Mr. James's offer. That letter of acceptance was addressed to Mr. James, and was received by him in the country, in due course of post, on 2d December. There is no question raised as to the formality of these writings, or as to their sufficiency to constitute a binding contract for the purchase and sale of Renniston, if the acceptance had been received by Mr. James before he had done any thing to withdraw the offer. But before Mr. James received the letter of acceptance he changed his mind; and on the 1st of December (being the day before the acceptance reached him) he posted at Jedburgh a letter addressed to Mr. Thomson recalling the offer. That letter was received by Mr. Thomson in Edinburgh on the 2d of December. As to all these facts the parties are agreed. The defender, Mr. James, makes some additional averments which are not admitted by the pursuers, and the relevancy of which is disputed. These additional averments are, — 1st, That the letter of recall was posted at Jedburgh, not only before the letter of acceptance was received, but before the letter of acceptance was posted at Edinburgh; and 2d, That the letter of recall was delivered to the pursuer at Edinburgh before the letter of acceptance was delivered to the defender in the country. It is contended for the defender, that either or both of these additional facts, if established, will be a sufficient defence against the action. The pursuers, on the other hand, dispute the relevancy of these averments; and they demand judgment in their favor on the undisputed facts of the case without further inquiry. The Lord Ordinary pronounced an interlocutor, of date 13th June, 1854, whereby he refused a motion made by the pursuers to have judgment pronounced in their favor without further inquiry; and directed that the case should be put in train for inquiry as to the first of the two averments to which I have

[1] See also Pandects, i. 14, 2; Grotius, *De Jure Belli et Pacis*, ii. 6, 1, 2; Pufendorff, iii. 6, 15; Brunneman; Bartolus, Com. on lib. xv., Digest, p. 94 of folio; Sugden's Vendors and Purchasers, p. 116; Story on Sale, 103.

alluded, — viz., the alleged priority of posting. It does not appear that the other averment was then so much, if at all, insisted on. That interlocutor of the Lord Ordinary in effect sustained the relevancy of the averment as to priority of posting, and of the defence founded on that averment; and the Lord Ordinary in a note explained the grounds on which he proceeded in taking that view of the case. The interlocutor of the Lord Ordinary having been submitted to review, and counsel having been heard against the interlocutor and in support of it, the Court, after deliberation, thought that the case had not been discussed in all its bearings quite so fully as was desirable, and it was set down for farther argument. In the course of that farther argument the case was discussed very fully and with remarkable learning and ability. Very great research was exhibited in bringing before us authorities, ancient and modern, and the *dicta* of writers not only of our own country, but of Continental Europe and of America. The ground then taken by the defender was not limited to the alleged effect of priority of posting on which he had first rested his defence. He took up also, and apparently with not less confidence, the other ground I have alluded to, namely, that his letter of recall had been delivered to the pursuers before their letter of acceptance had been delivered to him, as an additional or separate ground for holding that he was not bound by the acceptance.

The question thus raised (if the facts of the case are such as to present it pure for decision) is one of great importance, and of no small difficulty. I own that, at the conclusion of the last argument, the impression I had previously entertained in favor of the pursuers was materially weakened, especially by the argument submitted to us regarding the effect to be given to the fact, if established, that the letter of recall reached its destination before the letter of acceptance reached its destination. The subsequent consideration I have given to the case has however confirmed my first impression in regard to the general question of the completion of the contract by acceptance. But I have still some hesitation in holding that the case is free from specialty on one point, to which I shall presently advert, arising out of certain expressions in the defender's offer of 26th November, which may perhaps admit of being regarded as of the nature of special condition.

Assuming at present that there is no specialty in the case such as can materially affect the general question that has been raised and argued, I shall state the grounds on which I have formed the opinion, that the offer of purchase made by the defender in his letter of 26th November was effectually accepted by the pursuers' letter of 1st December, and that the contract was thereby completed.

The subject-matter of the transaction being the purchase and sale of land, I hold that writing on both sides was necessary to complete the bargain. But I hold that the two writings — the offer and acceptance in question — were sufficiently formal for that purpose; and that if the letter of acceptance had been delivered to the defender by post before he took any step towards the recall of his offer, the contract would have been complete, and the pursuers would have been entitled to enforce implement of it. That proposition I do not understand to be disputed. It was assumed in argument on both sides, and therefore it is unnecessary to refer to any authority in support of it. The real question in issue between the parties is, whether the offer was recalled before it was accepted. The defence against the action is, that the offer was recalled before it was accepted.

I hold that a simple unconditional offer may be recalled at any time before acceptance, and that it may be so recalled by a letter transmitted by post; but I hold that the mere posting of a letter of recall does not make that letter effectual as a recall, so as from the moment of posting to prevent the completion of the contract by acceptance. An offer is nothing until it is communicated to the party to whom it is made, and who is to decide whether he will or will not accept the offer. In like manner I think the recall or withdrawal of an offer that has been communicated can have no effect until the recall or withdrawal has been communicated, or may be assumed to have been communicated, to the party holding the offer. An offer, pure and unconditional, puts it in the power of the party to whom it is addressed to accept the offer, until by the lapse of a reasonable time he has lost the right, or until the party who has made the offer gives notice, — that is, makes known that he withdraws it. The purpose of the recall is to prevent the party to whom the offer was made from acting upon the offer by accepting it. This necessarily implies precommunication to the party who is to be so prevented.

The argument for the defender upon this branch of the case was rested upon what I cannot help regarding as a strained application of a rule or maxim, sufficiently sound in general application, but which cannot be applied in the most strictly literal sense that the words admit of. It was contended, that as the offerer had changed his mind, and had posted a letter announcing that change before the offeree had declared his mind by posting his acceptance, the intention or consent to purchase cannot be held to have continued until the consent to sell was declared, and consequently that at no one moment of time was there *in idem placitum consensus atque conventio*, which is said to be essential to a paction. It was argued, upon a rigid application of that definition, that the completion of the contract was interrupted by change of mind, though not yet communicated, just as it would have been by the death or insanity of the offerer, and that all these three events are classed together by some writers as being alike revocations of the offer. Death or insanity may prevent the completion of the contract as effectually as the most complete revocation, but they are not properly revocations of the offer. They are not acts of the will of the offerer, and their effect does not rest upon a supposed change of purpose. They interrupt the completion of the contract,—that is, the making of the contract,—because a contract cannot be made directly with a dead man or a lunatic. The contract is not made until the offer is accepted; and if the person with whom you merely intend to contract dies or becomes insane before you have contracted with him, you can no longer contract directly with him. You cannot, by adhibiting your acceptance to an offer, and addressing it to a dead man or a lunatic, make it binding on him, whether his death or insanity be or be not known to you. In such a case there is no revocation, in the correct use of the word, but there is an interruption—an effectual obstacle to the completion of the contract, equivalent in result to a revocation, though operating by very different facts and very different principles. Revocation or recall is an act of the offerer, by which he communicates his change of purpose, and withdraws from the offeree the right he had given him to complete the contract by acceptance. Having communicated his purpose to purchase, the offeree is entitled to regard that purpose as unchanged until a change is communicated. He has acquired a right, which he retains until it is withdrawn from him by a communication from the party who conferred it. If he exercises the right by a completed act of acceptance of the offer before notice has reached him, or ought in ordinary course to have reached him, the contract will be binding, although a change of mind on the part of the offerer had taken place, and although he had taken a step towards communicating that change of mind by writing a letter, or even putting it into the post-office. In a great many cases the maxim that there must be a concurrence of will at the moment of completion of the contract cannot be rigidly or literally applied. The very opposite may be the fact. Although one cannot, by accepting an offer, bind a dead or insane person, he may bind an unwilling person, one who has altogether changed his mind. Such cases are not unfrequent. If an offer bears that it is to be binding for a certain number of days or hours, the offerer may repent before the lapse of the given time, and yet at the end of it may find himself unwillingly bound; or if an offerer changes his mind, but does not take the proper steps to have his change of mind conveyed to the offeree,—either writes no letter, or writes a letter which he omits to send, or sends it by mistake to a wrong place,—he may find himself unwillingly bound. Other cases may be figured. Mere change of mind on the part of the offerer will not prevent an effectual acceptance,—not even although that change of mind should be evinced by having been communicated to a third party, or recorded in a formal writing, as for instance in a notarial instrument. In all these cases a binding contract may be made between the parties without that *consensus* or *concursus* which a rigidly literal reading of the maxim or rule would require.

Upon the grounds now indicated, I hold that the mere putting of the letter of recall into a distant post-office, before the acceptance was sent off, did not put an end to the offer and exclude the power of the offeree to bind the offerer by accepting the offer. I hold that a letter of recall has no effect till the recall has become known to the offeree, or should in due course have become known to him. In the present case the letter of recall reached its destination on 2d December, and on that day became known to the pursuers. The letter of acceptance had been posted on the preceding day, the 1st of December; but it is averred that it had not reached its destination when the recall was received on the morning of the 2d. I hold that, in the circumstances averred, the delivery and receipt of the letter of recall did not interrupt or prevent the completion of the contract. I do not think that the principle to which I have referred, as that applicable to the recall of an offer, applies equally to the acceptance of an offer; or that every thing which must be done, in order to effectuate the recall of an offer, must in like manner be done in order to give effect to the acceptance of an offer. The two things are in their nature different. The one consists in effectually undoing something that the party himself has already done, and which binds him unless it is effectually undone; the other consists in merely acceding to a proposal made. What it is that the acceptor must do in order to make his acceptance effectual, and to put it out of the power of the offerer to recall his offer, depends on circumstances. Some things he must do. He must make his acceptance in writing, and he must send forth or give up that writing to or for behoof of the offerer. It is not enough that he commits his acceptance to writing and locks it in his own repositories; and, on the other hand, it is not necessary that he shall deliver it personally to the offerer. When an offer is made by letter from a distance through the medium of the post, the offerer selecting that medium of transmission authorizes and invites the offeree to communicate his acceptance through the same medium. If the offeree avails himself of that medium of communication, and transmits his acceptance properly addressed through the post-office, and if the acceptance reaches its destination in the due and regular course of that medium of transmission, I am of opinion that the act of acceptance was completed by the putting of the letter into the post-office; and that a letter of recall, which did not arrive till after that act, cannot be held to have interrupted the completion of the contract. By putting the letter of acceptance into the post-office, the offeree did just what he was invited to do, and all that it was incumbent on him or possible for him to do in the way of acceptance, by the mode of communication which he was authorized, if not invited, by the offerer to adopt. This appears to me to be the general rule, and it is so laid down by Mr. Bell in his Commentaries, i. 327, and by the House of Lords in the case of Higgins. Mr. Bell says: "It is the act of acceptance that binds the bargain, and in the common case it is not necessary that the acceptance should have reached the person who makes the offer." In the case of Higgins, 6 Bell, 195, the Lord Chancellor laid down the same law, and held that the contract was completed by the posting of the acceptance. If the contract was completed by the posting of the acceptance, a letter of recall received afterwards could not annul the contract so completed. I think that the fair import of these authorities is, that an offer imports an obligation on the offerer conditional on acceptance; and that in the general case, if the offer has been sent by post, the offeree effectually avails himself of it, purifies the condition, and makes the bargain binding on the offerer by posting his acceptance. There may be extreme or extraordinary cases in which the offerer might not be bound by the fact that the letter of acceptance had been put into the post-office, as for instance if the mail was totally lost, and the letter never reached its destination; and the offerer, after waiting a reasonable time, and believing that the offer had not been accepted, sold the goods or property in *bona fide* to another. These are extraordinary occurrences, over which neither party has any control, and which neither of them was bound to anticipate or contemplate. Reasonable time may be given to cover such casualties or contingencies, but more cannot be required. The general rule, as laid down in the case of Higgins, is, that the writing and posting of the acceptance completes the contract so as to make it obligatory, and I think that the rule so laid down rests on principle.

The authority of Lord Stair was appealed to by both parties, but I think that inferences were deduced from the expressions used by that great authority which were not within the contemplation of the writer, and it is very certain that he had not in view that mode of making a contract by interchange of post letters which is so common in the present day, and which was adopted by the parties in the present case. At i. 3, 9, after treating of promises, Lord Stair says, "An offer hath the like implied condition of the other party's acceptance;" and again, "In mutual contracts the one party subscribing is not obliged till the other subscribe as being his acceptance." He is obviously there talking of a formal mutual contract in one writing to be subscribed by both parties. Again at i. 10, 6, he says, "If the promise be pendent upon acceptance, and no more than an offer, it is imperfect and ambulatory, and in the power of the offerer till acceptance." He does not there explain what constitutes acceptance; but somewhat further on, after noticing the formalities by which pactions were concluded among the Romans, and that with us writing is substituted in matters of importance, he goes on in § 9 to say, "In all which there is *locus pœnitentiæ* even after the agreement, and either party may resile till the writ be subscribed and delivered;" and one of the annotators on Stair (the present learned professor of law) in his note on this passage says, "Till such writings shall be exchanged, either of the parties is entitled to recede from the agreement, the rule being that in regard to such matters there can be no final or binding agreement till it shall be vouched by a regular and probative writing." From these and other passages I deduce the doctrine, recognized indeed by all our writers and authorities, that a simple offer is revocable till it be accepted; and that where writing is necessary, the writing, to make it available to the party in whose favor it is conceived, must be subscribed by the maker of it; and that even after subscribing it, the maker of it may withhold delivery, in which case also it will not be available to the opposite party; and although Lord Stair, in some of the passages to which I have referred, and especially in the passage regarding *locus pœnitentiæ*, is treating more particularly of dispositions and bonds, and such writings, following upon a previous agreement, I think that the principle is applicable to the written acceptance of an offer made in a separate writing, although there should not have been any previous agreement. But on these passages in Stair, I venture to make two observations: 1st, That he is treating of the case of the party who himself makes the writing and subscribes it, and of the requisites to initiating any obligation to be thereby imposed on him; and, 2d, That although he uses the word "delivered," he does not define that word, or say what is necessary to constitute delivery. He does not say that the writing must be delivered by the hand of the writer into the hand of the opposite party. That certainly is not necessary. It is not even necessary that it be delivered to the party in whose favor it is conceived: it may be placed in the custody of a third party, and then the question of delivery or non-delivery may depend on this other question, *quo animo* was it placed there? The doctrine means that while the maker of the writing abstains from handing it over, retains it in his own custody, his act of acceptance (if the writing be an acceptance) is not complete. Lord Stair certainly does not say that putting the writing into the post-office addressed to the offerer completes the contract, but as little does he say the reverse. He does not write in contemplation of such a mode of transacting. If the question is to be solved by the inquiry *quo animo* was the letter delivered into the custody of the post-office, there can be no doubt that it was so delivered for behoof of the party to whom it was addressed. If the letter constituting the offer had been sent by a messenger, and had requested that the answer should be returned by the bearer (which, I think, is implied in an offer sent by post), and if the offeree had accepted the offer, and delivered a sealed letter of acceptance to the bearer of the offer, and if while the bearer was on his journey back with the acceptance another messenger had brought a letter of recall of the offer, I think that the recall would have been too late to interrupt the completion of the contract.

In support of the contention that the acceptance was not complete till the letter of acceptance reached its destination, it was urged that until that event the acceptor might have interrupted or prevented the completion of the contract by recalling or revoking his acceptance,— that he might have sent the recall by the same or a more rapid conveyance, so that it would be received as soon as, or sooner than, the acceptance; and upon the authority of the case of Lady Dunmore, it was argued that if this had been done, the acceptance would not have been binding. Then, combining that proposition with the general rule that in matters of contract both must be bound or neither, it was argued that, as the acceptor was not irrevocably bound till his acceptance was received, neither could the offerer be bound. I think that here the argument for the defender partook of ingenious subtleties, and a straining of general rules to extremes. In the first place, the authorities we have on the subject of the power of an acceptor to revoke or recall his acceptance are very scanty, if indeed the doctrine of revocation or recall is at all applicable to an acceptance, which I much doubt. In strict language recall or revocation, which applies to an act already complete, but which the party is entitled to annul, cannot be applicable to an acceptance, which, once it is fully made by the acceptor, completes the contract, and leaves nothing more to be done or agreed to by either party. In the second place, I think there is a manifest distinction in principle between the mere abstaining from doing a thing which would be necessary to be done before you could be held to have completed your act, and that conduct which consists in a subsequent active interference set on foot for the purpose of undoing or counteracting the legal consequences of a thing you have already done, to the full extent that was required of you. When the letter of acceptance was put into the post-office there was nothing more to be done by the acceptor personally; whether he could interfere so as to counteract or annul the legal consequences that would have flowed from what he had already done if he had thenceforth remained inactive, may be a question, and may depend on circumstances, and on the character of the interference;—we have no such question here. But in the case of Lady Dunmore effect is said to have been given to something of that kind as sufficient to prevent the completion of the contract; that was a very peculiar case. In the first place, the correspondence there was not between the principals directly; there was an interposed person acting in some respects for both. In the second place, the two letters from the same party were received at the same time, the second undoing what the first proposed to do; and it appears to have been held that both were to be regarded as one writing,—the second letter as a postscript to the first,—and that so regarding them, the construction of the writing, taken as a whole, was hostile to the idea of a contract. But where there is no such postscript, no question as to the writing which is to be taken as the answer to the offer, no interference by the acceptor to undo or explain what he had already done, — when he has given away his written acceptance to the messenger to whom he was invited or authorized to intrust it, and has done so not for the purpose of being retained as for himself, but for the opposite purpose of being held for the offerer until given into his own hands; when that purpose has never been departed from, I think that we are out of the case of Lady Dunmore, and of any principle on which that decision can be held to have proceeded.

These are the grounds on which I think that if the offer of 26th November is to be regarded as free from any condition except the implied condition of accepting, the acceptance posted on 1st December must be held to have completed the contract, and that the letter of recall, which was in due course received the day after the acceptance had been posted, did not interrupt the completion of the contract, although the recall may have been posted before the acceptance was posted, or may have been received before the acceptance was received.

But I have said that there are expressions in the offer which may perhaps admit of being read as a condition. I allude to the last sentence, which is thus expressed: "Upon hearing from you that these terms are to be acceded to, the form necessary in such transactions will be gone through." These words appear to be suspensive and conditional upon hearing that the terms of the proposal are to be acceded to, and it becomes a question whether that suspensive condition is, or is not, applicable to the contract of sale. If it be applicable to the contract of sale, I think that there is authority for holding that the power to recall the offer continued until the actual receipt of the answer acceding to the terms, and consequently that if the letter of recall reached its destination before the letter of acceptance was received, effect would be due to the recall. In that view the defender's averment that his letter recalling the offer was despatched and reached its destination before he received Mr. Thomson's letter acceding to the terms of the offer, would, I think, be a relevant averment, and if proved or admitted, would be very material in the defence. But I doubt whether the expressions to which I have alluded can be held to apply to the contract of sale. I think they have reference rather to those formal proceedings which were to be consequent on the contract of sale, and which in all such transactions are necessary to complete the formal transference of the property to the purchaser, such as the executing of a formal disposition or deed of conveyance by the seller, &c. That I take to be the true meaning of the sentence; and when so understood, it does not raise any such specialty in the case as can affect the opinion I have expressed. I therefore think that judgment should go in favor of the pursuers.

LORD IVORY. I have given very anxious attention to this case, and the result is, that I am of the same opinion as your Lordship. Perhaps I should have contented myself with announcing that entire concurrence with your Lordship's opinion, because I not only agree in its result, but in the whole argument by which it is supported. I shall not attempt to detain the court by going over all the notes I have taken, but I shall endeavor to bring out the substantial view of the law as it has occurred to me.

With regard to the facts, it appears to me that there are only three of importance in the general question: 1st, That there was an offer to purchase an estate on the 26th of November; 2d, That there was an acceptance of that offer on the 1st of December; and, 3d, That there was a retractation dated the same day, but not reaching the acceptor till his acceptance had been posted. There is no other fact of any moment. It was a condition that this bargain was to be conducted by means of correspondence, and it is that circumstance which has occasioned the difficulty of the question. The question is simply this: Where an offer of sale has been accepted, no notice of the revocation of the offer having at that time come to the acceptor's knowledge, is there a completed contract by that offer and acceptance? or, whether the fact of acceptance may not be rendered ineffectual by an act of revocation by the offerer before the acceptance has reached him?

It is necessary before coming to the question of revocation to ask and to decide precisely what it is that constitutes the contract of sale when entered into in such circumstances, what is necessary for its completion, and what the *punctum temporis* at which it is to be considered as completed.

With reference to the argument we had as to the *punctum temporis*, if the contract is not completed till the acceptance has been received and notified, the power of revocation must exist till then; but if the completion of the contract rests upon the act of acceptance, it is this act that completes the contract, and from that moment there can be no retractation. It is perhaps an inaccurate expression to speak of revocation or retractation; this power comes more within the meaning of our words *locus pœnitentiæ*.

In discussing the question, I think the parties ran into confusion by mixing up what constitutes the contract and what empowers one or other of the parties to get quit of it or prevent its completion.

There is no doubt of the correctness of the general maxim, that in all mutual contracts there must be *consensus in idem placitum*,—that is to say, both parties must be agreed as to all conditions essential to the contract; otherwise the one party would have in view one contract, and the other a different one. So also both parties must be bound or neither, that is, to such conditions as have been agreed upon, so that one shall not be bound to any one thing which is intended to be mutually binding, and the other free. It does not, however, follow that there may not be stipulations and conditions as to which one may be bound, and to which it has never been intended that the other should be bound. In order to explicate this phase of the case, we must inquire what is the meaning of the parties, and the mutual though diverse obligations here made, these obligations being the considerations given for each other.

As to what was further maintained, that there must be a simultaneous concourse of the two wills, it must not be taken too absolutely, and much fallacy lurks in the argument used on this head by the defenders. For example, *inter absentes* the offer must necessarily be of one date, and the acceptance of another. It is the *concursus* of both of these which forms the contract, and the question is, — When does this *concursus* take place? Now, naturally speaking, there is no offer *quoad* the acceptor until the letter containing it reaches him. An offer by letter is, in some sort, *ad longum manum*, and until it reaches its destination there is only one will at work. If acceptance is then made, there is an instant *concursus*, and the offer hitherto in suspense takes effect, — the acceptance, when the offer comes to hand, merging with it into the completed contract.

But, according to the defender, there is no contract till the acceptance reaches back to the offerer. If so, when is the acceptor bound? It is his act of acceptance that binds him; but if the offerer be free till that acceptance reaches him, how is the acceptor to know whether he is bound at all, or when? And if the acceptor also be free till his acceptance has reached the offerer, how does the offerer know that his consent to the contract has so long continued?

On the contrary, if the acceptor be bound from the moment that he accepts, while the offerer remains free for a course of post later, how is this more consistent with the theory of simultaneity than the view which holds that the offerer is bound at the date of the acceptance? Accordingly, almost all the authorities concur in this, — that when the offer continues to be a subsisting offer at the date of the acceptance, the *concursus* which then takes place between the two matures the transaction into a completed contract.

It is clear to me, therefore, that had there been no retractation the sale would have been complete on the 1st of December. Upon this footing, the question was raised before the Lord Ordinary whether the retractation or the acceptance was prior in date. Had notice or delivery of the acceptance been supposed to be necessary, the case would have been wholly with the defender. In support of this view it is said that every part of the mutual contract, in order to take effect, must have *suum signum;* that the inner act of one mind is nothing in its relations and bearing upon another mind; and that in law an act of the mind, uncommunicated, is no act at all.

I see no reason to dispute these propositions, if properly understood.

But how do they apply to the present case? The offer, it is admitted on all hands, is nothing till it reaches the other party; it only becomes an offer by communication. The acceptance, according to the above propositions, must be in *pari casu* so long as it remains *sine signo suo.* But is it really in that predicament here? There is here constructive delivery. If it had been delivered to a messenger of the offerer, sent for that purpose, the case would have been clear. If delivered into the hands of a third party, as *quasi* trustee, it would also have been clear. Now, delivery into the post-office is in its circumstances clearly analogous. The post-office is in some sort a middleman between the parties, and has a recognized effect in other transactions.

In the second place, as to the effects of the retractation taking place before acceptance, there can be no doubt that a party may in a certain sense recall his offer, so long as there is no contract, — that is to say, so long as it is a mere offer; but after there is a complete contract, he cannot do so. Thus, if the preceding reasoning is sound, and if the contract was completed by the act of acceptance, though unknown to the offerer, the latter cannot revoke after the date of the acceptance.

This, however, is not the *species facti* which occurs here. The revocation bore as its date, in point of fact, the same day as the acceptance. The former contention related to the question, which of the two was earliest despatched. But postponing that question for the present, which is at any rate one of fact, the question now discussed has rather been, whether the retractation could in law have any effect before it was received by the acceptor. If it had not, it is plain that the acceptance was good, because the retractation was certainly not delivered until after the act of acceptance took place, according to the view of the latter which I have just supported.

This state of the question renders it necessary to resume consideration of the nature and effects of the offer. Now we have seen that the offer is *habile*, as such, only upon its receipt, and the party sending it must be held to be aware that, from that date alone could it have either meaning or operation. He must therefore have intended that it should subsist up to that date. He could certainly have given the acceptor a specific time for consideration; and it is no objection to say, that during this time he is held to be bound while the other is free. It is the same relation of parties as that which accrues in cases of sale and return, or of taking upon trial. But if *per expressum* such a state of matters may arise, it may do so no less by implication. Now, *inter absentes*, the existence of such implication is clearly rested upon principle. It arises necessarily *ex natura rerum* in such circumstances, and if it were otherwise commerce would be rendered impossible.

The tendency of courts and writers on jurisprudence in modern times has accordingly been all in this direction. Even the older authorities are divided, and many of their *dicta* appear to be ill-considered, amounting to little more than an *ipse dixit*, — an assertion without reasoning. As to Pothier, the exceptions to his rules, which he admits, themselves are destructive of his rules. He admits that damages may be due, if an offerer changes his mind; but why give damages if no wrong is done? And no wrong can be held to be done, if an offer is a thing essentially subject to recall as much as if the power of recall were an expressed condition of it when made.

But if I offer to sell, there can be no room for damage, provided between my offer and the ratified acceptance I have not changed my mind. *A fortiori*, as to actual shipments being binding, this is an effectual evidence of acceptance, which is the view of Troplong and other writers. The whole question resolves, in every other shape which it can take, into a matter of evidence, — whether or not a *jus quæsitum* has been created in favor of the offerer.

In questions of mandate consent is held to continue if once given, and the mandatory is instantly entitled to act and to bind his principal, and a revocation of the mandate goes for nothing. So much so, that in this case, had the sale been to be effected through a mandatory, it would have been perfectly good. The same holds good in the case of orders to commission agents, and orders to ship goods. In all these cases consent is capable of being recalled before it has been acted on, but after this has taken place a *jus quæsitum* has been created.

Accordingly, as in the first branch of the question, I hold that the acceptor is bound from the date of his acceptance, and that, from that date, he is entitled to incur charges, to purchase, if necessary, in order to fulfil, to borrow, or to alter the most important arrangements on the faith of the contract as completed.

As to the specialties of this case, the words "upon hearing from you" might be argued to imply a condition affecting the contract. But it does not appear to be so. These words rather imply that the agreement, previously complete as the [a] personal obligation, would be carried out into a real contract as soon as the other party should write.

In regard to its being a sale of heritage, I shall merely remark that we are here entirely in the question of a personal contract. The principles which hold good as to the effect of revocation are not peculiar to the sale of either heritage or movables. They are common to all consensual contracts, and there is here no ground for distinction or exception.

Lord Curriehill. The conclusion of the summons in this case is, that the defender should be ordained "to implement his part of the following letters or missives, — viz., letter or missive of offer from the defender to the said Alexander Thomson on behalf of the pursuers, dated 26th November, 1853, offering or agreeing to purchase the lands of Renniston at the sum of £6,400 sterling, payable at Whit-Sunday, 1854; and letter or missive from said Alexander Thomson on behalf of the pursuers to the defender, dated 1st December, 1853, accepting of said offer of 26th November, 1853," and that by accepting of a disposition of the subjects and paying the price. In the record accordingly the contract of sale, upon which this demand is founded, is stated to have been entered into by the parties having interchanged these documents. And the plea in law in which the pursuers embody the ground of their action is, that "the correspondence between the parties, and particularly the letters of 26th November and 1st December, 1853, constitute a valid contract of sale." The defender does not deny that he made the offer contained in the former of these letters, and that the latter of them, if it had been delivered to him *tempestive*, would have been a binding acceptance of that offer; but maintains that that acceptance did not take place until after the offer had been effectually retracted by him.

In considering the question thus raised, two things should be kept in view: 1. That the subject of this alleged contract consisted of an heritable estate; and consequently that, according to a familiar rule of the law of Scotland, it was essential to the validity of such a contract not only that the parties should be fully agreed as to the terms of the bargain, but that their consent should be embodied in writing, — the mental act of volition being ineffectual, unless it be indicated in writing according to certain established rules (Erskine, iii. 2, 2); — and, 2. That this alleged contract of sale is said to have been constituted not by a unilateral deed, but by two different writings, of which one was written by the defender in Roxburghshire on the 26th of November, and the other was written five days later by the pursuers' agent in Edinburgh, and that there is no allegation that such contract was entered into by any act or deed whatever other than the interchange of these letters. Such being the nature of the present case, it must be distinguished from other kinds of cases which are subject to the operation of different rules, — such, for example, as contracts of sale of goods, which may be constituted by mere consent, without writing or any other security, — or mere promises, which may become effectual without acceptance by the donee, — or mere orders, which become effectual by being obeyed or performed without any other acceptance. The contract which it is the object of the present action to enforce, is not alleged to belong to any of these classes of transactions, but is said to have been entered into only by the defender sending a missive of offer to the pursuers, and by the latter five days afterwards sending a missive of acceptance to the former; and the question must be decided according to those rules of law which are applicable to a case of that kind.

The first step in this inquiry is to ascertain what were the relative positions of the parties when the defender had sent to the pursuers his missive of offer of the 26th of November, and before either the retraction by the one party or the acceptance by the other was written.

And one thing at least is clear enough, that so long as matters remained in that state there was no concluded contract of sale between the parties, and no binding obligation was actually incurred by even the offerer to receive a disposition of the subjects and to pay the price. The trite rule of law as to this matter is thus stated by Lord Stair, i. 3, 9, when treating of implied conditions in contracts: "An offer hath the like implied condition of the other party's acceptance (and in that it differs from an absolute promise), so that if the acceptance be not adhibited presently, or within the time expressed in the offer in which the other party hath liberty to accept, there ariseth no obligation, as was found 25th June, 1664, Allan *contra* Collier." And the same author afterwards (i. 10, 3) thus discriminates this implied condition in offers from other things with which it is sometimes confounded: "We must distinguish betwixt promise, pollicitation or offer, paction, and contract,— the difference amongst which is this, that the obligatory act of the will is sometimes absolute and pure, and sometimes conditional, in which case the condition relates either unto the obligation itself, or to the performance, such as are the ordinary conditional obligations which, although they be presently upon the granting thereof binding and cannot be recalled, yet they are only to be performed and have effect when the condition shall be existent; but when the condition relateth to the constitution of the obligation, then the very obligation itself is pendent till the condition be purified, and till then it is no obligation; as, when an offer or tender is made, there is implied a condition that before it becomes obligatory the party to whom it is made must accept." And in contradistinction to such an offer his Lordship, in the next section (i. 10, 4), says: "A promise is that which is simple and pure, and hath not implied in it the acceptance of another."

But the defender's offer to the pursuers, although it did not create a binding obligation on him so long as nothing followed upon it, had then the twofold effect of conferring one power upon the pursuers, and of reserving another power to the defender himself. On the one hand, the power which was thereby conferred upon the pursuers was to accept the offer at any moment, within a reasonable period, so as to bind themselves to perform the counterpart of the proposed contract of sale. That was an implied condition of the offer, and there was placed in the pursuers the option of purifying that condition by accepting the offer within due time. As the period of time which was allowed for acceptance is not stated in the offer, it might have been a question of some nicety how long it was to endure; but that question is not raised in the present case.

On the other hand, the power which the defender reserved to himself was to retract that offer, and thereby put an end to it at any moment, so long as the pursuers did not exercise their power by accepting of the offer to the effect above mentioned. That such an implied power is reserved to the offerer is another fundamental principle in the Scottish law of mutual contracts, which is thus expressed by Lord Stair, i. 10, 6: "If the promise be pendent upon acceptation, and no more than an offer, it is imperfect and ambulatory, and in the power of the offerer till acceptance; and if he die before acceptance, it is revoked, as a commission or mandate, which necessarily imports acceptance, and expires by the mandator's death." The implied power of retractation, thus reserved by the law itself to an offerer, may indeed be competently renounced by him; and this is sometimes done by his stating in his offer that he will be bound by it only for a certain definite period of time. But as the defender in his offer did not, in this or any other way, renounce his implied power of retractation, it remained with him.

Holding then, that at the time when the defender's offer of 26th November reached the pursuer Mr. Thomson, the positions of the respective parties were, that the latter had the power of concluding the bargain by accepting of the offer, so as to bind themselves to perform the counterpart thereof,—but that so long as they did not effectually exercise that power, there remained with the defender a reserved power to retract his offer,—the question comes to be, Which of these powers was first effectually exercised? The solution of this question has been rendered puzzling by the circumstance, that both the retractation and the acceptance were transmitted through the post-office, and they crossed each other in the course of their transit. According to the statements of the defender (the truth of which must be assumed in this discussion as to their relevancy, he being willing to undertake a proof of them), his letter of retractation was written and posted at Jedburgh before or about the hour of noon of the 1st of December, and arriving in Edinburgh in the course of that day, was delivered to Mr. Thomson early on the morning of the 2d of December, whereas the pursuers' letter of acceptance was written and posted at Edinburgh not sooner than half-past two o'clock on the 1st of December, and remaining in the post-office of Edinburgh all night, was delivered to the defender in Roxburghshire on the evening of the 2d of December. And thus, if either the time of writing and posting of these letters by the writers of them—or the time of the actual delivery of them to the parties to whom they were addressed—be held to be the *punctum temporis* when they became effectual, the retractation was prior in date to the acceptance.

When I pronounced the interlocutor now under review, I thought that the time of posting the letters was the criterion; as it then appeared to me that the posting of a letter was in effect delivery of it to or for behoof of the party to whom it is addressed. And if that opinion as to the effect of posting a letter be well founded, I still think that the conclusion I deduced from it was a sound one, inasmuch as even on that assumption the missive of retractation must be held to have been first completed by delivery. And although, in consequence of the able and more ample discussion which the case has undergone since the interlocutor was pronounced, I have changed my opinion as to the effect of posting letters in such a case as the present, and I now think that such letters require to be actually delivered to the parties to whom they are addressed, or to those acting for them, the result appears to me to be the same, because the delivery of the letter of retractation preceded the delivery of the letter of acceptance by a still longer period of time than the posting did. The pursuers cannot escape from this dilemma, unless they establish not only that the mere posting of their letter of acceptance rendered it binding on both parties, but also that the posting of the defender's letter of retractation had not a similar effect. I do not think that they have established that proposition either on principle or on authority.

At the debate, the counsel for the pursuers was requested to state the precise ground on which the mere posting of such a letter of acceptance made it binding on the party to whom it is addressed, although he be then in ignorance of such a proceeding; and I did not hear any satisfactory answer to that question. So far as I could gather from the argument, the proposition was attempted to be supported on two different grounds: 1st, That the posting of the letter of acceptance being sufficient evidence of the pursuers having consented to accept of the defender's offer, the condition of the offer was purified by such acceptance, even although the defender was in ignorance of the proceeding until a late period of the following day; and, 2d, That the posting of the letter is to be held as having been delivery thereof on behalf of the defender. But I do not think that either of these propositions is consistent with the established principles of the law of Scotland.

1. Even assuming that the posting of the letter of acceptance on the afternoon of the 1st of December was sufficient evidence of the pursuers having then consented to accept of the offer, that consent was not such as could conclude this bargain until the letter was delivered to the defender; because until it was communicated to the offerer, it was not in legal effect acceptance of an offer. An offer is effectually accepted only by the offeree doing that which binds himself to perform the counterpart of the offer. What is tendered by an offerer is to undertake to give or to do something on the offeree undertaking to give or to do something in return; and although the offer conferreth on the latter the conditional power of binding the former, this power can be exercised so as to purify that condition, and to deprive the offerer of his reserved power of retractation, only by the offeree binding himself to perform what is required of him in the offer. In short, so long as the offeree does not so bind himself, but reserves entire

his option of being free from the bargain, the offerer also retains his reserved power of retractation, and neither party is irrevocably bound until both parties be so. And hence the pursuers' letter of acceptance, so long as it did not effectually impose an irrevocable obligation on them to sell the estate of Renniston to the defender on the terms stated in his offer, could not deprive him of his legal reserved right to retract that offer.

But the letter of the pursuers had not that effect so long as it was not delivered to the defender. Even if it had not been essential to the efficacy of the acceptance that it should be in writing, it would not have been irrevocable by the pursuers so long as it was kept from the knowledge of the defender. The writer of the letter might have destroyed it so long as it remained in his own hands. After despatching it by his clerk, or servant, or any person in his employment, he might have recalled it before it arrived at its destination, and have still destroyed it. Or after so despatching it, he might still have sent an express with a refusal of the offer, and if it had been first delivered, he would still have been free, and the treaty would have been at an end. In short, until the acceptance reached the offerer, there was not that *conventio in idem placitum* which is necessary to constitute a mutual contract.[1] Until then, the pursuers had not conferred upon the defender that power of exacting performance of the counterpart of the offer, which was essentially necessary to constitute a binding obligation upon them, and to render their acceptance effectual; and their consent

[1] "What is the precise moment when the concourse of the two wills effects the extinction of the debt, and when the creditor can no longer revoke the offered release? Is it necessary that the acceptance be known to the creditor? M. Pardessus (*Cours de Droit Commercial*, tom. i. p. 252, *et seq.*) thinks that, immediately upon the acceptance of the offer, the contract is perfect, and that it can no longer be revoked by the creditor, though he does not yet know of the acceptance. I have held, on the contrary (tom. vi. No. 29, pp. 32, 33), that he who has made an offer can revoke it up to the moment when the acceptance is known to him, because an acceptance which is not known is in law as if it did not exist. I have followed in that particular the doctrine of Heineccius, which seems to me the most correct, and which besides is sanctioned by the Code, art. 932, since it permits a donor to revoke his donation until he has knowledge of its acceptance. The reader can weigh the reasons of two professors, who both seek the truth in good faith without claiming to make their opinion prevail." — Toullier, *Droit Civil*, liv. iii. tit. iii. chap. v. No. 321, note 3.

"Quæri etiam solet, *sufficiatne acceptionem factam esse, an præterea requiratur, ut innotescat illa promittenti?* Subtiliter auctor resp. videndum esse, quid actum sit, nam posse utraque sub conditione conveniri, si alter acceptet, et si innotuerit illum acceptasse. Deinde videndum ait, an promissio sit mutua, an unilateralis. Ibi necessarium esse, ut mihi innotescat acceptatio, hic præsumi illum acceptasse.

"Sed non opus est his ambagibus. Semper requiritur, ut acceptatio mihi innotescat. Non esse et non apparere in jure pari passu ambulant. Sed innotescit mihi vel per signa alterius expressa, e.g. verba, litteràs, cet. vel per præsumtionem, si alter tam sit indigus, ut non possit adspernari promissum." — Heineccius, Prælect. in Grotium, lib. ii. cap. xi. § 15. — ED.

was merely a resolution, which has no such effect. This fundamental principle in the law of Scotland is clearly stated thus by Lord Stair, i. 10, 2: "We must distinguish three acts of the will, — desire, resolution, and engagement. 1. Desire is a tendency or inclination of the will towards its object, and it is the first motion thereof, which is not sufficient to constitute a right; neither is resolution (which is a determinate purpose to do that which is desired) efficacious; because whatsoever is resolved or purposed may be, without fault, altered, unless by accident the matter be necessary, or that the resolution be holden forth to assure others, the alteration whereof, without evident ground, importeth levity and inconstancy, and sometimes deceit and unfaithfulness; but still resolution is but an act of the will with itself, as deliberation is of the understanding acting within itself; and it is unquestionable nothing can be obliged to itself, though it be obliged to God, or to another in relation to itself; and, therefore, if a party should express a resolution to give unto, or to bestow upon, another any thing, though that resolution related to the good of another, yet it is not obligatory, nor can that other compel the resolver to perform, though it were never so fully cleared or confirmed by word or writ. So it was found that a resolution expressed both by word and writ in favor of near relations did not confer an obligation. — February 27, 1673, Kincaid *contra* Dickson, 12, 143. It remaineth, then, that the only act of the will which is efficacious, is that whereby the will conferreth or stateth a power of exaction in another, and thereby becomes engaged to that other to perform."

The pursuers' letter of acceptance, so long as it was undelivered and unknown to the defender, was ineffectual to bind them, not only according to the principle of that law of mutual contracts, but likewise according to another rule of the law of Scotland, — that delivery of a writing to the grantee, or to some person for his behoof, is, in the general case, necessary to make it binding on the grantor. As already stated, writing was as essential as consent itself to constitute the alleged contract, in respect that the subject of it was land. And although writing on one side may be effectual when it is followed by implement or *rei interventus*, importing that the parties were acting upon it, yet as the present action is not laid upon any such medium, but expressly on the ground of the defender's missive of offer having been accepted by the pursuers' missive of 1st December, 1853, the latter writing required to be validated according to the established rules of law. And while the want of the statutory rules of authentication is of no importance in consequence of its having been holograph of the grantor, yet so long as it was not delivered to the grantee it was not binding on the former, and consequently did not deprive the latter of his right of retracting his offer. Delivery is, in such a case, as indispensable a solemnity to validate a writing, as are the statutory solemnities in cases in which writing is not holograph nor privileged. And had the pursuers' missive not been holograph, it would not have been effectual as an acceptance without the statutory solemnities, even although the offer itself had been holograph or duly authenticated. This was decided in the case of Barron, 23d January, 1794, Mor., p. 8463, where one of the mutual missives by which a contract as to heritable property was entered into was neither attested nor holograph, and the court held that "a bargain concerning heritage may indeed be completed by an unilateral obligation. But the present is not a case of that kind. It is a mutual contract entered into by mutual missives, which must be binding on both or neither of the contracting parties. This is the rule in all bargains concerning heritage, as has been solemnly decided." And accordingly Erskine, iii. 2, 2, states: "Where an agreement concerning heritage is executed in the form of mutual missives, both missives must be probative, otherwise either party may resile." And as the delivery is as necessary to the validity of such a writing as is any of the statutory solemnities, it follows that, so long as one of the writings by which alone this alleged contract is said to have been constituted was not delivered, it was of no effect, and it remained in the power of either party to resile. And for this reason, as well as on the more general rule in the law of mutual contracts above stated, I think that, until the missive of acceptance was delivered to the defender, the pursuers had not become irrevocably bound to him, and he had not been deprived of his power of retractation.

2. Nor is there any authority in the law of Scotland for holding that the posting of the letter of acceptance by the pursuers, is to be dealt with as delivery thereof to or on behalf of the defender. If this were the rule, there appears to be no good reason why that rule should not be applied also to the defender's letter of retractation; and if it were, then, as already stated, the retractation was completed by delivery thereof to or on behalf of the pursuers before the acceptance was so delivered.

But the pursuers have failed, as I think, to show that the posting of their letter had such an effect in law. The postmaster-general and the subordinate officers and servants of the post-office establishment, are not constituted by law the agents or mandatories of the parties to whom posted letters are addressed, and are not even in the position, nor subject to the rules, of common carriers; and a party to whom a letter is addressed is not placed in the position of having received delivery of it, by its being merely dropped into the receiving-box of a distant post-office, and before he actually receives it, or has any knowledge of its existence. And although the writer of a posted letter may not be entitled to obtain redelivery of it from the officers of the post-office, this is only in consequence of a regulation for the benefit of the public, which equally forbids these functionaries to deliver the letter to the party to whom it is addressed until it reaches its destination. In short, the writer of a posted letter, although he may have lost command over the document itself, has no more lost his control over the act of his will which he therein expresses, than if that document were still in the hands of his own servant or messenger. That this is the true view of the matter appears to me to be established by the case of Lady Dunmore, 15th December, 1830, where a letter, written in order to conclude a contract of hiring, was placed in a post-office, and some hours afterwards another letter was posted retracting the former one, and both of the letters were received at the same time by the party to whom they were addressed. If the mere posting of the letters had been equivalent to delivery, then the bargain would have been irrevocably concluded the moment the first one was posted; and the second one containing the retractation would have been too late and ineffectual. But the court held that neither of them were binding until they were delivered; and that the first one was duly retracted, and the bargain was not concluded. Lord Newton, who pronounced the judgment, which was affirmed by the Inner House, stated the ground of the judgment. After stating the necessity of delivery to make a missive of offer binding, he proceeds: "Nor will the writing of a letter of acceptance be sufficient if this letter is never sent. The Lord Ordinary conceives that if, after writing such a letter, the author should add a postscript, stating that, on farther consideration, or in consequence of new intelligence, he did not choose to accept the offer, and if, from the letter's referring to other matters, he still thought it necessary to send it, the acceptance would be effectually recalled. But if this be the case, the same effect would follow when a second letter retracting the offer is transmitted by the same post, so as to be received at the same time, or where a communication to this effect is made, by express or otherwise, to the offerer before the acceptance reaches him. In short, each party may resile so long as his offer or acceptance has not been communicated to the other party."

Nor was a different principle established, as the pursuers maintain, in the case of Dunlop *v.* Higgins, 2d July, 1847, affirmed on appeal 24th February, 1848. In that case the question was — not whether the offer had been retracted before it was accepted? because there had confessedly been no retractation of the offer, either delivered, or posted, or even written, before the letter of acceptance of it was actually received by the offerers — but whether the acceptance had been made within the period limited by the usage of trade for that purpose? The offer was sent from Glasgow to Liverpool, and the acceptance was not only posted in Liverpool, but received by the offerers in Glasgow, without the latter having in the mean time retracted the offer; and the ground on which the latter attempted to resile from the bargain was, that according to usage of trade the time within which such a mercantile offer may be accepted is limited to the return of post; and the offeree had not accepted it (as was alleged) by the return of post, inasmuch as, although he had posted his letter at Liverpool on the very day he had received the offer, it had been detained on its journey to Glasgow in consequence of the road having been obstructed by frost. It was held that the acceptance was made according to that rule of commercial usage, as it was duly sent by return of post, although the return of the post was so accidentally delayed. But the question, whether the offer could not have been retracted by the offerer before it was actually delivered to the offeree, not only was not decided in the affirmative in that case, but was expressly held to be left open, as appears from the following remarks of Lord Fullerton, which were acquiesced in by the other judges. He said: "I find it necessary to make a distinction which neither party were disposed to notice in the course of the argument. I mean the distinction between the binding effect of the acceptance when put into the post, as barring the offerer from founding on the implication that it was declined, and the absolute completion of the contract. I think the posting of the acceptance by the pursuers had most certainly the first effect. That having been done, there was no silence on their part, and consequently the pursuers were barred from arguing that the offer must be held to have been declined. But I am by no means prepared to go farther, and to say that in the larger question of the actual completion of the contract, the mere fact of the putting of the letter of acceptance into the post-office has the same effect as if it had not only been put into the post-office, but had been actually delivered to the other party." And his Lordship, after criticising Professor Bell's opinion, to which I shall afterwards advert, adds: "I do not see how there can be *in idem placitum concursus et conventio* between two parties, where one of them remains in entire ignorance of the fact — the acceptance — on which the *concursus et conventio* is supposed to rest." These remarks show that the principle of the case of Lady Dunmore was left untouched and entire by the decision in this case of Higgins.

As to the English case of Adams v. Lindsell, 1 Barn. and Ald. 681, founded on by the pursuers, it might be sufficient to state that, if the principle which has received effect in Scotland were at variance with the law of England, this would only be one of many particulars in which the principles of the two systems of law as to contracts, and particularly as to contracts for sale, differ from each other; and that of course this Scots case must be decided according to the law of Scotland. But in that case, as in the Scots case of Higgins, no retractation of the offer was either posted or written by the offerer before he received actual delivery of the offeree's acceptance; and there also the question was only whether the acceptance had been made within the time which in that case was expressly conditioned in the offer, — viz., by return of post. That question was decided in the affirmative, because the offeree despatched this acceptance by the first post after he received the offer, although that offer had not reached him in due time in consequence of a mistake by the offerer himself in misdirecting it.

It may be farther remarked, that as the reports of both the cases of Higgins and of Adams state that they proceeded upon what was held to have been a usage of trade in such commercial cases, these decisions could be of no authority in a question as to the completion of a contract of sale of land in Scotland, as such a transaction is not alleged to be subject to the operation of any such usage of trade.

The pursuers farther maintained that the mere posting of their letter of acceptance ought to be held as delivery of it to the defender, because he having sent his offer through the post-office constituted it the medium through which the answer was to be sent to him. But since the law itself did not place the officers of the post-office in the position of servants or mandatories of the defender in the management of this transaction, there appears to me to be no ground for holding that they were placed in such a position by his authority. Although he availed himself of that public mode of conveyance to transmit his letter to the pursuers, he did not tell them how to transmit their answer, and left them at full liberty to do so by sending it by their clerk, or servant, or by delivering it personally, as well as by sending it through the post-office. Not only did the defender not authorize the officers of the post-office, or any other third party, to receive an acceptance on his behalf, but on the contrary he appears to me to have expressly excluded any such pretence by his having stated in his letter of offer that the acceptance was to be delivered to himself, inasmuch as he stipulated, in his offer of 26th November, that "upon hearing from you that these terms are to be acceded to, the form necessary in such transactions will be gone through." I refer to this clause not as being a stipulation for what would not have been requisite by the ordinary rule of law although it had not been expressed, but as showing that the defender did not dispense with the ordinary rule of law, and required the pursuer, in conformity with that rule, to inform himself whether the terms of his offer were to be acceded to.

The pursuers found upon a remark in Professor Bell's Commentaries, i. 326, that "in the common case it is not necessary that the acceptance shall have reached the person who makes the offer." But no authority is quoted in support of that remark; and although it is correct enough as to several classes of cases, such, for example, as those in which there is an unconditional promise, or in which orders for goods are given and implemented, it is not consistent with the principles of the law of Scotland relative to the completion of onerous contracts, which can be entered into only by writing, and where the writings are to consist of a conditional offer by one party, and such an acceptance by the other as binds him irrevocably to perform the counterpart of the offer.

This doctrine accordingly was not adopted in the case of Lady Dunmore; and in the case of Higgins it was stated from the bench to require some modification. And even Professor Bell himself does not appear to have thought that it applies to cases where writing or some other external act is essential to the constitution of a contract, as is the case here; for he states in the sequel, that (*ib.* p. 327) "the doctrine of *locus pœnitentiæ* is a corollary from the law, which appoints particular evidence or solemnities for the constitution of obligations. Till the final purpose to undertake an obligation be declared, and the pledge of faith conclusively given, there is no binding obligation, there is *locus pœnitentiæ*."

Both parties have quoted largely from the writings of jurists and commentators on the civil law. But the speculations of these learned authors are so much at variance as to make them of but little use as guides in such a question. And fortunately in Scotland we have those general principles of the law of contracts, which have been adopted in this country, stated in a very lucid manner by a most eminent jurist, who, after having taught philosophy as a professor in one of our universities for several years, was distinguished as a practising lawyer and a most eminent judge for a period of about half a century, and who, as he himself informs us (Preface to More's Stair, p. 22), as to his Institutes of the law of Scotland, "did derive it from that common law that rules the world, and compared it with the law civil and canon, and with the custom of neighboring nations." I am referring of course to Lord Stair, and it is in his Institutes I have looked for and found those principles of the law of Scotland, on which I have founded my opinion in this case. And I may add, that my confidence in the general principle, stated by Lord Newton as the ground of the judgment in the case of Lady Dunmore, is much strengthened by the circumstance that that eminent judge was for a considerable time professor of civil law in the University of Edinburgh. And unless the principles taught by these authorities are now to be relinquished as our guides in practice, I think that the relevancy of the defence in this case must be sustained.

LORD DEAS. In this case two questions arise: 1st, Whether the offer by Mr. James, of 26th November, 1853, imports an express stipulation that it was to be binding upon him only when Mr. Thomson's acceptance should reach him? and, 2d, If it imports no such express condition, whether it is to be held as duly accepted by the posting of Mr. Thomson's answer on 1st December, notwithstanding the posting on that same day of Mr. James's retractation?

The first is a mere special question upon the terms of the offer. The second is a question of general application and importance.

Upon the special question, I am of opinion that the offer does not import any express stipulation to the effect contended for. The words relied on are these: "Upon hearing from you that these terms are to be acceded to, the form necessary in such transactions will be gone through." I think these words are not suspensive of the bargain, but mean merely that the preparation of the formal deeds, necessary for carrying out a purchase of land, would be gone about so soon as the writer became aware that the bargain was concluded. It is a matter of form only which he assumes to remain behind, not the substance of the bargain. He might undoubtedly have stipulated that he should not be bound till the acceptance reached him. But he did not do so. He left this matter upon the general implication of law, whatever that may be. If any inference could be drawn from the special terms of the offer, it would rather be that, if the formal proceedings necessary for converting the personal contract into a legal right of property be alone spoken of as postponed till the acceptance should reach the offerer, the completion of the personal contract of sale itself was not understood to be so postponed. But I do not go upon this inference. I pass to the consideration of the second question, as arising in a pure and general form.

In reference to this second question we have had a very able argument and a most refreshing citation of authorities, — commentators, jurists, and civilians, as well as authorities in our own law and the law of England. After attentively considering the argument and authorities, I am humbly of opinion that the fair and legal import of Mr. James's offer of 26th November was that he should be bound by it if accepted within a reasonable time, — that the posting of Mr. Thomson's letter on 1st December was acceptance, — and that, as it is not disputed that this acceptance (laying retractation out of view) was within a reasonable time, the result is that Mr. James is bound, according to his own proposal and obligation, notwithstanding that, before the acceptance reached him, he had posted a retractation, which neither did nor could reach Mr. Thomson before the latter had posted his acceptance.

Such, I conceive, would have been the result if Mr. James had said expressly, "I shall be bound by my offer if accepted by you within a reasonable time." And this, I think, is implied in his offer equally as if it had been expressed.

There could admittedly have been no doubt about the matter if Mr. James had said, "I shall be bound by my offer provided you *post your acceptance* within a reasonable time." But between this and becoming bound, either expressly or by implication, provided the offer should be *accepted* within a reasonable time, I see no substantial difference. He sent his offer by post, and he expected the answer by post, the parties being forty or fifty miles distant. And when Mr. Thomson posted his answer within a reasonable time, he did all he could do, and consequently all he was bound to do in compliance with the implied stipulation as to acceptance.

Had the bargain been an ordinary mercantile transaction, there would have been the same implication that the offer was to be binding if accepted within a reasonable time; and the act of acceptance would have been the same, — viz., by posting the answer, — with this difference merely, that there a reasonable time would, by the usage of trade, have meant in course of post. Here, the transaction being a purchase of land, the limitation to the course of post is not contended for; and it is not disputed that the acceptance, had there been no other disturbing element, was within a reasonable time. It follows that, if posting the answer were not acceptance here, posting the answer, even in due course of post, never could be acceptance in any mercantile transaction. This would be a great impediment to mercantile dealings, where the party who receives an offer of goods, or for goods, and duly posts his acceptance, naturally goes into the market and deals with other persons upon the footing that this particular bargain has been concluded. And I do not see how the doctrine that, in a mercantile transaction, posting an affirmative answer is not acceptance, can be reconciled with the judgment of this court in Dunlop *v.* Higgins, as affirmed in the House of Lords.

But between a proper mercantile transaction and a transaction as to the sale of land where no objection is made to the form of the writings, which are here holograph on both sides, I know no distinction bearing upon the point now in dispute, except that a reasonable time in the one case is not limited to the course of post as it is in the other, — a distinction which plainly cannot affect the question, whether the posting of the affirmative answer be or be not acceptance.

In the law of Scotland, by which the contract of sale without delivery does not transfer the property of movable subjects, and does not transfer the property of heritable estate till conveyed by disposition, it seems of little practical importance whether the posting of the acceptance *debito tempore* merely bars the offerer from resiling, as Lord Fullerton suggested in the case of Dunlop *v.* Higgins, or absolutely completes the contract. It is enough that the offerer has said, or is held to have said, that, if the offer be accepted *debito tempore*, he shall be bound. This being the nature of his offer, whether expressly or by implication, he cannot resile from it if the party to whom it is addressed, having the offer, and nothing but the offer, before him, has, by duly posting his acceptance *bona fide*, done all in his power to comply with the only condition contained or implied in the offer to make it absolutely binding on the offerer.

The observation may no doubt be made, that this implies a certain time, — namely, the period between the posting and receipt of the acceptance, — during which the offerer was bound and the acceptor not bound, if it be held that the acceptor, by telegraphing or otherwise outstripping or overtaking the post, may negative or recall his acceptance at any time before it reaches the offerer, which was the nature of the case of Alexander *v.* the Earl and Countess of Dunmore, 15th December, 1830, where Lady Agnew was held to be the mandatory of the Countess; and consequently the principle applied was, that, as the retractation reached the other party, Alexander, at the same moment with the acceptance, it negatived the effect of it, just as a postscript to the letter of acceptance itself would have done.

Undoubtedly there is some difficulty in reconciling this decision with the supposition, either that the posting of the acceptance, *eo ipso*, operated as a bar to the offerer resiling, or that it operates as an absolute completion of the contract. I can understand, however, that the implied condition of the offer may be held to be even broader than I have hitherto suggested, and to import an agreement by the offerer that both parties shall be bound from and after the posting of the acceptance, but with an option in favor of the acceptor to neutralize or rescind the contract, if, by outstripping the post or otherwise, he can prevent his acceptance from becoming operative upon the mind of the offerer, and consequently from being, even for a single moment, relied on by him, or in any way affecting his transactions. But upon this question I reserve my opinion till it again occurs; and all I say at present is, that if the decision in Alexander's case can be shown to be irreconcilable with the general doctrine I am now stating, I shall be disposed to abandon the decision, and to adhere to the doctrine.

For, whatever may be its difficulties, I think the difficulties attending the view contended for on the other side are infinitely greater. That view proceeds upon the footing that, in order to a completed contract, there must not only be a concourse of consenting wills upon both sides at the same moment, but that the existence of this concourse must be known to both parties.

Now, a concourse of wills, at the same moment, of two parties, even at opposite sides of the globe, is easily supposed. But that the one can know, at the time when notice of the will of the other reaches him, that that other has not then changed his mind, and posted or despatched a letter to that effect, is an impossibility.

If neither party changes his mind, then there is doubtless a moment of time at which the concourse of wills takes place. But, at that moment, neither party can know it; and consequently, in the case of parties at a distance, the mutually known concourse desiderated never can take place. The search after it, pursued I may say for ages with great learning and ingenuity, seems to me to be just a hopeless attempt to bring parties who are absent into the precise same predicament with parties who are present, in place of adopting the easy and natural rule that an absent offerer is understood to say, — "If you receive no notice to the contrary, you shall be entitled to hold me as continuing my offer up to the moment of posting or despatching your acceptance, which, if done *debito tempore*, shall bind the contract." If the offerer were thus to express himself, I see neither legal nor metaphysical difficulty in holding him bound by such express consent. And I see just as little legal or metaphysical difficulty in holding him bound to the same effect by his implied consent.

When pressed to explain at what time he held a contract between absent parties to be completed, the Dean of Faculty latterly said, — At the time when notice of the acceptance reaches the offerer. But this will never create the sort of mutually known concourse of wills contended for, except constructively. And, if it can only take place constructively, surely it may just as easily, and far more naturally, be held to take place at the moment when the acceptance is posted or despatched, as at the moment when the acceptance reaches the offerer. The *actual* concourse of wills can just as little take place, if the one party has changed his mind, as if the other has done so. And the offerer can just as little know, when the acceptance reaches him, whether the acceptor has or has not changed his mind and retracted, as the acceptor can know, when he posts or despatches his acceptance, whether the offerer has done so.

The principle, admittedly involved in the argument, that an act of the will of one party, unknown to the other, is to be held no act of the will at all, seems to me to receive its natural application when applied to the posting by the offerer of his retractation, unknown to the acceptor at the time of acceptance. The acceptor had neither expressly nor by implication agreed to dispense with the rule, that such an act of the will, while unknown to him, was to be held no act of the will at all; while, on the other hand, there is no difficulty in holding the offerer to have dispensed with that rule by the implied condition of his offer, to the effect that he should be bound by it so soon as the acceptance had been posted, although the act of posting could not be then known to him. The posting of the acceptance is constructive notice of the acceptance, and this constructive notice the offerer, according to my view of the meaning of his offer, virtually agreed to hold sufficient.

Such appears to me to be the sound doctrine of the law of Scotland. I cannot say that Lord Stair gives any express opinion upon it either way. He says, however, i. 10, 2, "The only act of the will which is efficacious is that whereby the will conferreth or stateth a power of exaction in another, and thereby becomes engaged to that other to perform." He then goes on to explain what it is, in the case of an offer, which confers the power of exaction, and binds the offerer, — namely, acceptance. His words are, i. 10, 3, "When an offer or tender is made, there is implied a condition that, before it becomes obligatory, the party to whom it is made must accept." He adds, "So then, an offer accepted is a contract, because it is the deed of two, the offerer and the acceptor." From the dissertation which follows, I think it clear enough that the words quoted are applicable to written as well as verbal contracts; and if he had explained what he held, in the case of parties at a distance, to constitute acceptance, his observations would have been complete. This, however, he does not do. But it is, to say the least of it, remarkable, in so philosophical and profound a writer, that, when he gives the reason why an offer accepted is a contract, — "because it is the deed of two, the offerer and the acceptor," — he does not suggest that any farther act, mental or physical, after the appropriate act of the acceptor, is necessary to the completion of the contract. If he had held that the act of acceptance, before becoming efficacious, must reach the mind of the offerer, I think it is rather to be presumed that he would have said so. In place of this, he gives at least one example to the contrary, — that of a mutual deed which, after being subscribed by one party, is completed by and at the moment of the subscription of the other, although without the presence of the first party, and unknown to him (i. 3, 9, and i. 10, 5). The consent under such a deed could obviously, I think, not be retracted by the first subscribing party after it had been signed by the second, and certainly not after it had been signed by the second and posted by him to the address of the first; and yet all the same difficulties about the want of a mutually known concourse of wills at the time of the completion of the contract might, so far as I can see, be raised in that case just as well as in this.

It is true that Lord Stair says (what we know to be trite law), that in unilateral deeds there must be delivery. But when this doctrine is applied to the case of a written acceptance of a written offer, the object, so far as I can discover, is not to bring home the acceptance to the knowledge of the offerer, but to obtain evidence by an overt act of the acceptance. Accordingly it cannot be doubted that, if the offerer had sent his servant with the offer, delivery of the acceptance to that servant would have completed the contract, although the servant, so far from acting the part of a mandatory, had been as ignorant of the contents of the letters and of the object of his mission as a carrier pigeon, or the *pica* of the commentators.

Mr. Erskine, iii. 3, 88, simply adopts the doctrine of Lord Stair, and it is unnecessary to repeat, as regards the one writer, the observations I have made upon the other. Mr. Bell, however, in his Commentaries, vol. i. pp. 326, 327, says expressly, "In the common case it is not necessary that the acceptance should have reached the person who makes the offer." And what he means by the common case is explained by the exception which follows of the case of the offerer "limiting it, so that the arrival of the acceptance only shall bind the bargain." In the last edition of his Principles, published many years after the Commentaries, he says, § 73, "An offer is an obligation provisional on acceptance. It is presumed to be continued till acceptance." And, after observing, § 74, that an offer may be either by parole or by letter, he says, § 78, "The acceptance completes the contract. The agreement is not suspended till the offerer has received notice of the acceptance; though contended for by some commentators: But this is under the qualification that there shall be no undue delay in notifying the acceptance." The English case of Adams *v.* Lindsell is quite in accordance with the views thus expressed by Mr. Bell. And I think the same doctrine is sanctioned, by necessary inference, by the case of Dunlop *v.* Higgins already referred to, both in this court and in the House of Lords.

I consider it unnecessary to say any thing of the effect of death or insanity, because our writers — and in particular both Lord Stair and Mr. Bell — limit the effect of these to their occurrence before acceptance; and if posting the affirmative answer be acceptance, then neither death nor insanity subsequently occurring could affect the contract. Besides, other considerations are involved in such occurrences, which it is unnecessary here to enter upon. On the question which really does occur, I have formed an opinion satisfactory to my own mind, — all the more so, that against that opinion I do not think we could have had a more logical and powerful argument than that with which the Dean of Faculty concluded what were throughout the able and elaborate pleadings in this case.

The court pronounced the following interlocutor: "Recall the interlocutor of the Lord Ordinary reclaimed against; repel the pleas stated for the defender, and decern against him conform to the conclusions of the libel: Find the defender liable in expenses to the pursuers," &c.

S—— *v.* F——, D——, AND OTHERS.

COURT OF CASSATION IN FRANCE, SEPTEMBER 1, 1813.

[*Reported in Merlin, Répertoire de Jurisprudence, Tit. Vente,* § 1, *Art.* III., *No.* XI. *bis.*]

IN the beginning of January, 1813, D., who was intending to purchase an English license, was at Paris with S. of Havre, who had recently purchased the ship Elisa of one M. Filleau.

S. proposed to transfer his bargain to D. for his firm, F., D. & Company.

To induce D. to treat with him, S. declared that he would assume, among other obligations, that of furnishing this vessel with fifteen men, comprising therein two captains and one master of perfectly good repute, and that the vessel should be ready to put to sea the 5th of February, 1813.

The bargain was not concluded; S. returned to Havre: it was agreed that D. should write to him, if he concluded to make the purchase in question.

The 21st of January, 1813, the Messrs. D. wrote to S. as follows: "You have guaranteed to us to furnish this ship with fifteen men, comprising therein two captains and one master of perfectly good repute, and that the ship shall be ready to put to sea the 5th of February next. . . . With these several assurances and guaranties, without which we should not treat, since this affair is based entirely on our confidence in your aforesaid assurances and guaranties . . . we consent to assume, in your place and stead, the payment to M. Filleau of the price of 55,000 francs," &c., &c.[1]

S. answered this letter by two others of the 23d, the one written, as he said, in the morning, and the other in the evening; but they both arrived at Paris on the 25th, at the same moment.

In the first of these letters he said: "The ship was still in my hands when your letter reached me: it is therefore yours *upon the conditions agreed upon between us.* You can act accordingly. I have only time to address you this word, so that you may receive it to-morrow evening. A longer letter, which I am going to write to you this evening, will reach you Monday morning by the diligence."

In the second letter, after announcing that the definitive act of sale would be passed on the morrow, he added: "The most difficult thing is the crew, with which I have occupied myself since the receipt of your letter. . . . It is very true that I said to you that I could have the ship ready to sail the 5th of February; she will be much sooner; but as to the crew, if you had come to a decision in time, I would have written from Paris to obtain one; and now it is going to be necessary to send an agent to look for one, and it is scarcely possible that this crew can be at hand at so early a date: I shall leave nothing undone, however, to accomplish it."

To this letter . . . the Messrs. D. replied, by letter of the 25th January, that they could not accept the purchase, since S. did not assure them of the provision of a crew of good character, and of two honest and intelligent captains, as he had offered and guaranteed to them, so as to put to sea the 5th of February, conditions specified in their letter of the 21st, and upon which they had made the purchase of the ship Elisa to depend.

The same day, the 25th, S. confirmed his letters of the 23d, announcing

[1] Messrs. D. added: "We shall expect your answer by return of post. . . . Please to deliver your answer to the conductor of the mail, promising him two or three francs."

that the act had been signed on the 25th, that he had received 55,000 francs in drafts, the price of the ship, &c.

S. added that he had sent a man to Ostend, Dunkirk, and Antwerp, for the crew; that it was necessary to be on the alert; and that he intended that every thing should be ready the 5th of February, *if it was possible.*

The Messrs. D. replied to this letter the 28th, confirming the positive refusal expressed in that of the 25th. They said they had only consented to the purchase upon the several conditions specified in their letter of the 21st; and that all the guaranties demanded not having been accorded, they were not bound.

Upon the presentation of the bills drawn by S. to the order of M. Filleau, who had sold the Elisa, the Messrs. D. & Co. refused to accept them.

Thereupon Filleau had recourse to S. as the drawer of the bills, and S. commenced proceedings before the Tribunal of Commerce of Havre against F., D. & Co., to enforce his alleged contract with them; and judgment was there rendered in the plaintiff's favor.

The defendants thereupon appealed to the Court of Appeal of Rouen, where the judgment was reversed; and from the decree of reversal the original plaintiff appealed to the Court of Cassation.[1]

In the latter court Merlin argued as follows in support of the decree appealed from: —

What law has the Court of Appeal of Rouen violated, in declaring that the two letters, for the reason alone that they reached the Messrs. D. at the same time, formed as to them only one indivisible whole?

It has, they say, violated law 65, D. *de acquirendo rerum dominio*, and law 14, § 17, D. *de furtis*, which decide that a letter addressed to a person ceases to belong to him who wrote it, from the moment when he delivers it to the individual whom the person addressed has charged with receiving it and bringing it to him. Whence it follows that the first letter of the 23d of January became the property of the Messrs. D. at the very instant that the demandant delivered it to the conductor of the mail, conformably to the direction which the Messrs. D. had given him on that subject; that from that instant the contract was formed between the Messrs. D. and the demandant; and that the demandant could neither break it nor modify it by the second letter of the same day. . . .

Assuming that the first letter became the property of the Messrs. D. at the very instant when the demandant delivered it to the person indicated to him for that purpose, would it follow that the Messrs. D., receiving the second letter at the same moment as the first, could not consider it as modifying the consent, pure and simple, given to

[1] All details as to the proceedings in the lower courts, and also portions of the argument of Merlin, have been omitted. — ED.

their propositions by the first, as putting upon that consent a restriction which left them at liberty to reconsider their propositions?

In order to decide this question, let us examine another connected with it: Could the demandant, having written and sent his first letter, revoke its contents before it reached the Messrs. D.; and if, having done so, his revocation had been notified to the Messrs. D. before they received the first letter, could the Messrs. D., on receiving afterwards his first letter, adhere to it in spite of him, and force him to execute the bargain to which by his first letter he had given his assent?

The demandant maintains that he could not revoke it; but he maintains it only because the interests of his cause oblige him to do it; and good sense and the most weighty authorities rise up against his assertion. What is a letter missive by which I announce to you that I accept the bargain which you have proposed to me? Nothing else than a dumb agent, which I send to declare to you my acceptance; and it is thus that Cujas considered it in his notes upon the title of the Code, *si quis alteri vel sibi emerit*, when he says: *Epistola non contrahit, sed nunciat dominum contrahere.*

Now it is an elementary maxim that I can recall my agent, so long as he has not executed his mandate.

I can therefore recall the letter which I have addressed to you, so long as it has not reached you, so long as it has not brought to you the words which I had given it in charge for you.

Grant that you are the owner of the material of my letter from the moment when I committed it either to your carrier or to a public messenger, who is the carrier of everybody, at the proper hour. That does not deprive my letter of the character of a dumb agent; it does not consequently prevent me from recalling it before you have received it.

Suppose we look at the letter missive under another aspect; suppose we say, with the demandant, that it is a series of words fixed upon paper: we shall still arrive at the same result.

Indeed, in what sense is it true, as the demandant says, that the words fixed upon the paper in the morning are as distinct from those which were affixed to it in the evening, as the words pronounced at mid-day are distinct from those which are pronounced six hours after?

It is true in this sense, that, if the words fixed upon the paper in the morning reach the person to whom they are addressed before those which were affixed to it in the evening, those of the evening cannot destroy those of the morning.

But it is false in this sense, that the words fixed upon the paper in the morning preserve their priority over those of the evening, if those of the evening reach the person to whom they are addressed either before those of the morning or at the same time.

Bartolus, whom all the authors have copied in this regard, establishes, upon law 4, D. *de donationibus*, a principle which puts this in the clearest light. A letter, says he, is for the absent to whom it is written what words are addressed to a person present; and he who sends a letter to another is considered as speaking to him as if he was present: Epistola absenti idem est quod sermo præsentibus; et qui mittit alteri litteras, intelligitur præsens præsenti loqui.

Now it is certain that words addressed to a person present can only bind him who uttered them, so far as the person to whom they were addressed heard them before they were retracted.

It is therefore the same of a letter written to an absent person. This letter therefore can only oblige its author, so far as the absent person to whom it is written receives it and reads it, things being still entire.

This is the necessary consequence of the very definition which the demandant gives of a letter missive. A letter missive is only a series of words fixed upon paper; but these words are addressed to an absent person; it is necessary therefore, in order that they should have their effect, that the absent person to whom they are addressed should understand them; they are, therefore, without effect so far as he to whom they are addressed has not understood them; as they would be without effect if, being addressed to a person present, that person was from a physical cause not in a condition to understand them. Now how can an absent person understand the words that are addressed to him? Certainly he can only understand them by reading the letter which contains them. The letter by which I contract an obligation can therefore only fulfil its object so far as I can be supposed to persist, at the moment when it arrives, in the will which I had in writing it. If, therefore, at the moment when my letter arrives, I have already in another way manifested and notified a contrary will, my letter can no longer bind me; it is paralyzed in advance.

That is so true that if, at the moment when my letter arrives, I am no longer able to speak to the person to whom it is addressed, or to persist in the will which I had in writing it, that will cannot be opposed to me, it cannot produce any effect against me; and it is upon this foundation that all the doctors teach that if, after having written to a person with whom I was in treaty for a bargain, that I accepted his proposition, I happen to die before my letter reaches that person, there is no contract between him and me.

"Epistola," says Surdus, lib. 1, Consilium 136, in accordance with a host of authors whom he cites, "obligare non potest scribentem, si is decedat antequam ad eum pervenerit cùm quo erat contrahendum, quia cùm per mortem deficiat scribentis consensus, non potest dici quod ejus scriptura loquatur; per epistolam enim præsens videtur absenti loqui; sed mortuus non loquitur; ideò cessat præsumptio seu conjectura." . . .

Alexander, lib. 5, Consilium 22, No. 9, professes the same doctrine: "Epistola," says he, "seu scriptura quæ mihi absenti à te dirigitur, non potest acceptari et ratificari per me, mortuo illo scribente seu illo qui scripturam ad me dirigebat. . . . Quia, mortuo eo, non potest dici quod scriptura ejus loquatur."

The same language is used by Benvenuttus Straccha, in his treatise *De Mercatura*, title *De Probationibus*, No. 16: "Quod diximus litteras quæ inter absentes mittuntur probare, non procedit ubi antequàm ei cui scriptæ sunt litteræ traditæ fuissent, decessisset is qui scripsisset. Cujus rei illa ratio redditur, quia per litteras absens absentem dicitur alloqui; non ergò dici potest alloqui qui misit, si antequàm traderentur decessit."

The same author, in his treatise *De Abjecto*, last part, No. 8, adverts again to this doctrine, and he opposes to it an objection: "Every one agrees," says he, "that he who contracts by letter is considered as binding himself at the moment when he writes; the contract is therefore perfect on his side at the instant when the letter leaves his hands: mittens epistolam consentit eo tempore quo mittit. But," he answers, "although he who writes a letter obligatory truly consents at the instant when he causes it to start, his consent only binds him because he persists in it up to the moment when his letter reaches its address: et huic objectioni respondeo quod licet mittens consentiat tempore quo mittit, verum est etiam consentire tempore quo litteræ tradentur, quia durat primus (consensus), et ex quod non reperitur mutata voluntas, præsumitur durare. And for this reason," continues he, "if death chances to overtake you before the letter by which you oblige yourself to me is delivered to me, your obligation falls, and I cannot avail myself of it against your heirs: undè si epistola à te missa mihi inscripta est, te mortuo cùm mihi traditur, acceptari à me non potest."

Baldus upon law 1, D. *Mandati*, explains himself in precisely the same manner: "Licet mittens consentiat tempore quo mittit, tamen consentit tempore quo epistola pervenit ad eum cui mittitur, quia durat primus consensus, ex quo non reperitur mutatus; voluntas præsumitur durare; et ideò putò quod si antequàm perveniat epistola, morietur mittens vel efficiatur furiosus, quod tunc non contrahatur obligatio per epistolam, quia non durat voluntas nec intervenit consensus tunc temporis."

Pothier, whom the demandant cites to you as teaching the contrary in his *Traité du Contrat de Vente*, says, however, neither more nor less. After having established that the agreement upon the thing and the price, of which the contract of sale is composed, can take place between the absent by letters, he adds: "In order that the agreement should take place in this case, it is necessary that the will of the party who writes to the other to propose to him the bargain should continue until the time when his letter shall reach the other party, and the latter shall declare that he accepts the bargain." Pothier, therefore, acknowledges very clearly that the consent written in a letter only becomes irrevocable by the delivery of the letter to him for whom it is intended; he acknowledges, therefore, very clearly that, so long as the letter has not reached that person, he who wrote it can revoke its contents.

Be it well observed, moreover, Pothier does not limit his decision to the case where the letter is carried by the messenger of him who wrote it; so far from it, he applies it specially to the case of a letter written from Orleans to Leghorn, that is to say, to a case where correspondence is very seldom carried on except by post, true messenger of the public, and consequently to a case where, by the terms of the Roman laws invoked by the demandant, he to whom a letter is addressed becomes proprietor of it at the instant when the writer parts with it; and therefore it is evident that Pothier, who, according to the expression of the demandant, knew well the text of those laws, himself condemns the inference which the demandant seeks to draw from them.

But, exclaims the demandant, Pothier does not say that it is necessary, for the completion of a contract of sale, that the answer of acceptance should reach the proposer.

No; he does not say it expressly, and why? Because there is no need of saying it, it being understood. And in fact the consent of him who accepts the proposed bargain is of no other nature than the consent of him who makes the proposal; both consents are equally necessary for the completion of the contract. If, therefore, he who proposes is not bound by the proposition, when he retracts it before it has reached its address, he who accepts can no more be bound by his acceptance, when he retracts it before it has reached the author of the proposition.

And here recurs the comparison, which we made just now, of the consent expressed by a letter addressed to an absent person, with the consent expressed by words addressed to a person present.

I find myself in the presence of a deaf person who says to me: Will you buy of me such a thing for such a price? I answer him: I will; but he does not hear me; he declares to me that he has not heard me, and he prays me to give him in writing the answer which he judges, by the movement of my lips, that I have made to him. Then I take a pen and trace for him these words: I said that I would, but on further reflection your proposition is not satisfactory. Could this man pretend that, by the answer which I admit that I made to him *viva voce*, I am bound to him irrevocably? Certainly not; and if he prosecuted me, the judge would dismiss him without hesitation.

Wherefore would it be otherwise in the case of a letter written to an absent person? Because the absent person has become proprietor of my letter from the moment when it left my hands? But let us take another comparison.

A man has in his cabinet an acoustic vault, constructed in such a manner that, by reason of the various and extremely multiplied windings of the tubes which compose it, the words transmitted through one of the extremities do not reach the other till after a space of five minutes. I am in the presence of that man, and in his cabinet in question. There, after saying to me: Will you buy of me such a thing for such a sum? he adds: Answer me by your [my] acoustic vault. Thereupon we take our places, I at one of the extremities of his vault, he at the other; and I say to him by this speaking trumpet: I will. But a minute after I change my resolution; I run to him, and before he has been able to hear my answer, I say to him: I will not. Could he, after having heard the answer which I made to him at first by his acoustic vault, pretend that this answer having been transmitted to him by tubes of which he was proprietor, and having consequently become his property at the very instant that it left my mouth, I could not retract it before it had struck his ear? No; emphatically no; a hundred times no.

For the same reason, the obligation which I contract by a letter to an absent person does not bind me, so long as the absent person to whom I have addressed that letter has not received it.

Therefore, we ought to hold it as very evident that, if the demandant had, before the arrival of the first letter of the 23d of January, caused a second letter to reach the Messrs. D., by which he had declared to them that he revoked the acceptance which he had made of their propositions by the first, the Messrs. D. would not have had any action against him to compel him to execute the bargain which was negotiating between him and them.

But what the demandant could do by a second letter arriving before the first, could he not do equally by a second letter which, without anticipating the first, reached the Messrs. D. at the same time? Yes, without doubt he could: the two letters arriving together, the Messrs. D. could not say that the consent expressed by the first still subsisted; they could not say that the dumb agent, whom the demandant had sent to them by the first, still had power to manifest to them his consent; they would have been forced to regard the second as taking from the first all credit.

Assuming that, our question resolves itself in the same manner. Since the demandant could, by a second letter arriving at the same time as the first, revoke in a definitive and absolute manner the acceptance contained in the first, it is clear that he could equally, by such second letter, modify that acceptance; that he could equally retract the assurance which he had given by the first, that the crew would be ready by the 5th of February, and substitute for it a simple promise to do every thing in his power to that end; that he could equally restore to a state of negotiation what by the first he had concluded definitively;

in a word, that he could equally give to the Messrs. D. the right to reconsider their propositions and retract them.

The decree of the court was in the following terms: —

Considering that the decree attacked has only interpreted a correspondence held between two parties upon commercial agreements; and that, therefore, it has not violated any law, —

The court rejects the appeal.

CHAPTER II.

CONSIDERATION.

SECTION I.

Nature of Consideration.

ELEANOR THOMAS *v.* BENJAMIN THOMAS.

IN THE QUEEN'S BENCH, FEBRUARY 5, 1842.

[*Reported in* 2 *Queen's Bench Reports,* 851.]

ASSUMPSIT. The declaration stated an agreement between plaintiff and defendant that the defendant should, when thereto required by the plaintiff, by all necessary deeds, conveyances, assignments, or other assurances, grants, &c., or otherwise, assure a certain dwelling-house and premises, in the county of Glamorgan, unto plaintiff for her life, or so long as she should continue a widow and unmarried; and that plaintiff should, at all times during which she should have possession of the said dwelling-house and premises, pay to defendant and one Samuel Thomas (since deceased), their executors, administrators, or assigns, the sum of £1 yearly towards the ground-rent payable in respect of the said dwelling-house and other premises thereto adjoining, and keep the said dwelling-house and premises in good and tenantable repair. That the said agreement being made, in consideration thereof and of plaintiff's promise to perform the agreement, Samuel Thomas and the defendant promised to perform the same; and that although plaintiff afterwards and before the commencement of the suit, to wit, &c., required of defendant to grant, &c., by a necessary and sufficient deed, &c., the said dwelling-house, &c., to plaintiff for her life, or whilst she continued a widow; and though she had then continued, &c., and still was, a widow and unmarried, and although she did, to wit, on, &c., tender to the defendant for his execution a certain necessary and sufficient deed, &c., proper and sufficient for the conveyance, &c., and although, &c.

(general readiness of plaintiff to perform), yet defendant did not nor would then or at any other time convey, &c.

Pleas: 1. Non assumpsit. 2. That there was not the consideration alleged in the declaration for the defendant's promise. 3. Fraud and covin. Issues thereon.

At the trial before Coltman, J., at the Glamorganshire Lent assizes, 1841, it appeared that John Thomas, the deceased husband of the plaintiff, at the time of his death, in 1837, was possessed of a row of seven dwelling-houses in Merthyr Tidvil, in one of which, being the dwelling-house in question, he was himself residing; and that by his will he appointed his brother Samuel Thomas (since deceased) and the defendant executors thereof, to take possession of all his houses, &c., subject to certain payments in the will mentioned, among which were certain charges in money for the benefit of the plaintiff. In the evening before the day of his death he expressed orally a wish to make some further provision for his wife; and on the following morning he declared orally, in the presence of two witnesses, that it was his will that his wife should have either the house in which he lived and all that it contained, or an additional sum of £100 instead thereof.

This declaration being shortly afterwards brought to the knowledge of Samuel Thomas and the defendant, the executors and residuary legatees, they consented to carry the intentions of the testator so expressed into effect; and after the lapse of a few days they and the plaintiff executed the agreement declared upon, which, after stating the parties and briefly reciting the will, proceeded as follows: —

"And whereas the said testator, shortly before his death, declared, in the presence of several witnesses, that he was desirous his said wife should have and enjoy during her life, or so long as she should continue his widow, all and singular the dwelling-house," &c., "or £100 out of his personal estate," in addition to the respective legacies and bequests given her in and by his said will; "but such declaration and desire was not reduced to writing in the lifetime of the said John Thomas and read over to him; but the said Samuel Thomas and Benjamin Thomas are fully convinced and satisfied that such was the desire of the said testator, and are willing and desirous that such intention should be carried into full effect: Now these presents witness, and it is hereby agreed and declared by and between the parties, that, in consideration of such desire and of the premises," the executors would convey the dwelling-house, &c., to the plaintiff and her assigns during her life, or for so long a time as she should continue a widow and unmarried: "provided nevertheless, and it is hereby further agreed and declared, that the said Eleanor Thomas or her assigns shall and will, at all times during which she shall have possession of the said dwelling-house, &c., pay to the said Samuel Thomas and Benjamin Thomas, their executors, &c., the sum of £1 yearly towards the ground-rent payable in respect of the said dwelling-house and other premises thereto adjoining, and shall and will keep the said dwelling-house and premises in good and tenantable repair:" with other provisions not affecting the questions in this case.

The plaintiff was left in possession of the dwelling-house and premises for some time; but the defendant, after the death of his co-executor, refused to execute a conveyance tendered to him for execution pursuant to the agreement, and shortly before the trial brought an ejectment, under which he turned the plaintiff out of possession. It was objected for the defendant that, a part of the consideration proved being omitted in the declaration, there was a fatal variance. The learned judge overruled the objection, reserving leave to move to enter a nonsuit. Ultimately a verdict was found for the plaintiff on all the issues; and in Easter term last a rule *nisi* was obtained pursuant to the leave reserved.

Chilton and *W. M. James* now shewed cause. It is sufficient if there be any legal consideration for this agreement. [E. V. Williams conceded that, in a court of law, he could not go into the adequacy of the consideration; and that, if the consideration was in part a legal and in part only a moral one, the latter part need not be stated in the declaration.[1]] The objection taken at the trial was, that the consideration for the agreement, instead of being that which is alleged in the declaration, was, as stated in the agreement itself, a respect for the testator's intentions, in which case this would be a mere voluntary agreement: the defendant now appears to contend that respect for the testator's intentions is a part of the legal consideration, and ought to have been set out. But it could not be so characterized. All that a plaintiff is required to do is to set out the legal effect of the contract, and to show performance on the plaintiff's part: here she was in possession for three or four years paying rent, under an undertaking to pay rent and keep the premises in repair: that is a good consideration; and if so, it cannot be necessary in pleading it to allege additional motives, which, in the eye of the law, do not enter into the consideration. Thus, in debt for rent on a demise of a messuage with the furniture, though in fact the furniture forms an important item in estimating the rent, yet, as in point of law the rent issues out of the real property, and not out of the furniture, it is sufficient to allege a demise of the real property. Farewell v. Dickenson.[2] Parties are often influenced by motives which form no part of the legal consideration, such as the character of a tenant, or the merits or distresses of the party intended to be benefited; and the circumstance that such motives happen to be stated in the agreement cannot affect the legal rights of the parties, nor make it necessary to state those motives in the declaration.

[1] On this point Chilton cited Bul. N. P. 147, and 1 Chitt. Plead. 295, 300, 6th ed.
[2] 6 B. & C. 251.

E. V. Williams, contra. The consideration alleged in the declaration is solely the promise to pay rent and repair: therefore it lay on the plaintiff to prove that to have been the true and sole consideration. Beech v. White.[1] But the evidence shews that the testator's declaration, as brought before and recognized by the executors, was part, if not the whole, of the consideration. It is conceded that where there is a good legal consideration conjoined with a moral one, it is not necessary to state both; but here regard for the testator's intentions was not, under the circumstances, a mere moral consideration; for the declaration had been made and reduced to writing so formally that it might well be thought valid in law, and so the agreement be made by the executors and residuary legatees to buy peace.[2] If the testator's expressed wish was part or the whole of the consideration, the declaration should have so alleged it, and a nonsuit ought to be entered. But in fact, if it be not the consideration, there is no legal consideration at all: this is a mere gift *cum onere;* and, had it been stated truly, the declaration would have been bad on general demurrer. [PATTESON, J. The rent, if issuing out of the house, might follow the gift; but the obligation to repair does not.] The expressions in the agreement with reference to the ground-rent, and the evidence of one of the witnesses, shew that the property was held under a superior landlord: the assignee's obligation to pay rent and repair would therefore be implied from the very nature and state of things which existed between the parties. Bayley, J., in Burnett v. Lynch.[3] [LORD DENMAN, C. J. There is nothing to show who was liable to pay the ground-rent. COLERIDGE, J. The £1 is reserved payable to the executors: it is quite different from an assignee's liability.] Still the annexing of such a payment cannot be regarded as the consideration. What is meant by the consideration for a promise, but the cause or inducement for making it? Plowden,[4] commenting on Sharington v. Strotton, says, "Note: That by the civil law *nudum pactum* is defined thus: Nudum pactum est ubi nulla subest causa præter conventionem; sed ubi subest causa, fit obligatio, et parit actionem." In Chitty on Contracts[5] the following passage is cited from the *Code Civil:* "L'obligation sans cause, ou sur une fausse cause, ou sur une cause illicite, ne peut avoir aucun effet." The rent and repairs cannot be said to have been the cause or motive which induced the executors to make this agreement: it must have been such a belief as is recited in the agreement itself, which, though a good moral consideration, and perhaps sufficient to raise a use, is not

[1] 12 A. & E. 668.

[2] See Haigh v. Brooks, 10 A. & E. 309, and Brooks v. Haigh, 10 A. & E. 323.

[3] 5 B. & C. 589, 605. See also the judgments of Holroyd, J., and Littledale, J., in the same case.

[4] Note to Sharington v. Strotton, Plowd. 309.

[5] P. 28, 3d ed., 1841. *Code Civil,* liv. 3, tit. 3, ch. 2, §§ 4 and 1131.

sufficient to support a promise. The proviso merely causes the donee to take the gift charged with the burthen of paying the rent and keeping the premises in repair; and she cannot turn these conditions into a consideration. It is clear that, if the proviso had not existed, the executors might have retracted at any moment; their right to do so cannot be qualified by the circumstance that the gift was *cum onere;* otherwise, when carried out to conveyance, it would be a conveyance on good, as distinguished from valuable, consideration. Suppose a subsequent sale; a purchaser for value would have been entitled, though he had purchased with notice of the gift. A consideration, to be sufficient against such a purchaser within the saving clause of the 27 Eliz. c. 4, s. 4,[1] must be such a consideration as would support an assumpsit. Were it otherwise, donees by voluntary gift would confirm their estates by covenanting to repair a monument, maintain a plantation, or the like. Here the donors in effect say, that the donee is to pay no purchase-money, but is to do what a purchaser for full consideration would have to do, pay the rent and maintain in repair. And it is to be observed that, in that part of the agreement where the purchase-money is usually mentioned, instead of any valuable consideration there is a mere reference to the testator's wishes; which is followed in a different part of the deed by a simple provision for the burthens commonly belonging and incident to the subject-matter. The defendant is therefore entitled to a verdict on the first issue.

LORD DENMAN, C. J. There is nothing in this case but a great deal of ingenuity, and a little wilful blindness to the actual terms of the instrument itself. There is nothing whatever to show that the ground-rent was payable to a superior landlord; and the stipulation for the payment of it is not a mere proviso, but an express agreement. (His Lordship here read the proviso.) This is in terms an express agreement, and shows a sufficient legal consideration quite independent of the moral feeling which disposed the executors to enter into such a contract. Mr. Williams's definition of consideration is too large: the word *causa* in the passage referred to means one which confers what the law considers a benefit on the party. Then the obligation to repair is one which might impose charges heavier than the value of the life estate.

PATTESON, J. It would be giving to *causa* too large a construction if we were to adopt the view urged for the defendant: it would be confounding consideration with motive. Motive is not the same thing with consideration. Consideration means something which is of some value in the eye of the law, moving from the plaintiff: it may be some benefit to the plaintiff, or some detriment to the defendant; but at all events it must be moving from the plaintiff. Now that which is suggested as the consideration here, a pious respect for the wishes of the

[1] See Newland on Contracts, c. 24, p. 392, *et seq.*

testator, does not in any way move from the plaintiff: it moves from the testator; therefore, legally speaking, it forms no part of the consideration. Then it is said that, if that be so, there is no consideration at all, it is a mere voluntary gift: but when we look at the agreement we find that this is not a mere proviso that the donee shall take the gift with the burthens; but it is an express agreement to pay what seems to be a fresh apportionment of a ground-rent, and which is made payable not to a superior landlord but to the executors. So that this rent is clearly not something incident to the assignment of the house; for in that case, instead of being payable to the executors, it would have been payable to the landlord. Then as to the repairs: these houses may very possibly be held under a lease containing covenants to repair; but we know nothing about it: for any thing that appears, the liability to repair is first created by this instrument. The proviso certainly struck me at first as Mr. Williams put it, that the rent and repairs were merely attached to the gift by the donors; and, had the instrument been executed by the donors only, there might have been some ground for that construction; but the fact is not so. Then it is suggested that this would be held to be a mere voluntary conveyance as against a subsequent purchaser for value: possibly that might be so: but suppose it would: the plaintiff contracts to take it, and does take it, whatever it is, for better for worse: perhaps a *bona fide* purchase for a valuable consideration might override it; but that cannot be helped.

COLERIDGE, J. The concessions made in the course of the argument have in fact disposed of the case. It is conceded that mere motive need not be stated; and we are not obliged to look for the legal consideration in any particular part of the instrument, merely because the consideration is usually stated in some particular part: *ut res magis valeat*, we may look to any part. In this instrument, in the part where it is usual to state the consideration, nothing certainly is expressed but a wish to fulfil the intentions of the testator; but in another part we find an express agreement to pay an annual sum for a particular purpose, and also a distinct agreement to repair. If these had occurred in the first part of the instrument, it could hardly have been argued that the declaration was not well drawn, and supported by the evidence. As to the suggestion of this being a voluntary conveyance, my impression is that this payment of £1 annually is more than a good consideration: it is a valuable consideration: it is clearly a thing newly created, and not part of the old ground-rent.

Rule discharged.[1]

[1] In a commentary on the *Code Civil*, in *Codes Français Expliqués*, &c., by J. A. Rogron, Paris, 1836, the words of the *Code*, "L'obligation sans cause, ou sur une fausse cause, ou sur une cause illicite, ne peut avoir aucun effet" (*ante*, p. 167), are discussed; and the note upon "sans cause" is as follows:—

"La cause est ce qui détermine l'engagement que prend une partie dans un con-

SECTION II.

What Contracts require a Consideration.

PILLANS AND ROSE *v.* VAN MIEROP AND HOPKINS.

IN THE KING'S BENCH, APRIL 30, 1765.

[*Reported in* 3 *Burrow*, 1663.]

ON Friday, 25th of January last, Mr. Attorney-General Norton, on behalf of the plaintiffs, moved for a new trial. He moved it as upon a verdict against evidence, the substance of which evidence was as follows: —

One White, a merchant in Ireland, desired to draw upon the plaintiffs, who were merchants at Rotterdam in Holland, for £800 payable to one Clifford, and proposed to give them credit upon a good house in London for their reimbursement, or any other method of reimbursement.

The plaintiffs in answer desired a confirmed credit upon a house of rank in London as the condition of their accepting the bill. White names the house of the defendants as this house of rank, and offers credit upon them; whereupon the plaintiffs honored the draft, and paid the money, and then wrote to the defendants, Van Mierop and Hopkins, merchants in London (to whom White also wrote about the same time), desiring to know whether they would accept such bills as they, the plaintiffs, should in about a month's time draw upon the said Van Mierop and Hopkins's house here in London for £800 upon the credit of White; and they, having received their assent, accordingly drew upon the defendants. In the interim, White failed before their

trat; il ne faut pas la confondre avec la cause implicite du contrat, autrement le motif qui porte à contracter. La cause de l'engagement d'une partie est le fait ou la promesse de l'autre partie; elle peut aussi consister dans une pure libéralité de la part de l'une des parties: ainsi, lorsque je m'oblige à payer mille francs à Paul, pour tels services que son père m'a rendus, la cause déterminante du contrat, ce sont les services qui m'ont été rendus; le motif qui m'a porté à contracter, c'est le désir de m'acquitter envers lui des services de son père; si celui-ci ne m'a jamais rendu les services dont il a été parlé dans l'acte, le contrat est sans cause. Je m'oblige à donner mille francs à Paul pour qu'il suive une affaire pendante devant le tribunal de la Seine: la cause déterminante est la promesse de Paul qu'il suivra mon affaire; si elle est jugée irrévocablement au moment où nous avons stipulé, le contrat est sans cause. Autre exemple: je vous vends ma maison; la cause de la vente est, d'un côté, la maison elle-même, de l'autre, le prix. Enfin je donne, dans la forme de dispositions entre vifs, ma maison à Paul, qui l'accepte: ma libéralité est ici la seule cause du contrat." p. 209.

draft came to hand, or was even drawn; and the defendants gave notice of it to the plaintiffs, and forbid their drawing upon them,—which they nevertheless did: and therefore the defendants refused to pay their bills.

On the trial, a verdict was found for the defendants.

Upon shewing cause, on Monday, 11th February last, it turned upon the several letters that had respectively passed between the plaintiffs, and defendants, and White. The letters were read: first, those[1] from White & Co. in Ireland to the plaintiffs in Holland (by which it appears that Pillans and Rose had accepted the bills drawn upon them by White, payable to Clifford); then those of the plaintiffs to the defendants, and also White's to the defendants; then those of the defendants to the plaintiffs,[2] agreeing to honor their bill drawn on account of White; the letter from the defendants to the plaintiffs informing them that White had stopped payment, and desiring them not to draw, as they could not accept their draft; and lastly, that which the plaintiffs wrote to the defendants, that they should draw on them, holding them not to be at liberty to withdraw from their engagement.

The counsel for the defendants were Mr. Serjeant *Davy* and Mr. *Wallace*. They observed that the plaintiffs had given credit to White above a month before the defendants had agreed to accept their draft. For it appears by White's letter of 16th February, 1762, that Pillans and Rose had then actually accepted Clifford's bills, but Van Mierop and Hopkins did not agree to honor their drafts till 19th of March, 1762; therefore the consideration was past and done before their promise was made. And they argued and principally insisted, that for one man to undertake to pay another man's debt was a void undertaking, unless there was some consideration for such undertaking; and that a mere general promise, without benefit to the promiser or loss to the promisee, was a *nudum pactum*. And they cited 1 Bulstr. 120, Thorner *v.* Field; Dyer, 272, pl. 31, Hunt *v.* Bate; 2 Vern. 224, 225, Cecil et al. *v.* Earl of Salisbury; 1 Ro. Abr. 11, pl. 1, letter Q, "Consideration executed;" Yelv. 40, 41; and 2 Strange, 933, Hayes *v.* Warren; where a past consideration was holden insufficient to raise an assumpsit.[3]

The counsel for the plaintiffs were Mr. *Attorney General*, Mr. *Walker*, and Mr. *Dunning*. They denied this to be a past consideration, and insisted that the liberty given to the plaintiffs to draw upon a confirmed house in London (which was prior to the undertaking by the defendants) was the consideration of the credit given by the plaintiffs to White's drafts, and that this was a good and sufficient consideration for the undertaking made by the defendants. It relates back to the

[1] Dated 16th Feb. 1762. [2] Dated 19th March, 1762.
[3] See likewise Hardres, 72, 73, 74.

original transaction. If any one promises to pay for goods delivered to a third person, such promise, being in writing, is a good one. And here White had had £800 from the plaintiffs upon this assurance; and the defendants undertake in writing, in pursuance and completion of this original assurance, to be answerable for White's reimbursing the plaintiffs. And a promise in writing is out of the statute.

This case does not fall within those that have been cited; for Van Mierop and Hopkins have made themselves originally liable. An *ex post facto* event cannot alter the nature of an original promise. Their original promise made them liable, and bound them; and they are obliged, both by law, and in honor and honesty, to perform it. It is a mercantile transaction; and it must be considered, upon the whole of it, as an admittance that the defendants either had, or soon would have, effects of White's in their hands.

LORD MANSFIELD. The objection is, that the letter whereby Van Mierop and Hopkins undertake to honor the plaintiffs' bills is *nudum pactum;* the other side deny it. This is the only question here.

But this is quite different from what passed at the trial: the *nudum pactum* was not mentioned at that time. The grounds it was argued upon there were: 1st, That this imported to be a credit given to Pillans and Rose, in prospect of a future credit to be given by them to White, and that this credit might well be countermanded before the advancement of any money; and this is so;—2d, That there was a fraud; for that Van Mierop and Hopkins had reason to think that White had sent goods to Pillans and Rose; whereas this was a mere lending of credit;—3d, That if Pillans and Rose had received goods from White, and retained them till he failed, the defendants' undertaking was revocable.

I was then of opinion that Van Mierop and Hopkins were bound by their letter, unless there was some fraud upon them; for that they had engaged under their hands, in a mercantile transaction, to give credit for Pillans and Rose's reimbursement. And I did not see it to be future, as had been objected; nor did I see any fraud. And nothing was then urged about its being *nudum pactum.* I have no idea that promises for the debt of another are applicable to the present case. This is, as Mr. Walker said, a mercantile transaction, and it depends upon these letters from merchant to merchant about honoring bills to such an amount; and this credit is given upon a supposition that the person who is to draw upon the undertakers within a certain time has goods in his hands, or will have them Here Pillans and Rose trusted to this undertaking; and there is no fraud. Therefore it is quite upon another foundation than that of a naked promise from one to pay the debt of another.

MR. JUSTICE WILMOT. I own the want of consideration at first occurred to me. But I now am satisfied that this case has nothing to do with the cases of undertakings by one to pay the debt of another. In those cases it is settled, that where the consideration is past the action will not lie. And yet this seems a hard case. The mere promise to pay the debt of another, without any consideration at all, is *nudum pactum.* But the least spark of a consideration will be sufficient. It seems almost implied that there must be some consideration; but if there be none at all, it is *nudum pactum.* The statute must mean such a special promise as would have supported an action. But all this is out of the present case. So also I think is all the precedent correspondence. It lies in a narrow compass. White, Pillans and Rose, and Van Mierop and Hopkins, had all a correspondence together. They have intercourse together, mutually, in mercantile transactions. Pillans and Rose write to Van Mierop and Hopkins to know whether they will honor their drafts for £800 in about a month's time. They say they will. Now it strikes me, as Mr. Walker said, that it admits that they either have assets or effects of White's in their hands, or that they have credit upon him. Now by this undertaking of a good house in London, and relying upon it, they are deluded and diverted from using any legal diligence to pursue White, or even not to part with any effects of his which they might have in their hands. Therefore this seems to be an irrevocable undertaking by Van Mierop and Hopkins, and they ought to be bound by it. Consequently there ought to be a new trial.

LORD MANSFIELD. A letter of credit may be given as well for money already advanced, as for money to be advanced in future. Let it be argued again the next term, and you shall have the opinion of the whole court. *Ulterius Concilium.*

Yesterday this matter accordingly came on again, and was argued by Mr. *Wallace* for the defendants, and by the same counsel as argued last term for the plaintiffs.

The latter repeated and enforced their arguments. They said the consideration moved from White to the defendants; not from the plaintiffs, Pillans and Rose, to the defendants. And as the defendants have undertaken for White, they can't revoke or retract their engagement. This case is not like the cases cited; some of which are strange cases and not founded on solid or sufficient reasons, and in others of them there was no meritorious consideration at all. And Mr. Walker cited Hardres, 71, Reynolds *v.* Prosser, where the consideration was adjudged sufficient, notwithstanding all the reasoning of Sir Thomas Hardres and all the cases cited by him. That was an assumpsit by a stranger, in consideration that the plaintiff would forbear to prosecute Lord Abergavenny upon a judgment, in the name of the original plaintiff, by virtue of a letter of attorney to receive it to his own use.

Serjeant *Davy* was heard this morning on behalf of the defendants, and urged that the plaintiffs gave credit to White upon his promising to reimburse them; and he said there was a fraudulent concealment of facts. White's first letter could have no influence on the plaintiffs, for they afterwards desired a confirmed credit upon a house of rank in London; so that they did not rely on White's first letter, which offered credit on the defendants or any other method of reimbursement. And nothing had then passed between White and the defendants. For the first letter between them was on the 16th of February (a fortnight after); and then the defendants were deceived into a false opinion that it was for a future credit, and not to secure a past acceptance of White's bills by the plaintiffs. And this concealment of circumstances is sufficient to vitiate the contract. The plaintiffs had accepted a bill of £800 of White's, a fortnight before the defendants' letter of 16th February; which bill the plaintiffs had accepted upon assurance of credit on a house in London to reimburse them. And this transaction was fraudulently concealed, both by White and the plaintiffs, from the defendants. If this had been disclosed, the defendants would have plainly seen that the plaintiffs doubted of White's sufficiency, by their requiring further security for his already contracted debt. All letters of credit relate to future credit, not to debts before incurred; nor can the advancer of money thereupon include an old debt before incurred. A bill cannot be accepted before it is drawn. This is only a promise to accept; for it is only a promise to honor the bill, not a promise to pay it. A promise to pay a past debt of another person is void at common law for want of consideration, unless there be at least an implied promise from the debtee to forbear suing the original debtor. But here was a debt clearly contracted by White with the plaintiffs on the credit of White; and there is no promise from the plaintiffs to forbear suing White. A naked promise is a void promise: the consideration must be executory, not past or executed.

Lord Mansfield asked if any case could be found where the undertaking holden to be a *nudum pactum* was in writing.

Serjeant *Davy*. It was anciently doubted whether a written acceptance of a bill of exchange was binding for want of a consideration. It is so said somewhere in Lutwyche.

LORD MANSFIELD. This is a matter of great consequence to trade and commerce, in every light. If there was any kind of fraud in this transaction, the collusion and *mala fides* would have vacated the contract. But from these letters it seems to me clear that there was none. The first proposal from White was to reimburse the plaintiffs by a remittance, or by credit on the house of Van Mierop: this was the alternative he proposed. The plaintiffs chose the latter. Both the plaintiffs and White wrote to Van Mierop and Company. They answered that they would honor the plaintiffs' drafts. So that the defendants assent to the proposal made by White, and ratify it. And it does not seem at all that the plaintiffs then doubted of White's sufficiency, or meant to conceal any thing from the defendants. If there be no fraud, it is a mere question of law. The law of merchants and the law of the land is the same. A witness cannot be admitted to prove the law of merchants. We must consider it as a point of law. A *nudum pactum* does not exist in the usage and law of merchants.

I take it that the ancient notion about the want of consideration was for the sake of evidence only: for when it is reduced into writing, as in covenants, specialties, bonds, &c.,[1] there was no objection to the want of consideration; and the Statute of Frauds proceeded upon the same principle. In commercial cases, amongst merchants, the want of consideration is not an objection.

This is just the same thing as if White had drawn on Van Mierop and Hopkins, payable to the plaintiffs. It had been nothing to the plaintiffs whether Van Mierop and Company had effects of White's in their hands or not, if they had accepted his bill. And this amounts to the same thing: "I will give the bill due honor," is in effect accepting it. If a man agrees that he will do the formal part, the law looks upon it (in the case of an acceptance of a bill) as if actually done. This is an engagement to accept the bill, if there was a necessity to accept it, and to pay it when due; and they could not afterwards retract. It would be very destructive to trade, and to trust in commercial dealing, if they could. There was nothing of *nudum pactum* mentioned to the jury; nor was it, I dare say, at all in their idea or contemplation. I think the point of law is with the plaintiffs.

MR. JUSTICE WILMOT. The question is, whether this action can be supported upon the breach of this agreement. I can find none of those cases that go upon its being *nudum pactum* that are in writing: they are all upon parol. I have traced this matter of the *nudum pactum*, and it is very curious.

He then explained the principle of an agreement being looked upon as a *nudum pactum*, and how the notion of a *nudum pactum* first came into our law. He said it was echoed from the civil law: *Ex nudo pacto non oritur actio.* Vinnius gives the reason, in lib. 3, tit. *De Obligationibus*, 4to edition, 596. If by stipulation (and *a fortiori*, if by writing), it was good without consideration. There was no radical defect in the contract for want of consideration. But it was made requisite, in order to put people upon attention and reflection, and to prevent obscurity and uncertainty; and in that view either writing or certain formalities were required. *Idem*, on Justinian, 4to edit., 614. Therefore it was intended as a guard against rash, inconsiderate declarations. But if an undertaking was entered into upon deliberation and reflection, it had activity; and such promises were binding. Both Grotius and Puffendorff held them obligatory by the law of nations. Grot., lib. 2, c. 11, *De Promissis*; Puffend., lib. 3, c. v. They are morally

[1] *Vide* 3 Burr. 1639.

good, and only require ascertainment; therefore there is no reason to extend the principle, or carry it further.

There would have been no doubt upon the present case, according to the Roman law; because here is both stipulation (in the express Roman form) and writing. Bracton, who wrote[1] *temp.* Hen. 3, is the first of our lawyers that mentions this. His writings interweave a great many things out of the Roman law. In his third book, cap. 1, *De Actionibus*, he distinguishes between naked and clothed contracts. He says that *obligatio est mater actionis*; and that it may arise *ex contractu, multis modis; sicut ex conventione*, &c.; *sicut sunt pacta, conventa, quæ nuda sunt aliquando, aliquando vestita*, &c., &c.

Our own lawyers have adopted exactly the same idea as the Roman law. Plowden, 308 *b*,[2] in the case of Sharington and Pledall *v.* Strotton and others, mentions it; and no one contradicted it. He lays down the distinction between contracts or agreements in words (which are more base), and contracts or agreements in writing (which are more high); and puts the distinction upon the want of deliberation in the former case, and the full exercise of it in the latter. His words are the marrow of what the Roman lawyers had said: "Words pass from men lightly." But where the agreement is made by deed, there is more stay, &c., &c. For, first, there is, &c., &c.; and, thirdly, he delivers the writing as his deed. The delivery of the deed is a ceremony in law, signifying fully his good-will that the thing in the deed should pass from him who made the deed to the other; and therefore a deed, which must necessarily be made upon great thought and deliberation, shall bind without regard to the consideration. The voidness of the consideration is the same in reality in both cases: the reason of adopting the rule was the same in both cases, though there is a difference in the ceremonies required by each law; but no inefficacy arises merely from the naked promise. Therefore, if it stood only upon the naked promise, its being in this case reduced into writing, is a sufficient guard against surprise; and therefore the rule of *nudum pactum* does not apply in the present case.

I cannot find that a *nudum pactum* evidenced by writing has ever been holden bad, and I should think it good; though where it is merely verbal, it is bad; yet I give no opinion upon its being good always, when in writing. Many of the old cases are strange and absurd; so also are some of the modern ones, particularly that of Hayes *v.* Warren.[3] It is now settled, that where the act is done at

[1] Sub ultima tempora Regis H. 3.

[2] This probably was Plowden's own argument. I suppose he was himself that apprentice of the Middle Temple who argued for the defendants.

[3] *Vide* 2 Sir J. S. 933. I have a very full note of this case. The reason of the reversal of the judgment was, that it did not appear by the declaration to be either for the benefit or at the request of the defendant.

the request of the person promising it will be a sufficient foundation to graft the promise upon. In another instance the strictness has been relaxed; as, for instance, burying[1] a son, or curing[2] a son. The considerations were both past, and yet holden good. It has been melting down into common sense of late times.

However, I do here see a consideration. If it be a departure from any right, it will be sufficient to graft a verbal promise upon. Now here, White, living in Ireland, writes to the plaintiffs to honor his draft for £800,[3] payable ten weeks after. The plaintiffs agree to it, on condition that they be made safe at all events. White offers good credit on a house in London, and draws; and the plaintiffs accept his draft. Then White writes to them to draw on Van Mierop and Hopkins; to whom the plaintiffs write, to inquire if they will honor their draft. They engage that they will. This transaction has prevented, stopped, and disabled the plaintiffs from calling upon White for the performance of his engagement; for White's engagement is complied with, so that the plaintiffs could not call upon him for this security. I do not speak of the money, for that was not payable till after two usances and a half. But the plaintiffs were prevented from calling upon White for a performance of his engagement, to give them credit on a good house in London for reimbursement; so that here is a good consideration. The law does not weigh the *quantum* of the consideration. The suspension of the plaintiffs' right to call upon White for a compliance with his engagement is sufficient to support an action, even if it be a suspension of the right for a day only, or for ever so little a time.

But to consider this as a commercial case. All nations ought to have their laws conformable to each other in such cases. *Fides servanda est; simplicitas juris gentium prævaleat. Hodierni mores* are such, that the old notion about the *nudum pactum* is not strictly observed, as a rule. On a question of this nature, whether by the law of nations such an engagement as this shall bind, the law is to judge.

The true reason why the acceptance of a bill of exchange shall bind is not on account of the acceptor's having, or being supposed to have, effects in hand, but for the convenience of trade and commerce. *Fides est servanda.* An acceptance for the honor of the drawer shall bind the acceptor; so shall a verbal acceptance. And whether this be an actual acceptance, or an agreement to accept, it ought equally to bind. An agreement to accept a bill to be drawn in future would (as it seems to me), by connection and relation, bind on account of the antecedent relation; and I see no difference between its being before or

[1] Church and Church's Case, cited in T. Raym. 260.
[2] *Vide* 2 Leon. 111.
[3] For between Ireland and Holland each usance is one month.

after the bill was drawn. Here was an agreement sufficient to bind the defendants to pay the bill; agreeing to honor it is agreeing to pay it. I see no sort of fraud. It rather seems as if the defendants had effects of White's in their hands; and it does not appear to me that the defendants would not have honored the plaintiffs' drafts, even though they had known that it was future credit. But whether the plaintiffs or the defendants had effects of White's in their hands or not, we must determine on the general doctrine; and I am of opinion that there ought to be a new trial.

Mr. Justice YATES was of the same opinion. He said it was a case of great consequence to commerce; and therefore he would give both his opinion and his reasons. The arguments on the side of the defendants terminate in its being a *nudum pactum*, and therefore void. This depends upon two questions: 1st question, — Whether this be a promise without a consideration; 2d question, — If it is, then whether this promise shall not be binding of itself, without any consideration.

First, the draft drawn by White on the plaintiffs, payable to Clifford, is no part of the consideration of the undertaking by the defendants. The draft payable to Clifford is never mentioned to the defendants. They are asked whether they will answer a draft from the plaintiffs upon them. They answer, they will honor such a draft on them. Whether the defendants had or had not effects of White's in their hands, is immaterial. Any damage[1] to another, or suspension or forbearance of his right, is a foundation for an undertaking, and will make it binding, though no actual benefit accrues to the party undertaking. Now here the promise and undertaking of the defendants did occasion a possibility of loss to the plaintiffs. It is plain that the plaintiffs would not rely on White's assurance only, but wrote to the defendants to know if they would accept their drafts. The credit of the plaintiffs might have been hurt by the refusal of the defendants to accept White's bills. They were, or might have been, prevented from resorting to him, or getting further security from him. It comes within the cases of promises where the debtee forbears suing the original debtor.

Second question, — Whether, by the law of merchants, this contract is not binding on the defendants, though it was without consideration. The acceptance of a bill of exchange is an obligation to pay it. The end of their institution, their currency, requires that it should be so. On this principle, bills of exchange are considered and are declared upon as special contracts, though legally they are only simple contracts. The declaration sets forth the bill and acceptance specifically, and that thereby the defendants, by the custom of merchants, became liable to pay it. This agreement to honor their bill was a virtual acceptance of the bill. An acceptance needs not be upon the bill

[1] *Vide* Coggs *v.* Bernard, 2 Lord Raym. 919.

itself: it may be by collateral writing. Wilkinson v. Lutwidge, 1 Strange, 648. A promise to accept is the same as an actual acceptance, and a small matter amounts to an acceptance; and so says Molloy, lib. 2, c. 10, § 20. And an acceptance will bind, though the acceptor has no effects of the drawer in his hands, and without any consideration. Symons v. Parminter,[1] Hil. 1747, 21 G. 2, B. R. And a bill accepted for the honor of the drawer will also bind.

Then he applied these positions to the present case. It was an acceptance of this very draft by relation and connection, though the bill was not then drawn by the plaintiffs on the defendants. But even if it did not amount to an actual acceptance, yet it would equally bind the defendants: they would be equally obliged to perform the effect of their undertaking. The plaintiffs apprised the defendants of their intention to draw, and the defendants promised to honor their draft; and the plaintiffs of course would regulate their conduct accordingly. Therefore, upon the whole circumstances of this transaction: 1st, There is a consideration; and, 2d, If there was none, yet in this commercial case the defendants would be bound.

MR. JUSTICE ASTON. I am of opinion that there ought to be a new trial. If there be such a custom of merchants as has been alleged, it may be found by a jury; but it is the court, not the jury, who are to determine the law. This must be considered as a commercial transaction, and is a plain case. The defendants have undertaken to honor the plaintiffs' draft; therefore they are bound to pay it. This cannot be called a *nudum pactum*. The answer returned by the defendants is an admission of having effects of White's in their hands, if that were necessary. And after this promise to accept (which is an implied acceptance), they might have applied any thing of White's that they had in their hands to this engagement, even though White had drawn other bills upon them in the interim. The defendants voluntarily engaged to the plaintiffs, and they could not recede from their engagement. As to its being a *nudum pactum* (which matter has been already so well explained), if there be turpitude or illegality in the consideration of a note, it will make it void, and may be given in evidence. But here nothing of that kind appears, nor any thing like fraud in the plaintiffs. Here was full notice of all the facts; a clear apprehension of them by the defendants; a question put to them, whether they would accept; and their answer, that they would. Upon the whole he concurred, that an action will lay for the plaintiffs against them; and that the plaintiffs ought to recover.

BY THE COURT unanimously the rule to set aside the verdict, and for a new trial, was made absolute.

[1] This was on a motion in arrest of judgment. The judgment was affirmed (*ex parte*) in Dom. Proc. with £100 costs, upon or soon after 20th Feb. 1748.

WILLIAMSON ET UXOR *v.* LOSH, *Executor*.

IN THE KING'S BENCH, MICHAELMAS TERM, 1775.

[*Reported in Chitty on Bills, 9th ed., p.* 75, *note* (*x*).]

THIS was an action of assumpsit against the defendant, as executor of John Losh, deceased, upon the following promissory note:—

"I, John Losh, for the love and affection that I have for Jane Tiffin, my wife's sister's daughter, do promise that my executors, administrators, or assigns, shall pay to her the sum of £100 of money, one year after my decease, and a caldron, and a clock, a wainscot chest, and a bed and bed-clothes, seven pudden-dishes: as witness my hand this 16th day of February, 1763.

"Witnessed by us, A. B., C. D."

Jane Tiffin afterwards intermarried with the plaintiff. Upon the trial, a verdict was found for the plaintiff, and a case reserved. The defendant admitted he had proved the will, and had assets sufficient to cover the damages, but contended that there was no consideration in point of law, and that the note could not be recovered upon, and that, as the testator was not bound, the executor was not. The court held that the instrument being in writing and attested by witnesses, the objection of *nudum pactum* did not lie, and ordered the *postea* to the plaintiff.

RANN AND ANOTHER, *Executors of* MARY HUGHES, *v.* ISABELLA HUGHES, *Administratrix of* J. HUGHES.

IN THE HOUSE OF LORDS, MAY 14, 1778.

[*Reported in* 7 *Term Reports,* 350, *note* (*a*).]

THE declaration stated that on the 11th of June, 1764, divers disputes had arisen between the plaintiffs' testator and the defendant's intestate, which they referred to arbitration; that the arbitrator awarded that the defendant's intestate should pay to the plaintiffs' testator £983; that the defendant's intestate afterwards died possessed of effects sufficient to pay that sum; that administration was granted to the defendant; that Mary Hughes died, having appointed the plaintiffs her executors; that at the time of her death the said sum of £983 was unpaid: by reason of which premises the defendant, as administratrix, became liable to pay to the plaintiffs, as executors, the said sum; and being so liable, she in consideration thereof undertook and promised to pay, &c. The defendant pleaded *non assumpsit*, *plene administravit*, and *plene administravit* except as to certain goods, &c., which were not sufficient to pay an outstanding bond-debt of the intestate's therein set forth, &c. The replication took issue on these pleas. Verdict for the plaintiff on the first issue, and for the defendant on the two last; and on the first a general judgment was entered in B. R. against the defendant *de bonis propriis*. This judgment was reversed in the Exchequer Chamber; and a writ of error was afterwards brought in the House of Lords, where, after argument, the following question was proposed to the judges by the Lord Chancellor: Whether sufficient matter appeared upon the declaration to warrant after verdict the judgment against the defendant in error in her personal capacity; upon which the Lord Chief Baron Skynner delivered the opinion of the judges to this effect: It is undoubtedly true that every man is, by the law of nature, bound to fulfil his engagements. It is equally true that the law of this country supplies no means, nor affords any remedy, to compel the performance of an agreement made without sufficient consideration. Such agreement is *nudum pactum, ex quo non oritur actio*; and whatsoever may be the sense of this maxim in the civil law, it is in the last-mentioned sense only that it is to be understood in our law. The declaration states that the defendant, being indebted as administratrix, promised to pay when requested; and the judgment is against the defendant generally. The being indebted is of itself a sufficient consideration to ground a promise; but the promise must be coëxtensive with the consideration, unless some particular consideration of fact can be found here to warrant the extension of it against the defendant in her own capacity. If a person indebted in one right, in consideration of forbearance for a particular time, promise to pay in another right, this convenience will be a sufficient consideration to warrant an action against him or her in the latter right; but here no sufficient consideration occurs to support this demand against her in her personal capacity, for she derives no advantage or convenience from the promise here made. For if I promise generally to pay upon request what I was liable to pay upon request in another right, I derive no advantage or convenience from this promise, and therefore there is not sufficient consideration for it. But it is said that if this promise is in writing, that takes away the necessity of a consideration, and obviates the objection of *nudum pactum*, for that cannot be where the promise is put in writing; and that, if it were necessary to support the promise that it should be in writing, it will, after verdict, be presumed that it was in writing; and this last is certainly true; but that there cannot be *nudum pactum* in writing, whatever may be the rule of the civil law, there is certainly none such in the law of England. His Lordship observed, upon the doctrine of *nudum pactum* delivered by Mr. J. Wilmot in the case of Pillans *v.* Van Mierop and Hopkins, 3 Burr. 1663, that he contradicted himself, and was also contradicted by Vinnius in his comment on Justinian.

All contracts are by the laws of England distinguished into agreements by specialty, and agreements by parol; nor is there any such third class, as some of the counsel have endeavored to maintain, as contracts in writing. If they be merely written and not specialties, they are parol, and a consideration must be proved. But it is said that the Statute of Frauds has taken away the necessity of any consideration in this case: the Statute of Frauds was made for the relief of personal representatives and others, and did not intend to charge them further than by common law they were chargeable. His Lordship here read those sections of that statute which relate to the present subject. He observed that the words were merely negative, and that executors and administrators should not be liable out of their own estates, unless the agreement upon which the action was brought, or some memorandum thereof, was in writing and signed by the party. But this does not prove that the agreement was still not liable to be tried and judged of as all other agreements merely in writing are by the common law, and does not prove the converse of the proposition, that when in writing the party must be at all events liable. He here observed upon the case of Pillans *v.* Van Mierop, in Burr., and the case of Losh *v.* Williamson, Mich. 16 G. 3, in B. R.; and so far as these cases went on the doctrine of *nudum pactum*, he seemed to intimate that they were erroneous. He said that all his brothers concurred with him that in this case there was not a sufficient consideration to support this demand as a personal demand against the defendant, and that its being now supposed to have been in writing makes no difference. The consequence of which is that the question put to us must be answered in the negative.

And the judgment in the Exchequer Chamber was affirmed.[1]

[1] In 7 Brown's Parliament Cases, 550 (vol. 4 of Tomlin's ed., p. 27), the arguments of counsel are given. Upon the question of consideration, F. Buller and J. Dunning for the plaintiffs in error argued as follows: —

"In the case of a promise in writing, which this must be taken to be [and which they said it was in fact], it is not necessary to allege any consideration in the declaration; but if it were necessary, there was a sufficient consideration for the promise appearing upon this declaration. In reason, there is little or no difference between a contract which is deliberately reduced into writing, and signed by the parties, without seal, and a contract under the same circumstances, to which a party at the time of signing it puts a seal, or his finger on cold wax. In the case of a deed, *i.e.*, an instrument under seal, it must be admitted that no consideration is necessary; and in the year 1765 it was solemnly adjudged in the Court of King's Bench, Pillans *v.* Van Mierop, 3 Burr. 1663, that no consideration was necessary when the promise was

SECTION III.

Sufficiency of Consideration in General.

SMITH AND SMITH'S CASE.

In the Queen's Bench, Michaelmas Term, 1583.

[*Reported in* 3 *Leonard*, 88.]

Lambert Smith, executor of Tho. Smith, brought an action upon the case against John Smith, that whereas the testator, having divers children infants, and lying sick of a mortal sickness, being careful to provide for his said children infants, the defendant, in consideration the testator would commit the education of his children, and the disposition of his goods after his death, during the minority of his said children, for the education of the said children, to him, promised to the testator to procure the assurance of certain customary lands to one of the children of the said testator; and declared further, that the testator thereupon constituted the defendant overseer of his will, and ordained and appointed by his will that his goods should be in the disposition of the defendant, and that the testator died, and that by reason of that will, the goods of the testator, to such a value came to the defendant's hands to his great profit and advantage. And upon *non assumpsit* pleaded, it was found for the plaintiff. And upon exception to the declaration in arrest of judgment for want of sufficient consideration, it was said by Wray, C. J., that here is not any benefit to the

reduced into writing. That opinion has since been recognized in the same court, and several judgments founded upon it; all which judgments must be subverted, and what was there conceived to be settled law totally overturned, if the plaintiffs in this cause were not entitled, to recover. But further: If a consideration were necessary, a sufficient one for the promise appeared upon the declaration in this case. The defendant was the administratrix of John Hughes, she had effects of his in her hands, she was liable to be called upon by the plaintiffs in an action, to show to what amount she had effects, and how she had applied them; and under these circumstances she promised to pay the demand which the plaintiffs had against her. But it was said, that it did not appear on the declaration that she had effects of John Hughes sufficient to pay all his debts. To what amount she had effects, or what debts were due from Hughes at his death, was known to the defendant only, and not to the plaintiffs. They applied to the person against whom they had a right of action; she promised to pay them, and under that promise they rested satisfied. This promise, if it did not import an admission of effects, must naturally be understood to mean that the defendant would pay the debt whether she had effects or not; and if it was not so meant, it could only be intended to amuse, mislead, and deceive the plaintiffs. And after such a promise, the defendant ought not to be permitted to say that she had not sufficient assets to pay this debt." —Ed.

defendant that should be a consideration in law to induce him to make this promise; for the consideration is no other but to have the disposition of the goods of the testator *pro educatione liberorum.* For all the disposition is for the profit of the children; and notwithstanding that such overseers commonly make gain of such disposition, yet the same is against the intendment of the law, which presumes every man to be true and faithful if the contrary be not shewed; and therefore the law shall intend that the defendant hath not made any private gain to himself, but that he hath disposed of the goods of the testator to the use and benefit of his children according to the trust reposed in him. Which AYLIFFE, J., granted; GAWDY, J., was of the contrary opinion. And afterwards by award of the court it was that the plaintiff *nihil capiat per billam.*

REYNOLDS *v.* PINHOWE.

IN THE QUEEN'S BENCH, TRINITY TERM, 1595.

[*Reported in Croke Elizabeth,* 429.]

ASSUMPSIT. Whereas the defendant had recovered five pounds against the plaintiff; in consideration of four pounds given him by the plaintiff, that the defendant assumed to acknowledge satisfaction of that judgment before such a day; and that he had not done it. And it was thereupon demurred; for it was moved that there was not any consideration, for it is no more than to give him a part of the money which he owed him, which is not any consideration. But all the COURT held it to be well enough; for it is a benefit unto him to have it without suit or charge; and it may be there was error in the record, so as the party might have avoided it. Wherefore it was adjudged for the plaintiff.

DIXON *v.* ADAMS.

IN THE EXCHEQUER CHAMBER, MICHAELMAS TERM, 1596.

[*Reported in Croke Elizabeth,* 538.]

ASSUMPSIT. For that J. S. and J. D. were obliged to Adams in £40, and thereupon he sued J. S. in the Queen's Bench, in which suit Dixon became bail. Adams recovered, and, upon a *scire facias* against Dixon the bail, had judgment against him; and he without other process paid the condemnation, and Adams *in consideratione inde* assumed to Dixon to deliver unto him the principal obligation, and a letter of attorney to sue it against J. D.: and for non-performance hereof the action was brought; and upon *non assumpsit* pleaded, and found for the plaintiff, he had judgment: and thereupon error brought, because it was not a sufficient consideration. And so it was held by the whole court; for Dixon had not done any act whereto the law would not have compelled him. Wherefore the judgment was reversed.

SIR ANTHONY STÜRLYN *v.* ALBANY.

In the Queen's Bench, Michaelmas Term, 1587.

[*Reported in Croke Elizabeth*, 67.]

Assumpsit. The case was, the plaintiff had made a lease to J. S. of land for life, rendering rent. J. S. grants all his estate to the defendant; the rent was behind for divers years; the plaintiff demands the rent of the defendant, who assumed that if the plaintiff could show to him a deed that the rent was due, that he would pay to him the rent and the arrearages; the plaintiff allegeth that upon such a day of, &c., at Warwick, he showed unto him the indenture of lease by which the rent was due, and notwithstanding he had not paid him the rent and the arrearages due for four years. Upon *non assumpsit* pleaded, it was found for the plaintiff, and damages assessed to so much as the rent and arrearages did amount unto. And it was moved in arrest of judgment, that there was no consideration to ground an action; for it is but the showing of the deed, which is no consideration. 2. The damages ought only to be assessed for the time the rent was behind, and not for the rent and the arrearages; for he hath other remedy for the rent; and a recovery in this action shall be no bar in another action. But it was adjudged for the plaintiff: for when a thing is to be done by the plaintiff, be it never so small, this is a sufficient consideration to ground an action; and here the showing of the deed is a cause to avoid suit; and the rent and arrearages may be assessed all in damages. But they took order that the plaintiff should release to the defendant all the arrearages of rent before execution should be awarded.

Nota. In this case it was alleged that it hath been adjudged, when one assumeth to another, that if he can show him an obligation in which he was bound to him, that he would pay him, and he did show the obligation, &c., that no action lieth upon this assumpsit; which was affirmed by the justices.

BRET *v.* J. S. AND HIS WIFE.

IN THE COMMON PLEAS, EASTER TERM, 1600.

[*Reported in Croke Elizabeth,* 756.]

ASSUMPSIT. The case was, that William Dracot, first husband to the *feme*, sent his son to table with the plaintiff for three years, and agreed to give unto him for every year £8, and died within the year. The *feme*, during her widowhood, in consideration of her natural affection to the son, and in consideration that the son should continue during the residue of the time with the plaintiff, promised to the plaintiff to pay unto him £6 13*s.* 4*d.* for the tabling of the son for the time past, and £8 for every year after that he should continue there with the plaintiff. Afterwards she married the defendant, and the plaintiff brought his action as well for the £6 13*s.* 4*d.* as for the tabling for the two years following.

Warburton moved, that this action lay not. First, because it was an entire contract by her first husband for the entire year, which cannot be apportioned. Secondly, because natural affection is not sufficient to ground an assumpsit without *quid pro quo*. Thirdly, that this is a contract for which action of debt lies, and not this action.

But all the COURT held, that it well lay. For as to the first, it is well apportionable; because it being for tabling which he had taken, there ought to be a recompense, although he departed within the year, or that the contractor died within the year. To the second they agreed, that natural affection of itself is not a sufficient consideration to ground an assumpsit; for although it be sufficient to raise a use, yet it is not sufficient to ground an action, without an express *quid pro quo*. But it is here good, because it is not only in consideration of affection, but that her son should afterwards continue at his table, which is good as well for the money due before, as for what should afterwards become due. And as to the third, true it is that, if the contract had been only for the tabling afterwards, then debt would have lain, and not this action; but in regard it is conjoined with another thing for which he could not have an action of debt (as it is here for this £6 13*s.* 4*d.*), an action upon the case lies for all (as debt with other things may be put into an arbitrament). Wherefore it was adjudged for the plaintiff.

KENT v. PRATT.

In the Common Pleas, Michaelmas Term, 1610.

[*Reported in* 1 *Rolle's Abridgment*, 23, *placita* 27, 28.]

If A. lease land to B. at will, and A. assume to B. that, in consideration that he will surrender the said estate at will to him, he will provide a parsonage for J. S., this is not a good consideration to support an action, because he could determine this estate at will at his pleasure. It was alleged in the declaration that B. was possessed of a term, without showing what term; and therefore the court took it to be a lease at will. But if it had been alleged that there was a controversy between A. and B. whether this was a lease at will or for years, and thereupon the assumpsit made as before, this had been a good consideration.

BARNARD v. SIMONS.

Writ of Error at Serjeants' Inn, Michaelmas Term, 1616.

[*Reported in* 1 *Rolle's Abridgment*, 26, *placitum* 39.]

If A. makes a void assumpsit to B., and afterwards a stranger comes to B., and, in consideration that B. will relinquish the assumpsit made to him by A., he promises to pay him £10, this is not a good consideration to charge him, because the first assumpsit was void.

TRAVER v. ——.

In the King's Bench, Michaelmas Term, 1661.

[*Reported in* 1 *Siderfin*, 57.]

A woman, after the death of her husband, said to one of his creditors that, if he would prove that her husband owed him £20, she would pay it; and upon this assumpsit the creditor brought an action on the case against the woman, without any proof made before the action brought; but in this action it was found by verdict that her husband owed him that amount. And it was moved in arrest of judgment that this action was not well brought, for he ought to have proved the debt to entitle himself to the action, and ought to have proved it before action brought.

But upon several debates the COURT held clearly that the action was well brought, and that the plaintiff should have judgment. And it is not requisite to make any proof of it before action brought, but it can more properly and more naturally be tried in this action. And Twisden, J., cited a case, 15 Jac., between Grinden and ——, which was, "In consideration you'll prove I have beaten your son, I'll pay you so much" (naming the sum), and adjudged that he can bring an action before any proof made, in which, if he proves it, he shall recover; and it was said that the law is the same in the case of a wager. Also it was not denied by any but that this is a good consideration to support an action against the woman, though she was not administratrix, *sed qua* stranger; for it is a trouble and charge to the plaintiff to make the proof, though it is not any benefit to the woman.[1]

PAYNTER *v.* CHAMBERLYN.

IN THE KING'S BENCH, TRINITY TERM, 1639.

[*Reported in* 1 *Rolle's Abridgment,* 22, *placitum* 21.]

IF A. be indebted to B. in £200, and appoints B. to receive it of C., and, for the better satisfaction of B., A. delivers certain bills of exchange to one D., the factor of B., for the payment of it, and thereupon C. promises B. that, in consideration that said bills of exchange so delivered to D. be delivered to him, C., he will pay the said £200 due by A. to B., this is a good promise, for the consideration is valuable; for though C. can do nothing with the bills, being a stranger to them, yet it may be of some advantage to him to have possession of them, and at least it may be a prejudice to B.; and therefore the consideration is good.

[1] "*Nota.* A., upon receipt of 1s. from B., assumed and promised that, if B. could prove that A. had beaten him in the chancel of such a church, he would pay him £20. B. brought assumpsit upon this promise. A. pleaded *non assumpsit,* and the issue was found for the plaintiff. And it was moved in arrest of judgment that he brought the action before any duty accrued to him: for there was no duty before he had proved a battery in the chancel; and if that be found, then an action accrues to him But Dodderidge and Chamberlaine (*absentibus* the other justices) held clearly that the action lies before, and this trial and proof of the battery shall be by the same jury which tries the assumpsit. Otherwise if he had said, "After that you have proved that I struck you, &c., then I do assume to pay you £20." And it was said that it was so in 18 E. 4, and that it was so adjudged in this court; and the clerk of the court so affirmed that it was ruled in this court." Anon., Palm. 160. — ED.

HAWES v. SMITH.

IN THE KING'S BENCH, HILARY TERM, 1675.

[*Reported in* 2 *Levinz*, 122.]

ERROR of a judgment in assumpsit in *Com. Banco* against the defendant, an executor, wherein the plaintiff declared that, whereas the testator was indebted to him, the defendant assumed, in consideration the plaintiff at his request had accounted with him, upon which he was found so much in arrear, to pay it. The plaintiff had judgment in *Com. Banco de bonis propriis* of the executor; and this was assigned for error, but overruled as no error; for the plaintiff was not bound to account with the executor, and yet he did account at the request of the executor. ET PER HALE. Though a bare account will not oblige an executor to pay *de bonis propriis*, yet a promise in consideration of forbearance will; and the case is all one, for it must be intended that an express request was made to account, and thereupon an express promise to pay; otherwise the evidence would not support the declaration. Whereupon judgment was affirmed *per totam curiam*.

ATKINSON v. SETTREE.

IN THE COMMON PLEAS, MAY 7, 1744.

[*Reported in Willes*, 482.]

THIS was a special action on the case. The first count stated that on the 11th of December, in the 16th year, &c., at Westminster, and within the jurisdiction of the court of our Lord the King of his palace of Westminster, the plaintiff, in order to procure the payment of the sum of £7 18*s.*, which Catharine Grimaldi then owed him, by a certain writ dated the 10th of December in the same year, duly issued out of the Court of Record of our said Lord the King of his palace of Westminster, at the plaintiff's request, and directed to the bearers of the virge of the household, &c., officers and ministers of the said court, commanding them to take the said Catharine by her body, if she should be found within the jurisdiction of that court, and have her at the then next court, to be holden on Friday the 17th of December then next, to answer, &c., and [*sic*] procured the said Catharine to be arrested, &c., and to be there kept and detained in prison, &c.; that afterwards, on the said 11th [*sic*] of December, in consideration that the plaintiff at request of the defendant undertook to release and discharge the said Catharine from her said imprisonment, the defendant promised to pay the plaintiff £7 18*s*., and also the costs and charges by the plaintiff expended in that suit; with an averment that those costs amounted to 15*s*. 4*d*., and that the plaintiff at the defendant's request discharged the said Catharine from her said imprisonment. There was a second count in the declaration, which, though it varied from the first in several particulars, was equally open to the objection afterwards made to the first. There was also a third count for money had and received.

The defendant pleaded the general issue, and at the trial the plaintiff obtained a verdict on all the counts, with £8 13*s*. 4*d*. damages.

A motion was made in Michaelmas Term, 1743, in arrest of judgment, which was opposed this day by *Prime*, King's Serjt., and *Wynne*, Serjt., and supported by *Skinner*, King's Serjt., and *Draper*, Serjt., and at a subsequent time *The rule was discharged.*[1]

1 The grounds of the judgment do not appear in Lord Chief Justice Willes's books; but the following account is taken from Mr. J. Abney's MS.: "*Skinner* and *Draper*, Serjeants, moved in arrest of judgment. First, it does not appear that any plaint was levied, and without that a *capias* ought not to issue. Secondly, it does not appear that the cause of action in the court below arose within the jurisdiction, and then the arrest was illegal, and there was no good consideration to support the promise. 1 Rol. Abr. 809; 2 Mod. 30, 197; 3 Lev. 23; 1 Saund. 74; 2 Ld. Raym. 1310. This is a void arrest, and therefore the discharge is no consideration. Godb. 358.

"*Prime* and *Wynne*, Serjts., for the plaintiffs, insisted that to support this action in the superior court it was immaterial whether or not there were a cause of action in the inferior court, or whether or not the court below had a jurisdiction. The declaration sets out the writ duly issued, commanding the bearer of the virge to arrest the party if found within the jurisdiction, and there to detain her. Salk. 201, 2. And the case of Peacock *v*. Roll in 1 Saund. 74, relates only to cases determined in the inferior court and brought up by error. The case of Randal *v*. Harvey is better reported in Palm. 394, than in Godb. 358. If the plaintiff's consent were necessary to release Grimaldi, and the officer could not discharge her without, then there is a good consideration to support the promise. They argued that it was not necessary that the arrest and detainer should be legal in order to make a good consideration; and for that purpose they cited 1 Rol. Abr. 12, pl. 12; 1 Rol. Abr. 19, pl. 6; Hob. 216; Sir T. Raym. 204; 1 Rol. Abr. 27, pl. 47; Sty. 459. Besides, this is after a verdict, it having been proved to the satisfaction of Mr. J. Abney, who tried the cause, that the arrest and promise were within the jurisdiction of the Palace Court. 1 Sid. 30. If a judgment be irregular or erroneous, to forbear to sue out execution is a good consideration to support an assumpsit. 2 Rol. Rep. 495; Yelv. 25; 1 Ventr. 120; 2 Lev. 3; 1 Lev. 257; 1 Sid. 392; Sir T. Raym. 211; Poph. 183; 1 Sid. 89; 1 Saund. 229; and 2 Ld. Raym. 795.

"THE COURT inclined to think that if the party were under an illegal arrest or imprisonment the promise was not good; but the question was whether, as this was after a verdict, it did not now sufficiently appear that the writ duly issued below, and consequently that the suit arose within the jurisdiction; and that this case greatly differed from writs of error on judgments in the inferior court where nothing shall be intended. But they ordered it to be spoken to again; and afterwards the plaintiff had judgment." — MS., Abney, J.

WILLIAMSON *v.* CLEMENTS.

IN THE COMMON PLEAS, APRIL 25, 1809.

[*Reported in* 1 *Taunton*, 523.]

THE plaintiff declared that the defendant was indebted to him in £39 15*s.* 2*d.*, by virtue of a bill of exchange drawn by the defendant, payable to his own order, and indorsed to the plaintiff, but which bill the plaintiff was then unable to produce, or deliver up to the defendant; and thereupon, in consideration of the premises, and that the plaintiff at the defendant's request had executed to him a bond conditioned for indemnifying the defendant against his afterwards being compelled to pay the said sum of money, and purporting to acknowledge its having been paid by the defendant to the plaintiff (although the same had not been actually so paid), the defendant undertook to pay the plaintiff the said sum of money upon request. After verdict for the plaintiff upon this count, Best, Serjt., had obtained a rule *nisi* for arresting the judgment, on the ground that no consideration was stated for the defendant's promise.

Shepherd, Serjt., now showed cause. The plaintiff has by this bond given the defendant a complete acquittance and discharge for his bill; for he has not only estopped himself from ever bringing any action upon the bill which was lost, so that the bill as between them is gone, and he could recover the sum due only upon the defendant's promise, but also, if a third person had recovered against the defendant on the bill, the plaintiff on this bond would be bound to repay him. It is a detriment to the plaintiff to relinquish his remedy on the bill, and the subjecting himself to a detriment at the defendant's request is a sufficient consideration: it is not necessary that any benefit should result to the defendant. By the statute 9 and 10 W. iii., c. 17, § 3, upon the loss of this bill the defendant was bound to give the plaintiff another of the same tenor, taking an indemnity against the former; and the plaintiff in fact accepts this promise in lieu of another bill, though he has not so stated it in his count. In 1 Rol. Abr. 22, pl. 21, it was held that the giving up the possession of bills of exchange was a good consideration, though they were given up at the request of one who was a stranger to the bills, and could never avail himself of them, because it was a detriment to the plaintiff to part with them. So in an anonymous case, 1 Sid. 31, a son promised J. S., in consideration that he would deliver up the bond of his deceased father, and make him, the son, a discharge of the debt, he would pay him £100; and it was objected that it did not appear that the son was liable to this debt;

but it was answered, that it should be intended that the discharge was made to the party entitled to it, and so a good consideration, but at all events it was a detriment to the plaintiff to deliver up the bond.

Best, contra. The plaintiff has all the advantage in this transaction, and the defendant none. It is sufficient for the defendant that it does not appear in this count that he was ever liable to pay this bill. By law a drawer is discharged if he has not notice of the dishonor of a bill, and no notice is here averred. It does not appear on this count but that the plaintiff might have negotiated the bill. The defendant could in no case have been liable for more than the amount of the bill: to that extent he is still liable; therefore he is not benefited. In the case cited the bills were delivered at the defendant's request; the nature of this transaction proves that the contract was entered into at the instance of the plaintiff, for it is in no respect either beneficial to the defendant, or prejudicial to the plaintiff, for whose convenience only it took place.

MANSFIELD, C. J. The count states that before and at the time of the promises the defendant was indebted to the plaintiff: that fact, therefore, must have been proved at the trial; but if he had been discharged for want of notice of the bill's dishonor, or if the plaintiff had negotiated the bill, the defendant could not have been found then indebted to the plaintiff: it therefore must be taken that he was bound in law to pay the bill. The count then states that in consideration that the plaintiff, being unable to deliver up the bill, had given a bond of indemnity and discharge, the defendant promised to pay. What then is it more or less than this: The defendant was indebted to the plaintiff on a bill of exchange, which was not then negotiated; the time of payment was arrived, for the money is stated to be then due. The bill could not afterwards pass into other hands with better rights than the plaintiff had: it must pass subject to all the equities which the defendant had on it. The agreement is, entirely to discharge the defendant from payment of the bill, on his engaging in a different way to pay the money therein mentioned. Is not this a sufficient consideration?

HEATH, J., concurred.

LAWRENCE, J. The argument goes on a supposition which the count does not warrant, — that all is done at the instance of the plaintiff: now the count states that the request comes from the defendant. I will give the defendant credit to suppose him an honest man, and that, being told the bill is lost, he had said, "Give me a bond of indemnity, and I will give you another bill." This is just as natural as if the plaintiff had found him unwilling to do this, and had requested it. It is a disadvantage to the plaintiff to execute the bond, if it is no advantage to the defendant. There is a case in 1 Sid. 57, Traver *v.* ——, where a woman, after the decease of her husband, promised a creditor that, if he would prove her husband had owed him £20, she would pay it; and it was held a good consideration, because it was trouble and charge to the creditor to prove his debt.

CHAMBRE, J., concurring, *The rule was discharged.*

BAILY v. CROFT.

IN THE COMMON PLEAS, NOVEMBER 10, 1812.

[*Reported in 4 Taunton, 611.*]

THE plaintiff having been partner in trade with Bennet, and having dissolved partnership, upon a statement of accounts between the parties, they agreed on a considerable balance as due from the plaintiff to Bennet, in part payment of which the plaintiff gave Bennet his acceptance of a bill for £1349 16*s.* Bennet had indorsed this bill and delivered it to the defendant, who advanced to him thereon £500, and it was agreed between them that £300 more should be raised on the bill for the use of the defendant, to whom Bennet was indebted in a greater amount than the whole contents of the bill. The plaintiff and Bennet afterwards, discovering that the real balance of accounts between them had not been correctly ascertained, were desirous to refer the accounts to arbitration; and in order to remove the obstacle which would arise from the bill which had been already given, and had been put into circulation, they agreed that that bill should be given up, and that a bill of the like date, and with the like securities, for such other sum of money as the arbitrators should award to be the balance due, should be accepted by the plaintiff and delivered to Bennet; and upon their application to the defendant to accede to this agreement, he agreed to deliver up the bill of £1349 16*s.* 1*d.*, and to accept a like bill for the amount to be awarded; whereupon the plaintiff and Bennet submitted their accounts to arbitration. The arbitrators awarded that the former supposed balance, secured by the plaintiff to Bennet, was too much by £318 1*s.* The bill not being given up to the plaintiff, he declared upon this transaction and stated that, in consideration of the mutual agreement, and in consideration that the plaintiff had undertaken to accept a bill for the sum to be awarded in exchange for the first bill, Bennet and defendant undertook to give up the first bill; and averred a request and refusal by the defendant. Upon the trial of this cause before Mansfield, C. J., at the sittings at Guildhall after Trinity Term, 1812, a verdict was found for the plaintiff.

Shepherd, Serjt., now moved to set aside the verdict and enter a nonsuit, upon the ground, which he had also urged at the trial, that there was no consideration moving from the plaintiff for the promise of the defendant.

MANSFIELD, C. J. The plaintiff agrees to give a new bill, which will impose a liability on him, and that is a consideration beneficial to the defendant.

HEATH and CHAMBRE, JJ., concurred in refusing the application.

GIBBS, J. Suppose the agreement had stood merely between the plaintiff and Bennet: no doubt there would have been sufficient consideration as between them. The defendant is included in the treaty, because he is the holder of the bill; he is taken in on Bennet's account, and in consideration of what the plaintiff agrees to do beneficial to Bennet, the defendant, on Bennet's account, agrees to do this. The plaintiff certainly would never have entered into this agreement to refer and give a new bill for the balance found, unless the defendant had come into the measure, and agreed to give up this bill; the plaintiff would never have left this bill outstanding in the hands of the defendant, exposing himself to have the amount of both bills recovered against him. In giving the second bill, the plaintiff gives that which is beneficial to Bennet; and the giving up the former bill is part of the equivalent paid for the doing that which is beneficial to Bennet: it appears to me, therefore, that there is a sufficient consideration for the promise. *Rule refused.*

BROOKS *v.* BALL.

SUPREME COURT OF NEW YORK, OCTOBER TERM, 1820.

[*Reported in* 18 *Johnson*, 337.]

IN error to the Court of Common Pleas of Orange County. Ball brought an action of assumpsit against Brooks in the court below. The declaration contained a special count, stating that the plaintiff claimed of the defendant the sum of one hundred dollars, which the defendant denied that he owed to the plaintiff, but promised that, if the plaintiff would make oath to the correctness of his claim, he, the defendant, would pay the amount thereof; and averred that the plaintiff did make oath to the truth and correctness of his claim, but that the defendant, notwithstanding his promise, refused to pay the one hundred dollars, &c. The declaration also contained the common money counts. The defendant pleaded the general issue.

After the plaintiff's counsel had stated his case, the defendant's counsel insisted that, admitting the facts stated to be proved, they were not sufficient to support the action, because the promise of the defendant was without consideration and void, and the plaintiff could not lawfully support his claim on his own affidavit. He therefore moved that the plaintiff should be nonsuited, but the objection was overruled by the court. The plaintiff then went into the evidence in support of his case. It was proved that the defendant made the promise alleged; that the plaintiff had made the affidavit, and demanded payment of the one hundred dollars; and that the defendant had admitted his liability to pay the money, and intended to pay, but was advised to the contrary.

The defendant's counsel then offered to prove that the plaintiff, in his affidavit, had sworn falsely, or was grossly mistaken. This evidence was objected to, and overruled by the court; and the counsel for the defendant tendered a bill of exceptions. The jury, under the direction of the court, found a verdict for the plaintiff for one hundred and ten dollars and fifty cents.

Wisner, for the plaintiff in error. This case is distinguishable from the cases which are to be found in the books. They will be found to be cases where the defendant promised to pay a precedent debt, if the plaintiff would prove it by a third person. Here the debt was to be created by the promise to pay on the oath of the plaintiff himself. It is against the fundamental principle of law, that a party should be a judge in his own cause, or give evidence in his own favor.

If such a promise can be a foundation for an action, it is at most *prima facie* evidence, and may be rebutted by showing that the plaintiff swore falsely, or was mistaken. 2 Comyn on Contracts, 449, 450.

Betts, contra. In Knight v. Rushwood, Cro. Eliz. 469, the defendant promised that, if the plaintiff and two witnesses would depose before the Mayor of Lincoln, as to a bond of a third person, the defendant would pay it. Bretton v. Prettiman, T. Raym, 153, is precisely in point to show that this action may be maintained. The defendant promised that, in consideration that the plaintiff would take an oath that money was due to him, he would pay it; and the plaintiff took an oath before a master in chancery, and brought assumpsit for the money, and recovered. S. C. 1 Sid. 283; 2 Keble, 44. In Stevens v. Thacker, Peake's N. P. Cases, 187, 188, the holder of a bill of exchange promised not to sue the acceptor, if he would make affidavit that the acceptance was a forgery. The affidavit was drawn, but the defendant did not swear to it. Lord Kenyon said that, if the defendant had sworn to the affidavit, he should have held that he had discharged himself from the action, though the affidavit had been false. 1 Mod. 166; Lloyd v. Willan, 1 Esp. N. P. Cases, 178, 179;

Delesline *v.* Greenland, 1 Bay's S. C. Rep. 458, S. P. One promise is a sufficient consideration for another promise. 8 Johns. Rep. 306.

SPENCER, C. J., delivered the opinion of the court. The principal question presented by this case is, whether a promise to pay a sum claimed to be due by one party and denied by the other, if the party claiming would swear to the correctness of the claim, and he does so swear, is a valid promise. Another question was made on the trial, whether it was competent to the defendant below to prove that the plaintiff below either swore falsely or was grossly mistaken in the affidavit which he made.

It has been frequently decided that a promise to pay money, in consideration that the plaintiff would take an oath that it was due, was a valid and binding promise. Thus, in Bretton *v.* Prettiman, Sir T. Raym. 153, the plaintiff declared that the defendant promised, in consideration that the plaintiff would take an oath that money was due to him, he would pay him; and the plaintiff averred that he swore before a master in chancery. On demurrer, it was adjudged for the plaintiff, and, as the reporter states, because it was not such an oath for which he may be indicted. In Amie & Andrews, 1 Mod. 166, there was a promise to pay, if the plaintiff would bring two witnesses before a justice of the peace, who should depose that the defendant's father was indebted to the plaintiff; and two judges against one thought it not a profane oath, because it tended to the determining a controversy, and the plaintiff had judgment. This case occurred before the Statute of Frauds. The promise would now be holden to be void, unless in writing, it being to pay the debt of a third person. The case of Bretton *v.* Prettiman is differently stated in 1 Sid. 283, and 2 Keb. 26, 44. It is there stated to be a promise to pay, if the plaintiff would procure a third person to make oath that the money was due. But this makes no difference in principle, for in either case the oath was extra-judicial.

In Stevens and others *v.* Thacker, Peake's N. P. Rep. 187, the defendant was sued as the acceptor of a bill, and alleged it to be a forgery, and offered to make affidavit that he never had accepted it. The plaintiff agreed not to sue the defendant, if he would make the affidavit. The affidavit was drawn, but not sworn to. Lord Kenyon said that, had the defendant sworn to the affidavit, he should have held that he had discharged himself, though the affidavit had been false; for the plaintiffs, who had agreed to accept that affidavit as evidence of the fact, should not, after having induced the defendant to commit the crime of perjury, maintain an action on the bill. In Lloyd & Willan, 1 Esp. Rep. 178, the defendant's attorney proposed to the plaintiff's attorney, that the defendant should pay the demand, if the plaintiff's porter would make an affidavit that he had delivered the goods in question to the defendant. The affidavit was made; and Lord Kenyon held it to be conclusive, and that the defendant was precluded from going into any defence in the case.

These cases, which stand uncontradicted, abundantly show that such a promise as the present is good in point of law, and that the making the proof or affidavit, whether by a third person or by the party himself, is a sufficient consideration for the promise. It is not making a man a judge in his own cause, but it is referring a disputed fact to the conscience of the party. It is begging the question to suppose that it will lead to perjury. If the promise is binding, because the making the proof or affidavit is a consideration for it, the defendant must necessarily be precluded from gainsaying the fact.[1] He voluntarily waives all other proof; and to allow him to draw in question the verity or correctness of the proof or affidavit, would be allowing him to alter the conditions of his engagement, and virtually to rescind his promise.

Judgment affirmed.[2]

WILKINSON v. BYERS.

IN THE KING'S BENCH, APRIL 24, 1834.

[*Reported in* 1 *Adolphus & Ellis*, 106.]

ASSUMPSIT. The declaration stated that an action had been commenced and prosecuted in the Palace Court by Thomas Rimmer, as the defendant's attorney, in the name of the defendant, against the plaintiff, for the recovery of a certain sum, to wit, £13 10*s.*, alleged to be due from the plaintiff to defendant; which action was depending,

1 Such is the principle of the civil law, as to the effect of the decisory oath (*le serment decisoire*) as the French lawyers term it, or the *oath of verity*, as it is called in the Scotch law. The Digest contains many just rules and distinctions as to the cases in which the oath may be deferred. It is considered as an agreement or contract between the parties (*transactio*), and as of greater force even than a judgment (*res judicata*). It might be deferred in regard to all matters of civil controversy, and in any stage of a cause; but it could be deferred to a party in respect only to his own personal acts. When taken, it constituted the *presumptio juris et de jure*, which precludes all proof to the contrary. The party became entitled to judgment in his favor, or to be for ever discharged from the cause of action. Either party might defer the oath to the other. If the party to whom the oath was deferred, refused to take it, or to refer it back to the other, he lost his cause; if the one to whom the oath was referred back took it, what he swore to was deemed conclusively proved. "Cum res jusjurandum demissa sit judex absolvit: referentem audiet, et si actor juret, condemnet reum: nolentem jurare reum, si solvat, absolvit: non solventem condemnat: ex relatione, jurante actore, absolvit reum." Dig. lib. 12, tit. 2, l. 34; Poth., *Trait. des Oblig.*, Part 4, ch. 3, s. 4, Nos. 912, 913, 914 Ersk. Inst. 779, Book 4 tit. 2, ss. 8, 9.

2 See 1 Vin. Abr. 298, pl. 22. — ED.

and costs had been incurred therein: and thereupon, in consideration that plaintiff would pay defendant the said sum of £13 10*s*., defendant promised plaintiff to settle with the said attorney for the costs of the action, and to indemnify plaintiff and bear him harmless from the same. Averment, that plaintiff confiding, &c., paid defendant the said sum, which he accepted; but that defendant did not settle with the attorney, &c., by means and in consequence whereof the attorney proceeded with the action, and judgment was signed against plaintiff, and he was obliged to pay £7 16*s*. for costs of the action, and £3 for costs of endeavoring to set the judgment aside; of which defendant, on, &c., had notice, but that he did not nor would indemnify plaintiff, &c. Plea, the general issue. At the trial before Patteson, J., at the sittings in Middlesex after Trinity Term, 1833, it appeared that the plaintiff had employed the defendant (who carried on business as a wood-turner) to do work for him; that Rimmer, as the defendant's attorney, served the now plaintiff with a writ at the suit of the present defendant; and that a conversation afterwards passed between the parties at the plaintiff's house, which the son of the latter stated in evidence as follows: "My father expressed his surprise that he should have been treated in that peremptory manner. Byers said he had given no orders that he should be treated in that way; that he had desired the attorney to write a letter demanding payment of the balance due, and that was all the instructions he had given: he was extremely sorry such conduct had been pursued by his attorney, he having worked for my father many years, and having no just cause of complaint. My father offered to pay him the amount of the balance of the debt, and, taking into consideration the unjustifiable nature of the proceedings, would not he himself settle with his attorney? to which Byers readily assented, for the reason that he, Byers, himself would not pay any thing, he not having given instructions. The money was paid, and a receipt signed by Byers. Subsequently Byers said he would go immediately to Rimmer and settle the question of costs." Another witness, deposing to the same conversation, stated the defendant to have said that, if the plaintiff would pay him the money, as he was in particular want of it that day, he would settle the lawyer's expenses, and the plaintiff should come to no trouble about it. The receipt given by the defendant was as follows: "Received, March 30th, 1832, of Mr. Wilkinson the sum of £13 10*s*., balance of account to this day. John Byers." The costs at this time amounted to £1 4*s*. The defendant refused to pay them to the attorney, alleging that he had not authorized him to issue the writ, upon which the further proceedings ensued, which were stated in the declaration. Upon these facts a verdict was found for the now plaintiff, with £10 18*s*. damages; but leave was given to move to enter a nonsuit, on the ground that the payment being merely the discharge of an admitted debt, was no consideration for a promise by the creditor to the debtor. A rule *nisi* was afterwards obtained for entering a nonsuit, or for reducing the damages to £1 4*s*.

Sir *James Scarlett* and *Platt* now showed cause. The objection, if any, is on the record. Assuming that the declaration was sustainable, of which no question is made, the evidence was sufficient. As to the particular objection taken, the evidence here showed a contract, good in all its parts, and consistent with recognized practice. It constantly happens that a verdict is entered by consent, in consideration that no costs shall be taxed; and if a party attempted afterwards to tax costs, the court would stay the proceedings. That cannot be bad as a contract between parties, which the court is in the daily habit of enforcing. Supposing the whole demand to be really due, the plaintiff avoids delay and risk, and the loss of extra costs, by a compromise of this nature. It is therefore a good consideration; and if there be any, it is sufficient: the court will not look into the adequacy of it. If the creditor agreed to allow a discount for immediate payment, such a consideration for the allowance would be good; and this is the same in principle. If a creditor, after action brought, were to say to the debtor, "Pay me now, and I will take no costs," the contract would be one which the debtor might enforce. It is true it could not be effectual without the sanction of the attorney; but that makes no difference in the case, considered as between the parties.

Kelly, contra. The question is not on the record. The consideration there stated is the payment of a debt alleged to be due; but it is clear, upon the evidence, that the debt was undisputed. Giving up a defence against a disputable claim may be a good consideration for a promise; but payment of an admitted debt is none. In the former case, undoubtedly, the court would not suffer its process to be used against good faith, nor would it inquire minutely into the adequacy of the consideration; but in the latter no such consideration can arise; and to say that it can be raised by any probable difficulty or delay in the prosecution of the claim, is a fallacy. If it be clear that the party is legally bound to pay, the question whether payment can be extorted from him in a shorter or longer time cannot affect the sufficiency of the payment as a consideration. In Selw. N. P. tit. Assumpsit, § 1, it is laid down that "the mere performance of an act which the party was by law bound to perform is not a sufficient consideration. Hence a promise made by the master, when a ship was in distress, to pay an extra sum to a mariner as an inducement to extraordinary exertion on his part, has been holden to be void; because a seaman is bound to exert himself to the utmost in the service of the ship;" to which point Harris *v.* Watson[1] is cited. [PARKE, J. How does it appear that the demand here was not upon a *quantum meruit?* In that case, payment of less than the sum claimed would be a consideration for a

[1] Peake, N. P. C. 72.

promise by the plaintiff.] The declaration states that the defendant had sued the plaintiff for a certain sum, to wit, £13 10*s.*; and in consideration that the plaintiff would pay the defendant the said sum of £13 10*s.*, he promised, &c.: and the evidence shows that a specific sum, the balance of account between the parties, and no other, was in question. [LITTLEDALE, J. In Reynolds *v.* Pinhowe[1] the declaration stated that, whereas the defendant had recovered £5 against the plaintiff, the defendant, in consideration of £4 given him by the plaintiff, undertook to acknowledge satisfaction of the judgment before such a day; and it was demurred to, on the ground that there was no consideration. But the court held otherwise; "for it is a benefit unto him to have it without suit or charge, and it may be there was error in the record, so as the party might have avoided it."] If in this case there was room for doubt, whether error might not have been brought on the record, the reasoning in the case cited was applicable; and so if, in an earlier stage of the cause, a doubt had existed whether or not the debt was due. But here no doubt existed: the debt was due or it was not, and the plaintiff admitted it; then in paying it, he only discharged a duty. [PARKE, J. It is not clearly made out that there was a specific demand of £13 10*s.* previous to the agreement. The plaintiff admitted a liability to pay what the defendant claimed as his balance; but that admission is to be coupled with the fact that the defendant at the same time agreed to pay his own costs; and it does not appear from the whole, that the sum of £13 10*s.* was a sum originally demanded by the defendant, or due from the plaintiff.] The case leaves no room for conjecture as to this. The sum of £13 10*s.* stated in the declaration is the sum paid by the plaintiff as due on his part, and admitted by the defendant in conversation and by his receipt to be the balance claimable by him. [PARKE, J. It might have been paid on a *quantum meruit.* In the absence of evidence, are we to assume that there was a demand certain? To support your case, there should have been a demand about which there was no dispute, and for a specified sum.] If there was a doubt upon this, it should have gone to the jury. But if the demand was uncertain at first, it became certain when the parties had agreed to fix it at £13 10*s.* [PARKE, J. That agreement was on a condition. PATTESON, J. The defendant's undertaking as to the costs forms part of the same transaction.] The "sum" or "balance due," and £13 10*s.*, appear as convertible terms throughout the proceeding; and there is no proof that the parties ever had any discussion on the subject.

LITTLEDALE, J.[2] I should prefer taking the case as it has just been put by Mr. Kelly; viz., that the sum of £13 10*s.* was originally due from the plaintiff, and was not fixed by arrangement at the time of the bargain in question. And, viewing it so, I still think the plain-

[1] Cro. Eliz. 429. [2] Lord Denman, C. J., was at the Privy Council.

tiff is entitled to recover. Reynolds *v.* Pinhowe is a direct authority on this point. There is indeed another case, Dixon *v.* Adams,[1] in the same volume of reports, which may appear contradictory. But the promise there was of a very different nature from that in the preceding case and in this. There the obligee of a bond had judgment on *scire facias* against the bail, "and he, without other process, paid the condemnation money; and Adams (the obligee), *in consideratione inde*, assumed to Dixon (the bail) to deliver unto him the principal obligation, and a letter of attorney to sue it against J. D." (the obligor); and it was held not a sufficient consideration, "for Dixon had not done any act whereto the law would not have compelled him." And if the promise, as in that case, be to do a collateral thing, the consideration may be insufficient. But here the debtor says, "You have sued me for a debt, and may have trouble in recovering it; if you will forego the costs" (for the stipulation as to paying the attorney amounts merely to that), "I will pay the debt now." If the creditor agreed to these terms, he could not afterwards enforce payment of the costs. To do so, he must have proceeded to final judgment; but it would have been against his duty and against law to take that course. We are not now taking into consideration the rights of the attorney, in respect of his lien for costs; but, looking at the case as between the parties, if, after such an undertaking, the plaintiff attempted to go on with the action, it would be a breach of faith, and a contempt, and the court would stay the proceedings. A promise which the court would enforce by restraining the plaintiff from proceeding contrary to the terms entered into, cannot be treated here as a promise made on insufficient consideration, and is quite unlike an undertaking to do something merely collateral, as in the case of Dixon *v.* Adams. I therefore think the rule must be discharged.

PARKE, J. I am of the same opinion. It is not necessary to consider the case on the ground upon which it has been put by my brother Littledale, though as to that I do not mean to say that I differ in opinion. But the case may be decided shortly on this ground: If an action be brought on a *quantum meruit*, and the defendant agree to pay a less sum than the demand in full, that is a good consideration for a promise by the plaintiff to pay his own costs, and proceed no further. Payment of a less sum than the demand has been held to be no satisfaction in the case of a liquidated debt; but where the debt is unliquidated, it is sufficient. Now here we cannot say that there was originally any certain demand. A jury, if asked, could not in my opinion have said so. In the great majority of actions of this nature, for work, labor, and goods sold, it is not a specific sum that forms the subject-matter of the action; and unless that could have been shown in the present case, there was a good consideration for the promise.

[1] Cro. Eliz. 538.

PATTESON, J. I am of the same opinion. If a question had been raised upon the record, the words "a certain *alleged* debt" would have been a complete answer to the defendant's objection; and, indeed, this seems almost admitted. It is consistent with the declaration that there may have been a dispute between the parties as to the sum actually due. The answer attempted is, that the evidence showed the contrary. But, looking to the whole evidence, I think that is not so. The expressions of the plaintiff's son do not support that view of the case; and it appears that the defendant admitted having instructed his attorney to write a letter, which is not usually done where the party is considered able to pay, unless there be some dispute as to the sum. I do not say that I differ from my brother Littledale in his view of the case, supposing that there had been an admitted demand, though on that point I am not quite sure; but it is unnecessary to go that length, because it is not clear in my opinion that there was a settled and admitted demand. There is no ground for the reduction of damages: the defendant, to fulfil his promise to the plaintiff, might have paid the £1 4*s.* to the attorney, and afterwards disputed the matter with him. Whether the Palace Court were right or not in refusing to set aside the judgment, it was by the defendant's own act that costs exceeding £1 4*s.* were incurred. *Rule discharged.*

WILKINSON *v.* OLIVEIRA.

IN THE COMMON PLEAS, JANUARY 27, 1835.

[*Reported in* 1 *Bingham's New Cases,* 490.]

THE declaration stated that divers disputes and controversies had arisen between the defendant and divers other persons respecting the disposition of the estate and effects of one Dominick Oliveira, then late deceased, and the right of the defendant to the possession of any and what part thereof: in which disputes and controversies it became and was necessary, for the termination thereof in favor of the defendant, that the defendant should prove that the said Dominick Oliveira was, at the time he made his will, and at the time of his death, an alien, and a native of Portugal; that the plaintiff was lawfully possessed of a certain writing and paper, being a letter written by the said Dominick Oliveira in his lifetime to the plaintiff, which said letter showed, declared, and proved, that the said Dominick Oliveira was, at the time he made his will, and at the time of his death, an alien and a native of Portugal; that the plaintiff, at the request of the defendant, gave to the defendant the said letter, to be used and employed by the defendant for the purpose of proving that the said Dominick Oliveira was such alien and native of Portugal at the time he made his will and at the time of his death; that the defendant used and employed the said letter for the said purpose; and that by means of the said letter and of the matters therein contained, the defendant was enabled to and did cause the said disputes and controversies to be determined in favor of him, the defendant; and did, by means of the said letter and of the matters therein contained, become lawfully possessed of and acquired a large portion of the estate and effects of the said Dominick Oliveira, of great value, to wit, of the value of £100,000, &c. And thereupon, to wit, on, &c., at, &c., in consideration thereof, and that the plaintiff, at the special instance and request of the defendant, had then and there given the said letter to the defendant, the defendant then and there undertook and faithfully promised the plaintiff to give him, the plaintiff, a certain sum of money, to wit, the sum of £1000.

Breach, — refusal to give the £1000 in conformity with the promise.

Plea, — that the defendant was not by means of the letter enabled to, and did not by means thereof, cause the said disputes to be determined in favor of the defendant; and that the defendant did not, by means of the letter, become possessed of a portion of the estate of Dominick Oliveira, of the value of £100,000.

Demurrer, — for putting in issue matter not properly issuable, and for not denying or confessing and avoiding the breach of promise. Joinder.

Kelly, for the plaintiff, was called upon by the court to support the declaration. The consideration, though past, is alleged to have arisen at the defendant's request, which renders it sufficient to impart validity to the defendant's promise; and though the letter in question is alleged to have been given to the defendant, the statement amounts to this: that in consideration the plaintiff had put the defendant in possession of a document by which the defendant was enabled to recover £100,-000, the defendant undertook to give the plaintiff in return £1000. For such an undertaking the delivery of the document was ample consideration.

Talfourd, Serjt., contra, contended that, taking the whole declaration together, it appeared plainly the letter had been handed to the defendant by way of a spontaneous gift; and such gift was no consideration for a promise to pay.

TINDAL, C. J. What would you say to the case of a man who, entering a shop, should say, "I'll give you £10 for such an article." Here the word "give" is used on both sides. It is a gift upon a mutual consideration.

PER CURIAM. There must be *Judgment for the plaintiff.*

BAINBRIDGE v. FIRMSTONE.

IN THE QUEEN'S BENCH, NOVEMBER 2, 1838.

[*Reported in* 8 *Adolphus & Ellis*, 743.]

ASSUMPSIT. The declaration stated that, whereas heretofore, to wit, &c., in consideration that plaintiff, at the request of defendant, had then consented to allow defendant to weigh divers, to wit, two boilers of the plaintiff, of great value, &c., defendant promised that he would, within a reasonable time after the said weighing was effected, leave and give up the boilers in as perfect and complete a condition, and as fit for use by plaintiff, as the same were in at the time of the consent so given by plaintiff; and that although in pursuance of the consent so given, defendant, to wit, on, &c., did weigh the same boilers, yet defendant did not, nor would, within a reasonable time after the said weighing was effected, leave and give up the boilers in as perfect, &c., but wholly neglected and refused so to do, although a reasonable time for that purpose had elapsed before the commencement of this suit; and, on the contrary thereof, defendant afterwards, to wit, on, &c., took the said boilers to pieces, and did not put the same together again, but left the same in a detached and divided condition, and in many different pieces, whereby plaintiff hath been put to great trouble, &c. Plea, *non assumpsit.*

On the trial before Lord Denman, C. J., at the London sittings after last Trinity Term, a verdict was found for the plaintiff.

John Bayley now moved in arrest of judgment. The declaration shows no consideration. There should have been either detriment to the plaintiff, or benefit to the defendant. 1 Selwyn's N. P.[1] 45. It does not appear that the defendant was to receive any remuneration. Besides, the word "weigh" is ambiguous.

LORD DENMAN, C. J. It seems to me that the declaration is well enough. The defendant had some reason for wishing to weigh the boilers; and he could do so only by obtaining permission from the plaintiff, which he did obtain by promising to return them in good condition. We need not inquire what benefit he expected to derive. The plaintiff might have given or refused leave.

PATTESON, J. The consideration is, that the plaintiff, at the defendant's request, had consented to allow the defendant to weigh the boilers. I suppose the defendant thought he had some benefit; at any rate there is a detriment to the plaintiff from his parting with the possession for even so short a time.

WILLIAMS and COLERIDGE, JJ., concurred. *Rule refused.*

[1] 9th edit.

HAIGH AND ANOTHER v. BROOKS.

IN THE QUEEN'S BENCH, JUNE 6, 1839.

[*Reported in* 10 *Adolphus & Ellis*, 309.]

BROOKS v. HAIGH AND ANOTHER.

IN THE EXCHEQUER CHAMBER, JUNE 29, 1840.

[*Reported in* 10 *Adolphus & Ellis*, 323.]

ASSUMPSIT. The first count of the declaration stated that heretofore, to wit, on &c., in consideration that the said plaintiffs, at the special instance and request of the said defendant, would give up to him a certain guaranty of £10,000, on behalf of Messrs. John Lees & Sons, Manchester, then held by the said plaintiffs, he the said defendant undertook and then faithfully promised the said plaintiffs to see certain bills, accepted by the said Messrs. John Lees & Sons, paid at maturity; that is to say, a certain bill of exchange, bearing date, &c., drawn by plaintiffs upon and accepted by the said Lees & Sons, payable three months after date, for £3466 13*s*. 7*d*., and made payable at, &c.; and also a certain other bill, &c., describing two other bills for £3000 and £3200, drawn by plaintiffs upon and accepted by Lees & Sons, and made payable at, &c. Averment, that plaintiffs, relying on defendant's said promise, did then, to wit, on, &c., give up to the said defendant the said guaranty of £10,000. Breach, non-payment of the bills, when they afterwards came to maturity, by Lees & Sons, or the parties at whose houses the bills respectively were made payable, or by defendant, or any other person, &c.

Third plea to the first count: "That the said supposed guaranty of £10,000, in consideration of the giving up whereof the defendant made such supposed promise and undertaking as therein mentioned, and which guaranty was so given up to the said defendant as therein mentioned, was a special promise to answer the said plaintiffs for the debt and default of other persons, to wit, the said Messrs. John Lees & Sons in the said first count mentioned; and that no agreement in respect of or relating to the said supposed guaranty or special promise, or any memorandum or note thereof, wherein any sufficient consideration for the said guaranty or special promise was stated or shown, was in writing and signed by the said defendant, or any other person by him thereunto lawfully authorized. And the said defendant further saith that the said supposed guaranty, in consideration of the giving up whereof the defendant made the said supposed promise and undertaking in the said first count mentioned, and which was so given up as therein mentioned, was and is contained in a certain memorandum in writing, signed by the defendant, and which was and is in the words and figures and to the effect following, that is to say: —

MANCHESTER, 4th February, 1837.

MESSRS. HAIGH & FRANCEYS.

GENT., — In consideration of your being in advance to Messrs. John Lees & Sons in the sum of £10,000 for the purchase of cotton, I do hereby give you my guaranty for that amount (say £10,000) on their behalf.

JOHN BROOKS.

And that there was no other agreement or memorandum or note thereof, in respect of or relating to the said last-mentioned supposed guaranty or special promise; wherefore the said defendant says that the supposed guaranty, in consideration whereof the said defendant made the said supposed promise and undertaking in the said first count mentioned, was and is void and of no effect; and therefore that the said supposed promise and undertaking in the said first count mentioned was and is void and of no effect." Verification.

Demurrer, assigning for cause, "that it is admitted by the plea that the memorandum, the giving up of which was the consideration of the guaranty in the said declaration mentioned, was actually given up to the said defendant by the said plaintiffs, and the consideration was therefore executed by the said defendant; and that, even if the original memorandum was not binding in point of law, the giving up was a sufficient consideration for the promise in the declaration mentioned." Joinder. The demurrer was argued in last Hilary Term.[1]

Sir *W. W. Follett* for the plaintiffs. The undertaking declared upon is, on the face of it, sufficient to satisfy the Statute of Frauds, 29 Car. 2, c. 3, § 4. It is said, however, that the consideration is really insufficient, because the guaranty delivered up was one which could not have been sued upon consistently with the statute. But assuming that to be so, a promise in consideration of delivering up such a guaranty might still be good. The defendant might for substantial reasons wish to have the guaranty back. His mercantile character was pledged by it. It might, on various other accounts, be important to him that such a paper should not remain in the plaintiff's hands; and, if the bargain was made upon any consideration, the court will not inquire into its adequacy. This principle was lately recognized in Hitchcock *v.* Coker.[2] Such a promise might be made in consideration of delivering up a letter; no one but the defendant might be able to judge how far the possession of it was valuable; but if the letter

[1] January 18th. Before Lord Denman, C. J.; Littledale, Williams, and Coleridge, JJ.

[2] 6 A. & E. 438. And see Archer *v.* Marsh, 6 A. & E. 959.

was given up at his request, the rule would apply that any thing so given, to the plaintiff's detriment or the benefit of the defendant, is consideration for an assumpsit. Suppose the undertaking given up had been one rendered unavailing by the Statute of Limitations, no action would have lain upon it; but the attempt to enforce it could not perhaps have been resisted without injury to the defendant's mercantile character; the relinquishment of it therefore would have been good consideration for a promise. The present is a similar case. Release from a moral obligation is consideration enough for an express promise. If it were necessary that something should be foregone to which there was a legal right, the delivery of the mere written paper which contained the first guaranty was sufficient in this case. The plaintiffs are entitled to put some value on the possession of such a paper, though not legally available; as they might on the possession of a cancelled bond, or bills accepted by the defendant on wrong stamps. It is not, indeed, clear in this case that the first guaranty was void. In Boehm *v.* Campbell[1] a similar guaranty was held to show a sufficient consideration, though the advance for which the security was given had been already made, and it did not appear more distinctly than in the present case that time was to be granted. Supposing it even questionable whether the former undertaking bound the defendant, yet the discharge from a claim or waiver of a defence, on which the promisee might or might not have been legally entitled to succeed, is consideration enough to support an assumpsit. Longridge *v.* Dorville;[2] Stracy *v.* The Bank of England.[3] Here, however, it appears at all events that the original guaranty may have been given under circumstances which rendered it morally binding; and that brings it within the principle of Lee *v.* Muggeridge,[4] and other cases in which promises supported by moral obligation have been held sufficient.

Sir *J. Campbell*, Attorney-General, *contra.* First, the original guaranty was void; and, if so, then, secondly, the promise declared upon is without consideration.[5] . . . Secondly, the guaranty being void, the undertaking substituted for it, without any new consideration, is void also. The case is no better than if a second guaranty had been given in the words of the first. A consideration, to support a promise, must have some value in point of law; Smith and Smith's Case,[6] and other authorities cited in note (*b*) to Barber *v.* Fox.[7] Rann *v.* Hughes[8] illustrates the same point. A man may have in his possession a letter of which improper use might be made; but his delivering

[1] 3 B. Moore, 15; s. c. 8 Taunt. 679.
[2] 5 B. & Ald. 117.
[3] 6 Bing. 754.
[4] 5 Taunt. 36.
[5] The argument upon the first question is omitted. — ED.
[6] 3 Leon. 88.
[7] 2 Wms. Saund. 137 *e*, 5th edit. See Jones *v.* Waite, 5 New Ca. 341.
[8] Note (*a*) to Mitchinson *v.* Hewson, 7 T. R. 350.

it up is no legal consideration. An unfounded action may create annoyance; but the renouncing it is no consideration in law for a promise. Where, indeed, there is a reasonable doubt, in point of law, whether the promisee would or would not succeed if the litigation were prosecuted, the case is different: that was so in Longridge *v.* Dorville, and Stracy *v.* The Bank of England. In Shortrede *v.* Cheek,[1] the consideration disclosed was, that the plaintiff should withdraw a promissory note on which he had an unquestioned right of action; and Parke, J., said, "There is no doubt that the giving up of any note upon which the plaintiff might have sued would be a sufficient consideration." It is argued that foregoing a security upon which the Statute of Limitations had attached would be a consideration; but there an action would lie on the security if the statute were not pleaded. Whether the giving up a bill drawn on a wrong stamp would be a consideration or not may be questionable; but the objection is not one of which the court would take judicial notice: here the court must take notice that the guaranty is invalid. It is contended here that the promise is binding, because grounded on a moral obligation; but that obligation rests on a promise which is itself not binding: the new engagement then cannot have more force than the original one. In the cases where a moral obligation has been held sufficient ground for an express promise, the obligation has been something more than a *nudum pactum:* thus, in Lee *v.* Muggeridge money had been advanced by the plaintiff at the request of the promisor. But the doctrine that a moral obligation is sufficient consideration for a subsequent promise is not free from doubt. Lord Tenterden said, in Littlefield *v.* Shee,[2] that it must be "received with some limitation." The instances which have been considered as establishing that doctrine are brought together in note (*a*) to Wennall *v.* Adney,[3] and seem to resolve themselves into these classes: First, where there has been a legal obligation antecedent to the promise; as the duty of overseers to provide for the poor; — secondly, where there was an antecedent equitable liability, as that of an executor to pay legacies; but the doctrine, as applicable to these cases, appears to have been overruled; — thirdly, where a debt existed before the promise, but the remedy was barred by statute, — as in the cases of certificated bankrupts or discharged insolvents, or where the Statute of Limitations has attached: in these instances the party indebted may waive the statutory bar, and oblige himself by a promise to pay the debt; — fourthly, where a promise merely voidable has been ratified; as in the case of a person of full age promising to pay a debt contracted during his infancy.[4] In all these cases, so far as the doctrine is established, there has been an actual benefit received, or a debt, or other ground of

[1] 1 A. & E. 57. See Wilkinson *v.* Byers, 1 A. & A. 106.

[2] 2 B. & Ad. 811.

[3] 3 Bos. & P. 249.

[4] See Meyer *v.* Haworth, 8 A. & E. 467.

legal obligation, antecedent to the promise relied upon; not merely a *nudum pactum*, as in the present instance, where the party originally promising had received no benefit, nor had the plaintiffs incurred any loss or prejudice at his request. The money had been advanced when the guaranty was given; then the defendant says, "Forego the guaranty, and I will see you paid." The prior moral obligation was only that which every man is under to keep his word. Nash *v.* Brown,[1] Holliday *v.* Atkinson,[2] and Bret *v.* J. S. and his wife[3] (cited in note (*b*) to Barber *v.* Fox), all show that moral considerations, where no actual benefit has been received by one party or prejudice sustained by the other, and no legal duty has attached, are not sufficient ground for an assumpsit. As to the delivery in this case of the mere paper, it is not pretended that the paper had any value: the contract of guaranty, not the paper containing it, was the object really in question.

Sir *W. W. Follett* in reply.[4] . . . If it was only doubtful whether such a guaranty was not available, the giving it up was a good consideration. If the invalidity of it was not a point as clear as that the eldest son inherits, the court will not measure the degree of doubt. It has scarcely been disputed that the giving up of bills drawn on wrong stamps, or a contract on which the Statute of Limitations had attached, would be sufficient consideration; but those cases do not essentially differ from the present. The bills are void from the first, and cannot be made valid, though the promisor may have good reason for wishing to get them into his possession. It is suggested that the bar created by the Statute of Limitations may be waived; but so also may that under the Statute of Frauds. It is clear that, to support a promise of this kind, there need not have been an original liability in the promisor; for that is not so in the case of the bills, or in that of the contract made during infancy. That a promise may be founded on sufficient consideration, though no benefit has accrued to the promisor, appears from Stevens *v.* Lynch,[5] where the drawer of a bill, knowing that time had been given to the acceptor, undertook to pay on the acceptor's default, and an action was held maintainable on that undertaking. But supposing the guaranty in this case to have been totally void, the giving up of a paper on which no action would lie may be sufficient consideration for a promise. Here the plaintiffs, though not entitled to recover on the guaranty, might have brought trover for the document, if unlawfully taken out of their hands. In considering whether or not such an action would lie, the value would be of no importance: it is enough for the present argument, if the plaintiffs could have recovered a shilling. Suppose the defendant had said, "If you will not bring trover, I will pay the bills;" an action would

[1] Chitty on Bills, 74, note (*x*), 9th edit. (1840), by Chitty & Hulme.

[2] 5 B. & C. 501.

[3] Cro. Eliz. 756.

[4] See *supra*, p. 207, note 5. — ED.

[5] 12 East. 38.

clearly have lain on such an agreement, and the case would not have differed from the present. The consideration here is, not the releasing of an action on the guaranty, but the giving it up; whatever its value may have been, the bargain is binding. [COLERIDGE, J. It is decided in Scott *v.* Jones[1] that trover lies for an unstamped document, *if* it is capable of being made good by stamping.] Any paper may be the subject of an action of trover. *Cur. adv. vult.*

LORD DENMAN, C. J., in this term (June 6th) delivered the judgment of the court.

This action was brought upon an assumpsit to see certain acceptances paid, in consideration of the plaintiffs giving up a guaranty of £10,000 due from the acceptor to the plaintiffs. Plea, that the guaranty was for the debt of another, and that there was no writing wherein the consideration appeared, signed by the defendant, and so the giving it up was no good consideration for the promise. Demurrer, stating for cause that the plea is bad, because the consideration was executed, whether the guaranty was binding in law or not. The form of the guaranty was set out in the plea: "In consideration of your being in advance to Messrs. John Lees and Sons, in the sum of £10,000, for the purchase of cotton, I do hereby give you my guaranty for that amount (say £10,000), on their behalf. John Brooks."

It was argued for the defendant that this guaranty is of no force, because the fact of the plaintiffs being already in advance to Lees could form no consideration for the defendant's promise to guarantee to the plaintiffs the payment of Lees's acceptances. In the first place, this is by no means clear. That "being in advance" must necessarily mean to assert that he was in advance at the time of giving the guaranty, is an assertion open to argument. It may possibly have been intended as prospective. If the phrase had been "in consideration of your *becoming* in advance," or "*on condition* of your being in advance," such would have been the clear import.[2] As it is, nobody can doubt that the defendant took a great interest in the affairs of Messrs. Lees, or believe that the plaintiffs had not come under the advance mentioned at the defendant's request. Here is then sufficient doubt to make it worth the defendant's while to possess himself of the guaranty; and, if that be so, we have no concern with the adequacy or inadequacy of the price paid or promised for it.

But we are by no means prepared to say that any circumstances short of the imputation of fraud in fact could entitle us to hold that a party was not bound by a promise made upon *any consideration* which could be valuable; while of its being so, the promise by which it was obtained from the holder of it must always afford some proof.

[1] 4 Taunt. 865.

[2] See the discussion on the words "for giving his vote," in Lord Huntingtower *v.* Gardiner, 1 B. & C. 297.

Here, whether or not the guaranty could have been available within the doctrine of Wain v. Warlters,[1] the plaintiffs were induced by the defendant's promise to part with something which they might have kept, and the defendant obtained what he desired by means of that promise. Both being free and able to judge for themselves, how can the defendant be justified in breaking this promise, by discovering afterwards that the thing in consideration of which he gave it did not possess that value which he supposed to belong to it? It cannot be ascertained that that value was what he most regarded: he may have had other objects and motives, and of their weight he was the only judge. We therefore think the plea bad; and the demurrer must prevail. *Judgment for the plaintiffs.*

The plaintiffs having signed judgment, error was brought in the Exchequer Chamber.

The writ of error set out the pleadings, of which the material part is stated in the preceding report. The errors assigned were, that the declaration is insufficient, and that the judgment was for the plaintiffs below, whereas it ought to have been for the defendant. The writ of error was argued in Trinity vacation, June 22d, 1840, before LORD ABINGER, C. B., BOSANQUET, COLTMAN, and MAULE, JJ., and ALDERSON and ROLFE, BB.

Sir *J. Campbell*, Attorney-General, for the plaintiff in error.[2] . . . No action would have lain on this guaranty; and if so, is the giving it up sufficient consideration for a new promise? Such an act is no consideration, unless the thing given up be of some merchantable value. Thus in Com. Dig., Action upon the Case upon Assumpsit (F. 8), (cited by Holroyd, J., in Longridge v. Dorville), it is said that the action does not lie upon a promise "in consideration of a surrender of a lease at will; for the lessor might determine it." There is indeed a qualification added: "unless there was a doubt whether it was a lease at will or for years;" but even then, unless the doubt were a very reasonable and well-grounded one, the action would fail. In Smith and Smith's Case the alleged consideration for an assumpsit was, that the promisee "would commit the education of his children, and the disposition of his goods after his death during the minority of his said children, for the education of the said children," to the defendant; and this was held not sufficient, the consideration being only to have the disposition of the goods for the benefit of the children, and not for the defendant's profit. There must be some advantage to the promisor, or detriment incurred by the promisee at his request. [MAULE, J. It need not be pecuniary. LORD ABINGER, C. B. In Smith and Smith's Case the suggestion in support of the consideration was, that the defendant was to reap a pecuniary advantage, which the court would not presume, because his

[1] 5 East. 10. [2] See *supra*, p. 207, note 5. — ED.

doing so would have been a breach of trust.] The advantage must be such as can be appreciated in a court of law. There are many cases in which promises, in consideration of forbearance to sue, have been held void where there was no suit that could have been forborne. Tooley *v.* Windham;[1] Barber *v.* Fox; Loyd *v.* Lee.[2] It is true that the giving up a doubtful point of law has been held a good consideration, as in Longridge *v.* Dorville; and it may be so where a reasonable doubt exists; but in this case there could be no doubt on the invalidity of the first guaranty. [ALDERSON, B. What is the ground on which the giving up a doubtful point of law is a consideration? To whom must it be doubtful? The court which decides upon the assumpsit must be supposed capable of deciding the point of law.] There is a degree of uncertainty which the courts will notice. [MAULE, J., referred to Jones *v.* Randall.[3]] In Stracy *v.* The Bank of England, the point which might have been litigated was one of great nicety and difficulty. Tindal, C. J., in his judgment, so describes it. The argument on moral obligation can apply only to the first guaranty; the terms of the declaration do not admit of its being extended to the second. And on the first guaranty no consideration appears, except the general obligation to perform a promise.

The court below, in their judgment, argue that the words "in consideration of your being in advance" might mean "on condition of your being in advance," and suggest, as rendering this probable, that the plaintiffs must have come under the advance at the defendant's request, a supposition not confirmed by any thing which appears on the record; and they ground upon it the observation: "Here is then sufficient doubt to make it worth the defendant's while to possess himself of the guaranty; and if that be so, we have no concern with the adequacy or inadequacy of the price." They also say: "Whether or not the guaranty could have been available within the doctrine of Wain *v.* Warlters, the plaintiffs were induced by the defendant's promise to part with something which they might have kept, and the defendant obtained what he desired by means of that promise." [MAULE, J. The record does not show that any document was in the plaintiffs' possession. "Giving up" the guaranty might be merely relinquishing the contract. ALDERSON, B. If they held a written guaranty, it might have been given up by cancelling merely.] The court below argue that the defendant cannot be justified in breaking his promise by discovering that the thing in consideration of which he gave it did not possess that value which he supposed to belong to it. "It cannot be ascertained," they say, "that that value was what he most regarded. He may have had other objects and motives; and of their weight he was the only judge." But this reasoning would support a promise even in such a case as Barber *v.* Fox. The plaintiffs contend

[1] Cro. Eliz. 206. [2] 1 Stra. 94. [3] 1 Cowp. 37.

that trover would have lain for the paper; but it may be inferred, even from Scott *v.* Jones, that this would not be so unless the paper had some real value.

Sir *W. W. Follett*, contra. As to the observation that no actual delivery of a written paper appears, if that were considered important, the plaintiffs would ask leave to amend. The point was not taken on the former argument; and, when the declaration speaks of giving up a guaranty, which it describes as "then held" by the plaintiffs, it cannot reasonably be supposed that nothing is meant but foregoing an engagement. Supposing that no action would have lain on the first guaranty, here is an agreement between persons competent to make contracts, without imputation of fraud on either side, by which one is to give up an undertaking signed by the other, and the other in consideration of it is to provide for certain bills. It is assumed without reason that the defendant's only object in desiring to have the guaranty back must have been to prevent an action. He might not choose that his name should remain abroad in the mercantile world, annexed to such a document. It implies an admission which he might think proper to recall. He might not wish, if sued, to be put to a defence on the Statute of Frauds. If he attached a value to the document from any cause, however inadequate, as a man might be willing to give an immoderate price for a picture or autograph, the court will not inquire into the goodness of the bargain. Giving up any thing of which they were possessed was a disadvantage to the plaintiffs; and the defendant here was benefited by it. The case therefore differs from that of a mere forbearance to sue, where nothing is given and received. The law of Smith and Smith's Case may be doubted. If the promisee there complied with terms by which the defendant obtained something from him, although those terms could not authorize the making of any illegal profit, it would seem that the defendant was bound.[1] . . .

Supposing, however, that an action would not have lain on the first guaranty, yet, if the law upon the subject was doubtful (though Boehm *v.* Campbell makes it clear on the side of the plaintiffs), and the parties upon that doubt entered into a bargain for the abandonment of the guaranty, such bargain, made with a knowledge of all the facts, is binding. Longridge *v.* Dorville; Stracy *v.* The Bank of England; Com. Dig., Action upon the Case upon Assumpsit (F. 8), referring to 1 Rol. Abr. 23, *Action sur Case* (V.), pl. 27, 28.[2] It is indeed asked, Who is supposed to entertain the doubt in point of law? But matters of law may be considered as doubtful to the courts; and arrangements in equity are often made on the ground of the law being doubtful.

[1] See *supra*, p. 207, note 5. — ED.

[2] Comyns refers to Kent *v.* Pratt, Brownl. & Gold. 6, the case cited by Rolle. But it does not appear that any doubtful point of *law* was contemplated.

[BOSANQUET, J. A point may be considered so, on which learned men differ. LORD ABINGER, C. B. It is carrying fiction too far to say that the courts must always know how the law will be.] The parties here have made their contract on a consideration which they, knowing all the facts, thought beneficial; and this is enough. Merchantable or pecuniary value, in any more limited sense, is not to be insisted upon. The case falls within the principle of Stevens *v.* Lynch, and also within that of Lee *v.* Muggeridge, and other decisions which have turned upon moral obligation. It results from all these authorities that if parties, having made an engagement which ought to bind them but is incapable of being enforced, replace it by another, that new engagement is valid in law. If the contrary doctrine could prevail, what limit would there be to objections? Would a second or third renewal of guaranties be void on account of the original defect?

Lastly, as was contended below, if the consideration amounts to no more than the delivering up of a paper at the defendant's request, the court cannot say that it is insufficient. If they do, at what point will they allow sufficiency of consideration to begin? Would the giving up an autograph, or a horse or dog of no merchantable value, be sufficient? [LORD ABINGER, C. B. The Attorney-General cited the case of a lease at will.] That relates to a surrender, not the giving up of a document. Papers, though ineffectual for the purpose contemplated in drawing them up, may have a value from the mere wish of a party to get them into his own hands. [ROLFE, B. The Lord Chancellor has said that he will never compel the giving up of an instrument which is void on the face of it.] An application in equity for that purpose is very different from the enforcing of a bargain to give up something which is considered valuable. [BOSANQUET, J. Is not the document property, however small the value?] Yes; and trover would lie for it. In Wikinson *v.* Oliveira[1] it was held sufficient consideration, for a promise to pay £1000, that the plaintiff, being possessed of a certain letter, had given it to the defendant. It is true that the defendant was alleged to have made a beneficial use of the letter; but that was not an essential part of the consideration. Here the defendant could judge of the value of the document, and using his judgment made the promise. He cannot now annul it on the ground that the instrument was of no value.

Sir *J. Campbell*, Attorney-General, in reply. The last argument rests on a fallacious assumption. The bargain declared upon was not for the delivery of a piece of paper, but for the release of a contract. It does not appear that the paper itself may not even now be in the plaintiffs' possession. The plea, that the guaranty was of no effect, agrees with this view of the case. The main argument on the other side, assuming the first guaranty to be void, is in effect that, because

[1] 1 New Ca. 490.

it was given up at the defendant's request, he is estopped from saying that such an abandonment was no consideration for his promise. But this is contrary to the principle of many *placita* in Com. Dig., Action upon the Case upon Assumpsit (F. 8), already cited. On those authorities, if the right foregone was in reality null, it cannot be material that the parties made their agreement on a contrary supposition.[1] . . .

Stevens *v.* Lynch, where the holder of a bill had given time to the acceptor, and the drawer waived the benefit of that circumstance, is not applicable to the present case. As to Lee *v.* Muggeridge and the other cases which have turned upon moral obligation, it is sufficient to say that here no moral obligation appears for the first guaranty, and the declaration does not allege any consideration for the second guaranty, but the abandonment of the first. *Cur. adv. vult.*

Lord Abinger, C. B., in the same vacation (June 29th) delivered the judgment of the court.

In the case of Brooks *v.* Haigh the judgment of the court is to affirm the judgment of the Court of Queen's Bench.

It is the opinion of all the court that there was in the guaranty an ambiguity that might be explained by evidence, so as to make it a valid contract; and therefore this was a sufficient consideration for the promise declared upon.

It is also the opinion of all the court, with the exception of my brother Maule, who entertained some doubt on the question, that the words both of the declaration and the plea import that the paper on which the guaranty was written was given up; and that the actual surrender of the possession of the paper to the defendant was a sufficient consideration, without reference to its contents.

Judgment affirmed.

ENGLAND *v.* DAVIDSON.

In the Queen's Bench, May 5, 1840.

[*Reported in* 11 *Adolphus & Ellis*, 856.]

Assumpsit. The declaration stated that heretofore, to wit, &c., the defendant caused to be published a certain hand-bill, placard, or advertisement, headed "Fifty pounds reward;" whereby, after reciting that, late on the night of, &c., the mansion-house of defendant, at, &c., was

[1] See *supra*, p. 207, note 5. — Ed.

feloniously entered by three men, who effected their escape; that two men had been taken into custody on suspicion of having been concerned in the felony; and that a third, supposed to belong to the gang, had been traced to Carlisle, and was of the following description, &c., the defendant did promise and undertake that whoever would give such information as should lead to the conviction of the offender or offenders should receive the above reward: that plaintiff, confiding, &c., did afterwards, to wit, on, &c., give such information as led to the conviction of one of the said offenders, to wit, one David Robson; and that afterwards, to wit, at the assizes for Northumberland, D. R., who was guilty of the said offence, to wit, the feloniously entering, &c., was in due course of law convicted of the said offence of feloniously entering, &c., in consequence of such information so given by plaintiff; of all which said several premises defendant afterwards, to wit, on, &c., had notice, and was then requested by plaintiff to pay him the said sum of £50; and defendant afterwards, to wit, on, &c., in consideration of the premises, then promised plaintiff to pay him the sum of £50: breach, that, although defendant, in part performance of his said promise and undertaking, to wit, on, &c., did pay to plaintiff the sum of £5 5*s*., in part payment of the said sum of £50, yet, &c. (breach, non-payment of the residue).

Third plea. That heretofore, and long before and at the time when the house of defendant was so feloniously entered, and continually from thence hitherto, plaintiff was, and now is, a constable and police officer of the district where the said house of defendant is situate, and the said offence was committed; and it then was the duty of plaintiff, as such constable and police officer to have given and to give every information which might lead to the conviction of the said offender, and to apprehend him and prosecute him to conviction, if guilty, without any payment or reward to him made in that behalf: that, by the said advertisement partly set out in the declaration, defendant gave notice and promised that whoever would give such information to plaintiff, therein described as police officer Hexham, as should lead to the conviction of the offender or offenders, should receive the said reward in the said advertisement mentioned, and in no other manner whatever: and that, by reason of the premises, the said promise was and is void in law. Verification.

Demurrer, assigning for causes that the plea amounts to the general issue, and does not deny, or confess and avoid, and is multifarious, and tenders an immaterial issue. Joinder.

Ingham now appeared for the plaintiff; but the court called on

Martin, for the defendant. No consideration is shown on this record for the defendant's promise; the plaintiff was bound to do that, the doing of which is stated as the consideration. The duty of a constable is to do his utmost to discover, pursue, and apprehend felons. Com.

Dig., Leet (M. 9), (M. 10); Justices of Peace (B. 79). It has been laid down that a sailor cannot recover on a promise by the master to pay him for extra work in navigating the ship, the sailor being bound to do his utmost, independently of any fresh contract. Harris *v.* Watson,[1] explained by Lord Ellenborough in Stilk *v.* Myrick.[2] The principle was recognized in Newman *v.* Walters,[3] where the case of a passenger was distinguished. [COLERIDGE, J. Those cases turn merely on the nature of the contract made by the sailor.] If the duty here incumbent on the plaintiff was to do all that the declaration lays as the consideration, the case is the same as if he had been under a previous contract to do all. The cases on the subject of consideration are collected in note (*b*) to Barber *v.* Fox.[4] [*Ingham.* The constable was not bound to procure evidence.] The contract here declared upon is against public policy.

LORD DENMAN, C. J. I think there may be services which the constable is not bound to render, and which he may therefore make the ground of a contract. We should not hold a contract to be against the policy of the law, unless the grounds for so deciding were very clear.

LITTLEDALE, PATTESON, and COLERIDGE, JJ., concurred.

Judgment for the plaintiff.

HERRING *v.* DORELL.

IN THE QUEEN'S BENCH, TRINITY TERM, 1840.

[*Reported in* 8 *Dowling's Practice Cases,* 604.]

R. V. Richards shewed cause against a rule *nisi*, obtained by *V. Williams* for arrest of judgment or a new trial in this case. The case had been tried before the sheriff of Brecon, and a verdict found in favor of the plaintiff for £2 10*s.* 1*d.* The ground of seeking to arrest the judgment was, that no sufficient consideration for the promise by the defendant was disclosed on the face of the declaration. The substance of the declaration was, that a person named Watkins and a person named Voss were joint debtors to the plaintiff. The plaintiff proceeded against them, and ultimately took Watkins and Voss in execution. An arrangement was made between Watkins and the

[1] Peake, N. P. C. 72.

[2] 2 Campb. 317; s. c. 6 Esp. 129.

[3] 3 B. & P. 612.

[4] 2 Wms. Saund. 137 *a.* See also Jones *v.* Waite, 5 New Ca. 341, 351, 356; Haigh *v.* Brooks, 10 A. & E. 309.

plaintiff, and accordingly the former was discharged out of custody. Voss remained in custody, and in consideration of the discharge of Voss, the declaration alleged that the defendant undertook to pay the sum of £2 10*s.* 1*d.* due from Voss to the plaintiff, and Voss was accordingly discharged. It was contended in support of the rule that, the plaintiff having discharged Watkins, who was jointly liable with Voss, that had the effect of entitling Voss to his discharge. *Richards* submitted that, even after the discharge of Watkins, some step being necessary in order to obtain the discharge of Voss, some portion of his imprisonment, until that step could be taken, must be considered as lawful. Suppose the prisoners had been confined in two different gaols, one in Cornwall and the other in Northumberland, and one of them was discharged in Cornwall, some time must be allowed in order to discharge the other defendant from the gaol in Northumberland. The detention of the second defendant until his discharge must be considered as lawful. The smallest consideration was sufficient to support the promise alleged in the declaration, and here was some consideration for that purpose. If the proceeding could be considered as a nullity, then the plaintiff would be liable to an action of trespass; but in Crozer *v.* Pilling,[1] it appeared that an action on the case was the proper remedy, and not an action of trespass. There it was held that a plaintiff is bound to accept from a defendant in custody under a *ca. sa.* the debt and costs when tendered in satisfaction of the debt, and to sign an authority to the sheriff to discharge the defendant out of custody; and that an action on the case will lie against the plaintiff for maliciously refusing so to do. The case of Smith *v.* Eggington[2] was an authority to the same effect. The imprisonment was legal in its commencement, and therefore the sheriff could not be liable as a trespasser. It was not therefore a void imprisonment. The case of Atkinson *v.* Bayntun[3] was an authority to show that sufficient consideration was disclosed on the face of this declaration to support the defendant's promise. The marginal note was: "M. being in custody on execution pursuant to a warrant of attorney, by which he had agreed that execution should issue from time to time for certain instalments of a mortgage debt, defendant, in consideration that plaintiff would discharge M. out of custody, undertook that he should, if necessary, be forthcoming for a second execution. Held, that defendant's was a valid contract." He cited Sturlyn *v.* Albany,[4] and Pullin *v.* Stokes.[5] There, A. having recovered judgment against B., and a *fi. fa.* being delivered to the sheriff, in consideration that A. at the special request of C. had requested the sheriff not to execute the writ, C. promised to pay A. the debt and costs, together with the sheriff's poundage, bailiff's fees,

[1] 4 B. & C. 26; 6 Dowl. & Ry. 129.
[2] 6 Dowl. P. C. 38.
[3] 1 Scott, 404; 1 B. N. C. 444.
[4] Cro. Eliz. 67.
[5] 2 H. Bl. 312.

and other charges. On a judgment by default and error brought, the promise was holden to be binding on C., though it was not averred that the sheriff did in fact desist from the execution, nor what the amount of the poundage, &c., was, nor that the defendant had notice of such amount. In the present case, Voss was not taken in execution after the discharge of Watkins, but both were legally in custody at the time of Watkins's discharge. The detention of one prisoner in such a case could not be considered as a trespass. But suppose it should be said that the plaintiff was bound to take steps to discharge Voss: if he was, he was entitled to a reasonable time for that purpose. During the time that elapsed before his actual discharge, he was in legal custody. That custody furnished a sufficient consideration to support the defendant's promise.

V. Williams, in support of the rule. This was an action on a promise alleged to have been made by the defendant to pay a certain debt due from Voss, who was in custody, if the plaintiff would release him. The joint debt of the two had in point of law been satisfied by taking the defendants, Watkins and Voss, in execution, and discharging Watkins out of custody. It was therefore no consideration for the plaintiff to consent to the discharge of Voss out of custody, since it was that to which he was absolutely entitled. Here was an execution against two joint debtors. They were both taken in execution. The plaintiff consented to the discharge of one of them. The authorities shewed that the legal operation of the discharge of one of two joint debtors, was the discharge of the debt. The imprisonment of the latter debtor, therefore, was clearly illegal. He cited Clarke *v.* Clement,[1] Nadin *v.* Battie,[2] Good *v.* Wilks,[3] Basset *v.* Salter.[4] In the last case, even an escape with the consent of the plaintiff was held to be sufficient to prevent him from ever taking the defendant in execution for the same matter. The discharge of Watkins operated as if there had been actual payment of the debt. If so, then it must be contended, on the other side, that if the whole debt had been paid, that would afford a good consideration for such a promise. In the case of Crozer *v.* Pilling it was held, that an action on the case would lie for detention of the defendant, after a tender of the debt and costs, in consequence of the plaintiff not signing a discharge. With respect to the sufficiency of the consideration in the present case, Atkinson *v.* Settree[5] was an authority to show that the consideration here was insufficient. There it was held that if A. be illegally arrested by B. for a debt, a promise by C. to pay the debt claimed by B., in consideration of B.'s releasing A. out of custody, is void. He cited Stilk *v.* Myrick,[6] Harris *v.* Watson.[7]

[1] 6 T. R. 525.
[2] 5 East. 147.
[3] 6 Mau. & S. 413.
[4] 2 Mod. 136.
[5] Willes, 482.
[6] 2 Campb. 317.
[7] Peake's Ca. 72.

COLERIDGE, J. The question in this case, whether this was a good consideration or not, depends upon the situation of Voss at the time of his discharge. Both he and Watkins had been taken under a joint execution. Watkins made certain terms with the plaintiff, and the latter voluntarily discharged him. No terms were made as to the situation of Voss; his rights were, therefore, to be considered according to the situation in which the law had placed him. Suppose Watkins alone had been in custody, it is clear that the voluntary discharge of him would have been a discharge of the debt, and no other proceedings could have been taken to recover it. It seems to me, in the same way, that the discharge of Watkins operated to release Voss, his co-debtor. I think therefore, both on principle and authority, that this rule ought to be made absolute. *Rule absolute.*

SMITH AND ANOTHER v. MONTEITH.

IN THE EXCHEQUER, NOVEMBER 18 & 20, 1844.

[*Reported in* 13 *Meeson & Welsby*, 427.]

ASSUMPSIT. The declaration stated that an action had been commenced by the plaintiffs against one Charles J. Dunlop, for the recovery of a certain sum of money, to wit, the sum of £83 6*s.* 11*d.*; that said Dunlop, being about to leave England, had been arrested and was in custody of the sheriff, under a writ of *capias* duly issued by the order of a judge in said action; that costs and charges to a certain amount, to wit, the amount of £20, had been incurred by the plaintiffs in the prosecution of said action and the arrest of said Dunlop; and thereupon, in consideration that the plaintiffs, at the request of the defendant, would discharge the said Dunlop from said custody, the defendant undertook and promised the plaintiffs to pay to them the sum of £88 for the debt, interest, costs and charges of the plaintiffs in said action, when he, the defendant, should be thereunto afterwards requested; that the plaintiffs, confiding in said promise, did discharge said Dunlop from said custody; (averment of notice and request to pay said sum of £88 for debt, interest and costs). Breach, non-payment.

Plea: That there was not any claim or demand, or cause of action against said Dunlop, in respect whereof the plaintiffs could or were entitled to recover in the said action the said sum which the defendant so promised to pay, or any other sum or sums, matter or thing; and the plaintiffs did not, by discharging said Dunlop from custody, give up or part with any available remedy against the said Dunlop, as the plaintiffs at all times well knew, but which the defendant, at the time of making said promise, did not know; and the defendant says that said arrest and detaining in custody, and the proceedings in said action, were on the part of the plaintiffs colorable only, and the same were not procured, commenced, or prosecuted by the plaintiffs for the purpose or with the intent of trying any doubtful or contested question of law or fact. Verification.[1]

Special demurrer, assigning for causes, among others, that the plea does not in any manner answer the declaration; that it neither traverses any allegation therein, nor confesses and avoids the cause of action therein stated; that the contract of the defendant stated in the declaration is an original contract, founded on a new consideration, altogether distinct and different from the cause of action against the said C. J. Dunlop, such consideration for the defendant's promise being an act done by the plaintiffs for the benefit of the said C. J. Dunlop, at the request of the defendant, and such benefit to the said C. J. Dunlop being precisely the same whether the plaintiffs had or had not any cause of action against him; and therefore the question, whether the plaintiffs had any cause of action against the said C. J. Dunlop, is in this action wholly immaterial.

The plaintiffs' points marked for argument were, that the plea is bad in substance, and is no answer to the declaration. The consideration alleged is, the discharge of Dunlop out of custody of the sheriff at the request of the defendant, which discharge was a benefit to Dunlop, which he could not have obtained without the act of the plaintiffs in giving the discharge to the sheriff, whether the plaintiffs could have proved their debt against Dunlop or not, and which discharge materially altered the situation of the plaintiffs by allowing Dunlop to leave the kingdom. And therefore the question as to whether there was another and what distinct consideration, not alleged in the declaration, is in this action immaterial. The plaintiff will also contend, that the plea, if it amounts to any thing, is an argumentative denial of there being any consideration for the promise of the defendant, and is therefore bad, as amounting to the general issue. Also that, supposing the want of consideration for the promise may be specially pleaded, the plea is bad because it negatives one particular species of consideration only, namely, that of damage to the plaintiffs, whereas damage to the plaintiffs is not alleged in the declaration; and it is quite consistent with the plea that there was a good consideration for the promise, either by benefit to Dunlop at the request of the defendant, which in fact there was, or benefit to the defendant himself. Also that the plea, consisting of matter in denial only, ought not to have concluded with a verification. Also that the plea is double, in alleging that there was

[1] In this and a few other cases the statement of the pleadings has been curtailed of some of its verbiage. — ED.

no debt due from Dunlop, and that the arrest was colorable only, such defences being separate and distinct, which cannot both be put in issue without rendering the replication double. And lastly, that the plea contains no matter upon which any material issue can be taken.

The defendant's points were, that the declaration is insufficient and bad; that it does not disclose any sufficient consideration to support the action; that it is not alleged therein that there was a good cause of action, or a doubtful claim, on which the action mentioned in the declaration was founded, or that the plaintiffs had any right to continue Dunlop in custody; and that it is not shown that the plaintiffs sustained any damage by his discharge from custody.

Crompton, in support of the demurrer. This plea is bad both in form and substance. The declaration shows a good consideration for the alleged promise. For even supposing no debt to have been due from Dunlop, and the plaintiffs to have known that at the time of the promise and discharge, still the consideration is sufficient, for Dunlop was legally in custody, and had no right to require the other party to procure his discharge. The consideration is the doing of a collateral act, namely, the discharging of Dunlop, which was a benefit to him and a prejudice to the plaintiffs. He was in custody under a judge's order, and the act of the plaintiffs in procuring his discharge is a good consideration for the defendant's promise. It nowhere appears that the arrest was illegal. It is no doubt alleged in the plea that the arrest was colorable only, but that word as here used has no definite or distinct meaning of itself; and the declaration shows that the arrest was obtained by the order of a judge, and that the proceedings were regular. [POLLOCK, C. B. Are you aware of the case of Longridge *v.* Dorville?[1]] Yes; in that case the giving up of a suit intended to try a question respecting which the law was doubtful, was held to be a good consideration for a promise to pay a stipulated sum; and the reason for that decision was, that the plaintiff relinquished a benefit which he might otherwise have had. So here, the plaintiffs lost the right to all claim in respect to the costs incurred. There was a positive benefit to Dunlop by his immediate discharge from custody, which he could not otherwise have obtained except by procuring himself to be bailed, supposing he could have obtained bail. This was not a case of mere forbearance, but of an act done by the plaintiffs at the defendant's request, which was a benefit to him, or to the person whose discharge was thus obtained. The position of the plaintiffs is altered by Dunlop's discharge out of custody. The circumstance of the sum for which he was arrested being less than that agreed to be paid by the defendant is quite immaterial, as the slightest consideration will in law support the heaviest promise. The plea discloses no ground of fraud or duress. In Butcher *v.* Steuart[2] the arrest was irregular, and yet

[1] 5 B. & Ald. 117. [2] 11 M. & W. 857.

the discharge from execution was held a sufficient consideration for the defendant's promise. In that case Parke, B., says: "The case states in substance that Robert Steuart was arrested under a writ, irregular in itself, and from which arrest he might possibly have been entitled to be discharged out of custody by virtue of his privilege as a member of Parliament (a point on which it will not be necessary for us to give any opinion, as I think the undertaking for his discharge was an ample consideration); that the plaintiff released him from his debt, without entering into any question as to his right to be discharged generally, and without putting the defendant to the trouble of applying to the court on the ground of the irregularity in the writ, an application which after all might not be successful, as the court would probably have amended it. A discharge from such an execution is an ample consideration for the promise." And in Edwards *v.* Baugh[1] Lord Abinger, C. B., said: "Where an action is depending, the forbearing to prosecute it is a sufficient consideration for a promise to pay a certain sum of money; for, besides other advantages, the party promising would save the extra costs which he would have to pay, even if he were successful."

Peacock, contra. The declaration is insufficient. It contains no allegation that the plaintiffs had a good cause of action, or even a doubtful claim against Dunlop, or that they had any right to detain him in custody. It does not state that the sum of £83 6*s.* 11*d.* was due, but merely that an action had been commenced and was depending for the recovery of it; and that, Dunlop being about to leave England, he had been arrested, and was in custody of the sheriff, under and by virtue of a writ of *capias* duly issued in the said action. The word "duly" only means that it was issued in due form. That was decided by Butcher *v.* Steuart. The consideration alleged here is not a forbearance to sue, but a mere discharge out of the custody of the sheriff. The declaration does not show that any debt was really due, or that there was any color for the arrest; but the plea does show that there was not, for it expressly avers that there was not any claim or demand or cause of action against Dunlop, in respect of which the plaintiffs could or were entitled to recover. It states, moreover, that there was no color or pretence for the arrest, and that the plaintiffs well knew they did not part with any available remedy by this discharge. If a party, knowing he has no ground of action, causes another to be arrested, his afterwards causing him to be discharged from custody is no consideration for a promise by a third person to pay him a sum of money for so doing. It is not every benefit that will form a good consideration; and if a man is illegally in custody, the law will not regard his discharge as any benefit. Here Dunlop was only released from custody when in fact the plaintiffs were not entitled to detain him. Suppose a tenant for

[1] 11 M. & W. 641.

life were to say he would commit waste, and put the party in remainder to the necessity of going into equity to obtain an injunction, unless he would pay him a sum of money; his not committing waste in pursuance of such an agreement would form no consideration for a promise to pay the money, either by the party entitled to sue for waste or by a third person; unless, perhaps, it were doubtful whether the act were waste or not, or whether the party about to do the act were or were not entitled to commit waste. Here it is admitted by the demurrer that the action against Dunlop was not brought with the intention of trying any doubtful question either of fact or of law, as in the case of Longridge *v.* Dorville,[1] which is therefore distinguishable. There was no loss to the plaintiffs if they were not entitled to recover any thing, and there was no benefit in law to Dunlop, or to any one else; for, being wrongfully detained, the law supposes he would obtain compensation. In the case of Atkinson *v.* Settree[2] it was held that, if a person be illegally sued by another for a debt, a promise by a third person, in consideration of the plaintiff's releasing him out of custody, to pay the debt claimed, is void. So in Herring *v.* Dorell,[3] where a plaintiff discharged one of two joint debtors, a promise by a third person to pay the debt, in order to obtain the discharge of the other defendant in custody, was held to be void for want of consideration. That is a stronger case than the present, because there the plaintiff was entitled to make the arrest, and the parties were rightfully in custody. In an action against the sheriff for the escape of a prisoner on mesne process, a debt must be stated and proved. Alexander *v.* Macauley.[4] And in declaring on a promise to pay the debt of a third person in consideration of forbearance, it is necessary to show a good consideration, which in a case like the present could only be a demand recoverable at law or in equity. Barrell *v.* Trussell.[5] The case of the Duke de Cadaval *v.* Collins[6] shows that money paid under compulsion of colorable legal process may be recovered back. [PARKE, B. The plea does not aver that the plaintiffs maliciously sued out the writ.] It is not necessary to show, in order to support the plea, that Dunlop could maintain an action for maliciously suing out the writ; it is sufficient that it was sued out without any color or ground of action.

Crompton, in reply. The plaintiffs' case has not been answered by the argument on the other side. The declaration discloses a good consideration and promise, and there is nothing to show that it was made under circumstances of duress or illegality. [PARKE, B. The argument for the defendant is, that the plea confesses a good consideration by the suspension of the action, but avoids it by showing that the action was brought without foundation, to the knowledge of the

1 5 B. & Ald. 117.
2 Willes, 482.
3 8 Dowl. P. C. 604.
4 4 T. R. 611.
5 4 Taunt. 117.
6 4 Ad. & Ell. 858; 6 Nev. & M. 324

plaintiff.] The question is, Does it so avoid the cause of action? The facts alleged in the plea do not show any want of consideration or illegality. [POLLOCK, C. B. The substance of the plea is, that there was no claim or demand in the action against Dunlop, and no disputed question of law or fact; and this the plaintiffs knew at all the times necessary to be stated in the plea, whereas the defendant knew nothing of it. If there was either a good claim, or a reasonable disputed ground of controversy, that is sufficient.] There is nothing alleged to show that the arrest of Dunlop was not legal. The plea is in truth a mere plea of general injustice, and constitutes no defence in point of law. It is a mistake to suppose that there is any relation of principal and surety between these parties. The contract between the present plaintiffs and the defendant is not limited by the amount or nature of the original debt. If A. agrees with B. that, if B. will go to York, A. will pay him a certain sum, it is no answer to an action on this agreement, that B. has already contracted with some other person to go to York, which A. did not know, and that he will be there at all events. The plea really amounts to no more than this, that the plaintiffs knew that in that precise form of action they might be precluded from recovering against Dunlop, although they had a *bona fide* claim, because in that action Dunlop might set up a plea of some colonial act, or of the Statute of Limitations. [PARKE, B. To sustain this plea, it is certainly necessary to show that the plaintiffs had no cause of action, and no possibility of recovering against Dunlop, whatever might be the form of pleading.] Surely any holding of another by the Queen's writ must operate to create a good consideration for its suspension. "Duress cannot be where a party is in prison by the King's writ." Anon., 1 Lev. 68. But it is impossible to tell what is the precise legal defence set up by this plea — whether it be duress, or illegality, or fraud. With respect to the cases cited on the other side, that of Atkinson *v.* Settree is no authority against the plaintiff, but rather the contrary. There the question was, whether the arrest in the inferior court was not wholly void and illegal; and the *dictum* is only that, if it was, — so that the party would be a trespasser by keeping the defendant in custody, — the discharging him from such arrest could be no consideration for a promise by a third party to pay the debt. Here the arrest was perfectly legal and regular. In that case there was no authority to arrest, and no legal custody whatever, by reason of the want of jurisdiction in the inferior court. The decision of Coleridge, J., in Herring *v.* Dorell, does not bear directly on the present case. There, the one defendant being discharged, the continuance in custody of the other was clearly illegal. He had strictly a right to his discharge on an *audita querela*, and the court would not put him to that remedy, but discharged him on motion. Barrell *v.* Trussell has no application to this case; it was a question on the Statute of Frauds, and it is only the *dictum* of Heath, J., that can be cited as having the least bearing on the question now before the court. In Edwards *v.* Baugh and Butcher *v.* Steuart, the point in decision was quite different from this. The case of the Duke de Cadaval *v.* Collins is rather in favor of the plaintiff. That not only was a case of gross extortion from the plaintiff, but the writ against him had previously been set aside for irregularity. In Greenleaf *v.* Barker[1] it is said that "every consideration must be for the benefit of the defendant or some other at his request, or a thing done by the plaintiff for which he laboreth or hath prejudice." The present case falls within that definition; for here there was a benefit to Dunlop at the defendant's request, and a "labor and prejudice" to the plaintiffs, who relinquished the benefit they had by his arrest. And the plea cannot mean more than this, that, in the form of proceedings actually adopted, there was something to prevent them from recovering against Dunlop, — not even an answer in merits or substance. The plea would be proved, if in that action there were a misjoinder which prevented the plaintiffs from recovering. If, instead of merely making a promise to pay, the defendant had actually paid the debt, he could not have recovered it back in an action for money had and received. Here Dunlop receives a benefit by his immediate release to which he was not entitled by law, because at all events he must have put in bail. It is not said that the arrest was malicious. [PARKE, B. No; the plea discloses nothing to show that the original defendant had any right of action for the arrest, because it neither avers that the plaintiffs knew the action to be unfounded, nor that the arrest was malicious.] That really makes an end of the case. Dunlop could not have had any compensation for the arrest, and so he obtained a benefit in law, as well as in fact, by his discharge. It is perfectly immaterial to the maintenance of the action how small is the consideration, or how large the promise.

POLLOCK, C. B. I am of opinion that the plaintiffs are entitled to the judgment of the court. This is an action against the defendant, founded on a promise by him to pay a sum of money, in consideration of the discharge out of custody of a defendant in a former action, who had been arrested at the suit of the plaintiffs. For aught that appears that arrest was legal, and the party was in lawful custody: this is not therefore a case of duress; neither can it be put as a case of fraud, for there is no sufficient allegation of fraud in any part of the plea. The substance of the plea is, that there was not any claim or demand, or cause of action, in respect of which the plaintiffs were entitled to sue the defendant in the former action; but there is no averment that the plaintiffs were aware of that; and, for any thing that is stated in the plea, the original inception of that action was perfectly *bona fide*, although the plaintiffs may have been mistaken as to their remedy, or

[1] Cro. Eliz. 194.

the form of proceedings adopted by them. The plea goes on to state that the plaintiffs did not, by discharging Dunlop, give up or part with any available remedy against him. The words "available remedy" are rather loose and vague; they may mean several things; they would be satisfied by the fact of Dunlop being a mere pauper, for it is not stated that the plaintiffs had no legal right or remedy which they gave up, but merely that they had no available remedy. So also those words would be satisfied if there were some latent defect which might appear in pleading, or come out in evidence; yet the action might be honestly commenced, and the claim founded in justice; and it cannot be said that, because the proceedings were open to such latent defect, the defendant's promise would not be founded on a good consideration. And this is the only part of the plea as to which there is any averment of the plaintiffs' knowledge. It then goes on to say, that the action against Dunlop was not brought for the purpose of trying any doubtful or contested right. It seems to me that the declaration in its form calls for an answer, and that this plea is no sufficient answer. I agree with the general scope of Mr. Peacock's argument. If a party does an illegal act, or if he abuses the process of the court, to make it the instrument of oppression or extortion, that is a fraud on the law; and if the original arrest, or the continuance of that arrest, were of that character, and were shown to be so by proper averments in the plea, that would very probably constitute a good defence to an action like the present. But this plea falls far short of that, the arrest being legal, and there being no averment of knowledge on the part of the plaintiffs, except that they knew they did not part with any available remedy by discharging Dunlop out of custody. It does not therefore contain a sufficient statement in fact to bring it within the scope of Mr. Peacock's argument, or the cases cited by him. The judgment must therefore be for the plaintiffs.

PARKE, B. I am also of opinion that the plaintiffs are entitled to judgment. In the first place, I think that the declaration is sufficient on general demurrer. It states that an action had been brought and was depending at the suit of the plaintiffs against a person of the name of Dunlop, and that he had been arrested and was in custody on a *capias* duly issued in that action. On such a statement it must be intended, *prima facie*, that the action was well founded, and the writ regularly and properly issued. That doctrine is laid down in the case of Bidwell v. Catton.[1] That was an action of assumpsit on a promise by the defendant to pay £50, in consideration of the plaintiff's forbearing to prosecute a suit; and after verdict it was objected in arrest of judgment, first, that it was not alleged that the plaintiff had any just cause of action, and, secondly, that the action still remained. But the court nevertheless gave judgment; "for, first, suits are not presumed

[1] Hob. 216.

causeless, and the promise argues cause, in that he desired to stay off the suit; secondly, though this did not require a discharge of the action, yet it requires a loss of the writ and a delay of the suit, which was both benefit to the one and loss to the other." Therefore I think, *prima facie*, this declaration is sufficient, the former action being presumed to be for cause, and the *capias* being presumed to have been properly issued. There is another case which I may advert to, to the same effect, of Pooly *v.* Lady Gilberd.[1] There it is stated, that "the plaintiff had preferred a bill in chancery against the defendant for marriage money by her received. The defendant upon this, in consideration that the plaintiff would stay the suit there by him commenced, did assume to pay him £100, and also to deliver up a bond of £40, which she had. Upon this promise the plaintiff made stay of his suit, but the defendant not performing the promise, upon this the action was brought, and a verdict found for the plaintiff. It was moved for the defendant, in arrest of judgment, that the declaration was not good, for that there was no good ground to raise the promise, there being no sufficient consideration for the same, for it doth not appear in the declaration that the suit in chancery was a lawful suit to be there determined, and so if the suit was not lawful, the consideration to forbear such a suit was no good consideration to raise a promise." But the court say that, "if the plaintiff had only a *subpœna* out of chancery against the defendant, and did not make the cause thereof known to him,—if he, in consideration that he would not prosecute any farther against him, did assume to pay him so much, this clearly is a good consideration to raise a promise." Upon these authorities, and upon principle, this declaration is sufficient.

Then the question is, whether the plea, which must be construed most strongly against the defendant, discloses any answer. I agree with Mr. Crompton, that it is difficult to see upon what principle the plea is constructed. No doubt it shows a *prima facie* case of hardship and injustice upon the defendant in the former action; but the question is, whether it discloses a legal defence to this action. It does not show that the arrest was illegal; and it certainly is not sufficient on the ground of fraud, because there is no averment of any false statement or misrepresentation of fact in order to procure the arrest; still less does it disclose any ground of duress, since all the averments show that the imprisonment was lawful. If it be good at all, it must be on the ground of want of consideration for the defendant's promise. Now, it seems to me that the plea does not disclose sufficient matter to show a want of consideration. Taking it most strongly against the defendant, in substance it is no more than this, that the plaintiffs had no claim or cause of action which could have been enforced against Dunlop; but it does not allege that the plaintiffs knew that fact. It

[1] 2 Bulstr. 41.

must be taken, therefore, that the *capias* on which Dunlop was arrested was regularly and duly obtained; and the plea does not show that the plaintiffs were guilty of any illegal conduct, that they acted illegally in making the arrest, or from malicious motives, or that the arrest was without reasonable or probable cause. Dunlop therefore, as it must be assumed, was in custody at the suit of the plaintiffs under process which was legal and regular; and that being so, the discharge from such an arrest is quite a sufficient consideration to support the promise laid in this declaration; and I entirely agree that we cannot inquire into the *quantum* or amount of consideration. Upon the face of the plea, therefore, there was a legal arrest; and the discharge from that arrest, under which the payment of the debt might have been obtained, was a benefit to Dunlop, quite sufficient to found a consideration for a promise to pay that debt. For these reasons I am of opinion that the plea furnishes no sufficient answer to the declaration, and that our judgment must be for the plaintiffs.

GURNEY, B. I am of the same opinion. To make the plea a sufficient answer, it ought to have shown, either that the plaintiffs acted illegally or fraudulently in making the arrest, or that they practised some fraud on the defendant. It shows neither, and therefore is no sufficient answer. *Judgment for the plaintiffs.*

SHADWELL v. SHADWELL AND ANOTHER, *Executors, &c.*

IN THE COMMON PLEAS, NOVEMBER 26, 1860.

[*Reported in* 30 *Law Journal Reports, C. P.* 145.]

THE declaration stated that the testator in his lifetime, in consideration that the plaintiff would marry Ellen Nicholl, agreed with and promised the plaintiff, who was then unmarried, in the terms contained in a writing in the form of a letter addressed by the said testator to the plaintiff, which writing was and is in the words, letters, and figures following, that is to say:—

11TH AUGUST, 1838, GRAY'S INN.

MY DEAR LANCEY,—I am glad to hear of your intended marriage with Ellen Nicholl; and, as I promised to assist you at starting, I am happy to tell you that I will pay to you one hundred and fifty pounds yearly during my life, and until your annual income derived from your profession of a chancery barrister shall amount to six hundred guineas, of which your own admission will be the only evidence that I shall receive or require.

Your ever affectionate uncle,

CHARLES SHADWELL.

Averment, that the plaintiff did all things necessary, and all things necessary happened, to entitle him to have the said testator pay to him eighteen of the said yearly sums of £150 each respectively; and that the time for the payment of each of the said eighteen yearly sums elapsed after he married the said Ellen Nicholl, and in the lifetime of the said testator; and that the plaintiff's annual income derived from his profession of a chancery barrister never amounted to six hundred guineas, which he was always ready and willing to admit and state to the said testator; and the said testator paid to the plaintiff twelve of the said eighteen yearly sums which first became payable, and part, to wit, £12, of the thirteenth; yet the said testator made default in paying the residue of the said thirteenth yearly sum, which residue is still in arrear and unpaid, and in paying the five of the said eighteen yearly sums which last became payable, and the said five sums are still in arrear and unpaid.

Fourth plea: That before and at the time of the making of the supposed agreement and promise in the declaration mentioned, the said marriage had been and was, without any request by or on the part of the testator touching the said intended marriage, but at the request of the plaintiff, intended and agreed upon between the plaintiff and the said Ellen Nicholl, of which the testator, before and at the time of making the supposed agreement and promise, also had notice; and the said marriage was, after the making of the supposed agreement and promise, duly had and solemnized as in the declaration mentioned, at the request of the plaintiff and without the request of the testator. And the defendants further say that, save and except as expressed and contained in the writing set forth in the declaration, there never was any consideration for the supposed agreement and promise in the declaration mentioned, or for the performance thereof.

Fifth plea: To part of the claim of the plaintiff, to wit, so much thereof as accrued due in and after the year 1855, the defendants say that, although the supposed agreement and promise in the declaration mentioned were made upon the terms then agreed on by the plaintiff and the testator, that the plaintiff should continue in practice and carry on the profession of such chancery barrister as aforesaid, and should not abandon the same; yet that, after the making of the said agreement and promise, and before the accruing of the supposed causes by this plea pleaded to and in the declaration mentioned, or any part thereof, the plaintiff voluntarily, and without the leave or license of the testator, relinquished and gave up and abandoned the practice of the said profession of a chancery barrister, which before and at the time of the said making of the said supposed agreement and promise he had so carried on as aforesaid; and although the plaintiff could and might, during the time in this plea and in the declaration mentioned, have continued to practise and carry on that profession as aforesaid, yet the plaintiff, after such abandonment thereof, never was ready and willing to practise the same as aforesaid, but practised only as a revising barrister, that is to say, as a barrister appointed yearly to revise the list of voters for the year for the county of Middlesex, according to the provisions of the statutes in that behalf, by holding open courts for such revision at the times and places in that behalf provided by the said statutes.

Second replication to the fourth plea: That the said agreement declared on was made in writing, signed by the said testator, and was and is in the words, letters, and figures following, and in none other, that is to say (setting out the letter as in the declaration above). Averment, that the plaintiff afterwards married the said Ellen Nicholl, relying on the said promise of the said testator, which at the time of the said marriage was in full force, not in any way vacated or revoked; and that he so married while his annual income derived from his profession of a chancery barrister did not amount, and was not by him admitted to amount, to six hundred guineas.

Second replication to the fifth plea: That the said agreement declared on was in writing, signed by the said testator, and was and is in the words, letters, and figures set out in the next preceding replication, and in none other; and that the terms upon which it is in the fifth plea alleged that the said agreement and promise were made were no part of the agreement and promise declared on, and the performance of them by the plaintiff was not a condition precedent to the plaintiff's right to be paid the said annuity.

Demurrers to the replications to the fourth and fifth pleas. Joinder in demurrer.

Bullar, in support of the demurrers (Nov. 9). The letter declared on discloses no consideration for the promise of the testator. It was nothing more than a voluntary kindness on his part; and no intention is expressed in the letter to make it binding on him. Hawes v. Armstrong.[1] The promise to pay the annuity is not in consideration that "you will marry Ellen Nicholl," but it refers to a previous promise to assist the plaintiff "at starting," and that more naturally refers to his starting in his profession than to his starting in married life. And even if it be taken as referring to his starting in married life, the marriage is referred to in the letter as an obligation already incurred on the part of the plaintiff; the consideration therefore on which the testator's promise was based, was a consideration that the plaintiff should do what he was already bound to do; and that is not sufficient. Wennall v. Adney,[2] Eastwood v. Kenyon,[3] Rann v. Hughes,[4] Hopkins

[1] 1 Bing. N. C. 761.
[2] 3 Bos. & P. 250.
[3] 11 Ad. & El. 438.
[4] 7 Term Rep. 350.

v. Logan,[1] Stilk *v.* Myrick,[2] Clutterbuck *v.* Coffin,[3] Cowper *v.* Green;[4] Pothier on Obligations, by Evans, 25; Crowhurst *v.* Laverack.[5] As to the fifth plea, the question is whether the plaintiff's continuance at the bar was made a condition precedent to his right to the annuity. It is submitted that it was, and that when the plaintiff voluntarily abandoned his profession, his right to the annuity ceased, just as a covenant to pay rent during a term may be put an end to by the covenantee putting an end to the term.

V. Harcourt, in support of the replications. It is true that where the contract must be in writing, the consideration must appear on the face of the contract; but that is not so where the contract need not be in writing, — Shortrede *v.* Cheek;[6] and it was not necessary that the contract in this case should be in writing, for the Statute of Frauds does not apply where the promise is founded on a consideration executed. Souch *v.* Strawbridge,[7] Green *v.* Saddington,[8] and Chitty on Contracts, 456. But assuming that the consideration must appear in the writing containing the promise, it sufficiently appears in this case. The plaintiff having made an engagement to marry, the testator promised to assist him on starting in married life, viz., by giving him an annuity; and the plaintiff, relying on that promise, married. It is said, on the other side, that the plaintiff had already incurred an obligation to marry, and that a promise based on the consideration that he would fulfil that obligation is void. But the *quantum* of consideration is not material; and it is quite consistent with these pleadings that the plaintiff changed his condition sooner than, but for the testator's promise, he would have done, or even that, but for that promise, he might have broken off the engagement altogether. Or the true construction may be, that the plaintiff received a promise from the testator that, if he married, the testator would assist him at starting, on the faith of which he made his engagement to marry, and then the testator writes the letter referring to the former promise, and on the faith of that the plaintiff married. In either view there is a sufficient consideration to maintain this action. England *v.* Davidson,[9] and Kennaway *v.* Treleavan.[10] Till the marriage was executed there was a good continuing consideration to support the promise. Warcop *v.* Morse,[11] Payne *v.* Wilson;[12] Rol. Abr. "Consideration," Q. 12; Com.

1 5 Mee. & W. 241; s. c. 8 Law J. Rep. (N. S.) Exch. 218.
2 2 Campb. 317.
3 3 Man. & G. 842.
4 7 Mee. & W. 633; s. c. 10 Law J. Rep. (N. S.) Exch. 346.
5 8 Exch. 208; s. c. 22 Law J. Rep. (N. S.) Exch. 57.
6 1 Ad. & E. 57.
7 2 Com. B. Rep. 808; s. c. 15 Law J. Rep. (N. S.) C. P. 170.
8 7 E. & B. 503.
9 11 Ad. & E. 856; s. c. 9 Law J. Rep. (N. S.) Q. B. 287.
10 5 Mee. & W. 498; s. c. 9 Law J. Rep. (N. S.) Exch. 20.
11 Cro. Eliz. 138.
12 7 B. & C. 423.

Dig., tit. Action of Assumpsit (B. 12). And when persons have been induced to change their position on the faith of a promise, the person promising is not allowed to say there was no consideration. Pickard v. Sears,[1] Crosbie v. M'Doual,[2] Montefiori v. Montefiori,[3] Bold v. Hutchinson.[4] As to the replication to the fifth plea, the plaintiff's continuance at the bar is not made a condition precedent. If it had been the intention of the testator to make it a condition precedent, he would have expressly so stipulated.

Bullar replied, and cited Wain v. Warlters,[5] Lampleigh v. Brathwait,[6] and Thomas v. Thomas.[7] *Cur. adv. vult.*

ERLE, C. J., now delivered the judgment of himself and KEATING, J. The question raised by the demurrer to the replication to the fourth plea is, whether there was a consideration to support the action on the promise to pay an annuity of £150 per annum. If there be such a consideration, it is a marriage; therefore the promise is within the Statute of Frauds, and the consideration must appear in writing containing the promise, that is, in the letter of the 11th of August, 1838, and in the surrounding circumstances to be gathered therefrom, together with the averments on the record. The circumstances are, that the plaintiff had made an engagement to marry Ellen Nicholl, his uncle promising him to assist him at starting, by which, as I understand the words, he meant on commencing his married life. Then the letter containing the promise declared on is said to specify what the assistance would be, namely, £150 per annum during the uncle's life, and until the plaintiff's professional income should be acknowledged by him to exceed six hundred guineas; and a further averment, that the plaintiff, relying upon his promise, without any revocation on the part of the uncle, did marry Ellen Nicholl. Then, do these facts show that the promise was in consideration either of the loss to be sustained by the plaintiff, or the benefit to be derived from the plaintiff to the uncle, at his, the uncle's, request? My answer is in the affirmative. First, do these facts show a loss sustained by the plaintiff at the uncle's request? When I answer this in the affirmative, I am aware that a man's marriage with the woman of his choice is in one sense a boon, and in that sense the reverse of a loss; yet, as between the plaintiff and the party promising an income to support the marriage, it may be a loss. The plaintiff may have made the most material changes in his position, and have induced the object of his affections to do the same, and have incurred pecuniary liabilities resulting in embarrassment, which would be in every sense a loss, if the income which had been promised should

1 6 Ad. & E. 469. 2 13 Ves. 148. 3 1 W. Bl. 363.
4 20 Beav. 250; s. c. 24 Law J. Rep. (N. S.) Chan. 285.
5 5 East, 10. 6 Hob. 105.
7 2 Q. B. Rep. 851; s. c. 11 Law J. Rep. (N. S.) Q. B. 104.

be withheld; and if the promise was made in order to induce the parties to marry, the promise so made would be, in legal effect, a request to marry. Secondly, do these facts shew a benefit derived from the plaintiff to the uncle, at his request? In answering again in the affirmative, I am at liberty to consider the relation in which the parties stood, and the interest in the *status* of the nephew which the uncle declares. The marriage primarily affects the parties thereto; but in the second degree it may be an object of interest with a near relative, and in that sense a benefit to him. This benefit is also derived from the plaintiff at the uncle's request, if the promise of the annuity was intended as an inducement to the marriage; and the averment that the plaintiff, relying on the promise, married, is an averment that the promise was one inducement to the marriage. This is a consideration averred in the declaration, and it appears to me to be expressed in the letter, construed with the surrounding circumstances. No case bearing a strong analogy to the present was cited; but the importance of enforcing promises which have been made to induce parties to marry has been often recognized, and the cases of Montefiori *v.* Montefiori, and Bold *v.* Hutchinson, are examples. I do not feel it necessary to add any thing about the numerous authorities referred to in the learned arguments addressed to us, because the decision turns on a question of fact, whether the consideration for the promise is proved as pleaded. I think it is, and therefore my judgment on the first demurrer is for the plaintiff. The second demurrer raises the question, whether the plaintiff's continuing at the bar was made a condition precedent to the right to the annuity. I think not. The uncle promises to continue the annuity until the professional income exceeds the sum mentioned, and I find no stipulation that the annuity shall cease if the professional diligence ceases. My judgment on this demurrer is also for the plaintiff; and I should state that this is the judgment of my brother Keating and myself, my brother Byles differing with us.

BYLES, J. I am of opinion that the defendant is entitled to the judgment of the court on the demurrer to the second replication to the fourth plea. It is alleged by the fourth plea, that the defendant's testator never requested the plaintiff to enter into the engagement to marry, or to marry, and that there never was any consideration for the testator's promise, except what may be collected from the letter itself set out in the declaration. The inquiry, therefore, narrows itself to this question: Does the letter itself disclose any consideration for the promise? The consideration relied on by the plaintiff's counsel being the subsequent marriage of the plaintiff, I think the letter discloses no consideration. It is in these words: [His Lordship read it.] It is by no means clear that the words "at starting" mean "on marriage with Ellen Nicholl," or with any one else. The more natural meaning seems to me to be "at starting in the profession;' for it will be observed that these words are used by the testator in reciting a prior promise, made when the testator had not heard of the proposed marriage with Ellen Nicholl, or, so far as appears, heard of any proposed marriage. This construction is fortified by the consideration, that the annuity is not in terms made to begin from the marriage, but, as it should seem, from the date of the letter. Neither is it in terms made defeasible if Ellen Nicholl should die before marriage. But even on the assumption that the words "at starting" mean "on marriage," I still think that no consideration appears sufficient to sustain the promise. The promise is one which by law must be in writing; and the fourth plea shows that no consideration or request, *dehors* the letter, existed, and therefore that no such consideration or request can be alluded to by the letter. Marriage of the plaintiff at the testator's express request would be, no doubt, an ample consideration; but marriage of the plaintiff without the testator's request is no consideration to the testator. It is true that marriage is, or may be, a detriment to the plaintiff, but detriment to the plaintiff is not enough, unless it either be a benefit to the testator, or be treated by the testator as such, by having been suffered at his request. Suppose a defendant to promise a plaintiff, "I will give you £500 if you break your leg;" would that detriment to the plaintiff, should it happen, be any consideration? If it be said that such an accident is an involuntary mischief, would it have been a binding promise, if the testator had said, "I will give you £100 a year while you continue in your present chambers"? I conceive that the promise would not be binding for want of a previous request by the testator. Now, the testator in the case before the court derived, so far as appears, no personal benefit from the marriage. The question, therefore, is still further narrowed to this point: Was the marriage at the testator's request? Express request there was none. Can any request be implied? The only words from which it can be contended that it is to be implied are the words, "I am glad to hear of your intended marriage with Ellen Nicholl." But it appears from the fourth plea, that that marriage had already been agreed on, and that the testator knew it. These words, therefore, seem to me to import no more than the satisfaction of the testator at the engagement as an accomplished fact. No request can, as it seems to me, be inferred from them. And further, how does it appear that the testator's implied request, if it could be implied, or his promise, if that promise alone would suffice, or both together, were intended to cause the marriage, or did cause it, so that the marriage can be said to have taken place at the testator's request, or, in other words, in consequence of that request? It seems to me, not only that this does not appear, but that the contrary appears; for the plaintiff before the letter had already bound himself to marry, by placing himself not only under a moral, but under a legal obligation to marry, and the testator knew it. The well-known cases which have been cited at the bar in support of the position, that a promise, based on the consideration of doing that which a man is already bound to do, is invalid, apply to this case; and it is not necessary, in order to invalidate the consideration, that the plaintiff's prior obligation to afford that consideration should have been an obligation to the defendant. It may have been an obligation to a third person: see Herring *v.* Dorell[1] and Atkinson *v.* Settree.[2] The reason why the doing what a man is already bound to do is no consideration, is not only because such a consideration is in judgment of law of no value, but because a man can hardly be allowed to say that the prior legal obligation was not his determining motive. But, whether he can be allowed to say so or not, the plaintiff does not say so here. He does, indeed, make an attempt to meet this difficulty by alleging, in the replication to the fourth plea, that he married relying on the testator's promise; but he shrinks from alleging, that though he had promised to marry before the testator's promise to him, nevertheless he would have broken his engagement, and would not have married without the testator's promise. A man may rely on encouragements to the performance of his duty, who yet is prepared to do his duty without those encouragements. At the utmost, the allegation that he relied on the testator's promise seems to me to import no more than that he believed the testator would be as good as his word. It appears to me, for these reasons, that this letter is no more than a letter of kindness, creating no legal obligation. In their judgment on the other portions of the record, I agree with the rest of the court.

Judgment for the plaintiff.

SCOTSON AND OTHERS *v.* PEGG.

IN THE EXCHEQUER, JANUARY 28, 1861.

[*Reported in* 6 *Hurlstone and Norman,* 295.]

DECLARATION. For that in consideration that the plaintiffs, at the request of the defendant, would deliver to the defendant a certain cargo of coals, then on board a certain ship of the plaintiffs, the defendant to take the same from and out of the said ship, the defendant promised the plaintiffs to unload and discharge the same at the rate of forty-nine tons of the said coals during each working day, after the

[1] 8 Dowl. P. C. 604. [2] Willes, 482.

said ship was ready to unload and discharge the same. And although the plaintiffs did afterwards deliver the said cargo to the defendant, and were always ready and willing to suffer and permit him to take the same from and out of the said ship as aforesaid, and although all things were done, and conditions precedent to be performed by the plaintiffs were performed by the plaintiffs, to entitle the plaintiffs to a performance of the said promise by the defendant,—yet the defendant did not unload and discharge the said cargo at the rate aforesaid during each working day after the said ship was ready to unload and discharge the same, and the defendant wholly neglected and refused so to do for five days longer and more than he ought to have done according to his said promise; and the plaintiffs were put to expense in and about the maintaining and keeping the master and crew of the said ship, &c.

Plea: That before the making of the said promise the plaintiffs, by another contract made by and between the plaintiffs and certain other persons, agreed with the said certain other persons, for certain freight therefore payable by the said other persons to the plaintiffs, to carry the said coals on a certain voyage in the said ship, and to deliver the said coals to the order of the said other persons, which contract was in full force thence until and at the time of the making of the said promise and the delivery of said coals. And the defendant says that before the making of the said promise, and after the making the said other contract, and while the last-mentioned contract was in force, he bought the coals of the said other persons, who thereupon ordered the plaintiffs to deliver the same to the defendant under and according to the said contract with the said other persons, of which the plaintiffs, before the making of the said promise, had notice. And the defendant says that the said order was in full force until and at the time of the making of the said promise, and thence until and at the delivery of the said coals, of which the plaintiffs always had notice. And the defendant says the then further delivery to the defendant of the said coals on the terms in the declaration mentioned, which was the consideration for the said promise, was the delivery of the said coals to the order of the said other persons, which the plaintiffs had by the said contract with such other persons so agreed to make as aforesaid, and which before and at the time of the making of the said promise, until and at the time of the said delivery, the plaintiffs were, by, under, and according to the said contract with the said other persons, bound to make as aforesaid. And the defendant says that there never was any consideration for his said promise other than the doing of that which by the said contract with the said other persons, they, the plaintiffs, before and at the time of the making of the said promise, and thence until the plaintiffs did it, were bound to do.

Demurrer and joinder.

Dowdeswell, in support of the demurrer. The plea is bad. It admits a promise by the defendant to unload the coal at the rate of forty-nine tons a day; and the delivery of the same by the plaintiffs is a sufficient consideration to support the promise. The defendant, having made an express promise, is not relieved from his obligation to perform it because the plaintiff has entered into a previous contract with another person to deliver to his order. The defence would be available under the general issue; but the plea was allowed on the authority of Shadwell *v.* Shadwell.[1] This is an attempt to question the decisions on this subject, which have been uniform from the time of Jesson *v.* Solly.[2]

The court then called on

C. Pollock, to support the plea. There is no consideration to support the promise. The plea shows that the consideration alleged in the declaration is the doing that which the plaintiffs, by their contract with other persons, were bound to do. The charter-party only specifies the time and mode in which the cargo is to be discharged, as between the charterer and shipowner. [MARTIN, B. You must establish this, that, if a person says to another, "The goods which I have in my ship are yours; but I will not deliver them unless you pay my lien for freight," which the latter agrees to do, the delivery of the goods is no consideration to support the promise to pay.] The cargo is the property of the defendant, and the agreement to deliver to him that which he was entitled to have was a *nudum pactum*. In Black. Com., vol. ii. p. 450, it is said: "If a man buys his own goods in a fair or market, the contract of sale shall not bind him, so that he shall render the price, unless the property had been previously altered by a former sale." [WILDE, B. That is the case of a purchase of goods, the property in them being already in the purchaser; but here the plaintiffs will not deliver the cargo to the defendant, whereupon the defendant says, "If you will deliver it to me, I will discharge it in a certain manner."] The plaintiffs were under a prior legal obligation to deliver the cargo, and therefore the promise to the defendant to do the same thing was void. Where a plaintiff discharged one of two joint debtors, it was held that a promise by a third person to pay the debt, in order to obtain the discharge of the other debtor, was void for want of consideration. Herring *v.* Dorell.[3] So, if A. be illegally arrested by B. for a debt, a promise by C. to pay the debt claimed by B. in consideration of B.'s releasing A. out of custody, is void. Atkinson *v.* Settree.[4] [WILDE, B. In those cases there was a legal right to the performance of the very act which was bargained for: it is not so here. MARTIN, B. Suppose a man promised to marry on a certain day, and before that day arrived he refused, on the ground that his income was not sufficient, whereupon the father of the intended wife said to him: "If you

[1] 30 L. J., C. P., 145. — ED.
[2] 4 Taunt. 52.
[3] 8 Dowl. P. C. 604.
[4] Willes, 482.

will marry my daughter, I will allow you £1000 a year." Could not the contract be enforced?] There would be no consideration for such a promise, the party being already under an obligation to marry. A promise by a captain to pay his sailors increased wages for performing their duty during a storm is void for want of consideration. [MARTIN, B. That proceeds on the ground of public policy. WILDE, B. It often happens that when goods arrive in a ship, and there is a lien upon them, a merchant who wants to get possession of the goods promises to pay the lien if the master will deliver them to him. A man may be bound by his contract to do a particular thing, but while it is doubtful whether or no he will do it, if a third person steps in and says, "I will pay you, if you will do it," the performance is a valid consideration for the payment. MARTIN, B. If a builder was under a contract to finish a house on a particular day, and the owner promised to pay him a sum of money if he would do it, what is to prevent the builder from recovering the money?] As the plaintiffs would be doing a wrong by not fulfilling their contract, it must be presumed that the prior legal obligation, and not the subsequent promise, was the motive for their delivery of the cargo.

MARTIN, B. I am of opinion that the plea is bad, both on principle and in law. It is bad in law because the ordinary rule is, that any act done whereby the contracting party receives a benefit is a good consideration for a promise by him. Here the benefit is the delivery of the coals to the defendant. It is consistent with the declaration that there may have been some dispute as to the defendant's right to have the coals, or it may be that the plaintiffs detained them for demurrage; in either case there would be good consideration that the plaintiffs, who were in possession of the coals, would allow the defendant to take them out of the ship. Then is it any answer that the plaintiffs had entered into a prior contract with other persons to deliver the coals to their order upon the same terms, and that the defendant was a stranger to that contract? In my opinion it is not. We must deal with this case as if no prior contract had been entered into. Suppose the plaintiffs had no chance of getting their money from the other persons, who might perhaps have become bankrupt. The defendant gets a benefit by the delivery of the coals to him, and it is immaterial that the plaintiffs had previously contracted with third parties to deliver to their order.

WILDE, B. I am also of opinion that the plaintiffs are entitled to judgment. The plaintiffs say, that in consideration that they would deliver to the defendant a cargo of coals from their ship, the defendant promised to discharge the cargo in a certain way. The defendant in answer says, "You made a previous contract with other persons that they should discharge the cargo in the same way, and therefore there is no consideration for my promise." But why is there no consideration? It is said, because the plaintiffs, in delivering the coals, are only performing that which they were already bound to do. But to say that there is no consideration is to say that it is not possible for one man to have an interest in the performance of a contract made by another. But if a person chooses to promise to pay a sum of money in order to induce another to perform that which he has already contracted with a third person to do, I confess I cannot see why such a promise should not be binding. Here the defendant, who was a stranger to the original contract, induced the plaintiffs to part with the cargo, which they might not otherwise have been willing to do, and the delivery of it to the defendant was a benefit to him. I accede to the proposition that, if a person contracts with another to do a certain thing, he cannot make the performance of it a consideration for a new promise to the same individual. But there is no authority for the proposition that where there has been a promise to one person to do a certain thing, it is not possible to make a valid promise to another to do the same thing. Therefore, deciding this matter on principle, it is plain to my mind that the delivery of the coals to the defendant was a good consideration for his promise, although the plaintiffs had made a previous contract to deliver them to the order of other persons.

Judgment for the plaintiffs.[1]

SECTION IV.

Forbearance.

STONE v. WYTHIPOL, *Executor* P. WYTHIPOL.

IN THE QUEEN'S BENCH, TRINITY TERM, 1588.

[*Reported in Croke Elizabeth*, 126.]

ASSUMPSIT. And declares that, whereas the testator was indebted to him for certain pieces of velvet, and for £5 of money lent, *et pro diversis aliis mercimoniis, bonis et catallis*, and promised to pay him at such a day, and died before the day; and the plaintiff having an intent to sue the defendant, he required him to stop his suit till such a day, and he would pay him or give him security; whereupon he stayed, &c. The defendant showed that, at the time of the delivery of the goods to the testator, he was within age; and thereupon it was demurred.—*Egerton*, for the plaintiff. That the consideration here is good, and consists of divers parts; the debt precedent, the testator's

[1] Pollock, C. B., and Channell, B., were absent.

promise though within age, and the defendant's promise. And the promise of the infant is not void, but for his nonage he may help himself by plea; but if debt had been brought against him, and he pleads *nihil debet*, it shall be found against him: and if at his full age he had promised payment, it had been good, and *in foro conscientiæ* the promise of the infant had been good. And 9 Eliz. the case was, Lord Gray was indebted to divers, and after his death Lord Gray his son, who was not his executor nor chargeable with the debts, when the creditors complained and demanded their debts of him, told them that, if his father was indebted to them, he would pay them; and upon this it was held an action lay; and the promise of the executor is upon good consideration; for the plaintiff surceased his suit, and the executor was freed of trouble; and this matter will maintain suit in chancery. — *Coke*, contra. That it is no consideration; for every consideration that doth charge the defendant in an assumpsit must be to the benefit of the defendant or charge of the plaintiff, and no case can be put out of this rule. And this contract by the infant was void; and staying of suit is no benefit to the defendant, nor any charge to the plaintiff more than was before. And this is no consideration to sue in chancery, for no suit there against an express rule of common law; and denied the case of Lord Gray; and the defendant being not chargeable to pay the money, the staying of suit was no benefit to him. And afterwards the COURT was clear of opinion the action did not lie; for the contract of the infant was merely void, and in debt against him he might plead *nihil debet*. — *Egerton* said it was adjudged in this court in Edmunds *v.* Burton, that where an infant was bound in an obligation, and at his full age he promised payment, an action was maintainable against his executor upon this promise: to which the COURT agreed; for the bond which was the ground of it was not void, but voidable, and he could not plead *non est factum*, or *nihil debet* to a bond; and if at his full age he had accepted a defeasance of the bond, this had made it good; and in the case cited the promise was by the infant himself, which in conscience he ought to pay; but the defendant is in a remote degree. — And it was adjudged against the plaintiff.

TOOLEY *v.* WINDHAM.

In the King's Bench, Michaelmas Term, 1590.

[*Reported in Croke Elizabeth*, 206.]

Assumpsit. For that there were controversies between him and the defendant for the profits of certain lands which the father of the defendant had taken in his lifetime, and that he had purchased a writ out of chancery against the defendant, to the intent to exhibit a bill against him. Upon the return of the writ for the said profits, the defendant, in consideration he should surcease his suit, promised to him that, if he could prove that his father had taken the profits, or had the possession of the said land under the title of the father of the plaintiff, he would pay him for the profits of the said land; and said *in facto* that, he had proved that the father of the defendant had taken the profits under the title of the father of the plaintiff; and upon *non assumpsit* it was found for the plaintiff. — *Coke.* This is no consideration; for the suit in chancery was unjust, and then the staying of it is no good consideration; and he showeth not how the father of the defendant did hold it, viz., by lease or otherwise. — Curia. It is no consideration; for if the father of the defendant did take the profits, it is not reason his son should answer for them; and so the suit in chancery unjust, and the staying of it no good consideration: but if the suit had been for evidences or otherwise, the staying of it had been a good consideration; but here it is for a personal *tort*, for which neither the executor nor heir are to answer. And Trinity Term, 33 Eliz., it being moved again, all the Court held it no good consideration; for he did not allege he was heir or executor, and so had no color to charge him; and if it had been so alleged, yet no cause to charge him for a personal *tort*. And it was adjudged for the defendant.

PHILIPS *v.* SACKFORD.

In the Exchequer Chamber, Easter Term, 1594.

[*Reported in Croke Elizabeth*, 455.]

Error of a judgment in an assumpsit. Where the plaintiff declares, that in consideration the plaintiff would forbear to sue one Brediman for twenty pounds' debt which he owed unto him, that he assumed to pay the aforesaid twenty pounds before Michaelmas, and allegeth *in facto*, that from the time of the assumpsit *abstinuit* from suing him, *et adhuc abstinet;* and after *non assumpsit* pleaded and found for him, it was adjudged for the plaintiff.

The first error assigned was, because he allegeth not any request, but generally *licet sæpius requisitus*, &c. *Sed non allocatur;* for where a time certain is limited for the payment of any thing, he never shall allege a request before the day; but otherwise it is where it is uncertain.

A second error assigned was, that the consideration that he would forbear, &c., and showeth not for what time, is not a sufficient consideration; for it may be that he forbore but for a quarter of an hour, or other small time: and although it were alleged *quod abstinuit, et adhuc abstinet*, that will not help it.—And of that point the JUSTICES doubted; but the greater part held that it was not a sufficient consideration. *Sed adjournatur.* And afterwards for this cause it was reversed.

MAY *v.* ALVARES.

IN THE KING'S BENCH, EASTER TERM, 1595.

[*Reported in Croke Elizabeth*, 387.]

ASSUMPSIT. And declares, whereas the defendant was possessed *de diversis bonis* of the plaintiff, that the defendant, in consideration the plaintiff would forbear the goods, promised to deliver them within six months; and allegeth *in facto* that he did forbear them for six months, and that the defendant had not yet delivered them. Upon *non assumpsit* pleaded and found for the plaintiff, it was moved in arrest of judgment: first, that there was not any consideration, for it is that he should forbear; and he doth not show for what time, which is not any consideration; for so he might forbear but for a quarter of an hour: and although it be alleged that he [did] forbear for six months, that helps not the consideration alleged. Secondly, he doth not show what goods they were, and so uncertain.

But the COURT held it to be well enough, notwithstanding these exceptions. For as to the first, it is a sufficient consideration that he forbear, and he ought to show for what time he forbore it; and when the defendant saith that he would deliver them within six months, therein is implied that the other should forbear them for six months; and therefore it is sufficiently shown that he forbore them for six months. Secondly, there need not any certainty of the goods to be shown, for he is not to recover them in specie, but damages, &c. Wherefore it was adjudged for the plaintiff.

WILMOT v. PRIGGET.

IN THE QUEEN'S BENCH, EASTER TERM, 1599.

[*Reported in* 1 *Rolle's Abridgment*, 29, *placitum* 60.]

IF B. be indebted to A. in £20, and C. be indebted to B. in the same sum, and C. promise A., in consideration that he is content to accept the said sum by the hands of C., and to forbear it for four days, that he will pay him the said sum, this is a good consideration for A. to maintain an action upon the case against C.

LORD GRAY'S CASE.

[*Reported in* 1 *Rolle's Abridgment*, 28, *placitum* 57.]

IF a man bind himself and his heirs in a bond, and die, and then the obligee sue the heir, who has no assets descended to him, upon the bond, and the heir say to him that if he will not sue him, then he will pay him the money, this is no consideration to maintain an action, because he was not chargeable without assets.[1]

SMITH v. JONES.

IN THE KING'S BENCH, MICHAELMAS TERM, 1610.

[*Reported in Yelverton*, 184.]

THE plaintiff declared that Gregory Smith, his father, was possessor of several goods and chattels, and by his will bequeathed £7 as a legacy to the plaintiff, and made Constance his wife executrix, and

[1] "But it should seem," says Serjeant Williams, "that this would not now be so considered; for in the principal case [Barber v. Fox], it appears that the verdict was founded upon the want of alleging in the declaration that the ancestor had bound himself and his heirs; and if the heir had been liable, it seems to follow that forbearance would have been adjudged a sufficient consideration to support the promise without regarding whether he had assets or not at the time. And in Lord Gray's Case, if the defendant had not any assets he ought to have pleaded it to the action upon the bond: but if, instead of so doing, he desires the obligee to forbear his suit, and in consideration thereof promises payment, that appears to be a sufficient consideration; for though the forbearance may be of no benefit to the defendant, it might have been attended with a loss to the plaintiff not to proceed in his suit." — 2 Wms. Saund. 137 *a*, note 2. — ED.

died, and that the defendant married with Constance; and that such a day, in consideration that goods of Gregory Smith came to the possession and were in the hands of the defendant sufficient to satisfy debts and legacies, and in consideration the plaintiff at the defendant's request would forbear the £7 till All-Saints following, the defendant promised to pay the plaintiff the £7 at All-Saints next; and showed *in facto* that he had forborne the £7 till, &c.; yet the defendant had not paid him according to his promise, to his damage, &c. The defendant pleaded that Constance, the executrix of Gregory Smith, died intestate at such a place, before the promise made; upon which the plaintiff demurred. And it was adjudged against the plaintiff; for the demurrer confessing the death of the executrix before the promise, it thereby appears to the court that there is not any consideration sufficient to charge the defendant: for the thing for which the plaintiff would have damage by his action is for a legacy, which must be sued for only in the spiritual court; and by the death of the wife the defendant is not chargeable with the legacy, for he is not executor nor privy to the will of Gregory Smith; and although he had possession of the goods, yet forasmuch as he came to it lawfully by the intermarriage with Constance the executrix, by her death the defendant has but a bare custody of the goods, for which he shall not be charged either in the spiritual court or at the common law, without employment or conversion of the goods to his own use after the death of the wife; then there is no reason to charge the defendant with any promise when it is not grounded upon any consideration, for the plaintiff could not charge the defendant with the legacy, but he might compel the defendant to deliver the goods to the ordinary, or to take letters of administration, to the intent that he might sue in the spiritual court for the legacy. The declaration was also held ill, because it does not show precisely what person the plaintiff was to forbear to sue for the £7; for it cannot be intended that he should forbear the defendant, because it appears by the law that he is not chargeable with it. *Quod nota. Per totam curiam.* Yelverton was of counsel with the plaintiff.

BAKER *v.* JACOB.

IN THE KING'S BENCH, MICHAELMAS TERM, 1610.

[*Reported in* 1 *Bulstrode*, 41.]

IN an action upon the case for a promise of forbearance, the case was this: The defendant, in consideration that the plaintiff would forbear him *pro aliquo parvo tempore*, *videlicit* for a fortnight or thereabouts, he did assume and promise then to pay him, and for non-performance of his promise the plaintiff brought his action, and shews in his declaration that he had forborne him two years, and yet he hath not paid him: upon *non assumpsit* pleaded, a verdict was given for the plaintiff. It was moved for the defendant, in arrest of judgment, that the declaration is not good, because there is no good consideration laid in the same to maintain the action, the consideration laid being that, in consideration that he would forbear him *pro parvo tempore;* this time of the forbearance, being the consideration and ground of the action, is altogether uncertain, and so void, and no good consideration; in consideration that he would forbear him *pro aliquo parvo tempore*, this hath been adjudged to be no good consideration in law for to ground an action upon. YELVERTON, J. The *videlicet* here hath well explained the matter, *pro aliquo parvo tempore*, *videlicit*, or *anglice*, for some small time, that is to say, for a fortnight; if he had said, forbear a while, and names one day, this had been good; here it appears that he had forborne him two years, *per spatium* of two weeks and *duorum annorum*. FLEMMING, C. J. Forbear a little time, that is to say, a fortnight, and the plaintiff lays the truth of his case, that he hath forborne him this time and more (that is to say, two years); this is sufficient, and a good consideration, and certain enough. YELVERTON, J. If it had been in consideration that you will forbear me a small time, and I will pay you, and the plaintiff shews in his declaration that he had forborne him a fortnight, this had not been good clearly, because that no certain consideration is here laid, for the incertainty of the time of forbearance, and the same being without any words of explanation; but if it had been, as it is here, with a *videlicet*, for such a time certain, this had been good clearly.

Another exception was taken because the action was brought against an executor, and it is not averred in the declaration that he hath assets, and therefore for this omission the declaration is not good. The whole COURT disallowed of this exception, for that, as the court agreed, it is not requisite for the plaintiff to shew this in his declaration, for that this ought not to be averred by him; and so the opinion of the whole court clearly was, that the declaration was good and the consideration well and certainly laid; and by the rule of the court judgment was given for the plaintiff.

WILLIAM BANES'S CASE.

In the Exchequer Chamber, Hilary Term, 1611.

[*Reported in* 9 *Reports*, 93 *b*.]

William Banes brought an action on the case upon an assumpsit against Edward Paine and Mary his wife, and declared that, whereas William Havert was indebted to the plaintiff in £77, which the plaintiff had lent him; and that the said William Havert made his will, and thereof made the said Mary executrix, and died, and that the said Mary took upon her the charge of the said will; and that she, being possessed as executrix of an interest of a term for divers years yet to come of certain gardens, and of a bowling-alley in Moorfields, in the parish of St. Leonard's, in Shoreditch, in the county of Middlesex, the said Mary, 28 *Junii anno* 7 *Jac.*, perceiving that the said William Banes would sue her for non-payment of the said debt, in consideration that the said William Banes, at the request of the said Mary, *non molestaret aut sectaret eandem Mariam pro præd'* £77, *sed deferre vellet solutionem inde usque festum Sti. Michaelis tunc proxim' sequen'*, assumed to pay the said debt at the said feast of St. Michael, or otherwise *eadem Maria adtunc et ibidem assignare vellet eidem Willielmo Banes pro securitate suâ in eâ parte pro solutione præd'* £77 *totum interesse termini annorum præd,'* &c., in default of payment of the said £77, and averred that the plaintiff did not molest or sue her, &c., and that at the said feast the defendant did not pay or make assignment of the said interest; and afterwards the said Mary married the said Ed. Paine. The defendants pleaded *non assump'*, and it was found against them to the damages of £80, &c. Upon which a general judgment was given against E. Paine and his wife, *sc.* that the plaintiff should recover against them his damages; upon which judgment the defendant brought a writ of error in the Exchequer Chamber by the statute of 27 El. c. 8. And the principal error assigned was, because the plaintiff had not averred that the executrix had assets in her hands, at the time of the assumpsit made, of the goods of the deceased, amounting to the value of the said debt; and if she had not assets, then it is *nudum pactum*, for there is no consideration to charge her, nor to bind her to her promise; and *eo potius* because she shall by this promise be charged generally, and not only of the goods of the deceased; and therefore, in regard the assumpsit charges herself, and transfers the charge of her as executor in another right to herself as for her proper debt, in respect of her promise, reason requires that there ought to be some good consideration thereof, which cannot be if she has not assets.

But it was resolved by all the Justices of the Common Pleas and Barons of the Exchequer, that the declaration was good enough, for it shall be intended *prima facie* that she had assets; and therefore, in debt against executor, or against the heir, the plaintiff shall never aver in his declaration that they have assets, for the law presumes that *prima facie;* for the law presumes that the testator or the ancestor would not leave a greater charge upon his executor or heir than he leaves benefit to discharge it. And the consideration in the case at bar is good; for it is as much as if a stranger had said to the plaintiff, forbear your debt, and do not sue the defendant till Michaelmas, and at the said feast I will pay you your debt; that is a good consideration, although it cannot be any benefit to him who makes the promise; yet because it is a damage to the creditor to forbear his suit and duty, it is a good consideration; and as in the same case he who makes the promise for another shall be charged generally upon his own promise, so when one is executor, and makes such a promise, the debt is due by him in right of his executorship, and the promise is made in his own right; and therefore without question he shall be charged in an action brought upon his promise generally, and yet the money which he pays in satisfaction of the debt of the testator shall be allowed him as parcel of his account as executor; for his promise extends to pay the debt with which he was chargeable as executor; but I conceive, if the truth of the case be that in the case at bar there had not been any debt, or if there had been a debt, and the executrix had nothing in her hands at the time of the promise, she might have given it in evidence, and thereupon have been helped, for then in truth there was not any consideration; for to forbear the debt where none was, or with which she was not chargeable, is not any benefit to the defendant nor damage to the plaintiff. Also the case at bar was stronger, because the defendant promised either to pay the money or to assign the interest of the lease which she had as executrix, for it was in her election to do which of them she would. And so note the principal point resolved by both courts.

SIR JOHN POOLY *v.* THE LADY GILBERD.

IN THE KING'S BENCH, MICHAELMAS TERM, 1612.

[*Reported in 2 Bulstrode,* 41.]

IN an action upon the case for a promise, upon *non assumpsit* pleaded, the case appeared to be this: The plaintiff had preferred a bill in chancery against the defendant for marriage money by her received; the defendant upon this, in consideration that the plaintiff would stay the suit there by him commenced, did assume to pay unto him £100, and also to deliver up a bond of £40 which she had; upon this promise the plaintiff made stay of his suit; but the defendant not performing the promise, upon this the action was brought, and a verdict found for the plaintiff. It was moved for the defendant, in arrest of judgment, that the declaration was not good, for that there was no good ground to raise the promise, there being no sufficient consideration for the same; for it doth not appear in the declaration that the suit in chancery was a lawful suit to be there determined; and so if the suit was not lawful, the consideration to forbear such a suit was no good consideration to raise a promise.

WILLIAMS, J. This was an apt and proper suit for the chancery. If money comes into the hands of the defendant, being part of a marriage portion, and the defendant refuseth to pay it, this is a very fit and proper suit for the chancery, to sue the defendant there to execute the trust reposed in her, the money being in her hands; and this is in itself but a trust; if the plaintiff had only a *subpœna* out of the chancery against the defendant, and did not make the cause thereof known unto him [her]; if he [she], in consideration that he would not prosecute any further against him [her], did assume to pay him so much, this clearly is a good consideration to raise a promise.

CROKE, J. The consideration here is good, and this was a fit suit for the chancery, being for a marriage portion with which the party was trusted and did not perform this trust; here the promise is mutual and reciprocal, and so the plaintiff had good cause of action, and ought to have his judgment.

FLEMMING, C. J. This is a very plain and clear case; here the promise is mutual; the plaintiff promised to stay and surcease his suit, and the defendant promised to pay the £100. As to the suit in chancery, the consideration to stay proceedings in this suit is a good consideration to raise a promise to pay money. The court of chancery is a mixed court; the defendant here had the money only in trust, but performed not the trust; and for breach of this trust the bill was fitly there preferred to have performance of the trust; the money with which the defendant was trusted was £1000, part for legacies, and part for marriage portions, £300 of which was in the defendant's hands for marriage portions; this was matter of trust, and a fit suit for the chancery to have this performed. The forbearance and stay of this suit is a great ease to the defendant, in regard of travel and expenses; and this is a good consideration. And so the whole court agreed clearly, the consideration as it is laid to be good, that the plaintiff had good cause of suit, that the declaration is good; and by the rule of the court judgment was entered for the plaintiff.[1]

[1] See 1 Vin. Abr. 302, pl. 5, and notes. — ED.

BIDWELL *v.* CATTON.

HILARY TERM, 1618.

[*Reported in Hobart*, 216.]

BIDWELL, an attorney, brought an action of the case against Catton, executor of Reve, and counted that, whereas he had in Michaelmas Term, 14 Jac., prosecuted an attachment of privilege against Reve the testator, returnable in Hil. Term; the testator knowing of it, in consideration that at his request the plaintiff would forbear to prosecute the said writ any further against the said testator, the testator did promise to pay him £50, and then avers, &c. And after a verdict it was excepted in arrest of judgment:

First, that it was not alleged that the plaintiff had any just cause of action.

Secondly, that this action still remains. . . .

But the COURT nevertheless gave judgment: For first, suits are not presumed causeless, and the promise argues cause, in that he desired to stay off the suit. *Quære*, if the defendant had averred that there was no cause of suit.

Secondly, though this did not require a discharge of the action, yet it requires a loss of the writ, and a delay of the suit, which was both benefit to the one, and loss to the other. . . .

POTTER *v.* TURNER.

IN THE KING'S BENCH, EASTER TERM, 1621.

[*Reported in Winch*, 7.]

IN the King's Bench, Pasch. 19 Jac., the case between Potter and Turner was, as I conceived, to this effect: A. was indebted to B. in £20, and C. was indebted to A. in £30, and A., in satisfaction of the debt which he owed to B., assigned the debt of £30 which C. owed to him, and made a letter of attorney to sue in his name; A. and B. acquainted C. with this agreement, and C. promises to B., in consideration that he will forbear till such a day, that he will pay him the money; and upon this promise he brought the action against C., and he pleaded *non assumpsit*, and it was found for the plaintiff. And it was moved in arrest of judgment, that the consideration was not sufficient, according to Banes's Case, Coke 9. If executors who had not assets promise to pay a debt of the testator, this shall not bind them, because they who made the promise were not chargeable; but on the other side it was said by Whitwick of our house, that this was a good consideration, for the assignment of that debt was lawful, and no maintenance at all, as appears by 15 H. 7, 6; and a recovery by B. against C. is a good plea in bar, in an action brought by A. against C.; but Dodderidge, Houghton, and Chamberlin only present to the contrary, for B. here had only an authority to sue, and this is at all times countermandable by A. As if I deliver goods to my servant to deliver over to J. S., and J. S. promise my servant that, in consideration that he will deliver them to him, he will give him so much money, this is no consideration, except that they are delivered accordingly; for this is only an authority to deliver goods, which is always countermandable by me. And judgment was entered for the defendant. *Vide* 4 E. 4, 14.

MAPES, *Executor of* HOLDICK, *v.* SIR ISAAC SIDNEY.

IN THE COMMON PLEAS, HILARY TERM, 1624.

[*Reported in Croke James*, 683.]

ASSUMPSIT. For that the defendant, in consideration the plaintiff would forbear to sue one J. S. on an obligation of eighty pounds, promised to pay to him the said debt; and allegeth in fact, in the writ, that he forbore to sue the said J. S. *per magnum tempus*, and that the defendant had not as yet paid it to him, *licet requisitus*.

The declaration was, that he forbore him *per magnum tempus;* viz., from such a time of the promise until such a day, which was for a year and a half after the promise; yet he had not paid it.

The defendant pleaded *non assumpsit;* and it was found against him to the damage of eighty pounds.

Hitcham moved in arrest of judgment:

First, That this assumpsit is not grounded upon a sufficient consideration, viz., that he should forbear for a certain time, so as it might appear to the court that there was a sufficient time of forbearance, and a sufficient consideration to maintain the action: as in Sackford's Case[1] it was adjudged that an assumpsit for the payment of a debt in consideration to stay a suit *per paululum tempus*, was void: so in another case,[2] that he should forbear *per breve tempus*, although

[1] Cro. Eliz. 455. [2] Tolhurst *v.* Brickinden, Cro. Jac. 250.

he allegeth forbearance for half a year, an action lies not, for the consideration is no sufficient ground for the action.

Secondly, Admitting that the consideration to forbear, &c., should be good, because it shall be intended to be a total and absolute forbearance, yet the declaration is not good, because the writ is, *per magnum tempus* he had forborne to sue, not mentioning any time; and the declaration, that he did forbear *per magnum tempus, scilicet* from the time of the promise until such a day, &c., and doth not shew that it was until the day of the writ, &c., for if he doth not perform the consideration on his part, there is not any cause of action; and then here it shall be intended that he did not forbear until the day of the writ, because the day of the writ is not shewn; and it shall be intended strongest against the plaintiff, that he did forbear but until such a day, and afterwards before the writ brought sued that action. And upon these exceptions it was argued at large.

Lord Hobart, Winch, and Hutton (Jones being absent in chancery) held that the plaintiff should recover; for they all conceived that a consideration to forbear to sue a person for such a debt is a good consideration, and it shall be intended a total and absolute forbearance (as Hutton and Winch held); and that if the defendant paid it before upon this promise, and after the plaintiff sued for the debt, the plaintiff is chargeable in an action upon the case, for it is an implied promise in the plaintiff that he should forbear his suit totally; but yet when the plaintiff hath forborne a convenient time (when there is no time mentioned), if the defendant do not pay the debt according to his promise, the plaintiff may well sue him upon his promise, and he needs not tarry all his life. And here, when he shews that he forbore *per magnum tempus*, viz., such a day and year, that well agrees with the writ; and when the date of the writ doth not appear, it shall be intended that he did forbear until the day of the writ; and so the action is well brought.

Hobart, C. J., agreed with them that the action was well brought and the declaration good, because he shews he did forbear it for a convenient time; and he held that he was not bound by this agreement to forbear totally; and denied that upon this agreement he is chargeable in an assumpsit, if he (after this debt recovered from the defendant) should sue for the same debt; for it is not a promise to restrain him totally, and without express words he is not chargeable by promise. Wherefore it was adjudged for the plaintiff.

HILL *v.* BAYLIE.

In the King's Bench, Michaelmas Term, 1624.

[*Reported in* 1 *Rolle's Abridgment,* 22, *placitum* 23.]

In an action upon the case, if the plaintiff declare that A., the husband of the defendant, was indebted to him, and died possessed of divers goods, which goods after his death came to the defendant *legitimo modo*, and that the defendant, in consideration that the plaintiff would forbear the said debt for a certain time, assumed and promised to pay the debt, this is a good consideration, for, though there is not any sufficient matter shown by which it can appear that the defendant will have any benefit by this promise, yet, as the words are that he will forbear the debt and not the defendant, so that the promise is to forbear all the world, and any stranger who can be sued, viz., the executor or ordinary, it is a good consideration, for it is a prejudice to the plaintiff and a benefit to the stranger.

JOHNSON *v.* WHITCHCOTT.

In the King's Bench, Michaelmas Term, 1638.

[*Reported in* 1 *Rolle's Abridgment,* 24, *placitum* 33.]

If A. (to whom the testator was indebted) come to the executor, and say that he intends to sue him for the debt, whereupon the executor promises that, in consideration that the plaintiff will forbear him for a reasonable time, he will pay him, and A. forbears for a reasonable time to sue him, this is a good consideration to charge the defendant in an action upon the case, *de bonis propriis*, without assets; for by this promise it is intended as well to forbear to sue the executor as to forbear the debt, and a forbearance of suit is a good consideration without assets at the time of the promise.

The defendant pleaded that he had no assets at the time of the promise, to which the plaintiff demurred.

ROSYER *v.* LANGDALE.

IN THE UPPER BENCH, HILARY TERM, 1650.

[*Reported in Style,* 248.]

ROSYER, an executor, brought an action upon the case upon an assumpsit against Langdale a *feme* administratrix, and declares that the defendant, in consideration that he would forbear suit until she had taken out letters of administration, did assume and promise to pay unto him the plaintiff a certain sum of money owing unto him by the intestate. Upon issue joined, and a verdict and a judgment for the plaintiff, the defendant brought a writ of error to reverse the judgment. And *Baldwin* of his counsel took these exceptions: I. That the plaintiff had set forth no consideration in his declaration for the assumpsit; for all that is alleged is, that the plaintiff should forbear suit till the defendant had taken out letters of administration, which is no consideration at all, for the defendant was not liable to be sued as administratrix until she had taken out letters of administration, except there were a cause depending, as here is not. And he cited Hob. Rep., Bidwell and Catton's Case, that if there be a suit commenced, though there be no cause for it, yet forbearance to sue is a good cause to ground an assumpsit upon. . . . ROLLE, C. J., held the first a good exception, for the defendant was not chargeable before letters of administration taken forth, if she do not intermedle with the goods of the intestate, and it doth not appear here that she did; neither is the defendant compellable to take forth letters of administration, for they may be granted to the next of kin, if the ordinary pleaseth, according as the statute ordains. JERMAN, NICHOLAS, and ASK, JJ., to the same intent; thereupon the rule was *reversetur, nisi,* &c. But because *Day* being of counsel on the other side took some exceptions to the writ of error and the return thereof, *It was adjourned.*

NEWCOMIN *v.* LEIGH.

IN THE UPPER BENCH, HILARY TERM, 1650.

[*Reported in Style,* 249.]

LEIGH did assume and promise unto Newcomin, that if Newcomin would take one Loe for his debtor, in the room of one Cooper, and would spare Loe until such a time for the money, that then he would pay the money to Newcomin, if Loe did not; and upon this assumpsit Newcomin brought his action against Leigh. The question was whether this were a good assumpsit. And the COURT held it was not, because it is a collateral thing, and he doth not say that he will discharge Cooper, and so Newcomin may sue Cooper notwithstanding the assumpsit; for though it may be it was the intention of the parties to discharge Cooper, yet it appears not so by the words of the assumpsit set forth: and it was then said by ROLLE, that if I promise to pay to John a Down a debt which John a Stile oweth to John a Down, this is *nudum pactum.*

PITT v. BRIDGWATER.

IN THE UPPER BENCH, EASTER TERM, 1651.

[*Reported in* 1 *Rolle's Abridgment*, 20, *placitum* 11.]

IF A. be indebted to B. in £20, and thereupon B. makes a letter of attorney to C. to put the debt in suit, and recover it to his own use, and to release it at his pleasure, and afterwards A. promises C. that, in consideration that C. will forbear to sue him for a certain time, he will pay the debt, this is a good consideration; for the forbearance of a suit of which he has control is a meritorious consideration.

HUME v. HINTON.

IN THE UPPER BENCH, MICHAELMAS TERM, 1651.

[*Reported in Style,* 304.]

HUME brought an action upon the case against Hinton, and declared that, whereas the son of the defendant did in his lifetime owe unto the plaintiff £8, and died intestate, the plaintiff did demand the said £8 of the defendant, being mother to the intestate; whereupon she, being satisfied of the justness of the debt, did assume and promise unto the plaintiff that if he would stay for the money till Michaelmas next, that then she would pay it. Upon *non assumpsit* pleaded, and a verdict found for the plaintiff, the defendant moved in arrest of judgment, that here was no consideration to ground the assumpsit upon, because it was not the debt of the party that assumed to pay it;

neither was she executor or administrator, nor consequently liable any way by law to pay it; and therefore an assumpsit to pay a remediless debt, if the plaintiff would stay for it, is no good assumpsit, as in 6 Car. in this court, in Morgan's Case. An assumpsit to pay the rent of the land behind, if the party would forbear to distrain corn in the shocks, was adjudged no good assumpsit, because such corn is not distrainable; and it appears not here what person the son was, or where he lived, or that he either had or left any goods; and the mere ground of the action is the piety of the mother, and no other matter. And here appears no person liable to pay this debt, neither plainly nor by intendment; and the ordinary is not chargeable if no goods come to his hands. And, secondly, there is now no ordinary, for it is taken away by the Parliament; and 9 Rep. Baines's Case is not like to this case; neither is Jones and Smith's Case, Trin. 8 Jac. rot. 192, like to this case, for there was a person liable to be sued, but it is not so here; so that this is a stronger case. But if there should be a good consideration, yet the averment of the performance of it is not good, for it is not certain how he stayed. *Wild*, for the plaintiff, held that here is a good consideration, because the plaintiff is hereby tied not to sue any person whatsoever for the debt till Michaelmas, and so it is a prejudice to him to forbear. And it shall be intended here that the intestate did leave sufficient goods to satisfy the debt; and though there be no ordinary, yet the party that takes the goods may be sued. And the case of Homes [Jones?] and Smith[1] cited is for the plaintiff in my report, and the judgment is not there entered in the roll, but in the margent only: it is entered *pro defendente*, and the case of Hill and Baily is since that, and that is with me, and is to be preferred before the other, because it is a later judgment. Secondly, the averment is good in substance, although it is not so express in words as it might have been, and it is now after a verdict. The COURT for the first point held, here was a good consideration, for it is that the plaintiff shall forbear to sue for the money generally, which goes to all the world; and it is not only to forbear to sue a particular person, but to forbear to sue for the money; and this forbearance may be a prejudice to the party, and a loss in not suing till that time. But for the latter exception, ROLLE, C. J., said: If the breach be not well assigned, the verdict will not help it; and you say that you stayed in expectation of the money, and do not say absolutely that you stayed. Therefore let us see a book, and speak to the last point again on Saturday next. — In this case ROLLE, C. J., said: Where there is nobody else to be sued for a debt, the ordinary is to be sued, although he is not to be charged if he have no goods, and in London it is usual to do it; and now Sir Nathaniel Brent is in place of the ordinary throughout all England. — Afterward judgment was given for the plaintiff, because the consideration and the averment were held both good.

[1] See 1 Vin. Abr. 326, pl. 2. — ED.

HAYWARD v. DUCKET.

IN THE UPPER BENCH, HILARY TERM, 1654.

[*Reported in Style*, 405.]

HAYWARD brought an action upon the case against Ducket that was executor to another, and declares that, whereas the testator did owe unto the plaintiff such a sum of money, which the plaintiff did intend to sue the defendant for, the defendant did assume and promise to the plaintiff that, if he would forbear to sue him for the money, and would suffer him to go into the country, he would pay the money; and for breach of this promise he brought his action, and obtains a verdict. It was moved in arrest of judgment, that there appears no consideration in the declaration to ground the promise upon, whereby to make the defendant liable to pay the money which he promised to pay, for it doth not appear that he is executor; and Rosyer and Langdale's Case, *anno* 1650, in this court, was cited. To this it was answered by the counsel on the other side, that a good consideration doth appear well enough, for when he saith that he was to forbear to sue him as executor, it shall be intended that he was executor at the time when he should so forbear to sue him, and the promise is so laid. Plow. 128. ROLLE, C. J. To say that I will forbear to sue one as executor is not an affirmance that he is executor;[1] and there was such a case as this ruled in the Exchequer, and it is no more, nay, not so much as if he had said that he would not sue him at all. Judgment *pro defendente, nisi.*

SAMUEL REYNOLDS, *Plaintiff*, JOHN PROSSER, *Defendant*.

IN ACTION SUR LE CASE.

IN THE EXCHEQUER, MICHAELMAS TERM, 1656.

[*Reported in Hardres*, 71.]

THE plaintiff declares that, whereas John Lord Abergavenny, the 1st of April, 1647, did by his writing obligatory become bound to one George Smithson in £800, with condition for the payment of £369 to the said George on the twenty-ninth day of March next ensuing the date of the said writing obligatory; that the said £369 was not paid at the day: And whereas the said George, in Easter Term, 1652, in

[1] But see 1 Vin. Abr. 323, pl. 8.—ED.

the Common Bench, had obtained judgment for £700 debt upon the said bond, and £6 damages, against the said Lord: And whereas, on the twenty-fourth day of May, 1654, the said George had appointed the said Samuel to receive the principal money in the condition of the said bond mentioned, with the interest thereon then unpaid, and in default of such payment to prosecute the said Lord, in the name of the said George, upon the said judgment for the recovery thereof, to the proper use of the said plaintiff: And thereupon the said plaintiff, the seventh day of June, 1654, intended to sue forth execution against the said Lord, in the name of the said George, of which intent the plaintiff, the said seventh day of June, gave notice to the defendant: Whereupon the defendant afterwards, the said 7th of June, 1654, at London, in consideration that the said plaintiff would forbear to prosecute the said Lord, in the name of the said George, upon the said judgment until the end of Michaelmas Term then next ensuing, did assume upon himself and faithfully promise that the defendant, at the end of the said Michaelmas Term, would pay the plaintiff so much of the principal money in the condition of the said bond mentioned, with so much interest thereof as should be then remaining due and unpaid; and the plaintiff in truth saith that he, giving credit to the said promise, from thenceforth hitherto hath altogether forborne to prosecute the said Lord upon the said judgment; and that at the end of the said Michaelmas Term there was due upon the said bond, for principal and interest, the sum of £400, whereof the plaintiff then and there gave notice to the defendant; which the defendant hath not paid, but refuseth so to do, to the plaintiff's damage of £700.

Upon *non assumpsit* a verdict was found for the plaintiff, and damages given.

Hardres pro defendente, in arrest of judgment. The consideration is laid to be that, in consideration that the plaintiff would forbear to prosecute the Lord Abergavenny upon the said judgment, in the name of the said George, by virtue of a letter of attorney to the plaintiff to receive to his own use from the said George, till the end of Michaelmas Term then next ensuing, the defendant promised then to pay the plaintiff all the money due for principal and interest upon the said bond.

This is no good consideration. 16 Eliz., Dyer, 336 *b*, in Sir Francis Calthrop's Case: A consideration is called a cause or occasion meritorious, requiring a mutual recompense in deed or in law; in all contracts and bargains there is *quid pro quo*.

11 Rep., Magd. College Case. Resolved, that the statute of 18 Eliz. for confirmation of the Queen's grants made for money, or in discharge of a debt or other consideration, does not extend to a grant made upon no consideration, which is grounded upon the nature and definition of a consideration.

Doct. and Stud., *lib.* 2, *cap.* 24, so far discusses the point as to hold that a spiritual consideration, or a promise to build an alms-house, or to do such an act for the honor of God, is not obligatory, nor that an action will lie for it; but the ground there laid down is that, if he to whom the promise is made have any charge laid upon him, or any real damage, or that the party who makes the promise has any benefit or profit, such a promise doth bind in law; but if neither of these happen, or the party be in a worse condition than before, it binds not.

10 Eliz., Dyer, 272. A master promiseth to two men that, in consideration they had bailed his servant out of prison, he would save them harmless; this bound him not, because he had no benefit nor they prejudice by his promise; but if a man promise to pay a sum of money if J. S. will marry his daughter or cousin, or because he has married her, the person who makes the promise here has a benefit, *sc.*, the advancement of his daughter, and the consideration is a continuing one.

Now let us examine the present case by this rule. Where is the cause or consideration meritorious which deserves such a recompense? Or where is the benefit that the promisor receives by it? Or where is the prejudice of him to whom the promise is made? That the promisor has no benefit is clear, for he is a stranger to the debt, and no way liable to the judgment; so that the validity of the consideration must consist in the prejudice that he sustains to whom the promise is made, or else it is nowhere to be found. Now his prejudice can be pretended to be no other than he receives by forbearance to prosecute, &c.

Now the plaintiff's promise of forbearance can be no good consideration, unless it be prejudicial to one or beneficial to the other. Mich. 6 Car. B. R., Morgan's Case: A lessee promised, in consideration the lessor would forbear to distrain his corn unshocked, he would pay his rent that was due; adjudged to be no consideration, because such corn is not distrainable.

Trin. 2 Car. B. R., Goodwin *v.* Willoughby.[1] A. promiseth to pay a debt upon account, and dies; his wife promiseth, in consideration of forbearance, to pay the money when she should have received such a debt. This does not bind the wife, unless she were executrix or administratrix, or chargeable with the debt.

Hil. 1650, B. R., Lee *v.* Newcombe.[2] In error of a judgment in an inferior court, the defendant promised that, if the plaintiff would accept the defendant for his paymaster for a debt due to the plaintiff by a stranger, and would forbear the defendant six months, that he would pay the debt; adjudged to be no consideration, because the plaintiff might sue the stranger notwithstanding, and therefore is at no prejudice; which is a strong case to our purpose.

[1] See 1 Vin. Abr. 311, pl. 34, note.—ED.
[2] See 1 Vin. Abr. 317, pl. 60, note.—ED.

Mich. 1651, B. Sup., Hummers v. Hunton.[1] *Action sur le case sur promise;* the defendant's son died indebted to the plaintiff, and the defendant, being his mother but not executrix nor administratrix to him, nor having any effects of her son's in her hands, promised, if the plaintiff would forbear to sue for his debt, that she would pay it. This was adjudged to be no consideration, because she was not liable to any suit, so that the plaintiff had no prejudice by such forbearance.

So that it appears clearly that, where the plaintiff is at no prejudice, nor the defendant receives no benefit by forbearance, there forbearance is no consideration to ground an action upon.

But now in our case the plaintiff has no real prejudice by such forbearance of suit by himself, who has but a letter of attorney to prosecute in another man's name, and receive the money to his own use; for though he forbear to prosecute, yet the party himself to whom the debt is owing may prosecute in his own name, and recover the debt, and may permit and suffer the plaintiff to have the benefit of it, according to the purport of his letter of attorney; so that neither the defendant has any benefit by this forbearance, nor the plaintiff a prejudice by his cesser, and therefore here is no good consideration, no more than in the case before cited betwixt Lee and Newcombe.

But if it had been in consideration that the party himself to whom the debt was owing would forbear suit, such a promise would have been good; but as it is, it is no more than if an obligor should promise to pay the debt due upon the bond, if a stranger would forbear to sue, for the plaintiff here is in effect a stranger.

Pasch. 1651, Pet v. Bridgewater[2] was our very case. The plaintiff there had a letter of attorney to receive a debt to his own use as here, and power to release and discharge it, which the plaintiff here has not (for aught appears); and there the defendant promised that, if he would forbear to prosecute the suit, he would pay him the debt; and it was moved in arrest of judgment there, as it is here, that there was no consideration, because what the plaintiff does must be in another man's name, and the debt remains due to another person, who may sue and prosecute for it in his own name, notwithstanding the letter of attorney. And the Chief Justice Rolle said, in that case, that it appeared that the plaintiff had power to discharge and release the debt, which is for the defendant's advantage, and therefore he held it to be a good consideration; but said it would have been otherwise, if the plaintiff had had no such authority, which in our case he has not, at least it does not appear that he has; so that this case is a case in point for the defendant; wherefore he prayed for the defendant that the judgment might be arrested.

Allen argued for the plaintiff.

And afterwards the COURT was of opinion that the consideration was sufficient, and the plaintiff had his judgment.

[1] See 1 Vin. Abr. 307, pl. 23, and note. — ED.

[2] See 1 Vin. Abr. 304, pl. 11, and note. — ED.

SCOTT v. STEVENS.

In the King's Bench, Michaelmas Term, 1662.

[*Reported in* 1 *Siderfin*, 89.]

The surety pays the money for the principal; the principal dies (having made his executor); the executor promises the surety that, if he will forbear to sue him for so long a time, he will pay; and for non-payment the surety brings an action upon the case, and it is found for him. And it was moved in arrest of judgment that this was a void assumpsit; for if a stranger says, "Forbear to sue me, and I will pay," this is void, inasmuch as no action lies against him; no more here. *Tamen per Curiam:* The action well lies against the executor upon this assumpsit, inasmuch as he was liable in equity, and shall be compelled to pay him in chancery.

HUNT v. SWAIN.

In the King's Bench, Easter Term, 1665.

[*Reported in Sir Thomas Raymond*, 127.]

The plaintiff declares that the father of the defendant was obliged to the plaintiff in an obligation, and that the defendant is his son and heir; and that the plaintiff notified to the defendant that he intended to sue him; and upon this the defendant, in consideration that the plaintiff would forbear the defendant, promised to pay the money due upon the obligation. The defendant pleads *non assumpsit*, and found for the plaintiff. And it was moved in arrest of judgment, that it is not said that the heir was obliged in the same obligation with his father.

Wild, Serjt., for the plaintiff. That it shall be so intended; and he cited the case of Seignior St. Paul and his wife against the Earl of Rivers.[1]

[1] Trin. 1656, B. R. The plaintiffs declare that, whereas the father of the defendant obliged himself to the plaintiff's wife, *dum sola fuit*, in the sum of £400 for the payment of £200, which father is now dead, and the defendant is his son and heir, to whom the plaintiff repaired, and intimated that he intended to sue the defendant as son and heir for the said debt; the defendant upon consideration of forbearance assumed to pay, &c. And upon *non assumpsit* pleaded, and a verdict for the plaintiff, Serjeant Twisden moved in arrest of judgment, because it is not said that the father obliged him and his heirs, and therefore it does not appear the defendant was liable to an action, and so the consideration is void. But adjudged that it should be intended, it being found by the jury, according to Bidwell and Catton's Case, Hob. 216; and the plaintiff had judgment upon my own argument; but otherwise adjudged between Barber and Fox, Trin. 22 Car. 2, B. R.

TWISDEN, J. By this way presumption shall aid any thing; but I confess that Rolle, when he was chief justice, was of the opinion that it was good in this case after verdict; but I conceive the material thing is omitted.

WYNDHAM, J. The defendant hath admitted himself to be bound by the desire to give time to pay; and therefore it shall be presumed that he was bound, and so the plaintiff shall have judgment.

KELYNG, J. The forbearance only will not maintain the action; for in the action against an executor he ought to shew that he is executor, but here it is laid that he is heir; as if I lay a man to be executor, although he hath no assets, it is good.

HYDE, C. J. There is a grand difference between an heir and executor; and it was adjourned.[1]

QUICK v. COPPLETON.

IN THE KING'S BENCH, EASTER TERM, 1665.

[*Reported in* 1 *Levinz*, 161.]

ASSUMPSIT. Whereas the defendant's late husband was indebted to the plaintiff, and she about to come to London, and being in fear to be arrested by the plaintiff, she promised him, in consideration that he would not trouble her, and would forbear till Michaelmas, to pay, &c. After verdict, it was moved that, she not being shown to be executrix or administratrix, forbearing her was not any consideration, which was agreed by the court. But the subsequent words, "forbear till Michaelmas," are distinct and general, not only to forbear her, but all others, and make a good consideration, whether she be liable or not; and they cited Heriot [Hume?] and Hinton's Case, [where it was] adjudged that a general forbearance is a good consideration, whether the party promising be liable or not. But KELYNG at first doubted that by the

[1] In the report of the same case in 1 Sid. 248, it is said: "The court doubted, because the heir cannot be bound without express words; but it was agreed that if one declare that J. S. was indebted to him and died, and the defendant, being his executor, assumed, &c., that this is good, because an executor is liable without express words." In 1 Lev. 165, s. c., it is said: "After verdict judgment was stayed, because it did not appear that the ancestor bound himself and his heirs, and the consideration is not to forbear generally, but to forbear him who does not appear to be chargeable; and the plaintiff, perceiving the judgment of the whole court against him, prayed *nil capiat per billam*, to the intent to begin *de novo*. And note that the case of Lord St. Paul was cited as having been recently adjudged to the contrary; but the court paid no regard to it, and Twisden, who was counsel in the case, said it was at the time taken to be a hard case." — ED.

copulative *et* all was one sentence, and that it was not only not to trouble her, but also to forbear her till Michaelmas; but afterwards he agreed with the others; and judgment was given for the plaintiff. And HYDE, C. J., held that a forbearance to sue one who fears to be sued is a good consideration; and he cited a case in the Common Pleas, when he sat there, where a woman, who feared that the dead body of her son would be arrested for debt, promised in consideration of forbearance to pay; and it was adjudged against her, though she was neither executrix nor administratrix. But of this the other judges here doubted.

RUSSEL v. HADDOCK.

IN THE KING'S BENCH, EASTER TERM, 1666.

[*Reported in* 1 *Levinz*, 188.]

ASSUMPSIT against an executor. That whereas J. S. had a judgment against the testator, and had made a letter of attorney to the plaintiff to recover and receive it to his own use; the defendant, in consideration that the plaintiff would forbear execution thereupon, promised to pay him. The defendant demurred on the declaration, supposing that it was no good consideration; for that although the plaintiff, who was but attorney, did forbear, yet the plaintiff himself in the judgment might sue execution. To which it was answered, that the plaintiff having authority to receive it to his own use, it shall not be intended that the plaintiff in the judgment would sue execution, for it shall be intended that it was assigned to the plaintiff in satisfaction of a debt; and a case between Pitts and Bridgwater, in Hilary, 1650, was cited to be so adjudged; and so held the court here, and gave judgment for the plaintiff.

CLIPSAM v. MORRIS.

IN THE KING'S BENCH, MICHAELMAS TERM, 1668.

[*Reported in* 1 *Levinz*, 248.]

ASSUMPSIT. That whereas A. was indebted to the plaintiff, and wrote a note to the defendant to pay it to the plaintiff; the defendant on receipt of the note promised to the plaintiff, that if he would accept of his promise for a fortnight, that he would pay it, and avers that he tarried a fortnight; after verdict for the plaintiff it was moved in arrest of judgment that it was no consideration, for the defendant is not the debtor, nor was the said A. obliged to stay a fortnight: whereto TWISDEN on the first motion inclined; but KELYNG and MORETON on the contrary held that it did amount to an agreement generally to forbear, not only for the plaintiff [defendant?] but also for A. for a fortnight. But afterwards in Hilary following it being moved again, and a case between Newcomb and Lee in Easter Term, 1650, rot. 62 in B. R., being cited to be the very case in point, the whole COURT held it to be no consideration, and gave judgment for the defendant.[1]

FORTH AND OTHERS *v.* STANTON, WIDOW.

IN THE KING'S BENCH, HILARY TERM, 1669.

[*Reported in* 1 *Williams' Saunders,* 210.]

ASSUMPSIT. The plaintiffs declare that one Robert Stanton, the late husband of the defendant, was indebted to John Neve and Timothy Alsopp in £100 for beer sold by them to him, and being so indebted, the said Robert Stanton died; after whose death the defendant took into her hands goods and chattels of the said Robert Stanton of the value of £100, and administered those goods and chattels as executor of the will of the said Robert; and that afterwards the defendant had paid £40 parcel of the said £100 to the said Neve and Alsopp. And whereas the said Neve and Alsopp afterwards had assigned to and appointed the plaintiffs to receive of the defendant £60, residue of the said £100, to the proper use of the plaintiffs, whereof the defendant had notice given to her: whereupon the defendant, in consideration that the plaintiffs, at the special instance and request of the defendant, would accept the defendant to be their debtor for the said £60, undertook and promised the plaintiffs to pay them the said £60. And the plaintiffs aver that they had accepted the said defendant to be their debtor. And they also declare upon an *insimul computasset* for £60 more. Yet the said defendant had not paid the several sums, to the damage of the plaintiffs.

[1] In the report of this case in 1 Vent. 9, it is said: "If it had been in consideration that the plaintiff would accept of the defendant for his debtor, that might have been good; for that is an implied discharge of the other, whom if he had sued, the defendant might have had an action;" citing Wilmot *v.* Prigget, 1 Rol. Abr. 29, pl. 60. In 1 Sid. 396, s. c., it is said: "After several motions and suggestions that it was good by the custom of merchants, inasmuch as the defendant had accepted it as a bill, judgment was arrested."

The defendant as to the *insimul computasset* pleaded *non assumpsit*, and upon the issue tried a verdict was found for the defendant. And as to the said special promise, the defendant pleaded in bar, that the plaintiffs did not show her any writing or deed, whereby the said Neve and Alsopp had assigned to them, or appointed them to receive, the said £60 to their own use; and this she is ready to verify, &c.: upon which the plaintiffs demurred in law.

And now after verdict for the defendant, the plaintiffs moved the matter in law upon the defendant's special plea, which was agreed by all to be bad; but the defendant's counsel insisted that the declaration was insufficient, because here is no sufficient consideration to found the promise. For the defendant before the promise did not owe any thing to the plaintiffs, but to Neve and Alsopp; and by their assignment they did not transfer any property or interest in the debt, being a *chose in action*, but only gave an authority to the plaintiffs to receive it, if the defendant would pay it. But if the defendant will not pay it, the plaintiffs cannot bring any action against her, but Neve and Alsopp must sue for it. It is true indeed that, if the defendant had paid the £60 to the plaintiffs, she would be discharged against the said Neve and Alsopp; but in this case the defendant refused to pay; therefore Neve and Alsopp ought to bring the action against her, and not the plaintiffs, who have not any interest in the debt. And this case is no more than if I promise a stranger, to whom I do not owe any thing, that if he will accept me to be his debtor for £60 I will pay it to him; yet this is but a *nudum pactum*, because I was not indebted to him before. And my promise to pay, if the other will receive it, is nothing but a mere voluntary promise, which does not bind me at all. And in the present case, if the promise should be good, the defendant would be charged *de bonis propriis*, where she was chargeable to Neve and Alsopp only *de bonis testatoris;* and yet here is no consideration at all so to charge her: and of this opinion was the whole court. And judgment at the prayer of the plaintiff's counsel was given for the defendant, that plaintiffs should take nothing by their bill. *Jones* for the plaintiffs. *Saunders* for the defendant.

BARBER v. FOX.

In the King's Bench, Trinity Term, 1670.

[*Reported in 2 Williams' Saunders*, 136.]

Assumpsit. That whereas one Anthony Fox, the father of the defendant, by his writing obligatory became bound to the plaintiff in £92 12*s*. upon condition to pay him £51 16*s*. at a certain day past, which was not paid, and so the obligation became forfeited; and afterward Anthony Fox the father died, and the defendant was his son and heir, wherefore the plaintiff intended to sue the defendant as son and heir on the said bond; and the defendant having notice of it, in consideration that the plaintiff at the special instance and request of the defendant would forbear his intended suit against the defendant as son and heir on the said bond, undertook and promised the plaintiff to pay him the said £51 16*s*. on request; and the plaintiff averred forbearance, and yet the defendant had not paid the said money, although on such a day and year he was requested, &c., to the damage of the plaintiff, &c. On *non assumpsit* pleaded a verdict was found for the plaintiff.

And now *Weston* moved in arrest of judgment, that here was no consideration; for it does not appear that the defendant was suable upon this bond as son and heir; for it is not shewn that Anthony Fox, the defendant's ancestor, whose son and heir he is, had bound himself and his heirs by the said bond; and if the heir is not bound expressly by name, he is not bound at all, and therefore here was no consideration to found this promise. Wherefore judgment was stayed until it should be moved on the other side.

And afterwards *Saunders* for the plaintiff moved for judgment, and said that though the declaration would have been had on demurrer, yet it is now made good by the verdict; for the jury have found that the defendant was bound as heir in the said bond, for otherwise there was no consideration; and they ought to have found that the defendant did not undertake, &c., if there was no consideration, or otherwise they may be attainted for a false verdict; but they having found that the defendant did undertake and promise as the plaintiff has declared, it ought of necessity now to be intended that Anthony Fox had bound himself and his heirs by the said bond.

Sed non allocatur; for by the COURT, though they would intend a personal lien against an executor, if he has assets in his hands, though it be not averred, yet they will not intend a real lien against an heir, though he be bound by the bond of his ancestor, unless it is expressly alleged; and therefore they would not intend it here, though it be after verdict. Wherefore judgment was arrested; *quod nota.*

DAVIS *v.* REYNER.

IN THE KING'S BENCH, EASTER TERM, 1671.

[*Reported in 2 Levinz,* 3.]

ASSUMPSIT. And declares that J. S. devised a legacy to the plaintiff, and made the defendant executor and the plaintiff intending to sue him for the legacy, the defendant in consideration of forbearance promised to pay him. The defendant pleaded divers bonds and judgments, and *nul assets ultra*, upon which the plaintiff demurred, and had judgment without argument; for it is not material whether he had assets or no, for he is charged upon his own promise in consideration of forbearance, and a forbearance of suit for a legacy is a sufficient consideration.

OBLE *v.* DITTLESFIELD.

IN THE KING'S BENCH, MICHAELMAS TERM, 1671.

[*Reported in 1 Ventris,* 153.]

IN an assumpsit the plaintiff sets forth that J. S. was indebted to him in £40, and that the defendant was indebted in the like sum to J. S., and that J. S. did appoint him to receive this £40 from the defendant in satisfaction for the debt due to him from J. S. Which he signifying to the defendant, he, *in consideratione præmissorum*, and that the plaintiff would forbear him a quarter of a year, promised that he would then pay him.

To this the defendant pleaded *non assumpsit*, and a verdict was found for the plaintiff.

It was moved in arrest of judgment that here was no sufficient consideration; for it doth not appear that the defendant was party to this agreement, whereby he should become chargeable by the plaintiff, and then the forbearance is not material, and in the mean time he is suable by J. S. his creditor. And Clipsam and Morris's Case was cited, which was adjudged in this court, Hil. 20 & 21 Car. 2, where the plaintiff in an assumpsit declared that J. S. was indebted to him in £50, and gave him a note directed to the defendant, whereby he required the defendant to pay him; who upon view of the note, in consideration that the plaintiff would accept of his promise, and forbear him a fortnight, promised to pay him the money. There (after verdict for the plaintiff) judgment was arrested, because that was held no consideration. *Sed non allocatur.*

For HALE said: When assumpsits grew first into practice, they used to set out the matter at large, viz., in such a case as this, *Quod mutuo agreatum fuit inter eos*, &c., and they should be discharged one against the other; but since, it hath been the way to declare more concisely. And upon the whole matter here it appears, that the defendant agreed to this transferring of the debt of J. S. to the plaintiff, and that it was agreed that he should be discharged against J. S. And he said that the case of Davison and Haslip [Hanslop] (*hoc termino*) was to the same effect; and for Clipsam's Case, that was said to be good in law; for there it did not appear that the defendant was at all indebted to him that sent the note.

DAVISON v. HANSLOP.

IN THE KING'S BENCH, MICHAELMAS TERM, 1671.

[*Reported in Sir Thomas Raymond*, 211.]

THE plaintiff declares that one Fenwick was in arrear to him in £100 for an annuity, and that the defendant was bailiff and receiver of the rents of the said Fenwick, who appointed the defendant to account with the plaintiff, and to pay all which should be found in arrear of the annuity, out of the next rents due at Martinmas; and that upon an account there was £100 found due to the plaintiff; and the defendant *adtunc existens receptor* of the rents of the said Fenwick assumed to the plaintiff, that if he would forbear the said arrears for a month after the said Martinmas, that he would pay the same; and avers that he stayed accordingly, and that yet the defendant hath not paid. Upon *non assumpsit* pleaded, a verdict was found for the plaintiff.

And *Weston* moved in arrest of judgment, for that it doth not appear that the defendant had effects in his hands at the time of the promise.

PER CURIAM. It shall be presumed that he had effects after a verdict, being alleged that he was *adtunc receptor;* and judgment was given for the plaintiff.[1]

[1] In the report of this case in 1 Vent. 152, it is said: "The taking of this promise did not discharge the principal debtor; but there might be resort to him so long as the money was unpaid." — ED.

LOYD *v.* LEE.

BEFORE PRATT, C. J., AT NISI PRIUS, 1718.

[*Reported in* 1 *Strange,* 94.]

A MARRIED woman gives a promissory note as a *feme sole;* and after her husband's death, in consideration of forbearance, promises to pay it. And now in an action against her it was insisted that, though, she being under coverture at the time of giving the note, it was voidable for that reason; yet by her subsequent promise, when she was of ability to make a promise, she had made herself liable, and the forbearance was a new consideration. But the C. J. held the contrary, and that the note was not barely voidable, but absolutely void; and forbearance, where originally there is no cause of action, is no consideration to raise an assumpsit. But he said it might be otherwise where the contract was but voidable. And so the plaintiff was called.

ANONYMOUS.

IN THE KING'S BENCH, JUNE 16, 1774.

[*Reported in Cowper,* 128.]

UPON a rule to show cause why upon filing common bail a *supersedeas* should not issue as to this action to discharge the defendant out of gaol, Mr. *Cowper* shewed for cause that though the debt was originally under £10, yet after judgment obtained and costs taxed the whole sum amounted to £17; and that upon a writ of execution being sued out, the defendant, in consideration that the plaintiff would stay the execution at that time, undertook and promised to pay the debt and costs; that several applications had been since made to the defendant for payment without effect, and therefore he was now held to bail upon his new assumpsit for the £17. . . .

LORD MANSFIELD. This is a new species of action, and an attempt to turn a judgment debt into a debt upon simple contract. If the undertaking had been by a third person in consequence of the forbearance, it would have been a good ground of assumpsit against such third person. But here the promise is by the defendant himself to pay a debt to which he was before liable upon record; for by the judgment he is liable to the costs as well as the debt. And therefore I am of opinion that such promise is no ground upon which to raise an assumpsit.

ASHHURST, J. I am of the same opinion. This promise is no waiver or extinguishment of the judgment debt; but it still remains a lien upon the land. *Rule made absolute.*

PULLIN, ONE, &c. v. STOKES, ONE, &c.[1]

IN THE EXCHEQUER CHAMBER, IN ERROR, JUNE 25, 1794.

[*Reported in* 2 *Henry Blackstone*, 312.]

IN this case, the second count of the declaration stated that the defendant in error had recovered judgment in the Court of King's Bench against one Mathias Taylor for a debt of £400, and 63*s*. costs, and had sued out a *fi. fa.* directed to the sheriff of Somersetshire, &c., &c.; and thereupon afterwards, and before the said last-mentioned sum of £400, together with 63*s*., were made of the goods and chattels of the said Mathias Taylor, and whilst the last-mentioned writ was in force, to wit, on, &c., at, &c., he the said James (the plaintiff in error), in consideration that the said Thomas (the defendant in error), at the special instance and request of said James, had then and there requested the said sheriff to forbear and desist from executing the said writ, undertook and to the said Thomas then and there faithfully promised to pay him the sum of £225 10*s*., being for principal, interest and costs due to him from the said Mathias Taylor, together with sheriff's poundage, bailiff's fees, and other incidental charges.

The plaintiff in error, having let judgment go by default in the court below, brought a writ of error.

Lawes, for the plaintiff in error, contended that the second count was bad for want of a consideration; and the damages being general, if either count were defective it was a good reason for reversing the judgment. A consideration necessary to support an assumpsit must be such as is either beneficial to one party or detrimental to the other. Now in the second count it is merely stated that the defendant, in consideration that the plaintiff at his special instance and request had requested the sheriff to forbear from executing the writ, promised to pay the debt and costs, together with the sheriff's poundage, bailiff's fees, and other incidental charges, &c.; but it is not averred that the sheriff did actually forbear; if he did not, there was no detriment to the plaintiff, and clearly the defendant in either case received no benefit. The plaintiff ought also to have shown that the sheriff was

[1] Only so much of this case is given as relates to the question of consideration. — ED.

bound to attend to his request, if it had been made; otherwise the consideration fails. But a sheriff is not bound to attend to such a request after the writ is delivered to him; as on the one hand he cannot refuse to execute the process of the court, so on the other he has a right to go on with the execution to secure his poundage, which arises on the fact of seizure. In 1 Rol. Abr. 23, pl. 27, it is said that "if A. lease land to B. at will, and A. promise B. that in consideration that he will surrender the estate at will to him, that A. will provide a parsonage for J. S., this is not a good consideration to have an action, because he may determine the lease at will at his pleasure;" so in the present case, the plaintiff might have revoked his request to the sheriff immediately after he had made it.

Praed, contra. There is a good consideration disclosed on the second count. The slightest detriment to the plaintiff is sufficient (3 Burr. 1673); and here it is to be presumed that the sheriff did not proceed, for if he had done so after the plaintiff's request, he would have been liable to have the proceedings set aside with costs.

THE COURT held that, as to the consideration of the promise in the second count, it was sufficient to state the request to forbear, if the contrary did not appear, that is, that the sheriff did not desist from proceeding in the execution.

Judgment affirmed.

JONES v. ASHBURNHAM AND NANCY, HIS WIFE.

IN THE KING'S BENCH, JANUARY 31, 1804.

[*Reported in 4 East, 455.*]

THE plaintiff declared that, whereas one S. F. Bancroft, since deceased, at the time of his death was indebted to him in £58 for goods before that time sold and delivered to the deceased, whereof the defendant Nancy had notice; and thereupon, after the death of Bancroft, the defendant Nancy, before her intermarriage with the other defendant, Ashburnham, in consideration of the premises, and also in consideration that the plaintiff, at the special instance and request of the defendant Nancy, would forbear and give day of payment of the said £58 as aftermentioned, she the said Nancy, by a note in writing signed by her according to the form of the statute, &c., on the 20th of March, 1801, undertook and promised the plaintiff to discharge the said debt so due and owing to him in a reasonable time, and to send him £20 in part payment in the July following; and although the same July is long since passed, during which the said Nancy continued sole, and a reasonable time elasped for the payment of the whole £58, according to the tenor and effect of the said promise; and though the plaintiff has always from the time of making the said promise hitherto forborne and given day of payment of the said debt, whereof the defendant Nancy before her intermarriage, and both the defendants since their intermarriage, have had due notice, yet the defendants have respectively, &c., refused to pay, &c. There were other counts in substance the same; one alleging the forbearance to be till July, &c. To all which there was a demurrer, assigning for special causes that it is not alleged in the declaration from whom the said sum of £58 therein mentioned was due and owing to the plaintiff at the time when the defendant Nancy is supposed to have made the promise and undertaking mentioned, or that any persons or person were or was then liable to pay the plaintiff that sum; and that it is not alleged to whom the plaintiff hath forborne and given day of payment of the said £58; and that the declaration does not disclose any legal and sufficient consideration for the supposed promise; nor does it thereby appear that the plaintiff has any good cause of action against the defendan's, &c.

Marryat, in support of the demurrer. This is a promise made by a stranger to the original contract or consideration for the supposed forbearance. But a promise to forbear generally is not a sufficient foundation for an assumpsit, without shewing a person who was liable to pay the debt. If the promise had been laid barely for forbearing to sue the defendant, it not appearing that she was before liable for any debt to the plaintiff, the action could not have been sustained: then it cannot aid the plaint that a debt is stated to be due to the plaintiff, without stating any person from whom he could have enforced payment. It is not enough that there may be some person liable to him *in rerum natura* who is unknown. All the cases upon the subject are collected in 1 Com. Dig. 160, Action upon the Case upon Assumpsit (F. 8), which shew that no action can be maintained upon an assumpsit in consideration of forbearance where the party was not chargeable; as in the case of an heir who has no assets. This case is not distinguishable in principle from those. To sustain such an action the plaintiff must shew that he was in a situation to forbear some person whom he might have sued, whom it would have been beneficial to him to have sued, and consequently whom it was detrimental for him to forbear suing. Here it is not shewn that any person was liable to the plaintiff at the time of the promise made; for the original debtor was dead, and no representation was taken out, nor, for aught appears, any assets, nor any suit surceased in consequence of the promise which the plaintiff could have supported. In Smith v. Jones [1] the plaintiff declared that his father bequeathed him a legacy of £7, and made C. his executrix, and died, and that the defendant intermarried with C.; and that, in consideration

[1] Yelv. 184.

that assets of the plaintiff's father came into the hands of the defendant, and in consideration that the plaintiff would forbear[1] the £7 till All-Saints following, the defendant promised to pay it at that time; and then the plaintiff shewed that he had forborne, &c., till the day, yet the defendant had not paid him. The defendant pleaded that C., the executrix of the father, died intestate at such a place before the promise made: upon which the plaintiff demurred; and judgment was given against him: for, by the death of the executrix before the promise, it appeared that there was not any consideration sufficient to charge the defendant, who was not chargeable with the legacy after the death of his wife, the executrix. The report states further, that the declaration was also holden ill "because it did not shew precisely what person the plaintiff was to forbear to sue for the £7; for it could not be intended that he should forbear the defendant, who it appeared by law was not chargeable with it." So in Rosyer v. Langdale[2] the plaintiff declared against a *feme* administratrix that she, in consideration that he would forbear suit until she had taken out letters of administration, promised to pay him a certain sum owing to him by her intestate. And after verdict and judgment, error was brought; for that the plaintiff had set forth no consideration for the assumpsit; for till administration taken out by the defendant she was not liable to be sued, except there were a cause depending, which there was not. And this was holden to be a good exception. The subsequent case indeed of Hume v. Hinton[3] may seem to contradict that, where it was holden that a general forbearance of the debt was in effect a forbearance to sue all the world, and was sufficient to uphold an assumpsit, without shewing that any particular person was liable to pay; but that, it is to be observed, was after verdict, when it might be presumed that some person was shewn to be liable. And further, it is said to have been decided upon the authority of a case of Hill v. Bailey, overruling that of Smith v. Jones. But in Hill v. Bailey, which is reported in 1 Rol. Abr. 22,[4] there was an averment that the goods of the plaintiff's debtor came *legitimo modo* after his death to the defendant, who, in consideration that the plaintiff would forbear his debt, promised to pay it. There was therefore a good consideration for the promise to forbear generally. And in Reynolds v. Prosser,[5] Hardres, in argument, cites the same case of Hume v. Hinton (under the name of Hummers v. Hunton), as having been adjudged to be no consideration to sustain the promise. There is another case which may be cited for the plaintiff, of Quick v. Copleton,[6] where the defendant's late husband being

[1] *i. e.* forbear to sue the defendant for the £7, according to the report of the s. c. in Cro. Jac. 257.

[2] Sty. 248, and *vide* Hayward v. Ducket, *ib.* 405.

[3] Sty. 304.

[4] And *vide* 1 Danv. Abr. 50.

[5] Hardr. 73.

[6] 1 Lev. 161, 1 Sid. 242, and 1 Keb. 866.

indebted to the plaintiff, and the defendant about to come to London, and in fear of being arrested by the plaintiff, she promised to pay him, in consideration that he would not trouble her and would forbear till Michaelmas. And after verdict, it was moved in arrest of judgment, that, she not being shewn to be executrix or administratrix, her forbearance was not any consideration; which was agreed by the court: but they held that the subsequent words, "forbear till Michaelmas," were general, not only to forbear her but all others, and made a good consideration. But the opinion afterwards delivered by Hyde, C. J., very much shakes the authority of this case; for he says that a forbearance to sue one who fears to be sued is a good consideration; which certainly cannot be maintained: and he cited a case in C. B. when he sat there, where a woman, who feared that the dead body of her son would be arrested for debt, was holden liable upon a promise to pay in consideration of forbearance, though she was neither executrix nor administratrix. But of this the other judges are said to have doubted. [LORD ELLENBOROUGH, C. J. It is impossible to contend that this last forbearance could be a good consideration for an assumpsit; for to seize a dead body upon any such pretence would be *contra bonos mores*, and an extortion upon the relatives.] The weight, then, of the authorities is with the defendant, as the principle clearly is with him. For as where the forbearance is stated to be of the defendant himself, the plaintiff must shew that he was before liable to be sued; so when the forbearance is general, of all the world, it is equally reasonable that the plaintiff should shew some one person who was liable to him: for the forbearance of a groundless suit has been holden to be no consideration for an assumpsit, as in Tooley *v.* Windham [1] and Lloyd *v.* Lee.[2] Here the defendant is not shewn to be executrix or administratrix, or to have assets; and a promise even by an executor, as such, is a mere *nudum pactum* without assets at the time.[3]

Jervis, contra. The consideration of general forbearance, as here laid, is sufficient to maintain the assumpsit. To sustain a promise, the consideration must either be beneficial to the defendant or detrimental to the plaintiff. In Pillans *v.* Van Mierop,[4] Yates, J., says: "Any damage to another, or suspension or forbearance of his right, is a foundation for an undertaking and will make it binding, though no actual benefit accrue to the party undertaking." He adds, that there "the promise and undertaking of the defendants did occasion a possibility of loss to the plaintiffs." It is part of the definition that there must be a right in the plaintiff; which furnishes an answer to the cases of Tooley *v.* Windham and Lloyd *v.* Lee, where no such right appeared. Now here the plaintiff shews a debt due, and a right to recover, though not against any person named; but it is enough that he shews a possibility

[1] Cro. Eliz. 206.
[2] 1 Stra. 94.
[3] Rann *v.* Hughes, 7 Term Rep. 350, note (*a*).
[4] 3 Burr. 1673.

of loss by the forbearance. [LORD ELLENBOROUGH, C. J. It is not entitled to the name of forbearance unless you shew something or somebody to be forborne. If there be a right which can be enforced against anybody, no doubt that a promise to forbear is a good consideration; but if there be no person liable, how is it entitled to the name or quality of forbearance?] The cases shew that it is sufficient if there be a right in the plaintiff which is forborne, though not shewn to be capable of being enforced at the time against any particular person; as in Quick v. Copleton, where the consideration relied on by the court was not the fear of being sued, but the general forbearance, "to forbear till Michaelmas." And yet it was not averred there that either the defendant or any other person was executrix, &c., of the deceased debtor; and consequently no person appeared to be liable to the plaintiff at the time. So in the case of Hill v. Bailey, in 1 Rol. Abr. 22, the consideration relied on was not that the goods of the deceased debtor came to the defendant's hands *legitimo modo*, for then there was no occasion to lay any forbearance; but the judgment turned on the sufficiency of the general forbearance to sue, to sustain the assumpsit. [LAWRENCE, J. The promise to forbear goes further than the lawful possession of assets; for it makes the defendant liable to judgment *de bonis propriis*, and not merely as far as the assets go.] Then the case of Hume v. Hinton is in point (which is merely misquoted by Hardres [1] in argument); and that was subsequent to Smith v. Jones,[2] which, it appears from all the reports of it taken together, was a promise not for forbearance generally but to forbear the defendant, which reconciles the authorities; and the same answer will apply to Rosyer v. Langdale,[3] which was a promise in consideration that the plaintiff would forbear suit until the defendant had taken out administration; which was taken to mean a forbearance to sue the defendant. But where a person is sued as executor, which was the case in Rann v. Hughes,[4] his liability on a promise to pay can only be coëxtensive with his original liability in respect of assets.

Marryat, in reply, was stopped by the court.

LORD ELLENBOROUGH, C. J. The way in which I am disposed to consider this case will break in upon no recognized rule of law, nor on the plain sense of what was laid down by Mr. Justice Yates in the case of Pillans v. Van Mierop. It is a known rule of law, that to make a promise obligatory there must be some benefit to the party making it, or some detriment to the party to whom it is made; otherwise it is considered as *nudum pactum* and cannot be enforced. I do not say that the opinion which I have formed will not break in on any of the cases which have been cited, but it entrenches on no general rule; and in order to shew that, I will examine the rule referred to as laid down

1 Hardr. 73.
2 Yelv. 184, Cro. Jac. 257, Owen, 133.
3 Sty. 248.
4 7 Term Rep. 350, note.

by Mr. Justice Yates, and see how it applies to the present case. He says that "any damage to another, or suspension or forbearance of his right, is a foundation for an undertaking," &c. Now how does the plaintiff shew any damage to himself by forbearing to sue, when there was no fund which could be the object of suit; where it does not appear that any person *in rerum natura* was liable to be sued by him? No right can exist in this vague, abstract, and indefinite way. Right is a correlative term: there must be some object of right, some object of suit, some party who, in respect of some fund or some character known in the law, is liable; otherwise there cannot be said to be any right. Has there been then any suspension of the plaintiff's right? Now unless a right is capable of being exercised, unless it can be put in force, there can be no suspension of it. And that it could have been exercised or put in force but for the promise made by the defendant, is not shewn. Then what forbearance is shewn? It must be a forbearance of a right which may be enforced with effect. It is true that a promise may be binding though there may be no actual benefit resulting to the party making it, because it is enough if the plaintiff may be damaged by it; but it does not appear here that the forbearance could produce any detriment to the plaintiff. It does not therefore appear that Mr. Justice Yates laid down any doctrine which does not square with the general received rule of law, that to sustain a promise there must be a benefit on the one hand or a detriment on the other. But here, whether there were any representative or any funds of the original debtor does not appear. Then, as to the cases cited, that of Rosyer *v.* Langdale is strong to the purpose; for it was there decided that a promise, in consideration that the plaintiff would forbear suit until the defendant had taken out letters of administration, was without foundation, because it did not appear that the party was liable before administration taken out. And this was rightly determined; for forbearance of an unfounded suit is no forbearance. But this case is attempted to be met by that of Hume *v.* Hinton in the same book, where a promise by the mother of an intestate indebted to the plaintiff, that if he would stay for the money till a given day she would pay it, was sustained. That, however, was after verdict; and that is material to be attended to, because it might be presumed to have been proved that the defendant had so intermeddled with the intestate's effects as to make herself liable as executrix *de son tort*, and had funds of the deceased in her hands for which, but for the promise made, she might have been sued in that character. But no such intendment can be made here. The case of Quick *v.* Copleton is also relied on. That too was after verdict; and it was moved in arrest of judgment for want of consideration. I think that even after verdict that declaration would be bad, being vicious on the face of it. It is stated that the defendant's late husband was indebted to the plaintiff, and that she (not stating her to be clothed with any representative character), about to come to London, and being in fear to be arrested by the plaintiff, promised, &c. Now an attempt to impose upon a person an unlawful terror (and the threatening of an unlawful suit is as bad) can never be a good consideration for a promise to pay; yet that ground is insisted on by the Chief Justice. And as to the case there cited by him, of a mother who promised to pay on forbearance of the plaintiff to arrest the dead body of her son, which she feared he was about to do, it is contrary to every principle of law and moral feeling. Such an act is revolting to humanity, and illegal; and therefore any promise extorted by the fear of it could never be valid in law. It might as well be said that a promise, in consideration that one would withdraw a pistol from another's breast, could be enforced against the party acting under such unlawful terror. Here, there being no consideration of benefit to the defendant, or of detriment or possibility of detriment to the plaintiff, shewn by him on the face of the declaration, and this coming on upon demurrer, where nothing can be intended as it may after verdict, I am clearly of opinion that the declaration is bad.

GROSE, J. It must be admitted that, if a consideration for the promise do not sufficiently appear upon the face of the declaration, it cannot be supported. There is a great difference between questions of this sort, arising upon demurrer to the declaration, and in arrest of judgment after verdict; in which latter case every thing is to be intended which can be in favor of the verdict: but not so on demurrer. It is however said that a detriment to the plaintiff will support an assumpsit as well as a benefit to the defendant, and that here the plaintiff alleges a forbearance. But it is a perversion of terms to call that a forbearance to sue, if there were no person who was capable of being sued; and here none is shewn. There can be no forbearance in such a case; and therefore there is an end of the consideration. This is too plain to require any thing further to be said upon it, and makes it unnecessary, after what my Lord has said, to enter into the consideration of the cases.

LAWRENCE, J. This question arises upon a special demurrer, which points out an objection to the declaration, that no person is stated who was liable to be sued at the time of the promise made, in respect to whom the plaintiff can be said to have forborne suit. And on this ground the case is distinguishable from those relied on by the plaintiff's counsel, which were after verdict; and in support of which it might be said that when the jury found that the plaintiff did forbear to sue, they must be presumed to have found, upon proof laid before them, that there was somebody who could have been sued. But no such intendment can be made upon demurrer. The argument proceeds upon a fallacy, in supposing that some person must exist liable to the plaintiff's suit, to forbear whom must consequently be a disadvantage to him, and a consideration for the defendant's promise. But that is not so. The deceased might leave no assets, and there might be no administration to him taken out: there would then be no person to sue. So he might be a bastard, and have no legal representatives entitled to take out administration of his effects, in which case the crown would be entitled to them; and still there would be nobody to be sued. It is not therefore true that there must be somebody liable to whom a forbearance to sue may refer. And I agree with the argument of the defendant's counsel that, if it be no consideration for the promise to forbear to sue the defendant, without shewing that the defendant was before liable to have been sued, it can be no consideration for a promise to forbear to sue all the world generally, without shewing that some person or other was liable to be sued: for without that, the plaintiff does not shew any detriment arising to him from the forbearance of his suit. The principle is admitted that the plaintiff must shew some benefit to the defendant or some detriment to himself. And I understand Mr. Justice Yates, in illustrating that principle in the passage cited, to say that where it appears on the face of the declaration that there is somebody whom the plaintiff may sue, it is not necessary to shew that he would be benefited by suing him; it is sufficient that there is some person whom he might sue, and from whom he might obtain satisfaction.

Le Blanc, J. The definition by Mr. Justice Yates of a consideration sufficient to maintain a promise is, that it be either of some benefit to the defendant or some detriment to the plaintiff. It is sufficient if it be a detriment to the plaintiff, though no actual benefit accrue to the party undertaking. So far only the definition goes. Afterwards indeed, in commenting on that definition, he says that the promise of the defendant did occasion a possibility of loss to the plaintiffs. They might, he says, have been thereby prevented from resorting to the original debtor, or getting further security from him. But all this latter part is only a comment on the definition, and shewing how the case then in judgment applied to it. But I do not take it to be any part of the definition itself intended to be laid down by him, that if any person stated that he had forborne suing on a cause of action which might (or might not) by possibility occasion a loss to him, that was a sufficient ground for an undertaking by another to pay him. Now here the plaintiff endeavors to make out a detriment to himself by shewing that one deceased was indebted to him; and that, in consideration that he would forbear and give day of payment, the defendant promised, &c. But it does not follow of course from thence that any detriment arose to the plaintiff from his forbearance, if it do not appear that there was any person whom he could have sued. And the general current of authorities shews that it is not sufficient to state a consideration to forbear generally, unless it be also shewn that there was some person to be forborne. Now here the declaration does not state that there was any representative of the debtor, or that any person had taken out administration to him, or that any person was going to administer to the effects and to satisfy the plaintiff's debt, but was prevented from so doing by the undertaking of the defendant. There therefore appears to be a want of consideration to sustain the promise. *Judgment for the defendant.*

PAYNE *v.* WILSON, ONE, &c.

IN THE KING'S BENCH, NOVEMBER 15, 1827.

[*Reported in 7 Barnewall and Cresswell*, 423.]

ASSUMPSIT. The declaration stated that, at the time of making the promise of the defendant thereinafter mentioned, one C. Vaux was indebted to the plaintiff in £103 8*s*., for the recovery of which the plaintiff had commenced an action against C. Vaux in K. B., and in which action C. Vaux had signed a *cognovit* for the payment of the said debt of £103 8*s*., together with the costs of the said action, at certain times therein mentioned, to wit, at, &c.; that before the making of the promise of the defendant, C. Vaux having made default in payment of the whole of the sum of £103 8*s*. at the time specified in the *cognovit*, he the plaintiff was about to take proceedings on the *cognovit;* and thereupon, to wit, on, &c., at, &c., in consideration that the plaintiff, at the request of the defendant, would consent to suspend proceedings against C. Vaux on the *cognovit* so signed by him, he the defendant undertook and promised the plaintiff to pay to him the plaintiff £30 on account of the said debt on the 1st of April then next, and a further sum at a subsequent day. Averment, that the plaintiff did suspend all further proceedings against the said C. Vaux on the *cognovit*, of which the defendant had notice. Breach, non-payment of the £30. Plea, the general issue. At the trial before Lord Tenterden, C. J., at the Middlesex sittings after Hilary Term, 1827, the plaintiff produced in evidence the following paper, signed by the defendant: "Mr. R. Payne having, at my instance and request, consented to suspend proceedings against the above-named defendant on the *cognovit* signed by him in this cause, and given for payment of the debt this day, I do hereby, in consideration thereof, personally undertake and promise to pay to the plaintiff the sum of £30 on account of the said debt, on the first day of April now next; and the urther sum of £53 3*s*. within four months next ensuing the first day of

April." It was objected, on the part of the defendant, that there was a variance between the contract proved and that alleged in the declaration; the consideration for the promise stated in the declaration being executory, whereas the consideration proved had been executed. Lord Tenterden, C. J., directed the jury to find a verdict for the plaintiff, but reserved liberty to the defendant to move to enter a nonsuit. Campbell, in Easter Term, obtained a rule *nisi*, first, for entering a nonsuit on the objection taken at the trial; and, secondly, for arresting the judgment, on the ground that no sufficient consideration for the promise was stated in the declaration, it not being alleged that the plaintiff had consented to forbear to sue for any definite time; and also that it was not properly averred that the consideration was performed.

The *Attorney-General* and *Wightman* now shewed cause. There was sufficient proof of the executory consideration stated in the declaration. The proof was that, in consideration of the plaintiff's having, at the request of the defendant, consented to suspend proceedings against Vaux, the defendant promised. Now that implies that the defendant's request to suspend the proceedings preceded the consent given by the plaintiff, and therefore this was evidence of a promise made by the defendant in consideration that the plaintiff would suspend proceedings.

Campbell, contra. The consideration proved in this case was executed, the consideration alleged was executory. There is a material distinction between considerations executory and executed. Executory considerations are traversable, and performance must be averred with time and place. It depends on the performance of the consideration, whether the promise be binding. If the consideration be executed, the promise is immediately binding; there is no condition or qualification. Here the consideration alleged in the declaration was executory, and it would depend upon the plaintiff's consent to suspend the proceedings, whether the defendant's promise were binding. In the contract proved, the consideration was executed. No subsequent consent of the plaintiff was necessary to make the defendant liable. But no sufficient consideration appears in the contract itself, nor is alleged in the declaration; for a forbearance to sue is a good consideration for a promise, only where it is absolute, Mapes *v.* Sidney;[1] or for a definite portion of time, Fisher *v.* Richardson;[2] or a reasonable time, Johnson *v.* Whitchcott:[3] forbearance for a little[4] or

[1] Cro. Jac. 683. [2] Cro. Jac. 47. [3] 1 Rol. Abr. 24, pl. 33.

[4] 1 Rol. Abr. 23, pl. 25. ["If A. be indebted to B. in £20, and B. says to A. that he will sue him for the debt, whereupon A. says to him that, if he will forbear him *per paululum tempus*, he will pay him, this is not a good consideration for an assumpsit, because he could sue him immediately." — ED.]

some time[1] is not sufficient. And even supposing this could be considered as a contract to suspend proceedings for some definite period, it is not alleged that the plaintiff did suspend his proceedings absolutely, or for any definite period of time.

LORD TENTERDEN, C. J. I think that the contract stated in the declaration was sufficiently proved by the paper produced in evidence; for it must be implied, from the contents of the paper, that the defendant's promise was made in consideration that the plaintiff would suspend his proceedings against Vaux. It states that the plaintiff had consented to do so at the request of the defendant. That request therefore must have preceded and induced the consent given to suspend the proceedings. Then, as to the objections in arrest of judgment, it is said that it does not appear that the plaintiff consented to suspend the proceedings for any definite time. The promise made by the defendant was to pay £30 on the 1st of April, in consideration of the plaintiff's consenting to suspend proceedings. That imports that the proceedings were at all events to be suspended until that period; and I think that the averment that the plaintiff did suspend the proceedings is sufficient after verdict, because it must be taken that it was proved at the trial that the plaintiff had suspended the proceedings, either for a time required by law, or for a definite or reasonable time.

BAYLEY, J. I think there was no variance in this case. The declaration states that, in consideration that the plaintiff would consent to suspend the proceedings, the defendant promised. Now I think that the fair meaning of that is, "in consideration that he would suspend proceedings, the defendant promised;" and I think that is proved by the paper produced in evidence. I think also that it must be taken, after verdict, that the agreement was to suspend until the 1st of April, and also that the allegation that he did suspend is sufficient.

LITTLEDALE, J. I am of the same opinion. There is a clear distinction between considerations executed and executory. In Com. Dig., tit. Action on the Case upon Assumspit (B. 12), it is laid down that "an assumpsit lies, though the consideration be executed in part, as in consideration that he had done a thing at my request;" and afterwards it is laid down, "so if the consideration is continuing though the act be executed, as in consideration that the lessee now in possession had paid his rent very well, to save him harmless; for prompt payment of the rent is a continuing consideration when he remains in possession." In the present case, there was a continuing consideration, for the plaintiff not only had consented to suspend the proceedings, but that they should be suspended until the 1st of April (until the instalments

[1] 1 Rol. Abr. 23, pl. 26. ["If A. promise B., in consideration that he will forbear to sue him for a certain debt *pro aliquo tempore*, that he will pay him, and it is averred that he forbore him for a year, this is not a good consideration, for *aliquod tempus* is at least as little as *paululum tempus*." — ED.]

became due). Therefore, this might be alleged in pleading either as an executed or executory consideration; and it was therefore properly described in the declaration. As to the objection in arrest of judgment, I think it must be taken, after verdict, that the defendant did suspend his proceedings absolutely, or for a reasonable time.

Rule discharged.

SMITH *v.* ALGAR.

IN THE KING'S BENCH, NOVEMBER 26, 1830.

[*Reported in* 1 *Barnewall and Adolphus,* 603.]

ASSUMPSIT. The first count stated that the plaintiff had obtained judgment against one Elizabeth Mackenzie for a debt of £57, and 65*s.* costs, and for satisfaction thereof had sued out a writ of *fieri facias* to levy the said debt and costs of the goods of the said E. M.; that the plaintiff was about to enforce the execution of the said writ, and to levy to the amount of £107 upon goods of E. M. of the value of £200, which the defendant had in his custody; and that afterwards, in consideration of the premises, and that the plaintiff, at the defendant's instance, would forego executing the writ against the said goods for the recovery of the said sum of £107, defendant undertook to pay plaintiff the last-mentioned sum in seven days then next following; that plaintiff forbore accordingly, but defendant did not pay. The second count stated the consideration to be, that the plaintiff would forbear executing a writ of *fieri facias* issued against the goods of E. M., not saying at whose suit or for what sum. The defendant demurred specially to each count; and there was a joinder in demurrer.

Platt, in support of the demurrer, confined his argument to the first count; the court holding the second to be clearly bad. No legal consideration is shewn for the promise. The judgment was for £57 debt, and 65*s.* costs; it does not appear, therefore, that the plaintiff could have any right to levy £107. Forbearance is no consideration where there was originally no cause of action. Lloyd *v.* Lee.[1] If a party is illegally arrested, his release is no consideration for a promise to pay the debt. Atkinson *v.* Settree.[2] To prove a forbearance, it is necessary to shew a right in one party which could have been exercised with effect against the other. Jones *v.* Ashburnham.[3] The undertaking here alleged is to pay £107; it was necessary to shew a consideration

[1] Stra. 94. [2] Willes, 482. [3] 4 East, 455.

equally extensive with the promise; but the forbearing to levy £107 was not a valid consideration, inasmuch as the judgment stated would not have warranted a levy to that amount.

Kelly, contra, was stopped by the court.

LORD TENTERDEN, C. J. I agree in the principles laid down in the cases which have been cited, but they do not appear to me to be applicable. It is true the plaintiff might not perhaps have been entitled to recover to the full extent of £107, though, it is to be observed, he might have levied the costs of the execution in addition to the sum given by the judgment. But he had a right at least to levy £60; and if, in consideration of his forbearing that, the defendant promised to pay him the larger sum,—if the inconvenience of an execution against these goods at the time in question was so great that the defendant thought proper to buy it off at such an expense,—I do not see that the consideration is insufficient for the promise.

PARKE, J. If a plaintiff has a *fieri facias* indorsed to levy £60, there is no reason why the forbearing to execute such writ should not be a good consideration for a promise by a third person to pay double the amount at the end of seven days. What damages the plaintiff may recover in an action on such a promise is another question.

TAUNTON and PATTESON, JJ., concurred.

Judgment for the plaintiff on the first count.

MORTON v. BURN AND VAUX.

IN THE KING'S BENCH, MAY 25, 1837.

[*Reported in 7 Adolphus and Ellis*, 19.]

ASSUMPSIT. The first count of the declaration stated that, whereas before and at the time of making the promise, &c., to wit, 12th April, 1834, the defendants were indebted to the plaintiff in £728 2*s.* 6*d.*, and interest thereon from 1st February, 1834, under and by virtue of a bond dated 14th July, 1832, and a certain indenture and deed of assignment thereof, dated 19th October, 1833; and that, according to the condition of the said bond, £228 2*s.* 6*d.*, part of the said sum of £728 2*s.* 6*d.*, ought to have been paid on the 1st February then last past; and thereupon, in consideration of the premises, and also in consideration that plaintiff would accept and receive payment of the said sums of money on the days and times after-mentioned, and in the mean time give time to defendants for payment, the defendants undertook, &c., that the whole of the said £228 2*s.* 6*d.*, with interest from

1st February, 1834, should be paid to plaintiff on or before 1st June then next, or in default thereof that defendants would sign a warrant of attorney to plaintiff to enter up judgment against them forthwith for the same; and that defendants would pay to plaintiff £50 quarterly, on 1st September, &c., in every year, until the further sum of £500 (residue of the said £728 2*s.* 6*d.*) with interest at £5 per cent. per annum, should be fully paid and satisfied; and in default of paying any of the last-mentioned instalments, defendants would execute a warrant of attorney to plaintiff forthwith to enter up judgment against them for the whole £500 and interest, or so much thereof as might then remain due. Averment, that plaintiff did forbear and give time to defendants for the payment of the said £728 2*s.* 6*d.* and interest, until and upon the respective days and times mentioned for payment thereof in the said promise and undertaking of the defendants; and although defendants paid plaintiff the said £228 2*s.* 6*d.* and interest thereon, yet they did not nor would pay plaintiff £50 quarterly, on the days and times abovementioned in that behalf, but therein wholly made default; and a large sum of money of the said instalments, viz., £250, for five several sums of £50, respectively due on 1st September, 1835, &c., now is wholly due and in arrear, &c.; and although defendants made default in payment of the respective sums on the days and times aforesaid, according to the tenor and effect, &c., of their said promise and undertaking, yet defendants did not nor would execute a warrant of attorney to enable plaintiff forthwith to enter up judgment against them for so much of the £500 and interest as then remained due, &c. There was a second count on an account stated, and for interest.

Pleas: 1. *Non assumpsit.* 2. To the first count, that there was not any good or valuable consideration for the promises in the first count mentioned; conclusion to the country. Issues on both pleas.

On the trial before Coleridge, J., at the Middlesex sittings after Michaelmas Term, 1836, a verdict was found for the plaintiff. In Hilary Term last, F. Edwards obtained a rule *nisi* for arresting the judgment.

Cresswell and *W. H. Watson* now shewed cause. It is objected that the action should have been shaped in debt on the bond, not in assumpsit; and that the declaration shews no consideration for the promise. In Com. Dig., Action upon the Case upon Assumpsit (B. 1), it is laid down that assumpsit may be supported upon "consideration of the forbearance of a suit against an heir upon a bond of his ancestor, if he was bound and had assets." Now there the obligee might have sued the heir on the bond. And again, "so, in consideration of forbearance by the assignee of a bond, if he has a letter of attorney to sue and release;" for which Pitt *v.* Bridgwater is cited from Rolle's Abridgment.[1] In Mowse *v.* Edney[2] it was held that, if A. be indebted

[1] 1 Rol. Abr. 20, *Action sur Case* (V.), pl. 11.

[2] 1 Rol. Abr. 20, *Action sur Case* (V.), pl. 12; 1 Vin. Abr. 304, Actions [of Assumpsit] (U.), pl. 12.

to B. by bill, and B. be indebted to C., and B., in satisfaction of his debt, assign A.'s bill to C., and before the day of payment A. promise C. that, if he will forbear payment for a week, he will then pay him, and C. do forbear accordingly, still there is no consideration for the promise; because, notwithstanding the assignment of the bill, yet the property of the debt remained always in the assignor. In that case it does not appear that the week would expire before the day of payment arrived; and if not, there would be no advantage to the defendant or detriment to the plaintiff. Without some explanation of this kind, the case is inconsistent with the authorities. In Potter *v.* Turnor[1] the defendant had given a bond for £30 to J. B., who had given a bond for £50 to the plaintiff; and J. B. assigned to the plaintiff the debt due from the defendant, and gave the plaintiff a letter of attorney to receive the money to his own use, with a power to sue for it, or release: the plaintiff demanded the £30 of the defendant, who promised him that, if the plaintiff would forbear and give him respite till Sturbridge fair, he would then pay him: and on motion in arrest of judgment, it was held that this was not a good consideration. This case is certainly against the plaintiff; but it is contradicted by all the other authorities, as is said in note (1) to Forth *v.* Stanton,[2] where the cases are collected; Reynolds *v.* Prosser;[3] Oble *v.* Dittlesfield;[4] Willmot *v.* Prigget;[5] Russel *v.* Haddock.[6] In the last case, and in Reynolds *v.* Prosser,[3] the debt forborne was on a judgment, which, being a higher security than a bond, seems more open to the objection against the form of action. It is sufficient consideration if there be either a benefit to the defendant or a detriment to the plaintiff. Here there are both. The assignee might here sue in the name of the obligee, and this court would not allow the obligee to release the action. The contract sued on is to pay the money or do a collateral act: no one but the plaintiff can take advantage of such a contract. Here too the declaration avers that the defendant was actually indebted to the plaintiff: after verdict it may be assumed that the defendant was a party to the indenture of assignment, and covenanted to pay the plaintiff; then it comes to the simple case of forbearance by a covenantee.

F. Edwards, contra. A detriment to the plaintiff or a benefit to the defendant is a good consideration: but here the agreement to forbear was not binding on the plaintiff; he therefore gave up nothing, and the defendant gained nothing. After the assignment the plaintiff might have sued in equity in his own name, or at law in the name of the obligee. And again the plaintiff's right is not strengthened by the parol agreement: the defendant was not less liable to these suits before the agreement than after; therefore he merely promised what he was

[1] Palm. 185; s. c. Winch. 7.
[2] 1 Wms. Saund. 210.
[3] Hard. 71.
[4] 1 Ventr. 153.
[5] 1 Rol. Abr. 29, *Action sur Case* (V.), pl. 60.
[6] 1 Lev. 188.

before liable to do, which was no consideration for a promise on the part of the plaintiff. Harris v. Watson.[1] Now, if the plaintiff was not bound to perform his part of the agreement, the defendant could not be liable. [PATTESON, J. That proposition seems too broad. Suppose I say, If you will furnish goods to a third person, I will guarantee the payment: there you are not bound to furnish them; yet, if you do furnish them in pursuance of the contract, you may sue me on my guaranty.] Here the contract could only be supported by a consideration perfect and definite at the time of the contract, and such that the party from whom it moved was at the time made incapable of retracting. This is the only principle upon which the mutual promises can constitute a consideration; and it is confirmed by East London Water Works Company v. Bailey,[2] Mowse v. Edney,[3] and Potter v. Turnor.[4] Fenner v. Meares[5] may be considered an authority the other way; but that case cannot be relied upon after Lord Kenyon's remarks in Johnson v. Collings,[6] and those of Lord Ellenborough in Williams v. Everett.[7] Further, the forbearance is no consideration, unless there was a good cause of action at the time of the contract. Now there was no legal cause of action between these parties. And if the plaintiff rely upon his right to sue in equity, he lets in every equitable answer to the claim, as for instance a set-off against the original obligee. But it is clear that no such set-off would be allowed in this action; the forbearance of the equitable suit can therefore be no consideration here. [PATTESON, J. You must contend that the defendant could have a set-off if the plaintiff proceeded in equity on the new agreement alone. For, if the proceeding were on the bond itself, the defendant would have a set-off at law as much as in equity.] Further, this is an attempt to vary an instrument under seal by a parol agreement. The obligation of the bond itself could not be directly released by parol; neither therefore can this be effected indirectly, either wholly or in part. Anonymous Case in Cowper.[8] It might be otherwise, if the contract sued on were to do something distinct from the obligation in the bond, as in White v. Parkin.[9] Again, if this were a good contract, the defendant would be liable to two actions on the same instrument; for there is nothing to prevent the original obligee, or an assignee of the present plaintiff, from suing the defendant on the bond at any time. [LITTLEDALE, J. That would be an action for a different cause from this: that would be on the bond; this is on the parol contract.] The case of forbearance toward the heir of an obligee

1 Peake, N. P. C. 72. See Lord Ellenborough's remarks on this case in Stilk v. Myrick, 6 Esp. 129; s. c. 2 Campb. 317.

2 4 Bing. 283.

3 1 Rol. Abr. 20, *Action sur Case* (V.), pl. 12.

4 Palm. 185; s. c. Winch. 7.

5 2 W. Bl. 1269.

6 1 East, 104.

7 14 East, 582. See p. 587, note (*a*).

8 1 Cowp. 128, 129.

9 12 East, 578.

has been relied on; but an heir is to pay only if he has assets by descent. That raises a question to be determined by parol evidence. And as the heir's liability is conditional, not absolute like that of the obligee, he may be supposed to promise to pay when he has assets, which creates a liability different from that of the party to the original bond.

Cur. adv. vult.

LORD DENMAN, C. J., in this term (June 12th) delivered the judgment of the court.

This is a motion in arrest of judgment. The question is, whether forbearance for a given time on the part of the assignee of a bond to sue the obligors is a good consideration for a promise by the obligors to pay the assignee at the expiration of that time, or give him a warrant of attorney for the amount.

It was objected that there is no mutuality in the agreement; for that, if the plaintiff had sued the defendants in the obligee's name, the promise to forbear would be no answer. Again, that this is a mere *nudum pactum*, being only a promise to do that which the defendants were already bound to do by their bond. And further, that, if this promise be binding, it amounts to varying a deed by parol contract, which is contrary to the rule of law. We do not think any of these objections sufficient to arrest the judgment.

As to the first, there is sufficient mutuality; for although the agreement to forbear would not be pleadable to an action in the name of the obligee, yet, unless the plaintiff did forbear according to his agreement, he would not be able to sue on the defendant's promise. He is obliged to aver, as he does in the present declaration, that he has forborne, which is a condition precedent to his suing.

As to the second objection, this is not a mere *nudum pactum*, for the defendants promise to pay the plaintiff, a third person, whom they were not bound to pay by their bond; and they promise, in consideration of a detriment sustained by the plaintiff at their request, namely, a forbearance to enforce his right in the name of the obligee.

As to the third objection, the bond is in no respect varied by this agreement. The new contract entered into by the defendants with the plaintiff leaves the bond just as it was before: it was forfeited before the agreement, and so it remains; and the agreement would be no answer to an action on it.

The cases on this subject are collected in Mr. Serjt. Williams's notes to Forth v. Stanton,[1] and to Barber v. Fox,[2] to which may be added Yard v. Eland,[3] and other cases collected in Comyns's Digest, Action on the Case upon Assumpsit (B), Consideration. They are all in favor of the action lying, with the exception of Potter v. Turnor,[4] which we

[1] 1 Wms. Saund. 210, note (1).
[2] 2 Wms. Saund. 137, note (2).
[3] 1 Lord Raym. 368.
[4] Palm. 185; s. c. Winch. 7.

think inconsistent not only with the current of authorities, but with established principles.

For these reasons we are of opinion that the rule to arrest the judgment in this case must be discharged. *Rule discharged.*

WADE *v.* SIMEON.

IN THE COMMON PLEAS, JANUARY 21, 1846.

[*Reported in 2 Common Bench Reports,* 548.]

ASSUMPSIT. The first count of the declaration stated that the plaintiff had commenced an action against the defendant in the Court of Exchequer for the recovery of the two sums of £1300 and £700, with interest; that he had declared therein, the defendant had pleaded divers pleas to his declaration, and divers issues had been joined in said action; that the plaintiff had given notice of trial in said action and entered the *nisi prius* record therein, and said trial was appointed to take place on the 7th of December, 1844; that the plaintiff had incurred costs and charges in said action to the amount of, to wit, £300; that on the 3d of said December the defendant had notified the plaintiff that he should apply to the Court of Chancery for an injunction to restrain the plaintiff from issuing execution on any judgment which he might obtain in said action; that thereupon, on the 6th of said December, in consideration that the plaintiff would forbear prosecuting and would stay all proceedings in said action until the 14th of said December inclusive, except as thereinafter stated, the defendant promised the plaintiff to pay him said sums and interest on said 14th of December, together with said costs and charges to be taxed; in default whereof the plaintiff should be at liberty to sign judgment in said action, and that a judge's order might be obtained in said action to secure such payment, and that said application to the Court of Chancery should be abandoned. Averment, that the plaintiff, confiding in said promise, withdrew the said record, and forbore prosecuting and stayed all proceedings in the said action until the said 14th of December, and since then continually hitherto, excepting the taxing of said costs and charges, and the obtaining of said order; that on the 11th of said December the said costs and charges were duly taxed at £81 1*s.* 10*d.*, whereof the defendant then had notice; and that although the said 14th of December had elapsed before the commencement of this suit, yet the defendant, though often requested, had not as yet paid the plaintiff the said sums of £1300 and £700 with interest, and the said costs and charges so taxed as aforesaid, or either of them, or any part thereof, and the same remained wholly due and unpaid; that from and after the said 14th of December, and thenceforward, the defendant had wholly hindered and prevented the plaintiff from signing judgment in the said action; that on the 27th of January, 1845, the defendant obtained a rule and order of said Court of Exchequer for setting aside a certain order made by Alderson, B., on said 6th of December, pursuant to said promise; and that by means of the premises the plaintiff had been delayed in and hindered and prevented from recovering the said sums and moneys so promised by the defendant to be paid as aforesaid.[1]

There was also a count upon an account stated.

Fourth plea, to the first count: That the plaintiff never had any cause of action against the defendant in respect of the subject-matter of the action in the Court of Exchequer in that count mentioned; which he the plaintiff, at the time of the commencement of the action, and thence until and at the time of the making of the promise in the said first count mentioned, well knew. Verification.[2] . . .

Special demurrer to the fourth plea, assigning for causes, that it does not confess and avoid, or traverse, or deny, any of the matters in the first count alleged; that the matter pleaded affords no defence to the cause of action in that count mentioned; that the plea sets up as a defence immaterial matter; that the plea does not allege or shew that the defendant, before or at the time of the making of the promise, was not aware that the plaintiff had no cause for the said action, nor does it allege or shew that the plaintiff concealed any thing from the defendant; that it is ambiguous and uncertain what is meant by the allegation in the plea that the plaintiff never had any cause of action against the defendant in respect of the subject-matter of the said action; that the plea does not exclude all other consideration for the promise in the said count mentioned; that it is ambiguous and uncertain from the plea what is the real defence the defendant intends setting up thereby; and that the plea should have concluded to the country. . . .

The defendant joined in demurrer.

Channell, Serjt., in support of the demurrer. The promise alleged in the declaration consists of four parts: first, that the defendant would pay to the plaintiff £1300 and £700, with interest and costs, on the 14th of December, 1844; secondly, that in the event of his not paying the same he would suffer judgment; thirdly, that a judge's order should be obtained by consent; fourthly, that the motion in chancery, of which notice had been given, should be abandoned. The breach assigned in the first count is the non-payment of the money and costs on the day

[1] See *supra*, p. 221, note 1. — ED.

[2] The original report contains a seventh plea to both counts, and a special demurrer thereto; but as they do not relate at all to the question of consideration, they are here omitted, as well as the arguments and decision upon them. — ED.

appointed. To this the fourth plea affords no answer. In Longridge *v.* Dorville[1] it was held that the giving up of a suit instituted to try a question respecting which the law was doubtful was a good consideration for a promise to pay a stipulated sum.[2] . . . [TINDAL, C. J. That was the case of a relinquishment of a doubtful claim. The present case is more like that put in 1 Rol. Abr. fo. 26, pl. 39: "Si A. fait un void assumpsit à B., et puis un estranger vient al B., et en consideration que B. relinquera l'assumpsit fait à luy per A., il assume à paier à luy £10, ceo n'est bon consideracion à luy charger, pur ceo que le primer assumpsit fuit void."[3]] The plea does not allege that the defendant knew [*sic*] at the time he made the promise that the plaintiff had no cause of action; and there is no allegation of fraud. [TINDAL, C. J. It states that there never was any cause of action, and that the plaintiff knew it.] At all events the defendant was relieved from the threatened proceedings in chancery. The plea does not in distinct terms negative any other consideration for the promise. It is in effect an informal plea of *non assumpsit.* [TINDAL, C. J. That is not pointed out as a ground of demurrer.] . . .

Kinglake, Serjt. (with whom was *Barstow*), contra. The fourth plea is good. Under no circumstances can the forbearance to pursue an unfounded claim be a good consideration to support an assumpsit. In Com. Dig., Action upon the Case upon Assumpsit (B. 1), it is said: "The consideration upon which an assumpsit shall be founded must be for the benefit of the defendant, or to the trouble or prejudice of the plaintiff. And therefore a promise in consideration of the forbearance of a suit is good; for that is for the benefit of the defendant, though the action is not discharged; for forbearance for a reasonable time is sufficient."[4] But "a promise in consideration of forbearance is not good, where there was originally no cause of action; as if a note is given by a *feme covert.*"[5] In Atkinson *v.* Settree[6] it was held that, if A. be illegally arrested by B. for a debt, a promise by C. to pay the debt claimed by B., in consideration of B.'s releasing A. out of custody, is void.[7] . . . Longridge *v.* Dorville was the case of a forbearance of a doubtful claim:[8] The defendants obtained the release of their ship, and the plaintiffs relinquished a security the law gave them: there was

[1] 5 B. & Ald. 117. [2] The learned counsel here stated the case. — ED.

[3] Mich. 14 Jac., en brief d'error al Serjeants Inn enter Barnard & Simons, mise per Altham et agree per curiam (translated, 1 Vin. Abr. 312, pl. 39).

[4] Semb. per Hob. 216; Cro. Eliz. 387.

[5] Lloyd *v.* Lee, 1 Str. 94. This, being inserted by a subsequent editor, is not citable as having the sanction of Comyns.

[6] Willes, 482.

[7] The learned counsel here stated the case of Jones *v.* Ashburnham, 4 East, 455. — ED.

[8] There, the matter in dispute was about to be decided in a tribunal governed by the civil law, with which the judges, *a fortiori* the lay parties to the compromise, might be presumed to be unacquainted.

therefore abundant consideration for the promise. [MAULE, J. That decision is hardly consistent with some of the cases, wherein it has been laid down that no law is doubtful. Jones v. Randall[1] is the earliest case in which a question of law is admitted to be of doubtful issue.] In Edwards v. Baugh[2] the declaration alleged that disputes and controversies were pending between the plaintiff and defendant respecting a sum of money, and that the defendant promised, in consideration of the plaintiff's forbearing to sue, to pay him £100; and it was held bad, for want of averment that any debt was originally due from the defendant to the plaintiff. So in Herring v. Dorell,[3] a plaintiff having discharged one of two joint debtors, a promise by a third person to pay the debt, in order to obtain the discharge of the other from custody, was held to be void for want of consideration. Forbearance of an unfounded suit is in law no forbearance at all. To avoid the difficulty suggested in Smith v. Monteith,[4] this plea distinctly alleges that there never was any cause of action in the former suit, and that the plaintiff knew it. . . .

Channell, Serjt., in reply. In nearly all the cases cited the alleged consideration was forbearing to sue, no action having been commenced; here the consideration is forbearing further to proceed with a suit already instituted. This distinction is recognized by Lord Abinger, C. B., in Edwards v. Baugh, where he says: "A man may threaten to bring an action against any stranger he may happen to meet in the street. Where an action is depending, the forbearing to prosecute it is a sufficient consideration for a promise to pay a certain sum of money; for besides other advantages, the party promising would save the extra costs, which he would have to pay even if he were successful."[5] . . . Here, the plea does not allege that the defendant did not know he had no defence to the original action. If good, it can only be so on the ground that it shows an entire absence of consideration, which it clearly does not; but if it does, it amounts to *non assumpsit*. [TINDAL, C. J. That is not pointed out as a cause of demurrer.] One ground of demurrer assigned is ambiguity, which lets in this objection. [MAULE, J. The better course probably will be to allow the defendant to amend the fourth plea, by alleging that the plaintiff never had any available cause of action; upon which the plaintiff may take issue. I incline to think the plea bad, but it is doubtful whether the blot is hit by any of the causes of demurrer assigned.]

Kinglake, Serjt., for the defendant, declined to amend.

1 Cowp. 37. See Rex v. Grosvenor, 2 Stra. 1193. And see Rex v. Justices of Buckinghamshire, 1 B. & C. 485. In Doe v. Avis, Chitty's Statutes, 964, Lord Tenterden is reported to have said at *nisi prius:* "The words of the (stamp) act are so ambiguous that the party objecting ought to make out the affirmative."

2 11 M. & W. 641. 3 8 Dowl. P. C. 604.

4 13 M. & W. 427; 2 Dowl. & L. 358.

5 The learned counsel here states the case of Smith v. Monteith. — ED.

TINDAL, C. J. The only question now remaining is upon the demurrer to the fourth plea. I am of opinion that the fourth plea is a good and valid plea on general demurrer. The declaration alleges that the plaintiff had commenced an action against the defendant in the Exchequer, to recover two sums of £1300 and £700 respectively, which action was about to be tried; and that, in consideration that the plaintiff would forbear proceeding in that action until the 14th of December then next, the defendant promised the plaintiff that he would on that day pay the money, with interest and costs; that the plaintiff, confiding in the defendant's promise, forbore prosecuting the action, and stayed the proceedings until the day named, but that the defendant did not pay the money or the costs. The fourth plea states that the plaintiff never had any cause of action against the defendant in respect of the subject-matter of the action in the Court of Exchequer, which he the plaintiff, at the time of the commencement of the said action, and thence until the time of the making the promise in the first count mentioned, well knew. By demurring to that plea the plaintiff admits that he had no cause of action against the defendant in the action therein mentioned, and that he knew it. It appears to me, therefore, that he is estopped from saying that there was any valid consideration for the defendant's promise. It is almost *contra bonos mores*, and certainly contrary to all the principles of natural justice, that a man should institute proceedings against another, when he is conscious that he has no good cause of action. In order to constitute a binding promise, the plaintiff must shew a good consideration, something beneficial to the defendant or detrimental to the plaintiff. Detrimental to the plaintiff it cannot be, if he has no cause of action; and beneficial to the defendant it cannot be, for in contemplation of law the defence upon such an admitted state of facts must be successful, and the defendant will recover costs; which must be assumed to be a full compensation for all the legal damage he may sustain. The consideration therefore altogether fails. On the part of the plaintiff it has been urged that the cases cited for the defendant were not cases where actions had already been brought, but only cases of promises to forbear commencing proceedings. I must however confess that, if that were so, I do not see that it would make any substantial difference. The older cases, and some of the modern ones too, do not afford any countenance to that distinction. In Tooley *v.* Windham[1] it is stated that the plaintiff had purchased a writ out of chancery against the defendant, to the intent to exhibit a bill against him. Upon the return of the writ, which was for the profits of certain lands which the father of the defendant had taken in his lifetime, the defendant, in consideration he would surcease his suit, promised to him that, if he could prove that his father had taken the profits or had

[1] Cro. Eliz. 206 (more fully reported, 2 Leon. 105).

the possession of the land under the title of the father of the plaintiff, he would pay him for the profits of the land; and the court held that the promise was without consideration and void. There the suit was in existence at the time of the making of the promise. So, in Atkinson v. Settree,[1] an action had been commenced at the time the promise was made. These cases seem to me to establish the principle upon which our present judgment rests; and I am not aware that it is at all opposed by Longridge v. Dorville. It may be that the peculiar circumstances of that case took it out of the general rule. The ship was under detention by virtue of process from the Admiralty Court. The event of the suit in that court was uncertain; neither party could foresee the result; and therefore the relinquishment by the plaintiff of his hold upon the ship might well be a good consideration for the promise declared on. Here, however, there was no uncertainty: the defendant asserts, and the plaintiff admits, that there never was any cause of action in the original suit, and that the plaintiff knew it. I therefore think the fourth plea affords a very good answer, and that the defendant is entitled to judgment thereon.

MAULE, J. I also am of opinion that the defendant is entitled to judgment on the fourth plea, though I think it extremely questionable whether that plea is not open to objection, provided it were rightly taken. Forbearance to prosecute a suit in which the plaintiff has no cause of action (and in which, as the Lord Chief Justice properly adds, he must eventually fail), according to the authorities, is no consideration. It is no benefit to the defendant, and no detriment to the plaintiff. Costs are considered by the law a sufficient indemnification for a defendant who is sued, where there exists no cause of action; consequently the defendant, in contemplation of law, derives no benefit from a stay of the proceedings. In Smith v. Monteith it seems to have been considered that the allegation in the plea, — that the plaintiff had not any claim or demand or cause of action against the original defendant, in respect whereof the plaintiff was entitled to recover the sum which the defendant promised to pay, — did not sufficiently shew that the plaintiff must necessarily have failed in the original action; and it may be doubted whether the fourth plea here does sufficiently shew that there was no consideration for the defendant's promise, by reason of the plaintiff having no cause of action in the former suit, and that therefore he must necessarily have failed in that suit. That objection would, I think, have shewn the fourth plea pleaded in this case to be bad, provided the objection had been properly pointed out as a cause of demurrer. But, on general demurrer, I think the plea must be taken impliedly to allege that the plaintiff must necessarily have failed, and is therefore sufficient, the absence of a direct allegation to that effect being only ground of special demurrer. It

[1] Willes, 482.

has been contended that this objection is specially pointed out by that part of the demurrer which objects to the plea on the ground that it is ambiguous. That, however, is not in my opinion a sufficient assignment of this cause of demurrer, within the statute. Though I feel bound to state my opinion, I confess I should not be much surprised if a court of error should come to a different conclusion upon the doubt suggested.

CRESSWELL, J. The declaration in this case is founded upon a promise by the defendant to pay certain moneys, in consideration of the plaintiff's forbearing to proceed with an action pending in the Court of Exchequer. The answer set up by the fourth plea is, that the plaintiff never had any cause of action against the defendant in respect to the subject-matter of that suit, which the plaintiff well knew. It has been surmised, in the course of the argument, that there is a distinction between abstaining from commencing an action, and forbearing to prosecute one already commenced. In the older cases I find no such distinction. Lord Coke lays it down broadly, that the staying of an action that has been unjustly brought is no consideration for a promise to pay money. I cannot help thinking, on general principles, that the staying proceedings in an action brought without any cause is no good consideration for a promise such as is relied on here. The plea in plain terms avers that the plaintiff never had any cause of action, and that he well knew it. Are we to assume that the defendant might, by some slip in pleading, have failed in his defence to that action if it had proceeded? I think not. On general demurrer, the plea appears to me to be sufficient; and none of the causes of demurrer specially assigned in my judgment hits the point made by my brother Channell.

ERLE, J. It appears to me also that the fourth plea is sufficient. The declaration states that the plaintiff had commenced an action against the defendant in the Court of Exchequer to recover certain moneys; that the defendant had pleaded various pleas on which issues in fact had been joined, which were about to be tried; and that, in consideration that the plaintiff would forbear proceeding in that action until a certain day, the defendant promised to pay. The issues joined on that record therefore were perfectly well known and ascertained. The defendant pleads that the plaintiff never had any cause of action against him in respect of the subject-matter of the action in the Exchequer, which he the plaintiff, at the time of the commencement of the action, and thence until the time of the promise, well knew. I think the plea must be read as importing a distinct allegation that, upon the issues joined in that action, whether of fact or of law, the plaintiff must have failed. Construing the plea in this way, I think it is a good plea, at least on general demurrer, and that the defendant is entitled to judgment thereon.

Judgment for the defendant on the fourth plea.

SEMPLE *v.* PINK.

IN THE EXCHEQUER, JUNE 3, 1847.

[*Reported in 1 Exchequer Reports*, 74.]

THE declaration stated that one J. Leigh made his promissory note in writing, and delivered the same to the plaintiff, and thereby promised to pay to the plaintiff or his order £200 for value received three months after the date thereof, which period had elapsed before the making of the promise of the defendant hereinafter next mentioned; but the said J. Leigh did not pay the amount of the said note when the same became due, and the amount of the said promissory note being wholly unpaid to the plaintiff, and the said note being then in the plaintiff's hands overdue and unpaid, thereupon, heretofore, to wit, on the 2d of November, 1844, in consideration of the premises, and that the plaintiff, at the request of the defendant, would hold over the said promissory note, and would forbear and give time to the said J. Leigh for the payment of the said moneys in and by said promissory note payable, to wit, for a reasonable time then next following, the defendant then guaranteed and promised the plaintiff to be answerable to him, the plaintiff, for the payment of the said moneys due and payable upon and by virtue of the said promissory note, and to pay him the same, in case the said J. Leigh should make default in paying the same. Averment, that although more than a reasonable time for the plaintiff's forbearing and holding over the said note had elapsed before the commencement of this suit, and although the plaintiff, confiding in the promise of the defendant, did then, to wit, on, &c., hold over the promissory note, and forbear and give time to J. Leigh for the payment of the said sum of money, and hath thence, and for more than a reasonable time in that behalf, to wit, from thence hitherto, held over the said note, and forborne and given time for payment of the said note: yet J. Leigh hath not paid the moneys in and by the said promissory note due and payable, whereof the defendant had notice, and was requested by the plaintiff to pay him, but the defendant hath not paid the same or any part thereof.

Plea, *non assumpsit.*

At the trial before Rolfe, B., at the Middlesex sittings in last Hilary Term, the following facts appeared: In July, 1844, the plaintiff agreed to discount a promissory note for £200 for J. Leigh, if the defendant would guarantee payment of the same when due; the defendant having agreed to do so, the note set out in the declaration was made, upon the back of which the defendant wrote the following words: "I do hereby guarantee the payment of the within promissory note by James Leigh, the maker, for the second day of November next. John Pink." The note became due on the 2d of November, and was dishonored; and whilst the plaintiff was the holder of it, the defendant signed the following memorandum, addressed to the plaintiff: —

BLOMFIELD ROAD, MAIDA HILL, NOV. 2, 1844.

I request you will hold over the promissory note in your favor of Mr. James Leigh, dated 31st July, 1844, for £200 at three months; and in consideration of your so doing, I undertake to continue in all respects my guaranty of the same.

I am, Sir, yours truly, JOHN PINK.

MR. A. SEMPLE, Jr.

It was objected, on the part of the defendant, that there was no evidence of the guaranty set out in the declaration, and that the plaintiff ought to be nonsuited. The learned judge was of that opinion and directed a nonsuit, reserving liberty to the plaintiff to move to enter a verdict for the amount of the note.

Miller having obtained a rule *nisi* accordingly,

Ogle shewed cause. The plaintiff was properly nonsuited. The plea of *non assumpsit* puts in issue not only the promise, but also the consideration on which it is founded. The consideration stated in this declaration is forbearance for a reasonable time, but there is no evidence of such consideration. The memorandum of the 2d of November mentions no time for which the plaintiff was to hold over the note, and the pleader is not warranted in treating it as a contract to forbear for a reasonable time. Even if the memorandum be read together with the indorsement on the back of the note, the two documents will not support the declaration; for the latter is merely an undertaking to pay the note when due, and the former an agreement to continue a guaranty not founded on any consideration. Mere forbearance is not a sufficient consideration to support a promise to pay the debt of another; but there must be a forbearance for a certain or reasonable time. Chitty on Contracts, p. 30; Cole *v.* Dyer.[1] The law will not imply any such consideration from the terms of these instruments.

Miller, in support of the rule. The memorandum of the 2d of November supports the declaration. It is a rule of law that, where no time is mentioned in a contract, the law implies a reasonable time. Where a party undertakes to deduce title to an estate, he has a reasonable time for that purpose. [ALDERSON, B. Making out a title is an act which necessarily requires some time; but suppose in this case the plaintiff had brought his action the next minute, would that be a forbearance? In a case like the present, what definite idea can you attach to forbearance for a reasonable time? The meaning of the words may depend upon the character of the party, — whether he is litigious, or

[1] 1 C. & J. 461.

whether he is mild and somnolent. It will be found that the cases in which the law implies a reasonable time are those in which the particular act requires some time to do it. ROLFE, B. The declaration seems to be bad. ALDERSON, B. The guaranty itself is defective.]

PER CURIAM. The rule must be discharged.

Rule discharged.

MARIA OLDERSHAW AND ROBERT MUSKET, *Executrix and Executor of* ROBERT OLDERSHAW, *v.* WILLIAM THOMAS KING.

IN THE EXCHEQUER, MAY 23, 1857. — IN THE EXCHEQUER CHAMBER, JUNE 22, 23, 1857.

[*Reported in 2 Hurlstone and Norman*, 399, 517.]

THIS was a special case stated for the opinion of the court.

The action was brought by the plaintiffs, as executrix and executor of Robert Oldershaw, to recover the sum of £731 9*s.* 3*d.* upon the defendant's guaranty.

In August, 1848, John and Joseph Francis King being indebted to the testator Robert Oldershaw, who was their attorney, in a considerable sum of money, applied to him for further advances, which he declined to make unless he had the defendant's guaranty. The defendant, after some correspondence, signed the following memorandum: —

21 MANCHESTER TERRACE, August 24, 1848.

DEAR SIR, — I am aware that my uncles J. and J. F. King stand considerably indebted to you for professional business, and for cash lent and advanced to them, and that it is not in their power to pay you at present; and as in all probability they will become still further indebted to you, though I by no means intend that this letter shall create or imply any obligation on your part to increase your claim against them, I am willing to bear you harmless against any loss arising out of the past or future transactions between you and my said uncles to a certain extent; and therefore, in consideration of your forbearing to press them for the immediate payment of the debt now due to you, I hereby engage and agree to guarantee you the payment of any sum they may be indebted to you upon the balance of accounts between you at any time during the next six years, to the extent of £1000, whenever called upon by you to pay the same, and after twelve calendar months' previous notice.

I remain, &c., WILLIAM THOMAS KING.

TO ROBERT OLDERSHAW, Esq.

The above guaranty was handed to the testator Robert Oldershaw on the twenty-fifth day of August, 1848, on which day he advanced to John and Joseph Francis King £170. Previously thereto he had advanced to them £513 in money. After the 25th of August, 1848, he paid to John and Joseph Francis King various sums, amounting in the whole to £520. The transactions went on till the 10th of July, 1849, when John and Joseph Francis King became bankrupts. At the date of the fiat there was due from the said John and J. F. King to the testator Robert Oldershaw £2184 16*s.* 4*d.*

After the realization of the securities in the hands of the testator, and the receipt of a dividend under the estate of John and J. F. King, there remained due to the plaintiffs, as executrix and executor of the said Robert Oldershaw, who died in May, 1851, the sum of £731 9*s.* 3*d.*; and on the 6th of June, 1854, the plaintiffs gave notice to the defendant that the said sum of £731 9*s.* 3*d.* was due and owing, and requested him, under the terms of his guaranty, to pay the amount of the same to them.

It is agreed between the parties that all things necessary to be done, and all conditions precedent, have been performed and fulfilled, and all times have elapsed necessary to enable the plaintiffs to recover the said sum of £731 9*s.* 3*d.*, provided the court shall be of opinion that the defendant, under said memorandum and facts stated, is liable to pay the same.

The questions for the opinion of the court are: first, whether on the above facts the defendant is liable or not; and, secondly, to what extent.

Knowles (with whom was *W. M. Cooke*) argued for the plaintiffs in last Michaelmas Term (Nov. 10).[1] . . . The forbearing to press for immediate payment of the debt is a sufficient consideration to support the promise. A reasonable construction must be put upon the words. It is a question of fact whether the testator did press for immediate payment. Waiting for a very short time, such as an hour, might be an illusory forbearance. But the court will not entertain any question as to the adequacy of the consideration. Indeed, forbearance for a day, or even a less time, might be a matter of importance to the parties. The word "immediate" need not be construed literally. Page *v.* Pearce.[2] [ALDERSON, B. "Pleading immediately" means pleading in twenty-four hours.] In Mapes *v.* Sidney[3] a promise in consideration that the defendant [plaintiff] would forbear, with an allegation that the plaintiff did forbear *per magnum tempus*, was held good. [ALDERSON, B. Here the word "immediate" shews that the forbearance is not to be perpetual.] It is enough if it amounts to an agreement to suspend the remedy. In Payne *v.* Wilson[4] an agreement to pay a sum of £30 on the 1st of April, in consideration that the plaintiff would "suspend proceedings," was held to be binding.

[1] Only so much of the case is here given as relates to the question of forbearance. — ED.

[2] 8 M. & W. 677. [3] Cro. Jac. 683. [4] 7 B. & C. 423.

Petersdorff, for the defendant. . . . Forbearance for a long or a short or for some time is not a good consideration to support a promise; it must be an absolute forbearance, or for a definite time. Com. Dig., Action upon the Case upon Assumpsit (B. 1). In Mapes *v.* Sidney the consideration was forbearance to sue for a debt, and that was held good, two of the judges being of opinion that it should be intended a total and absolute forbearance. Semple *v.* Pink [1] shews that forbearance generally, or for a reasonable time, is not a sufficient consideration. Bell *v.* Welch [2] is also an authority in the defendant's favor. . .

Knowles, in reply. Forbearance to press for immediate payment is a good consideration. In Payne *v.* Wilson it was held that a consent to stay proceedings on a *cognovit* was a sufficient consideration to support a promise to pay the debt. Littledale, J., there said, that after verdict it must be taken that the proceedings were suspended absolutely, or for a reasonable time. . . . *Cur. adv. vult.*

The Court having differed in opinion, the following judgments were delivered: —

BRAMWELL, B. My brother Watson and myself are of opinion that the defendant is entitled to judgment. The consideration mentioned for the defendant's promise is forbearing to press for the immediate payment of the debt now due; and this in our judgment is void for uncertainty. The authorities which have been referred to shew that a guaranty in consideration of forbearance "for some time," or "a little time," is void. In the present case the word is "immediate." That cannot mean "instantaneous," and any thing beyond is uncertain. It was argued that, no time being named, it was to be taken to be that a reasonable time was intended. That is not so, as it is to "forbear to press for immediate payment," not forbear for a reasonable time. However, assuming it were so, that is equally vague and uncertain. In the result, one may be able to say in each particular case if the creditor has waited a reasonable time; but it is impossible to lay down a rule as to what does or does not constitute such a time between a debtor and creditor; and accordingly it was so held in Semple *v.* Pink, where the reasoning of Baron Alderson and the remark of Baron Rolfe are to the effect that such a guaranty as stated in the declaration in that case, is void for uncertainty. Then, whether this consideration be read to be to forbear for a reasonable time, or to forbear to press for immediate payment, it is void. Mapes *v.* Sidney will not help the plaintiffs on either ground of its decision, for here the agreement to forbear is not absolute; nor is Lord Hobart's reason applicable, as the consideration for the agreement must now be in writing. . . .

We are of opinion, therefore, that the plaintiffs are not entitled to recover; and we cannot help adding that, though we doubt not that the

[1] 1 Exch. 74. [2] 9 C. B. 154.

intention of the testator was perfectly fair, as indeed is shewn by the indulgence he gave, and that he desired not to tie himself up only because of the loss which might thereby accrue, still that he did endeavor to get a binding promise without giving any consideration for it, and in reality fails in consequence. What the defendant substantially bargained for was forbearance to the principal debtor, and to this he never had a right, though it was granted in fact.[1]

Judgment for the defendant.

Error on the foregoing judgment.

COCKBURN, C. J. . . . Supposing that the sole consideration was the forbearing to press for immediate payment, I should not be prepared to assent to the doctrine laid down in Semple *v.* Pink. There are authorities for saying that an agreement to forbear for a short time, or a little time, is too indefinite to constitute a consideration for a contract; but I am not at all prepared to assent to the proposition that an agreement to forbear for a reasonable time would not be sufficient. I see no reason why the question as to what is reasonable time should not be considered and determined with reference to the circumstances of the case by a jury. As however, in the view I take of this case, the contract discloses a sufficient consideration independently of such forbearance, it is not necessary to go the length of overruling Semple *v.* Pink.

ERLE, J. . . . Looking at the whole letter, and the circumstances under which it was written, and considering the importance of further advances, I come to the conclusion that the consideration contemplated was that further advance should be made, and time given by the creditor before he would press for the payment of the existing debt. Though the contract did not bind the creditor to make further advances, or to give time unless he chose to do so, it is clear that if he did make the advances, and did give time, that which was contingent at the time when the instrument was written became an absolute and binding contract. I am also of opinion that, although the amount of further advances and of the time to be given is not defined, still, if time is given and advances are made, it is enough. These undefined terms ought to receive a construction in reference to the facts given in evidence *ut res magis valeat quam pereat.* If the guarantor has had the advantage he bargained for, we must hold him to his promise. That suffices for the judgment of reversal in the present case. I concur with the Lord Chief Justice with respect to the case of Semple *v.* Pink. I do not assent to the doctrine that a guaranty in consideration of an agreement to give time is void unless the time to be given is defined in the contract. But it is not necessary to decide that point.

CROMPTON, J. . . . The consideration was that Oldershaw should not press for immediate payment, and I think that the giving a reason-

[1] Pollock, C. B., delivered a dissenting opinion; but as it does not relate materially to the question of forbearance, it is here omitted. — ED.

able time is a sufficient consideration. In the old authorities mentioned in Comyns it is said to be sufficient if there is an agreement for forbearance for a definite portion of time, or for a reasonable time; and in Payne *v.* Wilson Lord Tenterden rests his judgment on the ground that it must be taken that the plaintiff had suspended proceedings for a "definite or reasonable time." I do not see any great difficulty in saying that what is a reasonable time may be determined at *nisi prius.* It may be difficult to say what a reasonable time is; but the difficulty is not greater than in many other cases where there is a promise to do a thing in a reasonable time. And the only distinct authority against that is the case of Semple *v.* Pink. The court, however, in that case had really to decide whether there was a variance between the guaranty proved and that set out in the declaration. If I had to decide that case now, I should be inclined to say that a reasonable time might be implied, because no time was mentioned in the contract. That was the point before the court.

WILLES, J. I am of the same opinion. Assuming that we are only to look to the words of the document, and to see what is there stated as the consideration for the contract without regard to the previous recital, the consideration would appear to be "forbearing to press for the immediate payment of the debt due." There are many authorities which shew that in cases like the present the word "immediate" may be construed to mean within a reasonable time to do the act in question.[1] Accordingly, I think that forbearing to press for immediate payment means forbearance for a reasonable time. Then it is said that that is not a sufficient consideration, because of the indefiniteness of the word "reasonable;" and because it might be competent to the person who enters into a contract, engaging to forbear for a reasonable time, to sue the next instant, or within a very short time. Looking for a moment to the mode in which the question of reasonable or unreasonable time would be determined, the difficulty vanishes. The question whether the creditor had forborne for a reasonable time or not would be determined by the jury. Now, suppose the consideration expressed had been forbearing for such a time as a jury who might try the question should consider reasonable, there can be no doubt but that it would be a perfectly good contract, and for a good consideration. That is what is tacitly expressed in this instrument. There are many cases in which, the reasonableness of the time in which to do a thing not being fixed by legal decisions, as in the case of the dishonor of a bill of exchange, it is left to the jury as a question of fact with reference to the circumstances of the particular case. I do not see on what principle an agreement to forbear for a time stipulated for by the parties should not constitute a good consideration. There

[1] See Thompson *v.* Gibson, 8 M. & W. 281; Page *v.* Pearce, 8 M. & W. 677. The learned judge referred also to Regina *v.* Brownlow, 11 A. & E. 119.

are authorities to that effect: Com. Dig., Action on the Case on Assumpsit (B. 1). In Payne v. Wilson, Lord Tenterden seems to treat it as clear that the forbearance for a reasonable time would be a sufficient consideration. No doubt there are authorities on the other side; but if we are to choose between authorities, one class of which tends to defeat, and the other class to uphold the intention of the parties, I should have no difficulty in adhering to the latter class. . . .

Judgment reversed.

THE ALLIANCE BANK (*limited*) v. BROOM.

In Chancery, November 14, 21, 1864.

[*Reported in* 2 *Drewry and Smale*, 289.]

This case came on upon a demurrer.

It appeared from the bill that, in June, 1864, the Alliance Bank opened a loan-account with the defendants, who are merchants at Liverpool, and that such loan-account was continued down to the 19th of September, 1864, when there was a balance due from the defendants to the bank on such loan-account to the amount of £22,205 15*s.* 1*d.*

On the 19th of September, 1864, the plaintiffs requested the defendants, Messrs. Broom, to give them some security for the amount so due; and the defendants, who stated that they were entitled to certain goods, wrote to the manager of the bank the following letter: —

Liverpool, 19th Sept. 1864.

Dear Sir, — We hand you the following particulars of produce, which we propose to hypothecate against our loan-account, and at the same time undertake to pay the proceeds, as we receive them, to the credit of the said account.

The letter then contained a list of goods and their values, and was signed by Messrs. Broom.

In pursuance of this letter the plaintiffs, on the 20th of September, 1864, applied to the defendants for the warrants for delivery of the goods mentioned in the letter, and the defendants promised to deliver the warrants to the plaintiffs as soon as they could obtain them from the warehouses.

The bill stated that the defendants refused to deliver the warrants, or other documents relating to the goods, to the plaintiffs, and threatened and intended to deliver them to other persons; and the bill charged that the plaintiffs were entitled to a lien or charge upon the goods mentioned in the letter by virtue of the agreement, and prayed for a declaration to that effect. The bill also prayed that the defendants might be ordered to deliver to the plaintiffs the warrants and other documents relating to the title of said goods, and cause the said goods to be delivered to the plaintiffs, by way of security for the amount due to them on the loan-account. The bill also prayed an injunction to restrain the defendants from dealing with the warrants or goods in the mean time.

To this bill the defendants filed a demurrer, on the ground that the agreement contained in the letter was without consideration; and therefore one which the court would not enforce.

Mr. *Daniel* and Mr. *J. N. Higgins*, for the defendants, in support of the demurrer, contended that the agreement contained in the letter was executory; being also without consideration, the court would not enforce it. The existence of a debt was no sufficient consideration to support the agreement. There was a distinction between a motive and a consideration, — what might be good as a motive might be bad as a consideration; and that was so in this case. And therefore the bill, which sought the specific performance of such an agreement, could not be sustained. They referred to Eastwood v. Kenyon,[1] Thomas v. Thomas,[2] Hopkins v. Logan,[3] Kaye v. Dutton,[4] Smith on Contracts,[5] Addison on Contracts.[6]

Mr. *Bevir*, for the plaintiffs, in support of the bill, submitted that there was a good consideration for the agreement; namely, forbearance on the part of the plaintiffs from calling in their money. Twyne's Case.[7]

Mr. *Daniel*, in reply.

The Vice-Chancellor reserved judgment.

The VICE-CHANCELLOR,[8] after stating the facts, said: —

The defendant demurs to the plaintiff's bill in this case, on the ground that the promise to give security, which the plaintiff seeks to enforce, was without any consideration, — that it is in fact a *nudum pactum*, which the court will not enforce; and in support of this proposition it is argued that the plaintiffs, so far from giving any consideration for the promise, could at any time have brought an action for the payment of the debt; and that they could have done so is perfectly true.

Now, according to the facts stated in the bill, a demand was made by the creditor for security; and upon that demand a promise and agreement was made by the debtor that he would give such security, and that, although it might take some time to get the warrants, he would hand them over to the creditor when he obtained them.

It appears to me, that when the plaintiffs demanded payment of their debt, and in consequence of that application the defendant

[1] 11 Ad. & El. 450. [2] 2 Q. B. 859. [3] 5 M. & W. 241.
[4] 7 M. & Gr. 815. [5] p. 89. [6] pp. 6 and 296.
[7] 3 Coke 80 *b*. [8] Sir R. T. Kindersley. — ED.

agreed to give certain security, although there was no promise on the part of the plaintiffs to abstain for any certain time from suing for the debt, the effect was, that the plaintiffs did in effect give, and the defendant received, the benefit of some degree of forbearance, not indeed for any definite time, but at all events some extent of forbearance. If, on the application for security being made, the defendant had refused to give any security at all, the consequence certainly would have been that the creditor would have demanded payment of the debt, and have taken steps to enforce it. It is very true that, at any time after the promise, the creditor might have insisted on payment of his debt, and have brought an action; but the circumstances necessarily involve the benefit to the debtor of a certain amount of forbearance, which he would not have derived if he had not made the agreement.

On this ground the demurrer must be overruled.[1]

CALLISHER v. BISCHOFFSHEIM.

IN THE QUEEN'S BENCH, JUNE 6, 1870.

[*Reported in Law Reports, 5 Queen's Bench, 449.*]

DECLARATION that the plaintiff had alleged that certain moneys were due and owing to him, to wit, from the government of Honduras, and from Don Carlos Gattierez and others, and had threatened and was about to take legal proceedings against the said government and persons to enforce payment of the same; and thereupon, in consideration that the plaintiff would forbear from taking such proceedings for an agreed time, the defendant promised to deliver to the plaintiff certain securities, to wit, bonds or debentures, called Honduras Railway Loan Bonds, for sums to the amount of £600, immediately the bonds should be printed. Averment, that the plaintiff did not take any proceedings during the agreed period or at all; and that all conditions had been fulfilled necessary to entitle him to sue in respect of the matters before stated. Breach, that the defendant had not delivered to the plaintiff the bonds or any of them.

Plea, that at the time of making the alleged agreement no moneys were due and owing to the plaintiff from the government and other persons.

Demurrer and joinder.

[1] See Boyd v. Freize, 5 Gray, 553.

James, Q. C. (*Rose* with him), in support of the demurrer. The plea is bad, and affords no answer to the declaration, which discloses a good cause of action. The consideration for the plaintiff's [defendant's] promise or contract is sufficient; it is sufficient if the contractor, or some third person, avoids some detriment or injury; here the annoyance and expense of an action are avoided. In Llewellyn *v.* Llewellyn [1] the declaration alleged that there were disputes concerning accounts between the plaintiff and defendant, and in consideration that the plaintiff would relinquish all claims the defendant promised he would pay the plaintiff an annuity. There was no allegation that any sum was due to the plaintiff; it might be that the plaintiff's claim could not be sustained; but it was held that the declaration disclosed a sufficient consideration. [BLACKBURN, J. We must assume, on this record, that the plaintiff believed that he had a valid claim against the Honduras government.] Cook *v.* Wright [2] is in point. There the defendant knew he was not liable to satisfy the claim made by the plaintiff; but the plaintiff, *bona fide* believing him to be personally liable, threatened to take proceedings, and a forbearing to take those proceedings was held a good consideration for the defendant compromising the claim by giving promissory notes. In Wade *v.* Simeon [3] it was expressly averred in the plea that the plaintiff knew he had no cause of action, and it was therefore held good. The plaintiff has fulfilled his part of the contract, he has abstained from enforcing his claim whether good or bad, and the defendant ought not to be allowed to say he will not fulfil his contract. The position of the parties is altered, and the plaintiff may have been put to expense in stopping the proceedings. The consideration is not an abandonment of an unfounded claim, but a postponement of the prosecution of the suit.

Pollock, Q. C. (*Joyce* with him) contra. Forbearance to prosecute a groundless action affords no consideration capable of supporting a promise. It is admitted on the record that no money was due to the plaintiff from the Honduras government; and if the declaration and plea are read together, it is clear that a cause of action does not exist. All the cases are consistent with this view except Cook *v.* Wright; [4] and that case is distinguishable. There the question was not whether a sum of money was due to the plaintiff, but whether it was due from the defendant or another person; whereas here the question, before the contract declared on was made, was whether a sum of money was due to the plaintiff from the Honduras government. In Edwards *v.* Baugh [5] the declaration was held bad because there was not any allegation that a debt was due, but merely that a dispute existed respecting it; and in

[1] 3 D. & L. 318; 15 L. J. (Q. B.) 4.
[2] 1 B. & S. 559; 30 L. J. (Q. B.) 321.
[3] 3 D. & L. 587; 2 C. B. 548.
[4] 1 B. & S. 559; 30 L. J. (Q. B.) 321.
[5] 11 M. & W. 641.

Wade *v.* Simeon [1] it was held that forbearance to prosecute a groundless claim gave no benefit to the promisor, and imposed no detriment on the promisee.

James, Q. C., replied.

COCKBURN, C. J. Our judgment must be for the plaintiff. No doubt it must be taken that there was in fact no claim by the plaintiff against the Honduras government which could be prosecuted by legal proceedings to a successful issue; but this does not vitiate the contract and destroy the validity of what is alleged as the consideration. The authorities clearly establish that if an agreement is made to compromise a disputed claim, forbearance to sue in respect of that claim is a good consideration; and whether proceedings to enforce the disputed claim have or have not been instituted makes no difference. If the defendant's contention were adopted, it would result that in no case of a doubtful claim could a compromise be enforced. Every day a compromise is effected on the ground that the party making it has a chance of succeeding in it; and if he *bona fide* believes he has a fair chance of success, he has a reasonable ground for suing, and his forbearance to sue will constitute a good consideration. When such a person forbears to sue he gives up what he believes to be a right of action, and the other party gets an advantage; and, instead of being annoyed with an action, he escapes from the vexations incident to it. The defendant's contention is unsupported by authority.

It would be another matter if a person made a claim which he knew to be unfounded, and by a compromise derived an advantage under it: in that case his conduct would be fraudulent. If the plea had alleged that the plaintiff knew he had no real claim against the Honduras government, that would have been an answer to the action.

BLACKBURN, J. I am of the same opinion. The declaration, as it stands, in effect states that the plaintiff, having alleged that certain moneys were due to him from the Honduras government, was about to enforce payment, and the defendant suggested that the plaintiff's claim, whether good or bad, should stand over. So far, the agreement was a reasonable one. The plea, however, alleges that at the time of making the agreement no money was due. If we are to infer that the plaintiff believed that some money was due to him, his claim was honest, and the compromise of that claim would be binding, and would form a good consideration, although the plaintiff, if he had prosecuted his original claim, would have been defeated. This case is decided by Cook *v.* Wright.[2] In that case it appeared from the evidence that the defendant knew that the original claim of the plaintiff was invalid, yet he was held liable, as the plaintiff believed his claim to be good. The court say [3] that "the real consideration depends on the reality of the

[1] 2 C. B. 548.

[2] 1 B. & S. 559, 570; 30 L. J. (Q. B.) 321, 324.

[3] 1 B. & S. at p. 570; 30 L. J. (Q. B.) at p. 324.

claim made, and the *bona fides* of the compromise." If the plaintiff's claim against the Honduras government was not *bona fide*, this ought to have been alleged in the plea; but no such allegation appears.

MELLOR, J. I am of the same opinion. If the plaintiff's claim against the Honduras government was fraudulent, the defendant ought to have alleged it.

LUSH, J., concurred. *Judgment for the plaintiff.*

SECTION V.

Compromise.

ANONYMOUS.

IN THE KING'S BENCH, HILARY TERM, 1661.

[*Reported in* 1 *Siderfin*, 31, *placitum* 9.]

FATHER and son: The father is indebted to J. S. in £100, and makes a fraudulent deed, and by it gives all his property to the son. The father dies; and upon discourse had of the fraudulent deed the son promises J. S., in consideration that he will deliver the obligation to him, and make to him an acquittance and discharge of the debt, that he will pay the £100. And upon this an action was brought; and it was now moved in arrest of judgment that the consideration was not good; because it does not appear that the son was liable to the payment of the debt, either as heir, executor, administrator, or executor *de son tort;* and therefore the delivery of the obligation and the making of the acquittance and discharge to him is not good.

But it was answered and resolved that the consideration was good; and it shall be intended that he was liable, or at least that the discharge shall be made to the party who was liable; for he promises to make a discharge of the debt, and this shall be intended to the party who was liable to the payment of it, or else it would be no discharge.[1]

1 "If that was in truth a fraudulent deed of gift of the goods by the father to the son, as stated in the case, the son after his father's death would be chargeable for this debt as an executor of his own wrong, though possession of the goods had been delivered to him at the time of the deed. For it is holden that if a man makes a fraudulent gift of his goods in his lifetime to oust his creditors of their debts, the vendee after his death shall be charged for them. 1 Rol. Abr. 549, (C.), pl. 3. And the only way in which he can be so charged is as executor of his own wrong. 2 Leon. 223, Stamford's Case; Cro. Jac. 271, Hawes *v.* Leader; Yelv. 197, s. c., where it is

LONGRIDGE AND OTHERS *v.* DORVILLE AND ANOTHER.

IN THE KING'S BENCH, OCTOBER 29, 1821.

[*Reported in* 5 *Barnewall and Alderson*, 117.]

DECLARATION alleged, "that before the making of the promise, &c., a certain ship called the Carolina Matilda had then lately in a certain place, to wit, in the river Thames, to wit, at, &c., run foul of a certain other ship called the Zenobia, whereby the said last-mentioned ship had received great damage. And the said last-mentioned ship having received such damage in consequence of being so run foul of as aforesaid, the plaintiffs being the agents in that behalf of one —— Symonds, the owner of the Zenobia, and the defendants being the agents in that behalf of the owners of the Carolina Matilda, the former, as such agents, detained the Carolina Matilda till the owners of the said last-mentioned ship should have made good to them the damage so done to the Zenobia." It then stated, "that in consequence of such detention, the defendants undertook that they would, on the plaintiffs renouncing all claims on the Carolina Matilda, and on proving the amount of the damages sustained by the Zenobia, indemnify the plaintiffs for any sum not exceeding £180, the exact amount to be ascertained when the said latter ship should have been repaired;" and then alleged that, in consequence of such undertaking, the plaintiffs did renounce all claim on the Carolina Matilda, and did permit and allow her to proceed on her voyage, and that the Zenobia had been repaired, and that the amount of such repairs was ascertained. There were also the common counts, and the defendants pleaded the general issue. The cause was tried before Abbott, C. J., at the sittings after Easter Term, 1820, when a verdict was found for the plaintiffs, subject to the opinion of this court upon the following case: —

said that the goods are liable to the creditors in the hands of the vendee, as an executor of his own wrong, if the deed of gift be fraudulent. And the reason is, because every intermeddling without authority after the death of the party makes the person so intermeddling an executor of his own wrong. Dyer, 166 *b*, Stoke's Case. And the same point was recognized in the case of Edwards *v.* Harben, 2 Term Rep. 587, where it is adjudged that, if a creditor takes an absolute bill of sale of the goods of his debtor which is fraudulent against creditors, and the debtor dies, and thereupon the vendee takes and sells the goods, he is liable to be sued as executor of his own wrong for the debts of the deceased. Hence it seems to follow that the son was in the case in 1 Sid. liable to the payment of the debt, at least to the extent of the value of the goods, as executor of his own wrong; and therefore the delivering of the bond to him, and giving him an acquittance, appears to be a sufficient consideration to support his promise. For which reason that case seems to differ materially from the principal one." Serjeant Williams, note (2) to Barber *v.* Fox, 2 Wms. Saund. 136. — ED.

The Norwegian ship, called the Carolina Matilda, on her voyage to Norway, in sailing down the river Thames in November last ran foul of the ship called the Zenobia, then lying at anchor, and in consequence of which the latter ship sustained considerable damage. The plaintiffs, acting as the agents of Mr. R. Symonds, the owner of the Zenobia, instituted a proceeding in the High Court of Admiralty against the ship Carolina Matilda, to compel her owners to make good the damages sustained by the Zenobia in consequence of being so run foul of. Process was issued against the Carolina Matilda, under which she was arrested at Gravesend on the 22d November last, and on the 24th day of the same month the defendants wrote a letter to the plaintiffs, of which the following is a copy: —

MESSRS. LONGRIDGE, BARNETT, AND HODGSON.

GENTLEMEN, — In consequence of your having detained the Norway ship Carolina Matilda till the owners make good to you the damage done to the Zenobia, bound to Smyrna, we hereby engage, on your renouncing all claims on the said ship Carolina Matilda, and on proving the amount of damages sustained by the Zenobia, to indemnify you for any sum not exceeding £180, the exact amount to be ascertained when the Zenobia is repaired.

The defendants were the agents of the owners of the Carolina Matilda; and upon the receipt of this letter the plaintiffs withdrew proceedings in the Admiralty Court, and the officer, then in possession of the Carolina Matilda, was then also withdrawn, and such possession delivered up to the defendants, acting on behalf of her owners. The Zenobia had been since repaired, and the amount of damages sustained by her had been ascertained. At the time the Carolina Matilda sailed, and while she was proceeding down the river and ran foul of the Zenobia, she had the regular Trinity House pilot aboard, who had been placed there by the defendants.

Puller, for the plaintiff. It is not necessary to consider the question whether the owners of the Carolina are liable for the damage done to the Zenobia, under the circumstances of the case; for the defendants have made themselves liable by an express promise, founded upon a good consideration. The plaintiffs agree to release the ship, which they might otherwise have detained until bail was given; and the defendants agree to pay a stipulated sum by way of damage; waiving all question as to the legal liability of the owners. That might be considered as doubtful, there having been contradictory decisions.[1] The defendants, or their principals, therefore have obtained a benefit by the immediate release of the ship; and that constitutes a good consideration for the promise laid in the declaration.

F. Pollock, contra. There is no sufficient consideration for the promise in the declaration, because the plaintiffs had no ground for

[1] Neptune the Second, 1 Dodson, Adm. R. 467; Ritchie v. Bowsfield, 7 Taunt. 309.

instituting the suit in the Admiralty Court against the Carolina. The question whether the defendants are liable upon their undertaking must depend upon this, whether the owners were liable for the injury, the ship at the time having on board a pilot, as required by the act of parliament. If they were not liable, the plaintiff had no right to institute the suit in the Admiralty Court; and the forbearance of a suit, where a party is not liable, is not a good consideration. Tooley *v.* Windham[1] and King *v.* Hobbs[2] are authorities in point.

Abbott, C. J. I am of opinion that there is a sufficient consideration in this case to sustain the promise, without inquiring whether the owners of the ship are liable under the circumstances of the case. It appears that a suit had been instituted by the plaintiffs in the Court of Admiralty against the Carolina Matilda, to compel her owners to make good the damage done by her running foul of another vessel. The ship might have been redeemed from that suit by the defendants' giving bail that proper care should be taken of the ship, and that those on board her should not leave the kingdom until means were taken to secure that evidence which would enable the judge to decide the suit; and the plaintiffs might have insisted on such bail. The defendants, as agents for the foreign owners of the ship, write a letter, in which they engage, on the plaintiffs' renouncing all claims on the ship, and on proving the amount of damages sustained by the Zenobia, to indemnify them for any sum not exceeding £180, the exact amount to be ascertained when the Zenobia is repaired. Now the plain meaning of that engagement appears to me to be this: Release the ship, and we will waive all questions of law and fact, except the amount of damage; we will pay you £180, if the damage done amounts to that sum. The plaintiffs, by not insisting upon the bail required, therefore relinquished a benefit which they might have had, if the law had been with them. The law might fairly be considered as doubtful, for there had been contradictory decisions on the subject; and the parties agree to put an end to all doubts on the law and the fact, on the defendants' engaging to pay a stipulated sum. I am of opinion that this case is distinguishable from those cited in argument, inasmuch as in this case the law was doubtful, and the parties agreed to waive all questions of law and fact. I am therefore of opinion that the plaintiff is entitled to recover.

Bayley, J. I am of the same opinion. Where a cause is depending, it is competent to a party to refer the questions of liability and damage jointly, or to acknowledge his liability, and refer the question of damage only; and in this case, I think, the effect of the agreement is, that they the defendants acknowledge the liability of the owners, and, in consideration of the plaintiffs releasing the ship, they agree to refer the question as to the amount of damage, and pay the same, provided

[1] Cro. Eliz. 206. [2] Yelv. 25.

it does not exceed £180. If it had appeared in this case that the owners of the Carolina could not have been liable at all, I agree that the consideration for the promise would have failed. But the facts stated in the case by no means shew that the owners would not have been liable; for by the pilot act the owners are only protected in those cases where the loss arises from the default, neglect, incapacity, or incompetency of the pilot. Now there is no fact in this case which shews that the misconduct of the pilot was the cause of the injury.

HOLROYD, J. I am of the same opinion. If a person is about to sue another for a debt, for which the latter is not answerable, the mere consideration of forbearance is not sufficient to render him liable for that debt. Any act of the plaintiff, however, from which the defendant derives a benefit or advantage, or any labor, detriment, or inconvenience sustained by the plaintiff, is a sufficient consideration to support a promise. Now the consideration of forbearance is a benefit to the defendant, if he be liable; but it is not any benefit to him, if he be not liable. The authorities cited proceed on that ground. This case differs materially from those; for here a suit actually commenced is given up, and a suit too the final success of which was involved in some doubt. The plaintiff might sustain a detriment by giving up all claim in respect of the expenses incurred, and the defendant might derive a benefit by having that suit put an end to, without further trouble or investigation. Now I am of opinion that the giving up of a suit instituted for the purpose of trying a doubtful question, and consenting to deliver up the ship, which might otherwise have been detained until the security required was given, is a good consideration to support a promise to pay a stipulated sum by way of damage, in case the actual damage amount to that sum. In Com. Dig., tit. Action upon the Case upon Assumpsit (F. 8); it is laid down that an action does not lie if a party promise in consideration of a surrender of a lease at will, for the lessor might determine it; unless there was a doubt whether it was a lease at will or for years; and 1 Rol. 23, l. 25, 35, and 1 Brownlow, 6, are cited. That is an authority to shew that the giving up of a questionable right is a sufficient consideration to support a promise. Here therefore the giving up of a suit, instituted to try a question respecting which the law is doubtful, is a good consideration to support a promise. I think therefore that this action is sustainable.

BEST, J., concurred.

SMART v. CHELL.

IN THE QUEEN'S BENCH, TRINITY TERM, 1839.

[*Reported in 7 Dowling's Practice Cases*, 781.]

Ryland and *Knowles* showed cause against a rule, obtained by Petersdorff, for arresting the judgment in the present case, on the ground that a sufficient consideration did not appear on the face of the declaration for the defendant's promise. The declaration stated that on the 1st day of October, 1837, the plaintiffs retained and employed the defendant, then being an attorney and solicitor, at his request and on his solicitation, as such attorney and solicitor, to prosecute and conduct a certain action on their behalf, on the terms and conditions that, in the event of his not getting his costs and charges in said action from the defendant therein, he would only charge such sum as he should be out of pocket in conducting said action; and the plaintiffs averred that the defendant on the same day commenced and prosecuted said action on the terms aforesaid; and thereupon, in consideration of the premises, and that the plaintiffs had promised the defendant, at his request, to allow him to receive, take, and retain such costs and charges as aforesaid and under the terms aforesaid, the defendant promised the plaintiffs to use due and proper care, diligence, and skill, as such attorney in prosecuting and conducting said action. The plaintiffs then assigned as a breach that, said action having been commenced by arresting the defendant therein on a writ of *capias* issued out of the Court of Exchequer, no correct copy of said writ of *capias* was delivered to said last-mentioned defendant upon his said arrest; by reason whereof said writ of *capias* and all other proceedings in said action were set aside by a rule of said Court of Exchequer on the 1st of November following, with costs to be paid by the plaintiffs; whereupon and whereby the plaintiffs were forced to pay and did pay to the defendant in said action the sum of £14, the amount of said costs; "of all which said several premises the defendant then had notice, to wit, on the day and year last aforesaid, and then in consideration of the premises promised the plaintiffs to pay them half the said costs," to wit, the sum of £7, on request; yet the defendant hath not paid said sum or any part thereof, though requested so to do.[1]

On the face of this pleading sufficient consideration was stated. A detriment to the plaintiff was alleged in consequence of the defendant's negligence. For half this detriment the defendant was alleged to have agreed to pay the plaintiff. Had the plaintiff commenced an action for the negligence against the defendant, the forbearance of

[1] See *supra*, p. 221, note 1.—ED.

that suit would be sufficient consideration for the defendant's promise. In substance the consideration alleged here was such a forbearance. In Longridge and others *v.* Dorville[1] it was held that, if a party gave up a suit instituted to try a question respecting which the law is doubtful, it is a good consideration for a promise to pay a stipulated sum. Here there was no kind of doubt as to the right of the plaintiff to sue the defendant for his negligence. Under these circumstances the present rule ought to be discharged.

Petersdorff, in support of the rule, contended that no sufficient consideration, moving from the plaintiff to the defendant, was alleged on the face of this declaration. Consistently with any of the allegations here, the plaintiff might immediately bring his action to recover the remaining £7 out of the £14, which was the amount alleged to have been paid by the plaintiff in consequence of the defendant's negligence. The case might have been different if it had been alleged that [the defendant's promise was made] in consideration of the plaintiff relinquishing his claim for the remainder of the £14, which he had been obliged to pay through the negligence of the defendant, or in consideration that the plaintiff would not sue him for his negligence. No such allegation, however, was introduced. The declaration merely substituted one remedy for another. *Cur. adv. vult.*

Coleridge, J. Several points were raised on arguing this case, but the only one on which I shall give an opinion is that in arrest of judgment. The declaration is singular. It is in assumpsit; and it states that the defendant was an attorney, and that he agreed to conduct certain actions on certain terms, and that he did accordingly prosecute an action, and that in consideration of the premises he promised the plaintiffs to use due and proper care, skill, and diligence, as such attorney in conducting the action. Here, one would have thought, was a sufficient promise alleged; and the declaration goes on and assigns a breach, and specifies what the exact failure was in properly conducting the cause, namely, that through the negligence of the defendant the writ of *capias* was set aside with costs, and that the plaintiff was thereby forced to pay £14 for those costs. Now I should have thought that that was stated by way of special damage; but the declaration then goes on to state another promise, that in consideration of the premises the defendant promised to pay half the amount of those costs, and alleged a breach by non-payment of the £7. Now no rule is more clear in law than that the consideration for a promise must move from the plaintiff; then I must see what this plaintiff has done or suffered, or what the defendant has gained; the detriment to the plaintiff must be the immediate consideration for the promises alleged. Suppose an assault had been committed, and an action of

[1] 5 B. & Ald. 117.

assumpsit was brought for non-payment of a sum of money agreed to be given for the injury done, and the declaration did not state a release of action for the assault. It is not therefore enough that there should be a collateral consideration for the promise, but there must be an immediate consideration. In this case the consideration stated is, that for the loss of £14 by the plaintiff, through the defendant's neglect, the defendant promised to pay £7; but there is nothing to shew that the plaintiff may not sue for the whole £14 the very next day. There is consequently no sufficient consideration alleged, and the judgment must be arrested.

Rule absolute accordingly.

EDWARDS v. BAUGH.

IN THE EXCHEQUER, MAY 31, 1843.

[*Reported in* 11 *Meeson and Welsby*, 641.]

ASSUMPSIT. The declaration stated that before and at the time of the making of the promise by the defendant hereinafter in this count mentioned, to wit, on, &c., certain disputes and controversies were pending between the plaintiff and defendant, as to whether or not the defendant was indebted to the plaintiff in, to wit, the sum of £173 2*s.* 3*d.*, for money before then lent to and paid for the defendant by the plaintiff, at her [*sic*] request, and for interest upon and for the forbearance by the plaintiff, at the defendant's request, of moneys before due and owing from the defendant to the plaintiff for divers long spaces of time elapsed, and for money found to be due from the defendant to the plaintiff on an account then stated between them; and thereupon heretofore, to wit, on the day and year last aforesaid, in consideration that the plaintiff, at the request of the defendant, would then promise the defendant not to sue the defendant at any time thereafter for the recovery of the said sum of, to wit, £173 2*s.* 3*d.*, so in dispute between the plaintiff and defendant as aforesaid, or any part thereof, or any damages in respect thereof, and would then accept of and from the defendant the sum of, to wit, £100, in full satisfaction and discharge of the same, and every part thereof, and all damages in respect thereof, he [*sic*] the defendant then promised the plaintiff to pay him, to wit, the sum of £100, within a reasonable time then next following, in such satisfaction and discharge; and the plaintiff avers that he, confiding in the said promise of the defendant, did then promise the defendant not to sue the defendant at any time thereafter for the recovery of the said sum of, to wit, £173 2*s.* 3*d.*, so in dispute between the plaintiff and defendant as aforesaid, or any part thereof, or any damages in respect thereof, and that he would then accept of and from the defendant the sum of, to wit, £100, in full satisfaction and discharge of the same and every part thereof, and all damages in respect thereof: and although a reasonable time from the time of the making of the promise by the defendant, to wit, the day and year last aforesaid, had elapsed long before the commencement of this suit, to wit, on the day and year last aforesaid, of which the defendant then had notice; and although the plaintiff hath at all times, from the making of the promise by the defendant in this count mentioned to the commencement of this suit, been ready and willing to accept the said sum of, to wit, £100 of and from the defendant, in such full satisfaction and discharge as aforesaid, of which the defendant hath always had notice; and although the plaintiff hath not at any time sued the defendant for or in respect of the said sum of, to wit, £173 2*s.* 3*d.*, or any part thereof, or any damages in respect thereof, &c., yet, &c.: — [Breach, non-payment by the defendant of the said sum of £100, or any part thereof.]

General demurrer, and joinder in demurrer.

The defendant's points marked for argument were: That there is no sufficient consideration for the defendant's promise; either, first, in respect of the forbearance to sue, because, although forbearance to sue when there is a well-founded claim, or the giving up of a suit actually commenced where the claim is fairly litigable, may be a sufficient consideration for such a promise, the declaration here neither shews that there was a debt or claim which could have been enforced, nor that the plaintiff had commenced an action, or taken any step to enforce it, or was even intending to do so; nor, secondly, in respect of the promise of the plaintiff to take £100 in satisfaction, because it does not appear that any thing was owing from the defendant to the plaintiff, much less that more was owing, or that there was any fair or reasonable doubt whether more was owing or not; that there was consequently, so far as appears, neither benefit to the defendant nor detriment to the plaintiff. The defendant will also contend that the promise of the plaintiff not to sue and to take £100 in satisfaction was not binding upon him, being an agreement to accept a less sum in satisfaction of a greater.

The plaintiff's points were: That the declaration discloses a sufficient consideration to support the promise laid therein, inasmuch as the avoiding litigation by a settlement of claims of right in controversy is a sufficient consideration to support a promise; and that it makes no difference that the count shews, as the consideration for the promise of the defendant therein laid, a promise by the plaintiff partly executory, as a promise binding upon a plaintiff is in law a sufficient consideration to support a promise by a defendant.

Kelly, in support of the demurrer. The declaration is bad. It states no sufficient consideration for the defendant's promise to pay the

£100; for it does not shew that any debt was due from the defendant to the plaintiff, or that any suit was pending, the termination of which would be a benefit to the defendant or any detriment to the plaintiff. An undertaking not to sue, or forbearance to sue, is no consideration, where there is no legal demand or cause of action. It is not sufficient that disputes and differences existed between the plaintiff and defendant, for such an allegation would be satisfied by proof that the plaintiff made an unfounded claim which the defendant wholly denied. There is nothing to shew that the plaintiff was entitled to maintain any action whatever. The old cases establish that the forbearance of a suit, where the party is not liable, is not a good consideration. Tooley v. Windham,[1] King v. Hobbs.[2] That doctrine was first broken in upon in Longridge v. Dorville,[3] where it was held that the giving up a suit, instituted to try a question respecting which the law is doubtful, is a good consideration for a promise to pay a stipulated sum. But that case is very distinguishable; for there a suit had been actually instituted for the purpose of trying a doubtful question, and a ship had been delivered up which might otherwise have been detained. But Holroyd, J., there says: "If a person is about to sue another for a debt for which he is not answerable, the mere consideration of forbearance is not sufficient to render him liable." Here no suit has been instituted, and no liability is shewn. It is not even stated that the plaintiff had any reason at all to believe that he had a cause of action against the defendant. Besides, the acceptance of £100 would be no satisfaction for a claim of £173 2*s.* 3*d.*, if that were really due.

J. Henderson, contra. The consideration alleged is sufficient. The circumstance of an action being brought or not makes no difference. If there be a *bona fide* claim, which is forborne to be put in suit at the request of the defendant, that is enough. The allegation here in substance is, that the plaintiff had made a claim against the defendant for a certain amount, which the latter had denied to be due, and thus a dispute existed between them; and the defendant agreed, in consideration that the plaintiff would forego his claim for £173 2*s.* 3*d.*, to pay him a definite sum of money of a smaller amount. Had the declaration averred that the defendant was actually indebted to the plaintiff in £173 2*s.* 3*d.*, and that the plaintiff had agreed to take £100 in satisfaction of that larger sum, it would have been bad on the face of it. The abandonment of the right to sue for the unascertained amount is a good consideration for the promise. [LORD ABINGER, C. B. That may be true where the question is only as to the amount of a debt; but must not the existence of some actual debt be shewn, as a foundation for the promise?] It is submitted that, there being a claim, and it being doubtful what is the amount due, or even whether any thing is due, that is enough. In Wilkinson v. Byers,[4] where an action was

[1] Cro. Eliz. 206.
[2] Yelv. 26.
[3] 5 B. & Ald. 117.
[4] 1 Ad. & Ell. 106; 3 Nev. & M. 853.

pending for an unliquidated demand, the defendant's agreeing to pay a fixed sum in lieu of the plaintiff's claim was held a good consideration for the plaintiff to stay proceedings and pay his own costs. [LORD ABINGER, C. B. There an action had been brought, and there was a good consideration for the plaintiff's agreeing to discontinue it. ROLFE, B. Is not the plaintiff bound to shew that there are at least reasonable grounds for believing that something is due to him from the defendant?] The parties have here constituted themselves the judges whether there was any thing due or not, and the legality of a claim to some amount is admitted by their agreement. The relinquishment by the plaintiff of his right, and a corresponding benefit derived by the defendant thereby, is a sufficient consideration.

Kelly, in reply, was stopped by the court.

LORD ABINGER, C. B. The question in this case is, whether there is on the face of this declaration a good consideration for the promise alleged; and I am of opinion that there is not. Mr. Henderson has treated the words used in the declaration as if they implied that a reasonable doubt existed between the parties as to the existence of a debt due from the defendant to the plaintiff; but the declaration does not shew, either expressly or by implication, any thing of that kind; it only alleges that certain disputes and controversies were pending between the plaintiff and the defendant, whether the defendant was indebted to the plaintiff in a certain sum of money. There is nothing in the use of the word "controversy" to render this a good allegation of consideration. The controversy merely is, that the plaintiff claims the debt, and the other denies it. The case might have been different, if the declaration had said, "whereas the defendant was indebted to the plaintiff in divers sums of money for money lent, and also on an account stated;" that a dispute arose as to the amount of the debt so due; and, in order to put an end to all controversies respecting it, it was agreed that the plaintiff, in consideration of receiving £100, should not sue the defendant in respect of his original claim. In that case the plaintiff would have been bound to prove at the trial the existence of a debt to some amount; he might not indeed be bound to prove the full amount, but simply to shew such a claim as to lay a reasonable ground for the defendant's making the promise; whereas, in the present case, he would not have to prove any thing beyond the fact that there had been a dispute between himself and the defendant as to the existence of a debt. A man may threaten to bring an action against any stranger he may happen to meet in the street. Where an action is depending, the forbearing to prosecute it is a sufficient consideration for a promise to pay a certain sum of money; for, besides other advantages, the party promising would save the extra costs which he would have to pay even if he were successful.

GURNEY, B., concurred.

ROLFE, B. I am of the same opinion. Mr. Henderson lays down the proposition much too broadly,—that if a party forbears to do something which he might have done, that forbearance would be a good consideration for a promise; so that, if it had appeared on the face of the declaration that nothing was due to the plaintiff, his forbearance to sue would even then be a consideration. I cannot subscribe to that. I think the plaintiff is bound to shew a consideration, in the shape of something either beneficial to the opposite party or detrimental to himself. *Judgment for the defendant.*

LLEWELLYN v. LLEWELLYN.

IN THE QUEEN'S BENCH, MICHAELMAS TERM, 1845.

[*Reported in 3 Dowling and Lowndes' Practice Cases*, 318.]

ASSUMPSIT. The first count of the declaration stated that, whereas heretofore, to wit, on the twenty-third day of June, in the year of our Lord 1837, there had been and then were divers accounts between the plaintiff and the defendant, which accounts were open and unsettled; and there were then divers disputes between the plaintiff and the defendant touching and concerning the said accounts; and the plaintiff then claimed of the defendant that the defendant was indebted to the plaintiff in divers large sums of money, amounting together to the sum of, to wit, £500; and the defendant then claimed of the plaintiff, that he the plaintiff was indebted to the defendant; and thereupon it was then agreed, by and between the plaintiff and defendant, that they should respectively give up their respective claims each upon the other; and thereupon, in consideration thereof, and that the plaintiff at the request of the defendant would give up, relinquish, and forbear to prosecute, to and against him the defendant, all claims and demands whatsoever which he the plaintiff then had upon or against the defendant, he the defendant then promised the plaintiff to pay him the plaintiff, during the lifetime of him the said plaintiff, a certain yearly sum of, to wit, £6, at and upon, to wit, the twenty-third day of June, in each and every year during the lifetime of him the said plaintiff; and the plaintiff avers, that although he hath performed all things by him to be done in pursuance of the said agreement and of his said promise, and hath given up, relinquished, and ceased and forborne to prosecute against the defendant the said claims and demands of him the plaintiff in that behalf, yet the defendant, disregarding his said promise, hath not paid to the plaintiff the said yearly sum of £6 or any part thereof, but hath hitherto wholly neglected and refused so to do; and on the contrary thereof, a large sum of money, to wit, the sum of £6, of the said yearly sums of money for one year ending on a certain day, to wit, on the twenty-third day of June, in the year of our Lord 1842, and then last elapsed, then became and was and now is due and in arrear, and unpaid from the defendant to the plaintiff, contrary to the said promise.

The defendant pleaded the general issue.

At the trial, which took place on the 29th of last April, before the under-sheriff of Breconshire, a verdict was returned for the plaintiff, with leave to the defendant to move to enter a nonsuit, on the ground that there was no such [sufficient?] consideration stated in the declaration.

A rule *nisi* had been accordingly obtained to arrest the judgment, or for a nonsuit, or a new trial.

Peacock now shewed cause. It is submitted that this declaration discloses a sufficient consideration for the defendant's promise. It is stated in the inducement, which is admitted on the record, that there had been and then were divers accounts open and unsettled between the plaintiff and the defendant, and that the plaintiff claimed divers sums from the defendant, and that, in consideration thereof, and that the plaintiff at the request of the defendant would forbear to prosecute against the defendant these claims, the defendant made the promise stated in the declaration. That is a sufficient consideration, and the case differs from one where the only consideration is the foregoing of disputes and controversies as to whether any sum is owing between the parties. Here it appears that there have been accounts between the parties which remain unsettled, and that the plaintiff claimed certain sums from the defendant. The allegation that the plaintiff claimed certain sums from the defendant, taken in conjunction with the statement that there were accounts unsettled between the parties, is equivalent to an allegation by the plaintiff that a debt was due from the defendant to him. If so, then the giving up the claim in respect of that debt is a sufficient consideration for the promise.

E. V. Williams, in support of the rule. Whatever doubt may have formerly existed on this subject, it is now sufficiently clear that the mere giving up a claim to a debt, without shewing that a debt exists, is not a sufficient consideration on which to found an assumpsit. In Longridge v. Dorville[1] it was held that the giving up a suit instituted to try a question respecting which the law is doubtful is a good consideration for a promise to pay a stipulated sum. But there a suit was actually pending, and the plaintiff might have sustained some detriment by giving up all claim in respect of the expenses incurred, and the defendant have derived some benefit by having that suit put an end to without further trouble or investigation. Here, however, there

[1] 5 B. & A. 117.

is no allegation of the existence of a debt, but only that the plaintiff "claimed" a debt as owing to him. That a party "claims" a debt, raises no presumption that the money is owing to him. The claim may be perfectly unfounded. It is true that it is alleged that there were accounts open and unsettled between the parties, but it does not say which party was debtor. The plaintiff therefore may have been the debtor to the defendant; and if so, his claim against the defendant could not be rested on the state of the accounts between the parties. There is, however, a case which is very much in point with the present. In Edwards *v.* Baugh[1] the declaration alleged that certain disputes and controversies were pending between the plaintiff and the defendant, whether the defendant was indebted to the plaintiff in a certain sum of money; and it was held upon demurrer, that it disclosed no sufficient consideration on which to maintain the action; and Lord Abinger, C. B., in delivering judgment, drew the distinction between foregoing a dispute as to the existence of a debt, and foregoing a dispute as to the amount of it. The true rule is, as is laid down by Rolfe, B., in the same case, that "the plaintiff is bound to shew a consideration, in the shape of something either beneficial to the opposite party or detrimental to himself." Here there is nothing beneficial to the defendant, for the claim may have been unfounded; nothing detrimental to the plaintiff, for the giving up an unfounded claim could have been no injury to him.

Peacock referred to the case of Smith *v.* Monteith.[2]

Cur. adv. vult.

PATTESON, J. This case appears to me to be very distinguishable from that of Edwards *v.* Baugh, upon the authority of which the learned counsel for the defendant relied. There the declaration merely stated that disputes existed between the plaintiff and defendant whether the defendant was indebted to the plaintiff; which might be true, although they might have been entire strangers to each other, and never have had any transactions together. If so, the ending of such disputes could neither be detrimental to the plaintiff nor beneficial to the defendant. Here, on the contrary, the declaration states as a substantive fact, which might have been traversed by the defendant, that there had been and were mutual accounts between the plaintiff and defendant, which were open and unsettled. It then states in substance that each party claimed the balance, and that it was agreed that each party should withdraw his claim, and that the defendant should pay the plaintiff an annuity of £6 for his life. It then states that, in consideration that the plaintiff would withdraw his claim, the defendant promised to pay the annuity. Here is a plain detriment to the plaintiff in foregoing his claim to the balance; a claim which was not

[1] 11 M. & W. 641. [2] 13 M. & W. 427.

made against a stranger, but which had a probable foundation arising from mutual accounts between the parties, which are admitted to have been open and unsettled.

Under these circumstances I am of opinion that a valid consideration for the defendant's promise appears on the face of this declaration, and that the rule obtained in this case must be discharged.

Rule discharged.

SMYTH v. HOLMES.

IN THE EXCHEQUER, NOVEMBER 12 AND 17, 1846.

[*Reported in* 10 *Jurist*, 862.]

ASSUMPSIT. The declaration set forth an indenture made between the plaintiff and defendant, by which certain matters in difference between them were referred to an arbitrator; the indenture providing, *inter alia*, that the costs incident to said reference and to the preparation of said indenture, and of all proceedings relative to the same, should be in the discretion of the arbitrator. The declaration then averred that the arbitrator took upon himself the burden of the arbitration, and having been attended on the 11th of February, 1845, by the respective solicitors of the parties, and having heard the said solicitors as well as the respective counsel of the said parties, it was thereupon, with the approbation of the said arbitrator, agreed by and between the plaintiff and defendant in manner following: that is to say, that the sum of £200 should forthwith be paid by the defendant to and accepted by the plaintiff, in full satisfaction of all claims and demands of the plaintiff in respect to the several matters so referred, &c.; and that each of them, the plaintiff and defendant, should abide by and pay his own costs of the reference, &c., and of the said indenture, and of all the proceedings under the same. The declaration then averred mutual promises to fulfil the last-mentioned agreement, and alleged as a breach the non-performance of it by the defendant. General demurrer.[1]

Martin, in support of the demurrer. The declaration discloses no cause of action against the defendant. It shews in substance that certain matters in difference between the plaintiff and defendant having been referred to arbitration, the parties, in the presence of the arbitrator, agreed that a sum of £200 should be paid by the defendant to the plaintiff in satisfaction of his claim against him, and that each party should pay his own costs of the reference. Now, that is a mere accord; and it is an established principle that an action will not lie on an

[1] See *supra*, p. 221, note 1. — ED.

accord unless satisfaction be shewn. Peytoe's Case, 9 Co. 77 *b*; Allen *v.* Harris, 1 Ld. Raym. 122; 1 Rol. Abr. 128, tit. Accord; Case *v.* Barber, T. Jones, 158; Vin. Abr., Accord (A.), pl. 11; Lynn *v.* Bruce, 2 H. Black. 317; James *v.* David, 5 T. R. 143, per Grose, J. Edwards *v.* Baugh, 11 Mee. & W. 641, comes very near the present case. [POLLOCK, C. B. In that case Lord Abinger says: "Where an action is depending, the forbearance to prosecute it is a sufficient consideration for a promise to pay a certain sum of money; for, besides other advantages, the party promising would save the costs which he would have to pay even if he were successful."] That was an extra-judicial opinion. [PARKE, B. There, there was no new consideration, but merely an agreement to do something in discharge of an existing debt; here part of the consideration is, that the parties will abandon a previous unexecuted agreement, by putting an end to which each of them gets some immediate advantage.] There is no real distinction between the present benefit of putting a stop to the proceedings before an arbitrator, and the paying down a sum of money. [He also cited Wilkinson *v.* Byers, 1 Adol. & Ell. 106; and POLLOCK, C. B., referred to the judgment of Holroyd, J., in Longridge *v.* Dorville, 5 B. & A. 117.]

Cowling, who appeared to support the declaration, was stopped by the court.

POLLOCK, C. B. This is an action brought to recover a sum of money which the defendant promised to pay to the plaintiff. There had been an agreement to refer certain matters in difference; and if the doctrine of accord and satisfaction applied to this case at all, some doubt might have arisen in consequence of the observation of Lord Abinger in Edwards *v.* Baugh, 11 Mee. & W. 641. But the present is a case where parties agree to abandon a reference, and so far is distinguishable from a mere action brought by A. against B. When before the arbitrator, they entered into a mutual agreement to abandon the reference and the contingent right to the costs of it, and agreed that one should pay to the other a sum of money in satisfaction of his claim. It is very difficult to distinguish an agreement that one shall pay a sum of money on such a consideration as this from any other consideration that is good in law. Here was an agreement to refer certain matters to arbitration, and that arbitration, if proceeded with, might have ended more disadvantageously for the defendant than the agreement; as, for example, the award might be that he should pay the costs of the reference. The plaintiff, in consideration of the defendant promising to pay a sum of money, agrees to forego his right to the chance of an award that the defendant should pay those costs; and the defendant, on entering into such a bargain, agrees to pay money on a consideration which is good in law. Our judgment therefore must be for the plaintiff.

PARKE, B. I am of the same opinion. If this had been an action brought on an accord only, the authorities cited by Mr. Martin, namely, 1 Rol. Abr. 128, Lynn v. Bruce, in the Court of Common Pleas, and the rest, would be decisive on the point, that no action can be supported on a mere accord. But here we have more than a mere accord, for there is an agreement between these parties to discharge each other from an agreement of reference; and such an agreement before breach of the original agreement is binding. Here then the plaintiff agrees to abandon the reference, and discharge the defendant from his promise to refer the matter originally in difference. That is enough to shew this action maintainable, for an action will lie on mutual promises; and this is such an action, and not an action on an accord.

ALDERSON and ROLFE, BB., concurred.

Judgment for the plaintiff.

HENDERSON AND OTHERS, *Official Managers of the North of England Joint Stock Banking Company*, v. STOBART.

IN THE EXCHEQUER, FEBRUARY 9, 1850.

[*Reported in* 5 *Exchequer Reports*, 99.]

ASSUMPSIT by the official managers of the North of England Joint-Stock Banking Company for winding up the said company. The declaration stated that before the making of the promise, &c., one G. Burdis had been public officer of the said company; and that an action had been commenced by Burdis against one F. Todd and W. Todd for the recovery of the amount of a bill of exchange drawn by F. Todd and W. Todd upon the owners of the Trindon Colliery, and accepted by the defendant for himself and the other owners of the colliery, for £1250, and indorsed to the Banking Company; that, whilst the action was so pending, it was agreed between the Banking Company, W. Todd, F. Todd, and the defendant, that the action should be settled as follows: £250 by the promissory note of W. Todd and F. Todd; £500 by the promissory note of W. Todd and F. Todd; and £500 to be paid by the defendant's promissory note of £500 at twelve months; the defendant consenting to the North of England Banking Company appropriating the securities held by them to the payment of such balance, and the defendant agreeing to give them a power to sell the properties mentioned in the securities; the company to forego all interest on receiving the three notes, and to guarantee to give up the bill sued on, and the £1000 bill received on account of the said bill. The declaration then stated mutual promises, and averred that, although the Banking Company had performed all things in the said agreement on their part to be performed, and had always been ready and willing to settle the said action, and to forego all interest on receiving the three notes, and to guarantee to give up the bill sued on, and the £1000 bill received on account of the said bill, yet the defendant did not nor would give to the Banking Company such promissory note for £500, nor such power of sale, &c.

Pleas: First, *non assumpsit;* Secondly, that it was not agreed between the Banking Company, W. Todd, F. Todd, and the defendant, *modo et forma.*[1]

A rule *nisi* having been obtained to arrest the judgment on a verdict in favor of the plaintiffs,

Martin and *Hugh Hill* shewed cause. . . . It is conceded that no action will lie upon an accord unexecuted. Lynn v. Bruce,[2] Reniger v. Fogossa.[3] But this declaration does not state that which merely amounts to an accord, for the company are to give up something besides the action. An accord is an agreement between the parties to the original contract, but here the defendant was no party to the action. This is a new agreement, which, if carried out, would prevent the company from proceeding with the action. The general averment of performance by the company of their promises is good after verdict. Varley v. Manton,[4] Kemble v. Mills.[5] Mere forbearance is a sufficient consideration to support an agreement. In Com. Dig., Action upon the Case upon Assumpsit (B. 2), in treating of what will be a good consideration, it is said, "So in consideration of surceasing his suit, for that is a benefit to the defendant, and a prejudice to the plaintiff, though the action is not discharged." This is tantamount to an agreement by the company to forbear their suit, which they have done on the faith of the defendant being a party to the agreement. The other debtors signed the agreement as well as the defendant, and it would be a fraud on them, if he were not bound by it. Good v. Cheesman[6] shews that an accord with mutual promises is binding, though unexecuted. In Wilkinson v. Byers[7] it was held that the payment by the defendant of an agreed sum, in discharge of an action for an unliquidated demand, was a good consideration for a promise by the plaintiff to stay proceedings and pay his own costs; and Littledale, J., expressed an opinion that such an agreement would be binding, even in the case of a liquidated demand, on the authority of Reynolds v. Pinhowe.[8] [PARKE, B. That was in effect an accord executed.] This is not like the cases of Tattersall v. Parkinson[9] and Down v. Hatcher,[10] where the

1 A third plea and other parts of the case, having no reference to the question of consideration, have been omitted. — ED.

2 2 H. Bl. 317. 3 Plowd. 6. 4 9 Bing. 363.

5 1 M. & G. 757. 6 2 B. & Ad. 328. 7 1 A. & E. 106.

8 Cro. Eliz. 429. 9 16 M. & W. 752. 10 10 A. & E. 121.

defence set up was the payment of a less sum in satisfaction of a greater; but it comes within the principle of the decision in Sibree v. Tripp.[1] [They also referred to Smyth v. Holmes.[2]]

Knowles and *Unthank*, in support of the rule. This agreement is a mere accord, and had no effect in putting an end to the original action. Good v. Cheesman proceeded on the ground that the agreement amounted to a valid new contract between the other creditors and the debtor, capable of being immediately enforced. The test in these cases is, whether the parties intended to accept the agreement as a satisfaction, or the performance of it. This declaration in terms alleges a performance, but is accompanied with language which shews that the agreement has not been performed; for it is averred that the company were "ready and willing to settle the action," &c. It is plain therefore that the parties did not rely upon the agreement, but upon the performance of it; and that distinguishes the case from those cited, and brings it within the rule that an accord unexecuted is no satisfaction. Carter v. Wormald.[3] This agreement could not have been pleaded in bar of the original action, if it had been proceeded with. Flockton v. Hall,[4] Bayley v. Homan.[5] [PARKE, B. There is a new party to the agreement; it is as if the company had said to the defendant, "If you will become a party, and pay us £500, we will agree to stay proceedings in the action."] Ford v. Beech[6] decided that there can be no suspension of a right of action. . . .

PARKE, B. The rule must be discharged. We are satisfied that this is an agreement which would have been broken if the company had gone on with the original action; for, a new person being made a party to the contract, it becomes a binding engagement, and not a mere accord. . . .

ALDERSON, B., ROLFE, B., and PLATT, B., concurred.

Rule discharged.

CROWTHER AND OTHERS v. FARRER.

IN THE QUEEN'S BENCH, JUNE 10, 1850.

[Reported in 15 Queen's Bench Reports, 677.]

ASSUMPSIT. The declaration stated that at the time of the making of the promise two actions, one in trover and the other in trespass, both at the suit of the present plaintiffs against the present defendant, were pending in the Queen's Bench; and thereupon it was agreed by

[1] 15 M. & W. 23. [2] 10 Jur. 862. [3] 1 Exch. 81.
[4] 19 L. J., Q. B., 1. [5] 3 Bing. N. C. 915. [6] 11 Q. B. 852.

and between the plaintiffs and the defendant in manner following, that is to say: that the said actions should be settled, and all proceedings therein stayed, and that the defendant should pay to the plaintiffs £40 in respect of the costs of the said two actions, and also £236 9*s.* in part of damages; and that the plaintiffs should receive from certain other persons, to wit, J. B. and J. P., £263 11*s.*; but in the event of J. B. and J. P. neglecting or refusing to pay to the plaintiffs that amount, or in the event of J. B. and J. P. giving up their contract with the defendant,[1] then, and in either of such cases, the defendant should pay to the plaintiffs what might remain unpaid to them of such sum of £263 11*s.*, in which case the defendant should be entitled to get the 1506 square yards of stone[1] in the said agreement mentioned, or to sell it as he might think proper, in the same manner as though a certain agreement of 1835 had never been made.[1] Averment of mutual promises: "and, although the plaintiffs have always performed the said agreement on their part, and although they, confiding in the said promise of the defendant, did then, to wit, upon the making of the said promise, wholly cease to prosecute the said actions and each of them, and have thence continually hitherto stayed all proceedings therein, and although a reasonable time for the defendant to pay the said sums of £40 and £236 9*s.* had elapsed long before the commencement of this suit;" breach, non-payment of these sums, or either of them, or any part thereof.

Plea: *Non assumpsit.* Issue thereon.

On the trial before Patteson, J., at the York summer assizes, 1849, it appeared that a contract to the effect set out in the count was made between the plaintiffs and the attorneys of the defendant. The main contest was, whether or not there was sufficient evidence of authority on their part to bind the defendant. The learned judge reserved leave to move to enter a nonsuit if there was no such evidence, and left the case to the jury. Verdict for plaintiffs.

Knowles, in Michaelmas Term last, obtained a rule *nisi* to enter a nonsuit, pursuant to the leave reserved, or to arrest the judgment. On this day cause was shewn.

It appeared, by the judge's notes, that there was evidence of an express ratification of the contract by the defendant; and the rule to enter a nonsuit was discharged on that ground. The argument relating to that portion of the rule is omitted.

Martin and *Hugh Hill*, as to the rule for arresting judgment. The rule has been obtained on the supposition that this is an action on a mere accord. But it is an action on an agreement in consideration of forbearance of suit, which is more than a mere accord unexecuted. The reason why an action shall not lie on a mere executory accord (or,

[1] The declaration did not state any thing further on this subject.

as it is there called, concord), is fully explained in Reniger v. Fogossa.[1] The mere executory concord which does not prevent the plaintiff from proceeding with his action is without consideration. But, when there is consideration for the agreement, an action will lie, though the agreement is an accord. In Com. Dig., Action on the Case upon Assumpsit (B. 1), it is said: "A promise in consideration of the forbearance of a suit is good; for that is for the benefit of the defendant, though the action is not discharged." In the present case there is much more consideration than in that put by Comyns; for the actions are by the agreement actually settled, so that the plaintiffs could not afterwards have proceeded with them. Cartwright v. Cooke,[2] Wilkinson v. Byers.[3] It is sufficient, however, that there should be any consideration. Henderson v. Stobart[4] is much in point.

Knowles and *Tomlinson*, contra. [LORD CAMPBELL, C. J. If the plaintiffs at the request of the defendant made a contract which they would break if they proceeded with the actions, is not that alone a consideration to support the defendant's promise?] Such is not the meaning of the agreement; the plaintiffs do not agree to stay the actions unless they are paid the money: it is a mere accord. And, if the construction of the agreement was that the actions should be stayed by a binding release on the plaintiffs' part, there is no averment of performance.

LORD CAMPBELL, C. J. The motion in arrest of judgment is made on two grounds: first, that the declaration discloses no consideration for the defendant's promise; secondly, that there are not proper averments of performance of conditions precedent. Now, as to the first objection, the count states that it was agreed between the plaintiffs and defendant that the two actions should be settled, and all proceedings therein stayed. The question is not what would form a good plea in bar to the further maintenance of these actions, but whether this is a good consideration for the defendant's agreement. Is it not an advantage to the promisor, and a disadvantage to the promisee, that two actions against the one at the suit of the other should be settled, and no proceedings taken therein? Then there is a general averment of performance, which after verdict is abundantly sufficient, though it might be bad on special demurrer; but the count goes farther, and alleges performance more particularly. I think, however, that the agreement does not contemplate that any further act should be done to settle these actions. It appears that, by those who framed the agreement, they were considered as settled by the agreement itself; and I think, rightly; for they were so settled. I cannot entertain any doubt that, if after such an agreement an attempt were made to pro-

[1] Plowden, 1, 5, 6.
[2] 3 B. & Ad. 701.
[3] 1 A. & E. 106.
[4] 5 Exch. 99.

ceed in the actions, the court would interfere summarily if the defendant was not in default.

PATTESON, J. The question is raised, whether on the face of this declaration there is any thing more than an accord. Now I own I think the meaning of what is stated in the declaration is that the actions are actually gone by the agreement, and that the plaintiff could not have gone on with them; but, even if it was no more than an agreement on the part of the plaintiffs to refrain from going on, I think that was a sufficient consideration to support the promise of the defendant.

COLERIDGE, J. It seems to me that the declaration discloses a mutual agreement, binding each party to the other, supposing that other to have performed his own part. I had more doubt as to the sufficiency of the averment of performance. Perhaps on a special demurrer it might not be sufficient: but this is after verdict; and then it is enough that there is an averment of the plaintiffs having always performed the agreement on their part.

ERLE, J. I shall only add one word as to the averment of performance. I take it that, when the plaintiffs and the defendant agree that the actions are settled, the very agreement puts an end to the actions; that the court would interfere if they were afterwards proceeded with; and that consequently no further performance of the agreement is required. *Rule discharged.*

NASH, *Administrator with the Will annexed of* JOHN BEATSON, *deceased*, v. ARMSTRONG.

IN THE COMMON PLEAS, MAY 11, 1861.

[*Reported in* 10 *Common Bench Reports, New Series,* 259.]

THE declaration stated that, by deed dated the 29th of February, 1860, the said John Beatson, being then possessed thereof for a term which had not yet expired, let to the defendant certain rooms, part of a house of the said John Beatson, therein described, from the 1st of March in that year to the twenty-fourth of June in that year, at rent to be ascertained by two valuers, one on the part of the said John Beatson, and one on the part of the defendant, or an umpire to be agreed on by the said two valuers, such rent to include the use of the fixtures and fittings then in and upon the said demised premises, and which then belonged to the said John Beatson, the expense of the valuer to be employed by the said John Beatson to be paid in the first instance by the defendant, and retained by him out of the rent for the said demised premises accruing due from him on the said 24th of June, 1860; and afterwards the said valuers were respectively accordingly duly appointed, but did not, without any default of the said John Beatson or the plaintiff in that behalf, ascertain the rent so to be paid as aforesaid, or appoint any umpire; and the defendant nevertheless, at his request, occupied the said rooms under the said demise until the said 24th of June, and afterwards as tenant thereof to the plaintiff as administrator as aforesaid, for a long time, to wit, until the 1st of September, 1860, the said John Beatson having previously died; that afterwards, and whilst the amount of rent to be paid by the defendant for and in respect of his said occupation of the said rooms to the said 24th of June, and thence to the said 1st of September, was and remained unascertained and not agreed upon, and unpaid, it was, at the defendant's request, mutually agreed between the plaintiff as administrator as aforesaid and the defendant, that, if the plaintiff as administrator as aforesaid would not insist upon such valuation as aforesaid, and would not require that the said valuers should be called upon to appoint an umpire to ascertain the amount of the said rent to be paid for the defendant's said occupation until the said 24th of June, and the said valuers should be instructed not to appoint such umpire as aforesaid, the defendant would pay to the plaintiff as administrator as aforesaid, for and in respect of his occupation of the said rooms under the said deed, and for and in respect of the said subsequent occupation thereof as tenant to the plaintiff as administrator as aforesaid, a reasonable sum in that behalf, to wit, the sum of £70; and that neither the plaintiff as administrator as aforesaid, nor the defendant should ever call upon the other of them to carry out or perform or fulfil the terms of the said deed. Averment, that the plaintiff did every thing, and every thing existed and had before suit happened to entitle the plaintiff, as administrator as aforesaid, to payment of the said sum of money last mentioned, to wit, £70. Breach, that no part thereof had been paid.

To this count the defendant demurred, the ground of demurrer stated in the margin being, "that a contract under seal cannot be varied or discharged by a parol agreement." Joinder.

R. G. Williams, in support of the demurrer.[1] There is no valid consideration for the promise stated in the declaration. [WILLIAMS, J.

[1] The points marked for argument on the part of the defendant were as follows:—

"1. That the plaintiff by the first count is seeking to recover upon a deed as varied by a parol agreement, whereas a deed can only be varied by a deed;

"2. That the alleged agreement could be carried out by deed only, and there is no allegation of the execution of any such deed;

"3. That the matters alleged in the first count disclose a claim which can be enforced only in equity, and not at law;

Why is it not a good consideration in assumpsit that the plaintiff foregoes his rights under the deed?] It is varying by parol the terms of a deed. [WILLIAMS, J. That is not so.] By the parol agreement, the defendant is to pay the rent ascertained in a way different from that provided by the deed. [WILLIAMS, J. The plaintiff is seeking to enforce an agreement founded upon a consideration that the plaintiff will not put in force his rights under the deed.] A deed can only be varied by deed. Would a recovery in this action be pleadable in bar to an action upon the deed? [WILLES, J. I should have thought it a good answer by way of equitable plea. The payment of the £70 under the agreement would surely be ground for an unconditional perpetual injunction against proceeding upon the deed.] The declaration, it is submitted, must be treated as it would have been before equitable pleas were known. Most of the cases upon this subject are cases where the parol agreement is set up as an answer to an action on the deed; but the grounds of the decision in White v. Parkin, 12 East, 578, are strongly in favor of the proposition contended for here.[1] . . . In the present case, it cannot be contended that the parol agreement does not conflict with the deed. There is an utter repugnance between the two instruments. In the course of the argument in White v. Parkin, a case of Leslie v. De la Torre was cited, where Lord Kenyon ruled that the agreement by charter-party being under seal, the plaintiff could not set up a parol agreement inconsistent with it, and which in effect was meant in a certain extent to alter it. [WILLIAMS, J. The difficulty in your way is, that there is here an undertaking on the plaintiff's part to forbear from enforcing the payment of rent under the deed.] A rent would be payable under the deed, to which this agreement would be no answer. White v. Parkin[2] was cited and approved of in Thompson v. Brown, 7 Taunt. 656, 672.[3] . . . A deed cannot be varied in any way by parol; and no action can be maintained on a parol agreement which varies the deed. In the case of a contract for the sale of goods within the 17th section of the Statute of Frauds, where another day for payment has been by parol substituted for that originally fixed by the contract, it has been held that the subsequent parol agreement cannot be made the founda-

"4. That there is no consideration for the alleged agreement, if it is to be considered as independent of the deed;

"5. That the alleged agreement would afford no answer to an action upon the deed, or prevent the plaintiff from calling upon the valuers to appoint an umpire, or upon the defendant to carry out the terms of the deed, and the consideration for it is wholly nugatory;

"6. That the alleged agreement is in the nature of an accord only, and cannot be enforced or sued upon."

[1] The learned counsel here stated that case. — ED. [2] Leslie v. De la Torre?

[3] The learned counsel here stated the case of Gwynne v. Davy, 1 M. & G. 857, 2 Scott, N. R. 29, 9 Dowl. P. C. 1. — ED.

tion of an action. Marshall v. Lynn, 6 M. & W. 109; Mechelen v. Wallace, 7 Ad. & E. 49, 2 N. & P. 224; Stead v. Dawber, 10 Ad. & E. 57. In Chitty on Contracts, 6th edit. 55, it is said: "If there be an entire consideration for the defendant's promise made up of several particulars, and one of these consist of an agreement by the defendant which the Statute of Frauds requires to be in writing, and which for want of such writing is void, the whole consideration is void, and the promise cannot be supported." Here, there would be nothing to prevent the plaintiff from bringing an action upon the deed, even after the money was paid under the agreement. To allow this declaration to be good would be promoting circuity of action.

Raymond, for the plaintiff, was not called upon.[1]

WILLIAMS, J. I am of opinion that there should be judgment for the plaintiff on this demurrer. I do not think it necessary to dispute the correctness of many of the doctrines contended for in the argument; for I do not consider that the conclusion we have arrived at in any degree conflicts with any of the rules of law adverted to. On the face of this declaration there is an admitted promise by the defendant to pay a certain sum of money at a stipulated time, and an admitted breach of that promise. That is a perfectly good promise if founded upon a sufficient legal consideration; and the simple question is, whether there is a sufficient legal consideration disclosed on the declaration. I am of opinion that there is. It appears upon the face of the declaration that the plaintiff, as the personal representative of the original contracting party, being in a condition to bring an action upon the original contract, or otherwise to put it in force, in consideration of his abstaining from enforcing the rights conferred on him by that contract, the defendant promised to pay in respect of the occupation of the premises under the deed referred to, and in respect of his subsequent occupation thereof as tenant to the plaintiff as administrator, a reasonable sum. It was not necessary, in order to make that a good consideration, that the mutual promises should amount to a release of the right of action flowing from the original contract. The plaintiff, having a right to enforce the benefits conferred on him by the contract, enters into an agreement not to do so, whereby he changes his situa-

[1] The points marked for argument on the part of the plaintiff were as follows: —

"1. That the contract disclosed by the first count does not infringe upon the rule that a contract under seal cannot be varied by parol agreement;

"2. That, although a contract under seal cannot be varied by parol, yet it is competent to the parties to enter into a fresh agreement by parol, and for a good consideration, not to put in force the original contract;

"3. That the contract declared on is collateral to that entered into by the deed, and leaves the force of the deed itself intact, and amounts merely to an agreement not to enforce the performance of the original contract under seal;

"4. That such new contract is founded upon a good consideration, and is therefore valid."

tion to this extent, that, whereas before he had a right to sue upon the deed, if he now exercises that right he renders himself liable to an action. He has therefore plainly given a good consideration for the defendant's promise, and there is a complete cause of action disclosed on the face of the declaration. Upon principle, this is in truth nothing more than the ordinary case to be found in the old books, of an action against an heir whose ancestor has made a bond binding himself and his heirs, and who has assets by descent; if he contracts with the obligee of the bond that, if the latter will forbear to put the bond in suit, he will pay the sum secured by a given day, — that is a good assumpsit, and the forbearance till the day named is a good consideration to support the promise. The bond is not released by that. The only result is, to subject the obligee to an action if he puts the bond in suit before the expiration of the time agreed on. To that extent the terms of the bond are varied, and yet the bond remains unreleased; nevertheless, the consideration which flows from the agreement of the obligee not to put the bond in suit is good, and furnishes a ground of action if it be broken. That principle is applicable here.

WILLES, J. I am entirely of the same opinion. It appears to me that this declaration is neither open to the objection that it is an attempt to vary by parol the terms of a deed, nor to the objection that it is an action upon an accord.

BYLES, J. I had at first some doubt whether the maxim *unumquodque dissolvitur eodem ligamine quo ligatur* was not applicable here; for, till satisfaction, the plaintiff might always have an action upon the deed, and one cannot but see that this would lead to circuity of action. Further, whatever may be the value of the decision in Leslie *v.* De la Torre, the reported observations of Lord Kenyon are very much in favor of Mr. Williams's argument. But Gwynne *v.* Davy is not so. Three of the judges there intimate an opinion that an action might be maintained on the parol agreement. And no other authorities have been cited to shew that the rule is applicable to a cross-action, and is not confined to an action on the deed.

KEATING, J. I concur with the rest of the court in thinking that the declaration discloses a promise founded on a good consideration, and that it is not open to the objection that the plaintiff is seeking by parol to vary the terms of an instrument under seal.

Judgment for the plaintiff.

COOK AND OTHERS *v.* WRIGHT.

IN THE QUEEN'S BENCH, JULY 9, 1861.

[*Reported in* 1 *Best & Smith,* 559.]

DECLARATION by the plaintiffs, as payees, against the defendant, as maker of two promissory notes, dated the 7th February, 1856. The first count was upon a note for £10 10s., payable twelve months after date; the second was upon a note for £11, payable twenty-four months after date. There was also a count upon an account stated. Claim, £50.[1]

First plea, to the whole declaration: That, after the passing and coming into operation of The Whitechapel Improvement Act, 1853, and after the passing and coming into operation of The Metropolis Local Management Act, 1855, the defendant made the several promissory notes in the said first and second counts mentioned at the request of the plaintiffs; and that, at the time of making the said promissory notes, the plaintiffs asserted and represented to the defendant, and the defendant believed such assertion and representation to be true, that there was then due and owing and payable from him, the defendant, as the owner of certain lands and buildings in certain streets called Finch Street, John Street, and Dowson's Place, situate within the parish of St. Mary, Whitechapel, to the trustees of the parish of St. Mary, Whitechapel, under the provisions of The Whitechapel Improvement Act, 1853, divers large sums of money in respect of paving the streets fronting, adjoining, and abutting on such lands and buildings. And the defendant says that at the time of making the said promissory notes no sum of money whatsoever was due, or owing, or payable, from the defendant as such owner to the said trustees, nor was the defendant such owner as aforesaid; and that there never was any consideration or value for the defendant making the said promissory notes in the first and second counts mentioned, or either of them, or for his paying the same, or any part thereof; and the plaintiffs never were, nor was any person ever a holder of the said notes or either of them for value or consideration; and that the account stated, in the declaration mentioned, was stated of and concerning the matters and things in this plea mentioned, and not of or concerning any other matter or thing whatsoever.

Second plea, to the first and second counts: That the defendant was induced to make, and did make, the promissory notes in those counts

[1] The suit was commenced in the Whitechapel County Court of Middlesex, and was removed by *certiorari* into this court.

mentioned, and each of them, by the fraud, covin, and misrepresentation of the plaintiffs and others in collusion with them.

On the trial, before Wightman, J., at the sittings in London during Easter Term, 1860, it appeared that the plaintiffs were four of the commissioners or trustees acting under and incorporated by § 27 of The Whitechapel Improvement Act, 1853, 16 & 17 Vict. c. cxli.; and the action was brought to recover the amount of the two notes mentioned in the declaration. The evidence as to what took place at the time of the giving of the notes was as follows: Mitchell, the clerk to the trustees, said that, certain parts of the district not being in repair in 1854, notices to do repairs were sent or left addressed to the owners; and in October, 1855, he wrote a letter to the defendant demanding £70 for expenses incurred by the trustees in doing paving works in front of houses, of which the defendant was the owner or occupier, situate in and abutting on public highways within the district of The Whitechapel Improvement Act. The defendant complained that the works done by the trustees had seriously injured the property, and that the tenants were dissatisfied, and requested him to get an abatement made. He informed the defendant that the trustees assented, and the balance to be paid by the defendant was agreed to at £30; the defendant then requested time, and time was given, upon condition that he paid interest; and three promissory notes were given by the defendant, the first of which was paid by him under protest. The defendant was called, and stated that Mrs. Bennett was owner of the three houses in question, and that he was tenant of one of them at a rack-rent under her, and collected the rents of the others for her; that he paid the paving rate of the house which he occupied, and the paving rates of the other houses he paid for Mrs. Bennett and in her name; that, upon receiving the notice of October, 1855, he went before the Board of Trustees and told them that he was not the owner of the property, and shewed them Mrs. Bennett's receipts for the rent. They replied that, as he paid the rates, they considered he was the owner within the meaning of The Whitechapel Improvement Act, 1853, and, if he did not give notes, they would serve him as they had served Goble, which was by levying an execution on him; that there was another case in which the question of the liability of the inhabitants was to be tried, and, if decided against the trustees, he should not be called on to pay. When the first note became due he complained to Mitchell that the trustees had not carried out their promise to try one of the cases. Mitchell said that, as the defendant had signed the notes, he must pay them, and that the promised trial should take place; thereupon the defendant paid the first note. The defendant was afterwards told by Mrs. Bennett that he was not the owner within the meaning of the act, and he thereupon went to a board meeting of the trustees and told them that he would not pay the other notes. It was contended for the defendant that the notes were given without consideration, the defendant not being an "owner" within § 7 of The Whitechapel Improvement Act. The jury, in answer to questions put to them by the learned judge, found that the defendant told Mitchell or the Board, before he gave the notes, that he was not the owner; that the defendant mentioned, before he gave the notes, that Mrs. Bennett was the owner; and that Mitchell, or some member of the Board, told the defendant in the board-room that, unless he gave the notes, he would be served as Goble had been. The verdict was thereupon entered for the defendant, leave being reserved to move to enter a verdict for the plaintiffs. In the same term, May 4,

Montagu Chambers obtained a rule to shew cause accordingly, on the ground that the evidence did not prove want of consideration for giving the notes, and that upon the evidence the plaintiffs were entitled to a verdict.

This rule was argued in this term, May 23d, before COCKBURN, C. J., WIGHTMAN, CROMPTON, and BLACKBURN, JJ.

Shee, Serjt., and *Barnard* shewed cause. There was no consideration for the notes. The defendant signed them upon the representation by the trustees that they considered him the owner of the houses because he collected the rents and was liable to pay the rates. But the defendant was not the owner within § 7 of stat. 16 & 17 Vict. c. cxli., by which "the word 'owner,' used with reference to any lands or buildings in respect of which any work is required to be done, or any rate to be paid under this act, shall mean the person for the time being entitled to receive, or who, if such lands or buildings were let to a tenant at rack-rent, would be entitled to receive, the rack-rent from the occupier thereof."

The existence of disputes and controversies between a plaintiff and defendant, as to whether the defendant is indebted to the plaintiff, is not a sufficient consideration for a promise: there must be a debt in existence. Edwards v. Baugh.[1] These notes were not given for the debt of another party: the trustees did not profess to take them in payment of the rates due from Mrs. Bennett. [CROMPTON, J. Suppose money had been paid by the defendant, could he have recovered it back? The maxim *quod fieri non debet factum valet* seems to apply. WIGHTMAN, J., referred to Southall v. Rigg, and Forman v. Wright.[2]] In Addison on Contracts, p. 15, 4th ed., it is said: "So if the consideration prove to be a nullity, the promise founded upon it is void, as if the consideration be the forbearance of a suit when there is no cause of action .... or a promise to pay a debt which never had an existence in point of law."

Hannen, in support of the rule. 1. The plea was not proved. The defendant did not believe the representation of the trustees that he

[1] 11 M. & W. 641. [2] 11 C. B. 481.

was liable as owner of the houses under the provisions of The Whitechapel Improvement Act, 1853.

2. The plea is not good. In Edwards v. Baugh the defendant might have been imposed upon as to there being a debt due from him to the plaintiff, but in this case there is no statement that the defendant yielded to the assertion that he was owner of the houses; it amounts to no more than that he thought it doubtful whether he was liable. [CROMPTON, J. Did the trustees put themselves in a worse position by taking the notes? Might they not the next day have said, "We have mistaken our position," and have returned the notes?] No. In Baker v. Walker,[1] Parke, B., said (p. 467), "If I give a promissory note for the debt of a third person, I am bound to pay it when due." [CROMPTON, J. The defendant gave the note in discharge of his own liability: he took the debt upon himself, whosesoever it was, if the trustees would give him time.] The defendant signed the notes because the trustees threatened to sue him, not because he believed himself to be liable; and he obtained time for payment of the debt of a third person, which is a sufficient consideration for giving the notes. Sowerby v. Butcher.[2] Suppose the trustees had sued Mrs. Bennett for the rates, she might have pleaded that the trustees had taken notes for the amount from her agent. The notes were given for the debt claimed to be due in respect of a particular property. [COCKBURN, C. J. The difficulty which I feel is that I do not see in what character the defendant acted when he gave the notes.[3] . . .]

Cur. adv. vult.

BLACKBURN, J. (July 9th), delivered the judgment of COCKBURN, C. J., WIGHTMAN, J., and himself; CROMPTON, J., having left the court before the argument was concluded.

In this case it appeared on the trial that the defendant was agent for a Mrs. Bennett, who was a non-resident owner of houses in a district subject to a local act. Works had been done in the adjoining street by the commissioners for executing the act, the expenses of which, under the provisions of their act, they charged on the owners of the adjoining houses. Notice had been given to the defendant, as if he had himself been owner of the houses, calling on him to pay the proportion chargeable in respect of them. He attended at a board meeting of the commissioners, and objected both to the amount and nature of the charge, and also stated that he was not the owner of the houses, and that Mrs. Bennett was. He was told that, if he did not pay, he would be treated as one Goble had been. It appeared that Goble had refused to pay a sum charged against him as owner of some houses, and the commissioners had taken legal proceedings against him, and he

[1] 14 M. & W. 465.

[2] 2 Cr. & M. 368.

[3] Wightman, J., here read from 16 & 17 Vict. c. cxli. — ED.

had then submitted and paid, with costs. In the result it was agreed between the commissioners and the defendant that the amount charged upon him should be reduced, and that time should be given to pay it in three instalments; he gave three promissory notes for the three instalments; the first was duly honored; the others were not, and were the subject of the present action. At the trial it appeared that the defendant was not in fact owner of the houses. As agent for the owner he was not personally liable under the act. In point of law, therefore, the commissioners were not entitled to claim the money from him; but no case of deceit was alleged against them. It must be taken that the commissioners honestly believed that the defendant was personally liable, and really intended to take legal proceedings against him, as they had done against Goble. The defendant, according to his own evidence, never believed that he was liable in law, but signed the notes in order to avoid being sued as Goble was. Under these circumstances the substantial question reserved (irrespective of the form of the plea) was whether there was any consideration for the notes. We are of opinion that there was.

There is no doubt that a bill or note given in consideration of what is supposed to be a debt is without consideration if it appears that there was a mistake in fact as to the existence of the debt; Bell *v.* Gardiner;[1] and, according to the cases of Southall *v.* Rigg and Forman *v.* Wright, the law is the same if the bill or note is given in consequence of a mistake of law as to the existence of the debt. But here there was no mistake on the part of the defendant either of law or fact. What he did was not merely the making an erroneous account stated, or promising to pay a debt for which he mistakingly believed himself liable. It appeared on the evidence that he believed himself not to be liable; but he knew that the plaintiffs thought him liable, and would sue him if he did not pay, and in order to avoid the expense and trouble of legal proceedings against himself he agreed to compromise; and the question is, whether a person who has given a note as a compromise of a claim honestly made on him, and which but for that compromise would have been at once brought to a legal decision, can resist the payment of the note on the ground that the original claim thus compromised might have been successfully resisted.

If the suit had been actually commenced, the point would have been concluded by authority. In Longridge *v.* Dorville[2] it was held that the compromise of a suit instituted to try a doubtful question of law was a sufficient consideration for a promise. In Atlee *v.* Backhouse,[3] where the plaintiff's goods had been seized by the excise, and he had afterwards entered into an agreement with the commissioners of excise that all proceedings should be terminated, the goods delivered up to the plaintiff, and a sum of money paid by him to the commissioners,

[1] 4 M. & Gr. 11. [2] 5 B. & Ald. 117. [3] 3 M. & W. 633.

Parke, B., rests his judgment, p. 650, on the ground that this agreement of compromise honestly made was for consideration, and binding. In Cooper *v.* Parker[1] the Court of Exchequer Chamber held that the withdrawal of an untrue defence of infancy in a suit, with payment of costs, was a sufficient consideration for a promise to accept a smaller sum in satisfaction of a larger.

In these cases, however, litigation had been actually commenced; and it was argued before us that this made a difference in point of law, and that though, where a plaintiff has actually issued a writ against a defendant, a compromise honestly made is binding, yet the same compromise, if made before the writ actually issues, though the litigation is impending, is void. Edwards *v.* Baugh was relied upon as an authority for this proposition. But in that case Lord Abinger expressly bases his judgment (pp. 645, 646) on the assumption that the declaration did not, either expressly or impliedly, show that a reasonable doubt existed between the parties. It may be doubtful whether the declaration in that case ought not to have been construed as disclosing a compromise of a real *bona fide* claim, but it does not appear to have been so construed by the court. We agree that unless there was a reasonable claim on the one side, which it was *bona fide* intended to pursue, there would be no ground for a compromise; but we cannot agree that (except as a test of the reality of the claim in fact) the issuing of a writ is essential to the validity of the compromise. The position of the parties must necessarily be altered in every case of compromise, so that, if the question is afterwards opened up, they cannot be replaced as they were before the compromise. The plaintiff may be in a less favorable position for renewing his litigation; he must be at an additional trouble and expense in again getting up his case, and he may no longer be able to produce the evidence which would have proved it originally. Besides, though he may not in point of law be bound to refrain from enforcing his rights against third persons during the continuance of the compromise, to which they are not parties, yet practically the effect of the compromise must be to prevent his doing so. For instance, in the present case, there can be no doubt that the practical effect of the compromise must have been to induce the commissioners to refrain from taking proceedings against Mrs. Bennett, the real owner of the houses, while the notes given by the defendant, her agent, were running; though the compromise might have afforded no ground of defence had such proceedings been resorted to.

It is this detriment to the party consenting to a compromise arising from the necessary alteration in his position which, in our opinion, forms the real consideration for the promise, and not the technical and almost illusory consideration arising from the extra costs of litigation. The real consideration therefore depends, not on the actual commence-

[1] 15 Com. B. 822.

ment of a suit, but on the reality of the claim made and the *bona fides* of the compromise.

In the present case we think there was sufficient consideration for the notes in the compromise made as it was.

The rule to enter a verdict for the plaintiff must be made absolute.

Rule absolute.

SECTION VI.

Moral Consideration.

EDMONDS' CASE.

IN THE COMMON PLEAS, MICHAELMAS TERM, 1586.

[*Reported in* 3 *Leonard,* 164.]

IN an action upon the case against Edmonds, the case was, that the defendant, being within age, requested the plaintiff to be bounden for him to another for the payment of £30, which he was to borrow for his own use; to which the plaintiff agreed, and was bounden, *ut supra.* Afterwards the plaintiff was sued for the said debt, and paid it. And afterwards, when the defendant came of full age, the plaintiff put him in mind of the matter aforesaid, and prayed that he might not be damnified so to pay £30, it being the defendant's debt: whereupon the defendant promised to pay the debt again to the plaintiff: upon which promise the action was brought. And it was holden by the COURT that, although here was no present consideration upon which the assumpsit could arise, yet the court was clear that upon the whole matter the action did lie; and judgment was given for the plaintiff.[1]

[1] In the report of the same case in Godb. 138, *nom.* Barton and Edmonds' Case, it is said: "But if a *feme covert* and another at her request had been bounden in such a bond, and after the death of her husband she had assumed to have saved the other harmless against such bond, such assumpsit should not have bound the wife." — ED.

TREWINIAN v. HOWELL.

In the Queen's Bench, Hilary Term, 1588.

[*Reported in Croke Elizabeth*, 91.]

Error of a judgment in assumpsit against the now plaintiff, as executor to T. Trewinian his brother; in which Howell declared that, whereas the testator was indebted to him in a certain sum, the said Trewinian, the then defendant, did assume, that if he had goods sufficient, that he would pay him, and alleged that he had goods sufficient. Upon *non assumpsit*, it was found for the then plaintiff who had judgment. Upon this, error was brought; and the principal error assigned was, that there is no sufficient consideration alleged; for the having of goods was no consideration; but in consideration he would forbear to sue, &c., this had been a good consideration. But it was said of the other party that he being executor, his promise (he having assets) doth bind him, for he is in duty to pay it. *Daniel* said it was adjudged in one Hudson's Case, that a promise of the executor to pay a debt is binding if he hath assets, otherwise not. And so *Coke* said it was adjudged in Sir William Cook's Case that such a promise is good without any other consideration, if he hath assets of the testator in his hands, otherwise not; for the consideration is only by reason of the act and debt of the testator; and, therefore, shall bind me no further than the goods of the testator amount. Second error: that the judgment was general, and not *de bonis testatoris*, as it ought to be; for by such a general judgment, he shall be charged of his own goods. The Court said they would advise. But at another day (*absente* Wray) it was adjudged the judgment should be affirmed; for it was a good assumpsit, and he shall be charged *de bonis propriis*, being of his own promise.

WATSON v. TURNER et al.

In the Exchequer, Trinity Term, 1767.

[*Reported in Buller's Nisi Prius*, 129.]

An action was brought by an apothecary against the overseers of a parish for the cure of a pauper, who boarded with her son out of the parish, under an agreement made with him by the defendant Turner, who was the only acting overseer of the parish. The pauper was suddenly taken ill, and her son called in the plaintiff, who had attended her for four months, and cured her. After the cure Turner was applied to, and promised to pay the plaintiff's bill. It was held, that though there was no precedent request from the overseers, yet the promise was good, notwithstanding the Statute of Frauds; for overseers are under a moral obligation to provide for the poor. Secondly, that as Turner was the only acting overseer, the other was bound by his promise.[1]

ATKINS ET UXOR v. HILL.

IN THE KING'S BENCH, EASTER TERM, 1775.

[*Reported in Cowper*, 284.]

IN assumpsit the plaintiffs declared against Charles Hill, being in the custody, &c.: For that whereas James Clarke, &c., by his last will, &c., did give and bequeath to the plaintiff's wife the sum of £60, &c., and of his last will and testament made the said Charles Hill sole executor, &c., and the said Charles Hill took upon himself the burthen and execution of the said will: And the said N. and A. further say that divers goods and chattels, &c., afterwards, &c., came to the hands of the said Charles Hill as executor of the said J. C., which said goods and chattels were more than sufficient to satisfy and pay all the just debts and legacies of the said J. C., &c., of which the said C. H. then and there had notice: By reason of which said premises, the said Charles Hill became liable to pay to the said N. and A. the said sum of £60; and being so liable, he the said C., in consideration thereof, afterwards, &c., undertook and faithfully promised to pay to them the said sum of £60, whenever, &c.

To this declaration the defendant demurred generally.

Mr. *Le Blanc*, in support of the demurrer.[2]

Mr. *Buller*, contra, for the plaintiff. The question is, whether the facts stated in this declaration, namely, that the defendant was executor and had assets, &c., are a sufficient consideration for a promise. As to that question, it is a settled point that, wherever an express promise is made upon a good consideration, an action lies. And the slightest ground is sufficient to maintain a promise. 1 Vent. 40, 41, Wells v. Wells; 1 Lev. 273, s. c.; Stone v. Withipool, Latch, 21, in which latter case it is laid down, "that it is an usual allegation for a

[1] See Paynter v. Williams, 1 Cr. & M. 810. — ED.

[2] Only so much of the arguments and decision is here given as relates to the question of consideration. — ED.

rule, that any thing which is a ground for equity is a sufficient consideration."

But here an express promise is made, and by the demurrer admitted. It is objected, however, that there is no averment that the funeral expenses are paid. The answer is, it is averred that he had assets to pay, which is alone sufficient, and so it was expressly held by Lord King in the case of Camden *v.* Turner, Sittings after Tr., 5 Geo. I., C. B.; Select Cases of Evidence by Sir John Strange.

LORD MANSFIELD. This is a case in which the declaration particularly states that assets have been received by the defendant, the executor, more than sufficient to pay all the testator's debts and legacies. If so, it most undoubtedly must be taken upon the pleadings that there was sufficient to discharge the funeral expenses, because they are payable first; consequently, if there was less than the amount of them, there could not be sufficient to discharge the debts and legacies. The declaration then goes on to state that, in consideration of there being full sufficient assets as aforesaid, the defendant undertook and promised to pay the plaintiff his legacy. No doubt then but, at any time after an executor has assented, the property vests; and if it be a pecuniary legacy, an action at law will lie for the recovery of it. Formerly, upon a bill being filed in chancery against an executor, one part of the prayer of it was, that he should assent to the bequests in his testator's will. If he had assets, he was bound to assent. And when he had assented, the legacy became a demand which in law and conscience he was liable to pay. But in the present case there is not only an assent to the legacy, but an actual promise and undertaking to pay it; and that promise founded on a good consideration in law, as appears from the cases cited by Mr. Buller, particularly the case of Camden *v.* Turner,[1] where acknowledgment by an executor, "that he had enough to pay," was held a sufficient ground to support an assumpsit. Here the defendant by his demurrer admits he had sufficient to pay; therefore this is not the case that Mr. Le Blanc has been arguing upon; but it is the case of a promise made upon a good and valuable consideration, which in all cases is a sufficient ground to support an action. It is so in cases of obligations which would otherwise only bind a man's conscience, and which, without such promise, he could not be compelled to pay. For instance, where an infant contracts debts during his minority; if after he comes of age he consents to pay them, an action lies. So a conveyance executed by an infant, which he was compellable to do by equity, is a good conveyance at law. Co. Lit., Attornment, 315 *a.* In this case the promise is grounded upon a reasonable and conscientious consideration; namely, that the defendant had assets to discharge the legacy. If so, he was compellable in a court of equity, or in the ecclesiastical court, to pay it. I give my opinion upon this

[1] Sittings after Trinity Term, 5 Geo. I., C. B., *coram* King, C. J.

case as it stands; that is, that it is an express promise made upon a good and sufficient consideration.

The three other judges concurred.

Per Cur. Judgment for the plaintiff.

Mr. *Le Blanc* then moved for liberty to withdraw the demurrer, and plead the general issue; but the court refused it.

TRUEMAN *v.* FENTON.

In the King's Bench, January 28, 1777.

[*Reported in Cowper*, 544.]

This was an action on a promissory note, bearing date the 11th February, 1775, payable to one Joseph Trueman (the plaintiff's brother), three months after date, for £67, and indorsed by him to the plaintiff.

The declaration contained other counts for goods sold, money had and received, and on an account stated. The defendant pleaded, first, *non assumpsit;* secondly, "that on the 19th January, 1775, he became bankrupt, and that the debt for which the said note was given was due to the plaintiff before such time as he the defendant became bankrupt, and that the note was given to Joseph Trueman for the use of, and for securing to the said plaintiff his debt so due." The cause was tried before Lord Mansfield at the sittings after Michaelmas Term, 1776, when the jury found a verdict for the plaintiff, damages £72 12*s.*, costs 40*s.*, subject to the opinion of the court upon a special case, stating the answer of the plaintiff in this action to a bill filed against him in the Exchequer by the present defendant for a discovery of the consideration of the note; the substance of which was as follows: "That on the 15th of December, 1774, the defendant Fenton purchased a quantity of linen of the plaintiff Trueman; and it being usual to abate £5 per cent. to persons of the defendant's trade, the price, after such abatement made, amounted to £126 18*s.* That at the time of the sale it was agreed that one-half of the purchase money should be paid at the end of six weeks, and the other half at the end of two months: And in consideration thereof, the plaintiff Trueman drew two notes on the defendant for £63 9*s.*, each payable to his own order, at six weeks and two months respectively. That the defendant accepted the notes, and thereupon the plaintiff gave him a discharge for the sum. He then denied that he had proved or claimed any debt or sum of money under the commission; but set forth that he acquainted the defendant he was surprised at his ungenerous behavior in purchasing so large a quantity of linen of him at the eve of his bankruptcy, and informed him he had paid away the above two notes: upon which the defendant pressed him to take up the two notes, and proposed to give him a security for part of the debt. That afterwards on the 11th February, 1775, the defendant called upon the plaintiff, and voluntarily proposed to secure to him the payment of £67 in satisfaction of his debt, if he would take up the two notes and cancel or deliver them up to the defendant. That the plaintiff agreed to accept this proposal with the approbation of his attorney, and desired the note to be made payable to his brother Joseph Trueman or order, three months after date. That he took up the two acceptances and delivered them to the defendant to be cancelled, and accepted the above note for £67 in satisfaction and discharge thereof. That a commission of bankruptcy issued against the defendant on the 19th of January, 1775, and that the bankrupt obtained his certificate on the 17th of April following." The question reserved was, Whether the facts above stated supported the merits of the defendant's plea? If they did not, then a verdict was to be entered for the plaintiff on the general issue; but if the merits of the second plea supported the defendant's case, then a verdict was to be entered for the defendant on that plea.

Mr. *Buller*, for the plaintiff, argued that the note, though given after the bankruptcy, was in this case binding upon the defendant, and therefore the certificate was no bar to the present action. First: Because the goods, though sold before the bankruptcy, were sold on credit, and not to be paid for till a future day. Therefore, if no security at all had been given, the debt could not have been proved under the commission; because such a case does not fall within the provisions of stat. 7 Geo. I., c. 31. If not, this is simply the case of a sale of goods on future credit, for which the vendor receives a note after the vendee is become bankrupt; because the two drafts drawn by the plaintiff on the defendant at the time of the sale, and accepted by the defendant, could not vary the agreement. It was still a sale on future credit, and no debt due till after the bankruptcy. Besides, they were afterwards delivered up. If no debt was due at the time of the bankruptcy, the merits of the plea are clearly not proved; for the merits are, that the debt was then due. Now it clearly was not due, and therefore the certificate was no bar to the demand. Secondly: Supposing it could be contended that there was any thing like a debt due before the bankruptcy, yet the plaintiff upon the facts stated is still entitled to recover upon the note in question. The consideration was for a fair *bona fide* debt, without any mixture of fraud or pretence of undue advantage by the plaintiff. On the contrary, there was a gross fraud on the part of the defendant, in obtaining the goods upon the eve of his becoming bankrupt; and the conviction of such his misconduct was the inducement with him to offer the security now in dispute. If he were to discharge the whole original debt, it would not be more than was due, and what in conscience he ought to pay. But here the plaintiff has agreed to accept much less than in conscience was due to him. If so, like every other debt which a man is bound in conscience to discharge, it is a good ground for raising an assumpsit. The slightest acknowledgment is sufficient to revive a debt barred by the Statute of Limitations. So, where a man after he comes of age promises to pay a debt contracted during his minority, assumpsit lies. As to the case of a promise by a bankrupt to pay a debt in consideration of a creditor's signing his certificate, that is made void by the stat. 5 Geo. II., c. 30, sect. 11. But even that would have been a good ground of action before the statute; and it is the only exception made. The certificate, no doubt, is a provision for the benefit of the bankrupt. But he may waive it; and here he has waived it for a good and valuable consideration. If so, he is bound by the contract. In addition to this general reasoning, he cited the case of Lewis *v.* Chase, 1 P. Wms. 620, and Barnardiston *v.* Copeland, argued in the Common Pleas, in Hilary and Easter Terms, 1761, MSS.

Mr. *Davenport*, contra, for the defendant, contended that the plaintiff had no other remedy for his debt, but by resorting with the rest of the creditors to the commission. That the transaction, though colored over, was clearly intended as an evasion of the bankrupt laws, and therefore manifestly illegal. That the plaintiff's taking up the two drafts, and accepting another security short of his real debt, could in no respect be a new consideration to the defendant; because he was at all events discharged from them by his certificate. And as to the objection that the original debt itself was not within the stat. 7 Geo. I., c. 31, and therefore could not have been proved under the commission, it clearly might, allowing a rebate of interest for the time of the credit given. That the question depended solely upon the construction of the bankrupt laws, and particularly the stat. 5 Geo. II., c. 30, by which it was clear that, where such a promise or undertaking is made by a bankrupt before his certificate obtained, it is void. That any other construction would open a door to that collusion respecting the certificate which the statute meant to avoid, and at the same time be highly injurious to the bankrupt. Therefore he prayed judgment might be entered for the defendant.

LORD MANSFIELD. The plea put in, in this case, is that the debt was due at the time of the act of bankruptcy committed; and on that plea, in point of form, there was a strong objection made at the trial that the allegation was not strictly true; because at the time of the sale, credit was given to a future day; which day, as it appeared in evidence, was subsequent to the act of bankruptcy committed. To be sure, on the form of the plea, the defendant must fail. But I never like to entangle justice in matters of form, and to turn parties round upon frivolous objections where I can avoid it. It only tends to the ruin and destruction of both. I put it therefore to the counsel on the part of the plaintiff to give up the objection in point of form, and to take the opinion of the court, whether, according to the facts and truth of the case, the defendant could have pleaded his certificate in bar of the debt in question; and in case they had refused to do so, I should have left it to the jury upon the merits. The counsel for the plaintiff very properly gave up the point of form. The question therefore, upon the case reserved, is worded thus: Whether the facts support the merits of the defendant's plea? That is, Whether, on the merits of the case, properly pleaded, the certificate of the defendant would have been a bar to the plaintiff's action? Now, in this case there is no fraud, no oppression, no scheme whatsoever on the part of the plaintiff to deceive or impose on the defendant; and as to collusion with respect to the certificate, where a creditor exacts terms of his debtor as the consideration for signing his certificate, and obtains money or a part of his debt for so doing, the assignees may recover it back in an action. But that is not the case here. So far from it, the transaction itself excluded the plaintiff from having any thing to do with the certificate. No man can vote for or against the certificate till he has proved his debt. Here the plaintiff delivers up the two drafts bearing date prior to the act of bankruptcy, and by agreement accepts one for little more than half their amount, bearing date after the commission of bankruptcy sued out. Most clearly, therefore, he could not have proved that note under the commission; and if not, he could have nothing to do with the certificate. That brings it to the general question, Whether a bankrupt, after a commission of bankruptcy sued out, may not, in consideration of a debt due before the bankruptcy, and for which the creditor agrees to accept no dividend or benefit under the commission, make such creditor a satisfaction in part or for the whole of his debt, by a new undertaking and agreement? A bankrupt may undoubtedly contract new debts; therefore, if there is an objection to his reviving an old debt by a new promise, it must be founded upon the ground of its being *nudum pactum*. As to that, all the debts of a bankrupt are due in conscience, notwithstanding he has obtained his certificate; and there is no honest man who does not discharge them, if he afterwards has it in his power to do so. Though all legal remedy may be gone, the debts are clearly not extinguished in conscience. How far have the courts of equity gone upon these principles? Where a man devises his estate for payment of his debts, a court of equity says (and a court of law in a case properly before them would say the same): All debts barred by the Statute of Limitations shall come in and share the benefit of the devise, because they are due in conscience. Therefore, though barred by law, they shall be held to be revived and charged by the bequest. What was said in the argument relative to the reviving a promise at law, so as to take it out of the Statute of Limitations, is very true. The slightest acknowledgment has been held sufficient; as saying, "Prove your debt, and I will pay you," — "I am ready to account, but nothing is due to you." And much slighter acknowledgments than these will take a debt out of the statute. So in the case of a man, who after he comes of age promises to pay for goods or other things, which during his minority one cannot say he has contracted for, because the law disables him from making any such contract, but which he has been fairly and honestly supplied with, and which were not merely to feed his extravagance, but reasonable for him (under his circumstances) to have; such promise shall be binding upon him, and make his former undertaking good. Let us see then what the transaction is in the present case. The bankrupt appears to me to have defrauded the plaintiff by drawing him in, on the eve of a bankruptcy, to sell him such a quantity of goods on credit. It was grossly dishonest in him to contract such a debt, at a time when he must have known of his own insolvency, and which it is clear the plaintiff had not the smallest suspicion of, or he would not have given credit and a day of payment *in futuro*. On the other hand, what is the conduct of the plaintiff? He relinquishes all hope or chance of benefit from a dividend under the commission, by forbearing to prove his debt; gives up the securities he had received from the bankrupt, and accepts of a note, amounting to little more than half the real debt, in full satisfaction of his whole demand. Is that against conscience? Is it not on the contrary a fair consideration for the note in question? He might foresee prospects from the way of life the bankrupt was in, which might enable him to recover this part of his debt, and he takes his chance; for till then he could get nothing by the mere imprisonment of his person. He uses no threats, no menace, no oppression, no undue influence; but the proposal first moves from, and is the bankrupt's own voluntary request. The single question then is, Whether it is possible for the bankrupt, in part or for the whole, to revive the old debt? As to that, Mr. Justice Aston has suggested to me the authority of Bailey *v.* Dillon, where the court would not hold to special bail, but thought reviving the old debt was a good consideration. The two cases cited by Mr. Buller are very material. Lewis *v.* Chase, 1 P. Wms. 620, is much stronger than this; for that smelt of the certificate; and the Lord Chancellor's reasoning goes fully to the present question. Then the case of Barnardiston *v.* Coupland, in C. B., is in point. Lord Chief Justice Willes there says, "that the revival of an old debt is a sufficient consideration." That determines the whole case. Therefore I am of opinion that, if the plea put in had been formally pleaded, the merits of the case would not have been sufficient to bar the plaintiff's demand.

ASTON, J. As a case of conscience, I am clearly of opinion that the plaintiff is entitled. Wherever a party waives his right to come in under the commission, it is a benefit to the rest of the creditors. In the case of Bailey v. Dillon, the court on the last day of the term were of opinion, "that the defendant could not be held to special bail, yet they would not say that he might [not?] revive the old debt which was clearly due in conscience." A bankrupt may be and is held to be discharged by his certificate from all debts due at the time of the commission; but still he may make himself liable by a new promise. If he could not, the provision in the stat. 5 Geo. II., c. 30, sect. 11, by which every security for the payment of any debt due before the party became bankrupt, as a consideration to a creditor to sign his certificate, is made void, would be totally nugatory.—Lord MANSFIELD added that this observation was extremely forcible and strong.

Per Cur. Judgment for the plaintiff.

HAWKES ET UXOR v. SAUNDERS.

IN THE KING'S BENCH, JANUARY 28, 1782.

[*Reported in Cowper*, 289.]

THIS action was brought against the defendant in her own right; and the declaration stated that George Saunders by his will bequeathed a legacy of £50 to the plaintiff; that he appointed the defendant his executrix; that she proved the will; that goods and chattels came to her hands more than sufficient to pay all the testator's debts and legacies, by reason whereof she became liable to pay the legacy, and being so liable, in consideration thereof she promised to pay it.

LORD MANSFIELD. This case does not at all involve in it the question whether a legatee has a general right to sue for a legacy in this court.

Two objections have been made: 1st, That there can be no judgment in this case *de bonis testatoris;* because the action is not brought against the defendant as executrix *eo nomine*, but is a personal demand against her generally in her own right. As to that, we are of opinion the objection is good; for the demand is certainly a personal demand against the defendant, in consequence of a promise made by her, she being executrix.

It is admitted at the bar, that after verdict it must be taken to have been a promise in writing, and that there were assets. If so, the whole case is reduced to this single point: Whether the circumstance of the defendant having assets sufficient to pay all the debts and legacies is or is not a sufficient consideration for her to make a promise to pay the legacy in question? As to that point, the rule laid down at the bar, as to what is or is not a good consideration in law, goes upon a very narrow ground indeed; namely, that to make a consideration to support an assumpsit, there must be either an immediate benefit to the party promising, or a loss to the person to whom the promise was made. I cannot agree to that being the only ground of consideration sufficient to raise an assumpsit.

Where a man is under a legal or equitable obligation to pay, the law implies a promise, though none was ever actually made. *A fortiori* a legal or equitable duty is a sufficient consideration for an actual promise. Where a man is under a moral obligation, which no court of law or equity can enforce, and promises, the honesty and rectitude of the thing is a consideration: as if a man promise to pay a just debt, the recovery of which is barred by the Statute of Limitations; or if a man after he comes of age promises to pay a meritorious debt contracted during his minority, but not for necessaries; or if a bankrupt, in affluent circumstances after his certificate, promises to pay the whole of his debts; or if a man promise to perform a secret trust, or a trust void for want of writing by the Statute of Frauds.

In such and many other instances, though the promise gives a compulsory remedy where there was none before either in law or equity; yet as the promise is only to do what an honest man ought to do, the ties of conscience upon an upright mind are a sufficient consideration. But an executor who has received assets is under every kind of obligation to pay a legacy. He receives the money by virtue of an office which he swears to execute duly. He receives the money as a trust or deposit to the use of the legatee. He ought to assent if he has assets. He has no discretion or election. He retains what belongs to the legatee, and therefore owes him to the amount.

An account of assets, or a judgment to pay out of assets, is only necessary when the sufficiency of assets is uncertain. Where the sufficiency of assets received is certain, the executor's duty to pay a legatee follows by necessary consequence.

The legacy in such a case is a demand clearly due from the executor upon various grounds of natural and civil justice, and may be recovered from him by process of law. In such a case a promise to pay stands upon the strongest consideration.

Let us see then what are the facts in the present case. The executrix knows the state of her testator's affairs, and of his property. It might consist of chattels which she might not choose to dispose of. It might consist of leases which she had no mind to sell; and having a full fund to pay the demand, which the plaintiff had a right to recover if he pleased, she, in consideration of that fund, promises to pay. I cannot think this is not a sufficient consideration. I am of opinion it is amply sufficient. It is not like the case of Rann *v.* Hughes; for there, there were no assets, nor any averment of assets stated in the declaration. But in this case there was a full fund; and therefore she was bound in law, justice, and conscience, to pay the plaintiff his legacy.

Mr. Justice WILLES and Mr. Justice ASHHURST were of the same opinion.

BULLER, J. I am entirely of the same opinion. That an action in the courts of Westminster Hall will under some circumstances lie for a legacy, is a question which I think can never admit of any serious doubt. For there are a number of cases in the books, from the time of Henry VI. to the present time, which prove that under different circumstances such action may be maintained. I think there is as little doubt but that the circumstances of the present case, as proved at the trial, were sufficient to sustain an action; for the legacy was to be paid out of land; and there was an express assent by the executrix to the legacy. But the evidence which was given at the trial is not now before the court. We are to decide this case upon the face of the record alone.

The plaintiff, in his declaration, has not stated that the legacy was payable out of land; neither has he stated any assent by the executrix.

The action is brought against the defendant in her own right; and the declaration is simply that George Saunders by his will bequeathed a legacy to the plaintiff, and made the defendant executrix; that she proved the will, and had assets sufficient to pay all the debts and legacies; and by reason thereof she became liable to pay the legacy, and being so liable she promised to pay it.

To this declaration two objections have been made in arrest of judgment. 1st, That the defendant is not sufficiently described as executrix, and therefore there cannot be judgment *de bonis testatoris.* 2d, No judgment can be entered *de bonis propriis*, because there was no consideration for the promise; and therefore it is *nudum pactum.* As to the first, I am of opinion that the plaintiff cannot upon this declaration take judgment *de bonis testatoris.* The action is brought against the defendant in her own right, and not as executrix. It charges her with a personal promise to pay the legacy, and not upon a qualified promise to pay as executrix, or out of assets. And the plaintiff having by his declaration made a personal demand against her, he must stand or fall by that, and cannot now resort to any demand that he may have upon her in the particular character of executrix.

The forms of pleading are very different where a person is charged as executrix and where she is charged personally. In the first case, she is always named as executrix in the beginning of the declaration. She is afterwards stated to be liable as executrix; and the promise alleged to have been made by her as executrix. But in the other case, she is charged generally as any other person; and a general charge is a personal charge.

This case therefore depends wholly upon the second question: whether there be a sufficient consideration alleged for the promise, or whether the defendant's promise be merely *nudum pactum* and void.

The consideration stated for the promise is, that the defendant was executrix, and that she had received assets more than sufficient to pay all the debts and legacies. The question is, whether that be not a sufficient consideration.

Under those circumstances, if there had been no promise, nor even an assent to the legacy, the defendant might have been compelled, in a court of equity, or in the ecclesiastical court, to have paid it. Whether without assent she could be compelled, in a court of law, to pay it or not, is a question which it is not necessary to give any opinion upon now: and therefore, though I have endeavored to trace out the jurisdiction and the authority of the ecclesiastical court from the earliest times; and though there is great reason to suppose that the jurisdiction which that court now possesses in matters of legacy, was originally got by usurpation on the temporal courts; and though there is a wide difference between allowing to the ecclesiastical court a jurisdiction in such matters, and saying it shall have that jurisdiction exclusive of all other courts; I purposely avoid giving any opinion, or even hinting what would be the result of my researches, where there is no promise or assent.

I shall give my opinion singly on this point: Whether an obligation in justice, equity, and conscience, to pay a sum of money, be or be not a sufficient consideration in point of law to support a promise to pay that sum.

If such a question were stripped of all authorities, it would be resolved by inquiring whether law were a rule of justice, or whether it were something that acts in direct contradiction to justice, conscience, and equity. But the matter has been repeatedly decided.

In Stone *v.* Withipool, Latch, 21, the court say: "It is an usual allegation for a rule, that every thing which is a ground for equity is a sufficient consideration." So in Wells *v.* Wells, 1 Vent. 41, the court presumed an equitable right in the plaintiff, which did not appear on the declaration; and held that to debar herself of that was a good consideration.

These authorities alone are sufficient to shew that the ground taken in the argument at the bar is not large enough.

But to come closer to the consideration now in question, in Camden *v.* Turner, C. B., Sittings after Trin., 5 Geo. I., King, C. J., held that an action for money had and received lay against an executor for a legacy, which he had owned lay ready for the plaintiff whenever he would call for it. In that case, according to the form of the declaration, the objection did not appear upon the record; but it was necessary for the plaintiff to prove a consideration at the trial; and if he had not, he must have been nonsuited or have had a verdict against him. But Lord King held that his owning the money lay ready was an assent, and admission of assets, and a sufficient consideration.

In Reech *v.* Kennegal, 1 Vez. 125, Lord Hardwicke expressly holds that assets coming to an executor's hands is a sufficient consideration to support a promise; and he puts that case upon the same footing as a promise in consideration of forbearance. His Lordship says: "At law, if an executor promises to pay a debt of his testator's, a consideration must be alleged, as of assets come to his hands, or of forbearance; or if admission of assets is implied by the promise; otherwise it will be but *nudum pactum*, and not personally binding on the executor."

In Trewinian *v.* Howell, Cro. Eliz. 91, it was adjudged that having assets is a good consideration for a promise; and the judgment, which was *de bonis propriis*, was affirmed. And two other cases are there cited where the same point had been so determined. Lastly, the case of Atkins *v.* Hill, Easter, 15 Geo. III.,[1] is in point. The declaration was the same, and the objection the same, as in the present case; and the court unanimously held that the promise was good, and that the action well lay.

I agree with my Lord that the rule laid down at the bar, as to what is or is not a good consideration, is much too narrow. The true rule is, that wherever the defendant is under a moral obligation, or is liable in conscience and equity to pay, that is a sufficient consideration. Some of the cases which I have mentioned go fully to that extent. But even if the narrow rule which has been mentioned were adopted as the true rule, yet in this case I think the consideration is sufficient; for here is both a loss to the plaintiff and a benefit to the defendant, arising from that which is the consideration of the promise. The loss to the plaintiff is, that the effects which are liable to the payment of the legacy have not been so applied; but the defendant has detained them in her own hands for other purposes. The benefit to the defendant is, that she has received those effects, and has them still. The defendant is bound in conscience to apply the effects towards the discharge of the debts and legacies. She is a trustee for that purpose, and is guilty of a breach of trust in not so doing; and it is admitted that a breach of trust is a good ground for action.

Therefore I agree in opinion with the rest of the court, that this rule in arrest of judgment ought to be discharged.

Per Cur. Rule discharged.

[1] Cowper, 284.

BARNES, DOWDING, AND BARTLEY, *v.* HEDLEY AND CONWAY.

IN THE COMMON PLEAS, NOVEMBER 24, 1809.

[*Reported in* 2 *Taunton,* 184.]

THIS was an issue between the plaintiffs who were the executors of William Webb, deceased, and the defendants, who were assignees under a commission of bankrupt which issued against William Harrè and Henry Suthmier, directed by order of the Lord Chancellor, in order to try whether the bankrupts on the 13th of August, 1802, were indebted to Webb in any and what sum of money. The trial came on at the sittings in London, Mich. Term, 1808, before Mansfield, C. J., when a verdict was found for the plaintiffs for the sum of £11,672 4*s.* 2*d.* subject to the opinion of the court on the following case: By a written agreement made on the 15th of May, 1800, between Webb and the bankrupts, the former agreed to advance money from time to time upon interest at 5 per cent. to Harrè and Suthmier, who carried on the business of sugar bakers in copartnership, in order to enable them to purchase raw sugars; and in consideration of such advances the bankrupts were also to pay to Webb a commission of 5 per cent. for all sugars which were to be bought of him, or provided for Messrs. Harrè and Suthmier; and in order to secure to Webb the balance which might become due to him on these transactions, Harrè and Suthmier executed and gave to him certain deeds and securities. Webb made out four several successive half-yearly accounts between him and Harrè and Suthmier, on the footing of this agreement, and various sums of money were paid to Webb on these accounts from time to time by the bankrupts; these accounts closed on the 10th of August, 1802, when a considerable balance was due from the bankrupts to Webb. These accounts comprised the principal moneys actually advanced, and interest at 5 per cent.; and also 5 per cent. on all sugars purchased by the bankrupts. Webb never purchased or procured any sugars for the bankrupts; but the same were always purchased by the bankrupts themselves in their own names. It was admitted on the trial that the original agreement of the 15th of May, 1800, was illegal and usurious, and that no part of the balance could have been recovered by Webb from Harrè and Suthmier, if they had set up the usury; and Webb was informed by the attorney of Harrè and Suthmier in July, 1802, that these transactions were usurious, and that his whole debt was in danger of being lost, and a writ of *latitat* was actually sued out by the bankrupts' attorney upon the Statute of Usury; but this fact was unknown to Webb. In consequence of this intimation, it was agreed between

Harrè and Suthmier and Webb, that Webb should make out fresh accounts, leaving out all the charges for commission; and should only charge them with the principal money, together with legal interest; and that the original deeds and articles in the possession of Webb should be given up by him and cancelled accordingly. Webb accordingly made out such fresh account, in which he omitted the whole charge for commission; and the balance due to him amounted to the sum of £11,672 4*s.* 2*d.*, which balance was composed of principal moneys actually advanced under the agreement of 15th May, 1800, and of interest at 5 per cent. fairly and legally calculated; the whole commission and evey objectionable charge being omitted. This account, so corrected, was, on the 12th of August, 1802, delivered to the agent of Harrè and Suthmier, and on the following day they acknowledged this balance to be due to Webb, and promised to pay the same; whereupon the deeds and securities executed to Webb by Harrè and Suthmier, when the original agreement was entered into, were produced by Webb or his agent, in the presence of Harrè and Suthmier, and were then cancelled and burnt. The question for the opinion of the court was, whether under the circumstances of this case the plaintiffs were entitled to recover the above balance of £11,672 4*s.* 2*d.* If the court should be of that opinion, a verdict for such sum was to be entered for the plaintiffs; if otherwise, the verdict to be entered for the defendants.

This cause was twice argued: first, in Easter Term, 1809, by *Best*, Serjt., for the plaintiffs, and *Vaughan*, Serjt., for the defendants; and again in Trinity Term, 1809, by *Shepherd*, Serjt., for the plaintiffs, and *Lens*, Serjt., for the defendants.

Arguments for the plaintiffs. There are two questions in this case: first, Whether the promise that has been made to repay the sum lent, with legal interest, is avoided by the Statute of Usury;[1] secondly, Whether there was any good consideration to sustain the promise. . . . Secondly, there is a good consideration for the new promise; for the money has been actually received by the defendants, and there is a foundation in justice for the new contract. Hill v. Atkins, Cowp. 284. Lord Mansfield held that, when an executor had assented to a legacy, "it became a demand which in law and conscience he was liable to pay;" that it was a case of a promise made upon good and valuable consideration, which in all cases is sufficient ground to support an action. It is so in cases of obligations which would otherwise only bind a man's conscience, and which, without such promise, he could not be compelled to pay. For instançe where an infant contracts debts during his minority, if after he comes of age he consents to pay them, an action lies. So Hawkes v. Saunders, Cowp. 289, "A legal or equitable duty is a sufficient consideration for an actual promise." And

[1] The arguments upon the first question are omitted. — ED.

though these cases have been since overruled, it has been on a ground which does not impeach this principle; namely, on the ground that the court has not jurisdiction in case of legacies. Buller, J., says in the last case: "If such a question were stripped of all authority, it would be resolved by inquiring whether law were a rule of justice, or whether it were something that acts in direct contradiction to justice, conscience, and equity. But the matter has been repeatedly decided." Trueman v. Fenton, Cowp. 544. A promise to pay made by a bankrupt after obtaining his certificate revives the debt. That, notwithstanding a usurious security given, the money lent is a debt in equity and conscience, and ought to be repaid with legal interest, has long been acknowledged in courts of equity. 2 Ves. 567, the Lord Chancellor says: "The court does not relieve against usurious contracts to make a man lose his principal as well as his legal interest." Scott v. Nesbit, 2 Bro. Ch. Ca. 649. Upon an application to set aside a judgment tainted with usury, it was held "that it could be displaced only by the plaintiff's doing what was just, and that it must stand for the money actually paid, with legal interest." Indeed the practice there is so well established, that if a bill, filed to set aside a usurious security, does not voluntarily offer to repay the principal and legal interest, it is cause of demurrer. The plaintiffs could not have had the original securities set aside in a court of equity, without offering these terms. This court not long since, on setting aside an annuity in the case of Burdon v. Browning, 1 Taunt. 520, required the defendant to submit to the terms of repaying the principal and interest. [MANSFIELD, C. J., observed that this was always by agreement of the parties; that the court had no power to prescribe the terms. LAWRENCE, J., observed that actions had been allowed to recover back the money, as paid without consideration: it was so held in Shove v. Webb, 1 Term Rep. 732.] And if it be objected that Wright v. Wheeler[1] was the case of a bond, for which no consideration needs to be shewn, it is sufficient to say it was not decided on that ground, but on the sufficiency of the consideration; and if there had not been a new consideration, the old consideration must have remained; which was illegal, and an illegal consideration would have avoided the bond, though no consideration was necessary. But there is another consideration for the present promise: the plaintiffs had deeds and securities for the money; it is true they were vitiated by the usury, but it might be uncertain whether the defendants could prove it, and unless for that proof the plaintiffs could enforce them; therefore the giving them up to be cancelled was a valuable consideration for the second contract.

Arguments for the defendants. . . . It is not contended, as the plaintiffs imagined it was, that the second contract is tainted with usury, but that there was no consideration for it; and in order to enforce a

[1] 1 Campb. 165, n.

promise, it is not sufficient that a man has given it upon his judgment that some obligation lies on him: contracts purely voluntary are not enforced either in law or equity. Here no ground for the promise is shewn, either of advantage to the maker or detriment to the other party. The old securities are not delivered up to be cancelled, but are actually destroyed, rather for the safety of the lender, against whom they would have been evidence to subject him to heavy penalties, than for the advantage of the borrower. This case, therefore, is distinguishable from the case cited of a bond, for which no consideration needs to be shewn. Besides, the issue to be tried in Wright *v.* Wheeler upon the defendant's plea, was whether the usury was committed in giving that very bond; and the fact was against him. In overruling Hill *v.* Atkins, and Hawkes *v.* Saunders, as was done in 5 Term Rep. 690, Deeks *v.* Strutt, the courts at least determined that not every conscientious motive for a promise will support an action at law. [MANSFIELD, C. J. The overturning of those decisions did not touch any principle which applies to the present case; it went on the ground that the ecclesiastical court was the only legal place where to sue for a legacy; it is not enough as to a legacy that an executor has at one moment received money sufficient to pay it; but debts are to be paid according to their priority, and it is often necessary to refund: but the decision in Deeks *v.* Strutt had nothing to do with the general ground of conscience.] The cases of conscientious considerations which have been cited are not analogous. In the case of bankruptcy the certificate merely destroys the remedy, and leaves the bankrupt a free man: free to pay or not to pay at pleasure. But the legal debt extinguished by bankruptcy is neither *malum prohibitum* nor *malum in se;* and for an illegal debt the debtor does not want the aid of a commission to relieve him from it. Here it is the intention of the statute not only totally to destroy the engagement, but to make usury an offence; and in order to deter persons from being guilty thereof, it meant that a sum of money once usuriously lent should never under any circumstances be repaid, although it was honestly due; and it would be a complete evasion of the statute, if a man who enters into a usurious contract may, when he fears the consequences, alter his contract, and defeat the provisions of the act. [LAWRENCE, J., observed that, if the borrower should repay money usuriously borrowed, he would have no means to get it back from the lender.] The case of the Statute of Limitations is merely a suspension of the remedy, which the debtor may remove by again acknowledging the debt. The case of an infant is on account of his want of discretion, and his election to annul or confirm his contract is postponed till a more mature age. The case of Ellis *v.* Warnes[1] was the case of an innocent third person. The ground of the practice in courts of equity is not, that they consider the defendant as entitled

[1] Cro. Jac. 33, Moor, 752.

to the money, but because, unless the complainant waives the penalties of the statute, and among them the forfeiture of the money lent, the defendant could not answer without criminating himself, and subjecting himself to penalties, which a court of equity will not compel him to do. It also is a very different thing whether a court shall aid a plaintiff who has the money of another in his hands to set aside usurious securities, instead of leaving him to his remedy at law, or whether it shall compel a defendant to repay the money borrowed. Here the court is called on, not to remain neuter, but positively to compel repayment. Lloyd *v.* Lee, 1 Stra. 94. It was held that a married woman who had given a promissory note, and after her husband's death had promised to pay it, was not liable. Yet there was as much consideration in that case as in this. [LAWRENCE, J. The ground of that case, I presume, was that, as the party could not previously be sued on the instrument, there was no forbearance to sue, and therefore no consideration for the promise. And the forbearance being the only consideration alleged in the declaration, though another good consideration might exist, proof of it would not be admissible.] 7 Term Rep. 348, Mitchinson *v.* Hewson: the wife was living; and an express promise of the husband to pay her debt was there averred, and after verdict must be taken as having been proved: that surely was a conscientious consideration; but the court held that the action could not be maintained.

Arguments in reply. Usury is not now held altogether criminal by the law, but only the excess of it; and things not *mala in se* are not to be carried beyond the very letter of prohibitory statutes. In Lloyd *v.* Lee it does not appear that the wife ever received any money on the note for her own benefit, or was at all bound in conscience to pay it; and the case only proves that forbearance is no consideration for a promise made under the influence of terror of an action which would not lie. Mitchinson *v.* Hewson is a decision merely on the form of action, that the husband cannot be sued alone for a debt contracted by the wife before marriage. So in the case of a father promising to pay the debts of his son; in numerous cases it is not consistent either with honor or morality that he should do it. This case is not distinguishable from that of a certificated bankrupt, which rests only on the ground of conscience. Nor is the offence of usury in fact complete till usurious interest has been actually paid; here the payments were made on account generally. It is admitted that where a specific contract on certain terms has been made, an implied contract on other terms cannot be raised: and it may also be safely admitted that the moral obligation to perform a promise merely because it has been given, is not sufficient to maintain an action; otherwise every *nudum pactum* would be good. But it does not thence follow that the naked fact of a loan having taken place, one man having received the money of another, is not a sufficient consideration for an express, separate, and independent promise to repay it. Courts of equity could not pursue their present practice, if the repayment of money usuriously borrowed was inconsistent either with law or morality: they could not either directly or collaterally enforce a thing contrary to law: they proceed on the principle that he who comes to them for aid must first do that which is equitable. Supposing that the destruction of the securities had been for the mutual benefit of both parties, still it would be a sufficient consideration for the promise, because it was for the benefit of the defendants. [LAWRENCE, J., observed that there was one other case which had not been mentioned, and which seemed to bear on the subject: Fitzroy *v.* Gwillim, 1 Term Rep. 153; where in trover for goods which had been pledged for money advanced on a usurious contract, Lord Mansfield, C. J., held that it was necessary for the plaintiff to prove a previous tender of the money actually due.] *Cur. adv. vult.*

In the course of the present term the judges of the court sent to the Lord Chancellor the following certificate of their opinion:—

"This case has been argued before us by counsel, and we are of opinion that under the circumstances the plaintiffs are entitled to recover the above balance of £11,672 4*s.* 6*d.*"

DAVIS *v.* DODD.

IN THE COMMON PLEAS, NOVEMBER 9, 1812.

[*Reported in* 4 *Taunton,* 602.]

THE plaintiff declared upon a bill of exchange for £96 9*s.* drawn by Allen, to his own order, and accepted by the defendant, and indorsed by Allen to the plaintiff. There were also the usual money counts. Upon the trial at the Maidstone summer assizes, 1812, before Lord Ellenborough, C. J., it was proved that the witness had lost the bill out of his pocket; whereupon, when the bill became due, he applied to the defendant, stating the circumstance, and requesting him to pay the bill, which until the time of the action had never been presented for payment by any other person, and the defendant repeatedly and expressly promised to pay it. Lord Ellenborough was of opinion that, as the plaintiff had not presented the bill for payment to the defendant, and as the bill was not produced at the trial, the plaintiff could not recover in this action, and directed a nonsuit.

Best, Serjt., now moved to set aside the nonsuit, and have a new trial: he contended that the express promise to pay the bill was upheld by the consideration of the moral obligation, to which the defendant was subject, to pay the sum due on his acceptance.

The Court denied that there was any moral obligation on the defendant to pay this sum to the plaintiff, who by his negligence had exposed the defendant to the danger of being compelled to pay the bill when produced in the hands of another holder. It was quite clear the plaintiff could not recover in this action. If he could recover at all upon this promise, which they much doubted, it must be in an action upon the special undertaking. The party might have proceeded to enforce the giving of a new bill under the statute, and that seemed to be his only course. The promise contained in the bill is the equivalent given for the consideration paid for the bill. No new consideration had been subsequently paid to sustain this new promise, which was therefore *nudum pactum*, and could not be enforced. *Rule refused.*

LEE v. MUGGERIDGE and Another, *Executors of* Mary Muggeridge, *deceased.*

In the Common Pleas, Trinity Term, June 29, 1813.

[*Reported in* 5 *Taunton*, 36.]

This was an action of assumpsit, brought under the following circumstances: In 1799, Joseph Hiller, the son of Mrs. Muggeridge, the defendants' testatrix, by a former husband, falling into embarrassed circumstances, she, in order to induce the plaintiff, his father-in-law, to relieve him, proposed by letter to become security to the extent of £2000 by a bond payable at her death. The plaintiff accordingly advanced the money to Joseph Hiller; and Mrs. Muggeridge by her bond, dated the 4th of August, 1799, became bound to the plaintiff in the penal sum of £4000; with condition that the heirs, executors, or administrators of Mrs. Muggeridge should, within six months after her decease, pay to the plaintiff £1999 19*s.*, with such part of the interest as Joseph Hiller should omit to pay; it being agreed that he should pay the interest half yearly. Joseph Hiller having neglected to pay the interest, the plaintiff in the year 1804 wrote to Mrs. Muggeridge, requesting payment of the arrears; to which she, after her husband's death, returned an answer by letter, stating "that it was not in her power to pay the bond off, her time here was but short, and that would be settled by her executors."

It appeared that Mrs. Muggeridge had a considerable separate estate when the bond was given, which she acquired from the father of Joseph Hiller, and the bulk of which she gave by her will to the defendant, Nathaniel Muggeridge. After an ineffectual attempt to establish that the bond constituted an equitable lien or charge upon the separate estate of Mrs. Muggeridge (see 1 V. & B. 118), the plaintiff brought the present action, founded upon the promise contained in the letter above referred to. The declaration stated (*inter alia*) that the testatrix, after the death of her husband, and whilst she was sole, to wit, on the 11th of July, 1804, "in consideration of the premises undertook to the plaintiff that the bond, that is to say, the principal money and interest secured by the bond, should be settled, that is to say, paid, by her executors." The defendants pleaded the general issue; and upon the trial of the cause at the sittings after Hilary Term, 1813, at Guildhall, before Gibbs, J., the jury found a verdict for the plaintiff.[1]

Shepherd, Serjt., in Easter Term last, moved in arrest of judgment, on the ground that no sufficient consideration was shewn for the promise of the deceased. The court granted a rule *nisi*.

Lens and *Best*, Serjts., in this term shewed cause. They admitted that when the deceased gave the bond, being covert, she had no power thereby to bind herself, but contended that, notwithstanding that, the promise which, after she was liberated from all restriction, she gave in confirmation of the bond, was obligatory on her. The same payment which was recited to be the consideration of the bond is a sufficient consideration for the subsequent promise. This differs nothing from the case of infancy, and the many other cases which subsist in the English law, where though a party is not compellable to make a promise, yet if he does make it, the promise shall be compulsory on him. In certain cases where the law destroys the remedy, as in the case of the Statute of Limitations, a subsequent promise, operating by the old consideration, will revive the remedy. So, if an estate be devised for payment of debts, the law will not intend that it is exclusively for the payment of such debts as are not barred by the Statute of Limitations, but will intend the devise to be for payment of all debts whatever, unless advantage is taken of the Statute of Limitations by plea. Lord Mansfield, C. J., thought the rule of *nudum pactum* was much too strict, and that it was competent for parties to make their own agreements on deliberation; and if they did so think fit to make them, that they must be subject to them. It is now fully recognized in the law, that if there be, even in the strictest morality, the foundation for a promise, and the promise be accordingly made, it is binding. It is a new *ligamen*, though not a new consideration; for if there were a new consideration, it would be clearly good. Goodright *ex dem.* Carter v. Straphan, Cowp. 201. Lord Mansfield held

[1] In the original report the declaration is set forth with much fulness; but as it is exceedingly prolix, and most of it is wholly irrelevant to the one question argued and decided in the case, it is here omitted, and a statement of the material facts is substituted in its place. Some of the facts stated have been obtained from the report in 1 V. & B. 118.—ED.

that an account stated by a widow, allowing interest on a mortgage executed by her during coverture, a direction given by her in writing to her tenant to attorn to the mortgagees, and a paper whereby she purported to surrender the possession, amounted to a delivery by her in her widowhood of the mortgage-deed, holding her previous delivery during coverture to be absolutely void. [MANSFIELD, C. J. That was certainly a very strong case, and I very well remember the surprise I felt at the time when it was decided, because it was making those acts of the widow equivalent to a formal redelivery of the deed; and others were much surprised at it; but it strongly recognizes the principle that a moral obligation is a good consideration. CHAMBRE, J., evinced doubts of this case. GIBBS, J. The position in Perkins, *s.* 154, is not that re-execution, but only redelivery was requisite; and Lord Mansfield held that her acts were tantamount to a redelivery. He begins by saying: "I thought it cruel to contend for the wife that the mortgage was void," "a security which was entered into for the maintenance of herself and her family," "and after so many solemn acts on her part, it is a proceeding against every principle of natural justice and equity."] The doubt on that case has always been on the form in which Lord Mansfield applies the principle, not on the principle itself; there cannot, however, be a stronger case of moral obligation than the present, for the giving this bond of the deceased was the inducement to the plaintiff to lend the money. Trueman *v.* Fenton, Cowp. 544. Lord Mansfield and the rest of the court fully recognize the principle, and found on it their decision, that a bankrupt, promising after he has obtained his certificate to pay a debt thereby barred, is bound by his promise. Barnes *v.* Hedley, 2 Taunt. 184. A promise to pay the principal money lent on an usurious security, with legal interest, was held valid; and many cases to the like effect are there cited. Although no reasons are assigned for the judgment, it must necessarily have proceeded on the ground that a moral obligation will support a promise to pay.

Shepherd and *Vaughan*, Serjts., *contra.* The case of Doe *v.* Straphan is favorable to the defendants. The court were obliged to hold that the deed of a married woman was absolutely void, and by a refinement in law they presumed a redelivery; but no consideration is necessary to give effect to a deed; therefore the case does not decide that an engagement made by the *feme covert*, or money paid for her use, was a good consideration for the subsequent act. It will not be contended that the letter amounts to a redelivery of this bond; if it does, let the plaintiff sue on the bond. [*Lens* disclaimed the redelivery.] Barnes *v.* Hedley was decided on the ground that the money advanced to the defendant was an old subsisting debt, and therefore a good consideration for the promise. [HEATH, J. In the case of usury there could be no subsisting debt. GIBBS, J. In this case there was an advance of money.] The *feme covert* never had the money; neither can a *feme covert* by any means create a debt from herself; so that on the declaration the case stands thus, that she, not being indebted, was not liable, and in consideration of her not being liable she undertook to pay. If this money had been advanced, not on her bond, but on her mere promise, a subsequent promise to pay, made when she became discovert, would be merely void. A bygone debt from a third person would be no consideration for a promise to pay. There must be an agreement not to sue, or some new consideration moving to the promisor or from the lender. The devise of the property to the executors is no consideration. There is no mutuality or connection between this consideration and this promise, for the whole transaction had an end before the deceased was discovert. The law does not recognize the principle to the extent stated, that every moral obligation of any sort or kind whatever would be a good consideration for a promise. There must be a mutuality. This cannot be a stronger case than if the money had been advanced to the *feme covert* herself; yet in Lloyd v. Lee, 1 Str. 94, it was held by Pratt, C. J., where a married woman gave a note as a *feme sole*, and after her husband's decease, in consideration of forbearance to sue, promised payment, that the note was not barely voidable, but absolutely void, and that forbearance, where originally there was no cause of action, is no consideration to raise an assumpsit. Barber v. Fox, 2 Saund. 134. Assumpsit by the heir to pay the bond of his ancestor, in consideration of forbearance to sue, was held void. [MANSFIELD, C. J., and GIBBS, J. Neither of those cases is applicable, for it did not appear in the last that the ancestor bound his heir in the bond: forbearance to sue is the forbearing of that which he may legally enforce, and as there was before the renewed promise no right of action, so there could be no forbearance. It might, we will suppose, have been the moral duty of the *feme covert* in Lloyd v. Lee to pay the note before; but as she was not legally liable without a promise made by her after she was discovert, the consideration so averred did not exist; but it does not follow that no other consideration could have been stated that would have supported the promise.] In the cases of bankruptcy, and the Statute of Limitations, the law only suspends the remedy, it does not extinguish the debt; but here no debt ever existed; the acts of a *feme covert* not being voidable like those of an infant, but actually void.

MANSFIELD, C. J. The counsel for the plaintiffs need not trouble themselves to reply to these cases; it has been long established, that where a person is bound morally and conscientiously to pay a debt, though not legally bound, a subsequent promise to pay will give a right of action. The only question therefore is, Whether upon this declaration there appears a good moral obligation? Now I cannot conceive that there can be a stronger moral obligation than is stated upon this record. Here is this debt of £2000 created at the desire of the testatrix, lent in fact to her, though paid to Hiller. After her husband's death, she, knowing that this bond had been given, that her son-in-law had received the money, and had not repaid it, knowing all this, she promises that her executors shall pay; if then it has been repeatedly decided that a moral consideration is a good consideration for a promise to pay, this declaration is clearly good. This case is not distinguishable in principle from Barnes *v.* Hedley: there not only the securities were void, but the contract was void; but the money had been lent, and therefore when the parties had stripped the transaction of its usury, and reduced the debt to mere principal and interest, the promise made to pay that debt was binding. Lord Mansfield's judgment in the case of Doe on the demise of Carter *v.* Straphan is extremely applicable. Here in like manner the wife would have been grossly dishonest, if she had scrupled to give a security for the money advanced at her request. As to the cases cited of Lloyd *v.* Lee and Barber *v.* Fox, there was no forbearance, and those cases proceeded on the ground that no good cause of action was shewn on the pleadings.

HEATH, J. I am of the same opinion. Promises without consideration are not enforced, because they are gratuitous, and the law leaves the performance to the liberality of the makers. The notion that a promise may be supported by a moral obligation is not modern; in Charles the Second's time it was said, if there be an iota of equity, it is enough consideration for the promise.

CHAMBRE, J. There cannot be a stronger or clearer case of moral obligation than this. The gentleman has done this lady a great favor, in going to this expense, and accepting an invalid security; and when she could give a better security, it became her duty so to do, and she has done it. In the cases cited it was the plaintiff's fault if, having it in his power to state a good consideration on the record, he neglected so to do.

GIBBS, J. I agree in this case the plaintiff is entitled to recover. It cannot, I think, be disputed now, that wherever there is a moral obligation to pay a debt, or perform a duty, a promise to perform that duty, or pay that debt, will be supported by the previous moral obligation. There cannot be a stronger case than this of moral obligation. The counsel for the defendant did not dare to grapple with this position, but endeavored to shew that there was no case in which a subsequent promise had been supported, where there had not been an antecedent legal obligation at some time or other; from whence he wished it to be inferred that, unless there had been the antecedent legal obligation, the mere moral obligation would not be a sufficient consideration to support the promise. But in Barnes *v.* Hedley certainly Hedley never was for a moment legally bound to pay a farthing of that money for which he was sued; for it appears to have been advanced upon a previously existing usurious contract; and whatever was advanced upon such a contract, certainly could not be recovered at any one moment. The borrower, availing himself of the law so far as he honestly might and no further, reducing it to mere principal and interest, does that which every honest man ought to do in like circumstances, promises to pay it, and that promise was held binding. As to the cases of Lloyd *v.* Lee and Barber *v.* Fox, they have sufficiently been answered by my Lord, and my brother Chambre; that if a man will state on his declaration a consideration which is no consideration, and shews no other consideration on his declaration, although another good consideration may exist, when that which he does shew fails, he cannot succeed upon the proof of the other which he has not alleged. Now in the first of those cases there was clearly no forbearance, because forbearance must be a deferring to prosecute a legal right; but no legal right to recover previously existed. Whatever other consideration might exist for the promise, it was not stated in the declaration; it is therefore clear that this rule must be discharged, upon the ground that wherever there is an antecedent moral obligation, and a subsequent promise given to perform it, it is of sufficient validity for the plaintiff to be able to enforce it.

Rule discharged.

KING *v.* MILL.

IN THE KING'S BENCH, NOVEMBER 11, 1817.

[*Reported in* 1 *Barnewall & Alderson*, 104.]

ACTION for work and labor as a surgeon and apothecary. Plea, general issue. At the trial before Holroyd, J., at the last assizes for the county of Leicester, it appeared that the defendant was overseer for the parish of Silk Willoughby, and that this action was brought by the plaintiff to recover the amount charged in his bill for professional attendance on one Richardson, a pauper, who during twelve months' illness (induced not by accident, but by gradual decay) received a weekly allowance of four shillings from the parish of Silk Willoughby, which was the place of his settlement; but during the whole of the plaintiff's attendance on him, he was actually resident in the parish of Easton, where he died. After his death the defendant desired the plaintiff to make out his bill to the overseers of Willoughby parish, and said that he should be paid; and upon these facts a verdict was found for the plaintiff.

Copley, Serjt., now moved for a new trial. There was neither legal liability nor moral obligation to provide for the pauper while resident in Easton, and the subsequent promise was without consideration, and therefore *nudum pactum*. The poor laws are mere arbitrary enactments, and do not carry moral obligations beyond the legal liability, which in this case attached on the parish which was the residence of the pauper.

LORD ELLENBOROUGH, C. J. In this case both the legal and moral obligation obtain. The parish of Willoughby have by their weekly allowance admitted that they were bound to provide for the pauper; and the defendant, one of the overseers, after the pauper's death, expressly desires the plaintiff to send his bill made out to the overseers, and promises that he shall be paid. The case of Watson *v.* Turner[1] is decisive on the subject, and I have no doubt that the plaintiff is entitled to recover.

BAYLEY, J. I am of the same opinion. If the payment of four shillings per week had not been made by the parish officers of Willoughby, Easton parish would have removed the pauper to the place of his settlement, and in that case the former parish must undoubtedly have provided him medical attendance. The conduct of the defendant as the overseer of Willoughby amounts to an acknowledgment on his part that the plaintiff had attended at the defendant's wish, and upon his responsibility. I therefore think that Willoughby and not Easton was bound to maintain the pauper, and that the promise made after his death is founded on a legal as well as a moral consideration, and therefore affords a good ground of action.

ABBOTT and HOLROYD, JJ., concurred. *Rule refused.*[2]

BINNINGTON *v.* WALLIS.

IN THE KING'S BENCH, JUNE 29, 1821.

[*Reported in* 4 *Barnewall & Alderson*, 650.]

DECLARATION stated that, before the making of the promise and undertaking, the plaintiff had cohabited with the defendant as his mistress, and an immoral connection and intercourse had existed between them for a long space of time, to wit, for the space of twelve years; and the plaintiff had thereby been greatly injured in her character and

[1] Bull. N. P. 130, 147, 281. [2] See Paynter *v.* Williams, 1 Cr. & M. 810.

reputation, and deprived of the means of honestly procuring a livelihood; and that, before the time of the making of the promise, to wit, on the 1st of January, 1816, at, &c., the plaintiff wholly ceased to cohabit with the said defendant as his mistress, and to have any immoral intercourse with him; and thereupon it was determined and agreed between them that no immoral intercourse or connection should ever again take place between them; and that the defendant, as a compensation for the injury so sustained by the plaintiff, should pay and allow to the plaintiff the quarterly sum of £10, while she should be and continue of good and virtuous life, conversation, and demeanor; and thereupon, in consideration of the premises, and that the plaintiff at the request of the defendant would resign and give up the said quarterly sum, he undertook to pay her so much money as the said quarterly sum was reasonably worth, in order to enable her to continue to live in a virtuous and decorous manner. The declaration then averred that the plaintiff did resign and give up the said quarterly sum, and the same from thence wholly ceased and determined; and that she had always, from the time of the cessation of the immoral connection, lived in a virtuous and decorous manner, and been of virtuous life, conversation, and demeanor. It then averred that the quarterly sum was reasonably worth £400; and then alleged as a breach non-payment by the defendant. The other counts omitted any mention of the quarterly allowance, and in other respects were similar to this. To this declaration there was a general demurrer.

Parke, in support of the demurrer. There is no sufficient consideration to support the promise laid in this declaration. It is not stated that the plaintiff was seduced. There is not even a moral obligation to provide for a woman for past cohabitation. As to the giving up of the annuity, mentioned in one count, that depends upon the same question, for the only consideration for that annuity was the past cohabitation.

Holt, contra. There was a moral consideration for the promise stated in this declaration, for it must be taken (as the contrary does not appear) that the defendant seduced the plaintiff; and if that be so, he was morally bound to make some provision for her. In The Marchioness of Annandale *v.* Harris[1] the court held a bond given to a seduced woman good; and if it were sufficient to support a bond, it must be equally so to support an express promise. So also past cohabitation was deemed sufficient consideration for a bond in the case of Carew *v.* Stafford there cited; and in the case of Turner *v.* Vaughan.[2] And, secondly, there is a valuable consideration in this case, inasmuch as the plaintiff gave up her annuity.

PER CURIAM. The declaration is insufficient. It is not averred that the defendant was the seducer, and there is no authority to shew

[1] 2 Peere W. 433. [2] 2 Wils. 339.

that past cohabitation alone, or the ceasing to cohabit in future, is a good consideration for a promise of this nature. The cases cited are distinguishable from this, because they are all cases of deeds; and it is a very different question whether a consideration be sufficiently good to sustain a promise, and whether it be so illegal as to make the deed which required no consideration void. There must therefore be judgment for the defendant. *Judgment for defendant.*

DANIEL MILLS v. SETH WYMAN.

SUPREME JUDICIAL COURT OF MASSACHUSETTS, OCTOBER TERM, 1825.

[*Reported in 3 Pickering, 207.*]

THIS was an action of assumpsit brought to recover a compensation for the board, nursing, &c., of Levi Wyman, son of the defendant, from the 5th to the 20th of February, 1821. The plaintiff then lived at Hartford, in Connecticut; the defendant, at Shrewsbury, in this State. Levi Wyman, at the time when the services were rendered, was about twenty-five years of age, and had long ceased to be a member of his father's family. He was on his return from a voyage at sea, and being suddenly taken sick at Hartford, and being poor and in distress, was relieved by the plaintiff in the manner and to the extent above stated. On the 24th of February, after all the expenses had been incurred, the defendant wrote a letter to the plaintiff, promising to pay him such expenses. There was no consideration for this promise, except what grew out of the relation which subsisted between Levi Wyman and the defendant; and Howe, J., before whom the cause was tried in the Court of Common Pleas, thinking this not sufficient to support the action, directed a nonsuit. To this direction the plaintiff filed exceptions.

J. Davis and *Allen*, in support of the exceptions. The moral obligation of a parent to support his child is a sufficient consideration for an express promise. Andover, &c., Turnpike Corp. v. Gould, 6 Mass. R. 40; Andover v. Salem, 3 Mass. R. 438; Davenport v. Mason, 15 Mass. R. 94; 1 Bl. Comm. 446; Reeve's Dom. Rel. 283. The arbitrary rule of law, fixing the age of twenty-one years for the period of emancipation, does not interfere with this moral obligation, in case a child of full age shall be unable to support himself. Our Statute of 1793, c. 59, requiring the kindred of a poor person to support him, proceeds upon the ground of a moral obligation.

But if there was no moral obligation on the part of the defendant, it is sufficient that his promise was in writing, and was made deliberately, with a knowledge of all the circumstances. A man has a right to give away his property. [PARKER, C. J. There is a distinction between giving and promising.] The case of Bowers *v.* Hurd, 10 Mass. R. 427, does not take that distinction. [PARKER, C. J. That case has been doubted.] Neither does the case of Packard *v.* Richardson, 17 Mass. R. 122; and in this last case (p. 130) the want of consideration is treated as a technical objection.

Brigham, for the defendant, furnished in vacation a written argument, in which he cited Fowler *v.* Shearer, 7 Mass. R. 22; Rann *v.* Hughes, 7 T. R. 350, note; Jones *v.* Ashburnham, 4 East, 463; Pearson *v.* Pearson, 7 Johns. R. 26; Schoonmaker *v.* Roosa, 17 Johns. R. 301; the note to Wennall *v.* Adney, 3 Bos. & Pul. 249; Fink *v.* Cox, 18 Johns. R. 145; Barnes *v.* Hedley, 2 Taunt. 184; Lee *v.* Muggeridge, 5 Taunt. 36. He said the case of Bowers *v.* Hurd was upon a promissory note, where the receipt of value is acknowledged; which is a privileged contract. Livingston *v.* Hastie, 2 Caines' R. 246; Bishop *v.* Young, 2 Bos. & Pul. 79, 80; Pillans *v.* Mierop, 3 Burr. 1670; 1 Wms. Saund. 211, note 2.

The opinion of the court was read, as drawn up by

PARKER, C. J. General rules of law established for the protection and security of honest and fair-minded men, who may inconsiderately make promises without any equivalent, will sometimes screen men of a different character from engagements which they are bound *in foro conscientiæ* to perform. This is a defect inherent in all human systems of legislation. The rule that a mere verbal promise, without any consideration, cannot be enforced by action, is universal in its application, and cannot be departed from to suit particular cases in which a refusal to perform such a promise may be disgraceful.

The promise declared on in this case appears to have been made without any legal consideration. The kindness and services towards the sick son of the defendant were not bestowed at his request. The son was in no respect under the care of the defendant. He was twenty-five years old, and had long left his father's family. On his return from a foreign country, he fell sick among strangers, and the plaintiff acted the part of the good Samaritan, giving him shelter and comfort until he died. The defendant, his father, on being informed of this event, influenced by a transient feeling of gratitude, promises in writing to pay the plaintiff for the expenses he had incurred. But he has determined to break this promise, and is willing to have his case appear on record as a strong example of particular injustice sometimes necessarily resulting from the operation of general rules.

It is said a moral obligation is a sufficient consideration to support an express promise; and some authorities lay down the rule thus broadly; but upon examination of the cases we are satisfied that the universality of the rule cannot be supported, and that there must have been some pre-existing obligation, which has become inoperative by positive law, to form a basis for an effective promise. The cases of debts barred by the Statute of Limitations, of debts incurred by infants, of debts of bankrupts, are generally put for illustration of the rule. Express promises founded on such pre-existing equitable obligations may be enforced; there is a good consideration for them; they merely remove an impediment created by law to the recovery of debts honestly due, but which public policy protects the debtors from being compelled to pay. In all these cases there was originally a *quid pro quo*, and according to the principles of natural justice the party receiving ought to pay; but the legislature has said he shall not be coerced; then comes the promise to pay the debt that is barred, the promise of the man to pay the debt of the infant, of the discharged bankrupt to restore to his creditor what by the law he had lost. In all these cases there is a moral obligation founded upon an antecedent valuable consideration. These promises therefore have a sound legal basis. They are not promises to pay something for nothing; not naked pacts, but the voluntary revival or creation of obligation which before existed in natural law, but which had been dispensed with, not for the benefit of the party obliged solely, but principally for the public convenience. If moral obligation, in its fullest sense, is a good substratum for an express promise, it is not easy to perceive why it is not equally good to support an implied promise. What a man ought to do, generally he ought to be made to do, whether he promise or refuse. But the law of society has left most of such obligations to the *interior* forum, as the tribunal of conscience has been aptly called. Is there not a moral obligation upon every son who has become affluent by means of the education and advantages bestowed upon him by his father, to relieve that father from pecuniary embarrassment, to promote his comfort and happiness, and even to share with him his riches, if thereby he will be made happy? And yet such a son may, with impunity, leave such a father in any degree of penury above that which will expose the community in which he dwells to the danger of being obliged to preserve him from absolute want. Is not a wealthy father under strong moral obligation to advance the interest of an obedient, well-disposed son, to furnish him with the means of acquiring and maintaining a becoming rank in life, to rescue him from the horrors of debt incurred by misfortune? Yet the law will uphold him in any degree of parsimony, short of that which would reduce his son to the necessity of seeking public charity.

Without doubt there are great interests of society which justify withholding the coercive arm of the law from these duties of imperfect obligation, as they are called; imperfect, not because they are less binding upon the conscience than those which are called perfect but because the wisdom of the social law does not impose sanctions upon them.

A deliberate promise in writing, made freely and without any mistake, one which may lead the party to whom it is made into contracts and expenses, cannot be broken without a violation of moral duty. But if there was nothing paid or promised for it, the law, perhaps wisely, leaves the execution of it to the conscience of him who makes it. It is only when the party making the promise gains something, or he to whom it is made loses something, that the law gives the promise validity. And in the case of the promise of the adult to pay the debt of the infant, of the debtor discharged by the Statute of Limitations or bankruptcy, the principle is preserved by looking back to the origin of the transaction, where an equivalent is to be found. An exact equivalent is not required by the law; for there being a consideration, the parties are left to estimate its value: though here the courts of equity will step in to relieve from gross inadequacy between the consideration and the promise.

These principles are deduced from the general current of decided cases upon the subject, as well as from the known maxims of the common law. The general position, that moral obligation is a sufficient consideration for an express promise, is to be limited in its application to cases where at some time or other a good or valuable consideration has existed.

A legal obligation is always a sufficient consideration to support either an express or an implied promise; such as an infant's debt for necessaries, or a father's promise to pay for the support and education of his minor children. But when the child shall have attained to manhood, and shall have become his own agent in the world's business, the debts he incurs, whatever may be their nature, create no obligation upon the father; and it seems to follow, that his promise founded upon such a debt has no legally binding force.

The cases of instruments under seal and certain mercantile contracts, in which considerations need not be proved, do not contradict the principles above suggested. The first import a consideration in themselves, and the second belong to a branch of the mercantile law, which has found it necessary to disregard the point of consideration in respect to instruments negotiable in their nature and essential to the interests of commerce.

Instead of citing a multiplicity of cases to support the positions I have taken, I will only refer to a very able review of all the cases in the note in 3 Bos. & Pul. 249.[1] The opinions of the judges had been variant for a long course of years upon this subject, but there seems to be no case in which it was nakedly decided, that a promise to pay the debt of a son of full age, not living with his father, though the debt

[1] See *infra*. p. 378, note 1. — ED.

were incurred by sickness which ended in the death of the son, without a previous request by the father proved or presumed, could be enforced by action.

It has been attempted to show a legal obligation on the part of the defendant by virtue of our statute, which compels lineal kindred in the ascending or descending line to support such of their poor relations as are likely to become chargeable to the town where they have their settlement. But it is a sufficient answer to this position, that such legal obligation does not exist except in the very cases provided for in the statute, and never until the party charged has been adjudged to be of sufficient ability thereto. We do not know from the report any of the facts which are necessary to create such an obligation. Whether the deceased had a legal settlement in this commonwealth at the time of his death, whether he was likely to become chargeable had he lived, whether the defendant was of sufficient ability, are essential facts to be adjudicated by the court to which is given jurisdiction on this subject. The legal liability does not arise until these facts have all been ascertained by judgment, after hearing the party intended to be charged.

For the foregoing reasons we are all of opinion that the nonsuit directed by the Court of Common Pleas was right, and that judgment be entered thereon for costs for the defendant.

LITTLEFIELD, *Executrix of* JOHN LITTLEFIELD *v.* ELIZABETH SHEE.

IN THE KING'S BENCH, NOVEMBER 4, 1831.

[*Reported in* 2 *Barnewall & Adolphus,* 811.]

ASSUMPSIT for goods sold and delivered. The fourth count stated that John Littlefield in his lifetime, at the special instance and request of the defendant, had supplied and delivered to her divers goods and chattels for the sum of £16; and thereupon, in consideration of the premises, and of the said sum of money being due and unpaid, the defendant, after the death of the said John Littlefield, undertook and promised the plaintiff as executrix of J. L. to pay her the said sum o money as soon as it was in her (the defendant's) power so to do. And although afterwards, to wit, on, &c., at, &c., it was in her power to pay the said sum, yet she did not do so. Plea, the general issue. At the trial before Gaselee, J., at the last assizes for Sussex, it appeared that the action was brought to recover £15 for butcher's meat supplied by the testator to the defendant, for her own use, between September, 1825 and March, 1826. During that time the defendant was a married woman, but her husband was abroad. After his death she promised to pay the debt when it should be in her power, and her ability to pay was proved at the trial. The learned judge held that, the defendant having been a *feme covert* at the time when the goods were supplied, her husband was originally liable, and consequently there was no consideration for the promise declared upon. The plaintiff was therefore nonsuited. *Hutchinson* on a former day in this term moved to set aside the nonsuit, and to enter a verdict for the plaintiff on the fourth count; on the ground that, the goods having been supplied to the defendant while she was living separate from her husband, she was under a moral obligation to pay for them, and such obligation was a sufficient consideration for a subsequent promise. It was not necessary that there should have been an antecedent legal obligation. Barnes *v.* Hedley,[1] Lee *v.* Muggeridge.[2] *Cur. adv. vult.*

Lord Tenterden, C. J., now delivered the judgment of the court. The fourth count of the declaration states that the testator had at the request of the defendant supplied her with goods, and that in consideration of the premises, and of the price of the goods being due and unpaid, the defendant promised. Now, that is in substance an allegation that those sums were due from her, and the plaintiff failed in proof of that allegation, because it appeared that the goods were supplied to her whilst her husband was living, so that the price constituted a debt due from him. We are therefore of opinion that the declaration was not supported by the proof, and that the nonsuit was right. In Lee *v.* Muggeridge all the circumstances which shewed that the money was in conscience due from the defendant were correctly set forth in the declaration. It there appeared upon the record that the money was lent to her, though paid to her son-in-law, while she was a married woman; and that after her husband's death, she, knowing all the circumstances, promised that her executor should pay the sum due on the bond. I must also observe that the doctrine that a moral obligation is a sufficient consideration for a subsequent promise is one which should be received with some limitation. *Rule refused.*

[1] 2 Taunt. 184.

[2] 5 Taunt. 36.

JOHN MEYER v. SARAH HAWORTH.

IN THE QUEEN'S BENCH, JUNE 1, 1838.

[*Reported in* 8 *Adolphus & Ellis*, 467.]

ASSUMPSIT for goods sold and delivered, goods bargained and sold, and at defendant's request delivered to W. J. R., work and labor, money paid, and interest, and on an account stated.

Plea, coverture at the time of the promise.

Replication, that defendant, at the time when the debts were contracted, was living separate from her husband, and in open adultery with W. J. R.; that the husband was not liable to pay, nor did pay, the debts so contracted by defendant while she was so living separate, &c.; that plaintiff, at the time of the sale and delivery, &c., did not know that defendant was the wife of, &c., nor that she was living in open adultery, &c., and dealt with her as a *feme sole;* and that, after the death of the husband, and before action brought, defendant, in consideration of the premises, promised to pay. Verification.

General demurrer, and joinder.

Streeten, for the defendant. A married woman is not liable for the debts she contracts, though she be living in open adultery, and separate from her husband. [PATTESON, J. I presume the plaintiff does not mean to impugn Marshall v. Rutton[1] and other cases to the same effect. The subsequent promise will probably be relied on.] The replication, if it insist on the subsequent promise, is a departure. It admits the promises stated in the declaration to have been made during coverture, and sets up a new promise. The considerations are different: the delivery of the goods, &c., form the consideration in the declaration; the consideration for the promise in the replication is "the premises," which seems to point to a moral consideration. Such a consideration appears not to be sustainable. Littlefield v. Shee.[2] Barden v. De Keverberg[3] shews what is necessary to make a *feme covert* liable as a *feme sole.*

Humfrey, contra. In Littlefield v. Shee the husband was originally liable: here he never was so. Rex v. Flintan.[4] Lee v. Muggeridge[5] supports the validity of such a moral consideration as this. Then this is not a departure: if it were, every replication to a plea of the Statute of Limitations, setting up an acknowledgment, would be so; for such an acknowledgment is merely evidence of a fresh promise. Tanner v. Smart.[6] [PATTESON, J. That is a promise to pay an existing debt: here there was no debt from the wife.] If there be any state of facts

[1] 8 T. R. 545. [2] 2 B. & Ad. 811. [3] 2 Mee. & W. 61.
[4] 1 B. & Ad. 227. [5] 5 Taunt. 36. [6] 6 B. & C. 603.

in which the debt would not be absolutely null in the first instance, that distinction would not apply. Now suppose the husband had been transported. [LORD DENMAN, C. J. That should be part of the statement of consideration. PATTESON, J. You are to support your declaration.]

Streeten, in reply. The declaration states the supply of goods at the request of the wife, who could not then contract. The doctrine in Lee *v.* Muggeridge has been qualified by later decisions; and there too the special contract was set out in the declaration.

LORD DENMAN, C. J. The record states that goods were supplied to a married woman, who after her husband's death promised to pay. That is not sufficient. The debt was never owing from her. If there was a moral obligation, that should have been shewn.

LITTLEDALE, J. If there was any moral obligation, it should have been stated. The replication does not support the declaration. The promise in the declaration was altogether void. This is not like the case of an infant, whose promise is voidable only.

PATTESON, J. For the reasons given this replication is bad as a departure. The promise originally stated was not merely voidable, like that of an infant. There is another fault in the replication: it does not allege positively the death of the husband.

WILLIAMS, J., concurred. *Judgment for defendant.*

EASTWOOD *v.* KENYON.

IN THE QUEEN'S BENCH, JANUARY 16, 1840.

[*Reported in* 11 *Adolphus & Ellis,* 438.]

ASSUMPSIT. The declaration stated that one John Sutcliffe made his will, and appointed plaintiff executor thereof, and thereby bequeathed certain property in manner therein mentioned; that he afterwards died without altering his will, leaving one Sarah Sutcliffe, an infant, his daughter and only child, and heiress at law, surviving; that after making the will John Sutcliffe sold the property mentioned therein, and purchased a piece of land upon which he erected certain cottages, but the same were not completed at the time of his death; which piece of land and cottages were at the time of his death mortgaged by him; that he died intestate in respect of the same, whereupon the equity of redemption descended to the said infant as heiress at law; that after the death of John Sutcliffe, plaintiff duly proved the will and administered to the estate of the deceased; that from and after the death of John Sutcliffe until the said Sarah Sutcliffe came of full age, plaintiff executor as aforesaid "acted as the guardian and agent" of the said infant, and in that capacity expended large sums of money in and about her maintenance and education, and in and about the completion, management, and necessary improvement of the said cottages and premises in which the said Sarah Sutcliffe was so interested, and in paying the interest of the mortgage money chargeable thereon and otherwise relative thereto, the said expenditure having been made in a prudent and useful manner, and having been beneficial to the interest of the said Sarah Sutcliffe to the full amount thereof; that the estate of John Sutcliffe deceased having been insufficient to allow plaintiff to make the said payments out of it, plaintiff was obliged to advance out of his own moneys, and did advance, a large sum, to wit, £140, for the purpose of the said expenditure; and, in order to reimburse himself, was obliged to borrow, and did borrow, the said sum of one A. Blackburn, and as security made his promissory note for payment thereof to the said A. Blackburn or his order on demand with interest; which sum, so secured by the said promissory note, was at the time of the making thereof and still is wholly due and unpaid to the said A. Blackburn; that the said sum was expended by plaintiff in manner aforesaid for the benefit of the said Sarah Sutcliffe, who received all the benefit and advantage thereof, and such expenditure was useful and beneficial to her to the full amount thereof; that when the said Sarah Sutcliffe came of full age she had notice of the premises, and then assented to the loan so raised by plaintiff, and the security so given by him, and requested plaintiff to give up to one J. Stansfield as her agent the control and management of the said property, and then promised the plaintiff to pay and discharge the amount of the said note; and thereupon caused one year's interest upon the said sum of £140 to be paid to A. Blackburn. That thereupon plaintiff agreed to give up, and did then give up, the control and management of the property to the said agent on behalf of the said Sarah Sutcliffe; that all the services of plaintiff were done and given by him for the said Sarah Sutcliffe and for her benefit gratuitously, and without any fee, benefit, or reward whatsoever; and the said services and expenditures were of great benefit to her, and her said property was increased in value by reason thereof to an amount far exceeding the said £140. That afterwards defendant intermarried with the said Sarah Sutcliffe, and had notice of the premises; and the accounts of plaintiff of and concerning the premises were then submitted to defendant, who then examined and assented to the same, and upon such accounting there was found to be due to plaintiff a large sum of money, to wit, &c., for moneys so expended and borrowed by him as aforesaid; and it also then appeared that plaintiff was indebted to A. Blackburn in the amount of the said note. That defendant, in right of his wife, had and received all the benefit and advantage arising from the said services and expenditure. That thereupon, in consideration of the premises, defendant promised plaintiff that he would pay and discharge the amount of the said promissory note; but that, although a reasonable time for paying and discharging the said note had elapsed, and A. Blackburn, the holder thereof, was willing to accept payment from defendant, and defendant was requested by plaintiff to pay and discharge the amount thereof, defendant did not nor would, then or at any other time, pay or discharge the amount, &c., but wholly refused, &c.

Plea, *non assumpsit.*

On the trial before Patteson, J., at the York spring assizes, 1838, it was objected on the part of the defendant that the promise stated in the declaration, and proved, was a promise to pay the debt of another, within the Statute of Frauds, 29 Car. 2, c. 3, s. 4, and ought to have been in writing; on the other hand it was contended that such defence, if available at all, was not admissible under the plea of *non assumpsit.*[1] The learned judge was of the latter opinion, and the plaintiff had a verdict, subject to a motion to enter a verdict for the defendant.

Cresswell, in the following term, obtained a rule *nisi* according to the leave reserved, and also for arresting judgment on the ground that the declaration shewed no consideration for the promise alleged. In Trinity vacation, 1839,[2]

Alexander and *W. H. Watson* shewed cause. . . . It has been distinctly held that a moral obligation will support an express promise. There must be something done by the plaintiff at the defendant's request, or an act done for the defendant's benefit must be ratified by an express promise to pay; in either case an action will lie. [COLERIDGE, J. How are we to know the difference between an express promise and an implied promise on the pleadings?] After verdict an express promise must be presumed. [COLERIDGE, J. The same question may arise on demurrer.] In Lee *v.* Muggeridge[3] executors were held liable on a promise by the testatrix, after the decease of her husband, to pay a bond made by her when under coverture, on the express ground that she was morally bound to pay it. The same doctrine was upheld in Seago *v.* Deane,[4] Atkins *v.* Hill,[5] and in several other cases cited in the note to Wennall *v.* Adney.[6] A stronger case of moral obligation can hardly arise than the present, where the plaintiff is admitted to have been for many years the faithful guardian and manager of the estate of the defendant while she was under age, and

1 The arguments and decision upon these points are omitted. — ED.

2 June 19th. Before Lord Denman, C. J., Patteson, Williams, and Coleridge, JJ.

3 5 Taunt. 36.

4 4 Bing. 459.

5 Cowp. 284.

6 3 B. & P. 247.

where the defendant and his wife have received great pecuniary benefit from the plaintiff's acts.

Cresswell, contra. . . . What is it that constitutes the moral obligation here? Not the expenditure on the estate, for no duty was cast on the plaintiff to lay out any thing on it, nor had he any right to interfere with the management; and if he had, the defendant had at that time no interest in it at all. If the honesty of the outlay causes the moral obligation, then it is indifferent whether it turned out profitable or not to the defendant or his wife. It would support a promise, though the property had been damnified by it. If the benefit constitutes the consideration, then whenever a party benefits another against his will, a subsequent promise will be a ground of action. If it had appeared that the wife was liable at the time of her marriage, then the consequent liability of the defendant might have supported his promise; but no liability of the wife is stated, nor is it said that she promised in consideration of the premises. As to the agreement of the plaintiff to give up the control and management of the property, he had no right to either, and therefore nothing to give up; and if he had, it is not alleged to have been the consideration of the wife's promise. The doctrine of moral obligation as a ground for a promise must be limited to those cases where the law would have given a clear right of action originally, if some legal impediment had not suspended or precluded the liability of the party. The ordinary instances are infancy, bankruptcy, and the Statute of Limitations; and these were the cases referred to by Lord Mansfield when he laid down the above doctrine. As a general rule, it cannot be supported. Littlefield *v.* Shee.[1] The law is correctly laid down and the cases explained in the note to Wennall *v.* Adney.[2]

In this term (January 16th) the judgment of the court was delivered by

LORD DENMAN, C. J. . . . The second point arose in arrest of judgment, namely, whether the declaration shewed a sufficient consideration for the promise. It stated in effect that the plaintiff was executor under the will of the father of the defendant's wife, who had died intestate as to his real estate, leaving the defendant's wife, an infant, his only child; that the plaintiff had voluntarily expended his money for the improvement of the real estate, while the defendant's wife was sole and a minor; and that, to reimburse himself, he had borrowed money of Blackburn, to whom he had given his promissory note; that the defendant's wife, while sole, had received the benefit, and after she came of age assented and promised to pay the note, and did pay a year's interest; that after the marriage the plaintiff's accounts were

[1] 2 B. & Ad. 811.

[2] 3 B. & P. 247. See also the argument of the Attorney-General in Haigh *v.* Brooks, 10 A. & E. 315, 316.

shewn to the defendant, who assented to them, and it appeared that there was due to the plaintiff a sum equal to the amount of the note to Blackburn; that the defendant, in right of his wife, had received all the benefit, and, in consideration of the premises, promised to pay and discharge the amount of the note to Blackburn.

Upon motion in arrest of judgment, this promise must be taken to have been proved, and to have been an express promise, as indeed it must of necessity have been, for no such implied promise in law was ever heard of. It was then argued for the plaintiff that the declaration disclosed a sufficient moral consideration to support the promise.

Most of the older cases on this subject are collected in a learned note to the case of Wennall *v.* Adney,[1] and the conclusion there

[1] 3 B. & P. 249. [The note referred to, which was first published in 1804, is as follows: —

"An idea has prevailed of late years that an express promise, founded simply on an antecedent moral obligation, is sufficient to support an assumpsit. It may be worth consideration, however, whether this proposition be not rather inaccurate, and whether that inaccuracy has not in a great measure arisen from some expressions of Lord Mansfield and Mr. Justice Buller, which, if construed with the qualifications fairly belonging to them, do not warrant the conclusion which appears to have been rather hastily drawn from thence. In Atkins *v.* Hill, Cowp. 288, which was assumpsit against an executor on a promise by him to pay a legacy in consideration of assets, Lord Mansfield said: 'It is the case of a promise made upon a good and valuable consideration which in all cases is a sufficient ground to support an action. It is so in cases of obligations which would otherwise only bind a man's conscience, and which without such promise he could not be compelled to pay.' And in Hawkes *v.* Saunders, Cowp. 290, which was a similar case with Atkins *v.* Hill, Lord Mansfield said that the rule laid down at the bar 'that to make a consideration to support an assumpsit there must be either an immediate benefit to the party promising, or a loss to the person to whom the promise was made,' was too narrow, and observed 'that a legal or equitable duty is a sufficient consideration for an actual promise; that where a man is under a moral obligation, which no court of law or equity can enforce, and promises, the honesty and rectitude of the thing is a consideration.' His Lordship then instanced the several cases of a promise to pay a debt barred by the Statute of Limitations, a promise by a bankrupt after his certificate to pay an antecedent debt, and a promise by a person of full age to pay a debt contracted during his infancy. The opinion of Mr. Justice Buller in the last case was to the same effect, and the same law was again laid down by Lord Mansfield in Trueman *v.* Fenton, Cowp. 544. Of the two former cases it may be observed that the particular point decided in them has been overruled by the subsequent case of Deeks *v.* Strutt, 5 T. R. 690. And it may further be observed, that however general the expressions used by Lord Mansfield may at first sight appear, yet the instances adduced by him as illustrative of the rule of law do not carry that rule beyond what the older authorities seem to recognize as its proper limits; for in each instance the party bound by the promise had received a benefit previous to the promise. Indeed it seems that in such instances alone as those selected by Lord Mansfield will an express promise have any operation, and there it only becomes necessary because, though the consideration was originally beneficial to the party promising, yet, inasmuch as he was not of a capacity to bind himself when he received the benefit, or is protected from liability by some statute provision, or some stubborn rule of law, the law will not, as in ordinary cases, imply an assumpsit against him. The same observation is applicable to Trueman *v.* Fenton, that being an action against arrived at seems to be correct in general, "that an express promise can only revive a precedent good consideration, which might have been

a bankrupt on a promise made by him subsequent to his certificate respecting a debt due before the certificate. There is, however, rather a loose note of a case of Scott v. Nelson, Westminster Sittings, 4 Geo. 3, *cor.* Ld. Mansfield (see Esp. N. P. 945), in which his Lordship is said to have held a father bound by his promise to pay for the previous maintenance of a bastard child. And there is also an anonymous case, 2 Show. 184, where Lord C. J. Pemberton ruled that 'for meat and drink for a bastard child an *indebitatus assumpsit* will lie.' Although the latter case does not expressly say that there was a previous request by the defendant, yet that seems to have been the fact, for Lord Hale's opinion is cited to shew 'that where there is common charity and a charge,' the action will lie; which seems to imply that if a charge be imposed upon one person by the charitable conduct of another, the latter shall pay; and though he adds, 'and undoubtedly a special promise would reach it,' that expression does not necessarily import a promise subsequent to the charge being sustained, but may be supposed to mean that, where a party is induced to undertake a charge by the engagement of another to pay, the latter will certainly be liable even though he should not be so where the charge was only induced by his conduct without such engagement. The case of Watson v. Turner, Bull. N. P. 147, has sometimes been cited in support of what has been supposed to be the general principle laid down by Lord Mansfield, because in that case overseers were held bound by a mere subsequent promise to pay an apothecary's bill for care taken of a pauper; but it may be observed that 'this was adjudged not to be *nudum pactum*, for the overseers are bound to provide for the poor;' which obligation, being a legal obligation, distinguishes the case. Indeed in a late case of Atkins v. Banwell, 2 East, 505, that distinction does not seem to have been sufficiently adverted to; for Watson v. Turner was cited to shew that a mere moral obligation is sufficient to raise an implied assumpsit, and though the court denied that proposition, yet Lord Ellenborough observed that the promise given in the case of Watson v. Turner made all the difference between the two cases, without alluding to another distinction which might have been taken; viz., that though the parish officers were bound by law in Watson v. Turner, the defendants in the principal case were not so bound, because the pauper had been relieved by the plaintiffs as overseers of another parish, though belonging to the parish of which the defendants were overseers. In the older cases no mention is made of moral obligation; but it seems to have been much doubted whether mere natural affection was a sufficient consideration to support an assumpsit, though coupled with a subsequent express promise. Indeed Lord Mansfield appears to have used the term, 'moral obligation,' not as expressive of any vague and undefined claim arising from nearness of relationship, but of those imperative duties which would be enforceable by law, were it not for some positive rule, which, with a view to general benefit, exempts the party in that particular instance from legal liability. On such duties, so exempted, an express promise operates to revive the liability and take away the exemption, because, if it were not for the exemption, they would be enforced at law through the medium of an implied promise. In several of the cases it is laid down, that to support an assumpsit the party promising must derive a benefit, or the party performing sustain an inconvenience occasioned by the plaintiff. *Per* Coke and all the Justices, Hatch and Capel's Case, Godb. 202; *per* Reeve, J., Mar. 203; *per* Coke, C. J., and Dodderidge, J., 3 Bulst. 162; and *per* Coke, C. J., 1 Roll. Rep. 61, pl. 4. And in Lampleigh v. Brathwait, Hob. 105, it was resolved 'that a mere voluntary courtesy will not have a consideration to uphold an assumpsit. But if that courtesy were moved by a suit or request of the party that gives the assumpsit, it will bind; for the promise, though it follows, is not naked, and couples itself with the suit before, and the merits of the party procured by that suit.' And in Bret v. J. S. and his Wife, Cro. Eliz. 756, where enforced at law through the medium of an implied promise, had it not been suspended by some positive rule of law; but can give no original

the first husband of the wife sent his son to table with the plaintiff for three years at £8 per annum, and died within the year, and the wife during her widowhood, in consideration that the son should continue the residue of the time, promised to pay the plaintiff £6 13*s.* 4*d.* for the time past, and £8 for every year after, and upon which promise the plaintiff brought his action; the court held that natural affection was not of itself a sufficient ground for an assumpsit; for although it was sufficient to raise an use, yet it was not sufficient to ground an action without an express *quid pro quo;* but that as the promise was not only in consideration of affection, but that the son should afterwards continue at the plaintiff's table, it was sufficient to support a promise. In Harford *v.* Gardiner, 2 Leo. 30, it was said by the court, that love and friendship are not considerations to found actions upon; and in Best *v.* Jolly, 1 Sid. 38, where a father was held liable for his own and his son's debt, because he had promised to pay them if the plaintiff would forbear to sue for them, yet the court said 'he was not liable for his son's debt,' but having induced forbearance, which is a damage to the plaintiff, he was held liable, 'though as to the son's debt it was no benefit to the defendant.' So in Besfich *v.* Coggil, Palm. 559, it was debated whether the defendant was liable upon an express promise to repay the plaintiff money laid out by him in Spain for the defendant's son, and the charges of his funeral; Hyde, C. J., and Whitelocke being of opinion that the action could not be maintained; Jones and Dodderidge *e contra* that it could. The former of which, it should seem, was the better opinion; for in Butcher *v.* Andrews, Carth. 446, on assumpsit for money lent by the plaintiff to the defendant's son at his instance and request, and verdict for the plaintiff, the judgment was arrested, Holt, C. J., saying, 'If it had been an *indebitatus* for so much money paid by the plaintiff at the request of the defendant unto his son, it might have been good, for then it would be the father's debt and not the son's; but when the money is lent to the son, it is his proper debt, and not the father's.' But in Church *v.* Church, B. R. 1656, cit. Sir T. Ray. 260, where defendant promised to repay the plaintiff the charges of his son's funeral, the latter was held entitled to recover, though no request was laid in the declaration. Of which case it may be observed, that possibly after verdict the court presumed a request proved; for in Hayes *v.* Warren, 2 Str. 933, though the court would not presume a request after judgment by default, yet they said they would have presumed it after verdict. However, in Style *v.* Smith, cited by Popham, J., 2 Leon. 111, it was determined that if a physician in the absence of a father give his son medicine, and the father in consideration promise to pay him, an action will lie for the money. But the case of Style *v.* Smith, if closely examined, will not perhaps be found so discordant with the principle laid down in Bret *v.* J. S. and his Wife, as may be supposed. From the expression 'in the absence of a father,' used in that case, it may be inferred that the son lived with the father, and that the medicine was administered to the son in the house of the father while the latter was absent, from whence it results that the physician's debt, though not founded on any immediate benefit to the father, or on his request, was most probably founded on his credit; which credit, if fairly inferred from circumstances by the physician, might operate to charge the father in the same way as his request would operate, the physician having sustained a loss in consequence of that credit. Indeed if any of the cases could be sustained on the principle that a father is, by the mere force of moral obligation, bound to pay what has been advanced for his son, because he has subsequently promised to pay it, by the same rule the son should be liable for the debt of the father upon a similar promise; for the same moral obligation exists in both cases. Yet in Barber *v.* Fox, 2 Saund. 136, the court arrested the judgment in an action of assumpsit on a promise made by the defendant to avoid being sued on a bond of his father, it not being alleged that the defendant's father had bound himself and his heirs; for they refused to intend right of action, if the obligation on which it is founded never could have been enforced at law, though not barred by any legal maxim or statute provision." Instances are given of voidable contracts, as those of infants ratified by an express promise after age, and distinguished from void contracts, as of married women, not capable of ratification by them when widows; Lloyd v. Lee;[1] debts of bankrupts revived by subsequent promise after certificate; and similar cases. Since that time some cases have occurred upon this subject, which require to be more particularly examined. Barnes v. Hedley[2] decided that a promise to repay a sum of money with legal interest, which sum had originally been lent on usurious terms, but, in taking the account of which, all usurious items had been by agreement struck out, was binding. Lee v. Muggeridge[3] upheld an assumpsit by a widow that her executors should pay a bond given by her while a *feme covert* to secure money then advanced to a third person at her request. On the latter occasion the language of Mansfield, C. J., and of the whole Court of Common Pleas, is very large, and hardly susceptible of any limitation. It is conformable to the expressions used by the judges of this court in Cooper v. Martin,[4] where a stepfather was permitted to recover from the son of his wife, after he had attained his full age, upon a declaration for necessaries furnished to him while an infant, for which, after his full age, he promised to pay. It is remarkable that in none of these was there any allusion made to the learned note in 3 Bosanquet

even after verdict that the bond was in the usual form, and consequently held the promise of the defendant *nudum pactum*, he not appearing to have been liable to be sued upon the bond. And this last case was confirmed in Hunt v. Swain, 1 Lev. 165, Sir T. Ray. 127, 1 Sid. 248. See note 2 to Barber v. Fox, by Mr. Serjt. Williams. Indeed it is clear from Lloyd v. Lee, 1 Str. 94, and Cockshott v. Bennett, 2 T. R. 763, that if a contract between two persons be void, and not merely voidable, no subsequent express promise will operate to charge the party promising, even though he has derived a benefit from the contract. Yet according to the commonly received notion respecting moral obligations and the force attributed to a subsequent express promise, such a person ought to pay. An express promise, therefore, as it should seem, can only revive a precedent good consideration, which might have been enforced at law through the medium of an implied promise, had it not been suspended by some positive rule of law, but can give no original right of action, if the obligation on which it is founded never could have been enforced at law, though not barred by any legal maxim or statute provision. In addition to the cases already collected upon this subject, it may be observed that in Mitchinson v. Hewson, 7 T. R. 348, the court of King's Bench, upon the authority of Drue v. Thorne, All. 72, held a husband not liable to be sued alone for the debt of his wife contracted before marriage, though the objection was only taken in arrest of judgment, and consequently a promise by him to pay the debt appeared upon the record. From whence this principle may be extracted: that an obligation to pay in one right, even though it be a legal obligation, and coupled with an express promise, will not support an assumpsit to pay in another right." — ED.]

[1] 1 Stra. 94.
[2] 2 Taunt. 184.
[3] 5 Taunt. 36.
[4] 4 East, 76.

and Puller above referred to, and which has been very generally thought to contain a correct statement of the law. The case of Barnes *v.* Hedley is fully consistent with the doctrine in that note laid down. Cooper *v.* Martin also, when fully examined, will be found not to be inconsistent with it. This last case appears to have occupied the attention of the court much more in respect of the supposed statutable liability of a stepfather, which was denied by the court, and in respect of what a court of equity would hold as to a stepfather's liability, and rather to have assumed the point before us. It should, however, be observed that Lord Ellenborough in giving his judgment says: "The plaintiff having done an act beneficial for the defendant in his infancy, it is a good consideration for the defendant's promise after he came of age. In such a case the law will imply a request, and the fact of the promise has been found by the jury." And undoubtedly the action would have lain against the defendant whilst an infant, inasmuch as it was for necessaries furnished at his request in regard to which the law raises an implied promise. The case of Lee *v.* Muggeridge must however be allowed to be decidedly at variance with the doctrine in the note alluded to, and is a decision of great authority. It should however be observed that in that case there was an actual request of the defendant during coverture, though not one binding in law; but the ground of decision there taken was also equally applicable to Littlefield *v.* Shee, tried by Gaselee, J., at N. P., when that learned judge held, notwithstanding, that "the defendant having been a married woman when the goods were supplied, her husband was originally liable, and there was no consideration for the promise declared upon." After time taken for deliberation this court refused even a rule to shew cause why the nonsuit should not be set aside. Lee *v.* Muggeridge was cited on the motion, and was sought to be distinguished by Lord Tenterden, because there the circumstances raising the consideration were set out truly upon the record; but in Littlefield *v.* Shee the declaration stated the consideration to be that the plaintiff had supplied the defendant with goods at her request, which the plaintiff failed in proving, inasmuch as it appeared that the goods were in point of law supplied to the defendant's husband, and not to her. But Lord Tenterden added that the doctrine that a moral obligation is a sufficient consideration for a subsequent promise is one which should be received with some limitation. This sentence in truth amounts to a dissent from the authority of Lee *v.* Muggeridge, where the doctrine is wholly unqualified.

The eminent counsel who argued for the plaintiff in Lee *v.* Muggeridge spoke of Lord Mansfield as having considered the rule of *nudum pactum* as too narrow, and maintained that all promises deliberately made ought to be held binding. I do not find this language ascribed to him by any reporter, and do not know whether we are to receive it as a traditional report, or as a deduction from what he does appear to have laid down. If the latter, the note to Wennall *v.* Adney shews the deduction to be erroneous. If the former, Lord Tenterden and this court declared that they could not adopt it in Littlefield *v.* Shee. Indeed the doctrine would annihilate the necessity for any consideration at all, inasmuch as the mere fact of giving a promise creates a moral obligation to perform it.

The enforcement of such promises by law, however plausibly reconciled by the desire to effect all conscientious engagements, might be attended with mischievous consequences to society; one of which would be the frequent preference of voluntary undertakings to claims for just debts. Suits would thereby be multiplied, and voluntary undertakings would also be multiplied, to the prejudice of real creditors. The temptations of executors would be much increased by the prevalence of such a doctrine, and the faithful discharge of their duty be rendered more difficult.

Taking then the promise of the defendant, as stated on this record, to have been an express promise, we find that the consideration for it was past and executed long before; and yet it is not laid to have been at the request of the defendant, nor even of his wife while sole (though if it had, the case of Mitchinson *v.* Hewson[1] shews that it would not have been sufficient), and the declaration really discloses nothing but a benefit voluntarily conferred by the plaintiff and received by the defendant, with an express promise by the defendant to pay money.

If the subsequent assent of the defendant could have amounted to a *ratihabitio*, the declaration should have stated the money to have been expended at his request, and the ratification should have been relied on as matter of evidence; but this was obviously impossible, because the defendant was in no way connected with the property or with the plaintiff, when the money was expended. If the ratification of the wife while sole were relied on, then a debt from her would have been shewn, and the defendant could not have been charged in his own right without some further consideration, as of forbearance after marriage, or something of that sort; and then another point would have arisen upon the Statute of Frauds which did not arise as it was, but which might in that case have been available under the plea of *non assumpsit.*

In holding this declaration bad, because it states no consideration but a past benefit not conferred at the request of the defendant, we conceive that we are justified by the old common law of England.

Lampleigh *v.* Brathwait[2] is selected by Mr. Smith[3] as the leading case on this subject, which was there fully discussed, though not necessary to the decision. Hobart, C. J., lays it down that "a mere voluntary courtesy will not have a consideration to uphold an assumpsit.

[1] 7 T. R. 348. [2] Hob. 105. [3] 1 Smith's Leading Cases, 67.

But if that courtesy were moved by a suit or request of the party that gives the assumpsit, it will bind; for the promise, though it follows, yet it is not naked, but couples itself with the suit before, and the merits of the party procured by that suit; which is the difference;" a difference brought fully out by Hunt *v.* Bate,[1] there cited from Dyer, where a promise to indemnify the plaintiff against the consequences of having bailed the defendant's servant, which the plaintiff had done without request of the defendant, was held to be made without consideration; but a promise to pay £20 to plaintiff, who had married defendant's cousin, but at defendant's special instance, was held binding.

The distinction is noted, and was acted upon, in Townsend *v.* Hunt,[2] and indeed in numerous old books; while the principle of moral obligation does not make its appearance till the days of Lord Mansfield, and then under circumstances not inconsistent with this ancient doctrine when properly explained.

Upon the whole, we are of opinion that the rule must be made absolute to arrest the judgment.

Rule to arrest judgment, absolute.[3]

JOSEPH VALENTINE *v.* JAMES FOSTER.

SUPREME JUDICIAL COURT OF MASSACHUSETTS, OCTOBER TERM, 1840.

[*Reported in* 1 *Metcalf*, 520.]

INDEBITATUS ASSUMPSIT for money paid, &c. The report of the Chief Justice, before whom the case was tried, was in substance this: The plaintiff was formerly owner of three-eighths of a vessel in his own right, and held two-eighths thereof in his name as trustee for the defendant. An action was brought against the plaintiff and others, as owners of the vessel, for a demand alleged to be due to one Vinal. In the trial of that action, the plaintiff called the defendant as a witness, who was objected to on the ground of interest; whereupon the plaintiff executed and delivered to him a release from all liability to contribution for any sum which might be recovered in that suit, and the defendant gave his testimony. Vinal recovered judgment in that suit,

[1] Dyer, 272 *a.*

[2] Cro. Car. 408.

[3] The opinion ascribed to Lord Mansfield respecting the rule of *nudum pactum* appears to be not an unreasonable deduction from the cases of Pillans *v.* Mierop, 3 Burr. 1663; and Williamson *v.* Losh, reported from the paper books of Ashhurst, J., in Chitty on Bills, 75, note (*x*), 9th ed. Both are commented on by the Lord C. B. Skynner, in Rann *v.* Hughes, 7 T. R. 350, note (*a*). See also Evans's General View of the Decisions of Lord Mansfield, vol. i. p. 422.

at the March Term of this court in Suffolk, 1836; and the present action was brought to recover a part of the amount paid by the plaintiff in satisfaction of that judgment.

To maintain the action, the plaintiff offered to prove that after the trial of Vinal's said action, it appearing that the defendant's testimony was of little importance, the plaintiff proposed to the defendant to give him back the release and take no advantage of it; and that the defendant, in reply, said it would make no difference — he would take no advantage of it.

It was admitted that the plaintiff had no other ground to avoid the release, but a subsequent parol promise without any new consideration.

A nonsuit was entered, subject to the opinion of the whole court.

H. H. Fuller, for the plaintiff. A promise to pay a debt once due operates as a waiver of any mere legal discharge. The original debt, when not in fact paid, constitutes a continuing moral obligation which is a sufficient consideration for such promise. Chit. Con., Perkins's ed., 40, and cases there cited. In Willing *v.* Peters, 12 S. & R. 177, a debtor, after he had been released on paying a part of the debt, was held liable on his promise to pay the balance. *A fortiori*, it would seem, is the defendant in this case liable on his promise, as he paid nothing for his release.

Welch, for the defendant. In Willing *v.* Peters the release was executed at the request and for the benefit of the defendant; which distinguishes it from the present case.

The doctrine of moral obligation, as properly understood, and as illustrated by recent decisions, does not apply to the defendant's promise. See 3 Bos. & Pul. 249, note; Chit. Con., Perkins's ed., 42; Littlefield *v.* Shee, 2 Barn. & Adolph. 811; Meyer *v.* Haworth, 8 Adolph. & Ellis, 467; Smith *v.* Ware, 13 Johns. 257; Mills *v.* Wyman, 3 Pick. 207; Cook *v.* Bradley, 7 Conn. 57; Loomis *v.* Newhall, 15 Pick. 159; Hawley *v.* Farrar, 1 Vt. 420.

It is against the policy of the law that the promise in this case should be enforced.

SHAW, C. J. The single question in this case is, whether a pre-existing liability to contribution, voluntarily released by the party to whom it is due to the party liable, in order to qualify him as a witness in a trial at law between the releasor and a third party, is a good consideration for a subsequent promise to pay such contribution.

This action is one of new impression, and attempts to carry the doctrine of legal liability, arising upon an express promise made in consideration of moral obligation, somewhat further than it has yet been carried.

It is difficult to reduce this principle to a rule sufficiently accurate for practical use, on account of the looseness and uncertainty attending the notion of moral obligation or moral duty.

In Mills *v.* Wyman, 3 Pick. 207, where the subject was largely discussed, it was attempted to restrain and limit the generality of the principle broadly laid down, that a moral obligation is a sufficient consideration for an express promise, by confining it to cases where there has been some pre-existing legal obligation, which has become inoperative by force of positive law; and the cases of debts barred by the Statute of Limitations, by a discharge under bankrupt and insolvent laws, and debts incurred by infants, are put by way of illustration. But it is difficult to reconcile all the cases on the subject upon this principle. Lee *v.* Muggeridge, 5 Taunt. 36.

In some other cases another distinction has been somewhat relied on, to wit, when there is or would be a legal obligation, but where the remedy is taken away by positive law, or where the obligor is exempted from legal liability on considerations of policy. The only case I have found, where an action has been held to lie upon an express promise to pay a debt which had been voluntarily released, is that of Willing *v.* Peters, 12 S. & R. 177. It was a case where the debtor, having become insolvent, made an assignment for the benefit of all his creditors, containing a clause of release on the part of the creditors, in consideration of the assignment. A dividend had been received by the plaintiff, the creditor, after which the debtor made an express promise to pay the balance of the debt when he should become able. There, although it was argued that the release was voluntarily made, and though it actually extinguished the whole debt by an instrument under seal, which imported a consideration, yet the analogy was so strong to the case of a discharge under a bankrupt or insolvent law, in which it had always been held that an action might be maintained on an express promise to pay the balance of the debt, that the court decided in favor of the plaintiff.

But we think there are several considerations which distinguish the present case from that cited.

We are then to consider that, in becoming party to an assignment made by an insolvent debtor, the release is executed at the request and for the benefit of the debtor. And it has an important bearing in all those cases that the discharge or exemption, by which the debtor is held not liable to an action, is created for his benefit. Then applying the rule, that a party may waive an exception made for his benefit, and that he does waive it by an express promise, it affords a strong legal ground for the maintenance of an action upon such express promise. 21 Amer. Jurist, 278; 3 Bos. & Pul. 249, note. But in case of a release given in court to qualify a person as witness, the act can in no sense be regarded as done at the request or for the benefit of the releasee. On the contrary, the act is for the benefit of the releasor, that he may have the advantage of the releasee's testimony; and the understanding in all such cases is, that he prefers relinquishing for ever any actual or contingent claim which he may have upon the releasee, rather than forego the advantage he expects to derive from his testimony.

We also think there is another distinction between the case at bar and the case cited, founded in obvious and strong considerations of policy. A release given to qualify a witness is usually given in open court, in presence of the jury. It must be full and complete, to the satisfaction of the court; it is exhibited and represented as an absolute and complete discharge of all interest in the event of the suit. If it should come to be considered that such a release merely took away a legal remedy, that it left the moral obligation subsisting in its full force, and that the legal obligation would be revived by expressions on which it might be left to a jury to find a promise, it would introduce an element of doubt as to the force and effect of such a release. It might well be argued that it was merely formal, and left the witness still substantially interested; and would have a secret injurious effect upon the credit due to released witnesses.

Without therefore giving an opinion in reference to a case where a creditor has executed a release, to enable an insolvent debtor to obtain his discharge under a general assignment, the court are of opinion that, where a release has been voluntarily executed and delivered by a creditor to his debtor, for the express purpose of discharging all interest and qualifying him as a witness for his own benefit, there remains no moral obligation to pay the debt, which is sufficient to afford a consideration for a new promise upon which an action will lie.

Nonsuit to stand.[1]

SAMUEL O. DEARBORN AND ANOTHER *v.* FRANCIS BOWMAN.

SUPREME JUDICIAL COURT OF MASSACHUSETTS, OCTOBER TERM, 1841.

[*Reported in* 3 *Metcalf*, 155.]

ASSUMPSIT on a note in these terms: "June 17, 1839. I promise to pay Dearborn & Bellows sixty dollars in ninety days, value received. Bowman." Defence, want of consideration. The case came before this court upon a statement of the testimony given in the trial thereof in the Court of Common Pleas, which the parties agreed should be taken as a statement of the facts of the case. That statement was as follows:—

1 See Shepard *v.* Rhodes, 7 R. I. 470, 474; Warren *v.* Whitney, 24 Maine, 561.—ED.

"The defendant, to show that there was no consideration for the note, introduced Gen. Thomas A. Staples as a witness, who testified that at the democratic county convention held in October, 1837, in the county of Middlesex, the defendant was nominated, as one of the candidates of the democratic party, for election to the State Senate from the county of Middlesex, at the following November election; and that at the same convention the witness was chosen a member, and made chairman, of the democratic county committee for said county, for the ensuing year; that it was the duty of said committee to procure and cause to be printed and circulated in the county, previous to the election, such papers, addresses and documents, as would best promote the success of the democratic party, and secure the election of its candidates to office; that the plaintiffs, by the request of the witness, furnished extra papers to the amount of $105 during the months of October and November; and on or about the 16th of November, 1837, they rendered their bill to him for the same, and the bill was charged to, and made out against, the democratic county committee. The witness said it was customary, he believed, for the committee after an election to collect the bills of expenses attending the canvass, and apportion the amount among the candidates of the party, who usually paid their respective proportions; especially if they were elected. The defendant was not elected to the Senate in 1837, but had been the year previous. The witness said that the defendant had not paid any thing on account of the expenses of the election in 1837; that he had never spoken to or had any acquaintance with him until since the commencement of this action; that he had never agreed to pay, nor given the witness to understand that he would pay any thing on account of said expenses; that there was no subscription paper, or other written or verbal engagement, by which he had promised to pay; that the witness had paid $142 from his own funds towards defraying the expenses of the election in 1837, and that he had no legal claim upon the defendant or any other person for contribution; that if the defendant should offer to pay him $60, or any other sum, he should take it. The witness said that the extra papers, furnished by the plaintiffs, [and in part payment of which it is agreed by the parties that the note in suit was given] were furnished by his order; that the plaintiffs had repeatedly called on him as chairman to pay the bill before the date of said note; that the defendant had never requested or authorized him to procure or furnish any printing or papers on his account or credit. He also said he could not say but that he had authorized the plaintiffs to collect of the defendant his proportion of the expenses.

"Aaron Dow testified that the plaintiffs, or one of them, had often called on the defendant for his share or proportion of the expenses of the election in 1837; that the defendant said he was not bound or was not liable to pay any thing, but would do what was proper, and would pay if it was right that he should. The witness was present when the note in suit was given. The defendant refused to make the note payable to order, because he doubted to whom he was bound to pay it; whether to Staples or the plaintiffs. At the time the note was given, or at one of the times when one of the plaintiffs called on the defendant, he (the plaintiff) said that the plaintiffs had no legal claim against the defendant; and he produced no bill. He said he was authorized to collect of the defendant his proportion of the expenses by the chairman of the county committee.

"B. E. Hale testified that he was chairman of a committee in 1839, appointed at a convention of the democratic party that year, to collect the arrearages of bills from the candidates for office, and pay the expenses of the elections held prior to that time; that he wrote to the defendant for his proportion, but received no answer; that he afterwards saw the defendant, conversed with him on the subject, and the defendant said he would pay if it was proper that he should; and in a conversation holden with the defendant subsequently, the defendant said he would pay. The witness after that gave Bellows, one of the plaintiffs, a written order on the defendant for his assessment sometime before the date of the note in suit. The witness said he heard Gen. Staples authorize the plaintiffs to collect of the defendant his proportion of the expenses; and the witness said it was customary for the candidates of the party to pay the expenses."

J. G. Abbott, for the plaintiffs.

Buttrick, for the defendant.

SHAW, C. J. The defence to the action to recover the amount of this note is want of consideration. It is manifest from the note itself that it is not a negotiable instrument, being payable neither to order nor to bearer; indeed it appears by the case that the defendant declined making it negotiable. But total want of consideration is a good defence even to an action on a negotiable note, when brought by the promisee against the maker. Then the question is, whether upon the facts shown any consideration appears for this promise. The note was given in consequence of services before that time performed by the plaintiffs, in printing and circulating extra papers and documents, previously to an election of State Senators at which the defendant was a candidate. Such services imposed no obligation, legal or moral, on the defendant; and it would be somewhat dangerous to hold that they created any honorary obligation on him to pay for them. Nor would it be aided in a legal view by a previous custom, if proved, for candidates to contribute to the payment of similar expenses, whether successful or otherwise in the election.

Nor were these services performed at the request of the defendant. On the contrary, it appears by the evidence that they were performed by [*sic*] Gen. Staples, chairman of the county committee, who alone was responsible for the payment, and between whom and the defendant there was no privity, nor even any communication until long after the services had been performed. The rule of law seems to be now well settled — though it may have formerly been left in doubt — that the past performance of services constitutes no consideration even for an express promise, unless they were performed at the express or implied request of the defendant, or unless they were done in performance of some duty or obligation resting on the defendant. Mills *v.* Wyman, 3 Pick. 207; Loomis *v.* Newhall, 15 Pick. 159; Dodge *v.* Adams, 19 Pick. 429. As the services performed by the plaintiffs were not done at the request of the defendant, as they were not done in the fulfilment of any duty or obligation resting on him, there was no consideration to convert the express promise of the defendant into a legal obligation.

Another ground, however, was taken in behalf of the plaintiffs, which was, that the discharge by the plaintiffs of their legal demand against Staples was a good consideration for the defendant's promise to them. If such discharge was in fact given, and given at the defendant's request; or if the defendant had promised to pay, if they would discharge Staples *pro tanto*, and they did discharge him; it would have been a good consideration for the defendant's promise. But there is no evidence to establish the fact.

The court are of opinion that there was no legal consideration for the defendant's promise, and that no action can be maintained upon it.

Plaintiffs nonsuit.

JENNINGS AND WIFE *v.* BROWN AND OTHERS, *Executors.*

IN THE EXCHEQUER, HILARY TERM (JANUARY 31), 1842.

[*Reported in* 9 *Meeson & Welsby*, 496.]

ASSUMPSIT. The declaration stated that, before the making of the promise of the said A. B. B. (the defendants' testator), to wit, on the 1st January, 1833, the plaintiff Mary, being then sole and unmarried, and having theretofore always conducted herself with chastity and decorum, was seduced by the said A. B. B., who then debauched and carnally knew the said plaintiff Mary, so being sole and unmarried as aforesaid, and by means of which said seduction and carnal knowledge the said plaintiff Mary then became pregnant, and afterwards, and in the lifetime of the said A. B. B., and before the making of the said promise, to wit, on the 3d November, 1833, was delivered of a bastard child, to wit, a daughter, which said child had been and was begotten by the said A. B. B., and is still living; and whereas also afterwards, and in the lifetime of the said A. B. B., and before the making of the said promise as aforesaid, the said plaintiff Mary, so being then sole and unmarried as aforesaid, and having wholly relinquished and given up all cohabitation and immoral intercourse with the said A. B. B., had at his request undertaken, and then had the care and nurture of the said child; and thereupon afterwards, and in the lifetime of the said A. B. B., to wit, on the day and year last aforesaid, in consideration of the premises, and that the said plaintiff Mary would continue to take charge of the said child, and would thenceforth conduct herself correctly and virtuously, and would also keep secret the said fact that the said A. B. B. had so seduced and debauched the said plaintiff Mary, and was the father of the said bastard child, he the said A. B. B. then promised the said plaintiff Mary, then being sole and unmarried as aforesaid, that he the said A. B. B., his executors or administrators, should or would punctually pay or cause to be paid to the said plaintiff Mary an allowance of £60 a year during her natural life, by four quarterly payments in every year, to wit, on, &c., in each year; and the said plaintiffs aver that the said plaintiff Mary hath always, from the time of the making of the said promise of the said A. B. B. as aforesaid, continued to take charge of the said bastard child, and that the said plaintiff Mary hath also, from the time of the making of the said promise hitherto, conducted herself correctly and virtuously, and did not at any time after the making of the said promise, and during the lifetime of the said A. B. B., cohabit or have any immoral intercourse with the said A. B. B., and hath also always hitherto kept secret the said fact that the said A. B. B. did so seduce and debauch the said plaintiff Mary, and was the father of the said bastard child as aforesaid; of all which several premises respectively the said defendants, executors as aforesaid, have continually had notice; and the plaintiffs in fact say that afterwards, and after the death of the said A. B. B., and after the said intermarriage of the plaintiffs, and before the commencement of this suit, to wit, on the 12th November, 1841, a large sum of money, to wit, the sum of £180 of the said yearly allowance of £60, for twelve quarters of a year, which then, and as well after the said death of the said A. B. B. as after the said intermarriage of the plaintiffs had elapsed, became due and payable to the plaintiffs under and by virtue of the said promise of the said A. B. B. in that behalf; nevertheless the defendants, executors as aforesaid, not regarding the said promise of the said A. B. B., have not at any time paid to the plaintiffs the said sum of £180 or any part thereof (although often requested so to do), but have hitherto wholly neglected and refused so to do, and the same is still wholly due and unpaid, contrary to the said promise of the said A. B. B. in that behalf made as aforesaid.

The defendants pleaded *non assumpserunt*, and other pleas; traversing the seduction; that the child was begotten by the testator; alleging that the plaintiff Mary had not, at the time of making the promise, relinquished cohabitation with the testator; nor had she undertaken nor had the care or nurture of the child; nor had she continued to take charge of the child, nor kept secret the fact that the testator did seduce the plaintiff Mary, and was the father of the child. But all these pleas, on which issues were taken, were negatived by the finding of the jury.

The cause was tried before Rolfe, B., at the London sittings in this term. It appeared that the action was brought to recover twelve quarterly payments of an annuity of £60 a year, under the following circumstances: The testator, in the year 1833, became acquainted with the plaintiff Mary, a servant in his establishment; and the result was the birth of a child in the month of November in that year, which by a letter to her father he acknowledged himself to be the father of, and said that she and her child were amply provided for. It appeared that he paid her an annuity of £60 a year, and refrained from further criminal intercourse with her. Shortly after, the plaintiff Mary entertained intentions of getting married, and applied to the testator for the purpose of getting the annuity previously settled upon her. In reply to which the testator wrote her the following letter:—

DEC. 31st, 1834.

MARY,—I received your letter of yesterday, and feel a little annoyed at the distrust you entertain for my not providing for your child while I live, and after my decease. You seem to have got some would-be cunning adviser, which, if you do not mind, will cause you to lose a friend, instead of making one. Your father, by writing an imprudent letter, was very near doing you harm. When I spoke of an annuity, I did not consider that, from your youth and good health, the office would require (to allow the sum of £60 a year) a large deposit of some thousands, and which, were you to die the day after, would be entirely thrown away, besides its being a sum I am neither willing nor able to lay down.

And after stating other matters, and that her marrying would not alter his intentions, he adds:—

Thus, then, as long as your future conduct is correct, and the situation you have been placed in remains a secret, my allowance to you of £60 a year will be paid with punctuality; but I must remind you, were it to become known, the allowance of a magistrate would be 4*s.* 6*d.* or 5*s.* per week, which is £13 per annum. Under these circumstances, I should recommend you to consider me your friend, and place that confidence in me which you never had reason to doubt. Should you marry, for your mutual happiness, I would never see you but in the presence of your husband.

Shortly after this the plaintiffs were married, and a letter of congratulation, dated January 31, 1835, was written to her by the testator, which contained, amongst others, the following passage: "The allowance I told you I would make for the maintenance of Emma shall always be punctually paid quarterly."

The annuity was accordingly paid up to the testator's death, in March, 1839; but his executors, not feeling themselves justified in paying the annuity without the sanction of a court of law, refused to pay it, and the present action was brought. It was proved that the child was now living with the plaintiffs. The above facts having been proved, and the letters read in evidence, the counsel for the defendants objected that there was nothing in the correspondence which made out the consideration as expressed in the declaration. The learned judge, however, overruled the objection; and the jury found a verdict for the plaintiffs, with £80 damages, leave being reserved to the defendants to move to enter a nonsuit.

Humfrey now moved to enter a nonsuit accordingly. The letters written by the testator, and produced in evidence, do not shew a sufficient consideration to support the action. This is not the case of an instrument under seal, but a mere assumpsit, which is invalid for want of a consideration, and cannot be enforced either at law or in equity. Binnington *v.* Wallis[1] is in point. There the declaration stated that the plaintiff had cohabited with the defendant as his mistress; that it was agreed that no further immoral connection should take place between them, and that the defendant should allow her an annuity so long as she should continue of good and virtuous life and demeanor; that afterwards, in consideration of the premises, and that the plaintiff would give up the annuity, the defendant promised to pay as much as the annuity was reasonably worth. The court, on general demurrer, held the declaration bad. The only difference between that case and this is, that here it is stated that the testator seduced her; but that makes no difference. [PARKE, B. No, that makes no difference; but here the woman has supported the child, and that is a good consideration. It is a matter of bargain that she is to take care of the child, and to exonerate the father.] In Binnington *v.* Wallis there was abundant proof of consideration, for the plaintiff had given up the annuity. [PARKE, B. No, that was not part of the consideration; it was a mere moral consideration, which is nothing.] The courts have never yet gone to the extent of holding such an agreement valid.

PER CURIAM. The father might have had the child affiliated on him, and the consideration must be understood to be for ordinary provision. We think that a sufficient consideration.

Rule refused.

[1] 4 B. & Ald. 650.

CAROLINE BEAUMONT *v.* HENRY REEVE.

IN THE QUEEN'S BENCH, JANUARY 27, 1846.

[*Reported in* 8 *Queen's Bench Reports,* 483.]

ASSUMPSIT. The first count of the declaration alleged that whereas, before the making of the promise of defendant after mentioned, defendant had seduced and debauched plaintiff, and had induced and procured her to cohabit with him as his mistress for a long term, to wit, five years, and plaintiff by reason of the premises had been and was greatly injured in her character and reputation, and prejudiced in and deprived of the means of procuring an honest livelihood, and otherwise damnified; and whereas, before and at the time of making the promise, &c., plaintiff had ceased to cohabit with and then lived apart and separate from defendant; and thereupon heretofore, to wit, on, &c., it was agreed between plaintiff and defendant that they should continue to live apart from each other, and that no immoral intercourse or connection should ever again take place between them; and defendant, as a compensation for the injury so sustained by plaintiff, and in consideration of the premises, then undertook and promised plaintiff to allow and pay her yearly, from the said day, &c., during her life, towards and for her support and maintenance an annuity of £60; that, although plaintiff and defendant did not, at any time after the making of the promise of defendant, reside or cohabit together, yet defendant, disregarding, &c., hath not allowed or paid the annuity, &c., although often requested; and a large, &c., to wit, £60 of the annuity, for one year, ending upon, &c., now is due, &c. Special demurrer, assigning for cause the grounds insisted on in the argument. Joinder.

Crompton, for the defendant. The declaration is bad in substance, as disclosing no legal consideration for the promise. In Binnington *v.* Wallis[1] the declaration recited that the plaintiff had cohabited with the defendant as his mistress, whereby she had been injured in her reputation; that they had ceased to cohabit; that the two had agreed that no immoral intercourse should again take place between them, and defendant, as a compensation for the injury sustained by plaintiff, should pay her an annuity while she continued of good and virtuous life; and thereupon, in consideration of the premises, and that plaintiff would give up the annuity, defendant undertook to pay her its worth: and it was held that no consideration was disclosed, the plaintiff giving up only that which was of no value, inasmuch as she could not have enforced the original agreement for want of consideration. [PATTESON, J. The defendant's counsel there pointed out that the declaration did

[1] 4 B. & Ald. 650.

not aver that the plaintiff had been seduced; and the court seemed to think that an averment of seduction by the defendant would have supplied the defect: here that appears.] That makes no difference. A promise to induce cohabitation would clearly be illegal: here the consideration is only void. Where a part of a consideration is illegal, it vitiates the whole; where it is simply void, the remainder of the consideration, if good, will support an assumpsit.[1] In Jennings *v.* Brown,[2] where a consideration appeared similar to that in the present action, the action was supported on the ground that there was also a good consideration, namely, that the plaintiff would support a child which was the fruit of the intercourse; and Parke, B., said that it made no difference as to the invalidity of the former consideration, that the defendant had seduced the plaintiff. [PATTESON, J., mentioned Gibson *v.* Dickie.[3]] There the consideration was future, that the plaintiff should not cohabit with a third party or any one else; and the court held that this was a valid consideration and would support the action, nothing illegal appearing: the case was compared to that of an annuity to a widow *dum caste vixerit.* The decisions on bonds are inapplicable: a bond needs no consideration: it is sufficient that there is not an illegal one. This explains Marchioness of Annandale *v.* Harris[4] and Turner *v.* Vaughan.[5] [PATTESON, J., referred to Walker *v.* Perkins.[6]] That was the case of a bond upon consideration positively illegal. [WIGHTMAN, J. The declaration here alleges that the plaintiff was injured in her character, and deprived of the means of procuring an honest livelihood.] That is a mere aggravation of the seduction; but the seduction raises no consideration. The word has no legal meaning. [WIGHTMAN, J. There is the word "debauched."] That does not necessarily mean that the plaintiff was chaste before her connection with the defendant. At the utmost, there is no more than what has been called a moral consideration, which it is now settled will not support an assumpsit even with an express promise; Eastwood *v.* Kenyon,[7] and other cases cited in note (*e*) to Barber *v.* Fox,[8] which support the doctrine in note (*a*) to Wennall *v.* Adney,[9] that even an express promise upon a mere moral consideration does not support an assumpsit, but "can only revive a preceding good consideration, which might have been enforced at law through the medium of an implied promise, had it not been suspended by some positive rule of law, but can give no original right of action, if the obligation on which it is founded never could have been enforced at law, though not

1 See note (*e*) to Barber *v.* Fox, 2 Wms. Saund. 137 *h*.
2 9 M. & W. 496.
3 3 M. & S. 463.
4 2 P. Wms. 432.
5 2 Wils. 339.
6 1 W. Bl. 517.
7 11 A. & E. 438.
8 2 Wms. Saund. 137 *e*. See note (*a*) to Osborne *v.* Rogers, 1 Wms. Saund. 264 *a*, and Kaye *v.* Dutton (there referred to), 7 M. & G. 807.
9 3 B. & P. 247, 252.

barred by any legal maxim or statute provision." Lee v. Muggeridge[1] must now be considered as overruled by Littlefield v. Shee,[2] and other authorities already referred to. (He was then stopped by the court.)

Banks, contra. It must be conceded that a promise to pay money in consideration of future cohabitation would be illegal; but it is otherwise when the consideration is past cohabitation. There, although the promises will be void if it does not appear that the defendant seduced the plaintiff, Binnington v. Wallis,[3] yet, as there pointed out, the invalidity results from the absence of such an allegation. Here the allegation is expressly made; and therefore the case falls within the authority of Marchioness of Annandale v. Harris.

Lord Denman, C. J. I think Binnington v. Wallis, connecting it with the *dictum* of Parke, B., in Jennings v. Brown, directly in point. The moral consideration which alone appears here cannot support an assumpsit. That principle has been lately acted upon by this court in Eastwood v. Kenyon, where we adopted the doctrine laid down in the note to Wennall v. Adney. The result is, that an express promise cannot be supported by a consideration from which the law could not imply a promise, except where the express promise does away with a legal suspension or bar of a right of action which, but for such suspension or bar, would be valid. This result we arrived at after much deliberation; and we now adhere to it.

Patteson, J. This declaration appears to be framed on a view suggested by some expressions in Binnington v. Wallis which point to a distinction between that case and cases where the defendant is the seducer of the plaintiff. But, looking at Eastwood v. Kenyon and Jennings v. Brown, it is clear that circumstance is of no consequence as to the legal right. The seduction could give the plaintiff no direct right of action, and can therefore create no liability of any kind from which a consideration can arise.

Coleridge, J. Eastwood v. Kenyon, which affirmed the doctrine in the note to Wennall v. Adney, has established the principle that a moral consideration will not support an assumpsit: there are certainly some apparent exceptions; but here we have only to act upon the general rule. In Binnington v. Wallis the court did indeed suggest that the previous fact of the seduction might make a distinction; but that clearly is not so. The circumstance of previous seduction adds nothing but an executed consideration resting on moral grounds only.

Wightman, J. I felt some doubt in this case; but, on considering the point, I agree that a precedent moral obligation, not capable of creating an original cause of action, will not support an express promise. And clearly, on the authorities, there is nothing here to raise any obligation beyond that. We therefore must act on the doctrine laid down in the note to Wennall v. Adney.

Judgment for defendant.

[1] 5 Taunt. 36. [2] 2 B. & Ad. 811. [3] 4 B. & Ald. 650.

FLIGHT *v.* REED.

IN THE EXCHEQUER, JANUARY 21, 1863.

[*Reported in* 1 *Hurlstone & Coltman*, 703.]

DECLARATION on six bills of exchange, drawn in the years 1855 and 1856 by the plaintiff upon and accepted by the defendant.

Plea. That before the making of the said bills of exchange in the declaration mentioned, or any or either of them, to wit, on the thirty-first day of October, A.D. 1845, it was corruptly, and against the form of the statute in that behalf made and provided, agreed between the plaintiff and defendant, and one —— Robinson, that the plaintiff should lend and advance to the defendant and the said —— Robinson a certain sum of money, to wit, £1500, and that the plaintiff should forbear and give day of payment to the defendant and the said —— Robinson until a day then to come, to wit, until the bills of exchange next hereinafter mentioned should become due and payable, and that for such forbearance the defendant and the said —— Robinson should pay to the plaintiff more than lawful interest at the rate of £5 per centum per annum upon the said sums of money so lent and forborne by the plaintiff to the defendant, that is to say, £100. And that for securing the repayment of the said sum of £1500 and interest, the defendant and the said —— Robinson should accept and deliver to the plaintiff certain bills of exchange drawn by the plaintiff upon them, whereby they should engage to pay to the plaintiff or his order £1600 ten weeks after the date thereof and of the said loan. And the defendant further says that, in pursuance of the said unlawful agreement, the plaintiff accordingly, to wit, on the day and year aforesaid, made the said loan and advance to the defendant and the said —— Robinson, and they then accordingly accepted bills of exchange drawn by plaintiff on them for the sum of £1600 payable as aforesaid. And that save as aforesaid there never was any consideration for the acceptance by the defendant of the said last-mentioned bills of exchange, or any or either of them. And the defendant further says that the said bills were dishonored at maturity, and that the bills of exchange in the declaration mentioned were accepted and given, after the passing of the statute 17 & 18 Vict. c. 90, by way of renewal of the said other bills of exchange, to secure the payment to the plaintiff of the money secured by the said other bills of exchange so given to the plaintiff as aforesaid, including the said sum of £100 heretofore mentioned, and in the said other bills included as interest as aforesaid; and that save as aforesaid there never was any value or consideration for the acceptance by the defendant of the bills of exchange in the declaration mentioned, or any or either of them.

Demurrer, and joinder therein.

Lush (*Philbrick* with him), in support of the demurrer. The 3 & 4 Wm. 4, c. 98, § 7, exempted from the operation of the usury law bills of exchange and promissory notes payable at or within three months after date. The 7 Wm. 4 & 1 Vict. c. 80 extended the exemption to bills and notes not having more than twelve months to run. That enactment was continued by the 2 & 3 Vict. c. 37, § 1, which excepted from its operation loans on the security of land. The 17 & 18 Vict. c. 90, which passed in the year 1854, entirely repealed the usury law. This plea is bad for not alleging that the original bills were given while the usury law was in force. Thibault *v.* Gibson.[1] But even assuming that they were, the bills declared on were given after the usury law was repealed, and therefore they are not affected by the previous illegal contract. [MARTIN, B. The 12 Anne, stat. 2, c. 16, rendered an usurious contract utterly void; then what consideration is there for the new bills?] By the second section of the 17 & 18 Vict. c. 89, it is provided "that nothing herein contained shall prejudice or affect the rights or remedies of any person, or diminish or alter the liabilities of any person, in respect of any act done previously to the passing of this act." Therefore, as the original bills were void at the time they were given, they could not now be enforced; but the receipt of money which the defendant was under a moral obligation to repay is a sufficient consideration to support a new contract after the usury law was repealed. Barnes *v.* Hedley [2] decided that, after usurious securities given for a loan have been destroyed by mutual consent, a promise by the borrower to repay the principal and legal interest is founded on a sufficient consideration, and is binding. Wicks *v.* Gogerley [3] is an authority to the same effect. So in Wright *v.* Wheeler,[4] where an obligee cancelled a bond by which usurious interest was payable, and the obligor gave him another bond for principal and legal interest only, Lawrence, J., ruled that it was valid. [MARTIN, B. It appears by the report in Campb. 157, that Barnes *v.* Hedley was first tried before Chambre, J.; and he ruled that, if money is lent at usurious interest, a subsequent contract to repay the principal with legal interest was void under the 12 Anne, stat. 2, c. 16.] Though the contract is void, the original debt is a sufficient consideration to support a new promise. [POLLOCK, C. B., referred to Fitzroy *v.* Gwillim.[5]] Mather *v.* Lord Maidstone [6] shews that a person may be liable on a new security, although the one for which it was substituted could not be enforced against him.

Macnamara, in support of the plea. At the time the original bills were given an usurious contract was not only void but also illegal, for

[1] 12 M. & W. 88. [2] 2 Taunt. 184. [3] Ry. & M. 123.
[4] 1 Campb. 165, note. [5] 1 T. R. 153. [6] 18 C. B. 273.

the person who received money under it was subject to a penalty of treble the value. The 3 & 4 Wm. 4, c. 98, § 7, and 7 Wm. 4 & 1 Vict. c. 80, do not affect this question, because they only created an exemption in certain cases from the penalties imposed by the 12 Anne, stat. 2, c. 16; and therefore it is sufficient for the defendant to shew that the contract was usurious within that statute, and if the plaintiff relies on the exemption, that should come by way of replication. Thibault *v.* Gibson, Washbourn *v.* Burrows,[1] Derry *v.* Toll.[2] It appears that the bills declared on were drawn and accepted in the years 1855 and 1856, and therefore after the usury law was repealed by the 17 & 18 Vict. c. 90; but the plea shews that they were accepted to secure the payment of money lent upon an usurious contract, and secured by bills given while the usury law was in force. Therefore the substituted bills were tainted with the original usurious contract, and that being void, there was no consideration for them. The case falls within the second section of the 17 & 18 Vict. c. 90, which preserves all rights and liabilities in respect of transactions previous to that act. There is no new contract, but merely a renewed security for payment of money under an usurious contract. [WILDE, B. If, before the usury law was repealed, the parties to an usurious contract destroyed the securities and made a new contract to pay the principal and legal interest, that contract was valid; then why is not a new contract valid since the usury law has been altogether repealed?] Barnes *v.* Hedley is distinguishable on two grounds: first, the destruction of the usurious securities by mutual consent was a sufficient consideration to support a new promise; and, secondly, the promise was to pay the principal and legal interest. Here the bills declared on were given to secure payment of the usurious interest. Where a bill of exchange tainted with usury was in the hands of an innocent holder, and, on being informed of the usury, he took a fresh bill in lieu of it, drawn by one of the parties to the usurious contract, and accepted by a third person for his accommodation, it was held that the holder could not maintain an action against the acceptor of the substituted bill. Chapman *v.* Black.[3] [POLLOCK, C. B. If the innocent holder of a promissory note, made for an usurious consideration, took from the maker of it a bond for payment of the amount, the bond was valid. Cuthbert *v.* Haley.[4] — CHANNELL, B. The 58 Geo. 3, c. 93, enacts that no bill of exchange or promissory note given upon an usurious contract shall be void in the hands of an indorsee for valuable consideration without notice.] Cuthbert *v.* Haley does not support the proposition contended for. There the court expressed an opinion that a substituted security given for a security tainted with usury is void if given to a party to the original contract. Wicks *v.* Gogerley[5] is an authority in favor of the defendant, for it decided that

[1] 1 Exch. 107. [2] 5 Exch. 741. [3] 2 B. & Ald. 588.
[4] 8 T. R. 390. [5] R. & Moo. 123.

a new promise to pay the principal originally lent on an usurious agreement is invalid, unless all payments beyond legal interest are repaid or deducted. Here the substituted security is for the principal and usurious interest. The receipt of the money under the usurious contract is no consideration for a new promise to pay it. There is a distinction between cases where there is a moral consideration for payment of a debt not enforceable at law, as where an infant after attaining his majority promises to pay a debt contracted during infancy, and where a statute has expressly declared that a particular contract shall be illegal and void. In the former case the duty constitutes a sufficient consideration for a promise to pay the debt; but in the latter, the contract being declared void and an offence at law, there can be no consideration for any new promise. *Cur. adv. vult.*

The learned judges having differed in opinion, in the ensuing term (May 8) the following judgments were delivered: —

MARTIN, B. This is a demurrer to a plea. The action is upon several bills of exchange. The plea is that, before the making of the bills declared on, it was corruptly and against the form of the statutes agreed between the plaintiff and the defendant and one Robinson that the plaintiff should lend them £1500, and that he should forbear and give day of payment to them until a future day, and that for such forbearance they should pay to him more than lawful interest at the rate of £5 per cent. per annum upon the sum so lent and forborne, and that for securing the repayment of the said sum of £1500 and interest, the defendant and Robinson should accept and deliver to the plaintiff certain bills of exchange drawn by the plaintiff upon them, whereby they engaged to pay to the plaintiff or his order £1600 ten weeks after the date thereof and of the loan; that in pursuance of the said unlawful agreement the plaintiff made the loan, and the defendant and Robinson accepted the bills, and that save as above there was no consideration for these acceptances; that these bills of exchange were dishonored at maturity, and the bills of exchange declared on were given, after the passing of the statute 17 & 18 Vict. c. 90, by way of renewal of the said first-mentioned bills, and accepted to secure the payment to the plaintiff of the money secured by the first-named bills so given to the plaintiff and the said usurious interest, and that save as aforesaid there was not any value or consideration for the acceptance by the defendant of the bills sued on.

The plea disclosed this state of things, viz., that when the loan was made and the first bills of exchange given the statute 12 Anne, stat. 2, c. 16, was in operation, but that when the bills of exchange declared on were given the statute 17 & 18 Vict. c. 90 had passed. The latter statute repeals the statute of Anne; but the second section provides that nothing in it shall prejudice or affect the rights or remedies, or diminish or alter the liabilities of any person in respect of any act done previous to its passing. The original loan and bills of exchange were therefore left unaffected by it. The statute of Anne enacts that no person upon any contract shall take for a loan of money above £5 per cent. for a year, and that all contracts for payment of any principal so lent shall be utterly void, and that any person who shall take above £5 per cent. for a year shall forfeit and lose for such offence treble the value of the money lent. The loan was therefore an illegal transaction, and the original contract to repay it and the bills of exchange given for it were utterly void; and the plea states that save these there was no other consideration for the bills declared on.

It is quite clear that a bill of exchange is a simple contract; it and promissory notes differ from other simple contracts in this, that *prima facie* they import consideration; but when it is proved that there was no consideration, or an illegal one, the bill of exchange or note is of no avail. It does seem superfluous to cite any authority for the above positions, but in my brother Byles's book upon Bills, page 111 (8th edition), it is stated that the defendant is at liberty in all cases (when the issue raised admits of it) to shew affirmatively, by his own witnesses, absence or failure of consideration; and again, page 124, the consideration given for a bill must not be illegal; and at page 132, if part of the consideration of a bill be illegal, the instrument is vitiated altogether; and at page 288 usury is said to be an indictable misdemeanor at common law, for which Comyns's Digest, title Usury, is cited. Now the consideration for the bills declared on was the usurious loan, and the bills of exchange given to secure it. But the statute of Anne has declared these to be utterly void; and, speaking for myself, I cannot understand how an utterly void and illegal contract or transaction can be a legal consideration for a new contract. But the case does not rest here; for at page 294 the same learned author states that if an usurious bill be in the hands of a holder who was a party to the usurious transaction, and he gives it up for a substituted security, the original usurious taint infects the subsequent security, and either is void. Now, applying the above statement of the law, the consequence seems to me inevitable that the bills of exchange sued on are not of avail in the hands of the plaintiff, who was the usurious lender, and that the plea is good.

But a case of Barnes *v.* Hedley was cited. According to the statement in the report, a person called Webb had agreed to lend money at £5 per cent. interest, but with a proviso that he should also receive a commission of £5 per cent. upon sugars to be bought of him or provided by him, and certain deeds and securities were given to him to secure the balance due. It was admitted at the trial that this was an usurious contract, but it was proved that in consequence of its being intimated to Webb that it was so, it was agreed that Webb should make out fresh accounts, leave out all the usurious charges, charge only for the principal money and legal interest, and that the original deeds and securities in the possession of Webb should be given up and cancelled. Webb accordingly made out such fresh accounts, in which he omitted the usurious charges, and the balance sought to be recovered in the action was composed of the principal moneys actually advanced, with lawful interest fairly and legally calculated, the whole commission and every objectionable charge being omitted. The account was delivered to the debtor, who acknowledged the balance and promised to pay it, and thereupon the deeds and securities originally given to Webb were produced and cancelled and burnt in the presence of the debtor. The Court of Common Pleas held that the balance so arrived at and promised to be paid was recoverable at law, and so certified to the Lord Chancellor, the case being an issue from chancery. I cannot myself see the application of this case to the present. If it had appeared upon the record that the plaintiff and defendant had accounted together and struck off the usurious interest, and the latter had given the bills declared on for the amount of the original loan and legal interest, it would have been an authority in favor of the plaintiff; but nothing of the kind appears upon the plea; indeed the contrary appears, for the bills declared on are stated to have been given to secure the payment to the plaintiff of the money secured by the bills of exchange given to him in furtherance of the illegal and corrupt contract, and that there was no other consideration for them. The case has been put thus: That when the bills declared on were given, there was no usury law, and it was competent for the defendant to pay or contract to pay interest to any extent, and that the bills were lawful, assuming them to have been given for a loan then made. This is quite true, but it has no application to the real and true case under consideration. There was no loan after the repealing statute was passed. There was no correction of the original unlawful transaction. There is nothing whatever shown on the record except bills given upon and in respect of a transaction which the law had declared to be utterly void, and which at one time seems to have been considered an indictable crime.

Another case was cited, Wright *v.* Wheeler, which will be found in a note to Barnes *v.* Hedley. This was an action upon a bond. There had been an usurious contract, but afterwards the parties agreed that some usurious interest which had been paid should be deducted from the principal, and a bond given for the balance of the principal, with lawful interest. Mr. J. Lawrence was of opinion at *nisi prius* that the bond was lawful. The parties, he said, had rectified their error, and substituted for an illegal contract one which was fair and legal. The case has no bearing upon the present. There is here no substitution of a legal contract for an illegal one; it is a mere continuance of the old unlawful contract. Cuthbert *v.* Haley is to the same effect.

A case of Wicks v. Gogerley was also cited by the leading counsel for the plaintiff; but according to the statement of the law laid down there by C. J. Best, the plaintiff is not entitled to recover. He says the principle is, that where parties to an usurious agreement "state an account and agree upon the sum which would be due for principal and legal interest, after deducting all that has been paid beyond legal interest, and a fresh promise is made to pay that sum, such promise is free from the original usury and is perfectly valid in law. But, in order to bring this case within the principle, all beyond legal interest must be repaid or deducted." In the report of Barnes v. Hedley in 1st Campbell, which I have before referred to, there is a judgment of Mr. J. Chambre, which seems to me to be well worthy of consideration by any one who desires to ascertain what is the true law upon this subject. There is also a case which was not mentioned in the argument, Preston v. Jackes,[1] which was tried before Mr. J. Holroyd, who held that a party could not recover on a note which operated as a security for any usurious interest. This case seems to me in point for the defendant; and any opinion of Mr. J. Holroyd, wherever given, is entitled to the greatest weight and is of the highest authority.

The result is, that in my opinion an usurious loan within the statute of Anne, and usurious interest contracted to be paid for it, is not a good consideration for a bill of exchange, and that a bill given upon such consideration is not of avail; and this opinion does not contravene the case of Barnes v. Hedley, reported in 2 Taunton, or any other case or authority which I have met with or has been referred to; but on the contrary, in my opinion, is in conformity with them all.

POLLOCK, C. B. The judgment which I am about to deliver is that of my brother WILDE and myself.

My brother MARTIN having stated the pleadings, it is not necessary to repeat them.

The real question raised by this demurrer is, whether there is a good consideration for the bills declared upon. The original bills were given for an advance of money with usurious interest at a time when such a transaction was forbidden by law, and were therefore void and of no legal obligation.

The bills sued on were given since the repeal of the usury law, and at a time when the giving or confirming an obligation to pay any amount of interest, however high, was perfectly legal and binding.

But the altered law did not render valid the original bills; they were void when given, and remained void and of no legal obligation up to the time when they were renewed by the bills in question.

The original bills therefore could not form a legal consideration for those now sued upon; indeed there was, when the fresh bills were given, no legal obligation whatever upon the defendant to repay a sin-

[1] 2 Stark. 237.

gle farthing of the large advance he had received. But for that advance he has voluntarily given those bills, and whether the law will permit and enforce such a contract is the question.

During the existence of the usury laws the courts of law were bound to enforce them, — to deal with interest above the statute rate as an unlawful and forbidden thing, — and to discover and defeat all attempts, direct or indirect, to give or enforce it.

But the legislature has since repealed the laws against usury, and upon a fuller and wider view of public policy declared the rate of interest on loans to be unlimited and free.

The courts of law are bound with equal fidelity to give effect to this new and opposite view of the legislature. Interest above £5 per cent. should no longer be regarded as of necessity illegal or unrighteous, and no facility should be given to escape from an obligation to repay a real advance of money, or evade a contract willingly made, though interest should have been contracted for at a rate which used to be called usurious.

We make these remarks, because in argument the expression "taint of an usurious transaction" was often repeated, and the court was pressed in language, commonly and properly used while the usury laws were in force, to give no countenance to a contract of which the origin was an advance of money with more than £5 per cent. interest.

Such remarks have no application to or bearing on a contract made like that in question since the usury laws have been repealed.

We therefore pass them by to consider the true question in the case, viz., whether an advance of money under such circumstances as to create no legal obligation at the time to repay it can constitute a good consideration for an express promise to do so.

Such a consideration has been sometimes called a moral consideration. And we think unfortunately so; for the term used as a definition tends to include too wide a range of objects.

And there are many conjunctures in which a man may feel himself morally bound to pay money and promise to do so, which the law would not recognize as forming a good consideration.

But a loan of money is a very different thing. The very name of a loan imports that it was the understanding and intention of both parties that the money should be repaid.

And though at the time of the advance the law, for reasons of public policy, forbid any liability, and incapacitate the parties from making a binding contract, there is no reason why a binding contract should not be made afterwards if the legal prohibition be removed.

And the consideration which would have been sufficient to support the promise, if the law had not forbidden the promise to be made originally, does not cease to be sufficient when the legal restriction is abrogated.

There is therefore reasonable ground, as it seems to us, for this qualified proposition, viz., that a man by express promise may render himself liable to pay back money which he has received as a loan, though some positive rule of law or statute intervened at the time to prevent the transaction from constituting a legal debt.

There is likewise authority for it. The general doctrine within which such proposition falls is, we believe, first found promulgated in Lord Mansfield's time. It is the subject of a long note to the report of the case of Wennall *v.* Adney.[1] It has been the subject of much discussion in many subsequent cases. It was stated most widely, and perhaps too widely, in the case of Lee *v.* Muggeridge.[2] And it has consequently been much qualified and sometimes disparaged since: see Eastwood *v.* Kenyon,[3] Beaumont *v.* Reeve,[4] Cocking *v.* Ward.[5]

But it was repeated and stated to be undoubted law by Baron Parke, in Earle *v.* Oliver,[6] who says: "The strict rule of the common law was no doubt departed from by Lord Mansfield in Hawkes *v.* Saunders[7] and Atkins *v.* Hill.[8] The principle of the rule laid down by Lord Mansfield is, that where the consideration was originally beneficial to the party promising, yet if he be protected from liability by some provision of the statute or common law meant for his advantage, he may renounce the benefit of that law; and if he promises to pay the debt, which is only what an honest man ought to do, he is then bound by law to perform it. There is a very able note to the case of Wennall *v.* Adney[9] explaining this at length. The instances given to illustrate the principle are, amongst others, the case of a debt barred by certificate and by the Statute of Limitations, and the rule in these instances has been so constantly followed that there can be no doubt that it is to be considered as the established law."

The case of Fitzroy *v.* Gwillim[10] is an example of the view that has been taken of the subject even in a court of law; but although that case is certainly not law, it is quite true that courts of equity have relieved (where their interference was wanting) only on the terms of the principal and legal interest being paid.

We think the view we have taken receives considerable support from the case of Barnes *v.* Hedley, which, if not a direct authority for the plaintiff, is somewhat similar in its circumstances; the usurious interest was in that case struck out, but now, since the repeal of the statute of Anne, there is nothing unlawful in usurious interest. Here the defendant says, "I could not then make the promise. I can now, and I am willing to do so."

[1] 3 Bos. & P. 249. [2] 5 Taunt. 45. [3] 11 A. & E. 447.
[4] 8 Q. B. 487. [5] 1 C. B. 870. [6] 2 Exch. 71, 89.
[7] Cowp. 290. [8] Cowp. 284. [9] 3 Bos. & P. 247.
[10] 1 T. R. 153.

The plaintiff is therefore, in our opinion, entitled to the judgment of the court. *Judgment for the plaintiff.*[1]

SECTION VII.

Gratuitous Bailment.

RICHES AND BRIGGS.

IN THE QUEEN'S BENCH, EASTER TERM, 1601.

[*Reported in Yelverton*, 4.]

IN an action on the case the plaintiff declared that, in consideration he had delivered to the defendant twenty quarters of wheat, the defendant promised upon request to deliver the same wheat again to the plaintiff. And adjudged a good consideration; for by POPHAM and *tot. cur.* the very possession of the wheat might be a credit and good countenance to the defendant to be esteemed a rich farmer in the country, as in case of the delivery of £1000 in money to deliver again upon request; for by having so much money in his possession he may happen to be preferred in marriage. *Quære*, for it seems an hard judgment; for the defendant has not any manner of profit to receive, but only a bare possession. *Nota*, the truth of the case was (which doth not alter the reason *supra*) that the plaintiff had delivered to the defendant the said twenty quarters of wheat to deliver over to J. S. to whom the plaintiff was indebted in so many quarters, and the defendant promised to deliver the same quarters of wheat to J. S. And because they were not delivered, the plaintiff brought his action *ut supra;* and adjudged *ut supra.* But *nota*, the judgment was reversed in the Exchequer, Mich. 44 & 45 Eliz., as Hitcham told Yelverton.

PICKAS *v.* GUILE.

IN THE KING'S BENCH, TRINITY TERM, 1608.

[*Reported in Yelverton*, 128.]

THE plaintiff declared that the defendant, in consideration the plaintiff *adtunc et ibidem* at the defendant's request *deliberavit* to the

[1] See Goulding *v.* Davidson, 26 N. Y. 604; Stafford *v.* Bacon, 1 Hill, 532, 25 Wend. 384; Hemphill *v.* McClimans, 24 Penn. St. 367; Paul *v.* Stackhouse, 38 Penn. St. 302. — ED.

defendant four broadcloths, and two packs and a half of wool of the plaintiff's to the value of £50, promised the same broadcloths and packs of wool to the plaintiff upon request to redeliver: the plaintiff said *in facto* that he did deliver them to the defendant; yet the defendant had not, although he was such a day, &c., requested, redelivered them. And on *non assumpsit* pleaded, it was found for the plaintiff. And *Yelverton* shewed in arrest of judgment, that there is no consideration laid in the declaration to draw a promise from the defendant, for the defendant had no benefit by the cloths, &c., but *nudam custod.*, which is rather a charge than a benefit; for the defendant could not use them; and therefore it is to be resembled to 9 E. 4, where delivery of the evidences to the true owner is no consideration, for the owner ought to have them of common right. *Quod fuit concessum per totam curiam.* And *nil capiat per billam* entered.

WHEATLEY *v.* LOW.

IN THE KING'S BENCH, TRINITY TERM, 1623.

[*Reported in Croke James*, 668.]

ACTION on the case. Whereas he was obliged to J. S. in forty pounds for the payment of twenty pounds; and the bond being forfeited, he delivered ten pounds to the defendant, to the intent he should pay it to J. S. in part of payment *sine ulla mora;* that *in consideratione inde* the defendant assumed, &c., and assigns for breach that he had not paid; whereupon the other had sued him for this debt, &c.

The defendant pleaded *non assumpsit;* and verdict for the plaintiff.

It was moved in arrest of judgment, that this is not any consideration, because it is not alleged that he delivered it to the defendant upon his request; and the acceptance of it to deliver to another *sine mora* cannot be any benefit to the defendant to charge him with this promise.

Sed non allocatur; for being that he accepted this money to deliver, and promised to deliver it, it is a good consideration to charge him. Wherefore it was adjudged for the plaintiff. — A writ of error being brought, and this matter only assigned for error, the judgment was affirmed.[1]

[1] "There has been a question made, if I deliver goods to A., and in consideration thereof he promise to redeliver them, if an action will lie for not redelivering them; and in Yelv. 4 judgment was given that the action would lie. But that judgment was afterwards reversed, and according to that reversal there was judgment afterwards

HART *v.* MILES.

IN THE COMMON PLEAS, APRIL 23, 1858.

[*Reported in 4 Common Bench Reports, New Series,* 371.]

THE first count of the declaration stated that, in consideration that the plaintiff would consent to the defendant's retaining possession of two bills of exchange, one for £25, and the other for £24 10*s.* 6*d.*, each drawn by the defendant upon and accepted by the plaintiff, and payable to the defendant's order, and to which bills the plaintiff was then entitled, and of which the defendant was then the holder, but not for value, the defendant promised the plaintiff that, if he should succeed in procuring the said bills or either of them to be discounted, he would pay to Messrs. Sotheron & Richardson the proceeds of such discounting, or a sufficient part thereof, in discharge of another bill of exchange for £45 5*s.* 10*d.*, or of so much thereof as such proceeds would satisfy; and the defendant succeeded in procuring the said first-mentioned bills to be discounted, and the plaintiff did all things necessary to have the defendant perform his said promise, and a reasonable time for the defendant so to do elapsed; yet the defendant broke his said promise in this, that he did not pay the proceeds, or any part thereof, to the said Messrs. Sotheron & Richardson, in discharge of the said bill of exchange for £45 5*s.* 10*d.*, or any part thereof; by reason whereof the said Messrs. Sotheron & Richardson obtained judgment in an action at law against the plaintiff for the amount of the last-mentioned bill, and damages and costs, amounting to a large sum, to wit, £51 4*s.* 2*d.*, and issued execution thereon, and caused the plaintiff's goods to be seized and sold in satisfaction of the said judgment, and of the poundage, costs, and expenses of the said execution, amounting in the whole to a large sum, to wit, £64 2*s.* 10*d.*, and of certain arrears of rent; and by reason thereof the goods of the plaintiff, to a much greater value than the amount of those moneys, were sold under the said execution for the purpose of raising the said moneys; and thereby the

entered for the defendant in the like case. Yelv. 128. But those cases were grumbled at, and the reversal of that judgment in Yelv. 4 was said by the judges to be a bad resolution, and the contrary to that reversal was afterwards most solemnly adjudged in 2 Cro. 667, Tr. 21 Jac. 1, in the King's Bench, and that judgment affirmed upon a writ of error. And yet there is no benefit to the defendant, nor no consideration in that case but the having the money in his possession, and being trusted with it, and yet that was held to be a good consideration. And so a bare being trusted with another man's goods must be taken to be a sufficient consideration, if the bailee once enter upon the trust, and take the goods into his possession." Holt, C. J., Coggs *v.* Bernard, 2 Ld. Raym. 920.

plaintiff was greatly injured in his expectations, and ruined in his business and circumstances, and greatly harassed and impoverished; and by reason thereof also the plaintiff became liable to pay the two first-mentioned bills, and may have to pay the same, and was put to costs and charges in and about endeavoring to procure the holder of those bills not to sue the plaintiff thereon.

The defendant pleaded, amongst other pleas, — secondly, that he did not succeed in procuring the said bills to be discounted as alleged. Issue thereon. The cause was tried before Williams, J., at the sittings in London after last term.

It appeared that the defendant received the two bills on the 30th of June, 1857, and paid them in to his account at his bankers', where they were entered short; but that, shortly afterwards, he obtained an advance from the bankers, upon an understanding that any bills in their hands belonging to him might be discounted. The execution took place on the 7th of August; and the bills became due in September.

On the part of the defendant, it was submitted that this was a mere naked bailment, and that the defendant was acting as agent for Messrs. Sotheron & Richardson.

The learned judge left it to the jury to say whether the defendant made the agreement upon his own responsibility, whether he did succeed in getting the bills discounted, and whether he knew of the discount before the date of the execution; telling them that if he did know of the discount before that event, there was an end of the case, except as to damages; but that if he did not, he would not be liable.

The jury returned a verdict for the plaintiff, — damages, £75.

Wordsworth, Q. C., now moved for a new trial, on the grounds of misdirection, and that the verdict was against evidence; and also in arrest of judgment as to the first count. He submitted that the question of agency ought to have been more pointedly put to the jury, and that they should have been told that the defendant was not responsible for the accidental passing of the bills to his debit [credit?] by his bankers without his authority. As to the arrest of judgment, he contended that the count disclosed no consideration whatever for the defendant's promise; and that, at the utmost, it disclosed a mere bailment without reward. [WILLES, J. If there be any consideration, we cannot inquire into the adequacy of it. Haigh *v.* Brooks, 10 Ad. & E. 309, 4 P. & D. 288.]

CROWDER, J. I am of opinion that there is no ground for arresting the judgment in this case. Looking at the whole declaration, though it certainly is somewhat vague, I think it may be supported, and that the consideration stated is sufficient. The statement is that, in consideration that the plaintiff would consent to the defendant's retaining possession of two bills of exchange (describing them), to which bills the plaintiff was then entitled, and of which the defendant was then the holder, but not for value, the defendant promised, &c. It is clear that the bills were the plaintiff's property, and that he was entitled to the possession of them; and it is equally clear that they were in the possession of the defendant without value. Instead of requiring him to give them up, the plaintiff consents that the defendant shall retain them for a given purpose, viz., to get them discounted. That is a sufficient consideration for the defendant's promise to dispose of the proceeds in the manner agreed upon, if he succeeded in getting the bills discounted. If the defendant had not made the promise he did, the plaintiff might have handed the bills over to somebody else for the purpose of procuring them to be discounted. I think the consideration was sufficient to support the promise. As to the alleged misdirection, I am at a loss to discover in what it consisted. It is said that the learned judge should have told the jury that the defendant got no benefit from the transaction; and further, that he had been pressed with an argument that the case was one of agency only, — that the defendant was acting merely as agent for Sotheron & Richardson, — and that that should have been put to the jury. The learned judge did ask the jury whether the defendant made the agreement upon his own responsibility. That was in effect putting the question of agency to them. The defendant clearly did not make the promise as agent: it was an original undertaking. I see no ground therefore for granting a rule upon this point. But, with regard to the evidence, we will speak to the learned judge.

WILLES, J. I agree with my brother Crowder that there was no misdirection. As to the arrest of judgment, I also agree with him in thinking that the declaration discloses a sufficient consideration for the defendant's promise. If the pleader had reflected a little, he would probably have stated it thus: in consideration of the plaintiff's consenting to the defendant's retaining possession of the bills, and getting the same discounted if he could, the defendant promised, &c. I rather think he was considering how the promise would have looked had it been gathered from a correspondence between the parties. If the defendant had written to the plaintiff thus: "In consideration of your consenting to my retaining the bills in my possession, I undertake, if I succeed in procuring them to be discounted, to hand over the proceeds to you;" and the plaintiff had answered, "I assent to the terms of your letter;" there would have been a contract between them that the defendant should procure the bills to be discounted if he could, and hand over the proceeds. That is the contract, which is to be implied here. It is *do ut facias*, or *facio ut facias*. That brings me to my last observation: if this be not a sufficient consideration, the defendant might have procured the bills to be discounted without being compellable to hand over the proceeds. Assuming that there was no consideration in the first instance, the fact of the defendant's getting the money in the end makes him liable; just as a man who gives a guaranty for goods to be supplied to a third person incurs no liability until the goods are supplied, — the contract being until then entirely unilateral.

BYLES, J. I am of the same opinion. The true meaning of the declaration I conceive to be this, that the plaintiff intrusts or continues to intrust the two bills, which are his property, to the defendant upon certain terms. I think, for the reasons given by my brother Willes, that was a good consideration moving from the plaintiff for the defendant's promise to hand over the proceeds if he succeeded in getting the bills discounted. And further, as my brother Crowder observes, if the defendant had not retained the bills, the plaintiff might have got them discounted elsewhere. The loss of that opportunity was a detriment to the plaintiff, which would be of itself a sufficient consideration. Further, the declaration alleges that the defendant afterwards succeeded in getting the bills discounted, but failed to pay over the proceeds. There is therefore a good consideration for the defendant's promise, at least in three ways.

CROWDER, J., on a subsequent day intimated that he had conferred with CRESSWELL, J., and that the court saw no ground for disturbing the verdict upon the evidence. *Rule refused.*

SECTION VIII.

Mutual Promises.

STRANGBOROUGH AND WARNER'S CASE.

IN THE QUEEN'S BENCH, 1588 OR 1589.

[*Reported in 4 Leonard*, 3.]

NOTE, That a promise against a promise will maintain an action upon the case, as in consideration that you do give to me £10 on such a day, I promise to give you £10 such a day after.

GOWER v. CAPPER.

IN THE QUEEN'S BENCH, HILARY TERM, 1597.

[*Reported in Croke Elizabeth,* 543.]

ASSUMPSIT. And declares, whereas the defendant was indebted unto him by bill in £20, the defendant, in consideration the plaintiff assumed unto him to deliver him the said bill, assumed to procure two sufficient sureties to be bound to the plaintiff for the payment of the said £20; and allegeth in fact that he delivered the said bill to the defendant; and that he, intending to deceive the plaintiff, produced two sureties to be bound that were of no value. The defendant pleads, that the plaintiff had not delivered unto him the said bill. And it was thereupon demurred. — And without argument adjudged for the plaintiff; for the alleging that he had delivered the bill was but surplusage; for the consideration was the promise to deliver it; and therefore he needed not have alleged that he delivered it. But a promise against a promise is a sufficient ground for an action. And although it be alleged that he found sureties, yet when it is alleged that they are insufficient (which is allowed by the defendant's plea and demurrer) it is all one as if he never had found sureties. Wherefore it was adjudged for the plaintiff.

NICHOLS v. RAYNBRED.

HILARY TERM, 1615.

[*Reported in Hobart,* 88.]

NICHOLS brought an assumpsit against Raynbred, declaring that, in consideration that Nichols promised to deliver the defendant to his own use a cow, the defendant promised to deliver him fifty shillings. Adjudged for the plaintiff in both courts, that the plaintiff need not to aver the delivery of the cow, because it is promise for promise. Note, here the promises must be at one instant, for else they will be both *nuda pacta.*

HARRISON v. CAGE AND HIS WIFE.

IN THE KING'S BENCH, MICHAELMAS TERM, 1698.

[*Reported in* 5 *Modern*, 411.]

THIS is an action on the case, wherein the plaintiff declares that, in consideration the plaintiff would marry the defendant, the defendant promised to marry him, and that he had offered himself to her, but that she refused him, and had married the other defendant.

First, This action does not lie. Indeed it might be otherwise in the case of a woman; for a marriage is an advancement to a woman, but not to a man, as appears in Anne Davis's Case,[1] and in the case of a feoffment *causa matrimonii prœlocuti*, which shews that there is a great difference between the two cases of a man and a woman; for it is a breach of a woman's modesty to promise a man to marry him, but it is not for a man to promise a woman to marry her.

Secondly, Here is no time laid when this marriage was to be; and it may be still.

Thirdly, The consideration is ill; it is no more than "I will be your husband if you will be my wife:" it is no more than this, "I will be your master, and you shall be my servant."

Fourthly, It is not reasonable that a young woman should be caught into a promise.

E contra. The action very well lies; and certainly marriage is as much advancement to a man as it is to a woman. And I am sorry that the counsel on the other side has so mean an opinion of a good woman as to think that she is no advancement to a man. We say that we have offered ourselves, and that she did refuse us; and though we do not mention the portion, it is well enough.

HOLT, C. J. Why should not a woman be bound by her promise as well as a man is bound by his? Either all is a *nudum pactum*, or else the one promise is as good as the other. You agree a woman shall have an action; now what is the consideration of a man's promise? Why, it is the woman's. Then why should not his promise be a good consideration for her promise, as well as her promise is a good consideration for his? There is the same parity of reason in the one case as there is in the other, and the consideration is mutual. As for the case of the *matrimonii prœlocuti*, that goes upon another reason, there being a feoffment of lands and a condition annexed to it; but this here is upon a contract. In the ecclesiastical court he might have compelled a performance of this promise; but here indeed she has disabled herself, for she has married another. Then you might have given in evidence

[1] 4 Rep. 16 *b*.

any lawful impediment upon this action; as that the parties were within the Levitical degrees, &c., for this makes the promise void; but it is otherwise of a precontract.

TURTON, J. There is as much reason for the one as for the other; and Halcomb's Case in Vaughan is plain.

ROKEBY, J. If a man be scandalized by words *per quod matrimonium amisit*, a good action lies; and why not in this case?

TURTON, J. This action is grounded on mutual promises.

HOLT, C. J. The man is bound in respect of the woman's promise; if she make none, he is not bound by his promise, and then it is a *nudum pactum;* so that her promise must be good to make his signify any thing to her; and then if her promise be good, why should not a good action lie upon it? *Judgment for the plaintiff.*

HOLT v. WARD CLARENCIEUX.

IN THE KING'S BENCH, TRINITY TERM, 1732.

[*Reported in 2 Strange,* 937.]

THE plaintiff declared that it was mutually agreed between the plaintiff and defendant that they should marry at a future day which is past, and that, in consideration of each other's promise, each engaged to the other; notwithstanding which the defendant did not marry the plaintiff, but had married another, which she lays to her damage of £4000.

The defendant with leave of the court pleaded double; viz., *non assumpsit*, and that the plaintiff at the time of the promise was an infant of fifteen years of age.

The plaintiff joins issue on the *non assumpsit*, and a verdict is found for her, with £2000 damages. And as to the plea of infancy, demurred.

This cause was several times argued at the bar: 1. By Mr. *Strange* for the plaintiff, and Serjeant *Chapple* for the defendant; when the court inclined strongly with the plaintiff, because though the defendant would not have the same remedy against her by action for damages, yet they thought he might have some remedy, viz., by suit in the ecclesiastical court to compel a performance, the plaintiff being of the age of consent; and that would be a sufficient consideration. And therefore appointed an argument by civilians, to see what their law would determine in such a case.

Upon the arguments of the civilians, no instance could be shewn wherein they had compelled the performance of a minor's contract. And they who argued for the defendant strongly insisted that in the case of a contract *per verba de futuro* (as this was) there was no remedy, even against a person of full age, in the spiritual court; but only an admonition. And the only reason why they hold jurisdiction in the case of a contract *per verba de præsenti* is because that is looked upon amongst them to be *ipsum matrimonium*, and they only decree the formality of a solemnization in the face of the church.

After their arguments it was spoke to a fourth time by Mr. *Reeve* and Serjeant *Eyre*. And now this term the Chief Justice delivered the resolution of the court.

The objection in this case is, that the plaintiff not being bound equally with the defendant, this is *nudum pactum*, and the defendant cannot be charged in this action. Formerly it was made a doubt by my Lord Vaughan whether any action could be maintained on mutual promises to marry; but that is now a point not to be disputed. And as to the present case, we should have had no difficulty in giving judgment for the plaintiff, if we could have been satisfied by the arguments of the civilians that, as the plaintiff was of the age of consent, any remedy, though not by way of action for damages, could be had against her. But since they seem to have had no precedent in the case, we must consider it upon the foot of the common law. And upon that the single question is, whether this contract, as against the plaintiff, was absolutely void. And we are all of opinion that this contract is not void, but only voidable at the election of the infant; and as to the person of full age it absolutely binds.

The contract of an infant is considered in law as different from the contracts of all other persons. In some cases his contract shall bind him; such is the contract of an infant for necessaries, and the law allows him to make this contract as necessary for his preservation; and therefore in such case a single bill shall bind him, though a bond with a penalty shall not. 1 Lev. 87.

Where the contract may be for the benefit of the infant, or to his prejudice, the law so far protects him as to give him an opportunity to consider it when he comes of age; and it is good or voidable at his election. Cro. Car. 502; 2 Rol. 24, 427; Hob. 69; 1 Brownl. 11; 1 Sid. 41; 1 Vent. 21; 1 Mod. 25; Sir W. Jones, 164. But though the infant has this privilege, yet the party with whom he contracts has not: he is bound in all events. And as marriage is now looked upon to be an advantageous contract, and no distinction holds whether the party suing be man or woman, but the true distinction is whether it may be for the benefit of the infant, we think, that though no express case upon a marriage contract can be cited, yet it falls within the general reason of the law with regard to infants' contracts. And no dangerous consequence can follow from this determination, because our opinion protects the infant even more than if we rule the contract to be absolutely void. And as to persons of full age, it leaves them where the law leaves them, which grants them no such protection against being drawn into inconvenient contracts.

For these reasons we are all of opinion that the plaintiff ought to have her judgment upon the demurrer.

LYNN AND ANOTHER *v.* BRUCE.

IN THE COMMON PLEAS, JULY 1, 1794.

[*Reported in* 2 *Henry Blackstone,* 317.]

THIS was an action of assumpsit. The first count of the declaration was on a forbearance to sue on a bond given by the defendant to the plaintiffs for £200. The second was as follows: "And whereas also, afterwards, &c., in consideration that the said Robert and Thomas (the plaintiffs), at the special instance and request of the said Charles (the defendant), had then and there consented and agreed to accept and receive of and from the said Charles a certain composition of fourteen shillings in the pound, and so in proportion for a lesser sum than a pound, upon a certain other sum of one hundred and five pounds five shillings and twopence, then due and owing from the said Charles to the said Robert and Thomas upon and by virtue of a certain other writing obligatory, bearing date, &c., made and executed by the said Charles to the said Robert and Thomas, whereby he became held and firmly bound to them in the sum of two hundred pounds, in full satisfaction and discharge of the said last-mentioned writing obligatory, and all moneys due thereon, he the said Charles undertook and then and there faithfully promised the said Robert and Thomas to pay them the said composition of fourteen shillings in the pound, and so in proportion for a lesser sum than a pound, upon the said last-mentioned sum of one hundred and five pounds five shillings and twopence, upon request; and the said Robert and Thomas in fact say that the said composition of fourteen shillings in the pound, and so in proportion for a lesser sum than a pound, upon the said last-mentioned sum of one hundred and five pounds five shillings and twopence, amounted to a large sum of money, to wit, the sum of seventy-three pounds thirteen shillings and sixpence, to wit, at Westminster aforesaid, whereof the said Charles afterwards, to wit, on the same day and year last aforesaid, at Westminster aforesaid, had notice; and although the said Charles hath paid to the said Robert and Thomas a certain sum of money, to wit, the sum of seventy pounds and six shillings, part of the said last-mentioned sum of seventy-three pounds thirteen shillings and sixpence, the amount of the said last-mentioned composition, yet the said Charles not regarding, &c., hath not yet paid the sum of three pounds seven shillings and sixpence, being the residue of the said sum of seventy-three pounds thirteen shillings and sixpence, the composition last aforesaid, or any part thereof," &c.

A verdict having been found for the plaintiffs on the whole declaration, a motion was made in arrest of judgment on the ground of the insufficiency of the second count; and after argument the opinion of the court was thus delivered by

LORD C. J. EYRE. This is a motion made in arrest of judgment, on an objection to the second count of the declaration. The substance of that count is that, in consideration that the plaintiff at the defendant's request had consented and agreed to accept and receive from the defendant a composition of fourteen shillings in the pound, and so in proportion for a lesser sum than a pound, upon £105 5*s.* 2*d.* due from the defendant to the plaintiff on a bond dated the 30th March, 1792, for £200, in full satisfaction and discharge of the bond and all money due thereon, the defendant promised to pay the said composition. It is then averred that the composition amounted to £73 13*s.* 6*d.*, and that the defendant had paid the plaintiff £70 6*s.*, part thereof. The breach is, that he did not pay £3 7*s.* 6*d.*, the residue. This will be found to be a very clear case, when the nature of the objection is understood. The consideration of the promise is, as stated in this count, an agreement to accept a composition in satisfaction of a debt. If this is an agreement which is binding, and can be enforced, it is a good consideration; if it is not binding, and cannot be enforced, it is not a good consideration. It was settled in the case of Allen *v.* Harris, 1 Lord Raym. 122, upon consideration of all the cases, that upon an accord, which this is, no remedy lies; it was said that the books are so numerous that an accord ought to be executed, that it was impossible to overturn all the authorities: the expression is, "overthrow all the books." It was added that, if it had been a new point, it might have been worthy of consideration. But we think it was rightly settled upon sound principles. *Interest reipublicæ ut sit finis litium:* accord executed is satisfaction: accord executory is only substituting one cause of action in the room of another, which might go on to any extent. The cases in which the question has been raised, whether an accord executory could be enforced, and in which it has been so often determined that it could not, have been cases in which it has been pleaded in bar of the original action. But the reason given in three of the cases in 1 Rol. Abr., tit. Accord, pl. 11, 12, 13, is because the plaintiff hath not any remedy for the whole, or where part has been performed, for that which is not performed, which goes directly to the gist of this action, as it is stated in the count objected to. This is an action brought to recover damages for that part of the accord which has not been performed. But an accord must be so completely executed in all its parts before it can produce legal obligation or legal effect, that in Peytoe's Case, 9 Co. 79 *b*, it was holden that, where part of the accord had been executed, tender of the residue would not be sufficient to make it a bar to the action, but that there must be an acceptance in satisfaction. There are two cases in Cro. Eliz. 304, 305, to the same effect. It was argued according to the cases in Rol. Abr. that an accord executory in any part is no bar, because no remedy lies for it for the plaintiff. Perhaps it would be a better way of putting the argument, to say that no remedy lies for it for the plaintiff, because it is no bar; but put either way, it concludes in support of the objection to the second count in this declaration, and consequently the judgment must be arrested.

Rule absolute to arrest the judgment.

SECTION IX.

Consideration Void in Part.

CRIPPS *v.* GOLDING.

IN THE QUEEN'S BENCH, MICHAELMAS TERM, 1586.

[*Reported in* 1 *Rolle's Abridgment*, 30.]

IF a man, in consideration of a surrender and of £10 paid, promises to do such a thing, although the surrender cannot be made, so that that consideration is void, yet the action is maintainable upon the other consideration.[1]

BRADBURNE *v.* ELIZABETH BRADBURNE.

IN THE QUEEN'S BENCH, MICHAELMAS TERM, 1589.

[*Reported in Croke Elizabeth,* 149.]

ASSUMPSIT. The court held where there are divers considerations alleged by the plaintiff, and some are frivolous and void, yet if any of them be good, the plaintiff shall recover. And it was so adjudged.

[1] In 1 Leon. 296, s. c., *nom.* Crisp and Golding's Case, it was said by Coke, *arguendo:* "Where two or many considerations are put in a declaration, although some be void, yet if one be good, the action well lieth, and damages shall be taxed accordingly." — ED.

COLSTON *v.* CARRE.

IN THE QUEEN'S BENCH, HILARY TERM, 1600.

[*Reported in* 1 *Rolle's Abridgment*, 80.]

IF A. promises B., in consideration that she will not sue an attachment out of chancery upon a decree which is there made against him, and in consideration that she will give him all her right and title of dower, that then he will pay her £20; though the second consideration is void, because it cannot be given to a stranger, but only released to the tenant of the land by way of extinguishment, yet the action upon the case lies upon the other consideration which is good.[1]

CRISP *v.* GAMEL.

IN THE KING'S BENCH, TRINITY TERM, 1606.

[*Reported in Croke James*, 128.]

IT was resolved that where, in an assumpsit, two considerations be alleged, the one good and sufficient, and the other idle and vain, if that which is good be proved, it sufficeth; and although he fails in the proof of the other, it is not material; because it was in vain to allege it; and it is as if it had not been alleged.

BEST *v.* JOLLY.

IN THE COMMON PLEAS, EASTER TERM, 1661.

[*Reported in* 1 *Siderfin*, 88.]

IN an action upon the case for the non-payment of £69, the case was as follows: The defendant was indebted to the plaintiff in £6,

1 "They all agreed that if two or three considerations be alleged in the declaration, and there be one of them sufficient, although the others be insufficient in matter or form, yet the one being sufficient, it is well enough; but if two considerations be alleged, and one of them is found false by the jury, the action fails." Cro. Eliz. 847, 848, S. C., 2d Resolution. — ED.

and the son of the defendant was indebted to the plaintiff for *diversa negotia*, amounting to £63. And the defendant, in consideration that the plaintiff would forbear to sue for the debts for the space of one month, undertook and promised to pay the plaintiff the said debts; and for the nonpayment he brought this action. And it was oftentimes argued at the bar, and this term it was adjudged *per totam Curiam*, that the action well lies, and the father shall be charged with this entire debt of £69; because, although the father was not liable for the debt of his son, nor was that debt reduced to certainty, yet when the father takes it upon him to pay it, he is liable, the consideration of forbearance being a damage to the plaintiff, although (as to part) no benefit to the defendant. . . .

Nota, that where there are two considerations, and one is good and the other is void, the damages given upon it shall be intended to be all given for the good consideration. . . . So in our case it shall be intended that the £69 are given as damages for the £6; and in this respect also the plaintiff has a good cause of action, for the assumpsit being to pay £69 is entire, and cannot be apportioned by the plaintiff, and therefore upon this assumpsit he cannot have an action for the £6 only, as was agreed *per omnes*. And the Chief Justice said, If I will put my barley with your heap of barley, you can take the whole.

And of void consideration there is a difference between considerations which are against law, and consideration *inutilis;* for the latter will not vitiate a good consideration, but it seems that a consideration against law will vitiate a good consideration. *Quod nota.*

MARY KING, JOHN KING, AND SILVANUS KING, *Executrix and Executors of the Will of* JAMES KING, *deceased, v.* MATTHEW URLWIN SEARS.

IN THE EXCHEQUER, EASTER TERM, 1835.

[*Reported in 2 Crompton, Meeson, and Roscoe,* 48.]

ASSUMPSIT. The first count of the declaration stated that the defendant was the administrator of William Sears, who died August 10, 1833; that the said William Sears was indebted to the plaintiffs in the sum of £13, being rent due and in arrear for the use and occupation of certain premises of the plaintiffs, used and occupied by the said William Sears by the sufferance and permission of the plaintiffs and at his request, under and by virtue of a certain demise thereof made, and at and under the yearly rent of £26 payable quarterly; that the said

William Sears deposited with the plaintiffs, as collateral security for the said debt, a certain bill of exchange, dated March 12, 1833, for £16 14*s.*, drawn by said William Sears on and accepted by one Joseph Fabian, payable five months after date to the drawer's order and by him indorsed; that the said William Sears, at the time of his death, was in possession of said premises under said demise, and after his death Winifred, his widow and the mother of said defendant, was in possession thereof, and was possessed of goods and chattels of the value of £50, which were upon said premises and liable to be distrained for said rent; and the said Winifred was desirous of quitting said premises at Michaelmas then next, and of removing said goods and chattels therefrom (of all which said premises the defendant had notice); and thereupon, on the 24th of September, 1833, in consideration of the premises, and that the plaintiffs would permit the said Winifred to quit the said premises at Michaelmas then next, and to remove her goods and chattels therefrom, and would forbear to distrain the same for said £13 rent so due as aforesaid and for the further quarter's rent to become due at said Michaelmas, the defendant promised the plaintiffs to pay them one quarter's rent immediately, and the remainder of the said rent within twelve months then next, the said bill of exchange being given up by the plaintiffs to the defendant. Averment, that the plaintiffs, confiding in said promise, did permit said Winifred as aforesaid and did forbear as aforesaid (whereof the defendant had notice); and although the said twelve months have long since elapsed, and the plaintiffs after the expiration thereof, to wit, on the 15th of October, 1834, requested the defendant to pay said rent, being the sum of £19 10*s.*, and tendered said bill of exchange to the defendant, which he refused to accept, yet, &c. Breach, non-payment of the sum of £19 10*s.*

General demurrer, and joinder.[1]

The grounds stated for argument in the margin of the paper book were: —

First, that by the first count it appears that the bill of exchange therein mentioned was at the time of making the defendant's supposed promise over-due, and it is not averred to have been dishonored; so that the rent of £13 supposed to have been in arrear from William Sears, deceased, appears to have been satisfied thereby; and the forbearance to distrain for that sum of £13, which forms part of the consideration stated for the defendant's promise, is therefore insufficient.

Secondly, that it does not appear on the first count that the plaintiffs had any right to distrain for the quarter's rent, which is supposed to have been becoming due to them at Michaelmas mentioned therein; and so the forbearance to distrain for the sum of £6 10*s.* in respect thereof, which forms part of the consideration stated for the defend-

[1] See *supra*, p. 221, note 1. — ED.

ant's promise, is insufficient to support such promise, and renders the same of none effect.

Thirdly, that the consideration expressed in the first count, as moving the defendant to the promise therein alleged, is not stated to have been at the defendant's request, as, to give the same any effect, it ought to have been.

Fourthly, that it does not appear, nor can it be collected from the first count, whether the plaintiffs seek to recover against the defendant as administrator of his late father, or personally.

Erle, in support of the demurrer. First, the bill of exchange, as appears by the declaration, was given as a collateral security for the rent; but the plaintiffs do not state that any steps were taken by them, on the bill becoming due, to obtain payment of it, nor do they aver any presentment, or shew that it was dishonored, which it was their duty as holders to have done; and, not having done so, it amounted to a satisfaction of the debt for which the bill was given, that is to say, the £13 for rent due from William Sears. It was the duty of the plaintiffs to have shewn on their declaration that they had done all the acts necessary to entitle them to recover on the bill. [LORD ABINGER, C. B. It is stated in the declaration to have been given as a collateral security. The action is not brought on the bill itself.] It is submitted that it was incumbent on them to shew that the bill was duly presented; and, if they fail to do so, then they must be taken to have made the bill their own, and it operated as a satisfaction for the rent of £13, and the forbearance to distrain for that sum, which formed part of the consideration for the defendant's promise, failed. [PARKE, B. Though the bill was not duly presented, that objection might have been waived afterwards.] If the consideration fails to that extent, then the whole promise is *nudum pactum*. Another part of the consideration stated is the agreement not to distrain the goods of the widow to recover the sum of £6 10*s*. for rent to become due the Michaelmas following; but, as the rent was not then due, the plaintiffs could have no right to distrain for it, and consequently that was no consideration whatever. [LORD ABINGER, C. B. Was it not a privilege granted to her to be allowed to give up the tenancy at Michaelmas?] The executors could not compel her to remain, as she was a stranger to them. The allegation is that, in consideration that the plaintiff would permit the widow to quit the demised premises at Michaelmas then next, and to remove her goods and chattels from the premises, and would forbear to distrain for the said rent so due and in arrear, and for the sum of £6 10*s*. to become due at Michaelmas then next, the defendant undertook to pay the £6 10*s*. immediately, and the remainder within twelve months, the bill of exchange being given up by the plaintiffs to the defendant; but the rent of £6 10*s*. was not due, and they had no right to distrain for that sum, and therefore there is a failure of consideration. [PARKE, B. The giving up the note is one consideration, and the forbearance to distrain the goods of the widow on the premises for the rent then due from the intestate is another consideration.] At all events the whole of the consideration stated for the defendant's promise is not shewn, and therefore the promise is not supported. [PARKE, B. If a sufficient consideration remains, it is enough to support the promise laid in the declaration. There is abundant consideration.] Then the consideration alleged as moving the defendant to make the promise is not stated to have been at the request of the defendant. [PARKE, B. That would only be material in the case of an executed consideration. An averment of request is only necessary in cases of executed consideration.]

Judgment for the plaintiffs.

SECTION X.

Executed Consideration.

HUNT v. BATE.

EASTER TERM, 1568.

[*Reported in Dyer*, 272.]

THE servant of a man was arrested, and imprisoned in the compter in London for a trespass; and he was let to mainprize by the manucaption of two citizens of London (who were well acquainted with the master), in consideration that the business of the master should not go undone. And afterwards, before judgment and condemnation, the master upon the said friendly consideration promised and undertook to one of the mainpernors to save him harmless against the party plaintiff from all damages and costs if any should be adjudged, as happened afterwards in reality; whereupon the surety was compelled to pay the condemnation, *sc.* £31, &c. And thereupon he brought an action on the case, and the undertaking was traversed by the master, and found in London at *nisi prius* against him. And now in arrest of judgment it was moved that the action does not lie. And by the opinion of the court it does not lie in this matter, because there is no consideration wherefore the defendant should be charged for the debt of his servant, unless the master had first promised to discharge the plaintiff before the enlargement and mainprize made of his servant, for the master did never make request to the plaintiff for his servant to do so much, but he did it of his own head. Wherefore, &c.

But in another like action on the case brought upon a promise of £20 made to the plaintiff by the defendant, in consideration that the plaintiff, at the special instance of the said defendant, had taken to wife the cousin of the defendant, that was good cause, although the marriage was executed and past before the undertaking and promise, because the marriage ensued the request of the defendant. And land may be also given in frank-marriage with the cousin of the donor as well after the marriage as before, because the marriage may be intended the cause, &c. And therefore the opinion of the court in this case this term was, that the plaintiff should recover upon the verdict, &c. And so note the diversity between the aforesaid cases.

SIDENHAM AND WORLINGTON'S CASE.

IN THE COMMON PLEAS, EASTER TERM, 1585.

[*Reported in* 2 *Leonard,* 224.]

In an action upon the case upon a promise, the plaintiff declared that he at the request of the defendant was surety and bail for J. S., who was arrested in the King's Bench upon an action of £30, and that afterwards, for the default of J. S., he was constrained to pay the £30; after which the defendant, meeting with the plaintiff, promised him for the same consideration that he would repay that £30, which he did not pay; upon which the plaintiff brought the action. The defendant pleaded *non assumpsit*, upon which issue was joined, which was found for the plaintiff. *Walmesley*, Serjt., for the defendant, moved the court that this consideration will not maintain the action, because the consideration and promise did not concur and go together; for the consideration was long before executed, so as now it cannot be intended that the promise was for the same consideration: as if one giveth me a horse, and a month after I promise him £10 for the said horse, he shall never have debt for the £10, nor assumpsit upon that promise; for there it is neither contract nor consideration, because the same is executed. ANDERSON. This action will not lie; for it is but a bare agreement and *nudum pactum*, because the contract was determined, and not *in esse* at the time of the promise; but he said it is otherwise upon a consideration of marriage of one of his cousins, for marriage is always a present consideration. WINDHAM agreed with ANDERSON, and he put the case in 3 H. 7. If one selleth a horse unto another, and at another day he will warrant him to be sound of limb and member, it is a void warrant, for that such warranty ought to have been made or given at such time as the horse was sold. PERIAM, J., conceived that the action did well lie; and he said that this case is not like unto the cases which have been put of the other side: for there is a great difference betwixt contracts and this case; for in contracts upon sale, the consideration and the promise and the sale ought to meet together; for a contract is derived from *con* and *trahere*, which is a drawing together, so as in contracts every thing which is requisite ought to concur and meet together, viz., the consideration of the one side, and the sale or the promise on the other side. But to maintain an action upon an assumpsit, the same is not requisite, for it is sufficient if there be a moving cause or consideration precedent; for which cause or consideration the promise was made; and such is the common practice at this day. For in an action upon the case upon a promise, the declaration is laid that the defendant, for and in consideration of £20 to him paid (*postea scil.*), that is to say, at a day after *super se assumpsit*, and that is good; and yet there the consideration is laid to be executed. And he said that the case in Dyer, 10 Eliz. 272, would prove the case. For there the case was, that the apprentice of one Hunt was arrested when his master Hunt was in the country, and one Baker, one of the neighbors of Hunt, to keep the said apprentice out of prison, became his bail, and paid the debt. Afterwards Hunt, the master, returning out of the country, thanked Baker for his neighborly kindness to his apprentice, and promised him that he would repay him the sum which he had paid for his servant and apprentice: and afterwards, upon that promise, Baker brought an action upon the case against Hunt, and it was adjudged in that case that the action would not lie, because the consideration was precedent to the promise, because it was executed and determined long before. But in that case it was holden by all the justices that if Hunt had requested Baker to have been surety or bail, and afterwards Hunt had made the promise for the same consideration, the same had been good, for that the consideration did precede, and was at the instance and request of the defendant. RHODES, J., agreed with PERIAM; and he said that if one serve me for a year, and hath nothing for his service, and afterwards, at the end of the year, I promise him £20 for his good and faithful service ended, he may have and maintain an action upon the case upon the same promise, for it is made upon a good consideration; but if a servant hath wages given him, and his master *ex abundanti* doth promise him £10 more after his service ended, he shall not maintain an action for that £10 upon the said promise; for there is not any new cause or consideration preceding the promise; which difference was agreed by all the justices; and afterwards, upon good and long advice, and consideration had of the principal case, judgment was given for the plaintiff; and they much relied upon the case of Hunt and Baker, 10 Eliz., Dyer, 272.

PEARLE AND EDWARDS' CASE.

IN THE QUEEN'S BENCH, EASTER TERM, 1588.

[*Reported in* 1 *Leonard*, 102.]

THE case was, that the defendant had leased lands to the plaintiff rendering rent for certain years; and after some years of the term expired the lessor, in consideration that the lessee had occupied the land, and had paid his rent, promised the plaintiff to save him harmless against all persons, for the occupation of the land past and also to come. And afterwards H. distrained the cattle of the plaintiff being upon the lands, upon which he brought his action. *Golding*. Here is not a sufficient consideration, for the payment of the rent is not any consideration, for the lessee hath the occupation of the land for it, and hath the profits thereof; and also the consideration is past. *Cook*. The occupation, which is the consideration, continues; therefore it is a good assumpsit; as 4 E. 3, a gift in frank marriage after the espousals, and yet the marriage is past, but the blood continues, so here; and here the payment of the rent is executory every year; and if the lessee be saved for his occupation, he will pay his rent the better. *Godfrey*. If a man marrieth my daughter against my will, and afterwards in consideration of that marriage I promise him one hundred pounds, the same is no good consideration; which CLENCH, J., denied. And afterwards the plaintiff had judgment to recover his damages.

MARSH AND RAINSFORD'S CASE.

IN THE QUEEN'S BENCH, TRINITY TERM, 1588.

[*Reported in* 2 *Leonard*, 111.]

IN an action upon the case, the case was, that a communication was had betwixt the parties, that the plaintiff should marry the daughter of the defendant, in consideration of which the defendant promised the plaintiff to give him £200, but they could not agree upon the days of payment of it; after which they [he ?] stole away the defendant's daughter, and secretly married her without the defendant's knowledge; yet afterwards the defendant gave his consent to it, and allowed of the said marriage; and in consideration of the said marriage promised to pay the plaintiff £100. *Egerton*, Solicitor General, for the defendant:

That the action upon this matter will not lie; for here the consideration is precedent to the promise, whereas the consideration in such cases ought to be future and subsequent; and as the case is here, the plaintiff is out of the course of consideration of marriage; for he hath stolen away and married his wife, without the knowledge or consent of her father. See such case, 10 Eliz., Dyer, 272. The servant of one A. is arrested in London, and two friends of his master bail him, and afterwards A. promiseth to them, for their friendship, to save them harmless from damages and costs, &c. It was holden that the action doth not lie, for here is not any consideration, for the bailment was of their own heads, and it is executed before the promise; but if the master before the enlargement of his servant had requested the plaintiff for to bail his servant, and he had so done, the action would have lien. WRAY, J. Although the consideration be precedent, yet if it were made at the instance of the other party, the action would have lien. But here the natural affection of the father to his daughter is sufficient matter of consideration. If one cometh to a serjeant at law to have his counsel, and the serjeant doth advise him, and afterwards the client, in consideration of such counsel, promiseth to pay him £20, an action lieth for it. And so POPHAM said it had been adjudged in the Exchequer; and it is a common action in this court, in consideration *quod querens deliberasset* to the defendant, &c., he promiseth to pay him so much; and as it was late adjudged betwixt Style and Smith:[1] If a physician who is my friend, hearing that my son is sick, goeth to him in my absence, and helps and recovers him, and I being informed thereof promise him in consideration, &c., *ut supra*, to give to him £20, an action will lie for the money. And afterwards in the principal case judgment was given for the plaintiff.

JEREMY v. GOOCHMAN.

IN THE COMMON PLEAS, MICHAELMAS TERM, 1595.

[*Reported in Croke Elizabeth*, 442.]

ASSUMPSIT. And declares that, in consideration *quod deliberasset et dedisset* to the defendant twenty sheep, he assumed to pay unto him five pounds at the time of his marriage; and allegeth *in facto* that he was married, &c. The issue was *non assumpsit*, and found for the plaintiff; and now moved in arrest of judgment, because it is for a consideration past; for it is in the preter tense *deliberasset*, and therefore no cause of action. And of that opinion was the whole court; wherefore judgment was stayed.

[1] See note (*a*) to Wennall *v.* Adney, 3 B. & P. 247, 252; Veitch *v.* Russell, 3 Q. B. 928, 934.—ED.

BARKER v. HALIFAX.

IN THE COMMON PLEAS, HILARY TERM, 1600.

[*Reported in Croke Elizabeth*, 741.]

ASSUMPSIT. Whereas the defendant, such a day and year, in consideration that the plaintiff, by the defendant's appointment and for his debt, *paulo ante tunc solvisset* to R. S. £60, that the defendant assumed to repay it upon request, &c. The defendant pleaded *non assumpsit;* and it was found against him. And after verdict, upon a motion in arrest of judgment, the judgment was stayed; because the payment of the £60 being a consideration past was not sufficient to maintain the action. But WALMSLEY said that an assumpsit, in consideration that you had married my daughter, to give unto you £40 was good; for the affection and consideration always continues.

RIGGS v. BULLINGHAM.

IN THE QUEEN'S BENCH, MICHAELMAS TERM, 1599.

[*Reported in Croke Elizabeth*, 715.]

ASSUMPSIT. Whereas he was seised in fee of the advowson of Beckingham, in the county of Lincoln; in consideration that he at the defendant's request, by his deed, *dedisset et concessisset* to the defendant the first and next avoidance of the said church, the defendant, 22 August, 37 Eliz., assumed to pay to the plaintiff £100, &c. Upon *non assumpsit* pleaded, it was found for the plaintiff, and damages assessed to an £100. And after verdict it was moved in arrest of judgment that this consideration is past, and therefore not sufficient to ground an assumpsit; for there is not any time of the grant alleged; and it might have been divers years before the assumpsit made; and being a thing executed and past, no assumpsit afterwards can be good: and in proof thereof Dyer, 272, Hunt v. Bate was cited. But all the COURT resolved to the contrary; for the grant being made at his request, it is a sufficient consideration, although it were divers years before; especially being to the defendant himself, the consideration shall be taken to continue. But if the grant had been to a stranger, and not at the defendant's request, it had peradventure been otherwise. . . . Wherefore it was adjudged for the plaintiff.

DOCKET *v.* VOYEL.

IN THE COMMON PLEAS, EASTER TERM, 1602.

[*Reported in Croke Elizabeth*, 885.]

ASSUMPSIT. Whereas the defendant, 10th May, 40 Eliz., in consideration that the plaintiff at a certain day then past, at the defendant's request, had lent unto him £30 for such a time; that the defendant assumed to lend unto the plaintiff upon request £30 for a year, or otherwise to give him 40*s*. The plaintiff allegeth that the defendant did not lend him £30 *licet requisitus*, &c., nor pay the said 40*s*. And it was thereupon demurred; because the consideration was past and executed, and the consideration and promise ought to go together; or else it ought to be a consideration continuing. Wherefore for this cause it was adjudged for the defendant.

BOSDEN *v.* SIR JOHN THINNE.

IN THE KING'S BENCH, MICHAELMAS TERM, 1603.

[*Reported in Yelverton*, 40.]

THE plaintiff declared, *quod cum ad specialem instantiam* of the defendant, he had procured credit for one Flud for two pipes of wine amounting to £51, and Flud, *super credentiam* and *per medium* of the plaintiff at the request of the defendant, *emisset* of one Roberts two pipes of wine for £51, and *superinde* the plaintiff with Flud entered into bond of £100 to Roberts for payment of the said £51 at a day to come, which was not paid at the day; and thereupon Roberts sued the plaintiff upon the bond, and recovered, and had a *capias* against him, whereby he *fuit coactus* to pay Roberts £67, *de solutione* of which £67 *causa prœallegata* he notified to the defendant, who *in consideratione prœmissorum* promised to pay the plaintiff the £67 at Michaelmas; and shewed the failure of payment of the £67 at the day, &c. And upon *non assumpsit* pleaded, it was found against the defendant. And *Yelverton* moved in arrest of judgment, that the action upon the matter shewn does not lie, because the consideration was past and executed before the promise, and the defendant had no profit by it, but all the benefit was to Flud a stranger; like the case 10 Eliz., Dy. 272, where J. S. was bail for the servant upon an arrest, and signified all to the master after the bail entered into, who promised to save him harmless; and although the bail was condemned, yet no assumpsit lay against the master, because the consideration was past before the promise: and it seems that upon the first request only to give credit to Flud for two pipes of wine, no assumpsit lies; for a bare request does not imply any promise; as if I say to a merchant, I pray trust J. S. with £100, and he does so, this is of his own head, and he shall not charge me, unless I say I will see you paid or the like. And it seems likewise that the promise shall not have relation to the first request of giving credit to Flud, because the entreaty for the credit was but for two pipes of wine amounting to £51, and the promise is for £67, and so they differ in the sums; as if I request J. S. to enter into bond for J. D. for £10, and I will see him paid; now if J. S. enters into bond of £20 for the payment of £10 for J. D., which £20 is recovered against him, he shall not charge me on my promise but £10. But *non allocatur per* FENNER, GAWDY, and POPHAM; for although upon the first request only assumpsit does not lie, yet the promise coming after shall have reference to the first request; and although the request was but for two pipes of wine amounting to £51, that Flud might have credit for that; yet when Roberts, who sold the wine, would not take (as appears) security but by bond of £100 for payment of £51, and all this matter is signified afterwards to the defendant, who agrees to it, and promises to pay the £67, this shall charge him; because it has its essence and commencement from the first request made by the defendant. As (*per* GAWDY) if I request one to marry my cousin, who does so, and afterwards tells me of it, and thereupon I promise him £100, this is a good promise to charge me, although the marriage was past, which is the consideration; because now the promise shall have reference to the request, which was before the marriage. *Vide* this case, Dy. 272 *b*. The same law (by him) if I entreat one to be bail for my servant, and he thereupon becomes bail, and is condemned, and afterwards tells me of it, and I promise him to save him harmless, it is good, and he shall recover his damage *in toto*. Wherefore judgment was given for the plaintiff. But YELVERTON, J., was *contra* clearly.

FIELD *v.* DALE.

IN THE EXCHEQUER CHAMBER, MICHAELMAS TERM, 1614.

[*Reported in* 1 *Rolle's Abridgment*, 11, *placitum* 8.]

IF A., in consideration that B. *barganizasset et vendidisset* to him certain tuns of strong beer at the request of A., assumed and promised to B. to pay him £4 for each tun *super deliberationem inde* of 30 tuns of strong beer, this is a good consideration, although passed, because the sale was at the request of him who made the promise.

LAMPLEIGH *v.* BRATHWAIT.

IN THE COMMON PLEAS, MICHAELMAS TERM, 1615.

[*Reported in Hobart,* 105, 1 *Smith's Leading Cases,* 67.]

ANTHONY LAMPLEIGH brought an assumpsit against Thomas Brathwait, and declared that, whereas the defendant had feloniously slain one Patrick Mahume, the defendant, after said felony done, instantly required the plaintiff to labor and do his endeavor to obtain his pardon from the king; whereupon the plaintiff upon the same request did, by all the means he could and many days' labor, do his endeavor to obtain the king's pardon for the said felony; viz., in riding and journeying at his own charges from London to Roiston, when the king was there, and to London back, and so to and from Newmarket, to obtain pardon for the defendant for the said felony. Afterwards *scil.*, &c., in consideration of the premises, the said defendant did promise the said plaintiff to give him £100,[1] and that he had not, &c.; to his damage £120.

To this the defendant pleaded *non assumpsit*, and found for the plaintiff, damage £100. It was said in arrest of judgment that the consideration was passed.

But the chief objection was, that it doth not appear that he did any thing towards the obtaining of the pardon but riding up and down, and nothing done when he came there. And of this opinion was my brother WARBURTON; but myself and the other two judges were of opinion for the plaintiff, and so he had judgment.

First, it was agreed that a mere voluntary courtesy will not have a consideration to uphold an assumpsit. But if that courtesy were moved by a suit or request of the party that gives the assumpsit, it will bind; for the promise, though it follows, yet it is not naked, but couples itself with the suit before, and the merits of the party procured by that suit, which is the difference. Pasch. 10 Eliz., Dyer, 272, Hunt & Bates. See Onely's Case, 19 Eliz., Dyer, 355.

Then, to the main point, it is first clear that in this case, upon the issue *non assumpsit*, all these points were to be proved by the plaintiff:

[1] "In Lampleigh *v.* Brathwait, it was assumed that the journeys which the plaintiff performed at the request of the defendant, and the other services he rendered, would have been sufficient to make any promise binding if it had been connected therewith in one contract; the peculiarity of the decision lies in connecting a subsequent promise with a prior consideration after it had been executed. Probably at the present day, such service on such request would have raised a promise by implication to pay what it was worth; and the subsequent promise of a sum certain would have been evidence for the jury to fix the amount." — Erle, C. J., Kennedy *v.* Broun, 13 C. B., N. S., 677 740. — ED.

1. That the defendant had committed the felony, *prout*, &c.
2. Then that he requested the plaintiff's endeavor, *prout*, &c.
3. That thereupon the plaintiff made his proof, *prout*, &c.
4. That thereupon the defendant made his promise, *prout*, &c.

For wheresoever I build my promise upon a thing done at my request, the execution of the act must pursue the request, for it is like a case of commission for this purpose.

So then the issue found *ut supra* is a proof that he did his endeavor according to the request, for else the issue could not have been found; for that is the difference between a promise upon a consideration executed and executory, that in the executed you cannot traverse the consideration by itself, because it is passed and incorporated and coupled with the promise.[1] And if it were not indeed then acted, it is *nudum pactum*.

But if it be executory, as in consideration that you shall serve me a year I will give you £10, here you cannot bring your action till the service performed. But if it were a promise on either side executory, it needs not to aver performance; for it is the counter-promise, and not the performance, that makes the consideration; yet it is a promise before, though not binding, and in the action you shall lay the promise as it was, and make special averment of the service done after.

Now if the service were not done, and yet the promise made, *prout*, &c., the defendant must not traverse the promise, but he must traverse the performance of the service, because they are distinct in fact, though they must concur to the bearing of the action.

Then also note here, that it was neither required nor promised to obtain the pardon, but to do his endeavor to obtain it: the one was his end, and the other his office.

Now then he hath laid expressly in general that he did his endeavor to obtain it, viz., *in equitando*, &c., to obtain. Now then, clearly the substance of this plea is general, for that answers directly the request; the special assigned is but to inform the court; and therefore clearly, if upon the trial he could have proved no riding, nor journeying, yet any other effectual endeavor according to the request would have served; and therefore if the consideration had been that he should endeavor in the future, so that he must have laid his endeavor expressly, and had done it as he doth here, and the defendant had not denied the promise, but the endeavor, he must have traversed the endeavor in the general, not the riding, &c., in the special; which proves clearly that is not

[1] Harris *v.* Ewer, 1 Rol. Rep. 401. Harris brought an action on the case against Ewer, and the plaintiff counted that for such a consideration (which was not executory, but executed) the defendant promised, &c. The defendant traversed the consideration, upon which it was demurred. *G. Croke.* It seems that he cannot traverse a consideration executed, *quod fuit concessum per Curiam;* and judgment was given for the plaintiff, no one appearing for the defendant. — ED.

the substance, and that the other endeavor would serve. This makes it clear that, though particulars ought to be set forth to the court, and those sufficient, which were not done, which might be cause of demurrer, yet being but matter of form, and the substance in the general, which is herein the issue and verdict, it were cured by the verdict. But the special is also well enough; for all is laid down for the obtaining of the pardon which is within the request; and therefore suppose he had ridden to that purpose, and Brathwait had died, or himself, before he could do any thing else, or that another had obtained the pardon before, or the like, yet the promise had holden.

And observe that case 22 E. 4, 40, condition of an obligation to shew a sufficient discharge of an annuity, you must plead the certainty of the discharge to the court. The reason whereof given by Brian and Choke is, that the plea there contains two parts, one a trial *per pais, scil.* the writing of the discharge, the other by the court, *scil.* the sufficiency and validity of it, which the jury could not try, for they agree that if the condition had been to build a house agreeable to the state of the obligee, because it was a case all proper for the country to try, it might have been pleaded generally; and then it was a demurrer, not an issue as is here.

JANSON *v.* COLOMORE.

In the King's Bench, Trinity Term, 1616.

[*Reported in* 1 *Rolle's Reports*, 396.]

Janson brought an action upon the case against Colomore, and counted that, whereas the defendant was indebted to him, upon an accounting he was found in arrears to such an amount, and *in consideratione inde* the defendant *tunc et ibidem* promised to pay the said money at a certain day then to come, and for non-payment the action is brought. After a verdict for the plaintiff, it was moved in arrest of judgment that this action upon the case does not lie; for it is only in effect that a man who is indebted to me assumes to pay the debt at a day to come, in which it is clear that an action on the case does not lie, because the contract was before the promise and executed, and this promise to pay at a day to come cannot make it a contract executory.

Houghton. It seems that this action lies in this case, because it is that, upon his being found in arrears, the defendant *tunc et ibidem* assumpsit; so that, at the instant of the finding of the arrears, then commenced the duty in certain, and therefore the assumpsit at the same time is good; *quod fuit concessum per* CROKE and DODERIDGE; and DODERIDGE said that Slade's Case is that every debt executory includes an assumpsit. . . .

HODGE *v.* VAVISOR.

IN THE KING'S BENCH, MICHAELMAS TERM, 1616.

[*Reported in* 1 *Rolle's Reports,* 413.]

HODGE brought an action upon the case against Vavisor, and declared *quod cum* the defendant was indebted to him on such a day, &c., in a certain sum for divers things in certain sold to him, and being *sic indebitatus, postea,* on a day afterwards, *in consideratione inde* promised to pay it at a day certain afterwards, and for non-payment at the day he brought the action; and after verdict for the plaintiff, *J. Harris* moved in arrest of judgment that the declaration is not good, because this assumpsit does not commence with the debt, but is made at a day after, for which there is no consideration; for here is no promise by the plaintiff that he will forbear the defendant until the day of payment, and so no consideration, for he could sue him the next day after; so if a man promise another, in consideration that he has built a house for him, to give him £20, this is not good, because the consideration is past; but it is otherwise in the case of marriage, because that consideration continues; and he shewed a precedent where an exchange was made by a goldsmith for a certain sum, and afterwards such assumpsit was made as here, and adjudged no good cause of action because the consideration was past.

HOUGHTON. That is not like our case, because that is fully executed, it being an exchange; but *tota curia, scil.,* CROKE, DODERIDGE, and HOUGHTON: It seems that the action well lies, because the continuance of the debt to the time of the promise made is a good consideration continuing until the promise made to support this action; and DODERIDGE said the promise of payment included a forbearance until the day; and HOUGHTON said it was a usual declaration *quod cum indebitatus fuit* such a day, *postea eodem die assumpsit,* &c., and it is good, which seems to be all one with our case. *Harris.* "Ceo fuit un question en temps Popham pur ceo que peradventure cest promise puissoit estre al auter temps, scilicet en le Sommer, et le dett en le Matin del' jour, mes al darren fuit adjudge bon." HOUGHTON. That is all one with our case; and judgment was accordingly given for the plaintiff. (R. *quære* of this case; for it seems that here is no consideration for a new promise, inasmuch as no forbearance is promised; for it has been held that a consideration to forbear *per paululum temporis* is not good, because he can sue him notwithstanding; so in our case. And in this case it does not lie as upon a future contract, because the contract was executed before, and it does not make a new contract.)

HOWLET'S CASE.

In the King's Bench, Trinity Term, 1626.

[*Reported in Latch*, 150.]

The plaintiff declared that such a day, *anno* 21 Jac., he sold to the defendant so much barley, part of which he delivered immediately, and by agreement was to deliver the remainder afterwards; and afterwards on the same day the defendant promised to pay so much by such a day.

Serjt. *Hitcham*. Here the promise is made after the sale; and so, being upon a consideration executed, it is bad. But *per* Curiam: It is well enough, being on the same day, since no division shall be made in this case.

TOWNSEND *v.* HUNT.

In the King's Bench, Trinity Term, 1635.

[*Reported in Croke Charles*, 408.]

Assumpsit. The plaintiff declares, whereas Francis Townsend made his will, and thereby devised to the plaintiff £60 to be paid at his age of one-and-twenty years; and made Anne his wife his executrix, and left assets to pay his debts and legacies; and that the said Anne took the defendant to husband, and afterwards the plaintiff came to full age; and the defendant and his wife paid to the plaintiff, in part payment of the said legacy, upon the 23d of April £53, who gave to the defendant and his wife a general release; that the defendant, 28 September, 5 Car. 1, in consideration that the plaintiff at the defendant's request had made a general release to the defendant and his wife, assumed to the plaintiff that, if his wife did not pay the seven pounds' residue of the said legacy in her lifetime, that he would pay it after his wife's death; and alleges in fact that the defendant's wife did not pay the said seven pounds in her life, and that he had required it of the defendant; and he had not paid it, *per quod actio accrevit.*

Upon this declaration the defendant demurred; and it was argued at the bar by *Farrer* for the plaintiff, and by *Calthrop* for the defendant. And he shewed for cause of his demurrer that this promise, being for a consideration past, is a void promise; and here is not a continuing consideration, but *nudum pactum unde non oritur actio;* and compared it to the case in 10 Eliz., Dyer, 272, where one promised to one who was bail for his servant to save him harmless, [and] it was adjudged a void promise.

BERKLEY, J., for this reason was of that opinion; but if it had been a consideration continuing, as in consideration of marrying his daughter or cousin, which is a gift in frank marriage, it had been good; but not here, no more than if in consideration you gave him an horse a year since he had promised to pay you ten pounds, which is void because past.

But Justice JONES and myself, upon the first motion, conceived it good; for if this promise had been made at the time of the release made, it had been clearly a good promise and a good consideration; then being made after the release, forasmuch as the release is made at the defendant's request, and the defendant hath the continuance of the benefit thereof, the promise upon this consideration is good enough: for so the case imports in Dyer, 272. If the bail had been entered into at the master's request, and afterwards he had made the promise, it had been well enough. And for this purpose they vouched the case of Marsh *v.* Rainsford,[1] and another case here of Rigges *v.* Bullingham,[2] where, in consideration that the plaintiff at the defendant's request had granted the next avoidance of such a church, the defendant at a day after promised to pay to the plaintiff one hundred pounds. After verdict upon *non assumpsit,* it was moved in arrest of judgment, first, because there was no time or place mentioned when that grant was made. — *Sed non allocatur;* because it was but an inducement to the action. — A second exception; because it was a consideration past, and it might be twenty years before. — *Sed non allocatur;* because it was made at the defendant's request.

Afterwards in Michaelmas Term, 11 Car. 1, the principal case being moved again, all the JUSTICES, *seriatim,* delivered their opinions that it was good; and it was adjudged for the plaintiff.

[1] 2 Leon. 111. [2] Cro. Eliz. 715.

BARTON *v.* SHURLEY.

IN THE KING'S BENCH, MICHAELMAS TERM, 1639.

[*Reported in* 1 *Rolle's Abridgment,* 12, *placitum* 16.]

IF the defendant on the 30th of June was indebted to the plaintiff in £20 for money lent by the plaintiff to him, and the defendant being so indebted afterwards, viz., on the 30th of July thereafter, promised to pay him at a day to come, this is good, for it is a continuing consideration.

OLIVERSON *v.* WOOD.

IN THE COMMON PLEAS, TRINITY TERM, 1693.

[*Reported in* 3 *Levinz,* 366.]

ASSUMPSIT. And declares that whereas the defendant was indebted to the plaintiff in £20 for wares sold, *cumque etiam* in consideration that the plaintiff had sold other goods to the defendant, he promised to pay; *cumque etiam* the defendant was indebted to the plaintiff in another £20 for moneys by the plaintiff lent to the use of the defendant (but says not at his request), the defendant promised to pay it. After verdict for the plaintiff on *non assumpsit* and entire damages, it was moved in arrest of judgment, and the judgment stayed for this cause only, that the moneys in the last promise were not said lent at the defendant's request; for it may be lent to his use, contrary to his desire. Dy. 272, Hunt's Case; where the master promised in consideration that the plaintiff had bailed his servant, to save him harmless, which being laid without a request was ill; but the case there put, of a promise upon the marriage of his daughter, was admitted to be good, because for the apparent benefit of the father, it continuing. Also they agreed a case between Tiere and Langly, lately adjudged in this court; where the consideration was, that the plaintiff in an action had prosecuted a suit for the defendant, without saying at his request, and resolved good after two or three motions in arrest, &c., after a verdict, because it is necessarily to be so intended after a verdict; for otherwise it would be maintenance. *Levinz* for the plaintiff.

HAYES v. WARREN.

IN THE KING'S BENCH, EASTER TERM, 1732.

[*Reported in 2 Strange, 933.*]

ERROR of a judgment in C. B., in an action upon the case upon several promises; and after judgment by default and entire damages, it was objected that the fourth count was for work and labor done by the plaintiff for the defendant, in consideration whereof he promised to pay. And it was objected that this was a past consideration; and not being laid to be done at the request of the defendant, it could be no consideration to raise an assumpsit; and 1 Rol. Abr. 11, pl. 1; Cro. El. 442, 741; 3 Leon. 91; Dyer, 272, were cited by *Hussey.*

Strange, contra, cited 2 Leon. 111, 225; Raym. 260; Hutt. 84, where assumpsits have been maintained on a past consideration; and though formerly courts were strict, yet now they draw nearer to common sense. There was a time when assumpsit *pro bonis et mercimoniis* generally would have been wondered at; and Holt used to say he was a bold man that first ventured on them; but now they are every day's experience: and why should not gratitude be a good consideration? He further insisted that this is not to be taken as a past consideration, because the work and promise are both laid on the same day, and the law makes no fractions of a day, and cited Latch, 150, in point. He further insisted that upon the whole it appeared to be at the request of the defendant, it being laid to be done for him, and that the plaintiff *proinde* deserved from the defendant so much, which he has not paid, *ad damnum* of the plaintiff, and cited Latch, 112, 274.

Sed per CURIAM: It does not appear that this work was for the benefit of the defendant, and we must take it to be a past consideration, being laid that *postea* he promised to pay. If this was after a verdict, we should think the inferences from the words *pro* and *meruit de def'* would be material; but the statutes of jeofails do not protect judgments by default against objections that are cured by a verdict at common law, but such as are remedied after a verdict by the statutes. The judgment of C. B. was reversed.[1]

[1] According to the report of this case in 2 Barnard. 71, the Chief Justice and Page, J., said: "The present action is not for goods sold and delivered; if it had [been], it would have been a much more favorable case for the plaintiff; because, by the acceptance of the goods, there seems to be an agreement to pay for them. But here the defendant might be no ways privy to the work done at the time of the doing it." At p. 140 Strange is reported to have said, *arguendo:* "Wherever the consideration past concerned the benefit of a stranger only, a request is necessary to charge the defendant. But wherever the consideration is for the benefit of the defendant, no such request is

HOPKINS AND WIFE v. LOGAN.

IN THE EXCHEQUER, EASTER TERM, 1839.

[*Reported in 5 Meeson & Welsby*, 241.]

ASSUMPSIT. The declaration stated that, after the intermarriage of the plaintiffs, and before the commencement of this suit, to wit, on the first day of October, 1838, at the request of the defendant, an account was stated by and between the said Richard Hopkins, for and on behalf of himself and his said wife Ellen, on the one part, and the defendant on the other part, of and concerning certain moneys amounting to a large sum of money, to wit, the sum of £1000, by the said Ellen while she was unmarried lent and advanced to the defendant at his request, and remaining unpaid before, at, and after the time of said intermarriage; and of and concerning certain other moneys, amounting in the whole to a large sum of money, to wit, to the sum of £555 3*s.* 11*d.*, by the defendant before the stating of the said account paid to the plaintiff; and which said last-mentioned moneys the said plaintiff Richard Hopkins, for and on behalf of himself and his said wife, at the time of the said stating of the said account, and at the request of the defendant, agreed should be taken and considered as satisfying and discharging so much of the first-mentioned sum of money; and upon the account so stated as aforesaid the defendant was then found to be and then was in arrear and indebted to the plaintiff in a large sum of money, to wit, the sum of £444 16*s.* 1*d.*, residue of the said first-mentioned sum of money; and being so found in arrear and indebted as aforesaid, the defendant, in consideration of the premises, promised the plaintiffs to pay them the said last-mentioned sum of money on the tenth day of October then next ensuing, which period had elapsed before the com-

necessary when there is an express promise laid in the declaration." But "the court declared that they took the rule of law to be, that no past consideration is sufficient to support a subsequent promise, unless there was a request of the party, either express or implied, at the time of performing the consideration. Some acts," they said, "were of such a nature as that the law could imply a request; as the being bail for one, curing one's child of a sudden sickness, performing the part of a servant, &c.; and therefore in those cases they did allow that a subsequent promise might be well founded upon such past consideration. They did agree likewise, that where there was an express request at the time of the past consideration being performed, that might in all cases be sufficient to support a subsequent promise. And therefore the Chief Justice said he could not agree the case cited out of 3 Cro. 741 [Barker v. Halifax] to be law. But in the present case the act done by the defendant was by no means of such a nature as to be sufficient for the law to create a request upon it; and therefore an express request was necessary to have been laid." And see W. Kelynge, 117, s. c. — ED.

mencement of this suit. Breach, in non-payment of the last-mentioned sum of money.[1]

LORD ABINGER, C. B. I am of opinion that this declaration is bad, for that the contract declared upon is not binding on both parties, the consideration being executed upon which the new premise is attempted to be founded. The promise, it is true, proceeds both on the accounting and on the payment of the £555 by the defendant; but both those considerations are executed. The liability of the defendant on the account stated would be to pay the amount on request; to render him liable on the promise here alleged to pay on a future day, there ought to be some new consideration. . . .

PARKE, B. . . . The promise as laid cannot be supported, because there is no consideration for any promise different from that which the law implies. The promise which arises in law upon an account stated is to pay on request, and any other promise is *nudum pactum*, unless made upon a new consideration. At the time of the alleged promise the party is liable to pay *in præsenti* on request; and if by a simple promise, without fresh consideration, there can be a contract for future payment, the Statute of Limitations may be defeated by a mere verbal promise. Any promise to pay money *in futuro*, which is payable *in præsenti*, is bad, unless it be on a new consideration. The plaintiff here proceeds on an executed consideration, which constitutes an existing debt; and no such new consideration appears in the present case.

ALDERSON, B. If it were necessary to give an opinion upon the plea, I should wish to take some time to consider it; but I concur with the rest of the court in thinking that the declaration is bad. The consideration is clearly executed, and the promise which the law implies thereon is to pay on request. In order to convert that promise into a promise to pay at a future day, there must be a new consideration. Here there is none, and on that ground the declaration is bad. If it were otherwise, the consequence would follow that, as such a promise may be by word of mouth, the Statute of Limitations might always be evaded without a writing.

MAULE, B. I agree that an executed consideration is no consideration for any other promise than that which the law would imply; if it were, there would be two co-existing promises on one consideration. On this ground, without adverting to the objections raised to the plea, I think that the defendant is entitled to judgment.

Judgment for the defendant.

[1] The defendant pleaded a special plea, which was demurred to; and the question thus arose whether the declaration was good. Only so muth of the case is here given as relates to the latter question. — ED.

ROSCORLA *v.* THOMAS.

IN THE QUEEN'S BENCH, MAY 30, 1842.

[*Reported in* 3 *Queen's Bench Reports,* 234.]

ASSUMPSIT. The declaration stated that, whereas heretofore, to wit, &c., in consideration that plaintiff at the request of defendant had bought of defendant a certain horse, at and for a certain price, &c., to wit, &c., defendant promised plaintiff that the horse did not exceed five years old, and was sound, &c., and free from vice; nevertheless defendant did not perform or regard his said promise, but thereby deceived and defrauded plaintiff in this, to wit, that the said horse at the time of the making of the said promise was not free from vice; but, on the contrary thereof, was then very vicious, restive, ungovernable, and ferocious; whereby, &c.

Pleas. 1. *Non assumpsit.* Issue thereon.

2. That the horse, at the time of the supposed promise, was free from vice, and was not vicious, restive, ungovernable, or ferocious, in manner, &c.; conclusion to the country. Issue thereon.

On the trial, before Wightman, J., at the Cornwall spring assizes, 1841, a verdict was found for the plaintiff on both the above issues. In Easter Term, 1841, *Bompas*, Serjt., obtained a rule *nisi* for arresting the judgment on the first count. In last term

Erle and *Butt* shewed cause. The objection is, that the first count states only a *nudum pactum.* But there is an executed consideration, which with a request will support a promise. Now the request need not be express; wherever the law will raise a promise, a request by the party promising will be implied; note (*c*) to Osborne *v.* Rogers.[1] Payne *v.* Wilson[2] was the converse of the present case: there a consideration, which in its form was executed, was declared on as executory; and this was held to be no variance, because in reality the consideration was continuing. Here the declaration states an executed consideration in form; but it is practically executory because the sale and warranty would be coincident. In Thornton *v.* Jenyns[3] the declaration charged that, in consideration that plaintiff had promised to defendant, defendant then promised plaintiff. It was objected that this was an executed consideration without a request, which was insufficient where the law would not raise a promise; and Brown *v.* Crump[4] was cited; but the court held that the two promises might be considered

[1] 1 Wms. Saund. 264 *a.*
[2] 7 B. & C. 423.
[3] 1 Man. & G. 166.
[4] 1 Marsh. 567.

as simultaneous, and that the objection therefore could not be sustained.[1]

Bompas, Serjt., and *Slade*, contra. The warranty ought to be given at the time of the sale: if made after, it is without consideration. 3 Blackst. Com. 166; Com. Dig., Action upon the Case for a Deceipt (A. 11); Roswel *v.* Vaughan,[2] Pope *v.* Lewyns.[3] Thornton *v.* Jenyns was a case of mutual promises, which can never literally be made at the same moment: here the declaration definitely lays the perfect sale as antecedent to and distinct from the warranty. And the warranty is a matter not implied by the law upon a sale. Parkinson *v.* Lee.[4] Even an express promise without a legal consideration is invalid. Collins *v.* Godefroy.[5] In Hopkins *v.* Logan[6] there was an executed consideration from which a promise to pay on request would have arisen; and it was holden that this did not support a promise to pay on a future day named. [PATTESON, J., referred to Hunt *v.* Bate,[7] as cited in Eastwood *v.* Kenyon,[8] and to Lampleigh *v.* Brathwait.[9]] *Cur. adv. vult.*

LORD DENMAN, C. J., in this term (May 30) delivered the judgment of the court.

This was an action of assumpsit for breach of warranty of the soundness of a horse. The first count of the declaration, upon which alone the question arises, stated that, in consideration that the plaintiff at the request of the defendant had bought of the defendant a horse for the sum of £30, the defendant promised that it was sound and free from vice. And it was objected, in arrest of judgment, that the precedent executed consideration was insufficient to support the subsequent promise. And we are of opinion that the objection must prevail.

It may be taken as a general rule, subject to exceptions not applicable to this case, that the promise must be coëxtensive with the consideration. In the present case, the only promise that would result from the consideration as stated, and be coëxtensive with it, would be to deliver the horse upon request. The precedent sale without a warranty, though at the request of the defendant, imposes no other duty or obligation upon him. It is clear therefore that the consideration stated would not raise an implied promise by the defendant that the horse was sound or free from vice.

But the promise in the present case must be taken to be, as in fact it was, express; and the question is, whether that fact will warrant the extension of the promise beyond that which would be implied by law;

[1] It was also argued that the warranty might here, after verdict, be taken to be coincident with the sale: to which it was answered that if it were so, the evidence negatived the declaration.

[2] Cro. Jac. 196.

[3] Cro. Jac. 630.

[4] 2 East, 314.

[5] 1 B. & Ad. 950.

[6] 5 M. & W. 241.

[7] 3 Dyer, 272 *a*.

[8] 11 A. & E. 438, 452.

[9] Hob. 105, 5th ed. See s. c. 1 Smith's Leading Cases, 67.

and whether the consideration, though insufficient to raise an implied promise, will nevertheless support an express one. And we think that it will not.

The cases in which it has been held that, under certain circumstances, a consideration insufficient to raise an implied promise will nevertheless support an express one, will be found collected and reviewed in the note (*a*) to Wennall *v.* Adney,[1] and in the case of Eastwood *v.* Kenyon.[2] They are cases of voidable contracts subsequently ratified, of debts barred by operation of law subsequently revived, and of equitable and moral obligations which, but for some rule of law, would of themselves have been sufficient to raise an implied promise. All these cases are distinguishable from, and indeed inapplicable to, the present, which appears to us to fall within the general rule, that a consideration past and executed will support no other promise than such as would be implied by law.

The rule for arresting the judgment upon the first count must therefore be made absolute. *Rule absolute.*

KAYE *v.* DUTTON.

IN THE COMMON PLEAS, JUNE 29, 1844.

[*Reported in 7 Manning and Granger*, 807.]

ASSUMPSIT. The first count of the declaration stated that, by a certain instrument in writing made by the defendant on the 22d of September, 1836, — after reciting that one Whitnall, since deceased, had mortgaged certain freehold property to R. Rockliff and H. Bullen to secure £3500; that said mortgagees had required the said Whitnall to obtain the plaintiff to join him in a bond as a collateral security further to secure said sum of £3500 and interest; that, since the death of said Whitnall, the defendant had taken upon himself the management of his estate, and had paid £3370 on said mortgage, and that the plaintiff had been called upon to pay and had paid the sum of £130 remaining due thereon; that the defendant had repaid to the plaintiff the sum of £48, and had agreed to repay him the remaining sum of £82 out of the moneys arising from the sale of said property when sold, and in the mean time to appropriate the rents of said property to the payment of said sum, as the plaintiff had a lien on said property therefor; and that the defendant had requested the plaintiff to release and convey all his estate and interest in said property to Alison and Lenox, which he had done, reserving to himself a lien on the said property as aforesaid, — it

[1] 3 Bos. & Pul. 249. [2] 11 A. & E. 438.

was witnessed that, in consideration of the plaintiff's having paid said sum of £130, and released and conveyed all his estate and interest in said property (reserving to himself the said lien), and in order to secure to the plaintiff the repayment of said sum of £82, the defendant undertook and agreed with the plaintiff to pay him said sum of £82, with interest thereon, out of the proceeds to arise from the sale of said property when sold, and in the mean time to appropriate the rent of said property to the payment of said sum. Averment, that the defendant, in consideration of the premises, after the making of said agreement or instrument in writing, to wit, on the said 22d of September, 1836, promised the plaintiff to observe and perform the same in all things on his part to be observed and performed; that after the making of said agreement and before said sale was effected, the defendant received rents of said property to an amount sufficient to pay said sum of £82; yet the defendant, though requested, had not appropriated said rents or any part thereof to the payment of said sum of £82, and the same is wholly due and unpaid to the plaintiff.[1]

To this count the defendant pleaded amongst others two special pleas, to the replications to which he demurred specially. Upon the argument in Easter Term last, however, the defendant abandoned the pleas, and objected to the declaration.

Dowling, Serjt., for the defendant. Three objections arise on the declaration: first, it discloses no consideration for the promise alleged; secondly, the consideration (if any) is a mere moral consideration; thirdly, the consideration being executed, it can only sustain an implied promise;[2] whereas the promise alleged is a different one, being an express promise.

Construing the declaration most favorably for the plaintiff, it appears that he, having become surety for Whitnall the mortgagor, paid £130 to the mortgagees; that the defendant — who had taken upon himself the management of Whitnall's estate — had repaid him £48, and promised to pay him the residue out of the proceeds thereof; and that the plaintiff at the request of the defendant released and conveyed all his interest in the premises to Alison and Lenox, reserving to himself a lien on the property. This statement of facts does not disclose any consideration whatever for the defendant's promise. The only interest the plaintiff ever had in the premises was the lien, which entitled him in equity to stand in the position of the mortgagees. Copis *v.* Middleton.[3] The recital that the defendant had released all his estate and interest in the property except his lien, is in effect to say that he had released nothing. Possibly the consideration might have been good if it had been alleged that the plaintiff had executed some instrument purporting to convey an interest. In Wilkinson *v.* Oliveira[4] the dec-

[1] See *supra*, p. 221, note 1. — ED.

[2] *Quære.*

[3] Turn. & Russ. 224.

[4] 1 N. C. 490, 1 Scott, 461.

laration stated that, in consideration that the plaintiff at the request of the defendant had given the defendant a letter written by O., since deceased, by means of which letter the defendant was enabled to, and did, determine controversies, and obtain a large portion of O.'s effects, the defendant promised to give the plaintiff £1000; and it was held that the declaration disclosed a sufficient consideration to sustain an action on the promise. So here, if the declaration had stated that the plaintiff had executed an assignment, it might have been sufficient; but the only consideration alleged is the assigning of his interest; whereas he had none to convey.

Secondly. The only consideration that appears upon the face of the declaration (if any) is a mere moral consideration, to which the law will give no effect. A past consideration will not support a subsequent promise. Jeremy *v.* Goochman,[1] Barker *v.* Halifax,[2] Docket *v.* Voyel.[3] The law does not in truth give effect to any but an executory[4] consideration. It may be said that the consideration here is not simply an executed consideration, because it is stated that the defendant had requested the plaintiff to convey. But a mere request is of no avail. Lampleigh *v.* Brathwait.[5] The promise alleged and the promise implied by law must be coëxtensive. Veitch *v.* Russell.[6] [TINDAL, C. J. That case shews that a subsequent express promise will not convert that into a debt which of itself was not a legal debt.] It establishes that an express promise cannot be supported by a moral consideration.

Thirdly. If the court think that any promise can be implied from the facts stated, it will not be the promise alleged. It is clear that an executed consideration will only sustain such a promise as the law will imply. Brown *v.* Crump.[7] . . .[8]

Channell, Serjt., contra. The declaration is good. The defendant's promise being laid to have been made in consideration of the premises, that is, of all that is stated in the foregoing part of the declaration, it is submitted that the facts alleged disclose a sufficient legal consideration. Admitting that a mere moral consideration ordinarily will not sustain a promise, here a legal consideration is apparent. If the defendant had any estate or interest to convey, his parting with it at the defendant's request would be an ample consideration; and upon this declaration it is not competent for the defendant to say that the plaintiff did not release some interest in the mortgaged premises. Having paid money as surety for the mortgagor, he would stand in his

[1] Cro. Eliz. 442. [2] *Ib.* 741. [3] *Ib.* 885.
[4] *i. e.*, executory in its inception. [5] Hob. 105, Sir F. Moore, 866.
[6] 3 Q. B. 928, 3 G. & D. 198. [7] 1 Marsh. 567, 6 Taunt. 300.
[8] The learned counsel here cited the cases of Granger *v.* Collins, 6 M. & W. 458; Hopkins *v.* Logan, 5 M. & W. 241; Jackson *v.* Cobbin, 8 M. & W. 790; Roscorla *v.* Thomas, 3 Q. B. 234.

place, and if any interest can be inferred beyond the lien, there is a good consideration. The difficulty arises on the words "reserving to himself a lien on the said property." The fair meaning of that is, that the plaintiff had given up his lien so far as regarded Alison and Lenox, but preserved it as between himself and the defendant. As to the second point, the rule upon this subject is well laid down in 1 Wms. Saund. 264, note, where it is said that "a past consideration is not sufficient to support a subsequent promise, unless there was a request by the party, either expressed or implied, at the time of performing the consideration;[1] but where there is an express request at the time, it will in all cases be sufficient to support a subsequent promise." Here, what is treated as a past consideration is stated to have been done because of the defendant's request. Cases have been cited to shew that the past consideration here stated does not support the particular promise alleged in the declaration; but those cases are distinguishable, as in all of them the promise implied by law differed widely from that alleged on the face of the declaration. The question how far a moral consideration will support a subsequent express promise is discussed by Lord Denman in Eastwood *v.* Kenyon.[2] Here, looking at the whole declaration, a sufficient consideration appears for the promise laid.

TINDAL, C. J., now delivered the judgment of the court. This was a declaration in assumpsit upon a special agreement, to which the defendant pleaded amongst others two special pleas, namely, the fourth and fifth pleas, to which the plaintiff demurred; and the defendant demurred specially to the plaintiff's replication to the third plea. But it is unnecessary to advert to the particular state of the pleadings, as it was admitted by my brother Dowling, on the argument for the defendant, upon an objection taken to the fourth and fifth pleas, that he could not support those pleas, and the whole argument before us turned on the sufficiency of the declaration.

Two objections were made to the declaration: first, that it did not shew any consideration for the promise by the defendant; secondly that the promise was laid in respect of an executed consideration, but was not such a promise as would have been implied by law from that consideration; and that in point of law an executed consideration will support no promise, although express, other than that which the law itself would have implied. The cases cited by the defendant, viz., Brown *v.* Crump, Granger *v.* Collins, Hopkins *v.* Logan, Jackson *v.* Cobbin, and Roscorla *v.* Thomas, certainly support that proposition to this extent, — that, where the consideration is one from which a promise is by law implied, there no express promise made in respect of that consideration after it has been executed, differing from that which by law would be implied, can be enforced. But those cases may have

[1] *Vide* 1 M. & Gr. 266, n.

[2] 11 Ad. & El. 438, 3 P. & D. 276.

proceeded on the principle that the consideration was exhausted by the promise implied by law, from the very execution of it; and consequently any promise made afterwards must be *nudum pactum*, there remaining no consideration to support it. But the case may perhaps be different where there is a consideration from which no promise would be implied by law; that is, where the party suing has sustained a detriment to himself or conferred a benefit on the defendant at his request, under circumstances which would not raise any implied promise. In such cases it appears to have been held, in some instances, that the act done at the request of the party charged is a sufficient consideration to render binding a promise afterwards made by him in respect of the act so done. Hunt *v.* Bate,[1] and several cases mentioned in the margin of the report of that case, seem to go to that extent; as also do some others collected in Rol. Abr., Action sur Case (Q).[2] But it is not necessary that we should pronounce any opinion upon that point;[3] for, assuming it to be sufficiently alleged that the plaintiff released and conveyed his interest at the request of the defendant, yet it does not appear that he had any interest which passed by such release and conveyance. The declaration is founded on an agreement which recites that a certain estate had been mortgaged by one Whitnall, since deceased; and that the plaintiff had joined in a bond as a collateral security for the mortgage-money, and had afterwards been compelled to pay off a portion of it; that the defendant had taken upon himself the management of Whitnall's affairs, had repaid to the plaintiff part of the money which he had paid, and had agreed to pay him the residue out of the proceeds of the mortgaged property when sold, and in the mean time to appropriate the rents of the premises to the payment of the same sum as that for which the plaintiff had a lien on the said premises. Thus far there is nothing to shew that the plaintiff had any other interest than this lien. The agreement then recites that the defendant had requested the plaintiff to release and convey his interest to Alison and Lenox, and that he had done so, reserving to himself a lien on the property as aforesaid; that is, reserving to himself the only interest that he is shewn to have had. The

[1] Dyer, 272.

[2] 1 Rol. Abr. 11, translated 1 Vin. Abr. 279.

[3] In Elderton *v.* Emmens, 4 C. B. 496, Maule, J., said: "An executed consideration will sustain only such a promise as the law will imply. Thus, if goods are sold or work is done without any special agreement as to price, the law implies a promise to pay so much as the goods or the work may be reasonably worth. If the promise is alleged beyond that, it is not sustainable in law." To which Serjeant Manning appended the following note: "This must be understood with reference to those considerations from which, as in the case put by the learned judge, the law infers a precise promise. But A. may declare that, in consideration that he had, at the request of B., conferred a benefit on C., B. promised him, A., to pay him so much money, or to deliver to him a certain horse, a promise which would not be implied by law from such executed consideration." — ED.

agreement then proceeds to state that, in consideration of the plaintiff having paid the money and having released and conveyed all his estate and interest to Alison and Lenox, reserving to himself the said lien, the defendant undertook and agreed, &c. Now the payment of the money by the plaintiff would be no consideration for the defendant's promise; and the alleged release and conveyance was again no consideration, for it does not appear that the plaintiff parted with any thing by it. For the plaintiff it was contended that he must be taken to have parted with his lien on the property, reserving only his right to call upon the defendant to pay the residue still due to the plaintiff out of the proceeds of the estate when sold, and in the mean time to appropriate the rents to the same object. But we cannot put that construction upon the agreement, which expressly speaks of the lien reserved as the same lien which the plaintiff had before.

Such being in our judgment the effect of the agreement set out in the declaration, the case resembles that of Edwards *v.* Baugh.[1] There the declaration alleged that certain disputes and controversies were pending between the plaintiff and defendant as to whether the defendant was indebted to the plaintiff in a certain sum of money; and that thereupon, in consideration that the plaintiff would promise the defendant not to sue him for the recovery of the said sum in dispute, but would accept a smaller sum in full satisfaction, the defendant promised to pay such smaller sum. On general demurrer the declaration was held bad, because it did not allege that any debt was due from the defendant to the plaintiff, or that an action had been commenced for the recovery of any sum claimed. So in the present case, as the declaration does not shew that the plaintiff had any interest in the premises except that which he reserved, it does not appear that his release and conveyance, although executed at the defendant's request, formed any legal consideration for the promise alleged to have been made by the latter. Our judgment must therefore be for the defendant.

Judgment for the defendant.

VICTORS *v.* DAVIES.

In the Exchequer, April 22, 1844.

[*Reported in 12 Meeson & Welsby,* 758.]

Assumpsit. The declaration stated that the defendant, on the 6th of March, 1844, was indebted to the plaintiff in the sum of £10 for money lent by the plaintiff to the defendant.

[1] 11 M. & W. 641.

Special demurrer, assigning the following causes: That it is not alleged in the declaration that the money was lent to the defendant at his request, and that therefore there is no consideration to support the promise; nor does it sufficiently appear that the defendant was indebted to the plaintiff.

Pearson, in support of the demurrer. The declaration is insufficient for want of the averment that the money was lent to the defendant "at his request." [ALDERSON, B. How can there be a lender unless there be also a borrower?] A plaintiff is bound to allege a request wherever the consideration is executed. In the notes to Osborne *v.* Rogers[1] it is said that "a past consideration is not sufficient to support a subsequent promise, unless there was a request of the party, either express or implied, at the time of performing the consideration." And in a note by the learned editors of the fifth edition it is added, "So even an affidavit (to hold to bail) of debt for money lent, and for goods sold and delivered, and for work and labor, has been held irregular because it omitted to state that it was 'at the instance and request of the defendant,' although it stated that it was 'to and for his use and on his account;'" for which they cite Durnford *v.* Messiter.[2] In Chitty on Pleading[3] it is also said, "In each of these counts upon an executed consideration, except that for money had and received, and the account stated, it is necessary to allege that the consideration of the debt was performed at the defendant's request, though such request might in some cases be implied in evidence." [PARKE, B. There is a very learned note of my brother Manning on this subject,[4] in which he goes into the whole law with respect to alleging a request, and points out the error into which Mr. Serjeant Williams appears to have fallen in his comment upon Osborne *v.* Rogers. The note is thus: "The consideration being executory, the statement of the request in the declaration, though mentioned in the undertaking, appears to have been unnecessary. In Osborne *v.* Rogers the consideration of a promise is laid to be, that the said Robert, at the special instance and request of the said William, would serve the said William, and bestow his care and labor in and about the business of the said William; and the declaration alleges that Robert, confiding in the said promise of William, afterwards went into the service of William, and bestowed his care and labor in and about, &c. Here the consideration is clearly executory, yet Mr. Serjeant Williams, in a note to the words 'at the special instance and request,' says, 'these words are necessary to be laid in the declaration in order to support the action. It is held that a consideration executed and past — as in the present case the service performed by the plaintiff for the testator in his lifetime for several years then past — is not sufficient to maintain an assumpsit, unless it

[1] 1 Saund. 264, note 1.
[2] 5 M. & Selw. 446.
[3] Vol. i. p. 353 (7th ed.).
[4] 1 Man. & Gr. 265.

was moved by a precedent request, and so laid.' The statement, according to modern practice, of the accrual of a debt for, or the making of a promise for the payment of, the price of goods sold and delivered, or for the repayment of money lent, as being in consideration of goods sold and delivered, or money lent to the defendant at his request, is conceived to be an inartificial mode of declaring. Even where the consideration is entirely past it appears to be unnecessary to allege a request, if the act stated as the consideration cannot from its nature have been a gratuitous kindness, but imports a consideration *per se.* It being immaterial to the right of action whether the bargain, if actually concluded and executed, or the loan, if made and the moneys actually advanced, was proposed and urged by the buyer or by the seller, by the borrower or by the lender. *Vide* Rastall's Entries, tit. Dette; and Co. Ent., tit. Debt." There cannot be a claim for money lent unless there be a loan, and a loan imports an obligation to pay. If the money is accepted, it is immaterial whether or not it was asked for. The same doctrine will not apply to money paid; because no man can be a debtor for money paid unless it was paid at his request. What my brother Manning says, in the note to which I have referred, is perfectly correct.]

POLLOCK, C. B. There cannot be a doubt about this case; the statement that the money was lent implies that it was advanced at the request of the defendant. There must be judgment for the plaintiff.

PARKE, B., ALDERSON, B., and ROLFE, B., concurred.

Judgment for the plaintiff.

BRADFORD *v.* ROULSTON.

IN THE IRISH EXCHEQUER, MAY 6, 7, AND JUNE 12, 1858.

[*Reported in* 8 *Irish Common Law Reports,* 468.]

THIS was an action for breach of a contract by the defendant to pay a sum of £55, the balance of the purchase-money of a vessel sold by the plaintiff to a third person.

The summons and plaint contained four special counts, and a count upon an account stated. No question arose upon the first, third, and fifth counts; but the second and fourth, which were framed upon a guaranty, were as follows: — Second count: That in consideration that the plaintiff, at the express instance and request of the defendant, would execute to one James Gribben and John M'Teague a bill of sale of a certain vessel of the plaintiff, the defendant contracted and agreed with the plaintiff to guarantee the payment to the plaintiff on the day following the making of such contract of the sum of £55, being the balance of the purchase-money payable by the said John M'Teague in respect of such bill of sale; and the plaintiff avers that, relying on the said contract and agreement by the defendant, he did execute such bill of sale, and did perform all things on the part of him the said plaintiff in relation to the said contract to be performed; but the plaintiff avers that neither of them, the said James Gribben or John M'Teague or the defendant, did pay the said sum of £55 or any part thereof on the day aforesaid or since, and the same still remains wholly unpaid; of all which said defendant had notice.

Fourth count: That it had been agreed between the plaintiff and one James Gribben and John M'Teague, that the plaintiff should execute to them a bill of sale of a certain other vessel of the plaintiff for the price or sum of £230; and the plaintiff avers that at the time of executing such last-mentioned agreement the said John M'Teague omitted to pay over to or for the plaintiff the sum of £55, being the balance of the purchase-money payable by the said John M'Teague in respect of such last-mentioned agreement; and the plaintiff avers that he the said plaintiff was thereupon unwilling to execute such bill of sale; and the plaintiff says that defendant then expressly requested the plaintiff to execute the said bill, and that in consequence of such request the plaintiff did actually execute the same; and the plaintiff avers that the defendant did afterwards, in consideration of the plaintiff having so executed said bill of sale at the instance and request of the defendant, guarantee to the plaintiff the payment to him by the said John M'Teague of the sum of £55 on the day following the execution of such bill; but the plaintiff says that neither the said John M'Teague or the defendant did pay the said sum of £55 or any part thereof on the day agreed on or since, but same still remains wholly unpaid; of all which the defendant had notice.

The defendant, by his defences, traversed the making of the contract stated in the summons and plaint; and the issues settled upon the pleadings were in substance whether the defendant contracted as alleged?

At the trial before Ball, J., at the spring assizes of 1858 for the county of Antrim, a letter of the defendant, which it appeared was written subsequently to the transaction stated in the pleadings, was relied upon by the plaintiff as a guaranty for the payment of the £55. The jury, upon a question submitted to them, found that this letter was a guaranty; and his Lordship thereupon directed a verdict for the plaintiff on the second and fourth counts, reserving liberty to defendant to move to have a verdict entered for him upon the second count. Upon the other counts the jury found a verdict for the defendant.

R. Andrews having on the part of the defendant obtained a conditional order to have a verdict entered for him on the second and fourth counts, or that judgment upon the fourth count should be arrested,

The *Solicitor-General* and *F. R. Falkiner* now showed cause.

R. Andrews and *M. Harrison*, contra.

A full statement of the material facts of the case, the arguments of counsel and the cases cited, will be found in the judgment of the Lord Chief Baron. *Cur. adv. vult.*

PIGOT, C. B. By the conditional order in this case the defendant seeks to have a verdict entered for him as to the second and fourth counts of the plaint, or (as to the fourth count) that judgment be arrested. It appears from the report of the learned Judge, that the reservation made by him, and the objection to the evidence on which it was founded, applied to the second count only. The questions before us therefore are, Whether the verdict shall be entered for the defendant on the issue as to the second count? and Whether judgment shall be arrested as to the fourth? The plaintiff desiring to retain his verdict on both counts it becomes necessary to determine both questions.[1] . . .

The defendant by the conditional order also seeks to arrest the judgment on the fourth count. The plaintiff obtained a verdict upon the issues joined on that count; and as to this no point was saved, and no objection was made at the trial. The fourth count states an agreement, by which the plaintiff agreed to execute a bill of sale of a vessel to Gribben and M'Teague for £230. That at the time of executing that agreement M'Teague omitted to pay the plaintiff £55, being the balance of the purchase-money payable on that agreement; that the plaintiff being unwilling to execute the bill of sale, the defendant expressly requested him to do so, and that in consequence of that request the plaintiff executed the bill of sale; and the count then states that "the defendant did afterwards, in consideration of the plaintiff having so executed said bill of sale, at the instance and request of the defendant, guarantee to the plaintiff the payment to him by the said John M'Teague of the sum of £55 on the day following the execution of such bill of sale." The question is Whether this count is bad? — the contract alleged being upon an executed consideration, and not being a contract which, from such consideration, the law would imply.

It is clearly established that, where a past consideration, that is, a thing previously done by the plaintiff at the request of the defendant, is one from which the law implies a promise, an express promise different from, or in addition to, that which the law implies, is *nudum pactum*, on the ground that the whole consideration is exhausted by

1 Only so much of the opinion is here given as relates to the second question. — ED.

the promise which the law implies. Among those authorities are Brown *v.* Crump,[1] Granger *v.* Collins,[2] Hopkins *v.* Logan,[3] Roscorla *v.* Thomas.[4] And this principle of law was recognized and approved in Kaye *v.* Dutton[5] by Lord Chief Justice Tindal, and also in all the stages of Elderton *v.* Emmens.[6] This is in exact conformity with the opinion of Rolle, expressed at the end of his report of Hodge *v.* Vavisor,[7] and it is involved in the decision of Docket *v.* Voyel.[8] But it has also been held, in a long series of decided cases, that where there is a past consideration, consisting of a previous act done at the request of the defendant, it will support a subsequent promise; the promise being treated as coupled with the previous request. The leading authority for this proposition is Lampleigh *v.* Brathwait.[9] But it has been so laid down in a great number of ancient authorities. In Hunt *v.* Bate,[10] called in several of the books Hunt *v.* Baker, the defendant's servant was arrested and imprisoned in the Compter in London for trespass. The plaintiff and another, in order that the defendant's business "should not go undone," bailed the servant. The defendant afterwards promised the plaintiff to save him harmless from all damages and costs that might be adjudged against him in consequence of becoming the servant's bail. The plaintiff brought an action upon this promise for the amount of damages he was compelled to pay as the servant's bail; and after verdict for the plaintiff the judgment was arrested, "because" (the report states) "there is no consideration wherefore the defendant should be charged for the debt of his servant, unless the master had first promised to discharge the plaintiff before the enlargement and mainprize made of his servant; for the master did never make request to the plaintiff for his servant to do so much, but he did it of his own head. But," the reporter adds, "in another like action on the case, brought upon a promise to pay £20, made to the plaintiff by the defendant, in consideration that the plaintiff at the special instance of the defendant had taken to wife the cousin of the defendant, that was good cause, although the marriage was executed and past before the undertaking and promise, because the marriage ensued the request of the defendant." Several cases are referred to in the notes (ascribed to Chief Justice Treby) which are appended in 3 Dyer, p. 272, to the report of the case of Hunt *v.* Bate. In two of these, Halifax *v.* Barker[11] and Sandhill *v.* Jenny[12] (not reported elsewhere), it is stated that a promise founded

1 1 Marsh. 567.
2 6 M. & W. 458.
3 5 M. & W. 241.
4 3 Q. B. 234.
5 7 Man. & G. 807; s. c. 8 Scott, N. R. 495.
6 4 C. B. 479; s. c. 6 C. B. 160; s. c. 4 H. L. Cas. 624.
7 1 Rol. Rep. 413.
8 Cro. Eliz. 885.
9 Hob. 105; s. c. 1 Sm. L. C. 118.
10 3 Dyer, 272 *b*.
11 Cro. Eliz. 741.
12 "H. 2 Jac. B. R. The plaintiff declared that, in consideration that the plaintiff had formerly married his daughter at his especial request, the defendant promised the

upon a previous matter done by the plaintiff at the defendant's request, was held insufficient; but such a promise was held binding in each of four other cases, one of which was decided by all the judges. These were Riggs v. Bullingham,[1] Baxter v. Read[2] (not reported elsewhere), Gale v. Golsbury[3] (the history of which is given in the note, 3 Dyer, 272 b), and Sidnam v. Worthington.[4] Sidnam v. Worthington was in substance the same as Hunt v. Bate, with only the difference that the plaintiff became bail at the request of the defendant. In Gale v. Golsbury, the defendant requested the plaintiff to deliver £600 worth of wine to J. S.; and the defendant, in consideration that the plaintiff at defendant's request had delivered the wine to J. S., promised to pay him if J. S. did not. The action was brought for £200 remaining unpaid; "and adjudged by all the judges of England that an action lies by Gale against Golsbury." If the law was truly declared in these decisions, they are direct authorities for the plaintiff in support of the fourth count of this plaint.

The report of the case of Hunt v. Bate in Dyer is referred to and recognized in a variety of subsequent cases, as laying down a principle of law with reference to past considerations by which those decisions were influenced. It was so referred to in Sidnam v. Worthington,[5] in Marsh and Rainsford's case,[6] in Dogget v. Dowell,[7] in Bosden v. Thinne,[8] in Jones v. Clarke,[9] in Townsend v. Hunt,[10] in the leading case of Lampleigh v. Brathwait,[11] and in Oliverson v. Wood.[12] The principle was applied in many of the old authorities collected in 1 Rolle's Abr., p. 11, *Action sur le Case* (Q.), and in the corresponding title, 1 Vin. Abr., p. 29, where the abstracts of the cases in Rolle's Abr. are translated, and several others are added: *placita*

plaintiff to pay him every year during the life of the defendant £10, &c. The plaintiff, upon *non assumpsit* pleaded, had judgment; but upon writ of error in the Exchequer Chamber the judgment was reversed, because the marriage was executed before the promise made, yet the declaration supposes that the defendant requested the plaintiff to the marriage." — ED.

[1] Cro. Eliz. 715.

[2] "M. 26 & 27 Eliz. Adjudged that where Baxter had retained Read to be miller to his aunt at ten shillings per week, debt does not lie upon this, but an action on the case; for in debt it is requisite that [the benefit] come to the party who promises; and so for the want of a *quid pro quo* debt does not lie: but by the court this will support an action on the case, for although it is not beneficial to Baxter it is chargeable to Read." — ED.

[3] Golsbury requests Gale to deliver to J. S. six hundred pounds' worth of wine: afterwards Golsbury promises Gale, in consideration that he at his request had delivered it to J. S., to pay him if J. S. did not; J. S. paid only three hundred pounds; and adjudged by all the judges of England that an action lies by Gale against Golsbury. — ED.

[4] Cro. Eliz. 42; s. c. Godb. 31; s. c. 2 Leon. 224.

[5] Godb. 31, 27 Eliz.

[6] 2 Leon. 111, 30 Eliz.

[7] Owen, 144, 43 & 44 Eliz.

[8] Yelv. 40, 1 Jac. 1.

[9] 2 Bulst. 73, 11 Jac. 1.

[10] Cro. Car. 408, 11 Car. 1.

[11] 1 Hob. 105; s. c. 1 Sm. L. C. 119, 13 Jac. 1.

[12] 3 Lev. 366.

2, 3, 4, 5, 6, 7, 8, 18, 19, 38, 40, 43, 49. Also in Com. Dig., Action on the Case upon Assumpsit (B. 12), where the cases are distinguished from those in which the action does not lie, collected at (F. 6). Coming down to later times, we find in Hayes *v.* Warren[1] a decision which has been repeatedly treated as the ruling modern authority for the proposition that assumpsit will not lie upon a promise for a past consideration, unless it be at the request of the defendant. In the report of that case in 2 Barnard., p. 141, the Lord Chief Justice (Raymond), in giving judgment, referred to the case in Cro. Eliz., p. 741 (Halifax *v.* Barker, one of the cases cited in the note to 3 Dyer, p. 272). There the action was assumpsit: "whereas, in consideration that the plaintiff, by the defendant's appointment and for his debt, shortly before paid to R. S. £60, the defendant assumed to pay it upon request." And it is reported in Cro. Eliz., p. 741, that the court held the consideration was past, and not sufficient. The Lord Chief Justice, according to the report of Hayes *v.* Warren,[2] states: "They," the court, "did agree likewise, that where there was an express request at the time of the past consideration being performed, that might in all cases be sufficient to support a subsequent promise; and therefore the Chief Justice said he could not agree the case cited out of 3 Cro., p. 741, to be law." And unquestionably that case is directly opposed (if it was not so decided upon the term "appointment," as not indicating request) to the express decisions in the same book, Cro. Eliz., pp. 42, 59, 807. It is clear that the court in Hayes *v.* Warren affirmed the principle of law laid down in Hunt *v.* Bate and Lampleigh *v.* Brathwait. And Mr. Justice Wilmot, who in Pillans *v.* Van Mierop[3] quarrels with the decision in Hayes *v.* Warren as too much restricting contracts, treats it as "now settled that, where the act is done at the request of the person promising, it will be a sufficient foundation to graft a promise upon."

This rule of law was the foundation of express decision in Wilkinson *v.* Oliveira.[4] It was recognized in Lord Denman's judgment in Eastwood *v.* Kenyon,[5] in that of Lord Chief Justice Tindal in Kaye *v.* Dutton,[6] and in that of Mr. Justice Littledale in Payne *v.* Wilson.[7] But in Roscorla *v.* Thomas[8] Lord Denman intimated an opinion which, in one construction of the language, would seem to lay down as a general rule of law, that a past or executed consideration will support no promise save one which the law would imply from it; that proposition importing, not merely that where a promise would be implied by law, and would therefore exhaust the consideration, no other

1 2 Str. 933; s. c. Ke. 117; s. c. 2 Bar. 140, 5 G. 2.
2 2 Barnard. 141.
3 3 Burr. 1671.
4 1 Bing. N. C. 490; s. c. 1 Scott, 461.
5 11 Ad. & Ell. 452.
6 7 Man. & G. 815, 816; s. c. 8 Scott, 502.
7 7 B. & C. 427.
8 3 Q. B. 234.

express promise will be sustained by the same past consideration, but, further, that no promise at all will be sustained by such consideration unless a promise would be implied from it by law, and then only such a promise as would be so implied.

The proposition in that extended sense has never been the subject of express decision. It did not arise in Brown v. Crump,[1] in Hopkins v. Logan,[2] in Granger v. Collins,[3] in Eastwood v. Kenyon,[4] in Beaumont v. Reeve,[5] in Jackson v. Cobbin,[6] in Lattimore v. Garrard,[7] in Elderton v. Emmens[8] in any of its stages, nor even in Roscorla v. Thomas. In each of these cases (except Beaumont v. Reeve) the law implied from the consideration a promise which exhausted it. In Elderton v. Emmens the Court of Common Pleas held that the express promise went beyond the implied one, and therefore could not be sustained. The Court of Exchequer Chamber and the House of Lords held that the express promise was only equivalent to the implied one, and they therefore sustained it. In Beaumont v. Reeve the declaration stated in effect that the defendant had seduced the plaintiff, and thereby rendered her incapable of procuring an honest livelihood; that they had parted, and agreed to live separate, and to have no further immoral intercourse together; and that as a compensation for the injury which the defendant had done to the plaintiff, and in consideration of the premises, he undertook and promised to pay her a yearly sum of £60. There was in that case plainly no consideration for the promise but the moral obligation to repair a wrong. No precedent request or solicitation, either express or involved in the fact of seduction, could have created any sufficient consideration; for the immoral intercourse, with or without an express request, could not have formed any legal consideration, either executory or executed, for a valid promise. It was therefore within the direct authority of Eastwood v. Kenyon,[9] in which, on a review of the authorities, it was determined that a mere moral obligation will not support an assumpsit; and this appears to be the ground of the judgments in Beaumont v. Reeve of Mr. Justice Patteson and Mr. Justice Coleridge. Lord Denman in Beaumont v. Reeve expounds his own meaning of the proposition which he states in Roscorla v. Thomas, thus: "The result is that an express promise cannot be supported by a consideration from which the law could not imply a promise, except where the express promise does away with a legal suspension or bar of a right of action which, but for such suspension or bar, would be valid;" a proposition which, by the generality of its terms, would exclude the case of a promise of a defendant, founded on a previous benefit rendered to the defendant at

[1] 1 Marsh. 567.
[2] 5 M. & W. 241.
[3] 6 M. & W. 458.
[4] 11 Ad. & Ell. 438.
[5] 8 Q. B. 483.
[6] 8 M. & W. 790.
[7] 1 Exch. 809.
[8] 4 C. B. 479; s. c. 6 C. B. 160; 4 H. L. Cas. 624.
[9] 11 Ad. & Ell. 438.

his request. I am not sure whether Baron Parke in Elderton v. Emmens,[1] or in Lattimore v. Garrard,[2] and Mr. Justice Maule in Emmens v. Elderton,[3] adopted the proposition in that extended sense, or meant to confine it, as it appears to have been confined by Lord Truro, in 4 Com. B., p. 494, and 4 H. of L. Cas., p. 672; by Mr. Justice Maule, in 4 Com. B., p. 496; by Mr. Justice Cresswell, in 4 Com. B., p. 497; and Mr. Justice Crompton, in 4 H. of L. Cas., p. 639; and as Lord Chief Justice Tindal appears to have done in Kaye v. Dutton,[4] to cases where the consideration is one from which the law does imply a promise, which therefore exhausts the consideration. The reporter certainly understood the language used in 4 Com. B., p. 496, to be so confined, as appears from his note at that page of his report; and it is perfectly plain that the decision or the judgment in which it was pronounced in Eastwood v. Kenyon, or the note to Wennall v. Adney,[5] to both of which Lord Denman refers in his judgment in Roscorla v. Thomas, give no sanction to a denial of the rule of law laid down in Hunt v. Bate, and Lampleigh v. Brathwait. Lord Denman in Eastwood v. Kenyon not only refers to that rule, and to both those cases as establishing it, but refers also to Townsend v. Hunt,[6] as recognizing and acting on the distinction which those cases establish and explain, between a past consideration with, and a past consideration without, a precedent promise; and he precedes those references by the following passage: "In holding this declaration bad, because it states no consideration but a past benefit, not conferred at the request of the defendant, we conceive that we are justified by the old common law of England." In the note to Wennall v. Adney the case of Lampleigh v. Brathwait, and the distinction there explained, is explicitly stated without any denial of its authority.

I have thought it necessary to enter into this detailed discussion, because the language of the judges, in some of the cases I have cited, is so general that it would seem to sustain the objection to the fourth count of the plaint before us. It is very much to be lamented that the language so used (as reported) was not accompanied with such explanation as would have clearly shown whether the learned judges intended to declare that in their opinion the rule laid down in Hunt v. Bate, Lampleigh v. Brathwait, and Wilkinson v. Oliveira, and in the multitude of other decided cases which I have mentioned, or the exposition of that rule in Kaye v. Dutton, was or was not law. In no one of the cases in which the language to which I have referred was used by them, was any one of those authorities named; in no one was it stated that the rule which those authorities expounded and applied was to be no longer treated as a rule of law. I own it appears to me that a rule so well and so long established, if inexpedient, ought to

[1] 6 C. B. 174. [2] 1 Exch. 809. [3] 4 H. L. Cas. 658.
[4] 7 Man. & G. 815, 816. [5] 3 Bos. & P. 249. [6] Cro. Car. 408.

be abrogated, if at all, by an act of the Legislature; or, if otherwise reversed, ought to be reversed only by the highest appellate tribunal, especially when the change would have the effect of narrowing the sphere within which mankind shall be permitted to bind each other by their deliberate dealings.

Notwithstanding then the expressions of opinion of the learned judges which I have referred to, unnecessary for determining the questions judicially before them (even if they conveyed the more extended meaning on which I have commented), I cannot, in deference to those expressions of opinion, pronounce a judgment reversing a series of decisions made by successive judges, and establishing a rule of law that has been understood to prevail for certainly more than two centuries.

We refuse to arrest the judgment on the fourth count, or enter a verdict on the second; and our order will therefore be to allow the cause shown against the whole of this conditional order.

PENNEFATHER, B., concurred.

RICHARDS, B. Wherever, in the case of a past or executed consideration, the law implies a promise, I take it that no promise can be supported other than that which the law so implies; for the promise implied by the law exhausts the whole of the consideration; and so I would explain the case of Roscorla *v.* Thomas, and some other like cases to which we have been referred. But where the law will not imply any promise, I am of opinion that in many cases an express promise, though founded on a past or executed consideration, may be supported; as if A. does an act for B. at his request, and more especially if he does it to his, A.'s, detriment, and B. afterwards, in consideration of such past act, promises to remunerate A., or the like, I am of opinion that such a promise would in a sense unite itself with B.'s previous request, and with the compliance by A. therewith, and would be perfectly valid and binding in law, though resting on a past or executed consideration.

There is a vast difference in fact and in law between a service gratuitously rendered and the like service performed or act done at the request of another person. A voluntary courtesy will not support a promise subsequently made; neither will a mere moral obligation, however sacred, where there has not been any previous request to do the act or render the service relied on. Eastwood *v.* Kenyon. But in this case the fourth count alleges that the act of the plaintiff, which is relied on as forming the consideration for the defendant's promise, was done at the request of the defendant.

No doubt it is on an executed consideration that the plaintiff relies; and if such a consideration be not sufficient in law to sustain the promise as laid in the fourth count, the motion in arrest of judgment, so far as the verdict is rested on that count, ought to prevail. But in my opinion the consideration, though a past act of the plaintiff's, is, as laid in the fourth count or paragraph, a perfectly good consideration for the defendant's promise. The cases bearing, or that could by any construction be supposed to bear, on this subject, have been already so fully and laboriously collected and observed upon by my Lord Chief Baron, in his very able and most elaborate judgment, that I think it unnecessary to refer to those cases again. Indeed the most of them, and I will say the most important of them, will be found collected and discussed in a note to Lampleigh *v.* Brathwait in the first volume of Mr. Smith's Leading Cases.

With regard to the case of Emmens *v.* Elderton, ultimately reported in 4 House of Lords Cases, there was in that case a manifest attempt on the part of the pleader to lay a promise in his declaration more extensive than the express promise contained in the agreement that it appeared in that case had been entered into between the parties; and no doubt in such a case the additional promise, I mean a promise not found within the contract of the parties (and supposing it to have been so expressed in the declaration), being, as I have mentioned, outside the agreement, and having no consideration to rest on save that which was exhausted by the previous special contract of the parties, ought not, if my view of the law be right, to be supported; and accordingly the Court of Common Pleas, before which court the case first came, taking that view of the pleading, arrested the judgment; and if the construction which the Court of Common Pleas put on the agreement as set out in the declaration in that case was correct, the decision of that court would have been upheld. But the Court of Error, and ultimately the House of Lords, reversed the decision of the Common Pleas, but expressly on the ground that the promise so relied on by the plaintiff was not necessarily to be construed as made subsequently to the agreement concluded between the parties, or as falling outside of that agreement. The promise in that case, or rather the pleader's statement of it, would admit of two different interpretations, at least so thought the House of Lords; and their Lordships, after a little straining, ultimately considered it right to give the pleading that construction that would support the verdict, rather than a construction that would defeat the action.

All I need say therefore with reference to Emmens *v.* Elderton is that the Court of Common Pleas understood the agreement as stated on the pleading in one sense, and so arrested the judgment; whereas the House of Lords, understanding the agreement as stated in the declaration in a different sense, ruled differently. But neither in the one court nor the other does the principle which I have ventured to express appear to me to have been overruled.

Upon the whole, I am of opinion that the fourth count or paragraph in the plaint is good, and that the motion in arrest of judgment ought to be refused.

I think it unnecessary to say any thing upon the other question that has been argued before us; and I fully concur in the judgment already expressed by my Lord Chief Baron upon the point, and indeed I could add nothing to his observations.

PIGOT, C. B. My brother GREENE has authorized me to state that, after some fluctuation of opinion, he concurs in the judgment of the court.

CHAPTER III.

CONDITIONAL CONTRACTS.

SECTION I.

Conditions precedent.

ANONYMOUS.

IN THE KING'S BENCH, TRINITY TERM, 1500.

[*Reported in Year Book, 15 Henry 7, folio 10 b, placitum 17.*]

NOTA PER FINEUX, C. J. If one covenant with me to serve me for a year, and I covenant with him to give him £20, if I do not say for said cause, he shall have an action for the £20, although he never serves me; otherwise, if I say he shall have £20 for said cause. So if I covenant with a man that I will marry his daughter, and he covenants with me to make an estate to me and his daughter, and to the heirs of our two bodies begotten; though I afterwards marry another woman, or his daughter marry another man; yet I shall have an action of covenant against him, to compel him to make this estate; but if the covenant be that he will make the estate to us two for said cause, then he shall not make the estate until we are married. And such was the opinion of the court. And REDE, J., said it was so without doubt.

BROCAS' CASE.

IN THE QUEEN'S BENCH, MICHAELMAS TERM, 1588.

[*Reported in 3 Leonard, 219.*]

BROCAS, lord of a manor, covenanted with his copyholder to assure to him and his heirs, the freehold and inheritance of his copyhold. And the said copyholder in consideration of the same performed, covenanted to pay such a sum. It was the opinion of the whole Court, that the said copyholder is not tied to pay the said sum before the assurance made and the covenant performed. But if the words had been, *in consideration of the said covenant to be performed*, then he is bounden to pay the money presently, and to have his remedy over by covenant.

ANONYMOUS.

IN THE COMMON PLEAS, MICHAELMAS TERM, 1590.

[*Reported in* 4 *Leonard*, 50.]

A LEASE for years is made by deed indented, rendering rent, and the lessor covenants that the lessee, paying his rent, shall enjoy the land demised for the whole term; the lessee did not pay the rent, and afterwards is ejected by a title paramount. By WALMESLY and WINDHAM, JJ., that the covenant is conditional, and that the lessee should not have advantage of it, if he did not perform the condition, which is created by this word "paying." PERIAM, J., was strongly to the contrary, viz., that the word "paying" did not create a condition.

RAYNAY *v.* ALEXANDER.

IN THE KING'S BENCH, MICHAELMAS TERM, 1605.

[*Reported in Yelverton*, 76.]

THE plaintiff declared that, whereas the defendant was possessed of seventeen tods of wool, and whereas *colloquium fuit* betwixt them for fifteen tods of the seventeen tods to be chosen by the plaintiff, the defendant, in consideration of £6 to be paid on such a day, &c., promised to deliver the plaintiff *prædictas* fifteen tods of wool; and said *in facto* that he was ready at the day to pay the £6, yet the defendant had not delivered the plaintiff the fifteen tods of wool, to his damage, &c. And upon *non assumpsit* pleaded, it was found for the plaintiff. And it was shown in arrest of judgment, that the declaration was not good, because the plaintiff had not shown that he had chosen fifteen tods out of the seventeen; and that is *quasi* a condition precedent, and an act to be first performed by the plaintiff, before the defendant is bound by his promise to do any thing. *Quod fuit concessum per totam Curiam.* But *per* POPHAM, C. J. If the defendant had sold one of the tods of wool before election made by the plaintiff, that had destroyed the election and made the promise absolute, and had been a breach of it. The same law if the defendant would not have permitted the plaintiff to see the wool that he might make election; for that had excused the act to be done by the plaintiff, and had been a default in the defendant. And the matter aforesaid is much enforced by the word *prædictas* in the declaration; for that can be referred to nothing but the communication, by which the plaintiff of his own showing ought to make election. Then the plaintiff, omitting it in his declaration, shows the fault is in himself, which ought to be removed before he can charge the defendant. But if the communication had been that the plaintiff should choose fifteen tods of the seventeen, and the plaintiff had declared the promise to be to deliver fifteen tods generally, without saying *prædictas*, there, if the promise had been found, the plaintiff should have judgment; for the *colloquium* might have been conditional and the promise absolute. *Quod nota.* But the judgment was *Nil capiat per billam.*

SLATER *v.* STONE.

IN THE KING'S BENCH, MICHAELMAS TERM, 1622.

[Reported in Croke James, 645.]

COVENANT. Whereas he by indenture let and demised a house in Barleyhurst to the defendant for twenty-one years from Michaelmas following, and the defendant covenanted, *quod ab et post emendationem et reparationem dicti messuagii* by the plaintiff, his heirs and assigns, he at his proper costs and charges, as need should require, *bene et sufficienter repararet et sustineret* the said messuages during the said term, and so at the end of the term would leave them well and sufficiently repaired; and allegeth the breach, that at the time of the demise and beginning of the term one dove-house, parcel of the premises, was in good and sufficient reparations; and that the defendant *voluntariè* during the term suffered it to stand uncovered for a year, whereby it became very ruinous, and afterwards pulled it down, so as it became of no value.

The defendant pleaded, that he did not suffer it to stand uncovered, nor pulled it down, &c.; and thereupon they were at issue, and found for the plaintiff.

It was moved, in arrest of judgment, that the breach is not well assigned: for the covenant is, "that *ab et post* the plaintiff hath repaired it, that he would maintain it in reparations;" so the defendant is not to repair it until the plaintiff hath first repaired it.

And the whole Court (*absente* LEA, C. J.) was of that opinion. And although it was objected that the plaintiff, having alleged it to be in good reparations *tempore dimissionis et in initio termini*, needed not to repair it when it was not necessary, but that refers to all parts of the house which require reparation, yet *non allocatur:* for the Court held, that the covenant being "*quod ab et post reparationem* by the plaintiff, then he would sustain," &c., it is conditional that the plaintiff ought first to repair it: so, although it were in good reparation at the beginning, if it afterwards happen to decay, the plaintiff is first to repair it before the defendant is bound thereto. Wherefore it was adjudged for the defendant.

HOLDIPP, *Executor of* DOWSE, *v.* OTWAY.

IN THE KING'S BENCH, EASTER TERM, 1670.

[*Reported in 2 Williams' Saunders*, 106.]

ERROR, by Holdipp, executor of Dowse, plaintiff, against Otway, defendant, to reverse a judgment in an action of debt in the Common Pleas, in which Otway, then plaintiff, declared against Holdipp as executor, &c., upon a bill obligatory, made by the testator, 24th Nov. 1650, whereby the testator acknowledged himself to be indebted to the plaintiff in £68, which he covenanted and promised to pay to the plaintiff, or his assigns, as soon as several bills of costs of the testator, expended in the prosecuting of several suits in law and equity for Mr. Robert Riggs and Margery Riggs, deceased, should be duly audited, debated, and settled by two attorneys, to be indifferently chosen between them to examine and state the accounts of the said bills of costs, the plaintiff paying to the testator his proportionable part, that is to say, the third part of the said bills, to be in form aforesaid debated and settled. And the plaintiff, by protestation that he was always ready to perform all things on his part, and also by protestation that there was not any sum of money due to the testator upon any bill of costs by him expended in prosecuting any suits for the said Robert Riggs and Margery Riggs, the plaintiff in fact said, that neither the testator in his lifetime, nor the defendant upon his death, did ever show or produce any bills of costs, expended in the prosecution of the said suits, to be audited, debated, and settled according to the tenor of the said bill; whereby an action accrued to the plaintiff to demand and have the said £68 of the defendant: and upon this declaration the plaintiff had judgment by default in the Common Pleas:[1] . . . whereupon the defendant brought a writ of error into the King's Bench; and *Saunders*, of counsel with the plaintiff in the writ of error, assigned an error in the declaration, that the plaintiff in the Common Pleas had not sufficiently entitled himself to his action for the £68 on the bill obligatory mentioned in the declaration; for it was not to be paid until the bills of costs were debated and settled by two attorneys, to be indifferently chosen by the testator and the plaintiff, Otway; and Otway, the plaintiff in the Common Pleas, has averred that the testator had not shown or produced any bills of costs: which is nothing to the purpose; for he was not bound to show or produce any bills, except only to the two attorneys to be chosen to examine and state them; but the plaintiff in the Common Pleas ought to have averred that there were two attorneys chosen, and the testator did not produce the bills of costs to them to be settled, or that the plaintiff had chosen one attorney, and required the testator to choose another, to examine and settle the bills, which he refused to do; whereby it might have appeared to the court that there was no fault in the plaintiff, but a fault in the testator. But now it does not appear upon the record that the moneys are yet payable; for they were payable upon the settling of the bills of costs by the two attorneys; and this does not appear to be done, nor that there was any fault in the testator why it was not done, and therefore the £68 does not appear to be yet due according to the tenor of the said bill obligatory. And of this opinion was the whole court; whereupon a rule was given to reverse the judgment *nisi*, &c., but *Jones*, of counsel with the defendant in the writ of error, said that he could not maintain the judgment; and therefore he prayed that it should be reversed for the expedition of his client, who intended to bring a new action; wherefore the judgment was reversed absolutely.[2]

THORPE *v.* THORPE.

In the King's Bench, Easter Term, 1701.

[*Reported in* 12 *Modern*, 455.]

Error from the Court of Common Pleas of a judgment in an action on the case, wherein the plaintiff declared, that the defendant had and held of him by way of mortgage two closes of copyhold lands;

[1] This case has been modified by the omission of irrelevant matter. — Ed.

[2] Cited and approved in French *v.* Campbell, 2 H. Bl. 178–80. — Ed.

and that there was a discourse between them concerning the plaintiff's releasing his equity of redemption therein to the defendant, and concerning divers sums of money due from the plaintiff to the defendant upon the said mortgage; upon which the plaintiff did agree with the defendant that he would release to him the said equity of redemption, in consideration of which the defendant did agree with the plaintiff to pay him seven pounds above all that was due; and that, in consideration that the plaintiff promised the defendant to perform all of his side, the defendant promised the plaintiff to perform of his side; and avers that he did perform all on his, the plaintiff's, side, but that the defendant paid one pound seven shillings of the said seven pounds, and no more, &c.

To this the defendant pleads in bar, that long after the promise, viz., 29th July, 1694, the plaintiff did, by indenture made between him and the defendant, release to the defendant "all manner of actions, suits, debts, duties, sum and sums of money, and all demands whatsoever, which ever he had, or he, his heirs, executors, or assigns ever should have, for or by reason of any thing, matter, or demand whatsoever."

Upon *oyer* of this deed of release, it recited the said mortgage, and released "all provisos therein, and all his estate, right, title, and interest in the said close, both in law and equity;" and then follows the foregoing clause.

And upon this the plaintiff demurred, and judgment for the plaintiff in the Court of Common Pleas.

Cowper for the plaintiff in error objected to the declaration, that the consideration set forth in it was not sufficient to support a promise; for, though equity of redemption be a thing pretty well known, and for the most part valuable, yet some may be not of any value, and this may be of them; and therefore it was necessary to show that it was of some value; and for an example of an equity of redemption without value, he put this case: If a mortgage be till so much money be raised by the mortgagee out of the profits; here the mortgagor has an equity of redeeming by payment of the money and charges, and yet it is of no value to the other to have it released; but to the contrary, the redemption there would be rather a benefit to him.

Secondly, he objected that it did not appear by the count that the mortgage was forfeited, and then the plaintiff had no equity of redemption. *Ergo*, no consideration for the promise; *ergo*, &c. *Vide* 2 Saund. 136; Style, 248.

Then the plea in bar is good, for the release is full in words, and subsequent to the promise. But, say they, the money was to be paid in consideration of the release; therefore the release, which created the duty, cannot *in eodem instanti* extinguish it. To this I answer, that the payment of the money does not arise from the release, but from the promise; and the promise, and not the release, being the consideration of the debt, action lies upon the mutual promises before the release. *Ergo*, the release comes after the cause of action, and consequently destroys it. March, 75. Where promises are their own mutual considerations, there needs no performance to support the action. Hob. 88. In consideration that the plaintiff promised to deliver the defendant a cow, the defendant promised the plaintiff fifty shillings; in an action for the money there needs no averment of delivery of the cow, or *vice versâ*. Cro. El. 543. A declaration, that in consideration A. was indebted to B. by bills, and that he promised to deliver him up the bills, he promised to give him good security by bond for the money, and avers the delivery of the bills; the defendant traverses the delivery, and on demurrer adjudged against him, because not material; and it was not the consideration of the assumpsit, but the promise to deliver was it. Cro. El. 703, *simile*.

But Cro. El. 889, the promise is, *super solutionem* of such a sum, to do, &c.; therefore the thing not demandable before payment. So is Cro. Car. 19. So that if here the cause of action did arise upon the promise before any release made, the release subsequent clearly discharges it; *secus* not, if there were no more in the case. And if the release be what gives them cause of action, then they should show a release made, or a tender of it; and not generally, as here, that they have performed all of their side.

But it is objected that, although an action had accrued to the plaintiff immediately upon the promise, yet this release should not discharge it; for that the release shall be taken according to the intent of the parties, which was only to discharge the equity of redemption; and the general words of it shall be restrained and qualified by the foregoing special words. But I answer, that after releasing the equity of redemption by express words, there are in the self-same clause general words of "all actions and demands;" which I agree are qualified by the special words and intent of the parties. And then comes the clause in question, distinctly and separately from the first, releasing "all actions and demands;" and this clause would be entirely useless if they be applied to the first, because the first has a general clause in itself to serve it as a wall or muniment, and so stands in no need of any more. 2 Roll. Ab. 409. The general words, that are restrained by the special words, are part of the same clause and sentence, and not, as here, distinct and separate. 3 Mod. 277. Suppose A. recited in a deed, that whereas B. owes him ten pounds, and releases thereby "the said ten pounds, and all actions and demands," and further proceeds and releases him "all debts, duties, actions, and demands," would this last clause be rather entirely rejected than extended to any thing but the ten pounds? and upon this diversity Hetley, 9 and 15, Aubry's Case, is distinguishable from the present case.

Cheshire, contra. As to the want of averring that we have made a release, they in their replication show that we have done it, and set it forth; and that supplies that defect, if any; for many times the fault of a declaration may be helped by the defendant's plea; as the want of a venue by pleading a release. Cro. Eliz. 68, Debt upon a bond. And it did appear by the bond that the day of payment was not yet come; the defendant pleaded a release, and found against him, and plaintiff had judgment; for that by pleading the release he waived the other advantage; and 9 Edw. 4, there cited, Debt by an executor; the defendant pleaded that the testator had made two executors, and that one of them released to him; and issue thereupon found for the plaintiff, who had judgment, though the defendant might have abated the action, because he waived that advantage by his plea. 3 Cro. 111; 2 Keb. 766; 1 Vent. 114, 126.

And this court will take notice what an equity of redemption is, as well as a court of equity of trusts and mortgages. 4 Leon. 225; 1 Vent. 41. That the court will take notice of an equitable consideration; and we need not show what our equity of redemption was, or how created. For first, they requested we should release such a thing to them; and it cannot be imagined they would do so if we had none. Indeed, if it had appeared to the court that our equity was of no value, it would have been the stronger against us; though even so, there being something to be done by us that would be a trouble to us, it would have been a good consideration of a promise. And if in the case quoted out of Saunders, the heir had recited that he was bound by the bond, the court would intend it so, and give judgment against him. And in all the cases that have been put of the other side, it did appear to the court that there was nothing of value, or any pain or trouble to the plaintiff, to be the consideration of the promise; and there is a diversity between a thing's appearing not to be valuable, and its not appearing to be valuable; for a recital of it will help it in the one case, but not in the other. Raym. 19. To make a promise good, the one party, viz., he that does promise, ought to have some charge or trouble by the performance, or the other some advantage.

And the words of release are not sufficient to discharge the promise, because it was not in demand at the time of the release; for the release was a condition precedent, whereupon the demand did arise to the plaintiff, and therefore the release could not destroy that to which it gave birth.

But suppose an action did arise upon the mutual promises, yet each party had a reasonable time to perform; and perhaps each had time for his life, if not hastened by request; and neither is alleged here. Indeed the promise as soon as made was releasable by the word "promise," but not by the words "actions or demands," at least till a convenient time after; which is not alleged to have been between the promise and release.

And it is not absolutely necessary the words insisted on in this release must be rejected as fruitless, without they are extended to release this demand; for it may be, the mortgagee might be accountable to the mortgagor for some of the profits of the lands, which might be released by the words.

HOLT, C. J. A release of an equity of redemption is a good consideration for a promise; and we can take notice of an equity of redemption, and that it is a valuable thing. But suppose it were not a thing valuable, and the case were this. A. is possessed of Black Acre, to which B. has no manner of right, and A. desires B. to release him all his right to Black Acre, and promises him, in consideration thereof, to pay so much money, surely this is a good consideration and a good promise, for it puts A. to the trouble of making a release. Then where the doing a thing will be a good consideration, a promise to do that thing will be so too; and though the want of an averment that a release was made would have been bad if demurred to, yet it is now helped by going over and pleading. If one covenant to do several things in a certain deed agreed on, and in the end bind himself in a penalty for so doing, and debt is brought for the penalty, and shows generally that he has done nothing of what is agreed on, this would be bad on demurrer, but a plea over cures it. So if one covenant that, if J. S. do such and such things, that he will pay him so much money, J. S. brings action, and says, generally that he performed all the things, this would be bad on demurrer, but curable by pleading over. Indeed, this being a general distinct clause seems to diversify this case from all the cases before put, where the general words, restrained by the precedent particular ones, are in the same clause with the particulars.

At another day this Term, after great consideration, the whole Court came to one resolution, which was thus delivered:

HOLT, C. J. We all agree that the promise was not discharged by this release. It was urged at the bar by Mr. Cowper that if the plaintiff might have founded an action upon the mutual promise and agreement before any performance on his part, that certainly this release would have barred him; and the consequence is very true and necessary, if that were the case. And by the same reason, if he could not bring an action before such time as he had made a release, there is no color for the release to bar him; for till he makes the release in this case, if he has no title to the seven pounds, then till release there is no right of action; and then they do not lie in demand till release; and that a release of "all demands" will not release a thing that does not lie in demand at that time, *vide* 2 Cro. 171; 5 Co. 70, Hoe's Case. A release to bail in the King's Bench before judgment against the principal, is not good, because till then the cause of action is uncertain, and therefore not demandable.

So the whole question will be here, Whether the plaintiff could have an action before the release? And as to that it has been urged, that in this case there were mutual promises, and the one promise is the consideration of the other, and that then he that brings the action needs not aver any performance of his side; and this likewise would be a true and necessary consequence, if the premises were true. But where the one promise is the consideration of the other, and where the performance, and not the promise, is it, is to be gathered from the words and nature of the agreement, and depends entirely thereupon; for if in this case there were a positive promise that one should release his equity of redemption, and on the other side that the other would pay seven pounds, then the one might bring his action without any averment of performance; but this agreement is not so, but that the plaintiff should release his equity of redemption, in consideration whereof the defendant was to pay him seven pounds; so that the release is the consideration, and therefore being executory is a condition precedent, which must be averred. And whereas there seems to be a variance in the books upon this learning, it will be fit on this occasion to settle it; and I agree the case in Hob. 88 to be good law, for there is a positive agreement that one shall deliver a cow to the other, and that the other shall give him so much money, and therefore the action lies for either side without performance of his promise; but if by the agreement A. were to deliver B. a cow, and that for it B. were to deliver him a horse, there the delivery of the cow would be a condition precedent, and therefore ought to be performed before A. can bring his action; and upon this diversity the books are reconcilable. 15 Hen. 7, 10, pl. 17. If A. covenant with B. to serve him for a year, and B. covenant with A. to pay him ten pounds, there A. shall maintain an action for the ten pounds before any service; but if B. had covenanted to pay ten pounds for the said service, there A. could not maintain an action for the money before the service performed. And there is great reason for this diversity; for when one promises, agrees, or covenants, to do one thing for another, there is no reason he should be obliged to do it till that thing for which he promised to do it be done; and the word "for" is a condition precedent in such cases. But upon this head some diversities are to be observed.

First. If there be a day set for the payment of money, or doing the thing which one promises, agrees, or covenants to do, for another thing, and that day happens to incur before the time the thing for which the promise, agreement, or covenant, is made, is to be performed by the tenor of the agreement; there though the words be "that the party shall pay the money," or "do the thing for such a thing," or "in consideration of such a thing," after the day is past the other shall have an action for the money or other thing, although the thing for which the promise, agreement, or covenant was made, be not performed; for it would be repugnant there to make it a condition precedent, and therefore they are in that case left to mutual remedies, on which, by the express words of the agreement, they have depended. *Vide* 48 Edw. 3, 2, 3, cited in Ughtred's Case,[1] where the diversity is taken when there are mutual remedies and not; it is thus put in that book: Sir Richard Pool covenants with Sir Ralph Tolcelser to serve him with three esquires in the wars of France. Sir Ralph Tolcelser covenants, in consideration of those services, to pay him so much money; and there, it is said, action will lie for the money without any services performed. But if you look into the book at large, you will find it was upon the diversity which I have taken; for the case in 48 Edw. 3, 2, 3, is, Richard Pool covenants with Ralph Tolcelser to serve him with three esquires in the wars of France, and Ralph Tolcelser covenanted with him to pay him so much money for the service; and it was further agreed that twenty marks of the money should be paid in England, at a day certain, before they went for France, and the rest by quarterly payments, which might likewise incur before the service; and upon action brought by Sir Richard Pool it was objected, that the service was not performed; but there was no room for that objection upon the diversity which I have taken, the money by the agreement being made payable at a day certain before the service was to have been performed. 1 Vent. 147. Covenant, that in case A. would let B. enjoy land for a certain term of years, for the enjoyment he would pay him so much money before the expiration of the years. 3 Leo. 156. Covenant to pay so much money, the other making him a good estate in such lands: held the making the estate to be a condition precedent, and therefore to be averred. 1 Saund. 319 is upon the same diversity: An agreement was to let a house to the plaintiff, with certain brewing vessels; the plaintiff covenants to pay so much money for it before Midsummer-day; and here, because a day certain was appointed for the payment, though no assurance was made of the house, &c., yet an action lay for the money. If A. covenant to make an assurance of lands to B., who covenants to pay him ten pounds in consideration thereof, there he is not bound to pay the money before the assurance made; but if he had covenanted to pay the money in consideration of the covenant to make the assurance, he would be liable to an action immediately.

Secondly. If there be a day for the payment of the money, or doing of other act for another, and that day is to be after the performance of the thing for which the promise, &c., was made, there, if the agreement be to pay the money, or do other thing, "for," or "in consideration," or such other words that would make a condition precedent, there such things, for the doing or performing of which the other agrees to pay the money, or do other thing, must be averred to maintain an action;

[1] 7 Co. 10 b.

and for this Sir W. Jones, 218. The executor of A. brought an action on the case against B., declaring, that in consideration A. in his lifetime did promise to assure certain lands to B. before Michaelmas next, B. promised to pay him so much money for the land; so the assurance was to be made before Michaelmas, and the money was to be paid for the land, and consequently after Michaelmas, for A. had time till Michaelmas to make the assurance; and because the assurance was to have been made first, and the money by agreement to be paid for the land, though there were mutual promises, yet it was adjudged the action would not lie for the money without making the assurance first. This case, as it is there reported, is intricate, and requires consideration to make this construction upon it; but upon examination it is a full authority in point. Dy. 76, pl. 30. A. agrees to deliver B. a hawk at Midsummer, for which he agrees to pay him a horse at Michaelmas; there, if a hawk be not delivered at Midsummer, there shall be no horse delivered at Michaelmas, nor any remedy for it. Ughtred's case has afforded a ground for a variety of opinions upon this question; but such as seem against these diversities laid down by me shall receive a full answer. And in 1 Roll. Ab. 414, are several cases which have been urged against me; the first is said to have been in Michaelmas Term, in the seventh year of James the First, and it was a charter-party between A. and B., by which A. covenants to go a voyage, and take in several ladings at several ports beyond the seas, and return with them home; B. covenants to pay A. for all that voyage £147 at a day, whether after or before the voyage is left in doubt by the book; and there it was adjudged, there might have an action lain for the money without averment of performance of the voyage; and this seems an authority in point against me. But first, it does not appear there, but that the day of payment was before the voyage performed; but a full answer to it is, that there was a writ of error brought, and that judgment reversed for want of an averment. *Vide* 1 Bulst. 167. Rolle reports the judgment in the Common Pleas, in the seventh year of James the First; but it seems had not seen the reversal thereof, which was in the ninth year of James the First, two years after, as it is in Bulstrode, where it is adjudged, that *pro totâ transfretatione* is a condition precedent, and that its being in mutual covenants makes no alteration. Then there is 1 Roll. Abr. 415, said to be in Michaelmas Term, in the fifteenth year of Charles the First; and it seems also against me in point: There were articles of agreement made by A. in behalf of B. of the one part, and C. of the other part, where it was covenanted by A., that B. for consideration hereafter expressed should convey certain lands to C.; C. on his part, for the consideration aforesaid, covenanted to pay B. £166; and it was adjudged, that the assuring the land was not a condition precedent. But this case does not come up to ours; for there is an express covenant, that (for consideration hereafter expressed) B. would convey to C., and C. (upon consideration aforesaid) covenants to pay the money; and that must be forasmuch as A. hath covenanted that B. should assure lands for consideration hereafter mentioned, that is, that B. hath covenanted to pay so much money; for it is *pro consideratione prædictâ;* and the question is, What is meant by the words *pro consideratione præd.?* It is not said, "for consideration of conveyance of the land," but *pro consideratione præd.*, which must be understood in consideration of the agreement that B. should convey, &c.; for the one covenants for consideration hereafter mentioned, which must be the covenant for payment of the money, and the other covenants for consideration aforesaid, which must be that A. covenanted that B. should convey. But I must needs say, there is another home case; it was also in the time of King Charles the First, and it was on mutual promises to stand to an award between A. and B., and laid in consideration A. on his part did promise to stand to the award, B. on his part did promise to stand to it; and the award was made, that A. should pay B. £10, in consideration whereof B. should enter into an obligation to release unto A. all actions; A. brings an action against B. for not entering into the obligation according to the award; and he did aver, that he had done all on his part, but that B. had not entered into the obligation; and the exception was taken, that there was no averment of the payment of the £10, in consideration whereof he was to have entered into the bond; but it was said, there needed no averment, and this is full against me. But Rolle himself there says, the court were divided. And 1 Cro. 384 gives a quite contrary report of the case, and says: Jones and Berkely held it a condition precedent against Croke; so I rather believe Croke, who was one of the judges, and tells you himself was of a contrary opinion. And as to Haye's case, which is also in 1 Roll. Abr. *ubi supra*, it is reported, 1 Cro. 433, and it has no such point in it. These authorities, therefore, are well answered. There are some other scattered authorities in the books of this kind. But let us now see the reason of the thing. What is the reason that mutual promises shall bear an action without performance? One's bargain is to be performed according as he makes it. If he make a bargain, and rely on the other's covenant or promise to have what he would have done to him, it is his own fault. If the agreement be, that A. shall have the horse of B., and A. agree that B. shall have his money, they may make it so; and then there needs no averment of performance to maintain an action on either side; but if it appear by the agreement that the plain intent of either party was to have the thing to be done to him performed before his doing what he undertakes of his side, it must be then averred; as, where a man agrees to give so much money for a horse, it is plain he meant to have the horse first, and, therefore, he says the money shall be given for the horse. And it would be very dangerous to make every cursory agreement of parties to amount to mutual promises to bear an action without averment of performance; and, therefore, if two meet, and the one has a horse to sell, and the other would buy one, and they agree on the price, and then part without any earnest, or reducing the matter solemnly into writing, there, though there be no words of condition precedent, such cursory agreement ought not to be admitted as evidence of a mutual agreement; and it ought not to pass for a contract, but rather for a bare communication. *Vide* Dy. 30; —, 24; Style, 32. But if there be a solemn transaction, as writing, as that A. would deliver his horse to B., and no time appointed, and that B. should pay so much money to A., there, if there be not the word "for," or other words of condition precedent, a mutual action will lie, without averment of performance; but if it be only a discourse, without the solemnity of writing, earnest, &c., it ought not to be allowed. There is a case in 2 Mod. 33. In assumpsit the plaintiff declared, that in consideration that he promised to assign to the defendant his interest in certain land, the defendant promised to pay him *proinde* so much money, and averred that he offered to assign the interest; but that matter being not well pleaded, the question was, whether it was necessary to aver performance; and held, on the reason of Ughtred's case, that it was not. And this will be a light to the reasons of North v. Wild [Ware v. Chappell?] there. *Vide* Style, 186. Covenants were between A. and B., that A. should bring 500 soldiers to such a place, by a day certain, to be transported; and that B. should attend there then with ships to transport them, and both parties failed; and the question was, Whether, though A. had brought no soldiers, B. had broke his covenant, in not being ready with ships? And held, that B. had broke his covenant, though A. had not brought the soldiers. But this differs from our case; for there are two distinct acts to be done, one is to be ready with the soldiers, and the other with ships; and the performance of the one does not depend upon the other; the doing of the one is not the reward for the doing of the other; but they are distinct acts, and each party to do his part; there was also a day appointed. And this is not a hard case, for they are mutual acts not depending the one on the other. But in our case the money was to be paid for the release, and a vast difference. And the £7 being to be paid in consideration of making the release, the words "in consideration" make a condition precedent, which, till performed, does not entitle the plaintiff to action. Then the £7 were not demandable here, and consequently not dischargeable by the general release of all demands.

Another objection was, that the plaintiff had not averred a release given, or tendered by him, as he ought to have done. But here sufficient appears that it was done; for he avers performance of all that was to be done on his side; and that general averment, though informal, and beside wants time and place, for which it had been bad on demurrer, is helped by the defendant's passing it over and pleading a release, whereby he admits the plaintiff had a cause of action. And there are stronger cases than this in the books, where pleading over has helped an insufficient declaration. 3 H. 6, 8. Debt upon indentures, in which there was a penalty in which the defendant did bind himself, if he did not perform all the covenants in the said indentures; and regularly in such cases the way is, for the plaintiff to set forth the indentures, and to assign breach of one of the covenants in certain; and in debt for the penalty he said generally that the defendant had broke all the covenants in that indenture, without showing any one in certain; the defendant pleaded a collateral matter in bar, and adjudged the declaration had been bad on demurrer, but that the plea over cured it, though the breach was double and uncertain. 9 H. 6, 16, 19. And it was so adjudged in this court, in Bernard *v.* Michel.[1] But a full authority is that of Vivian *v.* Shipping:[2] though they agreed the money awarded was to be paid before the other was to enter into the obligation to the plaintiff, yet the plaintiff did not expressly aver payment, but generally, as here, that he had performed all on his side; and that was adjudged good after plea pleaded. So we all agree the judgment ought to be affirmed; for there was no money due to the plaintiff till release of the equity of redemption, and therefore none demandable till then, and consequently a release of all demands could not bar it.

NOTE. In this case Cowper offered this diversity in relation to mutual promises, that where the promise is of a valuable thing to the defendant, there such promise, without any performance, may be a good consideration; but where the promise is not of a thing valuable, but may be a consideration because a trouble to the party promising, there such promise, without a performance, cannot be a consideration, because such promise cannot be a trouble.

But *per* HOLT, C. J. No diversity at all; but the cases are the same upon the learning laid down above.

LOCK *v.* WRIGHT.

IN THE KING'S BENCH, TRINITY TERM, 1723.

[*Reported in* 1 *Strange*, 569.]

THE plaintiff declares, that the defendant by his writing indented agreed with the plaintiff, that he (the defendant) would accept of the plaintiff £500 fourth subscription so soon as the receipts should be

[1] 1 Vent. 114, 126, 2 Keb. 754, 766.

[2] Cro. Car. 384.

delivered out by the company, and would pay for the same £950, on the 5th of November next after the date of the writing. Then he avers, that the defendant did not pay the money at the day.

The defendant demurs generally, and Mr. *Lingard*, *pro defendente*, objected that the plaintiff had not shown the delivery of any receipts, or an impossibility of doing it, and cited, 1 Lutw. 245; Salk. 171.

Probyn, contra, answered, that there were mutual remedies, and therefore it need not be shown. 1 Saund. 319; 1 Lev. 274.

EYRE, J., doubted whether here was a mutual remedy, for the plaintiff does not covenant to deliver, but the other only to accept; to which Fortescue, J., inclined. *Sed per* PRATT, C. J. The time for payment of the money is certain at all events; but as for the delivery of the receipts, that was left uncertain, because it was impossible to fix the time for that, and if the defendant has made a foolish bargain in undertaking to pay the money on the 6th of November, whether he had the receipts or not, we cannot help him. The nature of these contracts is for the other party to give a deed obliging himself to deliver the stock, but even upon this agreement I should think the defendant would have his remedy. In the case of a deed-poll, if the lessee enters and enjoys the land, the other shall maintain debt for rent, and yet the whole is the words of the lessor.

Pasch. 8 Geo. It was argued a second time by *West*, *pro defendente*. It will not be disputed but that generally speaking the word *pro* will create a condition precedent, 1 Vent. 147; 2 Mod. 33; 1 Lev. 87; Salk. 112, and that it will do so in this case, if I can clear it from two objections that have been made. 1. That here is a mutual remedy; and, 2. That here is a particular day fixed for the payment of the money.

As to the first, that is begging the question, for I take it there is not a mutual remedy, the words being the words of the defendant only, "That he will accept the subscription, and pay for the same;" which lays the plaintiff under no obligation to deliver the receipts. 1 Saund. 320.

2. As to the second objection, that here is a particular day appointed for payment of the money, I do admit, that if it appeared upon the contract that such a day must of necessity happen before the receipts could be delivered, it would then be very difficult to answer it; but that is not this case, for the company might if they pleased have given out the receipts; and that brings the case within the distinction laid down by Lord Chief Justice Holt in the case of Thorpe *v.* Thorpe, Salk. 171. Besides, it is observable that this is an entire covenant to accept and pay, so that he is not to pay till he can accept. Lutw. 490.

Reeve, contra. I admit the first part of Mr. West's argument, but insist on the two objections he has taken notice of, as sufficient to bring this case out of the reach of that general doctrine.

Here is a certain sum to be paid at a certain day, and that too before the other part of the contract could possibly be performed. The court will take notice of the South Sea Acts, and by that of 7 Geo. stat. 2, it appears the receipts could not be delivered by the 6th of November; so that this case falls within the first distinction of Thorpe *v.* Thorpe, that if a day be appointed for payment of the money, and that day is to happen before the thing can be performed, an action may be brought for the money before the thing be done; because it appears the party relied upon his remedy.

But then, say they, here is no mutual remedy. But I take it that, this being an agreement by indenture, the court will intend it was executed by both parties. As to the cases, they are all of parol agreements, where a consideration must appear to make it a binding promise; but here the action will be maintainable on the bare covenant to pay, without any consideration at all, and therefore the *pro*, &c., may be left out.

ADJOURNATUR. And this term PRATT, C. J., delivered the resolution of the court.

This is an action upon a deed-poll made by the defendant, and whereby he covenants to accept so much stock, and to pay for the same; and the plaintiff in an action for the money has not averred a delivery or tender of the stock, and for this fault we are all of opinion the declaration is not good.

The intent of the parties appears to be, that one should have the money, and the other the stock; and not that either should perform his part of the agreement, and lay himself at the mercy of the other for the equivalent. This is not a covenant entered into by both parties, upon which each will have his mutual remedy; but it is the deed-poll of the defendant only; and therefore, though upon delivery or tender of the stock the plaintiff will have his remedy for the money, yet the defendant on the other side, upon payment of the money, will have no remedy to compel the delivery of the stock; and having no such remedy he shall not be obliged to pay the money till the consideration for which it is payable is performed.

The word *pro* will be either a condition precedent or subsequent, as will best answer the intent of the parties: in this case it must be a condition precedent, because otherwise the intention of the defendant to have the stock for his money can never take effect; and this is proved by 7 Co. 10, and 1 Inst. 204, where the annuity *pro una acra*, says the book, supposes the acre to be first granted.

The case of Callonel *v.* Briggs (Salk. 112) was not so strong, for there was a promise to transfer, which gave a mutual remedy, but yet Holt, C. J., held the plaintiff to show a tender, because that was the consideration for the defendant's payment of the money. And the case he there puts, of the sale of a horse for £10, is exactly the same with this.

The resolutions that were mentioned at the bar of the case of Thorpe *v.* Thorpe, are all founded on great reason; and the first of them is agreeable to the resolution of this case, which is an executory contract, where one is to do the act, and for the doing thereof the other is to pay.

And this difference between a mutual covenant and a deed-poll is likewise taken and allowed in the case of Pordage *v.* Cole, 1 Saund. 320, where the court were of opinion the defendant had his remedy, "otherwise (says the book) it would have been, if the deed had been the words of the defendant only," which is this case.

For these reasons we are all of opinion the defendant must have judgment.

JOHN THOMAS *v.* MARGARET CADWALLADER, *Administratrix of* CHARLES CADWALLADER.

IN THE COMMON PLEAS, NOVEMBER 24, 1744.

[*Reported in Willes*, 496.]

COVENANT. The plaintiff declares upon an indenture dated 10th of February, 1720, whereby the plaintiff and one Rebecca Thomas, since deceased, demised to Charles Cadwallader a messuage and tenement in Bishop's Castle with the stable, mill, garden, and backside or yard thereto belonging (except as therein excepted), to hold the same from the 25th of March then next for twenty-one years under the rent of £10 a year, payable at Michaelmas and Lady-day. And the said Charles did thereby covenant for himself, his executors, administrators, and assigns, to and with the said John Thomas, his heirs and assigns, that he, the said Charles, his executors, administrators, and assigns, should and would from time to time, and at all times during the said term, uphold, maintain, repair, and keep the said messuage and other the demised buildings thereto belonging in good and sufficient repair, and the same, at the end or sooner determination of the said term, should and would surrender and yield up to the said John and Rebecca, their heirs and assigns in good and tenantable order and repair, he, the said John, his heirs and assigns finding, allowing, and assigning timber sufficient for such reparations during the said term, to be cut and carried by the said Charles, his executors, administrators, and assigns.

And the plaintiff sets forth that Charles entered by virtue of the said indenture, and being possessed of the said demised premises, died at Ludlow, on the 22d of April, 1735; and that administration of all his goods, &c., with his will annexed, was afterwards duly granted to the defendant, who by virtue thereof entered upon the demised premises, and was possessed thereof until the end of the said term, and that at the end of the said term of twenty-one years, and for the space of five years then before the said message and other the demised buildings thereto belonging, were greatly ruinous and in decay, and wanted necessary reparations and amendments; and that the defendant during her possession of the said messuage, &c., did not uphold, maintain, repair, and keep the same in good and sufficient repair, and the same at the end of the said term surrender and yield up in good and sufficient order and reparation, but at the end of the said term left the same so in decay, and wanting great reparations as aforesaid; contrary to the form and effect of the said covenant, &c.; and lays his damage at £100.

The defendant pleads that the plaintiff during the said term did not find, allow, or assign timber sufficient for upholding, repairing, maintaining, or keeping the said messuage and other the said demised premises in good and sufficient repair; to which the plaintiff demurs generally, and the defendant joins in demurrer.

And upon this it came in judgment before the court.

Bootle, Serjt., for the plaintiff, insisted on three things: —

1. That the plea was too general; it only saying that the plaintiff during the term did not find, &c.

2. That the finding of timber by the plaintiff was not a condition precedent, but a mutual or reciprocal covenant; and consequently that the breach of it cannot be pleaded to an action brought on the covenant of the lessee.

3. That if it could be insisted on by way of plea, yet that a request ought to have been pleaded.

And he cited the case of Warren *v.* Asters, Sir Tho. Jon. 206, where the lessor covenanted that the lessee should have liberty to cut trees for repairing,[1] he making good the fences and ditches, and it was holden not to be a condition, but a mutual covenant. That the word "paying" has been held to be a covenant and not a condition.[2] And he cited a case in B. R., reported in Lucas,[3] 153, 189, and 222, where it was held that, if a man covenanted to pay money due on a judgment to a person, he assigning the judgment, in an action of covenant brought for non-payment of the money, the defendant could not insist that the plaintiff had not assigned the judgment, it being a mutual covenant and not a

1 This case is not accurately stated. It was an action of trespass by a lessee for years; to which the defendant pleaded that Martin, who had leased to the plaintiff, excepted the trees with liberty to cut and carry them away, he mending the fences and filling up the pits, and that Martin afterwards granted the trees and the liberty to the defendant; and then he justified under this liberty, &c. The plaintiff demurred, and showed for cause that the defendant had not alleged that he had mended the fences and filled up the pits; but it was not allowed, because it was not a condition but a covenant for which the lessee had a remedy by action.

2 The case of Sir George Bickerstaffe, cited *ib.*

3 10 Modern.

condition precedent. He cited likewise 3 Lev. 41; the case of Pordage v. Cole, 1 Saund. 319; and 1 Rol. Abr. 518, the case of Holder v. Taylor; to show that these words in the present case are not to be considered as a condition, but as a mutual covenant. But in the case cited out of Rolle, the words are plainly words of covenant; and it is there said that if the words had been that the lessee should repair, provided the lessor find him great timber for it, they would not have been considered as a covenant on the part of the lessor, but as a qualification of the covenant of the lessee; so that this case is rather an authority against the plaintiff.

He insisted likewise that if this were necessary to be done by the plaintiff, yet that the first act was to be done by the lessee; for that he was to request the plaintiff to find the timber; and that he ought likewise to show that these were such repairs for which timber was necessary; for which purpose he cited 1 Rol. Abr. 465, pl. 28.[1]

Hayward, Serjt., for the defendant, did not much insist that the plea was good, but said that the declaration was bad; and that then it was immaterial whether the plea were good or not. He said that these could not be considered as mutual covenants, for that the finding of timber was a condition precedent, or the qualification of the lessee's covenant. That *ipso faciente* and *si ipse fecerit* have exactly the same meaning; and that if the words had been *si ipse invenerit*, it had undoubtedly been a condition precedent. That the breach therefore is not assigned upon the covenant in the deed; for the covenant to repair is a qualified covenant, and *sub modo*, and the breach is assigned of an absolute covenant to repair. He cited the case of Large v. Cheshire, 1 Ventr. 147; 1 Rol. Abr. 414; and 2 Danvers, 229, title "Covenant," (C), ss. 2 and 3, where it is holden that though the word "agreed" makes a covenant, yet that "provided always" makes no covenant, but is a condition precedent. And he put the case that a man should covenant with A. to go to York, A. finding him a horse for that purpose; where it was plain that the covenantor was not obliged to go to York unless A. provided him a horse; which case (he said) was exactly parallel with the present. He therefore insisted that the plaintiff ought to have set forth in his declaration that he was always ready to find and assign him timber, and that not having done so the declaration was insufficient.

We were all of that opinion, and gave no opinion upon the plea.

I thought that none of the cases, though in my opinion they had gone too far already, came up to the present case, for that this finding

[1] Holder v. Taylor. If a man lease a mill for years, and the lessee covenant to repair the mill, and the lessor covenant to find him great timber for it, the lessee ought to give notice to the lessor how much will suffice for the reparation, and not demand in general timber for reparation; otherwise the lessor is not bound to deliver any. — ED.

of timber was a thing in its nature necessary to be done first, and therefore must be considered as a qualification of the lessee's covenant. When two covenants in a deed have no relation to each other, I was clearly of opinion that the non-performance of one could not be pleaded in bar to an action brought for the breach of another covenant in the same deed; and for this plain reason amongst others that the damages sustained by the breach of one such covenant may not be at all adequate to the damages sustained by the breach of the other; and therefore I held that all the cases were right where nothing more was determined. The case of assigning the judgment is plainly different; for a man may pay the money before the judgment is assigned. The case of paying rent is also different, because a man may enjoy the land, nay ought to enjoy it, before he pays rent. The case of repairing the hedges and fences likewise stands on the same reason; for there the wood must be cut down before the hedges and ditches are mended. But a man cannot repair until the timber is assigned him for such repairs. And the case in 1 Rol. Abr. 518, and that in Danvers, 229, are strong authorities for the defendant; for the word "provided," which was there holden to make a condition, is not so strong an expression as the words "finding and allowing" in the present case. But I expressed my dislike of those cases, though they are too many to be now overruled, where it is determined that the breach of one covenant, though plainly relative to the other, cannot be pleaded in bar to an action brought for the breach of the other, but the other party must be left to bring his action for the breach of the other; as where there are two covenants in a deed, the one for repairing and the other for finding timber for the reparations; this notion plainly tending to make two actions instead of one, and to a circuity of action and multiplying actions, both which the law so much abhors. If therefore this were a new point, I should be inclined to be of opinion that, though where there are mutual covenants relative to one another in the same deed, a plaintiff is not obliged in an action brought for the breach of them to aver the performance of the covenant which is to be performed on his part, yet that the defendant in such action may in his plea insist on the non-performance of the covenant to be performed on the part of the plaintiff; but this has been so often determined otherwise, that it is too late now to alter the law in this respect. But where words make a condition precedent or a qualification of a covenant, as the present case plainly is, all the cases agree that the plaintiff in his declaration must aver the performance of such condition or qualification.

And my brothers Abney and Burnett being both of the same opinion with me,

Judgment was given for the defendant.

COLLINS *v.* GIBBS.

IN THE KING'S BENCH, NOVEMBER 27, 1759.

[*Reported in 2 Burrow,* 899.]

MR. BURLAND had moved on Thursday last in arrest of judgment, after a judgment by default and a writ of inquiry executed, in an action upon the case on assumpsit.

His objection was the want of an averment of performance of what he insisted to be a condition precedent.

The question was, whether it was a condition precedent or not.

It was an action upon the case wherein the plaintiff, having first recited the dependency of a former action brought by the defendant against him, and a compromise thereof, upon an agreement for the payment of the costs of it by the present defendant to the present plaintiff, on the now plaintiff's giving him a general release, lays the defendant's promise to pay him his demand in the present action to have been made, "in consideration that the said William (the now plaintiff), at the special instance and request of the said John (the now defendant), would execute to the said John a general release, to bear date on the 27th day of July in the year aforesaid" (which was the day before the agreement), "and to be filled up in the common and usual form of general releases; he, the said John (the present defendant), undertook and faithfully promised the said William (the present plaintiff) to pay him all the costs and expenses that he, the said William, had been at in defending the said suit, feeing counsel, subpœnaing witnesses, journeys, and all other charges and demands in the said suit whatsoever, as soon as a bill of such costs could be prepared and produced to him, the said John."

Then the plaintiff avers his costs and expenses in the said suit to have been £21 3*s.* 7*d.*; and that a bill of such costs and expenses was prepared, and produced to the defendant; whereof he had notice. But the said defendant, &c.

Mr. *Burland* urged that the plaintiff ought to have averred "that he had given or tendered to the defendant a general release executed." For that his giving such a release appeared to be a condition precedent; the defendant's promise being made in consideration that he would do so. In proof of which he cited Hobart, 106; Ro. Rep.; 1 Ld. Raym. 662, Thorpe *v.* Thorpe.

Mr. *Dunning*, contra, cited 1 Salk. 29, Roe *v.* Haugh in Cam. Scac., where the judges held that they ought to do what they could to help the declaration (which case he acknowledged to be after a verdict).

Mr. *Burland* replied that that was after a verdict. This is only after a judgment by default.

The release would be no bar to the demand in the present case; because it is agreed that it should bear date the day before the agreement. So that the cause of action was subsequent to it, and therefore could not be barred by it.

The plaintiff made no promise to execute the release. Therefore, we have no other method to oblige him to it. The payment of the money is to be on his executing it.

LORD MANSFIELD. The release is to be given "at the special instance and request of John" (the now defendant). But perhaps he may never request it. We will see if it can be made good by construction. *Cur. advis.*

LORD MANSFIELD now delivered the resolution of the court.

This is a motion made by the defendant in arrest of a judgment by default; so that it comes before the court exactly as if it had been upon demurrer, and is not like the cases of objections to judgments after verdict.

The plaintiff has not averred performance of what was to be done on his part, nor shown that he was ready to perform it.

Therefore, we are all of opinion that it cannot be made good, as laid in the declaration; and the true distinction as to supplying such defects is, whether the objection be made after a verdict or not.

Therefore, the judgment must be arrested.

Whereupon Mr. *Dunning* moved to amend, upon payment of costs, by inserting such an averment, as (he said) the fact really was; which was opposed by Mr. *Burland*, as being too late after judgment was arrested, and as having never been done.

LORD MANSFIELD. As it is doubtful whether this can be done or not; and as it is certain that the difference between paying costs to amend, and beginning afresh, is very trifling in this case, it is better to let the rule be as it was pronounced: and, accordingly, let the judgment be arrested. *Per Cur. Judgment arrested.*

THE DUKE OF ST. ALBANS v. SHORE.

IN THE COMMON PLEAS, JUNE 29, 1789.

[*Reported in* 1 *Henry Blackstone*, 270.]

DEBT for £500, the penalty of articles of agreement.

The declaration stated the agreement to have been made between the plaintiff and defendant on the 30th of March, 1787, by which the defendant was to purchase of the plaintiff a certain farm with the appurtenances, together with an acre and half of boggy land, at the price of £2594, which was to be paid at Lady-day then next in the following manner: the plaintiff was to accept of a conveyance and surrender of certain copyhold and leasehold premises of the defendant, at the price of £1820 (to be deducted from the before-mentioned sum of £2594), the defendant to convey those premises at the expense of the plaintiff unless a fine should be necessary, the expense of which the defendant was to pay; and the plaintiff to make a good title to the defendant at his (the defendant's) expense, unless a fine or recovery should be necessary, for which the plaintiff was to pay, who, on executing the conveyances, was to receive the rest of the purchase-money. All timber-trees, elms, and willow-trees, which then were upon any of the above estates, to be fairly valued by two appraisers, and the prices or values thereof to be paid by the respective purchasers of the estates at the time before mentioned; the rents of the respective estates to be received by the owners till the 24th of March then next. It was also agreed that, in case the plaintiff should not be enabled to make a good title to the said estate before the said 24th of March, that agreement should be void. And although the plaintiff had done and performed every thing on his part, &c., yet protesting that the defendant had not done any thing on his part, &c., "in fact, the said duke saith, that he the said duke always from the time of the making of the said articles of agreement, until and upon the said 24th day of March next ensuing the date thereof, and always since hath been, and is, capable, ready, and willing to make a good title to the said William Shore of the said farm and premises, and boggy land so agreed to be purchased by the said William Shore as aforesaid, and to execute and cause to be executed necessary and proper conveyances and assurances of the said farm and premises, and boggy lands, to the said William Shore, if the said William Shore would have drawn and prepared the same for execution, according to the form and effect of the said articles of agreement, to wit, at Hanworth aforesaid: And the said duke avers that he the said duke, before the 25th day of March, being Lady-day, 1788, to wit, on the 22d day of March, A. D. 1788, at Hanworth aforesaid, gave notice to the said William Shore, that he the said duke was ready and willing at any time to make a good title to the said William Shore of the said farm and premises and land, so agreed to be purchased by the said William Shore, and to execute and cause to be executed proper deeds, conveyances, and assurances for that purpose, if the said William Shore would prepare the same, he the said duke then and there being, and still being, enabled to make, and capable of making, a good title to the said William Shore of the said farm and premises and land, according to the form and effect of the said articles: yet the said William Shore did not, nor would, on or before the said 24th day of March next ensuing the date of the said articles of agreement, nor hath he at any time hitherto, drawn or prepared, or caused to be drawn or prepared to be executed any deed, conveyance, or assurance whatsoever, of the said farm and premises and lands mentioned in the said articles of agreement, and so agreed to be purchased by the said William Shore as aforesaid, nor did, nor would pay the said purchase-money or any part thereof, nor did, nor would accept the said title according to the said articles of agreement: but on the contrary thereof, the said William Shore hath wholly neglected and refused, and still doth neglect and refuse, to draw or prepare any deed, conveyance, or assurance of the said farm, premises, and land, unto the said William Shore, or to pay the said purchase-money or any part thereof, or in any wise to carry the said articles into execution, contrary," &c.

PLEA. "That the said duke was not capable, ready, and willing to make, nor could he the said duke make a good title to the said William of the said farm so agreed to be purchased, according to the tenor and effect of the said agreement, &c. And for further plea, &c., that, after the making of the said agreement, and before Lady-day then next following, to wit, on the 20th of March, A.D. 1788, the said duke cut down divers, to wit, 500 of the said timber trees, 500 of the said elms, and 500 of the said willow-trees, in the said declaration and agreement respectively mentioned, and by the said agreement agreed to be valued and paid for as in the said agreement is mentioned, whereby the said duke disabled himself from performing, and it became and was impossible for him to perform and fulfil the said articles of agreement, on his part, &c.; for which reason he the said William declined and refused to carry the said articles into execution on his part, as he lawfully might," &c.

REPLICATION. Issue on the first plea, and general demurrer to the second. Joinder in demurrer.

This was argued in Hilary term last, by *Lawrence*, Serjt., for the plaintiff, and *Bond*, Serjt., for the defendant, and a second time in Easter term, by *Le Blanc*, Serjt., for the plaintiff, and *Marshall*, Serjt., for the defendant.

The arguments in support of the demurrer were in substance as follow: —

The articles of agreement in this case divide themselves into two branches. First, that the defendant was to purchase of the plaintiff a farm, &c., for £2594, in part of payment for which the plaintiff was to accept a conveyance of other premises. Secondly, that the trees growing upon any of the estates should be valued and paid for by the respective purchasers. The object of the plea is to show that the plaintiff, having cut down trees on his estate, was incapable of performing his part of the agreement, and therefore that the defendant was not bound to perform the other part. In order to support the plea, it must be proved that the matter contained in it was a precedent condition; for if it were not such a condition, the non-performance of it cannot be pleaded in bar. Where one part of an agreement is not the consideration of the other, non-performance of one part cannot be pleaded as an excuse for the non-performance of the other. In this case, the agreement respecting the trees was no part of the consideration of the act which the defendant was to perform, namely, to convey his estate, and pay the residue of the purchase-money. Where there are mutual remedies, it would be unjust that the breach of one covenant should be alleged as a reason for the breach of another, because the damages arising from the one might be unequal to those occasioned by the other. The case of Boone *v.* Eyre[1] was similar to the present: there the covenant was for well and truly performing, &c., the breach was non-payment, and the plea in bar, that the plaintiff was not legally possessed of the negroes on the plantation. There Lord Mansfield said, if the plea were allowed, any one negro not being the property of the plaintiff would bar the action. So here, if this plea were allowed, any one tree being cut down would be a bar to the plaintiff's demand. In Hunlocke *v.* Blacklowe, 2 Saund. 155, the terms of the agreement were as strong as the present, but there a similar plea was not allowed. To the same effect also is Cole *v.* Shallett, 3 Lev. 41. Though these were actions of covenant, yet the statute of 8 & 9 Will. 3 c. 11, has put actions of covenant and debt for a penalty on nearly the same footing, as in neither more than the real damages sustained can be recovered.

On the part of the defendant, three objections were made to the declaration: 1st. That the plaintiff had not shown a sufficient performance of his part of the agreement to entitle him to bring an action for the penalty. The conditions in this case seem to be what Lord Mansfield calls "dependent conditions," in which the performance of one depends on the prior performance of the other; and therefore, till the prior condition be performed, the other party is not liable to an action for the non-performance of his part. Dougl. 691.[2] It is not enough for the plaintiff to aver that he is ready and willing to perform his part; the defendant is not obliged to convey his estate to the plaintiff before the plaintiff conveys to him. Even in covenant to recover damages for the non-performance of this agreement, the plaintiff must have shown that he had actually done all in his power to perform his part; but this being debt for the penalty, an action of a more harsh nature, the plaintiff must show a precise performance; which is made a condition precedent. A court of equity, on the same principle, will not decree a specific performance of an agreement, unless the party applying for the decree has exactly performed his

[1] B. R. East. 17 Geo. 3.

[2] Last edition.

part. Wherever performance is necessary to be averred, it must be shown with such certainty that the court may judge whether the intent of the covenant be performed. 5 Com. Dig. 43. To make a good title means to convey by a good title; and he who is bound to convey is bound to prepare and tender such conveyances as are proper to make a good title to the grantee. 1 Roll. Abr. 465, l. 3; 2 Lev. 95; 1 Ventr. 255; 1 Mod. 104. If it be said that the defendant must prepare the conveyances, because he is to pay the expense of them, the answer is that the law is otherwise. If nothing be said of the expense, it shall be defrayed by the grantor. 1 Roll. Abr. 422, l. 50. But where the grantee is to pay the costs, yet the grantor must prepare the conveyances. Cro. Eliz. 517. If he be bound to assure at the charge of the grantee, he must give notice what sort of conveyance he will make. Halling's Case, 5 Co. 22 b. In the present case, as neither party has done any act towards conveying their respective estates, neither can bring an action for the penalty. But if it should be holden that the defendant was bound to prepare the conveyances because he was to pay the expense, yet the plaintiff has not shown a sufficient performance, since, for any thing that appears, a fine might be necessary: and as such fine was to be at the expense of the plaintiff, and he was bound to levy it if necessary, he ought to have shown either that he had levied it or that it was not necessary. But supposing the defendant was bound to prepare the conveyance from the plaintiff, then must the plaintiff be bound to prepare the conveyance from the defendant. If so, the plaintiff ought to have stated, not only that he had offered to make a good title to the defendant, but also that he had prepared a conveyance from the defendant to him, had tendered it to the defendant to be executed, and demanded the difference in value; but that the defendant had neither prepared a conveyance from the plaintiff to him, executed the conveyance from him to the plaintiff, nor paid the difference.

The second objection to the declaration is, that the plaintiff only states that he was ready and willing to make a good title, but does not show what title. If he in fact had no title, or could not make one to the defendant, the agreement was void by the terms of it, and it would be impossible for him to recover; this title is therefore an essential part of the case. But the validity of the title is a matter for the cognizance of the court, and therefore it must appear on the record, that the court may judge of it, and the defendant take issue on any of the facts which support it, if untrue, or demur if it be insufficient. Here the performance is stated so generally, that no precise issue can be taken on it. In covenant, the breach may be assigned as large as the covenant, because damages only are to be recovered; but in debt for a penalty a precise breach must be shown, because a breach is a forfeiture of the whole bond. 1 Ld. Raym. 107. No issue can be taken on the word "patron" or "heir." 1 Ld. Raym. 202. But the word "title" is of much more vague signification than either "patron" or "heir." Where any thing is to be done as a precedent condition, an averment that the party was ready and willing to do it, is insufficient; neither is an averment *paratus fuit* and *obtulit* sufficient, unless he states that he was hindered by the other party, 2 Saund. 350; 1 Roll. Abr. 465, l. 40: but *paratus fuit* and *obtulit* is sufficient where nothing is to be done on his part before the other has done a prior act. *Ibid.* The plaintiff, therefore, ought here to have shown that he had actually made a good title to the defendant, and what that title was. Hob. 69, 77; Cro. Jac. 315, 425, 503; Cro. Eliz. 919; Yelv. 49; Sid. 467; Doug. 620.[1]

The third objection to the declaration is, that there are three breaches assigned in an action of debt, but it is not stated to be according to the form of the statute: for as before the stat. 8 & 9 W. 3, c. 11, only one breach could be assigned in an action of debt, if many be now assigned, notice must be taken of the statute in pleading. But the breaches themselves do not meet the covenant, not being breaches of the contract stated. They are: 1st. That the defendant did not draw or prepare any conveyance. 2d. That he did not pay the purchase-money. 3d. That he would not accept the title. Now a breach should be assigned in the words of the covenant; or at least it must contain the plain and obvious meaning of the covenant. But it has been proved that the defendant was not bound to prepare the conveyance. The agreement also was that he should satisfy the plaintiff, partly by conveying certain premises to him, and by paying him the remainder in money, not that he should pay the whole in money. This breach, therefore, ought to have been, that the defendant did not convey to the plaintiff the premises which he agreed to convey, nor pay the difference. As to the third breach, it would have been proper if the plaintiff had shown a sufficient performance on his part; but the defendant could not accept till the plaintiff had actually executed the conveyances.

With respect to the plea, it is to be observed that the agreement is not in two parts; the clause relating to the trees is not a new contract of sale, but the mode of valuation. It was understood that they were to go with the land. They were to be paid for by the respective purchasers; that is, by the purchasers of the land on which they grew, and were considered as part of the purchase. The value of land with timber growing on it, can only be fairly estimated by an appraisement of the timber. But a grant of land passes all woods and timber growing on it; Co. Lit. 4 a; the appraisement is only to ascertain the value. Small timber growing is of great value, which if cut would be worth nothing. Thriving timber will pay 10 or 15 per cent. for the purchase-money, and without it the land may be of no value. If there be a covenant to leave all timber on the land, it is a breach for the party to

[1] Last edition.

cut them down, though he leave them. Sir Tho. Raym. 464. If the plaintiff has cut down any of the trees, he is not entitled to the penalty, because he has deprived the estate of certain qualities which were an inducement to the defendant to contract. Admitting the authority of Boone *v.* Eyre, it is not applicable to the present case; there the value of the plantation was not altered by the loss of some of the negroes. No case has been adduced where the subject-matter of the contract was changed. This is one entire contract. The sale of the land is the sale of the timber. The defendant is called upon to pay for a thing different from that for which he agreed. Various cases might be put where there may be an agreement for the purchase of one entire thing, and a particular mode of valuing a part of it.

It was replied,

That although it was objected that the plaintiff had not shown a sufficient performance on his part, yet he had stated that he was capable, ready, and willing to make a good title, and of which he had given notice to the defendant. This was sufficient. The plaintiff was not bound to execute the conveyances, unless the defendant had drawn and paid for them. As to the cases cited, where it was holden insufficient to state that the party was ready and willing to perform his part, there some specific, certain act was to be done; in which case, performance was necessary to be averred. But here the plaintiff was to make no conveyance without the consent of the defendant. The first class of cases only shows at whose expense conveyances were to be made, where there was no express agreement; but here, by the covenant, the defendant was to pay it. As to the objection that a fine might have been necessary, that is answered by stating that the plaintiff gave notice to the defendant that he was ready and willing at any time to make a good title. If a fine were necessary, the defendant ought to show that it was necessary; the plaintiff agreed to levy it only if it were necessary. As to the case where the word "patron" was not sufficiently certain to take issue upon, it was in *quare impedit*, where the party was obliged to make out a title to himself, and show an actual presentation. In the other class of cases cited, where the words "ready and willing" were holden not sufficient, an absolute performance was necessary to be stated, because it was wholly in the power of the party to perform the act required. But where two things are to be done at the same time by different parties, it is enough for the party declaring to state that he was ready and willing to perform his part; especially where money is to be paid for the conveyance of an estate, in which case the party to whom the estate is to be conveyed is not forced to pay, unless the other is ready and willing to convey. The ground of the decision in Cro. Jac. 315 was, that the plaintiff ought to have shown by what title the plaintiff in ejectment recovered, since it might have been by his own conveyance, and then though the facts alleged were true, still there might be no breach of covenant. On this principle the case of Noble *v.* King[1] was decided in this court. So also in the other cases cited, where there were covenants for good title and quiet enjoyment, it was necessary to state the title of those by whom the parties were evicted or disturbed, because the facts alleged might be true, and yet the covenants might not be broken. The case cited from Yelverton, 49, was decided principally on the ground that the declaration ought to have shown that B., the person who was to become bound according to the agreement, was in fact bound.

As to the third objection to the declaration, namely, that the breaches are not stated to be assigned by virtue of the statute; that is matter of form, and not to be taken advantage of on a general demurrer. As to the objection that they are not breaches of the agreement stated, it is to be observed that they are in substance and truth breaches of the agreement. It sufficiently appears from them, that the defendant did not do what he was bound to do, that he neither prepared the conveyances, paid the purchase-money, or accepted the title of the plaintiff. He ought by some act on his part to have enabled the plaintiff to have done what he had agreed to do, namely, to convey, &c. No answer has been given to the case of Boone *v.* Eyre, where the negroes were to pass with the land, as the trees in this case. There the damages for the loss of the negroes were unequal to those which would have accrued to the other party. There also a gross sum was stipulated for the negroes, together with the plantation; here, there was only an agreement for a valuation. If any tree had been cut down, the defendant would have paid so much the less; and if there was any ideal value annexed to the growing timber, he ought to have stated it. The whole contract is not to be rescinded by an alteration in the trees on the land, which were to be the subject of a separate valuation.

Cur. vult. advis.

On this day the following judgment of the court was delivered by LORD LOUGHBOROUGH, who having stated the pleadings, said:—

It is clear in this case, that unless the plaintiff has done all that was incumbent on him to do, in order to create a performance by the defendant (if I may use the expression), he is not entitled to maintain the action. If he has not set forth a sufficient title, judgment must be against him whatever the plea is, and if the plea be a good bar, the same consequence must follow. It was argued on the part of the plaintiff, that the agreement respecting the trees was not a condition precedent, and therefore a breach of that agreement could not be pleaded in bar of the action. In support of this argument, the case of Boone *v.* Eyre was cited; but in that case, though the Court of King's Bench held the plea insufficient, yet they laid down a clear and well founded dis-

[1] 1 H. Bl. 34.

tinction, that where a covenant went to the whole of the consideration on both sides, there it was a condition precedent; but where it did not go to the whole, but only to a part, there it was not a condition precedent, and each party must resort to his separate remedy; and for this plain and obvious reason, because the damages might be unequal. The cases also of Hunlocke *v.* Blacklowe, 2 Saund. 155, and Cole *v.* Shallett, 3 Lev. 41, were cited as being in favor of the plaintiff. But it is unnecessary to enter into the discussion of those cases, though perhaps doubts may reasonably be entertained of the doctrine laid down in Saunders, and though the case cited by him in his argument may deserve full as much consideration as that which was the subject of the determination of the court. For we found our opinion on the present case on the ground of the distinction in Boone *v.* Eyre, which we think a fair and sound one. Then the question is, Whether the covenant of the plaintiff goes to the whole consideration of that which was to be done by the defendant? Now the duke clearly covenanted to convey an estate to the defendant, in which all the timber growing on the estate was necessarily included. The timber was not disjoined from the estate by the separate valuation of it. It was expressly agreed that all trees, &c., which then were upon any of the estates should be valued. But it is not to be permitted to a party contracting to convey land, which includes the timber, by his own act to change the nature of it between the time of entering into the contract and that of performing it. There may be cases where the timber growing on an estate is the chief inducement to a purchase of that estate. But it is not necessary to inquire whether it be the chief inducement to a purchase or not; for if it may be in any sort a consideration to the party purchasing to have the timber, the party selling ought not to be permitted to alter the estate by cutting down any of it. This is not an action of covenant where one party has performed his part, but is brought for a penalty, on the other party refusing to execute a contract. But to entitle the party bringing the action to a penalty, he ought punctually, exactly, and literally to complete his part. We are therefore of opinion that the plea is a good bar to the action, and on this we give our judgment. My brother Marshall made some exceptions to the declaration, which it is not necessary to go into, but which, speaking for myself, I think material. It is to be observed, that this is not a contract absolutely and at all events to convey. Where a man undertakes to convey, he undertakes to convey by a good title. There are cases where a court of equity has holden that a party so undertaking might make a title by procuring an act of Parliament, and that he was bound to purchase in all outstanding terms to make a good title. But in this case if the plaintiff was not enabled to make a good title before a certain day, the agreement was to be at an end, he might be off and was released from his engagement. He therefore undertook to make a good title before a given time; the breach assigned is, that the defendant refused to accept the title. But what title? What exhibition of title? What title was tendered to him? What was there for him to accept? This, perhaps, is rather *dehors* the question, though it might be material if it were necessary to take it into consideration. But the ground of our determination is, that the plea is good, as I before stated, within the distinction laid down by the Court of King's Bench in the case of Boone *v.* Eyre. *Judgment for the defendant.*

WORSLEY *v.* WOOD AND OTHERS, *Assignees of* LOCKYER AND BREAM, *Bankrupts;* IN ERROR.

IN THE KING'S BENCH, JUNE 7, 1796.

[*Reported in* 6 *Term Reports,* 710.]

THIS was an action of covenant brought in the Court of Common Pleas.[1] The declaration stated that by a policy of insurance made before Lockyer and Bream became bankrupts, namely, on the 9th of March, 1792, it was witnessed that Lockyer and Bream had paid £11 16*s*. to the Phœnix Company, and had agreed to pay to them, at their office, the sum of £11 16*s*. on the 25th of March, 1793, and the like sum yearly on the said day during the continuance of the policy for insurance from loss or damage by fire, not exceeding the sum of £7000. That Worsley covenanted with L. and B. that, so long as the assured should pay the above premium, the capital stock and funds of the Phœnix Company should be liable to pay to the assured any loss that the assured should suffer by fire on the property therein mentioned, not exceeding £7000, according to the tenor of the printed proposals delivered with the policy. That in the printed proposals referred to by the policy it is declared that the company would not be accountable for any loss by fire caused by foreign invásion, civil commotion, &c.; and also that all persons assured sustaining any loss by fire should forthwith give notice to the company, and as soon as possible after deliver in as particular an account of their loss as the nature of the case would admit, and make proof of the same by their oath and by their book of accounts, or other vouchers as should be reasonably required, and should procure a certificate under the hands of the minister and churchwardens and of some reputable householders of the parish, not concerned in the loss, importing that they were acquainted with the character and circumstances of the person insured, and knew or be-

[1] See 2 H. Bl. 574. — ED.

lieved that he by misfortune and without any kind of fraud or evil practice had sustained by such fire the loss and damage therein mentioned; and in case any difference should arise between the assured and the company touching any loss, such difference should be submitted to the judgment of arbitrators indifferently chosen, whose award should be conclusive, &c., and when any loss should have been duly proved, the assured should immediately receive satisfaction to the full amount of the same. The declaration then stated that on the first of July, 1792, a loss happened by fire in the house of L. and B., in which all their books of accounts were destroyed, to the amount of £7000. That L. and B. on the same day gave notice of it to the company, and on the same day delivered to the company as particular an account of their loss as the nature of the case admitted, and were then and there also ready and willing and then and there tendered to make proof of the loss by their oath, and to produce such vouchers as could be reasonably required in that behalf; that on the same day they procured and delivered to the said company a certificate under the hands of four reputable householders of the parish, to the effect required in the printed proposals, and applied to E. Embry, the minister, and H. Hutchins and J. Bellamy, the churchwardens of the parish, to sign such certificate, but that they, without any reasonable or probable cause, wrongfully and unjustly refused and have ever since refused to sign it. The declaration then stated that the funds of the company were sufficient to pay this loss, yet the company have not paid it, either to the bankrupts or to their assignees; nor have the company submitted the said difference to the judgment of such arbitrators, &c.

There was another count, in which it was not averred that the bankrupts either offered to make proof of the loss, or procured a certificate, or applied to the minister, &c., for one; and the breach in this count was, that the company had not submitted the said difference to the judgment of such arbitrators, &c.

The defendant pleaded (to the first count) that the bankrupts were not interested in the house or goods, &c., at the time of the loss, on which issue was taken in the replication. 2d. That the loss was occasioned by the fraud and evil practice of the bankrupts; on which issue was taken, &c. 3d. That the minister and churchwardens did not refuse wrongfully and injuriously, and without any reasonable or probable cause, to sign the certificate; on which issue was taken. (To the second count.) 1st. That the bankrupts were not interested, &c.; on which issue was taken. 2d. That the loss was occasioned by fraud, &c. (as above); on which issue was taken. 3d. That neither the bankrupts or their assignees procured such certificate under the hands of the minister and churchwardens and respectable inhabitants, &c., as required in the printed proposals.

To the last of these pleas, the plaintiffs replied, that the bankrupts as soon as possible after the loss, namely, on the 1st of July, 1792, procured and delivered to the company such certificate as is required in the printed proposals under the hands of four respectable inhabitants, &c., but that the minister and churchwardens wrongfully refused to sign it without any reasonable or probable cause for so doing.

The rejoinder stated that the minister and churchwardens did not wrongfully refuse, &c.; on which issue was taken in the surrejoinder.

The jury found all the issues for the plaintiffs, and gave a verdict for £3000.

The defendant below removed the record into this court by writ of error, and assigned for error that the declaration, the replication, and the other pleadings of the plaintiffs below, were not sufficient in law to maintain the action.

This case was twice argued in this court, the first time in last Easter Term by *Wood* for the plaintiff in error and *Lambe* for the defendants, and now by *Law* for the former and *Gibbs* for the latter.

ARGUMENTS FOR THE PLAINTIFF IN ERROR. The principal question is, whether a compliance with the printed proposals, which are referred to in the policy of insurance, requiring (*inter alia*) a certificate under the hands of the minister, churchwardens, and reputable householders, be or be not a condition precedent to the right of the plaintiffs below to recover; if it be, the plaintiffs below were not entitled to recover, and consequently the judgment of the Court of Common Pleas must be reversed. Now the proposals referred to in the deed constitute a part of the deed, and must be taken as incorporated into it. By those, the trustees for the Phœnix Office engaged to pay only on condition that the insured give notice of the loss, deliver in a particular of the loss, &c., and procure a certificate of the minister, churchwardens, and householders. In this case, the insured have only complied with the two former of these conditions, and therefore the trustees for the fire office are not answerable; the certificate of some of the householders alone, without the signatures also of the minister and churchwardens, not being sufficient. This stipulation is made in order to guard the insurance office from the manifold frauds that would otherwise be practised upon them by wicked and designing men; nor is there any thing illegal or even unreasonable in this precaution, the public as well as the insurance office being so deeply interested in the preservation of houses from losses by wilful fires. The language the office hold out to the public is this: "We will not insure any individual whose character is not known to the minister, churchwardens, and some of his neighbors." Individuals may or may not enter into this engagement at their option; it is a mere voluntary act on their part: but when they do enter into the contract, they must be bound by every part of it. If this were not to operate as a condition precedent, it could have no effect whatever; for as this is a deed-poll, in which there is no covenant by the assured, the insurance office would have no remedy against them if they did not comply with the condition. Then if this be a condition precedent, it is no excuse for the insured to say that he cannot procure the certificate required. They engaged at all events to procure it before they called on the insurance office to indemnify them for the loss they sustained, and nothing can be considered as a dispensation with that but some act of the insurance office themselves, which is not shown here. It will be contended, however, that the minister and churchwardens wrongfully refused to sign the certificate without any reasonable or probable cause; but that fact, even if true, is immaterial in this case, because the assured engaged that this certificate should at all events be produced before their right of calling on the insurers attached. If a party undertake that a condition shall be performed by a stranger, and the latter refuses, this is no excuse, unless such refusal be procured by the other party. 1 Rol. Abr. 415, 452; Doughty *v.* Neal, 1 Saund. 216; Hesketh *v.* Gray, Say. 185; Gruit *v.* Pinnel, 5 Vin. Abr. 207; Davis *v.* Mure, cited 1 T. R. 642; Pole *v.* Harrobin, cited *ib.* 644; and Campbell *v.* French, 6 T. R. 200. So, though the condition be highly improbable; 1 Rol. Abr. 420; Co. Lit. 201, 206 b; Com. Dig. "Condition," 325, 348; Godb. 76; and there is no distinction in this respect between commercial and other instruments; a condition precedent must be strictly performed as well in the one case as in the other; Campbell *v.* French. But it is not true that the minister and churchwardens did without any reasonable or probable cause refuse to certify; for they were requested to certify that they believed that the insured had sustained a loss amounting to £7000, whereas it appears by the verdict that their loss did not exceed £3000. And independently of all analogous cases, there are two determinations of the Court of Common Pleas on the policies of the Sun Fire Office, which are couched nearly in the same terms with the present policy, in favor of the insurance office. Routledge *v.* Burrell, 1 H. Bl. Rep. 254; and Oldman *v.* Bewicke,[1] Hil. 26 Geo. 3, C. B. In the last case the declaration stated that persons sustaining any loss by fire were to give notice, &c., to deliver in an account of their loss, &c., and procure a certificate under the hands of the minister and churchwardens, together with some other reputable inhabitants, &c., not concerned in such loss, &c., "but until such affidavit and certificate of such loss should be made and produced, the loss money should not be payable." The defendant pleaded, 1st. That the premises were wilfully set on fire; and 2d. That the bankrupt had no interest in the premises. After verdict for the plaintiff for £300, a motion was made in arrest of judgment, which after argument was made absolute; Gould, J., saying, "until such affidavit is made and certificate procured, the money is not payable; the time of payment therefore is not yet come. Though he be a *bona*

[1] See 2 H. Bl. 577, note (*a*). — ED.

fide sufferer, still he is not entitled without a certificate. The stipulation is a condition precedent, that there shall be a certificate that there was no kind of fraud." If then the procuring of this certificate be a condition precedent, as it is not alleged in the declaration that such a certificate was procured, it cannot be presumed even after verdict; for this is a defective title appearing in the declaration itself.

ARGUMENTS FOR THE DEFENDANTS IN ERROR. It may be admitted that, if the procuring of the certificate be a strict condition precedent, no right of action could accrue to the insured until they had procured it; therefore none of the cases cited of strict conditions precedent need be disputed. But on adverting to the printed proposals it will be seen that the procuring of the certificate is not a condition precedent, but a mere regulation of the fire office. There is a marked distinction in the penning of the proposals between the first, which speaks of a loss by invasion, and the others of which that respecting the certificate is one. In the former the insurance office expressly stipulate that they will not be answerable; but immediately afterwards, speaking of the other articles, they studiously change the language: "And also all persons insured shall give notice, procure a certificate," &c. But these are evidently mere regulations in the office; and in order to construe this to be a condition precedent, the court must vary the terms of the proposals, and instead of "and also," must substitute words like these, "and until all persons insured shall have given notice and procured a certificate, &c., the insurers will not be answerable." The variation of expression in these proposals strongly shows the intention of the parties, which, according to the case of Hotham *v.* The East India Company,[1] must be the rule of decision. The procuring of a certificate is not a fact on which the plaintiff's title is founded; it is merely evidence of that title; but here that title is made out without it. Taking the whole of the instruments together it appears to have been the intention of the parties that the assured should recover for any loss, provided there was no fraud on their part; here the loss by fire is ascertained by the verdict, and all fraud on their part is negatived. It may be admitted that these regulations must be complied with as far as the assured themselves can comply: but here was a compliance *cy pres;* the assured did every thing in their power to comply with them; they gave notice, delivered in an account, and procured a certificate by four reputable householders, and also required the signatures to it of the minister and churchwardens, which the latter wrongfully and without any reasonable or probable cause refused. But such improper refusal ought not to prejudice the right of the assured, who did every thing required on their parts to be performed. In Moser and another *v.* The Churchwardens and Overseers of the united parishes of St. Magnus and St. Margaret, in Trinity Term 1795, a bill for relief was brought against

[1] 1 T. R. 645.

the defendants, who had employed the plaintiffs to fix up two stoves in the church of St. Magnus, under an agreement by which the plaintiffs engaged to complete the work on or before a certain day, "to the satisfaction of Mr. Trecker, a surveyor," and the money was to be paid on a given day, "in case the said surveyor should certify that the same was completed agreeably to the contract." The bill stated that the work was finished according to the contract, but that the surveyor refused to certify, &c. On the hearing of the cause it was argued on behalf of the defendants that the bill should be dismissed because the plaintiffs had their remedy at common law, it being a fair and direct issue to try whether the certificate was or was not properly withheld by the surveyor, and the surveyor having no right to refuse the certificate arbitrarily; and upon this ground the Master of the Rolls dismissed the bill. It is clear also, from the possibility of a loss happening in extra-parochial places where there is no minister, or in small hamlets where there are no churchwardens, that it was not the intention of the parties that the procuring of a certificate should be considered as a condition precedent to the right of the assured to recover. This case is distinguishable from some of the analogous cases cited, and from the two cases of the Sun Fire Office. In Davis v. Mure, where the defendants had covenanted that if the ship (which was a merchants' ship) should be taken, &c., and it should appear to a court-martial that the ship's company had made the utmost defence they were able, they would pay the value, &c., Lord Mansfield directed an inquiry to be made at the Admiralty as to the usage, on whose requisition courts-martial were held on losses of merchants' ships. Now that inquiry was wholly immaterial, if the court thought that the procuring of a court-martial by the plaintiff was a condition precedent to his right of action. In that case as well as the case of Campbell v. French, the party had not done every thing in his power to perform the condition, and therefore he could not rely on a performance *cy pres*. And with regard to the two other cases of Routledge v. Burrell and Oldman v. Bewicke, the same answer may be given to both: there the words of the printed proposals differed from the words here in this essential article, that there it was expressly agreed that "until such affidavit and certificate of such the insured's loss should be made and produced, the loss money should not be payable." But the insertion of those words by the Sun Fire Office in their proposals, and the omission of them by the Phœnix Office, strongly show that the latter did not mean to insist on the production of a certificate as a condition precedent to the right of the assured. But in the case of Hotham v. the East India Company, the court expressly held that the procuring of a survey to be taken was not a condition precedent, and there the words are stronger than in the present case, "that no allowance should be made for short tonnage, unless it should be made to appear on a survey," &c.

But at all events the assured may recover on the second count in the declaration, where the breach assigned is for not referring the matter to arbitration, and it cannot be pretended that the procuring of the certificate was a condition precedent to the reference; the consequence of this is, that a *venire de novo* must issue to assess damages on that count.

In reply, as to the second ground, it was said that the same objection applied to the second as to the first count; that by the printed proposals the assured were to give notice of the loss, deliver in an account, and produce the certificate required, and in case (that is, after those conditions were complied with) any difference arose, the matter was to be referred; and that to the second count there was a plea that the assured did not procure the certificate, &c., which led to the same question as arose on the first count in the declaration.

LORD KENYON, C. J. The second point respecting the *venire de novo* is now for the first time started, no notice having been taken of it on the first argument here, or on the motion to arrest the judgment in the Court of Common Pleas; if there appeared to be any ground for it, we would desire to have the case farther investigated; but it seems to me to have no foundation, because the objection that the procuring of the certificate is a condition precedent is as applicable to the second as to the first count of the declaration.

This case requires our serious consideration, because the Court of Common Pleas have already given their opinion on it in favor of the plaintiffs' claim, though it has been suggested that it was not the unanimous opinion of that court.[1] We are called upon in this action to give effect to a contract made between these parties; and if from the terms of it we discover that they intended, that the procuring of the certificate by the assured should precede their right to recover, and that it has not been procured, we are bound to give judgment in favor of the defendant below. These insurance companies, who enter into very extensive contracts of this kind, are liable (as we but too frequently see in courts of justice) to great frauds and impositions; common prudence, therefore, suggests to them the propriety of taking all possible care to protect them from frauds when they make these contracts. The Phœnix Company have provided, among other things, that the assured should, as soon as possible after the calamity has happened, deliver in an account of their loss, and procure a certificate under the hands of the minister and churchwardens, and of some reputable householders of the parish, importing that they knew the character and circumstances of the assured, and believed that they had sustained the loss without any kind of fraud. That this is a prudent regulation, this very case is sufficient to convince us; for it appears on the record, that soon after the fire the assured delivered in an account

[1] Mr. J. Heath differed from the rest of the Court of C. B.

of their loss, which they said amounted to £7000, that they obtained a certificate from some of the reputable inhabitants that the loss did amount to that sum, and that the jury after inquiring into all the circumstances were of opinion that the loss did not exceed £3000; and yet it is also stated that the minister and churchwardens, who refused to certify that they believed that the loss amounted to £7000, wrongfully and without any reasonable or probable cause refused to sign such certificate. The great question here is, Whether or not it was the intention of these parties that that certificate should precede payment by the insurance office; now it seems to me from the printed proposals that it was their intention that it should precede payment. What is a condition precedent, or what a condition subsequent, is well expressed by my brother Ashhurst in the case of Hotham *v.* The East India Company, to which I refer in general. If there be a condition precedent to do an impossible thing, the obligation becomes single; but however improbable the thing may be, it must be complied with, or the right which was to attach on its being performed, does not vest. If the condition be, that A. shall enfeoff B., and A. do all in his power to perform the condition, and B. will not receive livery of seisin, yet from the time of Lord Coke to the present moment, it has not been doubted but that the right which was to depend on the performance of that condition, did not arise. In the case of Hesketh *v.* Gray, which has been cited as a determination in this court, there was also an application to the Great Seal at the time when Lord Chief Justice Willes was the first commissioner to dispense with the condition, which was, that the Bishop of Chichester should accept the resignation of a living; but it was held, that there was no ground for a court of equity to interfere. This court also held, when the case came before them, that it was a condition precedent, and must be performed.

In this case, however, it said that, though the minister and churchwardens did not certify, some of the inhabitants did certify, and that that was sufficient, it being a performance of the condition *cy pres*. But I confess, I do not see how the terms *cy pres* are applicable to this subject; the argument for the plaintiffs below goes to show that if none of the inhabitants of this parish certified, a certificate by the inhabitants of the next or of any other parish would have answered the purpose. But the assured cannot substitute one thing for another. In the case of Campbell *v.* French, we explained the grounds of this doctrine, and said that the party who had not complied with the condition could not substitute other terms or conditions in lieu of those which all the parties to the contract had originally made. So here it was competent to the insurance office to make the stipulations stated in their printed proposals; they had a right to say to individuals who were desirous of being insured, "Knowing how liable we are to be imposed upon, we will, among other things, require that the minister, churchwardens, and some of the reputable inhabitants of your parish shall certify that they believe that the loss happened by misfortune and without fraud, otherwise we will not contract with you at all." If the assured say that the minister and churchwardens may obstinately refuse to certify, the insurers answer, "We will not stipulate with you on any other terms." Such are the terms on which I understand this insurance to have been effected; and, therefore, I am clearly of opinion, that there is no foundation for the action, and that the judgment below must be reversed.

ASHHURST, J. The question is, whether the certificate required be or be not a condition precedent; if it be, the plaintiffs below cannot maintain their action. It is perfectly immaterial whether they have entered into an improvident contract; if they choose to take the burden upon themselves, they cannot call on the insurance office until they have complied with the condition. I think that it is a condition precedent, and that the assured engaged at all events to procure the certificate before they applied to the office for an indemnity. Nor is there any thing unreasonable in these terms. It is well known that great frauds are sometimes practised on the insurance offices; and, therefore, it behooves them to take all care to prevent frauds. In order to guard more effectually to protect the Phœnix Company, they insist on having a certificate from the minister and churchwardens, from persons who are not likely, from their situations in life, to assist in such frauds. But as the plaintiffs below have not procured that certificate, they cannot maintain this action.

GROSE, J. Four questions arise on this record: First, whether the printed proposals are to be taken as part of the policy of insurance; Secondly, whether that part respecting the certificate creates a condition precedent; Thirdly, if it does, whether the assured were bound to perform the conditions; Fourthly, whether they have performed it. These are the material points. On the first, the case of Routledge *v.* Burrell is decisive to show that the printed proposals are to be taken as part of the policy. The second point also seems to me to be decided by the case of Oldman *v.* Bewicke. For though the words in both proposals are not exactly similar, the substance is the same. And what my brother Ashhurst said in the case of Hotham *v.* The East India Company, is applicable here, that there are no precise words necessary to make either a condition precedent or subsequent, but that the question must depend on the intention of the parties. As to the third point, the cases alluded to by the defendant's counsel (to which another in 22 Edw. 4, 26 b, may be added) are strong to show that if a person engage for the act of a stranger, he must procure that act to be done. With regard to the last point, the assured have not obtained the certificate required, but they have procured a certificate which, under the circumstances of the case, they consider equivalent to it, namely, a certificate by some of the reputable inhabitants of the parish. It is true that the minister and churchwardens were not bound to certify but the assured undertook to procure such a certificate; that is a condition on performing which alone the Phœnix Company engaged to pay any loss that might arise. It is admitted that the assured did not procure such a certificate; but they say that the minister and churchwardens wrongfully and without any reasonable or probable cause refused it; but that, if true, is no ground for supporting this action; it is a misfortune to the plaintiffs, but it ought not to prejudice the defendant. It is not sufficient that there is no probable cause for not certifying, there ought to be a probable cause to induce the minister and churchwardens to certify; they ought to be satisfied with the truth of the loss before they certify. Here they were requested to certify that the plaintiffs had sustained a loss to the amount of £7000, but the jury found that the loss only amounted to £3000; therefore, the minister and churchwardens could not in conscience sign the certificate which was offered to them. If the certificate which the assured procured were considered as a compliance with this condition, a certificate by the inhabitants of any other parish might equally be substituted in lieu of that which was required; but it is not competent to the assured to substitute other terms for those which were the foundation of this contract.

With regard to the question relative to a *venire de novo*, if a *venire de novo* were awarded, the plaintiffs could not recover on the second count for want of a certificate.

LAWRENCE, J. If the matter were to go to arbitration, and no certificate were produced, the arbitrators ought to determine against the plaintiffs; therefore it would answer no purpose to grant a *venire de novo*.

With respect to the principal question, this is an action to recover a loss which the insurance office are only liable to make good according to the terms of their engagement. There is no ambiguity in those terms; they were perfectly well known to all parties, and the plaintiffs below must be considered as having assented to them. It has been argued however that the certificate was not a condition precedent, and that the plaintiffs' right attached on the happening of a fire without fraud, and that this may be collected from the difference of penning the different proposals. But it does not seem to me that a fire without fraud will give the assured a right of action; it must be a fire accompanied with the notice, affidavit, and certificate, specified in the proposals. And as to the wording of the different articles, that speaking of a loss by foreign enemies, &c., is an exception; it is a loss for which the insurance company are not answerable; and for other losses they are only liable on certain conditions. Then it was argued on behalf of the plaintiffs below that it was sufficient for them to perform the conditions in substance; even admitting that argument to be well founded, there was no substantial performance here. In some cases in the books respecting conditions precedent, where the thing agreed to be done was in effect performed, though not in the exact manner, nor with all the circumstances mentioned, it was deemed a substantial performance; as where the condition was to enfeoff, a conveyance by lease and release has been deemed a compliance. So if the condition be to deliver the will of the testator, and he delivers letters testamentary. 1 Rol. Abr. 426, pl. 2, 4. But this, instead of being a substantial performance of the condition, is only a substitution of one thing for another. Suppose the terms of this contract had been that the insurance office should not pay any loss unless A. B. and C. certified, it would not have been sufficient for E. F. and G. to certify. So here the agreement was that persons of certain characters should certify; and when the assured substitute, for such a certificate, one signed by persons bearing different characters, it is the same as a certificate signed by persons of different names from those required. Perhaps it is difficult to ascertain who shall be called reputable or substantial persons; and in order to avoid this difficulty, the insurance office insist on the certificate being signed by persons who hold public situations in the parish. These terms seem highly reasonable; it is a duty that the office owe to the public as well as to themselves to take every precaution to protect them against fraud; and unless some such check as the present were interposed, the office would be holding out a premium to wicked men to set fire to their own houses. Then as this is a condition precedent, even supposing that the refusal by the minister and churchwardens were a wrongful act in them (which I do not admit under these circumstances), the cases are uniform to show that if a person undertake for the act of a stranger, that act must be done. Therefore I agree that the judgment below must be reversed. *Judgment reversed.*

SHADFORTH *v.* HIGGIN.

AT NISI PRIUS, CORAM LORD ELLENBOROUGH, HILARY TERM, 1813.

[*Reported in* 3 *Campbell*, 385.]

ASSUMPSIT upon the following agreement signed by the plaintiff and defendant: —

"James Shadforth, part-owner of the ship Fanny, of 300 tons, coppered and armed, agrees to despatch said vessel immediately in ballast direct to Jamaica, and, on her arrival at Rio Nova Bay, Salt Gut, and St. Ann's, receive a full and complete cargo of produce, consisting of sugar, rum, coffee, and pimento. In return, Messrs. Higgin & Co. agree to provide a cargo at the above shipping places, to be taken on board in the usual manner, in time for July convoy, provided she arrives out and ready by the 25th of June, and the freight to be at the current rate as given to other vessels loading at the same time and same ports."

The declaration alleged that the plaintiff did immediately despatch the vessel in ballast to Jamaica, and that, on her arrival at Rio Nova Bay, she was afterwards, to wit, on the 3d of July, and from thence for a long space of time, to wit, for the space of three months from thence next ensuing, ready to receive at Rio Nova Bay, Salt Gut, and St. Ann's, aforesaid, a full and complete cargo of produce, according to the form and effect of the said agreement; yet that the defendant did not nor would provide a cargo for the said vessel at the above shipping places, or any or either of them, according to the form and effect of the said agreement, whereby the said ship was obliged to return from Jamaica without any cargo being loaded on board thereof.

The ship in point of fact did not reach Jamaica till the 3d of July; and the question was, whether under these circumstances the defendant was answerable for having failed to furnish her with a full cargo.

Garrow, S. G., for the plaintiff, contended that the defendant was bound to furnish a full cargo for the ship at all events. Provided she arrived out and was ready by the 25th of June, this was to be done in time to enable her to sail with the July convoy. The condition of her arriving by 25th June only applied to the time of her departure on the homeward voyage. If by any accident her arrival was delayed beyond the day specified, she was still entitled to a cargo in a reasonable time, as if the proviso and the mention of the July convoy had not been introduced into the agreement. It could hardly be meant, that where the owner was absolutely bound to despatch his ship to Jamaica, if she arrived a day later than was expected, the freighter might send her home empty.

Lord Ellenborough. I think the arrival of the ship by the 25th June was a condition precedent. The freighter might know that, if she arrived by that day, he could easily provide a cargo for her; but that afterwards it might be impossible. He might have had goods of his own, which it was essentially necessary should be shipped by that day, and which he was therefore compelled to load on board another vessel. It would be a great hardship upon the freighter, if he were bound to provide a freight for a vessel which arrives at a season of the year when there is no produce ready for shipping in the island. If the freighter is liable, although the ship does not arrive till a week after the day agreed upon, where is the line to be drawn? I think the fair interpretation of the instrument is that, unless the ship arrived by the 25th June, the defendant's liability was to be at an end.

The plaintiff likewise failed in establishing another agreement declared upon for the loading of the ship, and submitted to be non-suited.

FREEMAN v. TAYLOR.

In the Common Pleas, November 25, 1831.

[*Reported in* 8 *Bingham,* 124.]

Assumpsit to recover damages for the breach of a contract of charter-party, whereby the defendant chartered of the plaintiff "The Edward Lombe, for a voyage from London to Madeira and the Cape of Good Hope," thence "with all convenient speed" to Bombay, where the defendant was to load the ship with a cargo of cotton and other goods, and from Bombay back to London, the cabins and between-decks of the vessel being reserved for the benefit of the plaintiff. The plaintiff averred performance of the charter-party on his part, and alleged a breach by the defendant in refusing to furnish any cargo for the ship at Bombay.[1] The defendant pleaded the general issue.

At the trial before Tindal, C. J., London sittings after Trinity term, 1830, it appeared that the ship sailed from London on the 20th of May, 1828, with a cargo shipped by the defendant for Bombay, and arrived at the Cape of Good Hope on the 28th of September following. She might have proceeded on her voyage on the 30th; but the captain detained her till the 8th of October, being occupied in stowing the between-decks on his own account with a cargo of mules and cattle for the Mauritius. On the 4th of October, the defendant's agents at the Cape protested against the delay, and against the ship's going to the Mauritius, on the ground that it was out of her course. The captain, however, insisted that it was not out of the course, nor any violation of the terms of the charter-party. He proceeded accordingly, arrived at the Mauritius on the 10th of November, and remained there till the 19th, discharging his mules and cattle. On the 19th he sailed for Bombay, where he arrived on the 9th of Jan. 1829, — six or seven weeks later than he would have arrived, if, on the 28th of September, he had sailed direct from the Cape of Good Hope to Bombay. In the mean time, several ships had arrived at Bombay, which left England subsequently to The Edward Lombe; and the defendant's agents refused to procure a cargo of cotton to freight that ship back. The captain remained at Bombay till the 17th of March, during which time he took on board, on his own account, whatever goods he could procure, and then proceeded to Ceylon for further cargo, with which he returned to London.

The plaintiff by this action sought to recover the difference in value between the freight so earned and that which would have accrued

[1] The original report sets out the declaration with great prolixity; but as no question arose upon it, this short statement has been here substituted in its place. — Ed.

from the defendant's cargo of cotton. The freight for the voyage out had been paid, partly in advance.

The Chief Justice told the jury that, inasmuch as the freighter might bring his action against the owner, and recover damages for any ordinary deviation, he could not, for such a deviation, put an end to the contract; but if the deviation was so long and unreasonable that, in the ordinary course of mercantile concerns, it might be said to have put an end to the whole object the freighter had in view in chartering the ship, in that case the contract might be considered at an end; and he left it to the jury to decide whether the delay here was of such a nature as to have put an end to the ordinary objects the freighter might have had in view when he entered into the contract.

The jury found for the defendant.

Taddy, Serjt., obtained a rule *nisi* to set aside the verdict, on the ground that the defendant's remedy for the alleged deviation, if he had been injured by it, was by cross-action; and that he was not at liberty, in the exercise of his own discretion, to put an end to the contract between him and the plaintiff. The engagement to sail from the Cape with all reasonable speed was not a condition precedent, but an independent covenant, for the breach of which the defendant might be entitled to sue; it did not go to the whole of the consideration for the defendant's contract, as was manifest from the circumstance that the defendant had not shown that his object in hiring the ship had been defeated by the plaintiff's delay. Unless it went to the whole consideration, it was not a condition precedent, the neglect of which would entitle the defendant to determine the contract.[1] . . .

Wilde and *Bompas*, Serjts., showed cause. The verdict of the jury, coupled with the previous direction, amounts to a finding that the object of the charterer's contract was entirely defeated by the unjustifiable delay of the plaintiff; it follows, therefore, that the engagement to proceed from the Cape with all reasonable speed was a condition precedent, going to the entire consideration for the contract; and as such, while the contract remained executory, the breach of it was an answer to the plaintiff's demand. Boone *v.* Eyre,[2] Duke of St. Albans *v.* Shore.[3] The plaintiff having by his wilful act defeated the object of the defendant, has no longer any claim against him. Thus, in Soames *v.* Lonergan,[4] where the charterers of a ship for a voyage from Cadiz to St. Blas, and thence to Guayaquil, to take in a homeward cargo, caused another ship to be chartered on their account to go out in ballast and bring home a cargo from Guayaquil, with a proviso that, in the event of the non-arrival of the first mentioned ship at Guayaquil, then the second charter should be void: it was held, that "non-

[1] The learned Serjeant here stated the cases of Bornmann *v.* Tooke, 1 Camp. 377; Havelocke *v.* Geddes, 10 East, 555; and Davidson *v.* Gwynne, 12 East, 381. — ED.

[2] 2 W. Blacks. 1312. [3] 1 H. Blacks. 270. [4] 2 B. & C. 564.

arrival" meant non-arrival within such time as might answer the purposes of the charter of the second ship; and that the first ship not having arrived in time to answer those purposes, and the delay not having been attributable to the charterers, the charter of the second ship was void, and the charterers were not bound to provide a homeward cargo for her. In Touteng v. Hubbard,[1] where a British merchant chartered a Swedish ship on a voyage to St. Michael's for a cargo of fruit, and the charter-party contained the usual exception against the restraint of princes, the ship having been prevented from reaching St. Michael's within the fruit season by an embargo laid on Swedish vessels by the British government, it was held the Swedish owner could not, by proceeding on the voyage after the embargo was taken off, entitle himself to recover the freight against the British merchant. So in Shadforth v. Higgin,[2] where a ship was freighted to go in ballast to Jamaica, and bring home a cargo from thence, and the freighter undertook to provide a full cargo for her in time for the July convoy, provided she arrived out and was ready by the 25th of June, it was held that, as she did not arrive out till after the 25th of June, the freighter was entirely discharged from his contract to furnish a cargo.

In the cases relied on for the plaintiff, either the stipulation was no condition precedent, or it did not appear, as in the present case, that the party had been deprived of the benefit of the contract. Thus, in Bornmann v. Tooke, there was no finding that the object of the defendant had been defeated. In Havelock v. Geddes the defendant made use of the ship, and thereby waived the right of insisting on seaworthiness as a condition precedent. In Davidson v. Gwynne the benefit of the voyage was obtained, although the ship did not sail according to agreement with the first convoy. Whether or not a stipulation shall operate as a condition precedent, and goes to the entire consideration, depends, says Lord Ellenborough, not on any formal arrangement of the words, but on the sense and reason of the thing, as it is to be collected from the whole contract; Ritchie v. Atkinson,[3]; and on that principle all the cases may be reconciled: Thomas v. Cadwallader,[4] Goodisson v. Nunn,[5] Porter v. Shepherd,[6] Campbell v. Jones,[7] Cook v. Jennings,[8] Glazebrook v. Woodrow,[9] Smith v. Wilson,[10] Storer v. Gordon,[11] Fothergill v. Walton.[12] Com. Dig. Condition precedent, G. 5, is express that it ought to be performed within a reasonable time.

Taddy. The defendant having had the benefit of the outward voyage, and having adduced no proof of loss occasioned by the late arrival of the ship at Bombay, it was not competent to the jury to find

[1] 3 B. & P. 291. [2] 3 Campb. 385. [3] 10 East, 306.
[4] Willes, 496. [5] 4 T. R. 761. [6] 6 T. R. 665.
[7] 6 T. R. 570. [8] 7 T. R. 381. [9] 8 T. R. 366.
[10] 8 East, 437. [11] 3 M. & S. 308. [12] 8 Taunt. 576.

that the whole object of the contract was defeated. In Touteng v. Hubbard, Soames v. Lonergan, and Shadforth v. Higgin, nothing was done for the benefit of the charterers on the outward voyage; the ships went out in ballast. And in Havelock v. Geddes, Lord Ellenborough said, "Had the plaintiff's neglect precluded the defendants from making any use of the vessel, it would have gone to the whole consideration, and might have been insisted upon as an entire bar; but as the defendants have had some use of the vessel, notwithstanding the plaintiff's neglect, the plaintiff's covenant is to be considered as going to a part only; the consideration has not wholly failed, and the covenant cannot be looked upon as having raised a condition precedent, but merely gives the defendants a right under a counter action to such damages as they can prove they have sustained from such neglect." [TINDAL, C. J. The plaintiff here has been paid for the outward voyage.] Still Bornmann v. Tooke and Constable v. Cloberie[1] are express authorities to show that the stipulation here as to proceeding direct to Bombay was not a condition precedent. Goodisson v. Nunn, Glazebrook v. Woodrow, and Kingston v. Preston,[2] there cited, were all cases of sale and purchase, involving concurrent conditions, which could not be pleaded one against the other, and inapplicable to the present case; but Campbell v. Jones is in point for the plaintiff. There A., in consideration of £250 paid by B., and of the further sum of £250 to be paid, &c., covenanted that he would, with all possible expedition, instruct B. in a certain mode of bleaching linen (for which he had obtained a patent); and B. covenanted that he would, on or before the 25th of February, 1794, or sooner if A. should before that time have instructed him, &c., pay the further sum of £250; it was held that the covenants of A. and B. were independent covenants; and that A. might sue B. for the £250, without averring that he had taught B. the mode of bleaching linen, &c. *Cur. adv. vult.*

TINDAL, C. J. This was an action of assumpsit upon a charter by the plaintiff to the defendant of the ship Edward Lombe, from London to Madeira and the Cape of Good Hope, and thence to Bombay and back; the plaintiff claiming a compensation in damages against the defendant for not loading the ship with a cargo of cotton at Bombay.

At the trial it appeared in evidence, that, instead of proceeding by the direct and usual course from the Cape of Good Hope to Bombay, the captain made a deviation to the island of Mauritius; and that the defendant's agents at Bombay, in consequence of such deviation, refused to find a cargo.

The point left to the jury at the trial was, whether the deviation was of such a nature and description as to deprive the freighter of the benefit of the contract into which he had entered; the jury being told

[1] Palm. 397. [2] Cited at large in Jones v. Barkley, Dougl. 689.

that if such was their opinion, the defendant was excused, by the act of the plaintiff's captain, from furnishing a cargo.

The jury having determined that question in the affirmative, and having found a verdict for the defendant, a motion was made to set the verdict aside, and for a new trial, on the ground of misdirection.

But, after hearing the arguments against and in support of the rule, we are of opinion, upon the same principle as that which was laid down in the case of Mount *v.* Larkins,[1] and which we therefore think it is unnecessary to repeat, that the direction was right; and we therefore think the rule for a new trial must be discharged. *Rule discharged.*

MORGAN *v.* BIRNIE.

IN THE COMMON PLEAS, APRIL 17, 1833.

[*Reported in* 9 *Bingham*, 672.]

THIS was an action on a builder's contract, by which it was stipulated, among other things, that all the proposed erections should be done in a good and workmanlike manner, and with good sound and well-seasoned materials, and be completed to the reasonable satisfaction of A. B. Clayton, or other the architect for the time being of the defendant, his executors or administrators, on or before the 29th day of October next ensuing the date thereof, or such further day as the said A. B. Clayton, or such other architect, and the said plaintiff should mutually agree upon. It was further provided, that no additions or alteration should be admitted unless directed by the defendant, his executors or administrators, or his or their surveyor, in writing; nor should any additions to or alterations of the works thereby contracted for, and contained in the particulars therein specified, vitiate or vacate the contract thereby made, but the price or allowance to be made in respect of any agreed additions or alterations, should be added to or deducted from the moneys that should become payable by virtue of the said memorandum of agreement as the case might require, such price or allowance being first estimated or settled by the surveyor or architect of the said defendant, who should be sole arbitrator in settling such price or allowance, and all disputes that should or might arise in or about the premises: And the defendant thereby promised and agreed, in consideration of the buildings and works to be done and executed by the said plaintiff, in manner in the said memorandum of agreement mentioned, that the defendant would pay or cause to be paid to the plaintiff the sum of £1250 in manner following, that is to

[1] 8 Bing. 108.

say, that he would pay or cause to be paid such a sum of money as would be equal to three-fourth parts of the price of the works thereby contracted for, which should have been executed and performed according to the true intent and meaning of the said memorandum of agreement, upon receiving a certificate in writing signed by the said A. B. Clayton, or other the architect of the defendant, testifying that the flooring-joists of the first story of the said dwelling-house had been actually laid, and his approval of the works so executed; such further sum of money as would be equal to three-fourth parts of the price or value of the further works that should have been done subsequently to the date of the architect's said certificate, upon the completion of the carcase of the dwelling-house; and the balance or sum which should be found due to the plaintiff, after deducting the two previous payments, within two calendar months after receiving the said architect's certificate that the whole of the buildings and works thereby contracted for had been executed, and completed to his satisfaction.

The work having been completed, the plaintiff sought by this action to recover his charges for some additional work not contained in the original contract.

At the trial it appeared that Mr. Clayton, the architect, had examined and approved of the plaintiff's charges for the buildings mentioned in the agreement, and had written the following letter to the defendant, more than two months before the action:—

With this you will receive Mr. Morgan's account. My private statement, showing the variations of prices and qualities, shall be copied and forwarded to you. As regards to when and where executed, my only data exist in my measuring book, which shall be open for your inspection at any time at my office. I also forward you the drawings marked 6 and 7, and the original elevation and plan submitted to the commissioners of woods and forests.

I remain, &c. A. B. CLAYTON.

March 24, 1832.

This letter contained an account, headed, "Final statement of extras and omissions of the carcase of a house for George Birnie, Esq., by T. Morgan, builder."

A letter was also put in, addressed to Clayton by the defendant, April 4, 1832, in which he asked for Clayton's private statement of prices and quantities; expressed himself anxious to have the matter speedily settled, and made no objection on the ground of not having received a certificate. But as it did not appear that Mr. Clayton had ever given any certificate of his satisfaction as to the mode in which the work had been executed, Tindal, C. J., directed a nonsuit, on the ground that the delivery of such a certificate was a condition precedent to the plaintiff's right of action.

Spankie, Serjt., now moved to set aside this nonsuit on the ground that the agreement did not require the certificate touching the additions to be in writing; and that Mr. Clayton's allowance of the plaintiff's charges must be deemed an implied certificate, for he could not allow the charges to be correct without implying thereby that the building had been executed to his satisfaction. Besides, it might be doubtful whether any certificate were requisite with respect to charges for additional work; the certificate was to apply only to the building as originally contracted for, and the defendant had never objected to pay on the ground that a proper certificate had not been rendered.

TINDAL, C. J. I was of opinion at the trial, and am still of opinion, that the production of a certificate from Mr. Clayton was a condition precedent to the bringing this action. The agreement stipulates, that the price of additions or alterations should be added to the sum contracted for by the agreement, such price being first settled by the architect of the defendant, who should be sole arbitrator in settling such price, and all disputes that should arise about the premises. Then follows the stipulation for payment in proportion to the work done at two different periods upon receiving a certificate in writing of Mr. Clayton's approval, and for payment of the balance of the whole within two calendar months after receiving the said architect's certificate that the whole of the buildings contracted for had been executed to his satisfaction. That appears to involve not only the original but the additional or extra works. Unless the letter and delivery of the plaintiff's account, and the checking that account by Clayton, amount to a certificate, no certificate has been given. It appears to me, that the effect of a certificate would be altogether different; applying to the manner in which the work has been done, while the checking the accounts applies only to the propriety of the charges.

The rest of the Court concurring the rule was *Refused.*

THURNELL v. BALBIRNIE.

IN THE EXCHEQUER, TRINITY TERM, 1837.

[*Reported in 2 Meeson & Welsby,* 786.]

THE first count of the declaration stated, that before and at the time of making the agreement and the promise and undertaking of the defendant thereinafter mentioned, the defendant held, occupied, and enjoyed, at his request, certain rooms, apartments, and premises of the plaintiff, as tenant thereof to the plaintiff, the same then being part and parcel of a dwelling-house of the plaintiff, and in which there were certain goods and fixtures and chattels, to wit, &c., of the plaintiff of great value, to wit, of, &c.; and thereupon heretofore, to wit, on the 26th of December, 1836, it was agreed by and between the plaintiff and the defendant in manner following; that is to say, the plaintiff then agreed to sell and deliver to the defendant, who then agreed to purchase and take of the plaintiff, the said goods, fixtures, and chattels, at a valuation to be made by certain persons, to wit, Mr. Newton and Mr. Matthews, or their umpire; and the plaintiff said, that the said Mr. Newton was appointed by and on behalf of the plaintiff, and the said Mr. Matthews by and on behalf of the defendant, to value as aforesaid. The declaration then averred mutual promises, and alleged that Newton, on behalf of the plaintiff, was ready and willing to value the said goods, &c., and at the request and by the authority of the plaintiff requested Matthews to value the same, whereof the defendant and Matthews had notice; but that the defendant and Matthews then and thence continually neglected and refused so to do. And the plaintiff further said, that he, the plaintiff, afterwards, to wit, on the 2d of February, 1837, gave notice to the defendant that the plaintiff's said appraiser and valuer, the said Newton, was ready to meet the defendant's appraiser and valuer, the said Matthews, or any other person he might think proper to nominate for the purpose on the defendant's behalf, at any time within ten days from the said 2d of February which the defendant might fix, to value the said goods, &c., of which the defendant then had notice, but then and thence hitherto wholly neglected and refused to appoint any day for his appraiser, the said Matthews, to value, and wholly neglected and refused to nominate any other appraiser, and during all that time has wholly refused and neglected to take any steps to value as aforesaid, or to cause or procure the same to be valued according to his said agreement and promise, and has during all the time aforesaid wholly refused to value the said goods, &c., or to let the same be valued, according to his said agreement and promise. And thereupon the said Mr. Newton afterwards, and after the lapse of a reasonable period of time, to wit, one month from the day and the year last aforesaid, proceeded to value and did then value the said goods, &c., and the price thereof upon such valuation reasonably amounted to the sum of £500, whereof the defendant had notice, and was requested to pay the same to the plaintiff. And the plaintiff further says, that he hath always from the time of making such valuation as aforesaid been ready and willing to sell and deliver to the defendant the said goods, &c., and to receive payment by him of the value thereof, whereof the defendant hath always had notice; yet the defendant, not regarding, &c., did not nor would, although often requested, take the said goods, &c., so agreed by him to be taken as aforesaid, and pay the plaintiff the value thereof, but hath hitherto wholly neglected and refused so to do, whereby, &c.

There were also counts for goods and fixtures bargained and sold, and on an account stated.

Special demurrer to the first count assigning, amongst other causes, the following: that the count does not sufficiently allege a breach of the defendant's promise therein mentioned, for that it does not allege that the defendant hindered or prevented the said persons appointed and agreed on to make the said valuation, or either of them, from making such valuation. And also that it is alleged by way of breach that the defendant refused to take the goods, &c., agreed by him to be taken, and that he also refused to pay to the plaintiff the value of the said goods, &c., and no agreement or promise is stated in the said count to take the said goods, &c., at their value generally, or at the valuation made by the said Mr. Newton, but at the valuation only of the said Newton and Matthews, or their umpire. Joinder in demurrer.

Kelly, in support of the demurrer. There are many objections in point of form to this count; but the substantial question is, where two persons are by agreement appointed to make a valuation of goods, and one refuses, can either party be liable for a breach of the agreement? How could the defendant be bound to take or pay for the goods until they had been valued according to the agreement? [GURNEY, B. It is not said that Matthews omitted to value by the procurement of the defendant.] It is just as if an action were brought against a party to a submission, because one of the arbitrators refuses to make an award.

The court here called upon

Hoggins, to support the declaration. It is specifically averred in the count that the defendant had notice that the plaintiff's appraiser was ready to value, and the breach assigned is, that he then wholly refused to let the goods be valued according to the agreement. It is submitted that that is sufficient to render him liable for the price. In Hotham *v.* East India Company [1] it was held, that where the defendant by his neglect and default prevented the performance of a condition precedent in a charter-party, that was equivalent to a performance by the plaintiffs. In Raynay *v.* Alexander,[2] where the plaintiff declared in assumpsit for non-delivery of fifteen tods of wool purchased by him out of seventeen of which the defendant was possessed, the declaration was held bad for want of an allegation that the plaintiff had selected fifteen tods of the seventeen, which was an act to be first performed by him; but the court said if the defendant would not have permitted the plaintiff to see the wool, that he might make election, that had excused the act to be done by the plaintiff, and had been a default in the defendant. If these cases be law, the facts alleged in this declaration make the defendant liable as for goods bargained and sold.

LORD ABINGER, C. B. I am of opinion that this count is bad. The agreement stated is an agreement to purchase the goods on the valuation of Newton and Matthews. There is no distinct allegation that the defendant refused to permit Matthews to value on his part; but

[1] 1 T. R. 638.

[2] Yelv. 76.

only an obscure statement that he refused to appoint any day for his valuing, or to take any steps to value or to cause and procure the goods to be valued, according to his agreement, and that he has refused to value the goods or to let them be valued according to his agreement: all which comes after the allegation that Matthews had refused to value, there being no statement that he had changed his mind and was ready and willing to do so, but that the defendant would not permit him. I am of opinion, therefore, that enough is not stated to render the defendant liable for the price of the goods.

BOLLAND, B., concurred.

ALDERSON, B. I should refer the words "or to let the same be valued," &c., to the defendant's letting the goods be valued by another appraiser instead of Matthews, according to the notice which the plaintiff says he gave him.

GURNEY, B., concurred.

Leave to amend on payment of costs; otherwise judgment for the defendant.

GLAHOLM v. HAYS, IRVINE, AND ANDERSON.

IN THE COMMON PLEAS, HILARY TERM, 1841.

[*Reported in 2 Manning & Granger*, 257.]

ASSUMPSIT to recover damages for a refusal to perform a contract of charter-party, whereby the defendants chartered of the plaintiff the ship Pomona, to proceed to Trieste, and having there loaded a complete and full cargo of wheat or other lawful merchandise, to proceed therewith to a good and safe port of the United Kingdom (calling at Cork or Falmouth for orders), and deliver the same on being paid freight, &c. "The vessel to sail from England on or before the 4th of February then next." The declaration contained a general allegation of performance on the plaintiff's part, and alleged a total failure to perform on the defendants' part.

The defendants pleaded, *inter alia*, that although the said vessel was required by the said charter-party to sail from England on or before the 4th day of February next after the making of the said charter-party, yet the said vessel did not sail from England on or before the said 4th day of February; but, on the contrary thereof, the said vessel remained and continued in England, without the leave or license and against the will of the defendants, for a long time after the said 4th day of February, to wit, until and upon the 22d day of February in the year aforesaid. Whereupon the defendants then refused to perform and fulfil the said charter-party, as they lawfully might do for the cause aforesaid. Verification.

To this plea the plaintiff replied, and the defendant demurred specially to the replication.

The argument and decision of the demurrer turned entirely upon the validity of the plea, the replication being admitted to be bad.[1]

Shee, Serjt., in support of the demurrer. The replication is admitted to be bad. The court will therefore have to decide upon the validity of the plea; which depends on the question, whether the engagement on the part of the plaintiff that the vessel should sail from England on or before the 4th of February, is to be considered as a condition precedent. [TINDAL, C. J. Suppose the wind was directly contrary?] In Shadforth *v.* Higgin[2] the freighter had engaged to provide a cargo at a port in Jamaica in time for the July convoy, "provided she arrived out and was ready by the 25th of June." It was held by Lord Ellenborough, C. J., that the arrival of the vessel by the 25th of June, was a condition precedent to the obligation to provide any cargo. In Shubrick *v.* Salmond[3] the defendant covenanted that the vessel should proceed from the port of discharge in Madeira to Wynyard in South Carolina, directly as wind and weather would permit after the discharge of the outward cargo. The charter-party contained a clause releasing the plaintiff from the obligation to provide a cargo at Wynyard, in case the ship should not arrive there by the 4th of March. The declaration assigned a breach in not arriving at Wynyard on the 4th of March, or at any time afterwards; to which the defendant pleaded, that it was impossible, after the discharge of the cargo, to arrive at Wynyard by the 4th of March. It was held, upon demurrer to this plea, that the defendant's engagement that the ship should proceed to Wynyard was an absolute engagement. In Granger *v.* Dent,[4] upon a proviso in a charter-party, that if the ship did not arrive at her port of loading on or before a certain day, unless prevented by stress of weather or other unavoidable impediments, the freighter should not be obliged to provide a cargo; it was held, that if ordinary diligence were used to reach the port of loading, the case was within the exception, though the causes by which the ship was detained might by extraordinary exertion have been overcome. There, unless the arrival of the ship before the particular day had been held to be a condition precedent, it would have been unnecessary to consider whether the case fell within the exception. [MAULE, J. In Granger *v.* Dent the verdict for the defendant would have been wrong, supposing the stipulation not to amount to a condition precedent.] Soames *v.* Lonergan,[5] Stavers *v.* Curling,[6] McAndrew *v.*

1 The statement of the case has been materially abbreviated. — ED.

2 3 Campb. 385. *Sed vide* Deffell *v.* Brocklebank, 4 Price, 42, 43.

3 3 Burr. 1637.

4 Moo. & Malk. 475, Lloyd & Welsby, 270.

5 2 B. & C. 564, 4 D. & R. 74, Abbott, Law of Shipping, 5th ed. 195, 6th ed. 250.

6 3 New Ca. 355.

Adams,[1] Ritchie v. Atkinson,[2] Havelock v. Geddes,[3] Davidson v. Gwynne,[4] all show that this is a condition precedent. [MAULE, J. It will be said that if the sailing on the 4th of February is a condition precedent in this case, the sailing within a reasonable time would also have been held to be a condition precedent. There is a difficulty in saying that one is to be a condition precedent and not the other.]

Bompas, Serjt., contra. No authority has been adduced which proves this to be a condition precedent. All the cases cited show that it is not. None of the stipulations which precede and follow the clause in question can be contended to create a condition precedent. In Shadforth v. Higgins the terms of the proviso made it a condition precedent. Soames v. Lonergan and Shubrick v. Salmond are in favor of the plaintiff. The leading case upon this point is Constable v. Cloberie,[5] where it was held, that a breach of the covenant to sail with the first wind was no answer to an action for freight. This principle was acted upon in Boone v. Ayre,[6] and in Freeman v. Taylor,[7] Bornmann v. Tooke.[8] In Hall v. Cazenove[9] the opinion of the judges is directly in point: Ritchie v. Atkinson, Davidson v. Gwynne. The clause requiring the vessel to be ready to sail on a certain day is introduced for the benefit of the shipper. So in Fothergill v. Walton,[10] where the ship-owner covenanted with the freighter to take on board six pipes of brandy at Hâvre de Grace, and to proceed to Terceira, and there take on board a complete cargo of fruit; it was held that, though this amounted to a covenant on the part of the freighter to ship the brandy at Hâvre, yet that such engagement did not create a condition precedent. A covenant is not a condition precedent because it is prior in point of time to other stipulations. In Stavers v. Curling it was laid down very strongly by the court that the terms must be precise to create a condition precedent.

Shee, Serjt., in reply. The owner is not bound to wait from day to day, and look to his remedy by action against the freighter. The authorities cited for the plaintiff are all cases in which the parties had put their own construction upon the agreement. [TINDAL, C. J. That observation can hardly apply to those cases in which the agreement was by deed. Davidson v. Gwynne.] This is not a case of a deed. In Abbott on Shipping[11] it is said, "If either party is not ready at the time appointed for the loading of the ship, the other may seek another ship or cargo, and bring an action to recover the damages he has sustained."

Cur. adv. vult.

1 1 New Ca. 29.
2 10 East, 295.
3 10 East, 555.
4 12 East, 381.
5 Palmer, 397, 2 M. & Gr. 18; and see 1 Wms. Saund. 320 *b*.
6 1 H. Bla. 273, *n.*, 2 W. Bla. 1312.
7 8 Bingh. 124, 1 M. & Scott, 182.
8 1 Campb. 377.
9 4 East, 476.
10 8 Taunt. 576, 2 B. Moore, 630.
11 5th ed. 179, 6th ed. 232.

TINDAL, C. J., now delivered the judgment of the court.

The question raised upon this record is, whether the clause contained in the charter-party, set out in the declaration, viz., "the vessel to sail from England on or before the 4th day of February next," is a condition precedent on the part of the ship-owner, upon the non-compliance wherewith on his part, the defendants, the freighters, were at liberty to throw up the charter. The defendants in their plea have treated the clause as importing a condition; alleging in such plea that the vessel "did not sail from England on or before the said 4th day of February, but on the contrary remained and continued in England, without the leave and against the will of the defendants, for a long time after; whereupon the defendants refused to perform and fulfil the said charter-party, as they lawfully might;" and the plaintiff having demurred to this plea, the question on the legal construction of the charter-party is thereby raised.

Whether a particular clause in a charter-party shall be held to be a condition, upon the non-performance of which by the one party, the other is at liberty to abandon the contract, and consider it at an end; or whether it amounts to an agreement only, the breach whereof is to be recompensed by an action for damages, must depend upon the intention of the parties to be collected, in each particular case, from the terms of the agreement itself, and from the subject-matter to which it relates.[1] "It cannot depend," as Lord Ellenborough observes, "on any formal arrangement of the words, but (must depend) on the reason and sense of the thing as it is to be collected from the whole contract." See Ritchie v. Anderson.[2] And looking, in the first place, at the terms of this agreement, we think some distinction must have been intended by the contracting parties, between this particular clause and those which precede and follow it, as to the nature of the obligations thereby respectively created. All the clauses of the charter-party, both prior and subsequent to the clause in dispute, are framed strictly and properly in the language of agreement only. The charter-party states, "it is mutually agreed between the parties, that the ship being tight, &c., shall proceed to Trieste, and there load a complete cargo; that the said vessel being so loaded shall therewith proceed to a good and safe port in the United Kingdom; that the cargo shall be sent alongside; that the freight shall be paid in the manner therein stipulated; that forty running days shall be allowed the merchants." And then is interposed the clause now under discussion, viz., "the vessel to sail from England on or before the 4th day of February next." After which the charter-party continues in the same frame as before: That the vessel shall be addressed to the charterer's agents, &c. Referring, therefore, in the first place, to the variation between the language of the particular clause, and that of the clauses amongst which

[1] And see 1 M. & Gr. 851.

[2] 10 East, 295.

it is found, there is reasonable ground for surmising, that some distinction must have been intended between them; and no other distinction can exist, except that the one set of clauses sounds in agreement, and the other clause in condition.

The very words themselves, "to sail on or before a given day," do, by common usage, import the same as the words "conditioned to sail," or "warranted to sail on or before such a day;" and undoubtedly, if in the middle of a common bought and sold note for a cargo of corn, or any other goods, were found the words, "to be delivered on or before such a day," they would be held to amount to a condition; and the purchaser would not be bound to accept the cargo, if not ready for delivery by the day appointed.

And looking at the subject-matter of the contract, without regarding the precise words, we think that construing the words as a condition precedent, will carry into effect the intention of the parties with more certainty than holding them to be matter of contract only, and merely the ground of an action for damages.

Both parties were aware that the whole success of a mercantile adventure does, in ordinary cases, depend upon the commencement of the voyage by a given time. The nature of the commodity to be imported, the state of the foreign and home market at the time the contract of charter-party is made, and the various other calculations which enter into commercial speculations, all combine to show that despatch and certainty are of the very first importance to their success; and certainly nothing will so effectually insure both despatch and certainty, as the knowledge that the obligation of the contract itself shall be made to depend upon the actual performance of the stipulation which relates to them.

The present case appears to us to be distinguishable from those cited on the part of the plaintiff, in both the particulars to which we have adverted, viz., that in this case the form of the stipulation is more nearly in the language of condition than in that of agreement, whilst in the cases cited the stipulation is in the language of covenant only; and again, that in this case the performance of the stipulation goes more to the very root and the whole consideration of the contract. And indeed in most or all of those cases the objection has not been taken until after the voyage had been performed, nor in many cases until after the goods had been accepted; so that it is manifest, the breach of the agreement of which the defendant complained, and which he sought to set up as the non-performance of a condition precedent, could not go to the whole of the consideration of the contract.

Such was the case of Constable *v.* Cloberie,[1] where the ship-owner covenanted, that his ship should sail with the first fair wind; the case

1 Palmer, 397, Noy, 75, Abbott, L. S. 191, 2 M. & Gr. 18.

of Bornmann v. Tooke,[1] where the covenant was that the ship should sail with the first favorable wind; and the defence in each was set up against a demand for the freight, after the ship had performed her voyage and the merchant had accepted the cargo. So likewise in Davidson v. Gwynne,[2] the covenant to sail with the first convoy was held not to be a condition precedent, the voyage being in fact performed; and so of the rest.

Upon the whole, therefore, we think the intention of the parties to this contract sufficiently appears to have been, to insure the ship's sailing at latest by the 4th of February, and that the only mode of effecting this is by holding the clause in question to form a condition precedent, which we consider it to have been.

Judgment for the defendant.

COOMBE v. GREENE.

IN THE EXCHEQUER, MAY 8, 1843.

[*Reported in* 11 *Meeson & Welsby*, 480.]

COVENANT. The declaration stated, that theretofore, to wit, on the 23d of April, 1832, by a certain indenture then made between the plaintiff of the one part, and the defendant of the other part (profert), the plaintiff, for the considerations therein mentioned, did demise, &c., to the defendant, his executors, &c., all that messuage or tenement, with the barn, stable, and buildings, and several closes of land, &c., therein described, for the term of ten years, at the rent of £100 by four quarterly payments. And the defendant did, for himself, his heirs, executors, &c., thereby covenant with the plaintiff, her heirs, executors, &c., that he the defendant, his executors, &c., should and would lay out and expend the sum of £100, being equivalent to the first year's rent for the said demised premises, in substantial and beneficial improvements of and additions to the said messuage or dwelling-house, and in the substantial and permanent repairs thereof, under the direction or with the approbation of some competent surveyor, to be named by and on the part of the said plaintiff, her heirs and assigns. The lease also contained a general covenant to repair, which was set out. Breach, that the defendant did not nor would, after the making of the said indenture and during the continuance of the said demise, or at any other time, lay out and expend the sum of £100, or any part thereof, in substantial and beneficial improvements of and additions to the

[1] 1 Campb. 377.

[2] 12 East, 381.

messuage or dwelling-house, or in the substantial and permanent repairs thereof, under the direction or with the approbation of a competent surveyor, to be named by and on the part of the said plaintiff, her heirs or assigns, or otherwise according to the covenant in that behalf, but on the contrary thereof, the defendant, after the making of the said indenture, and during the continuance of the said demise during the said term, and since wholly neglected and refused so to do, although the said plaintiff always during the said term was ready and willing to appoint a competent surveyor to approve of such substantial and beneficial improvements of and additions to the said messuage, of which the said defendant during all that time had due notice.

Special demurrer, assigning for causes, *inter alia*, that it is not alleged in the said count, that the plaintiff has ever named a competent or any surveyor, under whose direction or approbation the defendant might or could have laid out and expended the said sum of money in repairing the said premises according to the said covenant; that it is not alleged or shown that the plaintiff was ready and willing to name a surveyor according to the said covenant; that it is not alleged that the plaintiff ever offered to name a surveyor, to direct or approve of the laying out and expenditure of the said money by the defendant, &c.

Joinder in demurrer.

The defendant's points marked for argument were as follows:—

The defendant will contend that the breach is bad, because, inasmuch as the improvements of and additions to the messuage mentioned in the declaration, were to be done under the direction of a surveyor to be named by the plaintiff; the naming of the surveyor by the plaintiff was a condition precedent to the performance of the covenant on the part of the defendant, and that the said first breach is bad for not averring performance, or some dispensation of performance, by the plaintiff of such condition precedent. That if the naming of a surveyor by the plaintiff was not a condition precedent to the defendant's performance of the covenant, still, if any improvements or additions were made by the defendant, the naming of a surveyor by the plaintiff, and the disapproval of such improvements or additions by such surveyor, were conditions precedent to any right of action in the plaintiff on the said covenant; and on the other hand, if no improvements or additions whatever were made, the said first breach is too large, uncertain, and ambiguous.

The plaintiff's points for argument were: The plaintiff will contend that the naming of a surveyor by the plaintiff was not a condition precedent, and that it was not necessary to aver performance or dispensation of performance by the plaintiff of the said supposed condition precedent, but that the breach assigned is good in all respects, and not open to the objections or any of them set forth in the demurrer and points for argument made by the defendant.

Bovill, in support of the demurrer. The objection is, that the declaration does not show that any surveyor was appointed, and until a surveyor was appointed, there could be no breach on the part of the defendant. The money was to be laid out under the direction of a surveyor to be appointed by the plaintiff, which was a condition precedent, and until he was so appointed, the covenant could not be performed by the defendant, and it is not enough to aver a readiness and willingness to appoint a surveyor, because the defendant had nothing to do with the appointment: it ought to have been shown distinctly that an appointment had been made. As it is, the declaration does not show that the defendant has broken his covenant.

Ogle, contra. The general covenant to repair is not controlled by the appointment of a surveyor, and there might be circumstances under which the plaintiff might be entitled to maintain an action, although a surveyor had not been appointed. Suppose the defendant had wilfully damaged or pulled down any part of the dwelling-house, could not the landlord have maintained an action for dilapidations, without a surveyor having been appointed? In such a case the tenant would be bound to rebuild it, and in the event of his neglecting to do so, he would be liable to an action on the covenant.

Per Curiam. The plaintiff has declared on a covenant by which the defendant undertook to expend the sum of £100 in substantial improvements of and additions to the dwelling-house, and in the substantial repair thereof under the direction and with the approbation of a surveyor. Now the appointment of a surveyor was a preliminary step, for until one was appointed he could not give directions as to how the money was to be expended. The defendant could not fulfil his part of the contract without the approbation of a surveyor, who was to direct and approve of his proceedings. The appointment of a surveyor is therefore a condition precedent to his liability to expend the £100; and as the declaration does not aver any such appointment to have taken place, it is bad, and there must be

Judgment for the defendant.

RAE *v.* HACKETT.

In the Exchequer, May 1, 1844.

[*Reported in* 12 *Meeson & Welsby*, 724.]

Assumpsit on a charter-party. The declaration stated, that, by articles of agreement made between the plaintiff and the defendant, owner of the ship Emma, it was agreed that the ship should sail and proceed in ballast to a safe and convenient port near to Cape Town, and there load a full cargo of merchandise, and therewith proceed to Cork or Falmouth, and the plaintiff agreed to load the said vessel with the said cargo, and to pay freight for the same to the defendant, &c. The declaration then averred, that although the plaintiff was ready and willing to appoint and put on board the ship a fit and proper person as supercargo, to take care of the merchandise to be loaded on board the said ship, to indicate and make known, and which supercargo would have indicated and made known, to the master of the ship, a safe and convenient port near Cape Town for receiving on board such cargo of merchandise, yet the defendant did not nor would suffer or permit the said ship to proceed in ballast on the said intended voyage, &c.

General demurrer and joinder.

The principal point stated for argument by the defendant was, that the declaration was defective and bad, in omitting to state, either that the plaintiff gave notice to the defendant of a safe and convenient port near Cape Town, to which the ship was to proceed, or any thing equivalent in law to such notice.

Crowder, in support of the demurrer. The question in this case is, whether it is not a condition precedent to the right of action on this charter-party, that the charterer should have indicated a safe and convenient port to which the ship might proceed to take in her cargo, and whether what is averred in this declaration, as to the appointment of a supercargo, is sufficient. It is submitted that it is not. It is of the utmost importance that the owner of the vessel should know, before the commencement of the voyage, whither she is going. The plaintiff does not state that he gave him that information; he avers, indeed, that he did something else instead, but he does not state that that was assented to by the defendant. If he had alleged that it was agreed between the parties that the indication of a port by the supercargo should be sufficient, that might have entitled him to sue; but the charter-party does not provide for that. There is no provision for the maintenance of a supercargo. That which by the charter-party is a condition precedent to the defendant's liability is not averred. [PARKE, B. The only question is, whether the owner may not be bound to go to a safe port selected by himself.] The selection of the merchandise must be by the shipper; and so the plaintiff has considered it in framing his declaration.

Tomlinson, contra. If the defendant was bound to go to a safe port selected by himself, the plaintiff is entitled to recover, but it must be admitted that the contract was not so understood by either party, but that the plaintiff had the option of naming the port. It is submitted, however, that from the whole of the charter-party it appears that the plaintiff was to go out, and have the control of the cargo; and if so, that the averment as to the supercargo would be sufficient. The charter-party does not name or allude to any agents of the plaintiff at the port near Cape Town. The plaintiff personally undertakes to load the vessel with a cargo. On the other hand, agents of the plaintiff at London and Liverpool are expressly named for the return cargo. There is no allegation that the defendant asked the plaintiff to name a port; and there are many things to be done which must be done either by the charterer himself or by a supercargo. The calling for orders rather imports the latter.

POLLOCK, C. B. I think this is a perfectly clear case. Calling to our assistance our knowledge of mercantile matters, it seems to me that the port to which the vessel was to proceed was to be selected by the charterer, and not by the owner. It is admitted, that it is either to be named by him, or that he is to send somebody with the vessel to name it. But if it was to be the latter, there should have been a stipulation to that effect in the charter-party.

PARKE, B. My only doubt arose from the omission of the charter-party to state whether the option of selecting the port was to be with the charterer or the owner. But, looking at the whole of it, I think the port was to be selected by the plaintiff, the charterer; therefore it should either have been named before the ship sailed, or there should have been an express stipulation for its being named afterwards. So, if it was intended that a supercargo should go for that purpose, there should have been an express stipulation to that effect. In the absence of any such agreement, the charterer is the party to select the port. The declaration, therefore, is bad for want of an averment that he selected a safe port, and gave notice thereof to the defendant.

ALDERSON, B. I am of the same opinion. It is clear that the charterer is the person to name the port, because he is to provide the cargo. How could he provide a cargo from all the places which the other party might choose to go to?

ROLFE, B., concurred. *Judgment for the defendant.*

OLLIVE v. BOOKER.

IN THE EXCHEQUER, NOVEMBER 13, 1847.

[*Reported in* 1 *Exchequer Reports*, 416.]

ASSUMPSIT to recover damages for breach of a contract of charter-party, which was in the following terms: "London, 24th December, 1844. Charter-party. It is this day mutually agreed between Messrs. Ollive, Nephew, & Co., original charterers of the good ship or vessel called the Dove, A 1, of the measurement of 149 tons or thereabouts, now at sea, having sailed three weeks ago, and Messrs. Booker

& Co., merchants, that the said ship, being tight, staunch, and strong, and every way fitted for the voyage shall with all convenient speed sail and proceed to Marseilles (after having delivered her cargo at Genoa for ship's account), or so near thereunto as she may safely get, and there load from the factors of the said charterers a full cargo of linseed or other goods, which the said merchants bind themselves to ship, not exceeding what she can reasonably stow and carry over and above her tackle, apparel, provisions, and furniture; and being so loaded, shall therewith proceed to one safe port in the United Kingdom, calling at Cork or Falmouth for orders, which are to be given in due course of post, or so near thereunto as she may get, and deliver the same on being paid freight at and after the rate of 5*s.* 6*d.* per imperial quarter for linseed, or other goods in full proportion, according to the London printed rates delivered, the act of God, restraints of princes and rulers, the Queen's enemies, fire, and all and every other dangers and accidents of the seas, rivers, and navigation, of whatever nature and kind soever, during the said voyage, always excepted. The freight to be paid on unloading and right delivery of the cargo, one-third in cash, and the remainder by an approved bill on London at three months' date. Thirty working days are to be allowed, Sundays excepted, the said merchant (if the ship is not sooner despatched) for loading the said ship at Marseilles, and unloading at the return port; mats and bulkheads to be found by the charterers, and dunnage by the ship, and ——— days on demurrage, over and above the said laying days, at £4 per day; the penalty for the non-performance of this agreement, £400; the vessel to be consigned to the freighters' agents at Marseilles; cash for usual disbursements at Marseilles, free of interest and commission but the insurance. Bills of lading to be signed for more or less freight, without prejudice to the charter-party. Per proc. Booker & Co., Thomas Booker, jun.; Ed. Ollive, Nephew, & Co.; John Aitkin, witness to the signature of Messrs. Booker & Co., and of Messrs. Ed. Ollive & Co. The commission on this charter-party is at £5 per cent, due ship lost or not lost. The vessel to be addressed to Alexander Howden or his agents at the port of discharge."

The first count of the declaration, after setting forth the provisions of the charter-party, averred mutual promises and performance on the part of the plaintiff, and assigned as a breach that "the defendant did not nor would, within the space of the said thirty working days in the said last-mentioned charter-party, ship a full cargo of linseed or other goods, according to the terms of the said last-mentioned charter-party, in or on board the said ship or vessel, according to the tenor and effect of the said last-mentioned charter-party and of his said promise aforesaid, but on the contrary the defendant both neglected," &c.

The eighth plea to the first count, after setting out the charter-party verbatim, proceeded as follows: And the defendant avers that upon the making of the said charter-party, time was an essential and material part of the contract, and that the probable situation of the vessel, with reference to the date of her sailing, was also a material and essential part of the contract, to wit, with reference to the object of the said voyage and the distance of the said port of Marseilles, and the nature of the said intended cargo and the time of year at which the said charter-party was made. And the defendant further says, that in point of fact at the time of the making of the said charter-party the said vessel had not sailed three weeks before, but on the contrary had sailed at a materially and unreasonably later time, to wit, one week later, which the plaintiff at the time of the making of the said charter-party knew, and whereof the defendant had no notice or knowledge; wherefore the defendant wholly declined to accept or employ the said vessel under the said charter-party, to wit, immediately upon learning and knowing that the said vessel had not sailed as in the said charter-party set forth, to wit, upon the 1st of February, 1845, and wholly neglected and refused to load any cargo on board her, to wit, upon the day and year last aforesaid, as he lawfully might for the cause aforesaid. Verification. Replication, *de injuria*.[1]

At the trial, at the sittings after last Hilary Term, before the Lord Chief Baron, a verdict was found for the plaintiff upon all the issues, except those raised by the eighth, ninth, and eleventh pleas, and upon these issues the defendant had a verdict; leave being reserved to the plaintiff to move to enter a verdict upon them also.

Crowder having obtained a rule *nisi* accordingly, and also for judgment *non obstante veredicto* upon the eighth plea,[2]

Watson and *Greenwood* now shewed cause. The plaintiff is not entitled to judgment *non obstante veredicto* upon the eighth plea. The statement in the charter-party, that the vessel was then at sea, and had sailed three weeks, is an essential and most material part of the contract, and was not a mere collateral agreement, for the breach of which an action should have been brought to recover any consequential damages. The defendant was not bound to complete his part of the engagement, as this condition was not performed by the plaintiff. The time at which a vessel sails is a most important matter in contracts of affreightment. This is a term which forms the basis of the contract. The case of Glaholm *v.* Hays[3] is a direct authority upon this very point. The words in that charter-party were these: "The vessel to sail from England on or before the 4th of February next," and it was

[1] The statement of the pleadings has been materially abbreviated. — ED.

[2] The argument upon that part of the rule relating to the issues upon the 9th and 11th pleas depended upon the facts, and is omitted. Watson, on the part of the defendant, had obtained a cross-rule to enter a nonsuit upon the plea of *non-assumpsit*, which was argued immediately after the present case, and was discharged.

[3] 2 Man. & G. 257, 2 Scott, N. R. 471.

held that the sailing of the vessel on or before that day was a condition precedent. The stipulation in that and the present case is the same; there the vessel was "to sail," here it is affirmed that it "had sailed" at a certain time. The judgment of the court in Glaholm v. Hays is most material, as laying down the principles for the government of the present question. Tindal, C. J., there says: "It cannot depend, as Lord Ellenborough observes, on any formal arrangement of the words, but (must depend) on the reason and sense of the thing as it is to be collected from the whole contract." And in a subsequent part of the judgment, the whole of which is applicable to the present case, his Lordship proceeds: "Both parties were aware that the whole success of a mercantile adventure, does, in ordinary cases, depend upon the commencement of the voyage by a given time. The nature of the commodity to be imported, the state of the foreign and home market at the time the contract of charter-party is made, and the various other calculations which enter into commercial speculations, all combine to shew that despatch and certainty are of the very first importance to their success; and certainly nothing will so effectually secure both despatch and certainty, as the knowledge that the obligation of the contract itself shall be made to depend upon the actual performance of the stipulation which relates to them." That doctrine governs the present case. The Lord Chief Justice then distinguishes cases where the cargo had arrived, and the objection, being made at that time, was too late. In Freeman v. Taylor,[1] which was an action on a charter-party, the defendant had refused to find a cargo in consequence of deviation. Tindal, C. J., there said, in the course of his direction to the jury: "If the deviation was so long and unreasonable, that in the ordinary course of mercantile concerns it might be said to put an end to the whole object the freighter had in view in chartering the ship, in that case the contract might be considered at an end." The court held this direction right. It is a condition in contracts on charter-parties, that the time at which a vessel shall sail, shall either be a reasonable time, or the time which is stipulated. M'Andrew v. Adams.[2] In cases where an article is warranted, a person is not bound to accept it unless it comply with the warranty. The time of the vessel's sailing is as much a condition of the charter-party as that she was staunch and strong. (They were then stopped by the court.)

Crowder and *Bovill* in support of the rule. This plea affords no answer to the action. The statement in the charter-party, upon which the plea is founded, is a mere representation, and not a condition. The plaintiff might be liable for the breach of it in a cross-action. The statement is treated as a representation in the plea, which alleges that the plaintiff, at the time the contract was completed, knew that the said vessel had not sailed three weeks before, but a materially and unrea-

[1] 8 Bing. 124. [2] 1 Bing. N. C. 29, 1 Scott, 98.

sonably later time. The case of Glaholm *v.* Hays is distinguishable from the present; there it was agreed (after several stipulations), "the vessel to sail on or before a certain day." The very position of the words distinguishes the two cases, and the time there was future; here it was past. If the word "warrant" had been in the clause, the question would have been different. In Glaholm *v.* Hays, Tindal, C. J., says: "The very words themselves, 'to sail on or before a given day,' do, by common usage, import the same as 'conditioned to sail,' or 'warranted to sail on or before such a day.'" Freeman *v.* Taylor is not like the present case, the question there being with respect to deviation. There is no statement in this plea that the defendant received any prejudice from the time when the vessel sailed. It is established, that if a matter in a covenant goes to part only of the consideration, the breach of it is only a ground for a cross-action.[1]

PARKE, B. I am of opinion that the rule for judgment *non obstante veredicto* on the eighth plea ought to be discharged. It seems to me that the averment in the plea, that at the time of entering into the charter-party the plaintiff knew that the vessel had sailed a materially and unreasonably later time than that which was stipulated for, is an immaterial averment, and might be struck out. The main question, however, in the construction of this plea, is, whether the allegation in the charter-party, of the vessel being "now at sea, having sailed three weeks ago," is a warranty or a representation. In the construction of agreements, as in the case of contracts under seal, we should endeavor to discover the intention of the parties. Here it is stated that the vessel was now at sea, having sailed three weeks; and if time is of the essence of the contract, no doubt it is a warranty and not a representation. Such also is the case in policies of insurance. It appears to me that it is a warranty, and not a representation, that the vessel had sailed three weeks. It is, therefore, a condition precedent. The rule depends upon each particular contract, and here time was of the essence of the contract, as much so as the statement that she was a sound vessel. This being a condition precedent, and not performed, the defendant was not bound to load the vessel. If he had loaded her, the breach of the condition would have been waived, and he would have been liable for the full freight. I entirely agree with the reasoning of Tindal, C. J., in the case of Glaholm *v.* Hays, which I think applies to the present case. There the stipulation was held to be a condition precedent. The defendant was entitled to say that he was not bound to load the vessel, as the condition had not been performed, and that the case was the same as if the vessel had not proved to be A 1, as she was warranted to be. I think, therefore, that the plea affords a good answer, and that the rule for judgment *non obstante veredicto* ought to be discharged.

ALDERSON, B. I am of the same opinion. The words which describe

[1] Stavers *v.* Curling, 3 Bing. N. C. 355, 3 Scott, 740.

the ship as being A 1, amount to a warranty, and the statement that she had sailed for three weeks is equally so. The question, whether these words amount to a condition precedent has been decided by Glaholm *v.* Hays; the reasonings there are applicable to the present case, and I am unable to distinguish the two cases.

ROLFE, B. I am of the same opinion. The stipulation in the present case is not collateral matter, but is a part of the contract. I agree with the rest of the court, that the case in the Common Pleas governs this. There the stipulation was that the vessel should sail, but that makes no difference. The condition was founded upon the object that she should load her cargo in a certain time, and if it had been that she should load in six weeks, that being the length of the voyage, that would be the same as a condition that she should load in the ordinary time, of which she had already been three weeks at sea. I think the case is governed by that in the Common Pleas, which is consistent with common sense and reason. The rule, therefore, for judgment *non obstante veredicto* must be discharged. *Rule discharged.*

OLIVER *v.* FIELDEN AND OTHERS.

IN THE EXCHEQUER, MAY 30, 1849.

[*Reported in 4 Exchequer Reports,* 135.]

ASSUMPSIT. The declaration stated, that by a memorandum of charter, made the 28th of March, 1848, by the plaintiff, therein described to be agent for the owners of the ship called the Lydia, then on the stocks, of the admeasurement of 1100 tons or thereabouts, then at Quebec, to be launched and ready to receive cargo in all May, A. D. 1848, guaranteed by the owners to sail in all June, A. D. 1848, and the defendants, therein described as Messrs. Fielden & Co., merchants, of the other part, it was mutually agreed between the plaintiff and defendants that the said ship, being tight, staunch, and strong, and every way fitted for the voyage, should with all convenient speed there load, from the factors of the said merchants, a full and complete cargo of timber, including deck load, as follows: — The charterer having the option of shipping 200 to 250 loads of red pine, &c.; and being so loaded, should therewith proceed to Liverpool, or so near thereunto as she might safely get, and deliver the same, on being paid freight, as follows, &c. (The declaration then set out the usual exception of dangers of the seas, and stipulation as to demurrage, and alleged mutual promises and performance on the plaintiff's part.) Averment, that, although the ship, in a proper and reasonable time in that behalf, to wit, on, &c., being tight, staunch, and strong, and every way fitted for the voyage, was ready to receive such cargo, having been theretofore launched, and that she was so ready, as aforesaid, in such a time as that she could and would have sailed; and the plaintiff says, that the said ship could and would have sailed on the voyage aforesaid, in June aforesaid, if the defendants had provided such cargo as aforesaid. And that, during the time aforesaid, and during the whole of the laying days, and days of demurrage in the memorandum of charter mentioned, the plaintiff, at Quebec aforesaid, was ready and willing to receive on board the said ship, from the factors of the defendants, such a full and complete cargo of timber, including deck load, as in the said memorandum of charter in that behalf mentioned, according to the terms of the said memorandum of charter, &c. Yet the defendants did not, nor would, during the said month of June, or at any time whatsoever, provide for the said ship, or load on the said ship, such a full and complete cargo of timber, including deck load, as in the memorandum of charter mentioned, but wholly refused so to do, &c.

Plea, that the said memorandum of charter was and is made in words and figures following (the plea set out the charter *verbatim*, the material part of which is as follows): — It is this day mutually agreed between Edward Oliver, agent for the owners of the good ship or vessel called the Lydia, new ship, now on the stocks, of the measurement of 1100 tons or thereabouts, now at Quebec, to be launched and ready to receive cargo in all May, guaranteed by the owners to sail in all June; and Messrs. Fielden & Co., merchants, that the said ship being tight, staunch, and strong, and every way fitted for the voyage, shall with all convenient speed sail and proceed to, &c., or so near thereunto as she may safely get, and there load, from the factors of the said merchant, a full and complete cargo of timber, including deck load, as follows: — The charterer having the option of shipping 200 to 250 loads of red pine, &c. Averments, that the month of May in the charter-party mentioned, was meant to be, and was, the month of May, 1848; and that the said ship was not launched and ready to receive cargo in all May, 1848. Verification.

General demurrer and joinder therein.

Crompton in support of the demurrer. The being ready to receive cargo in May was not a condition precedent to the plaintiff's right to recover. The terms "ready to receive cargo in all May," mean only that the parties expected that the ship would be ready at that time. The next clause, "guaranteed by the owners to sail in all June," excludes any other construction. The doctrine as to conditions precedent attaches only where the whole adventure is destroyed; if the failure goes to part of the consideration merely, the remedy is by a cross-action. That view is supported by the judgment of Tindal, C. J., in Glaholm v. Hays,[1] where this subject was much considered. In Constable v. Cloberie,[2] it was held that a breach of the covenant to sail with the next wind was no answer to an action for freight. In Stavers v. Curling,[3]

[1] 2 M. & G. 257. [2] Palm. 397. [3] 3 Bing. N. C. 355.

the plaintiff, a captain of a South Sea whaler, covenanted with defendants that he would proceed to the fishery and procure a cargo of sperm oil, and would return to London; and then, at his own costs, deliver it to the defendants, who covenanted, on the performance of the before-mentioned terms on the part of the plaintiff, to pay him a certain proportion of the net proceeds of the cargo; and it was held, that the plaintiff's covenants were independent, and consequently the performance of them not a condition precedent to an action on the defendant's covenant. Ollive v. Booker[1] is distinguishable, for there the defendant pleaded that time was an essential and material part of the contract.

Aspland appeared to argue in support of the plea, but was not called upon.

POLLOCK, C. B. There must be judgment for the defendants. The stipulation as to the vessel being ready to receive a cargo in May, is not mere description, but part of the contract, and forms a condition precedent to the plaintiff's right to recover.

ALDERSON, B. I am of the same opinion. The plaintiff avers that he was ready and willing to receive a cargo according to the terms of the charter-party. One of those terms, and a very important one, was that the vessel should be ready to receive a cargo in May.

ROLFE, B. The cases of Glaholm v. Hays and Ollive v. Booker are conclusive in favor of the defendants.

PLATT, B. In Constable v. Cloberie, the vessel had actually carried the goods. *Judgment for the defendants.*[2]

ARMITAGE v. INSOLE AND ANOTHER.

IN THE QUEEN'S BENCH, FEBRUARY 5, 1850.

[*Reported in* 14 *Queen's Bench Reports,* 728.]

ASSUMPSIT on an agreement, whereby plaintiff agreed to conduct the sale and disposal of the defendants' coals, to carry out their instructions, promote their interests, and extend their connection, to the utmost of his ability and power, throughout Ireland, for three years from 1st of January then next, and for that purpose to visit certain places in Ireland at stated times in each year; and defendants agreed to engage the services of the plaintiff as above described for three years, and to pay him the yearly sum of £120, namely, £60 every 1st day of July and 1st day of January, from the date thereof. And defendants further agreed to give yearly free to the plaintiff during the

[1] 1 Exch. 416.

[2] And see Weisser v. Maitland, 3 Sandf. 318, to the same effect.—ED.

said three years twenty tons of coals, to be put free on board ship at Cardiff for the use of the plaintiff, in lieu of all charges for stationery, and so forth.

The declaration, after alleging mutual promises and performance by the plaintiff of the conditions precedent on his part, as far as was necessary to support the breaches for discharging him from his employment by the defendants under the contract, and for their refusing to pay him the salary agreed on, assigned a further breach as follows: Nor did nor would the defendants give to the plaintiff yearly, or at any time during the said period of three years, twenty tons of coals, or any coals whatever, free on board ship at Cardiff, for the use of the plaintiff; but on the contrary thereof, they, the defendants, wholly neglected and refused so to do, and have not at any time delivered or given to the plaintiff, at Cardiff or elsewhere, any coals whatever, and there is now due and owing from the defendants to the plaintiff, under the said agreement, a large quantity, viz., sixty tons of coals, the same being of great value, viz., £24.

Demurrer. Joinder.

Mellish, for the defendants. This is a demurrer to part only of the breach, but the defendants are entitled to judgment, although the residue of the breach is sufficiently assigned; Lush *v.* Russell.[1] The defendants agree "to give yearly free to the plaintiff during the said three years twenty tons of coals, to be put free on board ship at Cardiff, for the use of the plaintiff." The ship then must be selected, and its destination fixed, before this part of the contract can be complied with. The agreement is silent on the subject; but it is clear that the port must be first selected either by the plaintiff or the defendants. But it is the duty of the plaintiff to select the ship and the port of discharge, as, until that is done, the defendants cannot comply with the contract by delivering the coals free on board. It is therefore a condition precedent to be performed by the plaintiff; and he should have averred that he was ready and willing to accept the coals, and that he had given the defendants notice thereof, and had named a ship and the port at which they were to be delivered; Rae *v.* Hackett.[2]

A. I. Johnston, contra. There is no condition precedent necessary to be noticed by the plaintiff. Reade *v.* Meniaeff[3] shows the general principle, that contracts of this kind should not be construed narrowly. The substance of the contract was, that the plaintiff should have the coals. The defendants would be at liberty to deliver them at any time within the year, even if a request had been made by the plaintiff; Startup *v.* Macdonald.[4] But notice ought to have come from the defendants that they were ready to give the coals on the plaintiff naming the ship. Something was to be done at a time to be ascertained by the defendants. He then referred to Heron *v.* Treyne,[5] and Halling's case.[6]

[1] 4 Exch. 637. [2] 12 M. & W. 724. [3] 7 Com. B. 152, 161.
[4] 6 M. & G. 593. [5] 2 Ld. Raym. 750. [6] 5 Rep. 22 *b*.

The plaintiff's readiness to accept the coals was a condition subsequent to notice by the defendants that they were ready to deliver them; Hudson v. Haslam.[1]

PATTESON, J. The contract clearly shows a duty cast on the plaintiff to name the ship at some time or other; but, it is argued, not until the defendants have given notice of their readiness to supply the coals, because no time is fixed for the delivery. If "yearly" mean at the end of the year, then the time is fixed, and the plaintiff should have named a ship at that time. Perhaps that is the meaning of the contract. But, if otherwise, and if the defendants could call upon the plaintiff at any time during the year to accept the coals upon reasonable notice (for notice must be reasonable), even then the plaintiff must have named the ship, and should have averred that he was ready and willing to accept the coals, and that he had a ship ready to receive them.

COLERIDGE, J. I am of the same opinion. Where circumstances, left uncertain by the contract, are of such a nature that one party cannot perform his part of the contract until they are fixed, the other party, insisting on the contract, ought to fix those particulars. Here both time and place should have been fixed by the plaintiff; but certainly place.

WIGHTMAN, J. The main difficulty arises from the uncertainty of the time when the coals are to be put on board. I should say, the agreement being silent as to time, that it must be at the option of the plaintiff. But however that may be, the defendants clearly cannot give the coals free on board, until they know the ship, and at what port it is to discharge. Whatever, therefore, the construction of the agreement may be as to time, the plaintiff must fail for want of averring that he was ready and willing to name a ship.

Judgment for defendants.

NEALE v. RATCLIFF AND ANOTHER.

IN THE QUEEN'S BENCH, JULY 6, 1850.

[*Reported in* 15 *Queen's Bench Reports*, 916.]

ASSUMPSIT. The declaration stated that, heretofore, to wit, on the 10th May, 1845, in consideration that defendants, at their request, had become and were tenants to plaintiff of certain premises, with the appurtenances, of the plaintiff, to wit, a messuage or public house called the Swan Inn, situate, &c., together with the house and stable and

[1] 7 Com. B. 825, 833.

other outbuildings thereto belonging, upon and subject to the terms that the defendants should maintain and keep in good tenantable repair and condition the said messuage or public house, buildings, and premises, the same being first put into good tenantable repair and condition by the plaintiff, and should deliver up the same in such repair and condition at the expiration of their said tenancy, defendants then promised plaintiff to maintain and keep in good tenantable repair and condition the said messuage or public house, buildings, and premises, the same being first put into such repair and condition by the plaintiff, and that defendants would deliver up the same in such repair, &c., at the expiration of their said tenancy: And although such tenancy continued from thence, to wit, until 11th October, 1847, and although plaintiff after the making of the said promise, and during the continuance of the said tenancy, and before the breach of promise, &c., after mentioned, to wit, on the day and year first aforesaid, did first put the said messuage or public house, buildings, and premises, into good tenantable repair and condition, whereof defendants then had notice, yet defendants did not nor would afterwards and during such tenancy maintain or keep the said messuage or public house, buildings and premises, or any part thereof, in good tenantable repair or condition, or deliver up the same in such repair, &c., at the expiration, &c.; and defendants afterwards, at the expiration of the said tenancy, which happened before the commencement of this suit, to wit, on, &c., wrongfully delivered up the said messuage, public house, buildings, and premises in bad and untenantable repair, &c., and greatly dilapidated, &c., for want of such repair as aforesaid, contrary to their said promise; and thereby, &c. (damage to plaintiff by expense of repair, &c.).

Particular of demand: £50 for dilapidations and non-repair of the premises mentioned in the declaration, and for the bad order and condition in which defendants left the same.

Pleas. 1. Non-assumpsit. 2. That defendants had not become nor were the tenants to plaintiff, &c., in manner, &c. 3. That plaintiff did not first put the said messuage, buildings, and premises in the declaration in that behalf mentioned into good tenantable repair and condition, in manner, &c. 4. That defendants did during the said tenancy maintain and keep the said premises in good tenantable repair and condition, and did deliver up the same in such repair and condition at the expiration of the said tenancy, according to the tenor, &c., of their said promise in that behalf. Issues to the country were joined on the several pleas.

On the trial, before Wilde, C. J., at the Norfolk Summer Assizes, 1849, the following agreement was put in, dated May 10, 1845, between plaintiff of the one part and defendants of the other.

"Articles," &c. "Whereby the said William Neale doth agree to let to the said Francis Ratcliff and Robert Reid, who do agree to hire of him, all that messuage or public house called the Swan Inn," situate, &c., "together with the barn, stable, and other out-buildings, and all the appurtenances thereto belonging, as the same are now in the occupation of the said F. R. and R. R. or their undertenant, from the 11th day of October, now last past, for one year thence next ensuing, and so on from year to year, so long as the said parties shall mutually agree; determinable," &c.; "at and under the clear yearly rent of £41, payable," &c. "And the said F. R. and R. R. do hereby agree with the said William Neale that they the said F. R. and R. R., or one of them, will pay unto the said W. N., his heirs or assigns, the said rent," &c.; "and also shall and will pay and discharge all the rates, taxes," &c.; "and also shall and will maintain and keep in good tenantable repair and condition the said messuage or public house, buildings, and premises, the same being first put into good tenantable repair and condition by the said William Neale, and in such repair and condition deliver up the same at the expiration of this agreement. In witness," &c.

It appeared in evidence that the plaintiff had done repairs to some parts of the premises before the alleged breach, but had not repaired the whole. It was proved also that the defendants had omitted to repair, both in those parts which had been repaired by the plaintiff, and in those which had not. The Lord Chief Justice left it to the jury to say, whether the plaintiff had at first put the premises into a tenantable state of repair, and whether the defendants had left them in such tenantable state. The jury were of opinion that the plaintiff had not put the whole premises into tenantable repair; and that the defendants had omitted to repair in parts which the plaintiff had repaired under the agreement. They found a verdict for the plaintiff on the first two issues; on the third issue they found a verdict for defendants as to part and for plaintiff as to part; and on the fourth for plaintiff as to so much as he had put in repair; for defendants as to the residue. Damages on the fourth issue £20. Leave was reserved to the defendants to move to enter the verdict wholly for them on the third issue.

Palmer, in Michaelmas Term, 1849, moved for judgment *non obstante veredicto* on the third issue. The landlord's contract to repair was not a condition precedent, but an independent covenant; although, therefore, he may have broken it, wholly or in part, he may still recover for the breach committed by the defendants. [ERLE, J. You say that the landlord omitting to put the premises in repair, might sue the tenant for that very non-repair.] The words must be looked to and construed according to the intention of the parties. They clearly meant to frame independent covenants, and not that the landlord's should be a condition precedent. [ERLE, J., mentioned Thomas v. Cadwallader.[1]] There the lessee could not repair until the timber was assigned to him for repairs. There are mutual remedies here on the respective agree-

[1] Willes, 496.

ments; the performance of the landlord's, therefore, was not such a previous condition that the fulfilment of it was necessary to his right to recover; Com. Dig. "Pleader," (C 56.) [WIGHTMAN, J. Your agreement here is a qualification upon that of the tenant; he is to keep in repair the premises which have been put in repair by you. COLERIDGE, J. The tenant is to repair the messuage and buildings, "the same being first put into" good repair by the landlord.] This case ought to be decided on the principles applied in Stavers v. Curling,[1] namely, that a condition precedent is not to be inferred against the intention of the parties; and that, where the covenant does not go to the whole of the consideration, it is not a condition precedent, but only the ground of a remedy in proportion to the actual injury. Ritchie v. Atkinson[2] and Boone v. Eyre[3] are also authorities on this latter point. [WIGHTMAN, J. Would it have been a good replication here that you had put part in repair?] It would. In Cannock v. Jones,[4] by agreement between lessor and lessee of a farm house and buildings, the lessee agreed to do certain repairs, &c., "the said farm house and buildings being previously put in repair, and kept in repair," by the lessor, and the lessor's promise was held to be an independent covenant. [WIGHTMAN, J. The action there was brought by the lessee upon the lessor's promise; and the question was whether or not that amounted to a covenant.] It could not be both an independent covenant for the purpose of such an action, and also a condition precedent. [WIGHTMAN, J. Have you any authority for that?] There is none for the opposite proposition. If the fulfilment of the plaintiff's promise here was not a condition precedent, he is entitled at least to keep the verdict given for him on the third issue, and in any view of the case he ought to retain his damages on the fourth. *Cur. adv. vult.*

O'Malley, on the same day, moved to enter the verdict wholly for the defendants on the third issue. He cited Thomas v. Cadwallader,[5] Sinclair v. Bowles,[6] and Coombe v. Greene.[7] *Cur. adv. vult.*

COLERIDE, J., in the same term (November 16), delivered the judgment of the court. After mentioning the cross-motions his lordship said:

The action was by landlord against tenant for non-repair. The premises were let under an agreement, by one clause of which the defendants were bound to maintain and keep the premises in repair, "the same being first put into good tenantable repair" by the plaintiff.

[1] 3 New Ca. 355. [2] 10 East, 295. See Mills v. Blackall, 11 Q. B. 358.

[3] Note (a) to Duke of St. Albans v. Shore, 1 H. Bl. 273; s. c. (mentioned in Campbell v. Jones), 6 T. R. 573. See Boone v. Eyre, 2 W. Bl. 1312.

[4] 3 Exch. 233, affirmed in Exch. C., Jones v. Cannock, 5 Exch. 713.

[5] Willes, 496. [6] 9 B. & C. 92. [7] 11 M. & W. 480.

The third plea denied that the plaintiff had put the premises into tenantable repair. It appeared that the premises were a public house and outbuildings; the plaintiff had repaired the latter, not the former; but the defendants had neglected to keep the latter in repair; and they assessed the damages for this at £20. The plaintiff contended that his obligation to put in repair was an independent covenant, and not a condition precedent to his right to call on the defendants to perform their agreement; or at all events that it was divisible, and that he was entitled to damages for the non-repair of that part which he had previously put in repair. The defendants controverted both propositions, and therefore contended that, as the plaintiff had not put the whole premises in repair, he could not recover damages for the non-repair of any part. We are of opinion that this was a condition precedent, and that the case is distinguishable from Cannock v. Jones.[1] This disposes of the plaintiff's application; but we think, as the pleadings are framed, that the defendants should have a rule.

Rule nisi granted to defendants. Refused to plaintiff.

In this vacation, June 22,

Palmer and *Worlledge* showed cause. The question is, whether a repair of the whole premises demised was a condition precedent to recovery for non-repair of any part. The stipulations were independent, and the subject of independent remedies. Dicker v. Jackson[2] is a recent authority in favor of the plaintiff's construction. The rule of interpretation in such cases is laid down by Tindal, C. J., in Stavers v. Curling.[3] [WIGHTMAN, J. You must argue here that the plaintiff might recover, though he had never put any part of the premises into repair.] Here a part was put into repair, and was not kept in repair by the defendants; and the verdict is taken as to that part only. To make performance in every particular a condition precedent would lead to the same extravagance of construction which was pointed out in Boone v. Eyre,[4] commented upon, among other authorities, in note (4) to Pordage v. Cole.[5] In Macintosh v. Midland Counties Railway Company[6] the plaintiff had covenanted to complete part of a railway within a certain time for a specified sum, he being provided by the defendants with rails and chairs, &c.; in an action for non-payment, the defendants insisted on a penalty incurred according to the contract, by not completing the work within the stipulated time; the plaintiff denied owing the penal sum, and, in support of his case, proved that he had not been properly supplied with rails, &c., which, he contended, was a condition precedent to the accruing of the penalty. But the Court said: "The

[1] 3 Exch. 233. Affirmed in Exch. C. Jones v. Cannock, 5 Exch. 713. See Friar v. Grey, 15 Q. B. 891, and Grey v. Friar, 15 Q. B 901.

[2] 6 Com. B. 103. [3] 3 New Ca. 355, 368. [4] 1 H. Bl. 273, note (*a*).

[5] 1 Wms. Saund. 320 *a*. [6] 14 M. & W. 548.

covenant on the plaintiff's part is absolute, to complete on a given day, or to pay £300 daily if he does not. Any other construction would lead to the conclusion, which we think an unreasonable one, that the non-supply of a single rail or chair by the time specified for its delivery, although in the result wholly immaterial to the facilities for completion, would entitle the plaintiff to receive the £15,000 given for expedition money, without his giving the expedition for it. On the other hand, by treating the covenants as independent, it is open to the plaintiff, if he has really been prevented from completing the railway in due time by the defendants' neglect, to bring his action against them for that breach of their covenant." Here, according to the argument on the other side, if one hovel was unrepaired by the plaintiff, any other building, though entirely reinstated by him, might be left in decay by the defendants. They entered under the agreement, acquiescing in the partial performance. The landlord's remedy accrued from that time, to the extent of their whole undertaking. It may perhaps be argued that the third issue here involves the whole premises; the words of the plea being, "did not first put the said messuage, buildings, and premises into good, tenantable repair." But the issue is distributable; and, if the proof given by the plaintiff be less extensive than his averment, the proof may be applied to the issue *pro tanto;* Tapley *v.* Wainwright,[1] Wood *v.* Peyton.[2] It was not essential to aver that the plaintiff did not repair the buildings, &c., or any part of them, more than it is to rejoin in support of a plea of infancy in assumpsit that goods supplied to the infant were not, nor were any part of them, necessaries; the plaintiff, therefore, in traversing the averment, does not undertake to disprove it to its full extent. The cases cited in moving for the rule show merely that the contract on one side may, by its nature, be a condition precedent; which it is unnecessary to dispute.

O'Malley and *Couch*, contra. The defendants are entitled to succeed on the whole issue. There is no instance in which a condition has been apportioned in the manner contended for here. That the courts have thought this impracticable is proved by the anxiety they have shown in many instances to construe stipulations as independent covenants, thus avoiding the hardship, otherwise inevitable, that a covenant on one side could not be enforced, because some portion, however minute, of a condition precedent was unfulfilled on the other; Macintosh *v.* Midland Counties Railway Company[3] is an example. The hardship, if any, here, is that which the plaintiff has imposed upon himself. And the same complaint might be made on either side. Suppose the landlord puts in repair only a single window, or some part of the building which is of little use to the tenant, and leaves every thing else in decay, it may be asked, whether the

[1] 5 B. & Ad. 395. [2] 13 M. & W. 30. [3] 14 M. & W. 548.

tenant is liable for not doing all the repairs. In Slater *v.* Stone,[1] the court held that a covenant by tenant to repair premises "*ab et post reparationem*" by the landlord, was conditional, and that a declaration on the covenant, alleging as a breach non-repair by the tenant of a part specified, with an allegation that, at the time of the demise and the beginning of the term, the part was in good repair, without adding "*ab et post*," &c., was bad. The position that the tenant ought at least to repair what has been put in repair by the landlord would be very difficult of application, where partial repairs had been done in a number of places. The issue on the plaintiff's part is, that he did first put the said messuage, buildings, and premises in the declaration in that behalf mentioned into good repair. A verdict cannot be entered for him on such an issue, upon proof that he first repaired some part only. If so entered, it would be conclusive in his favor as to the whole in a subsequent action. [WIGHTMAN, J. The finding here would prevent that, if the contract is divisible.] But, further, this is an action of assumpsit; and the consideration stated is that the defendants had become tenants to the plaintiff on certain terms, which are stated. If the terms are that the plaintiff shall put, not "the same" messuage and premises, but some part of them, into repair, a different consideration is proved from that declared upon, and the variance is fatal; for the terms, taken as a whole, are the consideration; Beech *v.* White:[2] and the plaintiff's promise is entire, and cannot be apportioned; Thomas *v.* Williams,[3] Head *v.* Baldrey.[4] [WIGHTMAN, J. You contend that the putting every part in repair is the consideration for repairing each part. That is the plaintiff's contract.] *Cur. adv. vult.*

WIGHTMAN, J., now delivered the judgment of the court. After stating the substance of the declaration, and the third issue, his lordship said:—

The jury found on this issue that the plaintiff had not put all the demised premises into repair, but part only; that the defendants had not kept that part in repair; and assessed the damages for the non-repair of that part at £20.

There were cross-rules applied for; but the questions raised were discussed on that applied for by the defendants, namely, to enter the verdict for them on this issue; and two grounds were relied on: the first, that the obligation on the landlord to put in repair, was a condition precedent to the tenant's obligation to keep in repair, to which we all agreed on the argument; the second, that, being a condition precedent, it was not divisible, and therefore that a part performance

[1] Cro. Ja. 645.
[2] 12 A. & E. 668.
[3] 10 B. & C. 664, 671.
[4] 6 A. & E. 459.

would not enable the plaintiff to recover as to that part. And upon consideration, we think the defendants are right in this also.

We do not mean to lay down that in no case may a condition precedent be divisible. Cases may easily be conceived in which the covenant or agreement to which it is attached may apply to two or more subject-matters, so distinct that the covenant or agreement, which is one in form, is several in fact; and the condition, in the same way attached to each, is several in fact, though one in form; and in such case it may be clear that, by the intention of the parties, *reddendo singula singulis*, the performance as to one part may entitle to an action for the non-performance of the corresponding part of the covenant. But the burden of showing this will clearly lie on the party who insists upon it, and who seeks to make that divisible which on its face is entire. Now, in the present instance, we see no ground for concluding this to have been the case. The defendants have taken, not two separate dwelling-houses, of which one may be completely enjoyed, though the other may not be in a condition for proper occupation, but they have taken a dwelling-house with appurtenant outbuildings; they have insisted that they shall not be bound to keep in repair till the landlord has put into repair; the performance of this by him is the consideration for the keeping in repair by them; and it seems to us that the unrebutted presumption is, that they intended to have, and the plaintiff agreed they should have, the whole premises in tenantable repair before they were bound to repair any part.

Nor will this raise any inconvenience different in kind from that which follows from holding the condition divisible. If it be divisible, still the whole of the part as to which the action is brought must be shown to have been put in repair: non-repair of a single room would show the condition not performed as to the house, if that part of the covenant were sued on. Inconvenience of this sort must attend every case of condition precedent. On the other hand, the intentions of parties may be defeated, and great injustice done, by allowing an action to be maintained for non-repair of some part, the previous condition of which might have cast little burden on the landlord to put in repair, while he has neglected to do more expensive repairs to another part, the complete repair of which may have been the tenant's principal motive for taking the premises at all.

We think it better to avoid all such questions, and that the verdict on the third issue should be entered for the defendants.

Rule absolute.[1]

[1] Approved and followed in Coward *v.* Gregory, Law Rep. 2 C. P. 153.—ED.

MILNER v. FIELD.

IN THE EXCHEQUER, NOVEMBER 25, 1850.

[*Reported in 5 Exchequer Reports*, 829.]

ASSUMPSIT for goods sold and delivered, work and labor, and materials, &c. Pleas: non-assumpsit, payment, and set-off. Issues thereon.

At the trial before Pollock, C. B., at the last Surrey Assizes, it appeared that the plaintiff sought to recover for work done under a written agreement, whereby the plaintiff agreed to build for the defendant thirty houses for the sum of £3130, to be paid by instalments as the work progressed. There were penalties for the non-performance of the works at certain stipulated periods; and also a proviso, that none of the instalments should be payable unless the plaintiff should deliver to the defendant a certificate signed by the surveyor for the time being of the defendant, that the works had been in all respects well and substantially performed, according to the specifications and plans. Some of the instalments had been paid, and the action was brought to recover the balance. No certificate was obtained; but the plaintiff's counsel tendered evidence to show that the defendant had appointed his own father as his surveyor, and that although the works were in all respects properly done, the certificate was withheld fraudulently and by collusion with the defendant. It was objected on the part of the defendant that this evidence was inadmissible; and the learned judge, being of that opinion, nonsuited the plaintiff, reserving leave for the plaintiff to take the opinion of the court upon the point, and if they should think the evidence admissible the cause was to be referred.

Lush in the present term (November 11) moved accordingly, and submitted, that the want of a certificate could not be taken advantage of under the general issue; but that the proviso should have been pleaded specially, or at all events the plaintiff ought to have been allowed to give evidence of fraud. *Cur. adv. vult.*

POLLOCK, C. B., now said: In this case there will be no rule. Where, by the contract itself the certificate of a surveyor is made a condition precedent to the right to payment, even if it be withheld by fraud, that is only the subject of a cross-action. The nonsuit therefore was right.

Rule refused.

STAUNTON AND ANOTHER v. WOOD AND OTHERS.

IN THE QUEEN'S BENCH, FEBRUARY 14 AND 15, 1851.

[*Reported in* 16 *Queen's Bench Reports*, 638.]

ASSUMPSIT. The count recited that plaintiffs agreed to sell to defendants "certain goods, to wit, fifty tons of good cable bars, at and for the price of £9 per ton, the said goods to be delivered forthwith by the plaintiffs to the defendants at the works, and the said price to be paid by the defendants to the plaintiffs in cash in fourteen days from the time of the making of the said contract." Mutual promises. Averment that fourteen days had elapsed, and that "plaintiffs have in all things performed and fulfilled the contract on their part." Breach: Non-payment. Plea: That a reasonable time, according to the tenor of the contract for the delivery of the goods, within which reasonable time the goods according to the tenor of the contract might and ought to have been delivered, elapsed before the expiration of fourteen days from the making of the contract; and that, although defendants were always ready and willing to accept the goods and pay for them, of which plaintiffs had notice, and were requested to deliver the goods, yet plaintiffs would not deliver the goods; without this, that plaintiffs have in all things performed and fulfilled the contract *modo et formâ*. Conclusion to the country.

General demurrer. Joinder.

The demurrer was argued in this vacation.[1]

Phipson, for the plaintiffs. The demurrer is to the plea; but the real question depends on the construction of the contract stated in the count, whether it makes it a condition precedent to the right to demand payment that the plaintiffs should be ready to deliver the goods. The agreement is to deliver "forthwith;" that cannot mean instantaneously. It means as soon as plaintiffs reasonably can deliver under the circumstances; Tennant v. Bell.[2] In truth the contract is no more than the law would have implied. The plaintiffs are to deliver the goods in an uncertain time, as short as they can reasonably make it, but which may be more or less according to circumstances. Then, as this uncertain time may be more than fourteen days, and the day of payment may come before that of delivery, the defendants must, according to the rule stated in note (4) to Pordage v. Cole,[3] be taken to have relied on the plaintiffs' promise, not upon the performance; Mattock v. Kinglake,[4] Wilks v. Smith.[5] The plea avers that this uncertain time has now been ascertained, and that it has turned out to be less than

[1] February 14. Before Patteson, Coleridge, Wightman, and Erle, JJ.

[2] 9 Q. B. 684. [3] 1 Wms. Saund. 320 *b*. [4] 10 A. & E. 50.

[5] 10 M. & W. 355.

fourteen days; but the question, whether the delivery is a condition precedent or not, depends on what was known and intended at the time of the contract, not on what happens afterwards. The plea does not aver that a reasonable time for the delivery of the goods must in all cases be less than fourteen days, or that the parties supposed that it must, and made their contract accordingly. If it had so averred, the plea would be good in substance, though probably amounting to non-assumpsit, as denying the legal effect of the contract declared upon. The court cannot know what a reasonable time for delivering bars at the plaintiffs' works may be. [WIGHTMAN, J. This is not a contract to manufacture the bars, but to sell them and deliver them forthwith. Is it a reasonable intendment that the parties thought that this could not be done within fourteen days?] The court cannot judicially know what might be reasonably expected; it must depend on all the circumstances; Simpson *v.* Henderson.[1] [ERLE, J. Has there ever been a decided case in which there have been mutual promises, and the time for the plaintiff's performance of his part has actually come before the time for the defendant's performance of his, and the plaintiff has been wholly in default, and nevertheless has recovered?[2] I do not wish to be understood to give an opinion, but ask the question for information, as on your construction of the contract the plea raises that point.] Where performance is not a condition precedent by the contract, a breach in fact is no plea; Dicker *v.* Jackson.[3]

Winston, contra. It appears by the plea that "forthwith" did, under the circumstances of this particular case, mean less than fourteen days. Simpson *v.* Henderson[4] shows that the circumstances might be legitimately taken into account; and, if so, there is a defence; and though the form of the plea ought perhaps to have been non-assumpsit, it is good on general demurrer; Kemble *v.* Mills.[5] No case has been cited in which it appeared on the face of the record that a reasonable time for the performance by plaintiff of what was alleged to be a condition precedent was in fact less than that for the performance by the defendant.

Phipson, in reply. The plea does not say that a reasonable time was necessarily, or probably, to be less than fourteen days. It says that it turned out afterwards to be less. The case is precisely within the words of Mr. Serjeant Williams in note (4) to Pordage *v.* Cole:[6]

[1] Moo. & M. 300.

[2] See New *v.* Swain, Danson & Lloyd's Mercantile Cases, 193, and Bunney *v.* Poyntz, 4 B. & Ad. 568; in which cases it appears to have been held, at *nisi prius*, that, where the period of credit has expired before an actual delivery, a readiness to pay the price is a condition precedent to the right to demand a delivery of the goods, though the purchaser has not failed, and no right analogous to that of stoppage *in transitu* has arisen. There does not appear to be any case, except the principa one, in which the converse has been discussed.

[3] 6 Com. B. 103.

[4] Moo. & M. 300.

[5] 1 M. & G. 757.

[6] 1 Wms. Saund. 320 *b*.

"If a day be appointed for payment of money, or part of it, or for doing any other act, and the day is to happen, or may happen, before the thing which is the consideration of the money or other act is to be performed," &c. *Cur. adv. vult.*

PATTESON, J., now delivered the judgment of the court.

We have considered this case and the authorities referred to on the argument, and are of opinion that, according to the statement of the contract in the declaration itself, the delivering of the goods was a condition precedent. Every contract must be construed according to the intention of the parties, which in the present case the demurrer calls upon the court to ascertain. We think it manifest that, by the use of the word "forthwith," as to the delivering of the goods, in connection with the payment in fourteen days, the parties intended that the goods should be delivered at some time within the fourteen days. Now the declaration alleges a general performance by the plaintiffs, and that is sufficient on general demurrer, and must be taken to mean a delivery or offer to deliver. It would be bad on special demurrer; but, being good on general demurrer, it becomes a material allegation, and is traversable. The plea has traversed it, and is good in that respect, without its being necessary for us to say how far the introductory matter of the plea could of itself have formed a sufficient answer to the declaration. *Judgment for defendants.*

ELLEN v. TOPP.

IN THE EXCHEQUER, APRIL 15, 1851.

[*Reported in 6 Exchequer Reports, 424.*]

COVENANT on an indenture of apprenticeship of the 21st of July, 1846, by the master against the father of the apprentice, the father being a party to the indenture. The material parts of this indenture (of which profert was made) were as follows: "This indenture witnesseth, that Richard Topp, an infant, of the age of sixteen years or thereabouts, by and with the consent of his father, George Topp, of, &c., farmer, doth put himself apprentice to Frederick Ellen, of, &c., auctioneer, appraiser, and corn-factor, to learn his art, and with him after the manner of an apprentice to serve from the 1st day of July now last past unto the full end and term of five years from thence next following, to be fully complete and ended; during which term the said apprentice his master faithfully shall serve, his secrets keep, his lawful commands everywhere gladly do." The indenture then proceeded to state, that the apprentice should do no damage to his master, &c., and that he "shall not absent himself from his master's service day or night unlawfully, but in all things as a faithful apprentice he shall behave himself towards his said master and all his during the said term. And the said Frederick Ellen, in consideration of the sum of £70 to him in hand paid by the said George Topp upon the execution of these presents (the receipt whereof the said Frederick Ellen doth hereby acknowledge), doth hereby covenant and agree to and with the said George Topp, his executors and administrators, and also the said Richard Topp, that he, the said Frederick Ellen, his executors and administrators, his said apprentice in the art of an auctioneer, appraiser, and corn-factor, which he useth, by the best means that he can, shall teach and instruct, or cause to be taught and instructed, finding unto the said apprentice sufficient meat, drink, and lodging, and other necessaries during the said term, except wearing apparel, medical attendance, and pocket-money; and the said George Topp, for himself, his executors and administrators, doth hereby covenant and agree with the said Frederick Ellen, his executors and administrators, that he the said George Topp, his executors and administrators, shall and will find and provide his said son Richard Topp with wearing apparel, medical attendance, washing, and pocket-money, during the said term; and for the true performance of all and every the said covenants and agreements, either of the said parties bindeth himself unto the other by these presents." The declaration then stated, that the said Richard Topp afterwards, to wit, on the said 21st of July, 1846, entered and was then received into the service of the plaintiff as such apprentice as aforesaid, and continued in such service under and by virtue of the said indenture for a long space of time, to wit, from the day and year last aforesaid until and upon the 22d of July, 1849; and laid as a breach that the said Richard Topp did not nor would faithfully serve the plaintiff according to the tenor and effect, true intent and meaning of the said indenture, but on the contrary thereof the said Richard Topp, during the said term of five years in the said indenture mentioned, to wit, on the said 22d of July, 1849, did unlawfully absent himself from the service of the plaintiff, and hath from thence hitherto remained and continued absent from the service of the plaintiff, contrary to the tenor and effect of the said indenture, and of the said covenant of the defendant in that behalf made as aforesaid, to the plaintiff's damage, &c.

The defendant, after setting out the indenture on oyer, pleaded that the plaintiff, at the time of the making of the said indenture as in the declaration mentioned, exercised the art and carried on the business of an auctioneer, appraiser, and corn-factor, as therein mentioned; and that the apprenticeship and covenants aforesaid were made with the plaintiff as such auctioneer, appraiser, and corn-factor, and not otherwise, and that, after the making of the said indenture, and before the accruing of the cause of action, &c., to wit, on, &c., the plaintiff voluntarily and of his own free will gave up, relinquished, abandoned, and ceased to exercise and carry on, and hath not, at any time since, exercised and carried on the art and business of a corn-factor as aforesaid. Verification.

Replication, that the plaintiff relinquished his business as a corn-factor aforesaid, with the full knowledge and consent of the defendant in that behalf; and that, from the time of such relinquishment continually until the accruing of the cause of action in the declaration mentioned, the said Richard Topp, with full knowledge of such relinquishment as aforesaid, continued, with the consent of the defendant in that behalf, to serve the plaintiff under the said indenture. Verification.

Special demurrer to the replication, *inter alia*, on the grounds that the consent of the defendant to the relinquishment by the plaintiff of his business of a corn-factor aforesaid, and to the continuing of the said Richard Topp to serve the plaintiff as in the replication mentioned, is not alleged to have been given or contained by or in any deed or instrument under the seal of him the defendant, and that the contract in the declaration mentioned could not in law be varied or altered by parol, or by any consent other than a consent given or contained in some deed or instrument under seal; and that the replication is a departure from the declaration; that the contract relied upon in the declaration is a contract to employ and serve in the art and mystery of an auctioneer, appraiser, and corn-factor; and the replication sets up some new alleged contract to employ and serve in the art and mystery of an auctioneer and appraiser only.

Joinder in demurrer.

The demurrer was argued in Easter Term last (April 26, 1850), before Pollock, C. B., Parke, B., Rolfe, B., and Platt, B., by *Macnamara* for the defendant, in support of the demurrer, and by *Taprell* for the plaintiff; and the court took time to consider their judgment: but afterwards Pollock, C. B., said that, as a difference of opinion existed among certain members of the court, they wished to hear the case re-argued. The case was accordingly re-argued in Hilary Term last (Jan. 20), before Pollock, C. B., Parke, B., Alderson, B., and Platt, B., by

Macnamara for the defendant in support of the demurrer. The replication is clearly bad as amounting to a departure from the declaration, and as setting up a parol discharge from an obligation under seal. The plaintiff, however, will contend, that the plea does not contain any defence to the action, and the question which the court will ultimately have to decide may be thus stated: A master who exercises three trades takes an apprentice, and covenants to instruct him in such trades, but during the term of apprenticeship abandons one of the trades; the apprentice thereupon leaves his service; can the master maintain an action upon the indenture of apprenticeship for the apprentice thus leaving him?

[1]... The exercise of the trades, or rather the non-abandonment of any one of them by the master, is a condition precedent to the service of the apprentice; or, in other words, they are dependent covenants. The non-exercise of the trades for a few days merely would not justify the apprentice in leaving; but the relinquishment of any of them would. The doctrine of dependent covenants is fully discussed in the notes to Pordage *v.* Cole, 1 Wms. Saund. 320 b, and Cutter *v.* Powell, 2 Smith's Leading Cases, 9; where the most important cases bearing upon the subject are cited. The principle was laid down by Lord Mansfield in Boone *v.* Eyre,[2] which has been often recognized and acted upon. "The distinction is very clear," said that learned judge; "where mutual covenants go to the whole of the consideration on both sides, they are mutual conditions, the one precedent to the other. But where they go only to a part, where a breach may be paid for in damages, there the defendant has a remedy on his covenant, and shall not plead it as a condition precedent." The question seems to be, whether, notwithstanding the breach, the contract can be substantially carried out, and whether adequate compensation can be obtained for such breach. The reason of the rule is, that the damages would be unequal if a breach of a comparatively unimportant part of the contract afforded a ground for rescinding it altogether. The chief tests to be applied appear to be the materiality and importance of the covenants broken, and the difficulty of assessing damages thereupon. There is a close analogy between these questions and those which relate to penalties and liquidated damages. In the latter instance, the importance of the matter, the performance of which is secured by a penalty, and the difficulty of estimating the damages for its breach, are the main points to be considered. Galsworthy *v.* Strutt.[3] The rule adopted for the construction of covenants as dependent or independent is this: That the good sense of the case, the nature of the instrument, and the intention of the parties are to decide the question. Applying these principles to the present case, the covenant by the apprentice to serve is dependent upon the implied covenant of the master not to relinquish any of his trades. The trades carried on by a master at the time when an apprentice is bound to him form the basis of the whole contract. It is of course a preliminary inquiry with the father or other guardian of the apprentice, what trades are exercised by this person to whom the apprentice is to be bound; are they such as I desire him to learn? This question affects the very position and status of one of the contracting parties, whose trading capacity forms the whole inducement

[1] A part of the case is omitted as not relating materially to the subject of conditions. — ED.

[2] 1 H. Bla. 273, *n.*, 2 W. Bla. 1312.

[3] 1 Exch. 659.

for the contract. If one trade may be given up, why may not all? Where is the line to be drawn? Suppose two out of the three had been abandoned, was the apprentice to continue in the service to learn the third trade alone? The one abandoned may have been the most material of the three; it may have been the only one which the father desired his son to learn; but yet it may have been necessary to bind him to a master who exercised the three, as it frequently happens in country towns that several trades must be followed by one person in order to gain a livelihood. Perhaps it was necessary for the son to learn and to exercise the three for himself in order to gain a livelihood. The master at one time thought proper to combine the three, why should not the apprentice have an opportunity of doing so? This plea must be considered as if it came before the court on general demurrer; and, in order to support it, the court will presume, if necessary, that the trade abandoned was the most important one. The consequences of compelling an apprentice to stay with a master who can teach him that only which is immaterial or insufficient for a livelihood, would be very serious. An apprentice may be bound for seven years, and the day after his binding the master may relinquish the most important trade. Can it be said that, in such a case, the apprentice must remain until the end of the term? If it should be contended that there may be a cross-action on the part of the apprentice, the answer is, that such a breach as this cannot be adequately paid for in damages. The injury done to a young man by forcing him to waste the best years of his life, does not admit of compensation. The only efficient remedy is afforded by allowing him to seek another service. The exercise of the trades is an entire consideration for the service, and is correlative with it. The covenants on the part of the master, after a breach like this, cannot be substantially performed, as it is a very different thing to exercise two trades instead of three. If the nature of the instrument be looked at, we shall find that its very object is the instruction and protection of the apprentice; this is its substance and its primary intent. The premium is paid in the first instance, and a long term of service is fixed. In some towns, to have served an apprenticeship to certain trades is a qualification required for the exercise of them; and it was necessary in order to obtain the freedom of the city of London. It was clearly the intention of the parties, that the apprentice was to learn and to be capable of following the same trades which his master followed at the time of the execution of the indenture.

The authorities are in favor of these views. The cases in which covenants have been held to be independent are distinguishable from this case. In Boone *v.* Eyre they were held to be so, because, as Lord Mansfield, C. J., said, "If the plea were allowed, any one negro, not being the property of the plaintiff, would bar the action;" showing that the importance of the covenant and of the breach were material points to be considered. Campbell v. Jones[1] may be upheld upon the ground that a time was fixed for the payment of the money, but not for the teaching. (See remarks in Glazebrook v. Woodrow.[2]) It seems the decision would have been different if the covenant had been to pay as soon as he should be taught. Again, the covenant broken by the plaintiff was not the most material part of the contract, as the defendant still had a right to use the patent, the specification whereof would give him full instruction regarding it. In Winstone v. Linn[3] it was held, that the absence of the apprentice, who offered to return, and his disobedience of his master's orders, did not afford an answer to an action for not teaching him. The grounds of the decision were, that otherwise the apprentice would lose the benefit of the contract, for which a premium had been paid, if he were guilty of a single act of misconduct, or were absent for two days; and that the statute relating to misconduct of parish apprentices showed that, at common law, the master had no power in such case to refuse to teach. The court, however, thought that there would have been a defence if the apprentice had absented himself during the whole of the term, or if an unreasonable time had elapsed before he offered to return.

The cases in which covenants have been holden to be dependent are clear authorities in favor of the defendant. Duke of St. Albans v. Shore,[4] and the judgment at page 280, Glazebrook v. Woodrow,[5] Kingston v. Preston,[6] Thomas v. Cadwallader,[7] Large v. Cheshire,[8] Oliver v. Fielden.[9] . . .

Taprell, contra. . . . Supposing the plaintiff to have broken his covenant in respect to that portion of the agreement by which he contracted to instruct the apprentice in the art and business of a corn-factor, yet, inasmuch as the covenant is independent, the defendant's true remedy is by a cross-action against the plaintiff for damages, and the plea, therefore, affords no answer to this action. 1 Wms. Saund. 320 c, Davidson v. Gwynne,[10] Stavers v. Curling,[11] Franklin v. Miller,[12] Cutler v. Bowen.[13] In Winstone v. Linn,[14] Bayley, J., in speaking of indentures of apprenticeship, says: "Such indentures generally contain reciprocal covenants by each party. Those covenants are not dependent, but are mutual and independent, entitling each party to his remedy for a breach of them. The master, therefore, is liable to an action for the breach of the covenant to instruct and maintain the apprentice during the term agreed upon." Here the master covenants to teach the apprentice three distinct trades. His neglect to teach one of them only

1 6 T. R. 570.
2 8 T. R. 366.
3 1 B. & C. 460.
4 1 H. Bla. 271.
5 8 T. R. 366.
6 8 T. R. 371, 1 Dougl. 689.
7 Willes, 496.
8 1 Vent. 147.
9 4 Exch. 135.
10 12 East, 389.
11 3 Bing. N. C. 355.
12 4 A. & E. 605.
13 11 Q. B. 973.
14 1 B. & C. 460.

goes to a part of the consideration. These trades are treated as distinct by several Acts of Parliament; the court is bound to take judicial notice that such is the fact. In the cases relied upon by the defendant, the consideration was indivisible, and the performance on the part of the plaintiff of the covenant on his part formed a condition precedent to his right of recovery. If the trade of a corn-factor formed the substantial part of the consideration, the plea ought to have contained an averment to that effect. If the plea is bad in part, it is bad altogether. 1 Wms. Saund. 28. The apprentice may obtain his discharge under the stat. 5 Eliz. c. 4, § 35, if he has been injured by the master's abandonment of one of the branches of his business; but it may be that the apprentice has received benefit rather than any injury from the relinquishment of this business. He also cited Morrison *v.* Chadwick[1] in support of this part of his argument. . . .

Macnamara, in reply. . . .

The plea need not contain the averment that the trade of corn-factor is essential to the plaintiff's business; for the deed on which the declaration is framed, treats the three trades as one art. The suggested remedy by cross-action presents many difficulties. There would not be any true rule by which to calculate the damages. At what time is the action to be brought? If it were to be delayed until after the expiration of the apprenticeship, the apprentice might sustain a loss for which he might not be able to receive adequate compensation. If the action is to be brought during the term, such a proceeding would militate against the relationship of parent and child, which has been suggested to exist between the parties. The remedy given by the 5 Eliz. is in favor of the apprentice, and is altogether cumulative. *Cur. adv. vult.*

The judgment of the court was now delivered by

POLLOCK, C. B. This was an action on an indenture of apprenticeship by the master against the father of the apprentice, the father having been party to the indenture. The breach assigned is, that the apprentice did not nor would faithfully serve the plaintiff according to the tenor and effect of the indenture; but on the contrary did on the 22d of July, 1849, unlawfully absent himself from the service of the plaintiff, and has thenceforth continued absent from such service. [The Lord Chief Baron, after stating the pleadings, proceeded:] On the part of the plaintiff it was scarcely contended that the replication could be supported. It is obviously bad. Such parol consent cannot entitle the plaintiff to maintain an action of covenant in this form, which is founded entirely on the deed under seal. The case therefore resolves itself into the only question really argued before us, which was whether the plea was good. . . . The objection taken by Mr. Taprell was, that the carrying on all the three trades was not a condition precedent to

[1] 7 C. B. 266.

the plaintiff's right to recover, but that his omission or refusal to carry on any one must be the subject of a cross-action.

This objection is founded on one of the rules for determining when covenants are dependent on each other; which is laid down in Boone v. Eyre,[1] and followed in Campbell v. Jones[2] and other cases collected in the note to 1 Wms. Saund. 320 c. That rule is, that when a covenant goes to part of the consideration on both sides, that is, forms a part of the consideration on the plaintiff's side for the defendant's covenant on the other, and a breach of such covenant may be paid for in damages, and the whole of the remaining consideration has been had by the defendant, the covenant is independent, and the performance of it is not a condition precedent.

"The reason of the decision in these cases is," as is observed by the learned editor, "that where a person has received a part of the consideration for which he entered into the agreement, it would be unjust that, because he had not had the whole, he should therefore be permitted to enjoy that part without either paying or doing any thing for it. Therefore the law obliges him to perform the agreement on his part, and leaves him to his remedy to recover any damages he may have sustained in not having received the whole consideration."

It is remarkable that, according to this rule, the construction of the instrument may be varied by matter *ex post facto*; and that which is a condition precedent when the deed is executed may cease to be so by the subsequent conduct of the covenantee in accepting less: as in the cases referred to, the defendant, in the first, might have objected to the transfer, if the plaintiff had no good title to the negroes, and refused to pay; in the second, he might have objected to the payment if the plaintiff had refused to transfer the patent, though he had been willing to teach the art of bleaching. But this is no objection to the soundness of the rule, which has been much acted upon. But there is often a difficulty in its application to particular cases, and it cannot be intended to apply to every case in which a covenant by the plaintiff forms only a part of the consideration, and the residue of the consideration has been had by the defendant. That residue must be the substantial part of the contract; and if, in the case of Boone v. Eyre, two or three negroes had been accepted, and the equity of redemption not conveyed, we do not apprehend that the plaintiff could have recovered the whole stipulated price, and left the defendant to recover damages for the non-conveyance of it.

Whether the rule can be applied to the present case, has been a matter of great doubt in the minds of some of us; but, after much consideration, we agree that it is not applicable. If this had been an action on a covenant to pay an apprentice fee at the end of the term, and the apprentice had served the whole period, and had had the

[1] 1 H. Bl. 273, note (*a*). [2] 6 T. R. 570.

benefit of instruction as such in two of the trades, it would, we are disposed to think, have been no answer to the action that the plaintiff had discontinued one. But this is an action for not continuing to serve as an apprentice; and although the later services of an apprentice are much more valuable than the early, and are in part a compensation to the master for his instruction in the commencement of the apprenticeship, and so are analogous in some degree to an apprentice fee payable *in futuro*, yet the immediate cause of action is the breach of the contract to serve, and the obligation to serve depends upon the corresponding obligation to teach as an apprentice; and, if the master is not ready to teach in the very trade which he has stipulated to teach, the apprentice is not bound to serve. To this particular covenant to serve, the relative duty to teach seems to us to be directly a condition precedent; and we are not able to distinguish between the three trades of auctioneer, appraiser, and corn-factor, so as to say that one is more the substantial part of the contract than another.

As the plaintiff by his own fault has disabled himself from acting as a master in all the three trades, he has no right to complain of the defendant's son refusing to continue to serve in any.

Our judgment will therefore be for the defendant.

Judgment for the defendant.

GRAFTON AND OTHERS v. THE EASTERN COUNTIES RAILWAY COMPANY.

IN THE EXCHEQUER, MAY 4, 1853.

[*Reported in* 8 *Exchequer Reports*, 699.]

THE declaration stated that by certain articles of agreement, bearing date the 30th of October, 1851, the plaintiffs and defendants covenanted and agreed with each other, amongst other things, in manner following: that is to say, that the plaintiffs would during a certain term of years therein mentioned supply to the defendants, and that the defendants would take from the said plaintiffs, all the coke the said company during the continuance of the said agreement should require at Lowestoft, equal to the reasonable capacity of certain ovens therein mentioned to manufacture for a certain district therein mentioned, at the price of 18*s.* 6*d.* per ton, laden into the said company's trucks, provided that the said coke should be of the best quality; the said plaintiffs on their part engaging that the same should be large and of the best quality, and equal to that made from the best Brancepeth coal, and to be to the satisfaction of the said railway company's inspecting officer for the time being; and agreeing that the said railway company should have power to refuse to accept coke of an inferior quality or small in its pieces, and to purchase what they might require elsewhere, if the plaintiffs did not supply coke of the best quality and equal to that above described, and to the satisfaction of the said railway company's said officer, and to charge the plaintiffs with the excess of price beyond the said contract price. And the plaintiffs say, that during the said term and continuance of the said agreement, they manufactured and supplied to the defendants in the manner provided by the agreement certain coke which they required at Lowestoft for the said district, which was of the quality required by the agreement, and equal to that made from the said Brancepeth coal, and large in its pieces, and of which the value amounted to the sum of £1100, but that the defendants then refused to take the same and pay for the same after the rate aforesaid, contrary to the said articles of agreement. And for that, during the said term and the continuance of the said agreement, the plaintiffs manufactured and supplied to the defendants certain other coke, which they refused, at Lowestoft for the said district according to the said agreement; and which was such coke as the plaintiffs engaged to supply according to the said agreement as aforesaid, and of which the value amounted at the rate aforesaid to the sum of £198 3*s.* 5*d.*, and in all things performed the said agreement on their parts; and although the defendants then accepted and received the said coke they have thence hitherto refused to pay for the same as aforesaid.

The defendants pleaded to the breach above assigned, secondly, that the plaintiffs did not during the said term manufacture and supply to the defendants in the manner provided by the said agreement any coke which they required at Lowestoft for the said district, which was of the quality required by the agreement and equal to that made from the best Brancepeth coal, and large in its pieces, as in and by that breach above alleged.

The defendants pleaded, thirdly, to the same breach, that no part of such coke was to the satisfaction of the defendants' inspecting officer for the time being; wherefore they refused to accept and pay for the said coke, or any part thereof, as in that breach alleged.

The plaintiffs replied to these pleas, that the coke, upon the refusal to take and pay for which the first breach is above assigned, was, during the said term, manufactured and supplied to the defendants in the manner provided by the said agreement, and was required at Lowestoft for the said district, and was of the quality required by the said agreement, and equal to that made from the best Brancepeth coal, and large in its pieces.

Demurrer and joinder.

H. T. Holland, in support of the demurrer. The pleadings do not show any cause of action; for, according to the terms of the agreement between these parties, the coke supplied by the plaintiffs ought to have been "to the satisfaction of the company's inspecting officer." This is a material part of the contract, and is a condition precedent to the plaintiff's right to recover for coke supplied. In Milner v. Field[1] a building agreement contained a proviso that no instalment should be paid unless the plaintiff delivered to the defendant a certificate signed by the surveyor of the latter that the works were performed according to the specifications; and it was there held, that the certificate was a condition precedent to the right to payment, and that the want of it was a good answer to the action. He was then stopped by the court.

Maynard, contra. According to the true construction of this agreement, either the obtaining of the satisfaction of the defendants' officer is not a condition precedent, or if it be so that condition is void. First, the meaning of this clause of the agreement is, that if the coke should not be large and of the best quality, the company should have the power to reject it. This is the subject to which the terms "to the satisfaction of the defendants' officer," is applicable. The inspecting officer was inserted as a person well qualified to form a proper opinion as to the quality of the coke supplied. It does not appear by the pleadings that he was dissatisfied, or that if he was his dissatisfaction was notified to the plaintiffs; and it does appear that the coke was of the quality stipulated for by the agreement. [PARKE, B. This stipulation empowers the company's officer to reject any coke whatever with which he may be dissatisfied. It is to be presumed that he will not be satisfied with the coke which may not be of the quality specified. The satisfaction of the officer is a condition precedent to the plaintiffs' right to insist upon the company's acceptance of the coke, and therefore the plaintiffs ought to have inserted an averment to that effect in their declaration.] Secondly. The condition is void and is not binding upon the plaintiffs. Here the party, upon whose decision the rights of the plaintiffs are made to depend, is the servant of the defendants, and consequently they have it in their own power to withhold payment from the plaintiffs. If the party named had been mutually agreed upon as the arbitrator between the parties, the case would have been different. The present case, however, falls within the principle of the decision in Dallman v. King,[2] where, under an agreement that the lessee should spend a certain sum in repairs, to be inspected and approved of by the lessor, and to be done in a substantial manner, the lessee was to be allowed to retain that amount out of the first year's rent of the premises; it was held that the lessor's approval was not a condition precedent to the lessee's retaining the rent. And the court there said that the case was distinguishable from that of Morgan v. Birnie,[3] where the defendant was to pay for a building upon receiving an architect's certificate that the work was done to his satisfaction; and the architect

[1] 5 Exch. 829. [2] 4 Bing. N. C. 105. [3] 9 Bing. 672.

having checked the builder's charges and sent them to the defendant, it was held that that did not amount to such a certificate of satisfaction as to enable the builder to recover, although the defendant had not objected to pay on the ground that no sufficient certificate had been rendered. In the latter case the architect was appointed by the parties the sole arbitrator in settling the amount to be expended on the premises and all disputes. And in Harrison v. The Great Northern Railway Company;[1] which is a similar case to the present, Williams, J., says: "There is a difference between the case in which the person who is to certify is made an arbitrator, and the case where he is a servant to do some act which the company might order him to do." Upon the defendants' construction of this contract, they have themselves an absolute power of discretion in the matter. [MARTIN, B. Parties therefore ought to be careful how they enter into contracts containing stipulations giving such powers.]

PER CURIAM. — The clause in question is a condition precedent to the plaintiffs' right of action and is binding upon them. They may amend, otherwise there will be *Judgment for the defendants.*

MASON v. HARVEY.

IN THE EXCHEQUER, JUNE 6, 1853.

[*Reported in* 8 *Exchequer Reports*, 819.]

ASSUMPSIT on a policy of insurance effected by the plaintiff, a pawnbroker, with the Norwich Union Fire Insurance Society. The declaration stated the insurance to be (*inter alia*) £150 on the shop of the plaintiff, and £1000 on pledges received under the 39 & 40 Geo. 3, c. 99; also that there was indorsed on the policy the following (among other) conditions:[2] "Eighth: Whenever any fire shall happen, the party insured shall give immediate notice thereof to one of the secretaries or agents of the society, and within three calendar months deliver to such secretary or agent, under his or her hand, accounts exhibiting the full particulars and amount of the loss sustained, estimated with reference to the state in which the property destroyed or damaged was immediately before the fire happened; and such accounts shall, if required by the directors, be supported by the oral

[1] 21 L. J., C. P., 89.

[2] Some of the conditions expressly declared that, in case of non-compliance with their requisitions, "the policy will become void."

testimony, and by the depositions or affirmations in writing of the claimant, and of his or her servants, and by the production of his or her books and vouchers." The declaration alleged that, whilst the property continued so insured, the "said shop and divers pledges received under the 39 & 40 Geo. 3, c. 99, and then being in the said shop, were damaged and destroyed by fire, &c. Breach, that the loss which so happened has not been made good to the plaintiff.

Plea, that the plaintiff did not, within the period of three calendar months after the said shop and pledges were so damaged and destroyed by fire, deliver to any secretary or agent of the said society, under his hand, any such accounts as are in and by the eighth condition mentioned and required, exhibiting the full particulars and amount of the loss sustained by the plaintiff as alleged, estimated with reference to the state in which the property damaged and destroyed was immediately before the fire happened by which the property was so damaged and destroyed.

Demurrer and joinder.

Unthank, in support of the demurrer. The plea is bad in substance. A compliance with the requisitions of the condition in question is not a condition precedent to the plaintiff's right to sue on the policy, but only renders him liable to an action for his breach of duty. The case falls within the principle of the decisions, that, where a person takes an estate or benefit under a contract, subject to a duty, the law will imply an undertaking to perform it; for the breach of which an action may be maintained: Burnett *v.* Lynch.[1] The language and sense of the condition are alike opposed to its construction as a condition precedent; and, moreover, it would be unjust so to construe it. Suppose the plaintiff delivered particulars of his loss, but some few of the pledges were omitted, is he on that account to be deprived of the whole benefit of the policy? [POLLOCK, C. B. The term "full particulars" must mean the best particulars the assured can reasonably give; otherwise it might happen that, if by some inadvertence a duplicate was omitted, or mentioned as lost when in fact it was not, the assured could not recover at all.] The only case on the subject is that of Worsley *v.* Wood,[2] where one of the conditions of the policy was, that persons insured should procure a certificate of the minister, churchwardens, and some reputable housekeepers of the parish, importing that they were acquainted with the character of the assured, and believed that he had really sustained the loss without fraud; and it was held that the procuring such certificate was a condition precedent to the right of the assured to recover; and that it was immaterial that the minister and churchwardens wrongfully refused to sign the certificate. In that case, however, the same injustice would not arise from construing the stipulation as a condition precedent, since it might be complied with at any time. [PLATT, B., referred to Oldman *v.* Bewicke.[3]]

1 5 B. & C. 589.
2 6 T. R. 710; s. c. in C. B., 2 H. Blac. 574.
3 2 H. Bla. 577, note.

Crowder (*Brewer* with him), contra. The delivery of particulars of the loss is a condition precedent to the right of the assured to recover. Worsley *v.* Wood in effect decides this case. The assured is bound to give the best particulars which he can under the circumstances. He was then stopped by the court.

POLLOCK, C. B. By the contract of the parties, the delivery of the particulars of loss is made a condition precedent to the right of the assured to recover. It has been argued that such a construction would be most unjust, since the plaintiff might be prevented from recovering at all by the accidental omission of some article. But the condition is not to be construed with such strictness. Its meaning is that the assured will, within a convenient time after the loss, produce to the company something which will enable them to form a judgment as to whether or no he has sustained a loss. Such a condition is in substance most reasonable; otherwise a party might lie by for four or five years after the loss, and then send in a claim when the company perhaps had no means of investigating it. The plaintiff may have liberty to amend by withdrawing the demurrer, otherwise judgment for the defendant.

ALDERSON, B., PLATT, B., and MARTIN, B., concurred.

Amendment accordingly.

GRAVES *v.* LEGG AND ANOTHER.

IN THE EXCHEQUER, MAY 9, 1854.

[*Reported in* 9 *Exchequer Reports*, 709.]

THE declaration stated, that it was on the 19th of May, 1853, through Messrs. H. & R., brokers at Liverpool, agreed between the plaintiff and defendants in manner following, that is to say, the plaintiff then agreed to sell to the defendants, and the defendants to buy of the plaintiff, about 300 to 350 bales white washed Donskoy fleece wool, to arrive, at 10½*d.* per pound, laid down either at Liverpool, Hull, or London, deliverable at Odessa during August then next, old style, to be shipped with all despatch, warranted fair average quality, but should they prove otherwise, to be taken with a fair allowance, which it was mutually agreed between buyer and seller should be assessed by the said Messrs. H. & R.; subject to the safe arrival of the wool in good condition at any of the ports stated, and the names of the vessels to be declared as soon as the wools were shipped; customary allowances, payment cash in fourteen days, less 1½ per cent discount, from the date of finishing loading. Which agreement being made, afterwards the said wool, being 333 bales of wool of the quality and description in the said agreement mentioned, was, during the said month of August, old style, delivered, to wit, by the growers thereof at Odessa, to wit, to the agents of the plaintiff in that behalf, and was with all despatch then shipped there on board a certain vessel called the Science, which said vessel then sailed from Odessa with the said wool on board thereof, and afterwards, to wit, on the 22d of November, 1853, arrived at Liverpool with the said wool on board safe and in good condition, and according to the terms of the said contract; and the plaintiff says, that the defendants have had notice of all the said premises, and that a reasonable time for the defendants to accept the said wools after the same arrived, and to fulfil their part of the contract, and pay for the said wools, has long since elapsed, and that he the plaintiff has at all times performed and fulfilled and been ready and willing to perform and fulfil all conditions precedent to his right to have the said wools accepted and paid for, and to his right to maintain this action. Yet the defendant would not at any time accept nor pay for the said wools, or any part thereof.

Plea, that the defendants agreed with the plaintiff to buy the said wool in the declaration mentioned, for the purpose of reselling the same in the way of their, the defendants', trade and business of wool-dealers, and thereby acquiring gains and profits. And further, that wool is an article that fluctuates greatly in price in the market; and that the defendants could only resell the said wool as aforesaid when, and not before, the defendants had notice of the same being shipped, and when and not before the name of the vessel in which it was so shipped had been declared, according to the said contract in the declaration mentioned; of all which premises the plaintiff, at the time of the making of the said agreement, had notice; and further that, although the plaintiff had such notice, yet the plaintiff did not declare to the defendants, or either of them, the name of the vessel in which the said wool was shipped, or within the time at or within which he was by the agreement bound to declare the same, that is to say, as soon as such wool was so shipped, but omitted so to do and delayed and omitted so to declare the name of the said vessel in which the said wool was so shipped as in the said declaration mentioned, or to give the defendants any notice of the same being so shipped, for a long and unreasonable time after the same was so shipped; and the defendants had not notice of the shipment of the said wool, or of the name of the vessel in which the same had been shipped, until after the expiration of a long and unreasonable time after the same had been so shipped, and after the plaintiff was bound and ought to have given and declared the same, and might and could have done so; and further, that between the time when the name of the said vessel ought to have been declared according to the said agreement in the said declaration mentioned, and the time when it was first declared to the defendants, or when they first had any notice of the said ship having sailed with the said wool on board thereof, the price of wool in the market had greatly fallen, and the said wool thence continually remained so fallen in price, and the same, when the name of the said vessel was first declared, and when the defendants first had notice or knowledge of the same having been so shipped, would sell or could be sold only for a much less sum of money than it would have done at the time when the plaintiff ought to and could have declared the name of the said vessel, or given the defendants such notice as aforesaid. Wherefore the defendants did not nor would accept or pay for the said wool, as in the said declaration mentioned.

Demurrer and joinder.

The case was argued in the present term (May 3), by

Blackburn, in support of the demurrer. The question is, whether, upon the true construction of the contract set forth in the declaration, the neglect on the part of the plaintiff to declare the names of the vessels in which the wools were shipped is a defence to this action; in other words, whether such matter is a condition precedent to the plaintiff's right of recovery. It is submitted that it is not. The principles upon which the decision of the question must turn can scarcely be disputed. Those principles are to be found in the notes to Pordage v. Cole, 1 Wms. Saund. p. 320 a, note (4); and also in the notes to the case of Cutter v. Powell, 2 Smith's Leading Cases, p. 1. If the matter goes to the very root of the contract, and is the pith and essence of it, such matter must be held to be a condition precedent; but if the non-observance by the plaintiff of that particular element of the contract may be compensated in damages, it is not a condition precedent. The fact stated in the plea, that the price of wool had fallen in the market, supports the plaintiff's construction of the contract, by showing that the neglect by him to declare the names of the vessels, by which omission the defendants have sustained an injury, is capable of being compensated in damages. [PARKE, B. Could the plaintiff contend that shipping the wools with all despatch is not a condition precedent?] That may be admitted to be so; but the language of the contract in speaking of the matter in question undergoes a change: the words being "the names of the vessels to be declared as soon as the wools were shipped." The shipping and delivery of the cargo is the substance and essence of the contract; and, by the nature of the transaction, the names could not be declared at once, as the advice would take time to arrive in this country. The time of the shipping of the wools may, therefore, be taken as a condition precedent; and the cases of Glaholm v. Hays[1] and Ollive v. Booker[2] seem to support that position; but the matter relied upon by

[1] 2 M. & Gr. 257. [2] 1 Exch. 416.

the defendants cannot be so treated. [PARKE, B., referred to Ellen v. Topp,[1] as laying down the rule upon the question of conditions precedent.]

C. E. Pollock, contra. The question turns upon the construction of this particular contract. The plea merely brings before the court the materiality of this element of it, by showing that the parties to the contract understood the matter to be a condition precedent, by stating the reason why the names of the vessels in which the wools should be shipped were required to be declared. In putting an interpretation upon this contract, the court will no doubt act upon the principle expounded by Lord Kenyon, C. J., in Porter v. Shephard,[2] by holding "that conditions are to be construed to be either precedent or subsequent, according to the fair intention of the parties to be collected from the instrument; and that technical words, if there be any to encounter such intention, should give way to that intention." If the shipping of the wools with all despatch, and their safe arrival, be conditions precedent, which they clearly are, the stipulation that the names of the vessels are to be declared is one also, inasmuch as that stipulation forms part of the same sentence. The word "subject" overrides the whole clause. The plaintiff cannot rely upon the performance of any portion of his part of the contract to the benefit of the defendants, as was the case of Boone v. Eyre,[3] the reason being as stated in 1 Wms. Saund. 320 e, that, "where a person has received a part of the consideration for which he entered into the agreement, it would be unjust that, because he has not had the whole, he should therefore be permitted to enjoy that part without either paying or doing any thing for it. Therefore the law obliges him to perform the agreement on his part, and leaves him to his remedy to recover any damage he may have sustained in not having received the whole consideration." If any portion of the wools had, on their arrival at the port of destination, been accepted by the defendants, the case would have fallen under the above-mentioned principle. But that was not done. On the other hand, where certain acts are to be performed on either side, and the contract remains open, and the defendant has received no benefit under it, the plaintiff must show that he has performed all these acts on his part which he was bound to perform, in order to sustain the action. The plaintiff may have incurred a disadvantage in having shipped the wools at Odessa, but the defendants have received no benefit therefrom. The defendants, therefore, are in a position to insist upon the non-performance of this condition precedent as an answer to this action.

Blackburn, in reply. It is admitted that there has been no waiver on the part of the defendants. In putting a construction upon the contract, the intention of the parties at the time of making it ought

[1] 6 Exch. 424. [2] 6 T. R. 668. [3] 2 Bla. 1313.

alone to be considered; and, consequently, what takes place *ex post facto* ought to be rejected, except for the purpose of shewing that the occurrence of what has happened might have been in the contemplation of the parties at the time of making the contract. The fact that the wools might be shipped in several vessels would go to shew that this matter was not a condition precedent. If such was the intention of the parties, mere words ought not to overrule it. Fishmongers' Company *v.* Robertson,[1] per Tindal, C. J. Kemble *v.* Farren[2] may be cited as one of those cases in which the courts, in putting a construction upon a written agreement, have held that mere words cannot overrule the intention of the parties. *Cur. adv. vult.*

The judgment of the court was now delivered by

PARKE, B. The pleadings in this case are these (his lordship stated them, and proceeded): The question raised by these pleadings is whether the provision, that the names of the vessels should be declared as soon as the wools were shipped, was a condition precedent to the defendants' obligation to accept and pay for the wools according to the contract stated in the declaration, and under the circumstances stated in the plea.

This contract, we think, is to be construed with reference to some of those circumstances. It is stated in the plea, that the wool was bought, with the knowledge of both parties, for the purpose of reselling it in the course of the defendants' business; that it is an article of fluctuating value, and not saleable until the names of the vessels in which it was shipped should have been declared according to the contract.

The declaration having averred, according to the 57th section of the Common Law Procedure Act, the performance of conditions precedent generally, the defendant proceeds in this plea to specify this condition of declaring the names of the vessels, as one on the breach of which he insists. The loss which he avers to have sustained by that breach is immaterial. The only question is, whether the performance of the agreement was a condition precedent or not to the defendants' contract to accept and pay for the goods.

In the numerous cases on the subject, in which it has been laid down that the general rule is to construe covenants and agreements to be dependent or independent according to the intent and meaning of the parties to be collected from the instrument, and of course to the circumstances legally admissible in evidence with reference to which it is to be construed, one particular rule well acknowledged is, that where a covenant or agreement goes to part of the consideration on both sides, and may be compensated in damages, it is an independent covenant or contract, and an action might be brought for the breach

1 5 M. & Gr. 197. 2 6 Bing. 141.

of it without averring performance in the declaration, under the old system of pleading; and under the new, the denial of such performance would be bad; and the cases of Campbell v. Jones [1] and Boone v. Eyre [2] are instances of the application of the rule. But then it appears, as Mr. Serjt. Williams observes in 1 Saund. 320 d (and the Lord Chief Baron, in delivering the judgment of this court in Ellen v. Topp,[3] adopts the observation), the reason of the decision in that and similar cases, besides the inequality of damages, seems to be, that where a person has received part of the consideration for which he entered into the agreement, it would be unjust that, because he had not the whole, he should therefore be permitted to enjoy that part without either payment or doing any thing for it. Therefore the law obliges him to perform the agreement on his part, leaving him to his remedy to recover any damage he may have sustained in not having received the whole consideration. Mr. Serjt. Williams goes on to observe that it must appear upon the record that the consideration was executed in part. This may appear by the instrument declared on itself, whereby a valuable right, part of the consideration, is conveyed, as in Campbell v. Jones or Boone v. Eyre, or by averment in pleading. When that appears, it is no longer competent for the defendant to insist upon the non-performance of that which was originally a condition precedent; and this is more correctly expressed, than to say it was not a condition precedent at all.

In this case, if the stipulation that the names of the vessels should be stated as soon as the wools were shipped was originally a condition precedent, it is so still. No other benefit was taken under the contract itself, as the consideration for the promise to pay the money, than the shipment and delivery of the goods by the named vessels; nor was any subsequently received by the acceptance of the goods or any part thereof. After such acceptance, the defendants would have been bound to pay the price, or the residue of it, and could not have insisted on the neglect to name in due time, but, if there had been any such neglect, would nevertheless have had their remedy for the damage by cross-action on the contract to declare the names. In the state of things on this record, the simple question is, whether this contract was originally a condition precedent or not. Looking at the nature of the contract, and the great importance of it to the object with which the contract was entered into with the knowledge of both parties, we think it was a condition precedent, quite as much indeed as the shipping of the goods at Odessa, with all despatch, after the end of August. And with respect to the shipment itself, Mr. Blackburn did not venture to contend that the performance of the plaintiff's contract in that respect was not a condition precedent.

[1] 6 T. R. 570. [2] 2 Black. Rep. 1312 and 1315.
[3] 6 Exch. 441.

The defendants, therefore, have a right to object to fulfil the contract on their part, as the plaintiff did not fulfil his, though they could no longer object to the plaintiff's non-performance had they afterwards taken any benefit under the contract.

Judgment for the defendants.

THOMPSON AND OTHERS *v.* GILLESPY.

IN THE QUEEN'S BENCH, JUNE 1, 1855.

[*Reported in* 5 *Ellis & Blackburn,* 209.]

THE first count of the declaration alleged that a charter-party was made and entered into by and between plaintiffs and defendant, of which the following is a copy: — "LONDON, 14th October, 1854. — It is this day mutually agreed between Messrs. R. Thompson & Sons, owners of the good ship or vessel called the Mary Graham, whereof is master, of the measurement," &c., "now at Sunderland, and Thomas Gillespy, of London, merchant, that the said ship, being tight, staunch, and strong, and every way fitted for the voyage, shall, with all convenient speed, at Sunderland load from the factors of the said merchant, in the customary manner and in regular turn, a full and complete cargo of Londonderry or Lambton's Walls End coals, whichever is readiest; which the said merchant binds himself to ship, not exceeding what she can reasonably stow and carry over and above her tackle," &c. "And, being so loaded, shall therewith proceed to Constantinople for orders, to deliver there, or Stenea or Beicos Bay, or at Varna, or a safe place in the Black Sea, or so near thereunto as she may safely get, and deliver the same, in her regular turn, into craft, steamer, or depot ship, at any wharf or pier where she may safely lie, as may be directed by the consignee, being paid freight on the quantity delivered in the manner after mentioned at the rate of £34 per kiel of 21½ tons, if discharges at Constantinople, Stenea, or Beicos," &c. (other rates for a discharge elsewhere), "in full of all port charges, consulages, pilotages, Ramsgate and Dover dues; the act of God, &c.," excepted. The balance of freight to be paid by an approved bill on London, at three months' date from the production of the consignee's certificate of the right delivery of the cargo at as aforesaid, agreeably to bills of lading, or in cash equal thereto, at charterer's option." Then followed stipulations as to rate of unloading, running days for the same, and demurrage for excess; and other clauses not now material. "One-fourth of the freight to be advanced to the owner's agent in London, on the ship having sailed, less five per cent. thereon for insurance, interest, and commission: penalty for non-performance of this agreement, the estimated amount of freight." Signed by defendant and plaintiffs. Averment: That the persons in the said charter-party mentioned and described as Messrs. R. Thompson & Sons, were and are plaintiffs, and that the person therein mentioned and described as Thomas Gillespy was and is defendant. That defendant caused the ship to be loaded with a full and complete cargo of coals, to wit, pursuant to the said charter-party; and that the said ship, being so loaded, sailed, to wit, for Constantinople, pursuant to the said charter-party. That plaintiffs did, and were ready to do, all things necessary on their part, and that all things necessary happened and were done, to entitle plaintiffs, to wit, by their agent in London, to receive, and to render defendant liable to pay to their agent in London, the one-fourth part of the said freight, by the said charter-party agreed to be advanced to the plaintiff's agent in London on the ship having sailed, less £5 per cent. thereon for insurance and commission. That the said one-fourth part of the freight, less £5 per cent. as aforesaid, amounted to a large, &c., to wit, £214. Yet defendant hath not paid the same, or any part thereof, to plaintiffs, or to their agent in London.

Second count, for money payable by defendant to plaintiffs for freight for the conveyance by plaintiffs for defendant, at his request, of goods in ships; and for money found to be due from defendant to plaintiffs on accounts stated between them.

Pleas: 1. To the first count: That the said ship did not sail as alleged.

2. To the first count: That the said ship was not, at the commencement of the said voyage, tight, staunch, and strong, and every way fitted for the voyage; and that, by reason of the premises, the said ship and the said cargo of coals were wholly lost.

3. To the first count: That the plaintiffs not only wrongfully and negligently sent the said ship, so loaded as in the said first count mentioned, out to sea in an unseaworthy state, and without a proper and sufficient crew to navigate her on the said voyage, and when she was not fitted for the said voyage, and at a time when it was very dangerous for the said ship to proceed to sea; but the defendant says that, after the said ship had been so as aforesaid sent to sea, and while she was on the high seas near to the sea-shore, the plaintiffs wrongfully and negligently caused and permitted the master of the said ship to leave the said ship, and go ashore, and wrongfully and improperly caused and permitted the said ship to be left there, to wit, on the high seas, near to the sea-shore, for a great length of time, without a master, without a proper and sufficient crew to manage and navigate her: during which time the said ship, by reason of the premises, sunk and was wholly lost; and the said cargo of coals was also, by reason of the premises, wholly lost.

4. To the residue of the declaration: Never indebted.

The plaintiffs joined issue on all four pleas, and also demurred to the second and third.

Joinder in demurrer.

The demurrer was argued in last Easter Term.

Atherton, for the plaintiffs. As to the second plea. The question on this demurrer is not whether the facts there stated afford ground for an action by defendant against plaintiffs, but whether they constitute a defence in this action. Now the first averment, that the ship was not seaworthy at the commencement of the voyage, is no answer to an action for freight, inasmuch as whether seaworthy or not she might still perform the voyage and earn freight; and the rules applicable to an ordinary action for freight, must be applicable to an action like this for a portion of the freight. But then does the additional averment that the ship was lost by reason of the unseaworthiness, aid the defence? Where a defendant sets up damage to himself as an answer to a declaration, he must at least show clear damage on his side equivalent to the damage sustained by the plaintiff. "A cause of action against a plaintiff will be no bar to an action by him for avoiding circuity of action, when the recovery in both actions is not equal." Note (2) to Turner *v.* Davies.[1] [*Manisty*, who was for the defendant, mentioned Charles *v.* Altin.[2] LORD CAMPBELL, C. J. The litigation is not put an end to unless the damages are equivalent.] Here the damage sustained by the loss of the cargo might be greater or less than the freight. It might happen that the cargo, on arriving at Constantinople, from the state of the market or other circumstances, was not worth the freight. [ERLE, J. Suppose the contract to be, if I give you a straw you shall give me £1000: the giving of the straw is a condition precedent to getting the £1000. I think that is the rule applied to such mutual contracts as this.] That would be to construe this charter-party as making the contract to pay the freight in advance dependent on the fulfilment of a warranty. There are three cases: first, where the act of one party is a condition precedent to his calling on the other to act; secondly, where there are simply mutual stipulations; thirdly, where the performance of the two acts is to be simultaneous. The utmost that can be said is, that this is a case of the third kind; but how can the right to the advance of freight be simultaneous with a right to have the use of the ship during the whole voyage which is to ensue? [ERLE, J. The case seems to me to fall within the class of simultaneous acts; and if the sailing were illusory, the plaintiff's right would not arise.] The defendant might raise that point on a traverse of the sailing. [LORD CAMPBELL, C. J. There is a great difficulty in resting the defence upon the ground of avoiding circuity; but it is a question whether the freight was ever earned. ERLE, J. Suppose the owner of the cargo had said, "I insist on the ship not sailing, for she is not seaworthy." I do not think the actual loss makes any difference.] Suppose the vessel to have sailed on the first of January, and not to have been lost till the first of March; would not the plaintiffs be entitled to recover the advanced freight? [ERLE, J. I am not prepared to answer in the affirmative: the loss is only evidence of the unseaworthiness.] According to

[1] 2 Wms. Saund. 150 *b*.

[2] 15 Com. B. 46.

that, the slightest want of completeness would be an answer? [ERLE, J. The question may be as to a substantial non-performance, as illustrated by the language of Lord Ellenborough in Havelock v. Geddes.[1] The condition precedent seems to be here a complex idea; the ship is to sail, being staunch, &c.] Suppose the action to have been brought the day after the ship had sailed, and the plea to have been that she did not sail, being staunch, &c., throwing the loss out of the question. [CROMPTON, J. There is an old case in Shower[2] which seems to show that where freight is advanced, if the ship be afterwards lost, the freighters cannot have their money back.]

The third plea shews only neglect subsequent to the vesting of the right of action. That, at the utmost, can be ground only for a cross-action.

Manisty, contra. As to the second plea. The contract was that the ship should sail in a state reasonably fit for the voyage. The quarter of the freight was to be advanced, subject to a deduction in respect of the insurance, interest, and commission, which would fall on the defendant. But the insurance would be worthless unless the ship was seaworthy when she sailed. [LORD CAMPBELL, C. J. It has been held that an advance like this may be insured under the name of freight, though it is not strictly freight.[3] You suggest that the contract contemplates the defendant's keeping up a contract of insurance.] Yes: the deduction is partly for the purpose of enabling the defendant to insure. [LORD CAMPBELL, C. J. Or to stand as his own insurer.] That would be the same thing, so far as relates to the construction of the contract. The contract therefore must be understood to contain a warranty by the plaintiffs that the ship would sail in a proper state. [ERLE, J. Perhaps, according to a distinction which has been drawn, it is not so much a warranty as an element of the contract.] Even in the case of an action for the price of goods sold, it is competent to show that there is nothing recoverable because of the breach of a warranty. If it be necessary to inquire whether the plea is good for prevention of circuity of action, it is to be observed that Charles v. Altin[4] is distinguishable. It was there held that a plea, in order to show a defence by way of avoiding circuity of action, must show that the cross-claim was for the same sum as that which the plaintiff demands. But that is so here; for the loss of the quarter freight to the defendant is that which the plaintiff, in respect of the identical contract, would have to make good in an action for sailing with the ship in an unseaworthy state; and to make two cross-actions necessary for the adjustment of this claim would be to incur what Lord Denman, in Walmesley v. Cooper,[5] calls "the scandal and absurdity of allowing A. to recover against B. in one

[1] 10 East, 555, 563. See Graves v. Legg, 9 Exch. 709, 716.
[2] Probably the Anonymous Case in 2 Show. 283.
[3] See Hall v. Janson, 4 E. & B. 500, 509.
[4] 15 Com. B. 46.
[5] 11 A. & E. 216, 221, 222.

action, the identical sum which B. has a right to recover in another against A." That something additional might be recovered in the cross-action can make no difference. [CROMPTON, J. What you would recover in the cross-action would be the value of the goods.] The jury would be bound to give the amount of the loss accruing from the payment of the quarter freight. [LORD CAMPBELL, C. J. That comes to a case of unliquidated damages; where the circuity of action principle applies, the cross-demand ordinarily sounds in debt.] Not invariably, as in the case of a covenant not to sue, or a contract to indemnify. [LORD CAMPBELL, C. J. It is certainly a reproach to our procedure that we cannot, as is done in other countries, always bring cross-demands to be settled at once.] Connop v. Levy [1] furnishes a good instance of the defence which a contract to indemnify supplies.

The principle of avoiding circuity of action applies to the third plea as well as to the second.

Atherton, in reply. The amount sought by the plaintiff here possibly might, but need not necessarily, be the same as that which the defendant would recover in a cross-action. Where that is so, the principle of avoiding circuity does not apply. As to the other point, the sailing in a proper condition was not a condition precedent, but was the subject of a mutual stipulation: the quarter freight, if it had been paid on the ship sailing, could not have been recovered back on its being discovered, before the loss of the ship was known, that she had sailed in an unseaworthy state. The only argument that can be raised from the deduction in respect of insurance is, that both parties took for granted that the ship would be seaworthy at the time of sailing; but that does not make the seaworthiness a condition precedent. The sailing is a condition precedent, but not the sailing in any particular state of fitness.

Cur. adv. vult.

LORD CAMPBELL, C. J., now delivered the judgment of the court.

This was an action by the owners of a ship on a charter-party, whereby it was agreed between them and the defendant that the ship being tight, staunch, and strong, and every way fitted for the voyage, should at Sunderland load from the factors of the defendant a full cargo of coals, and, being so loaded, should therewith proceed to Constantinople for orders, and deliver the cargo there or at some port in the Black Sea, being paid freight on the quantity delivered at certain stipulated rates: "one-fourth of the freight to be advanced to the owner's agent in London, on the ship having sailed, less 5 per cent. thereon for insurance, interest, and commission." The declaration alleged that the defendant caused the ship to be loaded with a cargo of coals, and "that the said ship, being so loaded, sailed, to wit, for Constantinople, pursuant to the said charter-party;" and that, although the plaintiffs

[1] 11 Q. B. 769.

had done every thing to entitle them to an advance of one-fourth of the freight, amounting to £214, the defendant had not paid the same or any part thereof to their agent in London.

The second plea was, "That the said ship was not, at the commencement of the said voyage, tight, staunch, and strong, and every way fitted for the voyage; and that by reason of the premises, the said ship and the said cargo of coals were wholly lost." To this plea there was a demurrer.

Upon the argument before us, in last Easter Term, the doctrine of circuity of action was relied upon. But we do not think it applicable, for the reasons stated in Charles *v.* Altin.[1] We are of opinion, however, that this plea is a bar to the action, on the ground that it shews that the advance of freight had never became payable.

Freight, generally speaking, is not payable till the goods have been delivered at the port of destination. Here, by special stipulation, one-quarter of the amount was to be paid in advance on a certain event, viz., the ship having sailed from Sunderland for Constantinople, in pursuance of the charter-party. The charter-party required that when she sailed, she should be "tight, staunch, and strong, and every way fitted for the voyage." If she sailed on the voyage in a seaworthy condition, the merchant was to advance one-fourth of the freight, which he could not recover back if the ship, having so sailed, should afterwards be lost by the perils of the sea without having delivered any part of her cargo. *Pro tanto* the risk was transferred from the ship-owners to the merchant; and the arrangement between them was that the amount to be advanced was to be insured by him, as appears clearly from the deduction of 5 per cent. for insurance, interest, and commission. By a policy of insurance, the merchant was to be indemnified to the extent of the sum he was to advance. But he could not have the benefit of this indemnity unless, at the commencement of the voyage, the ship was seaworthy. He must be considered to have promised to pay one-fourth of the freight in advance, if, when the ship sailed, she was in such a condition as that a policy of insurance on the freight would attach, and enable him to recover the money back in case of a subsequent loss. But the plea avers that the ship was not seaworthy at the commencement of the voyage, and that, by her unseaworthiness, the cargo of coals was wholly lost. It was argued, for the plaintiff, that the loss after the sailing is for this purpose immaterial, and that, although unseaworthy when she sailed, she might have completed the voyage and delivered the cargo in safety. In that case the full freight certainly would have been earned, and would have been payable: but still the conjuncture never would have arisen upon which a part of the freight was to be paid in advance. For these reasons we think that the second plea is sufficient.

[1] 15 Com. B. 46.

There is a third plea, upon which, as it is demurred to, we are bound to give our opinion. This plea has some introductory observations about the ship having been sent to sea in an unseaworthy state, but it contains no allegation to that effect, and we consider the substance and gist of the plea to be that, after the ship sailed and while she was on the high seas, the plaintiffs were guilty of negligent and improper conduct with regard to the management of the ship, by reason whereof the ship and cargo were wholly lost. This plea, we think, is bad, as it admits that the ship sailed on the voyage from Sunderland in pursuance of the charter-party. If this be true, one-fourth of the freight thereupon became payable in advance; and any subsequent default or misconduct of the plaintiffs would only be the subject of a cross-action.

Judgment for defendant on the second plea; for the plaintiffs on the third.

ROLT *v.* COZENS.

IN THE COMMON PLEAS, MAY 28, 1856.

[*Reported in 25 Law Journal Reports, Common Pleas, 254.*]

THE declaration stated that by a certain agreement made and entered into by and between the plaintiff and certain persons named Burlington B. Wale and G. Dawe, it was agreed by Wale and Dawe that in consideration of the plaintiff, by the said agreement, agreeing to supply one W. Fowler with timber and deal to the value of £200, the said Wale and Dawe severally agreed to guarantee to the plaintiff the due payment of any amount for such timber not exceeding £200, within six months from the sale of the said timber. That in pursuance of such agreement he the plaintiff did supply timber to the amount of £153 10*s.* 1*d.* to the said W. Fowler. That afterwards and whilst such timber was unpaid for, and before the period of six months from the date of the sale of the timber had elapsed, the plaintiff became and was dissatisfied with such guaranty so given by Wale and Dawe; and thereupon by another agreement (that on which the action was brought)[1] made and entered into by and between the plaintiff and the defendant in

[1] And which was in the following terms: "Memorandum of agreement made this twenty-second day of July, 1854, between Peter Rolt, of Clement's Lane, timber merchant, trading under the style or firm of Thomas Brocklebank & Rolt, of the one part, and Thomas James Cozens, of, &c., of the other part; whereas, on the 18th of June, 1854, B. B. Wale and G. Dawe, in consideration of the said Peter Rolt agreeing to supply William Fowler with timber to the value of £200, severally agreed and guaranteed to the said Peter Rolt the said amount; and the said Peter Rolt has accordingly delivered timber to the amount of £153 10*s.* 1*d.*, and is not satisfied with such guaranty; and accordingly the said Thomas James Cozens, at the request of the said B. B.

July, 1854, after reciting the said guaranty, and that the plaintiff had delivered timber to the amount of £153 10*s.* 1*d.* and that the plaintiff was not satisfied with such guaranty, the defendant at the request of the said Wale and Dawe, in consideration of the premises and of the plaintiff forbearing to take any proceedings against Wale and Dawe, guaranteed to the plaintiff the sum of £153 10*s.* 1*d.* on the 13th of December then next. Averment, that the plaintiff has done every thing, &c. Breach, non-payment.

Fourth plea. That the plaintiff has not done any thing on his part to entitle him to be paid by the defendant the said sum of £153 10*s.* 1*d.* as the plaintiff did not forbear to take the said proceedings in the declaration mentioned against the said Wale and Dawe, but on the contrary took such proceedings before the said 13th of December next after the making of the said alleged agreement.

At the trial before Alderson, B., at the Spring Assizes for Surrey, 1856, the plaintiff had a verdict on all the issues except that upon the fourth plea. It was proved that before the 13th of December, namely, on the 8th of December, a writ had been issued at the suit of the plaintiff against Wale and Dawe. The learned judge ruled that proceedings had been taken, but it was contended for the plaintiff, that the not taking proceedings against Wale and Dawe was not a condition precedent to his right to recover. The jury found a verdict for the defendant on the fourth plea, leave being reserved to the plaintiff to move to enter a verdict with damages *non obstante veredicto.*

A rule *nisi* was afterwards obtained to enter judgment for the plaintiff *non obstante veredicto;* or to set aside the verdict and enter a verdict for the plaintiff on the fourth plea, or for a new trial.

Garth (May 28) shewed cause. There are two questions in this case: first, whether judgment should be entered for the plaintiff on the issue on the fourth plea *non obstante veredicto;* and secondly, whether the plea was supported by the evidence. On the latter point the only ground of objection is, that issuing a writ is not "taking proceedings." The learned judge properly held that it was, and at all events the plaintiff is not entitled to a new trial. As to the judgment *non obstante veredicto*, it is moved for on the ground that not taking proceedings against Wale and Dawe was not a condition precedent to the plaintiff recovering, and the first rule in the note to Pordage *v.* Cole[1] is relied upon. But the proper construction of the guaranty upon which the

Wale and G. Dawe, has and does hereby agree, in consideration of the said Peter Rolt forbearing to take any proceedings against the said B. B. Wale and G. Dawe, to guarantee the payment of the said sum of £153 10*s.* 1*d.* on the thirteenth day of December next. This guaranty not to be prejudiced by the said Peter Rolt refusing and not delivering the remainder of the timber. As witness the hands of the parties, Thomas James Cozens." See 18 C. B. 676. — ED.

[1] 1 Wms. Saund. 320 *b.*

action is brought is this, that if the plaintiff would forbear taking proceedings till the 13th of December, then the defendant would pay on the 13th. The defendant meant to say to the plaintiff, "You are to forbear to sue Wale and Dawe till the 13th of December," and that is the only actual consideration. If it be contended that "forbearing" means "agreeing to forbear," and that that was the consideration, it may be answered that the plaintiff himself, in setting out the legal effect of the guaranty in the declaration, speaks of "forbearing." Whatever proceedings the declaration speaks of as not to be taken, the plea alleges to have been taken. Whether the meaning is that the forbearance is to be forbearance generally, or till the 13th of December, the plea fixes it. It is said that forbearance for ever so short a time would have supported the guaranty; Payne *v.* Wilson[1] and Edwards *v.* Roberts:[2] but if the forbearance is to be construed as general forbearance, it must at all events have been forbearance up to the 13th of December; Waters *v.* Glassop.[3]

Bovill and *C. Pollock.* Both branches of the rule bear upon the effect of the guaranty. The forbearing is not a condition precedent; the covenants are independent; and "forbearing" means agreeing to forbear. In the cases cited on the other side the forbearance was to be for a time named. Where no specific time for forbearance is named, the forbearance must be general. Here a time is named for payment, but not for forbearance. But it makes little difference whether the agreement be to forbear generally, or up to a particular time. If the agreement be to forbear for six months, and there has been forbearance for five months, part of the consideration has passed. The plaintiff did forbear for a time, and did no act causing damage to the parties. The case is therefore within the third rule in Pordage *v.* Cole. Covenants going to part of the consideration are independent, as they were held to be in Stavers *v.* Curling[4] and Boone *v.* Eyre.[5] [WILLIAMS, J. In Neale *v.* Ratcliffe[6] it was held that where the defendant undertook to keep premises in repair, the same being first put in repair by the plaintiff, it was a condition precedent to put the whole of the premises in repair, and the covenant could not be divided.] The agreement there was to perform something in respect of a subject-matter when it came into existence, and was therefore different from the present.

JERVIS, C. J. It seems to me that this rule ought to be discharged. To my mind the second point about part of the consideration having been given does not arise. It would arise only if we should be of opin-

[1] 7 B. & C. 423; s. c. 6 Law J. Rep. K. B. 107.
[2] 2 Mod. 24.
[3] 1 Ld. Raym. 357.
[4] 3 Bing. N. C. 355; s. c. 6 Law J. Rep. (N. S.) C. P. 41.
[5] 1 H. Bl. 273, *n.*
[6] 15 Q. B. Rep. 916; s. c. 20 Law J. Rep. (N. S.) Q. B. 130.

ion that the guaranty was general, and intended to impose on the the plaintiff continued forbearance. It seems to me that that is not so. The plaintiff said to the defendant, "if you will forbear till the 13th of December, and if Wale and Dawe do not pay you then, I will do so." The case is not distinguishable from Neale *v.* Ratcliffe.

CRESWELL, J., WILLIAMS, J., and WILLES, J., concurred.

Rule discharged.

ROPER *v.* LENDON.

IN THE QUEEN'S BENCH, APRIL 30, 1859.

[*Reported in* 1 *Ellis & Ellis,* 825.]

DECLARATION against the defendant, as secretary of the Kent Fire Insurance Company, on a policy of insurance against fire effected by the plaintiff with the said company on the household furniture and effects, stock in trade, fixtures, and fittings in his dwelling-house. The declaration set out the policy, which was granted subject to certain conditions thereon indorsed, also set out, of which the following only are material:—

"Condition 10. The amount of every loss will be paid, without any discount or deduction, immediately after the same shall have been established to the satisfaction of the directors; but they reserve to themselves in all cases the option of reinstating within a reasonable time."

"Condition 15. All persons insured by this company sustaining any loss or damage by fire, shall forthwith give notice thereof to the directors or secretary of this company, at their office in Maidstone, and within fifteen days after such fire deliver in as particular an account of their loss or damage as the nature of the case will admit of, and shall also make proof of the amount of such loss or damage, by his, her, or their solemn declaration or affirmation, by their books or accounts, and by such other proper vouchers as shall be reasonably required. In case any difference or dispute shall arise between the insured and the company, touching any loss or damage, or otherwise in respect of any insurance, such difference shall be submitted to the judgment and determination of two indifferent persons as arbitrators, of whom one shall be chosen by this company and the other by the insured, and such two arbitrators shall, previously to entering upon the reference, agree upon and nominate a third person to be an arbitrator with them; and the award in writing of any two of the three arbitrators so chosen shall be conclusive and binding on all parties; and if any fraud or false swearing shall appear on the part of the insured, and the same shall be certified in writing by any two of the said arbitrators, the party insured shall forfeit all claim under the policy."

The declaration then averred that, while the policy was in full force, the plaintiff sustained loss and damage by fire, on the property described in the policy, to the amount of the sums therein specified as the value thereof; that the plaintiff had done all things necessary to be done, and that all things had been done and had happened which were necessary to be done and to happen in order to entitle the plaintiff to have such loss and damage paid and made good to him by the company; and that the time for paying and making the same good elapsed before suit, of all which the company had notice; but that the company did not pay or make good the loss.

Demurrer to the declaration. Joinder in demurrer.

The defendant also pleaded six pleas, the second and sixth of which were as follows:—

Plea 2. That the plaintiff did not forthwith give notice of, or, within fifteen days after the said fire, deliver an account of his supposed loss or damage by fire as required by the said policy and condition in that behalf.

Plea 6. That this action is brought for and in respect of a difference and dispute between the said insured and the said company, touching the said loss and damage, within the meaning of the fifteenth of the the conditions indorsed on the said policy; and that the said company have never declined, but have always been ready and willing, to refer such difference and dispute to the judgment and determination of two indifferent persons as arbitrators, in manner provided by the said condition, of all which the plaintiff before suit had due notice; and the said dispute or difference and the amount of the plaintiff's supposed loss or damage have never been determined as by the same condition is provided.

Demurrer to the second and sixth pleas respectively. Joinders in demurrer.

T. Jones (Northern Circuit), for the plaintiff. The pleas are bad. The second plea is founded on the fifteenth condition indorsed upon the policy; but the delivery within fifteen days of particulars of the loss is not thereby made a condition precedent to the plaintiff's right to sue. The other side will rely upon Mason *v.* Harvey,[1] where the delivery of particulars of loss was held a condition precedent to the right of the insured to recover. But there is nothing in the judgment in that case to show that the court held that delivery within the time specified in the policy was essential; it may rather be inferred that they were of opinion that a delivery at any time before action would satisfy the

[1] 8 Exch. 819.

condition. So, here, it is admitted, on the part of the plaintiff, that, under the present policy, a delivery of particulars of loss before suit is a condition precedent to his right of action. The decision in Mason v. Harvey [1] is founded upon that in Worsley v. Wood,[2] in which case no fixed time was specified in the policy as that within which the certificate of the minister, &c., of the parish was to be procured. [HILL, J. The condition here requires merely that "as particular an account of" the "loss and damage as the nature of the case will admit of," shall be delivered within fifteen days after the fire. A full statement is not asked for. The condition, if taken to require that some statement shall be furnished within fifteen days, appears reasonable enough. It must be very important to the company to have some statement given in as soon as possible.] Perhaps so; but surely if a statement is furnished within a reasonable time, it is sufficient. Why should the precise period of fifteen days be held to be essential? In Wheelton v. Hardisty [3] the truth of the statement as to the health of the assured was held not to be a condition precedent to the right to recover on the policy, because there were no words in the policy to give it that effect. So, here, the policy contains no words making the delivery of particulars within the period of fifteen days essential. [LORD CAMPBELL, C. J. The condition must be taken as a whole; having admitted that the delivery of particulars is essential, you are not at liberty to reject the stipulation that they are to be delivered within the fifteen days.] Then as to the sixth plea. This plea is bad. The provision contained in the same fifteenth condition, and upon which this plea is founded, as to a reference of disputes to arbitration, is not compulsory. Scott v. Avery [4] is conclusive to that effect. That case shows, that although, where an agreement to refer provides that no action shall be brought, until arbitrators have decided what amount is due, a reference and ascertainment of the amount due are conditions precedent to the right to bring an action, the same effect is not to be given to a mere collateral agreement to refer, such as that in the present case, which contains no such provision. In Brown v. Overbury,[5] cited by Lord Campbell in his judgment in Scott v. Avery,[6] the race was, by the rules, to be decided by the stewards, so that their decision was necessarily a condition precedent to the right of either party to the stakes. The defendant here, had he chosen, might, before pleading, have taken out a summons under the Common Law Procedure Act, 1854, sect. 11, to refer the question of amount. Not having done so, he cannot rely upon the sixth plea as constituting any defence to the action.

Lush, for the defendant, admitted that the sixth plea was bad. The court did not call upon him to support the second plea.

[1] 8 Exch. 819.
[2] 6 T. R. 710.
[3] 8 E. & B. 232.
[4] 5 H. L. Ca. 811.
[5] 11 Exch. 715.
[6] 5 H. L. Ca. 811.

Lord Campbell, C. J. The second plea is clearly good. The whole of the fifteenth condition, relating to the delivery of particulars of loss, must be taken together, *tale quale.* When, therefore, it is conceded that a delivery of such particulars, before action, is essential, it follows, from the wording of the condition, that the delivery must be within fifteen days after the loss. And the condition so construed is a very reasonable one; it being obviously of great importance to the defendant's company to know as soon as possible after a loss the amount claimed by the assured. The sixth plea is as clearly bad. The agreement to refer, contained in the fifteenth condition, is merely collateral to the agreement to pay. The courts will not, therefore, treat the agreement to refer as ousting their jurisdiction until there has been a reference. The distinction between the present case and cases like Scott v. Avery[1] is plainly pointed out in the judgment there delivered in the House of Lords. The present case does not fall within that decision, and the defendant could have enforced the agreement to refer only by an application under the Common Law Procedure Act, 1854, § 11.

(Erle, J., and Crompton, J., were absent.)

Hill, J. I am of the same opinion. By the terms of the policy the conditions indorsed on the back are incorporated with it. The defendant's company agree to be liable only according to the tenor of those conditions. One of these conditions requires the assured, "within fifteen days after" a fire, to "deliver in as particular an account of their loss or damage as the nature of the case will admit of." The plaintiff has not done so; there must, therefore, be judgment for the defendant on the second plea. The sixth plea, however, is bad. The case is clearly not within the decision in Scott v. Avery.[2] Here the agreement to refer is collateral to the agreement by the company to pay; there, the agreement was to pay only such a sum as the arbitrators should award. On this plea, therefore, there must be judgment for the plaintiff.

Judgment for the plaintiff on the demurrers to the declaration and to the sixth plea; and for the defendant on the demurrer to the second plea.

[1] 5 H. L. Ca. 811. [2] 5 H. L. Ca. 811.

HOARE AND OTHERS v. RENNIE AND ANOTHER.

IN THE EXCHEQUER, NOVEMBER 14 & 16, 1859.

[*Reported in 5 Hurlstone & Norman*, 19.]

DECLARATION. First count: That, on the 21st of April, A. D. 1857, the defendants agreed to buy of the plaintiffs, and the plaintiffs then agreed to sell to the defendants, about 667 tons of hammered Swede bar iron of certain sizes, then agreed on between the plaintiffs and the defendants, the said iron to be shipped from Sweden in the months of June, July, August, and September next, and in about equal portions each month, at £15 10*s.* per ton, delivered in good condition ex ship, on arrival in the port of London; and it was thereby then further agreed, amongst other things, that no shipment should exceed 150 tons, which should be in proportionate quantities of each size; but that, if any variation therein it should not exceed one ton, and such variation to be corrected in subsequent shipments; that sellers should have the option of commencing shipments in May, 1857, and also of completing the whole by the end of July, 1857; that ships' names should be declared as soon as known to the sellers; that if any should be lost on the voyage the quantity lost should be null and void; and that there should be discount at the rate of two and a half per cent. for cash against each delivery. Averments: That plaintiffs had done all things necessary on their part to be done, &c.; and though all things had happened and all times had elapsed to entitle them to have the said iron accepted, yet the defendants have wholly refused to accept the said iron or any part thereof, or to pay for the same according to the terms of the said agreement, whereby the plaintiffs lost divers profits, &c.

Second count. That on the 21st of April, A. D. 1857, the plaintiffs agreed to sell to the defendants, and the defendants agreed to buy of the plaintiffs, about 667 tons of hammered iron, upon the terms in the first count mentioned; and that from the time of the making the agreement continually until after the refusal, notice, and discharge hereinafter mentioned, the plaintiffs did and performed all conditions precedent, and all things were done, and all times elapsed, necessary to entitle them to the performance of the agreement on the part of the defendants; and that at and after the refusal, notice, and discharge hereinafter mentioned, they were ready and willing to perform the agreement on their part; and although the plaintiffs, in part performance of the said agreement, did, in June, A. D. 1857, ship a certain portion of the said iron, and did, in further performance of such agreement, and within a reasonable time after such shipment, tender to the defendants, and offered to deliver to them the said portion of iron so shipped as aforesaid, yet the defendants refused to accept the said portion of iron so tendered and offered, and thenceforth wholly refused to accept the same or any of the residue of the said iron, and gave notice to the plaintiffs that they would not accept the residue of the said iron; and the defendants thenceforth wholly refused to observe the agreement on their part, and wholly discharged the plaintiffs from the further execution and performance of the agreement by them; and wholly waived such execution and performance; whereby, &c.

Third plea to the first count. That the plaintiffs did not avail themselves of the option given to them by the agreement of commencing shipments of the iron in the month of May; and that the plaintiffs in the month of June shipped from Sweden, on board a certain vessel, a quantity of the said iron so contracted for, to wit, 21 tons, 6 cwt., 1 qr., being a much less quantity than was required to be shipped during the said month of June according to the terms of the said contract, and gave notice to the defendants that the said iron was to be part of the iron so agreed to be sold as aforesaid; that the plaintiffs failed to complete the shipment for the month of June, according to the terms of the contract, and were never ready and willing to deliver to the defendants such a quantity of iron, shipped from Sweden in June, as is specified in the said contract, although none of the iron was lost during the voyage; and were not ready and willing to deliver to the defendants the said small quantity of iron which had been shipped during the month of June, until after the month of June had elapsed, and until after the defendants had notice that the plaintiffs were not ready and willing, and were unable to fulfil their part of the said agreement with reference to the quantity of iron to be shipped in June; and that the defendants having notice of all the premises in this plea mentioned did afterwards refuse to receive the said quantity of iron so shipped as aforesaid during the month of June, and did give notice to the plaintiffs that they refused to receive the residue of the said iron.

The sixth plea, to the second count, was similar to the third plea.

The plaintiffs demurred to the third and sixth pleas, and the defendants joined in demurrer.

Wilde (with whom was *Holland*), in support of the demurrer. The question is whether, upon the statement of the contract in the declaration, it appears that the shipment in about equal portions in each month is a condition precedent to the plaintiffs' right to sue for the non-acceptance by the defendants of what was actually shipped. The provision for the shipment in about equal proportions during each month is evidently not treated as being so essential as to go to the whole consideration of the contract. Great latitude is allowed to the sellers. They may begin the shipment in June and end in July, in which case they would ship about 333 tons in each month; or begin in May and end in September, when the quantity would be about 133 tons in each month. That shows that the gist of the contract was not that any definite quantity should be shipped in any particular month. If this is a condition precedent, though shipments had been made in due course in May, June, and July, if a short quantity was shipped in August, the defendants might say that the previous shipments were not under the contract. Therefore, according to the rules laid down on this subject in the notes to Pordage *v.* Cole[1] and Cutter *v.* Powell,[2] it will not be so construed. The price is £15 10*s.* a ton to be paid on delivery. The time for the payment for the first parcel shipped might therefore arrive before any failure of the condition alleged to be precedent. No condition can be precedent unless the whole thing which is to be done is to be done precedently. In Ritchie *v.* Atkinson,[3] on a contract that a ship should go to St. Petersburg and there load from the factors of the freighters a complete cargo of hemp and iron, and proceed to London and deliver the same on being paid freight after certain rates per ton named in the contract, it was held that the delivery of a complete cargo was not a condition precedent, and that the master might recover for a short cargo at the rates mentioned, the freighter having his remedy in damages. Lord Ellenborough there pointed out that the defendant's argument must go the length of saying that if the cargo wanted a single ton of being a complete cargo that would be a defence. Stavers *v.* Curling[4] was a similar decision upon a contract to procure a cargo of sperm oil, or as great a proportion as might be within the plaintiff's power to obtain. It is consistent with the allegations in the plea that the defendants have sustained no damage, because a parcel shipped on the 1st of July from one port might arrive before one shipped on the 30th of June from another port in Sweden. The plea should have shown or stated that the object of the contract was frustrated by the default: Tarrabochia *v.* Hickie,[5] Freeman *v.* Taylor,[6] Graves *v.* Legg.[7] In Glaholm *v.* Hays[8] the court thought that an express stipulation that a vessel "shall sail" on a day named shews that particular importance is attached to it. In Dicker *v.* Jackson[9] the delivery of an abstract, and deducing a clear title to an estate contracted to be sold, was held not to be a condition precedent to the right to maintain an action for the purchase-money, on the ground that the time for the payment of the money might happen before the time provided by the contract for the delivery of the abstract, &c., had arrived. [WATSON, B. Suppose no iron was shipped in June, July, or August, could the defendants have been compelled to accept the whole in September?] The substance of the contract is that the iron is to be delivered in four months, not month after month.

[1] 1 Wms. Saund. 320 *a*.
[2] 2 Smith's Lead. Ca. 1.
[3] 10 East, 295.
[4] 3 Bing. N. C. 355.
[5] 1 H. & N. 183.
[6] 8 Bing. 124.
[7] 9 Exch. 709.
[8] 2 Man. & G. 257.
[9] 6 C. B. 103.

Bovill, in support of the pleas. The defendants have agreed to pay for certain goods to be shipped in June; the plaintiffs contend that the defendants must accept goods not shipped in June. The argument for the plaintiffs must go this length, that if they shipped no iron in June, July, or August, and but ten tons in September, the defendants would be bound to accept those ten tons. Surely that would not be in any sense a performance of the contract on the part of the plaintiffs. [POLLOCK, C. B. If the first parcel sent might have been according to the contract, can it be contended that the defendants could refuse to accept it on account of any subsequent default, as for instance, if they afterwards discovered that the plaintiffs were not going to complete the June shipment?] In the present case, the defendants did not refuse to accept the shipment in question until after notice that the plaintiffs had broken their contract by not shipping the right quantities in June; in other words, "until after the defendants had notice that the plaintiffs were not ready and willing, and were unable to fulfil their part of the agreement?" The option being to accelerate the deliveries, any presumption that the plaintiffs were at liberty to retard the shipments is excluded. Under an ordinary mercantile contract for goods to be supplied in June, the buyer would not be bound to accept them if tendered in July. In Ritchie *v.* Atkinson [1] the cargo had been accepted by the defendants. In Stavers *v.* Curling [2] the agreed voyage had been performed, and the owners had had the benefit of the cargo. The breach of the agreement to be frugal of stores was a small part only of the consideration. Here there had been no tender before the plaintiffs had entirely failed to perform their part of the agreement. The quantity to be shipped, and the time in which it was to be shipped, were of the essence of the contract. That brings the case within the authority of Freeman *v.* Taylor,[3] and distinguishes it from Tarrabochia *v.* Hickie.[4] The cases on charter-parties are uniform that where a time is mentioned for the being ready to load or the like, it is of the essence of the contract. Glaholm *v.* Hayes,[5] Ollive *v.* Booker,[6] Oliver *v.* Fielden.[7] The principle which governed Ellen *v.* Topp [8] and Graves *v.* Legg [9] applies, because the tender was not a partial performance of the contract, but an offer or readiness to do something which was no performance of the contract at all. [POLLOCK, C. B. The principle of Boone *v.* Eyre [10] applies to the partial breach of a single contract, but surely not to a breach of a continuing contract, as to supply goods from day to day or from week to week, where during the contract one party becomes wholly incapable of performing his part. Suppose in June the plaintiff had shipped nothing, could he say, I will pay damages for that, and insist on going on with the

[1] 10 East, 295. [2] 3 Bing. N. C. 355. [3] 8 Bing. 124.
[4] 1 H. & N. 183. [5] 2 Man. & G. 257. [6] 1 Exch. 416.
[7] 4 Exch. 135. [8] 6 Exch. 424. [9] 9 Exch. 909.
[10] 1 H. Black. 273, *n.*

contract and supplying the rest of the iron in July, August, and September? In such a case, if one fails on his part, the other cannot insist that the contract shall go on. It may be different if a partial performance has been accepted.]

Wilde replied (Nov. 15). The doctrine of conditions precedent never has been applied where continuous acts are to be performed. In Withers *v.* Reynolds,[1] where the defendant had agreed to supply straw at a certain price per load, and the plaintiff always insisted on keeping one payment in arrear, it was held that, on the plaintiff's refusal to pay, the defendant was not bound to send any more; but Patteson, J., said, "If the plaintiff had merely failed to pay for any particular load, that of itself might not have been an excuse to the defendant for delivering no more straw; but the plaintiff expressly refuses to pay for the loads as delivered." In the present case the defendants cannot avoid the contract altogether because the shipments in some one month are not in all respects according to the contract. The quantity shipped in June is not said to have been an unreasonable quantity for shipment in that month. [POLLOCK, C. B. The expressions in the contract are loose and allow some latitude to the plaintiffs, but not so as to permit them to ship twenty tons in the month instead of 160. WATSON, B. The pleas aver that the shipment was not according to the contract.]

POLLOCK, C. B. We are all agreed that the defendants are entitled to judgment upon the pleas. The foundation of my opinion is shortly this, that a man has no right to say that which is a breach of an agreement is a performance of it. On that ground, this case is distinguishable from almost every other which has been cited. It does not turn upon any question of condition precedent. The only question is whether, if a man who is bound to perform his part of a contract does not do so, he can enforce the contract against another party. The plaintiffs contracted with the defendants to ship a large quantity of iron in June, July, August, and September, about one-fourth part in each month; but instead of shipping about 160 tons in June, as they should have done, they shipped little more than twenty tons, as a performance of the contract. The first count states that the plaintiffs performed all things necessary on their part to be performed, that they were ready and willing to do all things which according to agreement it was necessary they should be willing to do, and that all things happened to entitle the plaintiffs to a performance of the agreement on the part of the defendants. This is denied by the plea. The second count states that the plaintiffs, in part performance of the contract, shipped a certain portion of the iron, and in further performance of the agreement tendered and offered to deliver the said portion so shipped, yet defendants refused to accept the same. The pleas raise the question whether the defendants were bound to accept and pay for what was sent and tendered; the plaintiffs having, in June, shipped

[1] 2 B. & Ad. 882.

from Sweden a quantity much less than they were bound to have shipped, and the defendants having insisted that this was a breach of the contract, and given notice that they refused to accept the residue. The pleas expressly state that the plaintiffs were not ready to deliver such a quantity of iron shipped from Sweden in June as is specified in the contract, and were not ready and willing to deliver the small quantities shipped until after the month of June had elapsed, and until after the defendants had notice that the plaintiffs were not ready and willing to perform their part of the agreement. The only question we have to deal with is whether, on a contract like this, if the sellers at the outset send a less quantity than they are bound to send, so as to begin with a breach, they can compel the purchasers to accept and pay for that the sending of which was a breach and not a performance of the agreement. The argument on the part of the plaintiffs is that this was not a condition precedent. I do not think that is the test. It was said that if the plaintiffs had sent the one-hundredth part, instead of one-fourth part, in June, the defendants' remedy would have been by a cross-action. The case was put of the plaintiffs sending a short quantity after one shipment had been accepted. Possibly that might have made a difference. Where a person has derived a benefit from a contract he cannot rescind it, because the parties cannot be put *in statu quo*. Probably, therefore, in such case the defendants could not have repudiated the contract, and must have been left to their cross-action. Here, however, the defendants refused to accept the first shipment, because, as they say, it was not a performance, but a breach of the contract. Where parties have made an agreement for themselves, the courts ought not to make another for them. Here they say that in the events that have happened one-fourth shall be shipped in each month, and we cannot say that they meant to accept any other quantity. At the outset, the plaintiffs failed to tender the quantity according to the contract: they tendered a much less quantity. The defendants had a right to say that this was no performance of the contract, and they were no more bound to accept the short quantity than if a single delivery had been contracted for. Therefore the pleas are an answer to the action.

WATSON, B. I am of the same opinion. (His lordship read the contract stated in the declaration.) The contract is for the shipment of a quantity of iron in certain proportions, to be paid for on delivery. On performance of the contract the defendants agree to pay for the iron. The breach charged here is that the defendants shipped a small quantity in June, and declared that they would not ship more [*sic*]. The pleas aver that the shipment was not according to the contract. The obligation on the part of the defendants is merely to receive and pay for the goods according to the contract. Looking at the contract, the options given are all for the purpose of accelerating the shipments. Instead of shipping in June, the plaintiffs may ship a portion in May. The plaintiffs might have accelerated, but had no right to delay the delivering of the iron. Having done so, they have not performed their contract. The substance of the agreement in Ritchie v. Atkinson[1] was that the plaintiff should go to Russia and bring home a cargo; and that was done; though, in consequence of the embargo, a full cargo had not been loaded. A similar observation applies to Boone v. Eyre.[2] But on the sale of goods where the price is to be paid on delivery, can it be said that there is no condition to deliver them? Therefore, the defendant was not obliged to accept a small portion of that which should have been the shipment in June.

CHANNELL, B. On the pleas the defendants are entitled to judgment. The substantial question is, whether the defendants were bound to accept the portion which was tendered at the time at which it was tendered. That does not depend on the month in which it was tendered, but on the position of the parties at the time of the tender, by which the defendant was placed in the same situation as if, at the time of the tender, notice had been given to him that there would be no further shipment in all June. I think that there was not in the month of June such a shipment as was made necessary by the contract. Mr. Wilde admitted that the pleas might have been good if they had contained an averment to that effect. In some cases such an averment may be necessary. It would be so here, but that this is substantially a contract to ship one-fourth of the iron in June. There are options to vary the time of performance, which gave the plaintiffs the right to accelerate but not to delay it. The plaintiffs have not performed their part of the contract, and the defendants have not accepted any thing which can be construed as an imperfect execution of the contract by the plaintiffs. The defendants were thus at liberty to rescind the contract; and our judgment must therefore be for the defendants upon the demurrer to the pleas. *Judgment for the defendants.*

BEHN v. BURNESS.

IN THE QUEEN'S BENCH, JANUARY 21, 1862.

[*Reported in* 1 *Best & Smith*, 877.]

IN THE EXCHEQUER CHAMBER, FEBRUARY 24, 1863.

[*Reported in* 3 *Best & Smith*, 751.]

THE declaration alleged that the plaintiff and the defendant agreed by charter-party that the plaintiff's ship, called the Martaban, then

[1] 10 East, 295.

[2] 1 H. Black. 273, n.

in the port of Amsterdam, and being tight, staunch, strong, and every way fitted and ready for the voyage, should, with all possible despatch, proceed direct to Newport, Monmouthshire, and that the defendant should there load her with a full cargo of coals, which she should carry to Hong Kong and there deliver, in consideration of freight to be paid after the rate of sixty shillings sterling for every ton of twenty hundred-weight of coals so delivered, and at the times and in the manner following: that is to say, one-third by charterer's acceptance at three months' date from the final sailing of the vessel, or at the owner's option in cash, under discount of two and half per cent.; one-third by charterer's acceptance at six months' date, the charterer to insure the amount and deduct the cost of insurance; and the remaining one-third of the freight by the charterer's acceptance at three months' date from the delivery to the charterer in London of a certificate in writing, signed by the consignee, of the right and true delivery of the cargo agreeably to bills of lading, or in cash under discount of five pounds per cent. per annum, at charterer's option; and that the defendant should be allowed ten days for loading, and should receive the said cargo as delivered from on board at the rate of not less than thirty-five tons a working day, weather permitting, or in default should pay demurrage at the rate of four pence per ton register per like day. Averment of performance by the plaintiff and default by the defendant.

Plea. That at the time of making the charter-party time was an essential and material part of the contract, and the then situation of the ship was a material and essential part of the contract, as the plaintiff and defendant respectively then well knew, and that the said ship was not, at the time of making the said charter-party, in the port of Amsterdam, of which the defendant then had no knowledge or notice.

Issue.

The following special case, of which the pleadings were to be deemed part, was stated by consent of the parties under the order of a judge:—

By memorandum of charter-party, dated London, the 19th October, 1860, the plaintiff's ship, Martaban, was chartered to the defendant in the words and figures following, viz.: "It is this day mutually agreed between A. Behn, Esq., owner of the good ship or vessel called the Martaban, of 420 tons or thereabouts, now in the port of Amsterdam, and James Burness, Esq., of London, merchant, that the said ship, being tight, staunch, strong, and every way fitted and ready for the voyage, shall, with all possible despatch, proceed direct to Newport, Monmouthshire, addressing to Messrs. G. W. Jones & Co. for entering and clearing, and there load in the usual and customary manner in ten days at any one of the usual loading places. Freighter may name a full and complete cargo of coals, which said freighter binds himself to ship, not exceeding what she can reasonably stow and carry over and above her tackle, apparel, provisions and furniture (the captain to have a sufficient quantity of coal on board at port of loading for ship's use for the voyage, and have the same indorsed on bills of lading, independently of the cargo); and being so loaded, shall therewith proceed to Hong Kong, or so near thereunto as she may safely get, and deliver the same alongside any craft, steamer, floating depot, or pier named by the consignee, notice to be given to the agent or consignee of the vessel being ready to discharge (the act of God, the Queen's enemies, riots and strikes of pitmen, fire, and all and every other dangers and accidents of the seas, rivers, and navigation always mutually excepted); the freight to be paid on the quantity delivered in accordance with this charter, at and after the rate of sixty shillings sterling per ton of twenty hundred-weight in full of all port charges, wharfage, consulage, pilotage, Ramsgate and Dover dues, and to become due, say one-third by charterer's acceptance at 3 months' date from the final sailing of the vessel, or at owner's option in cash, under discount at 2½ per cent.; one-third by charterer's acceptance at 6 months, the charterer to insure the amount and deduct the costs of insurance; the remaining one-third of the freight, less the cost of any coals short delivered at the port of final discharge, and after deducting such cash as may be advanced by the agent of the charterer for ship's use, which the captain is at liberty to draw to extent of £200 on usual terms against captain's draft on charterer at 90 days' sight, to be paid by the charterer at 3 months' date from the delivery to the charterer in London of a certificate in writing signed by the consignee, of the right and true delivery of the cargo agreeably to bills of lading, or in cash under discount at 5 per cent. per annum, at freighter's option. The vessel to deliver as customary, and the cargo to be delivered by the captain and received by the consignee at the rate of not less than 35 tons a working day, weather permitting, or to pay a demurrage at the rate of four pence per ton register per like day. The vessel to be addressed to freighter's agents inwards only, at the port of discharge, free of commission, but paying 2 per cent. to charterer in London, same to be deducted from first payment of freight: any claim of average to be settled according to the custom at Lloyd's: a commission of 5 per cent. on amount of freight is due by the owner on signing this charter-party to David Brown, ship-broker, London, and to whom the ship is to be addressed on her return to London: penalty for non-performance of this agreement, estimated amount of freight."

The ship Martaban arrived on the previous 15th October, 1860, at Niewdiep, at the entrance to the Great Noord Hollandische Canal, on her way with a cargo from Sourabaya to the docks at Amsterdam, which, under favorable circumstances, she could have reached in twelve hours more; but, in consequence of strong gales from the opposite quarter, and the absence of steam-tug power, she was unavoidably prevented from reaching the place of discharge in the Amsterdam Docks before daybreak on the 23d day of the same month of October. Niewdiep, the place where the vessel was unavoidably detained by the circumstances aforesaid on the said 19th day of October, the date of the above recited memorandum of charter-party, is a place in the direct course of the said vessel to Amsterdam, and is sixty-two English miles from that place, but is not within the port of Amsterdam.

The ship Martaban, having discharged her cargo with all possible despatch, was immediately made ready for sea, and without any delay sailed on the sixteenth day of November, and proceeded direct for Newport, pursuant to the charter-party, and arrived there on the first December following. Notice was given to the defendant's agent at Newport, on the fifth day of the same December, that the ship was ready to receive cargo, and on the 16th December the stipulated lay days expired. The defendant continually, up to the expiration of the said lay days and afterwards, refused to load the ship. The plaintiff, as soon as possible thereafter, namely, on the 20th December, rechartered the vessel for Hong Kong from Newport, with a cargo of coals, at a smaller rate of freight than the defendant had agreed to pay, being at the time the highest that could be obtained; and thereupon the vessel, having loaded with all possible despatch, sailed without delay for Hong Kong.

The following statement is added at the request of the defendant's counsel, and under protest by the plaintiff's counsel:—

Before the charter was made, the defendant told the plaintiff's broker that he, the defendant, had a contract with the English government to supply coals at Hong Kong in China, and that he was taking up the ship for the purpose of fulfilling that contract. The defendant did not state that there was any limit of time for the performance of the contract with the government, but he said that there had been so much delay in the sailing of the ships previously taken up, he would not take up any which he was not certified was ready, or as near as possible ready.

The question for the opinion of the court is, Whether the words "now in the port of Amsterdam" in the said charter-party amount to a warranty; and, if so, whether the position of the ship Martaban on the nineteenth day of October amounted under the circumstances to a breach of that warranty.

If the court shall be of opinion, that the plaintiff is entitled to recover, the question of damages is to be referred to the master, and judgment to be entered for the plaintiff for such damages and costs of suit.

If the court shall be of opinion that the plaintiff is not entitled to recover, then judgment of *nolle prosequi*, with costs of defence, shall be entered up for the defendant.

Manisty (*Maclachlan* with him), for the plaintiff. The words in this charter-party, "now in the port of Amsterdam," do not constitute a warranty or condition precedent to the contract that the ship was there at the time of the execution of the instrument; and, if they did, here was no breach of it. The rule in construing contracts of this nature is to look to the intention of the parties as collected from the instrument. Here the intention was that the statement of the position of the ship should be mere matter of description, and if any damage resulted to the charterer from his object being frustrated in consequence of her not being in that position at the time, his remedy should be by a cross-action for damages; and this construction is in accordance with that put on instruments of this nature in Ritchie *v.* Atkinson,[1] Freeman *v.* Taylor,[2] Clipsham *v.* Vertue,[3] Barker *v.* Windle.[4] Dimech *v.* Corlett,[5] where the previous cases are reviewed, is an express authority on the point. [CROMPTON, J. Ollive *v.* Booker,[6] decided eleven years before, seems the other way. His lordship also mentioned Boone *v.* Eyre.[7] WIGHTMAN, J., referred to Kenyon *v.* Berthon[8] and Colby *v.* Hunter.[9]] Those two cases were on policies of insurance, which are a very different thing, for there the whole risk and premium depends on the representation. Great inconvenience would result from holding such matters as these conditions precedent; for if the statement as to the exact position of the ship or the time of her sailing is to be deemed part of the essence of the contract, the variance of a few yards or minutes would vitiate the whole. Moreover, if the words, "now in the port of Amsterdam," are to be construed as amounting to a condition precedent, a similar construction ought to be put on the other words in the same sentence, being "tight, staunch, strong, and in every way fitted and ready for the voyage," which is contrary to Tarrabochia *v.* Hickie.[10]

The verbal statement introduced into this case under protest ought not to be attended to: the doing so would have the effect of importing a verbal statement into a charter-party. Hurst *v.* Usborne.[11] [WIGHTMAN, J. The new matter introduced makes no difference, because it says, the ship must be "ready, or as near as possible ready."]

F. M. White (*Honyman* with him), contra. The statement of the position of the ship in this charter-party is a warranty that she was at that place at the time, and the facts shew a breach of it. The rule has been correctly stated by the other side, that the thing to be looked to is the intention of the parties as collected from the instrument. It is to be observed that the words here are not the usual ones, that the ship shall proceed on her voyage "with all convenient speed," but "with all possible despatch." Ollive *v.* Booker[12] is an authority in point for the

[1] 10 East, 295.
[2] 8 Bing. 124.
[3] 5 Q. B. 625.
[4] 6 E. & B. 675.
[5] 12 Moo. P. C. C. 199.
[6] 1 Exch. 416.
[7] 1 H. Bl. 273 (note).
[8] 1 Dougl. 12 note (4).
[9] 1 Mood. & M. 81.
[10] 1 H. & N. 183.
[11] 18 C. B. 144.
[12] 1 Exch. 416.

defendant; and there are several other instances where statements of this nature have been held to amount to conditions precedent: *e. g.*, that a ship shall answer a particular description, Hurst *v.* Usborne;[1] that she shall be seaworthy when about to sail, Thompson *v.* Gillespy;[2] that she shall sail on a particular day, Cranston *v.* Marshall;[3] Croockewit *v.* Fletcher;[4] that she shall be ready to receive cargo at a certain time, Oliver *v.* Fielden;[5] and that goods are on passage at the time of sale, Gorrissen *v.* Perrin.[6]

As to the authorities which have been cited by the other side, Dimech *v.* Corlett,[7] was decided on its peculiar circumstances; Ritchie *v.* Atkinson,[8] was an action for freight, and there had been a part-performance, and it is distinguished on that ground in Glaholm *v.* Hays.[9] Barker *v.* Windle, in the Exchequer Chamber,[10] is more fully reported, 25 L. J. Q. B. 349, *nom.* Windle *v.* Barker, from whence, and especially from the judgment of Martin, B., it appears that the question there was one of fact rather than of law; besides, the ship was only described as being of the specified size or "thereabouts," so that there could be no pretence for suggesting a warranty as to size.

Manisty, in reply. It is doubtful whether Cranston *v.* Marshall[11] and Croockewit *v.* Fletcher[12] will stand, if brought before a higher tribunal. If they do, it will be on the ground taken in Tarrabochia *v.* Hickie[13] and Seeger *v.* Duthie,[14] that a contract that a ship shall sail on a given day is a warranty, although a contract that she is to sail "within a reasonable time," or "with all possible despatch," is not. If the words here amount to a warranty, no qualification can be grafted on it, for a warranty must be taken *in omnibus.*

Cockburn, C. J. Our judgment should be for the plaintiff. I feel considerably embarrassed by the conflict of authority which we find in the cases that have been brought under our attention in the course of the learned arguments on both sides.

Ollive *v.* Booker[15] appears to me directly in point. The statement in the charter-party there was that the ship, relating to which the question arose, was then "at sea, having sailed three weeks ago;" and the Court of Exchequer held that that fact was a condition precedent to the enforcing of the contract by the ship-owner against the charterer. On the other hand, Dimech *v.* Corlett[16] appears also in point to this case, and is in conflict with the preceding one of Ollive *v.* Booker.[15] In Dimech *v.* Corlett,[16] the representation was that the vessel, the sub-

[1] 18 C. B. 144.
[2] 5 E. & B. 209.
[3] 5 Exch. 395.
[4] 1 H. & N. 893, 26 L. J. Exch. 153.
[5] 4 Exch. 135.
[6] 2 C. B., N. S., 681.
[7] 12 Moo. P. C. C. 199.
[8] 10 East, 295.
[9] 2 Man. & Gr. 257.
[10] 6 E. & B. 675.
[11] 5 Exch. 395.
[12] 1 H. & N. 893, 26 L. J. Exch. 253.
[13] 1 H. & N. 183.
[14] 8 C. B., N. S., 45, 29 L. J. C. P. 253.
[15] 1 Exch. 416.
[16] 12 Moo. P. C. C. 199.

ject of the charter-party, was then at anchor at a given place, and it appeared that, so far was that from being the fact, she was in dry dock and undergoing the process of being sheathed in copper; and the contract was that she, being in the position described, should sail "with all convenient speed." The Privy Council held that her being in that position was not a condition precedent; that if she was not there, it was merely matter of cross-action for damages; or that, if the object of the voyage was frustrated, it might be a good answer to an attempt of the ship-owner to enforce the contract against the charterer.

In this conflict of the decisions the right course for this court is to abide by the later decision, which is also that of a court of very high authority, and one or more of the members of which were particularly conversant with shipping law.

I own if this question were *res integra* I should be much disposed to think that the best mode of construing these charters, where there is a representation as to the place of a ship, or as to the time of sailing, or analogous matter, would be to hold that, if the fact represented turns out not to be correctly stated, and in consequence of it the charterer finds himself in a position where his speculation and enterprise may be frustrated, and the contemplated advantages of them converted into disaster and loss, that should justify him in repudiating the contract. But, on the other hand, where the representation is that the ship is at a given place, or is to sail on a given day, &c., and it turns out that she was not there, or could not sail for some short time after that specified, &c., and there is no real frustration of the objects of the charterer, and little or no damage has been done to him, he should be left to his action. I throw this out with a view to legislation rather than to interpretation of the law; supposing no authority on the subject. I do not feel it at all necessary to express judicially any opinion upon it; I only say that here is a conflict of authority, and I will abide by the latest decision. I sincerely hope that the parties will go to a court of error where the law may be satisfactorily settled.

I have to say on the part of my brother Wightman,[1] that he thinks we ought to abide by the cases referred to by Mr. White, and ought not to overrule them on the opinion of the Privy Council.

CROMPTON, J. The difficulty here is that there are so many of these decisions, and it is not easy to reconcile them. I join in the opinion of my Lord Chief Justice that this case should go to a court of error, which will be less hampered by contradictory decisions, and able to lay down the law more authoritatively than we can, who are only a court of co-ordinate jurisdiction. Many of the cases justify my brother Wightman in his doubts, but I agree with the view of my Lord Chief Justice. I think it lies on the party setting up this kind of statement as a condition precedent to shew that it is one, *i. e.*, that the parties

[1] Wightman, J., had left the court before the judgment.

intended that there was to be no contract unless the stipulation was performed to the letter. Now, looking at the earlier authorities, I cannot help thinking that the law on this subject is a branch of the general law as laid down in Boone v. Eyre.[1] Lord Mansfield there says, "The distinction is very clear, where mutual covenants go to the whole of the consideration on both sides they are mutual conditions, the one precedent to the other. But where they go only to a part, where a breach may be paid for in damages, there the defendant has a remedy on his covenant, and shall not plead it as a condition precedent." Here a very minute matter, such as a discrepancy of a day or an hour, would be a breach if the statement is to be taken as a condition precedent; which is the proper expression as stated by my brother Williams in Barker v. Windle,[2] in the Exchequer Chamber, who points out that "warranty" is not the correct one, for if there is a warranty the party must sue on it.

The early cases bear very much the aspect that things of this kind are to be looked on as matter of stipulation merely, unless you can see very clearly from the terms of the instrument that it was the intention of the parties not to be bound, unless they were performed to a hair's breadth. The words in the present charter-party, that the ship was to sail "with all possible despatch," created my chief doubt; but it is too slight to act on. Now Ollive v. Booker,[3] which was decided about eleven years ago, and some other cases, varied the old notion about independent stipulations. I was never quite satisfied with them, but should feel bound by them. Ollive v. Booker is very near the present case, but Dimech v. Corlett[4] is still nearer, for it is almost word for word. I should not like to found my judgment on any minute or fine-spun difference between those two cases; yet, when we look at the decisions which have taken place within the last two or three years, we must consider Ollive v. Booker as in some degree shaken, and that they are, I think, nearer to what the law ought to be. At all events, we must go by the latest authority, and leave the question to the Exchequer Chamber.

MELLOR, J. With very considerable hesitation I have arrived at the same conclusion with my Lord Chief Justice and my brother Crompton. I cannot distinguish this case from Ollive v. Booker. That case has, however, been broken in on by the subsequent decision in Dimech v. Corlett, and I shall therefore abide by that decision. I should have been glad if Ollive v. Booker had been alluded to in the judgment there, and the distinction between the cases pointed out. I consider that the onus of proving this statement to be a condition precedent lies on the person who asserts it to be such. Looking at the charter-party,

[1] 1 H. Bl. 273, note.
[2] 6 E. & B. 675, 679.
[3] 1 Exch. 416.
[4] 12 Moo. P. C. C. 199.

I do not think this is a condition precedent, and rather think it is not. *Judgment for the plaintiff.*

The defendant having brought error on the foregoing judgment,

Honyman (*Bovill* with him), for the defendant, cited Cockburn *v.* Alexander,[1] Glaholm *v.* Hays,[2] Ollive *v.* Booker,[3] Oliver *v.* Fielden,[4] Tarrabochia *v.* Hickie,[5] Croockewit *v.* Fletcher,[6] Hurst *v.* Usborne,[7] Cranston *v.* Marshall,[8] Bannerman *v.* White,[9] Van Baggen *v.* Baines.[10]

Manisty, (*Maclachlan* with him), contra, cited Freeman *v.* Taylor,[11] Seeger *v.* Duthie,[12] Barker, appellant, *v.* Windle, respondent,[13] Glaholm *v.* Hays,[2] Elliot *v.* Von Glehn,[14] Dimech *v.* Corlett.[15]

Honyman, in reply. *Cur. adv. vult.*

The judgment of the court was now delivered by

WILLIAMS, J. The question in this case is, whether the statement in the charter-party, that the ship is "now in the port of Amsterdam," is a "representation" or a "warranty," using the latter word as synonymous with "condition," in which sense it has been for many years understood with respect to policies of insurance and charter-parties.

It may be expedient to commence the consideration of this question by some examination into the nature of representations. Properly speaking, a representation is a statement or assertion, made by one party to the other, before or at the time of the contract, of some matter or circumstance relating to it. Though it is sometimes contained in the written instrument, it is not an integral part of the contract; and, consequently, the contract is not broken though the representation proves to be untrue; nor (with the exception of the case of policies of insurance, at all events, marine policies, which stand on a peculiar anomalous footing) is such untruth any cause of action, nor has it any efficacy whatever, unless the representation was made fraudulently, either by reason of its being made with a knowledge of its untruth, or by reason of its being made dishonestly, with a reckless ignorance whether it was true or untrue. (See Elliot *v.* Von Glehn,[14] Wheelton *v.* Hardisty.[16])

If this be so, it is difficult to understand the distinction which is to be found in some of the treatises, and is in some degree perhaps sanctioned by judicial authority (see Barker, appellant, Windle, respondent,[17]) that a representation, if it differs from the truth to an

[1] 6 C. B. 791. [2] 2 M. & Gr. 257. [3] 1 Exch. 416.
[4] 4 Exch. 135. [5] 1 H. & N. 183. [6] 1 H. & N. 893.
[7] 18 C. B. 144. [8] 5 Exch. 395. [9] 10 C. B. N. S. 844, 850.
[10] 9 Exch. 523. [11] 8 Bing. 124. [12] 8 C. B. N. S. 45.
[13] 6 E. & B. 675. [14] 13 Q. B. 632. [15] 12 Moo. P. C. C. 199.
[16] 8 E. & B. 232; on appeal, 8 id. 285.
[17] 6 E. & B. 680.

unreasonable extent, may affect the validity of the contract. Where, indeed, the representation is so gross as to amount to sufficient evidence of fraud, it is obvious that the contract would on that ground be voidable.

Though representations are not usually contained in the written instrument of contract, yet they sometimes are. But it is plain that their insertion therein cannot alter their nature. A question, however, may arise, whether a descriptive statement in the written instrument is a mere representation, or whether it is a substantive part of the contract. This is a question of construction which the court and not the jury must determine. If the court should come to the conclusion that such a statement by one party was intended to be a substantive part of his contract, and not a mere representation, the often discussed question may, of course, be raised, whether this part of the contract is a condition precedent, or only an independent agreement, a breach of which will not justify a repudiation of the contract, but will only be a cause of action for a compensation in damages. In the construction of charter-parties, this question has often been raised, with reference to stipulations that some future thing shall be done or shall happen, and has given rise to many nice distinctions. Thus a statement that a vessel is to sail, or be ready to receive a cargo, on or before a given day, has been held to be a condition (see Glaholm *v.* Hays,[1] Oliver *v.* Fielden,[2] Croockewit *v.* Fletcher,[3] Seeger *v.* Duthie[4]), while a stipulation that she shall sail with all convenient speed, or within a reasonable time, has been held to be only an agreement (see Tarrabochia *v.* Hickie,[5] Dimech *v.* Corlett,[6] Clipsham *v.* Vertue[7]). But with respect to statements in a contract descriptive of the subject-matter of it, or of some material incident thereof, the true doctrine, established by principle as well as authority, appears to be, generally speaking, that if such descriptive statement was intended to be a substantive part of the contract, it is to be regarded as a warranty, that is to say, a condition on the failure or non-performance of which the other party may, if he is so minded, repudiate the contract *in toto*, and so be relieved from performing his part of it, provided it has not been partially executed in his favor. If, indeed, he has received the whole or any substantial part of the consideration for the promise on his part, the warranty loses the character of a condition, or, to speak perhaps more properly, ceases to be available as a condition, and becomes a warranty in the narrower sense of the word, viz., a stipulation by way of agreement, for the breach of which a compensation must be sought in damages (see Ellen *v.* Topp,[8] Graves *v.* Legg,[9] adopting the observations of

[1] 2 M. & G. 257. [2] 4 Exch. 135. [3] 1 H. & N. 893.
[4] 8 C. B. N. S. 45. [5] 1 H. & N. 183. [6] 12 Moo. P. C. C. 199.
[7] 5 Q. B. 265. [8] 6 Exch. 424–441. [9] 9 Exch. 709–716.

Serjt. Williams on the case of Boone v. Eyre,[1] in 1 Saund. 320 d, 6th ed.; Elliot v. Von Glehn[2]). Accordingly, if a specific thing has been sold with a warranty of its quality, under such circumstances that the property passes by the sale, the vendee having been thus benefited by the partial execution of the contract, and become the proprietor of the thing sold, cannot treat the failure of the warranty as a condition broken, unless there is a special stipulation to that effect in the contract; see Bannerman v. White;[3] but must have recourse to an action for damages in respect of the breach of warranty. But in cases where the thing sold is not specific, and the property has not passed by the sale, the vendee may refuse to receive the thing proffered to him in performance of the contract, on the ground that it does not correspond with the descriptive statement, or in other words that the condition expressed in the contract has not been performed. Still if he receives the thing sold, and has the enjoyment of it, he cannot afterwards treat the descriptive statement as a condition, but only as an agreement, for a breach of which he may bring an action to recover damages.

In the present case, as the defendant has not received any benefit or advantage under the contract, but has wholly repudiated it, the question is simply, whether, in the true construction of the charter-party, the court ought to infer that the statement as to the ship's being at that date in the port of Amsterdam was meant to be a substantive part of the contract, or a representation collateral to it. And this question appears to be properly raised by the averment in the plea that time and the situation of the vessel were essential and material parts of the contract. On the trial of the issue joined thereon, it was no part of the judge's duty to leave to the jury any question as to the construction of the contract, or the materiality of any of its statements. It was his function to construe the contract with the aid of the surrounding circumstances found by the jury, and to decide for himself whether the statement that the ship was in the port, supposing it to be untrue, was an essential part of the contract, or a mere representation, and to direct the jury to find for the defendant or plaintiff accordingly. The question, it should seem, might also be raised by pleading the material circumstances (as was done in Graves v. Legg[4]) on which the defendant relies as leading to the construction which the plea seeks to put on the instrument. Unless one or other of these modes of pleading were adopted, the court, in case there should be a demurrer to the plea, or on an application for judgment *non obstante veredicto*, would be precluded from taking the surrounding circumstances into consideration in aid of the construction.

[1] 1 H. Bl. 273, note (*a*).
[2] 13 Q. B. 632.
[3] 10 C. B. N. S. 844.
[4] 9 Exch. 709.

It is plain that the court must be influenced in the construction, not only by the language of the instrument, but also by the circumstances under which and the purposes for which the charter-party was entered into. For instance, if it was made in the time of war, the national character of the vessel is of such importance that a statement of it in the charter-party might properly be regarded as part of the ship-owner's contract, and so amounting to a warranty; whereas the very same statement in the time of peace, being wholly unimportant, might well be construed to be a mere representation. So if it were shewn that the charter-party was made for a purpose such that, unless the vessel began her voyage from the port of loading, with her cargo on board, by a certain time, it was manifest that the object of the charter-party would, in all probability, be frustrated, the court might properly be led by this circumstance to conclude, that a statement as to the locality of the ship, coupled with a stipulation that she should sail with all convenient speed, was a warranty of her then locality. But we feel a difficulty in acceding to the suggestion which appears to have been, to some extent, sanctioned by high authority (see Dimech *v.* Corlett [1]), that a statement of this kind in a charter-party, which may be regarded as a mere representation if the object of the charter-party be still practicable, may be construed as a warranty if that object turns out to be frustrated; because the instrument, it should seem, ought to be construed with reference to the intention of the parties at the time it was made, irrespective of the events which may afterwards occur. It is true that in some of the cases, where the question has been whether a stipulation in a charter-party amounted to a condition, the court decided that question in the negative, and in so doing took occasion to suggest that neglect or delay on the part of the ship-owner to execute his part of the contract might be a breach of such an essential stipulation on his part as to justify the charterer in treating the contract as brought to an end thereby, and in refusing on that account to perform his part of it, and further suggested that, in deciding whether the breach on the ship-owner's part was of such an essential stipulation as that described, the court might advert to the fact whether such breach had frustrated the whole object which the charterer had in view (see Freeman *v.* Taylor,[2] Tarrabochia *v.* Hickie,[3] Dimech *v.* Corlett).[4] But the court did not, we apprehend, mean to intimate that the frustration of the voyage would convert a stipulation into a condition, if it were not originally intended to be one.

The question on the present charter-party is confined to the statement of a definite fact, — the place of the ship at the date of the contract. Now the place of the ship at the date of the contract,

[1] 12 Moo. P. C. C. 199.
[2] 8 Bing. 124.
[3] 1 H. & N. 183.
[4] 12 Moo. P. C. C. 199, 224, 227.

where the ship is in foreign parts, and is chartered to come to England, may be the only *datum* on which the charterer can found his calculations of the time of the ship's arriving at the port of loading. A statement is more or less important in proportion as the object of the contract more or less depends upon it. For most charters, considering winds, markets, and dependent contracts, the time of a ship's arrival to load is an essential fact for the interest of the charterer. In the ordinary course of charters in general, it would be so: the evidence for the defendant shows it to be actually so in this case. Then, if the statement of the place of the ship is a substantive part of the contract, it seems to us that we ought to hold it to be a condition upon the principles above explained, unless we can find in the contract itself or the surrounding circumstances reason for thinking that the parties did not so intend. If it was a condition, and not performed, it follows that the obligation of the charterer dependent thereon ceased at his option, and considerations either of the damage to him or of proximity to performance on the part of the ship-owner are irrelevant. So was the decision of Glaholm v. Hays,[1] where the stipulation in a charter of a ship to load at Trieste was that she should sail from England on or before the 4th February, and the non-performance of this condition released the charterer, notwithstanding the reasons alleged in order to justify the non-performance. So, in Ollive v. Booker,[2] the statement in the charter of a ship which was to load at Marseilles was that she was "now at sea, having sailed three weeks ago," and it was held to be a condition for the reasons above stated. And we would note that the marginal abstract of this case states the stipulation to have been, "having sailed three weeks ago, or thereabouts." If the statement had really been so indefinite, it may be that the court would have come to a different conclusion.

We think these cases well decided, and that they govern the present case. We think that the decision of Dimech v. Corlett[3] does not conflict with them; because it is immersed in the specific facts there set out, so as to be a precedent only for cases with very analogous specific facts. The statement in that charter, that the ship was "now at anchor in this port" (Malta), did not avail to release the charterer, because the ship was in the port in the dry dock; and, although the statement of the fact that she was at anchor in the port was definite, and indicated that she was ready for sea, while in truth she was in a dry dock being built, and was not completed for a month, yet, as the defendant was at Malta, and was presumed to have known the state of the ship, and also to have known of the delay, and did not insist that the charter-party was broken, but allowed the ship to sail from Malta for Alexandria without objection, his defence on this point failed.

[1] 2 M. & G. 257. [2] 1 Exch. 416. [3] 12 Moo. P. C. C. 199.

The court below in a manner referred the present case to a court of error, to say whether the decision should be governed by Ollive *v.* Booker, or Dimech *v.* Corlett. We are of opinion, for the reasons assigned, that the decision of Ollive *v.* Booker was sound, and that it governs our decision here; and we are further of opinion that, in so holding, we do not at all conflict with the decision in Dimech *v.* Corlett, as above explained.

On these grounds, we think that the judgment of the Queen's Bench should be reversed. *Judgment reversed.*

TIDEY *v.* MOLLETT.

IN THE COMMON PLEAS, MAY 2, 1864.

[*Reported in* 33 *Law Journal Reports, Common Pleas,* 235.]

THE second count of the declaration stated that an agreement was made between the plaintiff and the defendant, which said agreement was so made A. D. 1863, within six lunar months before midsummer of that year, and was contained in a certain letter and a paper therein inclosed, and the said letter, a letter written by the defendant, and by him addressed to the plaintiff, was in the words and figures following, that is to say: "13 Terrace, Camberwell. Sir, — Will you (meaning the plaintiff) be so good as to sign the inclosed, which contains in writing the agreement we (meaning the plaintiff and the defendant) made verbally, except that I have added the paragraph as to a lease at the end of three years. Return it to me, when signed, by post. Yours, John Mollett." And the said paper inclosed in the said letter was in the words and figures following, that is to say: "1. Mr. Tidey engages to complete the whole work necessary by the 14th of June next. 2. The stairs in the kitchen to be made less steep. 3. The division of the bath from the other part of the room to be made when required by Mr. Mollett. 4. A greenhouse is to be erected of respectable appearance and size, and to be warmed by hot-air flue. 5. A door from the garden to the road is to be made. 6. Bells are to be hung throughout the house, and finger plates to be affixed to all the doors, as may be required by Mr. Mollett. 7. In case of any of the work proving defective, such as doors opening badly, cracking, &c., within six months, all is to be made good by Mr. Tidey. This arrangement applies also to the drainage. The water is to be laid on to the upper part of the house, and other deficiencies which may appear are to be made good by Mr. Tidey, and as may be decided by Mr. Colchester. In consideration of these conditions being fulfilled, Mr. Mollett engages to take the house No. 51 Belsize Park, at the annual rent of £130 per annum, to be paid quarterly. At the expiration of the three years Mr. Mollett is to have the option of continuing possession by taking a lease for seven, fourteen, or twenty-one years, on the terms of this agreement. Rent to begin from midsummer next. London, 22d of May, 1863." And the plaintiff signed and returned to the defendant the said inclosed paper as requested by the said letter; and the plaintiff says that he has done every thing, and all things were done and happened necessary to entitle the plaintiff to have the defendant take the said house for three years at the said rent as agreed, yet the defendant did not nor would take the said house for three years at the said rent as agreed, but wholly refused so to do, whereby the plaintiff lost all the benefit of the said agreement and the said rent, and was prevented from letting the said house to other persons, and incurred great expenses in fitting up and preparing the said house for the defendant, and was otherwise injured and damnified.

Third count. For that the said agreement was made as and at the time in the second count mentioned; and the plaintiff says that all things were done and happened, and all times elapsed before the said breach, necessary to entitle the plaintiff to have the defendant take the said house for the said three years at the said rent as agreed, and to sue for the breach hereafter mentioned, except certain things which the defendant prevented the plaintiff from doing, yet the defendant did not nor would take the said house for three years at the said rent as agreed, whereby the plaintiff sustained similar damage to that in the second count mentioned.

Third plea to the second count. That the plaintiff did not fulfil the conditions on his part in the said agreement contained in this; that although required by the defendant so to do, the plaintiff did not complete the whole work necessary by the 14th of June, as in the said agreement provided.

Fourth plea to the third count. The defendant, to avoid repetition, pleads the same facts which are pleaded to the second count; and he further says, that he did not prevent the plaintiff as in the third count alleged.

Demurrer to the third and fourth pleas, and joinder in demurrer.

Macnamara (*C. A. Turner* with him), in support of the demurrers. The pleas are bad. They do not shew a non-performance of a condition precedent. The undertaking extends equally to all the provisions of the agreement; and it is quite clear that two of these provisions, one of which is to divide the bath from the other part of the room "when required," and the other, to make good deficiencies in the work "within six months," need not be carried out before the 14th of June;

and this shews that the words in the agreement are not to be taken in their literal sense. The pleas do not shew that the whole of the work was not done by the 24th, when the rent was to commence, or that the defendant gave notice to the plaintiff of the non-performance of a condition precedent. The agreement must be taken most strongly against the defendant. [BYLES, J. How do you understand the word "necessary"? The work could hardly answer the contract, unless it were all that was necessary.] If the conditions are to be fully and literally performed, the omitting to hang a single bell must defeat the plaintiff's right of action. The decisions which shew when an engagement is to be construed as a condition precedent are to be found in the notes to Pordage *v.* Cole.[1] In Lang *v.* Gale,[2] where conditions of sale provided that an abstract of title should be delivered within three months of the date of the conditions, the court said that this provision was not a condition precedent, but was meant only to secure a delivery within a reasonable time. And in Lucas *v.* Godwin,[3] where a contract to build cottages contained these words, "Mr. L. agrees to pay £210, on condition of the work being done in a proper and workmanlike manner, and to be completed by the 10th of October, 1836, together with the amount of one-half of the foundations, as before mentioned," and the cottages were not completed till the 15th of October, it was held, that the value of the work might be recovered in an action for work and labor. [WILLES, J. In Glaholm *v.* Hayes[4] these words in a charter-party, "The vessel to sail from England on or before the 4th of February next," were held to be a condition precedent. ERLE, C. J. Must not the case be decided by the intention of the parties to be taken from their own words, coupled with the circumstances in which they stood at the time these words were used?] There are several cases where similar clauses in charter-parties have been held not to be conditions precedent. In Ritchie *v.* Atkinson,[5] where the master agreed to load from the freighter's factors a complete cargo, and deliver the same on being paid freight, it was held that the delivery of a complete cargo was not essential in order to recover the freight. The late cases of Behn *v.* Burness[6] and Pust *v.* Dowie[7] are to the same effect. Then the pleas should have shewn that the defendant elected to rescind the contract on the 14th, and that he did not allow the plaintiff to go on and incur expense. In Carpenter *v.* Blandford,[8] where £30 had been deposited, to be forfeited in case the plaintiff did not perform his part of the agreement

[1] 1 Wms. Saund. 320 *b*. [2] 1 M. & S. 111.
[3] 3 Bing. N. C. 737; S. C. 6 Law J. Rep. (N. S.) C. P. 205.
[4] 2 Man. & G. 257; S. C. 10 Law J. Rep. (N. S.) C. P. 98.
[5] 10 East, 295. [6] 32 Law J. Rep. (N. S.) Ex. Ch. 204.
[7] 32 Law J. Rep. (N. S.) Q. B. 179.
[8] 8 B. & C. 575; S. C. 7 Law J. Rep. K. B. 58.

by a certain day, and the plaintiff, when that day arrived, gave notice that he should not be able to keep his engagement, but the defendant, without taking any notice of the default, allowed the plaintiff to proceed on the next day with the business which was the subject-matter of the agreement, it was held that the plaintiff might recover back the deposit. [WILLES, J. That is one of those numerous cases which shew that a deposit may be recovered back, unless the agreement shews that this was not the intention of the parties.] The pleas, at any rate, should have shewn that the repairs were necessary in order to make the house habitable, or that they were material and important repairs.

Bosanquet, for the defendant. The declaration is bad, as the instrument upon which it is founded is a lease, and therefore void, as not being under seal. With regard to the question as to whether the nonfulfilment of the condition is an answer to the action, in Jones *v.* Berkley[1] the rule is laid down that no person can call upon another to perform his part of the contract until he himself has performed all that he has stipulated to do as the consideration of the other's promises. The word "necessary" in the conditions must be taken to mean necessary in order to make the place fit for occupation. It could never be intended that the defendant should be compelled to move into a useless house, simply that he might recover damages. Lucas *v.* Godwin was not a case of tenancy. In Maryon *v.* Carter,[2] where the defendant covenanted to purchase one of a row of houses, and to pay a further sum of £80, provided the adjoining houses should be completed, *i. e.*, roofed, sashed, paved in front, inclosed with iron railings in front, and occupied by tenants for terms not less than yearly tenancies, by the 21st of April, 1829, and it was proved in an action to recover the £80 that, by reason of bad weather, the foot-pavement had not all been laid down before the 25th of April, Tindal, C. J., nonsuited the plaintiff. It is submitted that the intention of the parties, as it appears on the face of the contract in question, shews that the consideration for the defendant's promise was a strict performance of the stipulation as to the repairs of the house, and that the case is therefore brought within the rule laid down in Stavers *v.* Curling.[3] He also cited Bac. Abr. tit. "Leases," Chitty on Contracts, 6th ed. 644, and Gore *v.* Lloyd.[4]

ERLE, C. J. I am of opinion that our judgment should be for the defendant. I think that the writing upon which this case turns is an agreement and not a lease. The judges of this country were at one time not disposed to look upon writings such as this as agreements, but wishing to escape from the Statute of Frauds, they held them to be

1 Dougl. 684. 2 4 Car. & P. 295.

3 3 Bing. N. C. 355; s. c. 6 Law J. Rep. (N. S.) C. P. 41.

4 12 Mee. & W. 463; s. c. 13 Law J. Rep. (N. S.) Exch. 366.

leases. Now, however, since the Statute 8 and 9 Vict. c. 106, making leases not under seal voidable, it has been the practice, for a very similar reason to that which existed before, to hold them to be agreements. With regard to the pleas, it appears that the defendant is sued for breach of his agreement in not becoming a tenant of a house belonging to the plaintiff on the 24th of June. The words of this agreement are "in consideration of these conditions being fulfilled Mr. Mollett engages to take the house No. 51 Belsize Park, for three years, at the annual rent of £130 per annum." Now, these conditions are, that certain specified repairs are to be executed, and the whole work necessary is to be completed by the 14th of June. And the pleas say, that the plaintiff, although required, did not complete the whole work necessary by the 14th of June. I am of opinion that these pleas shew the non-performance of a condition precedent. What passed between the contracting parties seems to be this: The plaintiff was the owner of a house in the course of construction, and the defendant took the house for three years from the 24th of June, stipulating that what was necessary should be made ready by the 14th of June. I think that the defendant was quite right in insisting upon the repairs being completed some days before that fixed for the commencement of his tenancy and his taking possession of the house. It is, therefore, very probable that the 14th of June was a material day, and we all think that, in the absence of any thing in the agreement or the surrounding circumstances to remove this presumption, we ought to give effect to it. It is said that the meaning of the word "necessary" is undefined. But whatever may be the improvements which come under the word "necessary," the pleas take up the word in the same sense as that in which it is used in the agreement and in the declaration, and the demurrers admit that the right meaning has been given to it.

WILLES, J. I am of the same opinion. It has been ingeniously argued that the completion of the repairs by the 24th of June would have been sufficient; but a very proper answer to that was given by the learned counsel for the defendant, namely, that the proviso for the completion of the work by the 14th of June, might very well be inserted, in order to enable the defendant to establish himself within a reasonable time before the commencement of the tenancy. The proviso is made a condition precedent by the terms of the agreement, and I do not feel myself at liberty to say that the word "necessary" was not used in the sense contended for by the defendant.

BYLES, J. It ought now I think to be generally known from the cases of Bond v. Rosling [1] and Parker v. Taswell [2] that documents like

[1] 1 Best & Smith, 371; s. c. 30 Law J. Rep. (N. S.) Q. B. 227.
[2] 27 Law J. Rep. (N. S.) Chanc. 812; s. c. 2 De Gex & J. 559.

the one declared upon, though void as leases, may, nevertheless, be available as agreements. The construction put upon this agreement by my brothers is, I think, the proper one.

KEATING, J., concurred. *Judgment for the defendant.*

CLARKE, *Assignee of the Estate and Effects of* FRANCIS AYRES, *a Bankrupt*, AND OTHERS v. WATSON AND ANOTHER.

JANUARY 25, 1865.

[*Reported in* 18 *Common Bench Reports, New Series,* 278.]

THE first count of the declaration stated, that theretofore and before the said Francis Ayres became bankrupt, to wit, on the 9th of October, 1862, by an agreement in writing then made and entered into between the said Francis Ayres, William Mallows, and William Johnson, therein called "the contractors," of the one part, and the defendants of the other part, the said contractors agreed with the defendants to do certain works therein mentioned in conformity with certain plans, drawings, and sections therein mentioned; and also in conformity with certain specifications therein mentioned, as well as to the satisfaction and approval of the engineer to a certain board of health for the time, should such be found necessary, at or for £312 15*s.*, to be paid as follows: £156 7*s.* 6*d.* on production by the contractors to the defendants, or one of them, of the certificate of William Lambert, or other the surveyor for the time of the defendants, that they, the contractors, had duly and efficiently performed and completed such portion of the work as according to the judgment of the said surveyor should be not less than three-fourth parts thereof in extent and value; £78 3*s.* 9*d.* on the production by the said contractors to the defendants, or to one of them, of the certificate of the said surveyor as aforesaid, that the whole of the works mentioned and referred to in the said plans, drawings, and specifications, had been duly and efficiently performed and completely finished to his satisfaction, and also to the satisfaction of the said engineer for the time being of the local board of health, if necessary; and the balance of £78 3*s.* 9*d.* at the expiration of four months from the date of the said surveyor's certificate of completion; provided the therein-mentioned roads, pathways, drains, and culverts, and every part thereof, should be certified by the said surveyor to be in good repair and in perfect and sound condition in all respects; it being thereby intended and agreed that all the said works and materials should be so put and kept in good repair until the expiration of such four months from completion by and at the sole cost and expense of the said contractors; and the defendants thereby agreed with the said Francis Ayres, William Mallows, and William Johnson, in consideration of the due performance of the said agreements therein contained on their part, to pay to them the sum of £312 15*s.* at the times and in the manner thereinbefore mentioned: Averment, that although £156 7*s.* 6*d.*, part of the said sum of £312 15*s.*, had been paid, and all things necessary on the part of the said contractors to entitle them to have the certificate of the surveyor of the defendants, that the whole of the works in the said plans, drawings, and specifications had been duly and efficiently performed and completed to his satisfaction, and also to the satisfaction of the engineer of the said local board of health, had been done and performed by them; yet the said surveyor had not given such certificate, but had wrongfully and improperly neglected and refused so to do, nor had the defendants paid the said sum of £78 3*s.* 9*d.* payable on such certificate; and that, although more than four months since the said surveyor ought to have given such certificate had elapsed, and although all things had been done by the said contractors on their part to entitle them to a certificate by the said surveyor that the said roads, pathways, drains, culverts, and every part thereof, were at the expiration of the said four months in good repair, and in perfect and sound condition in all respects, yet the said surveyor had not granted such certificate, but had wrongfully and improperly neglected and refused to do so, and the defendants had not yet paid the said balance of £78 3*s.* 9*d.*

The defendants demurred to this count, and the plaintiffs joined in demurrer.

Henry James, in support of the demurrer.[1] Two breaches are alleged in the declaration. The first is, that the defendants have not paid the £78 3*s.* 9*d.* The answer to that is, that, by the terms of the contract, it was payable only upon production of the surveyor's certificate, which has not been produced. The second breach is, that the surveyor has wrongfully and improperly withheld his certificate. No fraud, however, or collusion is charged. It is not even alleged that the conduct of the surveyor was fraudulent; the allegation that he wrongfully and improperly neglected and refused to grant his certificate would be satisfied by shewing that he had been guilty of a mere error in judgment. Scott *v.* The Corporation of Liverpool, 1 Giffard, 216, is precisely in point. That was a bill for an account of certain

[1] The points marked for argument on the part of the defendants were as follows: 1. That the first count discloses no cause of action against the defendants; 2. That the plaintiffs are not entitled to recover without obtaining the several certificates of the surveyor; 3. That the defendants are not liable for the surveyor not giving such certificates; and that in the absence of such certificates, no breach of the agreement is shewn.

works constructed by Scott for the corporation of Liverpool, — the contract providing that, "if the contractors should fail in performing their contract, or, in the opinion of the engineer, not make due progress, it should be lawful for the corporation to seize the plant, and, in case any dispute should arise, the decision of the engineers should be final at law and in equity." The case was heard before Vice-Chancellor Stuart, assisted by Erle, J., and the bill was dismissed with costs, no case of fraud, misconduct, incapacity, or refusal to act being established against the engineer. In delivering his opinion there, Erle, J., says: "By the contract it appears to me that the engineer is interposed between the corporation and the contractors, and made the absolute judge of the performance of the works, and that there is no right in the contractors to demand payment, and no liability on the company to pay, throughout the contract, unless the condition of obtaining a valuation by the engineer and his certificate has been fulfilled." "The law can only enforce rights under a contract according to that contract. It is not necessary to cite authorities on such a subject. I refer only to some of those cited in the argument. In Grafton *v.* The Eastern Counties Railway Company, 8 Exch. 699, the contract was to deliver to the satisfaction of the agent of the defendants. It was held that the promise was on condition that the agent was satisfied, and that no action lay for the price of coke unless the condition was fulfilled. So in Milner *v.* Field, 5 Exch. 829, the same point prevailed. In Ranger *v.* The Great Western Railway Company, 5 House of Lords Cases, 72, the stipulation that the engineer should be the absolute judge during the progress of the works of the mode in which the contractor was discharging his duties, was recognized as both valid and reasonable, though the engineer was a shareholder in the company; and in pp. 106, 107 of the report, the notion that accounts of the work done under a similar contract to this might be taken by the Master in Chancery, instead of the engineer, on the ground that the contract has been abandoned, was repudiated as erroneous. The stipulation is of great importance, for, if the contractors can open this contract on account of alterations and additions with mutual disputes, and can insist that an account should now be taken before a stranger of the entire works, which can ill be examined after complete, they may inflict litigation, complicated, expensive, and doubtful in the extreme, — an evil which the stipulation is framed to avert. The question remains, whether the conduct of the parties affords any evidence of a right of action, either on the ground of waiving the conditions, or departing from the original contract and substituting another, either expressed or implied, or on the ground of a wrong. My answer is in the negative. I am not aware that the defendants are shewn to have committed any wrong, or any breach of their contract, or any departure from it." "I cannot discover that the corporation have by their conduct created a liability at law not imposed on them by the terms of the contract." And Vice-Chancellor Stuart, at p. 228, says, "This court has no right or power to impose upon either of the parties to the contract any other terms than those which have been prescribed by themselves, and by which they have agreed to be bound. It is the very essence of the contract that no sum should be considered due and owing to the plaintiffs on account of any of the works executed by them, unless the engineer shall certify the amounts."

Parry, Serjt., contra.[1] Substantially, this is an action for a tort. The plaintiff complains of a wrong done by the agent of the defendants. Lambert was not acting for the plaintiffs, but for the defendants alone, to protect them against overcharges by the contractors. The contract in effect is that the defendants will employ Lambert, "or other their surveyor for the time," to perform the duties of surveyor rightfully and honestly; and the defendants are responsible if the person so employed shall wrongfully or improperly withhold his certificate. [WILLES, J. The declaration states that the work was done to the satisfaction of the surveyor.] Yes. In Pawley v. Turnbull, 7 Jurist, N. S. 792, Vice-Chancellor Stuart held the conduct of the architect in withholding certificates to amount to improper conduct, and decreed payment of the money notwithstanding their absence. The defendants must be held to have dispensed with the condition of an engineer's or surveyor's certificate, if they appoint a man who wrongfully abstains from acting. [WILLES, J., referred to Harrison v. The Great Northern Railway Company, 11 C. B. 815, and The Great Northern Railway Company v. Harrison, 12 C. B. 576.] In Milner v. Field, 5 Exch. 829, there were negative words in the contract: the proviso was, that "no instalment should be paid unless the plaintiff delivered to the defendant a certificate signed by the surveyor of the defendant, that the works were performed according to the specifications." Batterbury v. Vyse, 2 Hurlst. & Colt. 42, is in reality an authority for the plaintiff, though the declaration alleged that the surveyor, in neglecting to certify, acted in collusion with the defendant and by his procurement. The point marked for argument on the part of the plaintiff there was, "that the defendant who employs the architect does contract with the plaintiff that he will do his duty and act fairly."

James was not called upon to reply.

ERLE, C. J. I am of opinion that the judgment in this case ought

[1] The points marked for argument on the part of the plaintiffs were as follows: 1. That the surveyor is the agent of the defendants, and they are bound to employ him to certify according to the said agreement; 2. That the surveyor is responsible to the defendants for improperly certifying or omitting to certify; and they are responsible to the plaintiffs; 3. That the wrongful refusal of the defendants' agent to certify is a dispensation of the condition precedent, and equivalent to the defendants' preventing the certificate being granted.

to be for the defendants. The contract which they entered into was, to pay to the contractors, the plaintiffs, certain sums on production by them to the defendants, or one of them, of the certificate of William Lambert, or other the surveyor for the time of the defendants. Many contracts are so made. Every man is the master of the contract he may choose to make; and it is of the highest importance that every contract should be construed according to the intention of the contracting parties. And it is important, in a case of this description, that the person for whom the work has been done should not be called upon to pay for it until some competent person shall have certified that the work has been properly done, according to the contract and specification. Here the contract is, that the money shall become payable on production by the plaintiffs to the defendants of the certificate of their (the defendants') surveyor, that the contractors have duly and efficiently performed and completed the work to his satisfaction. No such certificate has been produced. But it is said that the plaintiffs have done all things necessary to entitle them to have the certificate of the surveyor that the works had been duly performed and completed to his satisfaction, and that the said surveyor had "wrongfully and improperly" neglected and refused so to do. That, in my opinion, is not sufficient. If it had been alleged that the defendants wrongfully colluded with the surveyor to cause the certificate to be withheld, they could not have sheltered themselves by their own wrongful act. But the word "wrongfully," as used here, does not intimate any thing of that sort. If the plaintiffs had intended to rely on the withholding of the certificate as a wrongful act on the part of the defendants, they should have stated how it was wrongful. This is in effect an attempt on the part of the plaintiff to take from the defendants the protection of their surveyor, and to substitute for it the opinion of a jury. That is not the contract which the defendants have entered into. The allegations on the part of the plaintiffs are not in my judgment such as to entitle them to succeed.

WILLIAMS, J. I am of the same opinion. Notwithstanding the surveyor may have been wrong in withholding his certificate, the money is not due.

WILLES, J. I am of the same opinion. Consistently with the allegations in this declaration, the only wrong the surveyor has been guilty of may be an error in judgment, or he may have refused to exercise any judgment; in which case the proper course would have been to call upon the defendants to appoint some other surveyor who will do his duty.

KEATING, J., concurred. *Judgment for the defendants.*

ROBERTS v. BRETT.

JULIUS ROBERTS, *Plaintiff in Error.* JOHN W. BRETT, *Defendant in Error.*

IN THE HOUSE OF LORDS, FEBRUARY 13, 14, MARCH 16, 1865.

[*Reported in* 11 *House of Lords Cases,* 337.]

THIS was an action for damages for breach of a contract under seal entered into on the 15th of May, 1855. The defendant represented "The Mediterranean Submarine Electric Telegraph Company," and on its behalf entered into a contract with the plaintiff to lay down 150 miles of cable between Cape Tabaque, on the northern coast of Africa, and Cape Spartivento, in the island of Sardinia.

The declaration stated that by a certain indenture, &c., entered into on the 15th of May, 1855, the plaintiff, for the considerations therein mentioned, covenanted with the defendant "that he, the plaintiff, should and would forthwith, at his own expense, procure the Cornwall frigate, or some other suitable vessel, and stow or cause to be stowed on board the said vessel the submarine telegraphic cable, which was one hundred and fifty miles in length, and was then at Morden Wharf, Greenwich, &c., and also should and would, at the like expense, fit out, &c., the said vessel, and provide competent officers and crew, and place on board sufficient breaks and rollers, &c., and would, to the extent of £600, pay the expense of insuring the cable, and several other things; and should and would "have the ship fully equipped in all respects and ready for sea at the Nore on or before the 15th of July then next." There were several other acts which the plaintiff undertook to do. And if he made default in having the ship with the cable on board fully equipped and ready for sea before the 15th of July then next, the defendant should be at liberty to retain from any moneys payable by him, as and for liquidated damages, £200 per week, and at that rate for any less period than a week; but the power to enforce this payment by way of liquidated damages "should be without prejudice to the right of the defendant to exercise any other powers or remedies at law or in equity, by virtue of these presents, or the bond thereinafter referred to for enforcing the completion of the works before covenanted to be done, or for compensating himself for the damage occasioned by such default." And the defendant covenanted with the plaintiff that "he, subject to such rights of deduction, would pay the plaintiff £5000 by the instalments and at the times next mentioned, that is to say, the sum of £1000, part thereof, on or before the expiration of seven days after the arrival of the vessel alongside Morden Wharf," the sum of £2000 twenty-one days after such arrival, and £2000 when the ship should put to sea from the Nore; and at the expiration of twenty-one days from the time when the cable should have been laid down, the defendant covenanted to deliver to the plaintiff five hundred paid-up shares in the company of £10 each. And then "it was agreed and declared that for the true performance of the covenants by the plaintiff thereinbefore contained, and for securing any penalties which he might incur under these presents, the plaintiff and two responsible sureties should, within ten days after the execution of these presents, give and execute to the defendant, his executors, &c., a bond in the penal sum of £5000. And for the due performance of the covenants on the part of the defendant thereinbefore contained, the defendant and two responsible sureties should, within ten days from the execution of these presents, give and execute to the plaintiff, his executors, &c., a bond in the penal sum of £5000." And it was agreed and declared that the said bonds so to be given as aforesaid should not in any manner prejudice or affect the respective rights or liabilities of the plaintiff or the defendant.

The declaration then averred that the plaintiff did procure a vessel and fit it out, and was ready and willing to provide the officers and crew, and to perform all the acts covenanted to be performed, and to have the ship ready for sea at the Nore before the 15th of July; but before the time arrived for so doing, the defendant refused to perform the contract, and dispensed with the vessel being brought alongside the wharf; and the plaintiff alleged that he had performed all conditions stipulated on his part, and that every thing had taken place to entitle him to a performance by the defendant, of all which premises the defendant had notice, and was requested to stow the cable on board, &c., and for doing all which matters and things a reasonable time had elapsed before the commencement of this suit, yet that the defendant did not nor would stow, or allow to be stowed, the cable, &c., but wholly refused, &c., and stowed the cable on board another ship or vessel, and thereby broke his contract. And the plaintiff further assigned for breach, that the defendant did not, within ten days, &c., execute the bond,[1] but therein made default.

The defendant pleaded first, except as to the giving of the bond (an exception repeated in each of the other pleas but the fifth), that the plaintiff did not procure a suitable ship, &c., and place the same alongside Morden Wharf as alleged. Secondly, that he did not fit out the ship as alleged. Thirdly, that the plaintiff was not ready and willing to provide and pay the officers and crew as alleged: and, Fourthly, that the plaintiff did not within ten days from the execution of the indenture (such ten days expiring before the plaintiff placed the ship alongside the Morden Wharf), or at any time give and execute, nor within the ten days procure two responsible sureties to give and

[1] This was a new breach, added after the first argument on the demurrer. See 6 C. B. N. S. 611, 618.

execute, &c., a bond in the penal sum of £5000 for the true performance by the plaintiff of the other covenants in the indenture contained, and according to the meaning and effect of such indenture. Fifthly, as to the breach of covenant by the defendant so excepted as aforesaid, the defendant paid into court the sum of one shilling.

The plaintiff took issue on the first, second, third, and fifth pleas.[1] On these pleas issue was joined. On these issues of fact, the cause was tried in June, 1858, at Guildhall, and a verdict for £2300 was found (on all the issues) for the plaintiff.

The plaintiff demurred to the fourth plea, and the defendant joined in demurrer. On this demurrer, judgment was given for the defendant (18 C. B. 561), which judgment was affirmed in the Exchequer Chamber. This proceeding in error was then brought.

Mr. *Bovill* and Mr. *Massy Dawson* (Mr. *Beasley* was with them), for the plaintiff in error. It must be assumed on these pleadings, that the plaintiff was able to perform the work undertaken by him in this contract, and that he did perform it as far as in him lay, was a fact found by the jury. There is in the declaration an allegation of request to the defendant, and refusal by him to stow the cable. The declaration is therefore good. On the other hand, there is in the plea no allegation of request to the plaintiff, and refusal by him to give the bond. The plea is therefore bad. Besides, the covenants as to giving the bonds were mutual and dependent, and the defendant could not allege that the plaintiff did not give his bond without himself alleging that he was ready and willing to give his bond.

The proper construction of the contract is the question now to be considered. The intention of the parties must decide it. What is the first stipulation in the contract? It is that the plaintiff shall "forthwith," at his own expense, procure the "Cornwall frigate," or some other suitable ship, and stow the cable on board. And the first stipulation by the defendant is that he will pay the plaintiff the sum of £1000, part of the whole sum of £5000 "on or before the expiration of seven days after the arrival of the vessel alongside Morden wharf," £2000 more on the expiration of twenty-one days after that time, and the remaining £2000 as soon as the ship had put to sea from the Nore. There is nothing which justifies the argument that the bonds were to be given before any one of these acts was performed, or that if the first of them had been performed, the £1000 would not have been payable, and that no action would have lain for its non-payment. Nor is there any thing which justifies the argument that the work, which was the object of the contract, was to be delayed till after the giving of the bonds.

The stipulation is, that the plaintiff shall "forthwith" bring the ship

[1] The original pleadings were amended, see 6 C. B. N. S. 611, 618; they are here stated as they appeared when the case was brought up to this House.

alongside Morden Wharf. He might have done so the next day; if he had, must it have lain there uselessly till the expiration of the ten days given for the delivery of the bonds? It is absurd to suppose that the parties had any such intention. If the ship had been brought there within twenty-four hours of the signing of the contract, that would have been a performance of the stipulation within the meaning of the word "forthwith," a word which certainly does not in any way imply delay, but quite the reverse. In the court below it was assumed that the plaintiff would not be liable to do what he undertook, and that the stipulation respecting the bond was to be a security against that, but the contract does not warrant that assumption, and there is no plea alleging that he was requested to bring the ship alongside and failed to do so.

If the plaintiff was under an obligation to give the bond before beginning to perform the work, so was the defendant. The covenants to give bonds are mutual, and dependent on each other. In that respect each party is in default, and cannot set up the default of the other in his own defence. But the absence of the bond cannot affect the working of the contract. If the obligation of the defendant to give his bond was not a condition precedent to any thing being done under the contract, how could the giving of a bond by the plaintiff deserve that character? It might be that non-performance of an act by one contractor would be an answer to an action by the other [*sic*], but that would not shew that the act was a condition precedent; for example, in an action by the buyer of goods for non-delivery, the seller might aver that the plaintiff was not ready and willing to accept, and dispensed with the delivery of the goods, and proof of the plea might discharge the seller from his liability on the contract, but yet there would be no condition precedent in the case; Pordage *v.* Cole, and the notes,[1] which shew that where covenants are in form independent of each other, and the breach of any one of them may be compensated in damages, an action may be maintained for a breach of one without averring performance of the others. Suppose the plaintiff had laid down the cable, could it be said that he could not recover because no bond had been given. [LORD CHELMSFORD. He might, for work and labor.] It is clear that though the parties agreed to give bonds as further securities, they did not intend to prevent other modes of remedy. There is an express clause to that effect in the indenture. If there were ten things to be done, and nine were performed, it was not the meaning of the parties that the non-performance of one should invalidate the whole contract.[2] Stavers *v.* Curling[3] is in point. There A. undertook a whaling voyage, and covenanted to do certain things,

[1] 1 Wms. Saund. 319*l*, 320 *d*, n. 3, citing Boone *v.* Eyre. See also the notes to Cutter *v.* Powell, 2 Sm. Lead. Cas. 13–15.

[2] 1 Wms. Saund. 320 c, n. 3.

[3] 3 Bing. N. C. 355, 3 Scott, 740.

on doing which the defendant covenanted to pay him a certain share of the profits. The court held that these covenants were independent, and that the performance of them all was not a condition precedent to an action on the defendant's covenant. So in Boone v. Eyre,[1] the principle was established that where a covenant goes only to part of the consideration on both sides, and the breach of it may be compensated in damages, it is an independent covenant and cannot be treated as a condition precedent. [LORD WENSLEYDALE. Does not the application of that principle depend on the form of the words used in the indenture?] Not necessarily so. [LORD CHELMSFORD. In Stavers v. Curling,[2] Lord Chief Justice Tindal says, "The question whether covenants are to be held dependent [on], or independent of each other, is to be determined by the intention and meaning of the parties as it appears on the instrument, to which intention, when once discovered, all technical forms of expression must give way."] Even that test may be answered here in favor of the plaintiff, for the indenture nowhere shews that the whole business is to be stopped till the bonds are given; the fixing of a day for giving them is merely to prevent unnecessary delay in doing the work; but if part of the work had been done before the ten days elapsed, it would be contrary to the declared intention of the parties to prevent the plaintiff from having payment for it, by telling him that he ought previously to have gone through the formality of giving a bond.

In determining this question, regard must be had to the whole of the stipulations. The consideration here given by the plaintiff for the covenant of the defendant was not the execution of a bond, but the doing of the work. That was the principle acted on in Davidson v. Gwynne.[3] In Tarrabochia v. Hickie,[4] covenants that the vessel was tight, staunch, and strong, and should sail with convenient speed, were held not conditions precedent unless their breach frustrated the object of the voyage.[5] Kingdom v. Cox [6] and Clipsham v. Vertue,[7] Campbell v. Jones [8] and Mattock v. Kinglake,[9] established the same rule, even where there were fixed days for the performance of certain acts, the observance of those days not being held a condition precedent; and Dicker v. Jackson,[10] as to the delivery of an abstract of title in an agreement for the sale of lands, proceeded on the same principle. The defendant here had dispensed with the plaintiff's performance of the contract, and thereupon the plaintiff was entitled to maintain his action, Hochster v. De la Tour,[11] where after agreeing to pay a courier

[1] 1 H. Bl. 273, n. See 1 Wms. Saund. 320 b, n. 3.
[2] 3 Bing. N. C. 355, 368.
[3] 12 East, 380.
[4] 1 H. & N. 183.
[5] But see Behn v. Burness, 3 Best & S. 751.
[6] 2 C. B. 661.
[7] 5 Q. B. 265.
[8] 6 T. R. 570.
[9] 10 A. & E. 50.
[10] 6 C. B. 103.
[11] 2 Ellis & B. 678.

at and from a certain day, the defendant before the arrival of that day declined the plaintiff's services. So Lovelock *v.* Franklyn [1] decided that the defendant having incapacitated himself from assigning a lease to the plaintiff by having assigned it to another person, such act of the defendant was a good ground of action, and that it was not necessary for the plaintiff to aver a previous tender of the money, or a request, or plaintiff's readiness to accept the assignment. In Cort *v.* The Ambergate Railway Company,[2] there was a contract for the manufacture and supply of goods from time to time to be paid for after delivery, where the defendant accepted and paid for a portion, and then gave a notice to the plaintiff not to make or send any more, as he, the defendant, would not accept or pay for them; the plaintiff was held entitled to maintain an action for breach of contract, without manufacturing or tendering the rest of the goods.

By the terms of the contract the giving of the bonds is not to affect the rights and liabilities of the parties. [THE LORD CHANCELLOR. Did the defendant mean by that reservation, that if he suffered a greater amount of damage than £5000 he should not be barred from recovering for it? If so, he would be reserving equitable rights. If one person did so, would it be reasonable to deprive the other of that benefit?] It would not. If one made default, the other being ready to perform the covenant, the latter could have sued the defaulter; when both made default it had the effect of striking the covenant out of the indenture.

Two cases will be relied on by the other side. Ellen *v.* Topp [3] is the first; that was an action against a father for non-performance of the articles of his son's apprenticeship. The plaintiff had abandoned one of the three trades which he had engaged to teach the son, and that was held an answer to the action. But that case is distinguishable, for there the Lord Chief Baron in judgment distinctly pointed out that the plaintiff himself had rendered it impossible for the defendant's son to do what was stipulated for in the articles of apprenticeship. The other case is Graves *v.* Legg.[4] There the agreement was to ship Donskoy wool within certain times, and there was a provision that the names of the vessels were to be declared as soon as the wools were shipped. It was held that the provision was a condition precedent; but that was because of the established custom of the particular trade, which rendered the wool saleable only on the declaration of the names of the vessels. These cases have no application to the present.

Mr. *Mellish* and Mr. *Horace Lloyd*, for the defendant in error. This is a mere question of construction, and every thing depends on what was the intention of the parties. In the court below it was thought that their object was to secure the performance of the contract

[1] 8 Q. B. 371.
[2] 17 Q. B. 127.
[3] 6 Exch. 424.
[4] 9 Exch. 709.

by making the giving of the bonds a condition precedent. The other construction would frustrate that object. [THE LORD CHANCELLOR. How is the payment of £1000 within seven days consistent with the giving of the bond being a condition precedent, when that bond was not to be given till ten days?] No such thing as a payment of that kind was contemplated. It was known to be impossible to prepare and bring alongside a vessel within so short a period of time. The seven days meant seven days after the bond was given and the work begun. It was not intended, if the plaintiff did not perform the work, and should happen to become bankrupt, that the defendant should have to prove against the bankrupt's estate the damages sustained by non-performance of the contract; and a mere action for non-performance of the condition as to giving the bond would be valueless, for the damages to be recovered therein would be merely nominal. It was therefore matter of necessity that the giving of the bonds should be a condition precedent; and such was the intention of the parties. Their object could not be secured but by making the giving of the bond a condition precedent.

"Forthwith" never had any other meaning in this contract but that of a reasonable time. But even if the vessel had been ready the next day, the plaintiff might have refused to bring it alongside till he got the defendant's bond, and the defendant might have refused to put the cable on board till he got the plaintiff's bond. [THE LORD CHANCELLOR. Then if the parties had neither obligations nor rights till the bonds were given, does not that shew that the two acts are of necessity mutual obligations?] Giving one bond may or not be a condition precedent to giving the other bond; but it is a condition precedent to the performance of the other stipulations of the agreement. It appears to be so on the face of the indenture itself. The averments in the pleadings do not shew that the plaintiff was ready to give the bond and that the defendant was not, but that both made default. Either party was at liberty to rescind the agreement. If both had gone on, the condition might have been waived; but that is not so with one alone. If one had duly performed the contract, he must, in an action upon it, have averred performance of all the conditions. Even under the Common Law Procedure Act that averment must be made. Here the averment was only that of readiness and willingness; no actual performance was shewn, except by a general averment that the plaintiff had performed; nor was there any averment that there had been any dispensation with the duty of performing this condition of the contract. The pleas, therefore, rightly traversed the general allegation of the declaration, and specially alleged that the condition of giving the bond had not been performed.

The true construction of the covenant is, that neither party shall be called on to perform his part of the agreement until each has given his bond to perform it. It is for "the true performance of the covenants thereinbefore contained" that the bonds are to be given; and those covenants include the whole of the acts to be done under the contract.

Mr. *Massy Dawson* replied.

March 16.

THE LORD CHANCELLOR (LORD WESTBURY). My Lords, the question on this appeal is, whether having regard to the true construction and intent of the agreement of 15th May, 1855, the stipulation that the appellant should, within ten days after the date and execution of the agreement, give a bond with sureties for the due performance of the covenants on his part, was a condition, the previous fulfilment of which, unless waived or released, was necessary to enable the appellant to maintain any action upon the agreement.

The case has been learnedly argued at the bar, and many decisions were cited, but the question depends on simple principles. First, having regard to the subject-matter of the agreement between the appellant and the respondent, the latter the representative of a company, it is reasonable to suppose that the company which was about to intrust the appellant with the laying down of a very valuable telegraphic cable, should require from the appellant security for the due fulfilment of his contract, and the requisition that the bond should be given within ten days is sufficient to shew that it was intended to precede any material act under the agreement. The appellant indeed contends that if he had brought the "Cornwall frigate" or some other suitable vessel alongside Morden wharf on the day of the date of the agreement, or the next day, the sum of £1000 would have been payable to him by the respondent within a week afterwards; and thus he insists that a material part of the contract might have been performed before the expiration of the ten days allowed for the bond, and that therefore the giving of the bond is not a condition precedent.

I cannot think that any such great expedition, if it had been possible, was contemplated by the parties, or that the appellant was bound to act with any such rapidity. His engagement is that he will forthwith, at his own expense, procure the "Cornwall frigate" or some other suitable ship or vessel for the purpose required; the word "forthwith" does not necessarily imply that this was to be done by the appellant before he had received the bond of the respondent and his sureties, that is, before the expiration of ten days. But if the appellant had brought a suitable vessel alongside the wharf so expeditiously as to have entitled himself to the sum of £1000, and had received that sum (which must be the hypothesis) within the ten days and before the time for giving his bond expired, I should not have thought that it affected his liability to give the bond within the appointed time.

It is urged that in the state of things supposed, the £1000 might not have been paid as stipulated, and so a breach of covenant by the respondent might have occurred within the ten days. If it did, I should still be of opinion that the appellant was bound to give or tender his bond to the respondent within the prescribed time. The right to have the security of two responsible sureties for the performance of the appellant's covenant, was a very material thing to the respondent's company, and of the essence of the contract; and I do not think it could be affected by any thing voluntarily done by the appellant within the ten days.

It was also contended by the appellant that the covenants to give the bonds by the appellant and respondent respectively were mutual covenants dependent one on the other; and that there was no default by the appellant until that instant of time at which there was a like default by the respondent, and that the respondent being in like default, could not defend himself by pleading the default of the appellant.

But I fear that this is not the true meaning and effect of the contract. The engagements to give the bonds are not entered into in consideration one of the other; but the fulfilment of his own engagement by each of the parties, is a necessary preliminary to his right to recover on the agreement. It is the true intent and object of the agreement that each party should find security within the time prescribed. If this be not done by either party both may be in effect released from the contract, which may fall to the ground; but neither party can recover for breach of the covenants in the agreement, unless he has performed this precedent obligation. I therefore move your lordships that the judgment of the court below be affirmed.

LORD CRANWORTH. My Lords, I think that the judgment of the House ought to be for the defendant in error.

I agree with the opinions of the learned judges, that the giving of the bond must have been intended to be a condition precedent to any right of action for breach of any of the covenants contained in the indenture. On any other hypothesis the bond would be useless.

No doubt, as there was a covenant by each party with the other to give a bond with sureties within ten days, if default was made in giving a bond, a right of action would accrue for breach of that covenant, but such an action could produce no fruit to the party recovering in it. If brought before breach of any of the other covenants it could only result in nominal damages. If brought after a breach no damages could be recovered except such as would have been recoverable in an action founded on the breach itself. It would give no right against any sureties, the obtaining of which right was the sole object of the bond.

It was argued that the circumstance that the bonds were to be given not immediately, but within ten days, was inconsistent with the hypothesis of a condition precedent. A breach, it was suggested, might occur within the ten days, and so a right of action might accrue before any bond need have been given. This does not appear to me inconsistent with the hypothesis of a condition precedent. Probably the parties knew that, practically, no breach could occur within the ten days. But even if that is not so, the party injured by a breach of covenant within ten days might by giving his bond put himself in a condition to sue for the breach, for it would certainly be no answer on the part of the defendant sued for the breach to say that he had not given his bond.

Suppose, for instance, that the plaintiff had on the day of the date of the indenture moored a proper ship alongside Morden wharf, but that after the expiration of seven days the defendant refused to pay him the £1000. The plaintiff, if he had given a proper bond with sureties to the defendant, would then have been in a condition to maintain an action of breach of covenant against the defendant, whether he had or had not given a proper bond to the plaintiff.

But it was argued that, even assuming the giving of the bonds to be conditions precedent, still they must be treated as mutual and dependent conditions, and that the defendant, who had given no bond to the plaintiff, could not insist on the want of such a bond from him. I do not feel the force of this argument. There is nothing in the indenture making it obligatory on either party to apply to the other for his bond. By giving the required bond, the party giving it puts himself in a condition of enforcing, if he thought fit, the performance of the covenants. If neither party, as was the case here, gave any bond, neither party could sue for any breach of covenant. This was the opinion of the courts below, and in that view of the case I concur.

LORD CHELMSFORD. My Lords, I agree with the decision of the Court of Exchequer Chamber affirming the judgment of the Court of Common Pleas.

The question is, whether the fourth plea is an answer to the action, or, in other words, whether the giving the bond by the plaintiff was a condition precedent to his right to recover damages from the defendant for his non-fulfilment of his part of the agreement.

The parts of the deed necessary to be noticed are these. [His lordship stated them, see *ante*, 603, 4.]

The learned counsel for the plaintiff argued that the covenant on the part of the plaintiff to give the bond could not be intended to be a condition precedent, because he was forthwith bound to procure the ship or vessel, so that he was to do an act before the ten days had expired within which the bond was to be given; and also that the defendant, having covenanted to pay the plaintiff £1000 on or before the expiration of seven days after the arrival of the ship or vessel at

Morden wharf, and the money being appointed to be paid on a day which might happen before the expiration of the ten days within which the bond was to be given, the giving of the bond could not be a condition precedent, according to the first rule upon the subject of dependent and independent covenants laid down in the notes to Pordage *v.* Cole.[1] They also contended that the case fell within the third rule stated in these notes, as it was a covenant going only to part of the consideration, the breach of which might be paid for in damages. These rules are not proposed for the purpose of absolutely determining the dependence or independence of covenants in all cases, but merely as furnishing a guide to the discovery of the intention of the parties. For, as Lord Kenyon said in Porter *v.* Shepherd,[2] "conditions are to be construed to be either precedent or subsequent according to the fair intention of the parties to be collected from the instrument; and technical words (if there be any to encounter such intention) should give way to that intention."

Now what may fairly be considered to have been the intention of the parties upon the whole scope and object of the deed in question? Putting the agreement into a short form, it amounts to this: the defendant says to the plaintiff, in consideration of your doing certain acts, and giving me a bond with sureties to secure the performance of your covenant to do these acts, I will pay you a sum of £5000, and give you a bond with sureties to secure the payment. And the plaintiff, on the other hand, covenants to do the acts and to give the bond in consideration of the performance by the defendant of the covenants on his part to be performed.

Upon this short summary of the deed there could scarcely be a doubt that either party might refuse to perform his part of the agreement until he was secured by the bond of the other.

But the counsel for the plaintiff say that the particular terms of the deed shew that this could not be the intention. In particular, they lay great stress on the word "forthwith" in the plaintiff's covenant to procure the vessel, which they interpreted to mean "immediately"; and they urged this as a proof that the giving the bonds could not be meant to be conditions precedent, because this act of the plaintiff must necessarily have been done before the expiration of the ten days, to the last moment of which the defendant was at liberty to delay the execution of the bond. And they also insisted upon the clause for payment by the defendant of £1000 before the expiration of seven days after the arrival of the vessel at Morden wharf, which might have happened within the ten days; and therefore they argued that the case, in both these respects, was within the first rule in the notes to Pordage *v.* Cole.

It appears to me that too great force was attributed to the word

[1] 1 Wms. Saund. 320. [2] 6 T. R. 668.

"forthwith" in the agreement, and that all that was meant by it was, that the plaintiff was, without delay or loss of time, to procure a suitable vessel for receiving the telegraphic cable. And to quicken his diligence the defendant covenanted to pay him £1000 within seven days after the arrival of the vessel at Morden wharf. Out of regard to his own interest, too, the plaintiff would use all expedition in commencing the performance of the agreement, because unless he had the vessel with the cable on "board equipped and ready for sea by the 15th of July," he would have been liable to pay £200 per week for his default. I think that the plaintiff could not have been compelled to take a single step nor to incur the smallest expense towards procuring the vessel, till he was secured by having the defendant's bond, and that if he chose to proceed without having this security, every thing he did was at his own peril. If the defendant wished to obtain a right to urge the plaintiff's progress within the ten days, he might have executed and delivered his bond, and then he would have performed all that was required of him till the first instalment of the £5000 became due.

It is a strong circumstance indicative of the intention of the parties that the stipulations with respect to the mutual bonds should be conditions precedent, that these stipulations follow all the covenants entered into on both sides, and that they are agreed and declared to be given "for the true performance of the covenants hereinbefore contained." They are obviously intended, therefore, to be mutual securities for the performance of all the covenants by each of the parties respectively. This, I think, takes away all ground for saying that the covenants for giving the bonds go only to part of the consideration, and that a breach of them may be paid for in damages. Though strictly speaking they enter into and form part of the consideration on both sides, yet they extend to the whole of the covenants contained in the deed, and are an essential and vital part of the agreement between the parties. Nor is it easy to see how a breach of them could be compensated in damages, or what estimate could be formed of the measure of damages for their non-fulfilment.

I do not think that any thing in favor of the plaintiff can be made of the circumstance of the defendant not having given his bond. It appears to me that the mutual default of the parties had the effect of virtually putting an end to the agreement, because neither of them was in a situation to insist upon performance by the other.

A supposed case was put at the bar, of the plaintiff, after the ten days had expired without his bond having been given, going on to perform his covenants, and afterwards, in an action to recover the amount stipulated to be paid by the defendant, being met by a plea of the non-performance of the condition precedent. I have no difficulty in saying that in such a case the party who may avail himself of the non-performance of a condition precedent, but who allows the other side to go on and perform the subsequent stipulations, has waived his right to insist upon the unperformed condition precedent as an answer to the action.

Looking at the whole of the deed, I am satisfied that it was the intention of the parties that each should receive from the other a bond as a security for the performance of the covenants before either was bound to proceed to perform any of the stipulations contained in the deed. For these reasons, I think the judgment of the Exchequer Chamber ought to be affirmed.

Judgment affirmed.

RAYMOND v. MINTON.

IN THE EXCHEQUER, MAY 3, 1866.

[*Reported in Law Reports*, 1 *Exchequer*, 244.]

DECLARATION on a covenant by the defendant, contained in an indenture of apprenticeship of 18th Feb., 1864, by which the defendant covenanted to teach H. Page, the plaintiff's son-in-law, in the art, trade, or business of a builder, ornamental painter, and decorator, and to find him food, &c., during the five years of his apprenticeship, for a premium of £29, averring that the defendant did not nor would, during the term or the part of it already elapsed, teach the apprentice in the said art, &c., but wholly failed, neglected, and refused so to do; and did not nor would find him food, &c.

Third plea, as to the alleged breach in not teaching the apprentice, that at the time of the said alleged breach the apprentice would not be taught, and by his own wilful acts hindered and prevented the defendant teaching him in the said art, &c., and then, by his said acts, caused the breach pleaded to.

Demurrer and joinder.

Goddard, in support of the demurrer. The covenants in an apprenticeship deed are independent, and the non-performance of his duty by the apprentice may give a right of action to the master, but does not discharge him from the obligation to perform his own duty; Winstone v. Linn:[1] on the contrary it is the master's duty to make the apprentice obey and learn, and he has the power by law to compel obedience; per Watson, B., in Phillips v. Clift.[2] The contract is one of a peculiarly personal kind, and of great mutual trust, and its difference from the ordinary one of master and servant is illustrated by the case last

[1] 1 B. & C. 460. [2] 4 H. & N. 168, 28 L. J. (Ex.) 153.

cited, where the dishonesty of the apprentice was held not to form any answer to an action against the master for not fulfilling his side of the contract. This plea may only mean that the apprentice is idle. [MARTIN, B., referred to Mercer v. Whall.[1]] If it is contended that the apprentice's obedience is a condition precedent to the master's performance of his duty, independently of the covenants in the deed, the covenant in the deed for his obedience becomes superfluous.

Grantham, in support of the plea, cited Hughes v. Humphreys,[2] and pointed out that in both the cases relied on for the plaintiff, the action was brought for a total refusal to instruct the apprentice, which was not alleged here.

POLLOCK, C. B. It is evident that the master cannot be liable for not teaching the apprentice if the apprentice will not be taught, and the plea sufficiently shews that to be the case.

MARTIN, B. The master contracts to teach the apprentice by the best means in his power, and common sense points out that, if the apprentice will not be taught, the master cannot teach him by any means. The willingness of the apprentice to learn is naturally a condition precedent to the master's teaching him. Reduce the matter to a particular instance, and this becomes apparent. The master says to the apprentice, "get up on that ladder and I will teach you the business of a house decorator;" the apprentice refuses, and stands upon the floor; it is obvious that the cause of the apprentice not being taught is that he has made it impossible, and the master cannot be called upon to perform an impossibility.[3]

BRAMWELL and PIGOTT, BB., concurred.

Judgment for the defendant.

CUNNINGHAM AND ANOTHER v. MORRELL.

SUPREME COURT OF NEW YORK, MAY TERM, 1813.

[*Reported in* 10 *Johnson*, 208.]

J. DUER, for the plaintiffs, moved to set aside the report of the referees in this cause. It was an action of covenant. Articles of agreement were entered into between the parties relative to making a turnpike road. The material covenant was as follows: "The party of the first part agrees to pay to the party of the second part, for completing the whole of the aforesaid enumerated articles of covenant and

[1] 5 Q. B. 447.

[2] 6 B. & C. 680.

[3] *Vide* Ellen v. Topp, 6 Ex. 424, 20 L. J. (Ex.) 241.

agreement, the sum of 6000 dollars, to be paid on or before the 20th October, 1810, in instalments as the work progresses, in cash and stock of the said company, in the form and manner hereafter described, to wit, 1. The said party of the first part is to assign over to the said party of the second part the whole of the subscription books, which contain the number of shares of stock sold and the names of the persons to whom sold; likewise to furnish the said party of the second part with a proper power of attorney to collect the money due, at all times, from the stockholders, on such stock as they may have subscribed for."

On the hearing of the cause before the referees, it was admitted that the plaintiffs had entered on the performance of the work mentioned in the articles of agreement; and also that the defendant, before the 20th October, 1810, paid a part of the sum mentioned in the articles. The defendant then insisted that the plaintiffs were bound to shew the completion of the whole work mentioned in the agreement, or of some part thereof; and that under the true construction of the agreement, they were only entitled to recover in proportion to the work actually done: and the referees being of that opinion, and the plaintiffs refusing to produce any further proof, the referees reported that nothing was due from the defendant to the plaintiffs.

Duer relied on the cases of Sears *v.* Fowler and Havens *v.* Bush (2 Johns. Rep. 272, 387), as in point, and conclusive in this case, to shew that the decision of the referees was erroneous.

Fisk, contra, cited 1 Saund. 319, n. 3; 12 Mod. 455; 1 Ld. Raym. 662; Year Books, 48 Edw. III., 2, 3.

KENT, C. J., delivered the opinion of the court. — We cannot distinguish this case, so as to take it out of the operation of the cases of Sears *v.* Fowler and Havens *v.* Bush (2 Johns. Rep. 272, 387). Those cases were governed by the English decision in Terry *v.* Duntze, 2 H. Bl. 389, but from a more full consideration of the subject, we are now led to believe that the court of C. B. carried too far the principle of mutual and independent covenants. It is true, that if by the terms of the contract the money is to be paid by a day certain, and which is to happen before the performance of the service, or by a day certain, and there is no day certain for the performance, the performance is not a condition precedent; and the party may sue for the money, without averring or shewing performance. This is what was said by Lord Holt in the case of Thorpe *v.* Thorpe, 12 Mod. 455, 1 Ld. Raym. 662; and he went no further with the doctrine of mutual covenants. Where it would be repugnant to the contract to make the service a condition precedent, the parties, he observes, are left to mutual remedies, on which, by the express words of the agreement, they have depended. The cases which he cites of Pool *v.* Tolcelser, 48 Edw. III., 2, 3, and Pordage *v.* Cole, 1 Saund. 319, are to this effect; and in both of them the entire consideration was to be paid by a fixed time, and which might precede the service. Lord Holt further said in that case, "what is the reason that mutual promises shall bear an action without performance? One's bargain is to be performed according as he makes it. If he makes a bargain, and relies on the other's covenant or promise to have what he would have done to him, it is his own fault. If the agreement be that A. shall have the horse of B., and A. agree that B. shall have his money, they may make it so; and there needs no averment of performance to maintain an action on either side; but if it appear by the agreement that the plain intent of either party was to have the thing to be done to him performed before his doing what he undertakes of his side, it must then be averred."

After this rational explanation of the rule, we cannot but think that it was misapplied or carried to an unreasonable length in Terry *v.* Duntze. The covenant in that case was that the plaintiff should finish the building by a given day, and the defendant was to pay the consideration by instalments as the building should proceed, and according to a certain and specified state of advancement, and the remaining part of the consideration when the building should be completed. But because two several sums of money were to be paid before the whole was performed, and when only a part of the service was performed, the court held the covenants independent, and, as we understand the case and as the reporter understood it, that the plaintiff might maintain his action for the entire consideration without any averment of performance. This was contrary to the plain understanding of the parties, and was not warranted by any of the cases referred to. It was sufficient for the plaintiff to have shewn the advance of the building as stipulated to have entitled him to the instalment then to be paid, but to have entitled himself to the last instalment, he was bound to aver and shew a completion of the contract. The good sense and justice of the case, as it appears to us, required this construction, and the meaning of the parties could not have been mistaken. The error in that case, and in the two cases in this court which followed it, consisted in holding the covenants to be independent throughout, because a part of the consideration money was to be paid before the entire service was to be performed. This might have been the case if the contract in all those cases had not provided that a certain part of the consideration was to be paid on the completion of the service, and which rendered the service, *pro tanto*, a condition precedent. There is nothing unreasonable nor unusual in such an agreement. It has been the constant language of the English courts, that the dependence or independence of covenants depended on the good sense and meaning of the contract. "Their precedency," said Lord Mansfield, "must depend on the order of time in which the intent of the transaction requires their performance." A mechanic generally stands in need of advances, from time to time, in aiding him to procure materials to carry on his work, and the employer, if prudent, will generally reserve a considerable payment until the work be completed, and to depend on such completion. But if all these payments can be demanded without performance, merely because a part of them were to be made as the work advanced, it would be making the intention of the parties subservient to technical rules. The parties have an undoubted right, if they please, to make their covenants dependent or independent throughout, or to make the covenants independent as to one payment, and dependent as to another. They have a right to mould their contracts so as to suit their mutual convenience and interests, and when the courts can ascertain their meaning, they are so to construe the contract as to give effect to that meaning, provided the purpose be lawful. For these reasons I apprehend that we have yielded with too much deference to the decision in Terry *v.* Duntze, and did not sufficiently advert to the evil consequences of the doctrine in the extent there laid down. It becomes, then, our duty to limit the operation of that case, and of the two cases in this court which were founded upon it, so as better to fulfil the intention of the contract and the justice of the case; and in doing this we may be permitted to consider it some apology for those decisions, that we at the time reposed upon the authority of so respectable a tribunal as the C. B.; and, especially, when its decision was supported by so distinguished a judge as Buller, who was equally eminent for a clear and sound judgment and for diligent and profound inquiry.

Having thus freed ourselves from undue embarrassment in considering the real merits of this case, we say that, as the road was to be completed on or before the 20th of October, 1810, and as the defendant was to pay therefor the sum of 6000 dollars, to be paid on or before that day, in instalments as the work progressed, the just construction of the contract is that if the plaintiffs will go for the whole consideration money, they are bound to aver and show a performance of the whole work, and if they go for a ratable part of the money, they are bound to shew a ratable performance. The decision of the referees was accordingly correct, and the motion to set aside their report ought to be denied. *Motion denied.*

GRANT v. JOHNSON.

NEW YORK COURT OF APPEALS, JULY TERM, 1851.

[*Reported in* 1 *Selden*, 247.]

COVENANT on articles of agreement for the sale of land, between the plaintiff (Grant) of the first part, and the defendant (Johnson) of the second part. "The party of the first part, for the consideration of nine hundred and fifty dollars, to be paid as follows, to wit, two hundred dollars on the first day of April next, two hundred dollars on the first of April, 1847, the remainder in two annual payments of equal amount, to be paid on the first of April of the two succeeding years, together with interest from the first of April next, agrees to sell to the party of the second part a certain piece of land lying in the town of Neversink" (describing it). "And the party of the first part agrees to give to the party of the second part the quiet and peaceable possession of said premises on the first of November next, with the exception of certain privileges granted to Nicholas Wakeley, and certain other privileges granted to Teunis Misener," &c. "And the said party of the first part further agrees to give to the said party of the second part a good and sufficient deed for the same on the first of May next, if the above conditions are complied with."

The agreement contained a further stipulation, which it is unnecessary to mention, and was executed under the hands and seals of the parties on the 24th day of August, 1845.

The declaration assigned as a breach the non-payment of the second instalment of two hundred dollars, payable on the first of April, 1847; but it contained no averment of the tender of a deed of the premises, before, on, or subsequent to the first day of May, 1846, or a readiness or willingness to execute one, in accordance with the covenant of the plaintiff.

The defendant interposed several pleas, which, as no question arose upon them, it is unnecessary to mention more particularly.

At the trial the plaintiff proved the agreement, and rested. The defendant moved for a nonsuit, on the ground that the plaintiff was bound to shew the delivery or tender of a deed before he could recover the second instalment.

The judge decided that the covenants were independent, and that the plaintiff could recover without shewing either a delivery or tender of a deed. To this decision the defendant excepted.

It was then admitted that the defendant had received possession of the premises according to the contract, and had paid the first instalment. He then offered to prove that no deed of the premises in question had been tendered to him up to the 15th of July, 1846. The court rejected the evidence as not constituting a legal defence, and the defendant excepted. The jury, under the direction of the judge, found a verdict for the plaintiff for the amount of the second instalment, and interest. Upon a bill of exceptions presenting the above facts, a motion for a new trial was made before the Supreme Court in the third district, and denied. An issue of law, arising upon a demurrer to the replication of the plaintiff, presenting the same question, had previously been decided by the same court in favor of the plaintiff. The new trial was denied, and the defendant's demurrer overruled, upon the ground that the covenants were independent, and that the plaintiff could recover without averring or proving performance, or an offer to perform the covenant on his part.[1] From this decision the defendant appealed to this court.

N. Hill, Jun., for appellant.

S. Beardsley, for respondent.

GARDINER, J. The question in this case is, whether the plaintiff can sustain an action for the second instalment of the purchase-money secured by the agreement, without averring and proving the delivery, or an offer to deliver a deed of the premises.

The parties have declared that certain payments were to be made, and certain acts performed by them respectively, at the times specified in the agreement. They must be held to have intended the performance of these acts, when, and of course in the order of time indicated in their covenants. The plaintiff was to give the defendant possession on the first of November, 1845. The performance of this requirement preceded any thing to be done by the defendant, and it might consequently have been enforced without any offer upon the part of the defendant; but if no possession had been given, the plaintiff could not have recovered the two hundred dollars to be paid by the vendee on the first of April, 1846.

The possession, however, was given, and the first two hundred dollars paid, and on the first of May, 1846, the vendee was entitled to his deed, as the thing next to be done in the order prescribed by the parties in their agreement. It was not executed, nor a willingness to execute it either averred or proved. The payment of the two hundred dollars, for which the suit is brought, was fixed upon a day subsequent to that agreed upon for the delivery of the deed. The case is therefore brought directly within the letter and spirit of the second rule suggested by Serjeant Williams, in his note to Pordage v. Cole,[2] that, "when a day is appointed for the payment of money, &c., and the day is to happen after the thing which is the considera-

[1] See 6 Barb. 337.

[2] 1 Saund. 320 *b*.

tion is to be performed, no action for the money can be sustained without averring performance."

The plaintiff relies upon the third rule of Serjeant Williams in his note to the case above cited, that, "where a covenant goes only to a part of the consideration on both sides, and a breach of such covenant may be paid for in damages, it is an independent covenant, and an action may be maintained, without averring performance." The rule is not free from obscurity. It was given by Lord Mansfield originally in Boone v. Eyre.[1] The defendants in that suit, after having received a conveyance of the equity of redemption of a plantation, and the negroes upon it, when sued for a part of the consideration, set up a breach of a collateral covenant on the part of the plaintiff, relating to the title and possession of the negroes, in bar of the action. The warranty extended both to the estate and negroes.[2] The covenant of the plaintiff, it will be perceived, embraced the whole and every part of the subject conveyed. If the title failed to a single negro, or the defendant was evicted from an acre of the land, the covenant was intended to afford redress, and enable a jury to apportion the damages according to the agreement of the parties. A "breach of the plaintiff's covenant might be paid for in damages," because a failure of title as to any part of the consideration could be compensated according to the standard fixed by the parties. In other words, the consideration for the defendant's promise was divisible, and the damages arising from a breach of the covenant of warranty were apportioned to each parcel of that consideration by the agreement itself. This, it is supposed, is what is meant by the expression above quoted, that the breach may be paid for in damages.[3] Accordingly it is stated in the note to Pordage v. Cole,[4] that, "when the consideration for the payment of the money is entire and indivisible, so that the money payable is neither apportioned by the contract, nor capable of being apportioned by a jury, an action is not maintainable."

The doctrine is thus stated in Chanter v. Leese:[5] "The party contracting to pay his money is under no obligation to pay for a less consideration than that for which he has stipulated. If, indeed, he does accept a partial performance, and to a certain extent enjoys the benefit of that for which he has stipulated, it may become a question whether he may not be liable upon an implied contract to pay for what he has had. And when the consideration is in its nature capable of being divided, and the payment apportioned by the terms of the contract, there may be still a right to recover the portion due on the original contract." This decision was affirmed in the Exchequer Chamber,[6] in 1839, and may be considered as the established doctrine in England at that day.

[1] 1 H. Bl. 273, note *a*.
[2] 4 Mees. & Welsb. 311.
[3] 5 Mees. & Welsb. 701.
[4] *Supra.*
[5] 4 Mees. & Welsb. 311.
[6] 5 Mees. & Welsb. 701.

The rule of Lord Mansfield, according to its original application, and as expounded in the decision above mentioned, is reasonable. It brings us back to the contract to learn the intention of the parties. Courts are not required to speculate upon the inequality of loss to the parties, or to look beyond the agreement to its performance, in order to ascertain its character as suggested by some judges and commentators.[1] These inquiries are proper where the question arises, whether the plaintiff has any remedy for what he has done, or parted with, or whether the defendant is not estopped by his acts subsequent to the agreement from insisting upon a condition precedent in his favor. Much of the confusion in the books, it is believed, arises from confounding the doctrine of waiver by matters *ex post facto* with a rule of construction applicable to the agreement as it came from the hands of the parties. Havelock *v.* Geddes.[2] A defendant may waive the performance by the plaintiff, in case of a covenant clearly dependent, and thus render himself liable in some form of action (Mitchell *v.* Darthez,[3] Lucas *v.* Godwin[4]), but it is only when the consideration is divisible, and the payments are apportioned by the agreement to the different parts of the consideration, that the covenant becomes independent, and a recovery can be had upon the original contract without averring performance, or an excuse for non-performance.

A covenant, therefore, which goes only to a part of the consideration, is not necessarily independent. Nor is it conclusive upon this point that the consideration is divisible in its own nature, or that a part of it has been received by the defendant; nor will the circumstance that one or any number of covenants in an agreement are independent, render others so. In Chanter *v.* Leese[5] the agreement was that the defendants should have the exclusive use and sale of six different patents, and they were to pay £400 in half-yearly payments, for one of which payments the action was brought. The defence was a failure of title as to one of the patents. The grant of the exclusive right was an independent covenant, which the defendants could have enforced without any averment; the consideration for the undertaking of the defendants was divisible in its own nature. The undertaking upon which the action was brought went only to a part of the consideration to be paid; and the court remarked that, although it had appeared affirmatively that the other five patents had been enjoyed by the defendants, the plaintiff could not have recovered on the contract. Terry *v.* Duntze,[6] which was followed in our Supreme Court in Sears *v.* Fowler,[7] in Havens *v.* Bush,[8] and in Wilcox *v.* Ten

[1] 1 Saund. 320 *a*.
[2] 10 East, 555.
[3] 2 Bing. N. C. 555.
[4] 3 Bing. N. C. 737.
[5] 5 Mees. & Welsb. 311.
[6] 2 H. Bl. 389.
[7] 2 J. R. 272.
[8] 2 J. R. 387.

Eyck,[1] to the contrary, is not law in this State or in England. The two cases in 2 J. R. were expressly overruled in Cunningham *v.* Morrell,[2] and the court in Wilcox *v.* Ten Eyck observe, that that case could not be distinguished from Sears *v.* Fowler.

The decision in Bennett *v.* Pixley[3] is placed by the court on the same ground with that of Sears *v.* Fowler and Terry *v.* Duntze, and the reasoning of the court in that case is overruled by Cunningham *v.* Morrell, and by Dey *v.* Dox.[4] The case, I think, should be classed with Campbell *v.* Jones[5] and Tompkins *v.* Elliott,[6] all of which fall within the principle of the first rule in Saunders, "that if a day be appointed for the payment of money, or part of it, or the doing of any other act, and the day is to happen, or may happen, before the thing which is the consideration of the money, or other act, an action may be brought for the money, or for not doing such other act, before performance," &c.[7] The decisions in Term R. and in Wendell were placed distinctly upon that ground;[8] and what fell from Lord Kenyon and Judge Savage, beyond a mere recognition of the rule laid down by Lord Mansfield, was no way necessary to the determination of those cases. The judgments were unquestionably correct for other reasons assigned by those judges.

The question then returns, was the consideration in this case divisible, and were the payments apportioned by the agreement to the different parts of the consideration within the principles above stated? According to the contract, the $950 to be paid by the defendant, as therein stipulated, was the entire consideration for a complete title to the premises. The possession was incident to the title, the whole of which the defendant was to receive as the consideration for his payments. He received one element of a complete title, to wit, the possession, on the first of November, 1845. He then paid, on the first of the following April, all that he was to advance by the terms of the agreement, until the fee should be added to the possession by a conveyance from the plaintiff, and the title of the defendant be then perfected. The plaintiff refuses or neglects to convey, and yet by this action claims the purchase-money of the defendant.

If we assume that the consideration of the defendant's undertaking was divisible, yet by the terms of the agreement he was to receive both the possession and a deed of the premises before he could be called upon for the payment of the instalment in controversy. These things were "to be done to him," according to the rule of Lord Holt, adopted in 10 J. R. 206. He was not to trust to the personal responsi-

[1] 5 J. R. 77.
[2] 10 J. R. 203.
[3] 7 J. R. 249.
[4] 9 Wend. 129.
[5] 6 T. R. 570.
[6] 5 Wend. 496.
[7] 1 Saund. 320 *a*.
[8] 6 J. R. 572; 5 Wend. 499.

bility of the plaintiff.[1] The plaintiff had covenanted that the thing stipulated should be performed before the defendant could be required to pay. Nor by the contract were the payments to be made by the defendant apportioned to any particular part of the consideration. He was not to pay any thing for the possession as distinguished from the fee of the land, but a gross sum for both by separate instalments. If he had refused to accept a deed, all that the plaintiff could have recovered would have been the balance of the purchase-money with interest. On the contrary had the plaintiff refused to convey, the recovery on the part of the defendant would have been confined to the difference between the contract price and the actual value of the land with interest. In a word, the covenant sought to be enforced against the defendant in this action went to the whole consideration on the other side, and depended on it.

The judgment of the Supreme Court should be reversed.

FOOT, J. The question is, whether the covenants to pay the second and subsequent instalments are dependent.

So many decisions have been made on the vexed question of what are and what are not dependent covenants, and so many of them are irreconcilable that they rather perplex than aid the judgment in determining a given case. One rule is universal, and that is, that the intent of the parties is to control. On reading the covenant in this case, it is clear to my mind, that giving the deed was to precede the payment of the second and subsequent instalments. The parties have said so in so many words. The deed was to be given on the first of May, 1846; and the second and subsequent instalments paid on the first day of April in the following years. If each had fufilled his contract, the appellant would have had his deed when the second instalment was payable. The clause, "if the above conditions are complied with," can only apply to such conditions as were to be performed by the appellant before the deed by the terms of the contract was to be given. The possession is a mere incident which follows the title, and cannot be retained independently of it.

Judgment reversed.[2]

[1] 9 Wend. 134.

[2] Compare Bean v. Atwater, 4 Conn. 3. — ED.

PLINY CADWELL AND ANOTHER *v.* EZEKIEL BLAKE AND ANOTHER.

SUPREME JUDICIAL COURT OF MASSACHUSETTS, SEPTEMBER TERM, 1856.

[*Reported in* 6 *Gray*, 402.]

ACTION OF CONTRACT, commenced on the 5th of April, 1854, by the assignees in insolvency of David Ames and John Ames, upon an agreement in writing made by the latter with the defendants on the 26th of January, 1853.

The following are the material parts of that agreement: "The said D. & J. Ames hereby sell to the said Blake & Valentine all the right, title, and interest which the said D. & J. Ames have in the machinery and fixtures now at their paper-mill at Chicopee Falls. They also agree that said Blake & Valentine shall have the right which said D. & J. Ames have to manufacture white paper, made from straw and other materials; which right has been assigned to said D. & J. Ames by Jean Theodore Coupier and Marie Amadee Charles Millier, and as described in the application of said D. & J. Ames for letters-patent of the United States. They also agree to instruct the said Blake & Valentine fully in the art and mystery of preparing the straw and other materials, and manufacturing the same into paper, and to communicate to them from time to time all the improvements which they, the said D. & J. Ames, shall make in said art, and give them the benefit thereof; which instructions the said Blake & Valentine are to keep secret, so far as secrecy can be preserved consistently with their business."

"The said Blake & Valentine are to pay for said machinery and fixtures four thousand dollars, in four equal annual payments, with annual interest from date. Payment is to be made in paper, manufactured according to the process above mentioned, at the market price of such paper at the time when each payment shall become due, the paper to be delivered at the Western Railroad freight depot in Springfield. They also agree to take possession of said machinery and fixtures by the fourth of July next, and proceed as soon as may be with the manufacture; and to pay to said D. &. J. Ames for the right to manufacture said white paper" a certain share of the profits, if the profits exceed two cents a pound; otherwise nothing.

"If any dispute or disagreement shall arise between the parties in regard to the estimate of the profits, it shall be referred to three disinterested men, one to be chosen by each party, and the third by the two referees, and the award shall be binding on the parties."

"If the said D. & J. Ames shall, upon request, refuse to teach the said Blake & Valentine the art of making said paper as above mentioned, they shall forfeit, as liquidated damages, distinct from all the other liabilities under this contract, the sum of four thousand dollars.'

The declaration set forth the agreement, and averred that David Ames and John Ames delivered said machinery and fixtures to the defendants according to the terms thereof, and the defendants accepted and received the same; that the defendants owed the plaintiffs therefor the sum of one thousand dollars with interest, and also the interest due on four thousand dollars, as therein stipulated; and that the plaintiffs had been ready to receive the paper therein specified, yet the defendants had not delivered the same, but had refused so to do.

Answer, 1st. That the defendants entered into said agreement upon the consideration and for the purpose of securing the right to manufacture white paper from straw by the process therein named, and of obtaining the necessary instructions in said art and mystery; that D. & J. Ames and the plaintiffs had failed to fulfil their contract in this behalf, and had neglected and refused to secure to the defendants the right to manufacture according to said process, and to instruct them in the art and mystery thereof, although repeatedly requested by the defendants so to do, and had prevented the defendants from using said process. 2d. That there had been a failure of consideration for the contract on their part; that said machinery and fixtures were of no value to them without said instructions and said right to manufacture; and they had offered to return them. 3d. That D. & J. Ames were not the proprietors of said right to manufacture, and had not at the time, nor obtained since, any effectual assignment thereof, or any right to contract with the defendants therefor; or else had failed to avail themselves of such assignment, and had abandoned, lost, and suffered themselves to be deprived of the right to use said process, and of the patent issued therefor; whereby their agreement to give the defendants such right had been defeated, and the defendants prevented from using said process and from manufacturing said paper. 4th. That the defendants, by such failure to secure to them said right and to give them such instructions, had been prevented from fulfilling the agreement on their part. 5th. That D. & J. Ames were requested to teach the defendants the art and mystery of making said paper according to said process, but neglected and refused so to do, and thereby incurred a forfeiture under said agreement of the sum of four thousand dollars as liquidated damages; which the defendants claimed the right to apply to offset and cancel all claims of the plaintiffs under the agreement.

At the trial in this court the defendants admitted the execution of the agreement, and the delivery to them of possession of the paper-mill, machinery, and fixtures about the 1st of March, 1853. The plaintiffs then rested their case.

The defendants contended that the plaintiffs were not entitled to recover, without proving "1st. That D. & J. Ames had such an assignment of the right as their contract states; 2d. That they had availed themselves of it, and made it effectual to secure to themselves the patent, or at least a right to manufacture under it for themselves and the defendants; 3d. That they had conveyed or secured to the defendants the right to use the process; 4th, That they had instructed the defendants in the art of making said paper."

The plaintiffs denied that it was necessary for them to offer any further evidence, or that any of the matters alleged in the answer constituted a good defence to the action.

Bigelow, J., ruled that the plaintiffs had made out a *prima facie* case, and would be entitled to a verdict unless the defendants went forward and offered evidence of the matters set out in their answers; and reported the case for the determination of the full court upon these two questions: 1st. The correctness of his ruling as to the sufficiency of the case as presented by the plaintiffs; 2d. The sufficiency of the grounds of defence set forth in the answer; a new trial to be had if, upon either of these points, the opinion of the court should be in favor of the defendants.

The arguments and decision upon this report were had at the last September term.

W. G. Bates and *J. Wells*, for the defendants.

F. Chamberlin, for the plaintiffs, cited Boone v. Eyre, 2 H. Bl. 273, note; Stavers v. Curling, 3 Bing. N. C. 355; Campbell v. Jones, 6 T. R. 572; Lloyd v. Jewell, 1 Greenl. 356; Knapp v. Lee, 3 Pick. 452; Platt on Cov. 90, 106; Knight v. New England Worsted Co., 2 Cush. 271; Townsend v. Wells, 3 Day, 327; Couch v. Ingersoll, 2 Pick. 300; Pordage v. Cole, 1 Saund. 320, and note 4; Franklin v. Miller, 4 Ad. & El. 599.

SHAW, C. J. No question arises in the present case as to the pleading; the declaration is perhaps sufficient, under the new practice act, to enable the plaintiffs to recover, inasmuch as it does briefly aver the performance on the part of D. & J. Ames, and the plaintiffs, their assignees in insolvency, of all things on their part by the terms of the contract to be performed. But it is a question of proof; did the plaintiffs offer sufficient proof of performance on their part to enable them to recover? This again depends on the construction of the contract, and whether, according to its true interpretation, the stipulation for the payment of $4000 and interest, in paper to be manufactured by the process contemplated by the contract, was independent, and to be performed absolutely by such payment; or was it dependent and conditional, and to be performed only on condition that certain other things should be first performed on the part of the said D. & J. Ames?

The contract consists of several articles on both sides, is expressed in terms somewhat brief, and it is not easy to gather from it the full and clear intent of the parties. The great purpose of the contract seems to have been for D. & J. Ames to transfer to the defendants a right, a useful and beneficial right, to manufacture and sell white paper in so cheap a manner and in such quantities as to yield a profit, which right D. & J. Ames had acquired so far as it could be acquired by assignment before patent, and of which they were expecting to become the patentees by a patent to be regularly issued by the competent authority of the United States. The particular right is no otherwise specifically described and identified than as a right which had been assigned to them by Coupier & Millier, and as described in the application of D. & J. Ames for letters-patent. It manifestly looked to the expectation that D. & J. Ames were to be the patentees, because they were the assignees and had applied for a patent, and because they stipulated to extend to the defendants all the benefit of the improvements which they should make.

In construing a mutual agreement, in which there are several stipulations on both sides, the question, whether one is absolute and independent, or conditional and made to depend on something first to be done on the other side, does not depend on any particular form of words, or upon any collocation of the different stipulations; but the whole instrument is to be taken together, and a careful consideration had of the various things to be done, to decide correctly the order in which they are to be done.

It is contended that, as the machinery and fixtures were to become the property of the defendants at once, at a fixed price of $4000, payable at a certain time, they were to pay for them at all events, whether the manufacture of paper by the new process should go on or not. There would be more force in this argument if it appeared that the fixtures and machinery thus sold were adapted to the general purposes of paper-making, and had a market value, independently of the new process, and especially if the time for making the payment had been fixed at a time before the acts to be done on the other side.

But in this case, for aught that appears, the machinery and fixtures would be of little value except for manufacturing by the new process. And possibly the defendants may have stipulated to pay a sum greater than their value for these articles, in consideration of the advantages expected from the whole contract.

The stipulation, that the price of the machinery and fixtures should be paid at a fixed time, affords no criterion for determining that the stipulation is independent; because there was ample time before the first payment for D. & J. Ames to transfer the machinery, afford all the necessary instruction, execute and deliver a license conveying to the purchasers a right to manufacture, and do all other acts relied on as conditions precedent.

But the strong ground on which the court are of opinion that these acts of D. & J. Ames were conditions precedent is, that these payments were to be made by a delivery of paper, to be manufactured by this new process from straw and other materials, at the then market value. This process is recognized and represented in the contract itself as an art and mystery, to be kept secret as far as practicable, not yet patented, and of which, therefore, there was no specification in the patent-office, from which the process could be learned. The machinery sold may have been that of the inventors, adapted to the making of paper by this process.

It seems to us that these two stipulations, to deliver the machinery and to give the instruction, stand upon the same footing, because both were necessary to the making of paper by this process. The stipulation to instruct in the art and mystery was absolute and affirmative, like that to deliver the machinery, not dependent on request. There was a distinct stipulation, that if they should refuse to instruct on request, they should be liable to liquidated damages; but it has a distinct object, and does not supersede the other.

Without instruction in this art and mystery, the defendants might not know the method of preparing the straw and using the machinery; without these, this kind of paper could not be made, it could have no market price, the defendants could not make it, and of course could not deliver it.

When, in the order of events the act to be done by the one party must necessarily be done before the other can be done, it is necessarily a condition precedent, although there be a stipulation for liquidated damages for the breach on each side, and although there be a fixed future time for payment, sufficiently distant to have the work done in the mean time. Suppose B. agrees to build at his own shop a carriage for A., of A.'s materials; A. stipulates seasonably to furnish materials, and to pay B. in four months; and each, upon failure, stipulates to pay a sum as liquidated damages. The furnishing or tendering the materials by A. is a condition precedent. Without it B. cannot perform. He must build it of A.'s materials. Even building it of his own would not be a performance. B. has his shop, his tools, and his workmen all ready, but A. does not furnish the materials. If B. sues A., averring readiness to perform, he may recover. But if A. sues B. for not building the carriage, it would be a good answer that A. himself had not furnished the materials; because, whatever else the contract may contain, this is in its nature a condition precedent.

The court are therefore of opinion that the plaintiffs, as a part of their own case, should not only have averred, but should have offered proof at the trial, that D. & J. Ames gave full and ample and reasonable instruction to the defendants, or — which is of the same legal effect in matters of contract for doing specific acts — that they tendered and offered such instruction in regard to the preparation of the material and the use of the machinery, to enable them to make the paper in the manner and of the material proposed, which the defendants declined receiving.

The court are also inclined to the opinion that the legal effect of the stipulation of D. & J. Ames with the defendants was, that they should have a full right to manufacture paper by the process therein indicated, whatever the nature of the right then was or might become by the obtaining of a patent, which it appears by the contract they expected to obtain, or in failure of such patent, such right as they should hold from the assignment to them by Coupier & Millier. They were embarking in a new and expensive enterprise; and should another person obtain a patent, which might happen, they might be placed in a situation in which they could not carry on the manufacture without infringing the right of another. If the patent was obtained by D. & J. Ames, it seems to us that they should have tendered to the defendants an assignment of the patent, or at least a right under it; or that, if the application was still pending, or had been denied, and there was no patent, that fact should have been averred. But we have not placed our decision ordering a new trial mainly on that ground; but throw out the suggestion for the consideration of parties, should a new trial be had.

But there is another ground upon which the court are of opinion that a new trial ought to be had. Perhaps both points reserved in the report depend substantially upon the same question of construction of this contract, namely, whether any of the stipulations of D. & J. Ames constituted conditions precedent; because, if they did, and so far as they did, and the defendants have averred the performance of them, they would, if proved by the defendants, as they offered to do, be a good defence. Upon looking at the answer, we think that, even if the plaintiffs had made out a *prima facie* case, several of the facts stated in the answer would have been competent for the defendants to prove; and, if proved, would have been available in defence, either by way of bar, or in reduction of damages. *New trial ordered.*

The plaintiffs then amended their declaration by inserting an averment "that the said D. & J. Ames instructed the defendants in the art and mystery of preparing the straw and other materials, and manufacturing the same into paper, and offered them further instructions if they should need it, and full examination of the premises of the said D. & J. Ames, and permission to take dimensions, and to be shown the use and application of whatever they might desire to inquire about, and to give them all needful information which they should require."

The defendants demurred to the declaration, for that it did not state a legal cause of action, substantially in accordance with the rules contained in the Statute of 1852, c. 312; "because it does not allege that the plaintiffs, or said D. & J. Ames, had secured to the defendants the right to manufacture paper by the process named in said contract, nor that the defendants have the right to manufacture according to the terms of the contract."

Bates and *Wells*, for the defendants.

R. A. Chapman and *Chamberlin*, for the plaintiffs.

SHAW, C. J. The court are of opinion that this demurrer is well taken and must be sustained. It is true there is no warranty in terms of a right to manufacture paper by the process referred to; but we think such a warranty and condition results from the provisions of the contract, the whole of which must be taken together. D. & J. Ames agree that the defendants shall have the right to manufacture white paper from straw and other materials, which right has been assigned to D. & J. Ames by Coupier & Millier. It is not merely hypothetical, such right as they have, if they have any; but an express stipulation that they shall have the right, and an affirmative averment of the fact that it has been assigned to them, so that they have the power to assure it, with an intimation that the assignment is of such a character as to induce them to apply for a patent, which, if granted, would secure to them an exclusive right. If they had such an assignment, whether they obtained a patent or not, it would prevent any other person from obtaining a patent so as to exclude them from the right. Such a stipulation, accompanied with such an express undertaking that they held such an assignment, amounted to a stipulation that no other person should have such right as to exclude them therefrom; and that, either by a grant of the patent-right from D. & J. Ames if they obtained one, or by common right if none should be obtained, the defendants should have the right to manufacture by this new and peculiar process. When we consider that the whole object of the contract was to enable the defendants to manufacture by this process; that the consideration of the undertakings of the defendants was their right and power so to manufacture paper; that the debt was to be paid in paper thus to be manufactured; that without such right the machinery and fixtures might be of little value to them, and the teaching of an art they could not practise, without infringing the rights of others, wholly useless, the conclusion seems inevitable, that the enjoyment of a right to use this art and process, patented or unpatented, was regarded by the parties as a condition, without a performance of which on the part of D. & J. Ames, or those who claim under them, the defendants are not bound to make the stipulated payments. *Demurrer sustained.*

SECTION II.

Independent Covenants and Promises.

BETTISWORTH *v.* CAMPION.

IN THE KING'S BENCH, TRINITY TERM, 1608.

[*Reported in Yelverton,* 134.]

THE plaintiff as executor of J. his father declared against the defendant, that whereas there was a communication and agreement that the defendant should have all the iron made in such a furnace, paying *secundum ratam* of 40*s.* per ton, and that the testator *assumpsisset* to the defendant that he should have all the iron made in that furnace, *in consideratione inde* the defendant promised the testator to pay *secundum ratam* aforesaid; and shewed that the defendant had had so many tons and so many pounds of iron, which amounted according to the rate aforesaid to so much money; and confessed satisfaction of part, and £119 to be arrear and not paid to the testator or the plaintiff. The defendant pleaded payment; and issue thereon, which was found against the defendant, to the damage of £200.

And it was shewn in arrest of judgment that the plaintiff has not shewn the consideration was performed on his part, for the defendant was induced to make the promise in hopes and in consideration that he should have all the iron made there, and the plaintiff has not averred that the iron delivered was all, as, 13 H. 7 and 6 E. 4, a man is bound to enfeoff J. S. of all the land descended from his father; it is no plea that he has enfeoffed J. S. of 100 acres descended, without an averment that those 100 acres are all that descended. To which it was answered by the court, that the consideration *ex parte querentis* was not that defendant should have all the iron, but that the testator promised that the defendant should have all the iron, so that the consideration on each part was the mutual promise the one to the other; and, although the testator is now dead, whereby the defendant cannot have an action against the plaintiff as executor on the testator's breach, yet the promise *ex parte* of the defendant continues.

2. It was objected that the defendant promised to pay for every ton 40*s.*, and the plaintiff demands for pounds and sows of iron, which is not within the promise. To which it was answered by the court that the promise was to pay *secundum ratam*, and a ton amounting to 40*s.* the defendant must pay for pounds and sows according to the rate, computing how many pounds and sows will make a ton; and judgment was accordingly given for the plaintiff.

HOLDER *v.* TAYLOR.

IN THE COMMON PLEAS, TRINITY TERM, 1614.

[*Reported in* 1 *Rolle's Abridgment,* 518.]

IF lessee for years covenant to repair, &c., provided always, and it is agreed that the lessor shall find great timber, &c., this will make a covenant on the part of the lessor to find great timber by the word "agreed," and it will not be a qualification of the covenant of the lessee. But if lessee covenant to repair, provided always that the lessor shall find great timber, without the word "agreed," this proviso will not constitute any covenant on the part of the lessor, but will be only a qualification of the covenant of the lessee.

THE SPANISH AMBASSADOR *v.* GIFFORD.

IN THE KING'S BENCH, HILARY TERM, 1616.

[*Reported in* 1 *Rolle's Reports,* 336.]

THE Spanish Ambassador brought an action on the case against Gifford. It was moved in arrest of judgment by *Harris* that the declaration was not good, because it was, in consideration that he promised to pay so many ducats to the defendant to go such a journey before such a day, the defendant undertook to repay so many ducats if he did not go accordingly; and alleged that he did not go before the day, and for non-payment the action was brought; and it was not averred that the plaintiff delivered the ducats to the defendant according to his promise; and this was the consideration of the action. COKE. It is good, because there is a promise of both parties, and if he has not performed it the other can have his action; but if a man, in consideration of a future thing to be done by the plaintiff, undertake to do a thing, then in an action on the case he ought to aver the performance of it, for there is no remedy for it.[1] . . .

[1] "If in consideration of £10 I promise to deliver to you all the books of the law, this is good without alleging the payment of it, for the other can have an action for it; but if it be in consideration that you will (in the future tense) pay me £10, I will deliver you all the books of the law, this is not good without alleging payment of the £10." Per Coke, C. J., Everard *v.* Hopkins, 1 Rol. Rep. 124, 125. — ED.

VIVIAN *v.* SHIPPING.

IN THE KING'S BENCH, MICHAELMAS TERM, 1634.

[*Reported in Croke Charles,* 384.]

ASSUMPSIT. That in consideration the plaintiff assumed to stand to the award of J. S. and J. D. for certain matters and controversies betwixt them, and if he failed, to pay the defendant forty pounds; the defendant assumed in the same manner to pay forty pounds to the plaintiff if he did not perform. The plaintiff shews, that the said J. S. and J. D. made an arbitrament, that the plaintiff should pay to the defendant ten pounds upon the 18th August following; and in consideration thereof, that the defendant should be obliged to the plaintiff in an obligation of fourscore pounds, that the plaintiff should enjoy such copyhold lands during the life of the defendant, or that he would upon request pay him forty pounds; and allegeth *in facto*, that *licet* the plaintiff performed the award on his part, and that he, such a day and place, required the defendant to enter into such a bond, according to the said promise, the defendant had not sealed the said bond, nor had paid him the forty pounds, according to his promise. The defendant pleaded *nullum tale fecerunt arbitrium;* and found against him.

Rolle now moved in arrest of judgment, that this declaration is not good: First, because he doth not allege the payment of the ten pounds, and the award is conditional in consideration thereof; so if he hath not paid the ten pounds, the other is not bound to make the obligation. Secondly, because he doth not allege a special request for the payment of the said forty pounds; and the *assumpsit* is to pay upon request, and without request it is not payable; so not being specially alleged, the action lies not.

To the first JONES and BERKELEY held, that it is a conditional award, and that there is a precedent condition, which if not performed, the other is not bound to make the obligation.

But I held the contrary, that it is not a conditional award, for it only appoints that he shall enter into such a bond; and every one hath remedy upon the promise, the one against the other, if they do not perform the award.

But we all agreed, that although it be a condition precedent, yet when the plaintiff saith he hath performed the award on his side, it is intended that he hath performed it; and it is good in substance, though not in form; wherefore the defendant might, if he would, have demurred: and when he hath not demurred, but pleaded to the issue, denying the award, which is found against him, he shall not now have advantage of this matter of form.

To the second they all agreed, when it is an *assumpsit* to pay money, although it is upon request, the general allegation, *licet sæpius requisitus*, is a sufficient allegation; and the bringing of the action is a sufficient request for money. Whereupon it was adjudged for the plaintiff.[1]

THORPE'S CASE.

In the King's Bench, Michaelmas Term, 1639.

[*Reported in March*, 75.]

In an action upon the case upon *assumpsit*, it was agreed by the whole court, that where there is a mutual promise, viz., A. promiseth to B. that he will do such a thing, and B. promiseth to A. that in consideration thereof he will do another thing; if A. bring an action against B. and allege a breach *in non faciendo*, and saith that he is ready to do the thing which he promised, but that the other refused to accept of it: notwithstanding the breach is well laid, and the action well lieth; for it was idle, and more than the plaintiff was compelled to do, to shew that *paratus est* to do the thing which he promised: so that if there were a breach upon the part of the defendant, it is sufficient, and if there was a breach on the plaintiff's part, the defendant ought to bring his action for it. And the difference was taken by Bramston, where the promise is conditional, and where absolute, as in our case. And agreeing with this difference, it was said at the bar and bench that it was adjudged.

[1] Reported as follows in 1 Rol. Abr. 415, pl. 10: If an award be made by arbitrators between A. and B., that A. shall pay £10 to B., and *in consideratione inde* B. shall become bound in an obligation to A. to release all his right in certain land; in this case B. must become bound in the obligation, though A. has not paid him the £10, notwithstanding the latter is to be done first according to the intent of the arbitrators; for there is a mutual remedy on each side if the award be not performed; and the consideration was only the motive of the arbitrators to make the award, and not a condition precedent. Per Jones and Berkeley against Croke, this being moved in arrest of judgment; also, Hil. 11 Car. B. R., between Hayes and Hayes, the same case in effect, it was adjudged upon demurrer, that it is not any condition precedent, but that B. is bound to perform his part, though A. does not perform his part. — Ed.

CATON v. DIXON.

In the King's Bench, Michaelmas Term, 1639.

[*Reported in* 1 *Rolle's Abridgment*, 415, *placitum* 8.]

If by articles of agreement made between A. (in behalf of B.) and C., A. covenants that B., for the consideration afterwards in said deed expressed, shall convey certain land to C. in fee, and afterwards C. covenants on his part *pro considerationibus prædictis* to pay to B. £160, &c.; in this case, though B. do not assure the land to C., yet C. is bound to pay the money; for the assurance of the land is not a condition precedent, but these are distinct and mutual covenants. Adjudged upon demurrer.

BRAGG v. NIGHTINGALE.

In the King's Bench, Easter Term, 1649.

[*Reported in* 1 *Rolle's Abridgment*, 416, *placitum* 15.]

A. by indenture leased a messuage to B. in December (22 Car.) for twelve years, and covenanted with B. to repair it with all necessary repairs before midsummer following, and B. covenanted on his part *quod ab et post tale tempus quale A. repararet et emendaret prædictum messuagium, quod tunc prædictus B. sufficienter repararet prædictum messuagium ad omnia tempora durante dicto termino.* In an action of covenant, by A. against B., for non-repair of the messuage after midsummer, according to the covenant of B., the plaintiff declared that although he had performed all the covenants on his part to be performed (without any particular averment that he repaired it before midsummer, according to his covenant, with all necessary repairs), yet that the defendant did not repair it after the said feast, &c. Adjudged upon demurrer that this was a good declaration; for the covenant of A. to repair it before midsummer is not a condition precedent, but there is merely a division of time between A. and B., viz., that A. shall repair it before midsummer, and B. afterwards during the term; so that each of them can have his remedy by action against the other, for the ultimate time limited for A. to repair it is midsummer, and the covenant of B. refers to the said extreme time limited to A., and not to the fact, viz., the repairing by A., for the words are, *post tale tempus*, &c.

WARE v. CHAPPEL.

IN THE UPPER BENCH, MICHAELMAS TERM, 1649.

[*Reported in Style*, 186.]

WARE brought an action of debt for 500*l.* against Chappel, upon an indenture of covenants between them, viz., that Ware should raise 500 soldiers, and bring them to such a port, and that Chappel should find shipping and victuals for them to transport them to Galicia, and for not providing the shipping and victuals at the time appointed, was the action brought. The defendant pleaded that the plaintiff had not raised the soldiers at that time; and to this plea the plaintiff demurs. *Windham*, of counsel with the plaintiff, held, that the defendant ought to have provided the shipping and victuals against the time, though the soldiers were not raised; for the not raising of the soldiers can be only urged by way of mitigation of damages, and not pleaded in discharge of the breach assigned. *Yard*, of counsel with the defendant, held the plea was good in bar of the action, for the covenants of each part have relation one to the other, and there is a condition precedent made by the words, to find shipping for the soldiers; so that the defendant was not to find shipping, except the plaintiff raised the soldiers; neither is there any notice given us how many soldiers he had raised. ROLLE, C. J., held that there was no condition precedent; but that they are distinct and mutual covenants, and that there may be several actions brought for them: and it is not necessary to give notice of the number of the men raised, for the number is known to be 500; and the time for the shipping to be ready is also known by the covenants; and you have your remedy against him if he raise not the men, as he hath against you for not providing the shipping. JERMYN and NICHOLAS, JJ., held against ROLLE that there is a precedent condition. ASKE, J., was of ROLLE, the Chief Justice's opinion. NICHOLAS changed his opinion, and so judgment was given for the plaintiff, except better matter were shewn.

ANNE GIBBONS, *Plaintiff*, ANNE PREWDE, *Defendant.*

IN THE EXCHEQUER, EASTER TERM, 1657.

[*Reported in Hardres*, 102.]

In Action sur le Case.

THE plaintiff declared, that whereas it was upon the 18th of November, 1652, mutually agreed betwixt them, that the plaintiff should before Lady-day following convey over all her estate and interest in the real estate of William Prewde, deceased, to the defendant and her heirs, and that in consideration thereof the defendant should before that time pay the plaintiff £25, and convey unto her and her heirs so much of the said real estate as should amount to £50 per annum, and enter into a bond of £2000, the said defendant afterwards the same day and year, in consideration the plaintiff did promise to the defendant to perform her part of the said agreement, did promise to the plaintiff to perform her part of the same, and avers the real estate to be worth £500 per annum. Upon non-assumpsit, and verdict for the plaintiff, it was moved in arrest of judgment,

By Mr. *Atkins*, that as the case is, the plaintiff must perform her part of the agreement first, otherwise the defendant cannot convey to the plaintiff £50 per annum out of the said estate.

Answer. The performance on the defendant's part is not *submodo* or conditional, but absolute and reciprocal by reason of the agreement; for it is not in consideration that the plaintiff should convey all her estate, &c., but in consideration that the plaintiff did agree to it; and the consideration upon which the action is grounded is a mutual promise to perform the agreement. 15 H. 7, 10 *b*. As if I covenant to marry a man's daughter, and he covenants to give me a hundred pounds; so here, the agreement and promise, which is reciprocal and gives the defendant a remedy upon breach made by the plaintiff, is the consideration, and not the performance of any act by the plaintiff.

2. The plaintiff has as long time by the agreement to convey her estate, as the defendant has to convey part of the real estate of William Prewde.

3. The agreement and promise made by the defendant is not to convey to the plaintiff part of the estate conveyed by the plaintiff to the defendant, but to convey part of the real estate of William Prewde, which may be done though the plaintiff does not convey any part of her estate and interest therein to the defendant.

Second objection was, that the defendant's part of the agreement was promised to be performed in consideration of the plaintiff's performing her part of the agreement, which is not averred to be performed.

Answer. That is a mistake, for the defendant's agreement does not depend upon the plaintiff's performing of any act, but is, that in consideration that the plaintiff agreed to do such a thing, the defendant agreed to do another thing, and the consideration is no other than the reciprocal promise of one to the other, which is executory, and upon which the parties have mutual remedies; and it is a general rule, that when the defendant has a remedy for the consideration of a promise, that consideration needs not be averred to be performed, which is our case; and afterwards judgment was given *pro quer.*

PORDAGE *v.* COLE.

IN THE KING'S BENCH, MICHAELMAS TERM, 1669.

[*Reported in* 1 *Williams' Saunders,* 319.]

DEBT upon a specialty for £774 15*s*. The plaintiff declares that the defendant by his certain writing of agreement made at, &c., by the plaintiff by the name, &c., and the defendant by the name, &c., and brings the deed into court, &c., it was agreed between the plaintiff and defendant in manner and form following, viz., That the defendant should give to the plaintiff the sum of £775 for all his lands, with a house called Ashmole-house thereunto belonging, with the brewing vessels remaining in the said house, and with the malt-mill and wheelbarrow; and that in pursuance of the said agreement, the defendant had given to the plaintiff 5*s*. as an earnest, and it was by the said writing further agreed between the plaintiff and defendant, that the defendant should pay to the plaintiff the residue of the said sum of £775, a week after the feast of St. John the Baptist then next following (all other movables, with the corn upon the ground, except). And although the defendant has paid five shillings, parcel, &c., yet the said defendant, although often requested, has not paid the residue to the damage, &c. The defendant prays oyer of the specialty, which is entered *in hæc verba*, to wit.: "11 May, 1668. It is agreed between Doctor John Pordage and Bassett Cole, esquire, that the said Bassett Cole shall give unto the said doctor £775 for all his lands, with Ashmole-house thereunto belonging, with the brewing vessels as they are now remaining in the said house, and with the malt-mill and wheelbarrow. In witness whereof we do put our hands and seals: mutually given as earnest in performance of this 5*s*.; the money to be paid before midsummer, 1668; all other movables, with the corn upon the ground, excepted." And upon oyer thereof the defendant demurs. And *Withins*, of counsel with the defendant, took several exceptions to the declaration. 1. That the demand by the declaration is of £774 15*s*.; whereas the whole sum is £775; and the 5*s*. paid for earnest shall not be taken as part of the sum of £775. *Sed non allocatur*; for, *per curiam*, it shall be intended as part of the sum. 2. That the exception of the residue of the movables is not well recited, for the word (except) in the declaration is not good for want of sense. *Sed non allocatur*, for it is sensible enough in the declaration; and if it were not, the declaration is good; for an insensible clause does not make the rest of the deed vicious which is sensible in itself. 3. The great exception was, that the plaintiff in his declaration has not averred that he had conveyed the lands, or at least tendered a conveyance of them; for the defendant has no remedy to obtain the lands, and therefore the plaintiff ought to have conveyed them, or tendered a conveyance of them, before he brought his action for the money. And it was argued by *Withins*, that if by one single deed two things are to be performed, namely, one by the plaintiff and the other by the defendant, if there be no mutual remedy, the plaintiff ought to aver performance of his part; Trin. 12 Jac. I. between Holder *v.* Tayloe,[1] Ughtred's case,[2] and Sir Richard Pool's case there cited, and Gray's case,[3] and that the word (*pro*) made a condition in things executory.[4] And here in this case it is a condition precedent which ought to be performed before the action brought; wherefore he prayed judgment for the defendant.

But it was adjudged by the court that the action was well brought without an averment of the conveyance of the land; because it shall be intended that both parties have sealed the specialty. And if the plaintiff has not conveyed the land to the defendant, he has also an action of covenant against the plaintiff upon the agreement contained in the deed, which amounts to a covenant on the part of the plaintiff to convey the land; and so each party has mutual remedy against the other. But it might be otherwise if the specialty had been the words of the defendant only, and not the words of both parties by way of agreement as it is here. And by the conclusion of the deed it is said that both parties had sealed it; and therefore judgment was given for the plaintiff, which was afterwards affirmed in the Exchequer Chamber, Trin. 22 of King Charles the Second.[5]

[1] 1 Roll. Abr. 518 (C.), pl. 2, 3.

[2] 7 Rep. 10.

[3] 5 Rep. 78, 79; s. c. Cro. Eliz. 405.

[4] Co. Litt. 204 *a*.

[5] In a note to this case, Mr. Serjeant Williams states the following rules for distinguishing between dependent and independent covenants: 1. If a day be appointed for payment of money or part of it, or for doing any other act, and the day is to happen, or may happen, before the thing which is the consideration of the money or other act is to be performed, an action may be brought for the money, or for not doing such other act before performance; for it appears that the party relied upon his remedy, and did not intend to make the performance a condition precedent; and so it is where no time is fixed for performance of that which is the consideration of the money or other act. 2. But when a day is appointed for the payment of money, &c., and the day is to happen after the thing which is the consideration of the money, &c., is to be performed, no action can be maintained for the money, &c., before performance. 3. Where a covenant goes only to part of the consideration on both sides, and a breach of such covenant may be paid for in damages, it is an independent covenant, and an action may be maintained for a breach of the covenant on the part of the defendant without averring performance in the declaration. 4. But where the mutual covenants go to the whole consideration on both sides, they are mutual conditions, and performance must be averred. 5. Where two acts are to be done at the same time, as, where A. covenants to convey an estate to B. on such a day, and in consideration thereof B. covenants to pay A. a sum of money on the same day, neither can maintain an action without shewing performance of, or an offer to perform his part, though it is not certain which of them is obliged to do the first act; and this particularly applies to all cases of sale. — Ed.

HUNLOCKE v. BLACKLOWE.

IN THE KING'S BENCH, TRINITY TERM, 1670.

[*Reported in 2 Williams' Saunders*, 156.]

DEBT on bond dated the last day of July in the 16th year of the reign of the now king, conditioned to perform covenants in articles of agreement. The defendant, after oyer of the condition, sets out the articles, by which it appears that the plaintiff, being a tailor, had assigned his trade to the defendant, and all the benefit of the customers named in a schedule annexed to the articles, and the plaintiff covenants with the defendant, that he would from thenceforth leave off and desist from using and exercising the trade of a tailor with any of the customers named in the schedule, with several other covenants on the part of the said plaintiff to be performed, and the said defendant, in consideration of the performance thereof, covenants that he will pay the plaintiff £100 a year during his life by quarterly payments, with divers other covenants on the part of the said defendant to be performed; and the defendant, after he had shewn all the covenants, pleads in bar that the plaintiff, after the making of the said articles, to wit, on the first day of August in the aforesaid 16th year, at, &c., used and exercised the art and mystery of a tailor for and with the said Mr. Pierrepoint (namely, one of the customers named in the schedule), for the sole benefit of the said plaintiff, &c., to which plea the plaintiff demurred in law.

And it was urged by *Saunders*, for the defendant, that the words, "in consideration of the performance thereof," make a condition precedent, so that when the plaintiff had broken his covenant by using his trade with one of the customers, the defendant was not bound any longer to pay the £100 a year to the plaintiff. And here the plaintiff had used his trade with one of his customers before any payment of the £100 a year became due, and therefore the defendant was discharged from the payment of the £100 a year. And to prove that this was a condition precedent, he cited 3 Leon. 219, Brocas's case, where the lord of a manor covenanted to assure the freehold to one of his copyholders and his heirs, and the copyholder, in consideration of the same covenant performed, promised to pay a certain sum of money; and it was adjudged that the copyholder was not obliged to pay the money until the lord had first performed the covenant on his part; but it is otherwise, says the book, if the covenant on the part of the copyholder had been, in consideration of the covenant to be performed. And here the words are, in consideration of the performance of the plaintiff's covenant, which is as much as to say, in consideration of the covenant performed. Wherefore he concluded that here was a condition precedent, which being broken, the defendant is not bound to pay the £100 a year.

Sed non allocatur; for the plaintiff's covenant being in the nature of a negative covenant, namely, that he will not use his trade with the customers, if the words "in consideration of the performance thereof" should amount to a condition precedent, the plaintiff would never have the £100 a year during his life, because it is not possible for the plaintiff to perform his covenant in his lifetime; for at any time during his life he may break it, and a negative covenant is not said to be performed until it becomes impossible to break it; which impossibility can only happen here by the plaintiff's death. And therefore such a construction would entirely defeat the intention of the parties; for it plainly appears that their intent was that the plaintiff should have the £100 a year during his life, and therefore it is not a condition, but the defendant may have his action of covenant against the plaintiff for breach of the covenant on his part. And although it was urged that the £100 a year should be paid until the plaintiff has broken the covenant on his part, and no longer, and that such was the true meaning of the parties; and when the plaintiff has voluntarily broken the covenant on his part, he seems to be content that the £100 a year should not be paid any longer; yet this was overruled by the court. Wherefore it was adjudged for the plaintiff.

BEANY v. TURNER.

IN THE KING'S BENCH, TRINITY TERM, 1670.

[*Reported in* 1 *Levinz*, 293.]

ERROR of a judgment in the Common Pleas, where the plaintiff declares, that it was agreed between him and the defendant, that the plaintiff should surrender to the defendant certain copyhold lands, and that the defendant should pay to the plaintiff so much; and in consideration that the plaintiff had assumed to perform the agreement on his part, the defendant had assumed to perform the agreement on his part: and avers, that he had surrendered into the hands of two copyholders, according to the custom, to the use of the defendant, and that the defendant had not paid. On which the defendant demurs, and judgment was given in the Common Pleas for the plaintiff. And now the error assigned was, that the surrender into the hands of two copyholders was not a good performance on the plaintiff's part. . . .

To which it was answered, that on an agreement to surrender generally, a surrender by any way is sufficient. But TWYSDEN held, that this surrender was no performance, and KELYNGE, C. J., held the contrary. But by the whole court, here being mutual promises, there needs no averment at all of the performance, and therefore an ill averment of that which needs no averment, shall not hurt; and thereupon they all affirmed the judgment.

HAYS *v.* BICKERSTAFFE.

IN THE COMMON PLEAS, EASTER TERM, 1675.

[*Reported in* 2 *Modern Reports*, 34.]

IN covenant brought by the lessee, who declared that the lessor covenanted with him, that he, "paying the rent and performing the covenants on his part to be performed," shall quietly enjoy. The breach assigned was a disturbance by the lessor, who pleads that till such a time the plaintiff did quietly enjoy the thing demised without disturbance; but then he cut down wood, which was contrary to his covenant, and then and not before, he entered; and so by the plaintiff's not performing his covenant, the defendant's covenant ceases to oblige him; whereunto the plaintiff demurred.

The question was, whether the defendant's covenant was conditional or not? For if it amount to a condition, then his entry is lawful; but if it be a covenant, it is otherwise; for then he ought to bring his action.

Pemberton, Serjeant, for the plaintiff. That this covenant is not conditional, for the words "paying and performing" signify no more than that he shall enjoy, &c., under the rents and covenants, and it is a clause usually inserted in the covenant for quiet enjoyment; indeed, the word "paying" in some cases may amount to a condition; but that is where without such construction the party could have no remedy. But here are express covenants in the lease, and a direct reservation of the rent, to which the party concerned may have recourse when he hath occasion. A liberty to take pot-water, "paying so many turns," &c., is a condition. The words "paying and yielding" make no condition, nor was it ever known that for such words the lessor entered for non-payment of rent, and there is no difference between these words and the words "paying and performing;" in Bennet's case, in the King's Bench, it was ruled no condition; Duncomb's case, Owen Rep. 54.

Barrel, Serjeant, for the defendant, said, that the covenant is to be taken as the parties have agreed; and the lessor is not to be sued if the lessee first commit the breach: *modus et conventio* qualify the general words concerning quiet enjoyment.

The court took time to consider, and afterwards in this term judgment was given for the plaintiff, that the covenant was not conditional.

ATKINS, J., doubted.

COLE v. SHALLETT.

IN THE COMMON PLEAS, HILARY TERM, 1682.

[*Reported in* 3 *Levinz*, 41.]

COVENANT upon a charter-party, whereby the master of a ship covenanted to sail the first fair wind to Barcelona, and that his mariners should attend with his boat to relade the ship there, and that then he would return with the first fair wind to London, and would unload and deliver the goods. The merchants covenant to pay him so much for freight, and so much *per diem* during his stay there, and the master brought this action for the money due to him for the freight and for the demurrage, and declares that he sailed with the first fair wind, and so on according to the articles. The defendant *quoad* the freight pleaded that the ship did not return directly to London, but went to Alicante and Tangier, and made divers deviations, by which the goods were spoiled. And *quoad* the demurrage, that that was occasioned by the neglect of the mariners to attend with their boat to relade the ship. Hereupon the plaintiff demurred; *et per totam curiam* judgment was given for the plaintiff; for the covenants are mutual and reciprocal, whereupon each hath his action against the other, and cannot plead the breach of one covenant in bar of the other; and perhaps the damage of the one side and the other was not equal, and therefore the one not pleadable in bar of the other; but each party is by his action to recover against the other the certain damage he sustained, and so it was adjudged, Hil. 13 Car. 2 B. R. *inter* Thompson & Noel.[1]

[1] 1 Levinz, 15. — ED.

BLACKWELL v. NASH.

In the King's Bench, Michaelmas Term, 1722.

[*Reported in* 1 *Strange*, 585.]

In debt for a penalty, the plaintiff declares that he covenanted to transfer to the defendant on or before the 21st of September so much stock, and that the defendant *in consideratione præmissorum* covenanted to accept and pay for it; and then avers that he was at the books the 21st of September, *et paratus fuit et obtulit ad transferendum* to the plaintiff, who then and there refused to accept or pay.

On demurrer it was objected by *Acherley*, that "for it" made it a condition precedent; 14 H. 4, 19; 5 Co. 21; 15 H. 7, 18; Dy. 76; 2 Saund. 352. And therefore to entitle himself to this action, the plaintiff should have shewn an actual transfer of the stock, and the rather here, because the covenant was not to pay the money till the day of the transfer, which brings this case out of the distinction laid down in Thorpe v. Thorpe, Salk. 171.

Reeve, contra. Here are mutual covenants, and therefore we need not shew a performance of our part of the agreement; but if we were obliged, a tender is sufficient, especially a personal one, as this must be taken to be from the refusal which is alleged; and it being a personal tender, that helps the want of any averment of the usage of the company, and of staying till the books were shut, according to the case of Lancashire v. Killingworth, 1 Ld. Raym. 686; for this is like the tender of rent, where a refusal on any part of the day excuses the party from any longer attendance; besides, this declaration is according to the precedents. 1 Brownl. Ent. 14; Br. Red. 109; Lutw. 226; Lev. Ent. 30, 44.

Et per curiam: In consideratione præmissorum is in consideration of the covenant to transfer, and not of an actual transferring, for which the defendant has his remedy; or if it were, a tender and refusal would amount to a performance. In all these cases the great question is, who is to do the first act; but when the transfer is to be upon payment, there is no color to make the transfer a condition precedent.

Judicium pro quer' nisi, but enlarged to next term on the importunity of the defendant's counsel, who alleged he had new points. Hil. 9 Geo. the plaintiff had judgment without argument.

Trin. 10 Geo. the judgment was affirmed in the Exchequer Chamber.

MARTINDALE *v.* FISHER.

In the King's Bench, Easter Term, 1745.

[*Reported in* 1 *Wilson*, 88.]

This is a special action upon the case, wherein the plaintiff sets forth in his declaration that a horse-race was agreed to be run between a horse of the plaintiff and one of Sir Marmaduke Wyvill's; and that in consideration that the plaintiff had agreed to deliver to the defendant three yards and one eighth of cloth, the defendant agreed to pay to the plaintiff £5 12*s.* 6*d.* in case Sir Marmaduke Wyvill's horse should beat the plaintiff's horse, but if the plaintiff's horse beat Sir M. W.'s then defendant to pay nothing for the cloth; and avers that Sir M. W.'s horse won the race; upon the general issue there was a verdict for the plaintiff. It was now moved in arrest of judgment; and the exception taken to the declaration by Serjeant *Bootle* was, that it is not averred in the declaration that the cloth was delivered to the defendant; but to this it was answered by Mr. *Ford*, and resolved by the court, that this was an action founded on mutual promises, and that here was only promise for promise, and therefore it was not necessary for the plaintiff to make an averment in his declaration of the delivery of the cloth; and the court said the case of Nichols and Raynbred, Hob. 88, is in point. Dennison, J., said, that where a plaintiff declares that in consideration he the said plaintiff would deliver to the defendant a piece of cloth, that the defendant should pay such a sum of money for it, in that case an averment of the delivery of the cloth is necessary; but if plaintiff states an agreement, and then lays it that in consideration of such a promise or agreement, &c., there is no need of an averment. So N. B. the difference. And the *postea* was ordered to be delivered to the plaintiff. *Vide* Hob. 106; Yelv. 136; 1 Lev. 293; Hard. 103.

BACH *v.* OWEN.

In the King's Bench, November 15, 1793.

[*Reported in* 5 *Term Reports*, 409.]

This was an action of assumpsit. The declaration stated that on the 1st of May, 1792, it was agreed that the plaintiff should give the defendant a colt in exchange for the defendant's mare, and should pay the defendant two guineas to boot on the 17th of December following; that it was further agreed that the plaintiff should keep the colt until the 29th of September following; that mutual promises were made, &c.; that the defendant, "to make the agreement the more firm and binding, paid to the plaintiff one halfpenny in earnest of the bargain;" that the plaintiff kept the colt until the 29th of September, and that the plaintiff was ready and willing and offered to pay the defendant two guineas, and requested him to accept the same, but that the defendant would not receive the said money, and that he had not delivered the mare to the plaintiff although often requested so to do," &c.

To this the defendant demurred; and shewed for cause, that it did not appear by the declaration that the plaintiff was ready and willing, or offered, to deliver the colt to the defendant in exchange for the mare.

Burrow, in support of the demurrer, contended, that where the doing of one thing by one party is to be the consideration of another to be performed by the other party, the performance of the one must be averred before that party can maintain an action against the other for the non-performance of his part of the agreement. Co. Lit. 51 *b*; Callonel *v.* Briggs, Salk. 112; Thorpe *v.* Thorpe, Salk. 171; and Jones *v.* Barkley, Dougl. 684. In this case the plaintiff should have averred that he had delivered, or had offered to deliver, the colt to the defendant.

Walton, contra, admitted the cases cited, but denied their application to the present.

BULLER, J. There is no foundation for the objection taken by the defendant's counsel; the payment of the halfpenny vested the property of the colt in the defendant, and therefore it was unnecessary for the plaintiff to shew that he had tendered the colt to the defendant. But there seems to be another objection: the plaintiff has not alleged that he made any special request to the defendant to deliver the mare.

Walton. That is a mere matter of form; and as the defendant has not assigned it as a cause of demurrer, he ought not now to be permitted to take advantage of it. Besides, a request is stated at the conclusion: "that the defendant has not delivered the mare to the plaintiff, although often requested so to do."

BULLER, J. The want of a request is a substantial defect; and where it is necessary to allege a special request, the general words "though often requested" will not answer the purpose. It will be better to amend the declaration in this particular. Accordingly

The court gave the plaintiff leave to amend as to this point.[1]

[1] See Radford *v.* Smith, 3 M. & W. 254. — ED.

TERRY AND ANOTHER v. DUNTZE, BART.

IN THE COMMON PLEAS, FEBRUARY 4, 1795.

[*Reported in 2 Henry Blackstone*, 389.]

THIS was an action of debt, and the declaration stated, that by certain articles of agreement made on the 25th of March, 1789, between Sir George Yonge, Bart., the said Sir John Duntze (the defendant), one Henry Reed, and one Thomas Southcomb and the plaintiffs, the said plaintiffs, in consideration of the sum of £3800 to be paid as hereinafter mentioned, did jointly and severally covenant with the said Sir George Yonge, Sir John Duntze, Henry Reed, and Thomas Southcomb, and each of them, that the said plaintiffs, or one of them, would at their own proper costs and charges, finding all materials whatsoever, and with the best materials of every kind, and in a good substantial and workmanlike manner, build, erect, and finish a certain building for a manufactory, at Ottery Saint Mary, in the county of Devon, according to certain drawings and plans, and would erect the said building according to such rules, and in such manner, as by the particulars thereof there underwritten were mentioned and specified. And also that the said building, including the wheat case, to be adjoining or within the same, should be in every respect finished and completed on or before the 29th day of September then next. In consideration whereof they the said Sir George Yonge, Sir John Duntze, Henry Reed, and Thomas Southcomb, covenanted to pay the £3800 in the following manner, that is to say, the sum of £1266 13*s*. 4*d*. as soon as the second floor should be laid, the further sum of £1266 13*s*. 4*d*. as soon as the fourth floor should be laid, and the remaining sum of £1266 13*s*. 4*d*. as soon as the whole building should be covered in, and fully finished and completed, and the same building should be surveyed and approved of by such persons as should be by the said Sir George Yonge, Sir John Duntze, Henry Reed, and Thomas Southcomb, or either of them, appointed to examine the same, for that purpose, within one month after the same should be so as aforesaid finished and completed. And the said Sir George Yonge, Sir John Duntze, Henry Reed, and Thomas Southcomb, did, and each of them did also, agree to advance and pay unto the workmen and laborers employed by the said plaintiffs in erecting the said building, such sum or sums of money weekly as might be necessary for their weekly wages or subsistence, the same to be deducted and allowed out of the instalment, portion, or share of the said £3800 which should be by them next paid, according to the covenant and agreement aforesaid relating thereto; and also to pay unto the said plaintiffs at the time of paying the last of the three several sums of £1266 13*s.* 4*d.* in manner hereinbefore mentioned, the further sum of £150 for freight and carriage of materials, travelling expenses for workmen and laborers, and all other incidental charges, not included in the particulars thereunder written; provided always, and it was thereby also agreed between the said parties thereto, and each and every of them jointly and severally, that if the foundation should not prove good, so as that it should be necessary to put in sleepers, or a greater depth of brick work than was described in the plans annexed and the particulars thereunder written, then the said plaintiffs should be paid in addition to the several sums above mentioned as extraordinary work, but in a reasonable proportion, according to the extent of such extraordinary work; provided also, that neither such extraordinary work, nor any other variation which might be agreed on in the course of the carrying on the building, should make void that agreement, but the same should be binding and valid, notwithstanding such variation or extraordinary work as aforesaid, and the same should be allowed for or deducted at a proportionable estimate to the whole of the contract money, &c. It was then averred that the plaintiffs, after making the articles and before exhibiting their bill, did at their own proper costs and charges, finding all materials whatsoever, and with the best materials of every kind, and in a good substantial and workmanlike manner, build, erect, and finish the said building in the said articles of agreement mentioned, and so thereby agreed to be erected and built, for a manufactory as aforesaid, together with such wheat case as aforesaid, according to the said drawings, sections, and plans delineated in the two several papers thereunto annexed as aforesaid, and also according to such rules, and in such manner, as by the particulars thereof thereunder written were and are mentioned and specified as aforesaid, except as is hereinafter mentioned; and that the said building, including such wheat case aforesaid, would have been in every respect finished and completed by them the said plaintiffs, on or before the 29th day of September next after the making of the said articles of agreement, according to the tenor and effect of the said articles; but the said plaintiffs further said, that in erecting and building the said manufactory and wheat case, they the said plaintiffs by the direction, and at the special instance and request of the said Sir George Yonge, Sir John Duntze, Henry Reed, and Thomas Southcomb, made and caused to be made divers alterations and variations therein, and in many respects deviated from the said drawings, sections, plans, particulars, and rules in the said articles of agreement mentioned, and were thereby, and in consequence thereof, and without any neglect or default of the said plaintiffs, not only hindered and prevented from finishing and completing the same, upon or before the said 29th day of September next after the making of the said articles of agreement, but also forced and obliged to do and perform certain extraordinary work, in and about the said building and wheat case, over and besides what was originally designed and stipulated for as aforesaid. It was then averred that a surveyor was appointed who surveyed and approved of the building and the extraordinary work, &c., and that the plaintiffs reasonably deserved to have the sum of £7059 1*s.* 9¼*d.*, exclusive of the sum of £150, as a further allowance for divers expenses not included in the particulars written under the articles of agreement, according to the estimate of the surveyor, &c., and the breach assigned was the non-payment of any of the sums of money in the articles of agreement specified, &c.

There were also counts for work and labor, money paid, and on an account stated.

To the first count there was a general demurrer, and to the others *nil debet* was pleaded.

In support of the demurrer *Le Blanc*, Serjt., argued, that as the plaintiffs had positively agreed to complete the buildings on or before the 29th of September, it was necessary to shew that they were completed on or before that day. The excuse which is alleged, namely, that they made alterations deviating from the plan by the direction of the defendant, and were therefore prevented from finishing the buildings within the time, is not tantamount to a performance. The original undertaking was by deed, and cannot be dispensed with by the simple agreement of the parties. Thus, if a bond be conditioned to perform an award, provided the arbitrator make his award on or before a certain day, and afterwards both parties agree that the time shall be enlarged, yet unless the award be made within the time mentioned in the condition, the bond is void. Brown *v.* Goodman, 3 Term Rep. B. R. 592, *in notis;* Littler *v.* Holland, *ibid.* 590.

The counsel on the other side was stopped by

BULLER, J.[1] The only question in this case is, Whether the covenants were dependent, and whether the completing the buildings was a precedent condition. Now it is a rule long established in the construction of covenants, that if any money is to be paid before the thing is done, the covenants are mutual and independent. It is accordingly laid down by Lord Holt in Thorpe *v.* Thorpe,[2] that "if a day be appointed for payment of the money, and the day is to happen before the thing can be performed, an action may be brought for the money before the thing be done; for it appears the party relied upon his remedy; and intended not to make the performance a condition precedent;" and he cites the Year Book, 48 Ed. III., 2, 3; 7 Co. 10 *b*, Ughtred's case; 1 Ventr. 147; and 1 Saund. 319. The case in the Year Book, 48 Ed. III., 2, 3, is inaccurately stated

[1] Absent the Lord C. J.

[2] 1 Salk. 170, 1 Lord Raym. 662, Comyn's Rep. 98, and more at length, 12 Mod. 455.

by Lord Coke, in Ughtred's case, to be, "that Sir Ralph Tolcelser covenanted with Sir Richard Pool to serve him with three esquires of arms in the war with France, and Sir Richard covenanted therefor to pay him forty-two marks, and that each party had equal remedy, one for the service, and the other for the money." But it appears in the Year Book, that the covenant was that half the money was to be paid in England before they went to France: the principle therefore of that case agrees with the doctrine of Lord Holt in Thorpe *v.* Thorpe, as is observed by him, 12 Mod. 461. So also in Pordage *v.* Cole, 1 Saund. 319, where there was an agreement by the defendant to give a certain sum to the plaintiff for his lands and house, &c., to be paid at a fixed period, and only five shillings of the purchase-money was advanced at the time of making the agreement, an action on the agreement was holden to lie for the residue, amounting to £774 15*s.*, without shewing that he had either made or tendered a conveyance of the lands. Now let us apply this principle to the present case. The plaintiffs covenant to finish and complete the buildings on or before the 29th of September then next; in consideration of which the defendant covenants to pay £3800 by instalments, viz., a certain sum when the second floor should be laid, a further sum when the fourth floor should be laid, and the remainder of the money when the whole should be covered in and finished. By the terms of the contract then two several sums of money were to be paid before the thing to be done was done. The plaintiffs therefore were clearly entitled to their action for the money without averring performance, and the defendant to his remedy on the covenants.

HEATH, J., of the same opinion.

ROOKE, J., of the same opinion. *Judgment for the plaintiffs.*

MOGGRIDGE *v.* JONES.

IN THE KING'S BENCH, NOVEMBER 11, 1811.

[*Reported in* 14 *East*, 486.]

To an action upon a bill of exchange for £200, brought by the plaintiff as drawer against the defendant as acceptor, the latter set up by way of defence, at the trial before Lord Ellenborough, C. J., at Westminster, that there was no consideration for the drawing of the bill, for that the money for which it was drawn was agreed to be paid in consideration of the plaintiff's executing a lease of certain premises to the defendant, which he had not yet done, and avowed at the trial that he never meant to do. The terms of the agreement in this respect between the parties were to this effect: Memorandum of an agreement made 20th July, 1810. E. Moggridge agrees to let, and J. D. Jones to take (the messuage in question, being a house in Westminster) to hold from the 29th of December next for the term of twenty-one years, under the yearly rent of £120. "And the said E. Moggridge, for and in consideration of £500 to be paid by J. D. Jones by three bills to be drawn by E. M. and to be accepted by J. D. J., bearing date this day, to be payable thus, one bill for £200 payable eight months after date, &c., doth hereby agree to execute a lease of the said messuage for the said term," &c. And J. D. Jones agrees to take the said lease at the said yearly rent, &c., and execute a counterpart, &c. The defendant was immediately let into possession of the premises, and accepted the bill in question, with the other two, for the consideration money; after which the plaintiff refused to execute the lease. His lordship however held this to be no answer to the action on the bill; but that the defendant had another remedy; and the plaintiff recovered a verdict.

Garrow now moved upon this statement of facts for a new trial, on the ground that as between these parties the true consideration for giving the acceptance might be entered into; and that such consideration was not the mere letting of the defendant into possession, as the plaintiff now contended, but the performance of the agreement by the actual execution of a lease, which the plaintiff having since refused to do, the consideration had failed.

Lord Ellenborough, C. J. The money agreed upon for the premises would have been payable immediately, but for the convenience of the defendant the plaintiff agreed to take his acceptances at a future day. This bill must therefore be paid in course when due; and the defendant will have his remedy upon the agreement for the non-execution of the lease.

Per Curiam, *Rule refused.*

STORER v. GORDON and Others.

In the King's Bench, November 28, 1814.

[*Reported in* 3 *Maule & Selwyn*, 308.]

Covenant. The plaintiff declares upon a charter-party made 19th December, 1811, between the plaintiff of the one part and the defendants of the other, by which the plaintiff covenanted to let to freight the ship Concord, and take on board such cargo as the defendants should provide, and proceed therewith from London to Cagliari, and thence to Naples, and there make a right and true delivery of her outward cargo to the agents of the freighters if they should order the ship to unload there, and that having so done, the ship should receive on board such a return cargo as the agents of the freighters should provide at Naples, and being fully laden should depart from Naples and proceed to London (or first to Galipoli, if required), the perils and dangers of seas, rivers, and navigation, and capture, restraint, and detention of or by enemies, princes, rulers, and others, and all other inevitable accidents excepted. And in consideration of the premises the defendants covenanted that within the stipulated number of lay days, the outward cargo should be found and sent alongside at London, and received from on board at Naples, and that at Naples they would find and provide, as they did thereby warrant and assure unto the plaintiff, a full and complete return cargo of wine, &c., and that the same should be sent alongside, &c., and that they would pay for freight at the rate of £15 per ton for every ton of 252 gallons of wine, &c., and for any other goods a proportionate freight per ton, and that £1750 part of the said freight, &c., should be paid on the delivery of the ship's outward cargo (which was to be considered as earned and due for outward freight) by a bill of exchange, &c., and the remainder of the freight, &c., in equal moieties by two bills payable within a certain time after the ship should be reported inward at the custom-house in London; that it was covenanted that 85 running days should be allowed the freighters for receiving the outward cargo, touching at Cagliari, unloading and reloading at Naples, and delivering her return cargo at London, and 20 days more on their paying demurrage at the rate of £15 per day. The plaintiff then avers, that the ship with her outward cargo proceeded on her voyage and arrived at Naples, and that he gave notice of her arrival and readiness to unload, and was at all times ready and willing, as far as in him lay, to make a right and true delivery to the agents of the defendants at Naples of the said outward cargo; and that afterwards and during the time that the ship was remaining at Naples for the purpose of making such right and true delivery, the ship together with her said ca go was by the order and under the authority of certain persons exercising the powers of government at Naples, without any default of the plaintiff, with great force and violence, seized and taken, and her cargo unloaded, landed and delivered out of the said ship, by and to certain persons to the plaintiff wholly unknown, by the order and under the authority of the persons so exercising the powers of government at Naples; and that after the cargo had been so seized, &c., the plaintiff, having full possession of the ship for all purposes of loading the same according to the terms of the charter-party, was ready and willing, and then and there duly notified in writing to the agents of the defendants at Naples, that he was so ready and willing, either to receive on board such a return cargo as the agents should provide, or to proceed, &c., agreeably to the terms of the charter-party; and that afterwards and during the time that the ship was so lying at Naples the 85 running days expired, and the defendants detained the ship on demurrage 20 days. And the plaintiff assigns for breach, first, that neither the defendants nor their agents did within the 85 running days or 20 days of demurrage provide a full and complete cargo, &c., and send or cause the same to be sent alongside at Naples, &c., but wholly made default, and the ship was for want of such cargo compelled to remain at Naples, because by the laws and resolutions of the persons then exercising the powers of government there the ship was not allowed to depart from the port of Naples, without a sufficient cargo of such goods as by the charter-party was agreed to be furnished, and which goods, by the laws and resolutions above mentioned, were permitted to be exported from the said port, &c., whereby the ship was detained at Naples, over and above the 85 running days and the 20 days of demurrage, 430 days, during all which time the plaintiff was deprived of the use and advantage of the ship, and incurred divers great charges, &c. Second breach, that neither the defendants nor their agents have paid the £1750 in part-payment of the freight, &c., by bill or otherwise.

Plea to the first breach.[1] That the defendants, from the time of the arrival of the ship at Naples, were always ready and willing to receive there from on board the ship the said outward cargo, and upon a right and true delivery thereof to provide a full and complete return cargo, and to send the same alongside at Naples within the lay days or days of demurrage, whereof the plaintiff had notice, and was requested and ordered by the agents of the defendants to unload the ship at Naples, but before the outward cargo, or any part, was or could be delivered, and before any default or delay whatever was committed or incurred by the defendants or their agents in or about the receiving or sending for the same, the ship, with her outward cargo, at Naples, was without any default of the defendants or their agents forcibly seized and taken, and the cargo was unloaded and landed by the persons exercising the powers of government there, and was afterwards by those persons kept and converted to their own use, and never delivered or returned to or under the control of the defendants or the plaintiff, and the plaintiff never did or could make a right or true delivery of the said outward cargo, or any part thereof, to the defendants or their agents, and never was ready or able, after having so done, to receive on board any homeward cargo from the defendants or their agents, by reason of which premises the defendants were prevented and discharged from providing or sending alongside any return cargo, &c.

[1] This was the second plea upon the record.

Demurrer and joinder.

Pleas to the second breach.[1] 1st. That the plaintiff did not nor would at any time make any delivery of the outward cargo, or any part thereof, to the defendants or to their agents at Naples or elsewhere, nor did the defendants or their agents at any time receive the same or any part thereof, &c. 2d. That they, the defendants, from the time of the arrival of the ship at Naples, were always ready and willing to receive there from on board the ship the outward cargo, whereof the plaintiff had notice, and was requested and ordered by the agents of the defendants to unload the ship at Naples; and then pleaded the same facts as in the plea to the first breach.

Replication to the first of these pleas, that the ship proceeded with her outward cargo and arrived at Naples, and the plaintiff gave notice of her arrival and readiness to unload, and was at all times ready and willing, as far as in him lay, to make a right and true delivery to the agents of the defendants at Naples of the outward cargo, and that afterwards and during the time that the ship was duly remaining at Naples for the purpose of making such right and true delivery, the ship, together with her said cargo, was by the order and under the authority of certain persons exercising the powers of government at Naples, without any default of the plaintiff, with great force and violence, seized and taken, and her cargo unloaded and delivered out of the said ship by and to certain persons to the plaintiff wholly unknown, by the order and under the authority aforesaid, &c.

Demurrer to this replication and joinder.

To the 2d plea demurrer and joinder.[2] . . .

Puller, for the plaintiff, at the outset abandoned the claim to payment of the £1750 for outward freight, admitting that by the terms of the covenant the delivery of the outward cargo was a condition precedent to the payment of the £1750, so that the breach for non-payment thereof could not be supported. And this disposed of all further argument upon that breach, and the pleadings in answer to it. Upon the rest he made two questions, 1st, whether the delivery of the outward cargo at Naples was under the circumstances a condition precedent to the providing a homeward cargo; 2d, whether the subsequent charter-party amounted to a release of the former.[3] He argued that the delivery of the outward cargo was not a condition precedent to the providing a return cargo, the covenant being absolute to provide a return cargo, "as the defendants did warrant and assure to the plaintiff," and not like the covenant for the payment of the £1750 depending "on the delivery of the outward cargo." And this difference in the language of the two covenants shews that the parties did not intend

[1] These were the fourth and fifth pleas upon the record.

[2] See next note. — ED.

[3] So much of the case as relates to this question is omitted. — ED.

the same thing in both, and that when they did intend to make a condition precedent they knew how to express it so as to leave no doubt. The rule laid down in Ritchie v. Atkinson [1] and Atkinson v. Ritchie [2] is this, that whether a thing be a condition precedent depends on the reason and sense of the thing, as it is to be collected from the whole contract. Now here the plaintiff has covenanted to deliver the outward cargo, with an express exception of the restraint of princes, &c.; but if, as the defendants would have it, he cannot insist upon their covenant to provide a return cargo, by reason that he was prevented by the Neapolitan government from delivering the outward cargo, what is that but saying that though he has in express terms excepted a particular event, he shall nevertheless by construction be liable in that event? This exception has always been considered as an exception for the benefit of the ship-owner,[3] and the general covenant by him to make a true delivery has never been held to bind him to become an insurer for the delivery. If it were to be held that the delivery was a condition precedent, the consequence would be, that if the ship-owner were to be prevented from delivering but the smallest particle of the outward cargo, he would lose the whole benefit of his charter-party. Such a construction would be neither according to the sense or reason of the thing, as it is to be collected from the whole contract. . . .

Richardson, contra, argued that the delivery of the outward cargo was a condition precedent to the providing a homeward cargo, chiefly upon this ground, viz., that the plaintiff has covenanted to make a right and true delivery, &c., and that *having so done*, the ship should receive on board the return cargo, &c.; whence he concluded that the plaintiff's receiving on board a return cargo was to depend on his having made a right and true delivery, &c. And if that were so, the providing such return cargo must also depend upon the same condition, otherwise this hardship would follow, that the defendants would be obliged to provide a return cargo, although the plaintiff would not be obliged to receive it. Yet the defendants only covenant in consideration of the premises. The true construction, therefore, of these covenants, taking them together, is, that they are reciprocal, that the one shall deliver the outward cargo, and upon such delivery the other shall provide the homeward cargo; consequently whatever operates in excuse of the delivery of the outward cargo shall equally operate in excuse of the providing a homeward cargo. The non-delivery of the outward cargo goes to the whole consideration, and therefore falls within the rule in Boone v. Eyre;[4] for the produce of the outward cargo was to be the fund and means of obtaining the return cargo.

[1] 10 East, 295. [2] *Ibid.* 530.

[3] Blight v. Page, 3 Bos. & Pull. 295, *n.*; Touteng v. Hubbard, *ib.* 298, per Lord Alvanley, C. J.; Sjoerds v. Luscombe, 16 East, 201.

[4] 1 H. Bl. 273, *n.*, and cited in 6 T. R. 573.

And no such difficulty as suggested will occur in case the plaintiff should be prevented from delivering some small portion of the goods; for if he make a substantial delivery it will satisfy the covenant; in the same manner as in Davidson *v.* Gwynne,[1] a delivery of the entire quantity was held sufficient to satisfy a covenant to make a right and true delivery of the cargo, so as to entitle the covenantor to freight, though the quality of the cargo was deteriorated by his negligence, that being the subject of a counter remedy. . . . *Cur. adv. vult.*

LORD ELLENBOROUGH, C. J., on this day delivered the judgment of the court.

This was an action of covenant upon a charter-party between the plaintiff, as owner of the ship Concord, and the defendants the freighters. By the charter-party the ship was to proceed by Cagliari to Naples, and there make a delivery of her outward cargo; and having so done, she was to take on board a homeward cargo, and proceed therewith to London. There was an eventual stipulation for her going to Galipoli, but that became immaterial. The defendants covenanted that they would find and provide, as they did warrant and assure to the plaintiff, a full and complete homeward cargo, and they stipulated to pay freight by the ton, and that £1750, part thereof, should be paid on the delivery of the outward cargo, which was to be considered as earned and due for outward freight. The declaration assigned several breaches, the first of which was, that the defendants did not find and provide a homeward cargo, and another, that they did not pay the £1750 freight. The other breaches did not come in question. To the first of these breaches the defendants pleaded, that after the ship's arrival the outward cargo was, without any default of the defendants, forcibly seized and landed, and kept by the persons exercising the powers of government at Naples, and never was returned to the plaintiff or defendants, and the plaintiff never did or could make a right or true delivery of any part thereof; and to the plea stating these facts, viz., the 2d, there is a general demurrer. To the 3d plea there was a demurrer, upon which the plaintiff has had leave to amend. The 4th and 5th pleas, with the pleadings thereon, insist upon the same facts in answer to the 2d breach, and the plaintiff's counsel was satisfied upon the argument, and, we think rightly, that he could not support that breach. . . . The defendants contend that the right and true delivery of the outward cargo was a condition precedent, and that till the performance thereof by the plaintiff, they were under no obligation to provide a homeward cargo, and unless they can establish this position, the question upon the 2d plea must be determined against them. The covenant from them contains no words which import to make the delivery of the outward cargo a condition

[1] 12 East, 381.

precedent; they covenant generally, and without qualification, that the outward cargo shall be found and provided and sent alongside the ship, and received from on board at Naples or Galipoli, and that at one of those places they would find and provide, as they did thereby warrant and assure to the plaintiff, a full and complete cargo. It is contended, however, that from the wording of the plaintiff's covenant this condition precedent is to be implied. That covenant, as far as is material in this question, is that the ship should go to Naples, and there make a right and true delivery of her outward cargo, and that having so done she should take and receive a homeward cargo; and the argument is, that the words "having so done" would have excused the plaintiff from taking on board a homeward cargo, if he had not first delivered his outward cargo; and that whatever would have excused the plaintiff from receiving, would also excuse the defendants from loading. It does not appear to us, however, that these words would have been any excuse to the plaintiff; and admitting that they would, it by no means follows that they afford one to the defendants. The words seem rather intended to mark the time when the plaintiff's obligation to receive a homeward cargo should attach, viz., when his ship from being clear of one cargo should be in a condition to receive another, and they are unaccompanied with those express words of condition which would naturally have been used, had there been any intention of giving the plaintiff an option of terminating the contract, and refusing a homeward cargo, if he should have been prevented by any accident from delivering the outward cargo. But admitting that the plaintiff might have been discharged from his obligation to receive, does it follow that if the plaintiff is willing to receive, the defendants are discharged from their obligation to deliver? The plaintiff might wish to reserve an option to himself, and might therefore qualify his covenant; but he might not choose to give any option to the defendants, and might insist from them upon an unconditional and unqualified covenant. The plaintiff has in terms introduced as an exception into his covenants the perils of the seas, and capture, restraint, or detention, by enemies, princes, or rulers, but he has suffered no such exception to be in the covenant of the defendants. He did not therefore mean, that whatever would be an excuse to him should also be an excuse to the defendants; and we cannot therefore by implication from the wording of the plaintiff's covenant introduce an exception into that of the defendants. Nor is there any ground from the nature of the thing to imply such an exception. The outward cargo may be intended as the fund to procure the homeward cargo, but it by no means follows that it must be so, and in very many instances the homeward cargo is procured and in readiness to ship before the outward cargo arrives. We cannot therefore consider the right and true delivery of the outward cargo as a condition precedent; and the demurrer therefore to the second plea must be allowed. . . .

FOTHERGILL v. WALTON AND ANOTHER.

IN THE COMMON PLEAS, NOVEMBER 18, 1818.

[*Reported in* 8 *Taunton*, 576.]

COVENANT on a charter-party of affreightment, dated 28th Nov. 1816, between the plaintiff (ship's husband of the Elizabeth), then lying at the port of Havre de Grace, in France, of the one part, and the defendants, merchants and freighters of the said ship, of the other part; whereby it was witnessed that the plaintiff had letten, and that the defendants had hired and taken the ship Elizabeth, to freight upon the terms and conditions thereinafter mentioned; viz., the plaintiff covenanted with the defendants, "that the ship being staunch, &c., should take on board six pipes of brandy of good quality, with such other goods as the captain might procure on freight, and therewith proceed, with all possible despatch, to the island of Terceira, and either at the said island or the island of St. Michael, as might be ordered by the defendants or their agents, the master to take, load, and receive on board a complete cargo of green fruit in boxes, or such other lawful goods and merchandise as the defendants or their agents might think fit to send alongside, not exceeding what he could reasonably stow and carry over and above her tackle, &c.; and being so loaded and despatched, the said master should immediately depart with the ship and cargo on board, and proceed with all possible despatch into the port of London or into the port of Bristol, as might be ordered by the defendants or their agents, and at such ordered port or place of discharge, after giving due notice, should make a right and true delivery of all the fruit, or other lawful goods or merchandise thus to be loaded on board her, agreeably to bill or bills of lading that might be regularly signed for the same (the act of God, &c., excepted).. And the plaintiff also covenanted, promised, and agreed with the defendants, that for and during her homeward-bound voyage the said ship should be ballasted with stones or shingles, and not with sand, and the boxes to be stowed according to custom; and also that the said ship should, on her homeward voyage, if required, call at Falmouth for the purpose of receiving orders from the defendants or their agents; and furthermore, that for the purpose of loading the ship at the island of Terceira or the island of St. Michael, and discharging at her ordered port of discharge, the ship should stay and lie twenty-five running days in the whole, if required; the said running days to commence immediately on arrival in a proper place to discharge and receive her cargo. In consideration of the completion of the said voyage, the defendants or their agents agreed to pay, or cause to be paid, to the plaintiff, his executors, &c., the sum of £6 for every ton of 20 boxes, London size, or any quantity less than a ton, together with ten guineas gratuity to the captain, and five guineas more in case of completing the passage from the island in which he received his cargo in less than eighteen days, and average according to the custom of the sea, should any accrue; provided that it should be lawful for the defendants or their agents to keep the ship on demurrage ten running days, at the rate of four guineas a day, to be paid day by day as the same might grow due. The plaintiff engaged to ship, or cause to be shipped, at the aforesaid port of Havre de Grace, the aforesaid six pipes of brandy at the regular shipping price of the day; the defendants or their agents agreed to pay freight on the said brandy, at and after the rate of £4 sterling per ton, together with all brokerage, insurances, commissions, and expenses of the same, and to pay all port charges at Havre and Terceira, and differences arising between taking ballast and a full cargo; and also to pay all duties and expenses on the brandy at Terceira. The vessel to have the liberty of taking any cargo that might present itself for Terceira or the neighboring islands, the freight of brandy, together with the amount of same, insurance, &c., to be taken out in fruit, if at Terceira in all January, at 10*s.* per box free on board, if after that time at Terceira, at the shipping market price; if the vessel should load at St. Michael's, the price to be at the shipping-market price of the day of putting the same on board. The defendants or their agents in that case to pay a proportion of port charges, according to their proportion of cargo. The defendants or their agents also agreed to advance money at Terceira to the captain for the ship's use, and the defendants guaranteed that the ship should have a full and complete cargo home. If the ship should have taken at the port where she then lay any part of a cargo for London or any port of Great Britain, the vessel to be allowed to go to such port or place to deliver the same, and from thence to the aforesaid island, without detriment to that charter-party; and for the true performance of all and singular the articles, covenants, and agreements therein contained, and every part thereof, the said contracting parties bound themselves, their respective heirs, administrators, &c.; the owner, his said ship, with her freight, &c.; and the defendants, their goods and merchandises so to be loaded on board the said ship, in the sum of £500, &c."

The plaintiff having in the declaration set forth the charter-party, averred general performance on his part; and that the master, with the ship, on the 10th of February, 1817, proceeded to Terceira, according to the meaning and effect of the charter-party; and on the 1st of April, 1817, arrived there, and was then ready and willing to receive on board the ship a full and complete cargo of green fruit, either at Terceira or

St. Michael's as might be ordered by the defendants or their agents, according to the true intent, &c., of that charter-party; and that he was ready and willing to have performed all things in the same on his part to be done and performed, according to the true intent, &c., of the same; and then averred for breach, that the defendants did not, nor would, either at the said island of Terceira, or at the island of St. Michael, load or put on board the ship a full and complete cargo according to the meaning and effect of that charter-party, or any cargo or part of a cargo whatever.

The defendants craved oyer of the charter-party, which being set forth as above stated, they demurred generally, and the plaintiff joined in demurrer.

Lens, Serjt., in support of the demurrer. It is not sufficient for the plaintiff to aver performance generally. The specific performance of that which he was to perform as a condition precedent, viz., the shipping of the pipes of brandy at Havre, ought to have been averred. Ughtred's case.[1] A simple contract to bring fruit, absolutely and at all events to this country, was never contemplated by the parties; but the defendants agreed, that on being furnished with brandy by the plaintiff at the port of Havre, they would, on their arrival at Terceira or St. Michael, take in a cargo of fruit. If the ship had taken out the cargo of brandy, the defendants would have had it in their power to return with the fruit. The ship returned empty because the plaintiff neglected to ship the lading which would have been bartered by the defendants for fruit, had such lading been shipped. The answer, therefore, to the plaintiff's averment, that the defendants would not furnish the cargo of fruit at Terceira, is, that the plaintiff by neglecting to ship the outward cargo at Havre prevented them from doing so. [DALLAS, C. J. If the plaintiff had omitted wilfully to get more than five pipes of brandy, when he might have procured all the six, would that have discharged the defendants?] The plaintiff must, in that case, have averred that he could not get any more brandy. [BURROUGH, J. In the case of Storer *v.* Gordon[2] the outward bound cargo was never delivered.]

Vaughan, Serjt., contra. In Storer *v.* Gordon, though the covenant on the part of the ship-owner was to proceed to Naples, and there to deliver the outward cargo, and having so done, to receive on board a return cargo; it was held that the delivery of the outward cargo was not a condition precedent to the providing a return cargo. The argument for the plaintiff does not require that the case in Coke, cited on the other side, should be impugned. The supposition that want of goods in the market would excuse this condition precedent, if it exists, is totally without foundation. The inconvenience attending a condition precedent would form no reason for the non-performance of it. If such a condition here exists, the plaintiff is bound

[1] 7 Rep. 9 *a*. [2] 3 M. & S. 308.

to perform it; but the question as to conditions precedent does not depend on the order of the covenants, but upon the good sense of the whole agreement. If the plaintiff had put on board five pipes of brandy, and they had been accepted, and if a cargo of fruit had been brought back, the contract of the plaintiff would not have been fulfilled and he must have lost his freight, supposing the shipping of the brandy to be a condition precedent. The outward cargo may be intended as the fund to procure the homeward cargo; but it by no means follows that it must be so; and in very many instances this homeward cargo is procured and in readiness to ship before the outward cargo arrives. The delivery of the outward bound cargo cannot, therefore, be considered as a condition precedent.[1] In Boone *v.* Eyre,[2] which is recognized in the Duke of St. Albans *v.* Shore,[3] and subsequently in Campbell *v.* Jones,[4] Lord Mansfield lays down the distinction as clear, that where mutual covenants go to the whole of the consideration on both sides, they are mutual conditions, the one precedent to the other. But where they go only to a part, where a breach may be paid for in damages, then the defendant has a remedy on his covenant, and shall not plead it as a condition precedent. So here, the remedy should have been by a cross-action.

Lens, in reply, said, that he did not question the law as laid down in the cases cited on the other side; but in Storer *v.* Gordon the homeward voyage was perfectly unconnected with the outward voyage, whereas his argument was, that in the case before the court the return voyage was a branch of the outward voyage: he admitted that if the homeward voyage did not grow out of the outward voyage, the defendants must fail.

DALLAS, C. J. The only question here is, whether the shipping of the six pipes of brandy at Havre de Grace, and the delivery of them at Terceira, is a condition precedent. The plaintiff agrees to take out the six pipes, deliver them there, and take in fruit. Now does or does not this go to the whole of the consideration? Does it form a condition precedent, or are the covenants distinct and independent? If the plaintiff's covenant be a condition precedent, he cannot recover; if the covenants be distinct and independent, the defendants must resort to their action on the plaintiff's distinct and independent covenant. The argument for the defendants goes this length, that the plaintiff was bound to take on board the whole, that his covenant formed a condition precedent, and that the omission of shipping one pipe of brandy would have been a breach of the condition. The language of Lord Mansfield, in the case of Boone *v.* Eyre, is applicable to this argument: "If this plea," viz., that the plaintiff was not at the time of making the

[1] Per Ellenborough, C. J., Storer *v.* Gordon, 3 M. & S. 322.
[2] 1 H. Bl. 273, *n.* See also 2 W. Bl. 1312.
[3] 1 H. Bl. 270.
[4] 6 T. R. 570.

deed legally possessed of the negroes on the plantation, "were to be allowed, any one negro not being the property of the plaintiff would bar the action." The doctrine laid down in that case is, that "where mutual covenants go to the whole consideration on both sides, they are mutual conditions, the one precedent to the other. But where they go only to a part, where a breach may be paid for in damages, then the defendant has a remedy on his covenant, and shall not plead it as a condition precedent." Now here the covenant goes only to a part of the consideration; the breach of it may be paid for in damages; and the remedy of the defendants is, therefore, by action. The doctrine in Boone *v.* Eyre, on which this last proposition is founded, has all the weight which some of the greatest names in Westminster Hall can give it. That doctrine was laid down by Lord Mansfield, it was next recognized by Lord Loughborough, and formed the ground of the determination of the Court of Common Pleas in the case of the Duke of St. Albans *v.* Shore; it was then sanctioned by Lord Kenyon and the rest of the Court of King's Bench, in the case of Campbell *v.* Jones; and was afterwards eulogized by Lord Ellenborough in delivering the judgment of the court in Havelock *v.* Geddes.[1] But if more authority be required, we have the case of Storer *v.* Gordon, a case much stronger than this; for there the words "having so done" were immediately consequent on the covenant for the right and true delivery of the outward cargo. I am of opinion that the covenant in this case to ship the brandy was not a condition precedent, but a distinct and independent covenant.

PARK, J. The case of Boone *v.* Eyre, to the doctrine of which we now adhere, much resembles the case at present before the court. In Glazebrook *v.* Woodrow,[2] though the decision was that the covenants were dependent, the distinctions between dependent and independent covenants are well taken by Lawrence and Le Blanc, JJ., in commenting on the case of Boone *v.* Eyre. In Ritchie *v.* Atkinson[3] it was agreed that a complete cargo should be delivered on being paid freight; the master brought only a short cargo; yet there it was held that the master might recover freight for a short cargo at the stipulated rate; the freighter having his remedy in damages for the short cargo against the master on his distinct independent covenant.

BURROUGH, J. Storer *v.* Gordon, which was decided after the other cases, and which recognizes them all, applies in all its parts to this case.

Judgment for the plaintiff.

[1] 10 East, 564. [2] 8 T. R. 366. [3] 10 East, 295.

WINSTONE THE ELDER AND WINSTONE THE YOUNGER *v.* LINN.

IN THE KING'S BENCH, HILARY TERM, 1823.

Reported in 1 *Barnewall & Cresswell,* 460.

COVENANT upon an indenture of apprenticeship, bearing date the 11th April, 1820, whereby the defendant, in consideration of a premium of £90, covenanted with the plaintiffs that he, defendant, would, during four years, instruct Winstone the younger in the trade and business of a tobacconist, and also provide him with sufficient diet and lodging in the dwelling-house of the defendant. The declaration averred, that the son entered into the defendant's service, and then assigned a breach as follows: That the defendant did not, after the making of the indenture, instruct the apprentice in the trade of a tobacconist; but, on the contrary thereof, had hitherto altogether refused so to do. And after the making of the said indenture, to wit, on the 13th day of July, wholly refused then or at any other time to instruct the said Thomas Winstone the younger in the said trade, contrary to the covenant. And that the defendant did not, nor would, after the making of the said indenture, provide the said T. Winstone the younger with suitable diet and lodging, although he, the said T. Winstone the younger, at all times after the making of the said indenture, was willing to take his meals with the defendant; but, on the contrary thereof, he, the defendant, afterwards, to wit, on the 13th day of July, in the year aforesaid, compelled the said T. Winstone the younger to quit his service before the expiration of the time agreed upon for the said T. W. remaining therein, and refused to maintain and keep him, contrary to, &c. Plea first, as to so much of the breaches of covenant as related to the not instructing the said T. Winstone the younger, and not providing him with diet and lodging before the 10th day of July; that he did instruct him till that time, and did provide him with suitable and sufficient diet and lodging, according to the tenor of the covenant. Upon this, issue was taken and joined. And as to so much of the breaches of covenant as related to the not instructing the said T. Winstone the younger, and not providing him with diet and lodging, upon and after the 10th day of July aforesaid; that he, the defendant, was ready and willing to instruct the said T. Winstone the younger in the said business, and provide him with diet and lodging during the whole of the four years; but that the said T. W. the younger did not, nor would, after the making of the said indenture, serve the defendant as an apprentice in his said trade: but afterwards, on the 12th April in the year aforesaid, and on divers other days and times between that day and the said 10th day of July, wholly refused so to do; and on several of those days and times aforesaid refused to obey him in his said business, and to render him, defendant, a proper account of his moneys from time to time intrusted to the said T. W. the younger as such apprentice. And that when on the 10th of July he ordered the said T. W. the younger to add up the day-book used in his said business, which it was the duty of the said T. W. the younger as such apprentice to have done, he the said T. W. the younger refused so to do; and on the contrary thereof, then and there, against the positive orders of the defendant, absented and wholly withdrew himself from the service of the defendant in his said business; he, T. W. the younger, then and there declaring to the defendant that he never intended to return again to such service; whereby the defendant was prevented from instructing the said T. W. the younger, and from providing him with diet and lodging, according to the said indenture, as he the defendant would otherwise have done. Replication, that after the said T. W. the younger had been guilty of the said supposed misconduct and breaches of duty as such apprentice, as in the said second plea mentioned, and during the term in the indenture mentioned, and before the exhibiting of the plaintiff's bill, to wit, on the 13th day of July, he the said T. W. the younger returned to the defendant and tendered and offered himself to the defendant, to serve and obey him as such apprentice, and was then and there ready and willing and offered to the defendant, then and during the residue of the said term, well and truly to perform all things in the said indenture contained on his part to be performed; and then and there requested the defendant to receive him the said T. W. the younger as such apprentice, and to continue to instruct him in the said trade of a tobacconist, and provide him with sufficient diet and lodging in pursuance of the indenture; but that the defendant then and there wholly refused to teach or instruct the said T. W. the younger in the said trade, and wholly refused so to do, or any longer to provide him with suitable and sufficient diet and lodging according to the indenture.

Demurrer.[1]

E. Lawes, for the demurrer, contended that the master of an apprentice was not bound to take him back into his service under the circumstances disclosed in the special pleas, and admitted by the replication. Cuff v. Brown.[2] So an apprentice is not bound to return, if required so to do, after license from his master to leave his service. Anon.[3] The contract is entire, and imports mutual conditions to be performed at

[1] Special causes of demurrer were assigned, but as they relate to matters irrelevant to the purpose for which the case is here given, they have been omitted, as well as the argument and decision upon them. — ED.

[2] 5 Price, 297. [3] 6 Mod. 70.

the same time; and the plaintiffs having in every respect violated the contract, cannot sue the defendant upon it. Kingston *v.* Preston.[1] The defendant's performance is also prevented by the act of one of the plaintiffs.[2] This is like the case of a brewer who, having repeatedly furnished bad beer, cannot complain of a refusal to deal with him. Holcomb *v.* Hewson.[3] The case of Weaver *v.* Sessions[4] is very different from the present; the contract there not being entire, and there having been a liberty to buy of others; besides, the plea in that case did not connect the malt purchased with the orders given. The statutes respecting apprentices do not affect the case; and there is no distinction between contracts of apprenticeship under seal, and those between master and servant by parol. In several *nisi prius* cases between master and servant, misconduct on the part of the latter, and refusal to obey his master's commands, have been held sufficient to justify dismissal and non-payment of wages. Robinson *v.* Hindman,[5] Spain *v.* Arnott,[6] Williams *v.* Rice.[7] . . .

BAYLEY, J. . . . I am of opinion that the plaintiffs are entitled to the judgment of the court upon the question whether the master is at liberty to insist that the indenture is no longer binding upon him, because the apprentice has unwarrantably refused to obey the commands of his master. By the indenture the master covenants that he will for four years instruct and maintain the apprentice. Upon this record we are not at liberty to assume that there are any other covenants in the indenture than those set out. Such indentures generally contain reciprocal covenants by each party. Those covenants are not dependent, but are mutual and independent, entitling each party to his remedy for a breach of them. The master, therefore, is liable to an action for a breach of the covenant to instruct and maintain the apprentice during the term agreed upon. If the second plea be good in this case, there is a sufficient answer to this action. In that plea he relies upon a disobedience of orders, and upon the circumstance that the apprentice withdrew himself from his service, and declared his intention never to return. And if he had continued to absent himself to the end of the term, there can be no doubt that that would have been an answer to the action; but it appears by the replication that the apprentice did return, and offered to serve the master during the remainder of the term, and that the latter refused to receive him. I have entertained some doubt whether the replication ought not to have averred this offer to have been made within a reasonable time; but I am now satisfied that it lay upon the defendant to have rejoined that an unreasonable time had elapsed before the offer was made. That being so, the question arises upon these pleadings, whether disobedience of orders, or

[1] 2 Doug. 691. [2] 1 Roll. Abr. 455. [3] 3 Camp. 391.
[4] 6 Taunt. 154. [5] 3 Esp. 235. [6] 2 Star. 256.
[7] Middlesex sittings after Easter term, 3 G. 4, before Abbott, C. J.

other acts of misconduct by the apprentice, will entitle the master to put an end to the contract of apprenticeship. I am of opinion that it does not. If the parties had intended that the master should have such a power, they might have provided for it by the express terms of the deed. Not having done so, we must conclude that it was not intended that he should have any such power. In the case of parish apprentices, the legislature by 20 G. 2, c. 17, expressly provided, that the indentures may be discharged upon complaint made by the master to two justices, touching the misconduct of the apprentice in his service. The legislature must have thought, therefore, that without such an express provision the master of an apprentice would not, at common law, have the power of putting an end to the contract in case of the misconduct of the apprentice. The cases which have been referred to in argument, arising out of the relation of master and servant, do not apply to the present. In the case of apprentices a premium is usually given, in consideration of which the master expressly contracts to instruct and maintain the apprentice during a given term. The premium is a consideration for the instruction and maintenance during the entire term. Where the ordinary relation of master and servant subsists, it is a condition implied from the very nature of the contract, that the master should only maintain the servant so long as he continues to do his duty as servant; and the contract is to endure for a reasonable time if no specific time be fixed, and is determinable by a reasonable notice. For these reasons I am of opinion that the plaintiff is entitled to the judgment of the court.

HOLROYD, J. I am also of opinion that the plaintiff is entitled to judgment. The cases which have been referred to in argument, and which have arisen out of the relation of master and servant, do not bear upon the present question. Under that contract the master, in consideration of the servant performing his service, undertakes to maintain him and pay him wages. The moment the latter ceases to do his duty properly as a servant, the consideration for the maintenance and wages fails. The relation that subsists between a master and an apprentice is very different; under that contract all the acts are not to be done by the apprentice, but the master agrees to give him instruction; and the great object of the contract is, that a young person entering into li.e should receive instruction and protection from the master. The latter has a greater control over his apprentice than over a mere servant, for he may even correct his apprentice. The master, too, usually receives a premium, which is paid him as a consideration for instructing the apprentice during the term agreed upon. If the argument urged on the part of the defendant were to prevail, the effect would be to deprive the apprentice of that protection which it was the object of the indenture to give him, and to leave him at liberty to go where he pleased. The statute relative to parish apprentices tends strongly to shew that at common law the master had no power to put an end to the contract of apprenticeship. It is true, that this is not an indenture within the statute, and it must therefore be construed as if the statute had never passed; but the statute nevertheless shews, that the understanding of the legislature at that time was, that under indentures in the common form the master had no right to put an end to the contract in consequence of the misconduct of the apprentice.

BEST, J. I entirely concur in the opinions pronounced by my learned brothers. The argument is, that if the apprentice be guilty of a single act of misconduct, or be absent from the service of the master for two days, he is to lose the benefit of the instruction to which he was entitled by the indenture, and for which the premium of £90 was paid; and it has been said, that the act of going away, accompanied with the declaration that he would not return, deprived him of the protection of his master. But it would be most unjust if a single act of misconduct were to deprive a young person of the protection and instruction which he was to receive in virtue of the indentures, and for the continuance of which for a given time a valuable consideration has been paid. The master has at common law a complete remedy, if the apprentice misconducts himself, by an action for a breach of the covenants. The provisions contained in the statute relative to parish apprentices shew, that at common law the master could not determine the contract, if the apprentice misconducted himself. I am therefore of opinion that the plaintiffs are entitled to recover.

Judgment for the plaintiffs.

SPILLER AND ANOTHER v. WESTLAKE.

IN THE KING'S BENCH, APRIL 19, 1831.

[*Reported in* 2 *Barnewall & Adolphus*, 155.]

THIS was an action brought by the plaintiffs as payees, against the defendant as maker, of a promissory note for £200, bearing date the 5th of September, 1829, payable on the 2d of February, 1830. Plea, the general issue. At the trial before Taunton, J., at the last assizes for the county of Somerset, the plaintiff having proved the note, it was contended, on the part of the defendant, that there was no consideration for the note, inasmuch as the money for which it was drawn was, by agreement, to be paid in consideration of the plaintiffs executing a conveyance of a certain estate to the defendant, which they had not done. The agreement bore the same date with the note; and its terms, as to this matter, were to the following effect. The plaintiffs in consideration of £200, to them then paid or secured to be paid by the defendant, and of the further sum of £1140, to be paid to them by the defendant on the 2d of February then next, promised to surrender and convey to the defendant an estate in the agreement described, subject to two mortgages therein mentioned, in consideration whereof the defendant agreed to pay the plaintiffs, on the making and passing of such surrender and conveyance, the said sum of £1140, making with the sum of £200, that day paid or secured to be paid as aforesaid, the full consideration money agreed to be paid for the purchase of the estate. The note in question was given to secure the £200. A dispute having arisen between the plaintiffs and the mortgagee as to the precise sum due to the latter, he refused until that was settled to convey the legal estate, and the plaintiffs were thereby prevented from assigning the legal estate to the defendant on the 2d of February (on which day the note was payable), and informed the defendant they could not do so. The learned judge overruled the objection, but reserved liberty to the defendant to move to enter a nonsuit. A verdict having been found for the plaintiffs,

Merewether, Serjt., now moved as above, and contended that according to Jones *v.* Barkley,[1] Phillips *v.* Fielding,[2] and Glazebrook *v.* Woodrow,[3] the payment of the purchase-money and the execution and tender of the conveyance being concurrent acts, the vendor could not recover the purchase-money without having executed the conveyance or offered to do so. The conveyance of the estate was the only consideration for the note, and that consideration having failed, the plaintiffs were not entitled to recover. If the plaintiffs had paid the £200 as a deposit, they might now have recovered it back.

LORD TENTERDEN, C. J. Where, by one and the same instrument, a sum of money is agreed to be paid by one party, and a conveyance of an estate to be at the same time executed by the other, the payment of the money and the execution of the conveyance may very properly be considered concurrent acts, and in that case no action can be maintained by the vendor to recover the money until he executes or offers to execute a conveyance; but here the vendee by a distinct instrument agreed to pay part of the purchase-money on the 2d of February. I can see no reason why he should have executed a distinct instrument, whereby he promised to pay a part of the purchase-money on a particular day, unless it was intended that he should pay the money on that day at all events. In the cases cited the concurrent acts were stipulated for in the same instrument: here the payment of the £200 (which was part only of the purchase-money) was separately provided for.

LITTLEDALE, J., concurred.

[1] Dougl. 684. [2] 2 H. Bl. 123. [3] 8 T. R. 366.

PARKE, J. I incline to think that the defence to this action would have been maintainable, if the circumstances had been such that the defendant, having paid the £200 as a deposit, would have been entitled to recover it back; but it is perfectly clear that he could not have been so entitled as long as the contract remained open. Now here the contract remained open at the time when the action was commenced, for the plaintiffs agreed only to convey the estate subject to the two mortgages. They were never bound to convey the legal estate to the defendant, but merely the equity of redemption; and that they never had refused to convey. There can, therefore, be no rule.

TAUNTON, J., concurred. *Rule refused.*

DAWSON *v.* DYER, BARONET.

IN THE KING'S BENCH, NOVEMBER 8, 1833.

[*Reported in 5 Barnewall & Adolphus,* 584.]

COVENANT by lessee against lessor. The declaration stated a demise by the defendant to the plaintiff, *habendum*, for fourteen years, yielding and paying the yearly rent of, &c., by four equal payments on, &c.; and that the defendant covenanted that the plaintiff, his executors, &c., paying the yearly rent thereby reserved on the several days and times, &c.; and performing all the covenants, conditions, and agreements in the said indenture contained, and on his part and behalf to be performed, according to the true intent and meaning thereof, should and lawfully might peaceably and quietly have, hold, occupy, and enjoy the premises thereby demised, with the appurtenances, for and during the term thereby granted, without any let, suit, trouble, denial, eviction, or interruption of, from, or by the said defendant, his heirs, &c., or any person lawfully claiming or to claim by, from, or under him or them. Averment, that the plaintiff entered and performed all things, &c., but that he the plaintiff did not peaceably and quietly have, hold, &c., without any let, suit, &c., but on the contrary, after the making of the indenture and during the said term, to wit, on the 8th of January, 1833, H. B. then and there lawfully claiming by, from, and under the defendant, entered upon the premises, and there seized and took divers goods and chattels, to wit, &c., of plaintiff, as a distress for rent due to H. B. from one J. A. for use and occupation of the said premises, and remained on the premises for a long time, &c. The indenture was set out on oyer, containing a covenant by the plaintiff in the usual terms to pay the rent on the stated days; and a further covenant by him to insure the premises immediately after the execution of the indenture, and to keep the same insured: there was likewise a proviso that the landlord should be at liberty to re-enter if the rent should be unpaid for twenty-one days, or if default should be made as to any of the other covenants; and the covenant by the defendant for quiet enjoyment corresponded with the statement in the declaration. The defendant pleaded, among other pleas, that after the making of the indenture and during the term, and before the supposed breach of covenant, to wit, on the 26th of December, 1832, £40 of the rent therein mentioned, for a quarter of a year ending the preceding day, had become due from the plaintiff to the defendant, but the plaintiff did not nor would pay the same on the day on which it was reserved and appointed to be paid by the said indenture, but then and thenceforth continually for a long time, to wit, hitherto, neglected to pay the same or any part thereof. The defendant also pleaded in like manner that the plaintiff did not insure. Demurrer, assigning for cause, that the plaintiff's covenants in the pleas mentioned "are independent of the covenant of the defendant in the said declaration mentioned, and do not in any wise qualify, or constitute a condition precedent to the performance by the defendant of that covenant." Joinder in demurrer. The demurrer came on to be argued in this term,[1] and Follett, for the plaintiff, having mentioned the cases of Hays v. Bickerstaffe[2] and Warren v. Asters,[3] the court called upon

Barstow in support of the pleas. The earlier decisions which have turned upon the distinction between covenants and conditions, do not furnish any precise rule upon the subject; as is said in Platt on Covenants (p. 71). "So refined and subtle are the distinctions on which they have proceeded, that it is almost impossible to draw from them any reasons as a guide to discover with certainty whether covenants are dependent or not. Some of the determinations have incurred the censure of outraging common sense; others of deciding contrary to the real meaning of the parties and the true justice of the case;" and cases are there referred to which support this observation. In modern times the disposition of the courts has been to look, not at the particular clause only, but at the whole deed, and to collect from it the intention of the parties. Looking to that, and to the reason of the case, it will be evident here that the payment of rent was intended to be a condition precedent to the landlord's performance of the covenant for quiet enjoyment. That covenant is introduced for the purpose of limiting the liability of the landlord, who would otherwise be bound to warrant to the lessee an undisturbed possession generally. Noke's case.[4] The covenant in this case confines the landlord's liability to the acts of persons claiming under him; and also makes it dependent on

[1] Nov. 8th. [2] 2 Mod. 34. [3] Sir T. Jones, 205.
[4] 4 Rep. 80 *b*, Cro Eliz. 674.

the lessee's performance of every thing covenanted by him. The landlord reserves to himself a right of re-entry if the rent should be in arrear more than twenty-one days, which is admitted to have been the case here. The defendant might after that time have brought ejectment against the plaintiff; and it cannot have been intended by the deed of demise that the plaintiff should have an action against the defendant for disturbance of his possession at the very time when the defendant was entitled to treat him as a trespasser. [DENMAN, C. J. According to that argument, the tenant, if evicted while the rent was so in arrear, could not have maintained an action, though the landlord had waived the forfeiture.] The waiver might perhaps have been matter of reply, if the forfeiture had been pleaded. As to the cases: in Hays v. Bickerstaffe [1] there was no clause of re-entry. In an anonymous case, 4 Leon.,[2] the decision of two judges is in point for the present defendant. And in Simpson v. Titterell,[3] where land was let for years, "*proviso semper*, and it is further covenanted, that the lessee shall not assign his term" except in manner specified, the court held that the words amounted to a condition. [PARKE, J. The reason given there is against you; for it is said by the court, that a *proviso* always implies a condition, if there be not words subsequent which may change it into a covenant; as where there is a penalty annexed for non-performance. The *proviso* in the present case is introduced to reserve a power to the landlord on the particular occasion specified; if he, or any person claiming under him, enters on the tenant except by virtue of that power, the landlord is liable on the covenant for quiet enjoyment.]

Per Curiam, *Judgment for the plaintiff.*

FILLIEUL AGAINST ARMSTRONG.

IN THE QUEEN'S BENCH, NOVEMBER 21, 1837.

[*Reported in 7 Adolphus & Ellis*, 557.]

ASSUMPSIT. The first count of the declaration stated, that whereas heretofore, to wit, 24th June, 1835, in consideration that plaintiff, at the special instance, &c., of defendant, would enter into his employ in the capacity of a teacher of the French language and drawing, in a school of defendant, for one whole year then next following, at and for a certain salary or wages, to wit, at the rate of £60 per annum, together with the board and lodging of plaintiff, defendant undertook, &c., to

[1] 2 Mod. 34. [2] 4 Leon. 50, pl. 130. [3] Cro. Eliz. 242.

retain and employ plaintiff for and during the time aforesaid, in the capacity aforesaid, at and for the salary or wages and on the terms aforesaid; and although plaintiff confiding, &c., did afterwards, to wit, &c., enter into defendant's employ in the capacity, &c., and did duly and faithfully perform and execute the duties by him to be performed in the capacity aforesaid for a long space, &c., viz., until 3d February, 1836, and although plaintiff was on the day and year last aforesaid, and hath always been, ready and willing, and then offered, to remain and continue in defendant's employ, in the capacity, &c., for the remainder of the said year, yet defendant did not nor would continue plaintiff in his employ until the expiration of the said year; but, on the contrary thereof, during the said term of one year, viz., on 3d February, 1836, without any reasonable notice, wrongfully refused to suffer plaintiff to continue in his employ, and wrongfully discharged him therefrom, without any reasonable or probable cause whatsoever, and hath thence hitherto wholly neglected and refused to retain or continue plaintiff in his employ for the remainder of the said term: by means whereof plaintiff hath lost all the wages, &c., which he otherwise would have derived from being continued in the employ, &c., and which defendant hath from that time wholly refused to pay or allow to plaintiff; and plaintiff hath been, and is, by means of the premises, wholly unemployed. There was a second count.

Second plea to the first count. That, before and at the time when defendant retained plaintiff as in the first count mentioned, and when defendant made the promise in that count mentioned, plaintiff, in consideration of the premises therein mentioned in that behalf, promised defendant well and diligently and faithfully to serve defendant in the capacity of teacher at defendant's school, and not to absent himself therefrom without just and sufficient cause, except during the times appointed by plaintiff for vacations at the school; and defendant retained plaintiff, as therein mentioned, upon the faith and in consideration of plaintiff's said promise: that defendant was always ready and willing to continue to retain and employ plaintiff in the capacity aforesaid, for the period and on the terms in the first count mentioned, until plaintiff misconducted himself as after mentioned: that, after the making of the promise in the first count mentioned, and before plaintiff was dismissed, viz., 23d December, 1835, a vacation was appointed by defendant for the school, viz., from 24th December, 1835, until and upon 29th January, 1836; and it was then appointed by defendant that the vacation should cease, viz., on 29th January, 1836; and that, on a certain day, viz., 30th January, 1836, the school should recommence, and plaintiff as such teacher should return to the school and resume his duties as such teacher; of all which, &c. (notice to plaintiff): that plaintiff was absent from the school during the period appointed for the vacation; and that it became and was his duty as such teacher to return to the school and resume his duties, as such teacher as aforesaid, when the vacation ceased, viz., on 30th January, 1836; and, although divers of the pupils of defendant returned to the school on the said 30th January, 1836, and the school then recommenced, as plaintiff well knew, yet plaintiff, not regarding, &c., did not nor would return to the school, or resume his duties as such teacher on the day so appointed for that purpose; and, on the contrary thereof, plaintiff wrongfully absented himself from defendant's said service, and neglected to return to the school and to resume his said duties on the day so appointed, viz., on 30th January, 1836, and for a long and unreasonable period, viz., on that day and for the space of divers, to wit, two days from the day and year last aforesaid, without any just, sufficient, or reasonable cause or excuse for such absence, and without the consent and against the will of defendant; and thereby defendant was greatly delayed and injured in respect of divers matters and businesses, in which he would otherwise have employed plaintiff in his said situation and capacity during the last mentioned time, and was forced to endeavor to procure another person to serve him in the capacity aforesaid, and in place and stead of plaintiff; and thereupon it became and was lawful and necessary and expedient for defendant to discharge and dismiss plaintiff from his said service and employ as such teacher as aforesaid; wherefore defendant afterwards, viz., at the said time when, &c., in the first count mentioned, did refuse to suffer plaintiff to continue in his said employ in the capacity aforesaid, and then discharged him therefrom, being the supposed breach, &c.

Replication. That, after the absence of plaintiff and before defendant discharged him, plaintiff returned to the performance of his duties in such service and employ of defendant, as in the said first count mentioned, and defendant retained and employed him in such service and employ under the said agreement in the said declaration mentioned; and plaintiff afterwards remained and continued in such service and employ under the said agreement, and on the terms in the said first count mentioned, for a long space of time then next following, viz., until 3d February, 1836, when defendant wrongfully discharged plaintiff from his said service and employ. Verification.

Rejoinder. That after the said absence of plaintiff in the second plea mentioned, and before defendant discharged plaintiff from his said employment, as in the said second plea and in the said first count, &c., mentioned, plaintiff did not return to the performance of his duties, &c.; and defendant did not retain, &c.; and the said plaintiff did not afterwards remain, &c., in manner and form, &c. Conclusion to the country. Other issues of fact were joined.

On the trial before Lord Denman, C. J., at the Middlesex sittings after Easter Term, 1836, a verdict was found for the defendant on this issue. In Trinity Term, 1836, *Cresswell*, for the plaintiff, obtained a rule *nisi* for judgment *non obstante veredicto*, or for a new trial.

Gurney now shewed cause. As to the motion *non obstante veredicto*,[1] the record contains a sufficient justification of the dismissal. It will not be denied that a master may dismiss a servant for improper conduct: the question here is, whether the plea shews an impropriety of sufficient importance. The plaintiff complains that the defendant refused to retain him: the answer is, that he chose to absent himself; in effect, that he himself put an end to the contract. If such an absence as this be not a ground of dismissal, may an usher absent himself for a month, or a year? The master is compelled to insist upon dismissing as soon as the usher absents himself, for he must lose no time in engaging another to supply his place. In Winstone *v.* Linn[2] it was held that a master was not released from the covenant in an apprentice deed by the temporary absence of the apprentice: but there both Bayley and Holroyd, JJ., distinguished the case from that of master and servant, pointing out that a premium was received for taking an apprentice, and admitting that, in the ordinary case of hired service, the non-performance of the service was a good ground of dismissal. And, even in the case of the apprentice, judgment was given, as appeared by the language of Bayley, J., on the ground that the defendant had not rejoined that an unreasonable time had elapsed before the apprentice offered to return. Here there is such an averment: so that, if there can under any circumstances be such an absence as is unreasonable on the part of an usher, the defendant must have judgment.

Cresswell and *W. H. Watson*, contra. There may be some difficulty as to the form of the rule; for it does not seem quite clear what the effect of the plea is. It does not offer a traverse; yet it assumes to vary the contract in the declaration by adding new terms. [PATTESON, J. If the plea contain no confession, there must be a repleader.] If so, the rule might be moulded. That was done in Plummer *v.* Lee.[3] But there does appear to be a confession; for it may be contended that the term added is merely what the law would imply from the contract stated in the declaration, and that then the plea negatives the performance of the defendant's duty so implied. As to the general question, the plea shews no absence sufficient to justify the dismissal: it merely states an absence for a long and unreasonable time, to wit, two days. That may shew a breach of contract by the plaintiff, but such a breach does not authorize a dissolution of the engagement. It is not the case of a menial servant: and, even there, every

[1] This was the only question discussed on the present argument. See the end of the case.

[2] 1 B. & C. 460.

[3] 2 M. & W. 495.

breach of duty does not warrant a dismissal. The fault must involve either moral misconduct, wilful disobedience, or habitual neglect. Callao *v.* Brouncker.[1] In Atkin *v.* Acton[2] the party discharged was guilty of an immoral and indecent act, which made it impossible for the master to allow him to be in the house. In Ridgway *v.* The Hungerford Market Company[3] there was an act incompatible with the relation of the parties. Freeman *v.* Taylor[4] shews that one of two contracting parties cannot put an end to the contract on the ground of a breach by the other party, unless such breach go to the root of the contract. It is said that the defendant was compelled to engage a new usher; but that assumes the fact of the dissolution of the contract. (*Watson* was then stopped by the court.)

LORD DENMAN, C. J. I think the declaration is sufficiently confessed, although the defendant professes to add more terms to the contract. Then the question is, whether the defendant had a right to dismiss the plaintiff for any cause which he alleges. Now the defendant does not say that the plaintiff has been guilty of any immorality, nor does he shew that he was really obliged to hire another person, or that the plaintiff's department was not in fact adequately filled. He says, indeed, that he was delayed and injured in respect of matters and businesses in which he would have employed the plaintiff during the time; but he does not say that the instructions in French or drawing were impeded, or that the business of the school was suspended for a single hour. Although, therefore, the defendant might possibly be entitled to sue the plaintiff for absenting himself, the record shews nothing which puts an end to the contract.

PATTESON, J. I am of the same opinion. If the plea did not confess the declaration, it is clear that the rule might be moulded, and the court might order a repleader. But I think there is a confession. For the defendant says that, when he retained the plaintiff as in the first count mentioned, and when he made the promise in that count mentioned, certain other things took place. Then, next, from the contract stated in the declaration, and from the plea, it does not appear that the defendant had any power to put an end to the contract upon the plaintiff absenting himself, or that the contract thereupon became void. The assertion in the plea is, in effect, that the defendant put an end to the contract, not that the contract became void of itself. Now, even taking the case as between master and servant, the facts did not entitle the defendant to put an end to the contract. No moral misconduct is shewn, nor any failure on the defendant's part amounting to a dissolution of the engagement. The rule therefore must be made absolute for judgment *non obstante veredicto*.

WILLIAMS and COLERIDGE, JJ., concurred.

[1] 4 C. & P. 518. [2] 4 C. & P. 208.
[3] 3 A. & E. 171. [4] 8 Bing. 124.

A discussion afterwards arose respecting the finding of the jury upon the other issues; and finally the court on the last day of term (November 25th) made the rule absolute for a new trial.

MATTOCK, *Executor of* SOUTHWOOD, *v.* KINGLAKE.

IN THE QUEEN'S BENCH, APRIL 26, 1839.

[*Reported in* 10 *Adolphus & Ellis*, 50.]

DEBT by the plaintiff as executor of one Southwood.

The declaration stated that defendant was seised in fee of certain premises by virtue of a bargain and sale enrolled, dated 19th February, 1822, by which the Bishop of Winchester had bargained and sold the same to Southwood in fee to such uses as he (Southwood) by deed or instrument in writing, with or without power of revocation and new appointment, sealed and delivered by him in the presence of, and attested by, one or more credible witness, should from time to time, or at any time, appoint of or concerning the same; and in default of such appointment to the use of the defendant in fee, in trust for Southwood, his heirs and assigns for ever. That, defendant being so seised, it was afterwards agreed by and between Southwood and defendant, at defendant's request, that Southwood should convey to defendant all his estate and interest in the premises; that thereupon by articles of agreement, sealed and delivered by Southwood in the presence of a credible witness, and made between Southwood and defendant, Southwood agreed to sell and defendant to purchase the said premises for the sum thereinafter mentioned; and defendant thereby, for himself and his heirs, covenanted with Southwood, his heirs and assigns, to pay to him or them, on or before 19th of February, 1825, as the consideration for such sale and purchase, the sum of £11,206, with interest at five per cent., payable half-yearly, to the time of the completion of the purchase, Southwood allowing thereout the same rate of interest for so much of the purchase-money as had been, or might be, paid to him in the mean while; and defendant thereby also agreed to pay for the conveyance and stamp duty. Averment, that Southwood in his lifetime was always ready and willing to perform his part of the agreement, and did in fact offer to execute a conveyance to defendant of all his estate and interest in the premises, whereof defendant had notice; and that defendant had been ever since the agreement in possession of all the premises, and in receipt of the profits to his own use; yet defendant did not nor would pay or cause to be paid to Southwood in his lifetime the said sum and interest for the same, on or before the said 19th of February, 1825, although the purchase by and through the default of defendant had not been completed before that day; and although Southwood was living on and after that day; nor had defendant since the death of Southwood, paid the same to plaintiff, executor as aforesaid; but on the contrary a large sum, to wit, &c., for principal and interest, parcel of the above sum, was still due and unpaid, the rest having been satisfied; whereby an action accrued, &c.

Plea, that Southwood did not at any time tender to defendant any conveyance of the premises so agreed to be sold by him to defendant, or of any part thereof.

Verification. General demurrer and joinder.

Bere, in support of the demurrer. There is no obligation on the part of the vendor to tender a conveyance, where the expense of it and the stamp duty are to be paid by the purchaser. It is the purchaser's duty to prepare and tender it, even where the contract of sale is silent as to the expense. 1 Sugd. Vendors, &c., ch. 4, sec. 4,[1] where the authorities are collected. In Price v. Williams [2] a lessee, suing the party who had contracted to let, and who was to pay for the lease, was held not bound to aver a tender. Indeed, it is not clear that the vendor can recover the costs of the conveyance, if he incurs them without the direction of the vendee. At all events, the tender of a conveyance is not a condition precedent, where a time is fixed for payment of the purchase-money, and none for making the conveyance. Pordage v. Cole [3] is directly in point, and is not distinguishable from the present case. The rules for ascertaining the dependence or independence of covenants in a contract are all to be found in the note (4)[4] of Mr. Serjt. Williams on that case. The fact that the defendant is admitted on the record to be already seised in fee of the legal estate is alone enough to obviate the necessity of a tender, or, indeed, of any conveyance at all. The articles of agreement, executed in the manner set forth, operated as an execution of the power reserved to Southwood; so that the whole estate and interest, legal and equitable, was already in the defendant.

Manning, contra. Although it is alleged in the declaration that the defendant was seised in fee in trust for Southwood, yet the declaration also sets out the conveyance under which the defendant is supposed to have become seised, and that conveyance is an indenture of bargain and sale, by which the premises were conveyed to Southwood and his heirs, to uses to be thereafter appointed. A bargain and sale would at common law pass no estate to the bargainee, but in respect of the consideration they would create a use, and from the moment of the execution of the indenture of bargain and sale, the bargainor would stand

[1] Sect. 55, *et seq.* p. 374, &c., 10th ed.

[2] 1 M. & W. 6.

[3] 1 Saund. 319.

[4] 1 Wms. Saund. 320.

seised to the use of the bargainee. That use is now executed in the bargainee by the Statute of Uses; but after the statute has once operated to transfer the seisin, it can go no further, and all subsequent uses are void at law, and are merely cognizable as trusts. Here, therefore, the use appointed to the defendant by Southwood, by the articles of agreement, took effect only as a trust, not executed by the Statute of Uses.

But supposing the legal estate to have been vested in the defendant, there was an equitable interest in Southwood, which was the proper subject of a conveyance. It is true that for some purposes a bare contract is said to be an equitable conveyance; but it cannot be contended that a simple contract between a *cestui que trust* and his trustee, accompanied with merely such formalities as will satisfy the Statute of Frauds, will enure as a perfect conveyance. It was never supposed that a mere contract of sale between trustee and *cestui que trust* required the *ad valorem* duty of a conveyance; yet according to the doctrine contended for on the other side, the contract, followed by the fact of the payment of the purchase-money on the appointed day, would complete the defendant's legal and equitable title. It was never in contemplation that the defendant should rest satisfied with such an inferential conveyance; this is evident from the stipulation respecting the costs of the conveyance and the stamp duty; which stipulation would of itself be sufficient to entitle the defendant to call for a conveyance, even if the contract itself had conferred an unexceptionable title. As to the argument drawn from the fixed day of payment, it is not denied that parties may contract for a conveyance to be executed on one day, and the purchase-money paid on a precedent day; but the courts will not put such an interpretation upon a contract, unless the intention is plain. In Pordage *v.* Cole [1] the words "the money to be paid before midsummer, 1668," stand unconnected with any mention of conveyance or consideration. Here several expressions indicate an intention to make the conveyance and the payment concurrent and mutually dependent acts. The £11,206, or the balance, is to be paid on the 19th February, 1825, "as the consideration of such sale." Now, though the words "shall give" "£775 for all his lands" occur in Pordage *v.* Cole,[1] yet the words relied upon in that case (viz., "the money to be paid before midsummer, 1688"), as making the engagement to pay unconditional, occur in a different part of the deed. Again, interest is to be paid with the principal "to the time of the completion of the purchase." Now, the purchase (which means the acquisition of the land by the vendee) cannot be said to be complete until the land is conveyed. Unless, therefore, the two acts were intended to be concurrent, the purchase-money might be paid in February, 1823; and if, by death or incapacity of parties, the conveyance was delayed till 1833, the defendant might be called upon for ten years' interest on money which he

[1] 1 Saund. 319.

had paid, and of which Southwood was, in respect of the same period, receiving interest from other sources. The circumstance of the provision for payment of the expenses of conveyance being coupled with stipulation for paying the money and completing the purchase, is a further proof that the conveyance and payment of the purchase-money were to be contemporary. A bill in equity for a specific performance lies as well for vendor as vendee; Gibson *v.* Patterson,[1] Baxter *v.* Lewis[2]; yet such a bill would be absurd if the vendor might at law recover the amount of the purchase-money, although he had not conveyed, for the jurisdiction of equity proceeds on the ground that the plaintiff has no adequate remedy at law. If a vendee fail to pay the purchase-money on the stipulated day, the vendor may file a bill for a specific performance, or he may sue at law for the damage which he has sustained by reason of the breach of covenant, or of promise, on the part of the vendee; but if he choose to sue at law in a form of action in which he seeks to recover the price of the property sold, he must actually execute a conveyance, and tender it to the vendee; Standley *v.* Hemmington,[3] Heard *v.* Wadham,[4] Goodisson *v.* Nunn,[5] Glazebrook *v.* Woodrow,[6] Pincke *v.* Curteis.[7]

LORD DENMAN, C.J. None of the circumstances relied upon by Mr. Manning are sufficient to shew that the acts of payment and conveyance here were to be concurrent, or to distinguish this case from Pordage *v.* Cole[8] and the authorities cited in the note to it. If, as is contended on the part of the plaintiff, the legal and equitable estates are now united in the defendant, he requires no remedy against the plaintiff which he has not already in his own hands. If not, we cannot help him to a remedy which he has not secured for himself by his contract.

LITTLEDALE, J. A time being fixed for payment, and none for doing that which was the consideration for the payment, an action lies for the purchase-money without averring performance of the consideration. An action for not executing a conveyance of the premises might have been maintained by the defendant before the day of payment; and in such action no allegation of payment would have been necessary. The covenants are independent, and each party has relied upon his remedy by action against the other. The case therefore differs from Callonel *v.* Briggs,[9] and from Goodisson *v.* Nunn,[5] Glazebrook *v.* Woodrow,[6] and other cases cited, where both acts were to be done at the same time or on the same day.

PATTESON, J. Pordage *v.* Cole[8] is directly in point. We must overrule it if we decide in favor of the defendant. There is no express provision that the conveyance shall be executed before payment,

[1] 1 Atk. 12. [2] Forrest. 61. [3] 6 Taunt. 561.
[4] 1 East, 619. [5] 4 T. R. 761. [6] 8 T. R. 366.
[7] 4 Bro. C. C. 332. [8] 1 Saund. 319. [9] 1 Salk. 112.

nor any reasonable intendment that it was to be necessarily precedent to or concurrent with it. The words "completion of the purchase," which furnish the only plausible argument in the defendant's favor, only mean payment of the rest of the purchase-money. On the day specified, the defendant was to pay all the principal sum that remained due with interest up to that time; but he might have prevented the further running of interest by payment at any time before that day if he pleased.

COLERIDGE, J. We must collect the intention of the parties from the whole instrument. It fixes with precision the time of payment, which is expressed to be the consideration of the sale and purchase, and contemplates the possible payment before that time. It is possible that "the completion of the purchase" may have the meaning attributed to it by Mr. Manning; but I see no good ground for this construction. The defendant might have paid all the money, and called for a conveyance immediately. The acts are clearly independent, within the rule correctly laid down by Mr. Serjeant Williams in the note to Pordage v. Cole.[1] *Judgment for the plaintiff.*

WILKS v. SMITH.

IN THE EXCHEQUER, JUNE 17, 1842.

[*Reported in* 10 *Meeson & Welsby*, 355.]

ASSUMPSIT. The declaration stated that theretofore, to wit, on, &c., by a certain agreement then made between the plaintiff of the one part and the defendant of the other part, the plaintiff agreed to sell, and the defendant agreed to purchase, a lot of building ground, situate, &c., and which said lot of land the plaintiff agreed to sell, with all the rights and privileges thereto belonging, for the sum of £120, which sum the defendant agreed to pay to the plaintiff in manner following, that is to say, on or before the expiration of four years from the day of the date of the said agreement, with lawful interest at five per cent., half-yearly, until paid. The declaration then alleged mutual promises, and averred, that four years from the day of the date of the said agreement had not yet expired, and that the said sum of £120 had not yet been paid; and that after the making of the said agreement, and before the commencement of this suit, to wit, &c., a large sum of money, to wit, the sum of £12, for two years' interest on the said sum of £120, became and was due and payable from the defendant to the plaintiff

[1] 1 Wms. Saund. 320, note 4.

under and by virtue of the said agreement. Breach, in non-payment of the £12.

General demurrer, and joinder in demurrer.

The defendant's point was, that the first count of the declaration is insufficient, because it does not aver or shew that the plaintiff had any title to the ground in that count mentioned, or that there was any ability, or readiness, or willingness on the part of the plaintiff, to perform his part of the agreement.

The points marked for argument on the part of the plaintiff were, that it was unnecessary to aver or shew title to the ground or a readiness or willingness on his part to perform the agreement, as neither was a condition precedent to his right to recover the interest, which the defendant by his demurrer admits to have accrued due under the agreement. The plaintiff will also contend, that as a day is appointed for payment of the interest, and no time mentioned for performance of that which is the consideration for the interest, it was unnecessary to aver performance, and that the defendant's remedy is by cross-action, if any breach of the agreement has been committed by the plaintiff; and the plaintiff will also contend that it must be presumed he has performed his part of the agreement, and that if not the defendant should have pleaded the non-performance.

Warren, in support of the demurrer. First, the plaintiff ought to have shewn on the face of his declaration that he had a good title to the land. In Luxton *v.* Robinson [1] it was held that, in an action upon an agreement to deliver possession for certain considerations, subject to a forfeiture on failure by either party, the person who was to deliver possession could not sue for the forfeiture, without shewing in his declaration a possessory title in himself. The party must have that which he assumes to sell, to entitle him to sue, and therefore he was bound to shew he had a title to dispose of it. In Hallewell *v.* Morrell [2] the Court of Common Pleas recognized the doctrine that a vendor must shew a title to convey. That proposition was advanced by Stephen, Serjt., in argument, and though adverted to, was not denied by the court, who distinguished that case on the ground that it was not a contract for the purchase of an estate, but to execute a deed of covenant. In Souter *v.* Drake [3] it was held that in every contract for the sale of an existing lease, there is an implied contract by the seller (if the contrary be not expressed) to make out the lessor's title to demise; and without shewing such title, the seller cannot maintain an action at law against the buyer for refusing to complete the purchase. Roper *v.* Coombes [4] is also an authority to shew that a man is not bound to pay money on a contract for sale, before he is satisfied

[1] 2 Doug. 620. [2] 1 Man. & Gr. 367, 1 Scott, N. R. 309.
[3] 5 B. & Ad. 992, 3 Nev. & Man. 40.
[4] 6 B. & Cr. 534, 9 D. & R. 562.

that the vendor can make out a good title to the property sold. Secondly, there is no averment of performance; no allegation, either that the plaintiff had sold the land, or was ready and willing to make an actual sale of it. The declaration ought to have averred, either that he had done so, or was ready and willing to do so; otherwise he has no right to claim the purchase-money. That is a condition precedent. [He referred to Mr. Serjeant Williams's Notes to Pordage v. Cole,[1] and the language of Sir James Mansfield, C. J., in delivering the judgment of the Court of Exchequer Chamber in Smith v. Woodhouse.[2]] In Stavers v. Curling,[3] Tindal, C. J., says: "The rule has been established by a long series of decisions in modern times, that the question, whether covenants are to be held dependent or independent of each other, is to be determined by the intention and meaning of the parties as it appears on the instrument, and by the application of common sense to each particular case." It is plain, on such an agreement as this, that the party is to be put into possession at once of that which he is to pay for, for the four years; he was to be put into possesssion immediately, in order that he might commence building on the land, and until he was, he was not bound to pay the money. If the plaintiff had averred that he had put him into possession, the defendant might have traversed it. The plaintiff, after alleging mutual promises, ought to have averred performance on his part. In Laird v. Pim,[4] where, in assumpsit by the vendor against the purchasers of land, the declaration stated that in consideration of the plaintiff's selling to the defendants certain land, to be paid for as soon as the conveyance should be completed, the defendants promised to purchase and pay for the same; and there was an averment that, although the plaintiff had allowed the defendants to enter into possession of the lands, and had always been ready and willing to make a good title, and offered the defendants to execute a conveyance, and would have tendered a proper conveyance, but that the defendant discharged him from so doing. Breach, in non-payment of the purchase-money; and it was held that the declaration was good. There, there was an averment, of the absence of which in the present case the plaintiff complains. He also cited Mattock v. Kingslake [5] and Poole v. Hill.[6]

J. W. Smith, contra. The two questions resolve themselves into one; namely, whether the defendant's promise was in consideration of the plaintiff's promise, or of his performance. If the defendant promised in consideration of the performance of the contract by the plaintiff, performance must be averred; but if it was in consideration of the plaintiff's promise, the defendant has obtained that for which he contracted to pay the interest. In the present agreement no time

[1] 1 Wms. Saund. 320, note 4.
[2] 2 New Rep. 239.
[3] 3 Bing. N. C. 355, 3 Scott, 740.
[4] 7 M. & W. 474.
[5] 10 Ad. & Ell. 50, 2 Per. & D. 343.
[6] 6 M. & W. 835.

is fixed for delivering possession of the land, but a time is fixed for the payment of the purchase-money. In Mattock v. Kingslake, Littledale, J., says: "A time being fixed for payment, and none for doing that which was the consideration for the payment, an action lies for the purchase-money without averring performance of the consideration. An action for not executing a conveyance of the premises might have been maintained by the defendant before the day of payment; and in such action no allegation of payment would have been necessary. The covenants are independent, and each party has relied upon his remedy by action against the other." Here the defendant might at any time have brought an action against the plaintiff for non-performance of the agreement on his part. The promise is the consideration, and not the performance by the plaintiff. In Campbell v. Jones [1] the same principle is laid down; and that decision was recognized and approved by the court in Glazebrook v. Woodrow.[2] In Pordage v. Cole [3] the declaration was similar to the present, and there it was held that the covenant was an independent one, and that the vendor might bring an action for the money, before any conveyance by him of the land. In the notes to that case the rule is laid down thus: "If a day be appointed for payment of money or part of it, or for doing any other act, and the day is to happen, or may happen, before the thing which is the consideration of the money or other act is to be performed, an action may be brought for the money, or for not doing such other act, before performance; for it appears that the party relied upon his remedy, and did not intend to make the performance a condition precedent; and so it is where no time is fixed for performance of that which is the consideration of the money or other act."

Warren, in reply. The agreement being that the defendant was to pay interest for four years, or until the principal money was paid, shews that he was to be put into possession of the land; and the plaintiff should have averred that he had done that which on the face of the record it appears he had undertaken to do.

PARKE, B. I am of opinion that the declaration is good, and that it was not necessary for the plaintiff to aver his readiness and willingness to convey at every period of the contract. It is enough if he is ready and able to convey at the time when the title is to be made out. I also think that it is no objection that he has not averred that he had a title to the land. According to the terms of the agreement, no time is fixed for the sale; but a time is limited within which the principal money is to be paid, with interest in the mean time. The consideration for the defendant's paying the interest is the plaintiff's undertaking to sell the land, not the actual sale of it. The plaintiff is not bound to do any thing before the money is paid. The rule, as laid down in

[1] 6 T. R. 570.
[2] 8 T. R. 366.
[3] 1 Saund. 319.

the notes to Pordage *v.* Cole, applies strictly to this case. No time, then, being fixed by the agreement for the conveyance of the land, it cannot be a condition precedent; nor can we imply that a conveyance was intended to be made before the interest was paid, else we should be supposing that the plaintiff intended to part with his estate before the money was paid, and such an intention certainly cannot be implied from the nature of the contract. It may be that no conveyance need be made till the principal money is paid, that is, at the end of four years. The question here is whether or not interest is to be paid before the plaintiff has given up possession of the land. I think it is, and that the conveyance is not a condition precedent. The plaintiff is therefore entitled to our judgment.

ALDERSON, B. I am of the same opinion. If one act is to be done in consideration of another, the party suing for the non-performance must aver performance on his part. But if there be two acts, one fixed in point of time, and the other not, the latter is not a condition precedent. Here the defendant relied not upon the plaintiff's performance, but upon his promise to perform.

ROLFE, B. The case of Luxton *v.* Robinson, cited by Mr. Warren, is distinguishable from this case, because there possession was to be delivered to the defendant on a given day. But here there is no such obligation to deliver possession. No such intention appears on the face of the contract; and if we were to hold that possession was to be given by the plaintiff, our decision would be at variance with the meaning of the parties. The vendor was not to convey the estate before he got the purchase-money.

Judgment for the plaintiff.

GEORGE CLIPSHAM *v.* STEPHEN VERTUE AND HORATIO VERTUE.

IN THE QUEEN'S BENCH, NOVEMBER 14, 1843.

[*Reported in 5 Queen's Bench Reports,* 265.]

ASSUMPSIT. The declaration alleged that by a charter-party between the plaintiff and the defendants, dated May 28, 1842, it was agreed that the plaintiff's ship called the Emblem, then bound to Nantes, should load from the agents of the defendants at Nantes a full cargo of wheat and flour, &c., and being so loaded should forthwith proceed to London, and deliver the same on being paid freight, &c. Averment of performance by the plaintiff, and in particular that the said ship did afterwards, to wit, 16th June, 1842, proceed to Nantes aforesaid; and afterwards, to wit, 26th July, 1842, arrived at Nantes aforesaid; and being so arrived afterwards, to wit, 6th August, 1842, was ready to load her cargo in the charter-party mentioned. Breach, that the defendants did not nor would load on board the said ship at Nantes aforesaid a full cargo of wheat, &c., pursuant to the charter-party in that behalf, or any wheat, &c., but wholly neglected and refused so to do.[1]

Plea 3. That the charter-party was made and entered into by plaintiff and defendants at London aforesaid; and that the said vessel was, at the time of the making of the charter-party, lying in the port of London; that after the making of the charter-party, and before the said vessel set sail, or proceeded upon the said voyage to Nantes aforesaid, in pursuance of the charter-party, to wit, on the 29th May, 1842, plaintiff wrongfully, and without the knowledge or consent of defendants, set sail with the said vessel upon another and a different voyage from the said voyage to Nantes aforesaid, to wit, upon a voyage from the port of London aforesaid to the port of Newcastle in England, and proceeded with the said vessel upon the said last-mentioned voyage; and afterwards, to wit, 3d June, 1842, arrived at Newcastle aforesaid, and remained with the said vessel at Newcastle aforesaid for a long space of time, to wit, twenty-three days, for other and different purposes than the said voyage in the charter-party mentioned, to wit, for the purpose of chartering and engaging the said vessel to other persons than the defendants upon a voyage from Newcastle aforesaid to other places than Nantes, in parts beyond seas, and back to Newcastle aforesaid; which said sailing and proceeding to, and remaining at Newcastle aforesaid, were contrary to the form and effect, and true intent and meaning of the charter-party, and a breach thereof on the part of the plaintiff; by reason of which said sailing and proceeding to, and remaining at Newcastle aforesaid, the said vessel was prevented from arriving, and did not arrive at Nantes aforesaid as in the declaration mentioned within a reasonable and proper time in that behalf after the making of the said charter-party; but on the contrary thereof, the said vessel arrived at Nantes aforesaid a long and unreasonable time, to wit, thirty-eight days, after the said vessel would have arrived at Nantes, according to the usual length of the voyage from London aforesaid to Nantes aforesaid, if the said vessel had sailed direct from London aforesaid to Nantes aforesaid, according to the true intent and meaning of the charter-party. Verification.

Demurrer, assigning for cause that the plea neither denies nor confesses and avoids the promise in the declaration mentioned; that the plea amounts to the general issue, or to a traverse of the averments in the declaration; and that, although the plea is pleaded in confession and avoidance of the promise, &c., yet the plea does not set forth mat-

[1] The statement of the declaration has been materially abbreviated. — ED.

ters sufficient to discharge defendants from the performance of their promise in the declaration mentioned, as it does not shew that defendants were by the delay rendered unable to ship a cargo according to the charter-party, or that by the supposed deviation or delay the object of the voyage was lost.

Joinder in demurrer.

W. H. Watson for the plaintiff. The plea offers no answer to the declaration. The charter-party contains no stipulation that the vessel shall sail at any particular time, or without delay, or in a reasonable time. If loss has been caused by her reaching Nantes at an unreasonable time, that can be only matter for a cross-action. Mere delay does not avoid the contract; if it did, the smallest delay would put an end to the liability of the defendants. In Freeman v. Taylor [1] the charter-party contained a stipulation that the ship should proceed "with all convenient speed," and delay having been caused by a deviation, it was held that the proper question for the jury was, "whether the delay here was of such a nature as to have put an end to the ordinary objects the freighter might have had in view when he entered into the contract." It appears also from Fillieul v. Armstrong [2] that a partial failure by one party to perform the contract on his side does not exonerate the other party, unless the failure absolutely destroys the object of the contract. Bornmann v. Tooke [3] shews that the plea here discloses no more than a ground of cross-action. M'Andrew v. Adams [4] is an instance of such an action.

Cleasby, contra. The principle is as contended for on the other side; but the failure shewn in the plea does go to the root of the contract, because it appears that the defendants were prevented from loading in a reasonable time, so that no benefit has been received. If any cargo had been actually carried, and this action had been brought for the freight, the plea would afford no answer, because then some benefit would have been received by the defendants. But here the contract has not been acted upon at all. Therefore the principle of Freeman v. Taylor [5] applies, where the defendant was held to be exonerated because the object of the voyage was substantially defeated, though the defendant had received some benefit from the outward voyage; a point which does not clearly appear in the marginal note to the report. In Mount v. Larkins [6] it was held, that an unreasonable delay amounted to a deviation, and discharged the underwriter by varying the risk. If the contract here had been to arrive at Nantes on a given day, a failure so to arrive would have discharged the freighter; Shadforth v. Higgins; [7] but it is implied in every charter-party that the ship shall sail in a reasonable time. Touteng v. Hubbard [8] and Soames v. Lonergan [9] are

[1] 8 Bing. 124. See Benson v. Blunt, 1 Q. B. 870.
[2] 7 A. & E. 557. [3] 1 Camp. 377. [4] 1 New Ca. 29.
[5] 8 Bing. 124. [6] 8 Bing. 108. [7] 3 Camp. 385
[8] 3 B. & P. 291. [9] 2 B. & C. 564.

instances of the freighter being discharged by a delay substantially defeating the object of the voyage; and the principle was distinctly recognized in Havelock *v.* Geddes.[1] In Ritchie *v.* Atkinson[2] the owner of the vessel was held entitled to recover *pro rata*, though he had contracted to ship a complete cargo, and had in fact shipped only a short cargo; the principle relied upon there was, that freight in such a case is apportionable; but here, no cargo having been put on board, owing to the unreasonable delay, there can be no apportionment.

W. H. Watson in reply was stopped by the court.

LORD DENMAN, C. J. The plea is clearly bad. If issue had been taken on the term "unreasonable," we should have been required to put a construction upon it; and that, without further explanation, we have not the means of doing. It is quite possible that a vessel may arrive in a time which, in some sense of the word is unreasonable, and yet that the freighter may derive benefit from the voyage; so that the principle laid down by Lord Ellenborough, in Havelock *v.* Geddes,[3] may apply, namely, that the plaintiff's neglect shall not exonerate the defendant, unless it precludes him from making any use of the vessel; otherwise, as he says, the neglect in that case to put in a single nail might have been a breach of the condition forthwith to make the ship tight and strong. So this plea might, in one sense of the words, have been supported in evidence, if the slightest want of due expedition had been shewn.

WILLIAMS, J. The real question is, whether a plea, using only such expressions as this plea contains, can be supported. I find no authority in its favor; what is an "unreasonable" time is left matter of speculation. To what extent the unreasonableness went, whether so far as that the voyage was lost, or the cargo could not be put on board, we are not told.

COLERIDGE, J., concurred.

WIGHTMAN, J. The meaning of the allegation is simply that the vessel did not arrive so soon as she might have done; but not that she did not arrive in time to enable the defendants to perform the stipulations in the charter-party. *Judgment for the plaintiff.*

[1] 10 East, 555, 564. [2] 10 East, 295. [3] 10 East, 555.

JUDSON *v.* BOWDEN.

IN THE EXCHEQUER, JUNE 2, 1847.

[*Reported in* 1 *Exchequer Reports*, 162.]

COVENANT. The declaration stated, that by a certain indenture made on the 4th of March, 1845, between the plaintiff and the defendant (profert), the plaintiff and defendant did covenant and agree with each other in manner following, that is to say, that the plaintiff and the defendant would be and become partners in the profession or business of surgeons and apothecaries for the term of one year, to be commenced and be computed from the 1st of January, 1845, if the plaintiff and defendant should so long live; that the partnership should be carried on at the house situate at Water Row, Ware, in the county of Hertford, then in the occupation of the plaintiff, under the style or firm of "Judson & Bowden," to be printed or engraved or otherwise conspicuously posted and published on the principal outer door of the said house, and upon, under, and subject to the terms, conditions, and agreements following, that is to say, that the defendant should pay, and he did thereby covenant to pay to the plaintiff the sum of £800, at the times and in manner thereinafter mentioned, viz., the sum of £400 upon the execution of the said indenture, and the several sums of £100 on the 25th of March, in the years 1846–49 respectively, the said sums making together the sum of £800; that the defendant should, in consideration of such payments, be entitled to the entire profits of the said business from the 1st of January, 1845, the defendant paying all expenses of carrying on the said business from the said last-mentioned date; that the plaintiff should introduce the defendant to the patients and friends of the plaintiff, at first as a partner, and ultimately as his successor, with the view and for the express purpose of securing to the defendant the confidence of the said patients and friends, and of obtaining for the defendant their future employment in the said business; that the business of the said partnership should be carried on at the then residence of the plaintiff at Ware, and that the plaintiff should continue to reside and to practise as a surgeon and apothecary in the same residence till the 25th of June, 1845, and should at all reasonable times be ready and willing to attend and advise and prescribe for patients, and to assist the defendant in carrying on the said business of a surgeon and apothecary till the first of January, 1846, and at all subsequent times when the plaintiff should be at the said town of Ware or in its immediate vicinity; that the plaintiff should, from and after the first of January, 1846, introduce the defendant as his successor in the said business, and should use his best endeavors to establish him in his practice as a surgeon and apothecary in the said town of Ware; in consideration whereof the defendant thereby covenanted and agreed to pay to the plaintiff the further sum of £50 on the 25th of March, 1846, in addition to and beyond the said sum of £800; that the defendant should purchase from the plaintiff all the medical fixtures, drugs, and instruments then belonging to and used in the surgery of the plaintiff at Ware aforesaid, at a valuation to be made in the usual manner, the amount of such valuation to be paid within two months after the date of the said indenture. Averment of due observance and performance by the plaintiff of his part of the covenant. Second breach, non-payment of the said sum of £50, due on the 25th of March, 1846.

To this breach the defendant pleaded, that after the said first day of January, 1846, to wit, on, &c., and on divers other days and times between that day and the 25th of March, 1846, being proper and reasonable times in that behalf, he the defendant requested the plaintiff to introduce him as his the plaintiff's successor in the said business, to divers persons, to wit, T. C., F. E., W. C., and W. H., and divers other persons whose names are to the defendant unknown, and which said persons had been, and at the time of the execution of the said indenture, and up to the time when the plaintiff was requested by the defendant as aforesaid to introduce him, were respectively patients of the plaintiff. Yet the plaintiff did not nor would, at those several days and times when he was so requested as aforesaid, or at any or either of them, or at any other time hitherto, introduce the defendant to the said persons or any or either of them, but on the contrary the plaintiff then wholly refused and neglected, and from thence hitherto hath refused and neglected, to introduce the defendant to any of the said persons, nor has the plaintiff, from the said first day of January, 1846, hitherto, introduced the defendant at all to any person whomsoever as his the plaintiff's successor in the said business, nor has the plaintiff, at any time since the said first day of January, 1846, used any endeavor whatever to establish the defendant in the practice of a surgeon and apothecary in the said town of Ware, but the plaintiff has wholly neglected and refused so to do. And the defendant in fact saith, that the plaintiff hath not at any time hitherto performed any part whatever of the said alleged consideration for his the defendant's said covenant to pay the plaintiff the said further sum of £50, contrary to the terms of the said indenture in that behalf. Wherefore he the defendant did refuse to pay the said sum of £50, so by him covenanted to be paid in consideration of the plaintiff's introducing him the defendant, and using his endeavors to establish him the defendant in the practice of a surgeon and apothecary, in the said town of Ware, as in the said indenture and in the said declaration mentioned, as it was lawful for the defendant to do for the cause aforesaid. Verification.

Special demurrer, assigning for causes, that it is not stated in or by the plea, nor does it appear therefrom, that the plaintiff could or might, or that he had the means or opportunity of introducing the defendant to the patients in the plea mentioned, nor is it stated in or by the plea, that a reasonable time had elapsed for the plaintiff's so doing before the commencement of the suit, or before the 26th day of March, 1846; and that the plea is bad, inasmuch as the covenant on the part of the plaintiff to introduce the defendant to the plaintiff's patients, is not a condition precedent to the payment by the defendant to the plaintiff of the said sum of £50 in the declaration mentioned, but on the contrary thereof, the said covenant on the part of the defendant was and is a distinct and independent covenant, and in no way contingent on the performance by the plaintiff of his said covenant; and also that it does not appear by the plea that the defendant was ready and willing; and also that the plea is only good by reason of being an argumentative denial of plaintiff's performance of the condition on which he was to be paid, if any such condition there was; and lastly, that the plea improperly concludes with a verification instead of to the country.

Joinder in demurrer.

Willes, in support of the demurrer. The plea is bad. The introduction by the plaintiff of the defendant to his patients is not a condition precedent to his right to recover this sum of £50. If it were, the defendant would be absolved from payment of this sum if the plaintiff had neglected to do so in the smallest particular. It would also be unfair to the defendant if the covenant were to be considered as complete on the 25th of March, as the plaintiff would in that case be under no necessity of introducing him to any patient after the expiration of that time. The plaintiff is bound to use his best endeavors to introduce the defendant after the time fixed for the payment of the £50. Here the covenants are independent. The rule is correctly laid down in Saunders,[1] that, "If a day be appointed for payment of money or part of it, or for doing any other act, and the day is to happen or may happen before the thing which is the consideration of the money or other act is to be performed, an action may be brought for the money or for not doing such other act, before performance; for it appears that the party relied upon his remedy, and did not intend to make his performance a condition precedent; and so it is where no time is fixed for performance of that which is the consideration of the money or other act." The note contains the report of Sir Richard Pool's case, which is in point. The plea is also bad, as it is in fact a traverse, and therefore improperly concludes with a verification.

Hawkins, in support of the plea. The sum of £50 was added, that the plaintiff should use his best endeavors to introduce the defendant

[1] 1 Wms. Saund. 320 *b*, note 1.

to his patients, and to establish him in his profession as an apothecary, before the 25th of March; that is the consideration for the additional sum of money. [POLLOCK, C. B. It seems to me that it is quite consistent with this plea, that the plaintiff did use his best endeavors to introduce the defendant to other patients, though not the persons mentioned in the plea.] He cited Collins *v.* Gibbs.[1]

Per Curiam.[2] The introduction by the plaintiff of the defendant to his patients is not a condition precedent to the payment of the £50. The plaintiff would be under the obligation to introduce the defendant after the 25th of March. *Judgment for the plaintiff.*

DICKER *v.* JACKSON.

IN THE COMMON PLEAS, MAY 12, 1848.

[*Reported in* 6 *Common Bench Reports*, 103.]

ASSUMPSIT. The first count of the declaration stated that, by articles of agreement between plaintiff and defendant, dated September 2, 1844, the plaintiff agreed to sell, and the defendant agreed to purchase, for the sum of £5489 8*s.* 10*d.*, certain premises in said articles described; and the plaintiff thereby agreed, within one month from the date thereof or from being required so to do, at his own expense, to deliver to the defendant an abstract of his title to the said premises, and deduce a clear title thereto; and upon payment of the purchase-money of said premises together with all interest that might accrue due thereon, to execute a proper conveyance thereof (to be prepared by and at the expense of the defendant) to the defendant or as he should appoint; and the defendant thereby agreed to pay to the plaintiff said purchase-money as follows, that is to say, the sum of £548 18*s.* 10*d.* on the signing of said articles, and the residue or sum of £4940 10*s.* on or before the 2d of September, 1848, with interest thereon in the mean time, payable on the 2d of March and 2d of September in each year. The declaration then set out certain other stipulations contained in the articles which are not material to the question decided, and proceeded to allege that it was further agreed that possession of said premises should be forthwith given to the defendant, and that all taxes, rates, and other outgoings up to the date of said articles, should be paid by the plaintiff, and from and after the said date by the defendant. It then stated the terms of the agreement for entry and sale in case of default by the defendant, and after averring mutual prom-

[1] 2 Burr. 899. [2] Pollock, C. B., Alderson, B., Rolfe, B., Platt, B.

ises alleged performance on the plaintiff's part by delivering possession of the premises to the defendant, by paying all taxes, rates, and other outgoings up to the date of the articles, and by delivering to the defendant at his own expense an abstract of his title to said premises, and deducing a clear title thereto, as in and by said articles in that behalf specified and required; and it further alleged that the plaintiff, from the making of said contract to the commencement of this suit, did in all things perform, and was ready and willing to perform, said contract on his part. Breach, non-payment of the half-year's interest on said sum of £4940 10*s*., which became due on the 2d of September, 1846.[1]

The defendant, amongst other pleas, pleaded that the plaintiff did not deliver to him the defendant an abstract of title to the said premises, and deduce such a clear title thereto, as in and by the said agreement specified and required, *modo et forma*, &c.

To this plea the plaintiff demurred specially, assigning for causes, amongst others, that it tendered an immaterial issue, and that it was double, inasmuch as it offered to put in issue several material things averred in the declaration, viz., the delivery of an abstract of the plaintiff's title, and the deducing of such title.

Joinder in demurrer.

The demurrer was argued in Michaelmas Term last, before WILDE C. J., and COLTMAN, MAULE, and V. WILLIAMS, JJ.

Aspland, in support of the demurrer. It is submitted that this plea is double, inasmuch as it puts in issue two material allegations of the declaration, namely, the delivery by the plaintiff of an abstract of title to the premises, and the deducing of a clear title thereto. The contract here closely resembles in many respects the agreement set out in Sansom *v*. Rhodes.[2] Smith *v*. Dixon[3] is also in point. Secondly, the plea is bad in substance, and affords no answer to the declaration. By the contract the plaintiff undertakes, within one month from the date thereof, or from being required so to do, to deliver an abstract of title. It nowhere appears that one month had elapsed, or that the plaintiff had been required to deliver such abstract. It is true that the declaration alleges performance on the part of the plaintiff; but such averment is immaterial, and cannot be traversed; for, even if the plaintiff had broken his contract in this respect, it does not amount to a condition precedent. This case falls within the principle laid down in the note to Pordage *v*. Cole.[4] It is clear that here the time may arrive for the payment of the money by the defendant, before the plaintiff

[1] The statement of the declaration has been abbreviated. — ED.

[2] 6 N. C. 261, 8 Scott, 544.

[3] 7 Ad. & E. 1, 2 N. & P. 1.

[4] 1 Wms. Saund. 320 *b*.

can be called upon to perform his contract; and if so, there is no ground for calling it a condition precedent.[1] . . .

Rew, contra. As to the objection to the plea on the score of duplicity, the court must look at the agreement to see what was the meaning of the parties. Their intent clearly was, that the plaintiff should deduce a good title by the delivery of an abstract of title. The single point of defence sought to be raised by the plea is, that the plaintiff has failed to make out a good title in the way he undertook to do, namely, by delivering an abstract of such title. This case comes within the principle laid down in Bell *v.* Tuckett,[2] as to several allegations in a plea constituting only one defence. Sansom *v.* Rhodes is distinguishable, for there the time named did not govern the whole sentence.

As regards the point whether the plea discloses a substantial answer to the declaration, it is submitted that the deducing of a good title is such an essential part of an agreement for the sale of land, that if the plaintiff fails to do so he cannot enforce the agreement. In Flureau *v.* Thornhill,[3] Blackstone, J., in giving judgment, says: "These contracts are merely upon condition, frequently expressed, but always implied, that the vendor has a good title." If a good title cannot be shewn, the purchaser is entitled to rescind the contract; and here, the plea being admitted by the demurrer, the defendant had a right to put an end to the agreement. The case of Wilde *v.* Fort,[4] where it was held that, if the vendor of an estate by auction does not shew a clear title by the day specified, the purchaser may recover back his deposit and rescind the contract, without waiting to see whether the vendor may ultimately be able to establish a good title or not, is cited in Sugden on Vendors and Purchasers,[5] as an authority for the position that, "if the draft of the conveyance, for instance, is not delivered on the day appointed, the party who ought to deliver it has broken his agreement, and cannot therefore recover upon it at law. This works no injustice; for the further execution of the contract is at once stopped; the seller retains his estate and the purchaser his purchase-money; and the party making default is liable, as he ought to be, to an action for breach of his engagement." With respect to the note to Pordage *v.* Cole, the present case does not fall within the rule there laid down.

Aspland was heard in reply. *Cur. adv. vult.*

WILDE, C. J., now delivered the judgment of the court.[6] . . .

On the argument of this demurrer before us it was contended, on behalf of the plaintiff, that this traverse was bad in substance; for,

[1] The learned counsel here stated Mattock *v.* Kinglake, 10 Ad. & El. 50, and Stavers *v.* Curling, 3 Bing. N. C. 355. — ED.

[2] 3 M. & G. 785, 4 Scott, N. R. 402.

[3] 2 W. Bl. 1078.

[4] 4 Taunt. 334.

[5] 7th edit. p. 358.

[6] His lordship's statement of the pleadings has been omitted. — ED.

that the delivery of the abstract, and the deducing a clear title within one month from being required so to do, was not a condition precedent to his right to maintain the action, and therefore that the allegation in the declaration of his having performed it, was immaterial and superfluous; and that the traverse of it was consequently bad; and it was further contended that, even if the allegation was material and necessary, the traverse in question was bad for duplicity; for, that the true meaning of the part of the agreement in question was, not simply that a clear title should be disclosed on the face of the abstract, but that, moreover, a clear title in fact should be deduced; and that, consequently, a failure on the part of the plaintiff either to deliver an abstract, or to deduce a clear title within the appointed time, would be a good bar to the action, if the performance of that part of the contract were really a condition precedent.

On the other hand, it was argued on behalf of the defendant, that nothing more was required of the plaintiff than to deliver an abstract, deducing a clear title on the face of it; and that, therefore, the plea was not open to the objection of duplicity; and further, that the performance of this part of the agreement was a condition precedent.

It is not necessary for us to decide whether the plaintiff or the defendant is right in his construction of the terms of the contract in the former respect; because we are of opinion that the performance of this part of it was not a condition precedent to the plaintiff's right to enforce the payment which is the subject of the action.

The plaintiff, by the terms of the agreement, undertakes that he will, within a month from being required so to do, deliver an abstract, and deduce a clear title. And the time appointed for his performance of this part of the contract does not therefore arrive until he has been required to do so, and a month shall have expired after the date of such requisition. But the defendant undertakes to pay the interest upon the unpaid purchase-money, on certain specified days between the date of the agreement and the day fixed for the payment of the residue of the principal purchase-money; and the time appointed for him to make these payments may arrive before a month has expired after a requisition to the plaintiff to deliver the abstract and deduce the title, and consequently before the time appointed for the plaintiff to do so has arrived. The case, then, appears to fall directly within the rule laid down by Mr. Serjt. Williams in the note to Pordage v. Cole,[1] viz., that, "if a day be appointed for payment of money, or part of it, or for doing any other act, and the day is to happen, or may happen, before the thing which is the consideration of the money or other act is to be performed, an action may be brought for the money, or for not doing such other act, before performance; for it appears that the party relied

[1] 1 Wms. Saunders, 320 *b*.

on his remedy, and did not intend to make the performance a condition precedent."

If this rule be correctly laid down, as we think it is, it demonstrates that the performance of this part of the contract by the plaintiff is not a condition precedent to his right to maintain this action; and, consequently, the allegation in the declaration of such performance being immaterial and superfluous, the plea, which is merely a traverse of such allegation, is bad.

Our judgment must, therefore, be for the plaintiff.

Judgment for the Plaintiff.

SIBTHORP v. BRUNEL.

In the Exchequer, April 24, 1849.

[Reported in 3 Exchequer Reports, 826.]

Covenant on an indenture, whereby (after reciting that a company had been formed for the purpose of constructing a railway from Cheltenham to Oxford, and that the company was then applying to Parliament for an act of incorporation, and that the plaintiff was then the owner of an estate in the county of Oxford, which would be intersected by said railway and injuriously affected thereby, and that the plaintiff had petitioned Parliament against the said bill, &c., and that he had been requested by the defendant to desist from such opposition), it was covenanted (*inter alia*), "that within six months from the passing of the proposed bill into a law, and before the said company shall enter upon, take, or use any part of the said estate, &c., except for the purpose of setting out and ascertaining the land required to be taken, the said I. K. B. (the defendant) shall and will pay to the said C. D. S. (the plaintiff) the sum of £4000 sterling for the purchase of such part of the said estate as hereinafter described;" "and that, on payment by the said defendant to the plaintiff of the said sum of £4000 and interest after the rate of £5 per cent. per annum, after the expiration of six months after the passing of the said bill into a law, to the day of payment of the said sum of £4000, he the said plaintiff and all necessary parties shall convey to the said defendant, his heirs or assigns, or as he or they shall direct, so much of the said estate as shall be required for the construction of the said railway," &c. The declaration then contained an allegation, that, after the making of this agreement, &c., the said proposed bill, to wit, on, &c., passed into a law, and a general averment of performance, and that six months had elapsed since the passing of the said bill, and laid as a breach the non-payment of the purchase-money of £4000.[1]

The defendant, having craved oyer of the deed, and set it out, demurred generally to the declaration, on the ground that a general averment of performance by the plaintiff was not sufficient, but that he ought to have shewn by his declaration that he was ready and willing to convey the property to be purchased, and that the covenant to pay and the covenant to convey on payment were dependent covenants.

Joinder in demurrer.

Keating, in support of the demurrer, contended that the covenants were mutual and dependent covenants, and he cited the rule as laid down by Tindal, C. J., in Stavers *v.* Curling,[2] where he says, "The rule has been established by a long series of decisions in modern times, that the question, whether covenants are to be held dependent or independent of each other, is to be determined by the intention and meaning of the parties, as it appears on the instrument, and by the application of common sense to each particular case; to which intention, when once discovered, all technical forms of expression must give way;" and that, in the present case, the money was to be paid for the purchase of the estate. He also referred to Pordage *v.* Cole.[3]

[PARKE, B., referred to Mattock *v.* Kinglake.[4]]

Willes, contra, was not called upon.

POLLOCK, C. B. I am clearly of opinion that the plaintiff is entitled to the judgment of the court. This is a positive covenant to pay the amount of the purchase-money at a specified time. The case of Mattock *v.* Kinglake, to which my brother Parke has referred, is a decision expressly in point. Applying the rule as laid down by Tindal, C. J., in Stavers *v.* Curling, I think this covenant to pay the money is wholly independent of that to convey the estate; and that such was the intention of the parties at the time this instrument was executed, is perfectly clear from its terms. The rule as derived from Pordage *v.* Cole may be the technical one, but whether the language of these covenants be subject to a technical construction or to their natural one, the result will be the same, — that they are independent of each other.

PARKE, B. I am entirely of the same opinion. I think it is clear that these covenants are wholly independent, and that the case is a very plain one. The words of the covenant upon which this action is brought are, that the plaintiff shall pay the sum agreed for the purchase of the land; if they had been *upon*, or even *for*, the conveyance of the land, the defendant's argument might have been tenable, but they amount to a positive covenant to pay the money at a specified time.

ROLFE, B., concurred.

[1] The statement of the declaration has been abbreviated. — ED.

[2] 3 Bing. N. C. 368.

[3] 1 Saund. 320 *a*, n. 4.

[4] 10 A. & E. 50.

PLATT, B. The condition has occurred upon which the money became payable. There is no other condition precedent.

Judgment for the plaintiff.

TARRABOCHIA v. HICKIE.

IN THE EXCHEQUER, MAY 30, 1856.

[*Reported in* 1 *Hurlstone & Norman*, 183.]

THE declaration stated, that the plaintiff and defendant agreed by charter-party that the plaintiff's ship, called the Dominica, then lying at Fiume, being tight, staunch, and strong, and every way fitted for the voyage, should with all convenient speed sail and proceed to Cardiff, and there load from the factors of the defendants a full and complete cargo of coals in the customary manner, to be loaded in twenty days from the day on which the vessel was ready to load, which the defendants bound themselves to ship, and being so loaded should therewith proceed to Malta, Corfu, Smyrna, Athens, Alexandria, Constantinople, or Gallipoli, as ordered on signing bills of lading, or as near thereunto as she might safely get, and there deliver the same into craft alongside steamer or depot ship there, as might be directed by the consignee, being paid freight on the quantity delivered at the rate of 42*s*. 6*d*. per ton of twenty hundred-weight delivered, &c., and being in full of all port charges and pilotages (the act of God, the Queen's enemies, fire, and all and every other dangers and accidents of the seas, rivers, and navigation of whatever nature or kind soever during the said voyage always excepted), the freight to be paid on the right and true delivery of the cargo in cash at the current rate of exchange, &c. Averment: that the plaintiff did all things necessary on his part to entitle him to have the agreed cargo loaded on board the said ship at Cardiff, and that the time for so doing has elapsed. Breach, that the defendants made default in loading the agreed cargo.

Pleas. First, that the plaintiff's ship was not tight, staunch, or strong, or fitted for the voyage in the charter-party in that behalf mentioned, as she was required to be by the said charter-party, insomuch that by reason thereof the object of the said charter-party, and of the voyage therein mentioned, was wholly frustrated, and the defendants were prevented from deriving, and did not derive any benefit therefrom. Secondly, that the said ship did not with convenient speed, or in a reasonable time in that behalf, sail or proceed to Cardiff as required by the said charter-party, insomuch that by reason thereof the object of the said charter-party, and of the voyage therein mentioned, was wholly frustrated, and the defendants were prevented from deriving, and did not derive any benefit therefrom.

Replication. The plaintiff joins issue upon both the defendant's pleas.

At the trial before CRESSWELL, J., at the last Gloucester Assizes, it appeared that the charter-party was entered into on the 22d April, 1854. On the 29th of the same month, the vessel not being then ready to sail, an accident occurred while tightening the rigging, which rendered it necessary to have a new topmast, and the sailing of the vessel was in consequence delayed. On the 15th of May the vessel, being then about to sail, fouled her cable, whereby she was delayed until the 19th. On that day she sailed from Fiume; and, on the 20th, was compelled by stress of weather to enter the harbor of Sossino. She remained there until the 26th, when she proceeded on her voyage; and on the 16th of August arrived at Cardiff. The defendant then refused to load.

The learned judge left it to the jury to say whether the vessel was tight, staunch, and strong when she sailed from Fiume; and if not, whether the object of the voyage was thereby frustrated; also, whether the vessel sailed and proceeded to Cardiff with convenient speed or in a reasonable time; and if not, whether the object of the voyage was thereby frustrated. The jury found that the vessel was not tight, staunch, or strong when she sailed from Fiume, but that she was so when she arrived at Cardiff; and that the object of the voyage was not thereby frustrated. The jury also found that the vessel did not with all convenient speed, or in a reasonable time, sail and proceed to Cardiff, but that the object of the voyage was not thereby frustrated. A verdict was then entered for the defendant, leave being reserved to the plaintiff to move to enter a verdict for him.

Keating, in the following term, obtained a rule *nisi* accordingly, against which

Whately and *Huddleston* now shewed cause. The stipulations in the charter-party that the vessel, being tight, staunch and strong, shall sail with convenient speed and within a reasonable time, are conditions precedent to the plaintiff's right to enforce the contract. In Glaholm *v.* Hays [1] the charter-party provided that the vessel should proceed to Trieste, and there load a full cargo, "the vessel to sail from England on or before the 4th of February next;" and that was held to be a condition precedent on the part of the owner, upon the non-compliance wherewith the freighters were at liberty to throw up the charter. Tindal, C. J., in delivering the judgment of the court, said, "The very words themselves 'to sail' on or before a given day, do by common usage import the same as the words 'conditioned to sail,' or 'warranted to sail on or before such a day.'" So in Ollive *v.* Booker,[2] where the

[1] 2 Man. & G. 257. [2] 1 Exch: 416.

vessel was described in the charter-party as "now at sea, having sailed three weeks ago," that was held to amount to a warranty. In like manner the statement that the vessel is tight, staunch, and strong, is a warranty that she fulfils that description. In Oliver *v.* Fielden[1] the stipulation was that the vessel should be "ready to receive cargo in all May," and that was held a condition precedent. Cranston *v.* Marshall[2] is also an authority that a statement as to the time at which a vessel will sail is not a mere representation, but a warranty In Clipsham *v.* Vertue[3] there was no stipulation that the vessel should proceed in any particular time; and where no time is specified, the law implies a reasonable time. [They also referred to Ellen *v.* Topp.[4]]

Keating and *Phipson* appeared in support of the rule, but were not called upon to argue.

POLLOCK, C. B. The rule must be absolute. The first plea alleges that the vessel was not tight, staunch, or strong, and that by "reason thereof the object of the charter-party and of the voyage was wholly frustrated." The latter is a material allegation, and the jury have found it in the negative. The question then is, whether the fact of the vessel not being tight, staunch, or strong, is a condition precedent to the performance by the defendant of his contract. I think not. In like manner, it is not a condition precedent that the vessel should sail with convenient speed or in a reasonable time. Where, indeed, the charter-party provides that the vessel shall sail on a particular day, that is a condition precedent. The distinction is obvious: where a particular day is named it is evidently the intention of the parties that the vessel shall sail on that day; and if the ship-owner refuses to do so the merchant may decline to load, for the voyage is thereby altered, and the success of the adventure may depend on the vessel sailing on the day named. In Abbott on Shipping, part 4, c. 1, s. 5, it is said, "whether or not a particular covenant by one party be a condition precedent, the breach of which will dispense with the performance of the contract by the other, or an independent covenant, is a question to be determined according to the fair intention of the parties, to be collected from the language employed by them. An intention to make any particular stipulation a condition precedent should be clearly and unambiguously expressed." There can be no doubt about a particular day; but what is a "convenient speed" or a "reasonable time" must always be a subject of contention. We may therefore fairly say, that where a particular day is named the time is unambiguously expressed, but where the terms are so lax and ambiguous as to lead to a difference of opinion, then the stipulation is not a condition precedent. The general rule laid down by Lord Ellenborough in Davidson *v.* Gwynne[5] is, "that

[1] 4 Exch. 135.
[2] 5 Exch. 395.
[3] 5 Q. B. 265.
[4] 6 Exch. 424.
[5] 12 East, 381.

unless the non-performance alleged in breach of the contract goes to the whole root and consideration of it, the covenant broken is not to be considered as a condition precedent, but as a distinct covenant, for the breach of which the party injured may be compensated in damages." Applying that rule to this case, the jury have negatived an allegation which is the substance of each plea; consequently the pleas were not proved, and the rule must be absolute.

MARTIN, B. I am of the same opinion. The jury having negatived the allegation that "the object of the charter-party and of the voyage therein mentioned was wholly frustrated," that part of the pleas must be considered as struck out, and then all that remains is that the ship was not tight, staunch, or strong, or fitted for the voyage, and that the ship did not sail with convenient speed or in a reasonable time, which are mere traverses of those averments in the declaration. For at least twenty years, it has been considered that traverses of such averments are bad in law, as raising immaterial issues; and for the reasons stated by the Lord Chief Baron it is clear that if the latter allegation in the pleas was struck out, they would be bad on demurrer, and that the plaintiff would be entitled to the verdict though the jury found them against him. In the case of Hall v. Cazenove [1] the charter-party contained a covenant that the ship should sail on or before the 12th February, and LeBlanc, J., said, "If the defendant sustained any damage by reason of the ship's not having sailed on the particular day, he may recover it by bringing his action on the covenant; but at any rate, the objection does not go to the plaintiff's right of action on the ground of a condition precedent." But however that may be, my judgment is founded on this, that the terms used in this charter-party do not amount to a condition precedent.

BRAMWELL, B. I am of the same opinion. No doubt it is competent for the parties, if they think fit, to declare in express terms that any matter shall be a condition precedent, but when they have not so expressed themselves, it is necessary for those who construe the instrument to see whether they intended to do it. Since, however, they could have done it, those who construe the instrument should be chary in doing for them that which they might, but have not done for themselves. If the contract is to load at a particular port, the very language compels us to construe that as a condition precedent. So in the case of Glaholm v. Hays,[2] where the agreement was that the vessel should sail on a particular day. In the present case the only thing which made me doubt was an expression of Maule, J., in Glaholm v. Hays (which is a dictum rather than an authority.) He says in the course of the argument, "It will be said that if the sailing on the 4th February is a condition precedent in this case, the sailing within a reasonable time

[1] 4 East, 477. [2] 2 Man. & G. 257.

would also have been held to be a condition precedent. There is a difficulty in saying that one is to be a condition precedent and not the other." But the case of Freeman v. Taylor[1] is an express authority that the sailing within a reasonable time is not a condition precedent. *Rule absolute.*

PHILLIPS AND OTHERS v. CLIFT.

IN THE EXCHEQUER, JANUARY 24, 1859.

[*Reported in 28 Law Journal Reports, Exchequer,* 153.]

DECLARATION that, by an indenture of apprenticeship, dated the 28th of October, 1854, to which the plaintiffs and defendant and William Henry Ryde were parties, the said W. H. Ryde put himself apprentice to the defendant for the space of four and a half years; that the defendant, in consideration of £99 19*s.* to be paid to him by the plaintiffs, covenanted to and with Sarah Ryde, the mother of W. H. Ryde, and by a separate covenant with the plaintiffs that he, the defendant, his said apprentice in the art of a chemist and druggist, which he then carried on, by the best means that he could, should teach and instruct during the said term, and would during the said term, at his own charges, provide for the said W. H. Ryde proper and sufficient meat, drink, and lodging. Averment, that the said W. H. Ryde entered and the defendant received him into his service, and general performance of conditions precedent. Breach, that the defendant would not teach and instruct, &c., nor provide for the said W. H. Ryde proper and sufficient meat, drink, and lodging, and dismissed and discharged him from his service, and would no longer permit him to remain therein.

Plea. That after the making of the indenture, and after the said apprentice entered into the service of the defendant, the said apprentice did not, according to the covenants of the said indenture, faithfully serve the defendant, or behave himself towards the defendant as a faithful apprentice; but, on the contrary thereof, conducted himself in so improper and unfaithful and dishonest a manner in the defendant's said business, and defrauded and robbed the defendant, so that it became unsafe for the defendant to continue the said apprentice in his said business, or to permit him to reside or remain with him, the defendant; whereupon, as he lawfully might, he dismissed the said apprentice from his service, and refused any longer to permit him to remain therein, or to instruct him in his said business, or to provide any longer for the said apprentice meat, drink, and lodging.

[1] 8 Bing. 124.

Demurrer and joinder in demurrer.

Vernon Harcourt, in support of the plea. Winstone v. Linn[1] will no doubt be relied on by the plaintiffs. That is an authority to shew that slight misconduct of an apprentice affords no ground of justification for a dismissal. But the question here is, whether when his conduct is such that it becomes unsafe for the master to continue him in his service, the master may not dismiss his apprentice. In Wise v. Wilson,[2] Lord Denman, C. J., in summing up the case to the jury says: "If you think that from the conduct of the plaintiff's son real danger was occasioned to his master's business, you ought to find your verdict for the defendant, as the defendant was then in my opinion justified in dismissing him." There are provisions in several acts of parliament providing for the cancelling of indentures of apprenticeship in a summary manner before magistrates, but such provisions are confined to cases where the premium is under £50, so that the defendant is unable to avail himself of such remedy. Very serious injury might be done to the defendant's business, if he were bound under all circumstances to keep an apprentice in his service. Suppose an apprentice, having robbed his master, is convicted and sentenced to penal servitude, is the master bound to receive him back at the expiration of the sentence? [POLLOCK, C. B. The plea does not allege that the apprentice has been found guilty of felony. MARTIN, B. The judgment of Bayley, J., and Holroyd, J., in Winstone v. Linn, is against you.] In that case the action was in covenant; here there is no averment that the contract is under seal. Mercer v. Whall[3] is in favor of the defendant. [MARTIN, B. That was the case of a clerk. CHANNELL, B. There is this peculiarity in the case of an apprentice, that the father or mother would be liable, on their covenant, to recoup the master for any loss that he might sustain through the misconduct of his apprentice.] The covenants in a deed of this nature have been held not to be independent covenants. Ellen v. Topp,[4] Pordage v. Cole,[5] Cutter v. Powell,[6] Atkinson v. Smith.[7]

Garth, in support of the demurrer, was not heard.

POLLOCK, C. B. I think that this is a bad plea, and that the plaintiffs are entitled to our judgment. I give no opinion as to what would be the effect of a plea containing an allegation that the apprentice had feloniously stolen the property of his master, or had been found guilty of a felonious stealing, and had suffered punishment. This plea contains neither one nor other of these allegations. The authorities shew that

[1] 1 B. & C. 460. [2] 1 Car. & K. 662.
[3] 5 Q. B. Rep. 447; s. c. 14 Law J. Rep. (N. S.) Q. B. 267.
[4] 6 Exch. Rep. 424; s. c. 20 Law J. Rep. (N. S.) Exch. 241.
[5] 1 Saund. 320.
[6] 2 Smith's Lead. Cas. 14, in notes.
[7] 14 Mee. & W. 695; s. c. 15 Law J. Rep. (N. S.) Exch. 59.

this plea affords no answer to the declaration, and our judgment must be for the plaintiffs.

MARTIN, B. I am clearly of the same opinion. I give my judgment upon no abstract reasoning, but on the true construction of this indenture. If persons enter into improvident bargains, they must put up with them; and if a person puts his hand and seal to a deed, he must abide by it, and he cannot seek to be released from it because it afterwards turns out that the covenant is to his disadvantage, and is a burden to him. Indenture means a deed; it is so laid down in Sheppard's Touchstone, 50. All deeds are indented or polled; an indenture is therefore necessarily a deed. What, then, is this covenant? The mother and other parties covenant that the apprentice should serve the defendant for four and a half years, obey his lawful commands, and do him no damage; and the defendant, in consideration of £99 19*s.* to be paid to him by the plaintiffs, covenants to teach and instruct the apprentice in the art of a chemist, and at his own proper charges to supply him with meat, drink, and lodging. The defendant, therefore, has absolutely covenanted to do these things, and he must do them.

WATSON, B. I am entirely of the same opinion. It has long been considered that the covenants in an indenture of apprenticeship are independent covenants, and there are several authorities in the books to support that proposition. There is no analogy between the cases of master and servant and master and apprentice. In the former, the servant is bound to obey the lawful commands of his master, and if he misbehaves, the master may dismiss him. In the latter, if the apprentice misbehaves, the master may correct him, and it is laid down in the books to what extent he may go in punishing him. The plea here states that the apprentice robbed the defendant; this might be some trivial offence, for which, if the apprentice had been well whipped, he would never have done it again. Here, for aught that appears, there is only a misconduct on the part of the apprentice, for which he can be punished by his master.

CHANNELL, B. I am also of opinion that our judgment ought to be for the plaintiffs. I am unable to distinguish this case from Winstone *v.* Linn. The argument that has been addressed to us is founded on the *nisi prius* case of Wise *v.* Wilson, which Lord Denman treated as something between an apprenticeship and service; but this case presents no mixed character. With all deference to Lord Denman's opinion, I doubt whether he was correct in his ruling; and it is to be observed that the plaintiff obtained the verdict, and there was therefore no mode of bringing that ruling before the court above. It is, however, sufficient to say that this case, in principle, does not differ from Winstone *v.* Linn.

Judgment for the plaintiffs.

CHRISTIE *v.* BORELLY.

In the Common Pleas, January 17, 1860.

[*Reported in* 29 *Law Journal Reports, Common Pleas,* 153.]

The first count of the declaration stated that, in consideration that the plaintiff guaranteed to the defendant that two bills of exchange of £100 and £62, both drawn by Messrs. C. W. Olivier & Co. upon Messrs. Owen & Co., 75 Lower Thames Street, and both due on the 23d of January, 1859, would be paid and retired by the said Messrs. Owen & Co. when due, the defendant in return engaged and guaranteed to the plaintiff the repayment of the sum of £300 towards the payment of Scotch whiskeys, as follows: 6 puncheons, 5 hhds., 4 qr. casks, Auchtertool, 2 puncheons, 5 hhds., 8 qr. casks, Anderton, which Mr. B. Fisse, of Norris Street, had ordered, and was about to receive from the plaintiff. Averment, by the plaintiff, that he had performed all things on his part to be done and performed, in pursuance of the said agreement, to entitle him to the due performance by the defendant of his the defendant's part of the said agreement; and that the said two bills of exchange of £100 and £62 were duly paid and retired by the said Messrs. Owen & Co. when the same became and were due and payable; and that he the plaintiff delivered to the said Mr. B. Fisse the said Scotch whiskeys in the said agreement hereinbefore mentioned, and that the said Mr. B. Fisse, although requested to pay the said amount of £300 towards the payment of the said Scotch whiskeys, had not paid for the said Scotch whiskeys, nor the said sum of £300 or any part thereof, and the same still remained wholly due and unpaid; yet that the defendant had disregarded and broken his said promise in this, that he had not paid, or caused to be paid, to the plaintiff the said sum of £300 or any part thereof, but, on the contrary thereof, wholly neglected and refused so to do.

The defendant pleaded (*inter alia*) secondly, to the said first count, that, although the said debt and sum of £300 in the said first count mentioned, repayment whereof the defendant engaged and guaranteed to the plaintiff, was not payable, and, by the terms of the said order of the said Mr. B. Fisse, was not payable until after the said two bills drawn by Messrs. C. W. Olivier upon Messrs. Owen & Co., and guaranteed by the plaintiff, became due and payable, as the plaintiff and the defendant, at the time of the making of the said mutual agreement and guarantees, well knew; yet the said two bills of exchange of £100 and £62, in the said first count mentioned, were not duly or at any time paid or retired by the said Messrs. Owen, of which the plaintiff had due notice, but never at any time paid or retired the said bills. Issue thereon.

The defendant having, at the trial, obtained a verdict in his favor on the issue taken on the second plea, the court, in Michaelmas Term last, on the application of *Edward James*, granted a rule *nisi* to enter judgment for the plaintiff on such issue *non obstante veredicto*, on the ground that the said second plea was no answer to the action. Against this rule,

Petersdorff, Serjt., and *Garth* now shewed cause.

The performance of the defendant's engagement was to be after that which was the consideration for it, that is to say, after the bills which the plaintiff guaranteed became due, and, therefore, it is submitted that the performance by the plaintiff of his part of the contract was a condition precedent to his right to sue the defendant. The court, in all such cases as these, will always endeavor to ascertain from the terms of the contract the intention of the parties. Tindal, C. J., in Stavers *v.* Curling,[1] says, "The rule has been established by a long series of decisions in modern times, that the question whether covenants are to be held dependent or independent of each other is to be determined by the intention and meaning of the parties as it appears on the instrument, and by the application of common sense to each particular case." In Johnstone *v.* Nichols[2] the question was as to the sufficiency of the consideration to support the promise laid in the declaration. The promise was stated thus: namely, that in consideration the plaintiffs would continue certain dealings which they had had with Messrs. Claridge & Co., the defendant promised the plaintiffs to be responsible and guarantee them the payment of any sums of money in which Messrs. Claridge & Co. then were, or at any time thereafter might be, indebted to the plaintiffs in the course of such dealings; and Maule, J., (page 156) said, "These words, in fact, amount to this, that in consideration the plaintiffs would do something *in futuro*, the defendant promised to do something *in futuro* likewise." So here, looking at this agreement as it appears on the record, it means, if the plaintiff will pay the two bills drawn on Owen & Co., in case they are not duly honored, the defendant will pay the £300 in case the whiskeys are not paid for by Fisse. The averment in the declaration of performance by the plaintiff of all things on his part to be performed, in pursuance of the agreement, to entitle him to be paid the £300, shews that the plaintiff considered it to be a condition precedent to the defendant's liability. Inasmuch as the £300 could not be payable until after the bills on Owen & Co. were due, the case falls within the second rule laid down in the notes to Pordage *v.* Cole[3] for ascertaining

[1] 3 Scott, 754 ; S. C. 6 Law J. Rep. (N. S.) C. P. 41.

[2] 14 Law J. Rep. (N. S.) C. P. 151; S. C. 1 Com. B. Rep. 251.

[3] 1 Wms. Saund. 320 *b*.

what amounts to a condition precedent, where it is stated that "when a day is appointed for the payment of money, &c., and the day is to happen after the thing which is the consideration of the money, &c., is to be performed, no action can be maintained for the money, &c., before performance." To the same effect is the second resolution in Thorpe v. Thorpe.[1] [WILLES, J. In Thomas v. Cadwallader,[2] where there was a covenant by a lessee to repair, the lessor allowing and assigning timber for the repairs, it was held to be a condition precedent that the lessor should find and assign timber, but that was explained by Willes, C. J., to be because the one covenant related to the other, and the lessee could not repair until the timber was assigned him for such repairs; but, "when two covenants in a deed have no relation to each other, I was clearly of opinion," said Willes, C. J., "that the non-performance of the one could not be pleaded in bar to an action brought for the breach of another covenant in the same deed; and for this plain reason amongst others, that the damages sustained by the breach of one such covenant may not be at all adequate to the damages sustained by the breach of the other."] Here the plaintiff's engagement is the sole consideration for the defendant's promise, and there is an entire failure of performance by the plaintiff. Franklin v. Miller[3] shews the distinction between a partial and total failure of performance.

Grant, in support of the rule. The law is not disputed. The courts have ever since the case of Thomas v. Cadwallader endeavored to ascertain the object of the parties by looking at the contract itself. The apparent intention of the parties is the governing rule for the construction of the covenants. Glazebrook v. Woodrow.[4] (He was then stopped by the court.)

ERLE, C. J. I am of opinion that this rule should be made absolute; and that the plaintiff is entitled to have judgment entered for him *non obstante veredicto*. The real question is, whether the promises are independent promises, or whether they are mutual promises, their performance being mutually the consideration for each other. It appears to me that they are independent promises. The defendant guarantees the repayment of £300 towards the payment of certain whiskey being paid for when due; and the plaintiff guarantees that two bills of exchange of £100 and £62 shall be paid when due. It, therefore, appears that the damages in respect of the breach on one side must be very different from the damages arising from the breach on the other side; on the one side they would be £300, and on the other only £162; it is consequently apparent, on the face of the contract itself, that it was not intended by the parties that performance of the one stipulation should be a condition precedent to performance of the other. The

[1] 1 Salk. 171.
[2] Willes, 496.
[3] 4 Ad. & E. 599.
[4] 8 Term. Rep. 372.

question is, to my mind, one entirely of fact, namely, what was the intention of the parties to this contract? The rules of law are agreed on by both sides, and it is only a question of construction. On the construction of this contract, I am of opinion that the performance of the plaintiff's promise was not a condition precedent; and, therefore, that the second plea is no answer, and consequently that the rule ought to be made absolute.

WILLIAMS, J. The rules of law are now well established, and the object is to discover in each case what is the intention of the parties. If it had appeared from the contract in the present case, that the undertaking of the plaintiff had been to pay absolutely when the bills became due, the case would have been a very different one from what it is. What, however, the plaintiff undertakes is, only to pay if Messrs. Owen do not retire the bills; therefore, the compensation to be paid by the plaintiff, in consequence of such third party not doing their duty, is a matter which must have to be afterwards ascertained; and is it likely that it was the intention of the parties to this contract that the defendant's performance was not to take place until after such amount of compensation had been ascertained? It is, I think, obvious that such could not have been the intention of the parties; for Messrs. Owen might have retired the bills when due, and so there would have been nothing at all payable by the plaintiff.

WILLES, J. I am of the same opinion. It appears to me that the promise only on the one side is the consideration for the promise on the other side; and that the plea is, therefore, a bad plea.

Rule absolute.

SEEGER v. DUTHIE AND OTHERS.

IN THE COMMON PLEAS, MAY 1, 1860.

[*Reported in* 29 *Law Journal Reports, Common Pleas,* 253.]

IN THE EXCHEQUER CHAMBER, NOVEMBER 30, 1860.

[*Reported in* 30 *Law Journal Reports, Common Pleas,* 65.]

DECLARATION for freight for the conveyance by the plaintiff for the defendants, at their request, of goods in ships; and for the demurrage of a ship of the plaintiff kept on demurrage by the defendants; and for the defendant's use, by the plaintiff's permission, of ships of the plaintiff; and for the hire of ships by the plaintiff let to hire to the defendants; and for money agreed to be paid by the defendants to the plaintiff for the privilege of putting certain goods on board a ship of the plaintiff, to be conveyed to their destination, and which goods were shipped accordingly; and for a gratuity agreed by the defendants to be paid to the plaintiff, as master of a certain ship under a charter-party of such ship made between the plaintiff and the defendants; and for money paid, and on accounts stated.

Pleas: Never indebted; payment; set-off for goods sold and delivered, work and materials, money lent, money paid, and money agreed by the plaintiff to be paid by him to the defendants by way of demurrage for default in readiness of the said ship under the said charter-party, for interest, and on accounts stated. Issues thereon.

The particulars of set-off claimed various sums paid on ship's account, and also £330 received by the plaintiff, £168 for twenty-four days' demurrage, at £7 per day, as per charter-party, and various sums, amounting in the whole to £21 2*s.*, paid to shippers for delay and expenses, and to surveyors.

The cause was tried before the Lord Chief Justice and a special jury, at the sittings for London after last Michaelmas Term, when the claim of the plaintiff was confined to the £600, less discount, for freight payable in London, and the gratuity of £26 5*s.*, and credit was given for £330 admittedly paid; and in the course of the trial various payments on ship's account were proved or admitted, further reducing the plaintiff's claim to £188 19*s.* 10*d.* The following facts appeared in evidence.

The plaintiff was captain and part-owner of the Von Laffert Lehsen, chartered by the defendants to proceed to Geelong, in Australia, on the terms set out in the following memorandum of agreement, signed by both parties, but not under seal: Memorandum of agreement between Capt. William Seeger, captain of the good ship or vessel called the Von Laffert Lehsen, now in London, and Mr. William Duthie, and Adamson & Ronaldson, of London. Undertake that the said ship, being now tight, staunch and strong, and every way fitted for the voyage, shall load in the London Docks, in the river Thames, and there receive and take on board all such lawful goods as may be required by the said charterers; and being so loaded, shall therewith proceed to Geelong wharf, to be lightered over the bar at the charterers' expense, the ship being free from any charge for lighterage, and there deliver the said cargo agreeably to the bills of lading, which are to stipulate the cargo to be taken from alongside at the expense and risk of the consignees of the same (the act of God, the Queen's enemies, fire, and all and every other dangers and accidents of the seas, rivers, and navigation, of whatever nature and kind soever during the said voyage, always excepted); the captain to attend daily at the broker's office to sign bills of lading, as customary, and at any rate of freight, without prejudice to this charter. The whole of the ship to be at the disposal of the charterers for the conveyance of goods and specie, excepting cabin and such room as is requisite for officers and crew; and stores requisite for the voyage (not to exceed thirty tons in the whole, including lazarettes and coal-holes) are to be carried on deck, the master being guaranteed against the dangers and accidents of the seas. If gunpowder be shipped, the same is to be taken on board where ordered, below Blackwall, as customary. The captain to cause the cargo to be stowed in the best manner, and to take the measurements and other particulars as if for the owner's benefit, and a sufficient number of men to be engaged by him for that purpose; the stevedore employed to be approved of by the charterers. In consideration whereof the charterers agree to pay freight for the use and hire of the said ship the sum of £1400 sterling, with a gratuity of twenty-five guineas to the master, payable before leaving London. The ship to be consigned to the charterers' agents at the port of discharge (whom the owners hereby accept and appoint as agents), paying the usual commission, not exceeding £2 10s. per cent. on amount payable abroad, the vessel being subject to the usual and ordinary custom-house and publishing charges of a vessel loading outward, not exceeding £10. No goods are to be received on board without the permission of the charterers. In case of general average, the owners agree that the same shall be settled according to the custom at Lloyd's. The freight to be paid as follows: So much as may be payable in the colony by bills of lading, to the extent of £800, to be taken and received in part-payment, and balance, say £600, in cash, less seventy days' discount from date of clearing from London. Forty running days are to be allowed the said charterers, Sundays and holidays excepted (if the ship be not sooner despatched) for loading the said ship, to commence from the date of her being ready at her loading-berth to receive cargo. The owner further agrees that the ship shall be ready to sail for her destined port at the expiration of the said laying days, or sooner if required by the charterers. If the ship be not ready, either on the owners' or charterers' part, at the above-named dates, then demurrage to be paid by the party in default at the rate of £7 *per diem*. The ship to be ready on or before the 10th of November, or the charterers to have the option of cancelling this agreement; should government stores offer, the captain or owner to sign the usual tender, if required by the charterers. It is also agreed that the charterers' liability herein shall cease as soon as all the cargo is on board, except as to so much of the freight as is payable in London as above after the vessel's final sailing. Penalty for non-performance of this ageeement, £1400. Should the bills of lading not represent £800, payable in Geelong, to cover the balance due, the difference to be paid in cash before sailing from London.

(Signed,) WILLIAM SEEGER.
WILLIAM DUTHIE.
ADAMSON & RONALDSON.

The charterers to have the option of shipping acids on deck, to the extent of five tons' measurement, at shipper's risk, to which effect a clause to be inserted in the bill of lading.

On the 5th of November, 1857, the ship was ready to receive cargo at her berth in the London docks, and the plaintiff gave notice thereof to the defendants, and that the laying days would commence next day. Thereupon the loading of the ship began. The plaintiff, who was and continued to be captain of the ship, attended several times at the broker's office to sign bills of lading, as customary; but did not attend there daily, and was some time absent on the Continent. Amongst the lawful goods which the defendants required the plaintiff to load were a number of cases of lucifer-matches. These goods were brought alongside the ship on the 18th of December, and tendered for loading; but the plaintiff refused to receive them on board with acids, and they were therefore conveyed by the carman back to the warehouse. The defendants remonstrated, by letter, with the plaintiff on this subject, and next day these goods were again sent alongside and tendered for loading, and again refused by the plaintiff and conveyed back to the warehouse; some correspondence followed, and in the end the plaintiff allowed these goods to be loaded. With the exception of a ton and a half of acids, which the defendants had notified their option to have shipped on the deck, and three tons of gunpowder shipped below Blackwall, according to the charter-party, all the cargo was loaded by the 24th of December; and the ship was cleared at the custom-house on the 26th of December. The plaintiff refused to receive the acids and gunpowder, alleging that the ship could not safely stow and carry more cargo than was already on board, and gave notice to the defendants that the ship was ready to proceed to sea as soon as the ship's papers were handed to the plaintiff by the defendants. A correspondence ensued, during which the plaintiff called on the defendants, and demanded the ship's papers for the purpose of sailing on his voyage. The defendants refused to give the papers till the plaintiff took the acids and gunpowder, and said that the ship should not go till the acids and gunpowder were taken in. The ship was surveyed on behalf of the plaintiff and the defendants respectively; and on the 6th of January, 1858, in consequence of the surveyors previously employed having disagreed, Lloyd's surveyor was instructed to survey the ship, for the purpose of ascertaining whether she was sufficiently laden. The surveyor on that day certified that the ship would safely stow and carry ten tons more cargo; and thereupon the plaintiff signified his readiness to load the acids and gunpowder, and received on board and signed bills of lading for the acids, and afterwards the gunpowder, and then sailed with the ship, on the 14th of January, on her voyage to Geelong; and during that voyage this action was commenced. It was admitted by the defendants that the refusal of the captain to receive the acids and gunpowder was made *bona fide*. The defendants paid to different shippers of goods by the said ship on the said voyage, sums amounting in all to £16 18*s*., for demurrage and expenses in respect of the said delays in loading, and also paid to marine surveyors £4 4*s*. for surveys and reports incidental to the plaintiff's refusals to receive goods on board.

For the defendants, it was contended that the plaintiff was not entitled to recover on the charter-party, in respect of the money payable in London, because he had not performed the stipulations which, according to the charter-party, were previously to be performed on his part; nor on any implied contract, because such contract would enure to the owners, of whom he was only one; nor in *indebitatus assumpsit*, because the condition was not executed, and the express contract was still open and unperformed; that if he was entitled to recover in *indebitatus assumpsit*, it could only be on a *quantum meruit*, following the scale of remuneration stipulated for, with suitable deductions for the failure of performance of stipulations on the plaintiff's part; and that the defendants were entitled to set-off £168 for twenty-four days' demurrage, the laying days having expired on the 23d of December, 1857, and the ship not having sailed till the 14th of January, owing to the plaintiff's default.

All these points were reserved by the Lord Chief Justice for the opinion of the court; and under his lordship's direction, a verdict was found for the plaintiff for £188 19*s*. 10*d*., subject to leave reserved for the defendants to move to enter the verdict for them, or to reduce the damages; the court to have power to make all necessary amendments in the pleadings.

Grove (Jan. 16) moved[1] for a new trial, or to enter the verdict for the defendants, pursuant to the leave reserved, or to reduce the damages. The contract contained in the charter-party is special, and the consideration entire, and at the time of action brought it was not executed; and therefore no one can sue upon it in *indebitatus assumpsit*, treating it as an executed contract. If the declaration had been upon the special contract, the plaintiff must have averred the performance of all the conditions precedent, and the defendants could have succeeded on a traverse of that allegation. [WILLIAMS, J. I do not appreciate that argument. *Indebitatus assumpsit* is founded on a promise implied by law, and lies where nothing remains to be done but to pay. Where any thing else remains to be done, the law implies no promise to pay; and *indebitatus assumpsit* does not lie where conditions precedent remain to be performed. How then can the form of the declaration prejudice the defendants, if they could have pleaded to a declaration on the special contract the non-performance of conditions precedent?] Secondly, if *indebitatus assumpsit* lies, all the part-owners on whose behalf the contract was made ought to have sued, and

1 *Coram* Erle, C. J., Williams, J., and Willes, J.

not one only, the captain. Thirdly, the same objection lies to the plaintiff's recovering the gratuity of twenty-five guineas as to his recovering the freight. The action was commenced too soon, before the vessel had completed her voyage and earned the freight, and the consideration is entire and indivisible. Fourthly, the defendants are entitled to set off £7 a day for demurrage during the time the vessel was detained by the captain's default in refusing to take the matches and acids on board; Fletcher *v.* Dyche[1] and Valente *v.* Gibbs.[2] The defendants are also entitled to set off other expenses incurred by the employment of the surveyors and having to warehouse the goods, by reason of the captain's default in not performing his contract in not taking the acids, &c., on board. [ERLE, C. J. Any claim the defendants may have for unliquidated damages cannot be the subject of a set-off against a stipulated sum due.] The plaintiff has not performed his contract to entitle him to recover the full amount of his claim, and the defendants ought to be allowed to avail themselves, either by way of set-off or deduction, of all the damage and expenses incurred by reason of the plaintiff's delay; Turner *v.* Diaper.[3]

ERLE, C. J. We are of opinion that the defendants are entitled to a rule thus far, viz., as respects their claim for demurrage at the rate of £7 per day during which the captain delayed the loading of the ship, and, as the defendants contend, wrongly and in default of his contract under the charter-party; that the defendants are entitled to a rule to avail themselves of that claim, either as matter of set-off, if it is properly available in that way, or to defeat the plaintiff's claim altogether, in case it should turn out upon discussion that the loading of the ship according to the contract was a condition precedent to the right of the plaintiff under the contract to the £600 and the £25 gratuity, which sums by the contract were payable in London upon, at, or before the sailing of the ship.

We are of opinion that there ought to be no rule on the ground that the form of action is *indebitatus assumpsit*, because we are of opinion that if there was no failure of that condition precedent, but a contract to pay a specific sum of £600 on a given event, and £25 on a given event, when that event happened the money was payable on request, and *indebitatus assumpsit* will lie. We, therefore, think that if the defendants fail in making out the ground above mentioned, the action in this form is sustainable.

We are further of opinion that there ought to be no rule in respect of the action being brought by the plaintiff alone. The contract is made with the plaintiff in his own name, and with him, apparently, as the contracting party; and though it turns out that he made the contract for himself and other part-owners as well, and was acting partly

[1] 2 Term Rep. 32.

[2] 6 Com. B. Rep. N. S. 207; S. C. 28 Law J. Rep. (N. S.) C. P. 229.

[3] 2 Man. & G. 241.

as agent in the matter, yet the contract is one in which he had himself a personal interest, and was a contracting party. We think, therefore, if nothing remained to be done but payment of the money on the defendants' part, and every thing was done on the plaintiff's part to entitle him to the £625 under the contract, that he has a right to sue for it, and a right to sue in *indebitatus assumpsit.*

With respect to the claim of the defendants to set off the damages that fell upon them by reason of part of the cargo being prepared to be loaded on board and the captain's wrongful refusal to put it on board, thereby causing them to incur expense in warehousing the cargo, and also with respect to their claim for the money paid to the surveyors who were called in, by reason of the captain's refusal to load, to decide whether it was his duty to do so, we are of opinion that the defendants cannot avail themselves of either of those sums, either by way of set-off or deduction. They are not matter of set-off, because there is no contract or debt, they are only incidental damages, and whether the defendants could sustain any claim for the money paid to the surveyor, is doubtful; and with respect to the other sums incurred they are unliquidated damages, and not in the nature of a debt, and are not the subject of a set-off. Nor are they matter for deduction, as falling within the principle of those cases in which it has been held that a defendant can avail himself, in reduction of damages, of the failure on the plaintiff's part to perform his contract. Where there is a contract (say by a builder) to do work for £40, and he does only £35 worth, leaving the other £5 worth unperformed; if the party with whom the contract is made accepts that work he is bound to pay what it is reasonably worth. *Ex hypothesi* it is reasonably worth £35 and no more, and the builder who sues in *indebitatus assumpsit* cannot claim £40 as due to him upon the supposition that he has performed his contract, bcause, *ex hypothesi*, he left £5 worth unperformed; but that £5 is not a deduction from £40 due according to the terms of the contract, for the builder, failing to prove himself entitled to the full contract price, resorts to the implied contract to pay what the work is reasonably worth, that is, £35 and no more. The damages in question do not appear to me to fall within that principle, because the contract is to pay the £600 and the £25 on a given event, the sailing of the ship. The ship has sailed, and therefore the contract is entirely performed, subject to the reservation before given in respect of the captain's delay.

Grove. As to the gratuity of £25 to the captain there is another point, viz., that his misconduct disentitles him to it.

WILLES, J. It is clear the defendants can make nothing of that point, except by a cross-action. It was established in the year 1815, and if not much earlier, at least in that year, in the case of Shields *v.* Davis,[1] that the negligence of the master does not prevent his recovering money agreed to be paid, but is ground only for a cross-action.

[1] 6 Taunt. 65.

Upon these four points the rule was accordingly refused, and the rule granted was drawn up calling upon the plaintiff to shew cause why the verdict should not be set aside and instead thereof a verdict entered for the defendants, pursuant to leave reserved, on the ground that the plaintiff was not entitled to recover, he not having complied with the terms of the charter-party; or why the damages should not be reduced by £7 per day for demurrage or delay occasioned by the plaintiff's default.[1]

Lush and *Honyman* (April 26) shewed cause. Two questions now remain to be considered. First, is the plaintiff entitled to recover the £600? secondly, are the defendants entitled to set off £7 a day as demurrage? It is contended, on the other side, that the words in the charter-party, "in consideration whereof the charterers agree to pay freight for the use and hire of the said ship the sum of £1400," refer to all the preceding stipulations so as to make them all conditions precedent to the right of the ship-owner to receive the £1400 from the charterers. And then it is said that because the captain did not attend daily at the broker's office, and refused to take goods on board which he ought to have taken, these defaults on his part disentitle him to recover. [ERLE, C. J. In refusing to take the matches and acids he meant to do his duty, but he made a mistake.] Yes, he refused wrongfully, not wilfully. The delay occasioned by this default or the breaches of any one of the conditions of this charter-party, inasmuch as the conditions do not go to the whole of the consideration, are matters only for a cross-action. The present action is brought only for £600 of the £1400, and if the plaintiff cannot recover that now, he never can. The only condition precedent to his right to recover the £600 is the ship "clearing from London." All the other stipulations are independent within the rules recognized from Boone v. Eyre[2] to the present time. . . .

Grove and *Henderson* (April 28), in support of the rule. The plaintiff is not entitled to the £600, and the defendants can set off demurrage at £7 a day for the time the vessel was detained by the plaintiff's default. The action is not brought on the charter-party, but the declaration merely consists of *indebitatus* counts. [BYLES, J. The plaintiff is to be in the same situation as if he had declared specially.] The action was commenced immediately on the ship's sailing, and before she had earned her freight. The payment is indivisible, and the money does not become due when conditions precedent to its becoming due within the terms of the charter-party remain unperformed. This case falls within the second rule in Pordage v. Cole.[3] "When a day is appointed for the payment of money, &c., and the day is to

[1] So much of the arguments and decision as relates to the latter point is omitted. — ED.

[2] 2 W. Black. 1314; s. c. 1 H. Black. 273, n. (*a*).

[3] 1 Wms. Saund. 320.

happen after the thing which is the consideration of the money, &c., is to be performed, no action can be maintained for the money before performance." 1 Wms. Saund. p. 320 *c*, 6th edit. What is the object of the charter-party? If the breach of the contract is to be compensated by damages, why insert these stipulations? [BYLES, J. Would not your argument go to shew not only that the £600 was not payable here, but that on her arrival in the colony the £800 would not be payable there?] We need not shrink from that. In Glaholm *v.* Hayes[1] a stipulation in a charter-party that the vessel should sail on or before the 4th of February was held a condition precedent to the right to recover on the contract. There it might be said that if he sailed after twelve o'clock on the day named, it would be a breach of the condition. So it would be; but he could still recover for what he did, though not under the contract. [BYLES, J. In that case the party lost the very voyage he wanted.] So here. The parties measure the charge for freight with reference to what will be gained on the cargo at Geelong. Time is of the essence of the contract. [BYLES, J., referred to Constable *v.* Cloberie,[2] cited in Glaholm *v.* Hayes, 2 M. & G., p. 18, note *a*.] In Ollive *v.* Booker[3] a statement in a charter-party that a vessel then at sea had sailed three weeks was held a material part of the contract, and not a mere collateral agreement, for the breach of which an action for consequential damages should be brought. So, in Oliver *v.* Fielden,[4] a statement that a ship should be ready to receive a cargo in May was held a condition precedent to the plaintiff's right to recover for not loading a full cargo. In the present case the consideration is clearly indivisible, and a failure of part disentitles the plaintiff from recovering on the contract. The following portion of the judgment of the Court of Exchequer Chamber, in Chanter *v.* Leese,[5] is closely applicable to the present case: "But it was further contended that it must be taken on these pleadings that the other five (patents) are good, and also that the defendants have enjoyed the use of them, and consequently that they are bound to perform their part of the agreement by paying the annuity, and must bring a cross-action for damages in respect of the one void patent. This reasoning would undoubtedly apply, if the consideration had been divisible, and the money payable by the defendants had been apportioned by the contract to the different parts of the consideration; in which case the principles laid down in Boone *v.* Eyre and other authorities of that class would have governed the present decision. But here it is plain that the enjoyment of all the six patents is the consideration for every part of the defendant's promise, and that the annuity to be paid is

1 2 Man. & G. 257. 2 Palmer, 397.
3 1 Exch. Rep. 416; s. c. 17 Law J. Rep. (N. S.) Exch. 41.
4 4 Exch. Rep. 135; s. c. 18 Law J. Rep. (N. S.) Exch. 353.
5 5 M. & W. 701.

neither apportioned by the contract nor capable of being apportioned by a jury." In the present case, the consideration is entire, and the court has no means of saying how much is to be deducted on failure of a part. Lucas v. Godwin.[1] The plaintiff's claim rests entirely on special contract, and what he has himself undertaken to do is antecedent in date to what the defendants have to do, — the plaintiff has to attend daily at the office, to take goods on board, to clear his ship, and then the £600 is to be paid. These stipulations must be dependent, independent, or concurrent. They are clearly not concurrent; but on the other side it is said they are independent, and that each has his remedy for a breach by the other party. If that be so, and the obligation on each side is in contract only, then the owner might clear the ship, and sail, and refuse to receive any goods. [BYLES, J. The clearance meant by the charter-party is a clearance with cargo.] Not necessarily. A ship may be cleared in ballast. "Clearance" is, in point of fact, the permission to sail. Abbott on Shipping, p. 348, 8th edit. . . .

ERLE, C. J. This rule must be discharged. Speaking for myself, I am of opinion that the stipulation for the payment of the £600 was an independent stipulation; that is to say, each of the things to be done on the part of the ship-owner before clearance was not a condition precedent to the right to receive the £600. Certain things are to be done on the part of the ship-owner before clearance, and certain other things by him after clearance, such as sailing to the port of destination. For the whole of these, for what is done before and after clearance, £1400 is to be paid, £600 immediately after the ship has cleared, and £800 upon its arrival at the port of destination; the £600 is a part of the £1400, the reward for the entire service stipulated for. The construction to be put on these contracts depends on the terms of the individual contract, and what we have to look to is to ascertain the intention of the parties; and whether a particular stipulation is a condition precedent or an independent stipulation is to be ascertained by what we consider to have been the intention of the parties expressed in the instrument. Now, looking at this instrument, I think it was not intended by the parties that it should be a condition precedent that the captain should attend daily at the broker's office, or that the ship should be ready on any one particular day, or should never omit to take goods on board. I think that the intention of the parties was that these should be independent stipulations. In one of the cases cited there was a stipulation on the part of the ship-owner that the ship should be ready on the 14th of February, and in another that the ship was to go *viâ* Genoa to Marseilles: in each of those cases time was of the essence of the contract, and the court held the stipulations to be conditions precedent. In the present case there is a stipulation

[1] 2 Bing. N. C. 737.

which is of the essence of the contract, which the parties have made a condition precedent, shewing that when they intended a stipulation to have that effect, they knew how to express it. "The ship to be ready on or before the 10th of November, or the charterers to have the option of cancelling this agreement." Here time was of the essence of the contract, and the parties have rightly expressed the stipulation as to time, so as to make it take effect as a condition precedent. They have not used like language with respect to the other parts of the agreement; and therefore I think the right of the plaintiff to the £600 accrued independently of those stipulations. It may be that, according to the old form of declaring, the declaration could not have been sustained while part of the contract remained open and unperformed; but I think, if the whole of this contract had been set out, and the pleadings adapted to the facts, the plaintiff would have, under them, established his right to recover the £600. . . .

BYLES, J. I am of the same opinion. It is quite unnecessary to say what our decision on the declaration, as it now stands, would be. We may suppose a special declaration and proper pleas, and then the plaintiff in this action would be entitled to recover his £600 for freight, and it is agreed that he shall be in the same position as if that had been done. Now, it is said that, before the plaintiff can recover this £600, he must give proof of every iota of these alleged various conditions precedent having been satisfied by him. It seems to me that the case of Boone *v.* Eyre applies distinctly. I need not enlarge further on the observations which my lord has made on the general principles; but, in addition to the instance which my lord has cited of a distinct condition precedent appearing in the charter-party, and being, when intended, distinctly expressed, — I mean the condition which obliges the ship to be ready on or before the 10th of November, or the charterers to have the option of cancelling the agreement, shewing that where the parties intended a stipulation to be a condition precedent, they knew well enough how to express it, — there is also another condition precedent expressed in the charter-party, on which the stipulation to pay the £600 is in terms made dependent, and that is the clearing from London; whenever she has cleared the £600 becomes due. For these reasons, I think the plaintiff is entitled to recover the £600. . . .

There is one observation which I intended to have made on the first point. Where a charter-party contains a stipulation to sail on a particular day, that is of the essence of the contract. To sail on a day in the alternative is a different adventure. The weather may be different; the time of the year may be different; the market may be different. To sail in the same ship and on a different day may be as different an adventure as to sail from a different port, or with a different ship; but that rule has been very stoutly contended for. In giving judgment in Tarrabochia *v.* Hickie, Pollock, C. B., says, "It is not a condition precedent that the vessel should sail with convenient speed, or in a reasonable time. Where, indeed, the charter-party provides that the vessel shall sail on a particular day, that is a condition precedent. The distinction is obvious: where a particular day is named, it is evidently the intention of the parties that the vessel shall sail on that day, and if the ship-owner refuses to do so, the merchant may decline to load, for the voyage is thereby altered, and the success of the adventure may depend on the vessel sailing on the day named." Those cases, therefore, warranted to sail on a particular day, seem to stand on their own ground. If they are any exception to the rule laid down in Boone *v.* Eyre, this is a case within the rule, and not within the exception.

KEATING, J. No doubt the cases as to what stipulations are and are not conditions precedent run very fine. In Stavers *v.* Curling,[1] Lord Chief Justice Tindal expresses in a few words every thing that can be said on the subject. "The rule has been established by a long series of decisions in modern times, that the question, whether covenants are to be held dependent or independent of each other, is to be determined by the intention and meaning of the parties as it appears on the instrument, and by the application of common sense to each particular case; to which intention, when once discovered, all technical forms of expression must give way." And one of the means of discovering such intention has been laid down with great accuracy by Lord Ellenborough, in the case of Richie *v.* Atkinson,[2] to be this, "that where mutual covenants go to the whole of the consideration on both sides, they are mutual conditions, the one precedent to the other; but where the covenants go only to a part, there a remedy lies on the covenant to recover damages for the breach of it, but it is not a condition precedent." That was a very strong case in favor of the doctrine of holding covenants, however expressed, to be independent. Mr. Henderson has contended that the present case comes within the second rule in Pordage *v.* Cole; but it appears to me that it does not clearly come within that rule, because the £600 sought to be recovered here, and which, we must take it, is now sought to be recovered on a special declaration, is a portion of the £1400 freight which is expressed in the charter-party to be freight for the use and hire of the said ship, not only for what was to take place before clearance, but for what was to take place after clearance. That it is to be payable by the charterers after clearance, is provided, no doubt; but still that provision is only as to the mode of payment, and does not, in the slightest degree, make any distinction between the nature of the entire payment of the £1400 and of the different portions of it. Under these circumstances, it appears to me it does not come within that rule which Mr. Henderson pressed upon us with great force, but that here it is clearly, looking at the

[1] 3 Bing. N. C. 368. [2] 10 East, 295.

whole of the instrument, an independent covenant, and I need not add any thing upon that subject to what my lord has expressed. But there was an argument put forward by Mr. Henderson, to which I think it right to advert. He said, in answer to the argument pressed on the other side, if this is a condition precedent, if the captain omitted for a single day to attend at the office, freight never could be recovered. Mr. Honyman answers to that, that it could, but in a different way. When the voyage had been performed, the owner could bring *indebitatus assumpsit* for the freight, and could recover according to the rate of freight £1400, making those deductions which ought to be made as consequent upon the captain's default. But how is that to be done? The deductions consequent upon the captain's default would be unliquidated damages, and it would be extremely difficult in an action in *indebitatus assumpsit* to take that, if indeed it could be taken, into consideration. . . . *Rule discharged.*

An appeal having been taken from the foregoing decision to the Exchequer Chamber, the case was argued by

Grove, for the appellants the defendants below. The stipulations that the captain should receive all such lawful goods on board as might be required by the charterers, and that he should attend daily at the broker's office, were conditions precedent to the right of the plaintiff to payment, so far at least as the £600, the first part of the freight, is concerned. [BLACKBURN, J. According to the rule in Pordage *v.* Cole,[1] the stipulation does not go to the whole consideration, and is, therefore, not a condition precedent.] If any part of an entire consideration fails, the whole consideration fails. Chanter *v.* Leese[2] is in point. [COCKBURN, C. J. The £600 is to be paid when the ship is cleared.] If the receiving the goods is not a condition precedent, the captain might have sailed with one ounce of cargo, and then claimed the £600. [COCKBURN, C. J. No; there could not have been a clearing of the ship. That means that he should sail with a reasonable cargo.] . . .

Honyman, for the plaintiff, was not called upon.

COCKBURN, C. J. We are all of opinion that the judgment ought to be affirmed. With regard to the first point, the argument put forward by the defendants was entirely disposed of by the reasons given by the judges below. The appeal is one that ought never to have been brought. . . .

WIGHTMAN, J., concurred.

MARTIN, B. It has been laid down by Lord Tenterden, in his book, Abbott on Shipping, 266, 8th edit., "Whether or not a particular cov-

[1] 1 Wms. Saund. 319 *e*.

[2] 5 Mee. & W. 698; s. c. 9 Law J. Rep. (N. S.) Exch. 327.

enant by one party be a condition precedent, the breach of which will dispense with the performance of the contract by the other, or an independent covenant, is a question to be determined according to the fair intention of the parties to be collected from the language employed by them." And Tindal, C. J., says, in Stavers *v.* Curling,[1] "The rule has been established by a long series of decisions in modern times, that the question whether covenants are to be held dependent or independent of each other, is to be determined by the intention and meaning of the parties as it appears upon the instrument, and by the application of common sense to each particular case; to which intention, when once discovered, all technical forms of expression must give way." Applying the rule so laid down to this case, it is absurd to say that it was the intention of the parties that the non-receipt of these goods or the non-attendance of the captain at the broker's office were to cause the owner of the vessel to lose £1400. . . . .

BRAMWELL and CHANNELL, BB., and BLACKBURN and HILL, JJ., concurred. *Judgment affirmed.*

JONASSOHN AND ANOTHER *v.* YOUNG.

IN THE QUEEN'S BENCH, JUNE 24, 1863.

[*Reported in 4 Best & Smith*, 296.]

THE declaration stated that it was agreed by and between the plaintiffs and the defendant, that the plaintiffs should sell and deliver to the defendant, and that the defendant would purchase of the plaintiffs, as many of the plaintiffs' Nettlesworth Gas Coals, equal in quality to a certain cargo of them before then shipped on trial by a steam vessel called the Great Northern, as one steam vessel could fetch in nine months, proceeding to Sunderland, and after loading the cargo proceeding with it from thence to London, and after discharging the cargo at London proceeding back again to Sunderland for another cargo, and thence back again with the cargo to London, and so on until the expiration of the nine months; the steam vessel to be sent by the defendant for the coals, and the plaintiffs to ship them on board of it at Sunderland, at and for a certain price, to wit, 5*s.* 9*d.* per ton, to be paid by the defendant to the plaintiffs at the beginning of each month for the preceding month's supply, less £2 10*s.* per cent. discount. Averment, that the plaintiffs have always been ready and willing to sell and deliver to the defendants and ship the coals on the terms aforesaid, and

[1] 3 Bing. N. C. 355; s. c. 6 Law J. Rep. (N. S.) C. P. 41.

have done all things, and all things have happened, and all times have elapsed necessary to entitle the plaintiffs to have the agreement performed by the defendant on his part, &c.: Yet the defendant neglected and refused to send, and made default in sending a steam vessel to Sunderland to fetch divers cargoes, or the quantity of the coals which he ought, according to the agreement, to have fetched and accepted; and the defendant, before the expiration of the nine months, wholly and absolutely refused to send any other steam vessels for the coals, or to accept any more of the coals, and declared to the plaintiffs that he would not perform any more the agreement, and exonerated and discharged the plaintiffs from any further performance thereof on their part: and by reason of the premises the plaintiffs have been much injured.

Third plea. That, before any breach by the defendant of the agreement, the plaintiffs broke the contract by delivering and shipping to the defendant, in pretended fulfilment thereof, gas coal which was no part thereof equal in quality to the cargo shipped on trial, but was very inferior thereto, and wholly unfit for the defendant's purposes, as the plaintiffs well knew; whereupon and wherefore the defendant, immediately upon discovering the plaintiffs' default, and within a reasonable time in that behalf, refused to fetch or accept any more of the coal.

Fourth plea. That, before any breach by the defendant of the agreement, the plaintiffs broke their contract, to wit, by detaining the defendant's vessel an undue and unreasonable length of time, and far beyond the time permitted by the contract, and contrary to the defendant's will, upon divers occasions upon which the defendant had sent the same to the plaintiffs to be loaded with coal under the agreement, and by not loading the vessel with coal as aforesaid, on any or either of the occasions, until after the lapse of a long and unreasonable space of time after they had notice that such vessel was ready to receive coal, and thereby greatly injured and damnified the defendant; whereupon and wherefore he, immediately upon notice of the plaintiffs' default, refused to fetch or receive any more of the coal.

Demurrer to each plea, and joinder.

Hannen (*Bidder* with him), in support of the demurrer.

The substance of both pleas is, that, because the contract had been broken in part by the plaintiffs — whether in not delivering coals equal to sample, or in detaining the defendant's vessel beyond the time permitted by the contract, — the defendant is justified in refusing to carry out the contract for the remainder of the period to which it related: but such a plea is bad both on principle and authority; Weaver *v.* Sessions,[1] Franklin *v.* Miller.[2] In Withers *v.* Reynolds,[3] where there was a refusal by the plaintiff to complete the contract, Patteson, J.,

[1] 6 Taunt. 154. [2] 4 A. & E. 599. [3] 2 B. & Ad. 882.

said, p. 885, "If the plaintiff had merely failed to pay for any particular load, that, of itself, might not have been an excuse to the defendant for delivering no more straw; but the plaintiff here expressly refuses to pay for the loads as delivered; the defendant, therefore, is not liable for ceasing to perform his part of the contract." [WIGHTMAN, J. The plaintiff in effect said, "If you send a load of straw I will not pay for it." CROMPTON, J. If the purchaser of goods refuses to pay for them, or is insolvent, the vendor is not bound to deliver. But these pleas allege a breach of the contract by the plaintiff as to part only.] They do not shew that the plaintiffs were unable or unwilling to supply coals according to the contract. In Hoare *v.* Rennie[1] the plea alleged that the plaintiffs failed to complete a shipment of iron for the month of June according to the contract, and were never ready and willing to deliver to the defendants such a quantity of iron in June as was specified in the contract; and the plea was held good: there the refusal of the plaintiffs to supply the iron would have postponed the performance of the contract indefinitely. [CROMPTON, J. That case belongs to the class in which the breach alleged in the plea is an entire frustration of the contract. BLACKBURN, J., referred to Hochster *v.* De La Tour.[2]]

Keane, contra. Hoare *v.* Rennie supports the third plea. As soon as the defendant discovered that the plaintiffs had knowingly sent an inferior coal to that stipulated for, he was justified in throwing up the contract. [WIGHTMAN, J. Suppose the plaintiff intended in future to send such coal as was stipulated for? BLACKBURN, J. The third plea does not aver that the plaintiffs persisted in sending an inferior coal.] The contract is the employment of a vessel during a limited time, and for getting coal of a specified quality; the non-supply of that coal, and the unnecessary detention of the vessel by the plaintiffs, go to the root of the contract. [CROMPTON, J. The vice of both pleas is the same, that the breach goes only to part of the consideration. The argument for the defendant must go this length, that the supply of one chaldron of coal of an inferior quality, or the unnecessary detention of the defendant's vessel for one hour, would entitle him to put an end to the contract. In Hoare *v.* Rennie we must take it that time was of the essence of the contract. BLACKBURN, J. The reasoning of the judges in that case does not apply to the plea pleaded to the second count. As reported, it looks as if the court forgot the second count. CROMPTON, J. We must consider that the breaches alleged in the pleas in that case went to the root of the matter.]

Hannen was not called upon to reply.

Per Curiam. (WIGHTMAN, CROMPTON, and BLACKBURN, JJ.)

Judgment for the plaintiffs.

[1] 5 H. & N. 19. [2] 2 E. & B. 678.

MacANDREW and Others v. CHAPPLE and Another.

In the Common Pleas, May 29, 1866.

[*Reported in Law Reports*, 1 *Common Pleas*, 648.]

This was an action brought by the plaintiffs against the defendants for the recovery of damages for the loss sustained by them, by reason of the defendants having made default in shipping a cargo on board the plaintiffs' vessel, Ephesus; and by consent a case was stated without pleadings, of which the following were the material parts: —

The plaintiffs were the owners of the steamer Ephesus. On the 15th of October, 1864, the steamer was launched at Newcastle, and was immediately afterwards placed in the hands of Messrs. Randolph, Eldon & Co., engineers, for completion ready for sea. About the 1st of December, 1864, negotiations were opened between the plaintiffs and defendants for the purpose of the chartering of the Ephesus by the defendants. On the 7th of December these negotiations were concluded by a charter-party being made between the plaintiffs and defendants, containing the following terms: "It is this day mutually agreed that the said ship, being tight, staunch, and strong, and every way fitted for the voyage, shall with all convenient speed (on being ready), having liberty to take an outward cargo for owners' benefit, direct or on the way, proceed to Alexandria, Egypt, or so near thereunto as she may safely get, and there load from the factor of the said freighters, in the customary manner, a full and complete cargo of cotton . . . which the said merchants bind themselves to ship . . . and being so loaded shall forthwith proceed to London or Liverpool direct as ordered on signing bill of lading."

It is usual for steamers to make a trial trip before starting on their first voyage, and in order to have a satisfactory trial trip at Newcastle, it is necessary for steamers to put out to sea, having to cross and recross the bar at the mouth of the Tyne, an operation accompanied by some risk in the case of a steamer of the size of the Ephesus at that period of the year. It was arranged therefore that the vessel should make her trial trip from Newcastle to London, instead of returning to the Tyne, and that the deficiencies of her machinery, if any, should be made good in London. Accordingly on the 12th of January, 1865, the ship left Newcastle for London. While in London the ship took on board goods for Malta, Syra, Constantinople, Smyrna, and Alexandria, but no delay was thereby occasioned, the goods being shipped before the necessary repairs to the machinery were complete. The ship sailed from London on the 1st of March, 1865, for Malta, and after touching and unloading cargo there, and at Syra,

Constantinople, and Smyrna, arrived at Alexandria on the 29th of April, 1865, and was ready to load cargo on the 1st of May, 1865. The ship when she sailed from Newcastle was not complete and ready for the chartered voyage. There is no usage of trade by which vessels bound from Newcastle or London to Alexandria are justified in taking goods to Syra, Constantinople, Smyrna, or other ports, if the geographical position of such ports does not warrant such a course.

Had the Ephesus sailed direct from London to Alexandria, and discharged her outward cargo there instead of taking cargo to the various ports at which she touched on her way out, she would have been ready to load her homeward cargo at Alexandria a few days before the 1st of May, 1865.

Freight for cotton fell gradually and continuously from the month of January, 1865, to the month of May, 1865.

On the 5th of May, John Collings, the master of the Ephesus, not having received any cargo from Charles Grace, the person named by the defendants as their agent, formally demanded a cargo from him, whereupon the latter informed him that he had no cargo for him, and that he must therefore seek a cargo elsewhere for his vessel. The master accordingly did the best he could, but was unable to obtain more than a small freight.

The question for the opinion of the court was, whether, under the aforesaid circumstances, the plaintiffs had a right of action against the defendants for refusing to load the Ephesus at Alexandria as aforesaid. The court or court of appeal to be at liberty to draw all such inferences of fact as a jury would be entitled to do.

Mellish, *Q. C.* (*Cohen* with him), for the plaintiffs. The question is, whether there was such a delay in bringing the ship to Alexandria as entitled the charterer to refuse to load. The ship was only to sail when ready, and there was no unnecessary delay in getting her ready. The defendants, therefore, must rely on one of two breaches of the charter-party: either that the vessel was not any way fitted for the voyage at the time she left the Tyne, or that she did not proceed direct to Alexandria, but went to ports other than those to which she was entitled to go. It is clear on authority that where a vessel is chartered for a homeward voyage, a stipulation that she should be staunch, &c., at starting, is not a condition precedent to the duty of the charterer to provide a cargo, and the same is true of the stipulation that she shall proceed on the voyage with all convenient speed, otherwise an hour's delay in starting would entitle the charterer to throw up the charter-party. Some of the cases indeed seem to shew that if these stipulations are broken to such an extent as entirely to frustrate the object of the voyage, the charterer may throw up the agreement; but here the ship was seaworthy when she arrived at Alexandria, and the only effect of the delay (if there was any) was that freights were somewhat lower when she arrived. It did not prevent a cargo of cotton being shipped, which was the object for which the ship was chartered. Neither is the stipulation to proceed to Alexandria direct a condition precedent. The port of London was on the way, as the vessel necessarily passed the mouth of the Thames; and the vessel had a right to load as well as unload there. Proceeding to Constantinople was, no doubt, a deviation in terms; but Clipsham *v.* Vertue [1] and Tarrabochia *v.* Hickie [2] shew distinctly, that if the object of the voyage be not frustrated, the charterer is not relieved, either by deviation or delay, of his obligation to load a cargo. It is not necessary to support or disprove what has been said with respect to cases in which the object of the voyage is frustrated. Freeman *v.* Taylor [3] first gave rise to the opinion that the charterer would then be relieved from his engagements. [BYLES, J. We had all the cases on this subject before us in Seeger *v.* Duthie.[4]] The defendants may rely on Behn *v.* Burness,[5] in which the description of a ship in the charter-party as "now in the port of Amsterdam," was held to be a condition precedent that the ship should be there, but the words in that case were either a condition precedent or nothing; they clearly were not a stipulation upon which a cross-action could be brought. In the judgment in that case, Dimech *v.* Corlett [6] is referred to, and the judges intimate their dissent from the doctrine that a breach of a mere stipulation, even if it frustrates the object of the voyage, can therefore be treated as a warranty, and held to avoid the agreement.

E. James, Q. C. (*Watkin Williams* with him), for the defendants. Whether a stipulation be a condition precedent or not depends upon the intention of the parties, and not on any subsequent events. Behn *v.* Burness. It can make no difference whether the damage caused is great or small; whether the delay is one day or one hundred. The charter-party in the present case is one for a voyage from Newcastle to Alexandria, and the ship-owners agree to proceed on that voyage with all convenient speed. It is clearly a condition precedent that they should do so without deviating. In Clipsham *v.* Vertue there was no stipulation that the ship should proceed direct to London.

ERLE, C. J. In this case the charterers have not performed their part of the agreement, and defend themselves on the ground that a condition precedent has been broken by the ship-owners. A charter-party may contain either a stipulation or a condition precedent, and the question whether any provision in the contract is one or the other is a matter of construction, and depends on the judgment which the

[1] 5 Q. B. 265, 13 L. J. (Q. B.) 2. [2] 1 H. & N. 183, 26 L. J. (Ex.) 26.
[3] 8 Bing. 124, 1 L. J. (C. P.) 26.
[4] 8 C. B. (N. S.) 45, 29 L. J. (C. P.) 253; in error, 8 C. B. (N. S.) 72, 30 L. J. (C. P.) 65.
[5] 3 B. & S. 751, 32 L. J. (Q. B.) 204. [6] 12 Moo. P. C. 199.

court may form of the intention of the parties. This charter-party says that the Ephesus being every way fitted for the voyage, shall with all convenient speed proceed to Alexandria. I am of opinion that there is nothing to shew that it was the intention of the parties that this should be a condition precedent; if it were so, either of the deviations suggested — viz., to London in the first instance, and to Constantinople in the second — would be sufficient to render the contract void. I think the parties could not have intended that if it was broken ever so little the charterers should be free. The present case turns only on the construction of the charter-party, and I think the clause in question amounts to a stipulation for the breach of which the remedy is by cross-action, and not to a condition precedent. It is unnecessary to go into the cases which have been cited with reference to the doctrine that where the whole object of the voyage has been frustrated there is an answer to the action, as it is admitted that such was not the case in the present instance.

Willes, J. I am of the same opinion. The defendants seek to set up a deviation or delay in sending out the ship as an excuse for not having loaded a cargo on board it, as agreed by the charter-party. It seems to be now settled that delay by deviation is the same as a delay in starting; and it is also settled, at any rate in this court, that a delay or deviation which, as it has been said, goes to the whole root of the matter, deprives the charterer of the whole benefit of the contract, or entirely frustrates the object of the charterer in chartering the ship, is an answer to an action for not loading a cargo; but that loss, delay, or deviation short of that gives an action for damages, but does not defeat the charter. From the time of Boone *v.* Eyre,[1] Ritchie *v.* Atkinson,[2] and Davidson *v.* Gwynne,[3] this rule has been applied. In the present case I apprehend the breaches resolve themselves into such a delay as can be compensated for by damages. The vessel was not engaged for any particular cargo, but the contract was merely a speculation on the rise or fall of freight; and the object of the voyage, therefore, was in no sense frustrated.

Byles, J. I am of the same opinion. The principles upon which it is to be determined whether a stipulation in a contract is a condition precedent are laid down by Erle, C. J., in Seeger *v.* Duthie. Here there is the ordinary express stipulation that the ship shall proceed with all convenient speed. If the parties intended this to be a condition precedent, their intention must be implied, for there are no express words shewing such an intention. If such a stipulation was held to be a condition precedent, every actionable delay would avoid the contract, and a large number of charter-parties would be defeated. What would be the effect, if the delay was such as entirely to frustrate the object of

[1] 1 H. Bl. 273, *n.* [2] 10 East, 295. [3] 12 East, 381.

the voyage, is a question which does not arise here. Then, secondly, as to the deviation: this question is concluded by Freeman *v.* Taylor;[1] there the ship deviated to the Mauritius, but the stipulation was held not a condition precedent, and the charter-party not to be avoided. The deviation to Constantinople is no doubt an actionable breach of the stipulation that the ship should proceed direct to Alexandria, but is no answer to the action.

MONTAGUE SMITH, J. I am of the same opinion. Here the one question is, whether the stipulation to proceed with all convenient speed direct to Alexandria is a condition precedent or not. I am clearly of opinion that it is not, and that if we held that it was we should frustrate the intention of the parties. The loss does not go to the whole consideration, but may be compensated in damages; and the question as to what would have been the case if the object of the voyage had been frustrated does not arise. *Judgment for the plaintiffs.*

SECTION III.

Mutual and Concurrent Conditions.

CALLONEL *v.* BRIGGS.

AT NISI PRIUS, CORAM HOLT, C. J., TRINITY TERM, 1703.

[*Reported in* 1 *Salkeld,* 112.]

AN agreement was, that the defendant should pay so much money six months after the bargain, the plaintiff transferring stock. The plaintiff at the same time gave a note to the defendant to transfer the stock, the defendant paying, &c. *Et per* HOLT, C. J. If either party would sue upon this agreement, the plaintiff for not paying, or the defendant for not transferring, the one must aver and prove a transfer or a tender, and the other a payment or a tender; for transferring in the first bargain was a condition precedent; and though there be mutual promises, yet if one thing be the consideration of the other, there a performance is necessary to be averred, unless a certain day be appointed for performance. 1 Saund. 319. If I sell you my horse for £10, if you will have the horse I must have the money; or if I will have the money you must have the horse; therefore he obliged the plaintiff either to prove a transfer, or a tender and refusal within the six months.

[1] 8 Bing. 124, 1 L. J. (C. P.) 26.

GOODISSON v. NUNN.

IN THE KING'S BENCH, JUNE 19, 1792.

[*Reported in 4 Term Reports*, 761.]

THIS was an action of debt to recover £21 on certain articles of agreement, the substance of which was stated in the declaration. The defendant craved oyer of the agreement, by which the plaintiff agreed that he would, on or before the 2d of September then next, "by such conveyances, surrenders, assurances, ways, and means in the law, shall reasonably devise, advise, or require,[1] well and sufficiently grant, sell, release, assign, and surrender, or otherwise convey to the defendant all that copyhold tenement, lying," &c. In consideration whereof the defendant covenanted to pay to the plaintiff the sum of £210 on or before the 2d day of September next ensuing; on failure of complying with the before-mentioned agreement the defendant was to pay to the plaintiff the sum of £21; and if the plaintiff did not deliver the estate according to the before-mentioned agreement, then he was to pay to the defendant the sum of £21. It was further agreed between the parties that the plaintiff should take up the copyhold as follows, that is to say: "That the plaintiff should take it up either for the defendant or his wife, as they should agree at the time; that the plaintiff should take it up for himself; that each party should pay share and share alike towards the expenses attending the taking it up." The defendant then pleaded, 1st. *Non est factum*. 2d. That the plaintiff did not, on or before the 2d day of September next, &c., by such conveyances, assurances, surrenders, ways, and means, in the law reasonably devised, advised, and required, well and sufficiently grant, sell, and release, assign and surrender, or otherwise convey to the defendant the said premises in the said articles of agreement mentioned, &c. 3d. That the plaintiff did not on or before the 2d day of September, &c., or at any time since, well and sufficiently grant, sell, and release, assign and surrender, or otherwise convey to the defendant the said premises, &c. 4th. That the plaintiff, at the time of the making of the articles, &c., had nothing in the said premises, whereby he could be enabled to grant, &c., to the defendant the said premises, &c.

To the three last pleas the plaintiff demurred generally.

Wood, in support of the demurrer. The two first special pleas are drawn on a supposition that the conveyance by the plaintiff to the defendant is a condition precedent, and that the defendant is not liable on his covenant till the plaintiff has performed the covenant on his

[1] The agreement was drawn in this inaccurate manner.

part. But on the true construction of these articles, this was not a condition precedent on the plaintiff's part, but the covenants were mutual and independent, a breach of either of which gives the other party a right of action. If it had been agreed "that the defendant would on a particular day pay the money upon the plaintiff's conveying," that would have made the conveyance a condition precedent to the payment of the money. But here the parties have relied on the mutual covenants which each entered into with the other. Those covenants are general, not depending upon each other. The first is, that the plaintiff shall convey, &c., expressed in the most general terms; in consideration whereof (that is, in consideration of the plaintiff's covenant) the defendant covenanted to pay, &c., in terms equally general. In 1 Rol. Abr. 415, pl. 8, "If by articles of agreement between B. and C., by which B. covenants, for the consideration afterwards to be expressed, to convey certain lands to C. in fee, and after C. covenants on his part, for the consideration aforesaid, to pay B. £160, in this case although B. does not assure the land to C., still C. is bound to pay the money; for the assurance of the land is not a condition precedent; but they are distinct and mutual covenants." So in Pordage v. Cole,[1] the plaintiff declared on a specialty, by which it was agreed that the defendant should give the plaintiff £775 for all his lands, &c.; that the defendant had given the plaintiff 5*s*. as earnest; and that it was also agreed that the defendant should pay the plaintiff the residue of the £775 at a certain time; and the breach was the non-payment of that residue. To this the defendant demurred, and objected that the plaintiff had not averred a conveyance on his part, or a tender of one; and there too the word "pro" was used, which, it was said in Co. Lit. 204 *a*, makes a condition in matters executory; but it was held that the action was well brought, and that if the plaintiff did not convey, the defendant had his remedy against him on the covenant. Again in Blackwell v. Nash,[2] the plaintiff declared that he covenanted to transfer to the defendant at a certain time so much stock, and that the defendant in consideration of the premises covenanted to accept and pay for it; he then averred that he was ready and offered to transfer to the defendant, who refused to accept or pay, &c. On demurrer it was objected that "for it" made a condition precedent, and that the plaintiff should have shewn an actual transfer of the stock; to which it was answered that they were mutual covenants, and that the plaintiff need not shew a performance on his part; and it was held that in consideration of the premises was in consideration of the covenant to transfer, and not of an actual transferring, for which the defendant had his remedy. [In answer to a question from the court, whether this case could be distinguished from the late cases of Kingston v. Pres-

[1] 1 Saund. 319. [2] 1 Str. 535.

ton,[1] Jones *v.* Barclay,[2] and Lord Aldborough *v.* Lord Newhaven,[3] where the rule was established, that when two acts are to be done at the same time, neither party can maintain an action without shewing performance, or an offer to perform on his part; which rule applied to all cases of sale; he said]: This case may be distinguished from those, because here the conveyance was to be such as the defendant should require. The words are "by such conveyances, &c., shall reasonably devise, advise, or require;" which evidently mean such as the defendant should wish. The first act was therefore to be done by the vendee, who should have directed what conveyance he wished to have. And by another part of the agreement the plaintiff was to take up the copyhold either for the defendant or his wife, as they should agree; then they should first have elected to whom it should be made. Now if the first act were to be done by the defendant, this case differs from those alluded to.

Lord Kenyon, C. J. This case is extremely clear, whether considered on principles of strict law or of common justice. The plaintiff engaged to sell an estate to the defendant, in consideration of which the defendant undertook to pay £210; and if he did not carry the contract into execution, he was to pay £21. And now not having conveyed his estate, or offered to do so, or taken any one step towards it, the plaintiff has brought this action for the penalty. Suppose the purchase-money of an estate was £40,000, it would be absurd to say that the purchaser might enforce a conveyance without payment, and compel the seller to have recourse to him, who perhaps might be an insolvent person. The old cases cited by the plaintiff's counsel have been accurately stated; but the determinations in them outrage common sense. I admit the principle on which they profess to go; but I think that the judges misapplied that principle. It is admitted in them all that where they are dependent covenants no action will lie by one party, unless he have performed or offered to perform his covenant. Then the question is whether these are or are not dependent covenants? I think they are; the one is to depend on the other; when the one party conveyed his estate, he was to receive the purchase-money; and when the other parted with his money, he was to have the estate. They were reciprocal acts to be performed by each other at the same time. It seems from the case in Strange that the judges were surprised at the old decisions; and, in order to get rid of the difficulty, they said that a tender and refusal would amount to a performance. It is true they went farther, and said that "in consideration of the premises" meant only in consideration of the covenant to transfer, and not in consideration of the actual transferring of the stock; but to the latter part of that judgment I cannot accede. It is

[1] Dougl. 688, 3d edit.
[2] Dougl. 684, 3d edit.
[3] Mich. 21 Geo. 3, B. R.

our duty, when we see that principles of law have been misapplied in any case, to overrule it. The principle is admitted in all the cases alluded to that, if they be dependent covenants, performance or the offer to perform must be pleaded on the one part, in order to found the action against the other. The mistake has been in the misapplication of that principle in the cases cited. And I am glad to find that the old cases have been overruled, and that we are now warranted by precedent as well as by principle to say that this action cannot be maintained.

BULLER, J. The agreement was that the plaintiff should sell his estate, and that the defendant should buy it. In the nature of the thing, therefore, the two acts are to be done together. In Kingston *v.* Preston [1] Lord Mansfield said: "The construction contended for is, that in spite of his teeth the defendant shall be obliged to give personal credit to the plaintiff; whereas the essence of the agreement was that neither should trust the other personally." The next case was Jones *v.* Barclay; [2] there the plaintiff, who was the seller, stated that he had offered to assign and execute and deliver a general release, and had tendered a draft of an assignment and release, and offered to execute and deliver such assignment, but that the defendant had absolutely discharged him from executing the same, or any assignment and release whatsoever. The effect of that was to put an end to the contract; and therefore it was held that the plaintiff was entitled to damages; Lord Mansfield saying, "that the plaintiff had done every thing in his power to perform the agreement, and that the defendant only had been guilty of the neglect." Then followed the case of Lord Aldborough *v.* Lord Newhaven, in which it was said that the plaintiff must shew either that he had assigned the house, or that he had tendered an assignment, before he could insist on payment, because both acts were to be done at the same time. And, in truth, if there had been no case in opposition to the ancient ones, I should not have been afraid of making a precedent, the principle on which our decision is founded being universally admitted in all the cases. A distinction, however, has been made between this case and those of Kingston *v.* Preston, &c., by saying that the defendant was to do the first act here, namely, to elect to whom the estate should be conveyed, whether to him or his wife. But there is no foundation for this distinction; for the first act was to be done by the plaintiff; the words are, "the said R. Goodisson shall take it up for himself;" he was first to be admitted, before he could surrender to the defendant.

GROSE, J. In a case in Hobart [3] there is a good deal of comment on the word *pro*, shewing in what cases it operates as a condition pre-

[1] Dougl. 688, 3d edit.
[2] Dougl. 684, 3d edit.
[3] *Vide* Hob. 41.

cedent and where it does not. But, notwithstanding some of the old authorities, the courts of later times have considered whether in reality the first act is not to be performed by the seller, or at least whether they are not concurrent acts. There is so much good sense in the later decisions that it is too much to say that they are not law. There being several precedents in support of our decision, and those being founded in good sense and justice, I think we ought to take advantage of them. *Judgment for the defendant.*

Gibbs, who was to have argued for the defendant, mentioned the case of the Duke of St. Albans v. Shore, 1 H. Bl. Rep. 270, and Boone v. Eyre there cited.

MORTON v. LAMB.

In the King's Bench, February 1, 1797.

[*Reported in 7 Term Reports*, 125.]

In an action on the case, the plaintiff declared against the defendant, for that whereas, on the 10th February, 1796, at Manchester, in the county of Lancaster, in consideration that the plaintiff, at the special instance and request of the defendant, had then and there bought of the defendant 200 quarters of wheat, at £5 0*s.* 6*d.* per quarter, such price to be therefore paid by the plaintiff to the defendant, he the defendant undertook and then and there promised the plaintiff to deliver the said corn to him the plaintiff at Shardlow, in the county of Derby, in one month from that time, viz., of the sale; and then he alleged that, although he the plaintiff always, from the time of making such sale for the space of one month then next following and afterwards, was ready and willing to receive the said corn at Shardlow, yet the defendant, not regarding his said promise, &c., did not in one month from the time of the making of such sale as aforesaid, or at any other time, deliver the said corn to the plaintiff, at Shardlow or elsewhere, although he the defendant was often requested so to do, &c. The defendant pleaded the general issue; and at the trial the plaintiff recovered a verdict.

Holroyd obtained, in the last term, a rule calling on the plaintiff to shew cause why the judgment should not be arrested, because it was not averred that the plaintiff had tendered to the defendant the price of the corn, or was ready to have paid for it on delivery. He said this was necessary on the principle established in many cases, particularly in Thorpe *v.* Thorpe,[1] Callonel *v.* Briggs,[2] Kingston *v.* Preston,[3] Jones *v.* Barclay,[4] and Goodisson *v.* Nunn,[5] that when something is to be done by both parties to a contract at the same time, as in this case the tendering of the money and the delivery of the corn, there the party suing the other for non-performance of his part must aver an offer at least at the same time to perform what was to be done by himself.

Law, *Wood*, and *Scarlett*, now shewed cause. The covenants here are mutual and independent, and each party has a remedy by action against the other for non-performance of his part. But if there be any precedence between them, the delivery of the goods ought in the regular order of things to precede the payment of the price. In neither case can the averment contended for be necessary. The distinction is taken in many cases that where two things are to be done, and the time of doing it is mentioned for one and not for the other, there the thing for doing which the time is stipulated must be done first, and so averred to be. Pafford *v.* Webbe, 2 Rol. Rep. 88; Pordage *v.* Cole, 1 Saund. 319; Peters *v.* Opie, 2 Saund. 352, 1 Ventr. 177, 214; Elwick *v.* Cudworth, 1 Lutwitch, 493; Hilton *v.* Smith, ib. 496. So in Thorpe *v.* Thorpe,[6] it was said by Holt, C. J., that if by the agreement a day certain is appointed for the payment of money, and this day is to happen before the act can be performed for which the money is to be paid, there although the words are that he shall pay so much for the performance of the act, yet after the day appointed the party shall have his action for the money before the thing is performed. And that is a stronger case than the present, because the act for which the recompense is to be given ought in reason to precede the recompense itself. In Blackwell *v.* Nash[7] the plaintiff declared in debt for a penalty on a covenant that he should transfer so much stock to the defendant on or before the 21st September, and that the defendant in consideration of the premises covenanted to accept and pay for it; and then the plaintiff averred that he was ready and offered to transfer the stock on that day, but that the defendant refused to accept or pay for it. It was objected in arrest of judgment that the actual transfer of the stock was a condition precedent which ought to have been averred, but the court held that "in consideration of the premises" meant in consideration of the covenant to transfer, and not of an actual transferring, for which the defendant had his remedy; though if it did mean the latter, a tender and refusal would amount to performance. And they added that in all such cases the great question was, who was to do the first act? But that where the transfer was to be upon payment, there was no color to make the transfer a condition precedent. The

[1] Salk. 171.
[2] Salk. 113.
[3] Dougl. 3d edit. 688.
[4] Dougl. 3d edit. 684.
[5] 4 T. R. 761.
[6] 1 Salk. 171, 1 Lutw. 250.
[7] 1 Str. 535.

same doctrine was held in Dawson v. Myer.[1] These cases went on the ground that the parties had mutual remedies on their reciprocal promises, and therefore there was no need of the averment contended for. But the case of Merrit v. Rane[2] applies as strongly in another point of view. There the plaintiff declared on an agreement that in consideration of £252 paid to the defendant, he agreed to transfer £6000 South-sea stock to the plaintiff or his executors, &c., at any time before the 9th January, 1720, within three days after demand in writing, upon payment of the further sum of £9000; then he averred the demand in writing, and that he attended on the day, but that the defendant did not appear to transfer. One of the objections was, that the plaintiff had not averred that he had the money there on the day to have paid upon the transfer; but the court said that as to the plaintiff's not shewing a tender, that ought to have come from the defendant by way of excuse, that he was there ready to have transferred if the plaintiff had been there to have paid the money. To apply therefore the reasoning of all these authorities to the present case: Here the first act to be done was by the defendant, namely, the carrying of the corn to Shardlow; by not doing which he broke his agreement, and a cause of action accrued to the plaintiff according to that class of cases, wherein agreements of this sort have been construed to give mutual remedies to the parties. But admitting that he was not bound to deliver the corn there until the plaintiff was prepared to pay for it; still that ought to come from the defendant by way of excuse, and the tender of payment was not necessary to be averred by the plaintiff as a condition precedent to the right of action. The defendant might have shewn in excuse for the non-performance on his part, either that he carried the corn to the place, and was ready to have delivered it, but that the plaintiff was not there to receive it; or that the plaintiff refused to receive it; or that he was not ready to pay for it. Lancashire v. Killingworth, 12 Mod. 531, Salk. 624; Ughtred's case, 7 Co. 10. Where an action is brought for money due, the defendant may shew in his defence a tender and refusal, or that he was prepared at the day and place appointed to pay the money, but that the plaintiff was not there to receive it; yet it never was held necessary for the plaintiff to aver in his declaration that he was ready to receive it. And here, if the readiness to pay had been averred, it could have answered no purpose; because no issue could have been taken on it. Besides, in no case is tender of payment necessary to be averred when the contract is executory, as it is in this case, for there the parties necessarily rely upon the mutual remedies arising out of it; they give mutual credit to each other. All the cases cited on the other side are, if strictly considered, cases of condition precedent. Several of them, as well as the subsequent cases of Camp-

[1] 1 Str. 712. [2] 1 Str. 458.

bell v. Jones[1] and Porter v. Shepherd,[2] laid down the rule that whether covenants be or be not independent on each other must depend on the good sense of the thing; that is, who in the fair sense and meaning of the parties was required to do the first act. Now here there is no doubt that the first act was to be done by the defendant, which he neglected to do: and it would be absurd to require a person to pay for goods before he had received them; though if he were not ready to pay for them at the time when the other was ready to deliver them, that might be a reason for the non-delivery. But still that is only matter of defence and excuse on the part of the defendant, which it is incumbent on him to shew. And yet the effect of the averment required is, that the plaintiff was bound to tender the price before the goods were even offered to him.

Holroyd, contra. This action is not brought against the defendant for having omitted to carry the corn to Shardlow, even allowing that to be the first act to be done; and therefore much of the plaintiff's argument does not apply. But the ground of complaint is that it was not delivered to him there; and consequently upon this form of declaring it may be assumed that the defendant did carry the corn there. The question then comes to this, whether the defendant was bound to deliver his corn, the plaintiff not being there ready to pay for it. For if not, then it follows, according to all the late determinations, that he ought to have averred a tender of the price, or that he was there ready to pay for it, if the defendant had been there ready to receive it, and deliver the corn. And for this purpose it is not necessary to shew that the tender of the price was a condition precedent, strictly so considered; for according to Goodisson v. Nunn[3] and Kingston v. Preston,[4] if the acts are concurrent and in the nature of the transaction to be done at the same time, before one of the parties can maintain an action against the other for the non-performance of his part, he must aver that he performed or was ready to perform every thing on his own part. Callonel v. Briggs[5] is in point. That was an executory agreement, like the present, to pay so much money six months after the bargain, the plaintiff transferring stock. There Lord Holt said "if either party would sue upon this agreement, the plaintiff for not paying, or the defendant for not transferring, the one must aver and prove a transfer or a tender, and the other a payment or a tender; and this," says he, "though there be mutual promises. If I sell you my horse for £10, if you will have the horse, I must have the money; or if I will have the money, you must have the horse." Or according to Lancashire v. Killingworth,[6] the plaintiff should have averred that he was ready at the place to have received the corn on the last day of the

[1] 6 T. R. 570. [2] 6 T. R. 665. [3] 4 T. R. 761.
[4] Dougl. 3d edit. 688. [5] Salk. 113.
[6] Salk. 623.

time within which it was to be delivered, and ready and willing to have paid the price; but that no person was there on the part of the defendant to deliver the corn. The delivery of the corn and the payment of the price were concurrent acts to be done by the parties at the same time, the one depending on the other; and if so, then within the principle of all the modern cases, the plaintiff ought to have averred in his declaration a tender of the price, for want of which it is bad.

LORD KENYON, C. J. If this question depended on the technical niceties of pleading, I should not feel so much confidence as I do; but it depends altogether on the true construction of this agreement. The defendant agreed with the plaintiff for a certain quantity of corn, to be delivered at Shardlow within a certain time; and there can be no doubt but that the parties intended that the payment should be made at the time of the delivery. It is not imputed to the defendant that he did not carry the corn to Shardlow, but that he did not deliver it to the plaintiff; to this declaration the defendant objects, and says, "I did not deliver the corn to you (the plaintiff), because you do not say that you were ready to pay for it; and if you were not ready, I am not bound to deliver the corn;" and the question is, whether that should or should not have been alleged. The case decided by Lord Holt, in Salk. 112, if, indeed, so plain a case wanted that authority to support it, shews that where two concurrent acts are to be done, the party who sues the other for non-performance must aver that he had performed, or was ready to perform his part of the contract. Then the plaintiff in this case cannot impute to the defendant the non-delivery of the corn, without alleging that he was ready to pay the price of it. A plaintiff, who comes into a court of justice, must shew that he is in a condition to maintain his action. But it has been argued that the delivery of the corn was a condition precedent, and some cases have been cited to prove it; but they do not appear to me to be applicable. In the one in Saunders,[1] the party was to pull down a wall, and was then to be paid for it; there is no doubt but that the pulling down of the wall was a condition precedent to the payment; the act was to be done, and then the price was to be paid for it. So in the case in Salk. 171, where work was to be done, and then the workman was to be paid. And in ordinary cases of this kind the work is to be done before the wages are earned; but those cases do not apply to the present, where both the acts are to be done at the same time. Speaking of conditions precedent and subsequent in other cases only leads to confusion. In the case of Campbell v. Jones, I thought, and still continue of that opinion, that whether covenants be or be not independent of each other must depend on the good sense of the case, and on the order in which the several things are to be done; but here both things, the delivery of

[1] 2 Saund. 250.

the corn by one, and the payment by the other, were to be done at the same time; and as the plaintiff has not averred that he was ready to pay for the corn, he cannot maintain this action against the defendant for not delivering it.

GROSE, J. It is difficult to reconcile all the cases in the books on the subject of conditions precedent; but the good sense to be extracted from them all is, that if one party covenant to do one thing in consideration of the other party's doing another, each must be ready to perform his part of the contract at the time he charges the other with non-performance. Here the question is, what was the intention of the parties; they clearly intended that something should be done by each at the same time. The corn was to be delivered at Shardlow to the plaintiff for a certain price to be therefore paid by him, that is, at the time of the delivery; then the readiness to pay should have been averred by the plaintiff.

LAWRENCE, J. It has been argued, on behalf of the plaintiff, that this must be considered as a declaration on mutual promises, and that as this is a demand on the defendant on the ground of some mutual promise made by him, and which was the consideration of the plaintiff's promise, it was not necessary to aver performance on his part; but if so, the declaration is not adapted to the truth of the case in not stating that the defendant's promise was in consideration of the plaintiff's. But on this declaration I can only consider it as an agreement by the defendant to deliver the corn at Shardlow on being paid for it. The payment of the money was to be an act concurrent with the delivery; and then the case is like that of Callonel v. Briggs, which was on an agreement to pay so much money six months after the bargain, the plaintiff transferring stock; and there Lord Holt said, "If either party would sue upon this agreement, the plaintiff for not paying, or the defendant for not transferring, the one must aver and prove a transfer or a tender." He did not say that the not doing it should come from the defendant by way of excuse, but that the doing it must be alleged in the declaration; and that affords an answer to great part of the argument urged on behalf of the defendant in this case. The tendering of the money by the plaintiff makes part of the plaintiff's title to recover, and he must set out the whole of his title. The strongest case cited for the defendant was that of Merrit v. Rane;[1] but that does not appear to me of sufficient weight to overturn the authority of the case of Callonel v. Briggs. I do not quite understand what the court there said, that it was not necessary to allege a tender, for that it should have come from the defendant by way of excuse; for as it was stated that the plaintiff's agent was ready to receive a transfer of the stock, but that the defendant did not attend, it would have been absurd to state

[1] 1 Str. 458.

a tender of the money to a person who was not present to receive it. There is, however, another case, not referred to in the argument, Lea v. Exelby,[1] which is an authority to shew that the plaintiff in this case should have averred a tender. There the plaintiff declared that in consideration that he had promised to pay the defendant (who was possessed of a lease for years, the inheritance of which was in the plaintiff), a certain sum on such a day, the defendant promised on payment to surrender to him the lease; and that he had tendered the money at the time, but that the defendant had not surrendered; and on motion in arrest of judgment, because it was not alleged that the defendant refused as well as that the plaintiff tendered, the court held that the declaration was bad for that reason. Therefore, on the authority of that case, and of that of Callonel v. Briggs, I am of opinion that the declaration cannot be supported, and that the judgment must be arrested.

Rule absolute.

GLAZEBROOK, Clerk, v. WOODROW, Clerk.

In the King's Bench, November 19, 1799.

[*Reported in* 8 *Term Reports*, 366.]

In covenant the declaration stated that by articles of agreement under seal, made on the 10th of March, 1796, between the plaintiff and the defendant (after reciting that the plaintiff had established a grammar-school at Warrington in which he had many scholars, and for the purpose of conducting the said school with convenience had possessed himself of a piece of ground, on which he had erected a building appropriated to instruction, &c., and being about to leave Warrington had agreed with the defendant to sell him, not only his right, title, and interest in the said ground and building, subject to a yearly ground rent of 16*s.* 6*d.*, payable to J. Blackburne, in fee, but to surrender to him the pupils he then had under his care, so far as in him lay, together with all benefit arising therefrom, for the considerations thereinafter mentioned), the plaintiff covenanted and agreed to and with the defendant that he the plaintiff would on or before the 1st of August, 1797, convey to the defendant, his heirs, &c., the said ground with the buildings thereon erected, subject as aforesaid, and the fixtures therein, for all the plaintiff's right, title, and interest in the premises; and would on or before the 24th of June, 1796, surrender up the use and enjoyment of the said premises, and

[1] Cro. Eliz. 388.

deliver over as far as in him lay all the pupils he might then happen to have under his care to the care of the defendant, and all the profits arising from them; and also that he the plaintiff would in the mean time use his utmost endeavors with the parents and guardians of the children committed or to be committed to his care in Warrington to induce them to continue their children under the care and tuition of the defendant, &c.; and in consideration thereof the defendant covenanted and agreed to and with the plaintiff that the defendant, his executors, &c., would on or before the said 1st of August, 1797, pay the plaintiff, his executors, &c., the sum of £120 with lawful interest from the 1st of January next preceding the said 1st of August. The plaintiff then averred that in pursuance of the said articles he afterwards, viz., on the said 24th of June, 1796, surrendered up the use and enjoyment of the said ground with the buildings, &c., to the defendant, who thereupon entered upon and became and was and from thence hitherto hath been and still is thereof possessed, and also then delivered over as far as in him lay all the pupils he then had under his care and all the profits, &c.; and although the plaintiff had well and truly performed every thing else in the said articles contained on his part, yet protesting that the defendant had not performed any thing in the said articles contained on his part, the plaintiff averred that the defendant did not on the said 1st of August, 1797, or at any other time before or since, pay the said £120 with interest, &c., to the plaintiff, but wholly refused to pay the same, &c.; wherefore, &c.

To this the defendant pleaded, first, that from the time of making the said articles until and on the 1st of August, 1797, he the defendant was ready to accept a conveyance of the said ground in the declaration mentioned, with the buildings, &c., for and during all the plaintiff's right, title, and interest in the same, and at the same time to pay the said £120 in the declaration mentioned, with interest, &c., if the plaintiff would have made or procured any such conveyance or assurance, yet that the plaintiff did not on or before the said 1st of August, 1797, or at any time since convey to the defendant the said ground, with the buildings, &c., for and during all the plaintiff's right, &c.; wherefore the defendant had not paid to the plaintiff the said £120, &c. There was a second plea to the like effect; stating that the plaintiff had not tendered any conveyance of the premises, &c.

To these pleas there was a general demurrer, and joinder in demurrer.

Yates, in support of the demurrer. The question is whether the covenant to convey, and the covenant to pay the stipulated price, be dependent covenants, or whether they be mutual and independent covenants, for the breach of which the parties must respectively resort to their remedy by action. It may be admitted that if the performance of a covenant, for the breach of which the defendant is charged, depends upon a prior act to be done by the plaintiff, the non-performance of such prior act may be pleaded in bar of the plaintiff's action. But here the covenants are independent; and therefore it was not necessary in order to maintain the action for the £120 for the plaintiff to aver the execution or tender of a conveyance on or before the 1st of August, 1797; consequently the allegation of the non-performance of those acts by the defendant in his pleas is no bar to the plaintiff's recovery. It has been long settled that no precise form of words is necessary to make a covenant, precedent, mutual or subsequent, but it depends upon the intention of the parties and the good sense of the thing. Thorpe *v.* Thorpe.[1] It was there said that where the things to be performed by the parties respectively are to be done at different times, that shews that the covenants are not dependent one on the other, but that the parties look to different remedies to secure the performance of them. Now here the defendant was to be put in possession of the premises and of the pupils of the school on the 24th of June, 1796, and it was not until the 1st of August, 1797, that the conveyance was to be executed and the money paid. The defendant therefore has long ago had the advantage of the partial execution of the contract, by being put in possession of the school and of the emoluments arising from it, which is the material and substantial part of the contract. The same doctrine was laid down in Campbell *v.* Jones.[2] There one who had obtained a patent for an improved method of bleaching linen, &c., contracted with the defendant in consideration of £250 paid down, and of £250 more to be paid on a certain day or sooner, to instruct him in his art, and the defendant covenanted to pay the further sum on that day or sooner if the plaintiff instructed him before. There the court held that the times stipulated for the performance of the respective acts being fixed, the one could not be said to depend on the other; and accordingly the plaintiff had judgment in covenant for the £250, without averring that he had given the defendant the necessary instruction, in respect of which the money was to be paid. If it be objected that here the words of the covenant shew a condition precedent, for that the defendant only covenanted to pay the money "in consideration thereof," &c., *i. e.*, of all that the plaintiff had before engaged to do, the case of Boone *v.* Eyre[3] is an authority in answer to shew that those or the like expressions do not in themselves make a condition precedent, if on the whole the intention of the parties appears to have been otherwise. There the plaintiff had sold a plantation in Dominica, with the negroes thereon, to the defendant under certain covenants, in consideration of £500 and a certain annuity for lives; and the defendant covenanted with the plaintiff that, "he the said plaintiff well and truly performing

[1] Salk. 171. [2] 6 T. R. 570. [3] 2 Blac. Rep. 1312.

all the covenants in the said indenture of sale contained," the defendant should pay the said annuity; and in an action on the covenant for non-payment of the annuity the plaintiff averred performance generally of all the covenants on his part; the defendant in answer pleaded specially non-performance by the plaintiff of certain covenants contained in the indenture of sale, as that he had no title, and had not delivered possession, &c.; but the court on demurrer gave judgment for the plaintiff, on the ground that those words did not make a condition precedent; but that the covenants were mutual and independent. Now that case cannot be distinguished on principle from the present; for there the annuity was in the nature of a payment for the estate, of which it was admitted that the plaintiff had not put the defendant in possession; whereas here the defendant has had the benefit of the estate, and has his remedy on the covenant for the non-execution of the conveyance.

Wood, contra, agreed in the general principle first stated, but contended that upon the plain sense and reason of the contract the conveyance and the payment were intended to be concurrent acts. The same day was named for the performance of both; and it would be unreasonable, merely because the defendant was put in possession of the premises, that he should be compelled to pay the purchase-money before a title was made to him; for he might be evicted by an ejectment immediately after, and would be driven to his remedy in a court of equity. In the cases cited the respective acts of the parties were to be performed at different times; but here, though the plaintiff was to do one act before, yet the material acts were to be done on the first of August, 1797, and the defendant only covenanted to pay the money on that day in consideration of the plaintiff having performed all that he had engaged to do on or before that day. This case is in effect the same as that of Goodisson *v.* Nunn,[1] where the plaintiff having agreed to sell the defendant his estate for £210 on a certain day, in consideration whereof the defendant covenanted to pay that sum on that day, and on failure to pay £21, the court held them to be dependent covenants, and that the plaintiff could not recover the £21 without shewing a conveyance or at least a tender of one on his part.

Yates, in reply, said that this case was different from that of Goodisson *v.* Nunn, inasmuch as there no part of the consideration was performed by the plaintiff, and all was to have been done at one and the same time; whereas here the material and beneficial part has been performed, namely, the putting the defendant in possession of the premises and of the emoluments arising from the school, and a different day was appointed for the performance of what was stipulated to be done by the defendant.

[1] 4 T. R. 761.

LORD KENYON, C. J. The cases which have been mentioned are in my recollection; and, although I have not the least doubt what the sense and justice of this case require to be done, yet if I found that I should thereby transgress any technical rule of law which had been established, I would not set up my opinion against the wisdom of those who are gone before me. But I am fully satisfied that what justice requires to be done in this case will not contravene any principle of law which has been established in those cases. The general rule which governs them all is that every man's agreement is to be performed according to his intent, as far as that is to be collected from the particular instrument. Now here the case is that the plaintiff, being in possession of a school, covenanted with the defendant to convey to him the good will of it (if I may use the expression) and the building itself on or before the first of August, 1797, and in the mean time he consented to put him in possession of the premises on some prior day; on the other hand, the defendant engaged to pay him a stipulated price, in consideration of all that the other had undertaken to do, on or before the same first of August. And now the plaintiff, who is to execute the conveyance, and who is also the person to pay for it, not having made it or made a tender of it to the defendant, nevertheless calls upon him by this action to pay the consideration money. The very statement of such a claim is enough to refute it. If these be not dependent covenants, it is difficult to conceive what covenants are so. The very substance of the consideration to entitle the plaintiff to receive the money was the making of the conveyance required; and it is admitted that he has not done it: that makes an end of the question. The case of Campbell *v.* Jones was very different from the present; for there the instruction to be given was not to be, and could not in the nature of the thing be, performed at the same time with the payment of the money by the defendant, for which a certain time was limited; whereas no time was limited for giving the instruction. But here the parties have stipulated for the conveyance and the payment to be performed at the same time. And if we were to hold otherwise in such a case as the present, the greatest injustice might be done; for supposing, in the instance of a trader who had entered into such a contract for the sale of an estate, that between the making of the contract and the final execution of it he were to become a bankrupt, the vendee might be in the situation of having had payment enforced from him, and yet be disabled from procuring the property for which he had paid. The injustice of such a procedure is too manifest to be insisted upon further.

GROSE, J. The question is whether these covenants be dependent or independent, and that must be collected from the apparent intention of the parties to the contract. There is certainly some confusion in the books on this subject, some of the older cases leaning to construe covenants of this sort to be independent, contrary to the real sense of the parties and the true justice of the case. But the later authorities convey more just sentiments; and the case of Kingston *v.* Preston[1] was the first strong authority in which they prevailed in opposition to the former. Nothing indeed could exhibit the doctrine which ought to prevail in these instances in a stronger point of view than the circumstances of that case; for there, if the plaintiff had prevailed, the most flagrant injustice would have been committed. The fact was that the defendant, being possessed of a very large stock in trade, covenanted with the plaintiff to assign the same to him and another person at the end of a twelvemonth at a fair valuation, when deeds of partnership were to be executed between the two last persons; and the plaintiff covenanted that he would at and before the sealing and delivery of the deeds procure good and sufficient security to be given to the defendant, and to be approved of by him, for the payment of a certain stipulated sum by monthly instalments; and there the attempt was by the plaintiff to get possession of the whole stock in trade of the defendant to a great amount, without giving him any security at all, to his inevitable ruin. But the absurdity and injustice of the thing struck the court so forcibly that they said it could never have been the intention of the parties that the defendant should surrender his whole fortune into the plaintiff's hands without the previous security which he had insisted upon, and that he should solely rely upon his remedy by action for the breach of the plaintiff's covenant: they therefore gave judgment for the defendant. I have since found that that was not the first case where those sentiments began to be entertained; for it appears from a late publication of reports from the manuscripts of Lord Chief Justice Willes that in a case of Thomas *v.* Cadwallader,[2] his lordship noticed the injurious tendency of the doctrine which had before that time prevailed in these cases; and seemed very desirous that the governing rule should be so to construe such covenants as that the real intention of the parties should be carried into effect, to attain the true justice of the case. This was afterwards done in the case of Kingston *v.* Preston; and that has since been settled to be the rule in many cases. Now here the plaintiff covenanted to convey on or before the first of August, 1797, though the defendant was to be put in possession before. And the reason why the conveyance was not to be executed before is obvious; because that was the day on which the money was to be paid. Then what is the true justice of this case and the evident meaning of the parties? It is plainly this, that the execution of the conveyance and the payment of the money should be concurrent acts, and even the

[1] Cited at large in Jones *v.* Barkley, Dougl. 689.

[2] Willes's Rep. 496.

payment of the interest was to be deferred till the first of August, though it was to run from the first of January preceding. Then there is an end of the question; because it is not pretended that the plaintiff had conveyed or was ready to convey at the time. How far the determination in Boone *v.* Eyre militates against the principles I have laid down may be a matter of doubt; but the intention of the parties is or is assumed to be the governing principle of all the late determinations.

LAWRENCE, J. The plaintiff's case is attempted to be maintained on the supposed intention of the parties and on authorities. 1st. On the intention of the parties, it is said that where one promises to another to perform a certain thing in consideration of several matters to be performed by himself, he is entitled to maintain an action against that other for non-performance of his engagement, if he himself has performed any one of the things stipulated by him to be done. Therefore, that in this instance the plaintiff, who has covenanted to put the defendant in possession and to convey the premises to him in consideration of a certain sum, is entitled upon performance of one of those things to maintain his action for the consideration money. But it is clear that if the agreement appears to be that the whole of what the plaintiff engaged for was to be done before the money was to be paid, it will not follow that, because a part only has been performed, he can recover the money, and leave the defendant to his remedy upon the agreement for the breach of the other part. For whether one promise be the consideration of another, or whether the performance and not the mere promise be the consideration, must be gathered from, and depends entirely upon, the words and nature of the agreement. Now, suppose the terms of the agreement had been that the plaintiff was to put the defendant in possession of and to convey the premises to him on or before the 1st of August; and that upon the defendant's being put in possession and the conveyance made to him he was to pay the purchase-money on or before that day; there could be no doubt but that the conveyance must be made as well as the possession delivered up before any right to the purchase-money would accrue. Whatever the form of the words may be, if we can collect from the face of the instrument that the whole was to be performed by the plaintiff before the money was to be paid, nothing short of the performance of the whole can enable him to sustain this action for the money. But authorities have been cited to shew that, where a certain time is fixed for the payment of money in consideration of certain acts stipulated to be done, a partial performance of such acts is sufficient to found an action for the money: but the cases cited do not warrant so general a conclusion. Part execution is only a circumstance from whence the intention of the parties is to be collected; but nothing is to be inferred from it in favor of the plaintiff in this case; for though the defendant was to be put in possession in June, 1796, and the money was to be paid in August, 1797, yet as that also was the time fixed for the execution of the conveyance, it is plain that the defendant did not intend to part with his money till his title was secure. In the case of Boone *v.* Eyre,[1] the plaintiff had sold to the defendant an estate in Dominica, with the negroes, under the usual covenants for a good title and quiet enjoyment and further assurances, in consideration of a sum in gross and a certain annuity for lives, which the defendant covenanted to pay, "he the plaintiff well and truly performing all and singular the covenants, clauses, recitals, and agreements in the said indenture of sale contained:" and in bar to an action of covenant for the arrears of the annuity, besides assigning breaches of specific and partial covenants, the defendant by his fourth plea pleaded "that the plaintiff at the time of making the said indenture had not in himself full power, true title, and good and lawful authority to bargain, sell, and release the said plantation, and negroes, &c., *in manner and form as in the said indenture mentioned*." The court said it would be strange if such a defence were to be allowed, when if any one negro on the plantation were proved not to have been the property of the plaintiff, it would bar his action for the annuity. The judgment of the court there went on the ground that, in the form the breaches were assigned the plea did not necessarily go to the whole of the consideration. But if the plea had been that the plaintiff had no title at all to the plantation itself, I do not know that it would not have been holden sufficient. So in Campbell *v.* Jones the defendant against whom the action was maintained had the whole of what was to be conveyed to him; and the substantial part of the consideration was the right of using the method of bleaching described in the patent; though in addition to that the plaintiff had also engaged to instruct him in the use of that method; the not doing of which might be recompensed in damages. That instruction might consistently with the plaintiff's covenant as well be given after as before the time specified for the payment of the money, and therefore it was not necessary to be averred in an action to recover the money. Therefore, neither upon the reason of the thing nor the authorities is the plaintiff entitled to recover.

LE BLANC, J. This case falls within the rule first laid down in Kingston *v.* Preston, that no person shall call upon another to perform his part of a contract until he himself has performed all that he has stipulated to do as the consideration of the other's promises. This rule, I think, applies to every case of a sale of property, where one

1 This was cited from the case reported in 1 H. Blac. 273, note *a.*; and also, from a MS. note which is referred to by Lord Kenyon in giving judgment in Campbell *v.* Jones, 6 T. R. 573, and not from the case reported by Mr. Justice Blackstone, 2 vol. 1312.

engages to convey on a certain day, and the other to pay at the same time; and this, whether the one be stated in terms to be in consideration of the other or not. In neither case will the court compel one party to perform his part until the other has done or has offered to do his own. This is the case of a covenant for the sale of a school-house, where the plaintiff covenanted to convey on or before a certain day, and the defendant on or before that day covenanted to pay him. The payment therefore is the consideration for the conveyance, and cannot be enforced till that be made, or at least offered to be made by the plaintiff. But an attempt has been made to bring this case within the distinction taken in some of the cases; where one party having had the advantage of all the material part of the agreement, the other has been permitted to sustain his action for the consideration, although there may not have been a literal performance of other parts. Thus in Boone *v.* Eyre, the substantial part of the agreement being the conveyance of the property in respect of which the annuity was to be paid, the court held it to be no answer to an action for the annuity to say that the plaintiff had not a good title in some of the negroes which were upon the plantations, because all the material part of the covenant had been performed, and the plaintiff had a remedy upon the covenant for any special damage sustained by the non-performance of the rest. So in Campbell *v.* Jones, the material part was the conveyance of the patent-right, and that being performed the court held that the giving of the instruction concerning the proper use of it, which might be given at any time afterwards, need not be averred in order to sustain the action for the recompense; but that a breach of that part of the agreement might be compensated in damages. So here the material part of the covenant being the conveyance, the plaintiff cannot entitle himself to the money until he has shewn that every thing was done which he had undertaken to perform on his part as the consideration of that payment.

Judgment for the defendant.

WITHERS *v.* REYNOLDS.

IN THE KING'S BENCH, NOVEMBER 14, 1831.

[*Reported in 2 Barnewall & Adolphus*, 882.]

ASSUMPSIT for not delivering straw to the plaintiff pursuant to agreement. At the trial before Lord Tenterden, C. J., at the sittings in Middlesex after last Hilary Term, the agreement proved was as follows:—

"John Reynolds undertakes and agrees to supply Joseph Withers with wheat straw of good quality sufficient for his use as a stable-keeper, and delivered on his premises as above" (*i. e.*, at Long Acre, London), "till the 24th of June, 1830, at the sum of thirty-three shillings per load of thirty-six trusses, to be delivered at the rate of three loads in a fortnight, in a dry state and without damage. And the said J. W. hereby agrees to pay to the said J. R. or his order the sum of thirty-three shillings per load for each load of straw so delivered on his premises from this day till the 24th of June, 1830, according to the terms of this agreement.

(Signed) "JOSEPH WITHERS, JOHN REYNOLDS."

The straw was regularly sent in from the 20th of October, 1829, when this agreement was made, till the end of January, 1830. At that time, the plaintiff being in arrear for several loads of straw, the defendant called upon him for the amount, and he thereupon tendered to the defendant £11 11*s.*, being the price of all the straw delivered except the last load, saying that he should always keep one load in hand. The defendant objected to this, but was at length obliged to take the sum offered; and he then told the plaintiff that he would send no more straw unless it was paid for on delivery; and accordingly no more was sent. On the part of the defendant it was submitted that there must be a nonsuit, inasmuch as the plaintiff, on his own shewing, had not performed his own part of the contract, which was, in effect, to pay for each load on delivery. Lord Tenterden, C. J., was of this opinion, but directed a verdict for the plaintiff, reserving the point. A rule *nisi* was afterwards obtained for entering a nonsuit.

Campbell and *R. V. Richards* now shewed cause. Two things independent of each other were stipulated by this contract to be done by the respective parties; the defendant was to deliver straw; the plaintiff to pay the price. No time of payment was specified. There appears nothing which could entitle the defendant to insist on receiving his money till the whole quantity of straw was delivered. Payment, then, was not a condition of the defendant's performance of his contract. His promise was given in consideration that the plaintiff promised to pay, not in consideration of performance. If the plaintiff was bound to pay for each load on delivery, still it does not follow that a refusal to pay for one load excused the defendant from any future performance of his contract. Weaver *v.* Sessions.[1] And according to that case, he ought at least to have shewn that he subsequently made a tender of executing his part of the agreement, which the plaintiff rejected. The defendant, therefore, upon his construction of the agreement may be entitled to bring a cross-action, but has no defence to this.

[1] 6 Taunt. 154.

Platt, contra. The only question is upon the construction of this agreement. It is true, no time of payment was specified, but in the absence of any express stipulation the money would be payable on demand as often as it became due; and here the words, "to pay thirty-three shillings per load for each load so delivered," intimate that the price of each load was to be due as soon as it was delivered. (Here he was stopped by the court.)

LORD TENTERDEN, C. J. I am of opinion that the plaintiff is not entitled to recover. There is, I think, no doubt that by the terms of this agreement the plaintiff was to pay for the loads of straw as they were delivered. If that were not so, the defendant would have been liable to the inconvenience of giving credit for an indefinite length of time, and in case of non-payment, bringing an action for a very large sum of money, which does not appear to have been intended by the contract. Then the only question is, whether upon the plaintiff's saying, "I will not pay for the goods on delivery" (for that was the effect of his communication to the defendant), it was incumbent on the defendant to go on supplying straw: and he clearly was not obliged to do so.

PARKE, J. The substance of the agreement was, that the straw should be paid for on delivery. The defendant clearly did not contemplate giving credit. When, therefore, the plaintiff said that he would not pay on delivery (as he did in substance, when he insisted on keeping one load in hand), the defendant was not obliged to go on supplying him.

TAUNTON, J. The contract does not say merely that so much straw shall be supplied at thirty-three shillings a load, but it adds that the plaintiff shall pay that sum "for each load of straw delivered on his premises" from the date of the agreement till the 24th of June, 1830. That *prima facie* imports that each load was to be paid for as delivered.

PATTESON, J. If the plaintiff had merely failed to pay for any particular load, that of itself might not have been an excuse to the defendant for delivering no more straw; but the plaintiff here expressly refuses to pay for the loads as delivered; the defendant, therefore, is not liable for ceasing to perform his part of the contract.

Rule absolute.[1]

[1] See Tipton v. Feitner, 20 N. Y. 423. — ED.

ATKINSON AND OTHERS v. SMITH.

IN THE EXCHEQUER, NOVEMBER 8, 1845.

[*Reported in 14 Meeson & Welsby, 695.*]

ASSUMPSIT. The declaration stated that heretofore, to wit, on the 22d of November, 1844, it was agreed between the plaintiffs and the defendant, that the defendant should sell to the plaintiffs, and the plaintiffs should buy of the defendant, a large quantity, to wit, twenty-four packs of noils, to be delivered by the defendant to the plaintiffs within a reasonable time, and to be paid for on delivery thereof; and thereupon, in consideration of the premises, &c., and that the plaintiffs had promised to defendant to accept and pay for the same, he the defendant promised the plaintiffs to deliver the said noils in a reasonable time. Breach, that although the defendant delivered to the plaintiffs part of the said noils, yet that he did not nor would, within a reasonable time, deliver the residue thereof. Plea, *non assumpsit.*

At the trial before ROLFE, B., at the last Yorke Assizes, it appeared that in November, 1844, the defendant's agent applied to the plaintiffs to sell to the defendant some Cheviot fleeces, and at the same time agreed on his part to sell to the plaintiffs a quantity of coarse woollen cloths called "noils." The following note was exchanged between the parties:—

Bought of Messrs. W. F. Atkinson & Co. about thirty packs of Cheviot fleeces, ewes and hogs, and agreed to take the undermentioned noils; also agreed to draw for £250 on account at three months.

16 packs No. 5 noils, at 10¾*d.*
8 packs No. 4 noils, at 12*d.*

S. & W. SMITH.
22d Nov., 1844. P. H. SIMPSON.

It appeared that the plaintiffs supplied to the defendant a part only of the fleeces agreed for, and on the other hand, that the defendant delivered to the plaintiffs part of the noils; but, on their rising in price, refused to deliver the remainder, on which this action was brought. It was contended for the defendant, under the circumstances, that the plaintiffs could not recover, for that they were bound, the whole being one contract, to have averred and proved, as a condition precedent, the delivery or tender of all the fleeces to the defendant; and the learned judge being of this opinion directed a nonsuit, reserving to the plaintiffs leave to move to enter a verdict for £25, if the court should think that the agreements of the parties were not dependent agreements.

Baines now moved accordingly. The only question in this case is, whether the agreements of the plaintiffs to sell the fleeces and to take the noils, are dependent or independent agreements. If they are independent, each party of course has his remedy against the other for the non-performance of either of them. If the word "take" is to be construed to mean "take in part-payment" for the fleeces, the ruling of the learned judge was correct; but it would rather seem to mean "take by way of purchase." The acts and conduct of the parties are to be looked at in aid of the construction of the contract, and the defendant's refusal to deliver the remainder of the noils because the market had risen, shews that he considered it a purchase of the noils. [ALDERSON, B. Surely it is all one contract. The one sale is a consideration for the other. The plaintiffs should have declared on a contract that, in consideration that they would sell wool, the defendant would deliver noils by way of part-payment, and give a cheque for £250 for the residue. PARKE, B. The plaintiffs say, "We will sell you wool at such a price, provided you will sell us noils at such a price." They are not independent contracts, but the whole is one entire contract; and if the plaintiffs do not supply the fleeces, the defendant is not bound to supply the noils. Even if the word "take" means to take by way of purchase, the result is the same, one stipulation being dependent on the other.]

Per Curiam,[1] *Rule refused.*

JOSEPH GILES v. HENRY GILES.

IN THE QUEEN'S BENCH, MAY 29, 1846.

[*Reported in* 9 *Queen's Bench Reports*, 164.]

ASSUMPSIT. The declaration stated that heretofore, to wit, 21st September, 1840, by an agreement then made, by defendant of the first part, plaintiff of the second part, and John Giles of the third part, reciting that Henry Giles, the elder (deceased), father of defendant and plaintiff, and of Ann Giles, wife of the said John Giles, made his will, dated 3d June, 1839, whereby, after giving an annuity of £30 to plaintiff, and to other parties two other annuities and a legacy, he devised to defendant all his freehold lands in Porthmeor, and all his leasehold lands in Rosemergee and Bojewyan, *habendum*, the freehold lands to defendant in fee, and the leasehold lands to defendant, his

[1] Pollock, C. B., Parke, B., Alderson, B., and Rolfe, B.

executors, &c., for all such term, &c., as might be to come at the time of testator's death, subject as to the freehold lands to the annuities and legacy, and appointed defendant sole executor and residuary legatee and devisee; reciting also that by indenture, dated 22d March, 1841, between the said H. Giles the elder of the first part, defendant of the second part, and Charles Paynter of the third part, H. Giles the elder demised to Paynter, his executors, &c., for two thousand years the aforesaid lands in Porthmeor, and assigned to him, his executors, &c., the said leasehold lands in Rosemergee and Bojewyan for the residue of the terms therein, in trust to pay to H. Giles the elder an annuity, and, subject thereto, upon trust for defendant, his executors, &c.; and reciting further, that by the revocation of the will by the indenture as touching the annuities and legacies charged on the lands, the annuitants and legatee were left wholly unprovided for: defendant, as well in consideration of the natural love and affection which he had and bore for and towards his brother the plaintiff, the other annuitants, and the legatee, and also for divers other good causes and considerations him thereunto moving, did, among other things, thereby agree to permit and suffer plaintiff to occupy all that part of the said lands and premises in Porthmeor aforesaid then in his possession, until 29th September, 1843, he, plaintiff, paying therefore on the last-mentioned day to defendant, as he thereby agreed to do, the sum of £30 as rent for the same, and then to deliver up the same premises to the defendant, his heirs, and assigns, in good tenantable repair, and in the mean time to manage, &c., the premises in a good husband-like manner, &c., and also to permit defendant, his heirs or assigns, to enter, &c. (for certain agricultural purposes); "and, upon the plaintiff, his heirs, executors, and administrators, so quitting the said premises, paying the said rent, and observing the other stipulations before mentioned, and releasing the defendant, his heirs, and assigns, from all claims of and under the said will; as also, releasing and quitting claim to the defendant, his heirs, executors, administrators, and assigns, all the freehold and leasehold lands and hereditaments which were of the said testator, devised or bequeathed, given, granted or demised, conveyed or assigned by or under any former will or settlement of the said Henry Giles, deceased, and which the plaintiff did thereby, for himself, his heirs, executors, and administrators, agree to do; he the defendant, his heirs, executors, administrators, or assigns, should and would well and truly pay unto the plaintiff the sum of £200 with interest," at £4 10*s.* per cent., to be calculated from 29th September then instant; "And it was by the said agreement further agreed between the parties thereto, that all deeds or releases to be required by the defendant from any or either of the other parties in pursuance of those presents should be prepared by the attorney of the defendant, his heirs, executors, administrators, or assigns, at his or their own expense." (The declaration then set out other stipulations on the part of defendant, not material to the decision of the court.) And the agreement having been so made, afterwards, to wit, on, &c., in consideration thereof, and that plaintiff at the request of defendant had then promised, &c.; averring mutual promises of performance. And plaintiff saith that he hath always from the making, &c., in all things on his part performed and fulfilled the same; and that afterwards, to wit, on the said 29th September, 1843, "he the plaintiff was ready and willing to quit and deliver up the said premises to the defendant, and to pay the said rent; and the plaintiff farther saith that, at all times from the making of the said agreement, he the plaintiff was ready and willing to release the defendant, his heirs and assigns, from all claim of and under the said will in the said agreement mentioned; and also, to release and quitclaim to the defendant, his heirs, executors, administrators, and assigns, all the freehold and leasehold lands and hereditaments, which were by the testator aforesaid devised or bequeathed, given, granted or demised, conveyed or assigned, by or under any former will or settlement of the said Henry Giles, deceased, aforesaid, and to complete and fulfil the said agreement; and although the said 29th September, 1843, did elapse a long time before the commencement of this suit, and although a reasonable time did elapse between the said last-mentioned day and the commencement of this suit, for the payment of the said sum of £200 and interest as aforesaid, according to the said agreement, of all which," &c. (notice to defendant); "and the plaintiff further says, that, although no release was prepared by the attorney of the defendant, on or before the said last-mentioned day, under and according to the said agreement, yet the defendant, not regarding the said agreement nor his said promise, hath not as yet paid the said sum of £200 with the interest," &c., although often requested.

Plea 2. That plaintiff was not ready and willing to quit and deliver up the said premises, so in the possession of plaintiff, as in the said agreement mentioned, and to pay the said rent, in manner and form, &c.: conclusion to the country.

Demurrer, assigning for causes that the plea is a traverse of an immaterial averment in the declaration, and tends to raise an immaterial issue: and that the delivery of possession of the premises mentioned in the agreement was an independent undertaking, and not a condition precedent to or concurrent with the payment of the money, in respect of the non-payment of which the action is brought. That the payment of the rent by plaintiff is not a condition precedent to or concurrent with the payment of the said money. That by the traverse two matters quite distinct in themselves are mixed up together, namely, the non-delivery of possession of the premises and the non-payment of the rent; whereas the denial of readiness and willingness ought to have been pleaded separately to each. That the plea is double.

Joinder in demurrer.

Plea 3. That plaintiff was not ready and willing to release the defendant, his heirs, &c., from all claim of and under the will in the agreement mentioned, and also to release and quitclaim to defendant, his heirs, &c., all the freehold and leasehold lands, &c. (as in the declaration), and to complete the said agreement, in manner and form, &c.; conclusion to the country.

Demurrer, assigning for cause that the plea is a traverse of an immaterial averment in the declaration, and tends to raise an immaterial issue: that the undertaking to release the defendant, his heirs and assigns, as in the agreement set forth, was a distinct and independent undertaking, and was not a condition precedent to or concurrent with the payment by defendant to plaintiff of the money. That it was defendant's duty to prepare and tender such release; and that this obligation on his part would not be waived or discharged by the mere fact that plaintiff was not ready or willing to execute it, and that, consequently, the averment of the plaintiff's readiness and willingness (taken *per se*) is wholly immaterial to the result of the action.

Joinder in demurrer.

The demurrer was argued in last Easter Term.

Butt, for the plaintiff. The pleas tender immaterial issues. The allegations which the pleas traverse were unnecessary, because they relate not to conditions precedent, but to independent stipulations. The authorities are collected in note (4) to Pordage *v.* Cole.[1] It is there laid down (rule 3) that, "where a covenant goes only to part of the consideration on both sides, and a breach of such covenant may be paid for in damages, it is an independent covenant, and an action may be maintained for a breach of the covenant on the part of the defendant, without averring performance in the declaration;" and Boone *v.* Eyre[2] is cited. There the defendant's covenant was, that "the plaintiff well and truly performing all and every thing therein contained on his part to be performed," the defendant would pay an annuity. The plaintiff, by the same deed, transferred an equity of redemption in an estate, with the negroes on it, in consideration of £500 and the annuity; and covenanted that he had title; and, in covenant for non-payment of the annuity, it was held no plea to traverse the title. So here there are several distinct stipulations on the part of the plaintiff; and an action might have been maintained for the breach of any one, even before the time arrived for payment of the money by the defendant. Thus the plaintiff is to pay £30 for rent; he is also to manage the land in a husband-like manner. The damages might be assessed independently for

[1] 1 Wms. Saund. 320 *a*, 6th ed.

[2] In K. B., note (*a*) to Duke of St. Albans *v.* Shore, 1 H. Bl. 273; and see, as to s. c., 6 T. R. 573 (in Campbell *v.* Jones); also, Boone *v.* Eyre, in C. P., 2 W. Bl. 1312.

any one breach by the plaintiff. Ritchie *v.* Atkinson,[1] Campbell *v.* Jones,[2] Carpenter *v.* Creswell,[3] and Dawson *v.* Dyer,[4] are instances of applications of the same rule. In the sixth edition of Saunders's Reports the following remark is appended to the note already cited:[5] "Where the consideration for the payment of money is entire and indivisible, as where the benefit expected by the defendant under the agreement is to result from the enjoyment of every part of the consideration jointly, so that the money payable is neither apportioned by the contract, nor capable of being apportioned by a jury, no action is maintainable, if any part of the consideration has failed; for, being entire, by failing partially it fails altogether." For this Chanter *v.* Leese[6] is cited, where the consideration was manifestly entire. Stavers *v.* Curling[7] is an instance in which the covenants were held to be independent, the plaintiff's covenants, insisted on by the defendants, going only to a part of the consideration; and Ritchie *v.* Atkinson was relied on.

Montague Smith, contra. The stipulations on the part of the plaintiff are either conditions precedent or conditions concurrent. In the former case the declaration is bad for not averring that the plaintiff had performed the conditions: an averment of readiness and willingness is insufficient. In the latter case the averment is indeed sufficient, but it is still material; and therefore the traverses in the two pleas answer the complaint. The plaintiff can succeed only on the assumption that the stipulations on his part and the contract of the defendant are independent of each other. The criterion suggested on the other side is correct, but when applied to this agreement it is in favor of the defendant. The agreement is, first, that the plaintiff shall occupy the land, paying rent, delivering up in good repair, and cultivating properly; secondly, that the defendant will pay money to the plaintiff, on his quitting, paying the rent, observing the stipulations, and releasing the claims on the defendant. The liability of the defendant is in express terms made dependent upon the performance on the part of the plaintiff. And that performance is the only consideration for the payment by the defendant, which otherwise is gratuitous. The case does not resemble those where the stipulations are held to be independent because the consideration is the covenanting to do something, not the doing it; such as Rose *v.* Poulton,[8] where this distinction is particularly insisted upon by Taunton, J. Nor again, are cases like Carpenter *v.* Creswell[9] applicable, where the consideration is abstinence for an indefinite time. In 1 Chitt. Pl. 331 (7th ed.), it is said, "In general if

[1] 10 East, 295. [2] 6 T. R. 570. [3] 4 Bing. 409.
[4] 5 B. & Ad. 584. [5] 1 Wms. Saund. 320 *d*, note (*c*).
[6] 4 M. & W. 295. Affirmed on error in Exch. Ch.; Chanter *v.* Leese, 5 M. & W. 698.
[7] 3 New Ca. 355. [8] 2 B. & Ad. 822, 831. [9] 4 Bing. 409.

the agreement be that one party shall do an act, and that for the doing thereof the other shall pay a sum of money, the doing of the act is a condition precedent to the payment." Glazebrooke v. Woodrow[1] is a strong authority for the defendant. No time for the payment by the defendant is here pointed out in the agreement, except the performance of the stipulations by the plaintiff. Even if the times were to be coincident, readiness should be shewn, as in Jones v. Barkley.[2] If that averment were struck out no breach could appear. [PATTESON, J. If the defendant had sued the plaintiff for non-performance, must the declaration have averred readiness to pay?] It should seem not; but, supposing that it must, the conditions are concurrent, and the pleas here answer the declaration. According to Goodisson v. Nunn[3] and Chanter v. Leese,[4] the performance by the plaintiff here was a condition precedent.

Butt, in reply. The argument that no time for the payment is fixed by the agreement, fails, for in all such agreements a reasonable time will be intended. [WIGHTMAN, J. At what time were you bound to release?] Whenever required. The right to insist upon each of the plaintiff's stipulations separately formed the whole consideration; and as in Hall v. Bainbridge[5] the result is that the conditions were independent. The words "upon the plaintiff" "so quitting," &c., are insisted upon, but they are not stronger than the words in Boone v. Eyre.[6] *Cur. adv. vult.*

PATTESON, J., in this term (May 29th) delivered the judgment of the court.

The first question in this case is, whether the declaration be sufficient. It is objected to on the ground that the plaintiff has only averred his readiness and willingness to deliver up the premises, to pay the rent, and to release the defendant; whereas the defendant contends that those things were conditions precedent to his paying the £200 under the agreement, and, therefore, that the plaintiff ought to have averred the actual performance of those things. The plaintiff, on the other hand, contends that those things to be done by him, and the payment of the £200 by the defendant, were independent acts altogether; and that his averment of readiness and willingness to do them was unnecessary and not traversable, and that the defendant, in traversing them, has tendered immaterial issues.

We think that the plaintiff is clearly wrong in his view, and that

1 8 T. R. 366. 2 2 Doug. 684. 3 4 T. R. 761.

4 4 M. & W. 295. Affirmed on error in Exchequer Chamber, Chanter v. Leese, 5 M. & W. 698.

5 5 Q. B. 233.

6 Note (*a*) to Duke of St. Albans v. Shore, 1 H. Bl. 273; Boone v. Eyre, 2 W. Bl. 1312.

these acts of each party are clearly not independent. The words are, "upon" the plaintiff doing so and so, the defendant promises to pay £200. The time for paying that £200 is not fixed by the agreement itself, and cannot be fixed otherwise than by the plaintiff doing the acts required on his part. The cases collected in note (4) to Pordage *v.* Cole[1] were cited on the argument, and are important; but there are also others cited in note (3) to Peeters *v.* Opie,[2] which are quite as important, and more strictly applicable to the present case. Upon consideration of those cases, and of the intention of the parties to the agreement in this case, as shewn by the agreement itself, we are of opinion that the acts to be done by the plaintiff were not conditions precedent, not independent, but concurrent with those to be done by the defendant; and, therefore, that it was sufficient for the plaintiff to aver readiness and willingness to do them.

But it was also necessary for him to make that averment. It follows that the averment was traversable; and therefore the plaintiff's demurrer to the pleas, on the ground that they tender immaterial issues, cannot be sustained, except indeed as to the third plea from other reasons.

But the plaintiff objects to the pleas on other grounds.

To the second, that it is multifarious, inasmuch as it puts in issue two distinct things, the plaintiff's readiness and willingness to pay the rent, and also to deliver up possession.[3] Now the plaintiff was bound to do both acts. The issue therefore has not cast upon him too great burden of proof; and although his non-readiness to do either would have been an answer to the action, yet it does not necessarily follow that the defendant was bound to traverse them separately. The principle laid down in Stubbs *v.* Lainson,[4] Drewe *v.* Lainson,[5] and Moore *v.* Boulcott,[6] is that a traverse is too large where it casts more proof on the other side than is necessary to maintain the pleading which contains the allegation traversed. That is not so here; and therefore we think the second plea is not objectionable on that ground. Judgment must therefore be given for the defendant on that plea.

To the third plea the plaintiff objects that, as it appears by the agreement set out in the declaration that the release to be given to the defendant was to be prepared by the defendant's attorney, and as it is averred in the declaration that no such release was prepared, the plaintiff's readiness and willingness to have executed the release, if prepared, becomes immaterial. And we think that this objection must prevail. If no release was prepared by the defendant's attorney, the plaintiff

[1] 1 Wms. Saund. 320 *a*, 6th ed.

[2] 2 Wms. Saund. 352.

[3] This ground, though specially assigned for demurrer, was not noticed in the argument.

[4] 1 M. & W. 728; s. c. Tyr. & G. 1000.

[5] 11 A. & E. 529.

[6] 1 New Ca. 323.

might sue the defendant for the money, whether he was ready to have executed it or not. Indeed, if none were prepared, it would be difficult for the plaintiff to prove his readiness to have executed; for he was not bound to call upon the defendant to prepare a release, or to offer to execute one. If, on the other hand, a release was prepared by the defendant, he should have pleaded that fact, and shewn a refusal by the plaintiff to execute.

Upon the demurrer to this plea, therefore, we think the issue is immaterial, and that the judgment must be for the plaintiff.

Judgment for defendant on demurrer to the second plea; for plaintiff on the demurrer to the third.

MARSDEN v. MOORE AND DAY.

IN THE EXCHEQUER, MAY 2, 1859.

[*Reported in* 4 *Hurlstone & Norman*, 500.]

DECLARATION. That the plaintiff agreed with the defendants to sell to them one-fourth part or share in a mining sett, situate and known by the name of Osom's Hill, for the sum of £250; and the defendants agreed with the plaintiff to purchase of him the said one-fourth part or share in the said mining sett at the price aforesaid; and it was further agreed that the plaintiff and defendants should form a company, with a capital of £20,000, for working the mining sett, &c.; and as soon as the company should be registered, with limited liability, the defendants would pay to the plaintiff £250. Averment: that all conditions precedent, matters and things, requiring to have been performed and to have happened and existed to entitle the plaintiff to the performance of the defendants' said agreement, and to maintain this action for the non-performance thereof, were performed and did happen and exist before the commencement of this suit; yet the defendants did not pay the said sum of £250 or any part thereof.

Second plea, by defendant Day. That the agreement was an agreement in writing signed by the defendants, as follows: "Memorandum of agreement entered into between W. Marsden of the first part, and Paul Moore and Edward Day of the second part. W. Marsden has agreed to sell to Paul Moore and Edward Day one-fourth part or share in a mining sett situate and known by the name of Osom's Hill, in the parish of Grindon, in Staffordshire, for the sum of £250, and Paul Moore and Edward Day agree to purchase at that price. And it is further agreed between the parties that they will forthwith form a company under the Limited Liability Act, with a capital of £20,000, for working or developing the said mining sett, with such rules and regulations as the promoters shall afterwards agree and determine; and as soon as the company is registered, with limited liability, we, P. Moore and E. Day, will pay to W. Marsden the sum of £250 as hereinbefore stated." Averment: that the plaintiff had not at the time of making the agreement, nor had he at any time afterwards, nor hath he now, any title to the said one-fourth part or share in the said mining sett in the declaration mentioned, nor any right or title to convey the same.

Third plea. That the agreement in the declaration mentioned was that set forth in the second plea; and that, according to the agreement, the plaintiff ought, before being entitled to call on the defendants for payment of the sum of £250 or any part thereof, to have been ready and willing to convey the said one-fourth part or share in the mining sett. But the plaintiff never has been at any time ready and willing to convey the same to the defendants according to the said agreement.

Similar pleas were pleaded by the defendant Moore.

Demurrers and joinders.

Karslake, in support of the demurrers. The agreement expressly stipulates that the defendants shall pay the £250 at a certain time, viz., as soon as the company is registered. [BRAMWELL, B. If a man agrees to buy an estate and pay for it on a certain day, that implies that the seller is to convey the estate at the same time to the purchaser.] Assuming that the plaintiff has no title, still he may be in actual possession. The plaintiff has gone to the expense of registering the company. The want of title therefore does not go to the whole consideration. The defendants would have a right of action against the plaintiff on the implied agreement to give a good title. The plaintiff may have had an agreement with the owners of the land enforceable by a court of equity. In Pordage v. Cole[1] it was held that, if it be agreed between A. and B. that B. shall pay a sum of money for his land, &c., on a particular day, these words amount to a covenant by A. to convey the land; but it is an independent covenant, and A. may bring an action for the money before any conveyance by him of the land.

Gray, for defendant Day. It is true that if a man agrees to sell an estate for £10,000, to be paid on the 10th of May, an action may be brought on the 10th of May, though the plaintiff is not then in a condition to convey, if he is ready to convey in a reasonable time. De Medina v. Norman.[2] But upon this agreement there is nothing to shew that the party purchasing the mining sett did not intend to have the property conveyed to him on payment of the purchase-money; therefore this case is not governed by Pordage v. Cole[3] and Dicker v.

[1] 1 Saund. 319. [2] 9 M. & W. 820. [3] 1 Saund. 319.

Jackson.[1] [MARTIN, B. Would not the pleas be proved if the plaintiff had an equitable interest and there was a trustee ready to convey? BRAMWELL, B. Or suppose he had an equity of redemption?] The effect of the pleas is that the plaintiff has not any title or any means of giving one. A traverse of the readiness and willingness to convey puts in issue the plaintiff's ability to do so. De Medina *v.* Norman.[2] As to the first plea, the plaintiff must answer the allegation in the plea; and if he has not a title he must shew that some one else has. [BRAMWELL, B. Surely that is not so. The plaintiff does not bargain for his own title, but that he will give a title to the defendant.] In Manby *v.* Cremonini [3] a day was named for the payment of money, as in the present case, and the question was whether there was an absolute contract to pay the residue of the purchase-money on such day. But the court thought that the defendant was not bound to pay the money upon that day unless the plaintiff had made out a good title and was ready to execute a conveyance.

Field, for defendant Moore, referred to Purvis *v.* Rayer,[4] and BRAMWELL, B., to Webb *v.* Austin.[5]

Karslake, in reply. The authority of the case of Pordage *v.* Cole is admitted. Now if, instead of the words "as soon as the company is formed, with limited liability," the words had been "on the 21st of June," that case would have been a direct authority. The words as to the time of payment are the words of the defendants. The time and the event upon which the money is to be paid, viz., the registration of the company, were fixed by the defendants. The pleas only allege that *plaintiff* had no title, and that *he* was not willing to convey.

POLLOCK, C. B. We are all of opinion that the pleas are good and that the defendants are entitled to judgment. The question is, what did the parties mean by the agreement declared on, whether each party is entitled to insist on performance by the other, without reference to his capacity to perform his own part of the agreement. The plea sets out an agreement by which, "as soon as the company is registered, with limited liability," the defendants agree to pay to the plaintiff the sum of £250 "as thereinbefore stated;" that is, as the purchase of a mining sett. I do not think that the reference to the uncertain period depending upon the registration of the company, brings the case within the rule laid down in Pordage *v.* Cole.[6] It is essential to a contract of buying and selling that one shall pay, the other sell or convey. On that ground this case is distinguishable from Pordage *v.* Cole. In such cases each party intends that the other shall perform his part, and not to rely on a right of action. Therefore, in the present case, the plaintiff is not in a condition to maintain the action.

[1] 6 C. B. 103.
[2] 9 M. & W. 820, 828.
[3] 6 Exch. 808.
[4] 9 Price, 488, 518.
[5] 7 Man. & G. 701.
[6] 1 Saund. 319.

MARTIN, B. I am of the same opinion. I think that the law is correctly laid down in Pordage *v.* Cole.[1] In order to see the meaning of this contract, the parts of it should be separately considered. First, the plaintiff agrees to sell to the defendant a share in a mining sett for £250, and the defendants agree to purchase at that price. The sale and payment of the money are to be contemporaneous acts. In the notes to Pordage *v.* Cole, 1 Wms. Saund. 320 *e*, it is said, rule 4, "Where the mutual covenants go to the whole consideration on both sides, they are mutual conditions, and performance must be averred;" and rule 5, "Where two acts are to be done at the same time, neither party can maintain an action without shewing performance of, or an offer to perform his part." This particularly applies to the case of sales, where the common understanding is, that one thing is to be exchanged for another. Then as to the other part, as soon as the company is registered, the defendants agree to pay the sum of £250 "as hereinbefore stated." That does not convey to my mind that the defendants meant, if it should turn out that the plaintiff had no title, to take their chance of being able to recover back the £250 in an action for money had and received.

BRAMWELL, B. I am of the same opinion. In the case of Pordage *v.* Cole the court construed the agreement as if it appeared on the face of it that there was no intention that the conveyance should take place on the day appointed for payment of the money. Assuming that to be so, the case is rightly decided; but whether I should have so construed the agreement is another matter. Here the plaintiff agrees to sell, the defendants agree to purchase; there is a clear present agreement for a future sale and payment. The subsequent part of the agreement merely postpones the time for performance; it does not alter the effect of the prior stipulation, which is, that the money is to be paid upon the conveyance. The sale and payment are to be contemporaneous. The last plea is clearly good. As to the other plea there is more difficulty. The question is, whether the defendant has sufficiently negatived the existence of such a title as would have enabled the plaintiff to convey the sett to the defendants. In the old days I think we should have said it was good in substance as an averment that there was no title.

CHANNELL, B. I entirely agree with the correctness of the propositions of law laid down in Pordage *v.* Cole. Whether they govern the present case depends upon the construction of the agreement. By the first part of the agreement the payment and conveyance are to be concurrent acts. The plaintiff is to sell, and the defendant is to buy, a mining sett at a price specified. Then is that altered by the subsequent part of the agreement? I think not. The true construction of the

[1] 1 Saund. 319.

whole is, that the conveyance and payment are to be concurrent acts; but a provision is made as to the time at which the concurrent acts are to be done. The pleas are good traverses of that which is alleged in the declaration. *Judgment for the defendants.*

BANKART AND ANOTHER *v.* BOWERS.

IN THE COMMON PLEAS, MAY 1, 1866.

[*Reported in Law Reports,* 1 *Common Pleas,* 484.]

THE first count of the declaration stated, that by an agreement dated the 31st of July, 1863, and made between the defendant of the one part and the plaintiffs of the other part, it was agreed that the defendant should sell to the plaintiffs, and that the plaintiffs should purchase from the defendant, the equity of redemption of and in certain lands, &c., known as the Turnhurst Hall estate, in Wolstanton, in the county of Stafford, save and except certain closes therein described, and of and in all the mines, beds, and veins of coal, ironstone and other minerals within and under the same, together with all the engines, colliery buildings, and plant then being upon the same estate; and that payment should be made for the same by the plaintiffs on the terms and in the manner therein mentioned: and the defendant by the said agreement, and in consideration of the premises, agreed with the plaintiffs that the defendant would purchase from the plaintiffs all coal that the defendant might require from time to time, at the fair market rate: Averment, that although all things on the plaintiffs' part had been duly performed and fulfilled according to the terms of the agreement, necessary to entitle the plaintiffs to sue for the breach thereinafter mentioned, and although the plaintiffs were and still continued, and always had been from the making of the said agreement, ready and willing to sell and supply to the defendant such coal as the defendant required, at the fair market rate, according to the terms of the agreement and the true intent and meaning thereof: Breach, that the defendant did not after the making of the agreement purchase or take from the plaintiffs all coal that he required, according to the agreement, or more than a very small and inconsiderable quantity of the coal which he required, and a much less quantity thereof than was by him so agreed to be purchased and taken, and on the contrary he took large quantities of coal from persons other than the plaintiffs, whereby the plaintiffs lost profits, &c.

Plea, that the agreement in the first count mentioned was and is an agreement in writing, in the words and figures following, that is to say:

"Memorandum of agreement made this 31st of July, 1863, between G. F. Bowers, of &c., china manufacturer, of the one part, and F. Bankart, of &c., and H. Bankart, of &c., copper-smelters, of the other part, as follows: 1. The said G. F. Bowers agrees to sell to the said F. Bankart and H. Bankart, and the said F. Bankart and H. Bankart agree to purchase from him, the equity of redemption in all the mines, beds, and veins of coal, ironstone, and other minerals within and under the estate called the Turnhurst Hall estate, situate, &c., containing in the whole 110 a. 3 r. 27 p., or thereabouts, together with all the engines, colliery buildings, and plant, now being upon the said estate, which together with the surface of the estate are subject to a mortgage of £1750 to Messrs. C. & J., and also all the rights and interests of the said G. F. Bowers under a contract entered into by him on the 9th of March, 1863, with T. F. H., for the granting by him to the said G. F. Bowers for the term of forty-two years from the 31st of January, 1863, of power and authority to use a certain railway or tramway to be constructed over lands of the said T. F. H., at, &c. 2. The consideration for such purchase shall be the payment by the said F. Bankart and H. Bankart to the said G. F. Bowers of £2000 in manner following: £500 in cash on the execution of the conveyance, and the remainder in bills of exchange for £1500 and interest extending over nine months from the execution of the said conveyance. 3. The said G. F. Bowers agrees to sell to the said F. Bankart and H. Bankart, and the said F. Bankart and H. Bankart agree to purchase of him, the equity of redemption in the whole of the said Turnhurst Hall estate, the mines and minerals in and under which are hereby contracted for, with the mansion-house called Turnhurst Hall, and the other buildings thereon (except the field called Big Brent, containing 8 a. 3 r. 11 p., or thereabouts, and also except such portion of the field called Delph Field as is marked off with a red outline on a certain plan, &c., for house-building purposes only). 4. The consideration for said purchase of the surface of the said estate, mansion-house, and buildings (except as aforesaid), shall be the payment by the said F. Bankart and H. Bankart to the said G. F. Bowers of the sum of £4000 in manner following: the sum of £2000 in cash on the execution of the conveyance, and the remainder in bills of exchange for £2000 and interest extending over two years from the execution of the conveyance. 5. The said F. Bankart and H. Bankart shall take upon themselves all the engagements and liabilities of the said G. F. Bowers under the said agreement with the said T. F. H., and shall protect and indemnify the said G. F. Bowers from and against all such engagements and liabilities. 6. The said F. Bankart and H. Bankart shall be entitled to the rent of the surface of the Turnhurst Hall estate as from the 24th June, 1863. 7. The said G. F. Bowers shall purchase from the said F. Bankart and H. Bankart all coal that he may from time to time require, at the fair market rate. 8. The said G. F. Bowers shall deduce a good title to all the property comprised in this agreement." Averment, that it was not agreed by and between the defendant and the plaintiffs as in the first count mentioned, save and except as in and by the said written agreement in this plea particularly set forth as aforesaid; and that the plaintiffs did not nor would purchase from the defendant, although the defendant was ready and willing to sell to the plaintiffs, the said equity of redemption, or the engines, colliery buildings, or plant in the first count mentioned, on the terms in the said agreement mentioned.

Demurrer, on the ground that the completion of the purchase was not a condition precedent to the performance of the contract declared on. Joinder.

Watkin Williams, in support of the demurrer, contended that it was not a condition precedent to the defendant's liability to the plaintiffs for the non-performance of the contract contained in the seventh clause of the agreement, viz., that he would purchase from them all the coal he might from time to time require, that the plaintiffs should perform the contract on their part contained in the first clause, viz., purchase and pay for the estate contracted to be sold to them; but that the two were totally distinct and independent covenants, giving to either party a remedy against the other by an action for a breach, according to the rules laid down in the notes to Pordage v. Cole.[1]

T. Jones, in support of the plea. This is an agreement for the purchase of an estate by the plaintiffs from the defendant, and for the purchase of coal by the defendant from the plaintiffs. The plaintiffs are not willing to take the estate, but seek to compel the defendant to take all his coal from them. It must be conceded that the acceptance of the estate is not a condition precedent, but it is a condition concurrent, and the plaintiffs must be ready and willing to execute the contract on their part before they can call upon the defendant to perform his part of it. The reasonable construction of the contract is, that the whole is to date from the conveyance of the estate. The case falls within the fifth rule given in the notes to Pordage v. Cole:[2] "Where two acts are to be done at the same time, as where A. covenants to convey an estate to B. on such a day, and in consideration thereof B. covenants to pay a sum of money on the same day, neither can maintain an action without shewing performance of or an offer to perform his part, though it is not certain which of them is obliged to do the first act; and this particularly applies to all cases of sale." As to the averment of readiness and willingness, it is said in the notes to Peeters v. Opie:[3] "The nature and necessity of such averments was much considered in a late case, — Rawson v. Johnson,[4] — which was assump-

[1] 1 Wms. Saund. 319 *l*.
[2] 1 Wms. Saund. 320 *e*.
[3] 2 Wms. Saund. 352 *a*.
[4] 1 East, 203.

sit for the non-delivery of 100 qrs. of malt, which the defendant had undertaken to deliver on request at a certain price; and the plaintiff averred that although afterwards, to wit, on, &c., he requested the defendant to deliver him the 100 qrs. of malt, and was then and there ready and willing to pay the said defendant for the same according to the terms of the said sale, and although he was then and there ready and willing, and offered to accept and receive the said 100 qrs. of malt from the defendant, yet he refused to deliver them. After verdict for the plaintiff, it was moved in arrest of judgment that the plaintiff did not aver the actual tender of the price agreed upon, the averment of a readiness and willingness only in the plaintiff to pay not being sufficient. But the court overruled the objection, and held the averment of the plaintiff's readiness and willingness to pay for the malt sufficient; that under that averment the plaintiff was bound to prove that he was prepared to pay or tendered the money, if the defendant had been ready to receive it and to deliver the malt." So here, to effectuate the intention of the parties, the plaintiffs should have been ready and willing to take a conveyance of the estate and to pay the money on the day stipulated. Again, in Morton *v.* Lamb,[1] also cited in the notes to Peeters *v.* Opie,[2] the court held, that "where two concurrent acts are to be done, the party who sues the other for non-performance must aver that he has performed, or was ready to perform, his part of the contract."

Williams, in reply. No doubt, if the two covenants or contracts be dependent the one on the other, neither can sue the other for a breach without shewing performance, or readiness and willingness to perform the contract on his part. Here the covenants are totally independent. The defendant bound himself to take the coal immediately. He could not delay till a perfect title to the estate had been made, which might take a considerable time. The court cannot speculate upon the intention of the parties. They can only deal with the agreement as they find it. Hale *v.* Rawson.[3]

ERLE, C. J. I am of opinion that our judgment upon this demurrer should be for the defendant. Where there is a contract by one party to sell an article, and by the other party to pay for it, no time being named, it would be a strong thing to say that the buyer shall pay the money before he gets the consideration. The effect of the agreement set out in the plea is, that the plaintiffs are to buy the mines and minerals from the defendant, and the defendant is to take all the coals he may require from the plaintiffs. These clearly are concurrent acts.

BYLES, J. The effect of Mr. Watkin Williams's argument is, that the defendant must keep the mines, and yet is bound to buy his coals of the plaintiffs.

[1] 7 T. R. 125. [2] 2 Wms. Saund. 352 *c*. [3] 4 C. B. (N. S.) 85.

KEATING, J. We must look to the whole agreement in order to ascertain what was the intention of the parties. We should obviously be frustrating that, if we were to yield to the argument of Mr Williams.

MONTAGUE SMITH, J., concurred. *Judgment for the defendant.*

EBENEZER HUNT v. EDWARD ST. LOE LIVERMORE.

SUPREME JUDICIAL COURT OF MASSACHUSETTS, APRIL TERM, 1828.

[*Reported in 5 Pickering, 395.*]

ASSUMPSIT on a promissory note from the defendant to the plaintiff, not negotiable, dated February 26, 1823, for $1400, payable on demand.

At the trial before Morton, J., the plaintiff called a witness, who testified that on the 2d of December, 1824, the plaintiff demanded of the defendant payment of the note, or a return of the bond hereafter mentioned; but that the defendant did not pay the note, nor return the bond, but replied that what is written is written.

The defendant then gave in evidence a bond from the plaintiff, dated February 26, 1823, conditioned that the plaintiff, upon the defendant's paying him the sum of $1400, should make and execute to the defendant a good and valid warranty deed of certain land which the defendant had agreed to purchase of the plaintiff for the sum mentioned.

The defendant also produced the following receipt, signed by the plaintiff: "February 26, 1823. Received of E. S. Livermore a note of hand for $1400, for which I have this day given him a bond for a deed of a certain piece of land; but provided the bargain is not carried into effect, I am to deliver up said note upon said Livermore's delivering up said bond."

The defendant contended that the plaintiff was not entitled to his action before he had tendered a deed of the estate described in the bond, and that the defendant now had a right to rescind the contract referred to in the bond and receipt, and to return the bond to the plaintiff, which he offered to do in court. But the judge, being of opinion that these facts did not amount to a defence against the note, directed the defendant to be called. If the whole court should be of a different opinion, the default was to be taken off and the plaintiff to become nonsuit.

Livermore and *Hoar*, for the defendant. The three writings, bearing the same date and relating to the same subject-matter, are to be considered as one transaction, and they shew a promise by the defendant to pay, provided the condition of the bond is performed. If the bargain was not carried into effect, the note was to be given up. The plaintiff therefore should have performed his part of the contract, or at least have tendered a deed of the land as a condition precedent to bringing an action on the note. Collins *v.* Gibbs, 2 Burr. 899; Thorpe *v.* Thorpe, 1 Ld. Raym. 662; s. c. 1 Salk. 171; Pordage *v.* Cole, 1 Wms. Saund. 320, note 4.

The note was a *nudum pactum.* No consideration was given for it; and independent of that objection, it is not recoverable, for when the land was to be conveyed the money was to be paid; so that whether the bargain for the land should be carried into effect or rescinded, the note was to be given up. It was in fact a nullity.

Stearns, contra. It is manifest, on the face of the papers, that giving the receipt was an after transaction. The payment of the consideration is a condition precedent to giving a deed, but the note is unqualified in its terms, and being on demand might have been sued immediately.

But if the several writings were one transaction, they do not constitute a defence against the note. If there was a mutual right to rescind, it was not without a limitation as to time, and nearly two years had elapsed before payment of the note was demanded; which allowed the defendant more than a reasonable time to make his election. Bothy's case, 6 Co. 31; Pothier on Obligations, No. 205.

The opinion of the court was drawn up by

PUTNAM, J. We think that the note, the receipt, and the bond should be construed as if they were parts of one contract.

The plaintiff on his part agreed to convey the land to the defendant when he should pay the purchase-money, and the defendant agreed to pay the purchase-money when the plaintiff should convey the land. As no time for the conveyance or for the payment is mentioned, the law supplies the deficiency by providing that the contract should be executed in a reasonable time. And an offer to do what the contract required of either party, and a demand and refusal of the other to do what was required of him, would entitle the party so offering to perform to a remedy upon the contract. It is clear to our minds, that the contract is to be construed as containing dependent stipulations. Neither party intended to trust to the personal security of the other. If Hunt had in a reasonable time offered to give a good deed of the land, and had demanded payment of the money mentioned in the note, and Livermore had refused to accept the deed and to pay according to his engagement, Hunt would have had his remedy at law against Livermore for the purchase-money. On the other hand, if Livermore had in a reasonable time offered to pay his note, and had demanded a deed, and Hunt had refused to accept the money and to give the deed simultaneously, Livermore would have had his remedy at law against Hunt for the damages sustained by his not conveying the land according to his agreement.

If the stipulation contained in the receipt of the plaintiff to deliver up the note upon the defendant's delivering up the bond, "provided the bargain is not carried into effect," were to be construed to give either party an election at his own pleasure to annul the contract, it is evident that the contract could never be carried into effect against him who should please to avoid it. It would in effect have no binding operation. It would not be what the civil law defines, "juris vinculum quo necessitate adstringimur." "It is of the essence of all agreements which consist of promising something, that they should produce an obligation in the party making the promise to discharge it; hence it follows that nothing can be more contradictory to such an obligation than the entire liberty of the party making the promise to perform it or not as he may please." Pothier on Oblig. No. 47, 48. The case at bar strongly illustrates that position. If it were that either party had the entire liberty of vacating it, the contract would be void for want of obligation. It would stand thus: Hunt engages to convey his land to Livermore for $1400, if Hunt shall please to do so; and Livermore engages to pay $1400 for the land, if he shall please to do so. We cannot suppose the parties intended to make such a vain bargain. We are satisfied that it was a valid contract, containing dependent stipulations to be performed by each before he could compel a peformance by the other. It follows, therefore, that the plaintiff was not entitled to the money or price of the land, inasmuch as he neglected to offer to convey the land by a proper deed.

We are all of opinion that the default should be taken off, and that the plaintiff should be nonsuited.

OLIVER KANE ET AL. v. JOHN HOOD.

SUPREME JUDICIAL COURT OF MASSACHUSETTS, OCTOBER 27, 1832.

[Reported in 13 Pickering, 281.]

ASSUMPSIT, brought by the executors of John Innis Clark. Trial before SHAW, C. J.

The plaintiffs rely upon an unsealed contract made by Clark and Hood, dated October 28, 1803, by which "it is mutually agreed that Hood is to have the land, &c. (describing certain land in Somerset); in consideration of which the said Hood is to pay the said Clark $700, $200 of which are to be paid in ten days, half the remainder in twelve months, and the other half in two years, from the above date, with the interest annually; and the deed to be executed at the completing of the last payment."

The two first instalments had been paid and received before the commencement of this action.

The plaintiffs neither allege nor prove that they ever made or tendered or offered any deed or conveyance of the land, but they aver that Clark, in his lifetime, and they, in their capacity of executors, since his decease, have always been ready to convey the land to Hood, and to execute to him a good and sufficient deed thereof, upon his complying with the terms of the contract on his part, and that they are here in court ready to execute such deed upon his complying with those terms.

The defendant contends that, the two first instalments being fully paid, the agreements of the parties in respect to the last instalment are mutually dependent and conditional, and neither is bound to perform without a tender of performance on the other side, to be made at the same time.

On the contrary, the plaintiffs contend, that the promise of the defendant is independent, and that he was bound to pay at the time and conformably to the terms of the contract, in consideration of the engagement of Clark, without any tender of performance on the part of the plaintiffs.

The plaintiffs became nonsuit, subject to the opinion of the court on the above question.

Cobb, for the plaintiffs, cited Terry *v.* Duntz, 2 H. Bl. 389; 1 Wms's Saund. 320, note 4; Gardiner *v.* Corson, 15 Mass. R. 500.

W. Baylies and *Battelle*, for the defendant, cited Callonel *v.* Briggs, 1 Salk. 112; Thorpe *v.* Thorpe, ibid. 171; Jones *v.* Barkley, 2 Doug. 684; Goodisson *v.* Nunn, 4 T. R. 761; Glazebrook *v.* Woodrow, 8 T. R. 366; Phillips *v.* Fielding, 2 H. Bl. 123; Martin *v.* Smith, 6 East, 555; Johnson *v.* Reed, 9 Mass. R. 78; Cunningham *v.* Morrell, 10 Johns. R. 203; Couch *v.* Ingersoll, 2 Pick. 292; Dana *v.* King, ibid. 155; Hunt *v.* Livermore, 5 Pick. 395; Bean *v.* Atwater, 4 Conn. R. 3; Parker *v.* Parmele, 20 Johns. R. 130.

SHAW, C. J., delivered the opinion of the court. This is a contract not under seal, but the same rules govern the construction of it as those applicable to cases of covenant. The only question which would seem to be presented by the facts is, whether in a contract between parties relative to the same subject-matter, some stipulations may be mutual and independent, and others dependent and mutually conditional; and this question was settled in the case of Couch *v.* Ingersoll, 2 Pick. 292. Indeed the point in question constituted distinctly the ground of decision in that case, because the plaintiff, without having tendered performance on his part, recovered on a breach of one covenant because it was independent, and failed on the other, because upon the construction put upon it by the court, it was independent.

In the present case, the two first instalments of the purchase-money were to be paid before the time fixed for the conveyance of the land, and therefore it is very clear they are independent. Had a suit been brought for either of them, no tender, offer, or averment of readiness, would have been necessary, and no defence could have been made. The obligation of the defendant to pay the money at the times stipulated, was absolute and unconditional. But it is shewn by the facts, that the two first instalments were fully paid; and though payment was not made at the times fixed, yet it was afterwards accepted, and the plaintiffs affirmed the contract by suing on it. Then the question is, whether the payment of the last instalment on the one side, and the execution and tender of the deed, upon payment being made, on the other, were not dependent and conditional; and we think they were. The words are, "and the other half in two years, with interest annually, and the deed to be executed at the completing of the last payment." Suppose the whole had been payable at once, instead of being payable by instalments, and the stipulation had been to pay seven hundred dollars in two years, the deed to be executed at the payment; upon this statement of the question, is there a doubt that the agreements would have been mutually dependent and conditional? I think not. The intent of the parties is to govern. And what difference is there, whether the final payment is the whole or part, the remainder of the purchase-money having been paid and accepted? Where the whole purchase-money is to be paid at once and the deed is to be then given, the covenants are held to be dependent, because it is unreasonable to presume that the purchaser intended to pay the whole consideration, without having the equivalent in a title to the land purchased. The same reason applies to the last instalment. An obvious reason why the first and second instalments should be paid without having a deed is, that the vendor was to withhold the title as a security for the purchase-money, and the vendee was content to rely on the vendor's contract for his future title; but no such reason applies to the final and complete payment of the purchase-money. Whether therefore we consider the particular language of the contract, or the general intent of the parties, we think these parts of the contract were mutually dependent and conditional, and the plaintiffs cannot recover without averring performance or an offer to perform on their part.

Plaintiffs nonsuit.

DUNHAM AND DIMON v. PETTEE AND MANN.

NEW YORK COURT OF APPEALS, JUNE TERM, 1853.

[*Reported in 4 Selden*, 508].

THIS was an action brought in the Court of Common Pleas of the city of New York, upon a contract made between the plaintiffs and the defendants in the following form:

"Sold to Messrs. Pettee & Mann, for account of Messrs. Dunham & Dimon, 155 tons (or thereabout) of English bar iron, as per specification of the same, now in public store in this city, at fifty dollars per ton, as per custom-house weigher's return, equal to six months' credit; but payment for said iron is to be made as follows, to wit, 750 dollars to be paid now, and the balance is to be paid within sixty days from this date, and discount is to be made on the bill at the rate of seven per cent. per annum, reckoning the time from the date of the average payment of the bill until the end of the six months above named. The sellers are to hold a policy of insurance on the iron until the whole amount is paid; and the buyers are to pay the insurance and all storage expenses from and after this date. It is understood that the iron is to be paid for on delivery (within the sixty days aforesaid), and should the full amount not be paid within the sixty days aforesaid, Messrs. Dunham and Dimon will be at liberty to sell the iron to other parties for account of Messrs. Pettee and Mann.

New York, 12th March, 1849.

NATHAN CASWELL, Broker."

The contract was set out in the complaint, and it was alleged that the defendants paid the sum of $750 mentioned in it, and that the plaintiffs were ready and willing to deliver the iron to the defendants and receive the balance of the price therefor, and in all respects to comply with the terms of the contract on their part, and that they within the sixty days mentioned in the contract offered and tendered to the defendants the iron, but that the latter were not ready and willing to receive it and pay the balance of the price, and wholly refused so to do. The defendants answered admitting the contract, but denied that the plaintiffs were ready or willing to comply with its terms, or that they offered or tendered the iron to the defendants, and alleged that the defendants were ready and willing to receive the iron and to pay for it on delivery, and that they demanded its delivery of the plaintiffs, but that they were not able to deliver it and refused to deliver it. The plaintiffs replied denying the allegations in relation to their refusal to deliver the iron.

The cause was tried in March, 1850. It was proved by the plaintiffs that at the time the contract was entered into, the iron was stored in the United States bonded warehouse, where it remained until it was delivered to D. M. Wilson & Co. in October or November, 1849; that after the 23d of May, 1849, the storage upon it up to that day was paid by the plaintiffs; that the storekeeper requires a permit from the custom-house before he will deliver the iron; that he always delivered goods stored without requiring payment of the storage where he knew and had confidence in the parties; that in this case he would have delivered the iron, and he ultimately did deliver it without payment of the storage. The plaintiffs also proved that on the 11th of May, 1849, their clerk went to the defendants' office and delivered to the defendant Pettee a bill of the iron. Mr. Pettee told him they wanted the custom-house permit so that they could get the iron; and that they had sold the iron to D. M. Wilson & Co., and wanted to deliver it and get their notes in order out of their proceeds to pay the plaintiffs. The clerk then went to the plaintiffs' office and obtained the custom-house permit and returned with it to the defendants' office at 25 minutes before 3 o'clock, when he was informed that Mr. Pettee was not in and would not be until 6 o'clock, and that he had left no check to pay for the iron. The clerk handed the permit to the defendants' clerk, but did not leave it with him, he having been ordered to bring it back if he did not get a check for the amount of the bill. It was also shewn that on the 15th of May, 1849, it was agreed between the plaintiffs and defendants that the plaintiffs might dispose of the iron to D. M. Wilson & Co., upon a sale which had been agreed upon between the latter house and the defendants, at $41 per ton payable in six months, and without prejudice to the claim of plaintiffs for the difference in the price to be paid by D. M. Wilson & Co. and that contracted to be paid by the defendants, or to the defendants' claim for a restoration of the advance of $750 made by them. The plaintiffs then shewed the weight of the iron and rested.

The defendants' counsel thereupon moved for a nonsuit upon the following grounds:

1. That there must be an actual delivery or tender of the iron before the plaintiffs can recover. 2. That a symbolical delivery is only good where the vendee accepts. That the worst construction that can be put upon the contract between the parties is, that payment and delivery are simultaneous acts. 3. That if a symbolical delivery is good, then the plaintiffs have not made such delivery or offer to deliver.

The motion for a nonsuit was overruled, and the defendants' counsel excepted.

The defendants' counsel then called Caswell, the broker who made the sale. He testified that on the 8th of May, at the request of the defendants, he made sale of the iron to D. M. Wilson & Co., at $41 per ton payable in six months; that at the defendants' request, on the 9th of May he told one of the plaintiffs that he was requested by Mr. Pettee to say that the defendants were ready to take the iron and wished it delivered, to which he replied, "Very well, he would attend to it." The defendants then proved that on the 11th of May, between 12 and 1 o'clock, they sent their clerk to the plaintiffs' office to get the permit so that they might obtain the iron, and that one of the plaintiffs told him that the defendant Dimon was gone to the custom-house for it, but that they would not deliver it until the money was paid, but that the clerk had no money to offer or tender.

The testimony being closed, the defendants' counsel requested the court to charge the jury as follows:

1. The contract taken together shews that the sixty days prescribed therein were given for the benefit of the buyers, and it cannot be so construed as to make payment for the iron a condition precedent to delivery. It cannot be construed more unfavorably for the buyers than to make the payment and delivery concurrent acts.

2. The defendants have all of the sixty days within which to take the iron, and the plaintiffs should be ready to deliver at all times within the sixty days.

3. There was a sufficient demand by the defendants within the sixty days to put the plaintiffs in default.

4. The rights of the parties were thereby determined, and the acts on the part of the plaintiffs in presenting the bill were nugatory.

5. The plaintiffs by their acts of the 11th of May did not put the defendants in default. There was no tender or offer by the plaintiffs to invest the defendants with the possession of the iron, or the right to its immediate possession.

6. The plaintiffs were bound to shew that they did offer and tender the iron within the time specified in the contract.

The court declined so to charge, and in charging the jury commented upon the various rules of law in relation to the performance of contracts of sale, and the rights of vendors and vendees, and instructed them that the principal question for them to decide was, "Have the defendants on their part during the sixty days demanded the iron, and in readiness to pay on their part, demanded the delivery: that going through the form of a demand without the ability or intention to pay, could not put the plaintiffs in default: that if under such directions they should find for the plaintiffs, they would give them the difference between what they had received on the sale to D. M. Wilson & Co. and the contract price, with the expenses." The defendants seasonably excepted to the charge and the omission to charge as requested. The jury found a verdict for the plaintiffs for $753.38, and judgment was entered thereon.

The defendants appealed to this court.

N. Hill, Jr., for appellants.

A. Taber, for respondents.

RUGGLES, C. J. Under the contract of sale, the delivery of the iron and the payment of the money were things to be done at one and the same time. The plaintiffs were not bound to deliver the iron unless the defendants at the same time paid the money; and the defendants were not bound to pay the price unless the plaintiffs at the same time delivered the thing sold or were ready to deliver it. The obligations to deliver on the one part and to pay on the other, were mutual and dependent. If the buyer in a case of this sort fails to pay or offer to pay within the time specified for mutual performance, the seller is discharged from liability to answer in damages for not delivering the thing sold. But it does not follow that the seller in such a case is entitled from the mere default of the buyer to recover the purchase-money. To entitle the seller to recover the price, he must shew not only that the purchaser failed to pay, but that he himself was ready and offered to deliver the goods. 12 Johns. 209, Porter *v.* Rose; 20 id. 130.

The issue between the parties was framed upon a correct view of the legal question between them. The plaintiffs averred that they were ready and willing and offered to deliver the iron within the time specified in the contract; and this averment was denied by the defendants in their answer: and this was the question which ought to have been put to the jury. Instead of that the judge charged the jury that the principal question for them to decide was, "Have the defendants on their part during the sixty days demanded the iron, and in readiness to pay on their part, offered to pay the money on delivery." If this had been an action by the purchaser against the seller for the non-delivery of the goods, the charge would have been right, because the purchaser is bound, on a contract of this kind, to shew a readiness and an offer to perform before he can require the seller to deliver. Whichever party seeks to enforce the contract against the other must shew performance or tender of performance. Until that be shewn he is himself in default. The plaintiffs in this case are seeking to enforce the contract, and the judge should have told the jury that to entitle them to recover, they were bound to shew an offer of performance, whether the defendants were ready or not. But the case was put to the jury on the question whether the defendants had offered to pay; and if they had not, the jury were instructed in effect to find for the plaintiff, whether he had offered to deliver or not, thus making the payment by the defendant a duty precedent to the delivery, when in truth it was concurrent merely; and allowing the plaintiff to recover in a case in which neither party had shewn a readiness and offer of performance. In this the judge charged erroneously, and on this ground the judgment below must be reversed and a new trial ordered.

This is not done without some reluctance, because if the case had been properly left to the jury on the question whether the plaintiffs were ready and offered to perform on their part, we think the jury might well have found in their favor.

The plaintiffs sent to the defendants' office the bill for the iron, and the custom-house permit authorizing the delivery of the iron to Dunham & Dimon. It is said that this permit should have been indorsed by the plaintiffs: in other words, that there should have been an order by Dunham & Dimon on the storekeeper for the delivery of the iron to the defendants. But the permit was not objected to on that ground. If it had been, the indorsement or order could have been immediately made or obtained. And without it, the offer seems to have been sufficient, because payment by the defendants would have given them a title to the goods; and the contract of which the purchaser must be supposed to have the counterpart, together with the clerk's receipt for the money on the bill, and the unindorsed permit, would have entitled the defendants to the iron from the public storekeeper. These papers were equivalent to an order on the storekeeper for the delivery of the iron. But the bargain was in fact broken off because the defendants refused to pay the money on the delivery of the goods, and not because the custom-house permit was unindorsed. Pettee, one of the defendants, told the plaintiffs' clerk that he wanted the iron to deliver to Wilson & Co., so that the defendants might raise the money by means of the notes which Wilson & Co. were to give for it. The plaintiffs were excused from doing more than was actually done towards performance on their part by the virtual refusal of Pettee to pay until he could raise the money on the notes he expected to get from Wilson & Co.; and by what was said by defendants' clerk after Pettee had gone, namely, that Pettee had left no check, and that it was useless to wait until he returned. It was shewn that the storekeeper would have delivered the iron without payment of the storage due previous to the date of the contract. It was not necessary to bring the iron to the defendants' office and tender it there. The offer to deliver seems to have been made in good faith, and to have been a substantial compliance with the duty under the contract.

But the defendants are entitled to have this question submitted to a jury, to be determined according to such evidence as may be produced on another trial.

Gardiner, Jewett, Johnson, and Taggart, JJ., concurred with the Chief Judge.

Morse and Willard, JJ., dissented, and were for the affirmance of the judgment.

Mason, J., did not hear the argument.

Judgment reversed and a new trial ordered.[1]

[1] See also Lester v. Jewett, 1 Kern. 453; Wheeler v. Garcia, 40 N. Y. 584, 588-591, per Daniels, J.—Ed.

BEECHER v. CONRADT.

NEW YORK COURT OF APPEALS, SEPTEMBER TERM, 1855.

[*Reported in 8 Kernan*, 108.]

ACTION commenced in the Supreme Court, in 1851, to recover the amount agreed to be paid by the defendant in and by the contract hereinafter mentioned. The complaint alleged the making of the contract; that it had been duly transferred to the plaintiff; that the party of the first part to the contract and the plaintiff had always fulfilled and kept all things therein contained on their part to be performed; that the defendant had neglected to pay the amount agreed to be paid by him; and that the whole amount of the principal and interest named in the contract was due and unpaid, and judgment for this amount was demanded. The answer put all the allegations of the complaint in issue. The cause was tried at the Oneida County Circuit, held by Mr. Justice Gridley. The plaintiff read in evidence the contract mentioned in the complaint. It was dated the third day of January, 1839, and executed by Abraham Varick, as surviving executor of the will of one Walker, deceased, as party of the first part, and by the defendant as party of the second part. By the terms of this contract the party of the first part, in consideration of one cent to him paid, and "upon the express condition that the party of the second part shall and do well and faithfully perform the covenants hereinafter mentioned, and to be performed on his part," covenanted for himself and his assigns to execute and deliver to the party of the second part a deed of conveyance in fee, containing covenants of warranty against the acts of the grantor, of and for a parcel of land which was described in the contract; and the defendant, the party of the second part, covenanted to pay to the party of the first part or his assigns "the sum of three hundred and ninety-six dollars in five equal annual payments, with interest annually on all sums unpaid." The plaintiff further proved that the land mentioned in the contract was conveyed and the contract assigned to him in December, 1850, and rested. Thereupon the counsel for the defendant moved the court to nonsuit the plaintiff, on the ground, among others, that inasmuch as the action was brought to recover the whole amount of the purchase-money after the same had become due by the contract, the plaintiff could not recover without proving that he tendered a conveyance of the land, or offered to convey the same to the defendant before the commencement of the action. The court overruled the objection, refused to nonsuit the plaintiff, and decided that he was entitled to recover the amount of the purchase-money mentioned in the contract. The counsel for the defendant excepted. The judgment rendered at the circuit was affirmed by the Supreme Court at a general term, held in the fifth district. The defendant appealed to this court.

Samuel Beardsley, for the appellant.

Charles A. Mann, for the respondent.

GARDINER, C. J. The plaintiff has neither averred nor was there proof of any other breach of the contract upon the part of the defendant, except the non-payment of the purchase-money. The plaintiff had a right to sue for each instalment as they severally became payable; but this right he has waived, and now seeks to recover the whole purchase-money in this action, without an averment or proof of a tender of a conveyance or a readiness or willingness to convey. It is not denied by the court below that, if the several payments had been made as they fell due, and the suit had been commenced for the last instalment alone, the plaintiff must have made such an averment and sustained it by proof, if questioned; the point is too plain to admit of discussion. It is, however, said that a right of action accrued as the instalments became payable, which the non-performance of the plaintiff would not discharge. This doctrine assumes a right, upon the part of the plaintiff, to divide his cause of action into as many suits as there were instalments. The first answer to this suggestion is, that the consideration for the conveyance by the vendor was an entire sum, to be paid by instalments; that the whole was due at the commencement of the action, and the plaintiff has sued for the whole purchase-money without attempting to distinguish, in his complaint or evidence, between the different instalments. The second answer is, that the plaintiff, having elected to wait until the fifth and last instalment became due, and upon the payment of which, as this case stands, the defendant would be entitled to a deed, cannot now sustain his action for either instalment without proof of performance or readiness to perform on his part. The covenants, as to the four first instalments, were originally independent; but the plaintiff, by his omission to insist upon a strict performance by the defendant, has lost the right to bring more than one suit for the money which formed the consideration for his conveyance. The defendant, by a tender of the whole, which he has now a right to pay, would be entitled to his deed. The plaintiff on the other hand must establish his right to the consideration as an entirety, or he cannot recover any thing. If he recovered in this action but $50, the judgment would be a complete bar to any further claim for the purchase-money, and when that judgment was paid the defendant would be entitled to his deed.

The defendant could not protect himself against an action by an offer to pay the first, or all of the four first instalments; as the consideration was entire, and all due, the plaintiff could insist upon the whole. And yet, if because the covenants were originally independent they must always continue so, the defendant must have the right to discharge by payments what the plaintiff could enforce by action.

The truth is, the parties by lapse of time are in the same situation as though the purchase-money was all payable at one time. The defendant has lost his right to pay the instalments separately, and the plaintiff his right to enforce collection by separate suits. There is but a single cause of action, one and indivisible. The defendant, if he would obtain his deed, must pay all, and the plaintiff, if he would recover, must shew such a performance on his part as would entitle him to all the unpaid consideration. The condition attaches to the whole debt and every part of it. The judgment of the Supreme Court should be reversed, and a new trial ordered.[1]

DENIO, JOHNSON, MARVIN, and DEAN, JJ., concurred.

CRIPPEN, J. (dissenting). The first and fifth grounds on which the motion for a nonsuit was asked may properly be resolved into one and considered together, as they both present the same identical question. If the plaintiff was bound to prove the tender of a deed, or an offer to give such a deed to the defendant as the contract called for, prior to bringing his action to recover the purchase-money, then he failed to maintain the action, and the court in that event erred in refusing the nonsuit. In order to determine this question, it will be necessary to refer with care to the terms of the agreement between Varick, the trustee, and the defendant. By this contract Varick agreed to convey lot No. 3, in Walker's patent, on the condition of a full and faithful performance of all the covenants contained in the contract to be performed by the defendant. On the part of the defendant, the first covenant made by him was that he would pay the trustee, Mr. Varick, his heirs or assigns, the just and full sum of $396 in five equal annual payments, with interest annually on all sums unpaid. The contract bears date on the 3d day of January, 1839; consequently, the last annual payment became due on the 3d day of January, 1844. This covenant of the defendant is not made to depend on any contingency or act of the other party, or of any condition to be found in the contract. When then, let us inquire, did the defendant become entitled to the deed of said premises? The parties, by the plain language of the contract, have said that the defendant shall be entitled to such deed on the express condition that he shall pay the sum of $396 in five equal annual payments from the 3d day of January, 1839 with annual interest. It is not easy to mistake the meaning of parties when they use language so plain and emphatic in making their contracts.

The defendant most clearly was not entitled to a deed when the first, second, third, or fourth instalments became due, even if they had been punctually paid by him. So, also, in relation to the last instalment,

[1] See Bean v. Atwater, 4 Conn. 3. — ED.

the time for its payment was fixed by the agreement; when the time arrived the money became due and payable from the defendant. No act was agreed to be performed on the part of the trustee or the plaintiff as assignee of the contract, in order to entitle him to the money due on the last payment. The premises were to be conveyed on the express condition of the payment of the whole amount of the purchase-money.

No act whatever was agreed to be done by the trustee to entitle him to the money; or, in other words, the defendant agreed that he had no right to call for a conveyance except upon the express condition that he paid the whole amount of the purchase-money. The case is clearly distinguishable from that of Grant *v.* Johnson, 1 Selden, 247. In that case the contract did not require the defendant to pay the whole amount of the purchase-money before obtaining a deed. He was entitled, by the terms of the agreement, to receive both the possession of the premises and a deed thereof before he could be called upon for the payment of the instalment in controversy in that action. Not so in the case at bar; and in this particular the cases are manifestly and clearly different. The defendant in this action had no right to ask for a deed, except upon the express condition that he first paid the full amount of the purchase-money. I have not been able to find any adjudged case conflicting with the plaintiff's right to recover in this action the amount due upon the contract.

The judgment should be affirmed.

HAND, J. (dissenting). I am of the opinion that the covenants to pay the purchase-money and to convey the land are independent. The defendant agreed to pay the purchase-money, and at certain specified times; and the vendor agreed to convey "upon the express condition" that he did so. No suit was commenced until all of the purchase-money became due. But that circumstance did not make the covenants dependent which before were independent. Where the last payment and the conveyance are to be simultaneous acts, and the prior payments have not been made, in a suit for the purchase-money, a performance or an offer to perform is necessary. Johnson *v.* Wygant, 11 Wend. 48; Grant *v.* Johnson, 1 Seld. 247. But that is not this case as I understand this contract. The payment of all the purchase-money was a condition precedent to the right of the defendant to demand a conveyance. Having covenanted absolutely to pay certain sums at the expiration of certain fixed periods, and the vendor having promised a deed on condition that the payments were made, the clear intention of the parties must have been that payment of all the money should precede the conveyance. There was no duty for the vendor to perform until the vendee had performed all the covenants on his part. By inserting the word "condition" or "*sub conditione*," a condition is created. 10 Co. 42 *a;* 2 Bac. Abr., "Condition," (A.); Platt on Covenants, 72.

"Upon condition" is an expression from which a condition precedent usually arises. (Platt on Covenants, *supra.*) The agreement here was not merely to convey "upon" payment being made, but "upon the express condition" that the vendee should perform; while the covenant to pay is without condition. And besides, the meaning of the words "upon condition" has been settled by construction, which should not be disturbed.

For this reason I think the judgment should be affirmed.

Judgment reversed.

SECTION IV.

Conditions Subsequent.[1]

ELLIOTT *v.* BLAKE.

IN THE KING'S BENCH, MICHAELMAS TERM, 1662.

[*Reported in* 1 *Levinz*, 88.]

COVENANT, and declares that the defendant covenanted to deliver to him 1500 measures of saltpetre before such a day, and that he had not done it; the defendant demands oyer of the deed, wherein the covenant was as aforesaid, provided that if any mischance happen by fire or water to disable him, that he should be excused; and pleads that he was disabled by accident of fire; issue thereupon and verdict for the

[1] "Resolutory conditions are those which are added, not to suspend the obligation until their accomplishment, but to make it cease when they are accomplished. An obligation contracted under a resolutory condition, then, is perfect from the instant of the contract, and the creditor may demand the payment of it. But if, before it is acquitted, or the debtor is put *en demeure*, the condition upon which it was agreed that it should be defeated, is accomplished, the obligation will cease.

"This difference between resolutory conditions and the suspensive conditions spoken of in the preceding article, may be illustrated by the following example: You lend Peter by my orders the sum of £1000, and I engage to return it if such a ship, on which he holds a bottomry interest, arrives safe. This is a suspensive condition, and I am not your debtor until the condition is accomplished by the arrival of the vessel; but if I engage for Peter until the arrival of the vessel, that is to say, upon condition that my obligation shall only continue until the arrival of the vessel, the condition in this case is only a resolutory condition, which does not prevent my engagement from being perfect immediately upon its being contracted, and consequently you may immediately demand the payment of the money. All the effect of this condition is, that if the vessel arrives before I have discharged, or been called upon to discharge my obligation, the accomplishment of the condition puts an end to it." *Pothier, Traité des Obligations,* No. 224, Evans' translation. — ED.

plaintiff. And it was moved in arrest of judgment, that there was a variance between the deed on which he declared and that produced in court; for the one is absolute and the other conditional. But judgment was given for the plaintiff, for he need not declare on more of the deed than the covenant, and it is on the defendant's part to shew the proviso, which goes by way of defeasance of the covenants.

CAGE *v.* ACTON.

IN THE KING'S BENCH, HILARY TERM, 1700.

[*Reported in* 1 *Lord Raymond*, 515.]

THE plaintiff brought an action of debt for rent against the defendant as administratrix to her husband, and he declared upon a demise made to the intestate rendering rent, and for rent arrear in the life of the intestate this action was brought, &c. The defendant pleads that, the intestate in his lifetime, in consideration of a marriage to be solemnized between the said intestate and the defendant, became bound to the defendant in a bond of £2000 *solvendis* to the defendant *cum ad inde requisitus esset*, upon condition that if the defendant should survive the intestate, if then the intestate should leave to the defendant £1000, or if his heirs, executors, or administrators, should pay to the defendant £1000 within, &c., after the death of the intestate, that then the bond should be void; and then the defendant avers that the marriage afterwards took effect; she avers also the death of the intestate, and that he had not left her £1000, nor had his heirs paid it to her; and then she shews, that she herself took out letters of administration of the goods, &c., of the intestate, and that assets to the value of £250 came to her hands, which she retains in part of satisfaction of the money due by this bond; and that she hath not assets *ultra*, &c. The plaintiff demurs. This case was argued several times at the bar by Mr. *Conyers* and Mr. Serjt. *Levinz* for the plaintiff, and by Mr. *Carthew* and Mr. *Northey* for the defendant. And now the judges pronounced their opinions in solemn arguments. And two questions were made in this case: 1. If debt for rent was not of a higher nature than debt due upon bond; for if it were, then this plea could not be good; because the administratrix cannot retain the assets for the debt due by the bond, when there is a debt of a higher nature, viz., a debt for rent, owing by the intestate. 2. Admitting that this retainer is well pleadable in bar in respect of the nature of the debts; yet whether there is here any debt due to the defendant upon this bond, in regard that there was an extinguishment of it upon the intermarriage or not.[1] . . .

As to the second point the court was divided, viz., TURTON and GOULD, JJ., were of opinion that this debt was not extinguished by the intermarriage, and therefore that the plea was good, and judgment ought to be for the defendant. But HOLT, C. J., held that this debt was extinguished, and therefore that judgment ought to be given for the plaintiff. And GOULD, J., argued for the defendant in this manner following: 1. He said, he agreed, that the wife before the marriage might have released this bond by a release of all actions, because she had the right of action in her. 2. That by the intermarriage all contracts for debts due *in præsenti*, or *in futuro*, or upon contingency, which may become due during the coverture, are extinct. 1. Because the husband and wife make but one person in law. 2. Because the action is suspended. 11 Hen. 7, 4 *b*; Co. Lit. 164 *b*; 8 Co. 136 *a*; Dyer, 140; Cro. Car. 373. 3. That if there was an express agreement that they should not be released by the intermarriage, it would be void, because it would be inconsistent with the state of matrimony, the husband and wife being but one person in law, and so there is not debtor and debtee, and therefore the debt is extinct in such case, notwithstanding such covenant. 4. He said, that he was at the beginning, when the case was first argued at the bar, of opinion that this bond was extinct by the intermarriage. But now after mature consideration he was of opinion that it might subsist by the rules of law; for the law does not love that rights should be destroyed, but on the contrary for the supporting of them invents notions and fictions, as abeyance, &c. Litt. sect. 646; Co. Lit. 342. Now in this case the express agreement of the parties created a right, and such a right as is not inconsistent with the rules of marriage, since the bond here ought not to have any effect till after the death of the husband; and therefore the law will not work a release, especially since there are two rules of law which would be broken by the destruction of this agreement: 1. *Modus et conventio vincunt legem.* 2. That the law will not work a wrong. But since a suspension of rights in personal duties does not always work an extinguishment, as appears by the cases hereafter put, he was of opinion that this bond was suspended only during coverture. As 8 Co. 136 *a*, Co. Lit. 264 *b*, the wife executrix of the debtee takes the debtor in marriage; the debt is not released, but the right is suspended *pro tempore.* And so here, the law preserves it from extinguishment, by interposing and taking it into its custody, for the making of the agreement of the parties effectual. If the obligee make the obligor executor, because it is his own act, it is a release of the debt; but otherwise if administration was committed. 8 Co. 136, Needham's case; Cro. Car. 373, Dorchester *v.* Webb. Besides that 26 Hen. 8, 7 *b*, proves that the law does not absolutely work an extinguishment; for it is held there, that if there be a divorce, the wife shall have her goods

[1] So much of the opinions as relates to the first question is omitted. — ED.

again; and Fitzherbert and Norwich put the case of a bond by the husband to the wife before the coverture, and said, that though it was in suspense during the coverture, yet after the divorce the wife might sue him upon it. So here he agreed that this debt was qualified and remediless during the coverture. And (by him) there is no solid difference between the cases of Clark *v.* Thompson, Cro. Jac. 571, and Smith *v.* Stafford, Hob. 216, Hutt. 17, Noy, 26, Hetl. 12, Litt. Rep. 32, of a promise made by the husband to the wife before the coverture to leave her £100 at his death, and this case of a bond; for as Hobart there observes, it is a promise presently, though futurely to be performed, and has a present lien. And therefore as the promise was held to be in suspense, so here the debt is suspended during the coverture, for preserving an honest agreement, which otherwise would be destroyed. For the difference taken in Noy, and there said to be agreed by the court, viz., that it would be otherwise in case of a bond; no such matter is reported in Hobart or Hutton, and therefore he could not say how far the said point of the bond was under their consideration. It is said in Hutton, that the law will not work a release contrary to the intent of the parties; because the marriage, which is the cause, will not destroy that which itself creates, which is the same in the case of the bond. And in Lit. Rep. 32, the same with Hetl. 12, the promise is said to be suspended by the marriage; which he said is done here in the case of the bond. And Hobart does not seem to make any difference between a promise and a bond; and he could not believe that there is any; and therefore he was of opinion that the plea was good, and that judgment ought to be given for the defendant.

TURTON, J., argued much to the same purpose. And he agreed that if this bond had been given for a precedent debt, it had been destroyed by the marriage, which had been a release in law. But a release in law will never destroy the provision that was intended for the wife by the express agreement of the parties. But such releases shall be taken strictly. And Hutt. 17, 18, Plowd. 184, Hutt. 94, Hob. 10, Moor, 855, were cited by him to prove it. And he said that this debt being in contingency during the coverture could not be released; for the bond and condition make but one deed; and upon oyer of the condition it appears that if the wife did not survive the husband, nothing would be due to her; and therefore being a contingency, and only a bare possibility, could not be released. As Hoe's case, 5 Co. 70 *b*, Cro. Jac. 171, a man cannot release to the bail in the King's Bench before judgment against the principal. And therefore if it could not be released by a release in fact, no more could it be released by a release in law. And a bond cannot be sued until the condition is broken, which in this case could not be during the coverture; and therefore this debt is qualified. Then he cited the aforesaid cases cited by Gould, Justice, concerning the promises, and also 2 Sid. 58, the roll of which he had seen, and which is entered Mich. 1657, *Rot.* 629, *Sup. Banc.*, Hoblin *v.*

Lupart, where the case was thus: debt was brought upon a bond by Hoblin, a stranger, against Lupart, of which the condition was that Lupart should perform covenants in certain marriage articles, in which Lupart covenanted with his wife before marriage to leave her, &c., if she should survive him; and if he should survive her, that he should pay to the executors of his wife £400. Lupart pleaded there, covenants performed; Hoblin replied, and assigned a breach, that he had not paid the £400, &c., and judgment was entered for the plaintiff, as appears upon the record. And this case he urged as strong in point, together with the arguments and reasons therein used in 2 Sid. 58. And as to the objection that this was *debitum in præsenti*, &c., he answered that that was rather sound than substance. And he cited Litt. Rep. 87, that by a release of all demands a bond with condition to perform covenants shall not be released before the covenants are broken; and yet it is *debitum in præsenti* as much there as in this case. But a release of the covenants would discharge the bond. Dyer, 57. And he cited the words of Henden, in Littleton's Reports, that it is not a *chose in action*, but the possibility of a *chose in action*. And he relied upon the case of Hancock *v.* Field there cited as a case in point. [But see Cro. Jac. 170, 2 Roll. Abr. 407, that the said case was an action of covenant, and not debt upon a bond with condition to perform covenants, as it is there cited.] And therefore he agreed with Gould, Justice, that judgment ought to be given for the defendant.

HOLT, C. J., argued *e contra* for the plaintiff, viz., that the bond was extinguished by the intermarriage. And the foundation of his opinion was because it is an immediate debt due from the sealing of the bond. Litt. sect. 512; and the reason which Coke in his comment upon Littleton, 292 *b*, gives why a release of all actions before the day of payment will discharge it, though no action can be maintained upon it until after the day of payment, is because it is a *chose in action*. And then if it is a present debt, the question will be whether the condition will make any alteration. The nature of the condition therefore ought to be considered; and the condition here is a subsequent condition, and therefore cannot diminish, alter, or qualify the debt; but the debt will have the same existence that it had before. And in its nature it cannot be a subsequent condition, unless there be a precedent debt to which it was annexed. And the difference is put in 5 Co. 70 *b*, Hoe's case, as to the matter of the release, between a duty certain with a condition subsequent and a duty uncertain to be reduced to a certainty upon a condition precedent; the first is releasable before the day, the second not. And to say here that this is not a present debt is expressly contrary to the words of the bond, viz., that the obligor binds himself in £200, to be paid when he should be required. The condition goes in defeasance, but does not suspend the debt, for that would make the condition repugnant. And if the breach of the condition were to raise the debt, it ought always to be shewn in the declaration, which is against constant experience; and yet it ought necessarily to have been shewn if it raised the debt, as they always do in case of a condition precedent. And as to the objection that the defendant might have oyer of the condition, and then it becomes part of the declaration, he answered that that did not compel the plaintiff to shew a breach of the condition; which nevertheless ought to be done, if the breach of the condition was necessary to raise the debt. But the reason why there is oyer of the condition is because it is part of the same deed; but that does not drive the plaintiff to alter his declaration. If the defendant says nothing, nor demurs, the court must give judgment upon the bond, without having any regard to the condition; but if it appears upon the whole matter that the condition is not broken, the court cannot give judgment for the plaintiff. Then, since it is an immediate debt, by the intermarriage it is discharged. 1. Because the husband cannot be indebted to his wife, for they are but one person in law. 2. The husband might pay the money due upon the bond without having respect to the condition, and that would discharge the bond, 11 Hen. 4, 43; which since he cannot do to his wife, such payment being impertinent, as if the right hand should pay to the left; for this reason it is released. 3. The intermarriage is an actual payment, because the husband is entitled to receive the money. And when the person who ought to pay the money is the same with the person who ought to receive it, it is in law a payment. Suppose a stranger, who was bound to the wife *dum sola*, would pay the money; he ought to pay it to the husband; then if the husband be debtor to the wife *dum sola*, and would pay, &c., after marriage he must pay himself. If a stranger had been bound to the wife in a bond with the same condition as here, a release by the husband would have discharged the bond. Co. Lit. 264 *b;* Plowd. 184, Woodward *v.* Darcy. The law books do not make any distinction between bonds in which there is a precedent duty, and others; *et ubi lex non distinguit, nec judices distinguere debent.* And therefore he held that the bond was discharged. If this had been a single bill, statute, or recognizance, with a defeasance of the same purport as the condition of this bond, he said that without doubt the intermarriage would have released them; yet the statute, &c., would have been as much qualified by the defeasance as the bond here by the condition; and the agreement of the parties had been the same in both. The only difference is that in the case of the bond the defeasance is contained in the same deed, and therefore the deed being in court, one may have oyer of the condition; in the other case the defeasance is in the hands of the defendant, being in another deed, and therefore there cannot be oyer of it; but yet in both cases the defendant ought to plead the condition or defeasance; and therefore in both cases the law is the same.

Objection. If the executor of the obligee marries the obligor, the debt is not extinguished.

Answer. That depends upon different reasons. For 1. The difference of the rights there preserves the debt from extinguishment. As where a man has a term as executor, and purchases the inheritance, the term is not extinguished. Co. Litt. 264 *b*, 338 *b*. 2. If that should be an extinguishment, it would be a wrong to creditors and amount to a *devastavit*, which an act in law will not do. 8 Co. 136 *a*. And things shall be extinguished between the parties, which yet shall remain and have existence as to strangers. As if a tenant for life grants a rent-charge, and then surrenders to the reversioner; or if a man who has a rent in fee acknowledges a statute, and then releases to the terre-tenant; the estate for life in the one case will continue as to the grantee of the rent, and the rent in the other case as to the conusee. But if the husband pays debts of the testator with his own money, amounting to the sum in which he was bound to the testator; that will amount to a release of the debt, because it is an honest payment, and prevention of a wrong.

Objection. The intermarriage will not destroy that which itself supports.

Answer. That the bond is not supported by the marriage, but by its own efficacy. The bond was made in consideration of an intended marriage, but it had its full force and effect instantly upon the sealing and delivery.

Objection. That the law will not do wrong.

Answer. That this was the act of the wife herself, and therefore she is not injured. And this is no more than that she did not well understand what she was going to do, and there is no third person in the case.

Objection. 26 H. 8, 7 *b*, that a wife after a divorce shall have her goods again, and the bond would revive.

Answer. He agreed the said case; because the divorce, being *a vinculo matrimonii* by reason of some prior impediment, as pre-contract, &c., makes them never husband and wife *ab initio*. But if the husband had made a feoffment in fee of the lands of his wife, and then the divorce had been, that would have been a discontinuance as well as if the husband had died; because there the interest of a third person would have been concerned; but between the parties themselves it will have relation to destroy the husband's title to the goods. And it proves no more than the common rule, viz., that relation will make a nullity between the parties themselves, but not among strangers.

And as to the objection made by Mr. Justice Turton, that there is nothing here to be released, because it is but a contingency and a bare possibility, he answered, that that avails nothing, because a release of the condition will not release the bond, but they must release the bond itself.

He agreed also the cases of Smith *v.* Stafford and Clark *v.* Thompson,[1] that the intermarriage would not extinguish such a promise, though Hobart is of a contrary opinion. But there is a difference between the said cases and this present case, because the promise must raise a future duty upon a contingency; so that there is nothing due there, nor ever was, and it is a question whether there ever will be. In an action upon the promise all the special matter must be shewn in the declaration, but otherwise in the case of a bond. Pleading, though it does not make the law, yet is good evidence of the law, because it is made conformable to it. If, therefore, in the one case there is no need to shew a breach, and in the other one must shew it, that proves that in the case of the bond the duty arises immediately, and is defeasanced by the condition; but in the other case it arises upon the performance of the condition, which ought to precede it; and consequently the cases are as different as a condition precedent and subsequent.

He said, also, that there is no difference between the case of Lupart *v.* Hoblin, which is covenant, 2 Sid. 58, and the case of a promise. For in covenant one must shew the special matter, and assign a breach, as one ought in that of a promise. And a release of all demands will not discharge the covenant before it be broken; as it will not discharge the promise before the time of performance; but it will discharge a bond before the condition broken: but the lien of the bond, if it was upon condition precedent, would be of the same nature. If a stranger promised to a woman that, in consideration that she would marry such a man, he would pay her so much if she survive her husband, the husband could not have released this promise, because nothing could become due during the coverture; but when the wife has a duty which may become due during the coverture, the husband may discharge that, according to Lampet's case, 10 Co. 46.

The reason given in Cro. Jac. 571, Clark *v.* Thompson, why the marriage of the promisor with the promisee is no discharge of the promise, viz., because the husband could not release it, ought to be understood of a promise made by a stranger; and those words ought to be added, as appears by the reason of it; but in case of such a bond the husband might release it. In Yelv. 156, Belcher *v.* Hudson, it is insinuated as if the husband might have released such a promise made by a third person; but the book there is nonsense; and in the same case, Cro. Jac. 222, the only question is there, whether it be released by a release of all demands, and no consideration had of the case upon the point of the marriage.

Noy, 26, in his report of the case of Smith and Stafford, reports that it was said by Warburton, that it would be otherwise in the case

[1] *Supra*, p. 784.

of a bond, and that the whole court agreed it; and nevertheless they resolved otherwise in the case of a promise; which proves that it must necessarily be, that they grounded themselves upon the difference between a bond and a promise, or otherwise their resolution will be contradictory. And one must consider the whole case, and not disallow the distinction, and agree the resolution; for that would be to agree the conclusion, and deny the premises.

Objection. The intent and agreement of the parties.

Answer. That the intent of the parties cannot alter the rules of the law, and make an immediate present lien not to have any efficacy.

Besides that, he said, in such a case as here the chancery will not give relief, as appears in 1 Cha. Cas. 21, Lady Darcy and Chute. Much less ought the King's Bench upon equitable considerations to give judgment against the rules of law. And therefore, for these reasons, he was of opinion, that judgment ought to be given for the plaintiff. But judgment was given for the defendant by the other two judges. Afterwards error was brought upon this judgment.[1]

SIR RICHARD HOTHAM, KNIGHT, AND ANOTHER v. THE EAST INDIA COMPANY.

IN THE KING'S BENCH, FEBRUARY 12, 1787.

[*Reported in* 1 *Term Reports*, 638.]

COVENANT on a charter-party of affreightment. The declaration, after stating several parts of the charter-party, by which it appeared that the plaintiffs had let their ship, the Royal Admiral, to the defendants for a voyage to the East Indies and back again, stated the following covenant on which the breach was assigned: "That, notwithstanding the ship was let to freight but for 903 tons, yet the company should lade

1 "But the plaintiff in error, perceiving the court above inclined to affirm the judgment, did not proceed," Carth. 513. And see Milbourn *v.* Ewart, 5 T. R. 381, in which the opinions of Gould and Turton, JJ., *supra*, were approved and followed. "A promise is sometimes called conditional, when it is subject to cease or be discharged by the happening of some event; which is then called a condition subsequent. Such is a bond, according to its literal construction, being the acknowledgment of a debt due from the obligor to the obligee, conditioned to be void on the performance of some act, or the happening of some event. The legal effect, however, of a bond is to secure the performance of the act, or the happening of the event, stipulated for in the condition; and in substance it constitutes a liability to pay, conditional on a breach of the condition, and the amount payable is restricted in law to the damages occasioned by the condition broken." Leake on Contracts, 833. — ED.

on board as many goods as the ship could bring, or was capable of taking in with safety, paying to the said owners freight for the same, according to the tonnage aforesaid." In a former part of the charter-party, stated in the declaration, is the following covenant: "And to the end the tonnage of the said ship, and the freight thereby payable, might be the better ascertained, it was thereby covenanted, that no claim should be admitted, or allowance made by the defendants, for short tonnage or deficiency in loading the said ship in or for her homeward bound voyage, unless the same should be certified by the defendants' president, agents, or chiefs and councils, or supercargoes, from whence she should receive her last despatch, which said certificate the said president, agents, or chiefs and councils, or supercargoes respectively, should give to the master for the time being, if reasonably demanded; and also, unless such short tonnage be found and made to appear on her arrival in the river Thames, upon a survey to be taken by four shipwrights or others to be indifferently named and chosen by the defendants and the plaintiffs; but no such survey should be taken, or allowance made, in case bulk should be found to have been broken before demand for such short tonnage was made.

The declaration then stated that, although the defendants loaded and put on board the said ship goods, &c., to the amount of 903 tons; and although the said ship could have brought, and was capable of taking in, with safety, goods, &c., to the amount of 100 tons more than the 903 tons, and more than were loaden and put on board the said ship by the defendants, their factors or assigns, from Bombay to London; and although the defendants, their factors and assigns, had notice of the premises last aforesaid before the ship sailed and departed from the East Indies on her voyage to England, and were then and there required to load the said ship with the residue of the said goods, &c., so as to complete her loading, and put on board her for the said voyage what she could reasonably and safely have carried; and although the plaintiffs offered to take in such loading, yet the defendants, their factors and assigns, absolutely refused fully to load the said ship, or to put any more goods, &c., on board her; and the said ship by means thereof was obliged to sail from Bombay to London deficient in her loading to the amount of 100 tons; neither have the defendants yet paid to the plaintiffs any freight or any sum of money for the said deficiency, but have refused, &c.

The defendants pleaded, first, that the ship was not capable of taking in more than 903 tons, on which issue was taken. And secondly, that the allowance claimed for short tonnage and deficiency in loading the ship was not certified by the company's president, agents, &c.

Replication, that the plaintiffs requested the company's president, agents, &c., to certify the deficiency, and that they wholly refused. Rejoinder, taking issue on that fact.

This cause was tried at the sittings at Guildhall after last term, when the jury found a verdict for the plaintiffs on both the issues.

A motion was made in arrest of judgment this term by *Law*, because the plaintiffs had not averred in their declaration, that a certificate of short tonnage was obtained from the defendants' servants before the ship sailed from India; and because it was not averred that, upon her arrival in the river Thames and before bulk was broken, a survey was had, and that such short tonnage was found and made to appear.

Erskine, *Mingay*, *Baldwin*, and *Watson* shewed cause. In an action of covenant, it is not necessary for the plaintiffs to set forth more in their declaration than that part on which the breach is assigned; and if there be any condition or proviso for the defendants' benefit, they must take advantage of it by pleading. 1 Lev. 88. The covenant, which was the foundation of the present rule, consists of two distinct parts; and the one which is pleaded by the defendants is independent of the other. Now nothing is more clear than that it was not necessary for the plaintiffs to aver that there had been a survey, because it is a proviso to be taken advantage of by the defendants. They have pleaded the first, and it was found against them; as to that, therefore, there is justification on the record. If the covenant had run, that short tonnage should only be recovered, provided there had been a survey, the not having had a survey would have been a condition precedent, and must have been averred by the plaintiffs. But standing in the form and place which it now does in the instrument, it is entirely distinct from the subsequent covenant on the part of the defendants to allow for more freight, if the ship would take more. But even supposing that it is necessary that a survey should have been had, after verdict the court will presume that there has been one. For the defendants having relied in their plea upon the other proviso, and taken no notice of this, they have waived taking advantage of it by their silence. In East and Essington [1] the plaintiff declared upon a bill of exchange set out in these words, "pray pay this my first bill of exchange, my second and third not being paid." A motion was made in arrest of judgment, that there was no averment that the second and third were not paid, which, it was contended, was a condition precedent. But the court were of opinion, that it must be intended after verdict. In the present case there is in fact an averment that the ship was short loaded, and that the defendants had notice of it, so that the survey was unnecessary; the fact must therefore be presumed after verdict, as the defendants have not taken issue upon it, and there is a verdict for the plaintiffs on the whole record. In Vivian *v.* Shipping [2] the declaration stated, that in consideration the plaintiff assumed to stand to the award of J. S. and J. D., and if he failed to pay the defendant £40, the defendant

[1] 1 Salk. 130; 2 Lord Raym. 810, s. c. [2] Cro. Car. 384.

assumed in the same manner to pay £40 to the plaintiff if he did not perform; the declaration then stated, that the arbitrators awarded that the plaintiff should pay the defendant £10, and in consideration thereof that the defendant should be bound in an obligation of £80 that the plaintiff should enjoy certain copyhold lands, &c., or that he would upon request pay him £40, and then alleged in fact, that although he had performed the award on his part, and had on such a day and place required the defendant to enter into such a bond, yet that he had not done it, nor had paid him the £40 according to his promise. The defendant pleaded no award, which was found against him. It was moved in arrest of judgment, that the plaintiff had not alleged payment of the £10, and the award is conditional for the payment thereof, and because it was not alleged that he had made special request for the payment of the £40. In that case, though the court differed as to whether the award was conditional, yet they all agreed that though it was a condition precedent, yet when the plaintiff says that he has performed the award on his side, it shall be intended that he hath performed it after verdict found for him, and it is good in substance, though not in form. These provisos are in the copulative, and not in the disjunctive, and the survey without the certificate would have been of no avail; therefore, the defendants have superseded the necessity of the former by depriving the plaintiffs of the latter.

Bearcroft, *Rous*, and *Law*, in support of the rule. In an action of covenant, a plaintiff, in order to entitle himself to damages, must state upon the face of the declaration a clear, legal demand. And though it is only necessary to set forth such parts of a deed of covenant as are essential to support his title, yet if he takes upon himself to state a proviso, which would have been a matter of defence for the defendant, he must aver performance of it. It is apparent on this record that the plaintiffs are not entitled to recover, unless they have performed two conditions which are precedent to their right of action. If therefore they be conditions precedent, the plaintiffs should have averred performance; but whether precedent or subsequent, as the plaintiffs have undertaken to state these conditions in their declaration, they have made it incumbent on themselves to shew that they have been performed. The true rule with respect to covenants precedent or subsequent, or whether distinct or not, is laid down by Lord Mansfield, in the case of Jones v. Berkley,[1] who said "that the dependence or independence of covenants was to be collected from the evident sense and meaning of the parties, and however transposed they might be in the deed, their precedence must depend on the order of time in which the intent of the transaction requires their performance." That both these are strict conditions precedent to the plaintiff's right of recovery, and, as

[1] Dougl. 665.

the plaintiffs have stipulated by their contract that they shall be performed, that before they can recover they must shew that they have been complied with (however difficult to be performed), appears from the cases of White *v.* Middleton[1] and Davis *v.* Mure.[2] The first of those was an action by the owner of a ship, employed in the government service, against the commissioners of the navy for freight. The plea stated a general proviso, inserted in all those charter-parties, "that on its being made appear that there had been a loss of time or negligence in the owner, a mulct by way of reduction of freight should be imposed, such as the commissioners should adjudge," &c. That the plaintiff had been guilty of a breach of orders; that it had been made appear, and that by the judgment of the commissioners this mulct had been assessed. The plaintiff in his replication traversed the breach; to this there was a general demurrer. The court thought the proviso was good, and said there could not be a doubt but that the commissioners were, by the proviso, judges of the delinquency as well as of the quantum. In that case the question was by the charter-party referred to the decision of a particular tribunal, and if the commissioners had imposed a mulct equal to the freight, the plaintiff could not have recovered at all; so here the plaintiffs are not entitled to recover under this contract entered into with the defendants, unless a certificate was given by the defendants' president, &c., and unless a survey was actually made, and it did appear that there was short tonnage. The case of Davis *v.* Mure was an action to recover the value of a ship against the person to whom she was let to freight. The declaration, after reciting (among other things) the following clause, "and it is further covenanted that if the said ship shall happen to be burned, sunk, or taken during the time she shall be in his majesty's service, and it shall appear to a court-martial that the master and ship's company have made the utmost defence they were able, the value of her shall be paid by the defendants," then stated that the ship sailed with provisions for the use of the army in America, under convoy of the Mercury, and was separated and taken; with an averment that the master of the ship and the ship's company did make the utmost defence they were able, and that it would have appeared to a court-martial, &c., if the defendants had thought proper to have had an inquiry made in that respect by a court-martial. To this the defendants pleaded: 1st, that she was not captured; 2dly, that she did not make the utmost defence; 3dly, that it would not have appeared to a court-martial, &c.; and, 4thly, that it hath not appeared, &c. The plaintiff took issue on the three first, which were found for him; and demurred generally to the fourth, which was argued. The court at

[1] Hil. 24 Geo. 3, B. R.

[2] Davis, otherwise Davidson *v.* Mure and others, M. 22 G. 3, B. R.

first doubted whether the ship was to be considered in the service of government at the time of her capture; but it was agreed on all sides that ships were considered in the service when they were laden for the king's use, and under orders of a king's ship. The court directed an inquiry to be made at the Admiralty as to the usage of holding courts-martial on such occasions, when it appeared that there were several instances in the war before the last of courts-martial to inquire of losses in the merchants' service, but none in the last war; and it did not appear on whose requisitions they were held. After argument by the plaintiff's counsel, that the inquiring by a court-martial was not a condition precedent, the court, without hearing the other side, were of opinion that the charter-party annexed an express condition that it should appear to a court-martial, &c., and therefore the plaintiff was bound to shew that it had appeared, or that it arose from the fault of the defendants that it had not; and judgment was given for the defendant. As it was necessary in that case for the plaintiff to shew that it had appeared, &c., to a court-martial before his right of action vested; so in the present case the production of the certificate, and the fact that short tonnage was found and had appeared upon a survey, were necessary to give the plaintiffs a right of action. In vain was it argued in that case that it was not in the plaintiff's power to procure a court-martial; for the answer to such argument was that if a person choose to make his debt arise on a contingency almost impossible, it is his own fault. Therefore here it is no answer to the objection against the plaintiff's recovering, arising from the want of a certificate and the neglect of having had a survey, that they could not procure a certificate, and that the defendants did not appoint their shipwrights to survey, because they have stipulated by their contract that a certificate should in fact be given by the defendants' agents abroad, and that short tonnage should appear upon a survey to be made at home, before their right of action should accrue. It was likewise held by the court, in the case of Pole v. Harrobin,[1] that if a party chose to make a debt depend on a condition, however difficult to be performed, he must take the consequences. If, however, the court should be of opinion that a sufficient excuse for not complying with the former part of this condition, with respect to the certificate, appears upon the record, because the plaintiffs did every thing they could in order to procure it; yet the same reason does not apply to the latter part; for the plaintiffs should have shewn that they had taken all necessary steps to have a survey, as by naming two surveyors on their part; and then if the defendants had not named two other surveyors, or had prevented the survey being made, there might perhaps have been the same excuse for not complying with the second part of the condition. But it does

[1] E. 22 Geo. 3.

not appear on the record that the plaintiffs took any steps to perform their part of the condition. In the case of East and Essington there was no previous act to be done by the plaintiff to entitle him to recover. It was not necessary to aver that the second and third bills had not been paid; for if nothing were shewn to the contrary, it was to be taken for granted that they were not paid. The objection there was requiring proof of a negative. And in fact, though the bills were three in number, yet the contract was one and the same; so that if the defendant had shewn that he had paid one, the court must have seen that he had discharged the others. But in the present case it was incumbent on the plaintiffs to do some act before they were entitled to make a demand; and that distinguishes it from the cases cited.

The court took time to consider; and now

ASHHURST, J., delivered their opinion (after stating the pleadings). The objections that have been made are that the certificate previous to the ship's sailing from the East Indies, and the survey after her arrival in the Thames, are conditions precedent to the plaintiffs' right to recover for short tonnage; and being such, and performance not being averred, it is a radical defect in the plaintiffs' title, and is not cured by a verdict, but is objectionable in arrest of judgment. And if they were right in their premises, namely, that these are conditions precedent, the conclusions which they draw from it would be right. It becomes necessary then to be considered whether these are conditions precedent or not? Now in order to clear this point, I would first premise that there are no precise technical words required in a deed to make a stipulation a condition precedent, or subsequent; neither does it depend on the circumstance, whether the clause is placed prior or posterior in the deed, so that it operates as a proviso or covenant. For the same words have been construed to operate as either the one or the other, according to the nature of the transaction. The merits, therefore, of the question must depend on the nature of the contract, and the acts to be performed by the contracting parties, and the subsequent facts disclosed on the record, which have happened in consequence of this contract. It is unnecessary to say whether the clause relative to the certificate be a condition precedent or not; for granting it to be a condition precedent, yet the plaintiffs having taken all proper steps to obtain the certificate, and it being rendered impossible to be performed by the neglect and default of the company's agents, which the jury have found to be the case, it is equal to performance. If it were necessary to cite any case for this, which is evident from common sense, it was so held in Rolle's Abridgment, 455, and many other books. If so, there was a right of action once fairly vested in the plaintiffs, from the defendants not having fully laden the ship before she left India, which they were by their covenant bound to do. For all that is necessary *prima facie* to found an action of covenant upon is, that the covenant should be broken. And this right of action, once vested, was only capable of being divested by a subsequent *non-feasance*, namely, by not taking the proper steps to procure a survey after the arrival of the ship in the river Thames. This, therefore, being a circumstance, the omission of which was to defeat the plaintiffs' right of action, once vested, whether called by the name of a proviso by way of defeasance, or a condition subsequent, it must in its nature be a matter of defence, and ought to be shewn by the defendants; and as they have not insisted on it, though they have insisted on the want of a certificate, we must, after verdict, take it that the fact did not exist; and it will follow as a consequence that there is no ground for arresting the judgment, and that the rule must be discharged. *Rule discharged.*

WILLIAM GRAY v. OLIVER GARDNER AND OTHERS.

SUPREME JUDICIAL COURT OF MASSACHUSETTS, MARCH TERM, 1821.

[*Reported in* 17 *Massachusetts Reports,* 188.]

ASSUMPSIT on a written promise to pay the plaintiff 5198 dollars, 87 cents, with the following condition annexed, viz., "on the condition that if a greater quantity of sperm oil should arrive in whaling vessels at Nantucket and New Bedford, on or between the first day of April and the first day of October of the present year, both inclusive, than arrived at said places in whaling vessels on or within the same term of time the last year, then this obligation to be void." Dated April 14, 1819.

The consideration of the promise was a quantity of oil sold by the plaintiff to the defendants. On the same day another note unconditional had been given by the defendants for the value of the oil, estimated at sixty cents per gallon; and the note in suit was given to secure the residue of the price, estimated at eighty-five cents, to depend on the contingency mentioned in the said condition.

At the trial before the Chief Justice, the case depended upon the question whether a certain vessel, called the Lady Adams, with a cargo of oil, arrived at Nantucket on the first day of October, 1819, about which fact the evidence was contradictory. The judge ruled that the burden of proving the arrival within the time was on the defendants; and further that, although the vessel might have, within the time, gotten within the space which might be called Nantucket Roads, yet it was necessary that she should have come to anchor, or have been moored, somewhere within that space before the hour of twelve following the first day of October, in order to have arrived within the meaning of the contract.

The opinion of the Chief Justice on both these points was objected to by the defendants, and the questions were saved. If it was wrong on either point, a new trial was to be had; otherwise judgment was to be rendered on the verdict, which was found for the plaintiff.

Whitman, for the defendants. As the evidence at the trial was contradictory, the question on whom the burden of proof rested, became important. We hold that it was on the plaintiff. This was a condition precedent. Until it should happen, the promise did not take effect. On the occurrence of a certain contingent event, the promise was to be binding, and not otherwise. To entitle himself to enforce the promise, the plaintiff must shew that the contingent event has actually occurred.

On the other point saved at the trial, the defendants insist that it was not required by the terms of this contract that the vessel should be moored. It is not denied that such would be the construction of a policy of insurance containing the same expression. But every contract is to be taken according to the intention of the parties to it, if such intention be legal and capable of execution. The contemplation of parties to a policy of insurance is, that the vessel shall be safe before she shall be said to have arrived. So it is in some other maritime contracts. But in that now in question, nothing was in the minds of the parties, but that the fact of the arrival of so much oil should be known within the time limited. The subject-matter in one case is safety, in the other it is information only. In this case the vessel would be said to have arrived, in common understanding, and according to the meaning of the parties.

F. C. Gray, for the plaintiff.

PARKER, C. J. The very words of the contract shew that there was a promise to pay, which was to be defeated by the happening of an event, viz., the arrival of a certain quantity of oil, at the specified places, in a given time. It is like a bond with a condition: if the obligor would avoid the bond, he must shew performance of the condition. The defendants, in this case, promise to pay a certain sum of money, on condition that the promise shall be void on the happening of an event. It is plain that the burden of proof is upon them; and if they fail to shew that the event has happened, the promise remains good.

The other point is equally clear for the plaintiff. Oil is to arrive at a given place before twelve o'clock at night. A vessel with oil heaves in sight, but she does not come to anchor before the hour is gone. In no sense can the oil be said to have arrived. The vessel is coming until she drops anchor, or is moored. She may sink, or take fire, and never arrive, however near she may be to her port. It is so in contracts of insurance; and the same reason applies to a case of this sort. Both parties put themselves upon a nice point in this contract; it was a kind of wager as to the quantity of oil which should arrive at the ports mentioned before a certain period. They must be held strictly to their contract, there being no equity to interfere with the terms of it.

Judgment on the verdict.

SECTION V.

Performance of Conditions, and how it should be averred.

LAMB'S CASE.

IN THE COMMON PLEAS, TRINITY TERM, 1599.

[*Reported in* 5 *Reports*, 23 *b*.]

IN debt on a bond by Lamb, executor of D., against Brownwent, with condition, "That if the defendant shall in the term of St. Michael next, in the Prerogative Court of the Archbishop of Canterbury, give unto the said D. his executors or assigns such sufficient release and discharge, &c., as by the judge of the said court shall be thought meet, that then," &c. The defendant shewed, that Doctor Lewyn was judge of the court, *et quod idem judex nec devisavit, nec appunctuavit aliquam relaxationem, seu exonerationem, &c., secundum formam, &c.;* upon which the plaintiff did demur in law. And it was adjudged for the plaintiff; for inasmuch as the judge was a stranger to the condition, and the condition is for the benefit of the obligor, and the performance thereof shall save his bond, he hath taken upon him to perform it at his peril; and therefore he ought not only to have done the first act, but ought also to have procured the judge to have devised and directed it. Otherwise it is, if the obligee himself or his counsel should devise.

BLANDFORD *v.* ANDREWS.

IN THE QUEEN'S BENCH, MICHAELMAS TERM, 1599.

[*Reported in Croke Elizabeth*, 694.]

DEBT on an obligation of £80, conditioned that if the defendant procured a marriage to be had between the plaintiff and one Bridget Palmer, at or before the feast of St. Bartholomew then next following, that then, &c. The defendant pleaded that the plaintiff, before that feast, came to the said Bridget Palmer and called her whore; and told her, that if he married her, he would tie her to a post; and used other opprobrious words unto her; by reason whereof the defendant could not procure the said marriage before the said feast. Whereupon the plaintiff demurred. *Williams*, Serjeant, moved, that this was not any plea; for he hath not shewn that he used his endeavor to procure the marriage; for it may be that, notwithstanding these words, they would have intermarried. And of that opinion was all the court; for the defendant ought to shew that there was not any default in him, and that he did as much as in him lay to procure it; otherwise he doth not save his obligation; and these words spoken before the day, at one time only, are not such an impediment but that the marriage might have taken effect. Wherefore it was adjudged for the plaintiff.

MORE AND BAKER v. MORECOMB.

IN THE COMMON PLEAS, MICHAELMAS TERM, 1601.

[*Reported in Croke Elizabeth*, 864.]

DEBT upon an obligation conditioned to deliver to the plaintiff before such a feast, such a ship, and all the tackling thereto, or in default thereof to pay at the same feast such a sum as John Norris and J. S. shall value them to be worth. The defendant pleaded, that before the said feast the said J. Norris and J. S. did not make any valuation of them. It was thereupon demurred, and resolved by all the court for the plaintiff; for although he hath election to do the one or the other, yet the condition being for his benefit, he ought to provide that the value should be assessed, otherwise he is to deliver the goods themselves; for if one be obliged to make such an assurance of such land as the counsel of the obligee before such a day shall advise, or to pay there and then £100; if the counsel devise not any assurance, he ought to pay the £100, for it being to his advantage when it is performed, he ought to provide that he performs the one. And WALMESLEY said, if one be obliged to pay £20 before the first day of May, or to marry A. S. before the first day of August next ensuing, if he doth not pay the £20 before the first day of May, and A. S. dies before the first day of August, so as the condition is become impossible by the act of God in this part, yet the obligation is forfeited, because he hath undertaken to perform the one of them; and it was his folly that he did not perform it when it was in his power and election to have done it. Wherefore, &c. And afterwards it was adjudged for the plaintiff.

LEA v. EXELBY.

IN THE QUEEN'S BENCH, TRINITY TERM, 1602.

[*Reported in Croke Elizabeth*, 888.]

ASSUMPSIT. Whereas the defendant was possessed of such a lease for years, the inheritance being the plaintiff's, in consideration the plaintiff promised to pay unto him such a sum of money, such a day and place, that the defendant promised *super solutionem inde* to surrender unto him his lease; and allegeth that he at the day and place tendered the money, and that the defendant had not surrendered his lease. The defendant pleaded *non assumpsit*, and found against him; and it was moved in arrest of judgment, that the defendant was not to make the surrender, but upon the payment of the money, or an express tender and refusal. And the plaintiff here hath alleged *quòd obtulit;* but he saith not that the defendant refused, which is material and issuable; and he might have taken issue upon the refusal, if it had been alleged; and although he hath pleaded *non assumpsit*, yet the declaration being ill in substance, the defendant may well take advantage thereof. *Coke*, Attorney-general, moved, that the declaration was good, and there needed not any tender and refusal to have been alleged, for it sufficeth to allege that in consideration he assumed to pay such a sum, the defendant assumed to surrender; so there being an *assumpsit* against an *assumpsit*, it had been well enough. But all the court held, that if the promise had been in consideration he assumed to pay such a sum, that the defendant had assumed to surrender, that had been sufficient; for then he is to make his surrender, and he ought to take his remedy against the other for the non-performance of his promise; but here it is, that he assumed to pay, and the other assumed to surrender it upon the payment, so as he would not trust to his promise; but when he had paid, he would then surrender it. And in the first case, he needed not allege the performance of the promise; but here in this he ought. And when he saith *quòd obtulit*, and saith not that the other accepted it or refused it, his allegation of the tender is not to any purpose; for he shall never say *quòd obtulit* only, but he ought to plead further that none was there to receive it, or that he refused; or he ought to allege payment; and here it is matter of substance, for want whereof the declaration is not good. Wherefore it was adjudged for the defendant. And afterwards *Coke* said, that Willenhall's case was adjudged, that tender without alleging a refusal was not good.

AUSTIN *v.* JERVOYSE.

In the Common Pleas, Trinity Term, 1615.

[*Reported in Hobart*, 69.]

S. C. *nom.* AUSTEN *v.* GERVAS.

[*Reported in Hobart*, 77.]

John Austin, being within age, brought an *assumpsit* by *prochein ami* against Jervoyse, and declared, whereas he bought of the defendant a horse for a piece of gold of twenty-two shillings paid in hand, and for eleven pounds more to be paid at the death or marriage of the said John, for which he should become bound with sufficient surety by their writing obligatory; the defendant in consideration thereof promised to deliver him the horse when he should be required, and says that afterwards he offered to become bound to him (but says not by his writing obligatory, with a sufficient surety, for the payment of the said eleven pounds as aforesaid), but yet he hath not delivered him the horse, though he were required.

The issue *non assumpsit*, and the verdict for the plaintiff. But he could not have judgment, for he should have tendered the obligation sealed; he should set down the sum, that the court might judge if it were sufficient for the eleven pounds; the surety should have been named.

In the *assumpsit* before, by Austen, plaintiff, against Gervas, judgment was given against the plaintiff, because he did not aver that he did offer the bond ready sealed, and to deliver the same to the said Gervas, neither did set down the sum in which he should be bound for the same ten pounds; for though it were expressed in the consideration laid, only that he should be bound for the payment, yet the law required that he should be bound in a competent sum, which is under the judgment of the court, and therefore must be pleaded expressly, that the court may judge of it.

ANONYMOUS.

IN THE KING'S BENCH, MICHAELMAS TERM, 1622.

[*Reported in* 2 *Rolle's Reports,* 238.]

A MAN named —— was bound in an obligation, and the condition of it was that he should deliver to the obligee a release of, &c. In debt upon this obligation the obligor pleaded that he *paratus fuit* at the day to seal and deliver to the plaintiff the release; that it was written and the wax fixed to the label; and that the plaintiff refused to accept it: whereupon it was demurred.

CHAMBERLAYNE. If it was a thing that could not be done without the plaintiff, and the plaintiff refused to accept it, he would be discharged if he did all he could, as if the obligee refuses to accept a feoffment which the obligor offers. But in this case he has not done all he could, for he ought to have sealed it without the plaintiff, which he did not do; and thereupon the plaintiff rightfully refused to accept it. . . .

BALL *v.* PEAKE.

IN THE KING'S BENCH, MICHAELMAS TERM, 1660.

[*Reported in* 1 *Siderfin,* 13.]

IN an action on the case the plaintiff shewed that the defendant promised, in consideration that the plaintiff would pay him so much money, to assign over his term to the plaintiff; and upon *non assumpsit,* &c., it was moved in arrest of judgment that the declaration was bad, because he said he tendered the money, but did not shew that the defendant refused; and *W. Wyndham,* Serjeant, said the refusal was the issuable thing; 6 E. 3, 31; and there ought to be a payment in fact or in law, and it is the refusal that is payment in law, and not the tender. TWYSDEN, J., said, that if the defendant had demurred, the declaration would have been bad; but as it is after verdict, it is good enough. And he cited a case ruled in this court, where a *feme* brought an action on the case against J. S. upon a promise that J. S. would marry her; and she did not say that she tendered herself to be married. But, it being after verdict, it was held good enough; wherefore it was ruled accordingly in this case. *Vide* 17 E. 3, 11 a, pl. 35.

DOUGHTY v. NEAL.

IN THE KING'S BENCH, HILARY TERM, 1669.

[*Reported in* 1 *Williams' Saunders*, 215.]

DEBT on bond; the defendant prayed oyer of the condition, which is, "That in a suit depending in Chancery between Elizabeth, Alexander, Priscilla, Mary, and Charles Fraiser, children of Elizabeth Fraiser, deceased, by the defendant, their guardian and administrator during their minority, to the use of the infants, plaintiffs, and the said Doughty, the now plaintiff, and others, defendants, it was decreed that the said Doughty, the now plaintiff, should pay to the said infants, or to their guardian for their use, the sum of £850 in satisfaction of all their right, title, and interest to a lease of the manor of Martley, and other lands, in the county of Suffolk; if therefore the defendant shall procure Doctor Alexander Fraiser, or the plaintiffs, Elizabeth and Priscilla Fraiser, to perform the decree, and that he and they shall at their several and respective ages of one-and-twenty years release the right, title, estate, interest, and claim which he or they, or either of them, have, hath, or may pretend to have, in and to the said lease of the said manor and lands, and to all the rents and profits due for the same, and had and received or not received by the said now plaintiff, then the obligation shall be void," &c. Upon which the defendant pleaded, that the said Alexander Fraiser, and the said infants Elizabeth and Priscilla, never had, nor ever pretended to have, any right, title, interest, estate, or claim to the said manor and lands which they could release; and this, &c.; wherefore, &c. To which plea the plaintiff demurred.

And judgment was given for the plaintiff by the whole court, because the defendant at his peril ought to have procured them to make a release *de facto*, although they had not any right, &c.; and the rather, because it appears by the condition that they had a pretence in equity, although they had no right, title, or interest at law. *Saunders* of counsel with the defendant. *Winnington* with the plaintiff.

PEETERS v. OPIE.

IN THE KING'S BENCH, TRINITY TERM, 1671.

[*Reported in* 2 *Williams' Saunders*, 350.]

ASSUMPSIT. The plaintiff declares that it was agreed between the plaintiff and defendant, that the plaintiff should pull down and prostrate the walls of three houses, and in the places in which the said walls were erected should build for the said defendant a malt-house, and a linny or dry-house, and cover them with slate or tile, and that the said defendant should pay to the said plaintiff, for his work in and about the pulling down and prostrating the said walls and building and erecting the said malt-house and linny-house, £8 of lawful money, &c. And then the plaintiff lays mutual promises, namely, that in consideration that the plaintiff had undertaken to perform his part of the said agreement, the defendant promised to perform the said agreement on his part to be performed; and the plaintiff also lays another promise in his declaration, and then he makes this averment, namely, "And the said plaintiff in fact says that he always from the time of making the said agreement hitherto was ready and offered to perform the said agreement in all things on his part to be performed, yet the said defendant" has not paid the £8 nor the other sums of money contained in the other promise, to the plaintiff's damage of £20. The defendant pleads *non assumpsit*, and the issue was found for the plaintiff on both promises, and entire damages assessed.

And now in this term *Saunders* moved in arrest of judgment that the plaintiff has not well entitled himself to the action on the said promise for want of averring that he has performed the work which he was to do, or that he was prevented from doing it by the defendant; for he only says that he was ready and offered, but he does not say that he performed, or that he was hindered or prevented by the plaintiff from doing it. And therefore he ought not to have the £8, for he was to have it for his labor, &c.; which implies that he first ought to do the work before he can demand his wages for his labor. For though it be laid by way of agreement and mutual promise, yet it appears by the very agreement itself that the plaintiff was to do the work and to have the £8 *for his work;* and therefore the mutual promise is only to perform the agreement, which the defendant has not broken on his part by the non-payment of the said £8, if the plaintiff has not performed the work, which was to be precedent to the payment of the money. And although the plaintiff has laid it by way of mutual agreement, yet in fact it is no more than that the defendant desired the plaintiff to do the work, and he would pay him £8 for it, which is a common contract between parties; and the meaning of it is that the work should be done first before payment: for the party who is to pay the money does not intend to pay it unless the work be performed; he does not mean to pay his money, and then to bring an action for not performing the work against one who perhaps is not responsible, or after he has got the money, will run away; but if the plaintiff has offered to do the work and the defendant has hindered him, the defendant will be in such case bound to pay the money, because he ought not to take advantage of his own wrong. And therefore the judgment was stayed until it should be moved on the other side.

And afterwards at another day *Pollexfen* moved for judgment for the plaintiff, because, as he said, there was here a promise on each side, and if the plaintiff has not performed the agreement on his part, the defendant has remedy against him by action; and here the agreement is not that the money is to be paid after the work is done, but it is to be paid generally whether the work be done or not; but if the work is not done the defendant has his remedy on the promise as aforesaid; and therefore he prayed judgment for the plaintiff.

And TWYSDEN, J., was of opinion that the plaintiff should have judgment for the reason given by Pollexfen; and also because the words 'for his labor' are no more than what the law would have implied. And he said that if the agreement had been that the plaintiff should do the work and the defendant should pay the plaintiff £8, without saying for his work, there had been no doubt that the plaintiff might maintain an action for the money although he had not done the work; yet the law implies that the £8 was to be paid for his work, and therefore the addition of the words 'for his work' will not alter the case at all, for they would be intended if they had been omitted, *et expressio eorum quæ tacitè insunt nihil operatur;* wherefore he concluded that the plaintiff ought to have his judgment.

HALE, C. J., contra; and that the declaration was insufficient, and judgment should be arrested; for he said that the words 'for his labor' make a condition precedent, so that the plaintiff ought of necessity to have the work done, or at least that he was hindered from doing it by the defendant, before he can demand the money. And he further said that if the said agreement had been put into writing under the seals of the parties, it had been clear that the plaintiff could not maintain an action of covenant for the £8 without such an averment; and no more can he do so here; and although there were mutual promises in the case, yet the defendant's promise was on the performance of the agreement, which in itself was only conditional on the defendant's part, namely, that if the plaintiff performed the work, then the defendant was to pay him £8 for his labor, but otherwise not; and here it appears that the plaintiff has not performed the work; wherefore the defendant is not bound to pay him the £8 notwithstanding the mutual promise.[1]

[1] "In contracts containing executory considerations, that is to say, in which a promise on the one side is given in consideration of a promise on the other, the mere promise, and not the performance of it, constitutes the consideration strictly so called; and the obligation of the one promise may be quite independent of the performance of the other. But when the matter of such mutual promises is examined, it may appear, upon the correct construction of their terms, that the obligation of the one promise is made expressly or impliedly conditional upon the due performance of the other; and then the performance of the promise, constituting the executory consideration, is a condition precedent to the liability to perform the other promise; in the latter case the mutual promises are called dependent, and in the former they are called independent." Leake on Contracts, 844. — ED.

But he said, that if by the agreement it had been that the £8 should be paid on any certain day, perhaps the law would be otherwise; because then it might be construed that the defendant relied on the plaintiff's mutual promise for his security; but here no certain time being limited when the money should be paid, the law makes a construction that it shall be paid when the work will be finished and not before, unless the defendant himself was the cause why it was not finished, which does not appear here in this record.

RAINSFORD, J., agreed with HALE; MORTON, J., being absent on account of ill health; wherefore the judgment was not absolutely arrested, but the plaintiff had leave to move it again; but his counsel perceiving the opinion of HALE and RAINSFORD, did not move it again, and consequently judgment was arrested. *Vide* Co. Lit. 204 *a*, that the word *pro* makes a condition in things executory, &c.

Afterwards, in Trinity Term, in the twenty-fourth year of the now king, it was moved again; and TWYSDEN retaining his former opinion, the court gave judgment for the plaintiff, because then HALE, C. J., and the other judges held, that "he was ready and offered to perform," &c., was a sufficient averment after verdict. *Quod nota.*

LARGE *v.* CHESHIRE.

IN THE KING'S BENCH, TRINITY TERM, 1671.

[*Reported in* 1 *Ventris,* 147.]

IN covenant the plaintiff declared upon articles of agreement between him and the defendant, whereby the defendant covenanted to pay him such a sum, the plaintiff making to him a sufficient estate in such lands before the feast of St. Thomas next ensuing the date of the deed; and then he saith, that *licet* he the plaintiff *semper a tempore confectionis scripti paratus fuit ad performand'* all the agreement of his part *usque ad diem exhibitionis billæ*, the defendant had not paid him the money.

The defendant pleaded, *quod ipse obtulit solvere* the money aforesaid, *apud Derby, si le plaintiff faceret ei bonum et sufficient' statum de et in præmissis, &c.*

The plaintiff replied, *protestando* that the defendant did not offer the money, *pro placito* that he the 21st of December *apud Derby fecit et sigillavit quandam Chartam Feoffamenti*, whereby he conveyed the premises to the defendant, and that he came to the premises an hour before sunset the same day, *paratus ad deliberand' seisinam, &c., et quod defendens nec aliquis ex parte illius venit ad recipiend'*, *&c.*, to which the defendant demurred and adjudged for him.

It was held, that these words, *ipso faciente bonum statum*, were a condition precedent to the payment of the money; therefore the plaintiff in his declaration should have averred the performance of it particularly, and not by such general words, that he had done all on his part.

And it differs from the case where in assumpsit the plaintiff declared, that the defendant in consideration the plaintiff should permit him to enjoy such land for seven years, that he would pay him *pro quolibet anno* 20s., and the action was held well brought within the seven years, for that it was an executory contract for every of the years, according to the intention of the parties.

It was resolved also, that the replication was insufficient; for that the plaintiff having election to make what conveyance he pleased, he ought to have given notice to the defendant that he would execute this charter of feoffment by livery, for it might have been by enrolment. But HALE said, the time when, in this case, was not necessary to be in the notice, because the charter was sealed and delivered upon the extreme day limited by the agreement, so the defendant knew it must be upon that day; so for the place, because it is a local thing, and must be done upon the land.

But because he had set forth no notice given to the defendant, that he would make livery, the replication is insufficient; as if a man be bound to levy a fine, he must shew whether he will do it in court, or by *dedimus;* and the court said, if the defendant had refused to accept of livery, the plaintiff might as well have brought the action as if he had actually made it.

LANCASHIRE v. KILLINGWORTH.

IN THE KING'S BENCH, TRINITY TERM, 1701.

[*Reported in* 1 *Lord Raymond*, 686, 12 *Modern*, 529.]

IN covenant for £2000 the plaintiff declared that the defendant's testator covenanted with the plaintiff, upon two days' notice to be given to him, to accept at any time within the year £1000 of the joint stock of the Hudson's Bay Company at the Hudson's Bay house in, &c., and upon the transfer thereof to pay to the plaintiff £2000; and the plaintiff avers, that upon the second of November, 1692, he left notice in writing at the testator's house, requiring him, the fourth of November following (which was within the year) at the Hudson's Bay House to accept the £1000 stock; and that the plaintiff was ready there at the day, and offered to transfer the stock, but that the testator did not come to accept it; nor hath the said testator or the defendant paid to the plaintiff the £2000. Upon demurrer to the declaration, and argument at the bar two or three times, the whole court held the declaration ill, and that judgment ought to be given for the defendant. 12 Mod. 529.

And HOLT, C. J., who delivered the opinion of the court, argued thus: It does appear that the money was to be paid upon transfer of the stock; and it is to be admitted, that when the money was to be paid upon the transferring of the stock, or doing any other thing, if he that is to make the transfer or do such other thing, make tender, and the other refuse, then he is as much entitled to the money, as if the transfer or other thing had been actually done; for though the words be, that the money shall be paid upon the transfer, yet if the party does all that lies in him, he is thereupon as much entitled to the money as if he had done all effectually.

But the question will be, whether there be a sufficient tender here? And we all hold that there is not, but that it is defective, and therefore the plaintiff cannot recover: he avers that he was ready, and did at the time and place appointed offer to make a transfer, but the defendant did not accept it; and in this is the fault of his declaration. Suppose the defendant had been there, and he had tendered it to him, and the other refused, he ought to have averred the tender and refusal; and in that case, to aver a tender, without averring a refusal likewise, would not do. . . .

Then there is another way of pleading a tender, if time and place be appointed for the doing of the act. If the party that is to do it come, and he to whom it is to be done do not come, there he ought in his declaration to allege that he was at the time and place, and tendered, but nobody came to receive. Yelv. 38. And if the party to whom the thing is to be done, be absent, there is this further considerable in averring a tender, that is, the time of day to make the tender: if there be time and place appointed, the party cannot come at any time of the day to make a tender; but in such case the law hath appointed the last time of the day on which the thing can be conveniently done, for the tender to be made; for it cannot be in the morning, nor at any time of the day but the last time on which it may conveniently be done, and the party must stay till then. . . .

If he had averred a refusal to accept, such refusal would be good evidence of a tender to his person, and that would have been good at any time of the day; and averring of such tender and refusal on the plaintiff's side would have been well, without telling on what time of the day the tender had been; because the averring a refusal implies the defendant's being present, who ought to accept it; but if the party were not present, it ought to be shewed that he did not come, and that you were there, and made tender on the time of the day on which the law appoints it to be done; and that is the last time of the day on which it may be done conveniently.

It was heretofore questioned whether it should not be alleged, that neither the party himself, nor anybody for him, was at the place to receive; because if anybody else had been there for him, it had been as well as if he himself had been there; and therefore ancient precedents are, that neither he nor anybody for him was there. But a tender being pleaded, and that he was not there ready to receive it, was held good, without saying that nobody else was there for him. 3 Cr. 734; 2 Cr. 13; Yelv. 38. For if anybody had been there on his behalf, that ought to come of his side, and it shall not be intended if they do not shew it. And what is the reason of this? This is it: when a man has covenanted and agreed to do a thing, in excuse of himself, for not doing thereof according to agreement, he ought to shew that he has done his utmost endeavor to perform it, and shew how it came to pass that he did not or could not do it. And here was an agreement by the plaintiff to transfer his stock; and hereupon the money was to be paid: the plaintiff indeed says he tendered the transfer, and so shews he did whatever he could do towards the performance of his agreement; but that is not enough, for he ought likewise to shew how it came to pass that it was not performed; as that the defendant was there and refused to accept, or was not there at all, or on the last convenient time of the day which the law appoints for doing the matter. And all this the plaintiff ought to shew to entitle himself to this action. . . .

There is one thing of what I have said may be liable to exception, especially in a case of transferring a company's stock, which is mentioned in the case of Shales and Seignoret;[1] this transfer was to have been made in the book of the Hudson's Bay Company, and they have set hours on which their books are open; and to say that he was there to make transfer, and tendered it at a time which is the last convenient time of the day, might be in vain; because by the usage of the company, the books are not then open, and therefore no transfer could be; and a tender, when no transfer could be, would be void.

Answ. If the agreement leaves it indefinite at such a day, the law knows no other time but the last convenient time of that day; but if a usage be averred, that the time for transferring is between such an hour and such an hour, there it ought to be averred, that he came within the ultimate convenient time by the usage, and that will be well; as if the usage be, that the books are open till six o'clock only, the proper time to come will be about five, and to stay till six.

And judgment for defendant *per totam curiam.*

[1] 1 Ld. Raym. 440. — ED.

HESKETH v. GRAY.

IN THE KING'S BENCH, HILARY TERM, 1755.

[*Reported in Sayer*, 185.]

AN action of debt being brought upon a bond in the penalty of five thousand pounds, and oyer being prayed of the bond, it appeared from a recital therein that Robert Hesketh, the plaintiff, had presented John Gray, the defendant, to the vicarage of Steyning, in the County of Sussex; and that it was agreed betwixt them that the said John should, within three months after the expiration of six years, to commence from the day of the date of the bond, at the request of the said Robert, his heirs, executors, administrators or assigns, resign and deliver up the said vicarage into the hands of the proper ordinary, so that it may become vacant, and the said Robert, his heirs, executors, administrators or assigns, may present anew. It likewise appeared that the condition of the bond was, that if the said John shall, within three months after the expiration of six years, to commence from the day of the date of the bond, at the request of the said Robert, his heirs, executors, administrators or assigns, resign and deliver up the said vicarage into the hands of the proper ordinary, whereby it may become vacant, and the said Robert, his heirs, executors, administrators or assigns, may present anew, then the obligation to be void.

The defendant pleaded, that he did, within three months after the expiration of the six years mentioned in the condition of the bond, at the request of the said Robert, offer to resign and deliver up into the hands of Matthias, Lord Bishop of Chichester, who was the proper ordinary, the said vicarage, for the said ordinary to accept the same, whereby the said vicarage might become vacant, and the said Robert might present anew; and that the said ordinary did then refuse, and from thenceforth hitherto hath refused to accept such resignation.

Upon a demurrer to this plea, it was holden to be bad; because it is not therein averred that the bishop accepted the resignation.

And by RYDER, C. J. The defendant, by undertaking to resign, so that the vicarage may become vacant, and the plaintiff may present anew, has undertaken for the bishop's acceptance of a resignation; which, according to what is laid down in Fane's Case, Cro. Ja. 198, is necessary to the completion of a resignation.

Several cases have been cited, in which it has been holden, that if a third person, who is a trustee for the obligee, refuse to do an act, for the doing of which the obligor has undertaken, the penalty of the bond is saved: And in order to bring the present case within the reason of those cases, it has been said, that the bishop is to be considered as a trustee for the obligee. If the bishop were a trustee for the obligee, it would be in the obligee's power to compel him to accept a resignation; it being always in the power of a *cestui que trust* to compel his trustee to execute the trust: but it is not in the present case in the power of the obligee to do this; and consequently the bishop is not to be considered as a trustee for the obligee.

We are of opinion, that the bishop is in the present case a stranger to the obligee; and if this be so, it was incumbent upon the obligor to procure his acceptance of a resignation. In 1 Roll. Abr. 452, 5 Rep. 23, and 1 Saund. 216, it is laid down, that if the obligor undertake for the act of a third person, who is a stranger to the obligee, it is incumbent upon the obligor to procure the act to be done; unless there were at the time of entering into the bond an impossibility of doing the act, or unless the doing thereof have been since rendered impossible by the act of God, or by the act of law.

PHILLIPS v. FIELDING.

IN THE COMMON PLEAS, NOVEMBER 26, 1792.

[*Reported in 2 Henry Blackstone*, 123.]

IN this action of assumpsit, for the non-performance of a special agreement, the declaration contained nine counts, the first of which stated that the plaintiff on the 10th of September, 1791, at Westminster, in the county of Middlesex, "was about to expose to sale, and to sell by way of public auction, a certain copyhold estate of him the said William (the plaintiff), that is to say, a certain copyhold messuage or dwelling-house, consisting of two parlors, a kitchen, and useful offices, with a garden behind the same, then in the occupation of one Edward Corey, situate and being in the parish of Titchfield, in the county of Hants, under the following conditions of sale, to wit: First, that the highest bidder should be the purchaser, and if any dispute should arise between two or more bidders, the estate should be put up again. Second, that no person should advance less than £2 at each bidding. Third, that the purchaser should pay down immediately a deposit of £20 per cent. in part of the purchase-money,[1] meaning the sum of £20 upon each and every £100 of the sum at which he should purchase such estate, and sign an agreement for payment of the remainder on

[1] But see 4 Co. 17 *b*, as to the office of an innuendo.

or before Christmas day then next, meaning the 25th day of December which was in the year of our Lord, 1791, on having a good title. Fourth, that the purchaser should have a proper surrender of the estate at his own expense, on payment of the remainder of the purchase-money according to the third condition, at which time the purchaser would be entitled to the rents and profits of the estate. Fifth, there being a duty on all sales of estates by auction of threepence half-penny in the pound, to be levied on the buyer or seller, as may be thought most proper, the said estate should be sold, subject to the buyer paying the said tax, exclusive of the sum the said estate should sell for. Sixth, if the purchaser should neglect or fail to comply with the conditions before mentioned, the deposit money should be forfeited, the proprietor should be at full liberty to resell the said estate, and the deficiency (if any) by such second sale, together with the charges attending the same, should be made good by the defaulter at such sale. Lastly, the purchaser should pay the auctioneer one guinea at the fall of the hammer; of all which said premises he the said George (the defendant) afterwards, to wit, on the said 10th day of September, in the year 1791 aforesaid, at Westminster, in the said county of Middlesex, had notice; and thereupon afterwards, to wit, on the same day and year last aforesaid, at Westminster aforesaid, in the said county of Middlesex, in consideration that the said William, at the special instance and request of the said George, had then and there undertaken and faithfully promised the said George to perform and fulfil every thing contained in the said conditions of sale on his part and behalf, as the vendor of the said estate, to be performed and fulfilled, he the said George undertook and then and there faithfully promised the said William to perform and fulfil the said conditions of sale in all things therein contained on the part and behalf of the buyer or buyers of the said estate to be performed and fulfilled, if he the said George should buy the same at the said sale. And the said William further saith, that the said intended sale of the said estate, afterwards, to wit, on the same day and year last aforesaid, at Westminster aforesaid, in the said county of Middlesex, was accordingly begun, made, and ended under the aforesaid conditions of sale; and the said George at the said sale became and was the highest bidder for the said estate, and then and there under the said conditions of sale bought and purchased the said estate, with the appurtenances, at and for the price or sum of £170 of lawful money of Great Britain, and then and there signed a certain agreement in writing, bearing date on the day and year last aforesaid, whereby he agreed to become the purchaser of the said premises, subject to the aforesaid conditions of sale, at and for the price or sum of £170, whereby and according to the said conditions of sale, and the said promises and undertakings of the said George, and the said agreement so by him in this behalf made as aforesaid, he the said George then and there became liable to pay to the said William the said sum of £170, according to the aforesaid conditions of sale; and the said William further saith, that although he the said William hath well and truly performed and fulfilled the said conditions of sale in all things therein contained, on his part and behalf to be performed and fulfilled, according to his said promises and undertakings, yet the said George, not regarding the aforesaid conditions of sale, nor his said promises, undertakings, and agreements so by him in this behalf made as aforesaid, but contriving and fraudulently intending craftily and subtilely to deceive and defraud the said William in this respect, did not pay down immediately on such purchase being so by him made as aforesaid, to the said William, or any other person or persons for his use, a deposit of £20 per cent. in part of the said purchase-money, or any deposit whatsoever; nor did he, on or before the 25th day of December, in the year 1791 aforesaid, pay, nor hath he at any other time whatsoever yet hitherto paid to the said William, or to any other person or persons to or for his use, the said sum of £170, being the purchase-money for the aforesaid premises, according to the aforesaid conditions of sale and according to his said agreement, or any part thereof, although so to do he the said George was requested by the said William, afterwards, to wit, on the day and year last aforesaid, and often afterwards, to wit, at Westminster aforesaid, in the county of Middlesex, and although the time limited by the said conditions of sale for the payment of the said purchase-money hath long since elapsed, and although the said William hath always been ready and willing, and hath frequently offered to make out a good title to the said estate, and to make a proper surrender of the said estate to the said George on payment of the said purchase-money; but the said George to pay any deposit, or to pay the said purchase-money or any part thereof to the said William, hath hitherto wholly refused, and still refuses so to do, and the said purchase-money still remains and is wholly due and unpaid to the said William, contrary to the aforesaid conditions of sale, and the said promise and undertaking of the said George, and his said agreement so by him in this behalf made as aforesaid, to wit, at Westminster aforesaid, in the said county of Middlesex; by means of which said several premises the said William hath wholly lost and been deprived of the benefit of the said sale by auction, and of the selling of his said estate, and the said William was thereby put to great and unnecessary expense of his money, and delay in the sale of his said estate, and by reason of the premises aforesaid, was, and hath been, and is otherwise much injured and damnified, to wit, at Westminster aforesaid, in the said county of Middlesex."

In the second, third, fourth, and fifth counts the respective estates which the plaintiff was about to sell were described as being really different from each other, but in all other respects those counts were similar to the first, reciting the same conditions of sale, and containing the same allegations. The remaining four were the common money counts.

To the first five counts there was a general demurrer, and to the four last *non assumpsit* was pleaded.

In support of the demurrer, *Marshall*, Serjt., argued as follows: —

There are two objections to this declaration. 1. The plaintiff has not shewn a sufficient performance of the agreement on his part, by stating an actual surrender to the defendant, or a tender and refusal, which is equivalent. 2. Though he states that he was ready and willing, and offered to make a good title to the estate, and a proper surrender, yet he does not shew what title.

1. By the third condition of sale, the purchaser is to pay down £20 per cent. in part, and to sign an agreement to pay the remainder on or before Christmas-day, on having a good title; and by the fourth, he is to have a proper surrender of the estate, at his own expense, on payment of the remainder. These two conditions taken together amount to this: the purchaser is to pay the money at or before Christmas, on having a good title; the seller is to make a good title on payment of the money. No terms could have been used more explicit to frame concurrent conditions. The promises are to be fulfilled at the same time, each being the condition upon which the other is to be performed; and though it is not certain that either party is bound to do the first act, yet, if either would have a remedy at law for the non-performance of the other, he must perform his own part; for unless he can shew a performance of his part, or an offer to perform and a refusal by the other party, he cannot support an action. Instead of this, the plaintiff in the present case brings an action against the defendant for not doing the first act; he says he has been always ready and willing, and frequently offered to "make out a good title to the estate, and a proper surrender, on payment of the purchase-money;" so that the allegation imports that if the defendant had previously paid him the money, he would afterwards have made out a good title, thus making payment a condition precedent. The general rule laid down by Lord Holt has never been departed from but in cases which have been afterwards overruled. That rule is, that in executory contracts, if the agreement be, that one shall do an act, and for doing it the other shall pay, &c., the doing the act is a condition precedent to the payment, for the party who is to pay shall not be compelled to part with his money till the thing be performed for which he is to pay. Thorpe *v.* Thorpe, 1 Salk. 171, 1 Lutw. 245, 12 Mod. 455, 1 Ld. Raym. 662; and S. P. 1 Salk. 112, Callonel *v.* Briggs. The rule indeed is subject to some distinctions; as if a day of payment be appointed which falls before the thing can be performed, an action may be brought for the money before the thing be done, it then appearing that the party relied on his remedy, and did not mean to make the performance a condition precedent. It fol-

lows, therefore, that though the conditions be concurrent, yet if either party would bring an action against the other for non-performance, he turns his part of the contract into a condition precedent, and he must aver performance or a tender and refusal; the reason of which is, that when a man undertakes to do a thing, he ought to shew his utmost endeavor to do it, and if it be not done, the reason why it is not done. Bro. tit. Condition, pl. 62; Lea *v.* Exelby, Cro. Eliz. 888; Lancashire *v.* Killingworth, 1 Ld. Raym. 686, Com. Rep. 116, 12 Mod. 529, 2 Salk. 623. Thus in Large *v.* Cheshire, 1 Ventr. 157, the plaintiff declared on an agreement, whereby the defendant covenanted to pay him such a sum, the plaintiff making to him a sufficient estate in certain lands, before such a day, and avers, that although he was always ready to perform the agreement on his part, yet the defendant had not paid the money. The defendant pleaded that he offered to pay the money if the plaintiff would make him a good estate in the premises. The plaintiff replied, that he sealed a deed of feoffment, and came on the premises before sunset on the day to deliver seisin, but neither the defendant, nor any person for him, came to receive it. On demurrer to this replication, the court held, that the words "making him a sufficient estate" were a condition precedent, and therefore the plaintiff should have averred performance particularly, and not in such general words. Thus, also, in Russell *v.* Ward, Sir W. Jones, 218, cited by Lord Holt in Thorpe *v.* Thorpe, 1 Ld. Raym. 665, the executor of A. declared against B., that in consideration A. in his lifetime had promised to assure certain lands to B. before Michaelmas next, B. promised to pay him so much for the land; that is, the assurance was to be made before Michaelmas, and the money was to be paid for the land; it was adjudged that the action would not lie for the money, without making an assurance of the land.

Even where the promises are mutual and independent, yet if one be the consideration of the other, each is a condition precedent to the other, and performance must be averred, unless a certain day be appointed for the performance. Thus, if A. agree to pay £100 to B. in six months, B. transferring so much stock to A., and B. gives a note to transfer the stock to A., he paying the £100. If B. sues for the £100 he must aver that he transferred, or a tender and refusal, and if A. sues for not transferring, he must aver and prove payment or a tender and refusal of the £100. Wyvill *v.* Stapleton, 8 Mod. 68, 381. And the manner of the performance must be shewn. Thus, in Austin *v.* Jervoyse, Hob. 69, 77, the plaintiff declared that he had bought a horse of the defendant for 22*s.* paid down, and £11 more to be paid at the death or marriage of the plaintiff, for which he should become bound with sufficient surety by writing obligatory, and that the defendant, in consideration thereof, promised to deliver the horse when he should be required, and averred that afterwards he offered to become bound to him, but the defendant had not delivered the horse. On *non assumpsit* and verdict for the plaintiff, the judgment was arrested, because the plaintiff had not stated that he had tendered the obligation sealed, nor what security he had offered. This doctrine, viz., that either a performance, or a tender and refusal, which is equivalent to it, must be shewn, is fully recognized by recent authorities. Jones *v.* Barkley, Dougl. 684, 8vo. edit.; Kingston *v.* Preston, there cited; and Goodisson *v.* Nunn, 4 Term Rep. 761.

2. But supposing the plaintiff had stated explicitly and formally, that he had offered to make a good title to the defendant, and that the defendant had refused to accept it; yet the declaration would still be bad, because it does not shew what title. If the plaintiff had no title, he could not recover damages against the defendant for not paying for an estate to which the seller could not make a title, though the defendant would have had a remedy against him for his breach of contract. The title, therefore, is an essential part of the case. But whether a title be good or not, is a question for the court to decide, and therefore it ought to appear with sufficient certainty on the face of the record. If it be so stated, the defendant will be able to take issue on any fact alleged if untrue, or demur if the title set forth be defective. But the merely alleging that he was ready and willing to make a good title, is not an averment of his title upon which an issue can be taken either of law or fact. If it be stated that a person is patron of an advowson or heir, it must be shewn how he is patron or heir, for no issue can be taken on "patron" or "heir." 1 Ld. Raym. 202. Still less can an issue be taken on the word "title," being much more vague and less appropriated in its signification. In an action upon a covenant to enjoy without eviction, the breach must shew what title the person had who recovered. Cro. Jac. 315, Kirby *v.* Hansaker; s. P., Broking *v.* Cham, Cro. Jac. 425. So in covenant for quiet enjoyment, the breach assigned was, that A. B. *habens legale jus et titulum* entered upon the plaintiff; after verdict for the plaintiff, this was holden to be no breach without shewing what title A. B. had. Wootton *v.* Hele, 1 Sid. 466, 2 Saund. 177. Thus, also, where the plaintiff declared that in consideration he would acquit one T. O. of a debt, and permit him to carry his goods off the premises, the defendant promised to pay the plaintiff £10 at a certain day; and averred that he acquitted and discharged the said T. O., and suffered him to carry away his goods, but the defendant had not paid the £10; after verdict for the plaintiff the judgment was arrested, because the plaintiff did not shew how he acquitted T. O., for it could not be without deed, which ought to have been particularly shewn. Cro. Jac. 503, Leneret *v.* Rivet. So in debt on an obligation, the defendant pleaded that it is indorsed that if the defendant should come to Bristol such a day, and shew the plaintiff a sufficient discharge of an annuity, that then, &c., and averred that he came to Bristol on

the day, and tendered to shew a sufficient discharge of the annuity, and that the plaintiff refused to see it. The plaintiff demurred, and after great argument it was held to be no plea by all the justices, because the defendant did not shew what discharge he tendered. Bro. tit. Condition, pl. 183.

So too the plaintiff declared that in consideration that he would relinquish a rent-charge which he had out of the defendant's land, the defendant promised to pay him £30, and averred that he did relinquish it. After verdict for the plaintiff this was held insufficient, without shewing how he relinquished it; for it might be by parol, which is no discharge. Cro. Eliz. 292, Gregory *v.* Nevill. Thus likewise in assumpsit on an agreement by which the defendant was to take of the plaintiff certain premises with the fixtures, &c., or else to forfeit a deposit of £5 5*s.*, with a penalty of £5 to be paid by the party who should fail; the plaintiff averred that he was ready and willing to deliver the premises, &c., to the defendant at such an appraisement, in pursuance of the agreement, but the defendant did not accept the said premises, &c. On demurrer, the court (without hearing the defendant's counsel) held that [as] the plaintiff was to deliver possession, he ought to do so, and to do that, he should have shewn that he had an interest in the premises. Luxton *v.* Robinson, Dougl. 620. And nearly the same objections as are now taken to this declaration were made in the case of the Duke of St. Albans *v.* Shore, 1 H. Bl. 273, and though the court in that case gave judgment on the plea, yet a strong opinion was intimated that those objections would of themselves have been fatal.

Cockell, Serjt., contra. It appears on the face of the declaration that there is a sufficient inducement to the promise of the defendant, for the breach of which he is liable. It is stated that the plaintiff was about to sell by auction "an estate of him the said plaintiff," and afterwards that, "although he hath frequently offered to make a good title," yet the defendant refused to perform his part; and it is objected that these allegations are insufficient. Now, supposing the objection to be well founded, it, being a matter of form, ought to have been pointed out by a special demurrer, but cannot be taken advantage of on a general demurrer. But in truth the allegations are sufficient to enable the plaintiff to maintain his action. It is not necessary to set out the title particularly, unless the defendant makes it so by pleading; it is sufficient, *primâ facie*, to state the contract; and if the defendant object to the want of title, it lies upon him to impeach it. Here the defendant was to do the first act, to pay for and consequently prepare the surrender; a more distinct averment therefore was not necessary on the part of the plaintiff, but *paratus fuit et obtulit* is sufficient. Davies *v.* Ridgeway, 1 Roll. Abr. tit. Condition, 465, pl. 31. And that *licet* makes an express averment appears from Com. Dig. tit. Pleader (C. 77), and the authorities there cited. But if it be not certain which party is to do the first act, but both are to do something at the same time, and one refuses to do his part, in that case he who was ready and offered to perform his part may maintain an action against the other, according to the mode of reasoning adopted in Jones *v.* Barkley and Kingston *v.* Preston.

Marshall, in reply. These cannot be considered as independent conditions, where each party relies on his remedy for the performance of the other; for if they were, then the plaintiff might bring an action for the money without conveying, and the defendant might sue for a conveyance without paying. As to the argument that *paratus fuit et obtulit* is sufficient, the true distinction is that, if the consideration is to be performed before the action is brought, performance must be expressly and fully averred, and the general allegation *paratus fuit et obtulit* is not sufficient; Cro. Jac. 583; but if nothing is to be done on the part of the plaintiff till the defendant has done a prior act, there it is sufficient; as if the plaintiff, being a bailiff, agree for £10 to arrest J. S. at the suit of the defendant, it is sufficient to aver that he was ready and willing and offered, but the defendant did not deliver him the writ, which was the case of Davis *v.* Ridgeway, 1 Roll. Abr. tit. Condition, 465, cited for the plaintiff. So also if a request be part of an agreement, and the debt or duty is to commence on the request, it must be specially alleged with time and place; as if in consideration that the plaintiff would assure certain lands to I. S., the defendant promised that, if I. S. did not pay so much on request, he would pay it; it is not enough to say that I. S. *licet sæpius requisitus* did not pay, for the request to I. S. is material to make the defendant chargeable, and must be specially alleged. Cro. Eliz. 85. But where the debt or duty exists before any request, there the general request *licet sæpius requisitus* is sufficient; and even that is not necessary, because the bringing the action is itself a request.

LORD LOUGHBOROUGH, after censuring in very strong terms the length of the declaration,[1] held that it was clearly bad, on both the grounds insisted on in the argument; first, because the plaintiff had not distinctly averred a sufficient performance of his part of the agreement, by stating an actual surrender to the defendant or a tender and refusal; and, secondly, because he had not shewn what title he had to the estate; for whatever his interest was, it ought to have been specially set forth.

GOULD, J., was of the same opinion. He remembered the case of an indictment for forgery, in which there were three counts for the forgery and three for the utterance; in the first count the prisoner was particularly described, and the grand jury having rejected the three

[1] But the fact was stated in court to be, that there were five different estates sold in five separate lots, for the purchase of which the defendant signed five separate agreements.

first counts, an objection was raised that the remaining counts described him "the said A. B." by reference to the first; but all the judges held that the description was good, and that the latter counts might refer to the former. So in the present case, the declaration, which was swelled to a very improper and unnecessary length, might have referred generally to the conditions of sale set forth in the first count, without repeating them over again in the subsequent counts.

HEATH, J., was of the same opinion.

Judgment for the defendant.

RAWSON AND OTHERS v. JOHNSON.

IN THE KING'S BENCH, JANUARY 31, 1801.

[*Reported in* 1 *East*, 203.]

THIS was an action on the case, to recover damages for the breach of a contract, whereby the defendant undertook to sell and deliver to the plaintiffs a certain quantity of malt at a given price. This was laid differently in different counts, and at the trial at the last assizes at York the plaintiff obtained a verdict, which was entered generally on all the counts. The two first counts, in which was averred a part delivery of the malt, were admitted to be good; but a rule was obtained calling on the plaintiffs to shew cause why the judgment should not be arrested for the defect of the third count, in only averring a readiness and willingness in the plaintiffs to pay for the malt, and not averring the actual tender of the price agreed upon. The count in question was as follows:—

And whereas also afterwards, to wit, on the 12th of November, 1799, to wit, at Leeds, in the county of York, in consideration that the plaintiffs, at the instance and request of the defendant, had then and there bought of the defendant a certain large quantity (to wit), 100 quarters of malt, at and for a certain price then and there agreed upon between them, he the defendant undertook and then and there faithfully promised the plaintiffs well and truly to deliver to them the said 100 quarters of malt whenever he the defendant should be thereunto afterwards requested; and the plaintiffs in fact say, that although the plaintiffs afterwards, to wit, on, &c., at, &c., requested the defendant to deliver to them the said last-mentioned 100 quarters of malt, and were then and there ready and willing to pay the said defendant for the same, according to the terms of the said sale, and although the plaintiffs were then and there ready and willing and offered to accept and receive the said last-mentioned 100 quarters of malt of and from the said defendant, yet the defendant, not regarding his said last-mentioned promise, &c., did not, when he was requested as aforesaid, or at any other time before or since, deliver to the plaintiffs the said last-mentioned 100 quarters of malt, or any part thereof, but hath hitherto wholly refused and still doth refuse, whereby, &c.

Law and *Lambe* shewed cause against the rule. The two first counts are out of the question, because there being an averment of a part-delivery of the malt without payment, and the contract stated being entire, the defendant is precluded from saying that such a delivery of the rest ought not to have been made, or that the payment was a condition precedent. As to the third count, the averment that the plaintiffs were ready to pay the defendant is sufficient; and distinguishes this from the case of Morton *v.* Lamb,[1] where the opinion of the court turned upon the want of such an averment. A readiness to pay implies an ability as well as a willingness to do the act; and it could only be satisfied in proof by shewing that the plaintiffs had the money by them to pay for the malt if the defendant had been ready to deliver it. The case cited was stronger than the present, because there a particular time was fixed, so that a formal tender might more easily have been made; but even there some of the judges thought that an averment of this sort would have done; whereas here no time being mentioned, a performance of the contract by the defendant within any reasonable time would have been sufficient; and a tender by the plaintiffs could not be necessary till the defendant might be expected to be ready to do the act.[2] It is not required in all cases to make an actual tender, where from the nature of the thing it would be nugatory. In Merrit *v.* Rane,[3] which was finally decided in the House of Lords, the agreement was, that in consideration of £250 paid to the defendant he was to transfer certain stock to the plaintiff before a certain day, within three days after demand in writing, upon payment of the further sum of £9000. The plaintiff averred that he appointed one J. M. to demand the stock and pay the price, that the defendant was required by note in writing to transfer the stock on a certain day, when J. M. attended all the while the books were open, but that the defendant did not appear to transfer, &c. It was objected (*inter alia*), that the plaintiff should have shewn that he had the money there to have paid on the transfer; but Lord C. J. Pratt said, "the payment of the money is no condition precedent, but a concurrent act; and if the defendant had been there the plaintiff must have laid down his money, though not so as to part with it till the transfer." And the court afterwards said, "as to the plaintiff's not shewing a tender, we think that ought to come from the

[1] 7 Term Rep. 125.

[2] *Vide* Ferrand *v.* Pearson, E. 2 Geo. 1, C. B., Bull. Ni. Pri. 156.

[3] 1 Stra. 458.

defendant by way of excuse, that he was there ready to have transferred if the plaintiff had been there to have paid the money." The ground therefore of the determination was, that as the actual performance of the act was disappointed by the party's non-appearance, such performance in fact was unnecessary. So here, it being uncertain when the defendant would be ready to deliver the malt, it could not be necessary that the plaintiffs should carry the money constantly with them. Besides, it is averred that the defendant refused to deliver the malt, and a refusal to deliver generally where no time is fixed for the delivery is a renunciation of the contract, and dispenses with a tender. All the cases cited in Morton v. Lamb, in support of the necessity of a strict averment of a tender, were cases upon demurrer, except the case of Callonel v. Briggs,[1] which was only a *nisi prius* decision. But this being after verdict, every thing will be intended that was necessary to support the facts laid in the declaration; and therefore it must now be presumed either that the plaintiffs were prepared to have paid the money on the spot if the defendant had been ready to deliver the malt, or that he refused to do so, in which case no tender was necessary. If a party say he will not receive the money, that has been ruled to dispense with the necessity of a tender. So here a general refusal to deliver the malt is the same in effect. The objection to the sufficiency of this averment may be resolved into this, that the defendant had a right to require the plaintiffs' money to be paid to him first, and then he might determine whether or not to deliver the malt. In covenant for non-payment of rent it is sufficient to aver that the tenant was on the land the last day ready to pay, but that nobody was there to receive it on the part of the landlord; but there never is any averment in such case that he tendered it.

Holroyd, contra. Where mutual acts are to be done, one party cannot maintain an action against the other for non-performance without averring either an actual performance or a direct tender or offer to perform his own part. The case of Morton v. Lamb only decided that a declaration without such an averment was bad: and Lawrence, J., there said, that the plaintiff must either aver performance or a tender; and that is the result of all the cases collected in the report of that case. It was expressly so decided by Lord Holt in Callonel v. Briggs;[2] also in Thorpe v. Thorpe,[3] Kingston v. Preston[4] and Goodisson v. Nunn.[5] It is not enough to be ready and willing to pay unless that be made known to the other party; this may be done without actually parting with the money, which is not necessary, according to what is said in Merrit v. Rane, unless the defendant had been ready to have delivered the malt at the same time; but such a readiness amounts to a tender, and ought to be so pleaded. It is different, as in that case, where an

[1] Salk. 113. [2] Salk. 113. [3] Salk. 171.
[4] Dougl. 688. [5] 4 Term Rep. 761.

act is to be done at a particular time and place; there if the party does not attend a tender is impossible, and therefore not necessary to be shewn; but such non-attendance must be pleaded in order to excuse the necessity of the tender.

LORD KENYON, C. J. However technical rules are to be attended to, and in some cases cannot be dispensed with, yet in administering justice we must not lose sight of common sense, and the common sense of this case will not be found to militate against any rule of law. No doubt can be entertained how this case should be decided; one man agrees to do a certain act in consideration of another man doing another act; the acts are to be done at the same time and place; one of the parties goes there intending to do his part, and the other stays away altogether; the former is obliged to bring his action for this breach of the agreement, and he pleads according to the truth of the fact, that he was at the time and place appointed ready to have received the other's goods and to have paid the stipulated price for them, which is all that he was bound to do, and that nobody was there on the part of the defendant, or that the goods were not there ready to be delivered: would it be any answer to say that he ought to have pleaded a tender of the money? Now this case is the same in effect: the defendant undertook to deliver the malt when he should be requested, and the plaintiffs plead that they made the request to him, and were ready and willing to have accepted and paid for it, but that he did not deliver it when requested, or at any other time, but refused so to do. To be sure under this averment the plaintiffs must have proved that they were prepared to tender and pay the money if the defendant had been ready to have received it and to have delivered the goods: but it cannot be necessary in order to entitle them to maintain their action that they should have gone through the useless ceremony of laying the money down in order to take it up again. It would be repugnant to common sense to require it. It is reported in the case of Morton *v.* Lamb, that I said that the plaintiff should have averred a performance or a readiness to perform his part of the contract; I do not doubt that I said so, and I still think it was rightly said: and if so it would decide this case. However, if it were necessary I see no reason why we should not avail ourselves of another argument urged at the bar, namely, that this is after verdict, when every thing may be presumed to have been proved which was necessary to sustain the declaration. It is true that a verdict will not cure a defective case, but it will cure a case defectively stated.

GROSE, J. The doctrine in question was much discussed in the case of Morton *v.* Lamb; and we there held that where mutual acts are to be performed, the plaintiff in order to maintain his action for the non-performance by the other party, must shew that he was ready to do whatever was required to be done by himself. And I have lying before me the ground of objection that was made in arrest of judgment in that case, namely, that the plaintiff had not averred "that he had tendered to the defendant the price of the corn, or was ready to have paid for it on delivery;" and the court afterwards adopted the suggestion, and considered that an averment of a readiness to pay would have been sufficient as well as an actual tender. Now this averment I consider under the circumstances as tantamount to a tender of the money; for the plaintiffs say they were ready to pay for the malt, but the defendant refused to deliver it. If these parties had met for the purpose of settling the business, and the plaintiffs had expressed their readiness to pay the price agreed on upon delivery of the malt, but the defendant had not got the malt there to deliver to them, there could have been no necessity for the plaintiffs to make a tender of the money, because they were not bound to part with it until the defendant was ready to deliver them the malt. Therefore I do not think that this is a defective averment, but that it was sufficient under the circumstances to aver a readiness to pay.

LAWRENCE, J. The rule in this case was moved for on the authority of Morton *v.* Lamb; the ground of that determination was, that where a man had agreed for a certain price to deliver corn to another at a certain place within a month, the payment of the money and the delivery of the corn were concurrent acts to be performed at the same time; and that it was not sufficient to enable the plaintiff to maintain an action for damages for the non-delivery of the corn to aver merely that he was ready and willing to receive it. But the court did not hold it necessary in such a case that the plaintiff should part with his money into the other's hands, and then endeavor to get the corn as he could. I alluded there to some cases in order to shew that the plaintiff must state in his declaration that he was ready to do every thing that was required on his part to be done; but I did not mean to say, nor was the attention of the court called to it, that that averment was to be made in any particular form. In the case before the court there was no averment whatever of the kind. It is urged that this is after verdict, and that it is sufficient that there is an allegation of the fact of a readiness to do that which was required of the plaintiff; and to be sure, if it were necessary to resort to that, so much strictness in the manner of pleading a fact is not necessary after verdict as on demurrer. But since this rule was obtained I have looked more particularly into the precedents to see in what manner averments of this sort have been made; and I have found one in particular in Plowd. 180, on which probably the pleader who drew this declaration had his eye. The case is that of Norwood *v.* Norwood and Read, executors of Gray; wherein the plaintiff declares that in consideration that he had paid the testator in his lifetime 40*s.* he promised to deliver to the plaintiff at Ramsgate 60 quarters of wheat in certain proportions and for a given price, to be paid immediately after the delivery of the same. The declaration then avers that Gray, though often requested to deliver the corn, and though the plaintiff at the several times aforesaid when the wheat should have been delivered was ready at Ramsgate to receive it, and to pay to Gray the several sums which he ought to pay immediately after the said receipts of the wheat, hath not delivered, but the same to deliver to the plaintiff hath wholly refused, &c. And upon demurrer the plaintiff had judgment. There indeed the only question made was, how far the executors were liable, but it was never questioned but that supposing they were liable the form of the declaration was good. There are similar precedents to be found in Hearne's Pleader, 131, and in Clift, 97. It appears therefore upon the whole, that this form of declaration agrees with the current of authorities; that it is not impeached by the case of Morton *v.* Lamb, on the authority of which the question was brought forward, and that it is warranted by the precedents I have quoted.

LE BLANC, J. According to the cases which have been determined on this question, neither of the parties was bound to do the first act or to perform his part of the agreement before the other. If so, then neither can be bound to state that in pleading which is equivalent to performance. Now a tender and refusal has always been deemed to be equivalent to performance; therefore as performance in this case was not necessary, neither was it necessary to aver that which was equivalent to it. But all that is required of the plaintiffs to shew is, that they did every thing which they were bound in fact to do. Then if they shew that they were ready to pay the price provided the defendant were ready to deliver the malt, that is all that was necessary for them to do, and consequently their pleading a readiness to perform is equivalent to every thing that they were bound to perform where the defendant refused to perform his part. Therefore I consider this averment sufficient; and that it must be taken after verdict that they had the money ready to have paid it, if the defendant had been ready to perform his part. *Rule discharged.*

WATERHOUSE *v.* SKINNER.

IN THE COMMON PLEAS, MAY 18, 1801.

[*Reported in 2 Bosanquet & Puller*, 447.]

ASSUMPSIT. The declaration stated that the plaintiff, at the instance and request of the defendant, bargained with the defendant to buy of him, and the defendant agreed to sell to the plaintiff a quantity of oats, at the price of twenty-one shillings per quarter, to be delivered any time between Michaelmas day, 1799, and Lady day, 1800; and in consideration thereof the plaintiff undertook to accept and receive the oats, and pay for them at the above-mentioned price, and the defendant undertook to deliver them some time between the above-mentioned days; "and although the said defendant afterwards, to wit, on, &c., at, &c., did in part-performance of his said promise deliver to the plaintiff a part, to wit, five quarters of the said oats, and although the time for the delivery of the residue of the said oats to the said plaintiff according to the defendant's promise aforesaid is long since elapsed, and the plaintiff was for and during all that time, and still is ready and willing to accept and receive the residue of the said oats, and to pay for the same at the rate or price aforesaid, to wit, at," &c. Yet defendant, not regarding, &c., had not delivered, &c., but had refused, &c. The defendant pleaded *non assumpsit*, and a verdict having been found for the plaintiff, a rule *nisi* was obtained in Michaelmas term last, calling upon him to shew cause why judgment should not be arrested, because it was not averred in the declaration that he had performed his part of the contract by tendering the price of the corn.

Shepherd and *Best*, Serjts., shewed cause, and distinguished this case from that of Morton *v.* Lamb, 7 Term Rep. 125, by observing, that in that case there was no averment of the plaintiff's readiness to receive and pay for the corn; which is all that is necessary to support the action, as appears from the words of Lord Kenyon, in Morton *v.* Lamb, that "where two concurrent acts are to be done, the party who sues the other for non-performance must aver that he has performed, or was ready to perform, his part of the contract."

Marshall, Serjt., in support of the rule, contended that the meaning of the contract was that the money should be paid on the delivery of the corn; that the payment and delivery therefore were concurrent acts, and consequently that neither party could maintain an action against the other without averring performance on his part, or a tender and refusal; that the averment in this declaration of the plaintiff's readiness to pay was introduced in order to avoid the necessity of proving an actual tender, without which the plaintiff was not entitled to maintain his action. He cited Callonel *v.* Briggs, 1 Salk. 112, and Pordage *v.* Cole, 1 Saund. 320. *Cur. adv. vult.*

On this day the opinion of the court (present ROOKE and CHAMBRE JJ.) was delivered by

HEATH, J. The only doubt which we entertained on this case arose from the decision of the Court of King's Bench in Morton *v.* Lamb. But that decision has been explained by the subsequent case of Rawson *v.* Johnson, 1 East, 203, where in a declaration on a contract similar to the present an averment of the plaintiff's readiness and willingness to pay for the article to be delivered by the defendant, without any allegation of an actual tender of the money, was held sufficient. With the determination of this last case we are perfectly satisfied, and therefore think that the judgment ought not to be arrested.

Per Curiam, *Rule discharged.*

MARTIN AND OTHERS v. SMITH.

IN THE KING'S BENCH, JUNE 28, 1805.

[*Reported in* 6 *East*, 555.]

IN assumpsit against the vendee of land, for not performing his agreement to purchase on certain terms, the first count of the declaration stated, that whereas the plaintiffs on the 10th of March, 1804, were seised in their demesne as of fee of and in certain lands, &c., in the parish of Bluntisham, in the county of Hants, and being so seised caused P. C., &c., auctioneers, to sell by auction the said lands, &c., subject to certain conditions of sale, viz. (*inter alia*), first, that the highest bidder should be the purchaser; third, that the purchaser should pay down immediately a deposit of £20 per cent. in part of the purchase-money, and sign an agreement for payment of the remainder on or before the 24th of June, 1804, on having a good title; fourth, that the purchaser should have proper conveyances, together with such attested copies as might be thought necessary, at his own expense, on payment of the remainder of the purchase-money, conformably to the third condition, &c.; and lastly, that should the purchaser fail to comply with these conditions, the deposit money should be forfeited, and the vendors be at liberty to resell the estate; and the deficiency, if any, together with all charges, should be made good by the defaulter, &c. And whereas the defendant attended at the sale, and was the highest bidder and purchaser of, and did at such sale accordingly purchase certain of the said lands, &c., viz., a parcel of freehold woodland, called Bluntisham Low Wood, &c., in the parish of Bluntisham, in the said county, for £1500; and thereupon, in consideration that the plaintiffs at the request of the defendant had promised the defendant to perform the conditions of sale on their parts as sellers, &c., the defendant promised the plaintiffs to perform the said conditions of sale on his part as the purchaser, &c. The count then alleged, that the defendant in part-performance of the said conditions of sale and of his promise, &c., made a deposit of £300 at the sale in part of the purchase-money, and signed an agreement that he would comply with all the other conditions, &c. And then the plaintiffs averred that though after the sale, and the promise of the defendant, and before the 24th of June, 1804, in the said conditions mentioned, the title to the said lands, &c., was made good and perfect and satisfactory to the defendant, according to the said conditions of sale as aforesaid, and that they have always from the time of the said sale, and the said promise, &c., hitherto been ready and willing, and afterwards, to wit, on, &c., offered to convey the said lands, &c., to the defendant, according to the said conditions of sale, and have been always ready and willing to do and perform all things on their parts to be done and performed according to their said promise, &c.; and of all which premises the defendant had due notice; nevertheless the defendant, not regarding his said promise, &c., did not on or before the said 24th of June, 1804, or at any other time whatsoever pay to the plaintiffs the said £1200, the residue of the said £1500, the purchase-money, &c., in violation of his promise, &c. There were two other special counts, which it was admitted on the argument could not be supported, and there were also common money counts. To the first special count the defendant pleaded, that though after the sale and before the 24th of June, 1804, viz., on the 1st of June, &c., he requested the plaintiffs to deliver to him a good and sufficient abstract of their title to the lands mentioned to have been purchased by him, yet the plaintiffs did not nor would when requested as aforesaid, nor at any time before or afterwards, deliver to the defendant such good and sufficient abstract, but wholly refused, &c., and therein made default. To the second and third special counts there were special demurrers, shewing for cause principally, that it did not appear by those counts what estate, title, or interest the plaintiffs had in the premises. And to the common counts the defendant pleaded *non assumpsit*. Replication to the plea to the first count, that the plaintiffs did not refuse and neglect to deliver such good and sufficient abstract as in the said plea is mentioned when requested by the defendant in manner and form as he has alleged. To which there was a demurrer, assigning for special causes; 1st, that the plaintiffs ought in their replication to have alleged that they did deliver to the defendant a good and sufficient abstract of a good and sufficient title to the lands in question, and to have shewn therein what estate, title, or interest they had in the lands; 2d, that the plaintiffs have by their replication attempted to put in issue a negative allegation, when by the rules of pleading the issue ought to be upon some affirmative matter, viz., whether or not the defendant requested the plaintiffs to deliver to him an abstract as in the first plea mentioned; or whether or not the plaintiffs did comply with such request; 3d, that the plaintiffs have attempted by their replication to put in issue two facts, the one, whether or not the defendant made the request in the first plea mentioned; the other, whether or not the plaintiffs complied with the said request, &c. It was admitted that the plea to the first count and the replication to such plea were both bad; and the question turned wholly on the sufficiency of the first count.

Symonds in support of the demurrer objected to that count, that it was not sufficient to aver in general that they were seised in fee, and that their "title to the land was made good, perfect, and satisfactory to the defendant," and that they "were always ready and willing to convey;" but they should have set forth what their title was, in order that the court might see whether it were valid in law; and should have pleaded a tender of the conveyance. And he cited Reynoldson *v.* Blake,[1] where in *quare impedit* for hindering the plaintiffs from presenting to a church, an averment that Sir T. Gouge, from whom they claimed, was the true patron thereof, was deemed insufficient without shewing how he was patron. Also the Duke of St. Albans *v.* Shore,[2] where in debt for a penalty against one who had articled to purchase land, one objection was, that the plaintiff only stated that he was "ready and willing to make a good title," but did not shew what title; which Lord Loughborough, C. J., in delivering the judgment thought was material, and that the plaintiff ought to have exhibited his title. Also Phillips *v.* Fielding,[3] where the purchaser of a copyhold had agreed to make a deposit and to pay the remainder of the purchase-money at a certain time, on having a good title, and a proper surrender made to him. And in an action by the seller for the non-performance of the conditions on the part of the purchaser, wherein the seller alleged "that he had been always 'ready and willing' and frequently offered to make a good title to the estate, and to make a proper surrender of it on payment of the purchase-money," it was holden not to be sufficient, but that he ought to have averred that he actually made a good title and surrendered the estate to the purchaser, or a tender and refusal; and ought also to have shewn what title he had. And in Glazebrook *v.* Woodrow,[4] where the plaintiff covenanted to sell to the defendant a school-house, and to convey the same to him by a certain day, in consideration whereof the defendant covenanted to pay the plaintiff a certain sum on or before the day; it was determined that the conveyance and the payment of the money were concurrent acts, and the covenants dependent on each other; and that the seller could not recover the money without averring that he had conveyed or tendered a conveyance to the purchaser.

Donaldson, contra, contended that the averments of the plaintiffs' seisin in fee of the estate, and that the title to it was made good and perfect and satisfactory to the defendant, were sufficient averments of title, and a sufficient compliance with the condition of the sale to make a good title to the purchaser, to entitle the plaintiff to recover without

1 1 Ld. Ray. 192.
2 1 H. Blac. 270–5, 280.
3 2 H. Blac. 123.
4 8 Term Rep. 366.

setting forth the title particularly; and that admitting that the making a good title by the plaintiff, and payment of the purchase-money by the defendant, were concurrent acts, the averment that the plaintiff had always been ready and willing, and had offered to convey the estate to the defendant according to the conditions of sale, was sufficient to entitle him to recover in this action without averring an actual tender of the conveyance. He observed, that however strict the rule of pleading might formerly have been in requiring the party who averred title in himself to shew what his title was, yet that strictness had long been laid aside in practice, in actions upon contracts like the present, on account of the manifest inconvenience of it; and he distinguished this from the cases cited, by shewing that the averments here went much farther than in those. The case of the Duke of St. Albans v. Shore [1] was decided upon a different ground, for there the plaintiff by his own act had rendered himself incapable of performing his part of the contract, by having cut down the timber which was to have gone with the estate stipulated to be conveyed to the defendant. And in Phillips v. Fielding [2] there was no averment that the plaintiff had a good title, but only that he had been always ready and willing, and had frequently offered to make out a good title to the estate, and to make a proper surrender of it to the defendant, on payment of the purchase-money; whereas here the plaintiff avers not only that he was seised in fee of the estate, but that his "title was made good, perfect, and satisfactory to the defendant, according to the conditions of sale." Then, if there be a sufficient averment of title, the allegations that the plaintiffs "have always from the time of the sale hitherto been ready and willing," and that they "offered to convey the lands to the defendant," &c., are sufficient without an actual tender of the conveyance, according to the last decided cases on this subject, Rawson v. Johnson,[3] and Waterhouse v. Skinner,[4] wherein the prior authorities were considered; the agreement to make a good title and convey on the one hand, and to pay the purchase-money on the other, being concurrent and dependent contracts. [LORD ELLENBOROUGH observed, that the defendant's counsel had laid no stress on this objection.]

Symonds in reply relied principally on Phillips v. Fielding, as having been expressly decided on the ground that the abstract of the seller's title ought to have been set forth in the declaration.

LORD ELLENBOROUGH, C. J. It is too much to contend for, that it is necessary for a party alleging title in all cases to display his whole title on the record. In many instances, title is put in issue generally; in a writ of right the *mise* is joined on the mere right; in a [writ of] dower the issue is, that the party *ne unques seisie que dower*; though how a person is seised may involve important questions of law; it may

[1] 1 H. Blac. 270.
[2] 2 H. Blac. 123.
[3] 1 East, 203.
[4] 2 Bos. & Pull. 447.

be in fee, or in tail, or it may be by wrong; but these questions are not displayed upon the record. It seems indeed to have been considered by the noble judge, whose opinions in the Duke of St. Albans *v.* Shore, and in Phillips *v.* Fielding have been quoted, that it was necessary for the plaintiff to set forth the abstract of his title specially, but I am not convinced that that is necessary. At any rate however the question here is, whether sufficient has not been set forth by the plaintiffs to enable them to call upon the defendant for the non-execution of his part of the agreement, when, besides averring themselves to be seised in fee, they allege that their title to the lands in question was made good, perfect, and satisfactory to the defendant. If made satisfactory to the defendant, what further can the plaintiffs be called upon to do; it is all that can be expected of them. This averment, therefore, removes any difficulty which might arise from the cases in the Common Pleas, from which cases the present is distinguishable.

GROSE, J. There would be great inconvenience if in such a case as this it would be necessary for a plaintiff to set forth all the particulars of his title in the declaration. It stands admitted that the plaintiffs are seised in fee, and that their title to the land was made "good, perfect, and satisfactory to the defendant;" and what more can be required?

LAWRENCE, J. I cannot find any printed precedents of this sort of action by a vendor against a vendee of an estate for not accepting the title and paying the purchase-money. I have manuscript precedents like the present; but those I do not rely upon in the consideration of the question. The opinion delivered by Lord Loughborough upon this point in the Duke of St. Albans *v.* Shore, I collected at the time to be merely his own, and not that of the other judges. And as to the case of Phillips *v.* Fielding, it does not appear to me to be so exactly like the present as is supposed: there were no such averments there as are in this declaration, that the plaintiffs were seised in fee, and that their title was made good and satisfactory to the defendant.

LE BLANC, J. This is distinguishable from the case of Phillips *v.* Fielding, which has been most relied on, in the two particulars mentioned; that the plaintiffs were seised in fee, and that their title was made out good and satisfactory to the defendant. I do not see what else was to be stated; any thing beyond this is merely evidence of title, which cannot be necessary to be stated.

LORD ELLENBOROUGH, C. J., then said, that the court would give judgment *nisi*, &c., for the plaintiffs; and if any doubt occurred to them during the term, they would mention it; if not, the judgment would stand. And no further mention of the case being made, there was *Judgment for the plaintiffs.*

STANDLEY, Esquire, v. HEMMINGTON.

In the Common Pleas, May 21, 1816.

[*Reported in* 6 *Taunton*, 561.]

It having been referred to arbitration to determine whether a contract subsisted between the plaintiff and the defendant for the purchase of certain allotments of land under an inclosure act, and the arbitrator having on the 19th of August, 1815, awarded that such a contract subsisted, and directed the defendant forthwith to perform the contract, and to pay £1652 on the conveyance of the land by the plaintiff to the defendant, the plaintiff furnished his abstract in September, which, on the 1st of November, was returned with queries; the abstract with answers thereto was redelivered on the 11th of November, and on the 11th of December the plaintiff pressed for an early answer. On the 18th of January the defendant repeated in substance the same objections. On the 30th of January the abstract was again sent to the defendant with answers, and despatch was requested. A personal demand of performance had on the 11th of May been made on the defendant, and notice, that unless he complied in ten days, his silence would be construed as a refusal to perform, and the court would be moved for an attachment; but he had not yet given any answer.

Lens, Serjt., now moved for an attachment for non-performance of this award. The defendant, he said, being in possession of the allotments, the vendor could get neither his land nor his money, and the usual practice being that the purchaser prepares the conveyances, it was unnecessary for the plaintiff to tender a deed executed. If any plausible objections had been taken to the title, he would not have asked the court to try its goodness on affidavits; at least the court would direct an issue whether the title were good.

Gibbs, C. J. I think the plaintiff must do something more. He might file a bill in equity for a specific performance. The title would then be considered in a court of equity; it is impossible we should try a title here on affidavits. But before the plaintiff can have an attachment, he must execute and tender to the defendant a conveyance, and ask for the purchase-money awarded. The modern practice, indeed, has gone thus far, that in an action where the defendant has dispensed with the plaintiff's tendering the deed executed, the plaintiff may nevertheless recover; but even that was a relaxation of the law. Jones v. Barkley[1] was the first case that relaxed the rule, which was admirably argued by my brother Le Blanc; but there it was averred he informed

[1] Doug. 684.

the party that he was ready to convey, and tendered a draft of an assignment and release for the purchaser's approbation, and offered to execute and deliver the deed pursuant thereto, and the other declared, if the plaintiff had tendered, he would not accept it, and that he wholly discharged and exempted the plaintiffs from executing the same. In the present case the plaintiff could not maintain an action on his agreement, nor on a bond for performance of the award, if he had such, because he does not shew performance on his part. I think there is not enough to bring the party into contempt, and the plaintiff's much better course is to apply to a court of equity.

DALLAS, J. The plaintiff does not shew even a refusal by the defendant, nor whether he has decided on the objection taken.

The rest of the court concurring, the *Rule was refused.*

FERRY AND ANOTHER v. WILLIAMS.

IN THE COMMON PLEAS, NOVEMBER 4, 1817.

[*Reported in* 8 *Taunton*, 62.]

IN assumpsit, the plaintiffs declared, that they caused to be put up to sale by public auction (amongst other things) a certain leasehold estate, subject to the following (amongst other) conditions of sale, that is to say, "that the purchasers should pay down immediately a deposit of £25 per cent. in part of the purchase-money, and sign an agreement for payment of the remainder within twenty-eight days from the day of sale, when possession should be given of the part in hand; that the purchasers should have proper conveyances and assignments of the leases at their own expense, without requiring the lessor's title, on payment of the remainder of the purchase-money; and that all out-goings should be cleared to midsummer then last; that the duty of sevenpence in the pound should be equally borne between the vendor and purchaser; that, if the purchaser should neglect or fail to comply with the above conditions, the deposit-money should be forfeited, the proprietor should be at liberty to resell the estate by public or private sale, and the deficiency, if any, attending such sale, with all incidental charges, should be made good by the defaulter. And the plaintiffs averred that the defendant afterwards became the purchaser of the said estate, subject to the said conditions, for the sum of £2835; and the defendant then paid £200 in part of the purchase-money, and signed an agreement for payment of the remainder within twenty-eight days from the day of sale. And after averring mutual promises of performance, they alleged, that although the plaintiffs did give the defendant possession according to the said conditions, and were also ready and willing to give and make to him proper conveyances and assignments of the leases of the said estate at the defendant's expense, on payment of the remainder of the purchase-money, and to clear all outgoings to midsummer, according to the conditions, and well and truly performed, fulfilled, and kept the conditions on their parts, according to the tenor and effect, true intent and meaning thereof, yet the defendant did not nor would pay them the remainder of the purchase-money, or pay or bear his share of the duty of sevenpence in the pound, or accept such conveyances and assignments as aforesaid; but wholly refused to comply with the conditions, or complete or perform his contract of purchase or agreement. Whereupon the plaintiffs afterwards resold the estate by public sale for the sum of £1438 10*s.*, and were put to great trouble and expense about such resale; and that on the second sale there was a deficiency, which, with the said duty (which was wholly borne and paid by the plaintiffs), and all incidental charges, amounted together to £1600. In their second count, the plaintiffs stated, that they had contracted and agreed with the defendant to sell to him, and that the defendant contracted and agreed with the plaintiffs to purchase of them, a certain other leasehold estate, for the sum of £2835, and that, in consideration thereof and that the plaintiffs had undertaken to convey to the defendant the said last-mentioned estate, he the defendant undertook to accept the conveyance thereof and pay the plaintiffs the last-mentioned purchase-money in a reasonable time; and although the plaintiffs were ready and willing and offered to convey and assign to the defendant the last-mentioned estate, and although a reasonable time for accepting such conveyance and paying the said last-mentioned purchase-money had long since elapsed, yet the defendant would not, within such reasonable time or afterwards, accept or execute such conveyances and assignments as last aforesaid, or pay the said last-mentioned purchase-money or any part thereof, or in any manner perform the last-mentioned contract for the purchase of the last-mentioned estate; whereby the plaintiffs not only lost and were deprived of all the benefit which might and would have accrued to them by the defendant's performance and completion of his last-mentioned contract, but were put to great charges and expenses in respect thereof, amounting to the sum of two hundred pounds; and were also put to further charges, amounting to the further sum of two hundred pounds, about the resale of the said last-mentioned estate to another purchaser. The declaration also contained counts for leasehold premises bargained and sold, and the money counts. At the trial before PARK, J., at the London sittings after Trinity Term, 1817, the jury found a verdict for the plaintiffs.

Best, Serjt., had obtained a rule *nisi* in the last term to arrest the judgment in this case, on two grounds: first, because the declaration set out no title in the plaintiffs; and secondly, because there was no averment in the declaration that any conveyance or assignment had been prepared and tendered, but merely that the plaintiffs were ready and willing and offered to convey and assign. He cited Luxton v. Robinson,[1] the Duke of St. Albans v. Shore,[2] Phillips v. Fielding,[3] and Martin v. Smith.[4]

Vaughan, Serjt., on a former day in this term, shewed cause against the rule. As to the second objection, the averment contained in the declaration is sufficient, and it is not necessary to aver an actual tender as a condition precedent. This may be collected from Pordage v. Cole,[5] and the elaborate note of Serjt. Williams on that case. That case is not much unlike the present; for here the money is to be paid at all events within twenty-eight days of the sale, but no precise time is fixed for the execution of the assignment or conveyance. If either of the covenants forms a condition precedent, the payment of the money is a condition precedent. But whether that is to be considered as a precedent or concurrent act, is immaterial, for the parties come before the court after verdict, standing in a very different situation from that which they would have occupied if this question had come before the court on demurrer. Where two concurrent acts are to be done, it is sufficient for the party who sues for non-performance to aver that he was ready to perform his part of the contract. Morton v. Lamb.[6] So, in an action for the non-delivery of malt, an allegation that the plaintiffs were ready and willing to receive the same, and pay for it according to the terms of the sale, was held sufficient, without averment of actual tender of the price agreed on. Rawson v. Johnson.[7] But the allegation in this declaration is nearly as strong as an actual allegation of tender made, and the refusal averred comes within the case of Jones v. Barkley.[8] Even if the defendant were entitled to a tender, his refusal amounts to a dispensation of it; and, after verdict, it must be taken that the plaintiffs proved the matters averred. Moreover, here is an allegation that possession was delivered; and wherever a contract is executed in part, it is no longer executory, and such part-execution amounts to an absolute acceptance of the plaintiff's title. Boone v. Eyre,[9] Campbell v. Jones.[10] In Wilkes v. Atkinson[11] (an action for non-delivery of goods according to agreement), it was held unnecessary, after demand made, to adduce evidence in support of the averment that the plaintiff was ready and willing to pay for the goods. It is un-

[1] Doug. 620. [2] 1 H. Bl. 270. [3] 2 H. Bl. 123.
[4] 6 East, 555. [5] 1 Wms. Saund. 320, n. 4.
[6] Per Lord Kenyon, 7 T. R. 129. [7] 1 East, 203.
[8] Doug. 684; and see Kingston v. Preston cited therein, 689.
[9] 2 W. Bl. 1312; s. c. 1 H. Bl. 273, n. *a*. [10] 6 T. R. 570.
[11] 6 Taunt. 11; s. c. 1 Marsh. 412.

just that the defendant should retain the possession, and not do what he has covenanted to do; his remedy is by action. [BURROUGH, J. Maxwell v. Sharp[1] was an action on an agreement to transfer stock, and the declaration was objected to, because it was not therein stated that there was an actual transfer of the stock. But it was there held that a sufficient tender was averred to support the action, and that these contracts were mutual and independent. So, here, the defendant is not to be put in possession of the legal estate without paying the money.] Lord Loughborough's expression in Phillips v. Fielding, of the necessity of specifically setting out the title, is cavilled at in other courts, e. g., in Martin v. Smith; but at all events, in this case the defendant has dispensed with it. Then, in the second count, an actual offer to convey, and refusal on the defendant's behalf, is averred. He cited Vivian v. Shipping,[2] and concluded by observing, that the averment was sufficient, and at all events could not be taken advantage of after verdict.

Best and *Copley*, Serjts., supported the rule. In this case each count forms a separate declaration, and is to be considered separately; and upon general damages, if any one count cannot be supported, the judgment is gone. Both the counts in this declaration are bad; the second clearly so. In the first place, on a contract of sale, the vendor must shew a title to sell; in the next place, he must shew that he tendered a conveyance; it is true that, by the conditions of sale, he is relieved from shewing the title of the landlord; but he does not shew whether he is lessee or assignee, whether there is even any lease, or whether he is in any way related to the premises. If a man simply undertakes to convey land, he thereby impliedly undertakes to convey a good title. It is quite nugatory for a man to go through the farce of conveying, when he has no title; and, if he has no title, the purchaser is not bound to pay the money, nor can the vendor sue him for non-payment. Phillips v. Fielding. [DALLAS, J. Phillips v. Fielding was in a degree doubted in Martin v. Smith. Lord Ellenborough there speaks of the rule in the former case as being the opinion of Lord Loughborough only, and so speaks Lawrence, J.] Phillips v. Fielding is not the decision of Lord Loughborough only, but of the whole court; and in Martin v. Smith the only question was, whether it was necessary to set out all the particulars of the title. In Luxton v. Robinson, Buller, J., says, "The plaintiff was to deliver possession, and therefore he ought to have shewn that he had a right so to do." If in strictness the title ought to be set out in detail, and if it is not so set out, the verdict will cure the defect of a general averment; but, on this record, no averment of title whatever is made. It cannot, therefore, be assumed to be proved that the plaintiffs had a title, for nothing can be assumed as proved which is not alleged. The

[1] Sayer, 187. [2] Cro. Car. 384.

second count is still more deficient. There is, indeed, in that count an averment of an offer to convey and assign; but this is a sale of leasehold property, and no excuse is stated for not setting forth the title of the landlord; nor is there even an averment that the plaintiffs had a title. In none of the cases cited in Serjt. Williams's note to Pordage v. Cole is any principle stated, which bears out the argument of the counsel for the plaintiffs. For here, though the money is to be paid within twenty-eight days, it cannot be shewn that the plaintiffs were not bound to make a good title till the thirtieth day. If it could be so shewn, then, and then only, the cases cited for the plaintiffs would apply. In Jones v. Barkley, Glazebrook v. Woodrow,[1] and Goodisson v. Nunn,[2] the conveyance was to be made on the same day; and it was held, that the conveyance must first be made or tendered, though the agreement was in the same terms with these. Campbell v. Jones is entirely inapplicable to the present case; there, part of the covenant was to be performed on one day, and part on another; for the instruction in bleaching must be gradual, and Lord Kenyon's judgment proceeded on that ground. Rawson v. Johnson and Wilkes v. Atkinson are with the defendant; for in those cases the plaintiffs had done every thing which, in the nature of the cases, they could be required to do. So in Maxwell v. Sharp the plaintiff had done all in his power to transfer the stock: and in a subsequent case, Merrit v. Rane,[3] which was an action on an agreement for the transfer of stock, the plaintiff averred, that he attended all the while the books were open on the day on which the stock was to be transferred, but that the defendant did not appear: the court there held, that if the defendant had been there to transfer, the plaintiff must have laid down his money, though not so as to part with it until transfer; and in the argument was cited Turner v. Goodwin.[4] In Vivian v. Shipping the point of condition precedent was not decided, nor is it clear whether that case came on on demurrer or after verdict. [The court here observed that, in the first count there was an averment that the plaintiffs were ready and willing to give and make to the defendant proper conveyances and assignments of the leases of the estate, and that the defendant refused to accept the same; that this averment, as the case stood, was, as they were then advised, sufficient, and that the first count was good. They directed the counsel for the defendant to confine themselves to the second count.] The second count is entirely defective, for there is not even a premise in that count, from which it can be inferred that the plaintiffs had a title, or from which a tender of a conveyance can be presumed. If an averment of actual conveyance is, strictly speaking, unnecessary, it is absolutely necessary for the plaintiffs to shew that they were ready and

[1] 8 T. R. 366. [2] 4 T. R. 761. [3] 1 Str. 458.
[4] Fort. 145; s. c. 10 Mod. 154.

willing to convey, and not only to convey simply, but to convey at the time and place stipulated. No such averment appears on this count, not even that he offered to convey within a reasonable time. All the matters necessary to be proved will, after trial, be supposed to have been proved; but if such matters be not averred, there could be no need to prove them; and, therefore, it cannot be inferred that they were proved. Rushton *v.* Aspinall.[1] The verdict, therefore, will not cure the second count. Phillips *v.* Fielding is expressly with the defendant in this case, and Callonel *v.* Briggs[2] is strong to shew that performance must be averred and proved. Neither of the special counts states the plaintiff's title, nor a tender of the conveyance; the latter does not aver that the plaintiffs were ready to convey within a reasonable time; both are evidently bad, and the latter, at least, is pregnant with such defects that it cannot be cured after verdict.

DALLAS, J., now delivered the judgment of the court. This was a motion in arrest of judgment. The declaration consisted of two special counts, and the common counts. To the special counts objections have been raised. The first count, in substance, states that a leasehold estate was put up for sale, subject to certain conditions, of which one was, that the purchasers should have proper conveyances and assignments of leases, without requiring the lessor's title. What the buyer, therefore, did not stipulate for or require, the lessor [seller] was not bound to state. The want of such an averment, therefore, constitutes no objection. It was next urged, that the tender of a proper assignment was not alleged; and it is true that such a tender is not alleged in terms; but the allegation is, that the plaintiffs were ready and willing to give a proper assignment on payment of the remainder of the purchase-money, according to the intent, tenor, and effect of the agreement; but that the defendant refused to accept of such assignment, and to perform his agreement according to such intent and meaning. Now the rule is clear, that if performance of an act be rendered impossible by the default of the one party, it dispenses with the necessity of the other party's averment or proof of such fact; and if that rule be applied to this case, the objection vanishes. There is, then, a substantial right of action on the record; and whether the pleadings are so formally drawn as to be good on demurrer, it is not necessary now to consider; for this motion is in arrest of judgment, when the omission of form, and even of substance, is aided by the verdict.

The second count differs from the first: in the second count nothing is said of the purchaser having conveyances, without requiring the lessor's title; but the agreement set forth is, that the one party shall assign, and that the other shall accept; and then comes an averment, not merely that the plaintiffs were ready and willing to convey and

[1] Doug. 679. [2] 1 Salk. 112.

assign, as in the first count, but that they actually offered to convey and assign, and that the defendant refused to accept. To this count it is objected, first, that there is no title specially set forth; secondly, that title is not even generally alleged; and, thirdly, that there is no averment of the actual tender of any conveyance or assignment; and, it is true, that title in the lessor is not alleged. It becomes, therefore, unnecessary to consider the distinction between title specially set forth and title generally alleged. If it be urged that, under the facts of this case, such allegation would be necessary, and that the want of it would be bad on demurrer, the answer is, that we are now not to decide on demurrer, but on a motion in arrest of judgment; to that ground, therefore, and to that only, must our consideration be confined. And this makes it unnecessary to go into the various cases which have been cited; every one of which, if it were necessary to examine them, would be found to differ from the case before the court in many respects; but, for the present purpose, one broad ground of distinction is sufficient: they were all cases on demurrer. Being so distinguished, I need not say that they depend, not only upon different, but upon opposite principles to those which govern the present case. On demurrer, in favor of correct pleading, every objection is to be strictly considered, after verdict, matter whether of form or substance is to be aided by the verdict in favor of the justice of the case. Confining ourselves, therefore, to the consideration of this point, as arising on a motion in arrest of judgment, it becomes necessary to refer to the agreement and breach, as stated in the second count of the declaration. The contract alleged is an agreement by the defendant to purchase, and by the plaintiffs to assign and to convey, a certain leasehold estate of them the plaintiffs; and, after verdict, it must be taken that the contract alleged was proved. Nothing is said as to a title or right to convey; but it is insisted that, in legal construction, an agreement to assign and convey imports a right to assign and convey. Be it so, for the purpose of argument; for if such be the construction which the law will put upon the contract, it must be taken that the assignment offered was of such a description. It is sufficient to set forth in the declaration the agreement in the terms in which it exists. The same construction must be applied to the contract, and to the statement of the contract in the declaration, and this is done in the present case. Supposing it necessary to prove, under such an agreement, an offer legally to assign, it must be taken, after verdict, that this was proved at the trial, inasmuch as, without such proof, in the present view of the case, the plaintiffs could not have recovered. As to the remaining objection, viz., the want of an actual tender, it will be sufficient to say, that the objection becomes weaker when applied to the second count than it was when applied to the first; for in this second count is alleged an actual offer to convey by the plaintiffs, and an actual refusal to accept such conveyance by the defendant. What, therefore, has already been said on this subject, as applied to the first count, becomes much stronger as applied to the second. The case seems sufficiently clear; but if any illustration be required, it may be derived from Mason *v.* Corder,[1] the last case decided on this subject in this court. There, in an action upon an agreement to assign a lease, it was urged in arrest of judgment that the plaintiff should have averred and proved, not only that he was ready to make a good title, but that it was in his power to have done so. A new trial was granted on the merits, so that the case did not turn on the point whether the judgment ought to be arrested. But in delivering the judgment of the court, Gibbs, C. J., said, "The action cannot be maintained unless the plaintiff did offer, and was able and shewed that he was able, to do that for which he had agreed. Possibly the plaintiff may prove that circumstance on another trial which does not appear in this report, that the plaintiff was in a condition to procure and did procure that which he was bound to procure, the assent of the lessor." Now, it could not be done on a future occasion, if the want of such an averment would have excluded such proof: nor would it, on the same ground, have been proved on the trial had; and yet for want of such proof the new trial was ordered. Without, therefore, being in terms averred, the ability to make, is involved in the averment of being ready and willing to make, an assignment, and of having tendered and offered to assign, and becomes matter of necessary proof on the trial, to enable the plaintiff to recover. The rule being that, whatever is sufficiently alleged to let in proof, and without which proof the plaintiff must have failed, will be intended after verdict to have been proved; such intendment must be made in the present case, and consequently the plaintiffs are entitled to our judgment. *Rule discharged.*

POOLE *v.* HILL.

IN THE EXCHEQUER, TRINITY TERM, 1840.

[*Reported in 6 Meeson & Welsby*, 835.]

COVENANT on articles of agreement, dated Oct. 11, 1839, for the purchase by the defendant of the plaintiff of a certain messuage, lands, and premises, the defendant agreeing to complete the purchase, by paying the purchase-money and accepting a conveyance, on or before the 1st day of January, 1840. The declaration, after setting forth the

[1] 7 Taunt. 9; s. c. 2 Marsh. 332.

articles of agreement in detail, concluded thus: and although the plaintiff hath performed and fulfilled all things in the said articles of agreement contained on her part to be performed and fulfilled, and although she hath always from the time of the making of the said articles of agreement been ready and willing to execute and make the defendant a conveyance of the said purchased premises, so to be executed and made as aforesaid, and although the said 1st day of January, 1840, the time for the payment of the said purchase-money, had elapsed before the commencement of this suit, nevertheless the plaintiff in fact saith, that the defendant hath not yet hitherto paid the said purchase-money so by the defendant agreed to be paid as aforesaid or any part thereof, and the said purchase-money remains wholly due and unpaid.

General demurrer and joinder. The points stated in the margin of the demurrer were as follows: The defendant intends to argue that the declaration is bad in not averring that the plaintiff conveyed or executed any conveyance, or tendered any conveyance to the defendant, such conveyance being a condition precedent, or a concurrent act to be done by the plaintiff.[1]

Whitehurst, in support of the demurrer. First, the declaration is bad for not stating a conveyance, or an offer to execute one. There is nothing in the declaration to shew that the purchaser was bound to prepare the conveyance; but even assuming that the defendant was the party to do so, the plaintiff should have averred that she was ready and willing and offered to execute it. It never could be the intent of the agreement, that the defendant should pay before having a conveyance. Where mutual covenants go to the whole consideration, they are mutual conditions, and the plaintiff cannot recover in respect of any breach, unless he proves performance on his part. Com. Dig. "Covenant," (A. 2), (D. 1): Pordage *v.* Cole.[2] It is clear there is an implied covenant by the vendor to convey. If it be held to be sufficient to state merely that the vendor is ready and willing to convey, the purchaser may be saddled with an action, although he may be ever so desirous to complete the purchase. The declaration must state all that is necessary to the due performance of the covenant; and the plaintiff was bound at least to have shewn that she made an offer or tender of a conveyance. The allegation of readiness and willingness does not imply any step taken on her part. In Com. Dig. "Covenant," (A. 2), it is said, "Where something is covenanted or agreed to be performed by each of two parties at the same time, he who was ready and offered to perform his part, but was discharged by the other, may maintain an

[1] The statement of the case has been abbreviated, and a small portion of the argument and decision omitted as irrelevant to the subject of conditions. — ED.

[2] 1 Saund. 320 *b*.

action against the other for not performing his part." In Peeters v. Opie,[1] which was an action upon a covenant that the plaintiff should do certain work for the defendant, for which the defendant was to pay him £8, the declaration contained an averment, that the plaintiff "always from the time of making the agreement hitherto was ready, and offered to perform the said agreement in all things on his part to be performed." In Goodisson v. Nunn,[2] which was debt on an agreement by the plaintiff to sell the defendant an estate for a certain price before a day named, in consideration whereof the defendant agreed to pay that sum on that day, and in failure thereof to pay £21; it was held that these were dependent covenants, and that the plaintiff could not recover the £21 without proving that he had executed or tendered a conveyance. Glazebrook v. Woodrow[3] and Jones v. Barkley[4] are authorities to the same effect. The court then called on

Crompton to support the declaration. It was not necessary to aver a tender of the conveyance. No doubt where the party suing is by the agreement, to do some concurrent act, the performance of it must be averred in the declaration; but that rule cannot be applicable to a case like the present where the initiative is to be done by the other party. The purchaser is always the party to prepare the conveyance, unless it be otherwise expressed in the contract, Baxter v. Lewis[5]; he, therefore, and not the vendor, is the party who is bound to tender the conveyance for execution. Sugd. Vendors and Purchasers (6th edit.), 222. The averment, therefore, that the plaintiff was ready and willing to execute the conveyance is quite sufficient. In Price v. Williams,[6] where in an agreement for a lease it was stipulated that the lease should be drawn, prepared, and executed by and between the parties, if required by either of them, at the sole expense of the lessor, it was held that it was not necessary for the lessee to tender a lease for execution by the lessor. It is sufficient that the plaintiff is ready and willing to execute the conveyance when the defendant, whose duty it is to prepare it, puts him in a situation to do so.

Whitehurst, in reply. . . . Even if it were the defendant's duty to prepare the conveyance, *non constat* that it was not prepared; the objection is, that the plaintiff should have shewn that she had offered to execute it. Here the concurrent acts are, payment by the purchaser and the execution of a conveyance by the vendor. Whether the defendant could have brought an action for the non-completion of the contract, without averring a tender of the conveyance, is a different question. The cases of Goodisson v. Nunn and Glazebrook v. Woodrow clearly decide, that a conveyance must be either made or tendered

[1] 2 Saund. 346.
[2] 4 T. R. 761.
[3] 8 T. R. 366.
[4] 2 Dougl. 684.
[5] Forrest, 61.
[6] 1 M. & W. 6.

by the vendor before he can sue for the purchase-money. He cited also Phillips *v.* Fielding [1] and Ferry *v.* Williams.[2] . . .

Cur. adv. vult.

A few days afterwards the judgment of the court was delivered by

LORD ABINGER, C. B. [Having stated the declaration, his lordship continued:] We were at first disposed to think that the averment that the plaintiff was ready and willing to convey was insufficient; but after hearing the point discussed by Mr. *Crompton*, we are satisfied that it was not necessary to aver more than this. On a contract for the sale of lands, unless it be expressly stipulated otherwise, the conveyance is to be at the expense of and to be prepared by the purchaser. Here it was for the purchaser to make out the conveyance in the usual course; that being done, his agreement is on a given day to pay the purchase-money, and the plaintiff's to execute the conveyance and complete the title. The defendant could not have maintained an action for the non-completion of the purchase, without averring that he had tendered a conveyance. He was to perform the initiative before the plaintiff could be called upon to offer a conveyance, and the plaintiff was not bound to execute a conveyance until the defendant had prepared and tendered it for execution. The declaration is therefore good, and the judgment will be for the plaintiff.

Judgment for the plaintiff.

BRAUNSTEIN *v.* THE ACCIDENTAL DEATH INSURANCE COMPANY.

IN THE QUEEN'S BENCH, NOVEMBER 26, 1861.

[*Reported in* 1 *Best & Smith,* 782.]

ACTION on a policy of insurance, whereby the defendants agreed to insure the plaintiff against any bodily injury he might receive from any railway accident directly affecting himself, while travelling by a passenger train propelled by steam on any line of railway in Great Britain or Ireland. The amount agreed to be paid by the defendants, in case such accident should cause the death of the plaintiff within three calendar months after the occurrence thereof, was £1000; and in case such accident should not cause the immediate death of the plaintiff, but should cause any bodily injury to the plaintiff of a serious nature, such sum by way of compensation as should appear just and reasonable, and

[1] 2 H. Bl. 123. [2] 8 Taunt. 62.

in proportion to the injury received, such sum to be ascertained, in case of difference or dispute, in manner provided by the stipulations and conditions indorsed on the policy. Among other provisos contained in the policy, was one to the effect that the policy and the insurance thereby made should be subject to the several regulations and conditions printed on the back thereof, so far as they might be respectively applicable, in the same manner as if such regulations and conditions were repeated and incorporated in the policy with reference to the plaintiff. Among the regulations and conditions last referred to was one to the effect that, in case of difference of opinion as to the amount of compensation payable in any case, the question should be referred to the arbitration of a person to be named by the secretary for the time being of the Master of the Rolls, and all expenses and costs should be subject to the decision of such arbitrator, and the award made on such arbitration was to be taken as a final settlement of the question, and might be made a rule of court; and another to the effect that every policy granted by the company was granted upon the terms and conditions in the deed of settlement upon which the company was formed, the provisions of which should have the same force and effect as if inserted in the policy. After setting forth the terms of the contract, the declaration averred that the policy remained and continued in force up to and until, and upon and after the 21st of August, A. D. 1859, and that, whilst the policy was in full force as aforesaid, the plaintiff, to wit, on the day and year last aforesaid, while travelling on a line of railway in Great Britain by a passenger train, propelled by steam power, received and suffered bodily injury of a serious nature from a railway accident, directly affecting himself within the meaning of the policy, which accident greatly injured the plaintiff's health and constitution, and he thereby became sick, sore, lame, and disordered, and so remained and continued for a long space of time, during all which time the plaintiff was hindered and prevented from attending to his affairs and business.

The declaration concluded by averring performance by the plaintiff, and breach by the defendants.[1]

Fourth plea. That by the deed of settlement of the said company, mentioned in the said conditions printed on the back of the said policy, it was declared and provided that, before payment of the sum insured by any policy, proof satisfactory to the directors of the said company should be furnished by the claimant of the death or accident together with such further evidence or information, if any, as the said directors should think necessary to establish the claim. And the defendants say that, after the plaintiff had sustained the said injury by the said accident, and had made his claim in writing under the said policy upon the

[1] The statement of the declaration has been materially abbreviated. — ED.

said company for compensation in respect thereof, the directors of the said company thought it necessary that the plaintiff should furnish to the said company certain evidence or information to establish the said claim, of which the plaintiff, in a reasonable time after making the said claim and before the commencement of this action, had notice, and was then required by the said directors to furnish the said evidence or information to them; which the plaintiff wholly neglected and refused to do, although he could and might have obtained and furnished the same, nor did he furnish any proof satisfactory to the said directors of the said injury sustained by him.

Fifth plea. That after the plaintiff had sustained the said injury, and had made his claim in writing under the said policy upon the said company for compensation in respect thereof, and before this suit, the amount or sum of money to which the plaintiff was entitled, by way of compensation for the said injury, became and was and still is a matter in dispute and difference between the plaintiff and the defendants, and although the defendants then were and ever since have been willing to refer the same to arbitration in manner mentioned in the conditions indorsed on the back of the said policy, yet the amount of the said compensation has never been settled or ascertained by arbitration as in the said conditions mentioned.

To the fourth plea the plaintiff replied that the said evidence or information which the plaintiff was required by the said directors to furnish to them, was not evidence or information which the said directors ought properly or reasonably to have required the plaintiff to furnish. And that the plaintiff did, duly and in accordance with the said policy and conditions, furnish, supply, and provide the defendants, the said directors, and all other persons, with all due, reasonable, proper, and sufficient evidence and information to establish the said claim, and such as ought reasonably to have satisfied the said directors and the defendants. And that the said directors unreasonably and capriciously refused to be satisfied with the said evidence and information so furnished, supplied, and provided by the plaintiff as aforesaid; and in thinking it necessary that the plaintiff should furnish, and in requiring the plaintiff to furnish the said evidence or information in the said fourth plea mentioned, they the said directors acted in an unreasonable and capricious manner.

To the fifth plea the plaintiff demurred, and the defendants demurred to the replication to the fourth plea.

Joinders in demurrer.

Horace Lloyd, for the plaintiff. The fourth plea is bad. The directors are not empowered by the policy to exact from the assured any evidence they please. The clause requiring evidence satisfactory to the directors to be produced, was meant as an instruction to the directors for their guidance between them and their shareholders.

Besides, every clause in a deed should if possible receive a reasonable construction, and such as shall not be inconsistent with the general intention of the parties: *Expressum facit cessare tacitum.* This clause must therefore be understood to mean such evidence as the directors may reasonably require. In Dallman *v.* King,[1] Tindal, C. J., in delivering judgment, says, "admitting this clause of the agreement to constitute a condition precedent, the next question is, whether the condition has been substantially performed. The stipulation consists of two parts: 1st, that the work should be done in a substantial manner; 2d, that it should be done to the satisfaction of the lessor. The gist of the agreement is, that the work should be done in a substantial manner; the approval of the lessor was added, for the purpose of enabling him to ascertain that the work had been done. It never could have been intended that he should be allowed capriciously to withhold his approval; that would have been a condition which would go to the destruction of the thing granted, and if so, according to the well-known rule, the thing granted would pass discharged of the condition." Taking for granted, however, that the plea is good on its face, the replication alleges, which is admitted by the demurrer, that the refusal of the directors to receive the evidence offered them, was unreasonable and capricious.

Then, as to the fifth plea, the words used in this case do not constitute the reference to arbitration a condition precedent to the plaintiff's right to recover. It is true that in Scott *v.* Avery [2] one of the conditions in a policy of insurance on a ship was that the sum to be paid for loss or damage should, in the first instance, be ascertained and settled by the committee of the association; and if a difference should arise between them and any suffering member "relative to the settling any loss or damage, or to a claim for average, or any other matter relating to the insurance," the difference was to be referred to arbitration in a way pointed out; "provided always, that no member who refused to accept the amount of any loss as settled by the committee, &c., should be entitled to maintain any action at law or suit in equity on his policy, until the matters in dispute should have been referred to and decided by arbitrators, &c., and then only for such sum as the said arbitrators should award;" and the obtaining the decision of such arbitrators was declared a condition precedent to the maintaining of an action; it was held that these conditions were lawful, and that (even should the difference relate to other matters than those of mere amount) till an award was made no action was maintainable. But the words here are not so strong. The company undertake, where the accident does not occasion the death of the assured, "to pay such sum by way of compensation as shall appear just and reasonable, and in proportion to the injury

[1] 4 Bing. N. C. 105, 109.

[2] 5 H. L. Ca. 811; on error from the Exchequer Chamber, 8 Exch. 487, 497.

received;" and it then merely provides, "such sum to be ascertained in case of dispute or difference in manner provided by the stipulations and conditions indorsed," *i. e.*, by reference to arbitration.

J. Brown (having been informed by the court that they considered the fifth plea good). In construing this policy, the intention of the parties is the thing to be ascertained. A condition precedent does not require any particular words for its creation; Pordage *v.* Cole,[1] Poole *v.* Hill.[2] In Hotham *v.* The East India Company,[3] Ashhurst, J., in delivering the judgment of the court, says, "There are no precise technical words required in a deed to make a stipulation a condition precedent, or subsequent; neither doth it depend on the circumstance, whether the clause is placed prior or posterior in the deed, so that it operates as a proviso or covenant. For the same words have been construed to operate as either the one or the other, according to the nature of the transaction." The design of the clause on which the fourth plea is founded was to protect the company from being imposed upon by false representations as to the existence or extent of accidents. In Worsley *v.* Wood, in error,[4] which was an action on a policy of insurance against fire, in the proposals of an insurance company which were to be considered part of the policy, it was stipulated that persons insured should forthwith give notice of the loss, deliver in an account, &c., and procure a certificate of the minister, churchwardens and some reputable householders of the parish, importing that they knew the character and circumstances of the assured, and knew or believed that he had sustained the loss through misfortune and without fraud; and it was held that the procuring such a certificate was a condition precedent to the right of the assured to recover. [WIGHTMAN, J. That case is different. There the reference was to a third party.] Brown *v.* Overbury[5] was an action against the treasurer of a steeple-chase to recover the amount of the stakes, which the plaintiff alleged were won by his horse; according to the articles, any dispute as to the race was to be decided by the stewards: a dispute having arisen, it was held that the plaintiff could not recover unless he shewed that he either had obtained or was unable to obtain a decision from the stewards. In arrangements with railway companies, it is common to agree that all matters in dispute shall be determined by the certificate of an engineer. [CROMPTON, J. There the engineer is in effect the servant of both parties.] The object of the replication is to take from the directors the right given them by the policy of determining the existence and nature of a supposed accident, and transfer it to a jury. [WIGHTMAN, J. Suppose the directors were to require the claimant to furnish evidence as to the state of the weather, or something similar.] That would not be

[1] 1 Wms. Saund. 319 *l*, 6th ed. [2] 6 M. & W. 835. [3] 1 T. R. 638, 645.
[4] 6 T. R. 710. [5] 11 Exch. 715.

germane to the subject-matter. [CROMPTON, J. It never could have been intended to give the directors the right to act capriciously.] The directors act under the control of public opinion, for it is most injurious to companies of this kind to bring disputed cases before the world. Besides, juries may be capricious as well as directors. [WIGHTMAN, J. Perhaps so. But we cannot assume that they will be. BLACKBURN, J. If the directors are to settle all questions between the company and parties claiming compensation, what is the use of the clause providing for arbitration?] That clause is only applicable when the question is one of disputed amount.

WIGHTMAN, J. The question in this case is, what effect is to be given to a clause in a deed of settlement, which is incorporated by one of the terms of the policy in the policy itself, "that before payment of the sum insured by any policy, proof satisfactory to the directors of the company should be furnished by the claimant of the death or accident." And then there is this addition, "together with such further evidence or information, if any, as the said directors shall think necessary to establish that claim."

Now it is said that, by virtue of this clause, the directors have the power, if they please, wholly to withhold payment by capriciously, as asserted in the replication, and without any reasonable ground whatsoever, requiring further evidence perfectly immaterial to the matter in dispute. The question is, whether, giving a reasonable construction to the intention of the parties when the clause was introduced by reference into the policy, it can be understood that the assured did agree that, upon any ground whatsoever, capriciously or otherwise, which the directors, who are the parties to the suit, might think fit to urge, their decision should be binding? The clause must receive a reasonable construction, and the parties must be taken to have had in view any further evidence which the directors might reasonably require; such a construction would fulfil all the terms of that clause.

We have been referred to cases in which parties have agreed to refer the matter in dispute to the certificate of an arbitrator, that is to say, that no payment should be enforced by one against the other until a certificate was given that the work which was the subject-matter of the proceeding, had been completed; but in such a case the reference is to a third person, and not as here to one of the parties; and the effect of the clause, if it had the extensive construction contended for by Mr. Brown, would be that the directors might always refuse to pay, however improper or unreasonable such refusal might be, if they thought it inconvenient for the society to do so. It seems to me that a reasonable construction must be given to this clause; and I cannot but think that there is a good deal of weight in the observation that it is rather a clause directory as between the shareholders and directors of the company, that the latter shall take care that sufficient evidence be brought before them, than a clause amounting to a condition precedent to the right of the assured to recover that the assured must adduce such evidence as the directors might require, though without any reasonable ground, and which the assured might be wholly unable to produce. I cannot put such a construction upon the deed as that. It only requires the introduction of the word "reasonable," and that I say must be implied, to remove the difficulty. The replication raises the point that the directors have required something which is unreasonable, and that they have acted capriciously, and have acted therefore in a manner which disentitles them to set up such an answer as that which they have done. It is admitted that the assured might be required to produce a reasonable amount of evidence; but it is contended that the directors have no right to refuse, as the defendants admit by their demurrer that they have done, from capricious or unreasonable motives, to be satisfied with such evidence. It seems to me that that is an answer; that, by pointing out that they unreasonably and capriciously required evidence which was not necessary to satisfy them on any reasonable view of the case, it is shewn that they acted in contravention of what appears to me the proper and reasonable construction to be given to this clause. I therefore think that the fourth plea is bad, and the replication good. If it be necessary to give an answer to the plea, it is answered by the replication.

With respect to the fifth plea, it seems to me that the reference clause, as to the amount if disputed, is made a condition precedent to bringing an action, and I cannot read it otherwise. The clause in the policy is that they "should pay such sum by way of compensation as should appear just and reasonable." If the clause had stopped there, no doubt there would have been no difficulty; but it goes on to say "and in proportion to the injury received, such sum to be ascertained in case of difference or dispute in manner provided by the stipulations and conditions indorsed thereon," which is by reference to a gentleman who is to be named in a specified manner. Now there is clearly a difference and a dispute in the present case, to which, as it seems to me, the reference clause applies, and makes it a condition precedent to the right to bring an action that the sum shall first be ascertained in the manner pointed out.

On these grounds the judgment should be for the plaintiff in respect to the fourth plea, and for the defendants in respect to the fifth plea.

CROMPTON, J. The real question in all cases of this nature is that stated by Ashhurst, J., in Hotham v. The East India Company,[1] what was the intention of the parties? Now I cannot conceive that any company would put before a person desirous of effecting an insurance with them a stipulation that, in order to establish the occurrence of an

[1] 1 T. R. 638, 645.

accident insured against, their own directors might require any evidence, however chimerical, capricious, and unjust, the asking for it might be. The putting such a construction on a stipulation like this is opposed to the general rule, that when it is agreed that an act is to be done to the satisfaction of a party it must be understood to mean reasonably to his satisfaction. The cases where it is agreed between two parties that a disputed matter shall be determined by the certificate of a third person differ from the present, for there the act is to be done by a third person, whereas here it is to be done by one of the parties. The language of Tindal, C. J., in Dallman *v.* King,[1] is very important, where he says that stipulations in a contract going to the destruction of the contract are inoperative.

I do not however say that this fourth plea may not be good, but then comes the replication, that, in the exercise of the power conferred on them, the directors acted in an unreasonable and capricious manner. Perhaps the question could have been raised under a general traverse of the plea, and the jury might say that this stipulation, understood in the above sense, is so unreasonable that no one could suppose it was ever intended to be so understood. I think, however, that the sounder construction of the document is to hold that what is stated in the replication to have been done by the defendants, never could have been intended; and, consequently, the plaintiff is entitled to judgment on the demurrer to the replication.

Then as to the fifth plea. I think this case comes within the principle of Scott *v.* Avery.[2] In that case some of the judges thought, and the Court of Exchequer held, that parties must not be permitted by their agreement to withdraw cases from the jurisdiction of the courts of justice. But I think we may construe the having the amount determined by a third party as part of the cause of action; and a great judge, Mr. Justice Maule, was of this opinion.[3] It is said that the words of the contract in Scott *v.* Avery [2] are stronger than those before us; and they are so in some respects. Here is a contract that in an event specified the company will "pay such sum by way of compensation as should appear just and reasonable, and in proportion to the injury received, such sum to be ascertained, in case of difference or dispute, in manner provided by the stipulations and conditions indorsed thereon." It is said we must construe this as two sentences, and stop at the words "injury received." But "such sum" must have a word to govern it, and it evidently means such sum as shall be ascertained.

BLACKBURN, J. I agree with the rest of the court. I think the fourth plea is bad; and if it even were good, it is answered by the rep-

1 4 Bing. N. C. 105.

2 5 H. L. Ca. 811; on error from the Exchequer Chamber, 8 Exch. 487, 497.

3 See 8 Exch. 497, 498, 499.

lication. I quite admit that parties may make what they please a condition precedent, but it must be shewn that they so intended. Here the stipulation is the language of one party, the company, and *verba fortius accipiuntur contra proferentem.* No doubt they might have stipulated that no money should be payable under a policy unless the directors obtained any evidence they chose to ask for, but it would require very distinct language, and much stronger than any used here, to shew that the parties so intended. Here also is an express provision for reference to arbitration, which would be quite idle if there were a general clause compelling the party injured to furnish any evidence the directors should require. But I think the plaintiff's counsel right in saying that that stipulation was only introduced with reference to the duty of the directors towards the company, *i. e.*, that the directors were not to settle a claim against the company until they had got proper evidence. That is right in itself, but I do not understand the sixth condition indorsed on the policy to incorporate as part of the bargain such clauses in the deed as refer to the duties of the directors and shareholders towards each other.

As to the fifth plea, I quite agree that the parties have used sufficient words to make the reference to arbitration a condition precedent.

Judgment for the plaintiff on the fourth plea, and for the defendants on the fifth.

BATTERBURY *v.* VYSE.

IN THE EXCHEQUER, APRIL 22, 1863.

[*Reported in 2 Hurlstone & Coltman*, 42.]

DECLARATION. For that heretofore, to wit, on, &c., the plaintiff and the defendant agreed that the defendant should employ the plaintiff to do and provide for him, and that the plaintiff should do for the defendant certain specified works, and provide for the defendant certain specified materials, at No. 125 Oxford Street, upon the following terms and conditions, that is to say: "All the works hereinbefore described (meaning the description contained in a certain specification of the said works) are to be executed in the very best and most workmanlike manner, with the very best quality of materials of every description, under the superintendence and to the satisfaction of Mr. Vyse and his architect. The works described are intended to embrace every thing that may be necessary for the perfect completion of the several alterations. If, therefore, through any error or inadvertence, any matter or thing which may be deemed by the architect as essential to this end, be omitted, it is to be supplied and performed by the contractor in like manner as if it had been particularly specified; and if in the course of the work it should be found necessary to make any addition to or omission from the said works, such deviation is not in any way to vitiate the contract, but the value of such works shall be estimated by the architect, and the value thereof added to or deducted from the contract sum as the case may be, the decision of the architect being final and conclusive in all matters affecting the proposed works. The amount of the contract will be paid by instalments equal to the value of £80 per cent. of the value of the works executed, the balance within one month after final completion to the architect's satisfaction, but no payment will be considered due unless upon production of the architect's certificate." Then followed an agreement by the defendant to execute the works for £610. Averments: That pursuant to the contract the plaintiff did the specified works and provided the materials, with the exception of certain omissions which were duly required by the defendant and his architect; and that he also did divers and very many additional works which were duly required to be done by the defendant and his architect; and that the value of the said works and materials amounted to a large sum, to wit, £1000, whereof the defendant had due notice; and although the defendant paid to the plaintiff £600, on account of the said works, leaving a large balance, to wit, £400, of the fair and reasonable value of the said works, estimated according to the said contract, unpaid; and although the plaintiff had done all things necessary on his part to entitle him to have the value of the said extras and omissions estimated by the said architect, and to entitle him to the said architect's certificate for payment; and although he had completed the said works to the satisfaction of the defendant's architect; and although more than a month from such time had elapsed; and although the defendant and his architect had, at all times since the doing of the said works and the providing of the said materials, full knowledge that the plaintiff was entitled to be paid by the defendant a large sum of money over and above the money so paid; and although a reasonable time for the said architect to estimate the value of the said additions and omissions, and to certify as aforesaid, and for the defendant to pay for the said works, had long since elapsed; yet the architect had not estimated the value of the said additions and omissions, nor had he certified as aforesaid, but wholly neglected so to do, and had unfairly, improperly, and contrary to the true intent and meaning of the said contract, neglected to estimate the value of the said additions and omissions, and neglected to certify as aforesaid, and had so neglected in collusion with the defendant and by his procurement. By means of which premises the plaintiff has been unable to obtain payment of the balance justly due to him for the said works, and the said balance still remains wholly due and unpaid to the plaintiff.

Demurrer, and joinder therein.

Gates, in support of the demurrer. The declaration is bad. The production of the architect's certificate is a condition precedent to the plaintiff's right to claim any payment. [MARTIN, B. This is, in substance, a declaration in case, alleging that the defendant, acting in collusion with the architect, procured him unfairly and improperly to withhold his certificate.] Treated as an action of contract, the plaintiff cannot recover, because he has not complied with the condition which entitled him to payment; and it is not an action on the case, because it does not charge fraud, or allege any duty on the part of the defendant which he has neglected to perform. However unreasonable and oppressive a stipulation or condition may be, a court of law is bound to give effect to the terms agreed upon between the parties. Stadhard v. Lee.[1] [BRAMWELL, B. That case does not touch this. Here the complaint is not that something has been done, and done wrongly, but that there has been an improper refusal to do that which ought to have been done.] The opinion of Erle, J., in Scott v. The Corporation of Liverpool,[2] is an express authority that, in the absence of fraud, the withholding the certificate by the architect affords no right of action against the defendant, either on the ground of a waiver of the condition, or the substitution of a new contract, or on the ground of a wrong. This is an attempt to obtain indirectly that which the plaintiff is not entitled to by the terms of his contract. If, indeed, the certificate was withheld by fraud, the plaintiff might have a remedy by action. Milner v. Field.[3] But it is consistent with every allegation in this declaration that the architect was requested by the defendant not to certify because he was dissatisfied with the work. [WILDE, B. The declaration contains an averment that the plaintiff had done all things necessary to entitle him to the certificate, and that he had completed the works to the satisfaction of the defendant's architect; and that, although the defendant and his architect had knowledge that the plaintiff was entitled to be paid, the architect neglected to certify, "in collusion with the defendant and by his procurement."] There is no allegation that the works were done to the satisfaction of the defendant. [WILDE, B. There is an averment that the plaintiff had done all things necessary to entitle him to the certificate.] The word "collusion" does not necessarily imply fraud. [POLLOCK, C. B. In Webster's Dictionary one definition of "collusion" is "a secret agreement for a fraudulent purpose."]

J. Brown appeared in support of the declaration, but was not called upon to argue.[4]

[1] 3 B. & S. 364, 372. [2] 1 Giff. 216, 223. [3] 5 Exch. 829.

[4] The point for argument was: "That the defendant who employs the architect does contract with the plaintiff that he will do his duty and act fairly.

POLLOCK, C. B. We are all of opinion that the declaration is good, and that the plaintiff is entitled to judgment.

MARTIN, B., and BRAMWELL, B., concurred.

Judgment for the plaintiff.

SECTION VI.

Part Performance of Conditions, and Effect thereof.

CONSTABLE *v.* CLOBERIE.

IN THE KING'S BENCH, HILARY TERM, 1626.

[*Reported in Palmer,* 397.]

COVENANT upon a charter-party. The plaintiff covenanted that his ship should go a voyage to Cadiz with the next wind; and the defendant covenanted that if the ship went the intended voyage, and returned to the Downs, the plaintiff should have so much for the voyage. The defendant traversed that the ship went with the next wind, and upon demurrer the traverse was overruled; for the substance of the covenant was that the ship should go, and not that she should go with the next wind, for that may change every hour; and this is proved by the covenant of the defendant, viz., "if the ship went the intended voyage;" and this was the primary intention of the parties, and not that she should go with the next wind. But, per Justice JONES, if the defendant had covenanted that if the plaintiff went to Cadiz with the next wind, he would pay, &c., there the plaintiff ought to aver that he went with the next wind.

THOMPSON *v.* NOEL.

IN THE KING'S BENCH, HILARY TERM, 1661.

[*Reported in* 1 *Levinz,* 16.]

COVENANT brought, and declares that the plaintiff covenanted to go with a ship to D. in Ireland, and there to take in two hundred and eighty men from the defendant, and to carry them to Jamaica; and the defendant covenanted to have the two hundred and eighty men there ready, and to pay for the carriage of them £5 per man; and says that the defendant had not the two hundred and eighty men ready, but that he had one hundred and eighty, and those he took and carried, and the defendant had not payed for them. The defendant pleads that he had the two hundred and eighty men ready, and tendered them to the plaintiff, and that he would not receive them, but says nothing to the carrying of a hundred and eighty men, nor to the non-payment for them; and for that it was not a plea to the whole, but to the carrying only [*sic*], judgment was given for the plaintiff upon a demurrer.

BOONE *v.* EYRE.

IN THE KING'S BENCH, EASTER TERM, 1777.

[*Reported in* 1 *Henry Blackstone,* 273, *note.*]

COVENANT on a deed, whereby the plaintiff conveyed to the defendant the equity of redemption of a plantation in the West Indies, together with the stock of negroes upon it, in consideration of £500 and an annuity of £160 per annum for his life; and covenanted that he had a good title to the plantation, and was lawfully possessed of the negroes, and that the defendant should quietly enjoy. The defendant covenanted that the plaintiff well and truly performing all and every thing therein contained on his part to be performed, he the defendant would pay the annuity. The breach assigned was the non-payment of the annuity. Plea, that the plaintiff was not at the time of making the deed legally possessed of the negroes on the plantation, and so had not a good title to convey.

To which there was a general demurrer.

LORD MANSFIELD. The distinction is very clear, where mutual covenants go to the whole of the consideration on both sides, they are mutual conditions, the one precedent to the other. But where they go only to a part, where a breach may be paid for in damages, there the defendant has a remedy on his covenant, and shall not plead it as a condition precedent. If this plea were to be allowed, any one negro not being the property of the plaintiff would bar the action.

Judgment for the plaintiff.[1]

[1] Compare Boone *v.* Eyre, 2 Wm. Bl. 1312; and see Dakin *v.* Williams, 11 Wend. 67. — ED.

CAMPBELL *v.* JONES.

IN THE KING'S BENCH, FEBRUARY 9, 1796.

[*Reported in* 6 *Term Reports*, 570.]

THIS was an action of covenant, contained in an indenture dated 25th February, 1793, made between the plaintiff and the defendant. It recited that the plaintiff had obtained a patent for fourteen years from the 28th of November, 1792, for his invention of an improved method of destroying and taking away all the carbonic oleaginous and coloring elements and particles in linen, cotton, hemp, and in all colored rags and other materials used in making paper; and that the defendant, who then carried on the trade or business of a paper manufacturer, was desirous of bleaching and preparing the materials for making paper according to the improved method used by the plaintiff and as set forth in the specification, &c.; that it had been agreed between the plaintiff and the defendant that, in consideration of the sum of £500 to be paid by the defendant to the plaintiff in manner thereinafter mentioned, he the plaintiff should teach and instruct the defendant in the bleaching and preparing of all materials for making paper according to the said specification and improved method of the plaintiff, and should also permit and suffer the defendant during the continuance of the patent to bleach, &c., the materials for making paper according to the specification, &c., to the extent only and subject to such restrictions, provisos, and agreements as were and are thereinbefore mentioned, expressed, declared, and contained. That in pursuance of the agreement and for and in consideration of the sum of £250 to the plaintiff paid by the said defendant and of the further sum of £250 covenanted to be paid by the defendant to the plaintiff in manner thereinafter mentioned, and in consideration of the covenants and agreements of the defendant thereinafter contained, the plaintiff covenanted that he would to the best of his skill and with all possible expedition teach and instruct the defendant in the manner and method of bleaching, &c., linen and other materials used in making paper according to the direction of the specification, &c., and according to the method which he then used, or any improved method which he should or might thereafter use in bleaching, &c. That the defendant, in consideration of the plaintiff's covenants, covenanted that he would on or before the 25th of February, 1794, or sooner in case the plaintiff should before that time have sufficiently taught and instructed him in bleaching and preparing the materials for making paper, &c., pay to the plaintiff the further sum of £250. It then set forth a breach of covenant by the defendant in not paying the said further sum of £250 on or before the 25th of February, 1794, or at any time afterwards.

To this declaration there was a special demurrer, and these causes were assigned: that it appears by the declaration that the plaintiff had covenanted to teach and instruct the defendant in the manner and method of bleaching, &c., used in making paper in the manner set forth in and by the covenant stated in the declaration, and that the defendant in consideration thereof covenanted to pay to the plaintiff the said sum of £250, the breach of which covenant is alleged as the cause of action in the declaration, and yet it is not averred in the declaration that the plaintiff had taught and instructed the defendant in the manner and method of bleaching, &c., used in making paper, according to the specification or in any other manner, &c.

This case was argued in last Michaelmas Term by *Shepherd*, in support of the demurrer, and by *Lawes* against it. The former referred to these cases: Kingston v. Preston, cited in Dougl. 688; Duke of St. Albans v. Shore, 1 H. Bl. Rep. C. B. 270; Hotham v. The East India Company, 1 T. R. 638; and Goodisson v. Nunn, 4 T. R. 761. The latter cited these authorities: Martindale v. Fisher, 1 Wils. 88; Boone v. Eyre, 2 Bl. Rep. 1312, and 1 H. Bl. Rep. C. B. 273, n. a.; Callonel v. Briggs, Salk. 112; Thorpe v. Thorpe, Salk. 171, 1st point; Jones v. Barclay, Dougl. 684; Bach v. Owen, 5 T. R. 409; and 2 Saund. 156.

The court took time to consider of this case, and now their opinion was delivered as follows by

LORD KENYON, C. J., (after stating the case). In support of this demurrer it was said that the plaintiff's teaching the defendant his method of bleaching the materials used in making paper was a condition precedent to the plaintiff's right to demand payment of the last sum of £250; on the other hand it was insisted that they were mutual and independent covenants. Whether these kinds of covenants be or be not independent of each other must certainly depend on the good sense of the case. If one thing is to be done by a plaintiff before his right of action accrues on the defendant's covenant, it should be averred in the declaration that that thing was done. "Where there are mutual promises, yet if one thing be the consideration of the other, there a performance is necessary to be averred unless a day is appointed for performance." Per Holt, C. J., Salk. 113. "If a day be appointed for the payment of the money, and the day is to happen before the thing can be performed, an action may be brought for the payment of the money before the thing be done." Ib. 171. Upon the authority of these cases the judgment of the court must be in favor of the plaintiff, if upon the true construction of the deed a certain day be fixed for the payment of the money, and the thing to be done may not happen until after. The plaintiff in this case covenants with all possible expedition, not by any fixed time, to instruct the defendant in bleaching linen, &c., and in consideration of the plaintiff's covenants, "the defendant covenants that he will, on or before the 25th February, or sooner, in case the plaintiff should before that time have instructed the defendant, pay him the further sum of £250." To support the construction contended for by the defendant this covenant must be understood as if it had been written thus: "And the said Griffiths, the defendant, doth hereby covenant that he will, on or before the 25th of February, in case the plaintiff shall before that time have instructed him, and sooner in case the plaintiff shall before that time have instructed him, pay the further sum of £250," which is in effect covenanting to pay the money as soon as the plaintiff should have instructed him. Now had this been the intention of the parties, the natural and obvious way of expressing such intent would have been for the defendant to covenant to pay as soon as he should be taught; but if the design of the parties were that the plaintiff at all events should be paid on the 25th of February, and sooner in case the defendant should be sooner instructed, the expression here used is a natural expression, and the words "in case the said Hector, the plaintiff, should before that time have instructed the said Griffiths," the defendant, will be confined to the word "sooner." The intent of the parties appears to be that the payment might be accelerated, but should not, in any event, be delayed.

But another ground on which the plaintiff is entitled to judgment is this, that the teaching of the defendant is not the whole consideration of the covenant to pay. The agreement of the parties is, that in consideration of one entire sum of £500 the plaintiff should teach and instruct the defendant in the art of bleaching materials for making paper, and permit him, during the period of his patent, to bleach such materials according to his specification; and though this sum is divided into two sums of £250 each, and is to be paid at different times, no part is denominated to be the consideration of using the patent, nor any part as the consideration of teaching, but one integral sum is adapted to the whole. Under this agreement the defendant has a perfect title to use the patent, and the instruction of the defendant cannot be taken to be the most material part of the consideration, as the specification must be supposed to contain full instruction for that purpose though some advantage might arise from the assistance of the inventor. In the case of Boone v. Eyre, E. 17 Geo. 3, Lord Mansfield said, "The distinction is clear, where mutual covenants go to the whole of the consideration on both sides, they are mutual conditions; but where the covenants go only to a part, and where a recompense may be had in damages, it is a different thing." And Mr. J. Ashhurst added, "there is a difference between executed and executory covenants; here the covenants are executed in part, and the defendant ought not to keep the estate because the plaintiff has not a title to a few negroes." So here the covenant to teach is but part of the consideration of the £500; for not doing which the defendant may recover a recompense in damages. And the agreement of the plaintiff having been executed in part by transferring to the defendant a right to exercise his patent, he ought not to keep that right without paying the remainder of the consideration, because he may have sustained some damage by the plaintiff's not having instructed him.

For these reasons we are all of opinion that judgment must be for the plaintiff.

HALL v. CAZENOVE.

IN THE KING'S BENCH, FEBRUARY 3, 1804.

[*Reported in* 4 *East*, 477.]

THE plaintiff declared that whereas by a charter-party of affreightment, purporting to be indented, made, and concluded in London, on the 6th of February, 1801, between the plaintiff as owner of the ship Argo, then lying in the river Thames and bound on a voyage to Demerara, on the one part, and the defendant and one J. B. of London, merchants, on the other part; but which charter-party was in fact first indented, made, and concluded after the said 6th of February, &c., and also after the 12th of the same February, to wit, on the 15th of March, 1801; and not on the said 6th of February, or at any time before or on the said 12th of February in that year; and was also in fact sealed and delivered by the plaintiff and defendant only, and not by the said J. B. one part of which said charter-party sealed, &c., the plaintiff now brings here into court, the date whereof is the said 6th of February, 1801; it was witnessed that the said owner, for the considerations after mentioned, covenanted and agreed with the said freighters that the said ship should and would proceed from Deptford, where she then lay, on or before the 12th day of the said February to the port of rendezvous for the ships that were to join convoy for the West Indies, and proceed under convoy to Demerara; and on delivery of the cargo outwards, which was to be within ten days after arrival, she should and would receive on board from the agents of the freighters a full cargo, &c., and having received the same on board, should therewith proceed from thence, after the expiration of the lay days thereinafter mentioned, to the place of rendezvous for the convoy for England, and having joined the fleet should sail therewith for London, and there make true delivery of the cargo to the freighters, &c. And it was also in the said charter-party alleged that the said owner did thereby covenant and agree with the said freighters that the said ship should and would proceed on her intended voyage on or before the day before mentioned. And the plaintiff, as such owner of the ship, covenanted with the freighters that the ship should lay at Demerara, for unloading the outward and loading the homeward cargo, sixty running days (ten for unloading, and the remaining fifty only to be reckoned from unloading), and the usual time for unloading on her return to London, &c., in consideration whereof and of every thing therein above mentioned, the defendant covenanted and agreed that the said freighters should load, &c., in the port of Demerara within the time limited, and should pay the freight, &c., in two months after reporting at the custom-house at London. And the plaintiff thereby covenanted with the freighters that they might keep the ship on demurrage at Demerara twenty running days in the whole, on payment to the plaintiff of £10 a day for every day beyond the lay-days before mentioned. The plaintiff then averred that the ship did, after the making of the said charter-party, viz., on the 15th of March in the year aforesaid, proceed from Deptford upon the said voyage, under and upon the terms as by the charter-party, &c., to the port of rendezvous for the ships that were to join convoy in the West Indies with her outward-bound cargo, which had been shipped by the freighters, and afterwards proceeded under convoy to Demerara, where she arrived on the 29th of May following. That she delivered her outward-bound cargo within 10 days after, and received a full homeward cargo from the agents of the freighters, and lay at D. sixty running days for the purpose of unloading and reloading, and that the freighters kept the ship on demurrage at Demerara above the lay-days in the charter-party mentioned, which demurrage amounted to £200. That the ship afterwards joined convoy, &c.; and on the 27th of January, 1802, arrived at London with her homeward cargo, &c., and there ended the said voyage, and the freight, &c., amounted to £1888 6*s.*; and then the plaintiff averred that two months and upwards had elapsed from the time of reporting the ship at the custom-house, and that though he had performed and been ready and willing to perform every thing in the charter-party contained on his part to be performed, and which on his part and behalf could possibly be performed, according to the tenor and effect, true intent and meaning, of the charter-party, yet the defendant did not, at the expiration of two months from such report as aforesaid of the ship's arrival, &c., or at any other time, pay to the plaintiff the said sums for freight, &c., and demurrage, but made default, &c.

The defendant by his plea craved oyer of the charter-party, which was in these words: This charter-party of affreightment, indented, made, and concluded in London, this 6th day of February, 1801, between J. H. (the plaintiff), owner of the ship Argo, now lying in the river

Thames, and bound on a voyage to Demerara, of the one part, and C. T. C. (the defendant) and J. B., &c., of the other part, witnesseth that the said owner, for the considerations hereinafter mentioned, doth covenant, &c., with the said freighters, &c., that the said ship shall and will proceed from Deptford, where she now lies, on or before the 12th of this present February, to the port of rendezvous, &c., and proceed under convoy, &c., to Demerara, &c., and proceed from thence, &c., for London (as before set forth in the declaration), in witness whereof the parties have hereunto set their hands and seals the day and year first above written; and then the defendant demurred, and shewed for causes that it is not alleged, nor does it appear by the declaration that the said ship did proceed from Deptford on or before the 12th of the said February in the charter-party mentioned to the place of rendezvous, &c.; nor that the charter-party was first indented, made, and concluded after the 6th of February, 1801. But that it appears by the charter-party that the same was indented, made, and concluded on the said 6th of February in the year aforesaid; and that the plaintiff is by law estopped from making the said allegation, &c. Joinder in demurrer.

Giles, in support of the demurrer, after observing that the allegation in the declaration was not that the charter-party was sealed and delivered after the date of it, which is the 6th of February, but the allegation was of the time when it was indented, made, and concluded, argued that the plaintiff was estopped from alleging that the charter-party was indented, made, and concluded after the 6th of February, when it appears upon the face of it as stated to have been indented, made, and concluded on the 6th of February. And though it be competent to a party to aver that a deed was delivered after the date, yet he cannot make any allegation inconsistent with the deed. Goddard's case,[1] Bro. Abr. Obligation, pl. 40, Departure, pl. 14. [LORD ELLENBOROUGH, C. J. Stone *v.* Bale[2] is decisive to shew that a party may aver a delivery of a deed on another day than that on which it bears date.] The distinction taken is that a party cannot aver a delivery on a day prior to the date. But if the plaintiff be not estopped from making the particular allegation in the declaration, as being equivalent to an averment of the day of delivery of the deed; then, 2dly, the deed must be considered as delivered on the 15th of March, in which case it is void upon the face of it; because it appears from the whole scope of it, that it was a condition precedent to the payment of freight, &c., that the ship should proceed from Deptford, where it is stated that she then (*i. e.* on the 6th of February) lay, on or before the 12th of February, to the port of rendezvous, &c., and proceed under convoy to Demerara. And the allegation that the deed was executed

[1] 2 Rep. 4 *b*.

[2] 3 Lev. 348.

after the 12th will not supersede the necessity of alleging that a thing was done on the 12th, which by the terms of the deed is made a condition precedent. Co. Lit. 206.

Lawes, contra, was stopped by the court.

LORD ELLENBOROUGH, C. J. First, as to the objection that the party is estopped from saying that the deed was indented, made, and concluded on a different day from that on which it bears date, I see nothing inconsistent with the deed in such an allegation, any more than if he had alleged that it was sealed and delivered on a day subsequent. It is quite unimportant when it was indented, and equally so when it was made, by which may be understood when it was written. Then the only material word is concluded, and a deed can only be said to be concluded when it is delivered. The time of delivery is the important time when it takes its effect as a deed; and the case of Stone *v.* Bale[1] is in point to shew that the delivery may be averred to be after the date. There is therefore no repugnancy in the allegation. Then, 2dly, it is objected that the sailing on the 12th of February was a condition precedent, the performance of which was necessary to be alleged to entitle the plaintiff to recover. If it had been possible to have been performed at the time of the delivery, if the time itself had not then gone by, the inclination of my opinion at present is that it would have been a condition precedent. I do not, however, mean to give any opinion on that point. But here, when the deed was executed or concluded by the delivery, the stipulation, which was not impossible in its nature when the deed was first framed, had become impossible as between these parties from the time having passed. The stipulation therefore had then become wholly nugatory, and cannot be understood as having formed any part of the contract between the parties, without imputing to them the most manifest absurdity. Then the rest of the contract may take effect, which was prospective at the time when the deed was concluded.

GROSE, J., declared himself of the same opinion.

LAWRENCE, J. Though the allegation here be not in exactly the same words as in Goddard's case, yet it is the same in substance; and according to that case, though the deed appear on the face of it to have been made on one day, yet if in truth it were delivered on a subsequent day, that may be shewn by averment; and there is no more inconsistency in the one case than in the other. Then as to the second objection; I doubt whether the sailing on or before the 12th of February be a condition precedent on the part of the plaintiff to his recovery: it is a covenant that the ship should or would, &c., prospectively. But taking it, as my lord has said, to be a condition precedent in the terms of it, yet having become by the lapse of time altogether impossible when

[1] 3 Lev. 348.

the deed was executed, it could form no part of the agreement between the parties. But in construing instruments we must look to the substance of them in order to discover the meaning of the parties; and looking at the substance of this charter-party it is not unlike the case of Constable *v.* Cloberie,[1] where the plaintiff covenanted in a charter-party that his ship should sail with the next wind upon a voyage to Cadiz; and the defendant covenanted that if the ship went the intended voyage and returned to the Downs that the plaintiff should have so much for the voyage. The defendant traversed that the ship sailed with the next wind, and upon demurrer the traverse was overruled: for the substance of the covenant was considered to be that the ship should perform the intended voyage, that being the primary intention of the parties, and not merely that she should sail with the next wind, which might change every hour. And that this was shewn by the covenant of the defendant, who was to pay so much for the freight; that is, for performing the voyage, and not merely for sailing with the next wind. So here the substance of the covenant is that the ship shall go to Demerara on freight and return again. I take this to be rather a case of mutual covenants than a condition precedent, and in that view the case of Boone *v.* Eyre[2] is material to be attended to. That was where the plaintiff had conveyed a plantation in the West Indies, with the negroes upon it, to the defendant, in consideration of an annuity to be paid him for his life; and covenanted that he had a good title to the land, and was lawfully possessed of the negroes, and that the defendant should quietly enjoy. And the defendant covenanted that, the plaintiff well and truly performing all and every thing therein contained on his part to be performed, he (the defendant) would pay the annuity. The breach assigned was the non-payment of the annuity. The defendant pleaded that the plaintiff was not at the time of making the deed legally possessed of the negroes on the plantation, and so had not a good title to convey. But it was holden that these were mutual covenants, and that where mutual covenants go only to a part of the consideration on both sides, where a breach may be paid for in damages, there the defendant has a remedy on his covenant, and shall not plead it as a condition precedent. According to this case, therefore, it would not have been a condition precedent to the plaintiff's recovering on the covenant for freight, even if it had been possible for the ship to have sailed on or before the 12th of February, and she had not done so. And if the voyage has been performed, and the profit of it gained by the defendant, there can be no foundation for saying that the defendant shall not pay the freight for it; and he may recover damages for the not sailing in time, if any have been occasioned by it.

Le Blanc, J. The substance of the pleadings shews that the char-

[1] Palm. 397.

[2] 1 H. Blac. 273, *n.*, and in Campbell *v.* Jones, 6 Term Rep. 573.

ter-party was executed after the day on which it bears date, which, by all the authorities, the defendant is not estopped from doing. Then as to the other objection; if the defendant sustained any damage by reason of the ship's not having sailed on the particular day, he may recover it by bringing his action on the covenant; but, at any rate, the objection does not go to the plaintiff's right of action as on the ground of a condition precedent. *Judgment for the plaintiff.*

BORNMANN *v.* TOOKE.

AT NISI PRIUS, CORAM LORD ELLENBOROUGH, JUNE 15, 1808.

[*Reported in* 1 *Campbell,* 377.]

ASSUMPSIT to recover the sum of £2136 for freight upon a cargo of timber carried from Riga to Portsmouth for the defendant, by the ship Les Bons Enfants, whereof the plaintiff was master. Plea, the general issue.

The ship in question had been freighted by a charter-party, between the plaintiff and an agent of the defendant, dated 10th of April, 1807, and containing the following clause: "The freighter binds himself to load this ship with the greatest expedition with a full and fit cargo of masts, spars, and timber; with which cargo the captain must sail with the first favorable wind direct to the port of Portsmouth." The freight agreed upon was £3 5*s.* for each load of masts and spars, and £2 15*s.* for each load of timber.

It was allowed that the ship had arrived at Portsmouth, and that the cargo had been there delivered to and accepted by the defendant. His case was, that the ship had not sailed direct from Riga to Portsmouth, but had unnecessarily put into Copenhagen on the 19th of July, where she was detained until that place surrendered to the English arms; on account of which deviation the defendant was obliged to have fresh insurances done upon her cargo. But LORD ELLENBOROUGH intimated an opinion that these facts were no defence to the present action.

Park, for the defendant, contended that the plaintiff's sailing with the first favorable wind direct to Portsmouth, was a condition precedent to the freight becoming due; and that the damage suffered by the defendant from the imperfect execution of the contract might at any rate be given in evidence to reduce the plaintiff's demand.

LORD ELLENBOROUGH. I am of opinion that this was not a condition precedent, and that the defendant, having accepted the cargo, must pay the stipulated freight. To hold that any short delay in setting sail or trifling departure from the direct course of the voyage would entirely destroy the plaintiff's right to be remunerated for transporting the cargo, would indeed be going *inter apices facti.* If the plaintiff had proceeded merely on a *quantum meruit* for an indefinite sum, you might have reduced the damages by shewing a deficient performance of the contract. But here there is a specific agreement for specific freight. Therefore the defendant must bring his cross-action for any loss he may have suffered from the default of the plaintiff.

It was then suggested that the plaintiff, not having performed the charter-party on his behalf, was driven from it to a *quantum meruit*, so as to let in the proposed defence.

LORD ELLENBOROUGH, however, said, that if the sailing in the manner required by the charter-party was a condition precedent, then the plaintiff had no cause of action; but as it was not to be so considered, he had a right to recover for the freight according to the rate agreed upon. *The plaintiff had a verdict accordingly.*

RITCHIE *v.* ATKINSON.

IN THE KING'S BENCH, NOVEMBER 15, 1808.

[*Reported in* 10 *East*, 295.]

THIS was an action of *indebitatus assumpsit* for the freight of goods conveyed in the ship Adelphi, of which the plaintiff was master, from St. Petersburg to London, and delivered to the defendant or his order. There was also a count on a *quantum meruit* for freight, and the common counts for work and labour, and for money paid, &c. The defendant pleaded the general issue; and at the trial at Guildhall before Lord Ellenborough, C. J., a verdict was found for the plaintiff for £960 15*s.* subject to the opinion of this court on the following case.

The plaintiff being master of the ship Adelphi, in August, 1807, chartered her to the defendant by the following instrument: "Memorandum for charter. London, 12th August, 1807. It is this day mutually agreed between Captain J. Ritchie, of the ship Adelphi, burden 400 tons or thereabouts, now in the river, and W. Atkinson, of London, merchant, that the said ship, being tight, and every way fitted for the voyage, shall with all convenient speed sail and proceed to St. Petersburgh, or so near thereunto as she may safely get, and there load from the factors of Wm. Atkinson a complete cargo of clean hemp, and 80 tons of iron for ballast, not exceeding what she can reasonably stow, &c.; and being so loaded shall therewith proceed to Woolwich and London, and deliver the same, on being paid freight for clean hemp £5 per ton, for ballast iron 5*s.* per ton, with two-thirds port charges and pilotage as customary; restraint of princes and rulers during the said voyage always excepted: one half of the freight to be paid on unloading and right delivery of the cargo, and the remainder in three months following. Thirty running days are to be allowed the said merchant (if the ship is not sooner despatched), for loading her at St. Petersburgh, and thirty running days for delivery at Woolwich and London, and ten days on demurrage over and above the said laying days at £6 per day. Penalty for non-performance of this agreement £2000. The ship to sail with convoy from the Sound for England. Wm. Atkinson." The Adelphi sailed in ballast from Deptford on the 24th of August, 1807, and arrived at Cronstadt, the port of St. Petersburgh, on the 16th of September following; where the plaintiff proceeded to take in her cargo under the charter-party, and continued loading her with all due diligence until the 25th of September, and had then taken on board between 70 and 80 tons of iron for ballast, the same being a sufficient quantity for ballast, and a considerable quantity of hemp. On the 25th of September there was a general rumor of an embargo being intended to be laid by the Russian government on all British vessels; and there was every appearance that it would take place immediately; but it did not in fact take place then, nor until six weeks afterwards: but on the 25th of September Mr. Booker, the agent for the British factory at Cronstadt, and also the agent to the house of Hubbard & Co., the defendant's agents, in consequence of instructions that he had received from Sir Stephen Shairp, his Majesty's Consul-General at St. Petersburgh, desired the captains of such British vessels as were ready to proceed to sea, to do so as soon as possible, as he expected an embargo might take place immediately. [The case then set out a circular letter of advice to that effect, written to the captains of British vessels by the consul's agents.] In consequence of which the plaintiff gave directions to leave off screwing down any more hemp, which is the usual mode of loading, and to fill the ship up as fast as possible by hand; and the whole of this day was occupied in loading the vessel in this manner till 6 o'clock; at which time she was filled up as far as could be done by hand; and the ship sailed on the evening of the 25th of September with a cargo more than half what she could have carried, though there was at the time as much hemp of the defendant's lying in lighters alongside of the vessel as would have completely loaded her. The plaintiff acted *bona fide* and as an honest man under the existing circumstances, and there was a reasonable and well grounded apprehension for his acting as he did; and he brought home as complete a cargo as he could under the circumstances. Several other vessels sailed the same evening as the Adelphi. All or almost all the vessels which had passes sailed either the same evening or the next morning without full cargoes, under the apprehensions of an embargo: but some other British vessels did not sail from Cronstadt at that time, and were not detained, but completed their loading: and if the Adelphi had staid, she might have completed her loading. The plaintiff sailed without any previous communication with Hubbard & Co., the defendant's agents, to whom he was addressed; they residing at St. Petersburgh. As soon as they had notice of the circumstances they immediately came to Cronstadt with an intention to stop the ship, but it was too late; and they then formally protested against him for breach of his charter-party. The Adelphi arrived in London and delivered her cargo there to the defendant, who refused to pay the freight, as little more than a moiety of the quantity of hemp stipulated by the charter-party was brought by the plaintiff. The freight of the iron and hemp so brought to London and delivered to the defendant amounted, according to the rate stipulated in the charter-party, to £960 15*s*. And the verdict for that sum was to stand, if the court thought that the plaintiff was entitled to recover; otherwise a nonsuit was to be entered.

Littledale contended that the plaintiff was entitled to recover freight on the charter-party in proportion to the cargo, although he had not brought home a complete cargo; the delivery of a complete cargo not being a condition precedent, nor the payment stipulated for entire, but to be made at the rate of so much per ton on the different articles brought home and delivered, and therefore in its nature apportionable. The words, "and deliver the same," are equivocal, and may mean the cargo actually delivered, as well as the whole quantity stipulated for: and the former is the more reasonable construction, especially in a mercantile instrument, because the plaintiff would then be entitled to receive the just proportion of freight which he had earned: and if by negligence he did not bring home so complete a cargo as he might have done, the defendant would have a remedy against him upon his covenant. The true rule in these cases was laid down by Lord Mansfield in Boone *v.* Eyre,[1] that "where mutual covenants go to the whole of the consideration on both sides, they are mutual conditions: but where the covenants go only to a part, and where a recompense may be had in damages, it is a different thing:" and this was recognized in Campbell *v.* Jones,[2] and The Duke of St. Albans *v.* Shore.[3] That doctrine must at all events apply to a case where the amount of the freight was to be ascertained *pro rata*. As in Tompson *v.* Noel,[4] where the master of a ship covenanted to go to Ireland and there take in 280 men from the defendant and carry them to Jamaica, and the defendant covenanted to have the 280 men ready, and to pay £5 a man for their conveyance; though the defendant pleaded that he had all the men ready, and ten-

[1] 6 Term Rep. 573, and in 1 H. Blac. 273, *n*.

[2] 6 Term Rep. 573.

[3] 1 H. Blac. 278.

[4] 1 Lev. 16, and 1 Keb. 100.

dered them to be carried, and the plaintiff only took and carried 180 of them; yet it was held on demurrer to the plea that he might recover, because the plea was only an answer to part of the declaration: that is, though the plea in bar shewed that the plaintiff had not performed the whole of what he had covenanted to do; yet giving no answer to the part which he had performed, he was held entitled to judgment. But, 2dly, though the delivery of a complete cargo were a condition precedent, according to the terms and intent of the contract, yet the defendant having received that part of the cargo which was brought home, the plaintiff is entitled to recover upon a *quantum meruit* in respect of the service done, as upon a new cause of action. For though in Cook *v.* Jennings,[1] upon a covenant to pay so much freight for goods delivered at A., it was held that freight could not be recovered upon the covenant *pro rata itineris*, where the ship was wrecked at B. before her arrival at A., though the defendant had accepted the goods at B.; yet Lawrence, J., seemed to consider such receipt of the goods by the owner as evidence of a new contract between the parties. And Luke *v.* Lyde[2] went upon that principle; as did also Lutwidge *v.* Grey and others in Dom. Proc. 1733, there cited,[3] and the case of the Copenhagen, in the Court of Admiralty.[4] The case of Bright *v.* Cowper,[5] which seems to bear the other way, was an action of covenant, and it does not appear whether the action was brought for the whole or only a proportionable part of the freight. Besides, by the terms of this contract the plaintiff was not bound to deliver the cargo, without receiving payment of half of the freight at the time, and the remainder in three months afterwards: by receiving, therefore, less than the complete cargo, which the plaintiff was not bound to deliver without a tender of the half-freight, the defendant impliedly agreed to pay for the part so received. [LORD ELLENBOROUGH, C. J. I do not see how the receipt of the goods changes the situation of the parties; because these were the defendant's own goods; and unless freight were due upon them by the contract, the defendant was entitled to have his own goods without any consideration. It was therefore only taking peaceable possession of that for which, if wrongfully withheld, he might have brought trover. But on the other ground, the plaintiff may contend with strong effect, that the defendant's argument must go this length, that if the cargo wanted a single ton of being a complete cargo, it would be a defence to this action for the freight.] The plaintiff might have gone back again to St. Petersburgh for the remainder of the cargo, and was not bound to have delivered a part only of it: and the convenience of receiving the part brought home would be a good consid-

[1] 7 Term. Rep. 381.
[2] 2 Burr. 882, and 1 Blac. Rep. 190.
[3] This case is given at length by Mr. Abbott, in his Law of Merchant Ships, &c., 280.
[4] 1 Rob. Adm. Rep. 289.
[5] 1 Brownl. 21.

eration to the defendant from whence to imply a new promise to pay for it.

Taddy, contra. The covenant to bring home a complete cargo is a condition precedent to the plaintiff's right to recover freight upon the contract. It is necessary for the safety of merchants that these charter-parties should be strictly executed, and the late case of Smith *v.* Wilson[1] proceeded upon that principle, although the freight there was covenanted to be paid at so much per month during the voyage out to Monte Video and back again to the port of discharge. The case of Bright *v.* Cowper[2] was there relied on by the court; and it is immaterial whether the action was brought for the whole or a proportion *pro rata* of the freight; for the action of covenant sounding in damages, a part only might be recovered, though the plaintiff declared for the whole. And the same argument might have been urged in Cook *v.* Jennings;[3] but the court held the performance of the whole voyage a condition precedent to the recovery of any part of the freight. There is no difference in this respect between a contract under seal, or by parol. The construction in both cases proceeds on the ground, that if the parties have stipulated for themselves, whether reasonably or not, the court cannot stipulate for them. The substance of the contract in Boone *v.* Eyre was the conveyance of the estate; and the exact number of negroes on it was only the subject of an independent covenant; and any deficiency in the number might be compensated in damages without affecting the title to the estate. In Campbell *v.* Jones[4] a particular sum was covenanted to be paid on a given day at all events, which might arrive before the instruction covenanted to be given by the other party; and consequently such instruction could not in the nature of the thing be a condition precedent to the payment of the money on the day. Tompson *v.* Noel[5] seems indeed the other way; but there the covenant applied only to the number of men who were to be carried out at so much per head; which may perhaps make a difference; but a complete cargo, which was covenanted in this instance to be brought home, is in its nature an entire thing, depending on the capacity of the ship. [Grose, J. Does it not depend on the intention of the parties, to be collected from the whole instrument, whether the completion of the cargo was to be a condition precedent to the payment of any freight; and could it have been their intention that if the cargo wanted ever so small a quantity to complete the loading of the ship, that the plaintiff was to receive nothing for that which he brought home?] It may easily be conceived to have been the meaning of the parties, that if the master refused or neglected to take in any part of the cargo, however small, which was ready for him, he should not receive any

[1] 8 East, 437–445. [2] Brownl. 21. [3] 7 Term Rep. 381.
[4] 6 Term Rep. 570. [5] 1 Lev. 16.

freight; and that the only effectual way of preventing the omission, whatever the motive might be, was by making the completion of the cargo a condition precedent. Then if so, the acceptance here by the defendant of an incomplete cargo, being his own goods, cannot make any difference. And as to the argument that the plaintiff might have gone back to St. Petersburgh, and have refused to deliver any part of the cargo till he had completed the whole; the answer is, that he has brought his action before he has so done. Or at any rate he ought to have declared differently, by stating the partial performance of the original contract, and that in consideration that he would deliver the part of the cargo which had been first brought home, the defendant promised to pay freight *pro rata*. But a general *indebitatus assumpsit* cannot be maintained by a party under contract until the whole duty is performed. [LORD ELLENBOROUGH, C. J. There is a covenant by the plaintiff that the ship shall proceed with all convenient speed to St. Petersburgh, and there load a complete cargo; and that would not be satisfied by the plaintiff bringing part of the cargo at one time, and then going back and bringing the remainder of it; and therefore we may lay that, which is not the material part of the case, out of the question, and consider whether the completion of the cargo be a condition precedent.] In Hadley *v.* Clarke[1] the defendant, having contracted to carry the plaintiff's goods from Liverpool to Leghorn, was held liable in damages for the non-performance of his contract at the end of two years, during which time the ship was under an embargo of our own government at Falmouth in her way out. And Lawrence, J., referred to All. 27, "that where a party by his own contract creates a duty or charge upon himself, he is bound to make it good, if he may, notwithstanding any accident by inevitable necessity; because he might have provided against it by his contract." As to Lutwidge *v.* Grey,[2] and Luke *v.* Lyde,[3] the master in each had done all that he could, and had forwarded the goods or offered to complete the voyage; but the owner preferred to take them at another place. He then argued the case upon the marine law, as far as it could be collected from local ordinances and general opinions; and referred to 1 Valin, 626; 2 Poth. 393, 4; 2 Mag. 162; 1 Moll. 327; and Mal. Lex. Merc. 98, 100. Malynes, in one of these passages, mentions a case of five ships which were freighted out and home in 1587, but from some apprehension of being taken returned without their lading. Two of them having stayed out all their time in the foreign ports, and protested against the factors of the freighters from whom they were to have received their lading, were adjudged by the law of admiralty to have deserved their whole freight; but two others who had not stayed their abiding days, nor protested,

[1] 8 Term Rep. 259.
[2] Abbott's Law of Merchant Ships, 280.
[3] 2 Burr. 882.

were found not to have deserved any freight at all, though they were laden outward bound. The fifth ship, under the like circumstances as the two last, had half her freight by a particular proviso in her charter-party. In p. 100, treating on "Questions about freightings and their solutions," he says, "If freight be agreed upon for commodities to be laden for a certain price for every pack, &c., without regard to the burthen of the ship, but to give her the full lading, no man maketh doubt but that the same is to be performed accordingly." [LORD ELLENBOROUGH, C. J. No doubt if the master do not bring home a full lading, the other shall recover; but the writer does not say that that is a condition precedent to the claim of freight in proportion to what is actually brought home. In all the cases of conditions precedent the thing to be done is some indivisible thing; but the delivery of a cargo of goods is not one entire thing, but in its nature divisible.

Littledale, in reply, observed on the loose and doubtful opinions of the writers on the marine law, from whence no certain rule could be drawn; though in the very instance quoted, Pothier and the others admit that something is to be paid where the master is in no fault. But the intention of these parties (the material object of inquiry), that the freight should be paid in proportion to the quantity of the cargo, is manifest from fixing the rate of payment by the ton; for otherwise, if the cargo had been meant to be one entire thing of a given tonnage, the bringing home of which was to be made a condition precedent to the demand of any freight, one certain sum only would have been stipulated to be paid on the performance of the one entire duty. On the other point, if the expected embargo justified the carrying away the ship till the expectation of danger was removed, the returning afterwards for the remainder of the cargo would be a performance of the voyage with all convenient speed. But it has not been thought necessary in this case to argue the question of the embargo, which will arise in another case now standing for argument. As to Smith v. Wilson,[1] the owner did not do every thing in his power to earn the freight which he sought to recover, but merely offered to prosecute and complete the voyage, in the progress of which he had been interrupted for a time. That, therefore, was the case of a failure in the very substance of the contract, the performance of which was to entitle the plaintiff to freight. But a covenant to sail with the first fair wind has been held[2] not to be a condition precedent to the recovery of the freight.

LORD ELLENBOROUGH, C. J. If the delivery of a complete cargo were a condition precedent to the recovery of any freight, no doubt the defendant would be entitled to require the strictest performance of it: but the question is, Whether it be a condition precedent? and that

[1] 8 East, 437.

[2] Constable v. Cloberie, Palm. 397; Hall v. Cazenove, 4 East, 477, 483; and Bornemann v. Tooke, 1 Campbell's N. P. Cas. 377.

depends not on any formal arrangement of the words, but on the reason and sense of the thing, as it is to be collected from the whole contract: whether of two things reciprocally stipulated to be done, the performance of the one does in sense and reason depend upon the performance of the other. The rule was well laid down by Lord Mansfield in Boone *v.* Eyre,[1] that where mutual covenants go to the whole of the consideration on both sides, they are mutual conditions, the one precedent to the other; but where the covenants go only to a part, there a remedy lies on the covenant to recover damages for the breach of it; but it is not a condition precedent. That was a case where the plaintiff had conveyed to the defendant a plantation in the West Indies, with the negroes on it, and had covenanted that he had a good title, and was lawfully possessed of the negroes; and the defendant covenanted that, the plaintiff well and truly performing all and every thing in the deed contained on his part to be performed, he the defendant would pay a certain annuity. And to an action of covenant for non-payment of the annuity the defendant pleaded, that the plaintiff was not at the time legally possessed of the negroes, and so had not a good title to convey. But, on demurrer, Lord Mansfield said that if such plea were to be allowed, if any one negro were not the property of the plaintiff, it would bar the action. He must therefore have considered that such a covenant was in its nature apportionable according to the damage sustained by the breach of it, and did not make a condition precedent to the payment of the annuity. Now apply that to the present case. Here is a ship of about four hundred tons, which is freighted to go to St. Petersburgh, and to bring home a complete cargo of hemp and iron, and to deliver the same on being paid freight at so much per ton on each commodity. If the owner be not entitled to recover freight for any proportion of goods he may bring home short of a complete cargo, and it should appear by any subsequent admeasurement of the vessel, even after the delivery of the cargo, that there was wanting some small fraction of a complete cargo; if the ship had been supposed to measure four hundred tons, and a cargo adapted to that proportion had been loaded, and it turned out that she measured ten or twenty tons more; the owner would altogether be defeated of his remedy for the whole freight. But would not such a construction be contrary to common sense and the true nature of such a contract; and can any such meaning be fairly inferred from the terms of it? But it is said that a different construction will bear hard upon the merchant who has stipulated for the delivery of a complete cargo. It does not follow, however, from thence, that if there has been an imperfect delivery, he will be ousted of his remedy: for clearly an action on the case lies against the captain who has made an imperfect, when he could have made a perfect delivery. But I should require the strongest

[1] 1 H. Black. 273, and 6 Term Rep. 573.

authority to be adduced before I held that this was a condition precedent, when the consequences of such a construction would be such as I have before stated. There is no case, however, where the delivery of less than a complete cargo has been held not to be apportionable. Where, as in Smith v. Wilson,[1] the freight is made payable upon an indivisible condition, such as in that case the arrival of the ship with her cargo at her destined port of discharge, such arrival, &c., must be a condition precedent; because it is incapable of being apportioned; but here the delivery of the cargo is in its nature divisible, and therefore I think it is not a condition precedent; but the plaintiff is entitled to recover freight in proportion to the extent of such delivery; leaving the defendant to his remedy in damages for the short delivery. And all the cases of conditions precedent have been where the thing to be done was a strict indivisible condition. The same may be said of the case of the five ships mentioned from Malynes, which were freighted out to Leghorn and Civita Vecchia, there to remain a certain time and take in their lading and return home; and some of them came away without any lading, before the precise time stipulated for their abiding there to be laden had expired. In this case, however, the condition is divisible, and the real justice of the case will be attained by the plaintiff's recovering his freight in the proportion per ton of the goods delivered; and the remedy of the defendant will still be entire to punish the master for his imperfect and wrongful delivery.

GROSE, J. It is not a condition precedent to the claim of freight that a complete cargo should be delivered. The agreement, however, does contain a condition precedent in one part; for the payment of the freight is made a condition precedent to the delivery of the cargo; the master being to "deliver the same on being paid freight." This is strong to shew that the parties knew how to make a condition precedent where it was so intended: but they have not done so in the instance now in question. And to construe the delivery of a complete cargo to be a condition precedent to the right to recover any freight would be manifestly unjust; because if default were made in ever so small a proportion of that which would be a complete cargo, the master would not be entitled to any freight for however large a proportion of goods he may have delivered. The reasonable construction therefore is, that the plaintiff should receive freight according to the quantity per ton which he has delivered. But it is said that the intention of the parties was that the defendant should receive a complete cargo, as much as could be stowed in the ship; and that this was a material stipulation to be performed for his benefit. I will not say now that it was not so: but taking it to be so, the defendant has his remedy for the breach of it. If either of the parties break his part of what he has engaged to do, he will be answerable to the other. In

[1] 8 East, 437.

this way perfect justice will be done to both; but not so if the delivery of a complete cargo were made a condition precedent to the payment of any freight; and therefore I do not think that it was the intention of the parties to make it so. The cases, where acts stipulated to be done by one party have been held to be conditions precedent to the claim of the other, have been where it appeared upon the face of the contract to have been the intention of the parties that the one thing should not be done by one party till something else had been done by the other. But no such intention appears here.

LE BLANC, J. The question depends on the construction to be put upon this instrument; whether we can see from the whole of it that it was the intention of the parties that the delivery of a complete cargo should be a condition precedent to the recovery of any freight at all. This rule was laid down in one of the early cases, Kingston *v.* Preston,[1] which has been since followed in others. Now the delivery of the cargo was in its nature divisible; for it consisted of hemp and iron, the freight of which was to be paid for by the ton, according to a different rate of payment for the one and for the other: and therefore we cannot collect the intention of the parties to have been to make the delivery of a complete cargo a condition precedent to the payment of freight for any part which was delivered. The rule was laid down in Boone *v.* Eyre, and approved by this court in Campbell *v.* Jones, and by the Court of Common Pleas in The Duke of St. Albans *v.* Shore, that where a covenant goes to the whole of the consideration on both sides, there it is a condition precedent; but where it does not go to the whole, but only to a part, there each party must resort to his separate remedy for the breach of the contract by the other. Here it is clear that the delivery of a complete cargo does not go to the whole consideration of the freight; because the failure of bringing home one ton less than the full quantity of four hundred tons would prevent the plaintiff from recovering for the three hundred and ninety-nine tons which he might have brought over. The loss on his part by such a construction would bear no sort of proportion to the injury suffered by the defendant. The fair construction therefore is, that the plaintiff should recover freight for what he has performed; and that the defendant should have a remedy against him for that which he has not performed, and which he ought to have done.

BAYLEY, J. There would be great injustice done by holding this to be a condition precedent; and none by a different construction; because if the defendant has sustained any injury by the non-delivery of a complete cargo, he will recover a compensation in damages commensurate to such injury. It is necessary to look to the instrument to see whether this be a condition precedent; to see what the intention of

[1] Stated at length in Jones *v.* Barkley, Dougl. 689.

the parties was in this respect. It begins by stating that "it is this day mutually agreed," &c. That would have some little influence to shew that each of the parties had mutual stipulations to make. Not that those words would control the meaning of the subsequent words, if it clearly appeared that a condition precedent was intended by them. Then the captain engages that the ship shall be "tight, &c., and every way fitted for the voyage, and shall with all convenient speed sail and proceed to St. Petersburgh." Now if those were to be deemed conditions precedent, then if there were any defect in the fitting out, or an hour's delay in the sailing, the remedy for the freight would be defeated. Could that have been intended by the parties? Then the ship is to return with a complete cargo; and if that were a condition precedent, then if there were a deficiency of one ton only in the cargo, though all the rest were delivered, the defendant would have all the benefit of such delivery without being obliged to pay any thing for it. Is that reasonable? and can we collect any such intention from the instrument? In Cook *v.* Jennings the freight was to be paid for deals delivered at Liverpool: none were delivered at Liverpool; and therefore no freight could be due. In Bright *v.* Cowper an entire sum was to be paid; and therefore unless the plaintiff was entitled to recover the whole, he could not recover any part. Unless therefore there was a performance of the whole for which that entire sum was to be paid, which there was not, he could recover nothing. But there is nothing here to shew that it was the intention of the parties, that the delivery of a complete cargo should be a condition precedent to the recovery of any freight actually earned. Great injustice would ensue from holding it to be so; and no injustice to either party from holding it not to be so. *Postea to the plaintiff.*[1]

HAVELOCK *v.* GEDDES AND OTHERS.

IN THE KING'S BENCH, FEBRUARY 9, 1809.

[*Reported in* 10 *East,* 555.]

THIS was covenant upon a charter-party of affreightment, dated the 5th of September, 1806, whereby the plaintiff, owner of the ship Lord Duncan, of 933 tons burthen, of which A. Heartley was master, let her to freight to the defendants for twelve calendar months certain from the 24th of September, 1806, and from thence for such longer period, if any, as the defendants should think fit to keep and retain the same,

[1] See Atkinson *v.* Ritchie, 10 East, 530. — ED.

upon the conditions and covenants thereinafter contained. And the plaintiff covenanted that the ship should be navigated and furnished with fifty persons, and such further number, not exceeding one hundred, as should be required by the defendants; the owner being reimbursed by the freighters for such additional number, according to the average rate of wages and provisions expended on the whole. That the ship, during the time she should be navigated and employed under the charter-party, should be under the entire control of the defendants, so far as related to all orders for sailing, destination, and delay. And the defendants covenanted to pay to the owner, for the hire and service of the ship for the said term of twelve calendar months, and such longer period as they should keep the same, the freight and rate following, viz., 24*s.* per calendar month per ton, being £1119 12*s.* per month, commencing from the 24th of September, 1806, and ending when the ship should be returned to the river Thames, and there by the freighters declared to be discharged; it being understood that the freighter should not be at liberty to discharge the ship abroad, although she might be abroad at the expiration of the said twelve calendar months, or at any other place but within the port of London. And that the freight should be paid in the proportions and at the periods following, viz., two months freight at the execution of the charter-party either in cash or by accepted bills of the freighters at three months from the said 24th of September; two months more at the end of six calendar months from the said 24th of September; two months more at the end of ten calendar months; two months more at the end of fourteen calendar months, should the ship be so long employed; and in like manner two months more at the end of every succeeding two calendar months, until the ship should be discharged; and immediately upon such discharge, the balance to be paid by the freighters in cash or their acceptances at three months. That the freighters should pay all port charges, tonnage duties, dock dues, and all other duties and dues, except lights and pilotage, which were to be paid by the owner. That they would reimburse to the owner the charges for additional men beyond fifty as before mentioned; two calendar months allowance for such additional men to be added to the first payment of freight; but the residue of such allowance not to be paid until the ship's discharge or return from her first intended voyage; and in like manner for any other foreign voyage or voyages. By virtue of which charter-party the defendants on the said 24th of September took the ship into their service and kept and retained the same therein until she was afterwards, and whilst she was so in their service, and after the expiration of ten, but before the expiration of twelve months from the same 24th of September, viz., on the 22d of August, 1807, at St. Domingo, without any default of the owner, master, or mariners, consumed by fire and wholly lost, and was thereby prevented from returning to London. And then the plaintiff, after averring that the ship, during all the time she was so kept and detained in the service of the defendants, was navigated and furnished with fifty persons, and such further number, not exceeding one hundred, as was required by the defendants; and was during all that time under the entire control of the defendants as to all orders for sailing, destination, and delay; assigned three breaches; 1. That though the defendants paid the plaintiff the two months freight payable at the execution of the charter-party, and also the two months freight at the end of the first six calendar months; yet they did not pay the two months freight at the end of the said ten calendar months. 2. That the defendants have not paid to the plaintiff any subsequent freight. 3. That although on the 24th of October, 1806, the defendants required the plaintiff to put on board, and he did put on board, twenty additional men beyond the fifty, who all sailed in the ship on a foreign voyage to St. Domingo, and continued on board from thence until the loss of the ship; and although according to the average rate of wages and provisions expended on the whole, the defendants became liable to pay to the plaintiff £8 per month for every such additional man; yet the defendants had not reimbursed the plaintiff for any of them.

The defendants craved oyer of the charter-party, by which it appeared further that the plaintiff covenanted that the ship, at his expense, should be forthwith made tight and strong, and well and sufficiently equipped, manned, and fitted, &c., for a voyage or voyages of twelve calendar months to foreign parts, and should, during the continuance of the charter-party, be kept tight and strong, and well and sufficiently equipped, &c., and victualled; concluding with a mutual general covenant for performance, and particularly the plaintiff binding to the defendants the said ship, freight, tackle, &c. (the perils and dangers of the seas, rivers, &c., all inevitable accidents whatever, and capture by enemies, and the detention and restraint of rulers, &c., being excepted); and the defendants binding to the plaintiff the goods put on board the ship. The defendants then pleaded, 1. *Non est factum.* 2. That the ship was not at the expense of the plaintiff forthwith or within a reasonable time after the charter-party made tight and strong, and well and sufficiently equipped, &c., for a voyage or voyages of twelve calendar months to foreign parts, whereby she was delayed and hindered from proceeding on a voyage from London to St. Domingo, and was detained on her said voyage at Portsmouth for an unreasonable length of time, viz., for four months, during all which time the defendants lost the use and benefit of the ship, and were put to great expense in repairing her and making her tight and strong, and fitting her for such voyage; and also that thereby certain goods of the defendants on board the ship were wetted and damaged; wherefore they pray judgment of the plaintiff's action. 3. The defendants pleaded as to the first breach, that during the twelve calendar months therein mentioned, viz., on the 1st of November, 1806, certain goods of the defendants were shipped on board the vessel to be carried from London to St. Domingo; and that at the time of shipping them the vessel was not tight and strong, and well and sufficiently equipped, &c., but was decayed, leaky, defectively provided, and in an unseaworthy state for performing the said voyage; in consequence whereof it became necessary to unload and repair her, and she was afterwards unloaded and repaired before she could proceed on and perform her said voyage; and by means of the premises the ship was unemployed by and wholly unserviceable to the defendants for a great part of the six calendar months from the 24th of September, 1806, viz., for four calendar months part thereof. And then the defendants averred that they paid to the plaintiff for the hire and service of the ship for the residue of the said six calendar months the freight in the charter-party mentioned. The fourth plea was the same in substance as the last, omitting only to state that the defendants paid for all the time the ship was not wholly unserviceable to them or unemployed; and it avers that the ship was not in the actual service and employ of the defendants, or retained in such service under the charter-party, for ten calendar months in the whole from the 24th of September, 1806, until she was consumed by fire as in the declaration mentioned, and which fire happened without any default in the defendants. 7. The defendants pleaded (to the second breach) that the ship after the charter-party made was not employed by them or in their service until the end of fourteen calendar months from the said 24th of September, 1806; but while she continued in their service and employ, and before the end of fourteen calendar months, &c., viz., on the 22d of August, 1807, in parts beyond the seas near St. Domingo, the ship, without any default of the defendants, was consumed by fire and wholly lost. 8. (As to the last breach.) That the defendants did reimburse to the plaintiff two calendar months allowance for the additional men beyond fifty put on board, &c.; and further, that after making the charter-party the ship sailed on a voyage from London towards St. Domingo, being her first intended voyage outwards under the charter-party with a cargo of goods of the defendants' on board; and that afterwards, on the 22d of August, 1807, in parts beyond the seas near St. Domingo, the ship was, without default of the defendants, burnt and wholly lost, and never did return from St. Domingo aforesaid.

The plaintiff in his replication demurred to the 2d, 3d, and 4th pleas, and assigned for special causes of demurrer, that the defendants in each of those pleas had attempted to put in issue immaterial facts, and had insisted on divers covenants of the plaintiff as conditions precedent to the performance of their own covenant; whereas they were separate and independent covenants; and the breaches of covenants alleged against the plaintiff in these pleas were no answer to or justification of the breaches of covenant of which the plaintiff complains. To the 7th plea the plaintiff replied, that the defendants, after making the charter-party, viz., on the 18th of November, 1806, despatched the ship with a cargo on a voyage to the island of St. Domingo, and that the ship afterwards, and after the expiration of seven calendar months from the said 24th of September, 1806, and before she was so burnt and wholly lost, viz., on the 4th of May, 1807, arrived at St. Domingo, and delivered her cargo, and completed the said voyage. As to so much of the 8th plea as relates to the two calendar months allowance for the additional men, the plaintiff took issue on the reimbursement of such allowance. And as to the residue of the plea he replied, that before the ship was consumed by fire, to wit, on the 20th of August, 1807, the ship had arrived at St. Domingo and completed the said intended voyage.

The defendants joined in demurrer on the 2d, 3d, and 4th pleas; and demurred generally to the replications to the 7th and the latter part of the 8th pleas: on which there was also joinder in demurrer.

This case was argued on a former day in the term by *Gaselee* for the plaintiff, and *Marryat* for the defendants. The questions made upon the demurrer to the 2d, 3d, and 4th pleas were, whether the agreement in the charter-party that the ship should be made tight and strong, &c., were a condition precedent to the payment of any freight; and whether the matters alleged in those pleas were an answer to the action on the breach of covenant for non-payment of the freight, or were the ground of a cross-action against the plaintiff for damages. The next question arose upon the demurrer to the replication to the 7th plea, whether the ship not having returned from her voyage to St. Domingo back to the river Thames, and been there discharged, but having been burnt abroad before the end of fourteen calendar months from the date of the charter-party, after she had completed her outward voyage to St. Domingo (which was completed after the end of seven calendar months), the owner were entitled to any part of the freight accruing after the expiration of six calendar months, which is what he claimed upon the second breach of covenant. The last question arose upon the demurrer to the replication to the latter part of the 8th plea; whether the ship having been so burnt at St. Domingo, and not discharged in the river Thames or returned from her first intended voyage, the plaintiff were entitled to any part of the extra allowance claimed by the last breach of covenant beyond the part payment made in the first instance. The substance of the arguments on these points was afterwards fully stated by the court in giving judgment. And after time taken to consider,

LORD ELLENBOROUGH, C. J., now delivered judgment (after stating the declaration as before set forth).

The defendant craved oyer of the charter-party, by which it appeared that the plaintiff covenanted that the ship, at his expense, should forthwith be made tight, staunch, and strong, and well and sufficiently equipped, manned, &c., for a voyage or voyages of twelve calendar months, and should during the continuance of the charter-party be kept tight, staunch, &c., and well and sufficiently equipped, manned, &c.; and it is upon this covenant that the defendants have grounded several of their pleas. The first plea upon which any question arises, states that the ship was not forthwith after making the charter-party made tight, staunch, &c., and well and sufficiently equipped for a voyage or voyages of twelve calendar months; *per quod* she was hindered from proceeding on a certain voyage from London to St. Domingo, and detained an unreasonable length of time; during all which time the defendants were deprived of the use of the ship, and were put to great expense in making her tight, staunch, &c., and fitting her for her voyage, and divers goods of the defendants which were put on board her were wetted and damaged. To this plea, which is pleaded to the whole of the demand, the plaintiff has demurred, and the question upon it is, Whether the defendants are entitled to insist that the forthwith making the ship tight, staunch, &c., was a condition precedent? The defendants did not repudiate the ship because she was not immediately made tight, staunch, &c., but took her into their service and employed her; and after having navigated her for several months, they say that, because this was a condition precedent, and was not performed, they are not liable to pay any thing. They do not pretend that the non-performance has damnified them to the extent of the payment they wish to evade; and to be sure, if this were a condition precedent, the neglect of putting in a single nail for a single moment after the ship ought to have been made tight, staunch, &c., would be a breach of the condition, and a defence to the whole of the plaintiff's demand. We are clear, however, that the defendants, who took the ship into their service and employed her in an unimpaired state, have no right to insist that the forthwith making her tight, &c., was a condition precedent. Whether a particular covenant is to constitute a condition precedent depends upon the intention of the parties, as it is to be collected from the instrument in which the covenant is contained, as is laid down in Porter v. Shephard, 6 Term Rep. 668, and in Glazebrook v. Woodrow, 8 Term Rep. 370, 371. And it would be an outrage to common sense to say that it could have been the intention of these parties, that if the defendants took to this ship as a ship in their employ under the charter-party, they should be at liberty afterwards to insist that the making her complete in every particular, and that forthwith without any delay, was a strict condition precedent on the part of the plaintiff. The cases cited are also decisive upon the point. Constable v. Cloberie, Palm. 397, shews that a covenant to sail with the first wind is not a condition precedent. Bornmann v.

Tooke, 1 Campb. 377, proceeds upon the same principle. Boone *v.* Eyre, 1 H. Blac. 273, in the notes, lays down a very sensible general rule, that where mutual covenants go to the whole consideration on both sides, they are mutual conditions, the one precedent to the other; but where they go only to a part, and a breach may be paid for in damages, there the defendant has a remedy on the covenant, and shall not plead it as a condition precedent. Had the plaintiff's neglect here precluded the defendants from making any use of the vessel, it would have gone to the whole consideration, and might have been insisted upon as an entire bar; because the consideration for the defendant's covenant to pay the freight would then have failed *in toto;* but as the defendants have had some use of the vessel, notwithstanding the plaintiff's neglect, the plaintiff's covenant is to be considered as going to a part only; the consideration has not wholly failed, and the covenant cannot be looked upon as having raised a condition precedent, but merely gives the defendants a right, under a counter action, to such damages as they can prove they have sustained from this neglect. For these reasons we are of opinion that this plea cannot be supported, and that the demurrer to it must be allowed.

The next plea submitted to the consideration of the court is pleaded to the first breach only. It states that during the twelve months mentioned in the charter-party divers goods were shipped on board the vessel, to be carried from London to St. Domingo; that at the time of shipping them the vessel was not tight, staunch, &c., and sufficiently equipped, &c., but on the contrary was decayed, leaky, ill fitted, and in an unseaworthy state; that in consequence thereof it became necessary to unload and repair the ship; that by means of the premises the ship became unemployed by and unserviceable to the defendants for a great part of six calendar months; and that the defendants have paid for the hire and service of the ship for the residue of the said six calendar months. There is another plea similar to this, except that it does not state that the defendants paid for all the time the ship was not unserviceable to them, or unemployed; and it avers that the ship was not in their service or employ for ten calendar months in the whole. To these pleas the plaintiff has also demurred, and the question upon them is, whether the defendants have shewn such a neglect in the plaintiff as will excuse them from the payment of the freight which the first breach claims. These pleas are founded, not upon the stipulation forthwith to make the vessel tight, staunch, &c., but upon the stipulation to keep it so; and it is not alleged that there was any defect at the commencement of the twelve months for which the vessel was hired; but that at the time of shipping the goods during the twelve months she was not tight, &c. It is therefore perfectly consistent with the allegations in these pleas, that the ship had been put into a perfect state, and thoroughly equipped, immediately after the execution of the charter-party; that she was so when the defendants took her into their service; but that she became otherwise (which might be from one of the accidents to which all vessels are subject), whilst in the defendants' employ. It is indeed consistent with these pleas, that the vessel might have performed a voyage for the defendants before this defect occurred; and as it is a general rule that pleas are to be taken most strongly against the party pleading them, inasmuch as it is probable he would state his case as favorably for himself as the facts would permit, we should be warranted in assuming this to be the case. The pleas do not state that there was any delay in making the repairs, or that it was through any default in the plaintiff that the defect had occurred. The question then is, whether, because the plaintiff has undertaken to keep the vessel tight, &c., the defendants have a right to deduct any thing out of the freight they are to pay, in respect of the time which may be taken up in making good such defects as may occur during the period for which the vessel is hired? And we are of opinion they are not. From the accidents to which ships are liable, it was in the ordinary course of things to expect that this ship might want repairs in the course of her voyage; and when the defendants were making their bargain, they should have stipulated to deduct for the time which might be exhausted in making those repairs, if they meant to make that deduction. Without such a stipulation, we think the true construction of the charter-party is, that whilst those repairs are going on, the ship is to be considered as in the defendants' service, and the defendants liable to continue their payments. As these pleas, therefore, do not shew that it was owing to any default in the plaintiff that the defect in the ship occurred, or that there was any delay in repairing it, we are of opinion that no deduction is to be made from the freight on that account; that these pleas therefore are bad, and that the demurrer to them must be allowed.

The next plea upon which a question arises, is pleaded to the second breach (which claims freight beyond the expiration of six calendar months), and this plea is, that the vessel was not in the service or employ of the defendants until the end of fourteen calendar months, but within that time was without any default of the defendants consumed by fire. To this the plaintiff has replied, that the vessel sailed for St Domingo, delivered a cargo there after the end of seven calendar months, and was not burned till afterwards. To this replication there is a demurrer; and the defendants contend that the stipulations in the charter-party which fix the time for paying the freight, make the right to the portions of freight payable at those times depend upon the then safety of the ship; and that the loss of the vessel before any one of those periods destroys the right, except for such freight as was previously payable. That a loss, for instance, after the end of six months, but before the end of ten, would have precluded the plaintiff from claiming more in the whole than four months freight. And that a loss after ten months, and within fourteen, would have confined the plaintiff to six months freight. It is to be remembered, however, that the charter-party stipulates that the defendants should pay a given freight per calendar month, and the times fixed for its actual payment can only be considered as postponing for the defendants' convenience the actual payment of a sum then due to a future period; not as creating a contingency whether it should ever be paid at all. Each month's freight, therefore, was earned, and became completely due at the end of each month; and it was nothing but the actual payment that was postponed. We are, therefore, of opinion that this plea is also bad, and that the demurrer to the plaintiff's replication must be overruled.

The last question arises upon the last breach, which is for the allowance of the extra men: of that allowance two months was to be added to the first payment for freight, and the residue was not to be paid till the ship's discharge or return from her first intended voyage, and in like manner for any other foreign voyage or voyages. The defendants' plea to this breach is, as to the first two months allowance, payment; and as to the residue, that the ship sailed upon a voyage to St. Domingo, and was burnt and lost before her return. The plaintiff has taken issue upon the payment; and as to the residue has replied, that the ship arrived at St. Domingo, and completed that voyage. To this there is a demurrer; and the defendants insist that as the ship never was discharged, and never returned, nothing beyond the first two months allowance became payable. But we are of opinion that the destruction and loss of the vessel was, within the true intent and meaning of this charter-party, a discharge of the vessel from the further prosecution of the adventure and employment in which she was engaged; and that upon that event the residue of extra allowance became payable, as if the discharge had taken place by the act of the defendants themselves; and that the defendants must be understood to have discharged the vessel when they could by no possibility any longer employ her. We are therefore of opinion in favor of the plaintiff upon each of the several points raised by these pleadings.

Judgment for the Plaintiff.

DAVIDSON v. GWYNNE.

IN THE KING'S BENCH, MAY 25, 1810.

[*Reported in* 12 *East*, 381.]

THE plaintiff declared in debt on a charter-party of affreightment, made at London on the 17th October, 1808, between himself as master, and the defendant as freighter of the brig Pomona, then in the river Thames; whereby the master covenanted with the freighter, that the brig being tight, &c., and properly fitted, victualled, and manned for the voyage hereinafter named, should be at the disposal and direction of the freighter, his agents and assigns, for three calendar months certain, and longer if required for the voyage, under the following covenants, viz.: That the master should immediately load at London such goods as the freighter thought fit, and being despatched should immediately (wind and weather permitting,) proceed and join the first convoy that should sail after she should be so loaded from England for Spain and Portugal, or either, and should therewith proceed to any port or ports in Spain and Portugal, or either, as he should be ordered by the said freighter, his agents or assigns, and at any or either of such port or ports as he should be ordered as aforesaid should make a right and true delivery of the whole of the said outward goods, agreeably to bills of lading which should have been signed for the same; and having completed such delivery should load at any port or ports in Spain and Portugal, or either, as he should be directed by the freighter, his agents or assigns, such goods as the said freighter, his agents or assigns, should think fit, and return therewith to London, and there make a right and true delivery of the whole of the homeward goods agreeably to the bills of lading (the act of God, the king's enemies, restraint of princes, fire, and the dangers of the seas, &c., excepted). Also, the master thereby agreed to receive on board the said brig at London two supercargoes to be appointed by the freighter, and to convey them as cabin passengers to Spain or Portugal, or either, and back to London, free of passage-money. In consideration whereof, and of every thing above mentioned, the freighter covenanted that he, his executors, &c., agents or assigns, would employ the said brig under the conditions aforesaid, and would load the outward cargo and discharge the same in Spain and Portugal, or either; and would in Spain and Portugal, or either, load the homeward cargo and discharge the same at London; and would pay to the commander in full for the freight of the said vessel for the voyage aforesaid at the rate of £1 10*s.* per ton per month from the 5th of October, 1808, until the delivery of the homeward cargo at London; part of the freight to be paid before the brig left London, &c., and the remainder on the right and true delivery of the homeward cargo at London. And to the true performance of all and every the foregoing covenants on the part and behalf of the said parties respectively, they bound themselves, their heirs, executors, &c., each to the other in the penal sum of £1000. And by a memorandum at the foot of the charter-party it was agreed, that in case the freighter or his assigns should think proper to remove the brig to any other port than that in which she should have first arrived for the purpose of discharging her cargo, then he should pay all port-charges and pilotage arising therefrom.

The plaintiff then averred that he was ordered by the freighter to proceed with the said brig to Lisbon in Portugal; and thereupon the said brig being tight, &c., and properly fitted, victualled and manned for the said voyage, the plaintiff immediately received on board her at London such goods as the freighter thought fit to load, and being despatched, sailed with convoy (not saying with the first convoy) from England to Lisbon, and there made a right and true delivery of the whole of the outward cargo agreeably to the bills of lading that had been signed for the same; and that the plaintiff, having completed such delivery, afterwards took on board the said brig at Lisbon such goods as the freighter thought fit, and returned therewith direct to London, where he made a right and true delivery of the whole of the homeward cargo, agreeably to the bills of lading signed for the same: and then he averred that the freight amounted at the rate agreed upon by the charter-party to £1050, &c.

The second count was general, for so much money due for freight, &c. A third was for the use and hire of the vessel; and there were other common counts.

The defendant pleaded several pleas to the first count. 1. That after making the charter-party the plaintiff as master took on board the brig at London a cargo loaded by the defendant as freighter, and was therewith despatched and ordered by the freighter immediately to proceed and join the first convoy that should sail from England for Portugal, and to make a delivery of the whole of the said outward cargo, agreeably to bills of lading signed for the same, at Lisbon: and that after the brig was so loaded, the first convoy sailed from England for Portugal, to wit, from Portsmouth to Lisbon, whereof the plaintiff had notice: yet, though neither wind nor weather prevented the same, the plaintiff did not proceed and join such first convoy, but neglected so to do.[1] . . . 4. That though the plaintiff took on board the brig at Lisbon the goods mentioned in the first count, and returned therewith to London, yet the plaintiff did not then make a right and true delivery of the whole of the homeward cargo, agreeably to the bills of lading signed for the same. 5. That though the plaintiff took on board the brig at Lisbon the said goods, &c., and though the goods were shipped on board her in good order and well conditioned, and though the plaintiff thereupon signed bills of lading in respect of the said goods, and thereby undertook to deliver them to the defendant or his assigns in like good order and well conditioned at London (the dangers of the seas only excepted), and though the plaintiff did return with the said goods to London, and delivered the same there to the defendant; yet the plaintiff did not there deliver the goods to the defendant in like good order and well conditioned as the same were in when shipped on

[1] The second and third pleas, and all parts of the case relating to them, are omitted as irrelevant to the subject of this chapter. — ED.

board the said brig, but in a much worse order and condition, and in a damaged and injured state occasioned by the negligence of the plaintiff and his servants in the course of the voyage, whilst the goods were on board the brig, and not by the dangers of the seas, &c.: without this, that the plaintiff did make a right and true delivery of the whole of the said homeward goods, agreeably to the bills of lading which had been signed for the same, in manner and form as alleged in the first count. And to the general counts in the declaration the defendant pleaded *nil debet.*

To the first plea the plaintiff demurred generally. On the fourth plea issue was joined. To the fifth the plaintiff replied, as before, that he did make a right and true delivery of the whole of the said homeward goods, agreeably to the bills of lading signed for the same, in manner and form as alleged in the first count of the declaration: on which issue was joined. And issue was also joined on the *nil debet* pleaded to the common counts.

Taddy, in support of the demurrer to the first plea, contended that the sailing with the first convoy was not a condition precedent to the plaintiff's right to recover freight, as set up in defence by the first plea; the voyage having been performed, and the outward and homeward cargoes delivered to the freighter's orders. He referred to the rule laid down in Boone *v.* Eyre,[1] and recognized in Hall *v.* Cazenove,[2] that where mutual covenants go only to a part of the consideration on both sides, where a breach may be paid for in damages, there the defendant has a remedy on the plaintiff's covenant, and shall not plead it as a condition precedent: and likened this to Constable *v.* Cloberie,[3] cited by Lawrence, J., in Hall *v.* Cazenove, where the covenant being to sail with the next wind upon a certain voyage, the defendant traversed that the ship did sail with the next wind; which was overruled upon demurrer, as immaterial against a demand for freight after the voyage performed. And he also referred to Havelock *v.* Geddes,[4] the last reported case on the subject of a condition precedent in a charter-party, to the same effect. [LORD ELLENBOROUGH, C. J., then said, that the court would hear from the defendant's counsel, whether this case were distinguishable from those cited, where the question had been fully considered.] . . .

Lawes, contra . . . argued from the terms of the contract and the apparent intention of the parties, that the sailing with the first convoy was a condition precedent, and not an independent covenant: it might be an object of the first consequence to the success of the adventure; and the freight was to be regulated by time, and therefore it was material that the voyage should be performed as speedily as required by the contract. [LORD ELLENBOROUGH, C. J. That only goes to the ques-

[1] 1 H. Blac. 273, *n.*; and in Campbell *v.* Jones, 6 Term Rep. 573.
[2] 4 East, 484. [3] Palm. 397. [4] 10 East, 555, 562.

tion of damages; but is there any thing in that which goes to the whole consideration.] The freight is covenanted to be paid in consideration of every thing before mentioned, of which the sailing with the first convoy is one.

LORD ELLENBOROUGH, C. J. It is useless to go over the same subject again, which has been so often discussed of late. The sailing with the first convoy is not a condition precedent: the object of the contract was the performance of the voyage, and here it has been performed. The principle laid down in Boone *v.* Eyre has been recognized in all the subsequent cases, that unless the non-performance alleged in breach of the contract goes to the whole root and consideration of it, the covenant broken is not to be considered as a condition precedent, but as a distinct covenant, for the breach of which the party injured may be compensated in damages. It is useless to repeat all the cases, because we had the subject so fully before us very lately in Ritchie *v.* Atkinson,[1] and in the other cases mentioned. . . .

GROSE, J. The cases of Boone *v.* Eyre and Ritchie *v.* Atkinson, and all the others which have been mentioned, determine the first question, that the sailing with the first convoy was not a condition precedent, but one of several mutual covenants: and if either of the parties broke his covenant, the other might bring his action for it: but the plaintiff's right to freight was not to depend upon that. . . .

LE BLANC and BAYLEY, JJ., agreed in awarding judgment for the plaintiff on the demurrer to the first plea.

On the trial of the issues it appeared that the homeward cargo, consisting of chests of oranges, was in a good condition when shipped at Lisbon; but on the Pomona's arrival at London it was found when unpacked to be much heated and damaged; and this was made out in evidence to have been occasioned by the negligence of the master and crew in not having given it sufficient ventilation during the voyage. The deterioration was from 10*s.* to 20*s.* a chest.

On these facts it was objected that, the homeward cargo having been damaged and in part spoilt while on board by the negligence of the master and crew, the plaintiff had not made a right and true delivery of the whole of the goods as stipulated by the charter-party agreeably to the bills of lading, by which he undertook to deliver the same in like good order and well conditioned as when shipped on board; and therefore that the defendant was entitled to a verdict on that issue. To which it was answered, and Lord Ellenborough, C. J., ruled accordingly, that the allegation of having made a right and true delivery of the cargo was satisfied by the delivery made of the number of chests of fruit shipped on board; and that if the contents of any of them turned out to have been damaged by the negligent stowing or subse-

[1] 10 East, 295.

quent want of care and proper ventilation by the master and crew, the defendant had a cross-action to recover damages; but that it was no answer to an action for the freight. Though his lordship intimated further at the trial, that if there had been any special provision in the bills of lading for the care or against the negligence of the master and crew, the issue on the fourth special plea might have let the defendant into the proof of the negligence; but the issue being general on the fact of a right and true delivery of the goods according to the bills of lading, it was to be taken in a narrow and restrained sense, such as in his own experience it had always received, as meaning a right and true delivery of the entire number of chests or packages shipped on board, as specified in the bills of lading.

The jury having found a verdict for the plaintiff, a rule for a new trial was refused; all the court being satisfied that the right and true delivery of the goods according to the bills of lading was satisfied for the purpose of this action by the delivery of the entire number of chests which had been received by the owners; and that the deteriorated state of their contents, owing to the negligence of the master in not giving them sufficient ventilation, was no answer to this action. BAYLEY, J., added, that if the like good condition of the cargo when delivered as when shipped, were a condition precedent to the right to recover the freight, then if the goods were damaged to the extent only of a farthing, the master would not be entitled to recover any freight; which never could have been the intention of the contracting parties.

CARPENTER, ASSIGNEE OF THOMAS CRESSWELL, A BANKRUPT, v. H. R. CRESSWELL.

IN THE COMMON PLEAS, NOVEMBER 20, 1827.

[*Reported in 4 Bingham, 409.*]

COVENANT. Upon oyer it appeared that by a deed of 28th of October, 1825, between Thomas Cresswell, fish-factor, of the one part, and H. R. Cresswell, fishmonger, of the other, Thomas Cresswell, in consideration of the covenants in the deed contained, assigned to H. R. Cresswell all that branch or portion of the trade of him T. C. carried on at Billingsgate, consisting of purchases and consignments from Scotland, and also his interest in certain salmon fisheries there, and covenanted not to interfere or act in the branch of the business so assigned. H. R. Cresswell, in consideration of the assignment and covenants thereinbefore entered into by Thomas Cresswell, covenanted on his part to pay Thomas Cresswell an annuity of £250 by quarterly payments every year, to abstain from interfering in the branch of trade still carried on by Thomas Cresswell, and to refer differences to arbitration.

Breach, non-payment of £62 10*s.* for the quarter ending May 1, 1827.

Plea, that before the £62 10*s.* became due, Thomas Cresswell interfered, acted in, and intermeddled with the branch of trade assigned by him to the defendant.

Demurrer and joinder.

Taddy, Serjt., in support of the demurrer, was stopped by the court.

Wilde, Serjt., contra. The covenant by Thomas Cresswell not to interfere with the branch of the business he had assigned was a condition precedent to the payment of the annuity by the defendant, and the condition not having been observed, the plaintiff has no right of action. Wherever, as in the present case, a covenant relates to the whole consideration for the agreement between the parties, and not merely to a part of it, such covenant constitutes a condition precedent. Duke of St. Albans *v.* Shore,[1] Campbell *v.* Jones.[2] In Glazebrook *v.* Woodrow[3] Mr. Justice Le Blanc observed, that where one party has had the advantage of all the material parts of an agreement, the other has been permitted to sustain his action for the consideration, although there might not have been a literal performance of other parts. In Boone *v.* Eyre[4] and Fothergill *v.* Walton[5] the covenants on which the plaintiffs sued went only to a part of the consideration of the whole transaction. But in the present case the material part of the agreement, if not the entire consideration on which the defendant has engaged to pay the annuity, is, the undertaking by Thomas Cresswell not to interfere with the branch of business which he had assigned. The conveyance of the Scotch fishery was merely ancillary to that undertaking, and would probably have been worthless without it.

PARK, J. In this case our judgment must be for the plaintiff. Whatever confusion may prevail among the earlier cases on the subject of dependent or independent covenants, the rule seems now to be well understood, as ably and clearly laid down by Mr. Serjt. Williams in his note to Pordage *v.* Cole,[6] namely, "That where a covenant goes only to part of the consideration on both sides, and a breach of such covenant may be paid for in damages, it is an independent covenant, and an action may be maintained for a breach of the covenant [on the part of the defendant], without averring performance in the declaration." In the present case the engagement not to interfere in the Scotch fish business formed only a part of the consideration for the defendant's covenant. Another and most material part was the assignment of the Scotch fishery, and the case falls directly within the principle established by Boone *v.* Eyre.[7] . . .

[1] 1 H. Bl. 270. [2] 6 T. R. 570. [3] 8 T. R. 375. [4] 1 H. Bl. 273.
[5] 2 B. Moore, 630. [6] 1 Wms. Saund. 320 *b*.
[7] The learned judge here stated the cases of Boone *v.* Eyre, Campbell *v.* Jones, and Fothergill *v.* Walton. — ED.

The substantial part of the agreement, in the present instance, is the assignment of the fishery in Scotland; I am therefore of opinion that, according to all the cases, our judgment must be for the plaintiff.

Burrough, J. Upon examining the deed set out on oyer, I think it evident that the parties intended the covenant for payment of the annuity to be an independent covenant. The case of Campbell *v.* Jones is a most important authority, and expressly in point; for there the plaintiff having covenanted to teach the defendant to bleach, and to permit him to bleach during a certain time, in consideration of a certain sum, it was holden that, as the defendant at all events enjoyed the permission to bleach, the teaching to bleach was not a condition precedent to the payment of the money. In that case all the previous authorities were referred to, and among them Kingston *v.* Preston,[1] where the distinction between dependent and independent covenants was so satisfactorily laid down by Lord Mansfield. I am therefore clearly of opinion, that T. Cresswell's covenant not to interfere in the business is an independent covenant.

Gaselee, J. I am of the same opinion: the annuity to be paid by the defendant was in consideration of two things: one, the assignment of the fishery in Scotland; the other, Thomas Cresswell's giving up that branch of the business. Upon the authority of all the cases, therefore, the relinquishment of the business not forming the whole of the consideration for the payment of the annuity, the covenant not to interfere must be esteemed an independent covenant. The Duke of St. Albans *v.* Shore is distinguishable from the present case, and from the others which have been cited; because the vendor of an estate having cut down the timber after he had agreed to sell it with the timber standing, the state of the premises was so entirely changed that the vendee could never have that which he had contracted to buy.

Judgment for the plaintiff.

FRANKLIN *v.* MILLER.

In the King's Bench, January 26, 1836.

[*Reported in* 4 *Adolphus & Ellis*, 599.]

Assumpsit. The first count stated that defendant, being indebted to divers persons, undertook by a certain agreement to pay plaintiff the full amount of all accounts paid for defendant by him, with

[1] Dougl. 690.

the expenses, and further to pay over to plaintiff £40 per quarter of his (defendant's) salary, until the said debts should be fully settled; and that, by the said agreement, plaintiff agreed to advance a sovereign per week, and the rent of £5 5*s*., also Mr. Moxey £5 3*s*. 2*d*., and Mr. Morrison £5 per quarter out of the said £40, which would become due respectively on the first days of January, April, July, and October. And that, in consideration of the premises, and of plaintiff's promise to perform the agreement, defendant promised to perform, &c., on his part. And although plaintiff on, &c., and on divers other days, &c., paid for defendant to divers persons, to wit, &c. (naming them), divers accounts, being debts due and owing from defendant to those persons respectively, and amounting in the whole to a large, &c., to wit, £281, the full amount of which accounts defendant was liable to, and ought to have paid to plaintiff according to the agreement, whereof, &c. (notice to defendant): and although since the making of the agreement, and before the commencement of this suit, divers, to wit, five of the sums of £40 in the agreement mentioned, have become due from defendant to plaintiff according to the agreement, to wit, on October 1st, 1833, and the first days of January, April, July, and October, 1834, and although the debts mentioned in the agreement have not been fully settled, and although defendant hath paid a part, to wit, £160 of the amount of the said accounts so paid as aforesaid, and of the said sums of £40 so due as aforesaid, yet, &c., breach, that defendant hath not paid the residue of the full amount of the said accounts, or of the said sums of £40 which became due as aforesaid, though requested, to wit, on, &c., so to do; and there is now due to plaintiff, &c. The same count also charged a breach of contract by defendant in not paying expenses incurred by plaintiff in settling the accounts paid as aforesaid.

Third plea, as to the first three sums of £40, payment.

Fourth plea, as to the non-payment of two sums of £40, alleged in the declaration to have become due July 1st and October 1st, 1834: that long before the same or either of them became due, to wit, May 1st, 1834, and on divers other days and times afterwards and before the said 1st of July, 1834, there were persons, to wit, &c. (mentioning three persons different from those named in the declaration), the residue of the said persons to whom defendant, at the time of the making of the said agreement, was, and then still continued, indebted in divers sums of money, whereof plaintiff then had notice, and plaintiff could and might then have fully paid or otherwise settled their said debts, had he used due and reasonable care and diligence in that behalf; but plaintiff did not nor would fully pay or settle the same, and carelessly and negligently suffered and permitted the same to be and remain unpaid and unsettled. And defendant further saith that, although he did afterwards, to wit, April 1st, 1834, pay to plaintiff the said sum of £40 to be by defendant paid to plaintiff on that day for the purposes in the said agreement mentioned; yet plaintiff did not nor would, thereout or otherwise, at any time afterwards, although often requested so to do, advance to defendant a sovereign per week, but wholly neglected so to do; and thereupon defendant, within a reasonable time then next following, and before the said last mentioned sums of £40 became due and payable, to wit, May 20th, 1834, rescinded and put an end to and abandoned the said agreement, and gave plaintiff notice thereof, and that defendant should not require plaintiff to perform the same in any thing further on his part and behalf to be performed and fulfilled. Verification.

Replication to the fourth plea, that, before and at the time when defendant paid plaintiff the sum of £40 in that plea alleged to have been so paid, defendant was indebted to plaintiff in a large sum of money, to wit, £50 and more, for and in respect of the said money paid by plaintiff for defendant as in the said first count is mentioned; and that the said last-mentioned sum of £40, at the time when the same was paid by defendant to plaintiff, was of less amount than, and was insufficient to satisfy or discharge, the said money in which defendant was indebted to plaintiff as last aforesaid, and for which money the said agreement in the said first count mentioned was then a security to plaintiff. Verification.

Demurrer to the replication, assigning for causes, that, although the defendant hath in his fourth plea alleged that he paid plaintiff the £40 for the purposes of the agreement, the plaintiff hath not in his replication shewn any excuse for not applying it to those purposes, and hath endeavored to apply it to other purposes and debts which by law he could not do; that the replication does not specifically shew how the £40 was appropriated, nor what was the subject-matter of the debt due from defendant to plaintiff; that the replication is a departure; and that, although defendant in his fourth plea has shewn another breach by plaintiff of the said agreement sufficient to enable defendant to rescind the same, plaintiff hath not by his replication traversed or denied, or confessed and avoided the said breach, and hath admitted it. Joinder in demurrer.

R. V. Richards, in support of the demurrer. The replication admits that the sum of £40 was received, and was by agreement to be appropriated to a particular purpose. It could not be applied to a different one by making a set-off of the demand to which it was so applied. The question then may be, whether the fourth plea is one which would be bad on general demurrer. Now, whether the word 'rescinded' be correctly used in the plea or not, still, where two parties have agreed to do certain acts concurrently, and one seeks to enforce performance by the other, it is a sufficient answer that he himself has not fulfilled his part of the contract. The defendant here was not bound to go on paying the sums of £40 although they were not properly applied. In Withers v. Reynolds,[1] where the defendant agreed to supply the plaintiff with straw at so much per load, to be paid for (as the court construed the agreement) on delivery, it was held that, on the plaintiff's refusal to continue paying on delivery, the defendant might leave off sending straw, and that he was not obliged to go on with the supply and bring a cross-action. The judgments of the court in that case apply to the present. The plaintiff here was to pay a sovereign per week out of the £40 which the defendant was to advance. By ceasing to pay the sovereign, he virtually put an end to the contract. [COLERIDGE, J. Is not there a distinction between a partial and a total non-performance?] In Withers v. Reynolds[1] the plaintiff had only refused to pay for one load of straw; yet the defendant was held to be discharged from his contract.

W. Clarkson, contra. The replication is good. The declaration shews that the payments of £40 by the defendant were to be antecedent to those which the plaintiff was to make, but that the plaintiff had in fact paid a considerable sum, in advance, to certain persons named. Then the plea alleges that before July 1st, 1834, there were persons (naming them) whom the plaintiff might have paid but did not, and that, although the defendant on April 1st, 1834, paid the plaintiff £40, to be applied to the purposes of the agreement, yet the plaintiff did not afterwards advance the sovereign per week. To the new matter so alleged the replication is an answer. It states that, when the £40 was paid on April 1st, 1834, the defendant was indebted to the plaintiff in a large sum for money paid by the plaintiff as stated in the first count, that is, in discharge of the debts there referred to, beyond the amount advanced by the defendant. It does not (as is suggested on the other side) claim to appropriate the £40 to demands of the plaintiff on other accounts than those comprehended in the agreement. The replication here is like the sur-rejoinder in Calvert v. Gordon,[2] which was held good. The plaintiff shews that he has performed his contract as long as he had the means. The fourth plea discloses no act done by him which could warrant the defendant in rescinding the contract. On this point Withers v. Reynolds,[1] and particularly the judgment of Patteson, J., there, is an authority for the plaintiff.

R. V. Richards, in reply. One object of the agreement was, that out of the £40 the plaintiff should be enabled to pay the defendant a sovereign per week. The plaintiff cannot, in his replication, set up a right to retain, inconsistent with the stipulations of his agreement.

LORD DENMAN, C. J. The defendant by his plea says, "true it is, I did not pay the sums claimed, but there were some debts which you might have paid and have not, and you have not paid me the sovereign

[1] 2 B. & Ad. 882. [2] 7 B. & C. 809.

per week; therefore I have rescinded the contract." And this is said when the plaintiff is considerably in advance. It is clear that the defendant had no right to treat the contract as rescinded. That is illustrated by the judgment of Patteson, J., in Withers *v.* Reynolds,[1] where it is said, "If the plaintiff had merely failed to pay for any particular load, that of itself might not have been an excuse to the defendant for delivering no more straw." As therefore the defendant here has not shewn a valid excuse by his plea, it is unnecessary to consider whether or not the replication be bad.

LITTLEDALE, J. With respect to the plea, the plaintiff may say, "assuming that there has been a default made as to my part of the contract, it is only a partial breach, and the defendant's argument would go the length of insisting that if I had in any one week omitted to pay the sovereign, he might put an end to the contract, and deprive me of all the money I have paid in advance: for he states that he has rescinded the agreement altogether." It is a clearly recognized principle that, if there is only a partial failure of performance by one party to a contract, for which there may be a compensation in damages, the contract is not put an end to. In Boone *v.* Eyre,[2] which was an action of covenant on a deed whereby the plaintiff conveyed to the defendant the equity of redemption of a plantation with the stock of negroes upon it, in consideration of an annuity, and covenanted that he had good title and was lawfully possessed of the negroes, and the defendant covenanted that, the plaintiff performing every thing in the deed contained on his part, he would pay the annuity, and the breach alleged was non-payment, the defendant pleaded that the plaintiff was not lawfully possessed of the negroes. On demurrer to the plea, Lord Mansfield said, "The distinction is very clear. Where mutual covenants go to the whole of the consideration on both sides, they are mutual conditions, the one precedent to the other. But where they go only to a part, where a breach may be paid for in damages, there the defendant has a remedy on his covenant, and shall not plead it as a condition precedent. If this plea were to be allowed, any one negro not being the property of the plaintiff would bar the action." So here, it cannot be contended that, if in any one week the sovereign had been unpaid, that default would put an end to a contract made up of several stipulations, some of which have been executed. It is immaterial to consider whether or not the replication be good.

WILLIAMS, J., concurred.

COLERIDGE, J. I think both the replication and the plea bad. The plea is not good, unless one party to a contract like this may treat it as rescinded, if the other fails in the slightest degree to perform his part of it. The rule is that, in rescinding as in making a contract, both

[1] 2 B. & Ad. 882. [2] 1 H. Bl. 273, *n.*

parties must concur. In Withers v. Reynolds[1] each load of straw was to be paid for on delivery. When the plaintiff said that he would not pay for the loads on delivery, that was a total failure; and the plaintiff was no longer bound to deliver. In such a case it may be taken that the party refusing has abandoned the contract. The present case is different; and the plaintiff is entitled to judgment.

Judgment for the plaintiff.

STAVERS v. CURLING AND ANOTHER.

IN THE COMMON PLEAS, NOVEMBER 25, 1836.

[*Reported in 3 Bingham's New Cases,* 355.]

THE declaration stated that by certain sealed articles of agreement between the plaintiff and defendants, dated February 9, 1832, after reciting that the defendants, as owners of the ship Offley, then lying at Gravesend in the river Thames, had fitted out the same with all necessary stores, provisions, casks, and other implements for the prosecuting of a voyage to the southern whale fishery, and had appointed the plaintiff to be master of the said vessel on the terms and conditions thereinafter mentioned, it was witnessed that the plaintiff did thereby covenant, promise, and agree to and with the defendants to take upon himself the command of the said ship, and proceed in her, as soon as she was ready for sea, to the southern whale fishery, and procure a cargo of sperm oil, &c., or as great a proportion thereof as might be under all circumstances within his power to obtain; and having done so, to return with said ship to the port of London, and there at his own costs, together with the crew, discharge and deliver to the defendants whatever cargo the said vessel might have on board; and also to obey such instructions relative to the said vessel and her voyage as he might from time to time receive from the defendants, and be as frugal as possible with the stores and provisions of the said ship, and regularly enter in a book to be provided for the purpose the expenditure and appropriation thereof, and not dispose of any part of them without faithfully accounting with the defendants for the produce thereof, and not on any account or pretence whatsoever to smuggle or trade or permit it directly or indirectly, whereby the said ship or the owners thereof might be prejudicially affected, nor consent or suffer to be committed by his knowledge any illegal act or acts on board said

[1] 2 B. & Ad. 882.

ship, whereby the owners might be injured; and he engaged and bound himself to indemnify, in case of such an event, the said owners from and against any claims, loss, or damage which they might sustain thereby; and he engaged on all occasions to act for the interests of said ship and owners, according to the utmost of his judgment and abilities; and the defendants did thereby covenant, promise, and agree, on the performance of the before-mentioned terms and conditions on the part of the plaintiff, to pay to the plaintiff a sum of money equal to one-twelfth part of the net proceeds of the cargo; and also to allow him one per cent. on said net proceeds. And the plaintiff said that on the first of March, 1832, he took command of said ship, and proceeded in her for the southern whale fishery, and afterwards, to wit, on, &c., and on divers days between that day and the return of the said ship to the port of London as after stated, at and in the said southern whale fishery, procured for the said ship a cargo, to wit, 374 tons of sperm oil, &c., of great value, to wit, of the value of £10,000, being the best cargo that under all the circumstances it was in the power of the plaintiff to obtain; that the plaintiff arrived at the port of London with said ship and cargo on the first of January, 1835, and then and there at his own cost, together with the crew of said ship, discharged and delivered said cargo to the defendants. The plaintiff then averred in detail performance of the remaining covenants on his part, and alleged that said cargo was sold by the defendants for a large sum, to wit, £10,000, and that the net proceeds thereof amounted to a large sum, to wit, £6000, whereby an action had accrued to the plaintiff and against the defendants, to recover one-twelfth of the said net proceeds, and also one per cent. thereof. Yet, &c.

There was also a count for work and labor, money paid, and on an account stated.

The defendants pleaded, secondly, that after the making of said agreement, and on said 9th of February, 1832, the defendants had instructed the plaintiff, among other things, during the said voyage to pay the strictest attention to the preservation of the stores of all kinds belonging to the ship, and to be careful in bringing the ship and remaining stores home in the best possible order for undertaking a future voyage; to abstain cautiously himself, and strictly forbid all on board the said vessel from engaging in any sort of trade whatsoever; studiously to avoid putting in anywhere except when urgent and unavoidable necessity compelled him to do so; to use his best exertions to obtain in the least possible time a full cargo for the said ship; and to endeavor to maintain order and regularity therein, and to promote the health and comfort of all on board the said vessel during the voyage. The defendants then proceeded to allege disobedience to said instructions in detail, specifying in each instance in what the disobedience consisted; and concluded with a verification.

Thirdly. That the plaintiff during the said voyage did trade in such a manner that the owners of said ship were prejudicially affected thereby; concluding to the country. And

Fifthly. So far as related to the non-payment of the said sum of money, in which the defendants were alleged to be indebted to the plaintiff for the price and value of work done by the plaintiff for the defendants at their request, that such work was done and performed under said articles of agreement in the first count mentioned; and that the plaintiff did during the said voyage trade in such a manner that the owners of said ship were prejudicially affected thereby; concluding with a verification.

Demurrer and joinder.[1]

Whately, in support of the demurrer.

The pleas are ill. They disclose grounds for a cross-action, but no bar to the plaintiff's declaration; for the covenants which the plaintiff is alleged to have broken go only to a part of the consideration. Whether a covenant shall be deemed dependent and a condition precedent, or independent and merely the ground of a cross-action, must depend upon the intention of the parties, as it is to be collected from the whole of the instrument, and not from any particular expression. Where a covenant goes only to part of the consideration, and a breach of such covenant may be paid for in damages, it is an independent covenant, and an action may be maintained for a breach on the part of the defendant, without averring performance in the declaration. Boone v. Eyre.[2] According to the construction which the defendants propose to put on this deed, though the voyage should have been performed, and a large profit have been obtained upon the sale of the cargo, yet the plaintiff would not be entitled to any remuneration for three or four years' service, if he should have omitted to obtain a full cargo, minus only a single fish.[3] . . .

R. V. Richards, contra. Taking the whole of the agreement between these parties, as set forth by the declaration, it was their intention that the performance of the covenants into which the plaintiff has entered should be a condition precedent to his having any claim for remuneration; and this appears not only from the nature of the transaction, but from the express words employed. A whaling voyage is protracted through a period of several years; the ship and outfit absorb a heavy capital; and under the best management the risk is con-

[1] The statement of the pleadings has been abbreviated. — ED.

[2] 1 H. Bl. 273, *n.*; 1 Wms. Saund. 320, *n.* 4.

[3] The learned counsel here stated the cases of Davidson *v.* Gwynne, 12 East, 381; and Constable *v.* Cloberie, Palmer, 397; and cited Campbell *v.* Jones, 6 T. R. 573; Ritchie *v.* Atkinson, 10 East, 295; Puller *v.* Staniforth, 11 East, 282; Storer *v.* Gordon, 3 M. & S. 308; Carpenter *v.* Cresswell, 4 Bing. 409; Hunlocke *v.* Blacklowe, 2 Wms. Saund. 156. — ED.

siderable; the owners therefore could never ensure any return, if a rigid performance of his covenants were not a condition precedent to the captain's having any claim for remuneration of his services.

The demurrer admits the truth of the facts alleged in the pleas; according to the construction, therefore, put on this deed for the plaintiff, he is entitled to his pay as captain, notwithstanding he has done every thing to frustrate, instead of forwarding, the object of the voyage; has entered into prohibited trades; has lost his time in deviations; and has disorganized his crew by drunkenness. That never could have been the intention of the parties. No express form of words is necessary to create a condition precedent. It was at all events competent to the parties to annex such a condition to the contract if they wished it; and their language is free from doubt: it is not in consideration, but "on performance of the above-mentioned terms and conditions" that the captain is entitled to his reward. In Carpenter v. Cresswell the defendant's engagement was in consideration of the plaintiff's covenants, not as here on performance of them. And in Rose v. Poulton [1] Taunton, J., says: "There is a well known distinction between cases where the consideration for doing a thing is the doing of some other thing, and where it is merely the covenanting to do such thing." In none of the cases cited, with the exception of Hunlocke v. Blacklowe, where the covenant was negative, has the language been so strong. But they turned each on its peculiar circumstances, and therefore afford no guide for the present, in which the court may collect from the pleading that there has been a breach of the substantial covenants entered into by the plaintiff.[2] . . . In the present case, the material part of the plaintiff's covenant has not been performed, and the plaintiff therefore is not in a condition to sue.

Whately, in reply. This is not a question for a jury as to the materiality of the covenant which has been broken by the plaintiff, but for the court to determine whether that covenant constitutes a condition subsequent or precedent. That depends upon no technical expressions, but on the intention of the parties as deducible from the whole instrument. Hotham v. East India Company,[3] Porter v. Shephard.[4] And it cannot be imagined that the plaintiff would consent to lose all claim to remuneration if he deviated only for an instant from the strict line of his course. In Puller v. Staniforth it was urged that according to the terms of the charter-party, the captain was bound to come direct from Petersburgh to this country, and to bring his outward cargo with him; that his doing so was a condition precedent, without performing which he could not claim the freight or any part of it; and that his going into

[1] 2 B. & Adol. 831.

[2] The learned counsel here stated the case of Glazebrook v. Woodrow, 8 T. R. 366. —ED.

[3] 1 T. R. 645. [4] 6 T. R. 668.

Stockholm and disposing of part of his outward cargo there, was a breach of that condition: but Lord Ellenborough said, "Many circumstances might occur to make it prudent, and for the interest of all concerned, that the captain should touch at some port in his way home, should dispose of the outward cargo, and should get a freight home. Is such a construction then to be put upon the charter-party by implication as to take away from him all power of availing himself of those circumstances? If he were to do it improperly, he would be answerable in damages for whatever injury his misconduct should occasion: so that justice would be done to the freighters, though this were not held a condition precedent; and the holding it to be a condition precedent might, in the case I have just put, be extremely prejudicial to them." In Glazebrook *v.* Woodrow and Rose *v.* Poulton, the covenant was clearly dependent, and fell within the rule laid down in Thorpe *v.* Thorpe.[1] In Davidson *v.* Gwynne, after setting forth the covenants on the part of the master, and the course pointed out for him, the deed proceeded: "In consideration whereof, and of every thing above mentioned," the said freighter covenanted, &c. That amounts to the same thing as the language of the present deed, in which the consideration of the defendants' covenant is alleged to be the performance of the plaintiff's covenant; and yet in Davidson *v.* Gwynne the covenants of the master were held not to be conditions precedent. Hunlocke *v.* Blacklowe is in point. *Cur. adv. vult.*

TINDAL, C. J. The demurrer to the pleas of the defendants raises the question, whether the performance of the covenants entered into by the plaintiff in the articles of agreement on which this action is founded forms a condition precedent to the plaintiff's right to recover on the covenants entered into by the defendants.

The rule has been established by a long series of decisions in modern times, that the question whether covenants are to be held dependent or independent of each other, is to be determined by the intention and meaning of the parties as it appears on the instrument, and by the application of common sense to each particular case; to which intention when once discovered all technical forms of expression must give way. And one of the means of discovering such intention has been laid down with great accuracy by Lord Ellenborough, in the case of Ritchie *v.* Atkinson,[2] to be this, "that where mutual covenants go to the whole of the consideration on both sides, they are mutual conditions, the one precedent to the other; but where the covenants go only to a part, there a remedy lies on the covenant to recover damages for the breach of it, but it is not a condition precedent."

Now, applying that distinction to the consideration of the covenant

[1] 1 Salk. 171.

[2] 10 East, 295.

in question, we think the necessary inference is, that it was not the intention of the contracting parties that any of the covenants entered into by the plaintiff, the captain of the ship, should form a condition precedent to his right to recover on the covenant entered into by the defendants, the ship-owners, for his stipulated remuneration. Thus, for instance, if the covenant to procure a cargo of sperm oil, &c., or as great a proportion thereof as might be under all circumstances within the power of the plaintiff to obtain, be held to be a condition precedent, a very small and trifling deficiency from the best possible cargo, if attributable to any the slightest carelessness on the part of the plaintiff, would occasion the total loss of all his profits of the voyage, whereas if the breach of the covenant were made the subject of an action by the defendants, the compensation to them for such breach would correspond exactly with the extent of their injury. The same observation applies, in a still stronger degree, to the non-performance of the several other covenants set out and relied upon in the second and last pleas, which covenants might be broken, to the letter, with very little damage resulting therefrom to the ship-owner, whilst, on the other hand, by treating them as conditions precedent, a trifling injury to one party would occasion the loss of all the remuneration to the other for long and laborious service.

The parties to such a contract may undoubtedly, if they think proper, agree that the captain's right to recover any remuneration for his services shall be conditional only, and shall depend on his strict performance of the covenants he enters into; and if words are used in the contract so precise, express and strong, that such intention and such intention only, is compatible with the terms employed, however inconsistent it may be with general principles of reasoning, a court can only give effect to such declared intention of the parties. The only question in every particular case is, whether such intention is so declared. In this case it is insisted on the part of the defendants that such must be considered to be the intention; for that the defendants' covenant is entered into with the plaintiff, not simply in consideration of the plaintiff's covenants and agreements, but "on the performance of the before mentioned terms and conditions on the part of the plaintiff," which words it is argued must of necessity shew the intention that the performance by the plaintiff must be a condition precedent, and not rest in covenant merely. And if this were *res integra* the argument would undoubtedly be strong. But in the case of Boone v. Eyre,[1] the leading case on this subject, and in which the distinction before adverted to is first clearly established, the defendant covenanted that, "the plaintiff well and truly performing all and every thing therein contained on his part to be performed," he the defendant would pay the annuity.

[1] 1 H. Bl. 278, *n*.

In that case the performance of the plaintiff's covenant is made the consideration for the defendant's liability according to the strict technical frame of the agreement; but in that case it was held that the obvious intention of the parties was opposed to it, and such intention was allowed to prevail. The case also of Hunlocke v. Blacklowe[1] is strong to shew that courts of justice are more anxious to discover and to be governed by the intention of the parties, than to follow the strict and technical form of words used in the instrument.

We think, therefore, the authorities enable us to give effect in this case to that which appears to us the intention of the parties, namely, that the ship-owners should have their remedy in damages on the covenants entered into by the captain for any loss occasioned by the breach thereof; but that a failure in the full and literal performance of those covenants on the part of the captain should not be set up by the ship-owners as an answer to an action on their own covenants. And we therefore give *Judgment for the plaintiff.*

NEWSON v. SMYTHIES.

IN THE EXCHEQUER, NOVEMBER 15, 1858.

[*Reported in 3 Hurlstone & Norman, 840.*]

DECLARATION. That by indenture made between the plaintiff and the defendant, sealed with the seals of the plaintiff and the defendant, the plaintiff covenanted with the defendant that he the plaintiff would, on the 25th of March, 1857, quit and deliver up to the defendant specified parts of certain farms, and would, on the 29th of September, 1857, quit and deliver up to the defendant the residue of the several farms, and that in the mean time the plaintiff would cultivate the farms upon the four-course system, &c. And further, that upon delivery up of the residue of the several farms on the 29th of September, the plaintiff should surrender and yield up a certain agreement, in the indenture mentioned, to be cancelled; and would surrender and yield up all his unexpired term in the several farms, &c.; and, if the defendant should so require, the plaintiff should and would, at the expense of the defendant, at any time afterwards execute any further act or deed for the more effectual and absolute surrender of the residue of such unexpired term and interest in the said farms. And the defendant did thereby covenant that, if the plaintiff did and should, on the 25th, quit and deliver up to the defendant the parts of the farms mentioned in the

[1] 2 Wms. Saund. 156.

schedule, and did and should, on the 29th of September, quit and deliver up the peaceable possession of the residue of the several farms, and in the mean time cultivate the farms upon the four-course system, &c., and did and should well and truly observe, perform and keep all and singular other the covenants and agreements thereinbefore contained, and on his part to be performed, he the defendant should and would, upon the delivery up of the possession of the residue of the said farms, lands and hereditaments to him upon the 29th day of September, so farmed, cultivated and managed as aforesaid, and on such performance of such other covenants as aforesaid, pay or cause to be paid to the plaintiff for the manure, tillages, hay, clover, &c., usually paid for as between on outgoing and incoming tenant, such sum as the same should be said to be worth by the valuation of two persons, &c. Averment: that, though the plaintiff did quit and deliver up possession of the several farms in the parts, at the time and in the manner in the indenture covenanted, and did perform all other things by the said indenture on his part covenanted to be performed, and although the manure, tillages, hay, clover, &c., upon the said farms when the same were delivered up, as are usually paid for between an outgoing and an incoming tenant, were valued to be worth a large sum of money, &c.; and although the plaintiff had done all things necessary, &c., and a reasonable time had elapsed, &c., yet the defendant had not paid the said sum or any part thereof, &c.

Plea. That the plaintiff did not surrender and yield up the said agreement in the said indenture mentioned as covenanted by the plaintiff.

Demurrer and joinder therein.

Henry Mills, in support of the demurrer. The consideration for the defendant's covenant is not entire and indivisible. The plaintiff's covenant to deliver up the agreement does not go to the whole consideration; therefore, according to the authorities collected in the note to Pordage v. Cole,[1] the non-performance of it does not bar the action.

Hannen, for the defendant. Whether the performance of a covenant by one party constitutes a condition precedent to the right to enforce the performance of a covenant on the part of the other, must in every case depend on the intention of the parties to be collected from the whole instrument. In Stavers v. Curling[2] the defendant covenanted to proceed to a fishery and procure a cargo consisting of sperm oil in as great a proportion as possible, to deliver the cargo in London, to obey orders, to be frugal of provisions, &c., and not to smuggle or trade; and the defendants covenanted, on performance of the before-mentioned conditions on the part of the plaintiff, to pay him a certain proportion of the net proceeds of the cargo. Tindal, C. J., pointed out that if the matter were *res integra* the argument would be strong, that the words "on

[1] 1 Wms. Saund. 319 *h*, 320 *c*.

[2] 3 Bing. N. C. 355.

performance of the before-mentioned terms and condition on the part of the plaintiff," would shew that the intention was to make the performance by the plaintiff a condition precedent. The rule acted on in that case does not apply where the plaintiff covenants to perform a specific act on a particular day, and the defendant's covenant is to do something on the performance of that act. [BRAMWELL, B. It may be that by the word "if" the parties intended to make the performance of the plaintiff's covenant a condition precedent. He referred to Grey *v.* Friar.[1]]

H. Mills, in reply. Unless the covenants are treated as independent the plaintiff may get nothing, because he may fail in the performance of the covenant to give up possession of the agreement by reason of its performance having become impossible. Grimman *v.* Legge.[2]

POLLOCK, C. B. The plaintiff is entitled to our judgment. The decision of this case must turn upon the obvious intention of the parties rather than upon any strict construction of the language used. In Boone *v.* Eyre[3] and Pordage *v.* Cole[4] there was nothing in the language to prevent the acts to be done by the plaintiffs from being treated as conditions precedent. But common sense and justice dictated the decision in those cases. It is a general rule that covenants are to be treated as independent rather than as conditions precedent, especially where some benefit has been derived by the covenantor.

BRAMWELL, B. I am of the same opinion, though not without some doubt. The expressions "if the plaintiff did and should on the 25th quit, &c.; and did and should well and truly observe, perform, and keep all and singular other the covenants and agreements therein before contained," *prima facie* make the covenant of the defendant contingent on the performance of the plaintiff's covenants. I say, with Tindal, C. J., if this matter were *res integra* I should doubt. But Boone *v.* Eyre has established a principle which is fatal to Mr. Hannen's argument. The defendant's covenant appears to be made conditional upon the performance of all the covenants on the part of the plaintiff. But some of them, such as that for further assurance, are not to be performed until after the time for payment. Therefore it is impossible to construe the covenant literally. The reasonable construction is, that the plaintiff is entitled to recover for the manure; and that the breach of his covenant is the subject of a cross-action. I do not say that if possession of the farms had not been delivered up, that the plaintiff could have sued. That is of the substance of the consideration. I had some doubt whether the surrender of this document was not equally so. But there is an independent covenant by the plaintiff to surrender up all his unexhausted term and interest, which has been performed.

[1] 4 H. L. 565.

[2] 8 B. & C. 324.

[3] 1 H. Black. 273, note.

[4] 1 Saund. 319 *h*, 320 c.

WATSON, B. In cases of this kind we must look to the substance and real intention of the parties rather than to any particular expression. It is often difficult to say what covenants are conditions precedent and what are not; and it is well to adhere to the canons laid down by Mr. Serjeant Williams for determining the question. The delivery up of this piece of paper is immaterial, and not of the substance of the consideration.

CHANNELL, B. I think that the delivering up of this document is not of the essence of the consideration; and therefore the covenant to deliver it up is not a condition precedent unless expressly made so. Boone v. Eyre [1] seems to shew that the language of this deed is not sufficient for that purpose. *Judgment for the plaintiff.*

WHITE v. BEETON.

IN THE EXCHEQUER, JUNE 5, 1861.

[*Reported in 7 Hurlstone & Norman, 42.*]

DECLARATION. That an agreement was made between the defendant and the plaintiff in the words following, that is to say: "An agreement made the thirtieth day of June, A. D. 1856, between James Beeton, of, &c., of the one part (meaning the above-named defendant), and William White (meaning the above-named plaintiff), and Wilson Whitley, both of, &c., of the second part; whereby, in consideration of the sum of £8778 14*s.* of lawful English money, to be paid on or before the first day of July, 1860, in the following proportions, that is to say, to Mr. William White (meaning the plaintiff), for cash advanced by him to the Hull Loan and Discount Society, the sum of £698 14*s.*, also the sum of £480, being the value of and in full payment for sixty shares of £8 per share, held by him in his own name; also the sum of £40, being the value of five shares of £8 each now belonging to him, and originally held by Mr. Charles Todd, all in the said Hull Loan and Discount Society; and to Mr. William Whitley the sum of £160, being the value and in full payment for twenty shares of £8 each, held by him in the said society, and to Mr. John Goodburne the sum of £120, being the value of and in full payment for fifteen shares of £8 each, held by him in the said society, with interest at five per cent. per annum in the mean time, to be paid half yearly, &c. In consideration whereof the parties named herein as of the second part to this agreement do hereby covenant and

[1] 1 H. Black. 273, note.

agree, on account of the sums of money before named, that the entire property of and in the said Hull Loan and Discount Society, and all the sums of money now standing in the books to the credit of the said society, and all the interest, profits, and emoluments arising therefrom, and now due or to become due, shall from this day be vested in, and exclusively belong to, and be held by and to the uses of the said James Beeton, his heirs and assigns, and all promissory notes, bonds, or other securities shall be given up to him on the signing of this agreement, and all necessary assistance in the recovering, at law or in equity, of any sums of money owing on the said notes or other securities shall be given by the said William White as heretofore. And for the securing the payment of the sum of £8778 14*s*. as aforesaid, and the interest that may become due thereon, the said James Beeton hereby agrees to deposit with the said William White the title-deeds and conveyances of certain lots of land belonging to the said James Beeton, to remain with him until the said sum of £8778 14*s*. and interest thereon shall be fully paid. And the said William White hereby agrees, that on payment to him and them of the sums of money as above by the said James Beeton, he will deliver up to the said James Beeton or his assigns all the said title-deeds and conveyances of the said lots of land without injury done to them; and he will not in the mean time use them for any purpose but for their care and safe-keeping, according to the true intent and meaning of this agreement. Witness our hands, the day and year first before written, James Beeton, William White, Wilson Whitley." And although before suit, all conditions precedent were fulfilled, and all things had happened, and all times had elapsed necessary to entitle the plaintiff to a performance by the defendant of the said agreement, yet the defendant hath not paid the said principal sums of money by the said agreement to be paid to the plaintiff, or any part thereof, or any interest thereon.

Plea. That the said society was a common partnership, and was not constituted under any act of parliament; that the defendant entered into the contract in the declaration mentioned on the faith and in consideration of all the shares in the said society being vested in him: that neither the plaintiff nor the said William Whitley had any power or authority, nor were they or either of them ever ready or willing or able, to vest in the defendant the said five shares of the said Charles Todd, nor did the same ever vest in the defendant; and the said Charles Todd has wholly repudiated the said contract: that neither the plaintiff nor the said Wilson Whitley had any power or authority, nor were they or either of them ever ready or willing or able, to vest in the defendant the said shares of the said John Goodburne, nor did the said last-mentioned share ever vest in the defendant; and the said John Goodburne has wholly repudiated the said contract: that, with the exception of certain shares held by the defendant, the said shares in the said agreement mentioned were all the shares in the said society, and that the substantial part of the contract in the declaration mentioned was that the defendant should become the owner of all the shares in the said society, so that the defendant might become the sole partner in the said society, and so that he might carry on the business of the said society exclusively on his own account: that by reason of the premises in this plea mentioned all the shares in the said society never vested in the defendant, and neither the plaintiff nor the said Wilson Whitley, nor either of them, ever was ready, willing, or able to vest in the defendant all the shares in the said society, whereby the consideration for the defendant entering into the said contract failed.

Demurrer and joinder therein.

Mellish appeared in support of the demurrer; but the court called on

Quain to support the plea. The defendant entered into the agreement upon the faith and in consideration that all the shares in the society should be vested in him; but as two of the shareholders have refused to vest in him their shares, a substantial part of the consideration has failed. [MARTIN, B. Suppose a person says to another, "I have a debt due to me of £1000, and A. B. has a debt due to him of £500, in consideration of your paying me a sum of money, I will assign to you my debt immediately, and I undertake to assign to you the debt of A. B. at the end of one year;" if he assigns his own debt, and the assignee accepts the assignment, and has the benefit of it, is it any answer to an action for the consideration that he has not procured an assignment of the debt of A. B.?] The doctrine on this subject is founded on the case of Boone *v.* Eyre,[1] where Lord Mansfield said, "The distinction is very clear, where mutual covenants go to the whole of the consideration on both sides, they are mutual conditions, the one precedent to the other. But where they go only to a part, where a breach may be paid for in damages, there the defendant has a remedy on his covenant, and shall not plead it as a condition precedent." The authorities are discussed in 1 Wms. Saund. 319 *b*, note, where rules are laid down for ascertaining when covenants are dependent or independent. Here the defendant's bargain was that he should become the sole proprietor of all the shares in the society, and, as the bringing a cross-action would not effect that object, the breach could not be compensated by damages. In Ritchie *v.* Atkinson,[2] where it was held that the delivery of a complete cargo was not a condition precedent to the right to recover a freight, the sum to be recovered was apportionable. Glaholm *v.* Hays,[3] Croockewit *v.* Fletcher,[4] and Ellen *v.* Topp,[5] established this rule, that although part of the consideration has been

[1] 1 H. Black. 273, *n.*
[2] 10 East, 295.
[3] 2 Man. & G. 257.
[4] 1 H. & N. 893.
[5] 6 Exch. 424.

enjoyed, yet if a substantial part has not been performed the contract cannot be enforced. In Chanter *v.* Leese[1] the consideration for the defendant's contract was the exclusive use of six patents; but one of them being void for want of novelty, it was held that the contract could not be enforced, because he had not the *whole* benefit of that for which he contracted. So, here, the bargain was for an entire thing; viz., *all* the shares in the society. [BRAMWELL, B. In Ellen *v.* Topp there was a continuing duty to be performed: the case may be different where there is only a single act. The defendant might have refused to accept the other shares until he got an undertaking from the two shareholders that they would transfer to him their shares; and he should have returned the promissory notes and other securities, and said, "I will repudiate the contract unless all the shares are transferred to me within a reasonable time;" but instead of doing so he takes a benefit under it. CHANNELL, B. By not repudiating the contract does not the defendant affirm it?] If the defendant appropriated any portion of the property after he became aware that the plaintiff could not perform his undertaking, that should have been replied. [BRAMWELL, B. Suppose promissory notes to the amount of £2000 were handed over to the defendant, and he carried on the business for a long time, trying to negotiate with the two shareholders for the transfer of their shares, is he to pay nothing for the shares he has got?] If the defendant had carried on the business, he would be liable to account to the other partners in a court of equity. The authorities shew that the question, whether covenants are dependent or independent of each other, is to be determined by the intention of the parties as it appears on the instrument. Stavers *v.* Curling[2] and Macintosh *v.* The Midland Counties Railway Company[3] point out the distinction between covenants the breach of which may be compensated by damages, and covenants which go to the whole consideration.

Mellish, contra. There has been no such failure of consideration as to preclude the plaintiff from recovering in this action. The declaration contains a general averment of the occurrence of all things necessary to entitle the plaintiff to a performance by the defendant of his agreement. The plea alleges that the plaintiff has not performed that portion of his contract which relates to the vesting in the defendant the shares of two shareholders. Therefore it must be assumed that every thing has been done by the plaintiff except that which the plea alleges is not done. In this respect the case differs from Chanter *v.* Leese, because there the declaration contained no averment of performance of any condition precedent. This case is also unlike Ellen *v.* Topp, where there was to be a continual performance of the whole

[1] 4 M. & W. 295; in error, 5 M. & W. 698.
[2] 3 Bing. N. C. 355.
[3] 14 M. & W. 548.

agreement on both sides; so that when one party ceased to perform his part, the other was at liberty to do so. The cases are reviewed, and the rule laid down in Boone *v.* Eyre [1] is thus explained, in 1 Wms. Saund. 320 *d*, note: "Hence it appears that the reason of the decision in these and other similar cases, besides the inequality of the damages, seems to be that where a person has received a part of the consideration for which he entered into the agreement, it would be unjust that, because he has not had the whole, he should therefore be permitted to enjoy that part without either paying or doing any thing for it. Therefore the law obliges him to perform the agreement on his part, and leaves him to his remedy to recover any damage he may have sustained in not having received the whole consideration." Campbell *v.* Jones [2] was decided on that principle. Ritchie *v.* Atkinson [3] is an express authority that the transfer of all the shares was not a condition precedent to the plaintiff's right to payment for his shares. The plaintiff cannot, at law or in equity, recover back that which the defendant has received; and the defendant ought not to have taken any benefit under the agreement without first ascertaining that the plaintiff was in a position to transfer to him all the shares. The defendant, by accepting a part performance of the contract, has precluded himself from insisting upon the performance of the remainder as a condition precedent to the plaintiff's right to recover.

POLLOCK, C. B. I am of opinion that the plaintiff is entitled to judgment. The agreement is set out *in hæc verba*, and it appears to be made between the defendant of the one part, and the plaintiff and W. Whitley of the second part. The agreement then stipulates in substance that all the shareholders in a loan society shall give up their shares to the defendant at certain prices. He is to pay to the plaintiff a certain sum, to pay to Whitley another sum, and to pay to other persons, who do not appear to have signed the agreement, other sums. I can see nothing to prevent the fact that he had agreed with the other shareholders, and then came to the plaintiff and Whitley and said, "I have bargained with the other parties; if you will sign this agreement, you need not trouble yourselves about them;" whereupon the plaintiff and Whitley agree to give up their shares upon payment to each of them of a certain sum. After a lapse of more than four years the plaintiff wants to be paid, and then the defendant says: "I have not got the other shareholders to agree, and cannot get the whole of the shares in the society; therefore I am not in the position in which I ought to be, because I entered into the agreement upon the faith that I was to have the whole." It may be his misfortune or his fault that he has failed to carry out the arrangement, but that cannot affect the plaintiff's rights. It appears to me, therefore, that this case

[1] 1 H. Black. 273, *n.* [2] 6 T. R. 570. [3] 10 East, 295.

does not fall within the rule relied upon by Mr. Quain, where the parties have agreed that the performance of certain things shall be a condition precedent. It is clear that the defendant derived considerable benefit from the agreement, for all the property belonging to the society was vested in him.

BRAMWELL, B. I am of the same opinion. I think Lord Kenyon's remark in Campbell *v.* Jones [1] is perfectly correct, viz., that "whether these kinds of covenants be or be not independent of each other must certainly depend on the good sense of the case," except where the parties, by express agreement, have determined that something shall be a condition precedent. In the common case of building a house, the person who employs the builder says, "the money shall be paid when the house is built;" and if it is not built, the money is not payable because the contract has not been performed. But where there is no express stipulation making the performance of some act a condition precedent, Lord Kenyon's observation applies.

The question then is, What is the good sense of the case which we have now to decide? I cannot help thinking that the performance of an act may be at one time a condition precedent and not at another. For instance, if I bargain for the purchase of ten horses for a certain sum of money, and the seller delivers only nine, I may say to him, "I will not accept them; my bargain was for ten." But if instead of so doing I take the nine horses and use them, that which was at one time a condition precedent, by my own conduct has become no condition precedent. Therefore the delivery of ten horses was a condition precedent at one time and not at another. In the case of Ritchie *v.* Atkinson [2] the defendant might have said to the plaintiff: "You have not performed your condition precedent to sail on a particular day, and we will not load;" but, having loaded, they could not say, "the freight shall not be paid because it was a condition precedent that you should sail on a particular day." So, in this case, the defendant might have said to the plaintiff and Whitley, "I will not take from you any assignment of your shares until I am sure that you have the authority of the two other shareholders to vest in me their shares, so that I shall get the full benefit of the contract." However, he did not do so, but took all the property, credits, and securities of the society; for we must assume that the allegations in the declaration not controverted by the plea are the true facts.

Then, is it a condition precedent to the performance of his contract that the shares of the two refractory shareholders should be vested in him? We must look at the good sense of the matter, and I think that in cases of this kind there may be a part performance where there is no condition precedent. Suppose, for instance, the guardians of a

[1] 6 T. R. 570. [2] 10 East, 295.

union workhouse contracted with a baker to supply one hundred loaves every day for three months, and he supplied them, with one exception, when he delivered ninety-nine only, it would be preposterous to say that he is not entitled to be paid the contract price. Again, suppose the baker delivered the hundred loaves on one day only, is he entitled to be paid the contract price? It seems to me that would be equally unjust, and that the guardians, who had the hundred loaves for one day only, might reasonably complain that a new contract should be forced upon them; and as to retaining the loaves they might say, "We cannot help it, for they are consumed." Therefore it seems to me that there may be cases of partial performance in which the party would not be entitled to the contract price, and there may be other cases of partial performance in which he would be entitled to the contract price. Then where is the line to be drawn? If there is a substantial performance of the contract, the price must be paid, and the remedy is by a cross-action. . If one loaf only was missing out of three thousand which ought to have been delivered, there would be a substantial performance of the contract, but upon what deficiency there would cease to be a substantial performance is another question. Applying that reasoning, has there been in this case such a substantial performance of the contract that the plaintiff is entitled to the price and the defendant is driven to his cross-action? I am not sure that, upon demurrer and with the materials before us, that question can be correctly determined; but I think the answer is that the defendant has undertaken to make a good plea and has failed, and that it appears by the declaration that enough has been done by the plaintiff to entitle him to the contract price. I put it on this ground: the promissory notes, bonds, and other securities of the society are to be handed over to the defendant immediately on signing the agreement; and if he wanted guaranties that the shares of the two refractory shareholders should vest in him, he ought not to have signed an agreement whereby he was bound at once to take the assets with the securities of the society. Inasmuch as one act which the plaintiff had to do was to be done at one time, and another act, namely, the getting the assent of the two shareholders to vest their shares in the defendant, was to be done at a future time, there is good reason for supposing that the performance of the latter act is not a condition precedent. It may be that the defendant would have been at liberty, after the lapse of a reasonable time for procuring the assent of the two shareholders, to have returned to the plaintiff the property and securities received from him, and to have reinstated him so far as practicable; and then to have said, "You have not performed your contract, and you were bound to do so within a reasonable time; although I was obliged to take the property and securities at the time the agreement was signed, I now return them to you, and rescind the contract, as you have failed to perform the whole of your undertaking."

In whatever way the case is regarded, it seems to me that the plea is defective. It ought at least to have stated that a reasonable time had elapsed before the commencement of this suit for the plaintiff to get the consent of the two shareholders, and that he had failed; that in a reasonable time afterwards the defendant returned what he had received and rescinded the agreement. If a good plea could be made (and I doubt whether it could at law, because the plaintiff was to do one act at one time and another act at another time), it could only be done in the way I have stated. Further, that the substantial part of the contract could not be performed without the consent of the two shareholders to the vesting of their shares in the defendant, must be by reason of the property, securities, and shares delivered to the defendant being of no sensible value as compared with the vesting in him of those shares, but the plea fails to state that.

Upon the whole, therefore, I come to this conclusion: First, that inasmuch as the plaintiff was to deliver the securities to the defendant at one time, and at another time to get the consent of the two shareholders to the vesting of their shares in the defendant, the performance of the latter act is not a condition precedent to the plaintiff's right to recover in this action; but the non-performance of that act is the subject of a cross-action. Secondly, assuming that the performance of that act was a condition precedent, it was only so in the sense I have already described, where the party must insist on his right to the performance of that part of the contract before he accepts, or, having accepted, retains the benefit of the other part. Thirdly, if the performance of the act is to be treated as a condition precedent on account of the comparative worthlessness of that part of the contract which the plaintiff has performed, the defendant should have made that apparent on his plea. Therefore, upon all the three grounds on which it was suggested that the vesting of these shares in the defendant was a condition precedent, Mr. Quain has failed, that is to say, he has failed to shew that the performance of the act was in any sense a condition precedent; or, assuming it was, he has failed to shew that the defendant availed himself of his right to its performance, and, within a reasonable time, returned what he had received; and he has also failed to shew any condition precedent by alleging the comparative worthlessness of that part of the contract which the plaintiff did perform. For these reasons I think that the plaintiff is entitled to judgment. My brother Martin, who has left the court, requested me to state that he is of the same opinion.

Channell, B. I am also of opinion that the plaintiff is entitled to judgment. The agreement is also set out in terms in the declaration, and the plaintiff seeks to recover his proportion of the money payable under that agreement. No objection has been made to the declaration, and the question is, whether it is answered by the plea. The defendant relies upon this: that the plaintiff has not done any act by which he has vested in the defendant the shares of two of the shareholders in the society, and that they have repudiated the contract. Then, does that afford any answer to the declaration? Upon these pleadings it must be assumed that all the stipulations of the contract required to be performed before the time arrived for payment of the money to the plaintiff, have been performed, with the exception of the two particulars I have mentioned. The question then is, whether the defendant is liable to pay to the plaintiff these sums of money, which are the stipulated proportions which he was to receive, or whether the defendant can say that there has been an entire failure of the contract so as to preclude the plaintiff from recovering them. I am of opinion that he cannot, and that the vesting in the defendant the shares of the two shareholders who repudiated the contract, was not a condition precedent to the plaintiff's right to recover. I agree that in a certain sense it might have been, — the defendant might, if he had thought of it, have stood aloof from any acquiescence in a part performance of the contract by the plaintiff. I agree that the performance of certain stipulations might not give the plaintiff a right to recover this money when the rest have not been performed. But in this case there has been, not a mere partial performance by the plaintiff, but a partial performance which has been accepted by the defendant, and of which he has had the benefit: for on these pleadings we must assume that all the promissory notes, bonds, and other securities were delivered up to the defendant on signing the agreement, and that all necessary assistance has been rendered to him for the recovery, at law or in equity, of any moneys owing on the notes or other securities. It seems to me that the defendant should either have repudiated the contract before this action was brought, and have returned all that he obtained by it, or he should have averred in his plea that a reasonable time had not elapsed so as to enable him to see whether the plaintiff would perform the rest of the contract. For want of that averment, I think that the plea is bad.

It seems to me that the case falls within the principle of the decisions in Boone *v.* Eyre,[1] Ritchie *v.* Atkinson,[2] and Campbell *v.* Jones;[3] and is distinguishable from the cases of Chanter *v.* Leese[4] and Ellen *v.* Topp,[5] on the ground that it cannot be said that the plaintiff was to continue to do something, which was to be the consideration for the performance by the defendant of his part of the contract.

Judgment for the plaintiff.

[1] 1 H. Black. 273, *n.* [2] 10 East, 295. [3] 6 T. R. 570.
[4] 4 M. & W. 295; in error, 5 M. & W. 698. [5] 6 Exch. 424.

PUST *v.* DOWIE.

IN THE QUEEN'S BENCH, APRIL 28, 1863.

[*Reported in* 32 *Law Journal Reports, Queen's Bench,* 179.]

IN THE EXCHEQUER CHAMBER, FEBRUARY 4, 1865.

[*Reported in* 34 *Law Journal Reports, Queen's Bench,* 127.]

DECLARATION, setting out the following charter-party made between the plaintiff and the defendant: —

"Memorandum for charter, Liverpool, 30th of July, 1862. It is this day agreed between Captain Pust, of the good ship or vessel called the Der West, guaranteed 577 tons English, 3–3 *veritas*, whereof he is master, of the one part, and James Dowie, Esq., freighter or charterer of the said vessel, of the other part, witnesseth, that it is agreed that (sufficient room for the cables, ship's stores, provisions, water, captain, officers, and crew, throughout this charter-party being excepted, reserving, however, such room only for that purpose as the owners would, were the ship to be loaded for their exclusive benefit), the said vessel shall immediately be made ready, and receive and take on board from the said charterer (who is to have the full reach of the vessel's hold from bulkhead to bulkhead), a full and complete cargo of lawful merchandise, specie, gunpowder, acid on deck, the short number of steerage passengers, if necessary, the owners employing sufficient hands for that purpose; and thereupon, on being despatched, shall proceed to Sydney, N. S. W., and there deliver the said cargo in the usual and customary manner, agreeably to bills of lading, and so end the voyage; in consideration whereof the said affreighter shall deliver alongside the cargo to be laded on board the said vessel, and shall receive or cause the same to be received at her port of discharge in the usual and customary manner, and shall and will pay for the use and hire of the said vessel, in respect of the said voyage, the sum of £1550 in full, on condition of her taking a cargo of not less than 1000 tons of weight and measurement, payment to be made as follows, viz., the captain to receive the freight payable abroad, as per bills of lading, or an order handed over to him by the charterer at the current rate of exchange, and the balance to be paid in cash on sailing, less three months' interest; and the said charterer shall be allowed for the purpose of loading the said vessel forty-five running days (Sundays excepted throughout this charter-party), if not sooner despatched, to be computed from the arrival of the vessel at a proper place of loading in the Wapping or Prince's Dock; if she loads in Wapping, days not to commence before 8th of

August, having a clear hold, and being in readiness to load, and notice thereof being given in writing to the said charterer. . . . And that such goods only as the charterer may direct shall be received on board the said vessel, for which the mate shall give a receipt and measure when tendered alongside, as well as for weight of coals when weighed into the vessel; and no goods to be received in the cabin or any part of the vessel without the consent of the charterer. That the master shall at the charterer's request sign bills of lading for any rate of freight that may be filled in and made payable in any manner the charterer may choose, without prejudice to this charter, and that he shall attend at the broker's office at least once each day after the loading shall commence, for the purpose of signing such bills of lading. That the vessel shall be consigned to the charterer's agents at her port of discharge, the owners paying the outstanding compensation or freight payable abroad as per manifest. . . . The captain to have an absolute lien and charge for freight on the cargo, and to have no recourse on the charterer for any freight due abroad for bills of lading if not paid," &c.

The declaration then alleged that all things necessary to make the said charter-party a complete and binding agreement between the plaintiff and the defendant happened and were fulfilled; and further, that all conditions were performed, and all things happened, and all times elapsed necessary to entitle the plaintiff to maintain this action for the several breaches of contract hereinafter mentioned. Yet the defendant made default in loading the said ship with cargo as agreed, and did not pay the plaintiff the balance of the sum of £1550 in the said charter-party mentioned over and above the freight payable abroad as per bills of lading, and which in the whole amounted to a sum less than the said sum of £1550.

Third plea, as to so much of the declaration as relates to the non-payment of the balance of the said sum of £1550, that the vessel did not nor could take a cargo of not less than 1000 tons of weight and measurement pursuant to the said condition; but, on the contrary, could and did only take a cargo of very much less than 1000 tons of weight.

Demurrer and joinder.

Kemplay, for the plaintiff, in support of the demurrer. The agreement that the charterer will "pay £1550 in full, on condition of the ship taking a cargo of not less than 1000 tons," does not make the ship being of the burthen of 1000 tons a condition precedent. The promise is in consideration of her taking a full and complete cargo. [CROMPTON, J. It is a limitation on the promise to pay £1550.] Possibly, leaving the defendant to his cross-action. [CROMPTON, J. If it is a stipulation to reduce a proportionate part of the price if the ship cannot carry 1000 tons, it would go in reduction of damages.] There is a general allegation in the declaration of all the conditions precedent, &c., having happened; and the plea, therefore, is no answer. Even assuming that originally the burthen of 1000 tons was a condition precedent, yet as the defendant has had the benefit of a substantial part of the consideration, he cannot now avail himself of this stipulation as a condition precedent. [He cited Behn *v.* Burness,[1] Graves *v.* Legg,[2] notes to Pordage *v.* Cole,[3] notes to Cutter *v.* Powell,[4] and Stavers *v.* Curling.[5]]

No counsel appeared for the defendant.

Cockburn, C. J. I am of opinion that the plaintiff is entitled to judgment. If this clause in question is to be read as a stipulation only, then it gives the defendant the right merely to bring a cross-action for the plaintiff's non-compliance with it, or to a reduction of damages. But even if this were originally a condition precedent, still, under the circumstances of the case, the principle pointed out by Parke, B., in delivering the judgment of the court in Graves *v.* Legg would apply; and the defendant, having had the benefit of part of the consideration, cannot now be allowed to take advantage of the non-performance of the condition precedent, and to say that because the condition has not been performed he will pay nothing. The only way that justice can be done is, by holding the plaintiff entitled to maintain this action, leaving the defendant to one of two remedies, either by giving the failure of the full tonnage in reduction of damages, or by a cross-action. The vessel sailed, and has been used by the defendant, and he has had the full advantage of what she could carry, although the cargo carried was not up to the tonnage stipulated for; and it would be strange if the defendant, having had the use of the vessel up to the extent of her capability, could be compelled to pay nothing, simply because she did not come up to the stipulated amount of tonnage. The plea, therefore, which relies on this want of tonnage as a defence to the whole demand is bad, and judgment on the demurrer must be for the plaintiff.

Crompton, J. I am of opinion that the ship being of the tonnage named, was not a condition precedent to the defendant being called upon to pay any thing. I cannot think that if it was a condition precedent at all, it could have been intended as a condition precedent to any payment by the defendant in case the ship sailed. Now, the defendant has pleaded this (though in form to the balance, which is all that is claimed), not as a condition precedent to the payment of such balance, but as a condition precedent to any liability on the part of the defendant. It may possibly be that the use of the words "in full" may have some bearing on the construction of the contract. But without reference to this, I am inclined to think the clause was only a stipulation. There is

[1] 8 Law Times, (N. S.) 207; 32 Law J. Rep. (N. S.) Q. B. 204.
[2] 9 Exch. Rep. 709; S. C. 23 Law J. Rep. (N. S.) Exch. 228.
[3] 1 Wms. Saund. 320 *b*.
[4] 2 Smith's Lead. Cas. 1.
[5] 3 Bing. N. C. 355; S. C. 6 Law J. Rep. (N. S.) C. P. 41.

a great difference between a stipulation, warranty, and condition precedent; and the use of the word "warranty" has created some confusion. A warranty in insurance cases no doubt has the effect of a condition precedent. But the present is more like a warranty in horse cases. The plaintiff, however, pleads the failure of tonnage as a ground against the plaintiff's being entitled to recover any thing; so pleaded it is bad, though it might afford a good ground in reduction of damages. I am clearly, however, of opinion that, in the events that have happened, and looking at what must be taken to have been the intention of the parties, the defendant is not entitled to plead this as an answer to the action; and that, therefore, there must be judgment for the plaintiff.

BLACKBURN, J. I am of the same opinion. The first thing is to see what intention the parties express by the words they have used, and what the contract imports on the face of it. They say that the ship is to "take on board from the charterer a full and complete cargo," and for that the charterer is to "pay the sum of £1550 in full, on condition of her taking a cargo of not less than 1000 tons of weight and measurement;" and it is not easy to say what is meant by these latter words, unless they import a condition in some sense; and if, when the matter was still executory, the charterer had refused to put any goods on board, on the ground that the vessel was not of the capacity for which he had stipulated, I will not say that he might not have been justified in repudiating the contract altogether; and in that case the condition would have been a condition precedent in the full sense. In the recent case of Behn *v.* Burness, in the Exchequer Chamber, the law is stated, on the whole, rather favorably to conditions generally; adopting, however, the distinction put by Parke, B., in Graves *v.* Legg, Williams, J., in delivering the judgment of the Exchequer Chamber, says, "With respect to statements in a contract descriptive of the subject-matter of it, or of some material incident thereof, the true doctrine established by principle as well as authority, appears to be, generally speaking, that if such descriptive statement was intended to be a substantive part of the contract, it is to be regarded as a warranty, that is to say, a condition, on the failure or non-performance of which the other party may, if he is so minded, repudiate the contract *in toto*, and so be relieved from performing his part of it, provided it has not been partially executed in his favor. If indeed he has received the whole or any substantial part of the consideration for the promise on his part, the warranty loses the character of a condition, or to speak more properly perhaps, ceases to be available as a condition, and becomes a warranty in the narrower sense of the word, namely, a stipulation by way of agreement, for the breach of which a compensation must be sought in damages." No doubt that principle is adopted from the judgment of Lord Wensleydale, in Graves *v.* Legg, and this distinction will explain many of the cases in which, although there appears to have been a condition precedent not performed, a party having received part of the consideration has been driven to his cross-action. Now is not this a case in which a substantial part of the consideration has been received? And to say that the failure of a single ton (which would be enough to support the plea) is to prevent the defendant from being compelled to pay any thing at all, would be deciding contrary to the exception put in the case of Behn *v.* Burness.

MELLOR, J. I am of the same opinion. The failure of the ship in point of tonnage afforded no defence to the action. It must have been the intention of the parties that this should be or amount to a stipulation as to tonnage, so as to regulate the amount to be paid, and to no more. *Judgment for the plaintiff.*

From the foregoing judgment the defendant appealed to the Exchequer Chamber.

Baylis, for the appellant, the defendant below (*E. James* with him).[1] . . . By the terms of the charter-party no part of the balance of the freight was payable, unless the vessel could take 1000 tons. The words "on condition" in the charter-party import a condition precedent on their fair meaning. The court will give effect to the plain words of any contract importing a condition precedent. Stadhard *v.* Lee,[2] Tidey *v.* Mollett,[3] Behn *v.* Burness,[4] and Graves *v.* Legg.[5] The plaintiff, therefore, cannot recover on the charter-party at all. He may sue indeed on a *quantum meruit* for freight, having carried the goods; but in that action he would be met by the fact that the amount that the defendant would have to pay for freight, according to the rate per ton in the charter-party, is less than the sum actually paid by the defendant. The court below, in their decision on the demurrer, rely on the ruling in Behn *v.* Burness,[4] that when a party receives a partial benefit, a condition precedent loses that character and becomes a warranty. That principle does not apply to this case, for no part of the benefit had been derived by the defendant when the goods had been put on board the vessel.

Mellish (*Kemplay* with him), for the plaintiff, was not called upon.

ERLE, C. J. . . . The third plea states that the vessel did not nor could take a cargo of not less than 1000 tons of weight and measurement. Even if we were to construe the words as a condition precedent, the case falls within the principle laid down in Behn *v.* Burness,[4] that

1 Only so much of the case on appeal is given as relates to the demurrer to the third plea. — ED.

2 3 B. & S. 371; s. c. 32 Law J. Rep. (N. S.) Q. B. 75.

3 33 Law J. Rep. (N. S.) C. P. 235; s. c. 16 Com. B. Rep. (N. S.) 398.

4 3 B. & S. 751; s. c. 32 Law J. Rep. (N. S.) Q. B. 204.

5 9 Exch. Rep. 709; s. c. 23 Law J. Rep. (N. S.) Exch. 228.

where a part of the benefit of the contract has been received by the party, he cannot reject it *in toto.* Here the ship has been placed by the ship-owner at the disposal of the defendant, and loaded by the latter. Though the breach of a condition precedent might have given the defendant a right originally to repudiate the contract, it cannot now justify him in wholly refusing to pay any part of the freight. But he may have the benefit of the breach of contract, if any, in reduction of the amount claimed.

For these reasons, and also on the grounds stated by the court below, in which we fully concur, we are of opinion that the judgment of the court below ought to be affirmed.

The other judges concurred. *Judgment affirmed.*

SECTION VII.

Waiver of Performance of Conditions, and Effect thereof.

SIR ANTHONY MAYNE'S CASE.

IN THE QUEEN'S BENCH, EASTER TERM, 1596.

[*Reported in 5 Reports,* 20 *b.*]

THE case in effect was, that Sir Anthony Mayne did lease certain land to Scott for twenty-one years by indenture, and covenanted that at any time during the life of Scott, upon surrender of his lease, Sir Anthony, &c., would make a new lease during the residue of the years, and bound himself to perform the covenants, &c. And now in debt on the said obligation by Scott against Sir Anthony, he pleaded that Scott did not surrender, &c. To which Scott replied, and said, that after the said lease Sir Anthony had accepted a fine *sur conusans de droit come ceo,* &c., and by the same fine granted and rendered the land to the conusee for eighty years: upon which the defendant did demur in law. And it was adjudged for the plaintiff. And in this case three points were resolved:—

1. That Sir Anthony Mayne had broken his covenant without any surrender made; for, by the said fine levied by him for eighty years, he had disabled himself either to take a surrender or to make a new lease; and the law will not enforce any one to do a thing which will be vain and fruitless; *lex neminem cogit ad vana seu inutilia peragenda:* but it would be vain to compel him to make a surrender to him who cannot take it; and although the lessee in this case by the words of

the indenture ought to do the first act, *scil.* to make the surrender, yet when the lessor hath disabled himself, not only to take the surrender, but also to make a new lease according to the covenant, for this cause the lessor's covenant is broken without any surrender made. *Vide* 32 E. 3, Barre 264, and 21 E. 4, 55*a*. If you are bound to enfeoff me of the manor of D. before such a feast, if you make a feoffment of the said manor to another before the said feast, you have forfeited your obligation, although you repurchase the land again before the feast, because you were once disabled to make the feoffment. And therewith agreeth Temp. E. 1, Covenant 29. A man leased a manor for years, and the lessee covenanted to keep the houses of the manor and as much as was in the manor in as good plight as he found them; during the term the lessee committed waste in the houses, and in cutting of oaks; the lessor brought an action of covenant before the end of the term for the oaks, because for them it was impossible that the covenant should be performed; otherwise it is of the houses; and therewith agree F. N. B. 145 K, and 13 E. 3, Tit. Covenant 2.

2. It was resolved, if a man seised of lands in fee covenants to enfeoff J. S. of them upon request, and afterwards he makes a feoffment in fee of the said lands; now in this case J. S. shall have an action of covenant without request. And that in effect is all one with the principal case.

3. It was resolved that, in the case at bar, if the said term of eighty years were but an interest of a future term, so that Scott notwithstanding that might make the surrender, yet in such case Scott should have an action of covenant without making any surrender; for true it is that he may surrender; but also true it is that Sir Anthony after such surrender cannot make the new lease, which was the effect that the surrender should produce; and therefore inasmuch as the lessor hath disabled himself to make a new lease, which is the effect and end of the surrender, and that which he ought to do on his part, the lessee shall not be enforced to make the surrender, which is the first thing to be done on his part, for by the surrender he would lose his old term without a possibility of having the new according to the lessor's covenant. And therewith agreeth 14 H. 4, 19 *a*. J., parson of the church of G., was bound in an obligation of £100 to the prior of E.; the condition was that if the parson resign his church within certain time to the prior for a certain pension as they could agree, that then the obligation should be void; and afterwards and within the time the prior and parson agreed of a pension of £5, yet the parson did refuse to resign. And the opinion of the whole court was that, although they had agreed of the pension, yet the parson is not bound to resign until he be sure of the pension, and that he cannot be without deed. And

therefore in such case the parson is not obliged to resign until the prior hath tendered him a deed of the said pension, by which he might be sure of it.[1]

SHALES v. SEIGNORET.

IN THE KING'S BENCH, EASTER TERM, 1699.

[*Reported in* 1 *Lord Raymond*, 440.]

COVENANT upon articles of agreement. The plaintiff declares that it was covenanted and agreed between him and the defendant that he, in consideration of twenty guineas by the defendant to him then paid, should transfer to the defendant before or upon the 19th of November, 1695, £1000 of bank stock; and that the defendant covenanted with the plaintiff to accept it upon notice of three days, and to pay to the plaintiff for it £940; and then the plaintiff avers that no bank stock is transferable by law but in the office of the bank of England, in the presence of both the parties; and that he gave three days' notice to the defendant that he would transfer to him the bank stock in the office of the bank the 19th of November; and that he attended there the whole day to have transferred it; but that the defendant did not come to accept it; for which he brings this action for the £940, &c. The defendant after oyer of the articles pleads that the plaintiff nor none of his assigns had any interest in any bank stock upon the 18th of November, &c. The plaintiff demurs. And the whole court was of opinion that the plea was ill; because, though the plaintiff had not any bank stock upon the 18th of November, yet if he had it the 19th he might have performed the contract within the time; for the covenant was not that he should transfer any particular £1000 of bank stock which he had at the time of the covenant, but any £1000 of stock. But then the whole court held: 1. That this action will not lie for the plaintiff in this case, because it appears that the plaintiff has not transferred; and without transfer to the defendant, the defendant is not bound to pay the money, for the money was to be paid upon the transfer; and therefore no transfer, no money. Co. Lit. 304;[2] Dyer, 371; 2 Mod.

[1] "If a man binds himself to do certain acts which he afterwards renders himself unable to perform, he thereby dispenses with the performance of conditions precedent to the act which he has so rendered himself unable to perform." Per Maule, J., Sands *v.* Clarke, 8 C. B. 751, 762, citing Mayne's case, *supra;* and see Newcomb *v.* Brackett, 16 Mass. 161. — ED.

[2] "If a man plead performance of covenants, and the plaintiff reply that he did not such an act according to his covenant, the defendant saith that he offered to do it, and the plaintiff refused it; this is a departure, because the matter is not pursuant; for it is one thing to do a thing, and another to offer to do it, and the other refused to do it; therefore that should have been pleaded in the former plea." Co. Litt. 304. — ED.

266, Otway *v.* Holdips. But the matter in the declaration might have been a good excuse for the plaintiff, if the defendant had sued him for not transferring the bank stock; or the plaintiff might have assigned his breach in the non-acceptance of the stock by the defendant. 2. The court held that it did not appear to the court but that the bank stock was transferable at another place than at the office of the bank; for though the act says that no transfer shall be but as the king shall appoint, and the king has appointed it to be at the office of the bank, and not in any other place; yet that ought to have been pleaded, or otherwise the court cannot take notice of it; and therefore, notwithstanding any thing that appears here to the contrary, the transfer might have been in any other place; and then a tender ought to have been made to the person. Sir *Bartholomew Shower* and Mr. *Northey* argued for the plaintiff; *Darnall* and *Wright*, king's serjeants, for the defendant. *Judgment for the defendant.*

JONES AND ANOTHER, ASSIGNEES OF GARDINER, A BANKRUPT, v. BARKLEY.

IN THE KING'S BENCH, JUNE 19, 1781.

[*Reported in Douglas*, 684, 1*st ed.*, *p.* 659.]

THIS was a special action on the case for non-performance of an agreement. The first count of the declaration, after reciting that the plaintiffs, as assignees of Gardiner, were entitled to the equity of redemption of £1490 bank stock, which was in mortgage to one Lane for securing a sum of money lent by him to the bankrupt, and that the defendant was desirous that this equity of redemption should be assigned to Lane by the plaintiffs, and that they should execute to Lane a general release of all claims and demands which they, as assignees, had upon him; stated the agreement to have been, "That on Gardiner's having his certificate confirmed by the Lord Chancellor, and the plaintiffs assigning to Lane, or any person he should appoint, so far as in them lay, the equity of redemption of the said capital stock mortgaged to the said Lane, and also executing to him a general release of all claims and demands which they, as assignees, had on him, the defendant should pay, and promised to pay, (four months after the certificate should be confirmed by the Chancellor, and on the plainttiffs assigning the equity of redemption as aforesaid of the said stock to Lane or any person he should appoint, and executing and delivering such general release), the sum of £611 to the plaintiffs, for the benefit of the creditors of the bankrupt." Then, after stating that, in consideration of the promise and undertaking of the plaintiffs to perform all their part of the agreement, the defendant promised and undertook to fulfil all his part of it, the plaintiffs averred, "That afterwards, viz., on the 19th of July, 1774, the bankrupt's certificate was allowed and confirmed by the Chancellor; that the plaintiffs at all times since the making of the agreement had been ready and willing, and, at the expiration of four months from the time of the certificate being confirmed by the Chancellor, viz., on the 20th of November, 1774, offered to the defendant, to assign, as far as in them lay, the said equity of redemption, &c., and to execute and deliver to the said Lane a general release, &c., and did then and there tender to the defendant a draft of such assignment and release to the said Lane, for his the said defendant's approbation thereof, and did then and there offer to execute and deliver, and would then and there have executed and delivered to the said defendant such assignment and release, but that the said defendant then and there absolutely discharged the plaintiffs from executing the same, or any assignment or release whatsoever. Yet the defendant, not regarding, &c., did not, four months after the said certificate had been confirmed by the Chancellor, nor at any time before nor since, although often requested, pay the said sum of £611 or any part thereof to the plaintiffs." There was another count nearly to the same purpose. The defendant pleaded, 1. The general issue. 2. To the first count: "that the said plaintiffs did never execute an assignment of the said equity of redemption to the said Lane, or any person he appointed, and a general release to the said Lane of all claims and demands which they, as assignees, had on him at the time of making the agreement, and deliver or tender such assignment and general release so executed to the said Lane, or the said defendant." 3. A like plea to the second count. To these special pleas the ~~defendant~~ demurred, and shewed for cause, in the demurrer to the plea to the first count, that the defendant had not by his plea traversed or denied or attempted to put in issue any matter of fact alleged by the plaintiffs, but had introduced and attempted to put in issue matters of fact not alleged, nor necessary to be alleged, and that the plea was no answer to the said first count, but evasive and argumentative; and the same to the plea to the second count. The defendant joined in demurrer.

Le Blanc, for the plaintiffs. The averment of the plaintiffs, in the declaration, is equivalent to an averment of a performance of their part of the agreement, and, if it is, the plea is bad. 1. Wherever a man, by doing a previous act, would acquire a right to any debt or duty, by a tender to do the previous act, if the other party refuses to permit him to do it, he acquires the right as completely as if it had been actually done; and if the tender is defective owing to the conduct of the other party, such incomplete tender will be sufficient, because it is a general principle that he who prevents a thing from being done shall not avail himself of the non-performance which he has occasioned. Thus, it is laid down by Lord Coke, "that if a man make a feoffment in fee, upon condition that the feoffee shall re-infeoff him before such a day, and before the day the feoffor disseise the feoffee, and hold him out by force until the day be past, the state of the feoffee is absolute, for the feoffor is the cause wherefore the condition cannot be performed, and therefore shall never take advantage for non-performance thereof."[1] In Lancashire v. Killingworth, which is reported by Lord Raymond,[2] and in other books,[3] the plaintiff declared on a covenant by the defendant's testator, that upon two days' notice to be given to the testator to accept £1000 Hudson's Bay stock, at Hudson's Bay House, in, &c., and upon the transfer thereof to him, he would pay the plaintiff £2000, and the plaintiff averred that he gave notice, and was ready there at the day, and offered to transfer the stock, but that the testator did not come to accept it. This was held ill upon demurrer, because the plaintiff did not aver a refusal by the other party, or that he stayed till the last hour of the day, and the other did not come. But Lord Holt said, "that though the money were payable upon the transfer, yet if a legal tender had been made by the plaintiff, he would have been as well entitled to the money as if he had made an actual transfer." So in Blackwell v. Nash,[4] which was debt for a penalty, the plaintiff declared that he covenanted to transfer to the defendant, on or before the 21st of September, so much stock, and that the defendant, *in consideratione praemissorum*, covenanted to accept and pay for it, and then averred, that he was at the books the 21st of September, and *paratus fuit* and *obtulit* to transfer to the defendant, who then and there refused to accept or pay. On demurrer, it was objected that this was a condition precedent, and therefore to entitle himself to the action, the plaintiff ought to have shewn an actual transfer of the stock; but the court held that the expression "*in consideratione praemissorum*" meant, in consideration of the covenant to transfer, and not of an actual transfer, but that if it had meant an actual transfer, a tender and refusal would amount to a performance. Both of these cases prove that the refusal of the defendant excuses the non-performance, and completes the tender. In the case of Peeters v. Opie, reported by Ventris,[5] and Saunders,[6] the same principle is to be found. That was assumpsit on an agreement between the plaintiff and the defendant, that the plaintiff should pull down two walls, and build a house, &c., for the defendant, and that the defendant should pay him *pro labore suo in et circa divulsionem*, &c., £8, and that, in consideration that the plaintiff assumed to perform his

[1] Co. Litt. 206 *b*.
[2] 1 Ld. Raym. 686.
[3] Com. 117, 12 Mod. 529, 2 Salk. 623.
[4] 1 Str. 535.
[5] 1 Ventr. 177, 214,
[6] 2 Saund. 350.

part, the defendant assumed to perform his, and the plaintiff averred, that he was ready and offered to perform all on his part, but that the defendant had not paid him the money. After verdict the defendant moved in arrest of judgment, because there was no averment of performance or tender. But the court, after several arguments, and a discussion how far the words "*pro labore*" made a condition precedent, held that this was good after verdict. Now, the utmost that could be implied after the verdict was the refusal on the part of the defendant; for such an implication comes under the distinction in the rule on which a late case was decided,[1] being only a circumstance attending the facts on which the plaintiff's title was founded; but if nothing but performance would have done, then the very ground of action was not averred in the declaration, and that, according to the same rule, could not have been implied after verdict. To the same effect is a case stated in Rolle's Abridgment[2] from the Year Books,[3] where the condition of a bond being to raise a mill, the obligor came to the obligee and said, all is ready to erect the mill, and asked when he would have him come with it and put it up, and the obligee answered that he would not have it, and discharged him entirely of the mill. That was held to excuse him from the performance. And in the same book[4] it is laid down, that if a condition be, that the son of the obligor shall serve the obligee seven years, if he tenders his son, and the obligee refuses, or takes him, and within the term commands him to go away, the bond will not be forfeited. In like manner, where money is to be paid, tender and refusal is constantly held to be equivalent to performance. But, if it is said that the tender in the present case was defective and incomplete, still that cannot avail the defendant, because he has made it good by waiver, having discharged the plaintiffs from doing any thing farther. That such a waiver may make good a defective tender, is proved by many authorities, and particularly by the case of Austen *v.* The Executors of Sir William Dodwell,[5] where on a question whether interest should be allowed on a mortgage after an alleged tender of the principal, it appeared that the plaintiff had tendered a bank bill to one of the executors, for him to take out of the amount of it the principal and interest then due. The executor refused to take it, and the plaintiff asking if he objected to the legality of the tender, and saying that if he did he would presently turn the bill into money, he answered that he did not; upon which Lord King held, that the tender in a bank note was not strictly speaking a legal tender, but since it was proved that the defendant offered to turn it into money, that made it a good tender. Now, here, there was the most complete waiver of the irregularity by the discharge from executing any assignment or release whatsoever.

[1] Rushton *v.* Aspinall, Dougl. 679.

[2] 1 Roll. Abr. 453, N. pl. 5.

[3] 3 Hen. 6, 37.

[4] 1 Roll. Abr. 455, P. pl. 1.

[5] 1 Eq. Cases Abr. 318, pl. 9.

2. What I have hitherto submitted to the court, is upon the supposition that the execution of the assignment and release was a condition precedent; but I shall now contend that there is no condition precedent in this case, but that this is one of those middle agreements in which what each has undertaken to do, is to be performed at the same time. There are no words necessarily importing priority here, as "for, in consideration of, *proinde*," &c., but the agreement is, that the one party is to do an act on the other's doing another. Turner *v.* Goodwin,[1] reported in 10 Modern, is a case extremely applicable on this distinction. That was an action of debt upon a bond, by the condition of which, after reciting that A. was indebted to the plaintiff in a bond of £3000 conditioned for the payment of £1500, and had recovered judgment for that money, it was declared that the defendant, upon consideration that the plaintiff would forbear suing out execution upon A., promised to pay the money upon request to the plaintiff, "he assigning over to him the judgment he had against A." The defendant pleaded, that the plaintiff had not assigned the judgment; to which the plaintiff replied, "that he was ready to assign, and requested the defendant to pay the money, which he refused,"[2] and to this replication the defendant demurred. It was contended, on the part of the defendant, that the words "he assigning," &c., made a condition precedent. The case was argued several times, and there was on the first argument a difference of opinion, but at last judgment was given for the plaintiff, which could not have been if the court had not held that the assignment was not a condition precedent.[3] It may be said that 10 Modern is not a book of authority; but there is a recent case in this court which confirms the doctrine there laid down, and the distinction stated to have been taken by Lord Macclesfield. The case I allude to is that of Kingston *v.* Preston, determined in E. 13 Geo. 3.

"It was an action of debt for non-performance of covenants contained in certain articles of agreement between the plaintiff and the defendant. The declaration stated: That, by articles made the 24th of March, 1770, the plaintiff, for the considerations thereinafter mentioned, covenanted with the defendant to serve him for one year and a quarter next ensuing, as a covenant servant, in his trade of a silk-mercer, at 200*l.* a year, and, in consideration of the premises, the defendant covenanted that, at the end of the year and a quarter, he would give up his business of a mercer to the plaintiff, and a nephew of the defendant, or some other person to be nominated by the defendant, and give up to them his stock in trade, at a fair valuation; and that,

[1] 10 Mod. 153. [2] 10 Mod. 190.

[3] This case of Turner *v.* Goodwin, as stated in Viner's Abridgment, vol. 20, p. 183, pl. 9, is still more in point to the present, for there the words are "*upon* his assigning a judgment." But Viner cites the case from a book of still less authority than 10 Modern, viz., 2 Barnard, 308. [More fully reported in Fortescue, 145. — ED.]

between the young traders, deeds of partnership should be executed for fourteen years, and from and immediately after the execution of the said deeds the defendant would permit the said young traders to carry on the said business in the defendant's house. Then the declaration stated a covenant by the plaintiff, that he would accept the business and stock in trade, at a fair valuation, with the defendant's nephew, or such other person, &c., and execute such deeds of partnership, and, further, that the plaintiff should and would, at and before the sealing and delivery of the deeds, cause and procure good and sufficient security to be given to the defendant, to be approved of by the defendant, for the payment of £250 monthly to the defendant, in lieu of a moiety of the monthly produce of the stock in trade, until the value of the stock should be reduced to £4000. Then the plaintiff averred, that he had performed and been ready to perform his covenants, and assigned for breach on the part of the defendant, that he had refused to surrender and give up his business at the end of the said year and a quarter. The defendant pleaded: 1. That the plaintiff did not offer sufficient security; and, 2. That he did not give sufficient security for the payment of the £250, &c. And the plaintiff demurred generally to both pleas. On the part of the plaintiff, the case was argued by Mr. *Buller*, who contended that the covenants were mutual and independent, and therefore a plea of the breach of one of the covenants to be performed by the plaintiff was no bar to an action for a breach by the defendant of one which he had bound himself to perform, but that the defendant might have his remedy for the breach by the plaintiff in a separate action. On the other side, Mr. *Grose* insisted that the covenants were dependent in their nature, and therefore performance must be alleged. The security to be given for the money was manifestly the chief object of the transaction, and it would be highly unreasonable to construe the agreement so as to oblige the defendant to give up a beneficial business, and valuable stock in trade, and trust to the plaintiff's personal security (who might, and indeed was admitted to be worth nothing), for the performance of his part.

"In delivering the judgment of the court, LORD MANSFIELD expressed himself to the following effect: There are three kinds of covenants: 1. Such as are called mutual and independent, where either party may recover damages from the other for the injury he may have received by a breach of the covenants in his favor, and where it is no excuse for the defendant to allege a breach of the covenants on the part of the plaintiff. 2. There are covenants which are conditions and dependent, in which the performance of one depends on the prior performance of another, and therefore, till this prior condition is performed, the other party is not liable to an action on his covenant. 3. There is also a third sort of covenants, which are mutual conditions to be performed at the same time; and in these, if one party was ready and offered to perform his part, and the other neglected or refused to perform his, he who was ready and offered, has fulfilled his engagement, and may maintain an action for the default of the other; though it is not certain that either is obliged to do the first act. His lordship then proceeded to say, that the dependence or independence of covenants was to be collected from the evident sense and meaning of the parties, and that, however transposed they might be in the deed, their precedency must depend on the order of time in which the intent of the transaction requires their performance. That, in the case before the court, it would be the greatest injustice if the plaintiff should prevail. The essence of the agreement was, that the defendant should not trust to the personal security of the plaintiff, but, before he delivered up his stock and business, should have good security for the payment of the money. The giving such security, therefore, must necessarily be a condition precedent. Judgment was accordingly given for the defendant, because the part to be performed by the plaintiff was clearly a condition precedent."

But it is equally clear that, in the present case, the agreement falls within the third class, as defined by Lord Mansfield; and, therefore, absolute performance by the plaintiff was not necessary to entitle him to his action, nor had he occasion to aver any thing further than that he was ready to assign the stock and grant the release.

Wood, for the defendant. The plaintiffs' part of this agreement was a condition precedent. There cannot be a more emphatical term to express priority of performance, than the word "upon." The general principle is true, that tender and refusal is sufficient, but the plaintiffs ought to have done every thing they had engaged to do, as far as was in their power without any concurrence of the defendant; and after that, if they had tendered to complete their part and the defendant had refused his concurrence, such tender and refusal would have been equivalent to a performance. These plaintiffs had not proceeded so far. They might have executed a release, and tendered to deliver it to the defendant; for, as it was not required by the agreement that it should be such a release as the defendant should approve of, they might have gone that far without his concurrence. But, instead of doing so, they only tendered a draft of a release. It was the more necessary they should perform every thing in this case which they had bound themselves to do, as far as they could without any hindrance from the non-concurrence of the defendant, because there is no express mutual promise on their part to execute the release, so that the defendant could not have brought an action against them for not doing it. The two following cases are directly in point, viz.: 1. Austin *v.* Jervoyse,[1]

[1] Hob. 69, 77.

where the plaintiff declared, that he had bought a horse of the defendant for twenty-two shillings paid in hand, and for £11 more to be paid at the death or marriage of the plaintiff, for which he should become bound, with sufficient surety, by their writing obligatory, and that the defendant, in consideration thereof, promised to deliver him the horse when he should be required, and then averred, that afterwards he offered to become bound to him, but yet the defendant had not delivered the horse, though he had been required so to do. On *non-assumpsit* pleaded, there was a verdict for the plaintiff, but the judgment was arrested, because he had not averred that he had tendered the obligation sealed, nor stated what security he had offered; 2. An anonymous case in Rolle's Reports,[1] where, in an action on a bond conditioned for the delivery of a release on a certain day to the plaintiff, the defendant pleaded, that he was ready on the day to seal and deliver the release, that it was written and the wax fixed to the label, but the plaintiff refused to accept of it. The plaintiff demurred: And it was laid down by Chamberlayne, J., that if a defendant is bound to do a thing which cannot be done without the plaintiff, and the plaintiff refuse to accept it, there the defendant is discharged if he does what is in his power, but that in that case the defendant had not done all he could, for he ought to have sealed the release without the plaintiff, which he had not done. The same principle is to be gathered from the determination in Blandford v. Andrews;[2] for there, in an action on a bond conditioned for the defendant's procuring a marriage by such a time between the plaintiff and one J. P., the defendant pleaded that the plaintiff had gone to J. P., and abused her, and told her that, if he married her, he would tie her to a post, by reason whereof the defendant could not procure the marriage by the time stipulated; and the plaintiff having demurred to the plea, it was held to be bad, because the defendant had not alleged that he had used his endeavor to procure the marriage, and he ought to have shewn there was no default in him, and that he did as much as in him lay to procure it. Both this case and Austin v. Jervoyse are recognized by Lord Holt as law, in that of Lancashire v. Killingworth.[3] With regard to the payment of money, if the person who is bound to pay should bring money in bags, and say to the other, "Here, I am ready to pay you the money," and the other should discharge him, surely that would not be sufficient, but he still ought to make an actual tender of the money. This was expressly adjudged in the case of Suckling v. Coney.[4] As to the authorities relied on for the plaintiffs, they do not come up to the present case. In Lancashire v. Killingworth a tender of the transfer and refusal by the defendant would have been sufficient, because the plaintiff could not have gone further without the concur-

[1] 2 Roll. 238.
[2] Cro. El. 694.
[3] 1 Ld. Raym. 687.
[4] Noy, 74.

rence of the defendant. [LORD MANSFIELD. Yes, he might transfer stock without the presence of the other party.] The case of Peeters *v.* Opie was after verdict, and therefore does not establish what is or what is not good upon demurrer. In the case stated by Rolle from the Year Books, the plaintiff could not have come upon the defendant's premises to erect the mill without his concurrence. The tender of the bank-note, in Austin *v.* The Executors of Dodwell, was equivalent to a tender of cash, especially being accompanied with an offer to turn it into money.

Le Blanc, in reply, admitted that, unless there were a discharge by the other party from going farther, the plaintiff must take every step necessary for him to do, in which the defendant's concurrence is not requisite, before he can avail himself of a refusal by the defendant; but that none of the cases cited went so far as to controvert his position, that where the defendant stops the plaintiff by the way, he may take advantage of it. The case of Blandford *v.* Andrews was, he said, the strongest, but in that case there was only an averment that the defendant *paratus fuit*, and then particular facts stated, from which an inference was to be drawn that the plaintiff by his conduct had rendered it impossible for him to perform the condition; but no allegation of an express discharge by the plaintiff. As to the payment of money, in the case put of its being in bags, if the other party said, "I admit the money to be there, but I won't have it," he thought that would be a sufficient tender.

LORD MANSFIELD. If ever there was a clear case, I think the present is. One needs only state what the agreement, tender, and discharge were as set forth in the declaration. It charges that the plaintiffs offered to assign, and to execute and deliver a general release, and tendered a draft of an assignment and release, and offered to execute and deliver such assignment, but the defendant absolutely discharged them from executing the same, or any assignment and release whatsoever. The defendant pleads, that the plaintiffs did not actually execute an assignment and release; and the question is, whether there was a sufficient performance. Take it on the reason of the thing. The party must shew he was ready; but, if the other stops him on the ground of an intention not to perform his part, it is not necessary for the first to go farther, and do a nugatory act. Here, the draft was shewn to the defendant for his approbation of the form, but he would not read it, and, upon a different ground, namely, that he means not to pay the money, discharges the plaintiffs from executing it.

WILLES and ASHHURST, JJ., of the same opinion.

BULLER, J. The defence arises upon an objection to the declaration, and therefore the defendant should have demurred to it, and not have lengthened the record unnecessarily by two special pleas. None of the cases cited by Mr. Wood apply. The case in Hobart is very distinguishable from the present, for there was no refusal nor discharge in that case; the defendant was perfectly passive, and the plaintiff did not perform what he had undertaken, although there was nothing to prevent him. In the case of Blandford *v.* Andrews, the defendant had agreed to use his endeavors, and, notwithstanding what had been done by the plaintiff, he might have prevailed on the woman before the time elapsed to marry him. The questions on tenders are very different from this. They have arisen, not upon what shall excuse, but on what is a tender. If the party pleads a tender, he must prove one. But the decision would have been very different in the cases of that sort, if there had been any act of the one party stated on the record which had prevented the other from making a complete tender. The cases cited by Mr. Le Blanc are very strong on the present point. In Kingston *v.* Preston the principle is clearly laid down, that, where something is to be performed by each party at the same time, he who was ready, and offered to do his part, may sue the other for not performing his. I am sure there have been other cases since of the same sort.

Judgment for the plaintiffs.

SMITH *v.* WILSON.

IN THE KING'S BENCH, MAY 30, 1807.

[*Reported in* 8 *East*, 437.]

THIS case came on upon demurrers to the 4th, 5th, and 6th pleas to an action of covenant upon a charter-party of affreightment; and was argued in Easter Term last by *Richardson* in support of the demurrers, and by *Marryat* for the defendant. It was admitted that the 4th and 5th pleas were only intended to raise the question as to the validity of the declaration; and that if that were good the pleas were necessarily bad. But supposing the declaration to be sufficient in itself, it was contended that the matter disclosed by the 6th plea was an answer to it; setting out, as it did, certain proceedings in the Court of Admiralty, where the ship and cargo were libelled, which the defendant relied on as furnishing a legal excuse to him for not reshipping his cargo, which had been unshipped by the orders of that court, so as to enable the plaintiff's ship to proceed with the cargo on the destined voyage; but which plea the plaintiff contended to be merely argumentative and no answer to the breach assigned. It is unnecessary, however, to state the particulars of that plea, as the court waived giving any opinion upon it, and decided the case wholly on the insufficiency of the declaration. The case stood over for consideration till this term, when

Lord Ellenborough, C. J., delivered the judgment of the court. This was an action of covenant upon a charter-party of affreightment, made between the plaintiff, as agent of one James Clark of Baltimore, owner of the ship Portsmouth, of the one part, and the defendant, the freighter, of the other part. The covenants on the part of the plaintiff were, that the ship being properly fitted, &c., should receive and take on board at London or Portsmouth, at the option of the freighter, such goods as he might think proper to ship, and should sail and proceed therewith to Monte Video; and, being arrived there, should give due notice thereof to the agents of the freighter, and make a right and true delivery to them of all such goods, &c., as might be shipped as aforesaid; and after such delivery, should receive and take on board from the freighter, his agents, &c., a full and complete cargo of lawful goods, &c.; and having received the same, and being despatched, should and would (wind and weather permitting) immediately set sail from thence, and proceed to some one port of discharge in Great Britain, agreeable to the directions the commander might receive from the said freighter, his executors, &c.; and the said ship being arrived at her destined port, the commander should and would make a right and true delivery of the said cargo unto the freighter, his executors, &c., agreeably to the bills of lading that might be signed for the same, and there end his said intended voyage (the act of God, the king's enemies, and all and every the dangers and accidents of the sea, &c., excepted). The owner further covenanted that the ship should, if required, touch at the coast of Africa, on this side of the Cape of Good Hope, on her outward voyage to Monte Video, and take in passengers for that place, for whom water and provisions were to be provided and paid for by the freighter. In consideration whereof the defendant covenanted, that he, his executors, &c., would well and truly pay to the plaintiff £670 sterling per month, for every calendar month the ship should be employed by him the freighter during her said intended voyage to Monte Video and back to her port of discharge, and so in proportion for any less time, in full for the freight or hire of the said ship during her said intended service; such freight to commence from the day the ship should be ready to receive goods on board at Portsmouth, and end when she should have finally discharged the whole of her said cargo; and also should pay two-thirds of all pilotage and port-charges during the whole of the said voyage; and also two-thirds of all expenses of stowing the said ship's cargo at Monte Video; such freight, pilotage, and port-charges to be paid on the arrival and discharge of the said ship at her destined port in Great Britain. The declaration proceeds to state that the ship afterwards took on board at Portsmouth from the defendant, the freighter, such cargo as he thought fit to ship; and being despatched, proceeded on her outward voyage; and being required, touched at the coast of Africa for the purposes in the charter-party mentioned: and that whilst she was afterwards prosecuting her outward voyage, and before her arrival at Monte Video, the ship without the default of the plaintiff, the owner, commander, or crew, was, against their will, by force wrongfully seized, taken, and detained on the coast of Africa by persons unknown, and by them sent and conducted to London, and was by those persons forcibly kept and detained for a long time afterwards, until she was liberated and restored to the plaintiff. That in consequence of the seizure, detention, and other circumstances stated, the ship upon her liberation and restoration required certain necessary repairing and refitting to enable her to prosecute and complete the voyage; that the plaintiff caused such refitting and repairing to be done with all necessary despatch; and that the plaintiff always, from the time of the liberation, restoration, and refitting of the ship, was ready and willing to cause the ship to prosecute and complete the said voyage, and gave notice thereof to the defendant, and tendered and offered the ship to him to prosecute and complete that voyage, and requested him to give the necessary directions and instructions in that behalf, and to permit the said ship to prosecute and complete such voyage, and offered to observe such directions and instructions; and would have caused the ship to prosecute and complete that voyage: and avers that the ship was properly fitted, victualled, and manned for the purpose; and that the defendant had notice of it. The declaration further states that the defendant did not nor would give any directions or instructions respecting the ship, or the prosecution of that voyage; nor did nor would permit the ship to prosecute or complete the same; but refused to do so, and wholly renounced the charter-party and the further prosecution of the voyage, and wholly discharged the plaintiff from further prosecuting or completing that voyage, and dispensed therewith. The plaintiff then proceeds to state that the ship was employed during the voyage in the charter-party mentioned for twelve months, and that the freight thereof, according to the rate of the charter-party, amounted to £8040; and that the same ship would have been employed by the defendant, if he would have permitted her so to be, during the further prosecution and completion of the voyage for other twelve calendar months; and that the freight thereof, at the same rate, would have amounted to other £8040; and that two-thirds part of the pilotage and port charges of the ship, paid for and incurred by the plaintiff during the voyage, amounted to a further sum of £50; and then assigns a breach in the non-payment upon request of the freight, pilotage, and port charges, so claimed. To this declaration there were seven pleas pleaded on the part of the defendant; upon the three first of which issues were taken; to the 4th, 5th, and 6th of which there were demurrers and joinders in demurrer; and to the 7th there was a special replication upon which issue was taken by the rejoinder.

The question in this case arises upon the demurrers and joinders in demurrer to the 4th, 5th, and 6th pleas; the substance of which pleas it is unnecessary to state, because assuming them to be bad in law, the defendant is nevertheless entitled to judgment, if the declaration be bad in substance, as it appears to us to be. The breach assigned is in the non-payment of what is claimed by the plaintiff, *eo nomine*, as freight; viz., £8040 at the charter-party rate of £670 per month for twelve months that the ship was employed during the voyage; and the like amount of the like rate for freight for other twelve months that the ship would have been employed by the defendant (as alleged) in the further prosecution of the voyage, if the defendant would have permitted her so to be. But, by the terms of the charter-party, the freight, pilotage, and port charges, thereby covenanted to be paid on the part of the defendant, are all of them expressly covenanted to be paid, "on the arrival and discharge of the ship at her destined port in Great Britain;" and of course are made to depend on the event of such arrival and discharge at her destined port in Great Britain, as a condition precedent to the plaintiff's right to demand the same. But it is argued, on the authority of Jones *v.* Barkley, Doug. 685, last edit., and Hotham *v.* The East India Company, 1 Term Rep. 638, that the plaintiff having done all in his power towards earning the freight, pilotage, and port-charges in question, by the tender and offer of his ship to complete the voyage, by his request of necessary directions and instructions, and his offer to obey them, &c.; and the defendant having, as alleged in the declaration, refused to give any directions or instructions for the ship or the prosecution of the voyage, and having wholly renounced the charter-party and the further prosecution of the voyage, and having discharged the defendant from further prosecuting or completing the voyage, and dispensed therewith; that the plaintiff had acquired the right to the sums demanded as freight, &c., as completely as if the voyage had been performed, and the ship had arrived and been discharged at her destined port. But the decision of the court in neither of the cases cited sustains the argument urged on behalf of the plaintiff in this extent. The most that can be understood to have been there decided is (what was contended for by the plaintiff's counsel in the case of Jones *v.* Barkley), that where a man "by doing a previous act would acquire a right to a debt or duty; by a tender to do the previous act, if the other party refuse to permit him to do it, he acquires the right as completely as if it had actually been done." But the question still occurs whether, by actually doing the previous act tendered to be done in this case, the plaintiff would have acquired a right to the freight and other payments demanded? Here, if he had done all that he offered to do, and which the defendant discharged him from performing, still it would have amounted at most only to an *endeavor* on his part to prosecute and complete the voyage, and to procure, as far as in him lay, the arrival and discharge of her at her destined port; but the actual event of such an arrival and discharge did not depend upon him, nor was it within the reach of any efforts on his part to insure and to accomplish; but it was liable to be disappointed by the act of God, and all the various other accidents to which marine adventures are subject. But in the case put (*i. e.*, of Jones *v.* Barkley) no contingency but the immediate death of the party tendering the act could have disappointed its performance; and, being done, the party doing it would have instantly acquired, without any further act, either on his own part, or on that of any one else, a full right by the terms of his contract to the duty demanded; which in that case was the payment at a given time of a sum of money stipulated to be paid him. So that the difference between the two cases is this: in the one, by doing an act in the power of the party to have done, he would have acquired a full and instant right to the duty demanded: in the other, by doing the act tendered to the full extent to which the party tendering was able to perform it, he would still have only taken certain steps of remote and uncertain effect towards the attainment of the object and completion of the event necessary to be attained and completed, in order to vest a right to the duty demanded in the party demanding it. The same in effect may be said of the case of Hotham *v.* East India Company, 1 Term Rep. 638, where the only thing which stood in the way of the plaintiff's recovering the allowance claimed for short tonnage, according to the terms of his charter-party (after having taken all proper steps on his part to obtain the necessary certificate to entitle him thereto), was the neglect and default of the company's own agents in refusing to afford him such certificate. Covenants of this kind have always received a strict construction. In Bright *v.* Cooper, 1 Brownl. 21, the covenant made by the merchant with the master of a ship being to pay such a sum if he would bring his freight to such a port; and part of the goods being taken by pirates, and the residue brought to the place appointed and there unladed; the court held that the merchant was not bound to pay the money to the master, because the agreement was not performed by him. And the late case of Cook *v.* Jennings in this court (7 Term Rep. 381) proceeded upon the same principle. Adverting therefore to the declaration only, and the breach therein assigned, we are of opinion that, as the ship never arrived at her destined port within the terms of the charter-party, the freight claimed in the declaration never became demandable by law; and of course that the plaintiff cannot recover thereupon; which renders it unnecessary to consider the sufficiency of the several pleas demurred to, and the questions which might otherwise have arisen upon them.

Judgment for the defendant.

LAIRD v. PIM AND ANOTHER.

IN THE EXCHEQUER, JANUARY 18, 20, 1841.

[*Reported in 7 Meeson & Welsby, 474*].

ASSUMPSIT. The first count of the declaration stated, that on the 6th day of April, 1836, in consideration that the plaintiff, at the request of the defendants, would sell them a lot or parcel of land, situated between Bidston Road and Cleveland Street, in the county of Chester, at the price or rate of 7*s.* 6*d.* by the square yard, to be paid as soon as the conveyance thereof should be completed, with interest thenceforth on such purchase-money at the rate of £5 per cent. by the year until paid, the defendants to have the liberty of making bricks and erecting steam-engines on such lot or parcel of land, the defendants promised the plaintiff to purchase the said lot or parcel of land of the plaintiff, and to pay him for the same at the rate or price and on the terms aforesaid. And the plaintiff says, that although the plaintiff, relying on the said promise of the defendants, did, within a short and reasonable time from the making of the said promise, to wit, on the day and year aforesaid, allow and permit the defendants to enter into and take possession of the said lot or parcel of land, and the defendants did, to wit, then, take such possession thereof, and have continued in such possession for a long time, to wit, hitherto: and although the plaintiff, from the time of making the said promise to the commencement of this suit, has performed and fulfilled every thing on his part to be performed and fulfilled, and has always been ready and willing to make appear to the defendants a good and sufficient title in, and right and power to convey, the said lot or parcel of land in fee-simple, together with the liberty aforesaid, and to execute and complete a conveyance thereof in fee-simple to the defendants, together with the liberty aforesaid; and after the expiration of a reasonable time and before the commencement of this suit, to wit, on the 28th of October, 1837, offered the defendants to execute and complete a conveyance thereof, together with the liberty aforesaid, to the defendants, and would then have tendered to the defendants a draft of a proper conveyance, and also a proper conveyance for the purpose aforesaid, but that the defendants then discharged the plaintiff from so doing; of all which the defendants, from the time of making the said promise, have had notice: yet the defendants did not regard their said promise, and did not nor would pay the plaintiff the said purchase-money for the said lot or parcel of land, together with the said liberty, or any part thereof, at or after the expiration of the said reasonable time as aforesaid, or at any other time, but have wholly neglected and refused so to do; and the plaintiff has been and is wholly deprived of the said purchase-money, amounting to a large sum, to wit, £4125, together with interest thereon, to which he ought and otherwise would have been entitled as aforesaid. There were also counts for use and occupation, goods sold and delivered, and upon an account stated.

The defendants pleaded *non assumpserunt*, and several special pleas, of which the sixth plea (to the first count) was, that no conveyance of the said lot or parcel of land or any part thereof has ever been made or executed or completed to them the defendants or either of them, or to any person on their behalf, or in any manner whatsoever. Verification.

The plaintiff took issue on all the pleas except the above, to which he demurred generally, and the defendants joined in demurrer. The point stated for argument by the plaintiff was as follows: The plaintiff contends that the execution of a conveyance was not a condition precedent to his maintaining this action, and that if it were, it has been waived, and that consequently the plea demurred to is bad. The defendants' points were as follows: The defendants will contend that the plea is a sufficient answer to the first count of the declaration, and they will also contend that the first count is insufficient, inasmuch as it shews no sufficient breach of the contract stated in that count; and also that the statement in the declaration, that the plaintiff offered to execute a conveyance, and would have tendered one, but that the defendants dispensed with it, is no sufficient ground for alleging as a breach that the defendants did not pay the purchase-money; and that upon the promise stated in the first count, the non-payment of the purchase-money is no breach of contract as alleged in that count; and that the breach alleged in the first count and the claim to damages as therein stated are not warranted by the premises or allegations in that count.

The cause came on for trial upon the issues in fact before ROLFE, B., at the last Liverpool assizes, when it appeared that the defendants (who were directors of a company called the Saw-Mills and Timber Company, for which the purchase was made) had been put into possession of the land under the agreement, and had taken therefrom and sold a quantity of brick clay. They subsequently refused altogether to complete the purchase, upon which the plaintiff brought this action for the recovery of the purchase-money, and for the value of the clay so taken and sold. It was contended for the plaintiff at the trial that the amount of the purchase-money agreed on, with interest, was the proper measure of damages on the first count. For the defendants it was insisted, that the plaintiff could not be entitled to recover the purchase-money, as the land had never been conveyed, and the plaintiff still remained the owner of it as before the agreement for sale to the defendants. The learned judge was of opinion that the plaintiff could not recover the whole purchase-money, but was entitled on the first count to such damages only as had resulted from the defendants' breach of their contract: and a verdict was accordingly taken for the plaintiff for £750, made up as follows: £680 for interest on the purchase-money up to the commencement of the action, and £70 for the value of the brick clay. In last Michaelmas Term (Nov. 3d),

Cresswell moved, pursuant to leave reserved by the learned judge, for a rule to shew cause why the damages should not be increased by the sum of £4125, the amount of the purchase-money. The plaintiff is entitled to recover the full amount of the purchase-money. This is a contract for a specific plot of land, to which the plaintiff has shewn a good title, and which he has offered to convey to the defendants in pursuance of the contract. He has a right to consider them as the owners, and to insist on payment of the price. Sir E. Sugden[1] appears to consider that a vendor may recover the purchase-money without having executed a conveyance, where the purchaser has discharged him from so doing. [ALDERSON, B. It is like the case of goods bargained and sold, and an action brought for not accepting them, in which case the damages sustained by the breach of contract can alone be recovered.] There the plaintiff treats the goods as still his own. [PARKE, B. So here, the land is still yours at law; you might bring ejectment for it immediately after this verdict.] In Hawkins v. Kemp,[2] which was an action by the vendors of an estate against the vendee, who had refused to prepare any conveyance as required by the conditions of sale, or to pay the remainder of the purchase-money beyond the deposit, a verdict was given for the whole residue of the purchase-money. The defendants may afterwards go into equity to compel a conveyance.

PARKE, B. The measure of damages, in an action of this nature, is the injury sustained by the plaintiff by reason of the defendants not having performed their contract. The question is, How much worse is the plaintiff by the diminution in the value of the land, or the loss of the purchase-money, in consequence of the non-performance of the contract? It is clear he cannot have the land and its value too. A party cannot recover the full value of a chattel, unless under circumstances which import that the property has passed to the defendant, as in the case of goods sold and delivered, where they have been absolutely parted with and cannot be sold again. The direction of my brother Rolfe, therefore, was quite correct.

ALDERSON, B., GURNEY, B., and ROLFE, B., concurred.

Rule refused.

[1] 1 Vend. & P. 10th ed. 374. [2] 3 East, 410.

The demurrer was now argued by

Cowling, for the plaintiff. The execution of a conveyance is not a condition precedent to the plaintiff's recovering in this action; and if it were, it has been waived by the defendants. The plea is clearly bad. It states no more than is admitted on the face of the declaration; it amounts in effect only to a demurrer to the first count. But it will be argued that that count is bad. It is submitted, however, that although it may be somewhat more diffuse than was necessary, it is good. It states the contract, the possession taken by the defendants, the plaintiff's readiness to execute a conveyance, the expiration of a reasonable time, and that the plaintiff offered to execute a conveyance, and would have tendered a proper conveyance, but that the defendants discharged him from so doing. There is nothing to take this case out of the ordinary rule, that the purchaser is bound to prepare the conveyance; but nevertheless the plaintiff has offered a conveyance here, but the defendants have dispensed with it. That condition precedent, if it be one, has therefore been waived. Then it is said the plaintiff is not entitled to recover the whole purchase-money; but the declaration does not seek to do so; the breach is only for the damages sustained by the non-performance of the contract. But even if the declaration were wrong in seeking to recover the whole purchase-money, that would be no bar to the action; but the defendants undertake by this plea to say something in bar of the whole action. [He was then stopped by the court.]

Wightman, for the defendants. The first count of the declaration is bad. The breach alleged does not properly follow from the premises stated. The count alleges that, in consideration that the plaintiff, at the request of the defendants, would sell them a lot or parcel of land, &c., at the price of 7*s.* 6*d.* the square yard, to be paid as soon as the conveyance thereof should be completed, &c., the defendants promised the plaintiff to purchase the land of him, and to pay him for the same at the rate or price and on the terms aforesaid; and the breach assigned is that the defendants did not regard their promise, and did not nor would pay the plaintiff the said purchase-money, &c. There is no good breach, therefore, unless the defendants were bound under the circumstances to pay the purchase-money; if they were not, it is a bad breach, and the plaintiff cannot recover in respect of it. The rule as to dependent covenants is thus laid down in the notes to the case of Pordage *v.* Cole:[1] "It is justly observed that covenants, &c., are to be construed to be dependent or independent of each other, according to the intention and meaning of the parties, and the good sense of the case; and technical words should give way to such intention." The following rules are then enunciated: 1. "If a day be appointed for payment of money or part of it, or for doing any other act, and the

[1] 1 Saund. 320 *a*, n. 4.

day is to happen, or may happen, before the thing which is the consideration of the money or other act is to be performed, an action may be brought for the money, or for not doing such other act, before performance; for it appears that the party relied upon his remedy, and did not intend to make the performance a condition precedent; and so it is where no time is fixed for performance of that which is the consideration of the money or other act." A vendor, therefore, may declare for non-payment of the purchase-money on a certain day, although no conveyance have been executed. "But, 2, when a day is appointed for the payment of money, &c., and the day is to happen after the thing which is the consideration of the money, &c., is to be performed, no action can be maintained for the money, &c., before performance." The present case falls within the latter rule. It does not appear here that if the plaintiff were to recover the purchase-money, the defendants would have any remedy against him for the land; they only stipulate to pay as soon as the conveyance shall be completed. [PARKE, B. The conveyance and the payment are to be contemporaneous acts.] A tender of the conveyance is not sufficient; it must be executed before payment can be enforced. So, "if two men should agree, one that the other should have his horse, the other that he will pay £10 for him, no action lies for the money till the horse be delivered." Thorpe *v.* Thorpe.[1] [PARKE, B., referred to Knight *v.* Keech.[2]] It does not appear here that there were any mutual remedies, or, if there were, that the defendants intended to rely upon them; they stipulated to pay their money only when the purchase was completed; and although they may have subjected themselves to an action for damages, they are not liable to this action until after the execution of the conveyance. The plaintiff has therefore mistaken his remedy; he should have declared merely for damages for the non-completion of the contract, whereas here his only breach is the non-payment of the purchase-money, which, on this statement, he is not entitled to: Warn *v.* Bickford,[3] Phillips *v.* Fielding.[4]

The court then called on

Cowling to proceed with his argument. In the first place, the count does not claim to recover the whole purchase-money. The breach, it is true, states that the defendants did not nor would pay the plaintiff the said purchase-money or any part thereof, and that the plaintiff has been and is wholly deprived of it. But it would have been sufficient if it had alleged merely that the defendants did not regard their said promise, and then concluded to the damage of the plaintiff, &c. The special damage alleged cannot be traversed or demurred to, and the plaintiff may always recover for the damage properly alleged. Under

[1] 1 Salk. 171, Ld. Raym. 662.
[2] Skin. 344.
[3] 7 Price, 550.
[4] 2 H. Bl. 123.

that form of breach the plaintiff might have recovered all that he has actually recovered in this action; and upon this demurrer (the plea being to the whole count), the only question is whether the plaintiff is entitled to recover any thing. Jones v. Barkley[1] is an express authority for the plaintiff.[2] . . . Glazebrook v. Woodrow,[3] Goodisson v. Nunn,[4] and Martin v. Smith,[5] are authorities to the same effect. [PARKE, B. Your argument is, that nothing remains to be done which is beneficial to the plaintiff, but the payment of the money.] Yes: the plaintiff has perhaps even done more than was necessary. In Glazebrook v. Woodrow, Le Blanc, J., says: "The payment is the consideration for the conveyance, and cannot be enforced till that be made, or at least offered to be made, by the plaintiff." Here more than that is shewn to have been done.

Wightman. Unless the defendants are bound to pay the purchase-money, no damages can be recovered for the non-payment of it: the plaintiff therefore must shew, not only that the defendants did not pay, but also that they were bound to pay. The cases cited on the other side are distinguishable, and fall within the first rule cited from the note to Pordage v. Cole. In all of them the conveyance was to be executed, and payment to be made, on a certain day; and when the plaintiff had done all that it was incumbent upon him to do on that day, the non-payment was a breach of contract on the part of the defendant. But here the time for payment has not yet arrived. [PARKE, B. In Jones v. Barkley the payment depended on the previous act of assignment, as here of conveyance.] There was in that case a fixed day appointed; the defendant was not bound to pay until that day, although all the conditions precedent had been performed by the plaintiffs; but, on the other hand, he was bound to pay on that day, unless he could shew good cause to the contrary. [LORD ABINGER, C. B. The day was material until the four months had elapsed, but not afterwards. PARKE, B. After the expiration of the four months, Jones v. Barkley became identical with the present case; the money was then to be paid simply on the execution of the assignment. Lord Mansfield says: "The question is, whether there was a sufficient performance. The party must shew he was ready; but if the other stops him on the ground of an intention not to perform his part, it is not necessary for the first to go farther, and do a nugatory act."] But here the money is not to be paid until after the completion of the conveyance. True, it is by the defendants' default that it is not completed, and they may be liable in damages for that default; but not for non-payment of the money, until the time for payment of it has actually arrived. The case falls entirely within the rule laid

[1] 2 Dougl. 684. [2] The learned counsel here stated that case. — ED.
[3] 8 T. R. 366. [4] 4 T. R. 761. [5] 6 East, 555.

down by Lord Holt in Thorpe *v.* Thorpe. Then as to the breach, it is clear that it must be taken to be contained in the express allegation that the defendants did not pay the purchase-money after a reasonable time. Suppose the court held that on this declaration the plaintiff might recover the whole purchase-money, what counter remedy have the defendants? Mutual promises are not even alleged. [LORD ABINGER, C. B. It is certainly informal; but does it not amount in substance to a complaint against the defendants for not completing the purchase?] Assuming it to be so, still that does not entitle the plaintiff to recover the purchase-money; but the non-completion of the purchase is not assigned as a breach, but is stated before the allegation of the breach.

LORD ABINGER, C. B. I think that the breach is informally alleged, and that the words, "that the defendants did not regard their said promise" are not sufficient to constitute a good breach, so as to cure the defect; but the objection, as it arises on general demurrer, cannot prevail. With regard to the averment of the plaintiff's being ready and willing, and having offered to execute a conveyance, the case of Jones *v.* Barkley appears to be an express authority, and must govern the present case. The averment is, that the plaintiff offered to execute a conveyance, and would have tendered a proper conveyance, but that the defendants discharged him from so doing. That, coupled with the other allegations in the declaration, is substantially the same as if it had been averred that the defendants had refused to execute a conveyance actually tendered to them. Our judgment must therefore be for the plaintiff.

PARKE, B. I have had considerable doubt on this case in the course of the argument, but I have at length arrived at the same conclusion as that stated by my lord. This declaration is certainly informally drawn, but I think it is sufficient on general demurrer, upon the principle laid down in Jones *v.* Barkley. Upon the facts alleged in this declaration the plaintiff is substantially in the same situation, for the purpose of recovering the money, as if all had been done on his part which he engaged to do. It does not follow that he shall recover the whole purchase-money, but he is in the same situation for the purpose of recovering damages for the non-payment of the price, as if all had been done by him. The distinction which it has been attempted to draw between this case and Jones *v.* Barkley is no distinction at all; it proceeds altogether on the ground that there two contemporaneous acts were to be done on a particular day; but the case is just the same whether two contemporaneous acts are to be done at an indefinite time or on a specified day. The only distinction is, that in that case one simple act was to be done by the plaintiffs, which the defendant discharged them from doing; here, what the plaintiff has to do is somewhat more complicated; first, he is to make a good title, then the defendants are to prepare the conveyance, and the plaintiff to execute it; and the defendants having discharged him from doing that, it is the same as if it had been done. According to Jones *v.* Barkley, therefore, the plaintiff is in the same situation as if he had performed all his part of the agreement; that is, as if he had perfected a conveyance. That is the conclusion to which I have at length arrived, and to which, perhaps, I should not have come but for the case of Jones *v.* Barkley. This is all on general demurrer; had the question arisen on special demurrer, I doubt whether I should have come to the same conclusion.

GURNEY, B., and ROLFE, B., concurred.

Judgment for the plaintiff.

MARY SHORT *v.* STONE.

IN THE QUEEN'S BENCH, JANUARY 20, 1846.

[*Reported in* 8 *Queen's Bench Reports,* 358.]

ASSUMPSIT. The declaration stated that heretofore, to wit, on, &c., "in consideration that the plaintiff being then unmarried, at the request of the defendant, had then promised the defendant to marry him the defendant, he the defendant then promised the plaintiff to marry her within a reasonable time next after he should be thereunto requested by the plaintiff so to do; and the plaintiff avers that she, confiding in the said promise of the defendant, hath always hitherto remained and continued, and still is, sole and unmarried, and was always, from the time of the making of her said promise until the marriage of the said defendant as hereinafter mentioned, ready and willing to marry the defendant, whereof the defendant hath always had notice; yet the defendant, disregarding his said promise, after the making thereof and before the commencement of this suit, to wit, on," &c., "wrongfully and injuriously married a certain other person, to wit, one Edith Collins, contrary to his said promise; to the damage," &c.

Plea 2. "Defendant says that he was not at any time before the commencement of this suit requested by the plaintiff to marry her according to his said promise in that behalf." Verification.

Demurrer, assigning for causes, among others, that the plea confesses, but does not sufficiently avoid, and defendant has therein alleged a fact wholly immaterial to the merits: "for, inasmuch as it appears by the declaration that the defendant, before the commencement of this suit, had married another person, the plaintiff need not nor ought to have requested the defendant to marry her." Also, that the plea "tenders too large and an insufficient issue, to wit, whether a request were made before the commencement of this suit; whereas, if the request be material at all, it should have been alleged not to have been made before the marriage of the defendant: for, if the plaintiff were to traverse the allegation as it now stands in the said plea, and the same should be found for her, still it would not shew conclusively that she was and is entitled to maintain her action, as it would be consistent with the said issue, and verdict thereon, that the request found to have been made by the plaintiff was after the said marriage, and between it and the commencement of this suit." Also that the plea should have concluded to the country.

Joinder in demurrer.

Peacock, for the plaintiff. The want of a request is immaterial, since it appears that the defendant had put it out of his own power to comply with the request if made. This case was before the court in last Hilary Term, the plaintiff having signed judgment on the ground that the plea, denying a request, was not issuable, and the defendant was under terms to plead issuably. Wightman, J., set that judgment aside; and a motion was made here to rescind his order. The declaration did then aver a request, and the court intimated an opinion that the averment of non-performance on request was one distinct breach, and the averment that defendant had married another person was a second, and that a material traverse might be taken upon either. The learned judge's order was upheld; and the plaintiff then amended the declaration, leaving it in its present form. That form is good, according to Harrison *v.* Cage and wife,[1] where the plaintiff declared for breach of promise of marriage, stating that the defendant, Elizabeth Cage, after the promise, &c., married the male defendant; and it was objected that there is no time prefixed, and "he does not shew a request with a parson." But these exceptions were not regarded: "for, as to the time, it should be in convenient time; and as to the request with a parson, that was overruled in Dickenson and Holcroft's case."[2] "Besides that, in this case it appears that the defendant has disabled herself by marriage from the performance of her promise." Ford *v.* Tiley[3] affirms the principle on which the plaintiff relies.[4] . . . In Bowdell *v.* Parsons[5] the plaintiff declared in assumpsit for not delivering hay which the defendant had sold him and promised to deliver on request: the request was imperfectly alleged, but the declaration stated that the defendant did not deliver the hay to the plaintiff, and, "on the contrary, afterwards sold and disposed of" it

1 1 Ld. Raym. 386, 3 Ld. Raym. 268.
2 Holcroft *v.* Dickenson, Carter, 233; s. c. 1 Freem. 95, 3 Keb. 148.
3 6 B. & C. 325.
4 The learned counsel here stated that case. — Ed.
5 10 East, 359, 361.

"to other persons, without the consent and against the will of the plaintiff:" and Lord Ellenborough said: "There is clearly a sufficient breach laid in that count; for by the defendant's selling and disposing of the rest of the hay to other persons, he disqualified himself from delivering it to the plaintiff; and therefore no request was necessary." [COLERIDGE, J. The plea here denies, in effect, any request either before or after the marriage.] If there was a request before the marriage, and the defendant was ready to comply, but the plaintiff prevented it, that was matter to be stated in answer to the declaration. After the marriage a request could not be made. It may, indeed, be said that the defendant's wife might die, and a request be made then: but that supposition is too remote; otherwise it would have been an answer in Ford v. Tiley [1] that the new lease might have been surrendered, or in Bowdell v. Parsons [2] that the defendant might have repurchased the hay before request made. And in Ford v. Tiley [3] the court said, referring to 8 (5) Vin. Ab. 225, (224), tit., Condition (B. c) pl. 1, 2: "If a day be limited to perform a condition, if the obligor once disables himself to perform it, though he be enabled again before the day, yet the condition is broken, as if the condition be to enfeoff another before Michaelmas; if before the feast he enfeoff another, though he after repurchases, yet he cannot perform the condition." And it may be asked here if the suggested argument is admissible, how long the plaintiff's remedy is to be suspended on a supposition that the wife may die, and a request be then made?

Butt, contra. Harrison v. Cage [4] was decided, not on demurrer, but on motion in arrest of judgment; the contract to marry was averred generally.[5] Here it is to marry within a reasonable time after request, so that the request is a condition precedent. And the point there decided was that a request "with a parson" need not be averred; no dispute could arise on the necessity of a request generally, for the declaration did fully aver one.[5] Again, the declaration there shewed that the person whom the defendant married was still living. Here the declaration does not aver either that fact or a request made and lapse of a reásonable time afterwards, or that any reasonable time has elapsed since the promise. In Ford v. Tiley [6] the question arose, not, as here, on demurrer, but on the evidence at the trial, and appears, by the citation of authorities,[7] to have been decided without reference to the distinction between a feoffment on condition and a mutual contract. The Year Book, Mich. 21 Ed. 4, 54 B, 55 A, Pl. 26, cited in 5 Vin. Ab. 224, tit. Condition (B. c.) pl. 1, 2, speaks of a condition to enfeoff. If a feoffment be made on condition that the feoffee shall enfeoff another, and he enfeoffs a stranger, then, because he has disabled himself to

[1] 6 B. & C. 325. [2] 10 East, 359, 361. [3] 6 B. & C. 327.
[4] 1 Ld. Raym. 386. [5] 3 Ld. Raym. 269. [6] 6 B. & C. 325.
[7] See p. 327.

perform the condition, the feoffor may re-enter; Litt. s. 355, Co. Litt. 221 *a*; and Lord Coke makes a distinction between disability incurred in such a case by the feoffor and by the feoffee, observing (222 *a*): "If a man make a feoffment in fee upon condition, that, if the feoffor or his heirs pay a certain sum of money before such a day, the feoffor commit treason, is attainted and executed, now is there a disability on the part of the feoffor, for he hath no heir; but if the heir be restored before the day, he may perform the condition." "Otherwise it is if such a disability had grown on the part of the feoffee; and the reason of the diversity is, for that, as Littleton saith, *maintenant* by the disability of the feoffee the condition is broken and the feoffor may enter, but so it is not by the disability of the feoffor or his heirs, for if they perform the condition within the time it is sufficient, for that they may at any time perform the condition before the day. And so it is if the feoffor enter into religion, and before the day is deraigned, he may perform the condition for the cause aforesaid." But the law thus expounded does not apply to the case of ordinary contracts; nor does it result from the authorities that, if one contracts to deliver goods in twelve months, and parts with them within that time, there is a breach before the twelve months expire; or that, if a person agrees to enfeoff by a certain day, and before that day makes a different disposition, a breach of contract is then made. In cases of mere contract, if the thing is to be done on request, a request is material and must be specially averred; Com. Dig. Pleader (C. 69), 1 Chitty on Pl. 339, 340 (7th ed.). No question on this point was raised in Ford *v.* Tiley.[1] In the case of a promissory note payable at a specified time after demand, the Statute of Limitations begins to run from the demand; Thorpe *v.* Booth.[2] In Bowdell *v.* Parsons[3] a part of the chattel sold had already been delivered to the plaintiff: the residue might well be considered his property without any request. If, in the present case, the defendant, by marrying another, broke his contract with the plaintiff, though not requested to marry her, it must be assumed that he had impliedly contracted to remain single until requested, however long the time might be. Further, it is a good objection that the person whom the defendant married is not shewn to be still living, and such a point may be raised on general demurrer; Fryer *v.* Coombs,[4] Dayrell *v.* Hoare.[5] [COLERIDGE, J., mentioned Seymour *v.* Gartside,[6] but observed that the question in that case arose after verdict. PATTESON, J. The marginal note there states that the plaintiff alleged a promise to marry "within a reasonable time after the request," but the declaration, as stated in the report, says, "in a reasonable time then next following."] Where the contract is to marry within a reasonable time after a certain event, the court cannot conclude by inference that the event has happened.

[1] 6 B. & C. 325.
[2] Ry. & M. 388.
[3] 10 East, 359.
[4] 11 A. & E. 403.
[5] 12 A. & E. 356.
[6] 2 Dowl. & R. 55.

Butt also mentioned Caines *v.* Smith,[1] then depending in the Court of Exchequer.

Peacock, in reply. It is true that, in Harrison *v.* Cage,[2] request was not made a condition precedent; but the point on which the decision turned was the disability incurred by the defendant. Where there is a condition precedent, performance or a dispensing with it must undoubtedly be averred; but here a dispensation is averred. [WIGHTMAN, J. Suppose it appeared that the wife had died before the commencement of this action, and before request?] Still there was a breach. The defendant's situation was essentially changed. It might reasonably be asked in that case how long the plaintiff was bound to wait after the death of the wife. Or, on the other hand, if the defendant had at any time afterwards requested the plaintiff, whether she would have been liable to an action for refusing him. Suppose, in a case like this, the woman had married and had children, and her husband had died, could she then have required the man to marry her, and brought an action for refusal? As to the supposed inconvenience that the defendant might have been bound to remain single for an indefinite time if not requested, he might have requested the plaintiff to marry him, and brought an action if she had refused. The obligation was mutual. [*Butt* here pointed out that the declaration averred a promise by defendant to marry plaintiff within a reasonable time after request, in consideration that plaintiff had promised to marry him, not adding any words as to a request.] In 1 Sugd. Vend. 260, 261,[3] the author, after observing that "in agreements for purchase, the covenants are construed according to the intent of the parties, and they are therefore always considered dependent where a contrary intention does not appear," says: "If, therefore, either a vendor or vendee wish to compel the other to observe a contract, he immediately makes his part of the agreement precedent, for he cannot proceed against the other without an actual performance of the agreement on his part, or a tender and refusal." That, in principle, applies to the present case. The defendant here might have made his own request the condition precedent. The supposed hardship, therefore, need not arise. But here the defendant treats as the condition precedent a request by the plaintiff, which he has put it out of her power to make. As to the distinction between a contract and a feoffment on condition the authorities were much considered in Ford *v.* Tiley,[4] and this point was not adverted to; nor does it appear to have been noticed at the bar or on the bench in Bowdell *v.* Parsons.[5] Amory *v.* Broderick[6] is an additional authority

[1] 15 M. & W. 189, where the court afterwards decided in accordance with the judgment in the present case.

[2] 1 Ld. Raym. 386.

[3] 11th ed. chap. 4, s. 4, §§ 56, 58. [4] 6 B. & C. 325. [5] 10 East, 359.

[6] 5 B. & Ald. 712; s. c. 1 Dowl. & R. 361; Peacock read from the latter report.

for the general doctrine relied upon by the plaintiff.[1] . . . In Com. Dig. Condition (M. 3), under the general head, "What shall be a breach?" it is said: "So, if he be disabled to perform in the same plight and condition that it was when the condition was created."

LORD DENMAN, C. J. We must look at this case with a view to the feelings and intentions of the parties at the time of entering into such a contract; and the intention clearly is, to marry in the state in which the parties respectively are at the time. If either party puts himself out of that state, he must be taken to dispense with the contract so far that the other may have an action against him without a request to marry. It is unnecessary to inquire what cases among those which have been mentioned, are analogous to this, because here the intent must be considered; and, looking to that, the fact stated on the record is a necessary dispensation. According to this, which appears to me the true construction of the contract, the plaintiff shews a good right of action, and is entitled to judgment.

PATTESON, J. The only difficulty I had was on the averment of a promise to marry within a reasonable time after request. If the allegation had been of a promise generally to marry, or a promise to marry on request, or in a reasonable time, the application of the case in Lord Raymond would have been clearer. But, on consideration, I do not see any rational distinction between the averments of a promise to marry on request and a promise to marry in reasonable time after request. We must look to the intention, and, if a party puts himself out of the condition in which a request could properly be made, he dispenses with the request. Here it is alleged that the defendant married another person. It was not necessary to shew that that person was living when the action was commenced; there was a breach of contract at once when the defendant married.

COLERIDGE, J. The declaration is good, and the plea bad, for the same reasons. The promise to marry within a reasonable time after request must mean after request within a time when it might reasonably be made. If the defendant disables himself from fulfilling such a request, then, in the first place, he dispenses with the request, because it has become impossible to make the request effectually; and, secondly, he has broken his own contract, because he is no longer able to fulfil that. It is no matter how long the person whom the defendant has married lives, the contract having been once broken; and the averment of a request to fulfil it is immaterial.

WIGHTMAN, J. I am of the same opinion. The facts stated in the count shew a dispensation with the request to marry.

Judgment for plaintiff.

[1] The learned counsel here stated that case. — ED.

CAINES v. SMITH.

IN THE EXCHEQUER, JANUARY 26, 1846.

[*Reported in* 15 *Meeson & Welsby*, 189.]

ASSUMPSIT. The declaration stated that the defendant promised the plaintiff to marry her; that the plaintiff remained and still is sole and unmarried, and was during all the time aforesaid ready to marry the defendant; whereof the defendant always had notice: yet the defendant disregarded his said promise, and afterwards, to wit, on, &c., wrongfully and injuriously married a certain other woman.

Plea, that the defendant was not, at any time before the commencement of the suit, requested by the plaintiff to marry her. Verification.

Special demurrer, on the ground that the plea traversed matter not alleged in or implied by the declaration, and raised an immaterial issue. Joinder in demurrer.

Peacock, in support of the demurrer. The plaintiff was under no obligation to request the defendant to do that which he had put it out of his power to do by marrying another woman. The point was decided a few days ago by the Court of Queen's Bench in Short *v.* Stone.[1]

The court called on

Hawkins, contra. The plea perhaps cannot be supported; but the declaration is bad in substance. The averment that the defendant had married another woman, without an allegation of the lapse of a reasonable time for the performance of his agreement with the plaintiff, does not shew a breach of the express promise stated in the declaration. The defendant's wife may die before the lapse of the reasonable time, and he may still be able to perform his contract with the plaintiff. The declaration does not even aver that his wife is still alive. "A covenant shall not be broken, if a man does an act which by consequence may be a breach, if the breach does not actually follow." Com. Dig. Covenant (E. 3).

POLLOCK, C. B. Our judgment must be for the plaintiff. If a man were under a contract to deliver certain goods to another, and he had put it out of his power to do so by destroying them, it could not be necessary to request him to deliver them. We ought to put a reasonable construction on this declaration; and, doing so, a breach of contract is substantially alleged; and as the defendant has pleaded over, and the question arises as upon general demurrer only, I think the plaintiff is entitled to judgment.

[1] 15 Law J. (N. S.) Q. B. 143.

ALDERSON, B. I am of the same opinion. Why should we presume that the wife will die before the lapse of a reasonable time, or in the lifetime of her husband? We ought rather to presume the continuance of the present state of things; and while that continues, it is clear that the defendant is disabled from performing his contract.

PLATT, B., concurred. *Judgment for the plaintiff.*

RIPLEY v. M'CLURE.

IN THE EXCHEQUER, JULY 6, 1849.

[*Reported in 4 Exchequer Reports*, 345.]

ASSUMPSIT. The declaration stated, that on, &c., by a certain agreement in writing then made between the plaintiff, a merchant carrying on business at Liverpool, and the defendant, a merchant carrying on business at Belfast in Ireland, the plaintiff agreed to sell and the defendant agreed to buy, on arrival, one-third interest in a cargo of Congou tea by the ship called "The Mary Ann Webb," to include only such part as might be consigned to and for account of the plaintiff, or of certain persons carrying on business by and under the name, style, and firm of Thomas Ripley & Co.; and it was by the said agreement then further agreed between the plaintiff and the defendant, that the said cargo should consist principally of certain descriptions of tea, in and by the said agreement indicated by certain terms in that behalf, &c., that is to say, 430 chests Congou, &c. And it was thereby then further agreed, that the said tea should be delivered in Belfast from the said ship, to wit, to the defendant; and that the rate of freight should be £6 per ton; and that the cost of the said tea should be at invoice rate, with all charges in China, including a commission of not exceeding two and a half per cent. at an exchange of 5*s*. 3*d*. per dollar; and that insurance and charges of landing and warehouse in Belfast should be put to the debit of the account sales; and that payment for the same should be made equal to four months' cash from the last delivery in Belfast; and that the same agreement should be annulled and of no effect if the following circumstances collectively or separately occurred, that is to say, non-arrival, any engagement made in China that might prevent the plaintiff from carrying it out, the vessel being directed to another port without power of change on the part of the plaintiff, or any other cause that could not at the time of the making of the said agreement be explained, but what was then perfectly unknown to the plaintiff; and that the teas should be taken at the usual weights, taxes, and allowances in China as per invoice, and insurance to be done thereon at the rate of 5*s* per dollar, to pay average in the usual way; and that sales should be made by the defendant of the entire parcel as a joint concern through and through, in the proportions specified, — one-third the defendant's and two-thirds the plaintiff's, on usual terms; and that advice should be transmitted to the defendant, as soon as received, of the arrangements made in China respecting the lading and destination of the said ship, so that if there should be any obstacle to the carrying out of that contract in the vessel having been fixed without power of change, that agreement might be declared cancelled. The declaration then alleged mutual promises, and averred, that afterwards, to wit, on, &c., insurance was done by the plaintiff on the said tea at the rate of 5*s.* per dollar, to pay average in the accustomed way; and that afterwards, to wit, on the 20th of September, A. D. 1847, the said ship arrived at Belfast with a cargo of Congou tea consigned to and for account of the plaintiff, and consisting principally of such descriptions of tea as in and by the said agreement indicated as aforesaid, and amounting to a large quantity, to wit, 600 tons of Congou tea; that on the arrival of the said cargo at Belfast the plaintiff was ready and willing to deliver the said cargo in Belfast to the defendant, according to and for the purposes of the said agreement, and so that sales should and might be made by the defendant, upon the terms of and according to the said agreement, of the whole of the said cargo, as a joint concern through and through, in the proportions specified in the said agreement, to wit, one-third the defendant's and two-thirds the plaintiff's, on usual terms; and, although advice was transmitted by the plaintiff to the defendant, as soon as received by the plaintiff, of the arrangements made in China respecting the lading and the destination of the said ship, so that if there had been any obstacle to the carrying out the said agreement, or the said ship had been fixed without power of change, the said agreement might have been declared cancelled; and although no such obstacle ever existed; and although the circumstances, on the occurrence of which, collectively or separately, the said agreement was according to the terms thereof to be cancelled and of no effect, did not nor did any or either of them collectively or separately occur; and although, if the defendant would have observed the said agreement and his said promise, the said cargo of Congou tea would have been delivered in Belfast aforesaid to the defendant according to the said agreement, and the last delivery thereof would have been made more than four months before the commencement of this suit, and the sales of the cargo by the defendant would have been made and completed long before the commencement of this suit; and although the plaintiff, from the time of the said agreement and promise continually until and at and after the arrival of the said ship with the cargo at Belfast, was willing and desirous that the said cargo should be delivered in Belfast to the defendant, for the purposes of and according to the said agreement, and should be sold by the defendant according to the same agreement, and that the same agreement should in all respects be observed, performed, and fulfilled, yet the defendant, before the arrival of the ship with the cargo at Belfast, wholly discharged the plaintiff from delivering the said cargo, according to and for the purposes of the said agreement, in Belfast or to the defendant, and then and thenceforth continually wholly refused to buy the said one-third interest in the said cargo, or to pay for the same interest, according to the said agreement, or otherwise howsoever, or to receive or sell the said cargo, according to and upon the terms of the said agreement, or in any respect whatever to observe, perform, and fulfil the said agreement, and has not received or sold the said cargo, according to or for the purposes of the said agreement, nor paid or delivered any money, bill, note, or security whatsoever, for or in respect of the said third interest in the said cargo, or of any of the matters of the said agreement, &c.; concluding with special damages.

Pleas. First, *non assumpsit.*

Secondly, that the cargo of tea was not, nor was any part thereof, consigned to or for account of the plaintiff, *modo et forma.*

Thirdly, as to so much of the breach as relates to the discharging the plaintiff from the delivering the cargo, and refusing to buy and pay for the one-third interest in the cargo, to receive and sell the cargo, and to observe, perform, and fulfil the said agreement in manner as in the breach alleged, that the defendant did not discharge the plaintiff from delivering the cargo or any part thereof, or refuse to buy or pay for the one-third interest in the said cargo or any part thereof, nor did the defendant refuse to receive or sell the cargo or any part thereof, or to observe, perform, or fulfil the agreement or any part thereof, *modo et forma.*

Fourthly, as to so much of the breach as relates to the defendant having, before the arrival of the ship with the said cargo at Belfast, discharged the plaintiff from delivering the cargo, and refused to buy and pay for the one-third interest, and to receive and sell the cargo, and to observe, perform, and fulfil the said agreement in manner as in the breach alleged, that, within a reasonable time after the alleged discharge and refusal, and before the ship with the cargo arrived at Belfast, to wit, on, &c., the defendant retracted and withdrew the said discharge and refusal, whereof the plaintiff had notice; nevertheless, the plaintiff, from thence and on and ever after the arrival of the said ship with the cargo at Belfast, refused and neglected to deliver, and would not and did not deliver, to the defendant the said cargo or any part thereof according to the said agreement, although the defendant was then ready and willing to receive the same, and the plaintiff ought to, and could and might have then delivered the cargo to the defendant; and the defendant avers that, when he retracted and withdrew the said discharge and refusal, and also when the plaintiff had notice of such retraction and withdrawal of the said discharge and refusal, the ship with the cargo was on her voyage towards Belfast, and the plaintiff had not altered the voyage, course, or destination of the said ship or cargo or any part thereof, or sold or disposed of or dealt with the cargo or any part thereof; nor had the plaintiff in any manner acted on the said discharge and refusal in the said breach mentioned.

Fifthly, as to the residue of the said breach, that the plaintiff was not ready or willing to deliver to the defendant the said cargo or any part thereof, *modo et forma.*

Sixthly, that the agreement was made through the fraud of the plaintiff.

The plaintiff joined issue on the first, second, third, and fifth pleas, and replied to the fourth, that the defendant did not retract or withdraw the said discharge and refusal, or either of them, nor did the plaintiff refuse to deliver, nor was the defendant ready or willing to receive the said cargo or any part thereof, according to the said agreement, *modo et forma.* To the sixth he replied denying the fraud, on which last mentioned replications, issues were also joined.

At the trial before Coleridge, J., at the Liverpool Spring Assizes, 1849, the following facts appeared in evidence: The plaintiff was a merchant carrying on business at Liverpool in his own name, and also with another person at Ghanghæ, in China, as commission agents, under the firm of Thomas Ripley & Co. The defendant carried on business as a merchant and general commission agent at Belfast, under the firm of William M'Clure & Son. On the 20th of June, 1846, the plaintiff and defendant entered into a joint adventure for importing a cargo of tea from China, in which the defendant was to have one-third interest. An investment in goods was to be made to purchase the tea, which was to be brought by the ship Mary Ann Webb; and consigned to the defendant at Belfast for sale at the customary commission. On the 7th of October, 1846, the plaintiff wrote to the defendant inclosing invoice of shipment to China, and stating "the proceeds to be invested in tea for the Belfast market, in which you are to take one-third interest." The plaintiff subsequently wrote to the defendant, representing that the adventure was likely to prove a loss, and offering to release him from his engagement. Some correspondence then took place, and ultimately this contract was annulled by mutual consent, and on the 16th of March, 1847, the agreement set out in the declaration was substituted. The defendant became dissatisfied with this agreement, and proposed to the plaintiff to cancel it, and set up the first contract. A long correspondence ensued, in which the defendant alleged, that he had been induced to abandon the first contract and enter into the subsequent agreement by reason of the misrepresentations of the plaintiff. On the 1st of July, 1847, the plaintiff sent to the defendant copies of the invoices of the tea, in a letter containing the following passage: "I have had it from yourself, that you do not intend to comply with the conditions of the contract for the purchase of one-third of this cargo, a threat which I am inclined to believe you do not intend to act upon. On this subject you will please give me your opinion in writing, and I shall be glad if you will assign your reasons for choosing such a course, when the contract on my part will be fulfilled to the letter." No answer having been returned to this letter, the plaintiff, on the 26th of August, again wrote to the defendant thus: "As regards the Mary Ann Webb, there is nothing left for me to do but to send her to some other port than Belfast, since you have declined to fulfil your contract." On the 30th, the defendant wrote in reply: "As to the cargo of the Mary Ann Webb, to one-third of which we still think we are entitled under our first contract, we observe you now intend to send it to a different port. I am willing, and, such being the case, I am glad this unpleasant matter should be thus ended; and I am willing to waive any claim I may have under either the first or second contract." In reply, the plaintiff wrote that it was not his intention to release the defendant from his contract of purchase. On the 1st of September, the defendant wrote to the plaintiff as follows: "I give you notice, that I am entitled to have these teas delivered at Belfast, either under the first or second contract, and that, if you fail to deliver them accordingly, I shall hold myself released from all contracts respecting them." On the 21st of September, the Mary Ann Webb arrived in Belfast Lough with the cargo of tea on board; and the defendant, having been informed of it, wrote to the plaintiff, stating that he was "willing to dispose of the cargo and appropriate the proceeds according to the interests of both parties therein." The defendant also on the same day served the captain of the vessel with a copy of this letter. In consequence, however, of directions from the plaintiff, the vessel sailed from Belfast on the 24th of September for London, without delivering any portion of her cargo to the defendant. The copy of the invoice sent to the defendant was headed thus: "Invoice of Congou tea shipped on board the Mary Ann Webb, Silk, master, for Belfast; and consigned to Thomas Ripley, Esq., Liverpool." It afterwards appeared that, in the heading of the original invoice, the words "on account and risk of Messrs. M'Clure & Son and Thomas Ripley" were inserted after the word "Belfast." The bills of lading stated, that the goods were bound for Belfast market, and consigned unto Thomas Ripley or his assignee.

It was submitted, on the part of the plaintiff, that the above correspondence proved that the defendant had refused to perform the contract declared on, and had discharged the plaintiff from delivering the tea at Belfast. On behalf of the defendant it was contended, that he had not refused to perform the contract in question, and that, so far from discharging the plaintiff from delivering the tea at Belfast, he had insisted on the plaintiff delivering it there.

With respect to the second issue, the learned judge told the jury that the fact of the tea being stated to be shipped on the joint account did not preclude them from finding that they were consigned to the plaintiff, the invoicing them on the joint account having been done by mistake by the correspondent in China, who was ignorant of the fact of the first contract having been rescinded, and of the goods being consigned to the plaintiff, and coming home on the plaintiff's sole account.

The following questions were put by the learned judge in writing to the jury, who returned the accompanying answers:—

First, was the plaintiff guilty of any misrepresentation as to the circumstances connected with the former contract, by which the defendant was induced to enter into the second? No.

Second, did the defendant at any time refuse to perform the second contract? Yes, by implication.

Third, did the defendant ever withdraw that refusal before the ship arrived at Belfast? No.

Fourth, was the plaintiff willing to deliver according to the second contract down to the time of the defendant's refusal to perform the contract? Yes, but not after the arrival of the vessel at Belfast, the defendant having repudiated the contract.

Fifth, to and on whose account were the teas consigned? Thomas Ripley.

On these findings the learned judge directed a verdict for the defendant on the issue raised by the fifth plea, and for the plaintiff on the other issues.

Knowles, in Easter Term last, obtained a rule on the part of the defendant for a new trial, on the ground of the verdict being against evidence, and also upon the following alleged grounds of misdirection: First, that the learned judge had told the jury, with reference to the letter of the first of July, in which the plaintiff demanded that the defendant should state in writing whether he intended to comply with the contract, that the plaintiff had a right to an answer from the defendant. Secondly, that the learned judge was wrong in putting the question to the jury whether the defendant at any time refused to perform his contract; but the question ought to have been, whether he did so refuse after the arrival of the vessel at Belfast, and that the learned judge was not correct in directing a verdict to be entered for the plaintiff on the third issue, upon the answers which had been returned by the jury. Thirdly, that the mode in which the question was put to the jury as to the consignment of the teas to the plaintiff was improper. A rule was also obtained to arrest the judgment, on the ground that the fifth plea was found for the defendant, and was a complete answer to the action.

In the Vacation Sittings after the last Term (June 19 and 21),

Martin and *J. Henderson* shewed cause. As to the first alleged misdirection, it cannot fairly be contended that the learned judge told the jury, as a matter of law, and for the purpose of giving them a specific direction upon the point, that the plaintiff's request by letter required an answer; it was merely intended as an observation, that such a course ought to have been pursued. As to the second ground, the jury were not told that a refusal to perform the contract at any time was a breach of it; but the question left to them was, whether the defendant at any time refused to perform his contract, and whether that refusal had been withdrawn up to the time of the vessel's arrival; and the jury found there was no withdrawal of such refusal, and therefore the plaintiff was discharged from the delivery of the tea. The direction to the jury was, therefore, substantially correct. With respect to the application to arrest the judgment on the issue raised by the fifth plea, the answer is, that the plea in question raises an immaterial issue. That plea is pleaded to the residue of the breach, that is, as to so much of the breach as has not been pleaded to; but inasmuch as the third plea answers the whole breach, the residue of the breach is nothing. The breach was complete by the defendant discharging the plaintiff before the arrival of the vessel at Belfast. That the plaintiff was not ready and willing to deliver the cargo after the defendant had so discharged him, is wholly immaterial, for the plaintiff was not bound to deliver the cargo at Belfast after that discharge. [They also argued that the verdict was not against evidence.]

Knowles, *Crompton*, *Unthank*, and *Mellish*, in support of the rule. The learned judge misdirected the jury as to the issue raised on the third plea. That plea consists of a direct denial of that part of the alleged breach to which it is pleaded, and the finding of the jury does not warrant a verdict for the plaintiff on that issue. The refusal of the defendant on one occasion to perform the contract is not a repudiation of it. Such refusal was made under circumstances which rendered it unnecessary for the defendant to retract it. The important time to be looked at is the arrival of the vessel at Belfast; and the refusal to receive the goods or perform the contract before that time is no breach of the promise; Philpotts *v.* Evans.[1] Therefore the material part of the breach is, that the defendant refused to receive the cargo at Belfast; and it certainly does not follow that, because he may, at some previous time, have objected to perform the contract, therefore he committed a breach of promise by refusing to receive the cargo when it arrived at Belfast. A refusal necessarily implies a capability of acting; but after the arrival of the vessel at Belfast the defendant was never in a position to refuse, for the jury have expressly found that at that time the

[1] 5 M. & W. 475.

plaintiff was not willing to deliver the cargo. There are, therefore, inconsistent findings on the record; namely, that the plaintiff was not willing to deliver, and yet that the defendant refused to accept. A refusal to perform the contract before the vessel arrived at Belfast would at most be evidence only of a refusal to receive the cargo at Belfast; but such evidence is rebutted by the defendant's letter of the 1st of September, 1847, in which he requires the tea to be delivered to him at Belfast. Every thing to be done by the defendant contemporaneous with the delivery of the goods at Belfast was the same in the first as in the second contract; and therefore, although the defendant may have asserted that he considered the first, not the second contract to be the binding contract, that did not absolve the plaintiff from delivering the cargo at Belfast, if he intended to hold the defendant to the second contract. The defendant had nothing to do under the second contract until the tea was delivered at Belfast; so that his not being ready and willing to pay, or saying that he would not pay, did not afford the plaintiff a legal excuse for the non-delivery. The delivery of the tea at Belfast was a condition precedent to any obligation attaching on the defendant. A condition precedent can only be discharged by a readiness and willingness at the proper time to do the act; Jones *v.* Berkely,[1] Laird *v.* Pim;[2] in that respect it resembles a tender. Besides, the contract is in writing, and the waiver, if any, ought, under the Statute of Frauds, to be also in writing; Goss *v.* Lord Nugent,[3] Marshall *v.* Lynn,[4] Stead *v.* Dawber,[5] Giraud *v.* Richmond.[6] [PARKE, B., referred to Cuff *v.* Penn.[7]] The learned judge also misdirected the jury upon the issue as to the consignment of the tea. The invoice, not the bill of lading, is the important document, and that shewed that the consignment was for the plaintiff and defendant jointly.

The judgment ought to be arrested, inasmuch as the jury have found for the defendant on the fifth plea, which covers the whole of the substantial breach. The "residue" of the breach to which that plea is pleaded, is the portion left unanswered by the previous plea, which applies only to the discharging the plaintiff from delivering the cargo before the arrival of the vessel at Belfast. The "residue," therefore, points to the only material part of the breach, namely, a discharge after the vessel arrived at Belfast. [They also argued that the verdict was against evidence.] *Cur. adv. vult.*

The judgment of the court was now delivered by

PARKE, B. A motion for a new trial was made in this case, on the ground of misdirection, and the verdict being against evidence. Also a motion to arrest the judgment, on the ground that the issue on the

[1] Dougl. 684.
[2] 7 M. & W. 474.
[3] 5 B. & Ad. 58.
[4] 6 M. & W. 109.
[5] 10 A. & E. 57.
[6] 2 C. B. 835.
[7] 1 M. & Sel. 21.

fifth plea was found for the defendant, and was an answer to the action. (After stating the pleadings, his lordship proceeded): According to the statement of the contract in the declaration, and as it was proved, it was an executory contract to purchase one-third of a cargo of teas exported from China, capable of being ascertained, such purchase to be made on certain contingencies, viz., the arrival of the cargo at Belfast, the absence of previous contracts in China affecting the cargo, and other circumstances mentioned in the agreement. It is clear, therefore, that the property did not pass by the contract, and the delivery of the cargo by the plaintiff as vendor to the defendant as vendee,—not a mere readiness to deliver after arrival,—was a condition precedent to the plaintiff's right to recover the price, for that price was payable, not *on*, but *after* delivery. It also appeared on the trial, and is a most important element in the consideration of the case, and is a key to many ambiguous parts of the defendant's conduct in the transaction, that there had been before a contract of partnership in an outward adventure, and the cargo expected in return for it by the same vessel, for which the contract declared upon, being a contract of purchase and sale, was substituted. The liability to perform the contract of purchase, and its non-performance, not that for a partnership in a joint adventure, was the question in the case. One defence was fraud in obtaining the second contract by false representations as to the probable result of the first, which defence was not made out. The other is the one with respect to which a misdirection is alleged to have taken place. This was in two particulars; the first was, that the question which the learned judge left to the jury, as to the non-performance of the contract, was, whether the defendant refused at any time to fulfil the second contract, not whether he refused after the arrival; and secondly, that, as to the question whether he refused or not, the learned judge told the jury that the plaintiff had a right, before the arrival of the cargo, to a distinct answer whether the defendant would fulfil the contract or not.

As to the latter point, if this had been laid down as a proposition of law, it would certainly not have been correct. The defendant was not bound to do any thing before the arrival. But it was contended, that this was only an observation made by my brother Coleridge on the facts, and amounted merely to this, that, in the intercourse of merchants under the circumstances of the case, a letter from the plaintiff to the defendant, containing a request for such an answer, ought to have been answered; and we do not think that my brother Coleridge meant to say more, nor that the jury could have understood him to do so. The other objection requires more consideration.

It was contended, for the defendant, that to constitute a breach of the contract, a refusal at any time was insufficient; that it must be a refusal after the arrival of the cargo; and that the supposed refusal in

July, to which the attention of the jury was said to have been directed, and which was long before the contract to buy became absolute, was no breach, and nothing more than an expression of an intention to break the contract, not final, and capable of being retracted. And we think, that if the jury had been told that a refusal before the arrival of the cargo was a breach, that would have been incorrect. We think that point rightly decided in Phillpotts *v.* Evans.[1]

But we cannot collect that the learned judge ever told the jury that a refusal at any time was a breach. He left the questions in writing, whether there was a refusal at any time, and whether that refusal had been subsequently retracted; and the jury having found, as we think they were warranted by the evidence to do, that it had not, there was certainly evidence of a continual refusal down to and inclusive of the time when the defendant was bound to receive, which would render the defendant liable, if all the conditions precedent had been performed or waived. But then it was said, and rightly, that the delivery of the cargo being a condition precedent, the plaintiff was bound to perform it, unless the defendant waived or discharged him from so doing. In the declaration there is an allegation, though informal, of such waiver or discharge, coupled with the allegation of refusal, and an issue upon it in the third plea, and the plaintiff no doubt was bound to prove that waiver or discharge; we do not feel any difficulty in saying that there was ample evidence of such waiver in the conversation referred to in the plaintiff's letter of the 1st of July, coupled with the whole tenor of the defendant's letters.

By an express refusal to comply with the conditions of the contract of purchase, the defendant must be understood to have said to the plaintiff, "You need not take the trouble to deliver the cargo to me when it arrives at Belfast, as purchaser, for I never will become such;" and this would be a waiver at that time of the delivery; and, if unretracted, would dispense with the actual delivery after arrival.

And if we look to the correspondence, it is to be inferred from it that the defendant never did mean to perform the contract of purchase at all; and, consequently, never retracted the waiver of the delivery by the plaintiff as a vendor. It is true that the defendant insists that the cargo shall be delivered at Belfast; and even the alleged parol refusal was probably not intended to be, as Mr. Mellish in his able and ingenious argument with truth contended, any waiver of the delivery at Belfast; it may be taken that the defendant always meant that; but the true question is not, whether the delivery at Belfast was waived, but whether the delivery under the second contract, that is, the contract of purchase and sale, was waived; and we feel no doubt that the defendant, after he had formed the opinion that he had been deluded into a

[1] 5 M. & W. 475.

contract of purchase by false representations of the prospects of the original adventure in the first instance, wholly refused to be bound by the contract of sale, and thereby intended to waive the delivery under that contract, and never afterwards retracted the waiver.

This was a question for the jury; and we do not see any reason to think, from the report and the statements of the learned counsel on both sides, that the jury were not in substance properly directed as to the question for their decision; and we are all quite satisfied with their verdict. As to the issue with respect to the consignment to the plaintiff, we think that the learned judge's direction was quite right.

With respect to the motion in arrest of judgment, we think that the verdict on the issue as to the residue is immaterial. If this residue is that part of the breach which is not answered either by the third plea or the fourth, it is in effect no part of the breach at all, for the third plea answers all; there is nothing to plead to, and the plea is idle and irrelevant. If it means the residue not answered by the fourth plea, it is only the readiness and the willingness to deliver after the time that the delivery was excused, and the defendant refused to receive; and readiness and willingness after that time is wholly immaterial. The verdict for the defendant is, therefore, upon an immaterial averment in the declaration.[1] *Rule discharged.*

CORT AND GEE v. THE AMBERGATE, NOTTINGHAM, AND BOSTON, AND EASTERN JUNCTION RAILWAY CO.

IN THE QUEEN'S BENCH, MAY 27, JUNE 4, 1851.

[*Reported in* 17 *Queen's Bench Reports*, 127.]

CASE. The declaration stated that, on 14th December, 1846, defendants, then being about constructing the above-named railway, required in that behalf and advertised for certain railway chairs to be supplied to them according to a certain specification then made and published by defendants, and containing and stating therein, &c. The specification was then set forth, describing the required make, weight, and composition of the chairs, and that "the quantity of chairs required was to be 900 tons of joint and 3000 tons of intermediate chairs; and which were to be delivered at such places and in such proportions as hereinafter described, to wit, to be delivered out of barges and placed upon a wharf at Radcliffe upon Trent," &c. (other places of delivery for

[1] The judgment of the court was afterwards affirmed in the court of error upon the latter point. [5 Exch. 140.]

various quantities were then stated); "in the month of February, A. D. 1847, 60 tons at the Grantham Canal Wharf," &c. (naming quantities and places[1]); "in the month of March in the year aforesaid," &c.: the specification, as recited, then went on to require further deliveries at places and in quantities named, in April, and from thence monthly till November, 1847, inclusive; and again from January to May, 1848, inclusive. The tender was to state a price per ton; payments to be made by the directors of the company one month after delivery, on production of a certificate, from the person appointed by the company to receive and inspect the chairs, that the contract (for the portion) had been duly performed; the engineer to "have full power to alter the deliveries in any way or proportion to the different places before specified, by sending information to the contractor from time to time of the manner in which such deliveries were to be made";[2] the contractor to be paid according to the prices set forth in his tender. The declaration then averred that plaintiffs, having notice of the premises, did thereupon afterwards, viz., on, &c., propose to defendants to supply them with 3900 tons of cast iron chairs manufactured from strong mixed iron, subject to the conditions and stipulations set forth in the said specification, and in such proportion of joint chairs to intermediate or single chairs as described therein as aforesaid, and also to deliver the same at such places and in such quantities as stated and described as aforesaid, free from every other charge, and at the rate, &c. (specifying the rates); And thereupon afterwards, viz., on 28th December, 1846, by a certain contract or memorandum of agreement then made between plaintiffs of the one part and defendants of the other part, and then sealed with the common seal of the defendants, and delivered so sealed as aforesaid to the plaintiffs, and which, &c. (profert), it was agreed by and between plaintiffs and defendants that plaintiffs should and would execute and perform the said proposal according to the conditions and stipulations therein set forth and referred to as aforesaid, and subject to the said specification. And defendants did thereby agree to pay plaintiffs for the said chairs after the rate and in manner above-mentioned. Averment, that plaintiffs afterwards, viz., on, &c., and on divers other days, &c., did, in pursuance and part-performance of the said contract on their part, deliver to defendants, and defendants did accept and receive of and from plaintiffs, 1787 tons of such chairs as aforesaid; and, although one month from the said respective deliveries of the said chairs had respectively elapsed before the commencement of this suit, and plaintiffs afterwards, and after the expiration of one month as aforesaid, and before the commencement of this suit, viz., &c., produced such written

[1] The quantities were to be from 100 to 356 tons in the whole per month; places of delivery, Grantham Canal Wharf, Bottesford Wharf, Radcliffe Wharf, High Bridge Wharf, and Boston.

[2] These words were taken nearly *verbatim* from the specification.

certificates as aforesaid to the defendants in respect of the quantities of chairs so delivered as aforesaid, nevertheless defendants have not paid, &c., and a large sum, viz., £12,100, is due and unpaid from them to plaintiffs for and in respect of the said chairs so delivered, &c.

And plaintiffs further say that, although they were always, from the time of the making of the said contract until such refusal and wrongful discharge by defendants as hereinafter mentioned, and thence hitherto, ready and willing to execute and perform the said proposal according to the conditions and stipulations in that behalf aforesaid, and subject to the said specification, and to perform and fulfil the said contract in all things on their part and behalf to be performed and fulfilled, whereof, &c. (notice to defendants), and although defendants, in pursuance and part-performance of the said contract on their part, have accepted and received of and from plaintiffs a certain quantity of the said chairs, to wit, 1787 tons thereof, and although the time so limited and appointed for the execution and performance of the said contract by plaintiffs as aforesaid, hath long since elapsed, nevertheless defendants afterwards, to wit, during the time so limited and appointed for the execution and performance of the said contract by plaintiffs as aforesaid, to wit, the 31st January, 1848, wrongfully and injuriously and wholly refused, and have thence hitherto wholly refused to accept or receive of or from plaintiffs the residue of the said chairs so agreed to be supplied to and received by defendants as aforesaid, or any part thereof, according to the form and effect of the said contract or otherwise howsoever, and then and have thence hitherto wholly and wrongfully prevented and discharged plaintiffs from supplying the said residue, and from the further execution and performance of the said contract by them the plaintiffs. Whereby plaintiffs have lost all the profits, &c., and have been put to costs in providing, &c., for complete execution of the contract, and were obliged to discharge certain persons (named) from contracts which the plaintiffs had entered into with them for the supply of iron to be used by plaintiffs in making the said chairs, and to pay them compensation.

Plea 1. After oyer of the specification and agreement (the material parts of which appear sufficiently by the declaration): As to the first breach, except so far as the same relates to £159, parcel, &c., payment by defendants to plaintiffs, and acceptance by them in full satisfaction, &c.: verification.

Plea 2. As to the £159, payment into court of that sum: which the plaintiffs accepted, and gave a written admission that it covered the balance due for chairs actually delivered.

Plea 3. As to so much of the said declaration as alleges that plaintiffs were ready and willing to execute and perform the said proposal according to the conditions and stipulations in that behalf aforesaid, and subject to the said specification, defendants say that plaintiffs were not ready and willing to execute and perform the said proposal according to the said conditions and stipulations, and subject to the said specification in manner and form, &c. Conclusion to the country. Issue thereon.

Plea 4. As to so much of the declaration as charges defendants with having, during the time limited and appointed for the execution and performance of the said contract by the plaintiffs, refused to accept or receive the said residue of the said chairs, and prevented and discharged the plaintiffs from supplying the said residue, and from the further execution and performance of the said contract by them the plaintiffs, defendants say that they did not during the said last-mentioned time refuse to accept or receive the said residue, nor did they prevent or discharge the plaintiffs from supplying the said residue, and from the further execution and performance of the said contract by the plaintiffs in manner and form, &c. Conclusion to the country. Issue thereon.

Replication to plea 1. That defendants did not pay, &c., nor did plaintiffs accept, &c., in manner and form, &c. Conclusion to the country. Issue thereon.

On the trial before Coleridge, J., at the Nottingham Spring Assizes, 1851, it appeared that the plaintiffs, after the agreement declared upon, bought premises, made contracts for iron, and, at considerable expense and by incurring various liabilities, put themselves in a situation to supply the 3900 tons of iron chairs. The supply was begun; but in September, 1847, when the plaintiffs' bookkeeper, Smith, called upon the company's engineer for money, the engineer, who used to give directions on their behalf as to the delivery of the chairs, requested that the plaintiffs would go on very slowly with the supply, as he did not know how to do, the calls not being paid, and he did not know how far the line would be carried out. Part of the line for which the chairs had been ordered (ending at Boston) was ultimately abandoned. In January, 1848, the engineer stopped the supply for a time, saying he would let the plaintiffs know when more chairs were wanted. The plaintiffs' establishment for manufacturing the chairs was kept up during the suspension, which continued till August. Then the engineer said the company could take a few more, but plaintiffs were to go on slowly. They did so till February, 1849, and were then again stopped till April, when the engineer desired to have a boat-load (if plaintiffs had as many) sent to Radcliffe Wharf, which was done. No more were sent or asked for till December, 1849, when Smith called upon the engineer for money, and he inquired whether plaintiffs had any chairs. Smith replied that they had some which had been made a long time. The engineer said that if plaintiffs had 100 tons, they might send them, but they were not to make any more, as they would not be wanted, for the defendants had as many as were necessary to carry the line to Grantham. Plaintiffs sent all they had, about 53 tons, and no more were sent or required afterwards. During the supply the payments were not made punctually according to contract, nor had the plaintiffs delivered the stipulated quantities of chairs at the appointed times respectively; which omission on their part they attributed to the interruptions above stated. A large stock of iron remained on the plaintiffs' hands, and besides loss in the disposal of it they had to pay money for breaking off engagements which they had themselves made for the purpose of executing this work. The quantity of chairs delivered was 1787 tons.

In defence, an endeavor was made to shew that the plaintiffs had not the requisite means to complete their contract, and that the delays and final cessation took place with their concurrence. It was also urged that the engineer was not shewn to have had such authority as would make his acts binding on the company. These points were left to the jury, who decided them in favor of the plaintiffs.

It was further contended that the averment by plaintiffs, in the declaration, of readiness and willingness to perform their contract, was not borne out, inasmuch as the plaintiffs had not offered to deliver, nor had ever made, the residue of the chairs; nor was it proved that the defendants had prevented and discharged plaintiffs from supplying such residue, since it did not appear that the company had impeded the delivery by any active interference, or had countermanded it under their seal or by any authoritative communication. On the first of these points, Coleridge, J., said: There is no evidence of any refusal to accept; no evidence of their having said, for example, "We insist upon your completing the contract; and, if you do not, we shall bring an action." There is no offer to send the chairs, and no refusal to accept; nor is there the slightest ground for believing that the plaintiffs have ever made these chairs; but I think the law is not so unreasonable as to compel parties to be at the expense of making these chairs, if those who contracted to purchase have in truth told them they would not accept them; and I think the defendants had given very effective notice that they were not to be made. On the second point his lordship said, after reading the material statements of the witnesses: Upon this evidence you are to say whether or not the directors refused to accept. Why, they certainly have not in form; but do they, by any intervention on their part, cause the plaintiffs not to go on to complete the delivery. If you think that they did, then that issue, like the former, should be found for the plaintiffs; but if you think not, then that issue should be found for the defendants. With respect to the authority of the engineer to suspend and stop the work, and the responsibility of the company for his directions, though not warranted under their seal, the learned judge observed: This contract was entered into under seal by the Ambergate Railway

Company, a corporation, on the one part, who are under certain disabilities and disadvantages which do not attach to other people; but the corporation all the way through seem to have been represented by certain individuals; and the most important person with whom they (plaintiffs) have had to do is the engineer; and I think rightly and properly, and that he was a necessary man to go between these parties. Without his certificate the plaintiffs could not get any money; and before he would certify, he would have to be satisfied that they had a perfectly flat chair.[1] I shall advise ; ou very much to consider this case as one, in the particular parts to which I shall draw your attention, in which you should look upon every thing done by the engineer as if it was done by the company itself, as far as the plaintiffs are concerned. As to the damages, his lordship said that the plaintiffs, if they had a verdict, were entitled to be put into the same situation as if they had completed their contract; and he suggested modes in which the damage upon the whole quantity undelivered might be estimated, but without giving any actual direction upon this subject.

The learned judge read over to the jury the material parts of the evidence on all the points; and they found a verdict for the plaintiffs, damages £1800.

Macaulay, in the ensuing term, moved for a new trial on the ground of misdirection on the points of readiness and willingness, and of prevention; and he also objected to the summing up as to the authority of the engineer, and on the question how far the plaintiffs were shewn to have concurred in the stopping of their work. He cited West *v.* Blakeway,[2] Phillpotts *v.* Evans,[3] and Ripley *v.* McClure.[4] And he contended that the damages were excessive, inasmuch as the verdict was given in respect of all the chairs, whereas some had been undelivered on the appointed days before the final stoppage, and without any compulsion upon the plaintiffs not to deliver them. A rule *nisi* was granted.

Humfrey and *Willmore* now shewed cause.[5] The plaintiffs proved that they were ready and willing to deliver all the chairs, if the defendants had not prevented them. There could be no obligation to tender them, after the company had said that they would not be received. The defendants will be obliged to contend that their contract could not be broken but by an order under seal. [LORD CAMPBELL, C. J. That it could not be altered but under seal. PATTESON, J. The argument will apply only to the discharging.] The plaintiffs had no means of obtaining a discharge under seal. Discharge of the plaintiffs, or refusal to fulfil their own contract, are, for the present

[1] The specification required that the under side of the chair should be "perfectly flat and even on the surface."

[2] 2 Man. & G. 729.

[3] 5 M. & W. 475.

[4] 4 Exch. 345. See McClure *v.* Ripley, in Exch. Ch. 5 Exch. 140.

[5] Before Lord Campbell, C. J., Patteson, Coleridge, and Erle, JJ.

purpose, the same thing. To say that a seal was necessary to the discharge is to extend the law as to the making of contracts by a company to the breaking of them, and to require a formal contract for both. But, further, the averment put in issue here is that the defendants "refused to accept" the residue of the chairs, and "prevented and discharged" plaintiffs from supplying them. It is enough if the refusal and prevention be proved. They are an act *in pais* equivalent to a discharge. Otherwise the most formal tender of the chairs would not have entitled the plaintiffs to sue, unless there had been an express discharge by the company, and that regularly accepted by the plaintiffs. Refusal, and the continuance of it, were the questions which went to the jury in Ripley v. McClure;[1] and it was held that their finding for the plaintiff entitled him to recover in an action of assumpsit for discharging him from delivery of a cargo and refusing to purchase it according to contract. [LORD CAMPBELL, C. J. You say that it is not necessary here to shew that the contract was varied or put an end to: that the act of the defendants was a flat breach of the contract, which dispensed with your performance.] That is so. The ability of the plaintiffs, if they had not been prevented, was amply proved. (The plaintiffs' counsel commented upon the cases of West v. Blakeway,[2] and Phillpotts v. Evans,[3] cited in moving for the rule, but these are so fully discussed in the judgment of the court, who took the same view of them, that a further notice of this part of the argument is unnecessary.) As to the specific act of prevention here, the engineer was a person whose proceeding might bind the company, if he had their authority; and this fact was affirmed by the jury. The company's acts must be done through some individual agent: and the engineer, by refusing to certify for the purpose of warranting payment, might individually stop the further delivery. [LORD CAMPBELL, C. J. The company never interfered; and that seems to have justified the jury in finding that his act was theirs.] Glover v. London and North Western Railway Company[4] is an authority for the plaintiffs on this point. As to damages, the learned judge did not dictate to the jury any particular mode of estimating them, but only laid down as matter of law that the plaintiffs should be put into the same situation as if the contract had been fulfilled; which was correct.

Macaulay and *Denison*, contra. The plaintiffs, in order to recover, were bound to prove a delivery or something equivalent; the equivalent relied upon was a discharge or prevention, which appear to have been treated at the trial as the same thing. That a mere dispensation by parol would not suffice is clear from West v. Blakeway;[5] and the only modes in which the plaintiffs could exonerate themselves from

[1] 4 Exch. 345.
[2] 2 M. & G. 729.
[3] 5 M. & W. 475.
[4] 5 Exch. 66.
[5] 2 Man. & G. 729.

the condition precedent were either a competent dispensation or an actual prevention by the covenantee. "Discharge" in pleading is taken to mean a discharge legally operative; that is, where the obligation is by deed, a discharge by deed; Brymer v. Thames Haven Dock and Railway Company.[1] What amounts to legal prevention is shewn in Com. Dig. Condition (L. 6). "So the performance of a condition shall be excused by the obstruction of the obligee: as if a condition be to build a house; and he, or another by his order, hinders his coming upon the land." Other instances are then given; and it is added: "But it ought to be an obstruction which disables the performance." What would or would not amount to a disability appears by (M. 5) of the same title. [LORD CAMPBELL, C. J. The examples there regard conditions to enfeoff; I think they are not much to the present purpose.] There must be a prevention. [LORD CAMPBELL, C. J. Of what? COLERIDGE, J. Suppose a man said, "If you come for such a purpose, I will blow your brains out." That would be no physical prevention. LORD CAMPBELL, C. J. Such a threat might be used ten days before the act was to be done.] Its effect must be judged of by a jury. In West v. Blakeway,[2] Tindal, C. J., thought that, if the plea had disclosed "an act which the lessor had done, or which he had compelled to be done," it would have been good. Bosanquet, J., said: "I agree that if the covenantee prevent the performance of the covenant by an act of his own, his right of action for the breach of that covenant is destroyed. But the act, to constitute such a defence, must be the immediate act of the covenantee." And Coltman, J., said that the fallacy in the defendant's argument was its assuming "that there was an act done by the lessor by which the lessee was prevented from performing his covenant." Reference is there made to the case of the Master of St. Catherine's,[3] where the breach of condition by the lessee was caused by an actual ouster and force on the part of the lessor, who afterwards sought to take advantage of the condition; but it clearly was considered that nothing short of such force would be an excuse. No direct authorities as to prevention have been found; but it is evident that there ought to be a prevention in fact, when the party alleging it was ready, and did all that lay in him, to perform his part of the contract. [ERLE, J. There is prevention by a series of acts. COLERIDGE, J. You would not admit such a waiver as was allowed in Ripley v. McClure.[4] LORD CAMPBELL, C. J. According to your argument, even a notice under the common seal of the company to send no more chairs would have been insufficient.] That would be a discharge, not a prevention; and the proper mode of doing such act is pointed out by the Companies Clauses Consolidation Act, 1845, 8 & 9 Vict. c. 16.[5] In Ripley v. McClure[6] the point of time at which

[1] 2 Exch. 549.
[2] 2 Man. & G. 752.
[3] Cited in Frances's Case, 8 Rep. 91 *b*.
[4] 4 Exch. 345.
[5] See sect. 92, *et seq.*
[6] 4 Exch. 345.

the breach of contract took effect, was held to be the time when the ship arrived at Belfast, and the cargo was to be delivered and accepted, no intermediate act remaining to be done. A previous refusal, unless the evidence had shewn that it continued down to that time, would have been unimportant. The same conclusion may be drawn from Phillpotts *v.* Evans.[1] [LORD CAMPBELL, C. J. According to your view, if the party who contracted to purchase were to say, "I am insolvent, and your finishing the article will be of no use," the vendor could not recover unless he finished and tendered it. ERLE, J. Suppose the contract was that plaintiff should send a ship to a certain port for a cargo, and defendant should there load one on board, but defendant wrote word that he could not furnish a cargo: must the ship be sent, to return empty? LORD CAMPBELL, C. J. If it were law, it could not be sense.[2]] In Planché *v.* Colburn[3] the defendants had engaged the plaintiff to write a work for publication, but abandoned the publication when the work was partly completed; and the Court of Common Pleas held that he might recover for so much as he had done, without having tendered the work. There it must have been considered that the contract was rescinded, and that the plaintiff might recover upon it for so much as he had been allowed to execute: upon the facts here, a rescinding cannot be assumed, and the plaintiffs, in order to recover, must have carried out the contract. [COLERIDGE, J. Could the contract be rescinded without consent of both parties? The judgment of Bosanquet, J., in Planché *v.* Colburn[4] is against your view. ERLE, J. The court there do not say that the contract was rescinded.] (*Humfrey* referred to the observations on this case in Goodman *v.* Pocock;[5] and ERLE, J., cited Elderton *v.* Emmens.[6])

The learned judge in the present case told the jury to assume that the engineer's acts were authorized by the company; but there was no evidence of their sanction. [COLERIDGE, J. Not by orders under seal; but there was other conduct that shewed it.] (The discussion as to the evidence, and the words used by the learned judge, is omitted. LORD CAMPBELL, C. J., said: It was not a direction in point of law; and I should have advised the jury so myself.)

In considering what a corporation may authorize without seal, reference must be had to the nature and objects of the incorporation; that principle was acted upon in Beverley *v.* The Lincoln Gas Light and

[1] 5 M. & W. 475.

[2] Cook *v.* Jennings, 7 T. R. 381, was here cited; but Lord Campbell, C. J., said: That has nothing to do with this case.

[3] 8 Bing 14.

[4] 8 Bing. 14; See s. c. 1 Mo. & Scott, 51.

[5] 15 Q. B. 576, 582.

[6] 6 Com. B. in Exch. Ch., reversing the judgment of C. P. in Elderton *v.* Emmens, 4 Com. B. 479; judgment of Exch. Ch. affirmed in Dom. Proc.; Emmens *v.* Elderton, 4 Ho. L. Ca. 624.

Coke Company,[1] Mayor of Ludlow v. Charlton,[2] and Paine v. Strand Union;[3] and Ridley v. Plymouth Grinding and Baking Company[4] shews how strictly the courts will examine the authority of individuals to bind a joint-stock corporation instituted for the purposes of a special act of parliament. [LORD CAMPBELL, C. J. It appears here that, according to the course of the company's business, it was left to the engineer to manage the affairs in question; and that in those they were represented by him.] Cox v. The Midland Counties Railway Company[5] is another authority for the defendants on this point. [LORD CAMPBELL, C. J. There never was a case reported which admitted of less doubt.]

As to the damages. Until the first actual stoppage, in January, 1848, the plaintiffs might have delivered the chairs on the days specified; if any remained on hand by reason of their omission to do so, it was their own fault; and damages ought not to have been awarded to them for loss of profit on the whole amount finally undelivered, but only on that which they were prevented by express prohibition from delivering on the stated days. (They also contended that, on the amount for which damages might be claimed consistently with this objection, the assessment was not justified by the evidence).

Cur. adv. vult.

LORD CAMPBELL, C. J., on a later day of the term (June 4th), delivered the judgment of the court.

We are of opinion that the verdict found for the plaintiffs ought not to be disturbed. As to the supposed misdirection, the learned judge at the trial did not direct the jury that in point of law the engineer had authority to bind the company, but only left it to the jury to consider whether, in point of fact, the company by their mode of dealing had authorized and sanctioned his acts. His lordship intimated that he thought the evidence was strong to shew that they had done so, but that it was for the jury to give the evidence its due weight. The objection of misdirection therefore fails.

Next we have to consider whether the plaintiffs were entitled to a verdict on the issue whether they were ready and willing to execute and perform the said contract according to the said conditions and stipulations, in manner and form, &c.; and on the issue whether the defendants did refuse to accept or receive the residue of the chairs, or prevent or discharge the plaintiffs from supplying the said residue, and from the further execution and performance of the said contract. It is not denied that, if the defendants would have regularly accepted and paid for the chairs, the plaintiffs would have gone on regularly making and delivering them according to the contract; the objection

[1] 6 A. & E. 829. [2] 6 M. & W. 815.
[3] 8 Q. B. 326. [4] 2 Exch. 711. [5] 3 Exch. 268.

is that, although the plaintiffs were desirous that the contract should be fully performed, yet, after receiving the notice that the company did not wish to have any more chairs, and would not accept any more, they ceased to make any more, insomuch that the residue which the company are alleged to have refused to accept never were made. The defendants contend that, as the plaintiffs did not make and tender the residue of the chairs, they cannot be said to have been ready and willing to perform the contract; that the defendants cannot be charged with a breach of it; that, after the notice from the defendants, which in truth amounted to a declaration that they had broken and thenceforward renounced the contract, the plaintiffs, if they wished to have any redress, were bound to buy the requisite quantity of the peculiar sort of iron suited for these railway chairs, to make the whole of them according to the pattern, with the name of the company upon them, and to bring them to the appointed places of delivery and tender them to the defendants, who, from insolvency, had abandoned the completion of the line for which the chairs were intended, desiring that no more chairs might be made, and declaring, in effect, that no more should be accepted or paid for. We are of opinion, however, that the jury were fully justified upon the evidence in finding that the plaintiffs were ready and willing to perform the contract, although they never made and tendered the residue of the chairs. In common sense, the meaning of such an averment of readiness and willingness must be that the non-completion of the contract was not the fault of the plaintiffs, and that they were disposed and able to complete it, if it had not been renounced by the defendants. What more can reasonably be required by the parties for whom the goods are to be manufactured? If, having accepted a part, they are unable to pay for the residue, and have resolved not to accept them, no benefit can accrue to them from a useless waste of materials and labor, which might possibly enhance the amount of damages to be awarded against them.

Upon the last issue, was there not evidence that the defendants refused to accept the residue of the chairs? If they had said, "Make no more for us, for we will have nothing to do with them," was not that refusing to accept or receive them according to the contract? But the learned counsel for the defendants laid peculiar stress upon the words, "nor did they prevent or discharge the plaintiffs from supplying the said residue" of the chairs "and from the further execution and performance of the said contract." We consider the material part of the allegation which the last plea traverses to be, that the defendants refused to receive the residue of the chairs. But, assuming that the whole must be proved, we think there is evidence to shew that the defendants did prevent and discharge the plaintiffs from supplying the residue of the chairs, and from the further execution of the contract. It is contended that "prevent" here must mean an obstruction by physical force; and, in answer to a question from the court, we were told it would not be a preventing of the delivery of goods if the purchaser were to write, in a letter to the person who ought to supply them, "Should you come to my house to deliver them, I will blow your brains out." But may I not reasonably say that I was prevented from completing a contract by being desired not to complete it? Are there no means of preventing an act from being done except physical force or brute violence? Again, we are told there can be no "discharge" by a corporation, unless by deed under the corporate seal. Of a discharge in one sense of the word this is true. A discharge is sometimes used as equivalent to a release, which must be under seal; Brymer *v.* Thames Haven Dock & Railway Company.[1] But we conceive that, in the allegation traversed by the last plea, discharge only means, like prevent, that the act of the defendants was the cause of the residue of the chairs not being delivered, and of the contract not being further executed or performed. Taking the language employed in its natural and reasonable sense, there was abundant evidence to support the finding of the last issue for the plaintiffs.

It is averred, however, that there are express authorities to shew that there could be no readiness and willingness to perform the contract unless all the chairs were finished and tendered; that to prevent must be by positive physical obstruction, and that there can be no discharging unless by instrument under seal. The first case relied upon was West *v.* Blakeway,[2] in which, an action being brought by lessor against lessee on a covenant to yield up at the expiration of the term all erections and improvements set up or made during the term, assigning for breach the removal of the sashes and framework of a greenhouse erected during the term, it was held to be a bad plea that there was a subsequent parol agreement between the parties, that if the lessee would erect a greenhouse, he should be at liberty to pull it down and remove it. But this merely illustrates the well-known rule that a covenant under seal cannot be varied by parol: *Unumquodque ligamen dissolvitur eodem ligamine quo ligatur.* It has no application to a case where the covenantor is prevented from performing the covenant by the covenantee. In 1 Roll. Ab. 453, and in 5 Vin. Abr. 242, 3, tit. Condition (M. c.), will be found various instances of a covenant being discharged without deed by the act of the covenantee.

The next case relied on by the defendants' counsel was Phillpotts *v.* Evans.[3] That was an action of assumpsit for not accepting a quantity of wheat sold early in January, 1839, by the plaintiffs at Gloucester, "to be delivered at Birmingham as soon as vessels could be obtained for the carriage thereof." On the 26th of January the defendant gave notice to the plaintiffs that he would not accept the

[1] 2 Exch. 549. [2] 2 Man. & G. 729. [3] 5 M. & W. 475.

wheat if it were delivered. It was then on its way by canal to Birmingham; and on its arrival there the defendant was required to accept it, but he refused to do so. The only question at the trial was as to the time with respect to which the damages were to be calculated. The market having continued to fall from the day of the contract till the bringing of the action, the defendant sought to take advantage of his own wrong, and to calculate the damages according to the price in the market on the 26th January, when he gave notice that he intended to break the bargain; but it was very properly held that the plaintiffs were entitled to damages according to the market price when the wheat was tendered to the defendant for acceptance. The court cannot be considered as having decided that, if the notice had been received by the plaintiffs before the wheat was sent off from Gloucester, the plaintiffs might not at their pleasure have treated it as a breach of the contract, and commenced an action against the defendant for not accepting it, without tendering it to him at Birmingham.

The most recent case cited by the defendants' counsel was Ripley *v.* McClure.[1] This case is very complicated in its circumstances; but the second point decided in it is the only one applicable to the question which we have to consider. There being an executory contract, whereby the plaintiff agreed to sell and the defendant to buy, on arrival, certain goods, to be delivered at Belfast at a certain price, payable on delivery, it was held that a refusal by the defendant before the arrival of the cargo to perform the contract was not of itself necessarily a breach of it, but that such refusal, unretracted down to and inclusive of the time when the defendant was bound to receive the cargo, was evidence of a continuing refusal and a waiver of the condition precedent of delivery, so as to render the defendant liable for the breach of contract. But, in the case at bar, the refusal never was retracted; and therefore there was a continuing breach down to the time when this action was commenced.

Upon the whole we think we are justified, on principle and without trenching on any former decision, in holding that, when there is an executory contract for the manufacturing and supply of goods from time to time, to be paid for after delivery, if the purchaser, having accepted and paid for a portion of the goods contracted for, gives notice to the vendor not to manufacture any more as he has no occasion for them and will not accept or pay for them, the vendor having been desirous and able to complete the contract, he may, without manufacturing and tendering the rest of the goods, maintain an action against the purchaser for breach of contract; and that he is entitled to a verdict on pleas traversing allegations that he was ready and willing to perform the contract; that the defendant refused to ac-

[1] 4 Exch. 345.

cept the residue of the goods, and that he prevented and discharged the plaintiff from manufacturing and delivering them.

We are likewise of opinion that, in this case, the damages are not excessive, as the jury were justified in taking into their calculation all the chairs which remained to be delivered, and which the defendants refused to accept. They were all included in the declaration and in the issues joined: the time mentioned in the proposal for the delivery of some of them had arrived before the notice was given; but the time of delivery was not of the essence of the contract; and the obligation was still incumbent upon the defendants to accept the whole of the residue.

The rule must therefore be discharged. *Rule discharged.*

SECTION VIII.

Contracts Conditional upon Demand.

BANKS AND THWAITS' CASE.

IN THE QUEEN'S BENCH, MICHAELMAS TERM, 1579.

[*Reported in* 3 *Leonard,* 73.]

IN an action upon the case, the case was, That A. had pawned an indenture of lease for years of a messuage and lands to Banks; Thwaits, intending to purchase the same, required Banks to deliver him the said lease, and he would give Banks £10 whether he bought it or no, at what time he would request the £10. And Banks delivered the same to Thwaits accordingly; and afterwards brought an action upon the case, and declared upon the whole matter; and concluded, *licet sæpius requisitus, &c.*, without alleging a request express in certain, and the day and place of it. It was said by *Cook*, that here the moneys did not grow due before request, nor is payable before request, and therefore a request ought to be made *in facto.* And so, he said, it was ruled in this court, in an action upon the case betwixt Palmer and Burroughs; and he said that the money was not due by the promise, but by the request. And it was the opinion of the whole court, that although it be a duty, yet it is not a duty payable before request; and the request makes a title to the action. But if A. selleth to B. a horse for £10 there is a contract, and a request in fact need not be laid. And the opinion of the court was also, that upon this matter the plaintiff could not have an action of debt; for there is not any contract, for the thing is not sold, but it is a collateral promise grounded upon the delivery. And by CLENCH: here the request is traversable. And afterwards judgment was given against the plaintiff. And it was said, it was so ruled in Alderman Pullison's case in the Exchequer.

ESTRIGGE AND OWLES' CASE.

IN THE QUEEN'S BENCH, TRINITY TERM, 1588.

[*Reported in* 3 *Leonard*, 200.]

IN an action upon the case by Estrigge against Owles, it was holden by the justices, that forbearance *per paululum tempus* is a good consideration. Then it was moved, that in the action the request was not sufficiently laid in respect of the place and time.

And *Cook* said, that the difference had always been agreed, that where the promise is to do a collateral thing upon request, there in the declaration the place and the time ought to be certainly set down; as it was holden in the case of Alderman Pullison, where he promised to give a tun of wine upon request; in such case the request is traversable, and therefore it ought to be certainly shewed, for the request is parcel of the issue. But if such action be brought, and the plaintiff declares upon an *indebitatus*, then if the plaintiff prove the debt, it is not material to prove the promise; for every contract executory implies a promise; and in such case the request is not traversable. And the truth of the case was, that one Tickill was indebted to the plaintiff in £30, and died intestate. B., his wife, took letters of administration, and took to husband the defendant; and he, for the consideration aforesaid, and that the plaintiff would forbear his debt for a little time, promised to pay it: and further declared, that he had forborne, &c., from such a day until such a day; but yet the defendant would not pay it, *licet sæpius requisitus;* and upon this declaration the plaintiff had judgment. And now a writ of error was brought, and it was assigned for error, because that in the declaration it is alleged, that the wife administered the goods of the intestate, and did not shew that she was administratrix, &c., and took letters of administration. 2. It is not alleged that the wife had goods of the testator at the time of the promise, for otherwise she shall not be bound; for it is but *nudum pactum;* for executors or administrators, not having assets, shall not be charged. And it was holden here, that request is not necessary, for the debt was before the promise, so as the request is not any cause of the action.

THE CASE OF AN HOSTLER.

IN THE KING'S BENCH, TRINITY TERM, 1605.

[*Reported in Yelverton,* 66.]

IN an action on the case on assumpsit the plaintiff declared and shewed himself to be an hostler, and that the defendant brought his horse to him and agreed to give 6*d.* livery for day and night; and because the horse had been there for so many days and nights as amounted to £20, the plaintiff brought the action, and declared, *licet sæpius requisitus,* without alleging a request *in facto.* And it was adjudged good; for where the ground of the action is for a debt, in which case the law implies the promise, there the request is not issuable nor parcel of the consideration. Otherwise where the action is founded upon a mere collateral matter, and not upon a duty; for there the request is issuable and ought to be expressly alleged. . . .

SELMAN AGAINST KING AND OTHERS.

IN THE KING'S BENCH, MICHAELMAS TERM, 1607.

[*Reported in Croke James,* 183.]

ASSUMPSIT. Whereas upon a suit in the Star-chamber between the defendant and others, a commission issued for the examination of witnesses; that the plaintiff at the time of the commission kept an inn in Beningham; and in consideration that she promised to find horse-meat and man's-meat for the defendant and his company during the time of the sitting of the commission, that the defendant assumed to pay to the plaintiff all such sums as that diet and horse-meat amounted to, when he should be thereunto requested; and allegeth in fact that the commissioners sat there three days, and that she found the said horse-meat and man's-meat during the said time, which amounted to five pounds six shillings; and that the defendant, *licet sæpius requisitus,* hath not paid it.

The defendant pleads *non assumpsit,* and it was found against him; and now moved in arrest of judgment, that the promise being to pay when he should be requested, there ought to be a precise request alleged, and the year, day, and place of the request expressed; for the defendant is not otherwise chargeable in an assumpsit.

The whole court was of that opinion: for when the defendant chargeable upon a collateral promise, and not for a mere debt, there ought to be a request precisely alleged: but in an assumpsit for debt, where a duty was due before, that being but in nature of a debt, the general allegation, *licet sæpius requisitus*, is sufficient: and for that cause the judgment was stayed.

HARRISON v. MITFORD.

In the King's Bench, Easter Term, 1614.

[*Reported in 2 Bulstrode*, 229.]

In an action upon the case for a promise, upon *non assumpsit* pleaded, a verdict was found for the plaintiff. It was moved in arrest of judgment that the declaration was not good, the promise being for to save the plaintiff harmless, *cum inde requisitus esset*, and no special request laid in the declaration, as there ought to have been. The whole court agreed clearly in this, that for this cause the declaration is not good; for as this case is, being a promise to save harmless, a special request ought to have been in the declaration, and a *licet sæpius requisitus* will not here serve, and this verdict will in no ways aid or avail the plaintiff; otherwise it would have been, if the promise had been to have paid a certain sum of money, *cum inde requisitus esset;* there a *licet sæpius requisitus, non soluit*, will be good, without laying any special request, and so is the difference agreed by the whole court; and that this declaration, for want of a special request laid, is not good, and so the rule of the court was for the defendant. *Et quod querens nil capiat per billam.*

HILL v. WADE.

In the King's Bench, Hilary Term, 1619.

[*Reported in Croke James*, 523.]

Assumpsit; in consideration that he would buy such land of the defendant, and pay to him forty pounds for it, the defendant promised to pay to the plaintiff nine pounds which J. S. owed to the plaintiff, when he should be thereunto required; and allegeth in fact, that he bought the land and paid forty pounds for it, and that the defendant, *licet sæpius requisitus*, had not paid the nine pounds.

After verdict, upon *non assumpsit* pleaded, and found for the plaintiff, it was moved in arrest of judgment, that the declaration was not good, because there was neither time nor place alleged of the request.

Gwyn, for the plaintiff, oftentimes moved that it was not material, because the defendant pleaded *non assumpsit*, and so hath not taken advantage thereof.

The Court resolved, that forasmuch as it is a stranger's debt, and was no duty by the defendant before the promise, nor payable but upon request, and so no breach until request be made; therefore to enable the plaintiff to [maintain] the action, an express request ought to have been alleged, and a *sæpius requisitus* will not serve.

HOUGHTON, J., took this difference: where a request is upon a duty, as if I sell an house for five pounds, to be paid upon request, there a *licet sæpius requisitus* is sufficient; and where it is upon a collateral matter; for there he ought actually to allege a request, although issue be joined upon the assumpsit. And this difference was affirmed in Grigg's case in a writ of error; and so the opinion of the court was against the plaintiff; *et adjournatur*. Afterwards it was adjudged for the defendant.

LOWE AND KIRBY.

IN THE KING'S BENCH, MICHAELMAS TERM, 1624.

[*Reported in Sir William Jones*, 56.]

A MAN promised, in consideration that J. S. had delivered to him a horse, to deliver to J. S. a horse or a sum of money, upon request. J. S. brought an action upon the case upon assumpsit, and alleged that the defendant, *licet sæpius requisitus*, had not delivered the money nor the horse; and upon *non assumpsit* found for the plaintiff, he had judgment in the court of Rochester; but upon error brought the judgment was reversed, because a precise request was not alleged, for it is a part of the contract; but if a precise request had been alleged and no place of the request, and *non assumpsit* pleaded, and this found for the plaintiff, it would have been good enough; but if the request had been traversed it would have been otherwise, for then no venue would appear for the trial.

PECKE AND MITHWOLDE.

IN THE KING'S BENCH, MICHAELMAS TERM, 1625.

[*Reported in Sir William Jones*, 85.]

WILLIAM MITHWOLDE brought an action upon the case against William Pecke, and declared that the plaintiff and another were bound to the defendant by an obligation of £100, upon condition to pay £52 10*s*. upon a day passed, and that in consideration that the said plaintiff would pay to one William Playford to the use of the defendant the said £52 10*s*., the said defendant promised to deliver to the plaintiff the said obligation upon request; and he alleged that the said plaintiff paid to the said Playford to the use of the defendant the said £52 10*s*., and that the defendant, *licet sæpius requisitus*, had not delivered the bond to the plaintiff. The defendant pleaded *non assumpsit*, and found for the plaintiff; whereupon judgment was given in C. B. for the plaintiff, and the defendant Pecke brought a writ of error. The question was, whether the judgment was erroneous inasmuch as no special request was alleged by the plaintiff to deliver the obligation; and *tota curia* agreed, and so resolved, that the plaintiff ought to have alleged a special request, and the general allegation of *licet sæpius requisitus* was not sufficient; for, they said, where a request is material it ought to be alleged with certainty, for it is traversable; but where no request is necessary, the general allegation of *licet sæpius requisitus* is sufficient; and though the defendant took issue upon the assumpsit, and not upon the request, that does not help the matter, for the request is of the substance of the contract, and that being omitted no issue can make it good. *Judgment reversed.*

ALCOCK *v.* BLOFIELD.

IN THE KING'S BENCH, TRINITY TERM, 1627.

[*Reported in Latch*, 209.]

ALCOCK had judgment in an action upon the case against Blofield. The case was, Alcock brought an action against Bate, and Blofield promised Alcock, if he would forbear to sue Bate, that he would pay him £200 at the feast of St. John Baptist next following, and another £100 at any time after the said feast when he should be reasonably required; and the plaintiff alleged a failure of payment of the said £100, *licet postea* (viz.), 18 Octob. such a year, which in truth was before the day of the first payment; and this was assigned for error in a writ of error.

It was agreed by the court that the request was issuable, and therefore ought to be specially and certainly alleged, because there was no duty before the request, it being upon a promise of a stranger. But when the same party who is indebted promises to pay upon request, it is sufficient to say *licet sæpius requisitus;* for the debt is a debt without a promise.

BIRKS *v.* TRIPPET.

In the King's Bench, Michaelmas Term, 1666.

[*Reported in* 1 *Williams's Saunders,* 32.]

Assumpsit. The plaintiff declares, that there were divers differences between the plaintiff and defendant; and for the determining thereof, they submitted themselves to the award of one Barker, an arbitrator indifferently chosen between them to arbitrate, ordain, and finally adjudge of and upon the premises; and that the defendant, in consideration of the submission, and in consideration that the plaintiff had promised the said defendant to pay him £40 whensoever he should be requested, if the plaintiff should not perform the award to be made on his part, undertook and promised the plaintiff that if the defendant should not perform the award to be made on his part, then the said defendant would well and faithfully pay £40 to the said plaintiff when he should be thereunto requested. The plaintiff avers that the arbitrator made his award, and thereby awarded that the defendant should pay to the plaintiff 10*s.* in consideration of damages in an action of battery, and 20*s.* more for curing a horse, and 10*s.* more for curing an ox, and £4 more for the plaintiff's expenses in law, and that upon payment of the said sums amounting to £6 they should give to each other general releases, and that the defendant should deliver a fine to the plaintiff. And the plaintiff avers that the defendant hath not paid the £6 nor delivered the fine according to the award; yet the said defendant, not regarding his promise but intending to defraud the plaintiff of the said £40, had not paid the said £40 to the plaintiff according to his promise, nor contented him for the same, and so concludes the action to his damage, &c., without alleging any demand for the £40. The defendant pleads in bar, that the plaintiff was indebted to him being an attorney in £4 for fees and expenses, and before making the award he gave notice thereof to the arbitrator, and offered to make it appear to him, and prayed he would allow it in his award; but the arbitrator made his award without any allowance or consideration had of the said £4, notwithstanding such notice and proof. And this, &c. Wherefore, &c. Upon which the plaintiff demurred in law.[1] . . .

Saunders, of counsel with the defendant, said that he would not maintain the plea. But he took an objection to the declaration, that the plaintiff in his declaration had not laid any request of the penalty of £40. For the declaration is, that the defendant promised to pay £40 upon request, if he did not perform the award; and the request is material; for he took a difference between a mere duty and a collateral sum. For where a mere duty is promised to be paid upon request; as if in consideration of all moneys lent to the defendant, he promised to pay them again upon request, no actual request is necessary, but the bringing of the action is a sufficient request; but otherwise it is upon a promise to pay a collateral sum upon request; for there an actual request ought to be made before the action brought. Cro. Jac. 183, Selman *v.* King; 523, Hill *v.* Wade; 639, Waters *v.* Bridges. Now here the promise of payment of the £40 upon request is collateral, and is a penalty, and not a precedent duty, and therefore there ought to have been a request before the action brought. And so was the opinion of the whole court. And TWYSDEN, J., interrupted Saunders, and said to him, What makes you labor so? The court is of your opinion, and the matter clear. And thereupon judgment was given for the defendant, that the plaintiff should take nothing by his bill.

RUMBALL *v.* BALL.

IN THE QUEEN'S BENCH, MICHAELMAS TERM, 1711.

[*Reported in* 10 *Modern Reports*, 38.]

ACTION of debt upon a note to this effect: "I acknowledge myself indebted to such a one so much, which I promise to pay upon demand."

It was moved in arrest of judgment, that though upon a note acknowledging a debt it was not necessary to allege a demand, yet where it is part of the agreement, there a demand is necessary.

But the court was of another opinion, for it is a debt *in præsenti;* and the words "promise to pay" import no more than that I am ready

[1] The argument and decision upon the plea are omitted. — ED.

to pay the money at any time, and shall not restrain or qualify the other words, this being no debt arising upon the performance of a certain condition, but a debt plainly precedent to the demand. Besides, supposing the demand necessary, the action itself perhaps is a demand.[1]

WALLIS *v.* SCOTT.

IN THE KING'S BENCH, EASTER TERM, 1718.

[*Reported in* 1 *Strange,* 88.]

THE plaintiff declares that the defendant, in consideration the plaintiff would make him a set of sails worth £45, promised to pay so much for them upon request; and avers that he made the said sails; and the defendant although often requested refuses to pay. *Demurrer inde.* And *Branthwayte, Serjeant, pro defendente* argued that, the action being founded upon the breach of contract, there ought to be a special request laid. For this differs from the cases where there is a precedent debt or duty whereon to ground the promise, for there I admit the action is a request.[2] . . .

Yorke, contra. The *licet sæpius requisit'* is sufficient. But if not, yet the want of a special request ought to have been shewn for cause of demurrer. The cases in Croke can never be law, for they are after a verdict, when the court will intend a request proved, and so is Pop. 160.

Branthwayte replied. These cases as to the request being after a verdict, the argument holds *a fortiori* in this case, which is on a demurrer. The general request, as alleged, may be since the action brought, and this at most is but an executory promise.

EYRE, J. (*absentibus Parker et Pratt*). Where notice or a request are by law necessary, there the general averment will not be sufficient; but it must be particularly set forth, that the court may judge whether the notice or request were sufficient. But in this case I take it no request was necessary, for on the making the sails the money immediately becomes due. If I promise a tailor, that in consideration he will make me a suit of clothes, I will pay him so much; there needs no request, for as soon as he has done his part, there is a duty vested in him. And this differs from the cases where the payment is to be to a

[1] See Norton *v.* Ellam, 2 M. & W. 461. — ED.

[2] The learned counsel here cited the cases of Selman *v.* King, Cro. Jac. 183; Hill *v.* Wade, *id.* 523; and Birks *v.* Trippet, 1 Saund. 32.

third person, or where an award directs a request. Afterwards, the court being full, *Branthwayte* mentioned Cro. Eliz. 773, 91; Hutt. 107. And *Yorke* quoted Yelv. 66, 121; 3 Bulst. 258; 2 Cro. 639. And the former cases of 2 Cro. 183, 523, were denied per EYRE, J., and judgment given for the plaintiff.[1]

CARTER v. RING, *Widow, Administratrix of* JOSEPH RING, *deceased.*

AT NISI PRIUS, *coram* LORD ELLENBOROUGH, DECEMBER 3, 1813.

[*Reported in* 3 *Campbell*, 459.]

DEBT on bond, dated 1st of July, 1807, in the penal sum of £3800 to be paid by the said Joseph Ring to the plaintiff, when he the said Joseph Ring should be thereunto afterwards requested.

The bond had the following condition: "If the above bounden Joseph Ring, his heirs, executors, or administrators, do well and truly pay or cause to be paid to the above named Henry Carter, his executors, administrators, or assigns, the full sum of £1900 of lawful money current in Great Britain, on demand, with lawful interest at the rate of five per cent. per annum until paid, then," &c.

The defendant after oyer pleaded that no demand of payment of the said sum of money in the said condition mentioned, or of any interest thereupon, was ever made by the plaintiff. The plaintiff in his replication averred, that a demand was made by him upon the defendant as administratrix. Issue thereupon.

The question having arisen, whether express evidence of a demand was necessary, *Jervis*, for the plaintiff, insisted that the bringing of the action was a sufficient demand.

Abbott, contra. The bond must have been forfeited before action brought; and it could not have been forfeited till demand made of the sum of money mentioned in the condition. The stipulation as to the payment of interest clearly shews that the bond was not to be forfeited till default upon an actual demand. The plaintiff here seeks to recover the penalty, which is a collateral sum; and the cases with regard to payment of money on request, where there is an antecedent duty, do not apply.

1 This case has been modified by the omission of irrelevant matter. — ED.

LORD ELLENBOROUGH was of opinion, that the plaintiff was bound to prove a demand before action brought.

A witness was afterwards found who did so, and the plaintiff had a verdict.

GIBBS AND CLAYTON, *Executors of* ELIZABETH EDWARDS, *v.* SOUTHAM.

IN THE KING'S BENCH, JANUARY 17, 1834.

[*Reported in* 5 *Barnewall & Adolphus,* 911.]

DEBT on bond for £1512 given to the testatrix. The condition was as follows: "That if the above bounden Thomas Southam, his heirs, executors, or administrators, shall and do well and truly pay unto Elizabeth Edwards, her executors, administrators, or assigns, the full sum of £756, with interest after the rate of £5 for each £100 for a year, without fraud or further delay, then this obligation to be void and of none effect, or else to remain in full force." The defendant, in his fourth plea, pleaded that Elizabeth Edwards in her lifetime did not, nor have nor hath the plaintiffs or either of them, as executors, since her death, after the making of the said writing obligatory, and before the exhibiting the bill of the plaintiffs, &c., demanded payment of the said sum of £756 with interest, &c. General demurrer and joinder.

G. T. White was to have argued in support of the demurrer (Jan. 17th), but the court called on

Humfrey, for the defendants. The money was not payable before express demand. There could have been no doubt on this point if the money had, in the body of the condition, been expressed to be payable on demand; Carter *v.* Ring,[1] Simpson *v.* Routh.[2]. Here the stipulation for the payment of interest shews that the bond was not to be forfeited till default upon an actual demand. The plaintiff seeks to recover a penalty, which is a collateral sum; and the cases with regard to payment of money on request, where there is an antecedent duty, do not apply. This was the argument of counsel (Abbott) in Carter *v.* Ring. Birks *v.* Trippet[3] shews that where an undertaking is to pay a collateral sum on request, an actual request is necessary before action brought. Here the payment of the penalty is collateral to the payment of the money secured by the condition, just as where the condi-

[1] 3 Campb. 459. [2] 2 B. & C. 682.
[3] 1 Saund. 32.

tion is for the performance of any other kind of act. [LITTLEDALE, J. It is said in Co. Lit. 208 *a*, that "in case of a condition of a bond, there is a diversity between a condition of an obligation which concerns the doing of a transitory act without limitation of any time, as payment of money, delivery of charters, or the like, for there the condition is to be performed presently, that is, in convenient time; and when, by the condition of the obligation, the act that is to be done to the obligee is of its own nature local, for there the obligor (no time being limited) hath time during his life to perform it, as to make a feoffment, &c., if the obligee doth not hasten the same by request."] The convenient time cannot be fixed by the court, and should therefore be determined by the demand.

DENMAN, C. J. A bond given to secure the payment of a sum of money generally gives a cause of action which is not collateral. The obligation to pay arises upon the execution of the bond. I never heard that want of a demand was an answer to an action like this.

LITTLEDALE, J. The plea is no answer. In the case of a single bill the action is a demand. A different rule prevails where there is a bond with a penalty to secure the performance of a collateral act; there the question is, whether the defendant has shewn the performance of the condition. In Carter *v.* Ring [1] the money by the terms of the condition was payable upon demand, and issue was joined on the fact of the demand. The passage quoted from Lord Coke shews that here the money was payable immediately, that is, in convenient time. It is not necessary at present to determine how the convenient time is to be ascertained.

TAUNTON, J., concurred.

PATTESON, J. I am of the same opinion. The condition here says nothing as to a demand.

SECTION IX.

Contracts Conditional upon Notice.

ANONYMOUS.

IN THE COMMON PLEAS, MICHAELMAS TERM, 1478.

[*Reported in Year Book,* 18 *Edward* 4, *folio* 18*a*, *placitum* 23.]

IN debt upon an obligation, &c., the defendant shewed that the condition was, that if he accounted before an auditor assigned by the

[1] 3 Campb. 459.

plaintiff, when he should be required by the said plaintiff, concerning certain receipts from his manor of Dale, and paid to him the arrearages which should be found before the said auditor, that then the obligation should lose its force, &c.; *alioquin, &c.* And he in fact said that the said plaintiff assigned to him such a one, before whom he accounted, and that he had been at all times ready to pay the arrearages found before the auditor, if the said auditor had given him notice; and whether the defendant shall take notice at his peril, is the question. CHOKE. If I am bound to Catesby in an obligation upon condition that if I shall pay the damages which shall be recovered against the said Catesby in a writ of trespass brought against him by Jenney, that then, &c. In that case it is no plea for me to say that Catesby did not give me notice when the damages were recovered against him, but it is necessary for me to take notice at my peril; so here, &c. BRYAN *ad idem.* And where an arbitrament is made, the party ought to take notice of the award at his peril without notice, *quod Vavasour et Catesby concesserunt,* and they said the case which my Lord Bryan had put, was so adjudged in the King's Bench in the time of this king, &c.

ANONYMOUS.

MICHAELMAS TERM, 1485.

[*Reported in Year Book,* 1 *Henry* 7, *folio* 5*a*, *placitum* 8.]

A WRIT of debt was brought upon an obligation. The defendant said it was indorsed with a condition that if he should stand to the arbitrament of certain persons concerning all actions, trespasses, debts, and demands, &c., and fulfil the same on his part, provided that the arbitrament was made before a certain day, that then, &c.; and he in fact said that the arbitrators did not give him notice of any award made before such a day, &c. And the opinion was clear that it is no plea; for he has bound himself to perform the award, and therefore he is bound to take notice of it, &c. And it was said, if he had put in the condition, *Ita quod arbitrium fiat, et reddatur partibus in scriptis, &c.,* then it had been a good plea to say that they did not make any award in writing, or that they did not deliver any award in writing, &c. . . .

COLE'S CASE.

IN THE COMMON PLEAS, EASTER TERM, 1588.

[*Reported in Croke Elizabeth*, 97.]

ASSUMPSIT. And declared that whereas the defendant was indebted to J. S. in £20, in consideration that the plaintiff at the defendant's request agreed to give his bond to J. S. for the said debt, the defendant did assume to save him harmless; and allegeth in fact, that he did give his bond, &c., and he was sued upon it, &c. Upon *non assumpsit*, it was found for the plaintiff.

Shuttleworth moved that the plaintiff had not well declared, for that it is not alleged that he gave notice that he had made the bond, and was sued upon it. But it was adjudged for the plaintiff; for the defendant at his peril ought to take notice of the obligation, &c., as in a bond to stand to award, he is to take notice of it.

ANDERSON, C. J., said: If one be obliged to make such assurance as J. S. shall advise, he ought to take notice of the assurance devised at his peril, because a certain person is appointed to do it. But if it be such assurance as my counsel shall advise, I ought to give notice of the assurance; for he cannot take notice who is my counsel. And for the other point, he ought to save him harmless without request, viz., by payment of the money, or, &c.

FLETCHER v. PYNSETT.

IN THE COMMON PLEAS, MICHAELMAS TERM, 1605.

[*Reported in Croke James*, 102.]

COVENANT: That he should assure such a copyhold to the plaintiff, if he married with his daughter *secundum leges ecclesiasticas;* and allegeth that he *rité et legitimé* espoused the daughter of the defendant, &c. Issue was taken thereupon, and found for the plaintiff; and exception taken, because it ought to be tried by certificate from the bishop, and not by a trial *per pais. Sed non allocatur;* for the marriage is only in issue, and not whether he were lawfully espoused.

It was also held that it was sufficient for the plaintiff to allege *licet sæpius requisitus*, without giving notice of the marriage; for he at his peril ought to take notice thereof.

Also, that he need not shew a court to be holden; for he ought to procure a court to be holden. Wherefore it was adjudged for the plaintiff.

BRADLEY v. TODER.

In the King's Bench, Michaelmas Term, 1609.

[*Reported in Croke James*, 228.]

Assumpsit; in consideration he would marry such a one, his cousin, that he would give him £100; and alleges in fact that he married her such a day and place; and, although he requested the defendant such a day and place to pay, yet he had not paid.

Upon *non assumpsit* pleaded, and found for the plaintiff, it was moved in arrest of judgment that the declaration was not good; because it is not alleged that he gave notice of his marriage.

And upon the first motion the whole court was of that opinion; for a precise notice of the marriage ought to be given; and although it is alleged that he married the *feme*, and afterwards at such a day requested the money (which implies the notice alleged), yet it is not good in a declaration, which ought to be certain and is not to be maintained by intendment. But afterwards being moved again, upon a precedent shewn of Morley *v.* Hodges, in the Exchequer Chamber, where in this court in the like action *verbatim*, and no notice alleged, judgment was affirmed, the court resolved that it was good enough; for it is a necessary intendment that when after marriage he requested the payment of the money, that notice was given of the marriage. Wherefore it was adjudged for the plaintiff.

HAVERLEIGH v. LEIGHTON.

In the King's Bench, Hilary Term, 1610.

[*Reported in Jenkins' Centuries*, 311.]

A. upon good consideration assumes to B. that he will pay B. as much money as he B. will lend to C. before such a time; B. lends £100 to C. before the said time, which £100 C. does not pay to B. B. brings an action upon this promise against A., but gave no notice before the action brought that he had lent the said £100 to C.; yet the plaintiff had judgment, affirmed in error; for he had no need to give notice; the defendant might have notice by C. or otherwise; notice by suit and proof in this case is sufficient; B. is not bound to seek A. to give him notice.

Where the breach of the promise is so private that the defendant can by no possibility know it without notice, the action does not lie without notice; as upon the sale of a ton of woad for as much as another will give by a certain day, without naming any one; notice is necessary in this case before the action brought; such is also the law upon an assumpsit, where the action accrues upon a secret act of the plaintiff; in such a case notice is necessary; so of an obligation where the subject-matter of the notice is secret, and *ex parte* the plaintiff.

GABLE v. MORSE.

In the King's Bench, Michaelmas Term, 1610.

[*Reported in* 1 *Bulstrode*, 44.]

In a writ of error for to reverse a judgment given in the C. B. in an action upon the case for a promise, where the case was this: the defendant there did promise to pay such a sum of money unto the plaintiff when he should return from London; the plaintiff there did shew that he came from London, and the money was not paid unto him; upon this the plaintiff there brought his action upon the case for breach of promise, and, upon *non assumpsit* pleaded, a verdict was found for the plaintiff, and judgment for him given, to reverse which judgment a writ of error was brought. The error assigned was that the declaration was not good. First, because there was no special request of payment laid in the declaration, as it ought to have been. Secondly, because there was no notice laid to be given to the defendant in the action of the plaintiff's return from London, when the same was, that being the time of payment, which the defendant could not know of, without notice to him given of the same. Williams, J. In this case notice ought to have been given by the plaintiff in the action, of the time when he returned from London; for the defendant there could not, neither ought he to take notice thereof himself without particular notice to him given of the same. Yelverton, J. Notice in this case ought to be given of his return from London to the defendant, who by his promise was then to pay him the money, and herein the difference will be this: when it rests upon a matter to be done between the parties themselves, there notice is to be given of this unto the party who is to make payment upon an act to be done by the other to whom the payment is to be made; otherwise, where it is to be done by a stranger; for there he hath assumed upon himself to take notice, and so there at his peril he ought so to do, and so it hath been formerly adjudged upon this difference; and so in this case, the act to be done before payment of the money being to be done by the party himself to whom the money is by promise to be paid, he is himself to give notice of the time of the performance of this act by him, to the party that is to pay the money, before he is to pay the same; and there being no notice of this laid in the declaration, as the same ought to have been, for this cause the declaration is not good; and this is a good error, and so consequently the judgment for this cause is erroneous, and to be reversed. *Tota curia* clear of opinion that this is a good error, for that notice ought to have been given of the time of his return from London, and this ought to have been laid in the declaration; and so for this omission the declaration is not good, and the judgment for this cause erroneous, and for this error the judgment was reversed by the rule of the whole court.

HOLMES v. TWIST.

In the Exchequer Chamber, 1614.

[*Reported in Hobart*, 51.]

Thomas Holmes brought an assumpsit against John Twist, and declared that he was possessed of a heap of woad containing ten tons, and that Twist in consideration that Holmes would sell and deliver him one ton of the said woad, he would pay him for it within six months after the rate that he should sell the rest, and shewed that he sold and delivered unto Twist the ton of woad, and after sold unto one Collins the residue after the rate of twenty-three pounds a ton, and the defendant paid him not the twenty-three pounds according to the promise; and thereupon judgment was given for the plaintiff in the King's Bench. And now upon writ of error in the Exchequer Chamber, the judgment was reversed, because the plaintiff had not alleged that he had given notice to the defendant of the sale and price of the rest, being a thing of his private knowledge, and not like the case of a bond to perform the award. And some judges of the King's Bench allowed of the judgment.

BERESFORD v. GOODROUSE.

IN THE KING'S BENCH, EASTER TERM, 1616.

[*Reported in 1 Rolle's Abridgment*, 462, *placita* 3, 4.]

IF a man promise J. S., in consideration that he will marry A. W., his cousin, to pay him £10 on the day of his marriage, J. S. need not give notice to him who made the promise, before he marries A. W., on what day he will marry her; but the former ought to take notice of it at his peril, as he has taken upon himself to pay it on the day, although the marriage is to be made by J. S. himself; for it becomes a debt by the marriage. So, *a fortiori*, if a man promise to pay £10 to J. S. on the day of the marriage of W. N., for there the marriage is not to be made by him to whom the promise is made.

HENNING'S CASE.

IN THE KING'S BENCH, TRINITY TERM, 1617.

[*Reported in Croke James*, 432.]

ASSUMPSIT. Henning bought two weighs of barley, and assumed to pay for them as much as the plaintiff should have of any other, abating a penny only in every bushel. The plaintiff shews, that he sold to J. S. after this agreement two weighs of barley for eighteen pounds, which (abating the one penny in every bushel) amounted to £17 10*s*., and thereupon brought his action; and because it did not appear in the declaration that notice was given to the defendant that J. S. had given eighteen pounds, the judgment was arrested.

And for the same reason a judgment was reversed in Twist *v.* Holmes, and this difference taken: if the agreement be that he shall pay so much as J. S. in particular paid, in that case, *quia constat de personâ*, and he is indifferently named betwixt them, the defendant at his peril shall inquire of him, and the plaintiff is not bound to give notice; but when the person is altogether uncertain, there the plaintiff, to entitle himself to the action, ought to give notice.

HOUGHTON cited this case to be lately adjudged:[1] One assumes to save harmless J. S. of all obligations wherein he shall be bound for

[1] Somersall *v.* Barneby, Cro. Jac. 287. — ED.

J. N.; and in an assumpsit brought, he shews that he was bound in an obligation for J. N. from which he was not saved harmless, and doth not shew that he gave any notice to the defendant; yet held to be good enough.

POWLE AGAINST HAGGAR.

IN THE KING'S BENCH, TRINITY TERM, 1618.

[*Reported in Croke James*, 492.]

ERROR of a judgment in the Common Pleas in an assumpsit; where the defendant assumed, in consideration of divers sums paid to him, that if Cooper affirmed at his return beyond sea that he received of the plaintiff twenty pounds, that the defendant would pay the twenty pounds; and alleged in fact that Cooper returned from beyond sea, and on such a day, year, and place, affirmed that he received of the plaintiff twenty pounds, and that the defendant *licèt requisitus* such a day, year, and place, had not paid. The defendant pleaded *non assumpsit;* and it was found against him, and adjudged for the plaintiff.

The error was assigned, for that it is not shewn before whom he affirmed, nor that the defendant had notice given to him of this affirmation; for without notice given him he could not take cognizance thereof, nor is he bound to pay it.

Sed non allocatur; for the defendant is to take notice of this affirmation as well as the plaintiff; for the plaintiff is not bound to give him notice thereof; for the act being to be done by a stranger, and not by the plaintiff, the cognizance thereof lies as well in the notice of the defendant as in the plaintiff's, and therefore the plaintiff need not give him any notice; whereupon the judgment was affirmed.

JACKSON v. THORNELL.

IN THE KING'S BENCH, MICHAELMAS TERM, 1628.

[*Reported in* 1 *Rolle's Abridgment*, 464, *placitum* 20.]

IF, in an action upon the case upon a promise, the plaintiff declares that the defendant promised to pay for a passage over certain locks in a river made by the plaintiff on his own land so much as the Earl of Manchester should afterwards appoint to be paid for the passage of each boat, and alleges that the Earl of Manchester afterwards appointed so much in certain to be paid, &c., and that he requested the defendant such a day to pay it, this is a good declaration without alleging that he gave any notice to the defendant of the appointment of the sum made by the Earl of Manchester, because the plaintiff is as great a stranger thereto as the defendant, and it no more lies in his knowledge than in the knowledge of the defendant, the appointment being to be made by a stranger.

ANONYMOUS.

IN THE KING'S BENCH, MICHAELMAS TERM, 1646.

[*Reported in* 2 *Lilly's Practical Register,* 235.]

NONE is bound by the law to give notice to another of that which that other person may otherwise inform himself of; except he tie himself by special covenant and agreement to do it; for the law will not put an unnecessary trouble upon any man without his own consent.

CUTLER AND OTHERS *v.* SOUTHERN AND OTHERS.

IN THE EXCHEQUER, MICHAELMAS TERM, 1667.

[*Reported in* 1 *Williams' Saunders,* 116.]

DEBT on bond dated the 8th of March, in the sixteenth year of the reign of the now king. The defendants pray oyer of the condition, which recites, that whereas the plaintiffs, at the request of the defendants, stand bound to Thomas Cook for the payment of £103 10*s.* upon the first day of May next after the date of the bond; if therefore the defendants shall save, keep harmless, and indemnify the plaintiffs from all troubles, suits, inconveniences, damages, and molestations from or by the said Cook, or any other by his means and procurement, then, &c. Upon which the defendants plead affirmatively that they have saved harmless, &c. The plaintiffs reply, that before the time of the making of the bond brought into court, to wit, on the 1st of October, in the sixteenth year aforesaid, the plaintiffs, at the request of the defendants, by their bond became bound to the said Cook in £200 upon condition for the payment of £103 at a certain day specified in the same condition then to come and now past: and for that the said £103 were not paid to the said Thomas Cook on the said day in the condition mentioned, the said Cook afterwards, to wit, on the 12th of February, in the eighteenth year, at London, &c., sued the said plaintiffs at law for the recovery of the said penal sum of £200 and endeavored to arrest them for it, whereby the plaintiffs could not go about their necessary business through fear of being arrested. And so the plaintiffs say, that the defendants have not saved them harmless, &c. The defendants rejoin, that they had not any notice of the said damnification; and if they had they would have saved the plaintiffs harmless, &c. Upon which rejoinder the plaintiffs demurred.

And it was argued for the plaintiffs, that the rejoinder was bad for two reasons: 1. Because the defendants of themselves ought to take notice of the act of a stranger, as Cook in this case is; and the plaintiff has no need to give them notice of the damnification occasioned by Cook; 2. Because the rejoinder is a departure from the plea in bar; for in the bar the defendants plead that they have saved harmless the plaintiffs; and now in the rejoinder they confess that they have not saved harmless; but they had not notice of the damnification, which is a plain departure. And so was the opinion of the court.[1] . . .

KING v. ATKINS.

In the King's Bench, Hilary Term, 1670.

[*Reported in* 1 *Siderfin*, 442.]

Debt upon an obligation of £2000, conditioned to discharge, acquit, or otherwise save harmless the plaintiff from twelve bonds entered into by the plaintiff with the defendant's testator (concerning excise), and from all suits and troubles which should happen in consequence of them. After oyer the defendant pleaded performance. The plaintiff replied that he was sued and compelled to retain an attorney in the Exchequer, and that the defendant, *licet sepius requisitus*, had not acquitted him, &c. And thereupon the defendant demurred, and his cause of demurrer now shewn was that the plaintiff had not alleged particular notice to him of the suit, for *sepius requisitus* is too general. But all the court (except Morton) held that particular notice was not requisite in this case, for the defendant's testator took upon himself to do it, viz., acquit, &c., the plaintiff. . . .

[1] The remainder of the case relates to wholly different points. — Ed.

SIR CLEMENT CLERKE *v.* CHILD OF NORTHWICH.

IN THE COMMON PLEAS, EASTER TERM, 1678.

[*Reported in Freeman*, 254.]

THE defendant sold the plaintiff a parcel of wood, called the Ally Binde in Shrawley woods; and the defendant covenanted, that if the said wood did not upon measure amount unto forty acres, then he would make it up forty acres out of the woods next adjoining; and the plaintiff covenanted, that if it were more than forty acres, he would pay him £12 per acre for every acre above forty.

The plaintiff alleged for breach, that the said parcel of wood did not upon measure amount unto forty acres; and that he gave notice thereof to the defendant, but the defendant did not make them up.

The defendant pleaded, that the plaintiff did not give him any notice, &c.

The plaintiff demurred.

The question in this case was, whether or no notice was requisite?

And the court was of opinion, that notice in this case was not necessary; because the defendant had taken upon him by his covenant to make it up, and he might have measured as well as the plaintiff.

And per *Baldwin.* Whenever the defendant may, by any apparent means, come to the knowledge of the thing, there no notice is requisite; or if it be a thing that the defendant may as well come to the knowledge of as the plaintiff, there no notice is requisite; but if it be a thing that lies particularly in the knowledge of the plaintiff, there notice ought to be given; as if I give a bond to pay so much to A. when he cometh into Somersetshire, there A. ought to give notice, because he may come in the night, or so as it is impossible for me to know it; but otherwise it is, if it be when a stranger cometh into Somersetshire, for there I may take notice as well as he.

VYSE *v.* WAKEFIELD.

IN THE EXCHEQUER, EASTER TERM, 1840.

[*Reported in 6 Meeson & Welsby*, 442.]

COVENANT on an indenture, dated the 3d of March, 1827, whereby the defendant, in consideration of £3100, bargained, sold, and assigned to the plaintiff certain dividends, interest, and annual produce, from time to time due and payable or to arise from and after the decease of one Eliza Robson, during the natural life of the defendant, if he should survive her; to have, hold, receive, and take the dividends, &c., thereby assigned unto the plaintiff, his executors, &c., from and after the decease of the said Eliza Robson, for and during the natural life of the defendant, if he should survive her; and the defendant did thereby for himself, his heirs, &c., covenant, promise, and agree with and to the plaintiff, his executors, administrators, and assigns, amongst other things, that he the defendant should and would at any time or times thereafter, at the request of the plaintiff, his executors, administrators, or assigns, appear at an office or offices for the insurance of lives within London, or the bills of mortality, or before the agent or agents of any such office or offices in the county where he the defendant might happen to be resident or actually to be; and then and there truly answer such questions as should or might be asked or required touching or concerning his age and state of health, and do all other necessary acts in order to enable the plaintiff, his executors, administrators, or assigns, if he or they should think proper, to insure the life of him the defendant; and he should not afterwards do, or, as far as with him should lie, permit to be done, any act, deed, or thing whatsoever, whereby any such insurance might be avoided or prejudiced; as by the said indenture, reference being thereunto had, will, amongst other things, appear. And the plaintiff says, that he the defendant, in part performance of his said covenant, did afterwards, to wit, on the 8th day of March, 1827, at the request of the plaintiff, appear at an office for the insurance of lives within London, that is to say, the office of a certain company of persons, or office established for the purpose and carrying on the trade or business of and for the insurance of lives, under the name of, and called and known by the name of, the Rock Life Assurance Company, and did then and there answer certain questions then asked and required of him touching and concerning his age and state of health, and did then do all other necessary acts in order to enable the plaintiff to insure the life of him the defendant in and with the said company or office, he the plaintiff then thinking proper and intending to insure the life of him the defendant in and with the said company or office, according to the course and practice of the said company or office; the answering such questions as aforesaid, and the said other matters in that behalf aforesaid, being necessary and proper, according to the course and practice of the said company or office, to enable the plaintiff to insure the life of the defendant thereupon and therewith, and being reasonable in that behalf, of all which the defendant then had notice. And the plaintiff further says, that he the plaintiff did thereupon, and within a reasonable time then next following, to wit, on the day and year last aforesaid, according to the course and practice of the said company or office, insure the life of the defendant in and with the said company or office, by a certain policy or insurance, at and for the premium of £81 17*s.* 6*d.*, payable annually in that behalf, in order to and whereby the plaintiff then became and was entitled, if such premiums should be so paid, to be paid and satisfied out of the funds and property of the said company, according to the provisions of the company's deed of settlement, within three calendar months after satisfactory proof should have been received at the office of the said company of the death of the defendant, the sum of £3000, and such further sum or sums as might, under the regulations of the said company, be appropriated as a bonus to that policy, subject to and under the condition or proviso, amongst others, that, in case the defendant should go beyond the limits of Europe, the same should be null and void; and the plaintiff says, that the said condition or proviso, at the time of making the said indenture. and from thence hitherto, was and is usual and reasonable; and that although he the plaintiff has performed and observed every thing in the said indenture on his part to be performed and observed, yet the defendant has broken his covenant made with the plaintiff as aforesaid, in this, to wit, that he the defendant, after the making thereof, and after the making of the said policy or insurance as aforesaid, and after he the plaintiff had paid to the said Rock Life Assurance Company divers, to wit, twelve annual premiums as aforesaid, payable in respect of the said policy or insurance as aforesaid, and after the sum that, under the regulations of the said company, would have been appropriated as a bonus to that policy, in case of the death of the defendant, had amounted to a large sum, to wit, £2000, and had become of great value to the plaintiff, to wit, the value of £2000, and after the said policy had become and was of great value to the plaintiff, to wit, of the value of £3000, to wit, on the first day of June, 1838, he the defendant went beyond the limits of Europe, to wit, to the province of Canada, in North America, whereby and by reason of the premises the said policy became and was null and void, &c.

Special demurrer, assigning for cause that the declaration does not contain any specific averment that the defendant, before he went beyond the limits of Europe as in the declaration alleged, had received or had any notice from the plaintiff, or otherwise that the defendant had by any means been made or become aware of the fact, that the plaintiff had insured the life of the defendant as in the declaration alleged, or that such insurance was subject to or under the condition or proviso in the declaration alleged; whereas the defendant could not be liable for going beyond the limits of Europe, unless he knew at the time that the policy had been effected, and that it was subject to the condition or proviso stated in the declaration.

Peacock, in support of the demurrer, was stopped by the court, who called upon

Cowling to support the declaration. The declaration is sufficient. It was not necessary to allege any notice to the defendant; for the declaration states that the defendant did, at the request of the plaintiff, appear at the Rock Life Assurance Office, and did answer certain questions put to him; and he might, therefore, have informed himself of the fact of the insurance having been effected, and of the terms and conditions of it. The general rule is, that a party is not bound to do more than the terms of his contract oblige him to do; and here there is nothing in this covenant requiring him to give any notice. Therefore, unless the circumstances were such that the defendant had not any means of informing himself of it, no notice was necessary. This contract to insure is confined to insurance offices within the bills of mortality; and the defendant might readily have informed himself by inquiry of the fact of the insurance having been effected, and of the terms and conditions of it. In Com. Dig. tit. Condition, L. 9, many instances are given where parties are not bound to give notice, but the other parties must take notice at their peril. It is there said, "If a condition, covenant, or promise, be to do an act to a stranger, or upon performance of an act by a stranger, there needs no notice; for it lies equally in the knowledge of the obligor and obligee, and the obligor takes upon himself to do it; as if a condition be to pay when A. marries, there needs no notice when A. marries. So if a condition, covenant, or promise be to do upon the performance of any certain and particular act by the obligee himself, he ought to do it without notice by the obligee that the act is performed, for he takes it upon him to do it at his peril; as if the condition be to pay so much when the obligee marries, there need not be notice of his marriage." Notice is not necessary, unless where the party expressly contracts to give notice, or where it must necessarily be implied that notice is to be given, because the obligor cannot know or ascertain from the nature of the thing whether the act has been done or not. In Rex *v.* Holland[1] it was held, that where a public officer is charged with a breach of duty, which duty arises from certain acts within the limits of his government, it is not necessary to aver, in an indictment against him, that he had notice of those acts, as he is presumed from his situation to know them. In answer to the objection of want of notice, Wood says, in the argument, "Notice here merely means knowledge; and when the matter is as much in the knowledge of the defendant, or more, than of any other person, the law presumes that he had knowledge;" for which he cites 16 Viner's Abr. tit. Notice, p. 5, pl. 10, where it is said, "None is bound by the law to give notice to another of that which that other person may otherwise inform himself of;" and Lord Kenyon, in giving judgment, refers to that argument, and recognizes it as shewing "the true

[1] 5 T. R. 607.

grounds upon which notice is or is not required to be averred." So here, the defendant might have informed himself whether the insurance was effected or not, and was bound to do so at his peril; and the plaintiff not having undertaken by his contract to give the defendant notice that the assurance was effected, was not bound to do so. The defendant by his covenant undertakes to do nothing to vitiate an insurance effected with any person within the bills of mortality, without any stipulation whatever as to notice of the particular person with whom it should be effected. [PARKE, B. If the covenant had spoken of an insurance to be effected with A. B., there would be no necessity for notice; but if it were with any person that the plaintiff may choose, then it must surely be necessary that notice should be given. Is not notice equally necessary, when the covenant applies to an insurance in any one of the many public offices within the bills of mortality?] If five or six offices had been named, no notice would be necessary. If there are such a number of insurance offices in London as would render it unreasonable to expect the defendant to inquire of them all whether such an insurance had been effected, the defendant should have shewn that by his plea; not having done so, the court will not assume it to be the fact. In Doe *v.* Whitehead,[1] which was an ejectment by landlord against tenant on an alleged forfeiture by breach of a covenant to insure "in some office in or near London," it was held that the omission to insure must be proved by the plaintiff. There the same objection would have applied, as it would have been necessary for the landlord to make inquiry at every office in or near London. Lord Denman, C. J., says, "The proof may be difficult, where the matter is peculiarly within the defendant's knowledge; but that does not vary the rule of law; and the landlord might have had a covenant inserted in the lease to insure at a particular office, or to produce a policy when called for, on pain of forfeiture. If he will make the conditions of his lease such as render the proof of a breach very difficult, the court cannot assist him." Here the district is limited; but if the number of offices within it are so inconvenient as to render inquiry difficult, the court cannot calculate the balance of inconvenience. Suppose all the insurance offices were in one street, no notice would surely in such case be necessary. [PARKE, B. Have you any authority for that, or in any case where there is any choice as to where the insurance shall be effected?] The cases cited in Com. Dig., before referred to, are applicable in principle; but there is no case where the party's having a choice as to the office in which an insurance is to be effected, has been held to render notice necessary. In Viner's Abr., Condition (A. d.), pl. 15, it is said, "If A. sells to B. certain weys of barley or other things, and B. assumes to pay for every wey as much as he sells a wey for to any other

[1] 8 Ad. & Ell. 571, 3 Nev. & Per. 557.

man; if he after sells to others certain weys for a certain sum, he shall not have an action on the case against B. upon his promise till he hath given him notice for how much he sold the wey to others; for B. is not bound to pay it till notice, because it is uncertain and not known to him; and here he assumes in general and not in particular, *scilicet*, to pay so much as J. S. shall pay for a wey, and so he does not assume to take notice at his peril; "but," it is added in pl. 16, "if he had assumed to pay as much for every wey as he sold a wey for to J. S., if J. S. after bought a wey for a certain sum, he ought to take notice thereof at his peril without any notice given, otherwise he hath broke his promise." If, in the present case, the number of offices had been limited, it is quite clear that notice would not have been necessary, because the court cannot measure the inconvenience arising from a greater or less number; and the same argument will apply where the district is limited. The defendant might have remedied the inconvenience, if any inconvenience exists, by providing for it in his contract.

Peacock, in support of the demurrer. The principle established by the cases is, that where the act is to be done by a stranger no notice is necessary, because the fact is as much within the knowledge of the one party as the other; but where the act is to be done by the plaintiff himself, it is otherwise, and notice must be given. Powle *v.* Hagger.[1] There the court expressly drew the distinction between the case where the act is to be done by a stranger, and where it is to be done by the plaintiff himself. [PARKE, B. In Bradley *v.* Toder,[2] and in Fletcher *v.* Pynsett,[3] where the promise was, in consideration that the plaintiff would marry such a woman the defendant would give him £100, it was held that notice of the marriage was not necessary.] In Bradley *v.* Toder the court at first held that the declaration was not good, because it was not alleged that the plaintiff gave notice of the marriage; and though the court afterwards resolved that it was good, the reason given is, that it was a necessary intendment; that when, after the marriage, he requested payment of the money, notice of the marriage was given. But this is an act which lies entirely within the knowledge of the plaintiff, who effected the policy and who alone could know the conditions annexed to it. All the cases turn upon the question, whether the defendant had the means of knowledge or not; and if he had not, or not equally with the plaintiff, then notice is requisite. [LORD ABINGER, C. B. Suppose the defendant had promised to pay £1000 to any banker in London that the plaintiff chose to open an account with, must not the plaintiff give him notice of the bank in which he has opened an account? PARKE, B. Suppose the covenant had been, that the defendant would perform the terms and conditions of any policy that the plaintiff had entered into with the Rock Life Assurance

[1] Cro. Jac. 492. [2] Cro. Jac. 228. [3] Cro. Jac. 102.

Company, he must in that case have made inquiry as to the terms upon which the policy was effected.] In —— *v.* Henning[1] it is said, "If the agreement be, that he shall pay so much as J. S. in particular paid, in that case, *quia constat de personâ*, and he is indifferently named betwixt them, the defendant at his peril shall inquire of him, and the plaintiff is not bound to give notice; but when the person is altogether uncertain, there the plaintiff, to entitle himself to the action, ought to give notice." In this case the plaintiff had the option of selecting any one of the insurance offices, and he was not confined with respect to the time of effecting the insurance; and he ought, therefore, to have given notice. [PARKE, B. Suppose it had been a promise to pay the plaintiff £100 if he should go to Rome or Naples?] There it would be his duty to give notice. When the event depends upon the performance of one of two acts which are in the plaintiff's option, he is bound to give notice, because it could only be known to the plaintiff when he had exercised his option. [PARKE, B. In Haverley *v.* Leighton[2] the plaintiff promised J. S., that if he borrowed of one Powell £100, he would repay that sum to him upon the same day and upon the same conditions that they between them should agree upon, and it was there held that notice was not necessary.] That case shews that where the person or the act is certain, no notice is necessary; but when the person or the act is uncertain, and the option is to be exercised by the plaintiff, then it is necessary.

LORD ABINGER, C. B. I am of opinion that the defendant in this case is entitled to our judgment, on two grounds. The plaintiff having reserved to himself the liberty of effecting the insurance at any office within the bills of mortality, the number of which is limited only by the circumscription of the place, and having also reserved to himself the choice of time for effecting the insurance, it appears to me that he ought to give the defendant notice of his having exercised his option, and of the insurance having been effected, before an action can be maintained. But there is also another ground, which weighs strongly with me in coming to this conclusion. Even supposing the defendant were bound to go to all the insurance offices within the bills of mortality to ascertain whether such a policy had been effected, he would still be obliged to do something more, namely, to learn what were the particular conditions on which it was effected; because the covenant here is, not that the defendant shall not do any thing to evade the covenants or conditions usually prescribed by insurance offices, but that he shall not violate any of the conditions by which such insurance might be avoided or prejudiced; *i. e.*, he is bound to observe all the stipulations contained in any policy which the plaintiff may effect. Now, some conditions totally distinct from the conditions in general

[1] Cro. Jac. 432. [2] 1 Bulstr. 12.

use might be annexed by a particular insurance office; and in such case it would be most unfair to allow the plaintiff to keep the policy in his pocket, and without notice of them to call on the defendant to pay for a violation of the stipulations contained in it. Suppose one of the conditions imposed by the policy were, that the party whose life was insured should live on a particular diet, or at a particular place, or cease from some particular practice to which he was addicted, or that he should abandon some course of exercise which might, if persevered in, cost him his life, and the forsaking of which the insurance office might be fully justified in making a condition of insuring the life at all, it would be hard if the plaintiff could, without giving the defendant notice of the existence of such a condition, make him pay the amount of the policy on its violation. The rule to be collected from the cases seems to be this, that where a party stipulates to do a certain thing in a certain specific event which may become known to him, or with which he can make himself acquainted, he is not entitled to any notice, unless he stipulates for it; but when it is to do a thing which lies within the peculiar knowledge of the opposite party, then notice ought to be given him. That is the common sense of the matter, and is what is laid down in all the cases on the subject; and if there are any to be found which deviate from this principle, it is quite time that they should be overruled.

PARKE, B. My mind is not entirely free from doubt: but I am inclined, on the whole, to agree with the Lord Chief Baron. The defendant here is sued on a covenant by which he stipulates to do two things, namely, to appear at an office for the insurance of lives, within London or the bills of mortality, in order to enable the plaintiff to effect an insurance on his life; and, after it is effected, to perform the conditions which may be contained in it. And it does not appear that this is confined to an insurance to be effected at the particular office at which he should appear; the words "such insurance" in this covenant meaning simply an insurance on his life. The defendant is bound in the first instance to appear at an insurance office, and when the insurance is effected, he is then bound, as far as in him lies, to fulfil the stipulations which have been entered into by the policy. The question then is, whether an action can be maintained on this covenant, when notice of the effecting such insurance, or of its terms, is not averred in the declaration. The general rule is, that a party is not entitled to notice, unless he has stipulated for it; but there are certain cases where, from the very nature of the transaction, the law requires notice to be given, though not expressly stipulated for. There are two classes of cases on this subject, neither of which, however, altogether resembles the present. One of them is, where a party contracts to do something, but the act on which the right to demand payment is to arise is perfectly indefinite; as in the case of Haule v. Hemyng,[1] where a man

[1] Viner's Abr. "Condition" (A. d.), pl. 15; Cro. Jac. 422.

promised to pay for certain weys of barley as much as he sold them for to any other man: there the plaintiff is bound to aver notice, because the person to whom the weys are to be sold is perfectly indefinite, and altogether at the option of the plaintiff, who may sell them to whom he pleases; and in such cases the right of the defendant to a notice before he can be called on to pay, is implied by law from the construction of the contract. So where a party stipulates to account before such auditors as the obligee shall assign, the obligee is bound to give him notice when he has assigned them; for that is a fact which depends entirely on the option or choice of the plaintiff. On the other hand, no notice is requisite when a specific act is to be done by a third party named, or even by the obligee himself; as, for example, where the defendant covenants to pay money on the marriage of the obligee with B., or perhaps on the marriage of B. alone (for there are some cases to that effect), or to pay such a sum to a certain person, or at such a rate as A. shall pay to B. In these cases there is a particular individual specified, and no option is to be exercised; and the party who, without stipulating for notice, has entered into the obligation to do those acts, is bound to do them. But there is an intermediate class of cases between these two. Let us suppose the defendant in this case bound to perform such stipulations as shall be contained on a policy to be effected at some office in London. Now, my present impression is, that where any option at all remains to be exercised on the part of the plaintiff, notice of his having determined that option ought to be given; and if this had been a covenant by the defendant to perform the conditions to be imposed by any insurance company then existing in London, I think it would be the duty of the plaintiff to notify to the defendant the exercise of his option, as to which he had selected. But this principle holds even more strongly in the present case, for not only do the terms of the covenant apply to all actually existing companies of the sort, but to all that might at any future time, subsequent to the date of the deed, be established within the bills of mortality. Now that is a condition which appears to me so perfectly indefinite, that notice ought to be given by the plaintiff of his having determined his choice, and I think, therefore, that he was at least bound to give notice that a policy of insurance had been effected by him at such a particular office; it might then, perhaps, be the duty of the defendant to inquire at that office into the nature and terms of the policy which had been there effected. If, therefore, the more extended construction of this covenant is to be adopted, and the defendant's contract understood to extend to all existing and future companies, no doubt at all can exist upon the point. Supposing, however, that the covenant is to be construed in a limited sense, as restrained to any office where the party should have appeared to answer the questions relative to his health, &c., as the words "such insurance" seem, and perhaps with truth, to indicate, even then the option of the plaintiff is of such an indefinite nature that the defendant cannot be called on to account for the non-observance of it, unless notice be given to him. Now here none has been given; there is, it is true, notice of an intention to effect a policy, but none either of its having been made at all, or made with any particular conditions. Possibly, if it had been notified generally to the defendant that an insurance had been effected at a particular office, it would become his duty then to inquire into its nature and the conditions with which it was coupled; but I think that he was at least entitled to notice of the fact of its existence.

ALDERSON, B. I am of the same opinion; and my judgment is founded on the authority of Haule *v.* Hemyng, as reported in Viner's Abr. Condition (A. d.), pl. 15. In this case the defendant covenants that he will not do any act, deed, or thing, whereby any such insurance may be avoided or prejudiced. The insurance is to be effected at any time or times, or at any office or offices, within certain limits, and is not confined to the then existing offices. The plaintiff has the selection from an indefinite number; and it seems to me that the person who is to select the office must give notice of his having done so. If the defendant had received notice that an insurance was effected in the Rock Life Insurance Company, I by no means say that he would not be bound to inform himself of any conditions to which it might be subject.

ROLFE, B. I am of the same opinion. I own that when the case was first opened, my impression was in favor of the plaintiff; and for this reason, that when a party enters into a contract, he is bound to perform it, whether reasonable or not. Where the law casts an obligation upon him, it says that it shall be reasonable; but that is not so where a party contracts to do a particular act; for then it is his own fault for entering into such a contract. In the progress of the argument, my opinion changed; and I think that the plaintiff was bound to give notice. I find it stated in Viner's Abr. Condition (A. d.), pl. 10, "If I am bound to enfeoff such persons as the obligee shall name, he ought to give notice of those he names, otherwise I am not bound to enfeoff them;" and reason seems in favor of this principle of law. The question is, what is the meaning of the contract, where a party covenants to do something at the option of another? It must mean, provided he have notice of that option having been exercised.

Judgment for the defendant.[1]

[1] Affirmed on error, 7 M. & W. 126. And see Genesee College *v.* Dodge, 26 N. Y. 213. — ED.

MAKIN v. WATKINSON.

IN THE EXCHEQUER, NOVEMBER 22, 1870.

[*Reported in Law Reports, 6 Exchequer, 25.*]

DECLARATION upon a covenant contained in a lease of a mill and other buildings with machinery and fixtures, by which the lessors (of whom the defendant was one) covenanted with the plaintiff (the lessee), that they would at all times during the demise, at their own expense, maintain and keep the main walls, main timbers, and roofs of the said buildings in good and substantial repair, order, and condition; alleging performance of conditions precedent, and a default in repairing, whereby, &c.

Plea. That the plaintiff gave no notice to the lessors of any want of repair in the main walls, main timbers, and roofs, nor that the same were not in good and substantial order and condition.

Demurrer and joinder.

Wills was called upon to support the plea. The only direct authority for the plea is a *dictum* of Mansfield, C. J., and Gibbs, J., in Moore v. Clarke,[1] that "the lessor may charge the lessee without notice, for the lessor is not on the spot to see the repairs wanting; the lessee is, and therefore the lessee cannot charge the lessor for breach of repairs without notice, for the lessor may not know that repairs are necessary." The justice of this is the more obvious if its principle is applied to a similar case, that of a watch-maker selling a watch with an agreement to keep it in repair for six months; it is plain that he could not be sued for non-repair unless the buyer required repairs to be done. The lessor in the one case, and the watch-maker in the other, not only would not, but could not, know that repairs were wanted unless notice was given; for they would have no right to insist upon examining the premises or the watch, and would be guilty of a trespass if they did so against the will of the possessor. The *dictum* above cited is supported by several analogous cases. In Com. Dig. Condition, L. 10, it is laid down that "if a condition be that the lessee repair, and that the lessor find timber, the lessee ought to demand timber, and give notice how much will be sufficient." [BRAMWELL, B., referred to L. 8, "if a condition, covenant or promise be to pay as much for goods as every other pays; the obligee shall give notice how much another pays."] In Vin. Abr. Condition, (A. d.), pll. 13, 38, it is laid down that when the condition is an act to be performed by a stranger, the obligor must take notice at his peril; but in the case cited in the latter *placitum* (Pollen v. Kinges-

[1] 5 Taunt. at p. 96.

meal, as stated in the margin), and in Harris *v.* Ferrand, reported in Hardr. 41, and cited in Vin. Ab. Notice, A. 2, pl. 12, the principle is more fully and more correctly stated that "notice is not necessary where the thing lies as much in the cognizance of the one as the other; but where it lies more properly in the cognizance of the plaintiff than of the defendant notice is necessary." That principle was acted upon in Vyse *v.* Wakefield,[1] and is entirely applicable to this case. [MARTIN, B. A distinction has always been made between a condition and a covenant. CHANNELL, B. The principle has been laid down, that where notice or demand is merely formal, the bringing of the action is sufficient notice, but not otherwise.] Here the notice is essential; if the lessor is to have no notice, extensive repairs may have been executed by the tenant, of which the lessor knows nothing, and of the necessity of which he has, after they are done, no means of judging, but for which he may be compelled to pay; and he may be made liable for consequential damage which he had no opportunity of preventing. [BRAMWELL, B. The case would be different if the covenant were, on the making of the lease, to *put* in repair. But the plaintiff's contention would reduce the lessor to a dilemma; if he went on the premises to repair, and repairs were not needed, he would be liable to be sued in trespass; if he did not go and repairs were needed, he would be liable for consequential damage, and he could have no knowledge whether they were or were not needed.]

Kemplay, in support of the demurrer. If the defendant is right, there is no difference between a covenant to repair and a covenant to repair on notice. The rule is, that notice is not necessary unless it is stipulated for by the contract; see 1 Wms. Saund. 116, note to Cutler *v.* Southern, and 2 Wms. Saund. 62, n. (4), where all the authorities are collected; Cole's Case.[2] [BRAMWELL, B. The covenant in Cole's Case was to save harmless, but if it had been merely to indemnify, must not notice have been given of the damnification?] The defendant's view cannot be sustained without adding words to the covenant, and there is no authority for such addition. [BRAMWELL, B. Words were added in Vyse *v.* Wakefield.[3] The question is, whether in reason the covenant does not require the addition; we must construe it if possible as a covenant made by reasonable people.] It is not necessary for that purpose to add words; there is nothing unreasonable in it as it stands; the lessee being under an obligation to repair would have an implied license to do all things necessary. The *dictum* in Moore *v.* Clarke[4] was not necessary to the case; on the other hand, Coward *v.* Gregory[5] is in favor of the plaintiff. [BRAMWELL, B. There the covenant was to put the premises in repair, which implied they were out of repair.]

[1] 6 M. & W. 442.

[2] Cro. Eliz. 97.

[3] 6 M. & W. 442.

[4] 5 Taunt. at p. 96.

[5] Law Rep. 2 C. P. 153.

CHANNELL, B. I am of opinion that this is a good plea. The declaration is good, because it avers the performance of conditions precedent, which would include a request if a request is necessary. The question is, whether the plea denying the giving of notice is a good defence. I agree that the case of Moore v. Clarke[1] is not an authority; because, although what was said there upon this point was said by two very eminent judges, one of them (Gibbs, J.) peculiarly conversant with pleading, and was illustrative of the matter under discussion, yet it was not necessary to the determination of the case. We must, therefore, look at the question apart from direct authority, and upon general principles. And, looking at it in this way, Vyse v. Wakefield[2] is to some extent an authority, for it warrants the proposition that, when a covenant would, according to the letter, be an unreasonable one, words not inconsistent with the words used may be interpolated to give it a reasonable construction. This proceeds on the assumption that the contracting parties were reasonable men, and intended what was reasonable. If, however, the language of the covenant is clearly inconsistent with the words sought to be added, I agree that, however absurd the covenant may be, it cannot be varied.

Now here repairs are to be done to the exterior of the premises, as to which it is just possible that the lessor might by observation acquire a knowledge of their necessity. But the main timbers of the building, which must be within its carcase, and the roofs are to be kept in repair; and of the repairs required for these he could have no knowledge without notice. He could not enter to see the condition of those parts, even though, independently of his obligation under the covenant, it might be of great consequence to him to be acquainted with it. Here, therefore, by the rule of common sense, which is supported by the case of Vyse v. Wakefield, we ought to import into the covenant the condition that he shall have notice of the want of repair before he can be called on under the covenant to make it good.

BRAMWELL, B. I am also of opinion that the plea is good. To hold it to be so, we must hold the defendant's covenant to be a covenant to repair on notice. I have the strongest objection to interpolate words into a contract, and think we ought never to do so unless there is some cogent and almost irresistible reason for it, arising from the absurdity of the contract if it is read without them. Does such a reason, then, exist here? I think it does. I think that we are irresistibly driven to say that the parties cannot have intended so preposterous a covenant as that the defendant should keep in repair that of which he has no means of ascertaining the condition. The lessee is in possession; he can say to the lessor: "You shall not come on the premises without lawful cause;" and to come for the purpose of looking

[1] 5 Taunt. at p. 96. [2] 6 M. & W. 442.

into the state of the premises would not be a lawful cause. If the lessor comes to repair when no repair is needed, he will be a trespasser; if he does not come, he will, according to the plaintiff's contention, be liable to an action on the covenant if repair is needed, and will be liable, not only to the cost of repair, but to consequential damage for injury to chattels caused by want of the repairs he had no opportunity of effecting. This is so preposterous that we ought to hold that the parties intended the covenant to be read with the qualification suggested.

As to the authorities, we have, in the first place, an *obiter dictum* of two eminent judges, which was appropriate to the matter in hand, and is therefore of great value, though not binding. The authorities on analogous cases, collected in Comyns' Digest, are by no means clear; some seem one way, some another; and one, which occurs under the title Condition, L. 9, is very much in favor of the plaintiff. The case there referred to is Fletcher *v.* Pynsett,[1] where, it appears, the defendant covenanted with the plaintiff that, if he would marry the defendant's daughter, the defendant would assure to him a certain copyhold; and it was held that the plaintiff was entitled to sue without giving notice of the marriage. It seems to be suggested that, when the engagement is conditional upon the doing of an act by a third person, notice must be taken from that person. But this cannot be the reason of the rule; for in a case put under L. 8 of the title I have referred to, it is said that a promise to pay as much for goods as any other pays requires a notice of how much another pays.[2] But there seems no reason why the obligee should be less bound to give notice or the obligor more bound to take notice of the act of a stranger than of the act of the obligee himself, as in some of the cases put in L. 9, where it is said notice is not necessary.

If we look to the reason of the rule, it is that when a thing is in the knowledge of the plaintiff, but cannot be in the knowledge of the defendant, but the defendant can only guess or speculate about the matter, then notice is necessary.

[1] Cro. Jac. 102; see to same effect, Roll. Abr. Cond. C. 1, 2, 3, 4, under the heading "At what time performance should be when no time is limited."

[2] Holmes *v.* Twist, the case there referred to, was decided by the Exchequer Chamber, reversing the judgment of the King's Bench, some judges of the court below agreeing with the judgment of reversal (Hob. 51); the reason there assigned was, that the price was "a thing of his (the plaintiff's) private knowledge, and not like the case of bond to perform the award;" in Cro. Jac. 432, where the same case is referred to in a similar case of —— *v.* Henning (Haul *v.* Hemmings, in 1 Roll. Rep. 285), it is said a difference was taken "if the agreement be that he shall pay so much as J. S. in particular paid; in that case *quia constat de persona,* and he is indifferently named betwixt them, the defendant at his peril shall inquire of him, and the plaintiff is not bound to give notice." The latter reason seems to be adopted by Parke, B., in Vyse *v.* Wakefield (6 M. & W. at pp. 453, 454), as the *ratio decidendi* of these cases.

To have inserted a provision in the covenant requiring notice would certainly have been very reasonable. When it is a question of putting it into the covenant by implication, one must needs, as in all such cases, have great doubt; but upon the whole, looking to the authorities, and bearing in mind what is said in Moore *v.* Clark,[1] I think we are warranted in so reading the covenant.

Martin, B. I am of opinion that this plea is bad. I think that when we are construing a contract we ought to adhere to its words, and not insert words not to be found in it; otherwise it is impossible for the parties to know what are the obligations they have bound themselves to, or for counsel to advise with certainty. Now the declaration states a covenant by the defendant to keep in good and substantial repair, and that the defendant did not keep in repair. In answer to this the plea alleges that there was no notice of want of repair. I think this plea bad, and for the simplest reason, that no such stipulation is contained in the covenant, nor any thing from which such a stipulation can be inferred.

I cannot perceive that the covenant as it stands is so unreasonable as is alleged. Moreover, there are in leases covenants to repair generally, and covenants to repair on notice; but if this covenant is construed in the way proposed, it is idle to require notice in terms; the one covenant will do as well as the other.

The authorities appear to me directly against the plea. The proposition laid down by Mr. Cowling *arguendo* in Vyse *v.* Wakefield[2] is, I apprehend, perfectly correct: "The general rule is that a party is not bound to do more than the terms of his contract oblige him to do;" and all the judgments support what he says. Lord Abinger, C. B., says:[3] "The rule to be collected from the cases seems to be this, that where a party stipulates to do a certain thing in a certain specific event which may become known to him or with which he can make himself acquainted, he is not entitled to any notice, unless he stipulates for it." Now, the assumption in the present case that the defendant cannot know without notice is, in my judgment, idle. Parke, B., says:[4] "The general rule is that a party is not entitled to notice unless he has stipulated for it; but," he adds, "there are certain cases where, from the nature of the transaction, the law requires notice to be given, though not expressly stipulated for;" he proceeds to describe those cases as cases where the thing to be performed is indefinite, and at the option of the plaintiff; and he decides the case before him on the ground that an option still remained to be exercised by the plaintiff. The present transaction is not of such a nature. Lastly, Rolfe, B., says:[5] "I own that when the case was first opened my impression was

[1] 5 Taunt. at p. 96.
[2] 6 M. & W. at p. 446.
[3] 6 M. & W. at p. 452.
[4] 6 M. & W. at p. 453.
[5] 6 M. & W. at p. 456.

in favor of the plaintiff; and for this reason, that when a party enters into a contract he is bound to perform it, whether reasonable or not. Where the law casts an obligation upon him, it says that it shall be reasonable; but that is not so when a party contracts to do a particular act, for then it is his own fault for entering into such a contract." I entirely agree with the rule of law so stated, and therefore think we are not at liberty to import any such stipulation into this covenant as the defendant claims. *Judgment for the defendant.*

INDEX.

CONDITIONAL CONTRACTS.

CONDITIONS PRECEDENT.

In General.

In Leases.

In Policies of Insurance.

In Charter-Parties.

CONSIDERATION VOID IN PART.

DEMAND.

DEPENDENT AND INDEPENDENT COVENANTS AND PROMISES.

FORBEARANCE.

MUTUAL AND CONCURRENT CONDITIONS.

MUTUAL CONSENT.

MUTUAL PROMISES.

NOTICE.

OFFER.

REFUSAL.

REQUEST.

REVOCATION OF OFFER.

REWARD.

WAIVER OF PERFORMANCE OF CONDITIONS, AND EFFECT THEREOF.

Cambridge: Printed by John Wilson and Son.

www.ingramcontent.com/pod-product-compliance
Lightning Source LLC
LaVergne TN
LVHW100021220926
848483LV00002BA/262
9781584770015